A Bibliography of the Prairie Provinces

A Bibliography of the Prairie Provinces to 1953 with Biographical Index

compiled by
Bruce Braden Peel

second edition

University of Toronto Press

First edition

Second edition

Reprinted in 2018
Toronto and Buffalo
Printed in Canada
ISBN 978-1-4875-7909-8 (paper)
ISBN 0-8020-1972-2
LC 72-97930

Dedicated to
THE HOMESTEADERS
among whom were
my father and mother

Contents

Contents

Foreword

The first edition of Bruce Peel's *Bibliography of the Prairie Provinces* appeared in 1956. It quickly gained a deserved reputation as one of those basic bibliographical tools without which historian, librarian, social scientist researcher, Canadiana dealer, academic, could not, any longer, find his or her way through the literature on the prairie provinces of Canada. The late F. Hedley Auld, the then Chancellor of the University of Saskatchewan, wrote the Foreword to the first edition. He noted how the bibliography 'pictures kaleidoscopically the occupation and development of a region of great agricultural importance which became in the course of a few decades the new home of a multitude ...' He noted further that the events encompassed in the bibliography were so recent that many persons were still living who had a part in the actual occurrence.

It was a commentary on the interest sparked by Mr. Peel in Western Canadiana that many titles not listed in 1956 came to light in the years immediately following publication. A Supplement to the Bibliography was prepared by Mr. Peel and published by University of Toronto Press in 1963. Now, ten years later, a new, enlarged edition of the original work is to appear.

Bruce Peel's Preface to the Enlarged Edition is at once a comprehensive introduction to the bibliography and a general comment on the lure of bibliographical research. The bibliophile who would succeed must have patience, pertinacity, time, money, interest, friends, prestige – and a publisher – if he or she is to bring a project to fruition. Mr. Peel's interest, ability, pertinacity, and dedication shine through the piece. And what a piece it is! When the Northwest became a formal possession of Canada there was at once provided for the young nation a backdrop of nature's best, on which broad canvas man might trace out, and work out, and record his progress.

The *Bibliography of the Prairie Provinces* in its enlarged form carries forward the arrangement found so successful in the first edition. Chronology, subject, title, and author arrangements give added emphasis to the time factor, the rhythm of change from fur trade to agricultural pursuits, and the development of a regional literature written by prairie dwellers. The chronological arrangement is particularly helpful to the researcher who must find his way through eighteenth and nineteenth century writings, and who must weigh the relevance and importance of each work. No apology need be offered for the need of an addenda. A pioneer work such as the Peel bibliography will not be definitive and it is only to be expected that unlisted items will continue to appear. The value of the addenda far outweighs the minor irritation of a break in the serenity of the chronology.

Foreword

The Peel bibliography ranks and deserves to rank with the great bibliographical works of Canada. It is a tribute to devoted research, and it is a work of scholarship. The subject arrangement speaks of the basic ingredients of the western land - space, sun, wind, water, and man's coming to terms with these forces. Students of prairie society will ignore these environmental factors at their peril and come to terms with them to their advantage.

Prairie Canada is a young society as men count time. The memory of man is short and subject to erosion. Oral history, tradition, legend, and myth slide into time past, to be obscured and lost amidst the fastnesses of ridges of memory formed of times long spent. Were it not for signposts, no one could find his way back of beyond. The Peel bibliography provides a clear, well-marked, and dependable highway back through our history to our beginnings. This work is a contribution to scholarship and a landmark in our western cultural development.

J.H. Archer
Regina
2 May 1973

Preface to the Second Edition

With the presentation of this enlarged edition of the bibliography of the Prairie Provinces the bibliographer completes a project begun by happenstance twenty-six years ago. On a September afternoon on the University of Saskatchewan campus the president and secretary of the undergraduate English society, making their rounds of potential speakers for the winter roster, came upon me by chance and asked if I would speak on regional materials which creative writers might exploit. I was then the librarian in the Shortt Collection of Canadiana. In preparation for the talk to be given the following February, I began a card file of Western Canadiana titles, and have been collecting titles ever since.

To the regional bibliographer the nineteenth and early twentieth century literature of the Prairie Provinces presents a greater challenge than would the literature of most other geographic areas, since such a high percentage of the publications was ephemeral, printed and distributed outside the region. In the search for these, I have at one time or another visited most of the major research libraries of Canada and the United States. In 1971 a Canada Council grant made possible a 70-day tour of national and other research libraries in seventeen European countries. I searched for immigration literature and for reminiscences published in the homelands of early pioneers. This odyssey was a bibliographical success.

A long-time frustration was the inaccessibility of something described as the 'first document printed in Manitoba.' In 1875 it had been entombed, along with a miscellany of other things, in the cornerstone of the Winnipeg City Hall. Finally the wreckers caught up with the Victorian building, and No. 208 was added to the bibliography.

Since so many of the early pamphlets related to immigration into Western Canada, it was unfortunate for me that the voluminous files of the old Department of the Interior remain closed to public access until they have been inventoried by the archival staff. However, in the nick of time for this bibliography, Miss Juliette Bourque, Librarian of the Public Archives of Canada, arranged to have her staff search the Interior files for Western pamphlets. En route home after a last fling in the Library of Congress, I visited Ottawa and in one day with the help of a strong-armed young archivist slung some 300-400 jam-packed archival boxes off shelves, ran an exploratory finger along the letters' edges to feel for hard-edged pamphlets, and then tossed the boxes back up on the shelves. As anticipated, the files were a well-stocked cache of immigration pamphlets.

Among the sources listed in this compilation is one designated 'Tanghe.' This is a card catalogue located in the National Library containing 25,000 entries of publications relating to Canada from Confederation to 1900. The compiler was Mlle Madeleine Pellerin who combed many printed national catalogues and other bibliographical sources over several years. Through her searches Mlle Pellerin made a significant contribution to retrospective Canadian bibliography.

I regret that the symmetry of the sequential numbering of entries has been marred by the inclusion of about 150 last-minute discoveries to which it was necessary to add the suffix 'A.' This came about by the last-minute search of the Department of the Interior files as related above, and to a lesser extent because bibliographers, book dealers, and librarians, on hearing that an enlarged Prairie Provinces bibliography was about to go to press, rushed new titles to the compiler.

Since the bibliography was compiled over many years as a spare-time activity, and information was gathered from many sources and in many places, the work is not without inconsistencies in cataloguing and bibliographic styles. Some entries have copied the styles of printed catalogues and bibliographies in which they were found. Two source libraries have changed their names in response to the changing politics of our times, but 'R.E.S.' and 'St. Sulpice' have been retained as sources after individual entries. Likewise a few descriptive words and phrases with political overtones are less frequently used in Canada now than twenty years ago. The practical difficulties of making many changes in the text, rather than a bibliographical conservatism, account for the retention of the above features.

As in the original bibliography, the closing date of publication of entries is 1953. However, a minimal attempt at up-dating has been the inclusion at the end of some subject lists of an addendum of some significant post-1953 titles. The choice of titles for inclusion has been highly selective from the increasing number of scholarly regional studies to appear in recent years.

In the preface to the original bibliography I placed in the first rank of those to whom I acknowledged my indebtedness Miss Juliette Bourque and Mr. T.R. McCloy. Seventeen years later I again have occasion to thank these librarians. As explained earlier, Miss Bourque arranged access to the Department of the Interior archival files. Mr. McCloy, Librarian of the Glenbow Foundation (from which position he has recently retired), as he collected for his library sent me new catalogue entries. Another person who made this edition richer is Mr. Tom Williams, proprietor of Northland Books in Saskatoon (now of Calgary), who brought to my attention obscure pamphlets as these passed through his shop.

The success of my grand tour of European libraries in search of Western Canadiana was greatly aided by preliminary letters in the language of each country, addressed to chief librarians. I am grateful to the eleven members of the University of Alberta library staff who wrote these letters; in one country I was complimented on the purity with which I wrote the vernacular. The European librarians who assisted me, too numerous to name individually, made my excursion successful and pleasant.

With the assistance of the librarians of the leading newspapers in Western Canada the biographical information on several dozen authors in the first edition was enlarged. (One resourceful librarian, unable to find a man in her newspaper's 'morgue,' contacted the provincial Bureau of Vital Statistics and furnished me with an official death certificate.) I wish to thank all these librarians. Miss Ruth Buggey of the Free Press of Winnipeg was, as in the earlier edition, the biographical researcher to whom I am most indebted.

The Historian of the Royal Canadian Mounted Police, Mr. S.W. Horrall, proved that the famous force when put on the trail of an elusive individual can still get its man.

In the University of Alberta Library office I appreciate the various typing services of the secretaries and, in particular, of Mrs. Shirley Meyer and Mrs. Donna Mulholland.

Over the winter of 1971-72 Mr. Milton Pinsky was engaged to organize the enlarged bibliography, a tedious scissors-and-paste job. He made an important contribution to the preparation of this edition, and I thank him for the attention to detail which prevented many errors and inconsistencies. And finally I acknowledge the work of my wife Margaret whose careful reading of the manuscript has brought to it a higher degree of accuracy.

As the work goes to press I would thank M. Jean Houston, Executive Editor of the University of Toronto Press, who guided the first bibliography, the supplement, and now this enlarged edition through the editorial and printing processes. With great forbearance she incorporated copy from a compiler who continued to send bibliographical corrections and newly discovered titles up to the last possible moment.

This second edition has been published with the help of a grant from the Social Science Research Council of Canada, using funds provided by the Canada Council.

Preface to the 1963 Supplement

In the preface to the original bibliography, I wrote with some satisfaction, 'Within the limits here set forth an effort has been made to make the compilation complete.' Subsequent to publication I collected from time to time a few fugitive titles, but it was not until July of 1962 that I realized there were enough additional titles to justify publication of a supplement. While in Calgary during Stampede Week I sought refuge from the shouts of the cowhands and the bawling of the steers in the quiet coolness of the Library of the Glenbow Foundation. Here I saw many new pamphlets, strays missed in the earlier round-up.

In this Supplement, Glenbow is the library most frequently cited as location; that so many scarce titles are in a library which has existed so short a time bespeaks diligent searching and a bibliophile's acquisitiveness on the part of Mr. T.R. McCloy, the librarian. Another source was microfilmed correspondence and records of the Church Missionary Society which, while mostly manuscript material, contained a number of little-known pamphlets. On one microfilm reel I was delighted to find a sermon by the Bishop of Rupert's Land printed in Winnipeg in 1868, earlier than any Winnipeg imprint previously known. Later I had the satisfaction of holding a copy of the booklet, owned by an enthusiastic collector of Canadian Prairiana, Mr. Nathan Arkin of Winnipeg; a contractor friend had found the booklet on the floor of an old house being demolished for a building project. The Arkin collection, it will be noted in the Supplement, was a happy hunting-ground for the bibliographer.

When I checked the Library of Parliament I located some interesting pamphlets, and I wondered how I had overlooked such an obvious source; then I recalled the Library of Parliament's fire which had made it impossible to examine the holdings of the library in 1953.

The appearance in recent years of printed catalogues of major libraries and special collections has immeasurably assisted bibliographers and research students. When each batch of volumes of the British Museum's Catalogue of Printed Books arrives in our library, I hasten to examine it for Western Canadian items. And titles turn up in unlikely places; why does the Union Theological Seminary in New York own a unique pamphlet published in 1905 which encouraged the building up of treasures on earth by investing in Western Canadian lands?

Last but not least of the sources were the Canadiana book dealers, who over the years in their catalogues have made available and drawn attention to pamphlets which were not in my original bibliography.

I gratefully acknowledge the assistance of librarians and others in suggesting titles for incorporation in the supplement, or in supplying other information. Those who suggested titles were Mr. T.R. McCloy and Mr. Hugh Dempsey of the Glenbow Foundation, Mr. H.V. Dempsey of Ottawa, Mr. J.E.A. Macleod, Q.C., of Calgary, Mrs. June Fritch, editor of the Alberta Poetry Year Book, the Rev. Peter T. Ream of Fort Saskatchewan, Mr. Foster M. Palmer, Assistant Reference Librarian of Harvard University Library, and Mr. Guy Lyle, Librarian of Emory University. While Mr. Bernard Amtmann did not suggest titles directly certainly I am indebted to his catalogues as a source of titles. Others whom I wish to thank for assistance given by letter, or during visits to their libraries, are the following: Miss Marjorie Morley, Provincial Librarian of Manitoba, the Rev. T.C.B. Boon, Honorary Archivist of the Provincial Synod of Rupert's Land, Miss Edythe H. McCausland, University of Toronto Library, Mrs. Ginsberg of the United Church of Canada Archives, Miss Martha Shepard, Dr. Ian Wees, and staff of the National Library of Canada, Miss Dorothy Duke of the Dominion Department of Agriculture Library, and Mr. D'Arcy Beckstead of the Library of Parliament. Nor must I forget the contribution made by the typists, my secretary, Mrs. Shirley Meyer, Miss Josie Pochirowski, and particularly Mrs. Dorothy Sears, who typed from a difficult scissors-and-paste draft the final copy for the press. And finally I acknowledge the work of my wife whose careful proofreading has eliminated many an inconsistency or error in form and entry.

Preface to the First Edition

The compilation of this regional bibliography was begun in 1946. The nucleus for a bibliography of the Prairie Provinces was to be found on the shelves of the Shortt Collection of Canadiana in the University of Saskatchewan Library, which collection I was at that time engaged in cataloguing. While sleuthing for titles, I have at one time or another visited all the larger libraries in Western Canada, libraries in Ottawa, Montreal, and Toronto, and, in the United States, the New York Public Library and the Library of Congress in Washington. An important collection not examined was the Icelandic collection in the University of Manitoba Library. Printed catalogues of libraries such as that of the Royal Empire Society, and, in particular, catalogues of Canadiana collections, yielded additional books and pamphlets. Numerous books and bibliographies were also checked for Western Canadian items. In the case of the latter sources, I am reasonably sure that items included exist substantially as described. An exception, however, is the inclusion of some half-dozen titles about whose existence in book or pamphlet form I am not completely convinced; by listing them and giving sources I have alerted interested students.

The scope of this bibliography is books and pamphlets relating to the Prairie Provinces. Towards titles relating to border areas restraint was exercised, since to have included certain of these would have involved the bibliographer with other titles whose content spread even further into the Rocky Mountains, the Arctic, Hudson Bay, and the Precambrian Shield east of Manitoba. The emphasis in the bibliography is centrical, directed towards the prairie region, that agricultural arc resting on the international boundary.

A more difficult decision for the regional bibliographer had to do with books relating to Canada and containing material on the prairies. There are significant studies of national agriculture, marketing, economics, transportation, and politics which the student of the prairie region cannot ignore. Had these been included the bibliography would have had no limits. Accounts by early explorers en route to the Arctic or Pacific are, however, included; although only a small section of each might relate to the prairies, they contribute to our limited information on the period. Likewise, books by early transcontinental tourists are listed since most of them gave special emphasis to the agricultural possibilities of the region and doubtlessly influenced settlement. Pamphlets on the Canadian Pacific Railway during the period when it was being built have been included since it played such an important part in the opening of the West; but most books about the railway after it became established as a national institution have been excluded.

The hundreds of technical bulletins relating to prairie agriculture would, had they been included, have swamped the compilation. Students can find these bulletins listed in the Agricultural Index. The attention of students interested in the economic or social conditions of agricultural communities must be directed to the excellent regional surveys made by the regional branches of the Economic Division of the Dominion Department of Agriculture.

British blue books relating to the Prairie Provinces have been listed, as have also early Canadian Sessional Papers, undoubtedly the best source of information on the West for the period of settlement; no student of the period can ignore the annual reports of the Departments of the Interior and Indian Affairs, or those of the Commissioner of the North West Mounted Police. The publications of the governments of the three Prairie Provinces are excluded (with a few exceptions) because of their multiplicity. There is already available a check list, compiled by Miss Christine MacDonald, of publications of the Province of Saskatchewan and of the earlier North West Territories government.

In the field of literature the original plan was to include all the works of prairie writers, but because of the recency of settlement and the mobility of the writers, I found it impossible to define 'prairie writers.' Some writers are expatriates who write of the lands from which they came. Writers of certain racial groups and religious sects, conscious of the rapid assimilation of their young people, set their fiction or drama in the ancestral homeland, pointing to their cultural heritage; there are novels and plays about German colonies in southern Russia, and novels, plays, and poems about the Ukraine. Another group of writers are the half-dozen English yarn-spinners who in their adventurous youth lived in Western Canada and later used the region as the locale for their stories. The first of these was R.M. Ballantyne; the most prolific, Harold Bindloss. Regarding fiction, my final decision was that the sole criterion should be whether or not a work had a prairie locale. Thus, not all the writings of a prairie author are necessarily listed. The fact that such writers of international stature as Rudyard Kipling, Somerset Maugham, Moira O'Neill, Maurice Constantin-Weyer, and Sinclair Lewis are listed emphasizes the interest in the 'last, best West' during the early years of the twentieth century.

A decision on poetry was more difficult. An attempt has been made to include that poetry which describes the prairie region, or poetry whose creator was unquestionably influenced by the prairie environment. Thus, a poet who was a child of the prairie would have his works included even if he wrote about the moon, but more selectivity was exercised in choosing works by poets who came to the region after they had reached adult estate. This latter policy is exemplified in the choice of Icelandic poetry.

I have tried to collect the writings, published in languages other than English, of the many racial groups who settled on the prairies. First were the Indians; I have included translations of the Bible and religious works into Indian dialects because the work of translating was part of the early missionary endeavour and because these works are often little known and not infrequently rare. The user will notice the absence of some works relating to the Athapascan tribes which might rightfully claim a place in the bibliography, but to have included them would have involved as well the writings relating to all the tribes in the Mackenzie drainage basin as far as Aklavik. A significant feature of the writings in French is that so many of them were written by Old Country Frenchmen, the majority of whom were missionaries of the Oblate Order. To the items in French might have been added all the Canadian Sessional Papers, as these were printed in French as well as English.

Works by prairie writers on non-prairie topics have been regarded as outside the scope of this bibliography. Their inclusion would have involved, among other types of material, a shoal of school books from primers to arithmetic texts. Scholarly studies have been omitted. To indicate their significance and number, one has only to mention a few of the publications of persons associated with the University of Saskatchewan alone: R. Altschul's *Select Studies on Arteriosclerosis*, V.C. Fowke's *Canadian Agricultural Policy*, H. Neatby's *So Little for the Mind*, M. Timlin's *Keynesian Economics*, N. Ward's *Canadian House of Commons*, R.A. Wilson's *Birth of Language*, and *Essays in Honour of Arthur Moxon.*

Local imprints have been excluded as such. Little publishing is done in Western Canada with the exception of school texts, and writings in Ukrainian and Icelandic. Winnipeg is one of the important publishing centres of Ukrainian literature outside the Iron Curtain countries. Many of the publications relate to the question of the autonomy of the Ukraine or are reissues of the works of Old Country poets and writers. Winnipeg is also an important publishing centre of Icelandic.

Serial publications have in general been excluded, but exceptions have been made for a few significant works. In fact, exceptions may have been made in any category.

Within the limits here set forth an effort has been made to make the compilation complete. The largest number of fugitive items is probably in the fields of immigration pamphlets and privately printed verse.

The arrangement of the bibliography is chronological, with fur-trade journals placed in their historical period rather than listed by date of publication. In this chronological arrangement a small number of entries are not in strict order; these are items which were arranged before the publication date - or the correct author entry - was known, and when this missing information was subsequently established it was too late to rearrange in the numerical sequence.

For each entry full bibliographical details are given where the book has been examined, and as full as possible when the information was taken from other bibliographical sources. In a work compiled from many sources it will be appreciated that some inconsistency is inevitable. In the author entry, that portion of the name which does not appear on the title-page of a book has been enclosed in square brackets. In the matter of editions, the entries are usually for first editions with references to later editions and translations. For a few titles my information for a later edition was more complete, so I have chosen to give bibliographical details of that edition. My notes about editions are not always complete, particularly for twentieth-century titles; it is often difficult to ascertain that a work published in Toronto, New York, or London was also published in one or both of the other centres by the same or another publisher.

The second section of the bibliography is a subject index, with the subjects arranged in broad groups and the authors arranged chronologically under each subject. The chronological arrangement under subject is intended to enable the scholar to see the development of the literature in that field.

The biographical notes contained in the author index are intended to identify the authors whose works appear in the bibliography, and to show their association with the West or with the topics of their books. With this in mind, the emphasis has been strictly regional. Where biographical information is readily available in standard reference works, the reader has been referred to those sources. Thus, persons of significance in the national life of Canada have in many cases been dismissed with a phrase, while obscure Westerners have been treated at some length. Because of the difficulty of obtaining biographical information about some authors, their sketches are little more than clues which the interested student may follow up. Because of this difficulty, and because of the regional emphasis, the sketches are uneven. The biographical material contained in the author index is essentially a by-product of the bibliographical research.

Since the Shortt Collection of Canadiana is so frequently given as the location of items, a descriptive note is in order. The collection was originally the personal library of Adam Shortt, long associated with Queen's University, and later with the Dominion government as Civil Service Commissioner and as an archivist. As a collector, Dr. Shortt was in the enviable position of being personally acquainted with contemporaries who made and wrote Canadian history and with the families of Canadians prominent in an earlier generation. Through the foresight of Dr. W.C. Murray, first President of the University of Saskatchewan, and Dr. A.S. Morton, Librarian, this collection was purchased for the library of the University of Saskatchewan in 1918. However, the Western Canadian volumes now in the collection are mostly from the Prairie Provinces collection built up by Dr. Morton, who was an authority on the West in the fur-trade era. Many of the western ephemera were collected by Dr. Murray and Dr. E.H. Oliver – then professor of history at the University – while they were going about the province on official business. This collection owes much to the selective purchases made over the years by Dr. Jean Murray, professor of history. Miss Barbara Hobbs (now Mrs. Harcourt Smith) while in charge of the collection from 1951 to 1955 showed ingenuity in locating and adding scarce prairie items.

The assistance and co-operation I received from the many librarians and archivists whose libraries I visited is gratefully acknowledged; I wish to mention in particular the late Dr. J.L. Johnston, Legislative Librarian of Manitoba, Miss Juliette Bourque and Mr. T.R. McCloy of the Public Archives of Canada, and Dr. Willard Ireland and Miss Inez Mitchell of the Archives of British Columbia. My attention was directed to a number of items by Miss Edith Hilton of the Legislative Library of Alberta and Mr. Hugh Dempsey of the Alberta Department of Economic Affairs. Mr. Bohdan Kazymyra of the Ukrainian press suggested a score of Ukrainian titles and supplied me with biographical material for several Ukrainian writers. Of the librarians to whom I wrote for information I am especially grateful to the following for research on my behalf: Miss Georgina Thomson of Calgary, Mrs. J.C. Killen of Lloydminster, Miss Betty Carnie of Regina, Miss Ruth Buggey of the Winnipeg Free Press Library, Miss Elizabeth Dafoe and Mrs. Sigurbjornsson of the University of Manitoba, Miss Margaret Ray of Victoria University Library in Toronto, Miss Martha Shepard of the National Library, Dr. D.C.

Harvey of the Public Archives of Nova Scotia, Dr. Grace Lee Nute of the Minnesota Historical Society, Miss Ruth L. Butler of the Newberry Library in Chicago, Mr. R.D. Rogers of the New York Public Library, Mr. R.A. Wilson of the British Museum, and Mr. J. Packman of the Royal Empire Society Library in London. Dr. Carlyle King and Professor E.A. McCourt of the University of Saskatchewan, and Dr. Paul Yuzyk of the University of Manitoba, very kindly answered last-minute appeals from me. Inspector C.H. Bayfield, Headquarters Staff, Royal Canadian Mounted Police, tracked down some data on early members of the famous force.

Special thanks must go to Miss Christine MacDonald of the Legislative Library of Saskatchewan, and to Miss Barbara Hobbs, Librarian of the Shortt Collection of Canadiana, who cheerfully answered my many requests for information, bibliographic and biographic. To Dr. W. Kaye Lamb and Dr. Jean Lunn of the National Library, Mr. David C. Appelt of the University of Saskatchewan Library, and Mr. Bernard Amtmann, Canadiana dealer of Montreal, for examining the manuscript while in preparation and offering suggestions. I acknowledge my indebtedness.

Miss Marjorie Sherlock (now Mrs. H. Grayson-Smith) while Librarian of the Rutherford Library, University of Alberta, kindly granted time and library facilities for the completion of the manuscript; Miss Caroline B. Hicks, Chief Cataloguer, must also be thanked. And special mention must be made of the contribution of Margaret, my wife, who spent countless hours checking the copy.

I wish also to record my indebtedness to Miss M. Jean Houston, Assistant Editor of the University of Toronto Press, who guided a difficult manuscript through the press.

Dr. Lewis H. Thomas, Archivist of Saskatchewan, Dr. Geo. W. Simpson, Chairman of the Department of History, University of Saskatchewan, and Mr. John H. Archer, Legislative Librarian of Saskatchewan, by their interest in this compilation have assured its publication; I express my deep gratitude. The Canadian Social Science Research Council made a grant-in-aid in 1949 to assist in the preparation of the manuscript, and publication was made possible by the financial assistance of the University of Saskatchewan, the Saskatchewan Golden Jubilee Committee, and the Publications Fund of the University of Toronto Press.

[illegible] of the [illegible] Archives of Nova Scotia, Dr [illegible] of the Minnesota Historical Society, Miss [illegible] of the [illegible] in Chicago, Mr [illegible] Hunter of the New York Public Library, [illegible] of the [illegible], Mr [illegible] of the Royal Empire Society Library, [illegible] Dr [illegible] Professor [illegible] of the University of [illegible], and Dr Paul [illegible] University [illegible] kindly answered [illegible] from me, in particular [illegible] C.H. [illegible], Headquarters Staff, Royal Canadian Mounted Police, [illegible] information on [illegible] of the [illegible].

[illegible] to Miss [illegible] of the [illegible], and to Miss [illegible] the Sigmund Samuel Collection of [illegible], who [illegible] and [illegible]. Mr [illegible] and Dr [illegible] of the [illegible] and Library, Mr [illegible] of the University of Saskatchewan, and Mr [illegible] of [illegible] for [illegible] and [illegible] suggestions [illegible] acknowledge my [illegible].

Miss [illegible], [illegible] B. [illegible] of the [illegible] Library, University of Toronto, kindly [illegible] and [illegible]. [illegible] the [illegible] and Miss [illegible] who [illegible].

I wish [illegible] to Miss [illegible], Assistant Editor of the University of Toronto Press, who [illegible] through the press. Dr [illegible] of Saskatchewan [illegible] of the University of [illegible] and Mr John H. Archer, Legislative Librarian of Saskatchewan [illegible] the [illegible] of the Prime [illegible] and the [illegible] of [illegible].

Libraries, Collections, and Other Sources Cited

The library cited after each entry is the one in which a copy was originally located and examined. Printed catalogues of libraries and specialized collections, bibliographies, and a miscellany of printed references are also given as sources. In this bibliography when the location cited is a Canadiana dealer's catalogue, the first figure is the number of the catalogue, the second that of the item in the catalogue.

ACADIA	Acadia University, Wolfville, N.S., Library. Catalogue of the Eric R. Dennis collection of Canadiana. (Wolfville, 1928) Also a few titles listed in N.U.C.
ADELPHI	Adelphi Book Shop. Canadiana dealer, Victoria. Catalogues
AGRIC.	Canadian Department of Agriculture Library, Ottawa
ALTA. LEG.	Alberta Legislative Library, Edmonton
AMERICAS	New York. Public Library. Dictionary catalog of the history of the Americas. (Boston, 1961)
AMSTERDAM	Universteitsbibliotheek, Amsterdam, The Netherlands
AMTMANN	B. Amtmann. Canadiana dealer, Montreal Catalogues Contributions to a short-title catalogue of Canadiana. (Montreal, 1971-)
ANTIQUE	Antique Book Shop, Montreal. Catalogues
ANTWERP	Stadsbibliothek, Antwerp, Belgium
ARKIN	Nathan Arkin. Private collector of Western Canadiana, Winnipeg. Now part of the Lande collection in McGill University Library
AUSTRIA	Osterreichische Nationalbibliothek, Vienna, Austria
AYER	Newberry Library. Dictionary catalogues of the Edward E. Ayer collection of Americana and American Indians. (Boston, 1961)
B.C. ARCH.	Provincial Archives of British Columbia, Victoria
BAVARIA	Bayerische Staatsbibliothek, Munich, West Germany
BEGG VS. BEGG	M. Wolfenden. 'Begg vs. Begg' (in B.C. Historical Quarterly, 1937)
BELGIUM	Bibliothèque Royale Albert ler de Belgique, Bruxelles, Belgium
BENDER	H.S. Bender. Two centuries of American Mennonite literature. (Goshen, Ind., 1929)
BERKELEY	University of California, Berkeley Campus. Library. San Francisco
BIB. CAN.	H.J. Morgan. Bibliotheca canadensis. (Ottawa, 1867)
BIBLIOTHEQUE DE ST-BONIFACE	Bibliothèque de St-Boniface, Man.

BR. MUS.	British Museum, London Catalogue of printed books. (London, 1881-1900) Supplement, 1900-5 General catalogue of printed books. 1931– Subject index to the modern works. 1901– Also books and pamphlets examined during visits to London
BURPEE	L.J. Burpee. Sandford Fleming, empire builder. (Oxford, 1915)
CALGARY	Calgary Public Library
CAN. ANNUAL REV.	Canadian annual review of public affairs. (Toronto, 1901-38)
CAN. ARCH.	Canada. Archives. Catalogue of pamphlets prepared by Magdalen Casey. (Ottawa, 1931-32) Also books and pamphlets examined during visits to the Archives.
CAN. ARCH. (ms.)	Canada. Archives. Closed files of the Dept. of the Interior
CAN. CAT.	Canadian catalogue of books published in Canada, etc. (Toronto, 1923-48)
CAN. GOVT. OFF.	Scrap book catalogue of books in the library of the Canadian government offices in London in 1895. Copy from the Sir Charles Tupper papers in the possession of the Manitoba Legislative Library
CAN. IMPRINTS	D.D. Tod & A. Cordingley. A check list of Canadian imprints. (Ottawa, 1950)
CAN. JOURNAL	The Canadian Journal of Science, Literature, and History. (Toronto, 1855-75)
CAN. NOVEL	C. Thomas. Canadian novelists. (Toronto, 1946)
CANADA. BUREAU OF STATISTICS	Bibliographical list of references to Canadian railways, 1829-1938. (Ottawa, 1938)
CANADIANA	Canadiana. (Ottawa, 1951-)
CANNER	J.S. Canner & Co., Inc., Boston. Catalogues
C.H.R.	Canadian Historical Review. (Toronto, 1920-)
C.J.E.P.S.	Canadian Journal of Economics and Political Science. (Toronto, 1935-)
C.M.S.	Church Missionary Society. Records and correspondence. Microfilm, 52 reels. (The number following the symbol is that of the microfilm reel)
C.M.S. LIB.	Church Missionary Society Library, London, England
COLLECTION GAGNON	Bibliothèque Municipale, Montréal. Collection Gagnon. See also Gagnon below
COLUMBIA	Columbia University Library, New York
CONTRIB. TO CAN. EC.	Contributions to Canadian economics. (Toronto, 1928-34)
C.P.R.	Canadian Pacific Railway offices, Montreal. Library
CUM. CAT.	U.S. Catalog. Later the Cumulative book index. (New York, 1900-)
CUVERILLE	J.M.A. Cuverille. Le Canada et les intérêts français. (Paris, 1898)
CZECH	Narodni Knihovna Ceskoslovenské Socialisticke, Prague, Czechoslovakia
DALHOUSIE	Dalhousie University Library, Halifax
DAVIES	R.A. Davies. Canadiana dealer, Montreal. Catalogues
DENMARK	Det Kongelige Bibliotek, Copenhagen, Denmark
DIONNE	N.E. Dionne. Inventaire chronologique ... (Quebec, 1905-12)

D.N.B.	Dictionary of national biography. (London, 1885-1912) Also supplements
DOM. A.R.	Dominion annual register, ed. by H.J. Morgan. (Ottawa, 1878-86)
DORNBUSCH	C.E. Dornbusch. The Canadian army 1855-1955; regimental histories and a guide to regiments. (Cornwallville, N.Y., 1955-57) 3v.
EDMONTON	Edmonton Public Library
EDMONTON JOURNAL	(newspaper) (Edmonton 1903–)
EHRLICH	I. Ehrlich. Canadiana dealer, Montreal. Catalogues
EIRE	National Library of Ireland, Dublin, Eire
EMMANUEL COLLEGE	Emmanuel College, University of Saskatchewan, Saskatoon
FINLAND	Helsingin Yliopiston Kirjasto, Helsinki, Finland
FISKE	Cornell University. Library. Catalogue of the Icelandic collection bequeathed by Willard Fiske. (Ithaca, N.Y., 1960)
FRANCE	Bibliothèque Nationale, Paris, France
FRANCIS	E.K. Francis. 'Mennonite school problems in Manitoba, 1874-1919; bibliography on the Mennonites of Manitoba.' (In Mennonite Quarterly Review, July, 1953)
GAGNON	P. Gagnon. Essai de bibliographie canadienne. (Quebec & Montreal, 1895-1913) See also Collection Gagnon above.
GIRAUD	M. Giraud. Le métis canadien. (Paris, 1945)
GLENBOW	Glenbow Foundation Library, Calgary
HAIGHT	W.R. Haight. Canadian catalogue of books, 1791-1897. (Toronto, 1896-1904)
HAMILTON	Hamilton Public Library
H.B.C.	Hudson's Bay Company Library, London, England
HEENEY	W.B. Heeney. Centenary addresses and sermons. (Winnipeg, 1922)
HIGGINS	M.V. Higgins. Canadian government publications. (Chicago, 1935)
HISTORICAL ATLAS	J. Warkentin, ed. Manitoba historical atlas. (Winnipeg, 1970)
HORNING	L.E. Horning. & L.J. Burpee. Bibliography of Canadian fiction. (Toronto, 1904)
HOWARD	J.K. Howard. Strange empire. (New York, 1952)
HUDSON'S BAY HOUSE	Hudson's Bay House, Winnipeg
HUNGARY	Orszagos Szechenyi Konyvtar, Budapest, Hungary
IBIS	The Book Arts, Hamilton. Catalogues
INTERIOR	Canadian Department of the Interior. Annual Reports
KAPSNER	O.L. Kapsner. A Benedictine bibliography. 2d ed. (Collegeville, Minn., 1962)
KIRKCONNELL	W. Kirkconnell. Canadian overtones. (Winnipeg, 1935)
KNOX COLLEGE	Knox College Library. University of Toronto, Toronto
LANDE	L.M. Lande. The Lawrence Lande collection of Canadiana in the Redpath Library of McGill University. (Montreal, 1965)
	Rare and unusual Canadiana; first supplement to the Lande bibliography. (Montreal, 1971)
LAVALLEE	Camille Lavallee Inc., Canadiana dealer, Montreal. Catalogues
L.C.	Library of Congress. A catalog of books. (Ann Arbor, 1942) Supplements. Also books and pamphlets examined during visits to Washington, D.C.

LEHMANN	H. Lehmann. Das Deutschtum in Westkanada. (Berlin, 1939)
LEIDEN	Rijksuniversiteit Bibliotheek, Leiden, The Netherlands
LETHBRIDGE	Lethbridge Public Library
LIB. OF PARL.	Library of Parliament, Ottawa. Annual catalogues. (See also L. of P.)
LIVERPOOL	Brown, Picton, and Hornby Library, Liverpool, England
LOCAL COUNCIL	Local Council of Women of Saskatoon. Archival materials stored in the Shortt Collection, University of Saskatchewan Library, Saskatoon
L. OF P.	Library of Parliament, Ottawa
LORENZ	Otto H. Lorenz. Catalogue générale de la librairie française. (Paris, 1867-1945) 34v.
LYLE	Guy Lyle microfilm collection on the Barr Colony in the University of Alberta Library
MAN. LEG.	Manitoba Legislative Library, Winnipeg
MARBURG	Marburg. Universitat. Bibliothek. Katalog der Kanada-Bibliothek. (Marburg, 1963)
MARTIN	C.B. Martin. Lord Selkirk's work in Canada. (Oxford, 1916)
MATTHEWS	W. Matthews. Canadian diaries and autobiographies. (Berkeley, Cal., 1950)
McGILL	McGill University Library, Montreal
MONTREAL AUCTIONS	Montreal Book Auctions Ltd., Montreal. Catalogues
MOOSE JAW	Moose Jaw Public Library
MORGAN, 1912	H.J. Morgan. The Canadian men and women of the time. (Toronto, 1912)
MORICE	A.G. Morice. Histoire de l'Eglise catholique dans l'Ouest canadien. (St-Boniface, 1921-23)
MORTON	W.L. Morton. Progressive Party in Canada. (Toronto, 1950)
MR. LOVERIDGE'S PAPERS	Material in possession of a resident of Moosomin district, Saskatchewan
NAPRSTEK	Naprstkovo Musea, Prague, Czechoslovakia
NAT. LIB.	National Library of Canada, Ottawa
NEBENZAHL	Kenneth Nebenzahl, Inc., Chicago. Catalogues
NETHERLANDS	Koninklyke Bibliotheek, The Hague, The Netherlands
NEWBERRY	Newberry Library, Chicago. A bibliographical check list of North and Middle American Indian linguistics in the Edward E. Ayer collection. (Chicago, 1941) (Ayer purchased the J.C. Pilling collection for his library) Also pamphlets examined during visits to the Newberry Library
NORDMANNS	Nordmanns (periodical) office, Oslo, Norway
NORTHLAND	Northland Books, Saskatoon. Catalogues. (Now Tom Williams Books, Calgary)
NORWAY	Norges Riksbibliotek, Oslo, Norway
N.S. ARCH.	Nova Scotia. Archives. A catalogue of the Akins collection of books and pamphlets, compiled by S.I. Stewart. (Halifax, 1933)
N.U.C.	National Union catalog. (Washington, 1969-)
N.Y.	New York Public Library
OBLATES ARCH.	The Archives, Provincial House of the Alberta-Saskatchewan Province, Oblate Order, Edmonton
L'OEUVRE DES TRACTS	A series of pamphlets published in Montreal

OLD BOOK	Old Book Collector, Canadiana dealer, Kingston. Catalogues
PATRICK	Joseph Patrick, Canadiana dealer, Toronto. Catalogues
PILLING	J.C. Pilling. Bibliography of the Algonquin languages. (Washington, 1891)
POLAND	Biblioteka Narodowa, Warsaw, Poland
PRINCE ALBERT TIMES	(newspaper) (Prince Albert, 1892-1912)
PRIVATE	Various private sources
QUE. LEG.	Quebec Legislative Library
QUEEN'S	Queen's University, Kingston. Library. Canadiana, 1698-1900, in the possession of the Douglas Library. (Kingston, 1932) Also a few titles listed in N.U.C.
REAM	P.T. Ream. Fort on the Saskatchewan. (Edmonton, 1957)
REGINA	Regina Public Library
R.E.S.	Royal Empire Society, London. Subject catalogue of the library; v.3, Canada, etc. (London, 1932) Also pamphlets examined during visits to this Library, now called the Royal Commonwealth Society Library
R.H.P.	Review of historical publications relating to Canada. (Toronto, 1896-1918)
ROBERTSON	J.P. Robertson. A political manual of the province of Manitoba and the North West Territories. (Winnipeg, 1887)
RUPERT'S	Archives of the Diocese of Rupert's Land, in Manitoba Legislative Library, Winnipeg
RUPERT'S LAND	Church of England, Diocese of Rupert's Land. Triennial report on Indian missions. (Winnipeg, 1899)
RUTHERFORD	Rutherford Collection of Canadiana, University of Alberta Library, Edmonton
RYERSON	W.S. Wallace. The Ryerson imprint. (Toronto, 1954)
ST. ALBERT MUSEUM	St. Albert Museum, St. Albert, Alberta
ST. JEAN	College Universitaire St-Jean, Bibliothèque, Edmonton
ST. SULPICE	Bibliothèque Saint-Sulpice, Montreal. This Library is now part of the Bibliothèque Nationale du Québec
ST. THOMAS MORE	St. Thomas More College Library, Saskatoon
SASK. ARCH.	Saskatchewan Archives, Regina
SASK. HIST.	Saskatchewan History. (Saskatoon, 1948-)
SASKATOON	Saskatoon Public Library
SASKATOON SAN.	Saskatoon T.B. Sanatorium, Patients' Library, Saskatoon
SELECT	Winnipeg. Public Library. A selective bibliography of Canadiana of the Prairie Provinces. (Winnipeg, 1949)
SHORTT	Shortt Collection of Canadiana, University of Saskatchewan Library, Saskatoon
SLAVICA CANADIANA	J.B. Rudnyc'kyj, ed. Slavica canadiana. Slavistica proceedings of the Institute of Slavistics of the Ukrainian Free Academic of Sciences. (Winnipeg, 1952-)
SPECIALTY	Specialty Book Concern, Waterdown, Ont. Catalogues
STEVENS	Henry Stevens, etc. Short title list, 1956/no.6, Item 51. (London)
SVENSK	Svensk Bokkatalog. (Stockholm, 1878-)
SWEDEN	Kungliga Biblioteket, Stockholm, Sweden
SWISS	Schweizerische Landesbibliothek, Bern, Switzerland
TANGHE	A card catalogue, in the National Library, of publications relating to Canada, 1867-1900. The project was organized by Dr Raymond Tanghe, a former Assistant National Librarian; the compilation was by the late Mlle. Madeleine Pellerin

TORONTO	Toronto Reference Library
TORONTO (STATON)	F.M. Staton & M. Tremaine. A bibliography of Canadiana, being items in the Public Library of Toronto. (Toronto, 1935)
TRINITY	Trinity College Library, Dublin, Eire
TUREK	Polonica Canadiana; a bibliographical list of the Canadian Polish imprints, 1848-1957. (Toronto, 1958)
U.B.C.	University of British Columbia Library, Vancouver
U.C.	National Union Catalogue in the National Library of Canada
U.C. ARCH.	United Church of Canada Archives, Victoria University Library, Toronto
U. DE MONTREAL	La Bibliothèque Université de Montréal, Montréal
U. OF A.	University of Alberta Library, Edmonton
U. OF A. (Calg.)	The Library, University of Alberta in Calgary. Now the University of Calgary
U. OF A. (EDUC.)	Education Library, University of Alberta. Edmonton
U. OF A. (EXTENSION)	Extension Library, University of Alberta, Edmonton
U. OF M.	University of Manitoba Library, Winnipeg
U. OF N.B.	University of New Brunswick Library, Fredericton
U. OF S.	University of Saskatchewan Library, Saskatoon
U. OF S. (REGINA)	University of Saskatchewan, Regina Campus, Library
U. OF T.	University of Toronto Library, Toronto
U. OF T. QUARTERLY	University of Toronto Quarterly. (Toronto, 1931-)
U. OF TEXAS	University of Texas Library, Austin. (As listed in N.U.C.)
U. OF VICTORIA	University of Victoria Library, Victoria
U. OF W.	University of Washington Library, Seattle
UNION	Union Theological Seminary Library, New York. Shelf list ... in classification order. (Boston, 1960)
UNITED COLLEGE	The Library, United College, Winnipeg. Now the University of Winnipeg
UPPSALA	Universitetsbiblioteket (Carolina Rediviva) Uppsala, Sweden
VANCOUVER	Vancouver Public Library, Vancouver
VICTORIA COLLEGE	Victoria College Library, University of Toronto, Toronto. Now Victoria University
WAGNER	H.R. Wagner. The Plains and the Rockies. 2d ed. (San Francisco, 1937)
WALES	National Library of Wales, Aberystwyth
WATTERS	R.E. Watters. A check list of Canadian literature and background materials, 1628-1950 ... (Toronto, 1959)
WESTERN PRODUCER	The Western Producer (weekly newspaper) Saskatoon
WHO'S WHO IN CANADA	Who's who in Canada. (Toronto, 1922-)
WINNIPEG	Winnipeg Public Library
WINNIPEG CITY CLERK	Winnipeg City Clerk's Office
WOLFE	William P. Wolfe. Canadiana dealer, Montreal. Catalogues
YALE	Yale University. Library. Catalog of the Yale collection of Western Americana. (Boston, 1961)
YUZYK	P. Yuzyk. The Ukrainians in Manitoba. (Toronto, 1953)

A Bibliography
of the Prairie Provinces

1 **Kelsey**, Henry
The journal of Henry Kelsey (1691-1692): the first white man to reach the Saskatchewan River from Hudson Bay & the first to see the buffalo-grizzly bear of the Canadian plains; by Charles Napier Bell. Winnipeg, Dawson Richardson Publications, Ltd., 1928. 43p. front. (fold. map) illus. (incl. maps, double facsim.) 22cm. (Hist. & Sc. Soc. of Man., n.s., no.4) Shortt

2 **Kelsey**, [Henry]
The Kelsey papers, with an introduction by Arthur G. Doughty & Chester Martin. Published by the Public Archives of Canada and the Public Record Office of Northern Ireland. Ottawa, F.A. Acland, 1929. lxxxiii, 128p. incl. front. (facsim.) fold. map. 26 1/2cm.

Kelsey's journal was published in the report of the Committee on Hudson's Bay in 1749, but it was only in 1926 that the original ms. was found among the Dobbs papers in the Public Record Office of Northern Ireland. The first two papers cover his exploration, the third covers Indian beliefs and superstitions, while the remaining eight deal with events on Hudson Bay. Shortt

3 **Tyrrell**, J[oseph] B[urr] ed.
Documents relating to the early history of Hudson Bay. Toronto, The Champlain Society, 1931. xix, 419p. front., plates, maps (part. fold.) facsims. 25cm. (Champlain Soc., no.18) Shortt

4 **Bowery**, Thomas
A dictionary of the Hudson's-Bay Indian language. London, 1701. 7p. Not seen.

A compilation of about 600 Cree words.

It appears that Henry Kelsey compiled a dictionary some years later. The H.B.C. Letter Book 603 contains the reference in a letter to Kelsey: 'We have sent you your dixonary Printed that you may the better Instruct the young Ladds with you, in ye Indian Language.' Joseph Robson claimed that this was later suppressed by the H.B.C. See Kelsey Papers, p.xxvii. Br. Mus.

5 **Jérémie**, [Nicolas]
Relation du Détroit et de la Baie d'Hudson. Saint-Boniface, Imprimerie du Manitoba, 1912. 23p. 22cm. (Soc. Hist. de St-Boniface, no.2)

Jérémie's narrative was first published in Amsterdam in 1732 in 'Recueil de Voyages au Nord,' edited by Jean Frederic Bernard. Shortt

6 **Jérémie**, Nicolas
Twenty years of York Factory, 1694-1714; Jérémie's account of Hudson Strait and Bay. Translated from the French edition of 1720, with notes and introduction by R. Douglas and J.N. Wallace. Ottawa, Thorburn and Abbott, 1926. 42p. front., illus., plate, maps (part. fold.) 21 1/2cm.

Edition limited to 300 copies. Shortt

7 **Knight**, James
The founding of Churchill, being the journal of Captain James Knight, governor-in-chief in Hudson Bay, from the 14th of July to the 13th of September, 1717; edited with a historical introduction and notes by James F. Kenney. Toronto, J.M. Dent & Sons, Ltd. [1932] x, 213, [1]p. front. (plan) illus., plates, map, facsim. 19 1/2cm. Shortt

8 **Dobbs**, Arthur
An account of the countries adjoining to Hudson's Bay, in the north-west part of America: containing a description of their lakes and rivers, the nature of the soil and climates, and their methods of commerce, &c. shewing the benefit to be made by settling colonies, and opening a trade in these parts; whereby the French will be deprived in a great measure of their traffick in furs, and the communication between Canada and Mississippi be cut off ... The whole intended to show the great probability of a north-west passage ... London, Printed for J. Robinson, 1744. 1p.l., ii, 211p. front. (fold. map) 26 x 21 1/2cm.

An attack on the H.B.C. which led to the investigation of the monopoly by a parliamentary committee in 1749. Dobbs' information was largely based on French publications and Canadian sources, particularly that of a half-breed trader, Joseph La France. Shortt

9 [**Dobbs**, Arthur]
A description of the coasts, tides, and currents, in Button's Bay, and in the Welcome: being the north-west coast of Hudson's Bay ... taken from Serog's, Crow's, Napier's, and Smith's journals, made in the years 1722, 1737, 1740, 1742, 1743, and 1744. Also, from the discoveries made in 1742, in the voyage in the Furnace Bomb, and Discovery Pink, commanded by Captain Middleton and Captain Moor; showing from these journals, a probability, that there is a passage from thence to the Western Ocean of America. London, Printed for J. Robinson [1744] 24p. fold. map. 20cm. Glenbow

10 **Great Britain**. Parliament. House of Commons. Committee appointed to inquire into the state and condition of the countries adjoining to Hudson's Bay
Papers presented to the Committee appointed to inquire into the state and condition of the countries adjoining to Hudson's Bay and of the trade carried on there. [London] 1749. 79p. 30 1/2cm. Not seen. Toronto (Staton)

11 **Great Britain**. Parliament. House of Commons. Committee appointed to inquire into the state and conditions of the countries adjoining to Hudson's Bay
Report from the Committee, appointed to enqnire [sic] into the state and condition of the countries adjoining to Hudson's Bay, and of the trade carried on there. Together with an appendix. Reported by Lord Strange, 24th April, 1749. [London] 1749. p.213-86. 44 1/2cm.

An excerpt from the H. of C. Reports from Committees. The report embodies papers and evidence placed before the H. of C., but not the decision of the House. Evidence presented by the H.B.C. included Kelsey's journal. Shortt

12 **Robson**, Joseph
An account of six years residence in Hudson's Bay, from 1733 to 1736, and 1744 to 1747. Containing a variety of facts, observations, and discoveries, tending to shew, I. The vast importance of the countries about Hudson's-Bay to Great-Britain, on account of the extensive improvements that may be made there in many beneficial articles of commerce, particularly in the furs and in the whale and seal fisheries. And, II. The interested views of the Hudson's Bay Company; and the absolute necessity of laying open the trade, and making it the object of national encouragement, as the only method of keeping it out of the hands of the French. To which is added an appendix ... London, Printed by J. Payne and J. Bouquet [etc.] 1752. 2p.l., vi, 84, 95p. front (fold. map) fold. plate (map, 3 plans) 20 1/2cm.

A criticism of the H.B.C. and its policy by the company's surveyor and supervisor of buildings. Shortt

13 **La Vérendrye**, Pierre Gaultier de Varennes, sieur de
Journals and letters of Pierre Gaultier de Varennes de La Vérendrye and his sons, with correspondence between the governors of Canada and the French court, touching the search for the western sea; edited with introduction and notes by Lawrence J. Burpee. Toronto, The Champlain Society, 1927. xxiii, 548p. 7 fold. maps. 25cm. (Champlain Soc., no.16) French and English on opposite pages. Shortt

14 **Société Historique de Saint-Boniface**
[Documents sur la découverte du Nord-Ouest] Saint-Boniface, Imprimerie du Manitoba [1911] viii, 76, [205]-234p. illus., fold. map. 21cm. (Soc. Hist. de St-Boniface, no.1) Papers published as a supplement to the Cloches de Saint-Boniface.

Documents relating to the La Vérendryes. Shortt

15 **Henday**, Anthony
York Factory to the Blackfeet country; the journal of Anthony Hendry, 1754-55; edited by Lawrence J. Burpee. [Ottawa, Royal Society of Canada] 1907. p.307-59. incl. plates, maps (part. fold.) 24cm. Reprinted from Roy. Soc. of Can., Trans., 3d ser., v.1, sect.2, 1907.

Henday's name earlier appeared as Hendry. Shortt

16 **Wales**, William
Astronomical observations made by order of the Royal Society, at Prince of Wales Fort, on the north-west coast of Hudson's Bay, by William Wales and Joseph Dymond. Communicated to the Royal Society, November 16, 1769. London, Printed by W. Bowyer and J. Nichols, 1770. 24p. 24cm. H.B.C.

17 **Cocking**, Matthew
An adventurer from Hudson Bay; journal of Matthew Cocking; from York Factory to the Blackfeet country, 1772-73; edited with introduction and notes by Lawrence J. Burpee. [Ottawa, Royal Society of Canada] 1908. p.91-121, 361-64. fold. map. 24cm. Reprinted from Roy. Soc. of Can., Trans., 3d ser., v.2, sect.2, 1908. Shortt

18 **Henry**, Alexander
Travels and adventures in Canada and the Indian territories, between the years 1760 and 1776. In two parts. New York, Printed and published by I. Riley, 1809. vi p., 1 l., 330p., 1 l. front. (port.) 22 1/2cm.

One of the first 'pedlars' in the West under the British regime, Henry spent 1775-76 in the Saskatchewan country.

A reprint, edited with notes by James Bain, was published in Toronto and Boston in 1901; this edition was limited to 700 copies. Another edition was published in Chicago in 1921. Rutherford

19 **Hudson's Bay Company**
Cumberland House journals and inland journals, 1775-82; edited by E.E. Rich, assisted by A.M. Johnson, with an introduction by Richard Glover. London, Hudson's Bay Record Society, 1951-52. 2v. 25cm. (Hudson's Bay Record Soc., v.14-15)

Journals of the H.B.C.'s first inland post. See also Entry 22. Rutherford

20 **Umfreville,** Edward
Nipigon to Winnipeg; a canoe voyage through western Ontario by Edward Umfreville in 1784; with extracts from the writings of other early travellers through the region. Ottawa, R. Douglas, 1929. 63p. fold. map. 22cm.

The author was engaged by the N.W.C. to search for a new canoe route from Lake Superior to Lake Winnipeg. Shortt

21 **Umfreville,** Edward
The present state of Hudson's Bay. Containing a full description of that settlement, and the adjacent country; and likewise of the fur trade, with hints for its improvement, &c. &c. To which are added, remarks and observations made in the inland parts, during a residence of nearly four years; a specimen of five Indian languages; and a journal of a journey from Montreal to New-York. London, Printed for C. Stalker, 1790. 2p.l., vii, 230p. fold. tables. 20 1/2cm. Page nos.129-32 omitted in pagination; text continuous.

A criticism of the H.B.C. by an ex-employee who had joined the N.W.C. in 1784. Shortt

22 **Hearne,** Samuel
Journals of Samuel Hearne and Philip Turnor; edited with introduction and notes by J.B. Tyrrell. Toronto, The Champlain Society, 1934. xviii, 611p. maps (part. fold.) fold. plan, fold. facsim. 25cm. (Champlain Soc., no.21)

Hearne's journals cover his penetration of the interior in 1774-75, and the building of Cumberland House, the first permanent establishment of the H.B.C. in the interior. Turnor's journals include his surveys in the Saskatchewan-Athabasca region. Peter Fidler's journal covers his wanderings in 1791-92 from Lake Athabasca to Great Slave Lake. Appendices give biographical sketches of William Tomison, Humphrey Martin, and Malcolm Ross. Shortt

23 [**Turnor,** Philip]
Result of astronomical observations, made in the interior parts of North America. London, Printed for A. Arrowsmith by C. Buckton, 1794. 16p. 31cm.
Not seen. Toronto (Staton)

24 **M'Gillivray,** Duncan
The journal of Duncan M'Gillivray of the North West Company at Fort George on the Saskatchewan, 1794-5; with introduction, notes and appendix by Arthur S. Morton. Toronto, Macmillan Co. of Canada, Ltd., 1929. lxxviii, 79, 24, 6p. 2 maps (1 double) 24cm.

The introduction gives a sketch of the development of the fur trade with special reference to the Saskatchewan River. An appendix traces the later history of Fort George and of M'Gillivray. Shortt

25 **Mackenzie,** Sir Alexander
Voyages from Montreal, on the River St. Lawrence, through the continent of North America, to the frozen and Pacific oceans; in the years 1789 and 1793. With a preliminary account of the rise, progress, and present state of the fur trade in that country. London, Printed for T. Cadell [etc.] 1801. 2p.l., viii, cxxxii, 412, [2]p. front. (port.) fold. maps. 27 1/2cm. Errors in paging: p.ix numbered xi; 190 unnumbered; 212-16 numbered 214-18.

After the preface there follow 132 pages on the history of the fur trade in the North West. Some authorities think this was written by his cousin, Roderick Mackenzie. According to the D.N.B. the 'Voyages' was compiled by William Combe from Mackenzie's notes. Includes vocabularies of the Knisteneaux, Algonquin, Chepewyan, Nagailer, and Atnah Indian languages.

A 2-volume edition was published by Cadell in 1802, and the same year two American editions, a French and a German edition came out. Other editions were published in New York in 1803 and 1814. A number of reprints have appeared in the last fifty years. Shortt

26 **Maclauries,** Mr.
A narrative, or journal of voyages and travels through the northwest continent of America; in the years 1789 and 1793. London, Printed by J. Lee, 1802. 2p.l., 91p. 16 1/2cm.

Written in the third person about Maclauries, presumably a fictitious person. The text is taken from Mackenzie's 'Voyages.' Can. Arch.

27 **Johnson,** Alice M., ed.
Saskatchewan journals and correspondence; Edmonton House, 1795-1800, Chesterfield House, 1800-1802. London, Hudson's Bay Record Society, 1967. 368p. maps. 24cm. (Hudson's Bay Record Society. Publications, 26)

Journals of William Tomison and Peter Fidler. Limited edition, no.709. U. of A.

28 **Gates,** Charles M[arvin] ed.
Five fur traders of the Northwest; being the narrative of Peter Pond, and the diaries of John Macdonell, Archibald N. McLeod, Hugh Faries, and Thomas Connor. An introduction by Grace Lee Nute. [Minneapolis] Published for the Minnesota Society of the Colonial Dames of America, University of Minnesota Press, 1933. v p., 2 l., 3-298p. illus. (maps) 21cm.

Pond's narrative had appeared in print, but the diaries were published for the first time. Macdonell's diary describes a trip from Montreal to a post on the upper Assiniboine River in 1793. McLeod's diary is a description of the events of 1800-1 at Fort Alexandria on the Assiniboine. Faries was stationed at Rainy River fort in 1804-5, and Connor at Lake St. Croix at the same date. U. of A.

29 **Larocque,** [François Antoine]
Journal of Larocque from the Assiniboine to the Yellowstone, 1805, edited with notes by L.J. Burpee. Published by authority of the Minister of Agriculture under the direction of the Archivist. Ottawa, Government Printing Bureau, 1910. 1p.l., 82p. 24cm. (Publications of the Canadian Archives, no.3.)

A journey to the Mandans made with Charles Mackenzie, another fur trader, while in the service of the N.W.C. Shortt

30 **Selkirk,** [Thomas Douglas, 5th] earl of
Observations on the present state of the Highlands of Scotland, with a view of the causes and probable consequences of emigration. London, Printed for Longman, Hurst, Rees and Orme, 1805. 1p.l., [v]-vii, 223, lvi p. 23cm.

For this and the following pamphlets on Red River, published 1805-21, consult 'The Literature Relating to the Selkirk Controversy,' by W.S. Wallace, in C.H.R., v.13, 1932, p.45-50. Shortt

31 [**Brown,** Robert]
Remarks on the Earl of Selkirk's observations on the present state of the Highlands of Scotland, with a view of the causes and probable consequences of emigration. Edinburgh, Printed for John Anderson, [etc.] Alex Smellie, printer, 1806. 1p.l., 353p. 21 1/2cm. Not seen.

This was the second edition. Toronto (Staton)

The first edition had the same title, but prefaced by the words: Strictures and ... [etc.] Edinburgh, Printed by Abernethy and Walker, 1806. 120p. 21 1/2cm. (Copy in the Arkin collection)

32 [**Gordon**, James, of Craig]
Eight letters on the subject of the Earl of Selkirk's pamphlet on Highland emigration; as they lately appeared under the signature of Amicus in one of the Edinburgh newspapers. London, Longman & Co., 1806. 59p. Not seen.
C.H.R., 1932

33 [**Atcheson**, Nathaniel] supposed author
On the origin and progress of the North-West Company of Canada, with a history of the fur trade as connected with that concern, and observations on the political importance of the company's intercourse with, and influence over the Indians or savage nations of the interior, and on the necessity of maintaining and supporting the system from which that influence arises, and by which only it can be preserved. London, Printed by Cox, Son, and Baylis, 1811. 38p. map. 25cm.

The copy in the Toronto Public Reference Library has ms. note 'By Nathaniel Atcheson' written under the title, but Wallace in 'Documents Relating to the N.W.C.' attributes it to John Henry.

The pamphlet was written to further the efforts of the N.W.C. to obtain a charter for exclusive trade on the Pacific coast. Shortt

34 **Thompson**, David
David Thompson's narrative of his explorations in western America, 1784-1812; edited by J.B. Tyrrell. Toronto, The Champlain Society, 1916. xcviii, 582p. 21 plates, 2 fold. maps. 25cm. (Champlain Soc., no.12)

Part I covers Thompson's experiences and travels in the service of the H.B.C. and N.W.C. in the country east of the Rockies between 1784 and 1807. Part II covers in detail the years 1807 to 1812. This is a general account of the great geographer's travels written about 1847, many years after he had left the West. The ms. journal was owned by the editor. Shortt

35 **LeHaiye**
[Diary of a trip from Montreal to Lake Athabasca in 1811] Paris, 1813. 142p.

A private collector of Canadiana visited my office about 1967 and described a rare volume which he said he possessed. In Paris he had picked up a French book describing a journey with the Nor'West fur brigade taken by a Frenchman in 1811. It was my intention to verify this entry some time when in my informant's city by arranging to see the book. Finally, I made enquiries and learned that the collector had died unexpectedly and his collection had been dispersed. The discovery and verification of this book remains a challenge.
Private source

36 **Henry**, Alexander, [the younger]
New light on the early history of the greater Northwest, the manuscript journals of Alexander Henry, fur trader of the Northwest Company, and of David Thompson, official geographer and explorer of the same company, 1799-1814. Exploration and adventure among the Indians on the Red, Saskatchewan, Missouri, and Columbia Rivers; edited with copious critical commentary by Elliott Coues. New York, Francis P. Harper, 1897. 3v. front. (port.) fold. maps, fold. facsim. 24cm.

Contents: v.1, The Red River of the north; v.2, The Saskatchewan and Columbia Rivers; v.3, Index and maps.

A ms. copy of Henry's day-to-day journal, made by George Coventry of Montreal about 1824, is preserved in the Library of Parliament. Coues edited this in a somewhat condensed form using collateral information from Thompson's journals. Shortt

37 **Harrison**, Mr.
Proposal of Mr. Harrison for the application of part of the funds of the New England Company within the territories of the Hudson's Bay Company. London, Printed by S. Gosnell, 1815. 15p. Lande

38 **Hudson's Bay Company**
The royal charter for incorporating the Hudson's Bay Company, granted by His Majesty King Charles the Second, in the twenty-second year of his reign, A.D. 1670. London, R. Causton and Son, 1816. 19p. 25cm.

The charter was republished in 1865 as a 24-page pamphlet. Again, after the supplemental charter of 9 September 1884 was granted, the charter with the supplemental charter was issued as a 45-page pamphlet to which no date is attached. H.B.C.

39 **McAdam**, Adam
Communications from Adam McAdam, originally published in the Montreal Herald, in reply to letters inserted therein under the signature of Archibald Macdonald, respecting Lord Selkirk's Red River colony. Montreal, W. Gray, 1816. 57p. Not seen.

W.S. Wallace in his 'Literature Relating to the Selkirk Controversy' believes that the name is a pseudonym. C.H.R., 1932.

40 **McDonald**, Archibald
Narrative respecting the destruction of the Earl of Selkirk's settlement upon Red River, in ... 1815. London, Printed by J. Brettell, 1816. 14p. 21 1/2cm. B.C. Arch.

41 **McDonald**, Archibald
Reply to the letter, lately addressed to the Earl of Selkirk, by the Hon. and Rev. John Strachan, D.D. &c. Being four letters (reprinted from the Montreal Herald), containing a statement of facts, concerning the settlement on Red River, in the district of Ossiniboia, territory of the Hudson's Bay Company, properly called Rupert's Land. Montreal, Printed by W. Gray, 1816. 50p. Not seen.

See Entry 45. C.H.R., 1932.

42 **North West Company**
The memorial of Messrs. M'Tavish, Fraser, and Co. and Messrs. Inglis, Ellice and Co. on behalf of themselves and others, carrying on trade from Montreal in Canada, to the Indian territories, under the description or firm of the North-West Company ... [London, Printed by B. M'Millan, 1816?] 49p. 25 1/2 x 20 1/2cm. At head of title: To the Right Honorable Henry, Earl Bathurst. Not seen.

'On the subject of the proceedings of the Earl of Selkirk in the Indian territories of North America and towards the North-West Company.' L.C.

43 **Selkirk**, [Thomas Douglas, 5th] earl of
Lord Selkirk and the North West Company, a review; a sketch of the British fur trade in North America. (In Quarterly Review, v.16, 1816, p.129-72) Not seen. R.E.S.

44 **Selkirk**, [Thomas Douglas, 5th] earl of
A sketch of the British fur trade in North America; with observations relative to the North-West Company of Montreal. London, Printed for J. Ridgway, 1816. 3p.l., 130p. 22cm.

A second edition was published in New York in 1818. A French translation by Hugh Heney of the latter edition was printed by James Brown of Montreal in 1819. Shortt

45 **Strachan,** John
A letter to the Right Honourable the Earl of Selkirk, on his settlement at the Red River, near Hudson's Bay. London, Longman, Hurst, Rees, Orme, & Brown, 1816. 76p. 22 1/2cm.

Bishop Strachan thought it his duty to warn the public of the misery emigrants would experience in such a 'distant and inhospitable region' as Red River. Can. Arch.

46 [**Ellice,** Edward]
The communications of 'Mercator,' upon the contest between the Earl of Selkirk and the Hudson's Bay Company on one side, and the North West Company on the other. Republished from the Montreal Herald. Montreal, W. Gray, 1817. iv, [5]-99p. 20 cm.
Continuation of The communications of 'Mercator' ... etc. Montreal, W. Gray, 1817. 12, [1]p. 20cm.

A French translation was published by C.B. Pasteur and H. Meziere. Toronto

47 [**Gale,** Samuel]
Notices on the claims of the Hudson's Bay Company and the conduct of its adversaries ... Montreal, William Gray, 1817. 161, [1]p. 21 1/2cm. Not seen. Toronto (Staton)

48 [**Halkett,** John]
Statement respecting the Earl of Selkirk's settlement of Kildonan, upon the Red River, in North America; its destruction in the years 1815 and 1816; and the massacre of Governor Semple and his party. London, J. Brettell, 1817. 125, lxxxix p. fold. map.

This edition was printed for private circulation. A new revised and enlarged edition with the added 'Observations upon a recent publication entitled "A narrative of occurrences in the Indian country"' was published the same year by John Murray, with collation: viii, 194, [2], c p. front. (fold. map.) 23cm.
A New York edition was printed in 1818 and a French edition in Montreal the same year. Rutherford (Rev. ed.)

49 [**Halkett,** John]
Postscript to the statement respecting the Earl of Selkirk's settlement upon the Red River. [Montreal, 1818] 195-222p. Not seen. C.H.R., 1932

50 [**Wilcocke,** Samuel Hull] supposed author
A narrative of occurrences in the Indian countries of North America since the connexion of the Right Hon. the Earl of Selkirk with the Hudson's Bay Company, and his attempt to establish a colony on the Red River; with a detailed account of His Lordship's military expedition to, and subsequent proceedings at Fort William, in Upper Canada. London, Printed by B. McMillan, 1817. xiv, 152p., 1 l., [2], 87p. 22 1/2cm.

This anonymous pamphlet has also been attributed to E. Ellice, the elder; also to S. McGillivray.
In Montreal the following year an English edition, printed by Nahum Mower, and a French edition by James Brown, appeared. Shortt

51 [**Wilcocke**, Samuel Hull] supposed author
Notice respecting the boundary between His Majesty's possessions in North America and the United States; with a map of America, between latitude 40° and 70° north, and long. 80° and 150° west; exhibiting the principal trading stations of the North West Company and intended to accompany the Narrative of occurrences in the Indian countries of North America, connected with the Earl of Selkirk, the Hudson's Bay, and the North West Companies. London, Printed by B. McMillan, 1817. 12p. fold. map. 26 1/2cm.

This pamphlet has also been attributed to S. McGillivray. Man. Leg.

52 [**McKenzie**, Daniel]
A letter to the Rt. Hon. the Earl of Selkirk, in answer to a pamphlet entitled 'A postscript to the statement respecting the Earl of Selkirk's settlement on the Red River in North America.' Sandwich, 1818. 8p. 23cm.

One of the rarest pamphlets in the controversy. Shortt

53 **Reinhard**, Charles de, defendant
Report of the trials of Charles de Reinhard and Archibald M'Lellan for murder at a court of oyer and terminer, held at Quebec, May 1818. From minutes taken in shorthand, under the sanction of the court. Montreal, Printed by James Lane and Nahum Mower, 1818. xxiv, 652 (i.e. 656), 52, 159p. 22cm. Edited by S.H. Wilcocke. Shortt

54 **Boucher**, François Firmin
Relation donnée par lui-même des événements qui ont eu lieu sur le territoire des sauvages depuis le mois d'octobre 1815, jusqu'au 19 juin 1816, époque de la mort de Mr. Semple, avec les details de son long emprisonnement, jusqu'à son jugement. Montréal, 1819. Not seen. C.H.R., 1932

55 [**Gale**, Samuel]
Notices on the claims of the Hudson's Bay Company: to which is added a copy of their royal charter. London, John Murray, 1819. 69p. 24cm.

Reference on page 3 to these notices forming part of the larger work published in Montreal in 1817. See Entry 47. H.B.C.

56 **Graffenried**, Friedrich von
Sechs Jahre in Canada, 1813-1819. Aus dem Tagebuche und den Reiseerinnerungen des Leutenants Friedrich von Graffenried. Bern, Haller'sche Buchdruckerei, 1891. 71p. 22 1/2cm. (Separatabdruck aus dem X. Jahresbericht der Geographischen Gesellschaft von Bern.) Not seen.

An account by an officer of the Regiment de Meuron of his journey to the Red River Settlement in 1816, and his experiences in the country. Appended is an account by a fellow officer, Fauche, of events at Fort William in Aug. 1816. Toronto (Staton)

57 **Great Britain**. Colonial Office
Papers relating to the Red River Settlement: viz. Return to an address from the Honourable House of Commons to His Royal Highness the Prince Regent dated 24th June 1819; for copies or extracts of the official communications which may have taken place between the Secretary of State and the provincial government of Upper or Lower Canada, relative to the destruction of the settlement on the Red River, to any legal proceedings thereon in the courts of Upper or Lower Canada, or to any complaints made of those proceedings by Lord Selkirk or the

agents of the Hudson's Bay or the North-West Companies; also for copies or extracts of the reports made by the commissioners of special inquiry, appointed to inquire into the offences committed in the Indian territory so far as the same can be made public without prejudice to the public service, or to judicial proceedings now pending in Canada. Ordered, by the House of Commons, to be printed, 12 July 1819. [London, 1819] 2p.l., 287p. 2 fold. maps, plan. 33cm. (Parliament, 1819, no.584) Shortt

58 **Halkett**, J[ohn]
Correspondence in the years 1817, 1818, and 1819, between Earl Bathurst and J. Halkett, Esq., on the subject of Lord Selkirk's settlement at the Red River in North America. [London, J. Brettell, 1819?] 1p.l., 180p. 23cm. Not seen. Toronto (Staton)

59 **Macdonell**, Alexander [Greenfield]
A narrative of transactions in the Red River country; from the commencement of the operations of the Earl of Selkirk, till the summer of the year 1816 ... London, Printed by B. McMillan for Egerton, 1819. xix, 85p. front. (fold. map) 21cm.

On title-page author's name appears as M'Donell. Shortt

60 **McKeevor**, Thomas
A voyage to Hudson's Bay during the summer of 1812. Containing a particular account of the icebergs and other phenomena which present themselves in those regions; also a description of the Esquimeaux and North American Indians; their manners, customs, dress, language, &c. &c. &c. London, Printed for Sir R. Phillips & Co., 1819. 2p.l., 76p. front., plates. 22 1/2cm.

Written by the medical officer to Lord Selkirk's settlers of that year. Shortt

61 **Masson**, L[ouis] [François] R[odrique]
Les bourgeois de la Compagnie du Nord-Ouest, récits de voyages, lettres et rapports inédits relatifs au Nord-Ouest canadien publiés avec une esquisse historique et des annotations. Québec, A. Coté et Cie, 1889-90. 2v. fold. map. 23cm.

Contents: v.1 [pt.1] Les bourgeois ...; [pt.2]-v.2, Récits de voyage, lettres et rapports inédits relatifs au Nord-Ouest canadien.

Partial contents of Récits de voyage ... as follows: Reminiscences of the Honorable Roderic McKenzie; W.F. Wentzel, letters to Roderic McKenzie, 1807-24; John McDonnell, some account of Red River (about 1797); Larocque's Missouri journal; Charles Mackenzie, Mississouri Indians, a narrative of four trading expeditions, 1804-6; Liste des bourgeois, commis, engagés, et voyageurs; John McDonald of Garth, autobiographical notes, 1791-1816; S.H. Wilcocke, death of Benjamin Frobisher, 1819; Peter Grant, The Saulteaux Indians. Shortt

62 **Montgomery**, Sir James, bart.
Substance of the speech of Sir James Montgomery, bart., in the House of Commons, on the 24th of June, 1819, on bringing forward his motion relative to the petition of Mr. John Pritchard, of Red River Settlement. London, Printed by J. Brettell, 1819. 53p. 23cm. Arkin

63 **Pritchard**, John
Narratives of John Pritchard, Pierre Chrysologue Pambrun, and Frederick Damien Heurter, respecting the aggressions of the North-West Company, against the Earl of Selkirk's settlement upon Red River. London, John Murray, 1819. 2p.l., 91p. 21cm. Toronto (Staton)

64 **Pritchard,** John
To the Honorable the Commons of the United Kingdom of Great Britain and Ireland, in Parliament assembled, the humble petition of John Pritchard, of the Red River Settlement in British America. [London, Printed by J. Brettell, 1819] caption-title, 7p. 33 1/2cm. H.B.C.

65 **Reinhard,** Charles de, defendant
Report at large of the trial of Charles de Reinhard, for murder (committed in the Indian territories), at a court of oyer and terminer, held at Quebec, May, 1818. To which is annexed, a summary of Archibald M'Lellan's, indicted as an accessory. By William S. Simpson, esquire. Montreal, Printed by J. Lane, for the reporter, 1819. xii, 340p. 22cm. Shortt

66 **Selkirk,** [Thomas Douglas, 5th] earl of
A letter to the Earl of Liverpool from the Earl of Selkirk, accompanied by a correspondence with the Colonial Department (in the years 1817, 1818, and 1819), on the subject of the Red River Settlement in North America. [London, 1819] 224p. 23cm. 'Printed for private distribution only.' Shortt

67 [**Wilcocke,** Samuel Hull] ed.
Report of proceedings at a court of oyer and terminer appointed for the investigation of cases from the Indian territories, held by adjournment at Quebec, in Lower Canada, 21st October, 1819, at which the following gentlemen, partners of, and connected with, the North West Company, viz. Archd. N. McLeod, James Leith, Hugh McGillis, Simon Fraser, Alexr. Macdonell, Archd. McLellan, and John Siveright, who were under accusation by the Earl of Selkirk, as private prosecutor, for great crimes and offences, alleged to have been by them committed, made their appearance, in pursuance of official notices given to both parties, and demanded their trials, which they could not obtain, because the private prosecutor was not ready: with the speeches of counsel, the arguments held on the occasion, and the decision given thereon, from minutes taken in court ... Montreal, Printed by William Gray, 1819. vi, 120p. 21cm. Not seen. Toronto (Staton)

68 [**Wilcocke,** Samuel Hull] ed.
Report of the proceedings connected with the disputes between the Earl of Selkirk and the North West Company, at the assizes, held in York in Upper Canada, October, 1818. From minutes taken in court. Montreal, Printed by James Lane and Nahum Mower, 1819. xxiii, 300, 218, 55, 4, xlviii p. 20cm. Can. Arch.

69 **Amos,** Andrew
Report of trials in the courts of Canada, relative to the destruction of the Earl of Selkirk's settlement on the Red River; with observations. London, John Murray, 1820. 2p.l., [vii]-xxx, [2], 388, iv p. front. (fold. map) 22 1/2cm.

An English barrister examines the proceedings and denounces them as without parallel in a British colony. Shortt

70 **Franchère,** G[abriel]
Relation d'un voyage à la côte du Nord-Ouest de l'Amérique septentrionale, dans les années 1810, 11, 12, 13, et 14. Montréal, C.B. Pasteur, 1820. 284p. 21 1/2cm.

The original ms., in the possession of the Toronto Reference Library, was edited by Michel Bibaud. The 1820 edition is now rare. In 1854 Franchère brought out an English edition which was translated by J.V. Huntington. This English version was also published in 1904 in Thwaites' 'Early Western Travels, 1748-1846.'

Chapters 24-26 describe the author's return journey through the prairie region on his return from Astoria. The party travelled via the Saskatchewan River. Shortt

71 **Harmon**, Daniel Williams
A journal of voyages and travels in the interiour of North America, between the 47th and 58th degrees of north latitude, extending from Montreal nearly to the Pacific Ocean, a distance of about 5000 miles, including an account of the principal occurrences, during a residence of nineteen years, in different parts of the country. To which are added, a concise description of the face of the country, its inhabitants, their manners, customs, laws, religion, etc. and considerable specimens of the two languages, most extensively spoken; together with an account of the principal animals, to be found in the forests and prairies of this extensive region. Andover, Printed by Flagg and Gould, 1820. xxiii, [25]-432p. front. (port.) fold. map. 20 1/2cm.

Harmon spent about 10 years in what is today the Prairie Provinces.

The preface is signed by the editor Daniel Haskel. The accounts following the journal were evidently written by somebody else, probably the editor under Harmon's dictation. Contains 'A general account of the Indians on the east side of the Rocky mountain'; also 'A concise account of the principal animals which are found in the north western part of North America.'

Reprinted in New York in 1903, and again in 1922. Shortt

72 **Hudson's Bay Company**
Instructions relative to the administration of justice in the colony of Rupertsland. [London, J. Brettell, 182–] caption-title, 19p. 25cm. H.B.C.

73 **Hudson's Bay Company**
An ordinance for the more effectual administration of justice in the colony of Rupertsland. [London, J. Brettell, 182–] caption-title, 80, 4, 2p. 25cm. H.B.C.

74 On the civilization of the Indians in British America. [London, Printed by J. Brettell, 182–] caption-title, 16p. 22 cm.

Ms. note: 250 copies printed.

Advocates establishing a school to educate young Indians who would then go back and instruct their people. H.B.C.

75 **Garry**, Nicholas
Diary of Nicholas Garry, deputy-governor of the Hudson's Bay Company from 1822-1835. A detailed narrative of his travels in the North-west territories of British North America in 1821 ... (In Roy. Soc. of Can., Trans., 2d ser., v.7, sect. 2, 1900, p.3-204. illus., port. 24cm.)

Garry came to Canada to cement the union of the two companies, N.W.C. and H.B.C. He reached Red River by the eastern route and returned to England via Hudson Bay. U. of S.

76 **Hudson's Bay Company**
Copy of the deed poll under the seal of the Governor and Company of Adventurers of England, trading into Hudson's Bay, bearing date the twenty-sixth day of March, 1821, stating the appropriation of the forty shares reserved by the

principal deed for chief factors and chief traders, with their duties; the regulations relating thereto, and for carrying on the trade. London, Printed by H.K. Causton, 1821. 21p., 1 l. 24 1/2cm. Not seen.

The agreement for the amalgamation of the N.W.C. and H.B.C. See Entry 97.
Toronto (Staton)

77 **Simpson,** [Sir] George
Journal of occurrences in the Athabasca department by George Simpson, 1820 and 1821, and report; edited by E.E. Rich, with a foreword by Lord Tweedsmuir, and an introduction by Chester Martin. Toronto, The Champlain Society, 1938. lix, 498, xiii p. incl. tables. front. (port.) maps in pocket. 24 1/2cm. (Champlain Soc., H.B.C. ser., no.1) Shortt

78 [**Bulger**, Andrew H.]
Papers referring to Red River Settlement, Hudson's Bay Territories. Bangalore, India, Printed at the Regimental Press, 2nd Battalion, 10th Regiment, 1866. [24]p. 28cm. Not seen.

Contents: Pembina (from Ross's 'Red River Settlement'); letter from Governor Bulger to Andrew Colville, Esq., dated 7 Dec. 1822.

Bulger was governor of the colony of Assiniboia during 1822-23. Toronto (Staton)

79 **Robertson,** Colin
Colin Robertson's correspondence book, September 1817 to September 1822; edited with an introduction by E.E. Rich, assisted by R. Harvey Fleming. Toronto, The Champlain Society, 1939. cxxxi, 372, xiii p. front. 25cm. (Champlain Soc., H.B.C. ser., no.2)

The letters cover the final period of violence before the union of the two companies.
Shortt

80 **Franklin,** [Sir] John
Narrative of a journey to the shores of the polar sea, in the years 1819, 20, 21, and 22. With an appendix on various subjects relating to science and natural history ... London, John Murray, 1823. 2p.l., [vii]-xvi, 768p. col. front., 1 illus. (plan) plates, col. ports., fold. maps. 28cm.

Some members of the party wintered at Cumberland House in 1819-20. In chapters 2-5 a description of the people and events in the Saskatchewan country is given.

Murray brought out a two-volume edition in 1824. A one-volume edition was published in Philadelphia by H.C. Carey and I. Lea. A new edition was brought out in London and New York in 1910, and a re-issue in 1924. Shortt

81 **West,** John
The substance of a journal during a residence at the Red River colony, British North America; and frequent excursions among the north-west American Indians, in the years 1820, 1821, 1822, 1823. London, Printed for L.B. Seeley and Son, 1824. xi, [1], 210, [1]p. front., plates. 22cm.

Journal of a Church of England clergyman sent to the colony by the H.B.C. He was the first Protestant clergyman in the West.

Another edition was published the same year without the illustrations. A new edition appeared in 1827, containing in addition a journal of his travels among the Indians of Eastern Canada. Shortt

82 **Keating,** William H[ypolitus]
Narrative of an expedition to the source of St. Peter's River, Lake Winnepeek, Lake of the Woods, &c., performed in the year 1823, by order of the Hon. J.C.

Calhoun, Secretary of War, under the command of Stephen H. Long, U.S.T.E. Compiled from the notes of Major Long, Messrs. Say, Keating, & Colhoun. London, Printed by Geo. B. Whittaker, 1825. 2v. front., plates (2 col., incl. music) fold. map, fold. tables. 22cm.

Half of volume II relates to the Red River Settlement and to communications with Fort William on Lake Superior.

The first edition was published in Philadelphia in 1824. A later edition, London, 1828, appeared under title: Travels in the Interior of North America. Rutherford

83 **Simpson**, [Sir] George
Fur trade and empire; George Simpson's journal; remarks connected with the fur trade in the course of a voyage from York Factory to Fort George and back to York Factory 1824-1825; together with accompanying documents; edited, with an introduction by Frederick Merk. Cambridge, Harvard University Press, 1931. xxxvi p., 2 l., 3-370p. fold. map (in pocket) 23cm. (Harvard hist. studies, v.31) Shortt

83A **Douglas**, David
Journal kept by David Douglas during his travels in North America 1823-1827, together with a particular description of thirty-three species of American oaks and eighteen species of pinus; with appendices containing a list of the plants introduced by Douglas and an account of his death in 1834. Published under the direction of the Royal Horticultural Society. New York, Antiquarian Press Ltd., 1959. 3p. l., 364p. front. (port.) 24cm.

First published in 1914.

Journey overland from Fort Vancouver to Fort Garry and York Factory, 20 March–28 August 1827, p.242-93. U. of A.

84 **McGillivray**, Simon
Letter from Simon McGillivray, Esq., to the creditors of the firms of McTavish, McGillivrays & Co. and McGillivrays, Thain & Co., of Montreal, in the province of Lower Canada; dated London, 26th of February, 1827. London, 1827. 26p. 31 1/2 x 24cm.

Reprinted in W.S. Wallace's 'Documents Relating to the N.W.C.' Lande

85 **Mackenzie**, Henry
Letter to Simon M'Gillivray, Esq., in answer to one addressed by him to the creditors of the late firms of M'Tavish, M'Gillivrays & Co. and M'Gillivrays, Thain & Co. dated London, 26th of February, 1826 [sic]. Montreal, Printed at the Herald office, 1827. 1p.l., 24p. 23cm. Not seen.

Reprinted in W.S. Wallace's 'Documents Relating to the N.W.C.' Toronto (Staton)

86 **Nute**, Grace Lee, ed.
Documents relating to Northwest missions, 1815-1827. Saint Paul, Published for the Clarence Walworth Alvord Memorial Commission by the Minnesota Historical Society, 1942. xix, 469p. 23 1/2cm.

Early Catholic missionary endeavours at Red River and in the surrounding territory. Includes French and Latin documents, each followed by an English translation. U. of A.

87 **Wallace**, W[illiam] Stewart, ed.
Documents relating to the North West Company, edited with introduction, notes, and appendices. Toronto, The Champlain Society, 1934. xv, 527, xii p. front., ports. 25cm. (Champlain Soc., no.22)

Includes a biographical dictionary of the Nor'westers. Shortt

88 **Franklin,** [Sir] John
Narrative of a second expedition to the shores of the polar sea, in the years 1825, 1826, and 1827. Including an account of the progress of a detachment to the eastward, by John Richardson ... London, John Murray, 1828. xxiv, [xxi]-xxiv, 320, clvii p., 1 l. front., illus. (incl. plan) plates, fold. maps. 28 cm.

The expedition travelled from Fort William to the Mackenzie River valley on the journey to the Arctic coast and back.

Also published in Philadelphia by H.C. Carey and I. Lea. Murray brought out another edition the same year under the title 'Journey to the Shores of the Polar Sea.'
Rutherford

89 **Ermatinger,** Edward
Edward Ermatinger's York Factory express journal, being a record of journeys made between Fort Vancouver and Hudson Bay in the years 1827-1828. With introduction by Judge C.O. Ermatinger and notes by Judge C.O. Ermatinger and James White. (In Roy. Soc. of Can., Trans., 3d ser., v.6, sect. 2, 1912, p.67-132. port., fold. map. 24cm.)

The party travelled along the Saskatchewan and Hayes rivers. The journal is largely confined to weather, travel time, and freight list. The diary of George T. Allan, who accompanied Ermatinger over the same route, was published in Oregon Pioneer Assoc Trans., 9th Annual Reunion, 1881. (See Wagner, 3d ed.) U. of S.

90 **McDonald,** Archibald
Peace River. A canoe voyage from Hudson's Bay to Pacific, by the late Sir George Simpson (governor, Hon. Hudson's Bay Company), in 1828. Journal of the late chief factor, Archibald McDonald (Hon. Hudson's Bay Company), who accompanied him. Edited with notes, by Malcolm McLeod. Ottawa, J. Durie & Son, 1872. xix, 119p. fold. map. 22cm.

The editor's object in publishing the journal was to draw attention to the potentialities of the Peace River country, and the suitability of the Peace River Pass for the proposed Canadian Pacific Railway. Shortt

91 **Richardson,** [Sir] John
Fauna boreali-americana; or, The zoology of the northern parts of British America: containing descriptions of the objects of natural history collected on the late northern land expeditions under command of Captain Sir John Franklin, R.N. By John Richardson, assisted by William Swainson, and the Rev. William Kirby. London, John Murray, 1829. 4 pts. in 3v. illus., plates (part. col.) 26 1/2cm.

Contents: pt.1, Mammalia; pt.2, Birds; pt.3, Fishes; pt.4, Insects.

In the introduction Richardson states that he had spent seven summers and five winters in the country. The description of the animals are largely from Thos. Drummond, many of whose experiences are related in describing them. (v.1 only in Shortt) Toronto (Staton)

92 **Tanner,** John
A narrative of the captivity and adventures of John Tanner (U.S. interpreter at the Saut de Ste. Marie), during thirty years residence among the Indians in the interior of North America. Prepared for the press by Edwin James. London, Baldwin & Cradock, 1830. 426p. front. (port.) illus. 22 1/2cm.

Tanner spent part of his life in the Red River country and along the Assiniboine. Contains much information on the H.B.C., N.W.C., and Selkirk Settlement. Coues, by checking Tanner against Henry's journal, has been able to supply dates lacking in the narrative.

Part II, evidently prepared by the editor, contains information on Indian ways, languages, plants, and animals.

A French edition translated by Vicomte de Blosseville was published in Paris in 1835, and a German edition translated by K.T. Andree was published in Leipzig in 1840. Shortt

93 **Tanner**, John
Grey Hawk; life and adventure among the Red Indians. An old story retold by James Macaulay. London, Hodder & Stoughton, 1883. xv, 341p. front., illus., plates. 19 1/2cm. Not seen.

Editor Macaulay abridged and somewhat altered the Edwin James version. L.C.

94 **Belcourt**, G[eorges] A[ntoine]
Mon itinéraire du Lac des Deux-Montagnes à la Rivière-Rouge ... Montréal, Arbour & Dupont [1913] 57p. 22 1/2cm. (Soc. Hist. de St-Boniface, no.4) Reprinted from the Revue Canadienne.

A journey made in the company of Mgr Provencher in 1831. Shortt

95 **Cox**, Ross
Adventures on the Columbia River, including the narrative of a residence of six years on the western side of the Rocky Mountains, among various tribes of Indians hitherto unknown; together with a journey across the American continent. London, H. Colburn and R. Bentley, 1831. 2v. 22cm.

Cox left Oregon for the East in April 1817. Chapters 10-13 cover the journey from the mountains to Lake Superior. The book contains a description of the rivalry between the fur companies.

In London a third edition appeared in 1832, while in New York in the same year a one-volume edition was published. Rutherford

96 **Rupert's Land**. Northern Department. Council
Minutes of the Council, Northern Department of Rupert's Land, 1821-31; edited by R. Harvey Fleming; with an introduction by H.A. Innis. Toronto, The Champlain Society, 1940. lxxxii, 480, xiii p. front. (ports.) 24 1/2cm. (Champlain Soc., H.B.C. ser., no.3) Shortt

97 **Hudson's Bay Company**
Deed poll, by the Governor and Company of the Hudson's Bay, with respect to their chief factors and chief traders, for conducting their trade in Rupert's Land and North America: and for ascertaining the rights and prescribing the duties of those officers. London, Printed by H.K. Causton, 1834. 17p. 25cm.

Revised edition of original deed poll of 1821. See other editions. Glenbow

98 **King**, Richard
Narrative of a journey to the shores of the Arctic Ocean in 1833, 1834 and 1835; under the command of Capt. Back, R.N. London, Richard Bentley, 1836. 2v. fronts., plate, map. 23 1/2cm.

King was surgeon and naturalist of the expedition, which followed the trade route from Eastern Canada to Athabasca, and departed from York Factory. Chapters 2-4 and 18-19 relate to the prairie region. Shortt

99 **Provencher**, J[oseph] N[orbert]
Mémoire ou notice sur l'établissement de la mission de la Rivière-Rouge, et ses progrès depuis 1818, présenté à la Propagande, le 12 mars 1836. [Rome, 1836] caption-title, 11p. 29cm. Not seen.

The early years of the Catholic Church in the West, described by the first bishop of St. Boniface. Toronto (Staton)

100 [**Belcourt**, Georges Antoine]
Principes de la langue des sauvages appelés Sauteux. Québec, Fréchette et Cie, 1839. iv p., 1 l., 146p. p.133-42 fold. 17 1/2cm. Toronto (Staton)

100A **Hooker**, Sir William Jackson
Flora Boreali-Americana; or, The botany of the northern parts of North America: compiled principally from the plants collected by Dr Richardson & Mr Drummond on the late northern expeditions, under command of Captain Sir John Franklin, R.N. to which are added (By permission of the Horticultural Society of London) those of Mr Douglas, from North-West America, and of other naturalists. Published under the authority of the Right Honourable the Secretary of State for colonial affairs. London, Henry G. Bohn, 1840. 2v. illus., fold. map. 24 1/2cm.

Reprinted in 1960. U. of A. (Reprint)

101 **Wesleyan Methodist Church**
The Red men of the West; or, The North American Indians. London, J. Mason [184-?] 16p. illus. 16cm. ([Wesleyan Methodist Church?] Missionary series no.644)

Includes letters from James Evans and Robert Rundle. Glenbow

102 **Evans**, James
[Cree syllabic hymnary. Norway House, 1841] 16p. Not seen.

This was the first book printed in Western Canada, but no copies are extant. The missionary had invented a system of writing for the Cree nation. To produce books for the Indians to read, Evans made letter moulds from oak, type metal from the lead of bullets and tea-chest lining, and ink from chimney soot.

103 [**Evans**, James] tr.
[Hymns; the Swampies; their language. Jack River, 1841] 20p. 12 1/2cm.

Text in Cree syllabic characters. Bound in an elkskin wrapper, with a syllabary on front and back covers, with each sign repeated.

Published at Rossville Mission, near Norway House. Republished in the Facsimile Series of the Bibliographical Society of Canada in 1954.

For a listing of the imprints of the Rossville Mission press see Peel, Bruce. 'Rossville Mission press: press, prints and translators.' Papers of the Bibliographical Society of Canada, v.1, 1962, p.28-43. See also his 'Frustrations of the missionary-printer of Rossville: Reverend William Mason' in the Bulletin of the Committee on Archives of the United Church of Canada, No.18, 1965, p.20-25. Ayer

104 **Great Britain**. Colonial Office
Hudson's Bay Company ... Copy of the existing charter or grant by the Crown to the Hudson's Bay Company; together with copies or extracts of the correspondence which took place at the last renewal of the charter between the Government and the company, or of individuals on behalf of the company; also, the dates of all former charters or grants to that company. Colonial Office, 25 July, 1842. G.W. Hope. (Mr. Hume.) Ordered, by the House of Commons, to be printed, 8 August, 1842. [London, 1842] 32, [1]p. 32 1/2cm. (Parliament, 1842, no.547) Toronto (Staton)

105 [**Dumoulin**, Joseph Nicolas Sévère]
Notice sur la Rivière Rouge dans le territoire de la Baie-d'Hudson. Montréal, Bureau des Mélanges Religieux, 1843. 32p. Not seen.

Reprint of a pamphlet published in 1824, at Saint Pierre, Rivière-du-Sud (see Morice's 'Dictionnaire'). A reply to critics in Quebec who regarded as premature the consecration of Provencher, the head of an isolated mission, as a bishop and coadjutor to the Bishop of Quebec for the North West. Wagner

106 [**Hargrave**, James]
The Hargrave correspondence, 1821-1843; edited with introduction and notes by G.P. de T. Glazebrook. Toronto, The Champlain Society, 1938. 3p.l., v-xxvi, 472, xii p. front., plates, fold. map (in pocket) 25cm. (Champlain Soc., no.24)

A collection of letters from H.B.C. men, written from all parts of the company's territory, and mostly addressed to Hargrave, stationed at York Factory. Shortt

107 **Rupert's Land**. Northern Department. Council
The minutes of the Council of the Northern Department of Rupert's Land, 1830 to 1843, being the transaction and enactment of the rulers of the country during the period, with accompanying documents. [Introduction by] Isaac Cowie. [State Historical Society of North Dakota, 1913?] cover-title, 644-865p. 23cm. Reprinted from the Collections of the State Hist. Soc. of North Dakota. Shortt

108 **Simpson**, Thomas
Narrative of the discoveries on the north coast of America; effected by the officers of the Hudson's Bay Company during the years 1836-39. London, Richard Bentley, 1843. xix, 419p. fold. maps. 21 1/2cm.

Chapter 1 contains a description of the plains Indians. Chapter 2 describes an overland journey in winter from Red River to Athabasca, and chapter 16 describes his return journey to the settlement. Shortt

109 **Howse**, Joseph
Grammar of the Cree language, with which is combined an analysis of the Chippeway dialect. London, J.G.F. & J. Rivington, 1844. xix, 324p. front. (port.) 22cm.

Copy in Rutherford Library interleaved, with ms. notes on the blank leaves; grammatical phrases transliterated into Cree syllabic written in the margins throughout the volume; signature of William Mason on the title-page, and at the beginning of the introduction. Rev. Wm. Mason was one of the translators of the Bible into Cree (see note in Entry 227). Another link between Howse's grammar and the missionary translators at Rossville is a letter by Rev. James Evans, quoted in the preface, commending the grammar.

Reprinted in London by Trubner in 1865. Rutherford

110 **Lefroy**, Sir John Henry
Diary of a magnetic survey of a portion of the Dominion of Canada, chiefly in the North West Territories, executed in the years 1842-44. London, 1883. xxiv, 192p. maps. 25 1/2cm. Not seen.

Lefroy's 'Autobiography,' printed 'for private circulation only,' was published by his widow in 1895. Of this rare volume that portion which relates to the magnetic survey journey was published under the title 'Sir Henry Lefroy's Journey to the North-West in 1843-4' in the Roy. Soc. of Can., Trans., 3d ser., v.32, sect. 2, 1938, p.67-96. It was edited by W.S. Wallace. Br. Mus. D.N.B.

111 **Lefroy**, Sir John Henry
In search of the magnetic North; a soldier-surveyor's letters from the North-West, 1843-44. Edited by George F.G. Stanley. Toronto, Macmillan, 1955. xxviii, 171p. illus., port., map (on lining paper) 23cm. (Pioneer books) U. of A.

112 [**Mountain**, George Jehoshaphat]
The journal of the Bishop of Montreal, during a visit to the Church Missionary Society's north-west America mission. To which is added, by the secretaries, an appendix, giving an account of the formation of the mission, and its progress to the present time. London, Seeley, Burnside, and Seeley, [etc.] 1845. vii, [1], 236p. front., plates, double map. 17 1/2cm.

In 1849 through Bishop Mountain's efforts Rupert's Land was created an episcopal see of the Church of England. The appendix was also published separately. See Entry 126.
Shortt

113 **Simpson**, Alexander
The life and travels of Thomas Simpson ... London, R. Bentley, 1845. viii, 424p. front. (port.) fold. map. 21 1/2cm.

Contains information on the unsolved mystery of Thos. Simpson's death. Shortt

114 **Isbister**, A[lexander] K[ennedy]
A few words on the Hudson's Bay Company, with a statement of the grievances of the natives and half-caste Indians, addressed to the British Government through their delegates now in London. London, C. Gilpin [1847?] cover-title, 24p. 20 1/2cm. Hudson's Bay House

115 **Simpson**, Sir George
Narrative of a journey round the world, during the years 1841 and 1842. London, H. Colburn, 1847. 2v. front. (port.) fold. map. 24cm.

According to Gagnon this work was prepared by Adam Thom from Simpson's notes. The first three chapters relate to Simpson's journey on horseback across the prairies via Fort Carlton and Fort Edmonton.

The American edition, published by Lea & Blanchard of Philadelphia, had the title 'An Overland Journey round the World.' Shortt

116 **Smet**, Pierre Jean de
Oregon missions and travels over the Rocky Mountains, in 1845-46. New York, Edward Dunigan, 1847. 2p.l., [xi]-xii, 13-408p. col. plates, map.

This Catholic missionary visited what is now Alberta.

Another edition with new material, plates, and maps was published in French by Schelden in Ghent in 1848. (This edition is in Rutherford.) Still another edition was published in Paris by Poussielgue-Rusand in the same year. Wagner

117 **Sondermann**, Johann Samuel
Die Mission der Kirchlichen Missions-gesellschaft in England unter den heidnischen Indianern des nordwestlichen America. Ein Beitrag zur neuesten evangelischen Missionsgeschichte ... Nüremburg, F. Korn, 1847. xii, 139, [1]p. front. 21 1/2cm. Yale

118 **Wesleyan Methodist Church**. Liturgy and ritual. Cree
The Sunday service of the Wesleyan Methodists. Translated by John E. Harriott, Esq. ... Rossville, Mission Press, 1847. 17p. 17 1/2cm.

Title vignette: illus. of Rossville Church. Text in Cree syllabic characters. On the leaf before the t.p. inscribed ms.: 'Norway House, Prince Rupert's Land, 18 June 1847.'

For a reference to Harriott giving assistance in translating to Rev. Robt. Rundle see J.E.A. Macleod's 'John Edward Harriott' in Alberta Historical Review, v.6, no.2, Spring, 1958, p.14. Americas

119 **Ballantyne,** Robert M[ichael]
Hudson's Bay; or, Every-day life in the wilds of North America, during six years residence in the territories of the Honourable Hudson's Bay Company. 2d ed. Edinburgh, William Blackwood and Sons, 1848. xii p., 1 l., 328p. front., illus., plates. 20cm.

Based on a rough diary kept by the author.
The first edition was published in 1848; third and fourth editions were published in both London and New York by T. Nelson in 1859 and 1879. An edition was published in Boston by Phillips, Sampson Co. in 1859. Reissued by Nelson in 1904, and in print as late as 1928. Shortt

120 The Red-River settlement, and the Hudson's Bay Company. (In The Colonial Intelligencer; or, Aborigines Friend. London, July-August, 1848. Nos. III & IV. New series. p.35-47) H.B.C.

121 [**Smithurst,** John]
[English-Cree-Ojibway word book. Rossville, Mission Press, 1848] Not seen.

'Its object is to aid the Indians in acquiring the English language.'
'It was my intention to have sent to England this summer a small book to be printed for the use of our schools. Mr. Mason, the Wesleyan missionary at Norway House, has undertaken to get it printed for me on their press, so that a whole year will be saved.' C.M.S.

122 **Synge,** Millington Henry
Canada in 1848. Being an examination of the existing resources of British North America; with considerations for their further and more perfect development as a practical remedy, by means of colonisation, for the prevailing distress in the united empire, and for the defence of the colony. London, Effingham Wilson [1848?] 32, vii, [1]p. 21 cm.

Advocated a railway to protect what was left of Oregon territory, and to defend the long international boundary. A similar plan for opening up the West was apparently voiced as early as 1833 by Sir R. Broun in his 'A Line of Direct Elemental Intercourse between Europe and Asia by Route of British North American Possessions, and the Systematic Colonization of the Vacant Crown Territories over which it will pass.' Toronto

123 **Thom,** Adam
A charge delivered to the Grand Jury of Assiniboia, 20th February, 1845. London, Printed by E. Couchman, 1848. 44p. 21 1/2cm. Glenbow

124 **Thom,** Adam
A few remarks on a pamphlet entitled 'A few words on the Hudson's Bay Company,' in a letter to Alexander Christie, Esq., Governor of Assiniboia. London, Printed by E. Couchman, 1848. 21, [1]p. 21 1/2cm. Yale

125 **Warre,** [Sir] H[enry James]
Sketches in North America and the Oregon Territory. [London] Dickinson & Co. [1848] 2p.l., 5p. 16 col. plates (20 illus.) map. 53 1/2cm.

Warre, accompanied by Lieut. Vavassour, crossed the continent via the North Sask. River in 1845, and returned the following year. A few of the sketches are of the prairie region. Shortt

126 **Church Missionary Society**
An historical notice of the formation of the Church Missionary Society's north-west America mission, and its progress to August, 1848. London, Seeleys [1849] 4p.l., 81, [1]p. 17 1/2cm.

First published as an appendix to the Bishop of Montreal's journal of a visit to the North-West. See Entry 112. L.C.

127 **Fitzgerald**, James Edward
An examination of the charter and proceedings of the Hudson's Bay Company, with reference to the grant of Vancouver's Island ... London, Trelawney Saunders, 1849. xv, 293p. incl. front. (fold. map) 18cm. Shortt

128 **Great Britain.** Colonial Office
Hudson's Bay Company. (Red River Settlement.) Return to an address ... dated 9 February 1849. Copies of any memorials presented to the Colonial Office by inhabitants of the Red River Settlement, complaining of the government of the Hudson's Bay Company; of the instructions given to the Governor-General of Canada, for the investigation of those complaints; of the reports of the officers appointed by Lord Elgin, or by the Colonial Office, for the purpose of such investigation; and of any correspondence which has passed between the Colonial Office and the Hudson's Bay Company, and the inhabitants of the Red River Settlement respectively, upon the subject of the above memorial. Colonial Office, 20 April 1849. B. Hawes. (Earl of Lincoln.) Ordered, by the House of Commons, to be printed, 23 April 1849. [London, 1849] iv, 115p. 33cm. ([Parliament, 1849. H. of C. Reports and papers] 227)

As it became possible to trade with American settlements to the south, dissatisfaction with the monopoly increased at Red River. In 1847 a petition to Queen Victoria was drafted and sent to England, where A.K. Isbister forwarded it to the Colonial Secretary. This paper contains evidence, etc., compiled by Isbister. Shortt

129 **McLean**, John
Notes of a twenty-five years' service in the Hudson's Bay Territory. London, R. Bentley, 1849. 2v. in 1. 19 1/2cm.

Contains little information on the prairie region as the author spent most of his service on the Pacific slope and in Labrador, but is an authentic record of the H.B.C. activities.
Reprinted in 1932 by the Champlain Society with notes by W.S. Wallace. Shortt

130 **Martin**, R[obert] M[ontgomery]
The Hudson's Bay Territories and Vancouver's Island, with an exposition of the chartered rights, conduct, and policy of the Honble Hudson's Bay corporation. London, T. & W. Boone, 1849. vii, [1], 175p. front. (fold. map) illus. 22cm.

Written in support of the company's policy. Shortt

131 **Smyth**, Robert [Stewart] Carmichael
The employment of the people and the capital of Great Britain in her own colonies, at the same time assisting emigration and penal arrangements by undertaking a great national work; and thus opening the shortest road to the most extensive regions of wealth ever before at the command of any nation in the world (not regions of gold, but for commerce and industry), so that at no future period (within at least the imagination of man) will Great Britain have to complain either of too great a population on her soil, or too small a market for her labour. All this fully explained in a letter from Major Robert Carmichael-Smyth to his friend the author of 'The Clockmaker,' containing thoughts on the subject of a British colonial railway communication between the Atlantic and the Pacific, from the magnificent harbour of Halifax, in Nova Scotia (north-eastern America), to the mouth of the Frazer's River, in New Caledonia (north-western America), or such other port as may be determined upon ... London, W.P. Metchim, 1849.

viii, 68p. front. (fold. map) 21 1/2cm. Title on two leaves; second leaf begins: A letter ...

The Glenbow Library has a copy of 'The Employment ...' with collation: 75p.
Also issued the same year under title 'A Letter to the Author of the Clockmaker,' and without the author's name. Collation: 59p. Shortt

132 **Great Britain.** Colonial Office
Hudson's Bay Company. Papers presented by command of Her Majesty to the House of Commons, in pursuance of an address praying that Her Majesty would be graciously pleased to direct that such means as to Her Majesty shall seem most fitting and effectual, be taken to ascertain the legality of the powers in respect to territory, trade, taxation and government, which are, or recently have been claimed or exercised by the Hudson's Bay Company, on the continent of North America, under the charter of His Majesty, King Charles the Second, issued in the year 1670, or in virtue of any other right or title, except those conveyed by or under the Act 43 Geo. 3, c.138 (extending the criminal jurisdiction of Canadian courts) and 1 & 2 Geo. 4, c.66; intituled, 'An act for regulating the fur trade, and establishing a criminal and civil jurisdiction within certain parts of North America.' Colonial Office, 11 July 1850. B. Hawes. Ordered, by the House of Commons, to be printed, 12 July, 1850. [London, 1850] 15p. fold. map. 33cm. ([Parliament, 1850. H. of C. Reports and papers] 542)
Shortt

133 **Isbister,** Alexander K[ennedy]
A proposal for a new penal settlement, in connection with the colonization of the unhabited districts of British North America. London, Trelawney Saunders, 1850. 2p.l., 22p. 22cm.

With former penal colonies, such as New South Wales, reluctant to receive more convicts, the author asks what is to be done with 6,000 persons annually convicted in Britain, and suggests that Rupert's Land would make as satisfactory a penal colony as Russia's Siberia.
Shortt

134 **Smyth,** Robert [Stewart] Carmichael
A letter to the Right Honourable Earl Grey on the subjects of transportation and emigration as connected with an imperial railway communication between the Atlantic and the Pacific. London, W.P. Metchim, 1850. 27p. 21cm.
Can. Arch.

135 **United States.** War Department
Pembina Settlement. Letter from the Secretary of War, transmitting report of Major Wood, relative to his expedition to Pembina Settlement, and the condition of affairs on the north-western frontier of the Territory of Minnesota. [Washington, 1850] caption-title, 55p. 24cm. (House of Reps, 31st Congress, 1st Sess. Ex. Doc. No.51) L.C.

136 **Wilson,** F.A.
Britain redeemed and Canada preserved. By F.A. Wilson and Alfred B. Richards. London, Longman, Brown, Green, and Longmans, 1850. xxx p., 1 l., 556p. plates (1 fold.) fold. map. 22 1/2cm.

The plan included the building of a transcontinental railway by a grandiose scheme utilizing convict labour in spaced prison camps along the line of construction. Shortt

137 **Anderson**, David
A charge delivered to the clergy of the Diocese of Rupert's Land at his primary visitation. London, T. Hatchard, 1851. 48p. 21cm. Man. Leg.

138 **Anderson**, David
Seal of apostleship, an ordination sermon, preached at St. Andrew's Church, Red River, on Sunday, December 22, 1850. London, T. Hatchard, 1851. 31p. 21cm. Man. Leg.

139 **Bible**. New Testament. St. John. Cree
[The Gospel according to St. John, in the Cree language of Hudson Bay. Translated by Rev. William Mason. Rossville, Mission press, 1851] [54] 1. 20 1/2cm.

No title-page; text in Cree syllabic.
Pilling lists another roughly printed edition dated 1856, and still another edition with the colophon, Rossville Mission press, 1857; this edition runs to 75 pages. The B.C. Archives has a 52-page edition to which the date 1857 has been assigned. Newberry

140 **Doull**, Alexander
Employment and colonization for the million, based upon a proposed railway communication with the Atlantic to the Pacific in the territories of B.N.A. ... read before the British Association for the Advancement of Science at Ipswich, on the 7th July, 1851. London, Canada Land and Railway Association, 1851. 15p. Not seen.

A copy listed in the Nova Scotia Archives. Canada. Bureau of Statistics

141 **Laflèche**, [Louis François] Richer
Lettre de M. Richer Laflèche, missionnaire, à un de ses amis. Saint François de la Prairie du Cheval-Blanc, le 4 septembre 1851.
(In Rapport sur les missions du Diocese de Québec, mars 1853, no.10, p.44-70) Not seen.

An entertaining account of an excursion which Father Laflèche made in the summer of 1851 with the half-breeds on their annual buffalo hunt. Wagner

142 **MacDonell**, Allan
A railroad from Lake Superior to the Pacific: the shortest, cheapest and safest communication for Europe with all Asia. Toronto, 1851. 16p. 20 1/2cm. Not seen. Queen's

143 **Richardson**, Sir John
Arctic searching expedition: a journal of a boat-voyage through Rupert's Land and the Arctic Sea, in search of the discovery ships under command of Sir John Franklin. With an appendix on the physical geography of North America. London, Longman, Brown, Green, Longmans, 1851. 2v. col. fronts., illus., col. plates, col. port., fold. map. 22 1/2cm.

Dr. Rae and Sir John Richardson made the journey in 1848-49, crossing the Hudson's Bay Territory to Athabasca and Great Slave lakes. Shortt

144 **Tucker**, S[arah]
The rainbow in the north; a short account of the first establishment of Christianity in Rupert's Land by the Church Missionary Society. London, J. Nisbet and Co., 1851. 4p.l., [vii]-viii, 216p. incl. plates, fold. map. 18cm.

At least two more London editions and one New York edition were published. Shortt

145 [**Anderson**, David]
Notes on the flood at the Red River, 1852. By the Bishop of Rupert's Land. London, Hatchard [1852] 2p.l., 124p. front. 17 1/2cm.

In diary form, the notes cover the period 25 April–12 June.
A second edition by the same publisher appeared in 1873. Shortt

146 **Doull**, Alexander
Project for opening a north-west passage between the Atlantic and Pacific oceans by means of a railway in British territory. Also, outlines of a plan proposed by the Canadian Land and Railway system of employment & colonization in connexion with the railways of British North America. London, Canadian Land & Railway Association, 1852. 32p. 21 1/2cm. B.C. Arch.

147 **Hargrave**, Letitia (Mactavish)
The letters of Letitia Hargrave; edited with introduction and notes by Margaret Arnett Macleod. Toronto, Champlain Society, 1947. cliv, 310, xv p. plates, ports., map. 25cm. (Champlain Soc., no.28)

Gossip of the fur-trade as collected at York Factory: letters cover the period 1838-52. Shortt

148 [**Hunter**, Jean (Ross)] tr.
[A collection of 96 hymns in Cree, by Mrs. Jane Hunter. Rossville, Mission Press, 1852?] [172]p. 13cm.

Bound in a soft gray leather, probably deerskin. '11 sheets of 8 leaves each, without the page or pagination. This book is not listed by Pilling. Its contents agree very nearly with those of "A Cree hymn book of the Wesleyan Missionary Society, etc." described by him on p.248 of his bibliography.' The number of the hymn and the verse is indicated in Arabic numerals. See Entry 248. Br. Mus.

149 Project for the construction of a railroad to the Pacific, through British territories, with Report of the Committee of the Legislative Assembly of Canada, thereupon, 30th August, 1851; to whom was referred after its 2nd reading on the 2nd day of July, 1851, the Bill, authorising the incorporation of a company with power to construct such road. Toronto, Printed by Lovell and Gibson, 1852. 36p. 18 1/2cm.

Contents: Eighth report of standing committee on railways and telegraph, p.3-4; Observations upon the construction of a railroad from Lake Superior to the Pacific, by Allan McDonell, p.5-36.
Published also in Canada. Leg. Assembly. Journals, 1851, appendix UU.
Toronto (Staton)

150 **Provencher**, Joseph Norbert
Lettres de Monseigneur Joseph-Norrert [sic] Provencher, premier évêque de Saint-Boniface. Saint-Boniface, Imprimerie du Manitoba [1913] 286p. 21cm. (Soc. Hist. de St-Boniface, no.3)

The letters cover the period 1818-52. Shortt

151 **Synge**, Millington Henry
Great Britain one empire. On the union of the dominions of Great Britain by inter-communication with the Pacific and the East via British North America, with suggestions for the profitable colonization of that wealthy territory. London, John W. Parker & Son, 1852. vi p., 1 l., [v]-xxv, [27]-124p. fold. map. 19 1/2cm. Shortt

152 [**Synge**, Millington Henry]
Proposal for a rapid communication with the Pacific and the East via British North America. [n.p., 185-] half-title, 28p. fold. map. 22cm.

The author's proposal was that obstructions such as rapids on the waterways across Canada be removed or lessened. H.B.C.

153 **Bible**. New Testament. St. Matthew. Cree
Oo meyoo ahchemowin S. Matthew. London, Church Missionary House, 1853. 148p. 18cm. Not seen.

Text in Roman characters; translated by Rev. J. Hunter.
A second edition was printed by the British and Foreign Bible Soc. in 1877. 136p. Newberry

154 **Bond**, J[ohn] Wesley
Minnesota and its resources, to which are appended camp-fire sketches; or, Notes of a trip from St. Paul to Pembina and Selkirk Settlement on the Red River of the north. New York, Redfield, 1853. 364, 3p. front., fold. map. 18 1/2cm.

P. [335]-358 is Appendix: Prince Rupert's Land - The Hudson Bay and Northwest Company - The Esquimaux, Montagnes, Crees, Saulteaux, Sioux, Assiniboine, etc. [By Rev. G.A. Belcourt, translated from the French by Mrs. Letitia May]
Another edition was published in 1856 by Kien & Lee of Chicago and C. Desilver of Philadelphia. Shortt

155 **Jacobs**, Peter
Journal of the Reverend Peter Jacobs, Indian Wesleyan missionary, from Rice Lake to the Hudson's Bay Territory; and returning. Commencing May, 1852: with a brief account of his life; and a short history of the Wesleyan mission to that country. Toronto, Anson Green, 1853. iv, [5]-32p., 1 l. front., port. 25cm.

The journey took him to Fort Garry and York Factory.
A Boston edition of 55 pages was published the same year. The author brought out new editions in New York in 1855, 1857 and 1858. Toronto (Staton)

156 [**Tytler**, Patrick Fraser]
The northern coasts of America, and the Hudson's Bay Territories. A narrative of discovery and adventure. London and Edinburgh, T. Nelson and Sons, 1853. 2p.l., [iii]-vi, 409p. front., plates, port., fold. map. 19cm.

Chapters 1-4 (p.[1]-255) are a reprint of the corresponding chapters of P.F. Tytler's 'Historical View of the Progress of Discovery on the More Northern Coasts of America.' The remaining chapters were written by R.M. Ballantyne. Shortt

157 **Anderson**, David
A charge delivered to the clergy of the Diocese of Rupert's Land, at his triennial visitation, in July and December, 1853. London, Thomas Hatchard, 1854. 2p.l., 59, [1]p. 21cm. Man. Leg.

158 **Anderson**, David
Children instead of fathers; a Christmas ordination sermon, preached at St. John's Church, Red River, on Sunday, December 25, 1853. London, Thomas Hatchard, 1854. 32p. 21cm. Man. Leg.

159 **Bible.** New Testament. St. Mark. Cree
... The Gospel according to St. Mark; translated into the language of the Cree Indians, of the Diocese of Rupert's Land, north-west America. London, British & Foreign Bible Society, 1855. 87p. 16 1/2cm. Not seen.

Text in Roman characters; translated by Rev. J. Hunter.
A new edition was published in 1876. Newberry

160 **Bible.** New Testament. St. John. Cree
... The Gospel according to St. John; translated into the language of the Cree Indians, of the Diocese of Rupert's Land, north-west America. London, British & Foreign Bible Society, 1855. 108p. 16 1/2cm. Not seen.

Text in Roman characters; translated by Rev. J. Hunter.
A second edition was published in 1876; with it was bound the first epistle general of John translated by Mrs. Hunter. Newberry

161 **Bible.** New Testament. St. John, First epistle general. Cree
... The first epistle general of St. John; translated into the language of the Cree Indians, of the Diocese of Rupert's Land, north-west America, by Mrs. Hunter. London, British & Foreign Bible Society, 1855. 18p. Not seen.

Text in Roman characters. Pilling

162 **Church of England.** Book of Common Prayer. Cree
Ayumehawe mussinahikun. The Book of Common Prayer and administration of the sacraments and other rites and ceremonies of the church according to the use of the united church of England and Ireland. Translated into the language of the Cree Indians of the Diocese of Rupert's Land. [London] Printed for the Society for Promoting Christian Knowledge, 1855. iv, 274p. 18 1/2cm.

Printed in Roman characters; translated by the Rev. J. Hunter.
The following year the translator published 'Portions of the Book of Common Prayer' in Cree syllabic. In 1859 a new edition of the 'Book of Common Prayer' was published in which the Rev. W. Mason changed Hunter's translation into Cree syllabic. See Pilling. Man. Leg.

163 [**Hunter,** James] tr.
Oo tapwātumoowin mena oo tipetotumoowin ootayumehaw. The faith and duty of a Christian, translated into the language of the Cree Indians, of the Diocese of Rupert's Land, north-west America. [London] Society for Promoting Christian Knowledge, 1855. vi, [5]-54p. 17 1/2cm. Not seen.

Text in Roman characters. Remarks signed: J.H.
An edition in Cree syllabic was printed about 1858. A second edition in Roman characters was published in 1876. L.C.

164 **Ross,** Alexander
The fur hunters in the far west; a narrative of adventures in the Oregon and Rocky Mountains. London, Smith, Elder & Co., 1855. 2v. fronts., fold. map. 19 1/2cm.

Ross left Oregon in 1825 to settle in the Red River Settlement. The last two chapters, some 80 pages, give an account of his journey overland.
A new edition was published by Donnelley of Chicago in 1924. Shortt

165 **Ross,** Alexander
Letters of a pioneer. Edited by George Bryce. Winnipeg, Manitoba Free Press print, 1903. cover-title, 15p. 21cm. (Hist. & Sc. Soc. of Man., no.63)
Interesting excerpts from several letters written over a period of years. Shortt

166 **Ryerson**, John
Hudson's Bay; or, A missionary tour in the territory of the Hon. Hudson's Bay Company. Toronto, G.R. Sanderson, 1855. xxiv, 190p. illus. 18 1/2cm. Imperfect: front. & plates lacking.

In 1854 this Methodist clergyman travelled from Fort William to Red River, to the Methodist mission at Rossville, and thence to York Factory. Shortt

167 **Aborigines' Protection Society**
Canada West and Hudson's-Bay Company: a political and humane question of vital importance to the honour of Great Britain, to the prosperity of Canada, and to the existence of the native tribes; being an address to the Right Honorable Henry Labouchere, Her Majesty's principal Secretary of State for the Colonies, with an appendix. [London] Published for the Society by W. Tweedie, 1856. 2p.l., 19, [1]p. 20 1/2cm. Yale

168 **Anderson**, David
A charge delivered to the clergy of the Diocese of Rupert's Land, at his triennial visitation, May 29, 1856. London, Thomas Hatchard, 1856. 54p. 21cm. Man. Leg.

169 **Anderson**, David
The winner of souls; a New-Year ordination sermon, preached at Saint John's Church, Red River, on Tuesday, January 1, 1856. London, Thomas Hatchard, 1856. 32p. 21cm. Man. Leg.

170 **Ballantyne**, Robert Michael
Snowflakes and sunbeams; or, The young fur traders. A tale of the far north. London, T. Nelson and Sons, 1856. 2p.l., vi, 429p. front., plates. 18 1/2cm.

Juvenile fiction. Frequently reissued since 1901, sometimes with title and sub-title transposed. Shortt

171 **Bible**. New Testament. St. John, First epistle general. Cree
... The first epistle general of John, translated by Mrs. Hunter into the language of the Crees. Transmuted into the phonetic syllabic symbols of the Indians of Rupert's Land, north-west America, under the superintendence of the Right Rev. David, Lord Bishop of Rupert's Land. London, Church Missionary House, 1856. 13p. Not seen.

Text in Cree syllabic. Prior to this work the Hunters' translations had appeared in Roman characters. Pilling

172 **Church of England**. Book of Common Prayer. Cree
Portions of the Book of Common Prayer ... in the language of the Cree Indians, of the Diocese of Rupert's Land. (Transmuted into the phonetic syllabic symbols.) Published under the sanction and superintendence of the Rt. Rev. David, Lord Bishop of Rupert's Land. Specially designed as an aid to family and private devotion of the Indians, while at a distance from the public means of grace. London, Church Missionary Society, 1856. iv, 52p. 21 1/2cm. Not seen.

Translated by the Rev. J. Hunter; probably changed from Roman characters to Cree syllabic by the Rev. Wm. Mason. Pilling

173 **[Goodwin**, Joseph**]**
The north-west-America mission. [London, T.C. Johns, 1856] 2v. (3-20, 3-24p.) in 1. maps. 17 1/2cm. (Church Missionary Society, Tracts. nos. 17 & –) Caption title. B.C. Arch.

174 **Ross,** Alexander
Red River Settlement; its rise, progress and present state, with some account of the native races, and its general history to the present day. London, Smith, Elder and Co., 1856. xvi, 416p. front. 19 1/2cm.

A vivid word-picture of life in the colony. Shortt

175 **Scripps,** J[ohn] L[ocke]
The undeveloped northern portion of the American continent. A lecture delivered in the course before Bell's Commercial College, February, 1856. Chicago, 'Democratic Press' Steam Printing House, 1856. cover-title, 20p. 19 1/2cm. L. of P.

176 **Aborigines' Protection Society**
Memorial to the Right Honorable Henry Labouchere, Her Majesty's principal Secretary of State for the Colonies: with an appendix. [London? 1857?] caption-title, 19p. 21cm.

Recommended proper protection and provision for the education of the Indians when the H.B.C. charter was surrendered. H.B.C.

177 [**Anonymous**]
The Hudson's Bay Company, Canada west, and the Indian tribes. [n.p., 1857?] 12p. 21cm. Hudson's Bay House

178 [**Anonymous**]
The Hudson's Bay question ... London, W. Tweedie, 1857. 28, 8, 4p. 20cm.

Three articles reprinted from the Colonial Intelligencer. Preface signed F.W. Chesson. Articles hostile to the Hudson's Bay monopoly. The third article proposed that when Rupert's Land was thrown open for settlement, the Indians be settled in a large colony near Lake of the Woods. Winnipeg

179 **Bible.** New Testament. Selections. Cree
[Epistles in the Cree language, translated by the Rev. William Mason. Rossville, Mission press, 1857] 40p. Not seen.

Consists of the following: Paul to the Ephesians; General epistle of James; Second epistle general of Peter; First epistle general of John. Pilling

180 **Canada.** Governor-General, 1854-1861 (Head)
Return to an address from the Legislative Assembly to His Excellency the Governor-General, dated the 4th ultimo, praying His Excellency to cause to be laid before this House 'A Return of all lands sold to the Hudson's Bay Company ... also, for a Return of all lands leased to the Hudson's Bay Company ...' [Toronto, Printed by J. Lovell, 1857] [4]p. 24cm. Glenbow

181 **Canada.** Governor-General, 1854-1861 (Head)
Return to an address from the Legislative Assembly to His Excellency the Governor General, dated the 2nd instant, praying His Excellency to cause to be laid before the House 'copies of all correspondence between the government and Mr. Justice Draper, relative to his appointment as agent to England on the subject of the Hudson's Bay Territory ... and of all correspondence between the Imperial and Provincial governments on the subject of the said Territory.' [Toronto, Printed by J. Lovell, 1857] [6]p. 24cm. (Canada. Sessional papers, 1857. Appendix 17) Glenbow

182 **Canada.** Governor-General, 1854-1861 (Head)
Return to an address of the Honorable Legislative Assembly dated 16th March, 1857, requiring copies of any charters, leases, or other documents, under which the Honorable Hudson's Bay Company claim title to the Hudson's Bay Territory, or any maps relating thereto in the possession of the Government. [Toronto, Printed by Stewart Derbishire & George Desbarats, 1857] 75p. 24cm.
Shortt

183 **Canada.** Legislative Assembly. Select Committee appointed to receive and collect evidence as to the rights of the Hudson's Bay Company under the charter
Report. The Select Committee appointed to receive and collect evidence and information as to the rights of the Hudson's Bay Company under their charter, the renewal of the license of occupation, the character of the soil and climate of the territory, and its fitness for settlement, having the honor to present their first report ... [Toronto] 1857. 25p. 25cm.

Marks the beginning of official interest in acquiring Rupert's Land. Shortt

184 **Roman Catholic Church.** Liturgy and ritual. Chipewyan
Prières, cantiques et catéchisme en langue montagnaise ou chipeweyan. Montréal, L. Perrault, 1857. 144p. 15cm.

At head of title: L.J.C. & M.J. Text in syllabic characters. Glenbow

185 [**Draper**, William Henry]
Hudson's Bay Company. Copy of the letter addressed to Her Majesty's Secretary of State for the Colonies, bearing date the 6th day of May 1857, together with a copy of the memorandum therein referred to, relative to the Hudson's Bay Company. (Mr. Labouchere.) Ordered, by the House of Commons, to be printed, 16 June 1857. [London, 1857] 5, [1]p. 35cm. ([Gt. Brit. Parliament. H. of C. Reports and papers] 104- Sess. 2)

Title from p.[6] Glenbow

186 **Financial Reform Association**
The Hudson's Bay Company versus Magna Charta and the British people ... Liverpool, The Association [1857] 36p. double map (col.) 22cm. (Financial Reform Tracts, n.s., no.21) Rutherford

187 **Freeport**, Andrew [pseud.]
The case of the Hudson's Bay Company. In a letter to Lord Palmerston. London, Edward Stanford, 1857. 2p.l., 18p. 21 1/2cm. Rutherford

188 **Great Britain.** Parliament. House of Commons. Select Committee on the Hudson's Bay Company
Report from the Select Committee on the Hudson's Bay Company; together with the proceedings of the Committee, minutes of evidence, appendix, and index. Ordered, by the House of Commons, to be printed, 31 July and 11 August, 1857. [London, 1857] xviii, 547p. fold. maps. 33 1/2cm. ([Parliament, 1857. H. of C. Reports and papers] 224, 260)

An important document containing the evidence of many witnesses on the suitability of Rupert's Land for agricultural settlement. Shortt

189 **Kernaghan**, W[illiam]
Hudson's Bay and Red River Settlement; with a short account of the country, and the routes in 1857. London, Algar and Street [1857?] 14p. fold. map. 21cm.

A pamphlet hostile to the H.B.C. monopoly, by one of the witnesses before the parliamentary committee. Copy in H.B.C. Library is author's presentation copy to J.A. Roebuck, M.P. Man. Leg.

190 **Red River Settlement.** Inhabitants
Petition to the Honorable the Legislative Assembly of the Province of Canada, in Parliament assembled. The petition of the undersigned inhabitants and natives of the settlement situated on the Red River in the Assiniboine country, British North America. [Toronto, Printed by John Lovell, 1857] caption-title, 6p., 1 l. 35cm.

'Ordered by the Legislative Assembly, to be printed, 22nd May, 1857.' H.B.C.

191 Report on the North West Territories in Canada, the Hudson's Bay and the Indian territories; with questions of boundary and jurisdiction connected therewith. [Quebec, 1857] 36p. Not seen.

Gagnon describes this as 'Très intéressant rapport pour l'Ouest canadien.' Gagnon

192 [**Anonymous**]
The Hudson's Bay Company, and the late government.
(Detached from Financial Reform Tracts. Liverpool, 1858, n.s., no.24, p.[24]-32) Shortt

193 **Canada.** Governor-General, 1854-1861 (Head)
Message. The Governor-General transmits, for the information of the Honorable the Legislative Assembly, copies of despatches from Her Majesty's Secretary of State for the Colonies, and other documents, on the subject of the Hudson's Bay Territory. [Toronto, Printed by John Lovell, 1858] half-title, [16]p. 25cm. (Canada. Sessional papers, 1858. Appendix no.3) H.B.C.

194 **Canada.** Governor-General, 1854-1861 (Head)
Return to an address from the Legislative Assembly to H.E. the Governor General, dated 30th June, 1858, praying to cause to be laid before this House, all papers and correspondence respecting any grants of land to the Hudson's Bay Company from the Crown. By Command, T.J.J. Loranger, Secretary. Secretary's Office, Toronto, 5th July, 1858. [Toronto, Printed by R. Campbell, 1858] [45]p. 26cm. (Canada. Sessional papers, 1858. Appendix no.3) Glenbow

195 **Canada.** Legislative Assembly
Report on the exploration of the country between Lake Superior and the Red River Settlement. Printed by order of the Legislative Assembly. Toronto, John Lovell, 1858. 425p. illus. (diagr.) fold. map. 22cm.

The report includes reports of George Gladman (in charge of the expedition), S.J. Dawson, surveyor, H.Y. Hind, geologist and naturalist, W.E. Napier, engineer.
In June, 1859, this report was presented to the British Parliament, and was printed as a parliamentary paper, entitled 'Papers Relative to the Exploration ...' Collation: 163p. fold. map. 23cm. Shortt

196 **Ermatinger,** Edward
The Hudson's Bay Territories; a series of letters on this important question. Toronto, Maclear, Thomas & Co., 1858. 32p. 24 1/2cm.

Letters to the Hamilton Spectator, 1857-58, written in defence of the H.B.C. by a former servant. Shortt

197 **Great Britain**. Colonial Office
Hudson's Bay Company ... Copies or extracts of any correspondence that has taken place between the Colonial Office and the Hudson's Bay Company, or the Government of Canada, in consequence of the report of the Select Committee on the affairs of the company which sat in the last session of Parliament. Colonial Office, 22 February, 1858. H. Labouchere (Mr. Roebuck). Ordered, by the House of Commons, to be printed, 26 February 1858. [London, 1858]
7, [1]p. 32 1/2cm. ([Parliament, 1858. H. of C. Reports and papers] 99)
Shortt

198 **Hind**, Henry Youle
Report on a topographical & geological exploration of the canoe route between Fort William, Lake Superior and Fort Garry, Red River; and also of the valley of the Red River, north of the 49th parallel, during the summer of 1857 ... Toronto, Printed by Stewart Derbishire and George Desbarats, 1858. 16p. 24 1/2cm. Shortt

199 [**Hunter**, James] tr.
First reading book. Nistum ayumechekawe mussinahikun. [London, 1858?] caption-title, 16p.

Cree text in Roman alphabet. Americas

200 **MacDonell**, Allan
The North-West Transportation, Navigation, and Railway Company: its objects ... Toronto, Printed by order of the Board, by Lovell and Gibson, 1858. 55p. 21cm.

The promoter showed – on paper at least – that a railway would derive a lucrative revenue by exporting buffalo tallow and tongues from the western plains. A railway from Lake Superior would re-route the trade carried by cart between Red River Settlement and St. Paul. Shortt

201 **Minnesota**. House of Representatives. Select Committee on overland routes to British Oregon
Report from a Select Committee of the House of Representatives, on the overland emigration route from Minnesota to British Oregon. With an appendix ... St. Paul, Earle S. Goodrich, 1858. 100p. Not seen.

The object was to open a route to the new gold fields on the Fraser River. The report embraces p.3-6; the remainder is various documents, including excerpts from Simpson's 'Narrative of a Journey round the World.' Appendix no.7 is entitled 'Memoir of the Selkirk Settlement,' by J.A. Wheelock. Wagner

202 **Mueller**, Karl
Die jungen Pelzjaeger im Gebiet der Hudsonbay Compagnie. Ein Naturgemaelde zur Lust und Lehr fuer die reifere Jugend gebildeter Staende. Breslau, Eduard Trewendt, 1858. viii, 366p. col. front., col. plates. Not seen.

Juvenile fiction. Mueller also wrote another boys' story called 'Jungen Bueffeljaeger.' Amtmann, Oct. 1950

203 **North-West Transportation, Navigation and Railway Company**
Memoranda and prospectus of the North-West Transportation and Land Company ... Toronto, Printed at the Globe Office, 1858. 12p. 23cm.

Text in double column. Glenbow

204 **North-West Transportation, Navigation and Railway Company**
Prospectus ... Toronto, Printed by the Globe Book and Job Office, 1858. 12p. 18cm. Can. Arch.

205 [**Belcourt,** Georges Antoine]
Anamihe-masinahigan, Jesus ot yitt-wawin gaye anamihe-nakamunan takobihikatewan. Mik yittwawad ketolik-anamihadjik. Nittam andjibihigan. Québec, Coté, 1859. vi, 208p. 14 1/2cm.

A collection consisting of primer lessons, prayers, catechism and hymns in the Saulteaux dialect.
Originally published in 1839. (In Oblates Arch.) L.C.

206 **Bible.** New Testament. Cree
[The New Testament in the Cree language] London, British and Foreign Bible Society, 1859. 612p. 18cm.

Title in Cree syllabic. See note on translators under Entry 227. Newberry

207 **Dawson,** S[imon] J[ames]
Report on the exploration of the country between Lake Superior and the Red River Settlement, and between the latter place and the Assiniboine and Saskatchewan. Printed by order of the Legislative Assembly. Toronto, John Lovell, 1859. 45p. fold. maps, fold. plan. 34cm.

Also printed in Canada. Leg. Council. Sess. papers, 1859, appendix no.36. Includes a letter by Bishop Taché on the half-breeds, etc. Shortt

208 A few reasons for a Crown Colony. [Text] Broadside: 34 lines. Type-page, 31 x 16cm. Colophon: Headingley Press 1859

Eight reasons are enumerated. The broadside was by the Reverent Griffith Owen Corbett, as both author and printer. The printing was crudely done, the work of an amateur. The hand-press used has not been positively identified, but would seem to have been one brought to Fort Garry for missionary purposes.
For over fifteen years the bibliographer was aware of the existence of this 'first imprint' in the Red River Settlement but was unable to get access to the only copy known to be extant. The broadside had been entombed in 1875 with a miscellany in the cornerstone of Winnipeg's first city hall. Finally, 'progress' caught up with the old building. When it was demolished the broadside was given into the custody of the City Clerk's office.
Winnipeg City Clerk's office

209 **Great Britain.** Colonial Office
Papers relative to the Hudson's Bay Company's charter and license to trade. Presented to both Houses of Parliament by command of Her Majesty, April, 1859. London, 1859. v, 26p. 32cm. ([Parliament, 1859. Papers by command]) Rutherford

210 **Great Britain.** Laws, statutes, etc.
... An act to make further provision for the regulation of the trade with the Indians, and for the administration of justice in the north-western territories of America. 13th August, 1859. [London, Printed by G.E. Eyre and W. Spottiswoode, 1859] caption-title, [157]-159p. 32 1/2cm.

Victoria, 22 and 23., cap.26. Yale Library also has the printed bill dated 1 August 1859.
Yale

211 **Hind,** Henry Youle
North West Territory. Reports of progress, together with a preliminary and general report on the Assiniboine and Saskatchewan exploring expedition, made under instructions from the Provincial Secretary, Canada. Printed by order of the Legislative Assembly. Toronto, Printed by John Lovell, 1859. xii, 201p. illus. (incl. diagrs.) plates, fold. maps, fold. plans. 33cm.

In Aug. 1860, the report was presented to the British Parliament, and published under the title 'British North America. Reports, [etc.]' (219p. illus. (incl. diagrs.) fold. maps (part. col.) 33cm.)

Listed in Staton's 'Bibliography of Canadiana,' no.3912, is a supplementary volume 'Photographs acoompanying [sic] a report on the Assiniboine and Saskatchewan exploring expedition.' The portfolio contains 37 mounted photographs. These are apparently the photographs listed in the appendix of Hind's 'Narrative' as being available from J. Hogarth, London. Shortt

212 **Kane,** Paul
Wanderings of an artist among the Indians of North America, from Canada to Vancouver's Island and Oregon, through the Hudson's Bay Company's territory and back again. London, Longman, Brown, Green, Longmans, and Roberts, 1859. xvii, [1], 455, [8] p. col. front., illus., col. plates, col. ports., fold. map. 22cm.

In 1846 Kane crossed the continent studying and painting Indians as he went. Much of the summer was spent on the prairies. Kane made Fort Edmonton his headquarters during the winter of 1847-48. Forty of the 101 Kane paintings in the Royal Ontario Museum and five of the eleven pictures in Ottawa were painted on the prairies.

A French edition translated by E. Delessert was published in Paris in 1861. A German edition was published in Leipzig in 1862. The following year a Danish edition appeared in Copenhagen. The latter is extremely rare. A reprint edition was published by the Radisson Society of Canada in 1925. Shortt

213 **Mason,** [Sophia (Thomas)] tr.
... Watts's first catechism for children, the Lord's Prayer, the Apostles' Creed, and the Ten Commandments. Translated by Mrs. Mason into the language of the Cree Indians of Rupert's Land, north-west America ... [London] 1859. 8p. 20 1/2cm.

One word in Cree syllabic characters at head of title. On t.-p.: May 7th, 1859. 38, Craven Street, Strand.

An edition of 15p., 13 1/2cm, with identical t.-p., was published in 1862.

In the late 1840's the Wesleyan missionaries at Rossville Mission had a catechism, printed at their press, in circulation. This catechism may have been the work of Mrs. Mason. Rupert's

214 **Mason,** W[illiam] tr.
A collection of psalms and hymns; translated into the language of the York Indians in the Diocese of Rupert's Land, north-west America. London, Society for Promoting Christian Knowledge, 1859. 163p. 11cm.

Text in Cree syllabic.

Reprinted the following year. Rupert's Land

215 **Morris,** Alexander
The Hudson's Bay and Pacific territories; a lecture. Montreal, John Lovell, 1859. 57p. 21cm.

Appears as lecture 2 in his 'Nova Britannia' (Toronto, 1884) Shortt

216 **Murray**, Andrew
Contributions to the natural history of the Hudson's Bay Company's territories. Part II, Mammals - continued - and Part III, Birds. Edinburgh, Printed by Neill and Co., 1859. 24p. fold. plate. 21cm. Reprinted from the Edinburgh New Philosophical Journal, n.s., April, 1859. Man. Leg.

217 **[Palliser**, John]
Exploration - British North America. Papers relative to the exploration by Captain Palliser of that portion of British North America which lies between the northern branch of the river Saskatchewan and the frontier of the United States; and between the Red River and Rocky Mountains. Presented to both Houses of Parliament by command of Her Majesty. June, 1859. London, Printed by G.E. Eyre & W. Spottiswoode, 1859. 64p. maps (part. fold.) diagr. 34cm. Shortt

218 **Palliser**, John
Progress of the British North American exploring expedition. Under the command of Capt. John Palliser. Communicated by the Right Hon. Sir Edward Bulwer Lytton. (In Royal Geog. Soc., Journal, v.30. p.267-314. fold. map. 23cm.) Shortt

219 **Anderson**, David
A charge delivered to the clergy of the Diocese of Rupert's Land, in St. John's Church, Red River, at his triennial visitation, January 6, 1860. London, Hatchard and Co., 1860. 58p. 21cm. Man. Leg.

220 **Church of England**. Book of Common Prayer. Cree
The Book of Common Prayer, and administration of the sacraments, and other rites and ceremonies of the church ... translated into the language of the Cree Indians of the Diocese of Rupert's Land, North-West America. London, Printed for the Society for Promoting Christian Knowledge, 1860. [3], 190p. 19cm.

In Cree syllabic characters. 'Archdeacon Hunter's translation.' Changed from the Roman alphabet to Cree syllabic characters by Rev. Wm. Mason.

This edition of the Book of Common Prayer was first published in 1859. See note under Entry 162. Glenbow

221 **Hind**, Henry Youle
Narrative of the Canadian Red River exploring expedition of 1857, and of the Assiniboine and Saskatchewan exploring expedition of 1858. London, Longman, Green, Longman and Roberts, 1860. 2v. fronts., illus., plates (part. col.) fold. maps, plans. 22cm.

An edition, for popular use, of the reports published by the Canadian Legislature and the British Parliament (see 211). An index adds to its usefulness. Shortt

222 **[Palliser**, John]
Exploration - British North America. Further papers relative to the exploration by the expedition under Captain Palliser of that portion of British North America which lies between the northern branch of the river Saskatchewan and the frontier of the United States; and between the Red River and the Rocky Mountains, and thence to the Pacific Ocean. Presented to both Houses of Parliament by command of Her Majesty. 1860. London, G.E. Eyre and William Spottiswoode, 1860. 75p. illus. (diagr.) fold. maps. 34cm. Shortt

223 **Palliser,** John
The papers of the Palliser expedition, 1857-1860. Edited with an introd. and notes by Irene M. Spry. Toronto, Champlain Society, 1968. 694p. 25cm. (Champlain Soc., no.44)

See Entry 238. U. of A.

224 **Smithsonian Institution, Washington**
Circular to officers of the Hudson's Bay Company. [Washington, 1860] 4p. (Miscellaneous collections)

Informed officers how to prepare specimens for transmission to the Institution. H.B.C.

225 **Taylor,** James W[ickes]
Northwest British America, and its relations to the State of Minnesota. A report communicated to the Legislature of Minnesota by Governor Ramsey, March 2d, and ordered to be printed. St. Paul, Newson, Moore, Foster & Co., 1860. 41, [1]p. map. 24 1/2cm. Not seen.

Taylor was commissioned by Gov. H.H. Sibley of Minnesota in June 1859 to report on the country between St. Paul and the Red River Settlement and the Rocky Mountains. Supplementing the report are several appendices including: Central British America (also in Atlantic Monthly, Jan. 1860); Geographical memoir of the Red River and Saskatchewan districts (also in 'Report of a Committee of the St. Paul Chamber of Commerce, Jan. 22, 1859'); Itinerary of routes from St. Paul to Pembina, Fort Garry, Fort Ellice, and Edmonton House. Wagner. Toronto (Staton)

226 **Anderson,** David
The truth and the conscience; an ordination sermon, preached at St. Andrew's Church, Red River, on Sunday, July 21, 1861. London, Hatchard and Co., 1861. 35p. 21cm. Man. Leg.

227 **Bible.** Cree
[The Bible, translated into the language of the Knisteneaux, Kristeneaux or Crees of North America, by William Mason and others] London, British and Foreign Bible Society, 1861. 2p.l., 855p., 1 l., 292p. 22 1/2cm.

Title-page in Cree syllabic. The New Testament portion has a separate title-page with the imprint date 1862.

Although Mason's name appeared on the title-page as translator, it was a co-operative effort by the missionary group at Rossville. John Sinclair, a half-breed teacher, is said to have translated from Genesis to Esther, and from Matthew to Acts. Rev. H.B. Steinhauer, a full-blooded Indian, translated from Job to Malachi, and from the Acts of the Apostles to the end of the New Testament. Rev. W. Mason and his wife returned to England in 1858 to work on the revision of the text and to see the Bible through the press.

See bibliographical references under Entry 103. Rutherford

227A **Hector,** Sir James
On the physical features of the central part of British North America, and on its capabilities for settlement. Edinburgh, Printed by Neill and company; 1861. 1p.l., 35p. tables. 21cm.

From the Edinburgh New Philosophical Journal, n.s., Oct. 1861. B.C. Arch.

228 **Synge,** M[illington] H[enry]
The country v. the company; or, Why British North America may be peopled, and how it may be done. With suggestions towards a plan for doing so to the best advantage. London, Edward Stanford, 1861. 22p.

Hostile to the H.B.C. B.C. Arch.

229 **Taché,** [Alexandre Antonin]
Lettre de Mgr Taché, évêque de St-Boniface, donnant à Mgr de Montréal le recit des malheurs de son diocese depuis deux ans. [Montréal, 1861] caption-title, 11p. 20cm.

Letter dated 12 Oct. 1861. St. Sulpice

230 **Assiniboia.** Laws, statutes, etc.
Laws of Assiniboia. Passed by the Governor and Council of Assiniboia, on the 11th April, 1862. [Fort Garry, Printed at the office of 'The Nor'-Wester,' Red River Settlement, 1862] caption-title, 8p. 26cm.

The B.C. Archives also has another edition without publisher or date: 17p. 22cm. This second edition was printed in Ottawa in 1870 at the request of Lt.-Gov. Archibald of Manitoba and the North-West Territories. He said he had only been able to find one copy of the 1862 edition in the Red River Settlement. The new printing contained the accretions from 1862 to 1869. Canada. Dept. of Justice

231 **Fleming,** [Sir] Sandford
Suggestions of the inter-colonial railway and the construction of a highway and telegraph line between the Atlantic and Pacific oceans, within British territory, respectfully submitted to the Government of Canada. Toronto, W.C. Chewett & Co., 1862. 77-134p. 16 1/2cm. Not seen.

An excerpt from H.Y. Hind's 'Sketch of an Overland Route to British Columbia.' Can. Arch.

232 **Hind,** Henry Youle
A sketch of an overland route to British Columbia. Toronto, W.C. Chewett & Co., 1862. 128p. fold. map. 16 1/2cm. Can. Arch.

233 **United States.** Treasury Department
Relations between the United States and northwest British America. Washington, Government Printing Office, 1862. 85p. illus. (map.) fold. map. 22 1/2cm. (37th Cong., 2d Sess. House. Ex. doc., no.146)

Abstracts of the reports of James W. Taylor. Shortt

234 **Canada.** Governor-General, 1861-1868 (Monck)
All papers and documents, reports, despatches, etc., in relation to the opening up of the territory commonly called the North West Territories, which have come into the possession of the Government since the 1st January, 1862. [Quebec, Hunter, Rose & Lemieux, 1863] 11p., 1 l. 23 1/2cm. Shortt

235 **Canada.** Governor-General, 1861-1868 (Monck)
Copies of all communications made to any member of the Government – of any report or reports made by any member of His Excellency in Council – of any communication to or from the Imperial Government, and all orders in council passed in relation to the opening of a route to Red River, or to British Columbia and the Pacific, since the last session of Parliament. Quebec, Hunter, Rose & Lemieux, 1863. 19, [1]p. 23 1/2cm. Shortt

236 **Cheadle,** [Walter Butler]
Cheadle's journal of trip across Canada, 1862-63. With introduction and notes by A.G. Doughty and Gustave Lanctot. Ottawa, Graphic Publishers Ltd., 1931. 311p. illus. (incl. ports.) fold. map. 20cm. (The Canada series, v.1)

The popular 'North-west Passage by Land,' usually attributed to Viscount Milton, appears to have been based on this diary, which consists of jottings of daily occurrences. See Entry 249. Shortt

237 **Fleming,** [Sir] Sandford
A great territorial road to British Columbia. Quebec, 1863. 57p. Not seen.
Burpee

238 [**Palliser,** John]
Exploration. – British North America. The journals, detailed reports, and observations relative to the exploration, by Captain Palliser, of that portion of British North America, which, in latitude, lies between the British boundary line and the height of land or watershed of the northern or frozen ocean respectively, and in longitude, between the western shore of Lake Superior and the Pacific Ocean during the years 1857, 1858, 1859, and 1860. Presented to both Houses of Parliament by command of Her Majesty, 19th May, 1863. London, Printed by G.E. Eyre and W. Spottiswoode, 1863. 325, [1]p. diagrs. and atlas of 5 fold. maps. 33cm.

Palliser's final report contains a detailed account of the country he traversed, and of general economic and social conditions. Shortt

239 **Red River Settlement.** Citizens
Memorial of the people of Red River to the British and Canadian Governments, with remarks on the colonization of central British North America, and the establishment of a great territorial road from Canada to British Columbia. Submitted to the Canadian Government by Sandford Fleming. Printed by order of the Legislative Assembly. Quebec, Printed for the contractors by Hunter, Rose & Co., 1863. 57, [1]p. 24 1/2cm.

This 'people's petition' asked for a complete change of government and the development of the resources of the country. Shortt

240 [**Roche,** Alfred R.]
New disposal of convicts. Reprinted from the letter of the Canadian correspondent of the London Morning Post, April 3rd, 1856. [Toronto, W.C. Chewett & Co., 1863] 29p. 22 1/2cm.

Preface signed: A.R.R., Toronto, January 1863.
Excerpts from various newspapers on both sides of the Atlantic on the subject of penal colonies in Rupert's Land: p.18-29. Rutherford

241 **Synge,** Millington Henry
The colony of Rupert's Land: where is it, and by what title held? A dialogue on England: her interests in North America and in free intercourse, against certain contrary pretensions on the part of the Hudson Bay Company. London, Edward Stanford, 1863. 56p. fold. map. 20 1/2cm. Shortt

242 [**Synge,** Millington Henry]
[Rupert Land: the colony and its limits. London? 1863?] 19p. 21cm.
A reprint of a paper delivered before the Royal Geog. Soc., Feb. 23, 1863, and published in the society's Proceedings, v.7, no.2. Not seen.

P.11-19: Further arguments, including arguments by A.K. Isbister. Toronto (Staton)

243 **Anderson,** David
A charge delivered to the clergy of the Diocese of Rupert's Land, in St. John's Cathedral, Red River, at his fifth and last visitation, January 6, 1864. London, Hatchard and Co., 1864. vi, [7]-64p. 21cm. Man. Leg.

244 **Great Britain.** Colonial Office
Sioux Indians. Return to an address ... dated 6 May 1864, for 'Copies or extracts of all the correspondence between the commanding officers of the United States troops in Minnesota and the resident governor of the Hudson's Bay Company at Red River, respecting a tribe of Sioux Indians who were refugees within the British territory': 'Of report of the meeting of the governor and council of Assiniboine, on the 12th day of March 1864, including copy of the message which the governor is reported to have received from the Indians': 'And, of the correspondence between the Hudson's Bay Company, or any of the colonial authorities, and Her Majesty's Government in reference thereto.' Colonial Office, 16 June, 1864. Frederic Rogers (Mr. Hennessy). Ordered, by the House of Commons, to be printed, 17 June, 1864. [London, 1864] 18p. 33cm. ([Parliament, 1864. H. of C. Reports and papers] 401) Man. Leg.

245 [**Nelson,** Joseph]
The Hudson's Bay Company. What is it? London, A.H. Baily & Co., 1864. cover-title, v, 81p. 21 1/2cm. Running vertically on the cover in red type are the words: Important. This pamphlet refers to a great public question which will be brought before the House of Commons in a few days.

A rare pamphlet hostile to the company. For authorship see the title-page of Nelson's 'Proposed H.B. & Pacific Railway.' Shortt

246 **Canada.** Executive Council
Documents relating to the opening up of the North-West Territories to settlement and cultivation. [Ottawa, G.E. Desbarats, 1865] caption-title, 17, [1]p. 22cm.

On cover: North-West Territories. '4th Session, 8th Parliament, 29 Victoria, 1865.' Glenbow

247 **Hudson's Bay Company**
List of the Adventurers of England trading into Hudson's Bay, November, 1865. London, Henry Kent Causton and Son, 1865. 80p. 15cm.

These lists published in pamphlet form from 1836 to 1868. Earlier lists printed as broadsides. H.B.C.

248 [**Hunter,** Jean (Ross)] tr.
A Cree hymn book, for the use of the Christian Indians in the missions of the Wesleyan Missionary Society in North-West America. London, W.M. Watts [1865?] [1], 163p. 14cm.

Text of 96 hymns in Cree syllabic characters. Glenbow

249 **Milton,** [William Fitzwilliam] viscount
The north-west passage by land. Being the narrative of an expedition from the Atlantic to the Pacific, undertaken with the view of exploring a route across the continent to British Columbia through British territory, by one of the northern passes in the Rocky Mountains. By Viscount Milton and W.B. Cheadle. London, Cassell, Petter and Galpin [1865] xviii, 397p. front., plates, fold. maps. 23cm. Map in pocket.

This work attained an immediate popularity and ran through many editions, seven within two years. It was again reprinted in 1875 and 1901. A French edition was published in Paris in 1866, and an abridged version of the latter in 1872. Though published as a joint work, it appears to have been written by W.B. Cheadle.

The authors issued a preliminary report of 37p. with the title 'An Expedition across the Rocky Mountains into British Columbia, by the Yellow Head or Leather Pass.' Read before the British Association at Bath, 17 Sept. 1864, and before the Royal Geog. Soc. of London, 28 Dec. 1864. Printed for private circulation. London, Petter and Galpin. Shortt

250 **Rawlings,** Thomas
The confederation of the British North America provinces; their past history and future prospects; including also British Columbia & Hudson's Bay Territory; with a map, and suggestions in reference to the true and only practical route from the Atlantic to the Pacific Ocean. London, S. Low, Son, and Marston, 1865. ix, [1] p., 1 l., 244p. plates, fold. map. 24cm. Shortt

251 **Watkins,** E[dwin] A[rthur] comp.
A dictionary of the Cree language, as spoken by the Indians of the Hudson's Bay Company's territories. London, Society for Promoting Christian Knowledge, 1865. xxiv, 460p. 13cm.

Apparently only a small number was printed for it was soon out of print. See Entry 3654. Shortt

252 **Wesleyan Methodist Church.** Catechisms. Cree
The Wesleyan first catechism; translated into the language of the Cree Indians, Hudson's Bay Territory. London, W.M. Watts, 1865. 23 [1] p. 14cm.

This item, and Entry 248, may have been the work, at least in part, of the Rev. Thomas Woolsey, early Methodist missionary at Victoria mission near Edmonton. B.C. Arch.

253 [**Woolsey,** Thomas] tr.
Hymns and paraphrases, translated into the language of the Cree Indians, for the use of the Methodist congregation in the Hudson's Bay Territory. London, W.M. Watts, 1865. vi, 6-207, [1] p. 13 1/2cm.

Preface by the translator. Americas

254 [**Anonymous**]
A brief sketch of the life and labours of Archdeacon Cockran, late missionary in North-West America. London, Religious Tract Society [1866?] cover-title, 24p. 17 1/2cm. (Tract no.1029)

Illustration on cover entitled: Indian settlement at Red River.

The Rev. Wm. Cockran's name also spelled Cochran or Cockrane. C.M.S. Lib.

255 [**Anonymous**]
The Hudson's Bay Company. 'A million': shall we take it? Addressed to the shareholders of the company by one of themselves. London, A.H. Baily, 1866. 38p. 20cm.

Stressed the potential wealth of the territory when developed, and questioned the price of disposal. Shortt

256 **Dodds,** James
The Hudson's Bay Company, its position and prospects. The substance of an address, delivered at a meeting of the shareholders, in the London Tavern, on the 24 January, 1866. London, Edward Stanford and A.H. Baily, 1866. iv, 77p. front. (fold. map.) 21 1/2cm. Rutherford

257 **Rawlings**, Thomas
What shall we do with the Hudson's Bay Territory? Colonize the Fertile Belt, which contains forty millions of acres. London, A.H. Baily, 1866. 83p. 21 1/2cm. Rutherford

258 **Roman Catholic Church**. Catechisms. Cree
Catéchisme et cantiques à l'usage des sauvages de la Baie d'Hudson. Montréal, Louis Perrault et Cie, 1866. 108p. Not seen.

The text in Cree syllabic was translated by Rev. Louis Marie Lebret. Gagnon

259 **Roman Catholic Church**. Prayers. Cree
... Prières, cantiques, catéchisme, etc., en langue crise ... Montréal, Louis Perrault et Cie, 1866. 72p. 14cm.

Translated into Cree by the Rev. Jean-Baptiste Thibault. He published the following collections of prayers and hymns:
Quebec, 1855. 142p. Roman alphabet.
Montreal, 1857. 288p. Cree syllabic.
Montreal, 1866. 324p. Cree syllabic.
See Pilling. Shortt

260 **Taché**, Alex[andre Antonin]
Vingt années de missions dans le nord-ouest de l'Amérique. Montréal, Eusèbe Senécal, 1866. xiii, 245p. 22cm.

A sketch of Catholic missions arranged in the form of annals.
In 1888 a new illustrated edition was published in Montreal with a 14-page preface by T.A. Bernier. Collation: 238p., 1 l. front., plate, ports. 25 1/2cm. Shortt

261 **Church of England**. Diocese of Rupert's Land
Report of the Diocese of Rupert's Land, by the bishop and clergy at the Red River Settlement. [London, W.M. Watts, 1867] caption-title, 15p. 20 1/2cm.

The report is dated December 1865. C.M.S. Libr.

262 **Church of England**. Diocese of Rupert's Land. 2d conference, 1867
Report of the second conference of clergy and lay-delegates from parishes in the Diocese of Rupert's Land. Called by the Bishop, and held on May 29th, 1867. Cambridge, Printed by J. Palmer, 1867. 40p. 20cm. Shortt

263 **Conolly**, John, plaintiff
Superior court, Montreal. No.902. John Connolly [sic] plaintiff; vs. Julia Woolrich, defendant; and Thomas R. Johnson, et al., executors and defendants par reprise d'instance. [Montreal, Printed by the Montreal Printing & Publishing Co., 1867?] caption-title, 86p., 1 l. 21cm.

John Conolly was the son of chief trader William Conolly. His mother was an Indian woman, married according to the custom of the country, whom his father put aside to marry Julia Woolrich. After his mother's death he sued Julia Woolrich for a share of his father's estate. See Entry 267. U.B.C.

264 [**Klaucke, M.F.**]
Prospectus of a joint stock company to be formed under the name and style of the British North-West American Emigrants' Settlement Association (Limited) [Ottawa? 1867] caption-title, 23p. 19cm. L. of P.

265 **Klaucke,** M.F.
Supplementary appendix to Mr. Klaucke's pamphlet, concerning the formation of a joint stock company, under the name and style of the British North-West American Emigrants' Settlement Association. [Ottawa? 1867] caption-title, 22p. 19cm. L. of P.

266 Memorandum in support of an address to Her Majesty from the inhabitants of the Red River Settlement, praying to be formed into a crown colony. [London, John King & Co., 1867?] caption-title, 14p. 32cm. On verso of last leaf: The Red River Settlement. Memorandum to His Grace, the Duke of Buckingham, Secretary of State for the Colonies. B.C. Arch.

267 **Woolrich,** Julia
Testament solennel et codiciles de Dame Julia Woolrich. Renonciation de MM. McCarthy. Renonciation de M. Belle, Nomination de M. Smallwood. [Montreal? 1867?] [15]p. 34cm.

See also Conolly, John, plaintiff, Entry 263. H.B.C.

268 **Canada.** Department of the Secretary of State
Return to an address from the House of Commons, dated 18th November, 1867; for correspondence, report of proceedings, and other documents, in the possession of the Government relative to Hudson's Bay Territory. [Ottawa, 1868] 25, 2p. 25cm. (Canada. Sess. papers, 1867-68, no.19) U. of S.

269 **Corbett,** G[riffith] O[wen]
Notes on Rupert's America; its history and resources, enclosed with a letter to His Grace the Duke of Buckingham, Secretary of State for the Colonies. [Dulwich, E. Menge & Bros.] 1868. 1p.l., vi, 88p. 20 1/2cm.

The Bibliographical Society of Canada issued a facsimile reprint in 1967. U. of M.

270 **Dawson,** S[imon] J[ames]
Report on the line of route between Lake Superior and the Red River Settlement. Printed by order of the House of Commons. Ottawa, Printed by Hunter, Rose & Co., 1868. 44p. 23 1/2cm.

Discusses various routes, types of transportation, costs, and probable volume of freight. Shortt

271 **E., T.F.**
... Précis on the Hudson's Bay Company. [London, 1868] 7p.

At head of title: Confidential. Signed: T.F.E. L. of P.

272 **Great Britain.** Laws, statutes, etc.
Hudson's Bay Company. (H.L.) A bill intituled An act for enabling Her Majesty to accept a surrender upon terms of the lands, privileges, and rights of 'the Governor and Company of Adventurers of England trading into Hudson's Bay,' and for admitting the same into the Dominion of Canada. [London, 1868] 3, [1]p. 34cm.

Bill 240. Brought from the Lords 16 July 1868. Ordered by the House of Commons, to be printed, 16 July 1868. Glenbow

273 **Hudson's Bay Company**
Report of proceedings at a general meeting of the Hudson's Bay Company held in the company's house, Fenchurch Street, on Tuesday, 24th Nov., 1868, the

Rt. Hon. the Earl of Kimberly in the chair. London, Printed by H.K. Causton [1868] 31p. 22cm. Glenbow

274 [**Machray**, Robert]
Christian privilege and duty. A sermon preached in St. John's Cathedral, Red River Settlement, by the Right Rev. the Lord Bishop of Rupert's Land on Sunday morning, May 10th, 1868 ... Published by request of the members of the congregation. Town of Winnipeg, Printed at the Nor'Western Office, 1868. 11p. 19cm.

This pamphlet was probably Winnipeg's first imprint. Arkin; C.M.S. - 8

275 **Waddington**, Alfred
Overland route through British North America; or, The shortest and speediest road to the East ... London, Longmans, Green, Reader, and Dyer, 1868. 48p. front. (fold. map.) 21 1/2cm.

Describes route for a proposed railway in some detail, with tables of distances, etc. The route crossed the Yellowhead Pass, and ended at Bute Inlet. Shortt

276 **Ballantyne**, Robert Michael
Away in the wilderness; or, Life among the red Indians and fur-traders of North-America. Philadelphia, Porter & Coates, 1869. 144p.

Juvenile fiction. Ran through several editions. (A later edition in Rutherford) Br. Mus.

277 **Canada**. Delegates appointed to negotiate for the acquisition of Rupert's Land and the North-West Territory
Report ... Laid before Parliament by command of His Excellency the Governor General. Ottawa, 1869. cover-title, ii, 39p. 23 1/2cm. Also issued as sess. paper, no.25, 1869.

Correspondence between the Canadian delegation - consisting of Geo. E. Cartier and Wm. McDougall - and the Colonial Office and the H.B.C. The delegates were in England from Oct. 1868 to April 1869. Shortt

278 **Dawson**, S[imon] J[ames]
Report on the line of route between Lake Superior and the Red River Settlement. Printed by order of the House of Commons. Ottawa, Printed by I.B. Taylor, 1869. 32p. 23 1/2cm.

Proposed a railway to the height of land, the use of navigable streams to Lake of the Woods, and another railway to Fort Garry, a wagon road to be a preliminary step. Shortt

279 **Church of England**. Diocese of Rupert's Land
Report of the Synod of the Diocese of Rupert's Land. Called by the Bishop, and held on Feb. 24th, 1869, including the primary charge of the Bishop ... Cambridge, Printed by J. Palmer, 1869. 76p. 19 1/2cm. L. of P.

280 **Foster**, John
Railway from Lake Superior to Red River Settlement, considered in a letter to the Hon. Wm. McDougall, C.B., Minister of Public Works. Montreal, John Lovell, 1869. 16p. fold. map. 21cm.

The inventor of a wooden railway tries to sell the idea to the Minister of Public Works. Shortt

281 **Great Britain.** Colonial Office
Canada (Rupert's Land) ... Copy or extracts of correspondence between the Colonial Office, the Government of the Canadian Dominion, the Hudson's Bay Company, relating to the surrender of Rupert's Land by the Hudson's Bay Company, and for the admission thereof into the Dominion of Canada. Colonial Office, 11 August, 1869. W. Monsell. (Mr. Monk.) Ordered, by the House of Commons, to be printed, 11 August 1869. [London, 1869] iv, 76p., 1 l. 33cm. ([Parliament, 1869. H. of C. Reports and papers] 440) Shortt

282 **Great Britain.** Colonial Office
Hudson's Bay Company. Letter from the Colonial Office to the Governor of the Hudson's Bay Company, dated March 9th, 1869. London, Printed by J. Causton and Sons [1869] 9p. 21cm.

Signed: Frederic Rogers. Yale

283 **Hudson's Bay Company**
Hudson's Bay Company. Correspondence between Her Majesty's Government and the Hudson's Bay Company. London, Printed by Henry Kent Causton & Son, 1869. 228p. 19cm.

The correspondence covers the years 1862-69, and relates to the surrender of the title to Rupert's Land. Hudson's Bay House

284 **Hudson's Bay Company**
Report of proceedings at a meeting of the Hudson's Bay Company held at the company's house in Fenchurch Street, on Wednesday, March 24th, 1869, the Right Honourable Sir Stafford Henry Northcote, bart., in the chair. London, Joseph Causton & Sons, 1869. cover-title, 65p. 21 1/2cm.

At this fateful meeting, Sir Stafford Northcote endeavoured to make the shareholders accept the £300,000 for the surrender of the company's chartered rights. Verbatim report. Shortt

285 **Kingston,** William Henry Giles
Rob Nixon, the old white trapper; a tale of central British North America. Published under the direction of the Committee of General Literature and Education appointed by the Society for Promoting Christian Knowledge. London, Society for Promoting Christian Knowledge [n.d.] 133p. plates. 15cm. Glenbow

286 **Ottawa.** Board of Trade. Committee
Report ... on the settlement of the North-West. Submitted to the general meeting of the Board on Monday, 5th April, 1869, and ordered to be published. Ottawa, Printed by Hunter, Rose, and Co., 1869. 12p. 21cm. Rutherford

287 **Russell,** Alex[ander] J[amieson]
The Red River country, Hudson's Bay and North-West Territories, considered in relation to Canada, with the last report of S.J. Dawson ... on the line of route between Lake Superior and the Red River Settlement ... Ottawa, G.E. Desbarats, 1869. 4p.l., [vii]-xv, 202p. fold. map. 21 1/2cm.

Written in 1868, it was intended to influence public opinion on the acquisition of Rupert's Land, but the first edition was destroyed by a fire in Desbarats' printing office. An 1870 edition contains both of S.J. Dawson's reports. Shortt

288 **Taché**, [Alexandre Antonin]
Esquisse sur le nord-ouest de l'Amérique. Montréal, Typographie du Nouveau Monde, 1869. 146p. 21cm. In double columns.

A comprehensive essay including notes on the flora and fauna, Indians, fur trade and missionary activities.

An English edition, translated by D.R. Cameron, was printed by J. Lovell in 1870, while another French edition was published in Montreal in 1901. Shortt

289 [**Anonymous**]
Red River insurrection. Hon. Wm. McDougall's conduct reviewed. Montreal, Printed by John Lovell, 1870. 69p. 21 1/2cm.

Gagnon attributes this anonymous pamphlet to Sir F. Hincks. McDougall, in his pamphlet addressed to Howe (see Entry 307), said, 'I have no difficulty in filling the blank with the name of one of your colleagues, who has seldom, hitherto, lacked the courage to affix his name to his productions.' Shortt

290 **Begg**, Alexander
Red River journal and other papers relative to the Red River resistance of 1869-70. Edited with an introduction by W.L. Morton. Toronto, Champlain Society, 1956. xxiii, 636p. port., fold. map. 25cm. (Champlain Soc., no.34) U. of A.

291 [Broadsides of the Red River Disturbances, 1869-70]

a) Public Notice to the Inhabitants of Rupertsland. [Text] By order of the President. Louis Riel, Secty. Winnipeg, Nov. 6th 1869. Broadside: 24 lines. Type-page, 21 x 19cm.

Text: 'The President and Representatives of the French-speaking population of Rupert's Land in Council ... do extend the hand of friendship to you our friendly Inhabitants, and in doing so invite you to send twelve Representative from the following places' ...

The copy in the Manitoba Archives has a ms. word 'fellow' inserted before and above 'Inhabitants'; also brackets around the clause 'the Invaders of our rights being now expelled.'

Dr. Walter Bown, proprietor of the Nor'-Wester, refused to print the broadside and was held prisoner while it was run off by Riel's men. Man. Arch. - Can. Arch.

b) Governor Mactavish to the Inhabitants of Red River Settlement. [Text] Given under my hand and seal at Fort Garry, this sixteenth day of November, 1869. [L.S.] W. Mactavish, Governor of Assiniboia. Broadside: 77 lines. Type-page, 35 x 16.5cm.

Text: '... during the last few weeks large bodies of armed men have taken up positions on the public high road to Pembina, and, contrary to the remonstrances and protests of the public authorities, have committed the following unlawful acts:-' Five unlawful acts are enumerated.

Printed by William Coldwell on a press recently brought into the Settlement to print a new paper, The Pioneer. Man. Arch.

c) The Nor'-Wester and Pioneer Extra. Winnipeg, Wednesday, November 17th, 1869. The Crisis! Loyalty Triumphant! [Royal Arms] The Governor's Proclamation! Broadside: ? lines. In double column. 35 (x 2?) x 11cm.

The Extra carried the address of residents of Winnipeg to Governor Mactavish, and the Governor's Proclamation. The latter document was not wholly accurate in this version.

Printed at the Nor'-Wester office.

Copy in Public Archives of Canada missing lower half. Can. Arch.

d) The North-West [Royal Arms. 3 x 4.5cm.] Territories. L.S. William MacDougall. Victoria, by the Grace of God. To all to whom these Ptesent [sic] shall come Greeting: Proclamation. [Text] At the Red River in our aforesaid North-West Territories, the first day of December in the year of our Lord one thousand eight hundred and sixty-nine, and in the thirty-third year of our reign. By command. J.A.N. Provencher Secretary. Broadside: 71 lines. In triple column. Type-page, 26.5 x 16.8cm.

Text: '... Now know ye, that we have seen fit by our royal letters patent ... to appoint the Honourable William Macdougall, of the city of Ottawa ... to be during our pleasure the Lieutenant Governor of the North-West Territories ...'

William Macdougall, still at Pembina, sent this proclamation to Fort Garry with Col. J.S. Dennis. Surreptitiously printed by the 'planers process' with type smuggled out of the Nor'-Wester office by George B. Winship. He was assisted by Patrick G. Laurie. When the printers ran out of lower case 'j's they used inverted 'f's. 300 copies printed. The printing was probably completed on 2 or 3 December. Bibliothèque Nationale du Québec

e) The North-West [Royal Arms. 1 x 2cm.] Territories. Proclamation. By His Excellency the Honorable William Macdougall ... Lieutenant-Governor of the North-West Territories, etc., etc., etc. To all to whom these shall come, greeting. [Text] Given under my hand and seal at arms at Red River in the said Territories, the second day of December ... William Macdougall. By command. I.A.N. Provencher, secretary. Broadside: 44 lines. Type-page, 19.1 x 16.2cm.

Text: '... I do hereby require and command that all and singular the public officers and functionaries holding office in Rupert's Land and the north-western Territory at the time of their admission into the union as aforesaid, excepting the public officer or functionary at the head of the administration of affairs, do continue in the execution of their several and respective offices, duties, places and employments until otherwise ordered by me ...'

This broadside was printed at Lower Fort Garry on a disused mission press by P.G. Laurie on 8 December. Man. Arch. - Can. Arch.

f) The North-West [Royal Arms. 1 x 2cm.] Territories. L.S. By His Excellency the Honorable William Macdougall ... To John Stoughton Dennis ... [Text] Given under my hand and seal at arms at Red River in the said Territories, this first day of December ... William Macdougall by command. I.A.N. Provencher, Secretary. [Postscript appeal by J.S. Dennis] J.S. Dennis, Lieutenant and Conservator of the Peace in and for the N.W. Territories. Broadside: 51 lines in triple column. Postscript 6 lines. Type-page, 23.2 x 16.5cm.

Text: '... by virtue of the authority in me vested, I have nominated and appointed, and by these presents do nominate and appoint you the said John Stoughton Dennis to be my Lieutenant and a conservator of the peace in and for the North-west Territories, and as such to raise, organise, arm equip and provision a sufficient force within the said Territories, and with the said force to attack, arrest, disarm or disperse the said armed men so unlawfully assembled and disturbing to the public peace ...

[appeal by J.S. Dennis] By virtue of the above commission from the Lieutenant-Governor I now hereby call on and order all loyal men in the North-west Territories to assist me by every means in their power to carry out the same and thereby restore public peace and order, and uphold the supremacy of the Queen in this part of Her Majesty's Dominions.'

McDougall's proclamation is dated 1 December, Dennis' appeal is given as 6 December.

The proclamation was printed at Lower Fort Garry on the same handpress as the above broadside by P.G. Laurie on 3 December. Was the Dennis postscript printed on this date, or were the copies of the broadsides run through a second time to add the additional information?

The Manitoba Archives has another printing of this commission on oilskin, suggesting that it is Col. J.S. Dennis' actual commission. Type-page is 36.2 x 16.5cm. Man. Arch.

g) List of Rights. [Text – 14 points followed by 4 paragraphs describing the meeting at which these were approved] Winnipeg, December 4th, 1869. Broadside: 35 lines. Type-page, 18.2 x 16.7cm.

The fourteen points were adopted at a meeting held at Fort Garry on 1 December as conditions under which Rupert's Land would enter confederation. A revised and extended list was issued in French on 23 March 1870. Man. Arch. – Can. Arch.

h) Declaration of the People of Rupert's Land and the North West. [Text] Issued at Fort Garry this 8th day of December, in the year of our Lord, one thousand eight hundred and sixty-nine. (Signed) John Bruce, President. Louis Riel, Secretary. Broadside: 72 lines. Type-page, 32 x 17cm.

This broadside proclaimed the establishment of a provisional government.

A preliminary printed draft is also in the Manitoba Archives. Man. Arch.

i) Declaration des Habitants de la Terre de Rupert et du Nord-Ouest. [Text] Broadside: 68 lines. Type-page, 25.3 x 11.1cm.

This is the French version of the above broadside. A preliminary draft of this broadside was printed. Of the draft, Col. Dennis at Lower Fort Garry recorded in his diary for the evening of 7 December that Mr. William Coldwell had arrived from Fort Garry with a copy. 'Mr. Caldwell [sic] said that he had been forced to print it, that the French were not satisfied to keep his press from him but in addition, forced him to work for them by threats of armed men, who were placed in possession.' Man. Arch. – Can. Arch.

j) [Royal Arms. 3 x 5cm.] Lower Fort Garry, Red River Settlement, December 9, 1869. To all whom it may concern. [Text] Given under my hand at the Lower Fort Garry this 9th day of December, 1869. J.S. Dennis, Lieut., and Conservator of the Peace in and for the North West Territories. Broadside: 19 lines. Type-page, 12.5 x 16cm.

Text: '... I now call on and order the loyal party in the North-West Territories to cease further action under the appeal to arms made by me ...'

This broadside became known as the 'peace proclamation.'

The copy in the Manitoba Archives is printed on oiled paper. Man. Arch. – Can. Arch.

k) Orders of the Provisional Government of Rupert's Land. January 8, 1870. Broadside.

Mentioned by Alexander Begg in his journal. Begg said that three days after it was printed it was recalled.

No copy located.

l) Official Order. It is hereby ordered that the town of Winnipeg be and shall be hereafter the capital of the North West. March 5, 1870. Broadside.

Reference made to it by Begg in his journal.

No copy located.

m) Liste des Droits. Revendiques par le peuple de le Terre de Rupert et du Nord-Ouest, et conditions sous lesquelles ce peuple consentirait à entre dans la Confederations Canadienne. [Text] Maison du Gouvernement, Fort Garry, le 23 Mars, 1870. Broadside: 61 lines. Type-page, 29 x 17cm. Can. Arch.

n) Pour prouver aux nations sauvages que le peuple de la Riviere Rouge ne veut pas les laisser maltraiter par le Canada; [Text] Louis Riel. Maison du Gouvernement, Fort Garry, le 23 Mars, 1870. Broadside: 15 lines. Type-page, 9.5 x 11.1cm.

Lists two points of which the second and more important one stated that if Canada entered into any treaties with Indian tribes it would be with the approval of the provisional legislature. Can. Arch.

o) Maison du Gouvernement Provisoire, Fort Garry, 7 Avril, 1870. Aux Hábitants du Nord et du Nord-Ouest, Concitoyens, – [Text] Par ordre du President, Louis Schmidt, Asst. Secr. d'Etat. Broadside: 55 lines. Type-page, 24 x 16.8cm.

Broadside intended to conciliate the opponents of the provisional government. Can. Arch.

p) Proclamation to the People of the North West. [Text] Louis Riel. Government House, Fort Garry, April 9, 1870. Broadside: 50 lines. Type-page, 24.3 x 11cm.

In the text President Riel pardoned 'all those whom political differences led astray for a time,' declared the public highways open, and stated that the Hudson's Bay Company could resume business. Man. Arch.

q) Protestation des Peuples du Nord-Ouest. [Text] Louis Riel. Broadside: 75 lines. Type-page, 40 x 16.5cm. On two pages. Is this a proof intended to have been issued as a single sheet?

The date 14 May 1870 has been provisionally assigned to this broadside in two pieces. Alexander Begg, the observant diarist, does not mention it, and it is probable that the document is a draft which was never issued. It is a statement of the position of the French-speaking inhabitants of the Red River Settlement in their dispute with the Canadian government. Can. Arch.

r) [Royal Arms. 4.5 x 11cm. In first column] To the loyal inhabitants of Manitoba. [Text] G.J. Wolseley, colonel commanding Red River Force. [In second column] Au peuples loyal de Manitoba. [Text] G.J. Wolseley. Colonel. Commandant de l'expedition à la Riviere Rouge. Prince Arthur's Landing, 30 Juin 1870. Broadside: in double column. English text, 29 lines; French text, 35 lines; common text, 1 line. Type-page, 31.5 x 25cm. Colophon: Printed at New Nation office, Winnipeg, 21st July, 1870.

According to Alexander Begg this proclamation was 'issued and published by Riel, and the printing superintended personally by him during the last night at the New Nation office.'

The proclamation assured the inhabitants that the purpose of the militia force was to 'secure Her Majesty's sovereign authority,' that the strictest discipline of troops would be maintained, private property respected, and supplies for the troops duly paid for. Man. Arch.

292 **Canada**. Department of the Secretary of State
Copies of all reports made by the engineers of the Public Works Department on their examination, so far as made last fall, of Dawson's proposed line of canal or water communication through the North-West Territory. Ottawa, 1870. 9p. 24 1/2cm. (Canada. Sess. papers, 1870, no.12 [pt.6]) U. of S.

293 **Canada**. Department of the Secretary of State
Copies of instructions to surveyors sent to North-West Territory, and statement shewing the number of men employed, and the salaries to be paid; also copies of all orders in council relating to such surveys and reports of surveyors employed, with copies of all documents relative thereto. Ottawa, 1870. 21p. fold. map. 24 1/2cm. (Canada. Sess. papers, 1870, no.12 [pt.2]) U. of S.

294 **Canada.** Department of the Secretary of State
Reports of superintendents of roads, from Thunder Bay to Fort Garry on the Red River ... Ottawa, 1870. 78p. 24 1/2cm. (Canada. Sess. papers, 1870, no.12 [pt.3]) U. of S.

295 **Canada.** Governor-General, 1869-1872 (Lisgar)
Correspondence and papers connected with the recent occurrences in the North-West Territories. Printed by order of Parliament. Ottawa, Printed by I.B. Taylor, 1870. xvi, 157p. 23 1/2cm. (Canada. Sess. papers, 1870, no.12)

Documents relating to the Red River Rebellion. Shortt

296 **Canada.** Parliament. Senate. Select Committee on the subject of Rupert's Land, Red River, and the North-West Territory
Report ... together with minutes of evidence. Printed by order of the Senate. Ottawa, Printed by I.B. Taylor, 1870. 38p. 24cm.

The committee examined several persons familiar with Rupert's Land on the suitability of soil and climate for agricultural settlement. Shortt

297 **Chesson,** F[rederick] W[illiam]
The Red River insurrection; three letters and a narrative of events. London, The Aborigines Protection Society, 1870. 28p. 21cm.

The first two letters are by F.W. Chesson, the third by A.K. Isbister. Sask. Arch.

298 **Church of England.** Diocese of Rupert's Land
The by-law of the clergy widow and orphan's fund of the Diocese of Rupert's Land. [Winnipeg? 1870?] 1 l. printing on front and verso. 21cm.

The type used was very broken and uneven. C.M.S. - 25

299 **Corbett,** Griffith Owen
An appeal to the Right Hon. W.E. Gladstone ... respecting the suppression of certain papers by the Government; the Red River Rebellion, and the illegal transfer of the North-West Territories to the Canadian Government. London, Printed for the author by Cassell, Petter & Galpin [1870] 12p. 21cm. B.C. Arch.

300 **Corbett,** Griffith Owen
The Red River Rebellion; the cause of it. In a series of letters to the British Government on the importance of opening the overland route through Rupert's America from Canada to British Columbia. For the introduction of means for the administration of justice therein; the promotion of emigration; and earnest appeals to stop bloodshed in the Red River Settlement, by extending righteous rule to that country. London, Printed for the author by Cassell, Petter & Galpin, 1870. 36p. 21cm. B.C. Arch.

301 **Dawson,** Aeneas MacDonell
Our strength and their strength. The North West Territories, and other papers chiefly relating to the Dominion of Canada. Ottawa, Printed at the Times office, 1870. viii, 326, 7p. plate. 22cm.

Only about 30 pages deal directly with the West. Shortt

302 **Emslie**, John
Journal of expedition to Fort Garry. [n.p.] 1870. caption-title, 14p. 22cm.

A letter dated 'Fort Garry, Sept., 1870' and signed 'Your affectionate brother.' Presumably published by the recipient in Ontario. Toronto

303 **Great Britain.** Colonial Office
Correspondence relative to the recent disturbances in the Red River Settlement. Presented to both Houses of Parliament by command of Her Majesty, August, 1870. London, Printed by William Clowes & Sons, 1870. ix, 223p. 33cm. ([Parliament. Papers by command] c-207) Shortt

304 **Great Britain.** Colonial Office
Red River ... Copy of all petitions that have been addressed to Her Majesty or to Her Majesty's Government from the inhabitants of the Red River district or other settlements or districts within the boundaries of British territories in North America, from 1860 up to the present time. Colonial Office, 10 August 1870. W. Monsell. (Viscount Milton.) Ordered, by the House of Commons, to be printed, 10 August 1870. [London, 1870] cover-title, 11, [1]p. 33 1/2cm. ([Parliament, 1870. H. of C. Reports and papers] 443)

Includes memorials from Thomas Spence and his provisional government at Portage la Prairie. Shortt

305 **Great Britain.** Treasury
Canada (Rupert's Land). Statement of proceedings taken by the Lords Commissioners of Her Majesty's Treasury to give effect to the guarantee of a loan for £300,000 authorised by the Act 32 & 33 Vict., c.101. Treasury Chambers, 28 June 1870. James Stanfield. Ordered, by the House of Commons, to be printed, 29 June 1870. [London, 1870] 3, [1]p. 34cm. ([Parliament, 1870. H. of C. Reports and papers] 315) Shortt

306 **Great Britain.** War Office
Notes on the routes from Lake Superior to the Red River, and on the settlement itself, compiled from reports by Captain Palliser, Professor Hind, and Messrs. Dawson and Napier; with notes relating to the transport of troops, &c., by Colonel Crofton and Captain (now General) Lefroy, R.A.; compiled in the topographical department of the War Office, Colonel Sir Henry James, director. London, Printed at the War Office, 1870. iv, 58p. 33cm. Not seen.

At head of title: Confidential. Amtmann, no.24

307 **McDougall,** William
The Red River Rebellion. Eight letters to Hon. Joseph Howe, Secretary of State for the Provinces, etc., in reply to an official pamphlet. Toronto, Printed by Hunter, Rose & Co., 1870. iv, [5]-68p. 22cm.

A reply to the anonymous 'Red River Insurrection: Hon. Wm. McDougall's Conduct Reviewed.' See Entry 289. Shortt

308 **Major,** J.C.
The Red River expedition. Winnipeg, Printed by P.G. Laurie, News-Letter office, 1870. 28p. 22cm.

An account in verse of Major's experiences between Prince Arthur's Landing and Red River as a member of the 1200-man Wolseley expedition. This was probably the first pamphlet printed in English in Western Canada.

Reprinted in the facsimile series of the Bibliographical Society of Canada in 1953. Can. Arch.

309 The Memorial & petition of the people of Rupert's Land and North-West Territory, British America, to His Excellency, U.S. Grant, President of the United States. [n.p., 1870] cover-title, 11p. 22 1/2cm.

Dated 3 Oct. 1870 at Red River. (Photostat copy of original in Harvard Library)
Can. Arch.

310 **Morton,** W[illiam] L[ewis] ed.
Manitoba: the birth of a province. [Altona, Man., Printed by D.W. Friesen & Sons Ltd., 1965] xxx, 265p. col. front., plates (incl. ports.) 24cm. (Manitoba Records Society Publications, v.1)

A collection of reports, diaries, and letters, written by persons involved in 'disturbances of 1869-70' in the Red River Settlement. U. of A.

311 **Rupert's Land.** Legislature [Provisional government]
Bill ... [Winnipeg, Printed by the New Nation Printing Co., 1870] 5 broadsides. Text on recto, docket-title on verso. Leaf-size: 29.5cm.

Contents:
Bill No.1. A bill respecting the haying privilege.
Bill No.2. An act to provide for the administration of public justice.
Bill No.3. An act providing for a military force.
Bill No.4. An act respecting indemnity to members.
Bill No.5. A bill respecting the haying privilege. (Bill No.1 as revised in the Legislature).
'1st Session, 1st Parliament, March, 1870.' The bills were passed 24 to 26 March.
A copy of Bill No.3 found in the Public Archives of Canada, the others in the Manitoba Archives. Can. Arch. - Man. Arch.

312 **Rupert's Land.** Legislature [Provisional government]
Minutes of proceedings ... Wednesday, March 9th, 1870 ... [Winnipeg, Printed by H.M. Robinson & Company, 1870] head-title, [4]p. 23.5cm. [page 1] Head-title, plus list of members in attendance. Pages 2-3 are text. Docket-title: No.1, 1st Session, 1st Legislature, Fort Garry. Can. Arch.

313 [**Strathcona and Mount Royal,** Donald Alexander Smith, 1st baron]
North-West Territories. Report of Donald A. Smith. Ottawa, 1870. 13p. 24 1/2cm. (Canada. Sess. papers, 1870, no.12 [pt.4])

Report of his visit to the Red River Settlement during the winter of 1869-70. U. of S.

314 **Synge,** [Millington Henry]
On practical communication with Red River district, central British America; or, Alleged impossibilities solved by example. An illustration applied towards the unity of the empire of Great Britain. [London?] 1870. 20p. 21cm. Read before the Royal Colonial Society, Jan. 17, 1870. B.C. Arch.

315 **Taylor,** James Wickes
The James Wickes Taylor correspondence, 1859-1870. Hartwell Bowsfield [Editor] Altona, Man., Printed by D.W. Friesen & Sons Ltd., 1968. li, 185p. 24cm. U. of A.

316 **Thibault,** [Jean Baptiste]
North-West Territories. Report ... [Ottawa, 1870] 3p. 24 1/2cm. (Canada. Sess. papers, 1870, no.12 [pt.5])

Report on conditions in the Red River Settlement during the disturbance. U. of S.

317 **United States.** President. Grant
Message of the President of the United States communicating, in compliance with a resolution of the Senate of December 8, 1869, information relating to the presence of the Honorable William McDougall at Pembina, in Dakota Territory, and the opposition by the inhabitants of Selkirk Settlement to his assumption of the office of Governor of the Northwest Territories. [Washington, 1870] 52p. 23cm. (41st Cong., 2d Sess. House. Ex. doc., no.33) B.C. Arch.

318 [**Anonymous**]
The North-West Territories; being an account of their extent, soil, and natural resources; the routes of travel; with a sketch of their history down to the organization of the Province of Manitoba. Toronto, A.S. Irving, 1871. 1p.l., [9]-135p. fold. map. 22cm. B.C. Arch.

319 **Begg,** Alexander
The creation of Manitoba; or, A history of the Red River troubles. Toronto, A.H. Hovey, 1871. v, 408p. front. 19cm.

A valuable history of the rebellion because based on a diary in which the author recorded the occurrences and the movement of local opinion from day to day. Shortt

320 **Begg,** Alexander
Dot it down; a story of life in the North-West. Toronto, Hunter, Rose & Co., 1871. viii, 9-381p. front. 19cm.

A novel describing the experiences of a family from Ontario who emigrated to the Red River Settlement. The book was obviously written to attract immigrants. An appendix informs the prospective immigrant on routes to Red River. Shortt

321 **Butler,** [Sir William Francis]
Report by Lieut. Butler, (69th Regt.) of his journey from Fort Garry to Rocky Mountain House and back, during the winter of 1870-71. [Winnipeg? 1871?] 23p. 32 1/2cm.

Report was also printed as an appendix in his 'Great Lone Land.'
Butler was commissioned to report to Lieut.-Gov. Archibald on the smallpox epidemic raging among the Indians. Can. Arch. (photostat copy)

322 **Canada.** Department of the Secretary of State
Return: instructions to the Honorable A. Archibald, Lieutenant-Governor of Manitoba and of the North-West Territory, &c., &c. Printed by order of Parliament. Ottawa, Printed by I.B. Taylor, 1871. 135, 5, 5p. 25cm. (Canada. Sess. papers, 1871, no.20)

Consists of correspondence between the Dominion government and the Lieut.-Gov. on such topics as postal arrangements, customs, census and elections for House of Commons, international boundary, and laws of Assiniboia. Supplementary returns contain correspondence with the Imperial government over the Manitoba Act, and the survey system to be inaugurated in Manitoba. U. of S.

323 **Canada.** Department of the Secretary of State
Statement of claims made on the Dominion Government, consequent upon the insurrection in the North-West Territories. Ottawa, Printed by I.B. Taylor, 1871. 57p. 24cm. (Canada. Sess. papers, 1871, no.44) Shortt

324 Circulaire privée au clergé de toute la province ecclésiastique de Quebec. Archevêche de Québec, 1871. [Québec, 1871] caption-title, 3p.

A document signed by the Archbishop of Quebec and several other ecclesiastical representatives, in which a plea is made to French Canadian youths to migrate to Manitoba, rather than to the border states of the United States. Lande

325 [**Clarke**, Henry Joseph Hynes]
Report of the Honourable the Attorney-General to His Excellency the Hon. A.G. Archibald, Lieutenant-Governor of the Province of Manitoba and the North-West Territories, on the Immigration Conference held at Ottawa, 18th Sept., 1871. [n.p.] 1871. 14p. Not seen. Queen's

326 **Dawson**, S[imon] J[ames]
Report on the Red River expedition of 1870. Printed by order of the House of Commons. Reprint: with remarks on certain strictures published in England by an officer of the expeditionary force. Ottawa, Printed by the Times Printing & Publishing Co., 1871. 57p. fold. map. 24cm.

Dawson replies to statements made in an article which appeared in Blackwood's Magazine. Can. Arch.

327 **Great Britain.** War Office
Correspondence relative to the recent expedition to the Red River Settlement; with Journal of operations. Presented to both Houses of Parliament by command of Her Majesty, 1871. London, Harrison and Sons, 1871. cover-title, 96p. 33cm. ([Parliament. Papers by command] c-298)

The journal was written by Col. Garnet Wolseley, commander of the expedition. In his autobiography, 'Story of a Soldier's Life' (Westminster, 1903), some sixty pages are devoted to this expedition.

Glenbow Library has a second volume entitled 'Maps to illustrate the correspondence ... Papers by command.' c324. Shortt

328 **Hargrave**, Joseph James
Red River. Montreal, Printed for the author by John Lovell, 1871. xvi, [17]-506p. 20 1/2cm.

A valuable history based on papers belonging to the author's father, an H.B.C. employee, and written under the eye of his uncle, William Mactavish, another old company servant. Shortt

329 **Huyshe**, G[eorge] L[ightfoot]
The Red River expedition. London, Macmillan and Co., 1871. xi, [1], 275, [1]p. front., illus., port., fold. maps, fold. table. 22cm.

A member of Wolseley's staff describes the experiences of the troops en route. Shortt

330 **Irvine**, M[atthew] Bell
Report on the Red River expedition of 1870. Presented to both Houses of Parliament by command ... London, Harrison and Sons, 1871. 16p. fold. plate. 33cm. ([Parliament. Papers by command] c-391)

Report of the assistant controller of the expedition. Rutherford

331 **McLean**, John
Circular letter ... To the reverend the clergy and laity of the Church of England in the Province of Manitoba. St. John's College, Manitoba, November 8, 1871. [Winnipeg? 1871?] caption-title, [3]p. 28cm.

The Bishop of Rupert's Land issued a similar one in 1873. (See C.M.S. Reel 26.) C.M.S. - 14

332 **Mills,** David
The blunders of the Dominion Government in connection with the North West Territory. A speech ... at London, January 17th, 1871. London, Ont., Advertiser Steam Job Office, 1871. cover-title, 8, [1]p. 22 1/2cm. U.B.C.

333 **North West Emigration Aid Society**
Second circular of the executive committee of the North West Emigration Aid Society, May, 1871. [Toronto, 1871] caption-title, 11p. 22cm.
Rutherford

334 **Raymond,** Joseph Sabin
Discours sur le 20e anniversaire du sacre de Mgr Taché, archevêque de St-Boniface, prononcé à Boucherville, le 23 novembre 1871. [s.1., 1871?] 12p.
St. Sulpice

335 **Riddell,** H[enry] S[om.] H[utton]
The Red River expedition of 1870. A paper read before the Literary and Historical Society of Quebec, March 15th, 1871. (In Quebec Lit. & Hist. Soc., 1870-71, p.99-136. 23cm.)

An account by one of the officers of the expedition. Can. Arch.

336 **Spence,** Thomas
Manitoba and the North-West of the Dominion; its resources and advantages to the emigrant and capitalist, as compared with the western states of America; its climate, soil, agricultural and manufacturing facilities; its unparalleled salubrity, growth and productiveness, in comparison with the older provinces; and the elements of its future greatness and prosperity; and containing land policy, latest information, cheapest and best way to get to Red River, and what is required. Toronto, Hunter, Rose & Co., 1871. 46p. front., illus. 18cm.

The first of the flood of pamphlets written to advertise the agricultural possibilities of the West. Spence may be regarded as the father of prairie immigration literature.
A second revised and enlarged edition was published in Ottawa in 1874, and a French translation of it in 1875. Another English edition appeared in Quebec in 1876. Shortt

337 **Sulte,** Benjamin
L'expédition militaire de Manitoba, 1870. Montréal, Eusèbe Senécal, 1871. 50p. 24cm.

First appeared as two articles in Revue Canadienne, juillet et août 1871. Can. Arch.

338 **Waddington,** Alfred
Sketch of the proposed line of overland railroad through British North America ... 2d ed. Ottawa, Printed by I.B. Taylor, 1871. iv p., 1 l., [7]-29p. 21 1/2cm.

Published originally in London by Longmans [etc.] in 1868. Shortt

339 [**Anonymous**]
Ontario and Manitoba (North West Rebellion). By a Canadian who has visited Manitoba to discover the truth. [n.p.] 1872. 16p. 19 1/2cm. Title-page lacking.

Author critical of the attitude of the people of Ontario toward Riel and his followers during and after the rebellion. Can. Arch.

340 **Ballantyne,** Robert Michael
The pioneers; a tale of the western wilderness, illustrative of the adventures and discoveries of Sir Alexander Mackenzie. London, J. Nisbet & Co., 1872. viii, 150p.

Juvenile fiction. Ran through a number of editions. (A later edition in Rutherford.) Br. Mus.

341 **Bible.** New Testament. Cree
Le Nouveau Testament, en langue crise d'après les quatre Evangélistes, ou concordance des quatre Évangiles. Montréal, Imprimerie de l'asile de la Providence, 1872. 478p. 14 1/2cm.

Translated into Cree syllabic by Rev. A. Lacombe. Oblates Arch.

342 **Butler,** [Sir] W[illiam] F[rancis]
The great lone land; a narrative of travel and adventure in the north-west of America ... London, Sampson Low, Marston, Low, & Searle, 1872. x p., 1 l., 388p. front. (fold. map.) plates. 23cm.

After participating in the events of 1870 at Red River, the author was sent on a special mission across the prairies to report on the smallpox epidemic. This is one of the travel classics of the West.

By 1875 seven reprints or editions had been published; in 1924 Musson of Toronto published the nineteenth edition. Shortt

343 **Canada.** Department of the Secretary of State
Copies of all correspondence with Lieut.-Governor A.G. Archibald, of Manitoba, and Mr. McMicken, Land Commissioner, regarding the Fenian invasion of Manitoba, and the intercourse of the said Lieut.-Governor with Louis Riel, the leader of the rebellion in the territory, and one of the men charged with the murder of Thomas Scott. [Ottawa, 1872] 14p. 25cm. (Canada. Sess. papers, 1872, no.26, pt.2) U. of S.

344 **Canada.** Treaties, etc.
Copies of the treaties, made 3rd and 21st August, 1871, between Her Majesty the Queen and the Chippewa and Cree Indians of Manitoba and the country adjacent. Ottawa, Printed by I.B. Taylor, 1872. 10p. 24cm.

The Library of Parliament has an 1879 reprint. Can. Arch.

345 **Fleming,** [Sir] Sandford
Progress report on the Canadian Pacific Railway exploratory survey ... Ottawa, 1872. 80p. 25cm. Shortt

346 [**Griffin,** Justin Alonzo]
From Toronto to Fort Garry. An account of the second expedition to Red River. Diary of a private soldier. Hamilton, Printed at the Evening Times [1872?] 62p. front. 20 1/2cm.

The diary covers the period, Oct. 19–Nov. 18, 1871. The edition in Man. Leg. Library has no imprint date. The copy listed in Can. Arch. catalogue is dated 1893. Man. Leg.

347 [**Lacombe,** Albert]
Dictionnaire et grammaire de la langue crise, par un missionnaire de la Saskatchewan. Prospectus. Montréal, C.O. Beauchemin et Valois, 1872. cover-title, 17p. 21cm. N.Y.

348 **Lacombe**, Albert
[Lettre adressée à ses confrères, par le Père Lacombe; sollicitant une aide financière pour le diocèse de Saint Albert, Saskatchewan] Montréal, 1872. 7p. 22cm. Can. Arch.

349 **Ross**, P[atrick] Robertson
Report of Colonel Robertson-Ross, Adjt.-General of Militia, on the north-west provinces and territories of the Dominion. Ottawa, 1872. 33p. 23 1/2cm.

Advocated the establishment of military posts and units of mounted riflemen to preserve order, an idea which materialized as the North West Mounted Police. Shortt

350 **Tassé**, Joseph
Le chemin de fer Canadien du Pacifique. Montréal, Eusèbe Senécal, 1872. 62p. 22cm. Can. Arch.

351 **Wagner**, W[illiam]
Einwanderung nach Manitoba. Bericht des Regierungs-Landvermessers W. Wagner an die Deutsche Gesellschaft zu Montreal. [Montreal? 1872] caption-title, 24p. 23cm. Can. Arch.

352 **Wallace**, N[esbit] Willoughby
The rebellion in the Red River Settlement, 1869-70, its causes and suppression. A lecture delivered at Clifton, October 25th, 1871. Barnstaple [England] Henry T. Cook, 1872. 40p. fold. map. 18cm.

'It makes no pretence of being anything more than a familiar account of what (to use his [the author's] own expression) was a novel military-naval expedition – something in fact between a "sailor's yarn," and "a soldier's tale."' Published to raise money for the local church. Can. Arch.

353 **[Anonymous]**
Comments on the proceedings and evidence on the charges preferred by Mr. Huntington, M.P., against the Government of Canada. Montreal, Gazette Printing House, 1873. 1p.l., 16p. 22cm.

A pamphlet in support of the government, based on an examination of the evidence of the Royal Commission of inquiry. Shortt

354 **[Anonymous]**
A plea for the early development of our resources. Winnipeg, Kenny & Luxton, 1873. 5p. 21cm. Can. Arch.

355 **Blake**, Edward
Three speeches ... on the Pacific Scandal ... [n.p., 1873] caption-title, 66p. 21 1/2cm. Shortt

356 **Butler**, [Sir] W[illiam] F[rancis]
The wild north land; being the story of a winter journey, with dogs, across northern North America. London, S. Low, Marston, Low & Searle, 1873. x p., 1 l., 358p. front. (port.) plates, fold. map. 22 1/2cm.

A journey to Lake Athabasca, and to the Pacific via the Peace River in 1872-73.
By 1874 the publishers had brought out the fourth edition. New editions were published in New York in 1904 and 1922, and in Toronto in 1924. Shortt

357 **Canada.** Department of the Secretary of State
Copies of all communications from Indians or others in Manitoba, with the Government on the subject of the dissatisfaction prevailing among the chiefs, headmen, and Indians treated with in Manitoba, and adjacent territory in the year 1871. [Ottawa, 1873] 16p. 25cm. (Canada. Sess. papers, 1873, no.23, pt.2) U. of S.

358 **Canada.** Department of the Secretary of State
Copies of all reports from the Land Commissioner in Manitoba, regarding the sale or location of lands in that province; all reports from, or correspondence with, the Commissioner (or any other parties regarding the sales or location of lands in the province); also for copies of the letters of resignation of Mr. Canavan, and all correspondence between Mr. Canavan and the Government; also all correspondence with the Government of Manitoba on the subject of the complaints against the management of the land office in that province. [Ottawa, 1873] 24p. 25cm. (Canada. Sess. papers, 1873, no.45) U. of S.

359 **Canada.** Governor-General, 1872-1878 (Dufferin)
Message. Papers relative to the issue of a commission to inquire into certain charges made against members of Her Majesty's Privy Council for Canada, respecting the granting of a charter and contract to the Canadian Pacific Railway Company. Ottawa, Printed by I.B. Taylor, 1873. 10p., 1 l. 23 1/2cm. Shortt

360 **Canada.** Governor-General, 1872-1878 (Dufferin)
Message. Papers relative to the prorogation of Parliament on the 13th day of August 1873. Ottawa, Printed by I.B. Taylor, 1873. 99, [1]p. 23 1/2cm.

Relates to the Pacific Scandal. Shortt

361 **Canada.** Royal Commission to inquire into and report upon the several matters relating to the Canadian Pacific Railway
Report of the Royal Commissioners appointed by commission, addressed to them, under the Great Seal of Canada, bearing date the fourteenth day of August, A.D. 1873. Ottawa, 1873. xii, 220p. 24cm. (Canada. H. of C. Journal, 1873, appendix 1) Shortt

362 **Canadian Pacific Railway**
The Canadian Pacific Railway. Montreal, Gazette Printing House, 1873. 1p.l., vi, 113, [1]p. 22cm.

Contains royal letters patent incorporating the company, together with the legislation of the Parliament of Canada especially applicable. Shortt

363 **Canadian Pacific Railway**
Charter for the construction of the Pacific Railway, with papers and correspondence. Printed by order of Parliament. Ottawa, I.B. Taylor, 1873. [1], 40p. 25cm. Can. Arch.

364 **Correll,** Ernst H.
Mennonite immigration into Manitoba, Canada; sources and documents, 1872, 1873. [Goshen, Indiana, 1937] 50, [1]p. 25cm. Reprinted from the Mennonite Quarterly Review, July and October, 1937.

The article reprints many documents found in the Public Archives of Canada. A continuation of this series of documents relating to the years 1873-74 was published in the Mennonite Quarterly Review, Jan. 1948; other collections of documents edited by Dr. Correll in the same periodical are 'The Mennonite Loan in the Canadian Parliament, 1875,' Oct. 1946; 'Canadian Agricultural Records on Mennonite Settlements, 1875-77,' Jan. 1947; 'Sources on Mennonite Immigration from Russia in the 1870's,' Oct. 1950. Offprints of some or all of these were published. L.C.

365 **Cunningham**, Robert
Speeches on the Indian difficulties in the North-West; delivered by Robert Cunningham, M.P., & Hon. D.A. Smith, M.P., in the House of Commons, April 1st, 1873. Ottawa, Free Press Steam Publishing Establishment, 1873. 14p. 21 1/2cm. Queen's

366 [**Denison**, George Taylor] comp.
Reminiscences of the Red River Rebellion of 1869. [n.p., 1873] 7, 45p.

Consists principally of extracts from newspapers, with an introduction by G.T. Denison. Man. Leg.

367 **Grant**, George M[onro]
Ocean to ocean. Sandford Fleming's expedition through Canada in 1872. Being a diary kept during a journey from the Atlantic to the Pacific with the expedition of the Engineer-in-Chief of the Canadian Pacific and Intercolonial Railways ... London, S. Low, Marston, Low, & Searle, 1873. xiv p., 1 l., 371p. incl. front., illus. plates (incl. maps) 21cm.

One of the classics of Canadian travel.
Several editions appeared in the 1870's. A new edition was published in Toronto by the Radisson Society of Canada in 1925 with an introduction and bibliography by W.L. Grant. Shortt

368 **Great Britain**. Colonial Office
Correspondence re: question of an amnesty for acts committed during the disturbances in the Red River Settlement. London, 1873. 57p. R.E.S.

369 **Horetzky**, Charles
The North-West of Canada. Being a brief sketch of the north-western regions, and a treatise on the future resources of the country. Ottawa Printed at the office of A.S. Woodburn, 1873. 30p. 20cm. Can. Arch.

370 **Langelier**, J[ean] C[hrysostôme]
Étude sur les territoires du Nord-Ouest du Canada. Montréal, Eusèbe Senécal, 1873. iv, [5]-69p. 29cm. Rutherford

371 [**Machray**, Robert]
... Memorandum by the Bishop of Rupert's Land on the present state of the mission. [London, 1873?] caption-title, 6p. 20 1/2cm.

At head of title: Confidential, for the use of Committee [of the Church Missionary Society] C.M.S. Lib.

372 **Manitoba**. Executive Council
Report of the delegates of the Executive Council, to Ottawa, with regard to the claims of Manitoba on the Dominion. Winnipeg, Printed by Caldwell & Cunningham [1873] 5, xiii p. 21 1/2cm.

Another edition with imprint and pagination as follows: Winnipeg, Printed by John A. Kenny, Queen's Printer, Daily Free Press Steam Printing Office [n.d.] 5, xxvii p. 20 1/2cm. (Copy in the Arkin collection) Shortt

373 **Moore,** William
Report on the condition and working of the Prince Albert Presbyterian Mission to the Indians on the Saskatchewan ... Ottawa, Woodburn, 1873. 52p. 21cm.

The 2 Feb. 1872 issue of the Western Advertiser made statements reflecting on the Rev. James Nisbet's management of the mission. Rev. Mr. Moore, sent out by the Foreign Mission Committee of the Canada Presbyterian Church, found the statements 'made up of inferences from slender premises.' Acadia. Queen's

374 **Schultz,** Sir John Christian
Speech on Indian affairs in the North West Territories, delivered in the House of Commons, 31st March, 1873. [n.p., 1873] caption-title, 8p. 25cm.

From the Ottawa Times. Can. Arch.

375 **Scott,** D.H.
Guide; Ontario to Manitoba; being a diary kept during a journey from Toronto, Ontario, to Winnipeg, Manitoba, via the Lake Superior, Duluth and Moorehead route, during a tour through Manitoba, visiting the principal farming settlements, and returning to Ontario, via the Dawson route. Toronto, Troy & Co., 1873. 61p. 20cm.

Author remained one month in Manitoba. Queen's

376 **Shantz,** Jacob Y[ost]
Narrative of a journey to Manitoba ... together with an abstract of the Dominion Lands Act; and an extract from the government pamphlet on Manitoba. Published by Department of Agriculture. Ottawa, Printed by Robertson, Roger & Co., 1873. 31p. 22cm.

Shantz was sent out to inspect land for the Russian Mennonites who subsequently settled in southern Manitoba. Shortt

377 **White,** Thomas
Our great West. A lecture delivered under the auspices of the Young Men's Christian Association of Christ Church Cathedral, on the evening of the 27th February, 1873. Montreal, Dawson Bros., 1873. 32p. 20cm. Rutherford

378 [**Anonymous**]
The history of the Lake Superior ring. An account of the rise and progress of the Yankee combination, headed by Hon. Alexander Mackenzie, Premier of Canada, and the Browns, for the purpose of selling their interest and political power to enrich Jay Cooke & Co. and other American speculators, changing the route of the Canada Pacific Railway, with a view of breaking up our great Dominion, and severing our connection with the British Empire. Thorough exposé of Mackenzie's and Brown's treachery to their country. This pamphlet is stereotyped, so that generations to come may look back with contempt upon a Government that has united with the Republicans of the United States to destroy our prosperous country. Toronto, Printed at the office of the Leader & Patriot, 1874. 14p. 23cm. Can. Arch.

379 [**Anonymous**]
Rupland. Our northern empire. How to reach our vast possessions. The different routes analyzed and described. The Canadian Pacific Railway necessary for the development of our resources. St. Catharines, Printed at the Journal Printing House, 1874. 15p. 22cm. Can. Arch.

380 **Canada.** Department of Agriculture
Le Canada et l'emigration Européenne. Ottawa, Department of Agriculture, 1874. 48p.

Contains much material on the lands available in the Prairie Provinces. Canner - 474-179

381 **Canada.** Department of Agriculture
Province of Manitoba. Information for intending emigrants. Ottawa, Department of Agriculture, 1874. 56p. front. (fold. map.) 16 1/2cm.

First edition was published in 1872. Shortt

382 **Canada.** Department of the Interior
Annual report of the Minister of the Interior. 1874-1936. Ottawa, 1874-1936. v.

Branches of government connected with the West which were at one time or another under this department are as follows: Dominion Lands Branch, 1873- ; Indian and Indian Lands Branch, 1873-80; Geology Survey, 1873-90; North West Mounted Police, 1878-83; North West Territories Branch, 1873-98; Dominion Lands Survey, 1883-1922; Half-Breed Commission, 1885-90; Immigration, 1893-1917.

The annual reports of this department are a mine of information for the serious student interested in the opening up of the West. U. of S.

383 **Canada.** Department of the Secretary of State
Copies of all instructions on the practicability of a mixed land and water transcontinental communication with British Columbia, and for reports thereon. Ottawa, Printed by I.B. Taylor, 1874. 6p., 1 l. 23 1/2cm. (Canada. Sess. papers, 1874, no.51) Shortt

384 **Canada.** Laws, statutes, etc.
Acts respecting the administration of justice and for the establishment of a police force in the North-West Territories as consolidated for the purpose of reference. [n.p., 1874?] 19p. 17cm. Can. Arch.

385 **Canada.** Parliament. House of Commons. Select Committee on the causes of the difficulties in the North-West Territory in 1869-70
Report ... Ottawa, Printed by I.B. Taylor, 1874. ix, 208p. 24cm.

The committee took evidence on causes of the rebellion, the cause of the delay in granting an amnesty, and whether the promise of amnesty had ever been given. Twenty-eight witnesses were examined and many documents filed. Shortt

386 **Canada.** Treaties, etc.
Copy of Treaty no.4 and supplementary treaty made 15th and 21st September, 1874, between Her Majesty the Queen and the Cree and Saulteaux tribes of Indians at Qu'Appelle and Fort Ellice. [Ottawa, 1874?] 8p. 24cm. L. of P.

387 **Church of England.** Diocese of Rupert's Land
The provisional statutes and act of incorporation of St. John's Cathedral, Winnipeg. Winnipeg, Printed by W. Coldwell, 1874. cover-title, 16p. 20 1/2cm. C.M.S. Lib.

388 **L'Événement**, Québec
Au pilori. La trahison des chefs conservateurs démontrée par les témoignages recueillis devant le Comité du Nord-Ouest. (Extraits de L'Événement) Québec, Imprimerie de L'Événement, 1874. 22p. 21 1/2cm.

Refers to the amnesty question in Manitoba. Shortt

389 **Fleming,** [Sir] Sandford
Confidential memorandum on the Canadian Pacific Railway. Ottawa, Printed by I.B. Taylor, 1874. 59p. 20 1/2cm. Shortt

390 **Fleming,** [Sir] Sandford
Report of progress on the exploration and surveys up to January 1874. Ottawa, Printed by MacLean, Roger & Co., 1874. xi p., 2 l., 286 (i.e. 294)p. fold. plates (incl. maps) 25cm. At head of title: Canadian Pacific Railway. Sandford Fleming, Engineer-in-Chief. Plates no.8, 10-11, 13-16 were issued later in a case.

Appendices (partial contents): A., Expedition across the continent, notes on the character of the country; B., Peace River expedition, by Charles Horetzky; C., Botanical report, Lake Superior to the Pacific Ocean, by John Macoun; O., Navigation of lakes and rivers in the prairie region, by A.R.C. Selwyn. Shortt

391 **Foran,** T[homas] P[atrick]
Trial of Ambroise Lepine at Winnipeg for the wilful murder of Thomas Scott ... Montreal, Lovell, 1874. 15p. 21cm. Not seen. Acadia

392 **Great Britain.** Colonial Office
Correspondence relative to the Canadian Pacific Railway. Presented to both Houses of Parliament by command of Her Majesty, March, 1874. London, William Clowes & Sons, 1874. 1p.l., 266p. 33cm. ([Parliament. Papers by command] c-911)

Correspondence relative to the Pacific Scandal. Shortt

393 **Hunter,** Jane (Ross), tr.
Kukwāche̍toowe mussina̍hikun. A catechism for the Cree Indians of Rupert's Land (north-west America). London, Printed for the Society for Promoting Christian Knowledge, 1874. 8p. 16cm. Not seen.

A translation of Watt's catechism. Text in Roman characters. First published in 1855 by the Church Missionary Society. L.C.

394 **Lacombe,** Alb[ert]
Dictionnaire de la langue des Cris. Montréal, Beauchemin & Valois, 1874. 6p.l., [v]-xx, 700p. 23 1/2cm. Shortt

395 **Lacombe,** A[lbert]
Grammaire de la langue des Cris. Montréal, Beauchemin & Valois, 1874. 1p.l., iii, 190p. 23cm. Shortt

396 **Leidarvisir fyrir vesturfara til Canada.** [Reykjavik, Einar Thodarsson, 1874] folder. 5p. 10 x 43cm.

Printed on one side only.
About half the text relates to Manitoba. Denmark

397 **Lepine,** Ambroise Dydime, defendant
Preliminary investigation and trial of Ambroise D. Lepine for the murder of Thomas Scott, being a full report of the proceedings in this case before the Magistrates' Court and the several Courts of Queen's Bench in the Province of Manitoba. Specially reported and compiled by Messrs. Elliott and Brokovski. [Montreal, Printed by the Burland-Desbarats Lithographic Co.] 1874. 121p. front., ports. 22 1/2cm. Shortt

398 **Manitoba Club**
Constitution and by-laws. Winnipeg, Nor'West print [1874?] 15p. 13cm.
Can. Arch.

399 **Riel**, Louis
L'amnistie. Mémoire sur les causes des troubles du Nord-Ouest et sur les négociations qui ont amené leur règlement amiable. [Montréal] Bureau de Nouveau Monde, 1874. 22p. illus. (port.) 21cm.

Another edition with slightly different title was published in Ottawa in the same year.
Shortt

400 **Taché**, [Alexandre Antonin]
L'amnistie. Montréal, Imprimée par le journal Le Nouveau Monde, 1874. 72p. 19 1/2cm.

The Archbishop, acting on behalf of the Canadian government, helped to restore order in 1870, but he promised a general amnesty; the government claimed this promise exceeded his instructions. Shortt

401 **Taché**, [Alexandre Antonin]
Archbishop Taché, O.M.I., on the amnesty question with regard to the North West difficulty; communicated to 'The Times' on the 6th, 7th and 8th April, 1874. St. Boniface, Printed by the Canadian Publishing Co., 1893. 60p. 22cm.

An English edition of Entry 400. See also Entry 402. Shortt

402 **Taché**, [Alexandre Antonin]
The North West difficulty. Bishop Taché on the amnesty question, as appeared in The Times on the 6th, 7th and 8th April, 1874. [n.p., 1874?] cover-title, [3]-36p. 24cm.

Text in double column. Can. Arch.

403 **Wilson**, W[illia]m
The Dominion of Canada and the Canadian Pacific Railway ... Victoria, Rose, 1874. [2], 42p. tables. 24cm.

Rare item on the Prairie Provinces. B.C. Arch.

404 **[Anonymous]**
Revue de la session parlementaire de 1875. [n.p., n.d.] caption-title, 63p. 23cm. In double column.

Devoted mainly to the amnesty question. St. Sulpice

405 **Beaubien**, Louis
Les chemins de fer. Nos communications avec l'Ouest. Discours de M. Louis Beaubien. [Québec? 1875?] 1p.l., [5]-40p. 21cm. U. of A.

406 **Beaubien**, Louis
The Pacific Railway and its eastern connections. Speech delivered in the Legislative Assembly of the Province of Quebec on 18th January 1875. Montreal, Gazette Printing House, 1875. cover-title, 16p. 23cm. U. of A.

407 **Bryce**, George
The Presbyterian Church in Canada, and the Canadian Northwest. Toronto, British American Presbyterian Office, 1875. 21p. front. (fold. map.) 18 1/2cm.
Man. Leg.

407A **Canada.** Department of Agriculture
Dominion lands, in Manitoba, Keewatin and the Northwest Territories, open for sale and homestead entry. [Winnipeg] 1875-78. 12v. 21 1/2cm.

Title varies slightly. Issued periodically. Can. Arch. (ms.)

408 **Canada.** Department of Agriculture
Nýja Island. Nýja Island i Kanada. Areidanleg lysing a legu og ásigkomulagi lands pess, er Kanada stjórnin hefir afmarkad til Islendinga byggdar og full skyrsla um, med hverjum kostum land er veitt ókeypis, og um ferda kostnad pangad, o.s. frv. i tveim skýrslum ... Ottawa, 1875. cover-title, 24p. fold. map. 17cm. Denmark

409 **Canada.** Governor-General, 1872-1878 (Dufferin)
Despatches regarding commutation of Lepine's sentence and North-West amnesty. Ottawa, MacLean, Roger & Co., 1875. cover-title, [42]p. 24 1/2cm. Shortt

410 **Church of England.** Ecclesiastical Province of Rupert's Land
Journal of the Provincial Synod of the Church of England in Rupert's Land. First session. Tuesday and Wednesday, third and fourth days of August, in the year of our Lord, 1875. Winnipeg, 'Standard' Printing and Publishing House [1875] 30, [2]p. 26cm.

This journal was reprinted in 1904. C.M.S. - 27

411 **Conservative Party**
Les Rouges et leurs oeuvres. Déplorables resultats des dix huit mois de pouvoir des Libéraux. La province de Quebec abaissée, asservie, méprisée. [Ottawa, 1875?] 64p., orig. wrappers.

Relates to Riel amnesty. Canner - 434-438

412 **Dawson,** George Mercer
Report on the geology and resources of the region in the vicinity of the forty-ninth parallel, from the Lake of the Woods to the Rocky Mountains. With lists of plants and animals collected, and notes on the fossils. Montreal, Dawson Bros., 1875. xi, 387p. plates (part. fold.) fold. maps (incl. front.) 24cm.

The author accompanied the British section of the British-American Boundary Commission. Shortt

413 **Elliott,** George B[abington]
Winnipeg as it is in 1874; and as it was in 1860 ... Ottawa, Printed at the Free Press office, 1875. cover-title, 36p. fold. maps. 21cm.

The first edition, published in 1874, contained 56 pages. Shortt

414 Exemplification of the proceedings and judgment of outlawry of Louis Riel. Ottawa, Printed by MacLean, Roger, & Co., 1875. 4p. Hayter Reed

415 **Finney,** W.
Manitoba. London, Labour News, 1875. cover-title, 10p. 18 1/2cm. (Pioneer papers, no. x) Br. Mus.

416 **Hunter,** [James]
A lecture on the grammatical construction of the Cree language delivered by the Ven. Archdeacon Hunter before the Institute of Rupert's Land at the Court

House, Fort Garry, Red River Settlement on the 2nd April, 1862 ... Also paradigms of the Cree verb, with its various conjugations, moods, tenses, inflections, &c. London, Printed for the Society for Promoting Christian Knowledge, 1875. 2p.l., 267p. 30cm. Shortt

417 **J[ohnson]**, M.E., supposed author
Dayspring in the far west; sketches of mission work in north-west America, by M.E.J. London, Seeley, Jackson and Halliday, 1875. xi, [1], 215p. plates. 20cm.

Newberry Library copy has presentation inscription on the fly-leaf signed 'M.E. Johnson,' and a ms. note 'Presentation inscription by the author.' The writer was a woman.
Five chapters relate to missions in the region now the Prairie Provinces. An appendix contains a valuable chronology of missionary endeavours. Shortt

418 [**Lacombe**, Albert]
Instructions en langue crise sur toute la doctrine catholique, par un missionnaire oblat de la Saskatchewan. St-Boniface, Journal de Métis, 1875. 505, iv p. front. (Oblate seal) 15cm.

Text in Cree, with headings in French. L.C.

419 **Langevin**, [Sir] H[ector] L[ouis]
Chemin de fer Canadien du Pacifique. [n.p., 1875] 30p. Not seen. U. de Montréal

420 [**Machray**, Robert]
The Bishop of Rupert's Land submits the following statement to the thoughtful consideration of church men. [Winnipeg, 1875] caption-title, 2p. 27cm. C.M.S. - 27

421 [**Mackay**, John Alexander] tr.
[Church of England catechism in Cree syllabics. Stanley Mission, Mission Press, 1875]

'I have prepared and printed for the use of the (confirmation) candidates, the church catechism, translated idiomatically, and broken into short questions, in which shape I find it better adapted to the capacities and opportunities of our people than in the original form.' - Annual letter to Church Missionary Society, 16 Dec. 1875. C.M.S.

422 [**McLean**, John]
Notes from the Bishop of Saskatchewan's journal January to May, 1875. Winnipeg, Printed at the 'Standard' Office [1875] cover-title, 8p. 22cm.

Describes a winter journey from Winnipeg to Prince Albert via Lakes Manitoba and Winnipegosis, and concludes with a description of the Prince Albert district. C.M.S. - 27

423 [**McLeod**, Malcolm]
The Pacific railway. Britannicus' letters, from the Ottawa Citizen. Ottawa, Printed by the Citizen Printing and Publishing Co., 1875. cover-title, 42, [1] p. 22cm.

The author was concerned about the future of the Pacific railway scheme during the tenure of office of the Mackenzie government, and during those years sought to keep the project alive by letters in the press and by pamphlets. Shortt

424 **McLeod,** M[alcolm]
Pacific railway, Canada. Britannicus letters, &c., thereon ... Ottawa, Printed by A.S. Woodburn [1875?] cover-title, 36, 21p. 24cm.

Selection from series of letters by 'Britannicus' (from 1869 to 1875) on the subject, with additional remarks.

Part II has separate title-page: Pacific Railway routes, Canada. U. of A.

425 [**Mason,** Sophia (Thomas)] tr.
... A first catechism of Christian knowledge, the Lord's Prayer, the Apostles' Creed, and the Ten Commandments. For the Cree Indians of Rupert's Land, north-west America. London, Society for Promoting Christian Knowledge, 1875. 14p. 17cm.

Text in syllabic characters, with English captions. Probably another edition of Entry 213. Americas

426 **Millman,** Thomas
Impressions of the West in the early seventies from the diary of the Assistant-Surgeon of the British North American Boundary Survey, 1872-75. (In Women's Can. Hist. Soc., Toronto. Reports, 1927-28, p.15-56) Not seen. R.E.S.

427 The Queen vs. Louis Riel. Exemplification of the proceedings and judgment of the outlawry of Louis Riel. Winnipeg, 1875. Tanghe

428 **Sister of Charity of Montreal**
Notes and sketches collected from a voyage in the North-West, by a Sister of Charity of Montreal. For the furtherance of a charitable object. Montreal, F. Callahan, 1875. 23p. 21 1/2cm.

The sister was in charge of a party of Grey Nuns sent out in 1871 to the missions and hospitals of the order in the West. She travelled as far as Lac La Biche and Isle à la Crosse, before returning East in 1872. Shortt

429 **Smyth,** Edward Selby
[Report on the defences and mounted police in the North-West] (In Canada. Dept. of militia. Annual report, 1875, p.xxiii-xlvii) Shortt

430 **Southesk,** [James Carnegie] earl of
Saskatchewan and the Rocky Mountains. A diary and narrative of travel, sport, and adventure, during a journey through the Hudson's Bay Company's territories, in 1859 and 1860. Edinburgh, Edmonston and Douglas; Toronto, James Campbell and Son, 1875. xxx, 448p. incl. front., illus. plates, fold. maps, facsim. 22cm.

One of the classics of early western travel literature.

A small edition, privately printed, apparently appeared in Edinburgh the previous year, 1874. Shortt

431 **Taché,** [Alexandre Antonin]
The amnesty again; or, Charges refuted ... Winnipeg, Standard office, 1875. 31p. 22cm.

A 42-page French edition was published by Le Metis. Shortt

432 **Trow,** James
A trip to Manitoba. Quebec, S. Marcotte, 1875. 86p. 20cm.

A series of letters which appeared originally in the Stratford Beacon. Can. Arch.

433 Vingt-cinquième anniversaire de l'épiscopat de Sa Grandeur Monseigneur Taché, archevêque de St-Boniface. Montréal, J.A. Plinquet, 1875. 40p. 21cm. Shortt

434 **Anderson,** S[amuel]
The North American boundary from the Lake of the Woods to the Rocky Mountains. (In Royal Geog. Soc. Journal, v.46, 1876. p.228-62. fold. map. 22cm.)

Experiences with the British-American Boundary Commission by the Chief Astronomer of the British party. B.C. Arch.

435 [**Anonymous**]
Debate in the Senate on the Canadian Pacific Railway. The government policy criticized. Ottawa, 1876. 70p. 24cm. Not seen. Can. Arch.

436 **Bible.** Old Testament. Psalms. Cree
Nikumoowe mussinàhikun. The book of Psalms, translated into the language of the Cree Indians of north-west America, by the Ven. Archdeacon Hunter. London, British and Foreign Bible Society, 1876. 2p.l., 271p. 18cm.

Text in Roman characters. L.C.

437 **Bible.** New Testament. Cree
The New Testament translated into the Cree language, by the Right Rev. John Horden. London, British and Foreign Bible Society, 1876. 2p.l., 425p. 19cm. Title also in Cree. Shortt

438 **Canada.** Department of Agriculture
Province of Manitoba; and North-West Territory of the Dominion of Canada. Ottawa, The Department, 1876. cover-title, 79p. 19 1/2cm

By 1881 this pamphlet was in its 5th edition. Shortt

439 **Canada.** Department of the Interior
Copies of all orders of His Excellency the Governor-General in Council, and of all laws and ordinances of the Lieutenant-Governor and Council of the North-West Territories, made under the provisions of 34 Vic., cap.16, sec.1, submitted for the information of the Honorable the House of Commons [Ottawa, 1876] 11p. 25cm. (Canada. Sess. papers, 1876, no.70) U. of S.

440 **Canada.** Treaties, etc.
Copy of Treaty no.6, made 9th September, 1876, between Her Majesty the Queen and the Plain and Wood Cree Indians, and other tribes of Indians, at Fort Carlton, Fort Pitt and Battle River. [Ottawa, 1876?] 11p. 24cm. L. of P.

441 **Canadian Pacific Railway**
Description of the country between Lake Superior and the Pacific Ocean on the line of the Canadian Pacific Railway. Compiled from the best authorities, and

published by order of the Canadian Government. Ottawa, 1876. xxxix, [1], 143p. 23 1/2cm.

'Compiled primarily for the benefit of intending contractors to supplement the more technical reports of the engineer-in-chief.' Shortt

442 **Church Missionary Society**
Memorandum on North West America financial system. [London, 1876] 2p. 24cm.

Signed: Edward Hutchinson, Lay Secretary. C.M.S. Lib.

443 **Douglas**, George
Memorial of Rev. George McDougall, Indian missionary to the Saskatchewan, with his two last letters. Presented to the teachers and scholars of the St. James St. Sabbath School. Montreal, 'Witness' Printing House, 1876. cover-title, 8p. port. 22cm.

Caption-title: Memorial of the late Rev. George McDougall, by Rev. Dr. Douglass [!] Glenbow

444 **Featherstonhaugh**, [Albany]
Narrative of the operations of the British North American Boundary Commission, 1872-76. Woolwich, Eng., A.W. and J.P. Jackson, 1876. 69p. fold. map, diagrs. (part. fold.) 24cm. Reprinted from the 'Professional Papers' of the corps of Royal Engineers, v.23. Shortt

445 **Great Britain**. War Office
Correspondence respecting the determination of the north-western boundary between Canada and the United States. Presented to both Houses of Parliament by command of Her Majesty, 1875. London, Printed by Harrison and Sons [1875] 1p.l., 2p. 33cm. ([Parliament. Papers by command] 1131) At head of title: North America, no.1 (1875)

——Further correspondence ... 1876. 1p.l., 10p., 1 l. 33cm. ([Parliament. Papers by command]1552) At head of title: North America, no.8 (1876)

The second paper lists astronomical stations and location of boundary markers. Shortt

446 **Hamilton, J**[ames] **C**[leland]
The prairie province; sketches of travel from Lake Ontario to Lake Winnipeg, and an account of the geographical position, climate, civil institutions, inhabitants, productions and resources of the Red River valley ... Toronto, Belford Bros., 1876. vii, 259 (i.e. 255)p. incl. front., illus., plates. plates, fold. maps, fold. plan. 18 1/2cm. Error in paging nos.121-24 omitted. Shortt

447 **Manitoba**. Laws, statutes, etc.
Acte pour établir un système d'éducation dans la province du Manitoba. Avec ses amendements. Publié par autorité. St. Boniface, 1876. 41, 9p. Ehrlich - 36-1

448 [**McLeod**, Malcolm]
... Pacific railway. Extra tax for it, not necessary. British Columbia ... Ottawa, Printed by the Citizen Printing and Publishing Co., 1876. cover-title, 15p. 21 1/2cm. Caption title: Britannicus' letters published in the Ottawa Citizen. Shortt

449 **Royal Canadian Mounted Police**
Annual report of the Commissioner. 1876– Ottawa, 1876– v.

Appeared from 1876 to 1905 as report of the North West Mounted Police, from 1906 to 1920 as report of the Royal North West Mounted Police, and from 1920 as report of the Royal Canadian Mounted Police. No reports issued in 1874, 1875, 1877, 1878 and 1883.
The reports for the first thirty-odd years are a valuable source of information as they contain many references to Indians, ranching, incoming settlers, etc. U. of S.

450 **Wood**, Edmund Burke
Report of Chief Justice Wood respecting claims made to reward offered for apprehension of the murderers of Thomas Scott. Toronto, 1876. (Ontario. Sess. papers, 1875-76, no.58) Not seen. Howard

451 **Canada**. Department of the Secretary of State
Copies of all instructions to the Honorable A. Morris, Lieutenant-Governor of the North-West Territories; also copies of all orders in council relative to the said territories since their organization, and not already published; also, copies of all reports and official correspondence between the Lieutenant-Governor and the Dominion Government from the date of his appointment. [Ottawa, 1877] 78p. 25cm. (Canada. Sess. papers, 1877, no.121) U. of S.

452 **Canada**. Parliament. House of Commons. Select Standing Committee on immigration and colonization
Report ... Printed by order of Parliament. Ottawa, Printed by MacLean, Roger & Co., 1877. 257p. 23 1/2cm. (Canada. H. of C. Journal, 1877, appendix no.6)

Evidence on the agricultural potentialities of the West submitted by J.Y. Shantz, A.G.B. Bannatyne, Hugh Sutherland, Thos. Spence, Mr. Hill, Mr. Fuller, and Col. Dennis.
Shortt

453 **Canada**. Parliament. Senate. Select Committee appointed to inquire into and report on the route of the Canadian Pacific Railway from Keewatin westward, &c.
Report and minutes of evidence ... Printed by order of the Senate. Ottawa, Printed by MacLean, Roger & Co., 1877. 53p. 23 1/2cm. (Canada. Senate. Journal, 1877, appendix no.1) Shortt

454 **Church of England**. Diocese of Saskatchewan
Diocese of Saskatchewan. Bishop:– The Right Reverend John McLean, D.D., D.C.L. [n.p., 1877] caption-title, [3]p. 24cm.

An appeal for funds. C.M.S. - 29

455 **Dawson**, George M[ercer]
Notes on the appearance and migration of the locust in Manitoba and the North West Territories; summer of 1875. [Montreal? 1877?] 20p. 21cm. Reprinted from the Canadian Naturalist. Man. Leg.

456 **Down**, J.W.
The Manitoban and great North-West colony. Explanation of its advantages and objects, from personal visits and negotiations ... Bristol, Jeffries and Sons, 1877. 15p. diagr. 19 1/2cm.

The writer had obtained eight townships of land for an agricultural colony. L. of P.

457 **Fleming,** [Sir] Sandford
Report on surveys and preliminary operations on the Canadian Pacific Railway up to January 1877. Ottawa, Printed by MacLean, Roger & Co., 1877. xvi, 431p. fold. maps, fold. plans. 26 1/2cm. Shortt

458 [**Hunter,** Jean (Ross)] tr.
Kunache nikumoowina, ā kē mussinăhŭk nāheyowe keeswāwinik, Mrs. Hunter. [Hymns translated into the Cree language] London, Gilbert & Rivington, 1877. iv, 741-828p. 18cm.

Originally appended to and paged continuously with some copies of James Hunter's Ayumehawe mussinahikun, 1877. Glenbow

459 **Libertas** [pseud.]
National schools for Manitoba. A reply to a pamphlet entitled 'Denominational or free Christian schools.' Winnipeg, Printed by the Standard Book and job Office, 1877. 25p. 13cm. Not seen.

See also Entry 466. B.C. Arch.

460 **Mackay,** John Alexander, tr.
[Prayers compiled by Rev. David Anderson, Bishop of Rupert's Land, and translated into Cree by Rev. J.A. Mackay. Stanley Mission, Mission press, 187–] ... Not seen. Kirkby: Manual of prayer (in prefatory note) See Pilling

461 **Mackay,** John Alexander, comp. & tr.
Psalms and hymns in the language of the Cree Indians of north-west America. London, Society for Promoting Christian Knowledge, 1877. 108p. 10 1/2cm. Not seen.

In Cree syllabic.
Rev. H. Cochrane (Annual letter, 1875, to Church Missionary Society) 'I have not heard anything of the hymns my wife and I translated last winter 116 in a collection. I hope the Society will kindly have these printed; the people (of Devon, The Pas) are very fond of them. The Rev. Mr. McKay will print them in syllabic this winter, but we want them in the Roman character as well.' C.M.S., Reel 7. At this time Mr. Mackay was at Stanley Mission where he had a press. Newberry

462 Manitoba directory for 1877-78, containing the names of professional and business men and other inhabitants of the province, with advertisers classified business directory, and a miscellaneous directory. 2nd year. Winnipeg, Manitoba Directory Publishing Co. [1877] 147p. 22cm.

The earlier edition 'Manitoba directory for 1876-77' has the imprint and pagination: St. Boniface, La Riviere & Gauvin, 1876. 2-162p. 22cm. Shortt

463 **O'Donnell,** J[ohn] H[arrison]
Manitoba matters, being a short chapter devoted and dedicated to the Davis-Royal administration. The autonomy of provinces no longer respected. Ottawa dictates, Manitoba obeys. Winnipeg, Printed at the Herald office [1877] cover-title, 22p. 22cm. Man. Leg.

464 **O'Leary,** Peter
Travels and experiences in Canada, the Red River territory and the United States. London, J.B. Day [1877] vii, 226p. 19 1/2cm.

A journey undertaken in 1874 to ascertain the possibilities for Irish emigrants of the labouring class. Shortt

465 **Spence**, Thomas
The Saskatchewan country of the North-West of the Dominion of Canada, presented to the world as a new and inviting field of enterprise for the emigrant and capitalist, its comparison as such with the western states and territories of America ... Montreal, Printed by Lovell Printing and Publishing Co., 1877. 60p. front. (fold. map) 21cm. Pagination includes advertising. Shortt

466 **Taché**, [Alexandre Antonin]
Denominational or free Christian schools in Manitoba. Winnipeg, Standard Book and Job Printing Establishment, 1877. 126p. 21cm. Shortt

467 **United States.** Commission appointed to meet Sitting Bull
Report of the Commission appointed by the direction of the President, under instructions of the Honorables the Secretary of War and the Secretary of the Interior, to meet the Sioux Indian chief, Sitting Bull, with a view to avert hostile incursions into the territory of the United States from the Dominion of Canada. Washington, 1877. 12p. 23cm. Rutherford

468 **Begg**, Alexander
Practical hand-book and guide to Manitoba and the North-West ... Toronto, Belford Bros., 1878. vii, [9]-110p. 22 1/2cm. Contents listed on title-page.
First published in 1877. Man. Leg.

469 **Bible**. Paraphrases. Chipeweyan
Histoire Sainte en montagnais. Lac la Biche, 1878. Not seen.
The translator was Rev. Henri Faraud, who first published it in Paris in 1876. (This edition in Oblates Arch.) The Lac la Biche edition, Alberta's first imprint, was printed by Father Emile Grouard. The printing press is now in the St. Albert Museum.
Title and text in syllabic. Morice

470 [**Bompas**, William Carpenter]
Beaver Indian primer. [London, 187-] 36p. 16cm. Not seen. Newberry

471 **Canada.** Department of the Interior
Copy of ordinances made by His Honour the Lieutenant-Governor and the Council of the North-West Territories, on the 22 March, 1877, submitted for the information of the Honourable the House of Commons, as directed by Section 7, sub-section 3, of 'The North-West Territories Act, 1877.' [Ottawa, 1878] 48p. 25cm. (Canada. Sess. papers, 1878, no.45) U. of S.

472 **Canada.** Department of the Interior
Navigation of Hudson's Bay. Ottawa, Printed by MacLean, Roger & Co. [1878] 1p.l., 43p. fold. map. 25cm. Shortt

473 **Canada.** Department of the Secretary of State
Copies of all reports of engineers, memorials, &c., relating to the survey and location of the line of the Pacific railway between the Red River and Battleford, and not heretofore laid before Parliament; and also all reports, &c., relating to the proposed line of said railway between the same points, but south of Lake Winnipeg. [Ottawa, 1878] 6p., 1 l. 23 1/2cm. (Canada. Sess. papers, 1878, no.20 i) Shortt

474 **Canada.** Department of the Secretary of State
Copies of all specifications on which tenders were invited to construct the Lake Superior and Fort Garry section of the Canadian Pacific Telegraph; also copies of all correspondence between the government and persons tendering the same; also copies of all contracts for the construction of the several portions thereof. [Ottawa, 1878] 15, [1]p. 23 1/2cm. (Canada. Sess. papers, 1878, no.52) Shortt

475 **Canada.** Department of the Secretary of State
Report of surveys made of Lakes Manitoba and Winnipegoosis, the Waterhen River and Little Saskatchewan River. [Ottawa, Printed by MacLean, Roger & Co., 1878] 19, [1]p. 23 1/2cm. Shortt

476 **Canada.** Department of the Secretary of State
Return ... For copy of all correspondence between the Hudson's Bay Company and the Dominion Government, relative to alleged losses at the Red River Settlement, connected with the insurrection in 1869-70. [Ottawa, 1878] 17,[1]p. 26 1/2cm. H.B.C.

477 **Canada.** Parliament. House of Commons. Select Standing Committee on public accounts
Third report ... in reference to alleged irregularities in the awarding of contracts in Winnipeg. Printed by order of Parliament. Ottawa, Printed by MacLean, Roger & Co., 1878. 2p.l., 103p. 23 1/2cm. Shortt

478 Cinq années d'administration réformiste. La ruine à l'intérieur quand la fortune est à la porte. Choisissez! [Montréal, 1878?] cover-title, xxiii, 110p. fold. map. 21cm.

Caption-title: Quelques faits pour les electeurs du Bas-Canada.
Contains much on Riel and Lepine. U. of A.

479 **Codd,** Donald
The prairie lands of Canada. Montreal, 1878. 56p. Not seen. Dionne

480 **Dawson,** George M[ercer]
Notes on the locust in the North-West in 1876. [Montreal? 1878?] 16p. 21cm. Reprint from the Canadian Naturalist, v.8, no.7, April, 1878. Man. Leg.

481 **Dufferin and Ava,** Frederick Temple Hamilton-Temple-Blackwood, marquis of Canada. Lord Dufferin in Manitoba. Testimony of the settlers. Shipment of Manitoban wheat to Europe. Liverpool, 1878. 16p.

See also Entry 1720. Br. Mus.

482 **Fernon,** Thomas S[argent]
No dynasty in North America. The West between salt waters. Hudson Bay a free basin like the Gulf of Mexico ... Manitoba like Louisiana a maritime state. North America for citizens not for subjects. The West and its ways out to the coast and in from the ocean. Miscellany. Philadelphia, H.B. Ashmead, 1878. 88p. 25cm.

Advocated the annexation of Western Canada. Can. Arch.

483 **Frá Nýja Islandi,** Manitoba, Canada
Snúid úr ensku. Utgefend.: Sigf. Eymundarson, Gudm. Lambertsen. Reykjavik, 1878. 15, [1]p. 16 1/2cm. Denmark

484 **Henderson's directories**, Winnipeg
Henderson's Manitoba & North West Territories gazeteer & directory, 1878-1905?
Winnipeg directory, v.1- 1878- annual. (incorporated as part of above directory for several years)
Edmonton directory, v.1- 1904?- annual.
Calgary directory, v.1- 1905?- annual.
Regina directory, v.1- 1907?- annual.
Saskatoon directory, v.1- 1907?- annual.
Brandon directory, v.1- 1908?- biennial.
Moose Jaw directory, v.1- 1908?- annual.
Lethbridge directory, v.1- 1910?- biennial.
Prince Albert directory, v.1- 1910?- biennial.
Medicine Hat directory, v.1- 1914- biennial.
North Battleford & Battleford directory, v.1, 1913; v.2, 1929.
Swift Current directory, v.1, 1913; v.2, 1916-17.
Yorkton directory, v.1, 1913; v.2, 1921.
Alberta gazeteer and directory, 1914; 1924.

The bibliographer is not certain of the dates some city directories were first published as he has not seen copies, and there was some irregularity in the period between issues. The longest and most complete file of 'Man. & N.W.T. Gazeteer & Directory' is probably the one in the Manitoba Legislative Library; the file of directories in the Edmonton Public Library for the years since 1912 is quite complete. Edmonton

485 [**Taché**, Alexandre Antonin]
Pastoral letter of His Grace the Archbishop of St. Boniface, concerning the elections. [St. Boniface, 1878] cover-title, 15p. 17cm.
Amtmann - 189-826

486 **Tassé**, Joseph
Les Canadiens de l'Ouest. Montréal, Compagnie d'Imprimerie Canadienne, 1878. 2v. plates, ports. 24cm.

Biographies of prominent French Canadians in the western United States and Canada.
Shortt

487 **Trow**, James
Manitoba and North West Territories. Letters ... Together with information relative to acquiring Dominion lands; cost of outfit &c. Ottawa, Published by the Department of Agriculture, 1878. 100p. fold. map. 21cm.

The author travelled as far west as Prince Albert. Written originally as a series of letters to a local paper. Shortt

488 **United States**. Congress
Reports upon the survey of the boundary between the territory of the United States and the possessions of Great Britain from the Lake of the Woods to the summit of the Rocky Mountains, authorized by an act of Congress approved March 19, 1872. Washington, Government Printing Office, 1878. 624p. front., plates, fold. maps. 30cm. Rutherford

489 [**Anonymous**]
Chronicles by the way. A series of letters addressed to the Montreal 'Gazette.' Descriptive of a trip through Manitoba and the North-West. Montreal, Printed by the Gazette Printing Co., 1879. 58p. 21 1/2cm. Can. Arch.

490 **Barnes**, Harris H.
Journal of a trip to Manitoba and back, June and July, 1878. Halifax, J.W. Doley, 1879. cover-title, 22p. 21 1/2cm. Not seen.

'In Ontario prevails a tremendous excitement generally known as "the Manitoba fever," and to a lesser degree its influence is felt in Nova Scotia ... Some persons are under the impression that all they have to do is apply to the Dominion Government and receive free grants of farms of the very best quality free of charge ... This delusion was even published as a fact in a certain Halifax newspaper ...' N.S. Arch.

491 **Begg**, Alexander
Ten years in Winnipeg. A narrative of the principal events in the history of the city of Winnipeg from the year A.D. 1870, to the year A.D. 1879, inclusive. By Alexander Begg and Walter R. Nursey. Winnipeg, Printed at the Times Printing and Publishing House, 1879. 3p.l., [3]-226p. illus. (plan) 22 1/2cm. Shortt

492 **Canada**. Department of Agriculture
Dominion of Canada. The Province of Manitoba and North West Territory. Information for intending immigrants. Ottawa, Department of Agriculture, 1879. 23p. plates, fold. map. Nebenzahl - 16-143

493 **Canada**. Department of the Interior
Extracts from surveyors' reports of township surveys in Manitoba, Keewatin and North West Territories. [Ottawa?] 1879. iv p., 1 l., [5]-82p. 23 1/2cm. Shortt

494 **Canada**. Department of the Secretary of State
Copies of ordinances passed by the Lieutenant-Governor and Council of the North-West Territories, on the 2nd August, 1878, and laid before the Honorable the Senate and the House of Commons ... [Ottawa, 1879] 30p. 25cm. (Canada. Sess. papers, 1879, no.86) U. of S.

495 **Canada**. Parliament. House of Commons. Select Standing Committee on public accounts in reference to expenditure on the Canadian Pacific Railway between Fort William and Red River
First report ... Printed by order of Parliament. Ottawa, Printed by MacLean, Roger & Co., 1879. xv, 135p. fold. tables. 24 1/2cm. Shortt

496 **Canada**. Parliament. Senate. Select Committee appointed to inquire into all matters relating to the Canadian Pacific Railway and Telegraph west of Lake Superior
Minutes of evidence ... Printed by order of the Senate. Ottawa, Printed by MacLean, Roger & Co., 1879. 133p. diagrs. 24 1/2cm. (Canada. Senate. Journal, 1879, appendix no.1) Shortt

497 **Church of England**. Diocese of Rupert's Land
The Diocese of Rupert's Land. [London, 1879] caption-title, 3, [1]p. 26cm.

'The Bishop and Metropolitan of Rupert's Land requests the earnest consideration of the following facts respecting the Province of Manitoba and other fertile land in his diocese, into which emigration is largely entering.' C.M.S. - 29

498 **Church of England**. Diocese of Rupert's Land
Memorandum submitted by the Bishop of Rupert's Land to the church societies. [London, 1879] caption-title, 4p. 26cm.

At head of title: 2, Little Dean's Yard, Westminster, February, 1879.
Description of the diocese, and an appeal for funds. C.M.S. - 29

499 Dominion ldans [sic] in Manitoba, Keewatin & North-West Territories, open for sale and homestead entry. Winnipeg, Standard, 1879. cover-title, 24, [2] p. B.C. Arch.

500 Dominion of Canada, Manitoba and the North-West, the great wheat fields and stock-raising districts of Canada; facts and information for settlers. Montreal, 1879. 24p. fold. plan. Toronto

501 **Dowse**, Thomas
Manitoba and the Canadian North West. [n.p.] 1879. cover-title, 34p. illus. 29cm.

Reprinted from the Chicago Commercial Advertiser, 30 Aug. 1877. It appeared originally as a 31-page separate. Man. Leg.

502 **Fleming**, [Sir] Sandford
Rapport sur les arpentages et explorations préliminaires accomplis sur le Chemin de Fer Canadien du Pacifique dans les années 1877, 1878, 1879. Montréal, Imprimé par Dansereau & Cie, 1879. ci, 608p. fold. maps, fold. plans. 26 1/2cm. Shortt

503 **Fleming**, [Sir] Sandford
Report in reference to the Canadian Pacific Railway. Ottawa, Printed by MacLean, Roger & Co., 1879. 1p.l., ii p., 1 l., [5]-142p. fold. map. 25cm.

Appendix - p.25-142 - is a compilation of all known information about the Canadian West, this data arranged by longitude and latitude. Authorities are cited. Shortt

504 **Hewson**, M. Butt
Notes on the Canadian Pacific Railway. Toronto, Patrick Boyle, 1879. 39p. 22cm. Can. Arch.

505 **Hudson's Bay Company**. Land Commissioner
Manitoba and the North-West, the great wheat fields, and stock-raising districts of Canada. Facts and information for settlers, with a map of the country. Montreal, 1879. 24p. fold. map. 21 1/2cm.

At head of title: Dominion of Canada.
A pamphlet with the same title was published in London, Sir Joseph Causton & Sons, 1881. See Entry 557. Man. Leg.

506 **Kirkby**, William West
A manual of prayer and praise for the Cree Indians of north west America. London, Society for Promoting Christian Knowledge, 1879. 127p. 14 1/2cm. Not seen.

Contains hymns and sacred songs by Mrs. J. Hunter, and prayers from a compilation by D. Anderson, Bishop of Rupert's Land. Br. Mus. Newberry

507 **Lake Winnipeg Land and Colonization Association**
Lake Winnipeg Land and Colonization Association. Privately printed. London, Yates and Alexander, 1879. ... Not seen. Br. Mus.

508 **Lamothe**, Henri de
Cinq mois chez les Français d'Amérique. Voyage du Canada et à la Rivière Rouge du nord ... Paris, Librairie Hachette et Cie, 1879. 2p.l., iv, 373p. plates, ports., maps (part. fold.) 19 1/2cm.

The last hundred pages describe Manitoba. Shortt

509 **Robinson**, H[enry] M[artin]
The great fur land; or, Sketches of life in the Hudson's Bay Territory. With numerous illustrations from designs by Charles Gasche. New York, G.P. Putnam's Sons, 1879. x p., 1 l., 348p. illus. 20cm.

Most of the material appeared originally in American periodicals. The author supplemented personal knowledge with information from published travels, fur trade narratives, etc. Shortt

510 **Ross**, Ross & Killam, barristers, etc.
Important to intending settlers in Manitoba. Sixty thousand acres of select farming lands in the vicinity of Winnipeg, and the various settlements in the Province of Manitoba for sale. Winnipeg, 1879. 32p. 21cm.

Advertising matter included in pagination.
For a later edition see Entry 547. Can. Arch.

511 **Spence**, Thomas
Prairie lands of Canada; presented to the world as a new and inviting field of enterprise for the capitalist, and new and superior attractions and advantages as a home for immigrants compared with the western prairies of the United States ... Montreal, Gazette Printing House, 1879. 56p. 22cm. Shortt

512 **Winnipeg**. St. George's Society
St. George's Society, Winnipeg, Manitoba. [Office bearers, by-laws, list of members] 1879. Winnipeg, Daily Times Steam Printing House [1879] cover-title, 8, [2]p. 15cm.

Paging includes green paper covers. Glenbow

513 [**Anonymous**]
The Manitoba exhibit of 1879, as shown in the cities of Ottawa, London, Hamilton and Toronto; proving that the Province of Manitoba and the Canadian North-West is a fertile soil for willing hands. Winnipeg, Manitoba Free Press steam print, 1880. 31p. 21cm. Pagination includes advertising. Man. Leg.

514 [**Armstrong, L.O.**]
Southern Manitoba and Turtle Mountain country. [n.p., 1880?] cover-title, 32p. fold. map. 19 1/2cm. Advertising included in paging.

Describes a journey by a party of five from Emerson to Turtle Mountain.
N.Y. Pub. Lib. ascribes to Wm. Beach & Co., Emerson, Man. Shortt

515 **Blake**, [Edward]
Canadian Pacific Railway. Hon. Mr. Blake's speech. Ottawa, Printed by MacLean, Roger & Co., 1880. 24p. 29 1/2cm. Can. Arch.

516 **Blake**, Edward
Pacific railway. Speech delivered in the House of Commons ... on Thursday and Friday, 15th and 18th April, 1880. [Ottawa, 1880] 44p. 24 1/2cm. Can. Arch.

517 **Burrows,** Charles Acton
The Canadian Pacific telegraph route. [Winnipeg?] 1880 ... Not seen.
Robertson

518 **Burrows,** [Charles] Acton
North western Canada, its climate, soil and productions with a sketch of its natural features and social condition. A manual of reliable information concerning the resources of Manitoba and the North West Territories, and the inducements which they offer to persons seeking new homes and profitable investments. Land for the landless, homes for the homeless, offered in the future wheat field of the world. Hints as to how, when and where to go. Winnipeg [1880] 114p. fold. map. 21cm.

A 16-page pamphlet with the same title is listed in the N.S. Arch., Akins collection.
Man. Leg.

519 **Canada.** Department of Agriculture
Reports of tenant farmers' delegates on the Dominion of Canada as a field for settlement. Liverpool, Turner and Dunnett, Printers, 1880. 173p. tables. 22cm.

A second series of reports was published in 1881 under the title: Canada in 1880. See Entries 563 & 564. Glenbow

520 **Canada.** Department of Railways and Canals
Reports and documents in reference to the Canadian Pacific Railway. Sandford Fleming. Ottawa, Printed by MacLean, Roger & Co., 1880. xii p., 1 l., 30, 30a-30i, 31-373p. fold. plates (maps, plans) 26cm.

A report on the prairie region similar to the report of the previous year, but with some additional information. Shortt

521 **Canada.** Department of the Secretary of State
Articles of agreement entered into in connection with the Canadian Pacific Railway. Ottawa, Printed by MacLean, Roger & Co., 1880. 98p. 25cm.
Shortt

522 **Canada.** Department of the Secretary of State
Tenders for works on the Canadian Pacific Railway since January, 1879. Printed by order of Parliament. Ottawa, Printed by MacLean, Roger & Co., 1880. 2p.l., 2-203p. incl. fold. tables. 25cm. Shortt

523 The Canadian Pacific Railway. [n.p., 1880?] 64p. 24 1/2cm. 'The following papers, with slight modifications, and the exception of article no.xi, have lately appeared in the Morning Chronicle of Quebec.' Shortt

524 **Church of England.** Manual of devotion. Beaver
Manual of devotion, in the Beaver Indian dialect. Compiled from the manuals of the Venerable Archdeacon Kirkby, by the Bishop of Athabasca. London, Society for Promoting Christian Knowledge [1880] 48p. 14 1/2cm. Not seen.

Text in syllabic characters. Newberry

525 [**Currie,** David]
The letters of Rusticus. Investigations in Manitoba and the North-West, for the benefit of intending emigrants. A series of letters from the special commissioner

of the 'Montreal Witness.' Montreal, John Dougall & Son, 1880. 1p.l., 82p. front., illus., fold. map. 23cm.

A critical study of the possibilities for immigrants in Manitoba made by the author during a tour in 1879. In his conclusion he advises 'genteel people who hate manual labor,' 'gregariously disposed persons,' 'fickle-minded, changeable' people, etc., not to emigrate. 'Young men, whose moral character is not already fully established, should avoid Winnipeg as they would a den of rattlesnakes.' Shortt

526 **Duffield,** A.J.
Needless misery at home and abounding treasure in the west under our own flag; or, Old town and new domains; or, Birmingham and Canada revisited. Birmingham, 1880. 147p. Robert Russell. Cat. of Canadiana. Centennial issue of 1968. No.141

527 **Dugas,** G[eorges]
Manitoba et ses avantages pour l'agriculture. [Montréal? 188–] 27p. illus., fold, map. 22cm. On cover: Ho! lisez ce pamphlet sur le Manitoba ... Shortt

528 **Fitzgibbon,** Mary [Agnes]
A trip to Manitoba; or, Roughing it on the line. Toronto, Rose-Belford Publishing Co., 1880. 2p.l., [v]-xiv, [13]-267p. 19cm. Shortt

529 [**Fleming,** Sir Sandford]
Memorandum addressed to the Honourable the Minister of Railways and Canals by the Engineer-in-Chief of the Canadian Pacific Railway. Ottawa, Printed by Maclean, Roger, & Co., 1880. 17p. 25cm. U. of A.

530 **Gordon,** Daniel M[iner]
Mountain and prairie; a journey from Victoria to Winnipeg via Peace River Pass. London, S. Low, Marston, Searle & Rivington, 1880. x, 310p. front., plates, fold. maps. 20cm.

In 1879 the author accompanied a party which crossed northern British Columbia to explore possible routes for the C.P.R. Shortt

531 **Great Britain.** Colonial Office
Canada. Information for emigrants to the British colonies. [London, Andrews] 1880. cover-title, 16p. fold. map. 21cm.

Mostly about Manitoba. L. of P.

532 **Gunn,** Donald
History of Manitoba, from the earliest settlement to 1835, by Donald Gunn, and from 1835 to the admission of the province into the Dominion, by Charles R. Tuttle. Ottawa, MacLean, Roger & Co., 1880. xxii, [33]-482p. port. 22cm. Shortt

533 **Hall,** E[dward] Hepple
Lands of plenty in the new North-West. A book for all travellers, settlers and investors in Manitoba and North-West Territory. Toronto, Hunter, Rose & Co., [1880] 129p. plates, maps. 19cm.

Extracts from his 'Lands of Plenty: British North America for Health, Sport, and Profit' (London, 1879) Can. Arch.

534 **Hewson**, M. Butt
The Canadian Pacific Railway. Toronto, Patrick Boyle, 1880. vii, 56p. front. (fold. map) 22cm.

Hewson's proposed route led from Quebec city, due west to Norway House, and north of Cumberland House and Lac la Biche. Shortt

535 **Historical and Scientific Society of Manitoba**
Constitution and by-laws. Winnipeg, Tribune Printing Co., 1880. [1], 10, [1]p. 14cm.

'Incorporated 1879.' List of officers on back cover. Glenbow

536 **Horetzky**, C[harles]
Some startling facts relating to the Canadian Pacific Railway and the North-West lands; also, a brief discussion regarding the route, the western terminus and the lands available for settlement. Ottawa, Free Press, 1880. 76p. 21 1/2cm.

Arguments favouring a northern route and a northern terminus in B.C. Shortt

537 **Kingston**, W[illiam] H[enry] G[iles]
The frontier fort; or, Stirring times in the North-West Territories of British America. Toronto, The Musson Book Co. [188–] 1p.l., 160p. front., plates. 19 1/2cm.

Juvenile fiction. Shortt

538 **Livingston**, W[illiam] G[uy]
Farmer vs. Livingston. An appeal by W.G. Livingston to the members of the House of Parliament at Ottawa. [n.p., 188–] cover-title, 14p. plan. 22cm.

A disputed title to land. Can. Arch.

539 **Macdougall**, W.B.
Macdougall's guide to Manitoba and the North-West; a concise compendium of valuable information, containing the latest facts and figures of importance to the emigrant, capitalist, speculator, and tourist, including the latest governmental maps and official land regulations. [Winnipeg] W.B. Macdougall, 1880. 67, [1]p. front. (fold. map) illus. 21 1/2cm.

Three or four editions appeared over a period of years. The 1882 and 1883 editions are in Can. Arch. Shortt

540 **McLeod**, Malcolm
The problem of Canada. Ottawa, Citizen Printing and Publishing Co., 1880. iv, [5]-72p. 20 1/2cm. Errata slip inserted.

At a time when the future of the Pacific railway project was uncertain, the author stressed its importance in developing the British Empire. Shortt

541 **Macoun**, John
[Letter to the Deputy Minister of the Interior] Belleville, 1880. 5p. 34cm.

Relates to Manitoba. Shortt

542 **Mitchell**, P[eter]
The West and North-West. Notes of a holiday trip ... Reliable information for immigrants. Montreal, 1880. 63, [1]p. incl. illus., maps. 22cm. Shortt

543 **Moore**, Thomas
A tour through Canada, in 1879; with remarks on the advantages it offers for settlement to the British farmer ... To which is appended a report on Manitoba specially compiled from the reports of the farmers' delegates from Great Britain. Dublin, The Irish Farmer office, 1880. 48p. illus., map. 21 1/2cm.
Can. Arch.

544 **Morris**, Alexander
The treaties of Canada with the Indians of Manitoba and the North-West Territories; including the negotiations on which they are based, and other information relating thereto. Toronto, Bedfords, Clarke & Co., 1880. 375p. illus. 19 1/2cm.

A valuable source book by one who played a leading role in settling the Indians' claims.
Shortt

545 The Pacific railway. Speeches delivered by Hon. Sir Charles Tupper ... Hon. H.L. Langevin ... J.B. Plumb ... Thomas White ... during the debate in the House of Commons, session 1880. Montreal, Printed by the Gazette Printing Co., 1880. cover-title, 100p. 21cm. Shortt

546 **Roman Catholic Church**. Prayers. Saulteaux
[Livre de prières, etc., en sauteux] Montréal, Beauchemin & Valois, 1880. iv, 382p. illus., plates. 16 1/2cm.

Translated by Rev. A. Lacombe. L.C.

547 **Ross**, Ross, and Killam
... Sixty thousand acres of select farming lands in the vicinity of Winnipeg, and the various settlements of the Province of Manitoba, for sale by Ross, Ross & Killam ... Winnipeg, Manitoba. Toronto, C.B. Robinson, 1880. 32p. 20cm.

At head of title: Canada, Manitoba. L. of P.

548 **The Sun**, Winnipeg
Manitoba and the North-West. The land of immeasurable promise. Happy homes for the millions secured by tickling the rich prairie soil. Facts for actual settlers. What the men who have been there say. Winnipeg, The Sun [188–] cover-title, 19p. 20cm. Can. Arch.

549 **Tassé**, Elie
The North-West. The Province of Manitoba and North-West Territories, their extent, salubrity of the climate, fertility of the soil, products, regulations concerning lands, prices of cereals and farm implements, salaries and wages, travelling routes by land and water, etc., etc., etc. Ottawa, Printed at Le Canada office, 1880. 48, [2]p. 22 1/2cm.

Also published in French. See Entry 650. Shortt

550 [**Van Dyke**, Henry]
The Red River of the north. (In Harper's New Monthly Mag., v.60, May, 1880, p.[801]-817. illus.) Shortt

551 **Winnipeg Conservative Party**
Constitution and by-laws of the Winnipeg Conservative Party. Adopted A.D. 1879. Winnipeg, Daily Times, 1880. 12p. 15cm. U. of A.

552 **Winnipeg.** Selkirk Club
Rules and regulations. November, 1880. [Winnipeg, McIntyre, 1880] [1], 9p. 15cm. Glenbow

553 **Wyatt,** G[eorge] H.
A journey from Liverpool to Manitoba. [1880?] ... Not seen.

'An instructive sketch intended chiefly for the sportsman.' Dom. A.R., 1880-81

554 **Wyatt,** Geo[rge] H.
Manitoba, the Canadian North-West, and Ontario. Toronto, 1880. 98p. fold. map. 22cm. Rutherford

555 [**Anonymous**]
... Complete table of distances, and description of trails in Manitoba and the North-West Territories. Best camping grounds, stopping places, &c. Winnipeg, Manitoba Free Press steam print, 1881. 15, [1]p. 17cm. At head of title: Presented by James F. Ruttan, real estate agent, valuator, &c., Winnipeg Land Office. Man. Leg.

556 [**Anonymous**]
Letters on the anomalous position of Manitoba as a province of the Dominion. [Winnipeg?] 1881. 39p. 19cm. In double column.

A demand for provincial control of natural resources. Comments of the local press on the letters: p.25-39. Man. Leg.

557 [**Anonymous**]
Manitoba and the North-West, the great wheat fields and stock-raising districts of Canada. Facts and information for settlers ... London, Sir Joseph Causton & Sons, 1881. 17p. fold. map. 21cm. Man. Leg.

558 [**Argyll,** John George Edward Henry Douglas Sutherland Campbell, 9th duke of]
The Canadian North-West. Speech delivered at Winnipeg by His Excellency the Marquis of Lorne, Governor-General of Canada, after his tour through Manitoba and the North-West, during the summer of 1881. Ottawa, 1881. 22p. front. (fold. map) 21cm.

A 20-page edition was published in Ottawa, and a 9-page edition with a slightly different title by M'Corquodale of London. It was also translated into German. Man. Leg.

559 **Barrette,** J.E.T.
Récit d'aventures dans le Nord-Ouest, etc. Montréal, W.F. Daniel, 1881. 24p. 21cm.

Part I, Le coureur des bois (aventures de George St-Arnaud); Part II, Appel en faveur du Manitoba et de la Vallée de la Saskatchewan: Part III, Lettre de Manitoba (par T.A. Bernier). France.

560 **Begg,** Alexander
The great Canadian North West; its past history, present condition, and glorious prospects. Montreal, Printed by John Lovell & Son, 1881. 135p. 22 1/2cm. Man. Leg.

561 [**Begg,** Alexander, the elder]
Letters on the situation in the North West, by Julius, as they appeared in the Montreal Gazette. [Montreal?] 1881. 24p. 18 1/2cm. In double column.

For authorship see Can. Hist. Rev., Sept. 1956. Man. Leg.

562 **Bryan**, Mary (Edwards)
Wild work; the story of the Red River tragedy. New York, Appleton, 1881. vii, [3]-410p. 20cm.

Another edition: New York, Munro [1893] (On cover: The Laurel library, no.13) L.C.

563 **Canada**. Department of Agriculture
The agricultural resources of Canada. Reports of tenant farmers' delegates and other informations on Manitoba, North-West Territory and other parts of the Dominion of Canada ... [Ottawa?] 1881. 152p. Canner – 474-178

564 **Canada**. Department of Agriculture
Canada in 1880. Reports of tenant farmers' delegates on the Dominion of Canada as a field for settlement. 2d series. [Ottawa] 1881. viii, [9]-144p. fold. map. 21cm.

Also published in French. Shortt

565 **Canada**. Department of Agriculture
Manitoba und das Nordwestliche Landergebiet. Eine Landkarte und sechs kurze Kapitels. Ottawa, 1881. 16p. fold. map. 20cm. Not seen. Can. Arch.

566 **Canada**. Department of Agriculture
Puissance du Canada; le grand occident canadien ... Informations pour ceux qui veulent émigrer. 2d ed. Ottawa, 1881. 103, [1]p. plates, fold. map. 21cm. Glenbow

567 **Canada**. Department of Agriculture
What farmers say of their personal experience in the Canadian North West. Ottawa, 1881. 91, iv p. 21cm.

Several editions with new testimonials were published in subsequent years. Man. Leg.

568 **Canada**. Department of Indian Affairs
Annual report. 1881– Ottawa, 1881– v.

The department was preceded by the Indian Office which issued annual reports. These appeared as appendices in the reports of the Department of the Secretary of State, 1868-73, and of the Department of the Interior, 1874-79.

Reports were detailed from 1880 to 1913, the period of transition for the prairie tribes from nomadism to reservation life. U. of S.

569 **Canada**. Department of the Secretary of State
Returns and addresses to the House of Commons relative to the surveys and appropriations of lands for the construction of the Canadian Pacific Railway in the Province of Manitoba, North-West Territory and British Columbia. Printed by order of Parliament. Ottawa, Printed by MacLean, Roger & Co., 1881. 1p.l., 51p. 25cm. Shortt

570 **[Chisholm & Dickson]** compilers
The great Canadian North-West. Manitoba, Keewatin, and North West Territories. General features of the country: location and area of Manitoba – description of Keewatin – a glance at the North-West Territories – climate, seasons, etc. – production and capabilities – railways and navigation – the outlook. Winnipeg, Chisholm & Dickson, 1881. 32p. fold. map. 22cm. On cover: Farmers', miners', and tourists' guide. Man. Leg.

571 **[Chisholm & Dickson]**
Hand-book and practical guide for Manitoba and the North-West. Containing railroad time-tables of distances, concise gazetteer of cities, towns, and villages, Winnipeg, 1871 to 1881, best trails and stopping places, post office directory and steamboat communications. [Winnipeg, 1881] ...

Described on back cover of the compilers' 'Great Canadian North-West.' See Entry 570.

572 **Daluaine** [pseud.]
The Syndicate! What is it? A story for young Canadians. Ottawa, A.S. Woodburn [1881] caption-title, 23p. 21 1/2cm.

Written in support of the agreement between the government and the C.P.R. syndicate. Shortt

573 **Dawson**, Aeneas McDonell
The North West Territories and British Columbia. Ottawa, Printed by C.W. Mitchell, 1881. 2p.l., iv, 232p. 20 1/2cm. Advertisements: p.219-32. Shortt

574 The Duluth & Winnipeg Railway. [Boston, Rockwell & Churchill, 1881] 48p. U.C.

575 **[Galbraith, J.F.]**
A sketch of both sides of Manitoba perpetrated by Jeff. Gee, being a narrative of seven years' varied experiences in the prairie province of the Dominion of Canada. Something fresh on an interesting subject. Nelsonville, Manitoba Mountaineer Book and Job Printing Establishment, 1881. 4p.l., 143p. 20cm.

The preface states that it was written to while away a Manitoba winter. Man. Leg.

576 Glaubensbekenntniss der Mennoniten in Reinland, Manitoba, Nord Amerika. Elkhart, Ind., Mennonitische Verlagshandlung, 1881. 37p. Not seen.

Relates to the Mennonites. Bender (In Mennonite Publishing House Library, Scottdale, Pa.)

577 **Langelier**, [Sir] F[rançois Charles Stanislas]
Le Pacifique; historique de la question. – Plan de M. Mackenzie en 1874. – Syndicat de St-Paul. – Syndicat canadien. – Plan de l'opposition. Conférence donnée au Club de Réforme, à Québec, le 4 février 1881. Québec, Impr. de L'Électeur, 1881. 41p. 20 1/2cm. Shortt

578 **La Londe**, [A.] de
Trois mois au Canada et au Nord-Ouest. Rouen, France, Ch. F. Lapierre, 1881. 62p. plan. 21cm.

P.24-40 relate to Manitoba. B.C. Arch.

579 **McEachran**, D[uncan McNab]
A journey over the plains. From Fort Benton to Bow River and back. [Montreal, 1881] 23p. 19cm. Can. Arch.

580 **McEachran**, D[uncan McNab]
Notes of a trip to Bow River, North-West Territories. Montreal, 1881. 10p. 19cm. Reprinted from the Gazette.

Describes the first part of his journey - up the Missouri. As the ms. of this narrative had accidentally been left in Calgary, it was published after his first pamphlet. Can. Arch.

581 **Mackay,** J[ohn] A[lexander] comp.
... Family prayers for the use of the Cree Indians, compiled and translated into the syllabic characters of the Cree language. London, Society for Promoting Christian Knowledge, 1881. 32p. 14cm. Title in Cree & English. On cover: Cree family prayers. Shortt

582 **McLelan,** Archibald Woodbury
Speech on the second reading of a bill to incorporate the Pacific Railway Company, in the Senate, Ottawa ... Feb. 9 & 10, 1881. Reported by A. & Geo. C. Holland. [n.p.] 1881. 28p. diagr. 23cm. L. of P.

582A **Munro,** William F.
The backwoods of Ontario, and the prairies of the North-West. London, Simpkin, Marshall & Co., 1881. 127p. Br. Mus.

583 **Nelson Valley Railway and Transportation Company**
A new route from Europe to the interior of North America, with a description of Hudson's Bay and Straits. Montreal, Printed by John Lovell & Son, 1881. cover-title, 19p. front. (map) 21cm. Shortt

584 **Rae,** W[illiam] Fraser
Newfoundland to Manitoba, a guide through Canada's maritime, mining, and prairie provinces. Reprinted, with large additions from The Times ... London, Sampson Low, Marston, Searle & Rivington, 1881. 3p.l., [vii]-x p., 1 l., 294p. plates, fold. maps (incl. front.) 20cm. Shortt

585 **Roman Catholic Church.** Catechisms. Saulteaux
Abrégé du catéchisme dans la langue des Sauteux. Montréal, Beauchemin & Valois [1881] 1p.l., 43p. 13cm.

Translated by Rev. A. Lacombe. Text in Saulteaux syllabic with headings in French. Oblates Arch.

586 **Sutherland,** A[lexander]
A summer in prairie-land. Notes of a tour through the North-West Territory. Toronto, Printed for the author, at the Methodist Book and Publishing House, 1881. 2p.l., [iii]-x, 198p. illus. 18 1/2cm.

The superintendent of Methodist missions travelled up the Missouri to Fort Benton, and then overland to Morley and Edmonton. He then travelled eastward visiting the more important settlements on the journey to Winnipeg. Shortt

587 **Taylor,** J[ames] W[ickes]
Central British America, physical aspects and natural resources; extracts from the publications of J.W. Taylor. [n.p., 1881] caption-title, 18p. 22cm. Toronto

588 **Westbourne & North-Western Railway**
Prospectus of the Westbourne & North-Western Railway, Manitoba. Winnipeg, McIntyre Bros., 1881. 7p. 17 1/2cm. Man. Leg.

589 **Wyatt**, G[eorge] H., ed.
A reliable guide for settlers, travellers & investors in the city of Winnipeg, Manitoba, and the new North-West. [n.p., 1881] xvi, 59, [1]p. front. (fold. map) Toronto

590 **Allen**, C[harles] W[illiam]
The land prospector's manual and field-book, for the use of immigrants and capitalists taking up lands in Manitoba and North-West Territories of Canada. 2d ed. Ottawa, Printed by C.W. Mitchell, 1882. 8p.l., 62, [40]p. illus., fold. map, plans, diagrs. 12 1/2 x 17cm.

The first edition was published in London by Passmore & Alabaster in 1881. A fifth edition was published in 1889. Shortt

591 **Anglo-Canadian**
Canada. London, G. Street & Co. [1882] 36p. Br. Mus.

592 [**Anonymous**]
One awful night, Meadow Lea, Manitoba. [n.p. n.d.] caption-title, [4]p. 11cm.

Printed on cardboard.
Ballad describing the tragedy of the James Taylor family whose home burned down during a blizzard in March, 1882. Only one of six persons survived.
For an account of the Meadow Lea tragedy see Entry 1927. Private source

593 [**Armit**, William]
... Hudson's Bay Company. Report by the Secretary on matters relating to the Company's landed property. London, Sir Joseph Causton and Sons, 1882. cover-title, 9p. 19cm.

At head of title: Confidential.
Letter addressed to Eden Colvile from Montreal dated 21 September 1882 and pertaining to discussions with officials of the Canadian Pacific Railway re townsites and other lands.
Another printing with same type has larger margins, 22cm. H.B.C.

594 [**Armit**, William]
... Hudson's Bay Company. Report by the secretary on the Company's trade. London, Sir Joseph Causton & Sons, 1882. cover-title, 22p. 18cm.

At head of title: Confidential. H.B.C.

595 **Artigue**, Jean d'
Six years in the Canadian North-West. Translated from the French by L.C. Corbett and Rev. S. Smith. Toronto, Hunter, Rose and Co., 1882. viii, [9]-206p. 18 1/2cm.

The author was one of the original members of the North-West Mounted Police. This was the first autobiographical sketch of police life to appear in print. Shortt

596 **Beaty**, James
Statement of facts and opinions for Hon. Henry J. Clarke, Q.C., of Manitoba, relating to his title to river lots 7 and 9, in the parish of St. Agathe, Manitoba. [n.p., 1882] cover-title, 48p. 21cm. B.C. Arch.

597 Brandon, Manitoba, Canada, and her industries. Winnipeg, Steen & Boyce, 1882. 95, [1]p. 21cm. Toronto

598 **Bryce**, [George]
Manitoba: its infancy, growth, and present condition. London, S. Low, Marston, Searle & Rivington, 1882. viii, 367, [1]p. front., plates, port., maps (part. fold.) 18 1/2cm. Shortt

599 **Brydges**, C[harles] J[ohn]
Hudson's Bay Company, (Land Department). Report ... London, Sir Joseph Causton & Sons, 1882. cover-title, 21p. 18 1/2cm.

This report to the Company's secretary, Wm. Armit, is a letter dated 28 September 1882, describing a journey westward as far as Calgary. He was disappointed with the quality of the land westward from Moose Jaw. H.B.C.

600 **Butler**, Sir William Francis
Red Cloud, the solitary Sioux; a story of the great prairie. London, Low & Co., 1882. x, 327p. plates.

Fiction. A new edition was published by Macmillan of Toronto in 1910. Br. Mus.

601 **Canada**. Department of Agriculture
Canada. Free grants of land. Information for capitalists, farmers, mechanics, labourers, and others, as to the advantages offered to settlers in Manitoba, the North West, and other provinces ... [n.p.] 1882. folder. cover-title, [16]p. illus., maps.

Large brochure, folding (3 folds) to 16 folio pages. (nine numbered, two column pages of text) Four illus. maps of Canada. Patrick - 38-24

601A **Canada**. Department of Agriculture
... A map of the Province of Manitoba showing the Dominion lands surveyed; also lands disposed of and Half-Breed lands. Ottawa, 1882. folder. 18p. map on verso. folds to 22 1/2 x 9cm. Can. Arch. (ms.)

602 **Canada**. Department of the Interior
Extracts from surveyors' reports of township surveys in Manitoba, Keewatin, and North-West Territories. [Ottawa] 1882. [1], 89p. 25cm. Glenbow

603 **Canada**. Department of the Secretary of State
Return of all papers concerning the granting of a charter to the Hudson Bay Company, to construct a tramway around the north shore of the Grand Rapids of the Saskatchewan, and any information to shew if the tramway can be used by the public on paying certain tolls. [Ottawa, 1882] 6, [1]p. 24cm. (Canada. Sess. papers, 1882, no.139) Shortt

604 **Canada**. Department of the Secretary of State
Return showing the names and nationality of all the government land guides in the Province of Manitoba and North West Territories, the residence and former occupation of each ... etc. etc. [Ottawa, 1882] 6p. 25cm. (Canada. Sess. papers, 1881-82, no.44) U. of S.

605 **Canada**. Department of the Secretary of State
Returns relating to the Canadian Pacific Railway (48b to 48p). Printed by order of Parliament. Ottawa, Printed by MacLean, Roger & Co., 1882. 1p.l., 71p. 25cm. Shortt

606 **Canada.** Laws, statutes, etc.
The Canadian Pacific Railway. Contract between the Government of the Dominion of Canada and the Canadian Pacific Railway Company, also the Consolidated Railway Act (1879), and the act of 1881 amending it. Ottawa, Printed by MacLean, Roger & Co., 1882. xix, 155p. 25cm. Shortt

607 **Canada North-West Land Company**
Manitoba and the Canadian North-West. The Canada North-West Land Co. Limited offers for sale, without cultivation or settlement restrictions, 5,000,000 acres of choice farming lands ... Also town lots in the rising towns and cities on the ... Canadian Pacific Railway. [Toronto, 1882?] 4p. Patrick - 38-152

608 **Canada North-West Land Company**
Memorandum and articles of association of the Canada North-West Land Company Limited. Registered 24th July, 1882. [London, 1882] cover-title, 1 l., 30p. 24cm. U.C.

609 **Canada.** Parliament
Petitions and reply to the charges preferred against the Hon. E.B. Wood. Ottawa, MacLean, Roger & Co., 1882. 1p.l., 132p. 24 1/2cm. Shortt

610 **Canada.** Royal Commission on the Canadian Pacific Railway
Report. Ottawa, Printed by S. Stephenson & Co., Chatham, Ont., 1882. 3v. 25cm.

Includes a historical sketch of the development of the idea of a Pacific railway and its execution, written by N.F. Davin. Shortt

611 **Canadian Pacific Railway**
Canada veiledning for nybyggere og andre som vil söge et nyt hjem i Amerika ogsaa breskrivende Manitoba og det Canadiske Nordvesten hvor henimod to millioner acres af det rigeste prairieland er bleven aabnet af den nye Canadiske Pacific Jernbane og hvor 160 acres frit land anvises ankommende nybyggere af den Canadiske regjering. 1882. Liverpool, Turner and Dunnett, 1882. folder. 9p. illus., maps. folds to 19 x 28cm. Norway

612 **Canadian Pacific Railway**
Land grant; twenty-five million acres in Manitoba and the North West, the future wheat field of the continent. Information for intending settlers. Montreal, 1882. folder. (12p.) map. 25cm. Can. Arch.

613 **[Carle,** Frank Austin]
The British Northwest. Pen and sun sketches in the Canadian wheat lands. The illustrations from photographs taken upon the spot. St. Paul, The Pioneer Press Pub. Co. 1882. 1p.l., iii, [1], 85p. illus. 22 1/2cm.

'Recast ... from a series of letters printed in the Pioneer Press newspaper at St. Paul, Minn. in the midsummer of 1882.' Illustrated from photographs taken by F. Jay Haynes, of Fargo, Dakota, who accompanied the writer. Shortt

614 **Charlton,** John
Speech delivered on the government land policy in the North-West. From official debates. House of Commons, session 1882. Ottawa, Maclean, Roger, 1882. cover-title, 28p. 21cm. L. of P.

615 **Church of England.** Diocese of Saskatchewan
Report of the Synod of the Diocese of Saskatchewan, August 31, 1882, with an appendix containing the Notarial Act on consecration; the Bishop's commission from the Archbishop of Canterbury; act incorporating the Synod; and the sermon, preached before the Synod by Rev. Canon Mackay. [Prince Albert, Spink & Maveety, 1882] 14p., [4]l., [8]p. 21cm.

Probably Prince Albert's first imprint, and certainly the first printed report of the synod of this diocese. C.M.S. - 37

616 [**Craig**, John Roderick]
The grazing country of the Dominion of Canada. Reports of tourists, explorers, and residents of the grazing lands of the North-West Territories. February, 1882. Edinburgh, Colston, 1882. 39p. 20cm.

'Introduction' signed: John R. Craig. L. of P.

617 **Dart**, H.A.
Guide to the manufacturers & wholesale dealers in the city of Winnipeg, 1882. [Winnipeg, 1882] half-title, 80p. 21 1/2cm.

Pagination includes much advertising. R.E.S.

618 **Daunt**, Achilles
The three trappers; a story of adventure in the wilds of Canada. London, T. Nelson and Sons, 1882. ix, 256p. plates (part. double) 19cm.

A juvenile adventure story of fur-trade days along the Saskatchewan. Man. Leg.

619 **Diogenes** [pseud.]
The Canadian Pacific Railway and the schemes of the syndicate ... 2d ed. London, Bates, Hendy & Co., 1882. [6], [3]-30, [1]p. 21cm. Arkin

620 Emerson, Manitoba, and her industries ... Winnipeg, Steen, 1882. 71, [1]p. 23cm. Not seen. Acadia

621 **Ennis**, Nicholas Devereux
Important information for intending settlers in Manitoba, respecting a quarter of a million acres of select farming and stock raising lands in the County of Minnedosa, Little Saskatchewan. Liverpool, Turner & Dunnett, 1882. 46p. 21cm. Toronto

622 **Fleming**, Sir Sandford
Letter to the Secretary of State, Canada, in reference to the report of the Canadian Pacific Railway Royal Commission. Printed by order of Parliament. Ottawa, Printed by MacLean, Roger & Co., 1882. 1p.l., 50p. 25cm. Shortt

623 **Fleming**, Sir Sandford
... Observations by Mr. Sandford Fleming on the general land policy of the Hudson's Bay Company. London, Sir Joseph Causton & Sons, 1882. cover-title, 9p. 22cm.

At head of title: Confidential. H.B.C.

624 **Forster**, Joseph
Fat lands for lean tillers. A lecture. Reprinted, with additions, from the 'Weekly London Canadian, and Manitoba and Far-West Times.' London, John Heywood, 1882. 21p. 18cm. Can. Arch.

625 **Fraser**, Geo[rge] B.
Morris, Manitoba, growth and progress. With personal sketches. Morris, The Morris Herald Printing House, 1882. 31p. illus. 22cm. Can. Arch.

626 [**Goodridge**, Richard E.W., of Headingly] supposed author
A year in Manitoba, being the experience of a retired officer in settling his sons. With illustrations, observations on the country, and suggestions for settlers generally. 2d ed. London, W. & R. Chambers, 1882. xii, 116p. front. (fold. map) illus. 17 1/2cm.

Copy in Man. Leg. Library has ms. note in red ink on t.-p.: This is by Capt. Goodridge of Headingly. Shortt

627 [**Kendrick**, Edward]
Manitoba and the Canadian North-West. The land of promise. A few facts worth reading. What an English tenant farmer says about it – finds it more than all it was represented – farming there adds ten years to a man's life. [n.p.] 1882. 22p. illus., map. 21cm. Can. Arch.

628 **Kosmack**, Albert
Beschreibung einer Entdeckungsreise nach dem nordwestlichen Landergebiete von Canada. Ein Brief von Albert Kosmack an das Ministerium für Landwirthschaft [sic.] [Ottawa? 1882?] cover-title, 8p. 20cm. Can. Arch.

629 [**McAdam**, J.T.]
... Canada; the country, its people, religions, politics, rulers, and its apparent future, being a compendium of travel from the Atlantic to the Pacific, the Great Lakes, Manitoba, the North-West, and British Columbia, with a description of their resources, trade, statistics, etc., viewed in its business, social and political aspects. The various cities and resorts, salmon rivers, etc. ... By Captain Mac. Montreal, 1882. 3p.l., [3]-353p. incl. front., illus. 22cm. At head of title: Enlarged edition.

What little information this book contains about the prairies is unreliable. Shortt

630 **McArthur**, Alexander
Causes of the rising in the Red River Settlement, 1869-70. Winnipeg, 1882. 12p. 22cm. (Hist. & Sc. Soc. of Man., no.1) Man. Leg.

631 **Maclean**, J[ohn]
Lone land lights. (First series) Toronto, William Briggs, 1882. 4p.l., 75p. 18 1/2cm.

A series of religious tracts originally printed on the 'printograph' for local distribution among the white settlers in the Bow River district in Alberta. Shortt

632 **Macoun**, John
Manitoba and the great North-West: the field for investment; the home of the emigrant, being a full and complete history of the country ... to which has been added the educational & religious history of Manitoba & the North-West, by George M. Grant ... also Montana and the Bow River district compared for grazing purposes, by Alexander Begg ... also sketch of the rise and progress of Winnipeg, by J.C. McLagan ... Guelph, World Publishing Co., 1882. 3p.l., [v]-xxii, [17]-687p. fold. front., illus., plates, fold. maps, fold. plan, col. diagrs. 24 1/2cm.

An encyclopaedic work on the West of this period. Shortt

632A **Manitoba Land Company, Limited**
The companies' acts, 1862 to 1880. Company limited to shares. Memorandum and articles of association of the Manitoba Land Company, Limited. Trinders & Curtis-Hayward, solicitors. London, Waterlow Bros. & Layton, 1882. 33p. 24 1/2cm. Can. Arch. (ms.)

633 **Manitoba South-Western Colonization Railway Company**, Plaintiff. In the Queen's Bench. Manitoba
The Manitoba South-Western Colonization Railway Company and others against Doctor Schultz and others. Bill of complaint and judgment in full of Chief Justice Wood in pronouncing the judgment of the court, granting, on motion and notice to the defendants, order for interlocutory injunction in terms of the prayer of the bill of complaint. Winnipeg, Manitoba Free Press [1882] cover-title, 49p. 25cm. Can. Arch.

634 [**Patteson**, Thomas Charles] supposed author
The Canadian Pacific Railway and its assailants. Letters from 'Mohawk.' London, 1882. 16p. 22cm. Shortt

634A **Montreal and Western Land Company**
Manitoba lands ... [n.p., 1882?] folder. [12]p. large map on verso. 23 x 10cm. Can. Arch. (ms.)

634B **Montreal and Western Land Company**
Prairie farms in the Qu'Appelle Valley, North-West Territory, Canada. Farmers their own landlords. Free grant lands and lands for sale. [Montreal? 1882] cover-title, 15p. 19cm. Can. Arch. (ms.)

635 [**O'Halloran**, Joseph Sylvester]
Five weeks in Canada ... London, Printed by Spottiswoode & Co., 1882. cover-title, 6p. 18 1/2cm.

Reprinted from the Colonies and India of 15 Dec. 1882. R.E.S.

636 **Ontario**. Provincial Secretary
Correspondence, papers and documents, of dates from 1856 to 1882 inclusive, relating to the northerly and western boundaries of the Province of Ontario. Printed by order of the Legislative Assembly. Toronto, Printed by C. Blackett Robinson, 1882. xxvii, [1], 504p. 25cm. Shortt

637 **Panton**, J[ames] Hoyes
Gleanings from outcrops of Silurian strata in the Red River valley. [Winnipeg] Manitoba Free Press print [1882] cover-title, 10p. 21 1/2cm. (Hist. & Sc. Soc. of Man., no.3) Shortt

638 **Patterson**, William John
Report on water communications and commerce between the older provinces of the Dominion and Manitoba and the North West. 1882. ... Not seen. Dom. A.R., 1886

639 Portage la Prairie, Manitoba, and her industries. Winnipeg, Steen & Boyce, 1882. cover-title, 63, [1]p. 24cm. Man. Leg.

640 **Primitive Methodist Colonization Company**
The Primitive Methodist Colony in the North West Territory of Canada. Information for the use of intending settlers. Toronto, Office of the Primitive Methodist Co. Ltd., 1882. 19p. map. 22cm.

The colony was north of the Qu'Appelle Valley. Can. Arch.

641 **Pringle,** C.A.
Canada. Manitoba and the North-West. Notes on a visit. Ottawa, Department of Agriculture, 1882. 14p. 21cm. Shortt

642 **Qu'Appelle and Long Lake Land Company**
Prospectus. [Winnipeg, Times, 1882] 4 l. Tanghe

643 **Rae,** John
Arctic regions and the Hudson Bay Route. Winnipeg, Manitoba Free Press print [1882] cover-title, 11p. 23cm. (Hist. & Sc. Soc. of Man., no.2) Shortt

644 **Rae,** W[illiam] Fraser
Facts about Manitoba; from W. Fraser Rae's 'Newfoundland to Manitoba,' reprinted with large additions from The Times. London, Chapman & Hall, Ltd., 1882. 2p.l., 131p. fold. maps. 18cm. Shortt

645 **Rosmad,** Albert
Beschreibung einer Entdeckungsreise nach dem nordwestlichen Laendergebiete von Canada. Ein Brief. [Ottawa, 1882] cover-title, 8p. 21cm. Man. Leg.

646 **Society for the Propagation of the Gospel**
North-west Canada. [London, 1882] caption-title, 24p. 21 1/2cm.

An appeal for funds for the Dioceses of Rupert's Land, Saskatchewan, and Algoma. U.B.C.

647 **Spence,** Thomas
Useful and practical hints for the settler on Canadian prairie lands and for the guidance of intending British emigrants to Manitoba and the North-West of Canada. With facts regarding the soil, climate, produce, etc. And the superior attractions and advantages possessed, in comparison with the western prairie states of America. [2d ed., rev. & corrected. St. Boniface, 1882] 47p. illus. 21 1/2cm.

The first edition of 40 pages was published in 1881. Shortt

648 **Steen and Boyce, comp.**
Winnipeg, Manitoba, and her industries. Chicago, Steen & Boyce, 1882. 131p. Man. Arch.

649 **Stephenson,** Thomas
Notes of a tour through the provinces of Quebec, Ontario, Manitoba, and the North-West Territory of the Dominion of Canada ... Southern Manitoba, by Wm. M. Porritt ... Agriculture in Ontario: lecture by Dr. MacGregor. Crops in Manitoba, and letters from settlers. [Montreal? Allan Steamship Co., 1882] 40p. illus. 20cm. L. of P.

650 **Tassé**, Elie
Le Nord-Ouest; la province de Manitoba et les territoires du Nord-Ouest ... 2d ed., revue et augmentée. Ottawa, Imprimerie du Canada, 1882. 92p. tables. 23cm.

Imperfect: part of cover missing. Glenbow

651 **Temperance Colonization Society**
Charter and bylaws ... Toronto, Printed by Hunter, Rose & Co. [1882] cover-title, 19p. 18cm.

The society was responsible for the founding of Saskatoon. U. of S.

652 **Vekeman**, G[eorges]
Canada. Het groote Noord-Westen. De grootste en vruchtbaarste velden waar de landverhuizers sich kunnen vestigen. Inlichtingen voor de uitwijkelingen. Uit het fransch vertaald door G. Vekeman. Ottawa, 1882. 44p.

This Flemish pamphlet was printed by Le Pionnier in Sherbrooke, Que. Belgium

653 **Wiedersheim**, Eduard
Kanada. Reisebeschreibung und bericht über die dortigen land- und volkswirthschaftlichen derhältnisse. Stuttgart, Adolf Bonz, 1882. vii, 156p. 21cm.

The author travelled to Manitoba via Chicago and Minneapolis. Pages 31-66 describe Manitoba in 1881. France

654 **Williams**, W.H.
Manitoba and the North-West; journal of a trip from Toronto to the Rocky Mountains, via Lake Superior, Thunder Bay, Rat Portage, Winnipeg, Qu'Appelle, Prince Albert, Battleford, Fort Calgary and Fort McLeod. And return via Edmonton, Touchwood Hills, etc. Toronto, Hunter, Rose & Co., 1882. xi, [9]-258p. 23cm.

A newspaper man who accompanied the Marquis of Lorne's party through the West in 1881 gives an informative description of the country. It appeared first as a series of letters in the Toronto Globe. Shortt

655 **Allan Steamship Line**
Lectures and letters referring to Canada, Manitoba and the North-West Territories. Liperpool, 1883. cover-title, 24p. Tanghe

656 **[Anonymous]**
Kanadský severozápad a Manitoba ... Viden, Otto Maass, 1883. cover-title, 24p. illus., fold. map. 23cm.

Immigration pamphlet in Czech. Man. Leg.

657 **Bell**, Charles Napier
Hudson's Bay; the feasibility of the proposed route discussed. [Winnipeg, 1883] 4, 3p. 22cm. (Hist. & Sc. Soc. of Man., no.7) Man. Leg.

658 **Bryce**, George
In memoriam; notes and reminiscences of the late A.K. Isbister. [Winnipeg, 1883] 4p. 22cm. (His. & Sc. Soc. of Man., no.8) Man. Leg.

659 **Bryce**, George
Notes and comments on Harmon's journal 1800-1820. Winnipeg, Manitoba Free Press, 1883. 7p. 22cm. (Hist. & Sc. Soc. of Man., no.9) Shortt

660 **Bryce,** [George]
Winnipeg country, its discovery and the great consequences resulting. [n.p., 1883] 9p. 22 1/2cm. (Hist. & Sc. Soc. of Man., no.4) Shortt

661 **Burman,** W[illiam] A[lfred]
The Sioux language. [Winnipeg] Free Press print [1883] cover-title, 4p. 22cm. (Hist. & Sc. Soc. of Man., no.5) Shortt

662 **Canada.** Department of Agriculture
Canadian North-West. Climate and productions. A misrepresentation exposed. Ottawa, 1883. 32p. 20cm.

A reply to a pamphlet entitled 'Settler's Guide to the North-West' published in New York and distributed in Great Britain in the interest of an American railway company. The pamphlet described Manitoba's climate as 'seven months of winter and five of cold weather.' This reply was written by John Lowe, a member of the Department.
Reprinted the same year. Shortt

663 **Canada.** Department of Agriculture
En kort beskrifning öfver Manitoba, ett af Nordvesterns bördigaste hveteland. Hvarje person, man eller qvinna, som fyllt 18 år, kan fritt erhålla 160 acres, (130 tunnland) regeringsland ... Göteborg, Victor Boktryckeri, 1883. cover-title, 20p. 20cm. Sweden

664 **Canada.** Department of the Secretary of State
Sessional papers relating to the Canadian Pacific Railway, 1882-83. Printed by order of Parliament. Ottawa, Printed by MacLean, Roger & Co., 1883. 1p.l., 213p. 24 1/2cm. Shortt

664A **Canadian Pacific Railway**
The Canadian Pacific Railway, only route to Manitoba and the great North West. New York, American Bank Note Co. [1883] folder. [24]p. illus., map on verso. folds to 22 x 11cm. Can. Arch. (ms.)

664B **Canadian Pacific Railway**
The Canadian Pacific Railway to Manitoba and the North West Territories of Canada. New York, American Bank Note Company [1883] folder. [16]p. illus., map on verso. folds to 24 1/2 x 11cm. Can. Arch. (ms.)

665 **Canadian Pacific Railway**
Manitoba, the Canadian North-West. [n.p., 1884] cover-title, 1p.l., 24, 1p. 17cm.

This should appear under 1884. The 1883 edition had 28p. Shortt

666 **Canadian Pacific Railway**
Official guide book to the C.P.R. lands of Manitoba and part of the Northwest Territory. Winnipeg, 1883. 55p. maps. 25cm. Not seen. Queen's

667 **Corbett,** G[riffith] O[wen]
The vast resources and the great progress of Christianity and colonization in the southern parts of Rupert's America, with an earnest appeal for the immediate increase of missionary effort therein ... Copies may be had from the author. [London] Printed for the author at The Boys' Home [1883] 12p. 18cm.

Dedication dated 19 and 25 Dec. 1882. C.M.S. - 37

668 **David,** L[aurent] O[livier]
Mgr Alexandre Antonin Taché, archevêque de Saint-Boniface. Montréal, Cadieux & Derome, 1883. 111p. front. 19cm. Not seen. Queen's

669 **Dennis,** W[illiam]
The sources of north-western history. Winnipeg, Manitoba Free Press [1883] cover-title, 4p. 22cm. (Hist. & Sc. Soc. of Man., no.6)

A brief survey of the literature in the field. Shortt

670 **Dionne,** N[arcisse] E[utrope]
Etats-Unis, Manitoba, et Nord-Ouest. Notes de voyage. 2 éd. Québec, Léger Brousseau, 1883. 180p. 14 1/2cm.

First published in 1882. The last 30 pages is advice to immigrants. Man. Leg.

671 **Dugas,** [Georges]
Légendes du Nord-Ouest. Montréal, Librairie Saint-Joseph [1883] 141p., 1 l. front. 20cm. Author's name spelled 'Dugast' on title-page.

Tales of adventure on the plains handed down orally among the métis. Shortt

672 **Dugas,** G[eorges]
La première Canadienne du Nord-Ouest; ou, Biographie de Marie-Anne Gaboury, arrivée au Nord-Ouest en 1806, et décédée à Saint-Boniface, à l'âge de 96 ans. Montréal, Cadieux & Derome, 1883. 108p. front. 18 1/2cm. (Bibliothèque religieuse et nationale ... 1. sér.)

Author's name spelled 'Dugast' on title-page.
A second edition of 70 pages was published at Saint-Dizier, J. Thevenot, 1907. Shortt

673 **East Selkirk, Man.** Board of Trade
East Selkirk, Manitoba. Incorporated by government charter, 13th February A.D., 1883. One look at the facts contained in this pamphlet will convince the reader that East Selkirk, with its natural advantages, its shipping and railways is destined to be the Chicago of the North-West. [East Selkirk? 1883?] cover-title, 14p. 22cm. map on back cover.

The C.P.R. was expected to cross the Red River at Selkirk instead of Winnipeg. Man. Leg.

674 **Fargues,** Henri
... Les nouveaux territoires canadiens de l'Ouest; travail lu le 19 avril 1883 à l'assemblée générale mensuelle de la Société. Nantes, Mellinet, 1883. 1 l, 15p., 1 l. map. 23cm.

At head of title: Société de géographie commerciale de Nantes. L.C.

675 [**Ffolkes,** Edward G.E.] supposed author
Letters from a young emigrant in Manitoba. London, K. Paul, Trench & Co., 1883. viii, 181p. 18cm. Edited by C.H.E.

The 'young emigrant' spent a year at the Ontario College of Agriculture, Guelph, and then settled in Manitoba. The letters cover his sojourn in Guelph and his first year in Manitoba, and were edited by his uncle, C.H.E. The parents sign the introduction at 'Hillington Rectory.' Shortt

676 **Fraser,** Hugh
A trip to the Dominion of Canada. Halifax, Printed at the Morning Herald office, 1883. 1p.l., 96p. 21 1/2 cm.

A farmer from Scotland describes his tour of the North West. Shortt

677 **Hahn,** Otto
Canada. Die Berichte der vier deutschen Delegierten über ihre Reise nach Canada. Reutlingen, 1883. 96p. Not seen. Lehmann

678 **Hanswirth,** Jakob Emanuel
Bericht an das landwirtschaftliche Departement der Regierung von Canada. Zweite Auflage. Liverpool, Turner and Dunnett, 1883. 23, [1]p. illus., fold. map. 21 cm.

An immigration pamphlet designed for the Swiss. Man. Leg.

679 **Hind,** Henry Youle
Manitoba and the North-West frauds. Correspondence with the Department of Agriculture, &c., &c., &c., respecting the impostures of Professor John Macoun and others. Windsor, N.S., 1883. 40p. 21cm. Can. Arch.

680 The land of immeasurable promise, Manitoba, and the North-West. Happy homes for millions secured by tickling the rich prairie soil. Facts from actual settlers. What the men who have been there say. Winnipeg, Sun Printing Co. [1883?] cover-title, 21, [5]p. incl. advertising. Amtmann - 219-100

681 **Laurie,** William
The Battle River valley, a pamphlet describing the advantages of the country drained by the Battle and Saskatchewan rivers as a field for settlement. Battleford, Printed by P.G. Laurie, 1883. ii, 104p. 17cm.

Other than ordinances of the N.W.T. Council, this was probably the first pamphlet published in the future province of Saskatchewan. The Laurie press began publishing the Saskatchewan Herald in 1878. This pamphlet is largely a compilation of articles which appeared in the paper. Shortt

682 **Leacock,** E[dward] P.
Hudson's Bay route. Interesting and instructive lecture ... [Winnipeg? 1883?] half-title, 9p. 20cm. H.B.C.

683 **Macdougall,** W.B., comp.
The Canadian North-West Land Company, Limited. A practical hand-book for Manitoba and the North-West Territories, containing important information for intending settlers. London, Blades, East & Blades, 1883. 64p. plates, fold. map. 21cm.

A 28-page condensation was published in 1884. B.C. Arch.

684 **McLean,** John
The principles of church action. A sermon preached before the Provincial Synod of the Ecclesiastical Province of Rupert's Land in St. John's Cathedral, Winnipeg, on 8th August, 1883. By the Right Rev. John McLean, M.A., D.D., D.C.L., Bishop of Saskatchewan. Published by request of the Synod. Winnipeg, Printed at the office of the Manitoba Free Press [1883] cover-title, 4p. 23cm. C.M.S. - 37

685 Manitoba og det Nordvestlige-Canada. [London, H. Blacklock & Co., 1883] cover-title, 16p. illus., plates. 24cm.

A Norwegian emigration pamphlet. Amsterdam

686 **Manitoba Turf Club**
Racing rules of the Manitoba Turf Club, Winnipeg, Manitoba. Adopted June 22nd, 1883. Winnipeg, Richardson Print [1883] 24p. 14 1/2cm. Arkin

687 Mittheilungen uber Manitoba und das Nordwest Territorium (Nordamerika) ... Liverpool, Turner & Dunnett, 1883. 42p. front (map), illus. 22cm. Man. Arch.

688 **Moore**, J.G.
Fifteen months round about Manitoba and the North West; a lecture. [Stratford-on-Avon, Eng., Printed by G. Boyden, 1883] 28p. 19cm.

Xerox copy. Glenbow

689 **Munro**, W[illiam] F.
Emigration made easy; or, How to settle on the prairie. Glasgow, Macrone, 1883. cover-title, 10p. diagrs. 21cm.

An outline of the plan of the Canadian North West Land Company to settle immigrants on farms in village communities. B.C. Arch.

690 **North West Territories.** Council
Proposed school ordinance for the North-West Territories. Considered in committee during the session of Council, held at Regina, 1883, and ordered to be printed for consideration only. [Moose Jaw] Moose Jaw News print, 1883. 35p. 21 1/2cm. Can. Arch.

691 **Pearce**, John
The agricultural depression at home, and the resources, capabilities and prospects of the Canadian new North-West. A lecture delivered before the Balloon Society of Great Britain, at the Royal Aquarium, on Friday, February 9, 1883. With additional information in an appendix ... London, H. Sell, 1883. 1p.l., 32p. 21cm.

An 'earthy' topic for such a society, but part of the great publicity campaign to encourage emigration to Western Canada. Shortt

692 **Plumb**, J[osiah] B[urr]
The great Canadian North-West! Speech ... in Senate of Canada, on the Dominion Lands Bill, May 8th and 9th, 1883. [Ottawa, 1883] 14p. 25cm. Can. Arch.

693 **Pocock**, [Sir] Sidney J[ob]
Across the prairie lands of Manitoba and the Canadian North-West. A Wiltshire man's travels in the summer of 1882. London, E. & S. Hebert [1883] 54p., 1 l. front. 18cm.

Author visited his brother George, a Manitoba homesteader. Their trip to the Estevan coal fields forms the basis of the book. Shortt

694 **Prince Albert Young Men's Literary and Athletic Club**
... Constitution and by-laws, etc. [Prince Albert, Printed by Spink & Maveety, Prince Albert Times Office, 1883?] [11]p. 17cm.

'Established, November 16th, A.D. 1883.' Can. Arch.

695 **Primitive Methodist Colonization Company**
The Primitive Methodist Colony, North West Territory. [Toronto? 1883?] caption-title, 8p. 22cm.

Letters from colonists describing their experiences. Mr. Loveridge's papers

696 **Roman Catholic Church.** Liturgy and ritual. Cree
[Prayer book in the Cree language. Lac la Biche, Oblate Mission] 1883. 232p. illus. 18cm.

In syllabic characters.
Printed by Bishop Emile Grouard on a Stanhope printing press.
Autographed by J.C. Pilling. Americas.

697 **Royal Society of Canada**
Circular to officers of the Hudson's Bay Company, in relation to the collection of specimens in geology, natural history, ethnology, etc. Ottawa, 1883. 1 l. 27cm.

Circular signed: J.G. Bourinot, Honorary Secretary. H.B.C.

698 **St. Paul, Minneapolis & Manitoba Railway Company**
Fourth annual report ... Fiscal year ending June 30th, 1883. 32p. 23cm. H.B.C.

699 **Saskatchewan Land and Homestead Company**
The memorial of settlers in the tract granted to the Saskatchewan Homestead Company, in the Canadian North-West. John T. Moore, managing director. Toronto, 1883. cover-title, 8p. 19cm.

Memorialists declare the plan a good one, but say that it is being unjustly criticized; p.3-8, list of memorialists with location of their land, at Crescent Lake, Assiniboia. Can. Arch.

700 **A Shareholder**
The Canada North West Land Company. Facts vs. fiction. Toronto, Mail Printing Co., 1883. 16p. 21cm. On cover: For private circulation.

A criticism of an article on western land companies which appeared in the London Money Market Review. B.C. Arch.

701 **Spence,** Thomas
The question of the hour! 1883. Where to emigrate. Advice to intending emigrants from Great Britain. [n.p.] 1883. 32p. Not seen. Queen's

702 **[Sykes,** Richard] supposed author
Particulars of farms to be let or sold on the Edgeley estate, Qu'Appelle Valley, Assiniboia, North-West Territory of Canada. Manchester, I. Sowler and Co., 1883. 16p. fold. map. 22cm.

'The Edgeley estate, the property of Mr. Richard Sykes, of Edgeley, near Stockport, England, was purchased in May, 1882, from the Canadian Pacific Railway Co.' The estate consisted of 31 sections. Can. Arch.

703 **Tuttle,** Charles R[ichard]
A history of the corporation of Winnipeg giving an account of the present civic crisis with some suggestions as to what course should now be adopted. Winnipeg, 1883. 79p. 19cm.

A chronology of civic government. Man. Leg.

704 **Vekeman**, G[eorges]
Lettres d'un émigrant; ou, Voyage au Canada. Suivies d'un appendice sur le Manitoba. Bruxelles, Antoine Logé, 1883. iv, 131p. 21cm. Can. Arch.

705 **Vis**, Gerrit Willem
Translation of a letter from Mr. G.W. Vis to Messrs. Adolph Boissevain & Co. and H. Öyens & Sons, Amsterdam. [Amsterdam, 1883] 20p. fold. map. 21cm. Glenbow

706 **Winnipeg**. Board of Trade
Circular from Winnipeg Board of Trade. [Winnipeg, 1883] caption-title, 5p. 23cm.

Signed by Joseph Mulholland, President [and] L.M. Lewis, Secretary. U. of A.

707 **Abernethy**, W.J.
The Saskatchewan Fife wheat; a history of this remarkable grain from its first importation from the Saskatchewan valley in Manitoba till the present time. Minneapolis, Abernethy, 1884. 17p.

Another edition published in 1896. Tanghe

708 **Agnew**, N[iven]
Our water supply. Suggestions as to the water we drink, and where to get it from. Winnipeg, Manitoba Daily Free Press, 1884. cover-title, 4p. 21cm. (Hist. & Sc. Soc. of Man., no. [11]) Shortt

709 **Allan Steamship Line**
Practical and useful information for intending emigrants. [n.p., 1884] caption-title, 16p. 18cm.

The last four pages relate specifically to Manitoba. Belgium

710 [**Anonymous**]
A future for the deaf and dumb in the Canadian North-West. Being an account of a first attempt at colonization in the Canadian North-West by Miss J.E. Groom, and a plan of her future operations. London, Potter Bros., 1884. 29p. 20 1/2cm. Not seen. Br. Mus.

711 [**Anonymous**]
L'agriculture dans le Nord-Ouest du Canada. Résultats pratiques. Québec, Joseph Dussault, 1884. cover-title, 87p. 15 1/2cm.

Would seem to be the French edition of Entry 742. Can. Arch.

712 [**Anonymous**]
Report of a Select Committee of the Legislative Assembly of the Province of Keewaydin upon the boundaries of the adjoining Province of Ontario. With an appendix containing the evidence. Printed, before presentation, from a manuscript copy, without permission of the Legislature. Winnipegoosis, Knisteneaux Printing Co., 1884. iv p., 1 l., 54p. col. fold. map. 22cm.

A delightful satire on the Ontario-Manitoba boundary dispute. Shortt

713 [**Anonymous**]
Souvenir of the City of Winnipeg, presented to the members of the British Association for the Advancement of Science, 1884. Winnipeg, 1884. 47p. illus. 22cm. Man. Leg.

714 **Barneby**, W[illiam] Henry
Life and labour in the far, far West; being notes of a tour in the western states, British Columbia, Manitoba, and the North-West Territory. London, Cassell & Co., 1884. xvi, 432p. fold. map. 21 1/2cm.
About half of the book deals with the prairie region. Shortt

715 **Barwis**, Thomas [Shepard]
Calgary, Alberta, and the Canadian North-West. Valuable information for intending settlers. Report of Lt.-Col. Barwis, of Arthabaskaville, Quebec, and a delegation of practical farmers from the district of Arthabaska, Province of Quebec, who visited the North West, and the vicinity of Calgary in particular, in the summer of 1884. [n.p., 1884?] 13p. 22cm. Shortt

716 **Barwis**, Thomas [Shepard]
Memorial ... in support of his petition as stipendiary magistrate in the Northwest Territories ... Three Rivers, La Concorde, 1884. 20p. 22 1/2cm. Acadia

717 **Battleford Rifle Association**
Constitution, by-laws, and regulations. Battleford, Printed at the Saskatchewan Herald office, 1884. 19p. 17 1/2cm. Sask. Arch.

718 **Begg**, Alexander
Seventeen years in the Canadian North-West. A paper read on April 8, 1884, at the Royal Colonial Institute ... London, Printed by Spottiswoode & Co., 1884. cover-title, 35p. 18cm. Reprinted from the Colonies and India. Man. Leg.

719 **Bell**, Charles N[apier]
Our northern waters; a report presented to the Winnipeg Board of Trade, regarding the Hudson's Bay and Straits. Being a statement of their resources in minerals, fisheries, timber, furs, game and other products. Also notes on the navigation of these waters, together with historical events and meteorological and climatic data. Winnipeg, Board of Trade [1884] 1p.l., 78p., 1 l. plates (part. fold.) fold. maps. 21 1/2cm. Shortt

720 **Brooks**, George B.
Plain facts about the new city hall; its inside history from the first down to the present interesting disclosures. Winnipeg, Walker & May, 1884. 87p. Tanghe

721 **British North American Fire Insurance Company**
Prospectus and charter of incorporation of the British North American Fire Insurance Company of Manitoba. Winnipeg, Winnipeg Times Steam Book & Job Printing House, 1884. iv, 8p. Amtmann – 125-46

722 **Bryce**, George
Our Indians; delivered before the Y.M.C.A., Winnipeg, December 1st, 1884. Winnipeg, Manitoba Free Press print, 1884. cover-title, 9p. 22cm. In double column. Man. Leg.

723 **Bryce**, George
Presbyterianism. What it has done and what it may do in the Canadian Northwest. Being a sermon preached in Knox Church, Winnipeg, July 16th, 1884, at the opening of the first synod of Manitoba and the North West Territories.

Winnipeg, Manitoba Free Press print, 1884. cover-title, 7p. 22 1/2cm.
In double column. Man. Leg.

724 **Calgary District Agriculture Society**
District of Alberta. Information for intending settlers. Ottawa, 1884. cover-title, 16p. fold. map. 23cm.

A small edition of this pamphlet was printed in Calgary in the fall of 1884. The above entry is a reprint authorized by the Dominion Minister of Agriculture. The Calgary edition was the first pamphlet in English published in the future province of Alberta. The compiler was J.G. Fitzgerald; see the preface of his pamphlet published in 1888. Man. Leg.

725 **Canada.** Department of Agriculture
Dominion of Canada. A guide book containing information for intending settlers. 6th ed., rev. and cor. to date. Ottawa, The Department, 1884. x p., 1 l., 137, [2] p. incl. front., illus. fold. map. 23cm.

Nearly two-thirds of the contents relate to the Prairies. L.C.

726 **Canada.** Department of Agriculture
Landgunningen. Gids voor kapitalisten, landbouwers, ambachtslieden, arbeiders, enz., omtrent de voordeelen die met het vestigen van kolonisten te Manitoba het noord westen, en de andere provincien verbonden zijn ... [n.p.] 1884. 43p. illus., plates, fold. map. 22cm.

The Glenbow Library enters this pamphlet under the cover-title as follows:
Manitoba en het groote Noord Westen van Amerika; 200 millioen akkers voor kolonisatie eene vrije haardstede ... Liverpool [Printed by] Turner & Dunnett, 1884.
The Glenbow Library attributes the pamphlet to the Allan Steamship Line. Man. Leg.

727 **Canada.** Department of Agriculture
Llawlyfrau ymfudwyr. Canada: ei hanes, ei hansawdd, a'i hadnoddau, seiliedig ar bapyrau y llywodraeth; gyda chynghorion buddiol i ymfudwyr ... London [1884] 64p. 17 1/2cm. Wales

728 **Canada.** Department of the Interior
Extracts from surveyors' reports of township surveys in Manitoba and the North-West Territories. Published by authority of the Honorable Sir David Lewis Macpherson ... [Ottawa?] 1884. 183p. 24cm. Shortt

728A **Canada.** Laws, statutes, etc.
46 Victoria, Chapter 17, Dominion lands act, 1883, with the amendments and additions thereto, authorized by 47 Vic., Cap. 25, (1884). [Ottawa, 1884] cover-title, 68p. 24 1/2cm.

A further amendment was enacted in 1886, 49 Victoria, chapter 27. Can. Arch. (ms.)

729 **Canada North-West Land Company**
... A practical handbook for Manitoba and the North-West Territories ... London, Spottiswoode, 1884. cover-title, 28p. Tanghe

730 **The Canadian Gazette,** London
What settlers say of Manitoba and the Canadian North-West as published in the columns of 'The Canadian Gazette,' London. London, 1884. cover-title, 32p. 21cm. B.C. Arch.

731 The Canadian Pacific Company's method of financing, etc. [Montreal? 1884?] cover-title, 9p.

Can. Arch. II, 615. A letter addressed to the editor of the Witness. Signed 'An Observer.' There is a slight possibility that this was written by Sir Joseph Hickson, at that time general manager of the Grand Trunk Railway. Amtmann - 214-636.

732 **Canadian Pacific Railway**
An account of the work and results of the Canadian Pacific Railway Co.'s experimental farms. The wise policy of selecting the southern route for the C.P.R. endorsed by facts. Winnipeg, Manitoba Free Press print, 1884. cover-title, 15p. fold. map. 21 1/2cm. B.C. Arch.

733 **Canadian Pacific Railway**
Manitoba. The Canadian North-West. Testimony of actual settlers. [Montreal, Montreal Herald, 1884?] cover-title, 49p., 2 l. 20cm. At head of title: Queries and replies. Shortt

734 **Canadian Pacific Railway**
Manitoba ved Red River Dalen i det store Nordvestlige America hvor henimod 200 millioner acres af det rigeste prairieland det bedste hvedeland er bleven aabnet af den nye Can. Pacific Iernbane og hvor 160 acres frit land (Ca 600 maal) anvises ankommende nybyggere af regjeringen, 1884. Liverpool, Turner and Dunnett, 1884. 43p. fold. col. map. 21cm.

Includes a basic Norwegian-English vocabulary. Norway.

735 **Canadian Pacific Railway**
Official guide book to the Canadian Pacific Railway lands in Manitoba and part of the N.W. Territory, compiled from manual of survey and C P.R. land examination reports. Winnipeg, Bishop Engraving and Printing Co., 1884. 122p. plans. 25cm. Man. Leg.

736 **Canadian Pacific Railway**
Report of proceedings at a special general meeting of the shareholders of the Canadian Pacific Railway Company held at Montreal on the 3rd and 6th days of March, 1884. Montreal, Printed by Gazette Printing Co., 1884. 40p. 22cm. Shortt

737 **Chapman**, Edward John
Report on the coal area of the Medicine Hat Coal Mining Company, near Medicine Hat, North-West Territories, Canada. Toronto, Copp, Clark, general printers, 1884. cover-title, 19p. map. 20cm.

'Data of coal mining property in the North-West Territory of Canada,' reports by W.H. Ellis and others: p.[9]-18. List of provisional directors, in ms: p.[2] U. of T.

738 **Cliffe**, C[harles C.]
Manitoba and the Canadian Northwest as a field for settlement. A plain statement of facts for intending immigrants. Brandon, Printed by the Mail Steam Book & Job Printing Establishment, 1884. 96p. 21 1/2cm. In double column. Man. Leg.

739 **Cockburn**, James Seton
Canada for gentlemen, being letters from ... London, Army and Navy Co-operative Society [1884] 63p. fold. map.

Printed for private circulation. Lande

740 **Un Colonisateur de neuf ans d'expérience**
Le Nord-Ouest canadien. Brochure compilée par un colonisateur de neuf ans d'expérience. [n.p., 1884] caption-title, 31p. 23cm. St. Sulpice

741 **Davin,** Nicholas Flood
Eos; a prairie dream and other poems. Ottawa, Printed by the Citizen Printing and Publishing Co., 1884. 36p.

See also Entry 1101. Lande

742 [**Dussault,** Joseph] ed.
Farming in the North West of Canada. Actual results. [n.p.] 1884. 36p. fold. map. 17cm.

Statements by various settlers which had appeared in newspapers and pamphlets. L. of P.

743 **Foster,** [Sir] George E[ulas]
Professor Foster's speech on the Canadian Pacific Railway resolutions. [n.p., 1884] 16p. Nebenzahl - 16-184

744 **Four Year Resident**
Remarks on Manitoba & the North West with practical hints for intending emigrants, by a four year resident. Winnipeg, Time Steam Book & Job Printing House, 1884. 63p. 16cm.

Verso of every leaf blank, but counted as a page. Pencilled corrections in the text. Ms. note on cover: Advance copy with I.P.P.'s comp'ts. Man. Leg.

745 [**Grandin,** Vital Justin]
Noces d'argent de Monseigneur Vital-Justin Grandin, évêque de Saint-Albert, 1884. [Le Mans, Typographie Edmond Monnoyer, 1884] 68p. 24cm.

Consists largely of congratulatory messages to Bishop Grandin. Oblates Arch.

746 **Grant,** John Cameron
Prairie pictures, Lilith, and other poems. London, Longmans, Green and Co., 1884. xvii p., 1 l., 93p. 19cm. Rutherford

747 **Greenway,** Thomas
Province of Manitoba, its position in confederation; speech on budget debate ... on April 23rd, 1884. [Winnipeg, 1884] 24p. tables. 20cm. Glenbow

748 **Hall,** [Mary Georgina Caroline]
A lady's life on a farm in Manitoba. By Mrs. Cecil Hall. London, W.H. Allen & Co., 1884. 2p.l., 171, [1]p. illus. (incl. plan) plates. 17 1/2cm.

The author spent part of the summer of 1882 on a farm near Headingly, Man. The last part of the book describes her tour through United States. Shortt

749 **Hudson's Bay Company**
Bye-laws of the Adventurers of England trading into Hudson's Bay. London, Sir Joseph Causton and Sons, 1884. 15p. 18cm.

Reissued in 1892, and revised bye-laws in 1922; other issues were printed in 1948, 1952, 1956, 1957. H.B.C.

750 **Hudson's Bay Company**
The Governor and Company of Adventurers of England trading into Hudson's Bay ... Supplemental charter. [London, 1884?] 7, [1]p. 40 cm.

Title from verso of document. H.B.C.

751 **Imrie**, Peter
Canada as a field for settlement ... the report of ... [Glasgow? T. Graham? 188_?] cover-title, 15p. 22cm.

About half the pamphlet relates to Manitoba.
Last sentence: 'If the man had a wife, I cannot see but that he and she would be as well off as Adam and Eve.' Ayer

752 **Ives**, William B[ullock]
Speech on the Canadian Pacific Railway delivered in the House of Commons, Ottawa, on February 8, 1884. [Ottawa, 1884] 44p. 20 1/2cm. Can. Arch.

753 **James**, J[ohn] C[ollinson]
The western division of the Canadian Pacific Railway, by the late J.C. James and Alan Macdougall ... London, Institute of Civil Engineers, 1884. 26p. 22cm. Reprint from Inst. of Civil Engineers. Proceedings. v.76, pt. 2.

Describes the construction of the railway across the prairies in the season of 1882. Man. Leg.

754 **Jones**, Harry
Railway notes in the North-West; or, The Dominion of Canada. [n.p.] 1884. 115p. 18 1/2cm.

Printed for private circulation only. About half of the book deals with the prairie region. Toronto

755 **Langevin**, Sir Hector [Louis]
Une question de véracité; correspondance entre Sir Hector Langevin, George Stephen, et L.A. Sénécal sur l'achat du chemin de fer du Nord. [Ottawa? 1884?] cover-title [3]-23p. 22cm. U. of A.

756 **McNeill**, Robert
Practical tests on gardening for Manitoba & North-West Territories. Winnipeg, Wilson Bros., 1884. 58p. illus. 15cm. Can. Arch.

757 **Manitoba**. Legislative Assembly. Select Committee to procure evidence as to the practicability of the establishment of a system of communication with this province via Hudson's Bay.
Report ... presented by the Hon. Mr. Brown. Winnipeg, Queen's Printer, 1884. cover-title, 56p. U.B.C.

758 **The Manitoba and Northwest Farmers' Union**
Resolutions adopted at the farmers' convention held in the city of Winnipeg, 19th and 20th Dec., 1883. Instructions as to the formation of branch unions, etc. Issued by order of the provincial council, Brandon, 1st January, 1884. [Brandon, Printed at the office of the Sun Printing and Publishing Co., 1884] 13, [1]p. 18cm.

This was probably the first farmers' organization in the West.
The union's constitution, passed 5 June 1884, was printed as a 10-page booklet by the Manitoba Daily Free Press. (In B.C. Arch.) Man. Leg.

759 **Moore**, John T[homas]
The settler's pocket guide to homesteads in the Canadian North-West. Toronto, Saskatchewan Land and Homestead Co. Ltd., 1884. 48p. maps (1 fold.) diagrs. 18 1/2cm.

A pamphlet written by the managing director of the company describing the company's lands. Man. Leg.

760 **Morris**, Alexander
Nova Britannia; or, Our new Canadian Dominion foreshadowed. Being a series of lectures, speeches and addresses. Edited, with notes and an introduction by a member of the Canadian press. Toronto, Hunter, Rose & Co., 1884. xii, 187p. 18 1/2cm.

Contains 'Hudson's Bay and Pacific Territories' published in 1859, and a number of speeches delivered while the author was Lieut.-Gov. of Man. and the N.W.T. Shortt

761 **Murdoch**, W.
Report on the Winnipeg and Hudson's Bay R'y and Steamship Company. Winnipeg, Times Steam Book and Job Printing Establishment, 1884. 35p. 24cm. B.C. Arch.

762 **Nicholl**, Mrs. M.A.
Lays from the West, by 'Stella' M.A. Nicholl ... Winnipeg, Manitoba Free Press print, 1884. 103p. 16cm.

Contents are not specifically western and many poems are of a religious nature. The copy in the Sask. Leg. Library was presented by Mrs. Kate Simpson Hayes who claimed that it was 'the very first book written in Saskatchewan, or Assiniboia, as it was then known.' Sask. Leg.

763 [**Norquay**, John]
Memoranda and statements prepared by the Hon. the Provincial Treasurer, Manitoba. Ottawa, Press of A.S. Woodburn [1884] cover-title, 23p. 23cm. L. of P.

764 **Panton**, James Hoyes
Fragmentary leaves from the geological records of the great North-west. 1884. 9p. 22cm. (Hist. & Sc. Soc. of Man., no.10) Man. Leg.

765 **Plumb**, Josiah Burr
The opposition press on Manitoba and the North-West; speech in the Senate of Canada. [Ottawa, Woodburn, 1884] half-title, 22p. 24cm. Tanghe

766 **Prance**, Courtenay C.
Notes on America; being two lectures delivered before the Evesham Institute in December, 1884. Evesham, Eng., Printed by W. & H. Smith, 1884. 44p. 18cm.

Xerox copy. Includes descriptions of the prairie region. Glenbow

766A **Qu'Appelle Valley Farming Company**
Annual meeting of the Qu'Appelle Valley Farming Co. Limited, proprietors of the Bell Farm. President's report, January 9th 1884. Winnipeg, Times Steam Book and Job printing, 1884. cover-title, 14p. 21cm. Can. Arch. (ms.)

767 **Richardson**, R[obert] L[orne]
Report of the visit of the British Association to the Canadian North-West. Description of the trip to the Rocky Mountains, addresses presented, report of speeches delivered, doings in Winnipeg. Winnipeg, McIntyre Bros., 1884. 53p. 22cm. Shortt

768 **Ross**, A[rthur] W[ellington]
Speech on the Canadian Pacific Railway and the Canadian North-West, delivered in the House of Commons, Ottawa, on the 19th of February, 1884. [Montreal, Gazette, 1884?] 13p. 21cm. Can. Arch.

769 **Ross**, A[rthur] W[ellington]
Speeches on the Canadian Pacific Railway and the Canadian North West, by A.W. Ross and C.F. Ferguson. February, 1884. [Montreal, Gazette, 1884?] 23p. 21cm. Tanghe

770 **Scott**, Thomas
Statement in support of a general railway act for the North-West. Ottawa, Woodburn [1884] cover-title, 8p. 22cm. Winnipeg

771 **Semmens**, John
The field and the work; sketches of missionary life in the far north. Toronto, Methodist Mission Rooms, 1884. 3p.l., [9]-199p. front., illus. 18cm.

A Methodist missionary describes work among the Indians in northern Manitoba.
Shortt

772 [**Telfer**, John How]
Canadian North-West. Free homesteads of wheat & grazing land in the Temperance Colony. Land for sale, with or without conditions of cultivation. Rare inducements offered to emigrants from Great Britain. Freehold farms may be acquired on easy terms. [London, James Ivison, 1884] cover-title, 15p. 21cm. B.C. Arch.

773 **Temple**, Sir Richard
Address ... to the citizens of Winnipeg on the North West of Canada, September 1884. [Winnipeg? 1884] 23p. 21 1/2cm. R.E.S.

773A A tour through Canada, from Nova Scotia to Vancouver Island ... London, Printed by Cassell, 1884. viii, 72p. illus. B.C. Arch.

774 **Tuttle**, Charles R[ichard]
Open letter on the agitation in Manitoba ... to Joseph Mulholland, Esq., of Winnipeg. 1884. 8p. 22cm. Not seen. Can. Arch.

775 [**Burgess**, Henry T.] supposed author
Manitoba and confederation, by Veritas Vincit [pseud.] Winnipeg, Printed at the office of the Manitoba Free Press [1884] 23p. 21cm.

Title-page bears the seal of Daniel Carey, barrister, Winnipeg. Can. Arch.

776 **White**, Thomas
Speeches on the Canadian Pacific Railway and on the financial & industrial position of Canada delivered in the House of Commons on the evenings of the

8th February and the 4th March, 1884, respectively, by Mr. Thos. White, M.P. for Cardwell. Montreal, Gazette Printing Company, 1884. cover-title, 1p.l., 37p., printed in 2 columns. Lande

777 Winnipeg. [New York, Witteman Bros., 1884] pictorial strip folder in covers (12p.) Printed on one side only. Glenbow

778 **Winnipeg Daily Sun**
Manitoba and the North-West Territories: settlers' opinions. [Winnipeg, ca. 1884] 21p. 22cm.

Bound in paper covers with title: Settlers opinions. Glenbow

779 **York Farmers Colonization Company**
... York Farmers Colonization Company, guide and record ... [Toronto] Front & Todd, printers, Monetary Times Office [1884] cover-title, 22p. fold map, charts. 22cm.

On cover: A farm is the safest investment. Choice homesteads free to the settler: Contents. Charts are of townships showing the names of settlers. Introduction refers to an earlier pamphlet. Toronto

780 [**Anonymous**]
À la mémoire de Louis Riel: La Marseillaise canadienne. [n.p.] Carmel [1885?] cover-title, [4]p. 25cm.

A song to the music of La Marseillaise. Collection Gagnon

781 Batoche polka, by Miss Annie Delaney. Toronto, H.A. & S. Nordheimer, 1885.
The Battleford march, composed by Dingley Brown. Ottawa, F. Boucher, 1885.
The Otter grand march, by Mrs. John E.M. Whitney. Montreal, J.L. Lamplough, 1885.
Welcome home, brave volunteers, song by F.H. Torrington. Toronto, Imrie & Graham, 1885.

The above four pieces of music, inspired by the Saskatchewan Rebellion, are here listed together for convenience. These not seen. Lib. of Parl., 1885-86

782 **Adam**, G[raeme] Mercer
The Canadian North-West; its history and its troubles, from the early days of the fur-trade to the era of the railway and the settler; with incidents of travel in the region, and the narrative of three insurrections. Toronto, Rose Publishing Co., 1885. viii, [9]-390p. front., ports. 20 1/2cm. At head of title: From savagery to civilization.

A second edition, published after the Regina trials, contains an appendix describing the court proceedings. Shortt

783 **Allen**, C[harles] W[illiam]
Volunteer land grants, scrip, and pensions, with suggestions shewing how a grantee may realize to best advantage. Toronto, Toronto News Co., 1885. 13p. 21cm. Man. Leg.

784 **Bell**, Charles N[apier]
Some historical names and places of the Canadian North-West ... Winnipeg, Manitoba Free Press print, 1885. cover-title, 8p. 22cm. (Hist. & Sc. Soc. of Man., no.17) Shortt

785 **Bellerose**, [Joseph Hyacinthe]
Assemblée à Saint-Hyacinthe le 8 décembre 1885, pour protester contre l'exécution de Riel. Discours. [n.p., 1885?] 8p. 22 1/2cm. St. Sulpice

786 **Blake**, E[dward]
Disturbance in the North-West. Speech ... May 20th, 1885. Ottawa, Printed by MacLean, Roger & Co. [1885] 32p. 21cm. Can. Arch.

787 **Blake**, [Edward]
Disturbance in the North-West. House of Commons debates, third session, fifth Parliament, 48 Vic. Speech ... June 6th, 1885. Ottawa, MacLean, Roger & Co. [1885] 36p. 29 1/2cm. Can. Arch.

788 **Blake**, Edward
Speech ... on the Canadian Pacific Railway resolutions. Ottawa, June 16th, 1885. [Ottawa, Printed by MacLean, Roger & Co., 1885] caption-title, 34p. 28cm. (H. of C. Debates) Glenbow

789 **Blake**, Edward
Speech ... on the North-Western Coal and Navigation Company. Ottawa, June 11th, 1885. [Ottawa, Maclean, Roger & Co., 1885] caption-title, 5p. (H. of C. Debates) Amtmann - 176-22

790 **Broughall**, Geo[rge]
The 90th on active service; or, Campaigning in the North West. A musical and dramatic burlesque in two acts, with an introduction, interlude and final tableau. Written by Staff Sergeant Geo. Broughall. Songs by Major L. Buchan, Chaplain D.M. Gordon, Sergts. Jos. Tees and W.R. Colgate, and Privates W.H. D'Arcy and R. Pomeroy. Music by Bandmaster H. Gooding. As played in the Princess Opera House, Winnipeg, July 29th and 30th, 1885. Winnipeg, George Bishop, 1885. 1p.l., 42p. 18 1/2cm. Man. Leg.

791 **Bryce**, George
The mound builders. Winnipeg, Manitoba Free Press print [1885] cover-title, 20p. illus. 21 1/2cm. (Hist. & Sc. Soc. of Man., no.18) Shortt

792 **Bryce**, George
Old settlers of Red River. Winnipeg, Manitoba Daily Free Press, 1885. 9p. 22cm. (Hist. & Sc. Soc. of Man., no.19) Shortt

793 **Campbell**, Sir Alexander
In the case of Louis Riel, convicted of treason and executed therefor. Report. Ottawa, Printed by MacLean, Roger & Co., 1885. 1p.l., 10p. 24 1/2cm.
A French text also issued. Shortt

794 **Canada**. Department of Agriculture
Agricultural statistics for Manitoba and the North-West Territories. Ottawa, Printed by MacLean, Roger & Co., 1885. 78p. 24 1/2cm. At head of title: Annex to the report of the Minister of Agriculture for the year 1884. Shortt

795 **Canada**. Department of Agriculture
L'agriculture dans le Nord-Ouest du Canada; resultats pratiques. Ottawa, 1885. cover-title, 32p. fold. map. 22cm.
An earlier edition (Montreal, 1884) was published by Joseph Dussault. Rutherford

795A **Canada.** Department of Agriculture
Neu elsass. Diefe neue deutsche auhedlung in Nord-Amerika ... Liverpool, Turner & Dunnett, 1885. folder. 16p. illus., map. folds to 15 x 9cm. Can. Arch. (ms.)

796 **Canada.** Department of the Interior
Papers and correspondence up to the present time, with respect to the commission recently appointed to investigate and report the claims existing in connection with the extinguishment of the Indian title preferred by half-breeds resident in the North-West Territories outside the limits of the Province of Manitoba, previous to the 15th day of July, 1870. [Ottawa, 1885] 113p. 24cm. (Canada. Sess. papers, 1885, no.116)

Contains petitions, documents, letters, and telegrams dealing with half-breed grievances from 1878 to 1885. U. of S.

797 **Canada.** Department of Public Works
Copies of all reports, correspondence, and surveys, if any, in the Department of Public Works, as to the improvement of the North Saskatchewan River for the purpose of navigation. [Ottawa, 1885] 41p. 24cm. (Canada. Sess. papers, 1885, no.138) Shortt

798 **Canadian Pacific Railway**
Manitoba wheat. Its territorial area and superior quality. Verdict of one hundred milling firms in Great Britain and Ireland. Winnipeg, Printed at the office of The Commercial, 1885. 14p. 22cm. Shortt

799 **Canadian Pacific Railway**
Plain facts from farmers in the Canadian North West. [London, H. Blacklock & Co., 1885] cover-title, 48p. illus., plate. 19 1/2cm.

Tabulated replies from farmers. Man. Leg.

800 **Canadian Pacific Railway**
Practical hints from farmers in the Canadian North-West. [London, H. Blacklock & Co., 1885] cover-title, 48p. front., plates. 20 x 16 1/2cm. L.C.

801 **Chapleau,** [Sir Joseph Adolphe]
Discours ... sur les résolutions du Chemin de Fer Canadien du Pacifique. Chambre des Communes, 16 juin 1885. Ottawa, MacLean, Roger & Cie, 1885. cover-title, 68p. 22cm. Shortt

802 **Chapleau,** Sir J[oseph] A[dolphe]
La question Riel. Lettre. [Ottawa, 1885] cover-title, 14p. 22cm. Half-title: Aux Canadiens-Français. Shortt

802A **Chittenden,** Newton H.
Settlers, miners and tourists guide from ocean to ocean by the Canadian Pacific Railway, the great trans-continental short line through a region of unsurpassed attractions for settler, miner, and tourist. Circular 14 of the 'World's guide for home, health and pleasure seekers.' [n.p., 1885?] cover-title, 80p. 26cm.

From p.62 relates to British Columbia and is taken from his 'Travels in British Columbia and Alaska, 1882-83.' Can. Arch. (ms.)

803 **Christy**, Robert Miller
Manitoba described, being a series of general observations upon the farming, climate, sport, natural history, and future prospects of the country. London, Wyman, 1885. viii, 208p. maps. 19cm. Man. Leg.

804 **Church of England.** Diocese of Qu'Appelle
Constitution and canons of the Diocese of Qu'Appelle, Assiniboia, N.W. Canada, as formulated at a meeting of the synod of the Diocese, June 3rd, 1885. Together with acts of incorporation of Diocese, order of proceedings at meetings and other regulations. Winnipeg, Manitoba Free Press, 1885. 34 7p. 20cm. Can. Arch.

805 [**Collins**, Joseph Edmund]
The story of Louis Riel, the rebel chief. Toronto, J.S. Robertson & Bros. [1885] 192p. incl. front., illus. 18 1/2cm.

This fictional biography was accepted as factual by many readers. An edition was also published by Rose Publishing Co. of Toronto. Shortt

806 **Craigie**, P[atrick] G[eorge]
The Canadian North-West and its development. [London? Farmer & Country Gentleman's Almanac for 1885] caption-title, 4p. 23cm.

Describes a visit to Western Canada. R.E.S.

807 **Daunt**, Achilles
In the land of the moose, the bear, and the beaver; adventures in the forests of Athabasca. London, T. Nelson & Sons, 1885. 328p. illus.

A third edition was published in 1928. Br. Mus.

808 **Dawkins**, William Boyd
Canada and the great North-West. Salford [England] 1885. 16p.

'A talk delivered before the Society at Salford Town Hall, on Monday, April 20th, 1885.' Br. Mus.

809 **Deriares**, Jules
Riel. Patriotisme vs. loyauté. [n.p.] 1885. 11p. 16cm. St. Sulpice

810 **Dunlevie**, Horace G.
Our volunteers in the North-West. A ready-reference handbook. Ottawa, Printed at the office of the Daily Free Press, 1885. 52p. 17cm.

Consists of regimental lists. Man. Leg.

811 [**Elliott**, George Babington]
Calgary, Alberta, Canada, her industries and resources, compiled and edited by Burns & Elliott. Calgary, 1885. 96p. 21cm. Paging includes advertising.

Contains short sketches of prominent business men. Published about a month after Fitzgerald's 'Business Directory.' B.C. Arch.

812 **Family Man**
Shall we emigrate? A tour through the States of America, to the Pacific coast of Canada. Dublin, G. Herbert, 1885. 32p. Br. Mus.

813 **Fitzgerald**, J.G.
Business directory of Calgary, Alberta, Canada. March, 1885. [Calgary] Calgary Herald Printing & Publishing Co. [1885] cover-title, [24]p. 23 1/2cm.

Consists largely of advertisements by local business men. Toronto

814 **Fream**, W[illiam]
The prairie ... London, William Clowes and Sons, Ltd., 1885. 94p. front. (fold. map) illus. 21cm. In two parts, of which this is Pt.I. Acadia

815 [**Garrioch**, Alfred Campbell]
Beaver Indian primer. [London, Gilbert & Rivington, 1885?] caption-title, 36p. 16cm. Rupert's

816 **Garrioch**, Alfred Campbell
A vocabulary of the Beaver Indian language consisting of Part I: Beaver-English; Part II: English-Beaver-Cree. Cyclostyled by E.S. Brewer, Printed by Mrs. Garrioch. London, Society for Promoting Christian Knowledge [1885] 138p. 28cm. Not seen.

Fifty copies were printed from the copy made with a cyclostyle. Pilling

817 **German**, Orrin, tr.
Methodist hymns, translated into the Cree language. Toronto, Methodist Mission Rooms, 1885. xviii (i.e. viii), [9]-665p. 16 1/2cm.

Added title-page in Cree; text in English and Cree on opposite pages; in Roman characters. L.C.

818 **Girouard**, Désiré
Louis Riel. Assemblée de Lachine, 10 août 1885. Discours ... Sommaire complet corrigé par lui-même, du Monde, 12 août 1885. [n.p., 1885] 6p. 20cm. L. of P.

819 **Gowanlock**, Theresa
Two months in the camp of Big Bear. The life and adventures of Theresa Gowanlock and Theresa Delaney. Parkdale, Times office, 1885. 141p. incl. front., illus., plates, ports. 19cm.

Accounts by the two women survivors of the Frog Lake Massacre. Shortt

820 **Haultain**, T[heodore] Arnold
A history of Riel's second rebellion and how it was quelled. Toronto, Grip Printing and Publishing Co., 1885. 44 (i.e. 40)p. illus., 2 col. double plates. 37 1/2cm. Page 12 incorrectly numbered 16. At head of title: The souvenir number of the Canadian Historical and Illustrated War News. Shortt

821 **Hill**, Alex[ander] Staveley
From home to home; autumn wanderings in the Northwest, in the years 1881, 1882, 1883, 1884. Illustrated from sketches by Mrs. Staveley Hill, and photographs by A.S.H. London, Sampson Low, Marston, Searle, & Rivington, 1885. vii, [3], 432p. front., illus., plates, 2 fold. maps. 22 1/2cm.

The author was managing director of the Oxley Ranch, an unbusinesslike English company. The book should be read in conjunction with 'Ranching with Lords and Commons' by J.R. Craig, the ranch foreman. Shortt

822 **Irvine,** [Acheson Gosford]
Copy of official diary of Lieut.-Col. Irvine. (Confidential) [Ottawa, 1885] caption-title, 20p. 34cm.

Diary, 18 March to 23 May 1885, of the Commissioner of the North-West Mounted Police. Glenbow

823 **Laidlaw,** Alex[ande]r
From the St. Lawrence to the North Saskatchewan, being some incidents connected with the detachment of 'A' Battery, Regt. Canadian Artillery, who composed part of the NorthWest Field Force, in the Rebellion of 1885. [Halifax, 1885?] [5]-43p. [Montreal Book Auctions Sale No.2, Catalogue Item No.100, pamphlet No.3 (Bound in a collection relating to Riel Rebellion)]

824 **Lennox,** G.
Guide universel de l'émigrant. Amérique anglaise fédération canadienne. La province du Manitoba, d'après les derniers documents officiels. 2d ed. rev. et aug. Bruxelles, Librairie Universelle de Rozez, 1885. 64p. illus. 23cm. Belgium

825 [**Logan,** John Edward]
A cry from the Saskatchewan, by Barry Dane. [Montreal, J. Theo Robinson, 1885] cover-title, 13p. 23cm.

'A poem characterized by grandeur and pathos, though faulty in a wilful irregularity of metre.' See Dom. A.R., 1886, p.212. Glenbow

826 Louis Riel and the North-West Rebellion; a review, compiled from public records and other authentic documents. Question and answer. [n.p., n.d.] cover-title, 16p. 21cm. Glenbow

827 **McCharles,** Angus
The extinct cuttle-fish in the Canadian North-West. A paper read before the Canadian Institute, Toronto, March 14th, 1885. Toronto, Hunter, Rose, 1885. 1p.l., [5]-16p. front. (map) 20cm. L. of P.

828 Manitoba. [Amsterdam? Ellerman, Harms & Co., 1885?] cover-title, 39p. illus. 20cm.

A pamphlet in French designed for European circulation. Man. Leg.

829 **Manitoba and Northwest Farmers' Union**
Statement of the claims of the Province of Manitoba and the North-West Territories; to the constitutional rights of a province under the British North America Act, 1867. [n.p.] 1885. cover-title, xxii, 90p. 22cm. B.C. Arch.

830 **Mathews,** Percy W.
Notes on disease among the Indians frequenting York Factory, Hudson's Bay. Montreal, Gazette Printing Co., 1885. 20p. 22cm. Not seen. Can. Arch.

831 **Mennell,** Henry Tuke
Across Canada to the Rocky Mountains, from a botanist's point of view. York, Eng., William Sessions, 1885. cover-title, 12p. 21cm. Shortt

831A **Meyer,** R.
The rules of a co-operative society for cheese and butter making. [Whitewood, 1885] caption-title, [3]p. 26cm. Can. Arch. (ms.)

832 **Le Monde**
L'insurrection du Nord-Ouest, 1885. 2. éd. [Montréal] Publié par les propriétaires du Monde, 1885. 39p. illus. (incl. ports.) 30cm. Shortt

833 **Montpetit**, A[ndré] N[apoléon]
Louis Riel à la Rivière-du-Loup. Lévis, Imprimerie Mercier & Cie, 1885. lxii, 111p. 18cm. Ports. on covers.

A case of mistaken identity some ten years earlier, when Riel was known to be in Eastern Canada after he had signed the register of the H. of C. in Ottawa. Pranksters had a stranger surreptitiously entertained and fêted in a sympathetic Quebec community. U.B.C.

834 **Mulvaney**, Charles Pelham
The history of the North-West Rebellion of 1885. Comprising a full and impartial account of the origin and progress of the war, of the various engagements with the Indians and half-breeds, of the heroic deeds performed by officers and men, and of touching scenes in the field, the camp, and the cabin; including a history of the Indian tribes of North-Western Canada, their numbers, modes of living, habits, customs, religious rites and ceremonies, with thrilling narratives of captures, imprisonment, massacres, and hair-breadth escapes of white settlers, etc. Toronto, A.H. Hovey & Co., 1885. viii, [17]-424p. front., illus. (incl. ports., maps) 19cm. Shortt

835 **Netherlands American Land Company**
Official guide book to the lands of the Netherlands American Land Company. Select lands in Manitoba and the North West Territories. Winnipeg, Bishop Engraving and Printing Co. [1885] cover-title, 14p. maps. 25cm.

The lands of this company were chiefly between Virden and Wolseley in the mile belt of the C.P.R. John B. McKilligan was the general agent. Man. Leg.

836 **One Who Has Just Returned**
Emigrant's prospects in Manitoba. A few facts from one who has just returned from the great North-West. London, J. Wakeham & Sons [1885] 8p.
Br. Mus.

837 **Panton**, J[ames] Hoyes
Rambles in the North-West, across the prairies and in the passes of the Rocky Mountains. Guelph, Mercury Steam Printing House, 1885. cover-title, 20p. 22 1/2cm. Shortt

838 [**Jones**, Nehemiah]
Sketches, by Don Pedro [pseud.] Dedicated to the veterans of –85. Toronto, Hill & Weir [1885?] 32p. 21cm. U. of A.

839 **Presbyterian Church in Canada**
Manitoba and the North West Territory. Report of home mission work presented to the General Assembly of 1885. Winnipeg, 1885. 32p. map. Queen's

840 **La Presse**
Louis Riel, martyr du Nord-Ouest. Sa vie – son procès – sa mort. Publié par le journal La Presse. [3. éd.] Montréal, Imprimerie Générale, 1885. 96p. illus. (incl. ports.) 20cm.

Ran through at least six editions. Shortt

841 Regina directory for 1885. [Regina] Regina Leader Steam Print [1885] [29]p. 23cm.

Pagination includes advertising. L. of P.

842 **Ritchie**, James Ewing
To Canada with emigrants; a record of actual experiences. London, T.F. Unwin, 1885. vi, 269p. plates. 18 1/2cm. L.C.

843 **S., A.**
A summer trip to Canada, by A.S. London, City of London Pub. Co. [1885] 112p. Br. Mus.

844 **Scoble**, Thomas C[larkson]
Our crop markets. A paper read before the Manitoba Historical and Scientific Society. [Winnipeg, Manitoba Daily Free Press, 1885] 11p. 22cm. (Hist. & Sc. Soc. of Man., no.16) L.C.

845 **Sheldon**, J[ohn] P[rince]
To Canada and through it, with the British Association. Ottawa, Dept. of Agriculture, 1885. cover-title, 32p. illus., fold. map. 21cm.

A revised edition was published in 1886. L.C.

846 **Sherlock**, Robert A.
Experiences of the Halifax Battalion in the North West. Halifax, Printed by Jas. W. Doley, 1885. 22p. 18cm.

The battalion was stationed at Swift Current. Man. Leg.

847 **Sykes**, Richard
Guide to the Qu'Appelle Valley, Assiniboia, Canada. With description of farms to be sold or rented on the Edgeley estate, Qu'Appelle station. Manchester, I. Sowler & Co., 1885. 29, [1]p. front. (incl. fold. map) plates. 21 1/2cm. L.C.

848 **Taché**, Alexandre [Antonin]
La situation. [n.p., 1885] caption-title, [10]p. 20 1/2cm. In double column.

Relates to the Riel Rebellion.
A 22-page edition, Quebec, J.O. Filteau, 1885, is listed in the Can. Arch. catalogue of pamphlets. A 38-page edition, St. Boniface, Journal Le Manitoba, 1885, is listed by Amtmann - 277-391. Shortt

849 **Tanner**, Henry
The Canadian North West and the advantages it offers for emigration purposes. London, G. Kenning, 1885. 48p. illus. 21cm. At head of title: A sequel to 'Successful Emigration.' Shortt

850 **Temperance Colonization Society**
Interim report of the management of the Temperance Colonization Society Limited, containing important judgment re. scrip, and other information for shareholders and scripholders. September, 1885. Toronto, Hunter, Rose & Co. [1885] cover-title, 23p. 18cm. U. of S.

851 **Tremblay**, Ernest
Riel: réponse à Monsieur J.A. Chapleau. St-Hyacinthe, Des presses de Union, 1885. 80p. 22 1/2cm. Can. Arch.

852 **Tuttle**, Charles R[ichard]
Our north land; being a full account of the Canadian North-West and Hudson's Bay Route, together with a narrative of the experiences of the Hudson's Bay expedition of 1884, including a description of the climate, resources, and the characteristics of the native inhabitants between the 50th parallel and the Arctic Circle. Toronto, C. Blackett Robinson, 1885. xvi, [17]-589p. front., illus., fold. maps. 24cm. Shortt

853 200 millioen akkers voor kolonisatie in Manitoba en het groote Noord Westen van Amerika ... 1885. Liverpool, Turner & Dunnett, 1885. 46p. illus., fold. col. map. 21cm.

On cover: Landgunningen. Gids voor kapitalisten, landbouwers, ambachtslieden, arbeiders, enz ...
Flemish immigration pamphlet. Belgium

854 What British settlers in the Canadian North-West say about the country; the following are extracts from letters. [London, n.p., 1885] 26p. illus. U. of T.

855 **White**, Thomas
Facts for the people. The Northwest Rebellion, the question of the half-breeds and the government treatment of them. Ottawa, 1885. 18p. Not seen. Queen's

856 **White**, Thomas
North West administration. Speech ... at Weston, Ont., Wednesday evening, December 16th, 1885. (From the Gazette, Montreal) [n.p., 1885?] 14p. 21cm. In double column. Shortt

857 Winnipeg war sketches. Published by request by the bishop. Winnipeg, Engraving and Printing Co., 1885. 12p. illus., map. Not seen. Can. Arch.

858 **The Witness**
The Riel Rebellion, 1885. Montreal, Witness Printing House [1885] caption-title, 44p. illus. (incl. ports.) 30 1/2cm. Shortt

859 [**Anonymous**]
The Albany settlement, Qu'Appelle Valley, Canada, N.W.T.; colonial profits with home comforts. London, George Kenning, 1886. cover-title, 16p. illus., double plan. 21 1/2cm.

A colonization scheme centring on the Bell farm at Indian Head. U. of T.

860 [**Anonymous**]
A Canadian tour; a reprint of letters from the special correspondent of the Times ... London, G.E. Wright, 1886. cover-title, 1p.l., 58p. double map. 28 1/2cm.

Nearly half the pamphlet is devoted to Western Canada. Shortt

861 [**Anonymous**]
L'histoire d'un crime. [n.p., 1886?] 16p. 22cm.

Relates to the execution of Louis Riel. St. Sulpice

862 [**Anonymous**]
Manitoba and the North-West Territories. General description of the resources & capabilities of the Canadian North-West, as well as some experience of men and women settlers. [n.p.] 1886. 32p. illus., map. 21cm.

The author was probably A. Begg. Can. Arch.

863 [**Anonymous**]
Manitoba en het Noord westelyk gebied (Noord Amerika) Verslag omtrent het klimaat, den bodem, de producten en bronnen van inkomst voor kapitalisten, landbouwers, ambachtslieden, arbeiders, dienstboden, enz. Met bizondere betrekking op Hollandsche en vlaamsche kolonisten. Liverpool, Turner en Dunnett, 1886. 47, [1]p. illus., fold. map. 21 1/2cm.

A pamphlet in Dutch. Man. Leg.

864 [**Anonymous**]
Manitoba och Nordvest-territoriet (Nord-Amerika) En skildring af klimat, jordman, höstresultater, och ervärfskällor for kapitalister, gordbrukare, handverkare, vanliga arbetare, tzenstsökande, o.s.v., med specielt hänsyn till skandinaviska kolonister. Liverpool, Turner och Dunnett, 1886. 43p. illus. 22cm.

A pamphlet in Swedish. Man. Leg.

865 [**Anonymous**]
Le mot de la fin. Voici le vote! Conspiration armée contre les métis français. Le chef métis sacrifié aux Orangistes! Sa prétendue vénalité. Légitimité du provisoire. Ce meurtre de Scott! L'opinion de quelques évêques sur le débat. Celle des missionnaires. Evêques et missionnaires. Nouvelles indignités! Nouveau griefs! La folie de Riel. [n.p., 1886] cover-title, 40p. 22cm. Shortt

866 [**Anonymous**]
Le peuple vs. Sir John. [n.p., 1886?] caption-title, [14]p. In double column. Collection Gagnon

867 [**Anonymous**]
La question Riel. Les griefs des métis. [n.p., 1886?] caption-title, 66, [1]p. 22cm. Shortt

868 [**Anonymous**]
The Riel Rebellion. How it began - How it was carried on - and its consequences. Succinct narrative of the facts. Half-breed grievances. [n.p., 1886?] 31p. 21cm. Shortt

869 [**Anonymous**]
The true inwardness of the Canadian North West Rebellion of 1885 exposed; or, Who is to blame? 2d ed. [n.p., 1886?] 16p. 22cm.

Author critical of the Dominion government's policy, and of General Middleton's leadership. Toronto.

870 [**Argyll**, John George Edward Henry Douglas Sutherland Campbell, 9th duke of]
Our railway to the Pacific, by the Marquis of Lorne, with illustrations by H.R.H. Princess Louise ... London, Isbister & Co., Ltd., 1886. 32p. illus. 23 1/2cm. Reprinted from Good Words. Can. Arch.

871 **Ballantyne**, Robert Michael
The red man's revenge; a tale of the Red River flood. London, J. Nisbet & Co., 1886. viii, 264p. illus.

Fiction. First published in 1880. (A later edition by Musson of Toronto is in Rutherford) Br. Mus.

872 **Bayer**, Ch.
Riel; drame historique en quatre actes et un prologue, cinq tableaux, par Ch. Bayer et E. Parage. Montréal, Imprimerie de L'Étendard, 1886. 75p. 25cm. St. Sulpice

873 **Beauregard**, George
Le 9me bataillon au Nord-Ouest. (Journal d'un militaire) Québec, Jos. G. Gingras & Cie, 1886. 100p. illus. 20cm. B.C. Arch.

874 **Begg**, Alexander
Canada and its national highway. London, Trounce, 1886. ... Not seen.

Text of a paper delivered before the Society of Arts, London. Begg vs. Begg

875 **Begg**, Alexander
Emigration; a paper read at conference, Indian and Colonial Exhibition, London, July 23rd, 1886. London, H. Blacklock & Co. [1886] 28p. incl. illus. (plans) fold. tables. Toronto

876 **Begg**, Alexander
The great North-West of Canada. A paper read at conference, Indian and Colonial Exhibition, London, June 8th, 1886. London, H. Blacklock & Co. [1886] 23p. 22cm.

Lande lists another edition of 15p. published the same year. Toronto

877 **Bible**. New Testament. St. Mark. Beaver
The Gospel according to St. Mark. Translated by Alfred C. Garrioch into the language of the Beaver Indians of the diocese of St. [sic] Athabasca. London, Society for Promoting Christian Knowledge [1886] 3p.l., 47p. front., illus. 16cm. Added title in the Beaver dialect.

In syllabic characters.
Also published in the same year by the British & Foreign Bible Society, edition of 79p. in Roman. L.C.

878 **Bible**. Old Testament. Psalms. Tukkuthkutchin
David vi Psalmnut. Takudh tsha zit thleteteitazya Ven. Archdeacon McDonald ... Winnipeg, Printed by R.D. Richardson for the Society for Promoting Christian Knowledge, London, 1886. 1p.l., 195p. 16 1/2cm.

Included because published in prairie region. L.C.

879 **Blake**, E[dward]
Execution of Louis Riel. Speech ... Ottawa, March 19th, 1886. House of Commons debates. [Ottawa] Printed by MacLean, Roger & Co. [1886] 29p. 29 1/2cm.
See also Entries 881 & 883. Can. Arch.

880 **Blake**, Edward
General review - Riel ... N.W. maladministration - Riel ... Toronto, Hunter, Rose & Co., 1886. 48p. 21cm. (Hon. Edward Blake's speeches. Dominion election of 1886. ser.1, no.1)
Speeches delivered at London and Owen Sound. Shortt

881 **Blake**, Edward
Ministers on trial. Was the execution of Riel necessary or proper? Mr. Blake's great judgments, delivered in the House of Commons of Canada, on the 19th March, 1886. [n.p., n.d.] caption-title, 61p. 20 1/2cm. Amtmann - 176-17

882 **Blake**, Edward
North-West affairs. Neglect, delay, and mismanagement. Race and creed cries ... Toronto, Hunter, Rose & Co., 1886. [397]-424p. 21cm. (Hon. Edward Blake's speeches. Dominion election of 1886. ser.1, no.14)
A speech delivered at Lindsay. Shortt

883 **Blake**, E[dward]
North-West Rebellion. Speech ... Ottawa, April 5th, 1886. House of Commons debates. Ottawa, Printed by MacLean, Roger & Co. [1886] 6p. 29 1/2cm. Can. Arch.

884 **Boulton**, [Charles Arkell]
Reminiscences of the North-West rebellions, with a record of the raising of Her Majesty's 100th Regiment in Canada, and a chapter on Canadian social and political life ... Toronto, Grip Printing and Publishing Co., 1886. 5p.l., [7]-531p. front. (port.) illus., plates, plans, map. 18 1/2cm. Shortt

885 **Bowerman**, A[llan]
Chinook winds. [Winnipeg, 1886] 6p. 21cm. (Hist. & Sc. Soc. of Man., no.22) Man. Leg.

886 **Broughall**, George
The tearful and tragical tale of the tricky troubadour; or, The truant tracked. A topical and tuneful tradition told in travesty. A four-act burlesque in grand opera. Music from Verdi's opera 'Il Trovatore.' As played at the Princess Opera House, Winnipeg, September and October 1886. Winnipeg, Manitoba Free Press [1886] 34p. 21cm. Man. Leg.

887 **Bryce**, George
Souris country; its monuments, mounds, forts & rivers. [Winnipeg, 1886] 7p. 22cm. (Hist. & Sc. Soc. of Man., no.24) Man. Leg.

888 **Canada**. Auditor-General's Office
Expenditure under appropriation of $2,300,000 to defray expenses and losses arising out of troubles in the North-West Territories, from 1st July, 1885, to

15th March, 1886. Also subsidiary statement of expenditure under the same appropriations, &c., Hudson Bay supplies, &c. [Ottawa, Printed by Maclean, Roger & Co., 1886] 60p. L. of P.

888A **Canada**. Department of Agriculture
Canada. Map of the North West Territories & Manitoba ... Ottawa, 1886. folder. [23]p. large map on verso. folds to 20 1/2 x 10cm.
Can. Arch. (ms.)

889 **Canada**. Department of Agriculture
Census of the three provisional districts of the North-West Territories, 1884-5 ... Ottawa, Printed by MacLean, Roger & Co., 1886. xvii, 97p. 24 1/2cm.
Shortt

890 **Canada**. Department of Agriculture
Esquisse générale du Nord-Ouest du Canada où étendue, bois et forêts, richesses minérales et climatologie des quatres districts provisoires d'Assiniboia, Saskatchewan, Alberta et Athabaska. Trois Rivières, 1886. 86, ii p. front. (fold. map) 21 1/2cm. Shortt

891 **Canada**. Department of Agriculture
200 Millionen Acres Zu-Ansiedlungszwecken in Manitoba, und Dem Grossen Nordwesten Amerikas. Liverpool, Turner and Dunnett, 1886. ...
Hist. Atlas of Man. 1970

892 **Canada**. Department of Indian Affairs
The facts respecting Indian administration in the North-West. Ottawa, Printed by Department of Indian Affairs [1886] cover-title, 74p. 21cm.
Can. Arch.

893 **Canada**. Department of the Interior
Description of the townships of the North-West Territories, Dominion of Canada ... Compiled and arranged from the field notes, plans and reports of the surveyors. Ottawa, Printed by MacLean, Roger & Co., 1886. 3v. fold. maps. 26cm. Shortt

894 **Canada**. Department of the Interior
Detailed report upon all claims to land and right to participate in the North-West half-breed grant by settlers along the South Saskatchewan and vicinity west of Range 26, W. 2nd meridian, being the settlement commonly known as St. Louis de Langevin, St. Laurent or Batoche, and Duck Lake. Ottawa, MacLean, Roger & Co., 1886. 18p. 23 1/2cm. (Canada. Sess. papers, 1886, no.8, pt.7)

The report was prepared by Wm. Pearce. U. of S.

895 **Canada**. Department of Militia and Defence
The medical and surgical history of the Canadian North-West Rebellion of 1885, as told by members of the hospital staff corps. Montreal, Printed by John Lovell & Son, 1886. 60p. 24 1/2cm.

Largely the daily journal and final report of Deputy Surgeon-General T.G. Roddick.
Shortt

896 **Canada.** Department of Militia and Defence
Report upon the suppression of the rebellion in the North-West Territories, and matters in connection therewith, in 1885. Presented to Parliament. Ottawa, 1886. xii, 384p. front. (fold. map) col. plates (part. fold.) 23 1/2cm. (Canada. Sess. papers, 1886, no.6a) Also printed for distribution.
Contains General Middleton's report and that of the War Claims Commission. Shortt

897 **Canada.** Department of the Secretary of State
Copies of all documents forming the record in the cases of Her Majesty against the different parties tried in connection with the late rebellion ... [Ottawa, 1886] 408, 36p. 23 1/2cm. (Canada. Sess. papers, 1886, no.52) At head of title: 'Return ... to an address of the House of Commons, dated 5th March, 1886.' The last 36 pages is a supplementary return. Shortt

898 **Canada.** Department of the Secretary of State
Copies of all papers found in the council room of the insurgents or elsewhere at Batoche, especially including: 1. The diary of Louis Riel. 2. The minute book and order in council of the insurgent council. 3. The correspondence of Louis Riel. [Ottawa, 1886] 49p., 1 l. 23 1/2cm. (Canada. Sess. papers, 1886, nos.43h-i) U. of S.

899 **Canada.** Department of the Secretary of State
Copies of all the depositions or other evidence submitted in favor of the half-breeds or métis sentenced to imprisonment in the gaol at Regina, and in the provincial penitentiary of Manitoba; and also all depositions submitted in behalf of André Nault and Abraham Monteur, métis prisoners confined at Regina and Battleford. [Ottawa, 1886] 27, [1]p. 23 1/2cm. (Canada. Sess. papers, 1886, no.45c) U. of S.

900 **Canada.** Department of the Secretary of State
Copies of instructions to Major Bell, Major-General Laurie, S.L. Bedson and other non-combatants employed during the North-West campaign, from the Minister of Militia, Major-General Middleton or the Adjutant-General of Militia, and of correspondence between the last named authorities and such non-combatants. [Ottawa, 1886] 10-20p. 23 1/2cm. (Canada. Sess. papers, 1886, no.80b) U. of S.

901 **Canada.** Department of the Secretary of State
Copies of the commission or commissions, and instructions issued to the commissioners appointed to enquire into and report on the losses sustained in the North-West Territories during the recent rebellion. Ottawa, 1886. 5p. 23 1/2cm. (Canada. Sess. papers, 1886, no.52f) U. of S.

902 **Canada.** Department of the Secretary of State
A copy of the memorial to the North-West Council, presented to the government by Messrs. Wilson and Ross, members of said Council, and of any answer to said memorial, and of any correspondence between the government and the Lieutenant-Governor of the North-West Territories or other parties in reference thereto. [Ottawa, 1886] 6p. 23 1/2cm. (Canada. Sess. papers, 1886, no.79)
In addition to 10 resolutions passed by the N.W.T. Council, contains 25 resolutions passed in the Edmonton electoral district bearing on the problems of the N.W.T. U. of S.

903 **Canada.** Department of the Secretary of State
Epitome of parliamentary documents in connection with the North-West Rebellion, 1885. Printed by order of Parliament. Ottawa, MacLean, Roger & Co., 1886. cover-title, 389p. 24 1/2cm.

The epitome contains sessional papers 43, 43a-e, the trial of Riel and documents bearing on it; 45a-c, documents on the claims to title to land by half-breeds; 52a-c, other trials arising out of the rebellion.

No.45c is not the document with this number in the sessional papers; 45c in the latter is 'copies of all depositions in favor of half-breeds.' Shortt

904 **Canada.** Privy Council. Committee on pensions
Copy of a report of the Honorable the Privy Council, approved by His Excellency the Governor-General in Council on the 8th July, 1885, respecting regulations as to pensions and gratuities, rebellion, North-West Territories. [Ottawa, 1886] 10p. 23 1/2cm. (Canada. Sess. papers, 1886, no.80e) Sessional paper 80d (2 pages) lists names of persons awarded pensions. U. of S.

904A **Canadian Pacific Railway**
Canada. Free grants of land. 160 acres in Manitoba and the great North West, and from 100 to 200 acres in other provinces. The Canadian Pacific Railway is now open from ocean to ocean. [n.p., 1886?] folder. 16p. illus., col. map. folds to 15 x 9 1/2cm. Can. Arch. (ms.)

905 **Canadian Pacific Railway**
Manitoba. The Canadian North-West. Testimony of actual settlers. [Montreal, Montreal Herald, 1886] cover-title, 1p.l., 50p., 1 l. fold. map. 20cm. At head of title: 1886. Shortt

905A **Canadian Pacific Railway**
Manitoba and the Canadian North-West. Letters from actual settlers. [Winnipeg, 1886?] cover-title, [4]p. 28cm. Can. Arch.

906 **Canadian Pacific Railway**
Settler's index to golden Manitoba and Canadian North-West. [Montreal, n.d.] cover-title, 37p. tables 14cm. B.C. Arch.

907 **Canadian Pacific Railway**
... Upplysninger om Manitoba och det Canadiska nordvesten. [n.p., n.d.] 16p. illus. 18cm. B.C. Arch.

908 **Canadian Pacific Railway**
What settlers say of the Canadian North-West; a plain statement of the experiences of farmers resident in the country. [London, Blacklock] 1886. 47p. illus. 20cm.

A Canadian edition of 53 pages was published the same year in Montreal. Tanghe

909 **Canadian Pacific Railway**
What women say of the Canadian North West. [Montreal, Montreal Herald, 1886] cover-title, 50p., 1 l. 20cm. At head of title: 1886.

A London edition was published by H. Blacklock. See Br. Mus. catalogue. Shortt

910 **Caron,** Sir [Joseph Philippe René] Adolphe
Discours sur la question Riel prononcé le 17 mars 1886, à la Chambre des Communes. [n.p., 1886?] 32p. illus. (incl. ports.) 22cm. Shortt

911 **Chapleau,** [Sir] J[oseph] A[dolphe]
Speech ... on the motion made, before the House of Commons, on the 11th March, 1886, to blame the government for having allowed the execution of Louis Riel. (From the official debates) House of Commons, March 24th, 1886. Montreal, Imprimerie Générale, 1886. cover-title, 40p. 22 1/2cm.

Also published in French.
A 50-page edition, published by Maclean, Roger of Ottawa, has a slightly different title. Shortt

912 **Church of England.** Diocese of Rupert's Land
Report of the Synod, Diocese of Rupert's Land, August 5, 1886. With an appendix containing the acts of incorporation and other important documents. Winnipeg, Manitoba Free Press, 1886. 95p. 21 1/2cm. Shortt

913 **Church of England.** Manual of devotion. Beaver
Manual of devotion in the Beaver Indian language. Translated by Rev. Alfred C. Garrioch. London, Society for Promoting Christian Knowledge, 1886. 3p.l., 87p. front., illus. 16 1/2cm.

Text in syllabic characters. L.C.

914 **Clark,** William
The Canadian North-West ... Reprinted by permission from the Canadian Gazette. [London, Printed by Cassell & Co., 1886] cover-title, 12p. 18 1/2cm. Man. Leg.

915 **Collins,** [Joseph] Edmund
Annette, the métis spy; a heroine of the N.W. Rebellion. Toronto, Rose Publishing Co., 1886. viii, [9]-155p. front. 18 1/2cm. Addendum: Nancy, the lightkeeper's daughter, p.[145]-155.

Fiction. Shortt

916 **Comité de collaborateurs**
La mort de Riel et la voix du sang, par un Comité de collaborateurs. [n.p., 1886?] 19p. 23cm. St. Sulpice

917 La croisade anti-française et anti-Catholique dirigée par Sir John A. MacDonald. Montréal, L'Etendard [1886?] 21, [iii]p.

This pamphlet exemplifies the most extreme of Quebec reaction to the Riel execution. Canner - 474-353

918 **Curran,** J[ohn] J[oseph]
Debate on Louis Riel. Speech ... in the House of Commons, Ottawa, on Monday, the 15th of March, 1886. 16p. 22cm. Can. Arch.

919 **Daoust,** Charles R[oger]
Cent-vingt jours de service actif. Récit historique très complet de la campagne du 65ème au Nord-Ouest. Montréal, E. Senécal & Fils, 1886. 242p. incl. illus., plates, plan. front., ports. 19 1/2cm. Shortt

920 **De Molinari,** M.G.
Au Canada et aux montagnes rocheuses – en Russie – en Corse – à l'exposition universelle d'Anvers. Lettres addresseés au Journal des Debats. Paris, C. Reinwald, 1886. x, 334p.

Part I, p.1-146, describes a journey across Canada in the autumn of 1885 by a party composed of delegates of chambers of commerce. Appendix, p.319-332, contains considerable information on the trial of Louis Riel which was then in progress. Belgium

921 **Desaulniers**, Gonzalve L[esieur]
L'Absolution avant la bataille, dédié aux braves de la Butte-aux-Français. Montréal, L'Etendard, 1886. 16p.

Poetry relating to the engagement of a detachment of the 65th Battalion Mount-Royal Rifles, on 28 May 1885 at Frenchman's Butte during the North-West Rebellion. A list of the members of the detachment under command of Lt. Col. G.A. Hughes is given in introductory pages. Lande

922 **Dixon**, L.
Halifax to the Saskatchewan. 'Our boys' in the Riel Rebellion. A musical and dramatic burlesque ... Halifax, Holloway, 1886. 36p. 21cm. Dalhousie

923 Documents officiels constatant les nombreuses plaintes et réclamations des métis du Nord-Ouest. [n.p., 1886?] 32p. 22 1/2cm. In double column. Shortt

924 Dominion of Canada, Pacific railway, and North-West Territories. [n.p., 1886?] cover-title, 32p. fold. map, table. 22cm.

Articles by several people, including Professors Fream, Sheldon, and Tanner. L. of P.

925 **Elliott**, Charles
A trip to Canada and the far North-West. London, W. Kent & Co. [1886] 3p.l., 93p. front., illus., fold. map. 19cm.

P.72-93 relate to the prairies. B.C. Arch.

926 **Entragues**, L. de St. Hubert d'
The Soudan campaign. [Montreux, Peyrollaz, 1886.] 134p. 15cm.

P.84-134 deal with the Riel Rebellion of 1885. Can. Arch.

927 **L'Etendard**
Polémiques et documents touchant le Nord-Ouest et l'exécution de Louis Riel. (Extraits de l'Étendard) Premier fascicule se rapportant principalement aux événements antérieurs à 1885. Montréal, Imprimerie de L'Étendard, 1886. 2p.l., iii, [311]p. 22 1/2cm. Various paging. Shortt

928 **Faucher de Saint-Maurice**, N[arcisse] H[enri] E[douard]
Assemblée législative. Le chemin de fer projeté des comtes du sud. Dorchester, Bellechasse, Montmagny, l'Islet, Kamouraska ... Discours ... sur la question Riel. Québec, Demers, 1886. 32p. Canner – 474-445

929 **Flynn**, E[dmund] J[ames]
Affaire Riel. Discours ... prononcé devant l'Assemblée législative le 29 avril 1886. [Québec, A. Coté et Cie, 1886] 16p. 24 1/2cm. In double column. Shortt

930 **Fream**, William
Across Canada: a report on its agricultural resources. Rev. ed. Ottawa, Dept. of Agriculture, 1886. cover-title, 31p. illus., fold map. 22cm.

Copy in Can. Arch. Ms. Division has ink corrections and insertions in text, presumably for a further revision. Can. Arch. (ms.)

931 Free homes in Manitoba and the Canadian North West ... [n.p., 1886?] cover-title 11, 32, 13-22p. fold. map. 24cm. Can. Arch.

932 **Galt**, Frank James
Alia delectant alios. A few notes from jottings on my journey to Winnipeg, Manitoba, via New York, Port Hudson, Chicago, etc. St. Leonards-on-Sea, 1886. 23p. 22cm. N.Y.

933 **Girouard**, [Désiré]
Discours ... sur l'exécution de Louis Riel. Chambre des Communes, 24 mars 1886. [Ottawa] Maclean, Roger, et Cie, 1886. 21p. 21cm. St. Sulpice

934 **Goodridge**, R[ichard] E.W.
On the proposed change of time marking to a decimal system; a plea that the duodecimal system can be retained. [Winnipeg, 1886] 10p. 21cm. (Hist. & Sc. Soc. of Man., no.21) Man. Leg.

935 **Grogan and Pettit**
[Settlers' guide to southern Alberta. Calgary, 1886] ... Not seen.

The Calgary Herald for 21 and 28 August 1886 contains references to Mr. W. Hanson Boorne collecting pictures for the projected pamphlet. No evidence that it was ever published.

936 **Holt**, David G., comp.
Souvenir of the Province of Manitoba and the city of Winnipeg. Winnipeg, H. Buckle & Sons, 1886. 47p. illus. 22cm. Man. Leg.

937 **Hubbard**, J.H.
Sport in the Canadian North-West. A paper, on the game birds and wild animals of Manitoba and the North-West Territories, read ... at a conference held in the Colonial and Indian Exhibition, July 29th, 1886. Also an appendix, giving practical information for the guidance of sportsmen. [London? 1886?] 37p. Can. Arch.

938 **Hunter**, Jane (Ross)
Nikumoowina. Hymns translated by Mrs. Hunter into the language of the Cree Indians of the Diocese of Rupert's Land, North-West America. London, Society for Promoting Christian Knowledge, 1886. 1p.l., 102p. 17cm.

'The translators ... were Mrs. Hunter, the Rev. H.B. Steinhauer, and Peter Erasmus, a native interpreter': Pilling, p.248.

The first edition appeared in 1855 appended to her husband's translation of the Book of Common Prayer, and contained 33 hymns. By 1876 the hymnary had grown to a hundred hymns. The first edition published as a separate was the above issue. Man. Leg.

939 **Jackson**, Thomas Wesley
The views of a leading Conservative in the North-West on the late rebellion. [n.p., 1886] 4p. L. of P.

940 **Lacombe**, Albert
Chemin de la croix. Montréal, 1886. ... Not seen. Morice

941 [**Lacombe**, Albert]
First reader in the English and Blackfoot languages with pictures and words. Prepared by order of the Department of Indian Affairs for the use of industrial

schools among the Blackfoot tribes in the North West Territories. Montréal, C.O. Beauchemin & Son, 1886. 88p. front., illus. 18 1/2cm.

The introduction is signed A.L., i.e. Albert Lacombe. Shortt

942 [**Lacombe**, Albert]
Petit manuel pour apprendre à lire la langue crise. Small manual to learn the reading in the Cree language. Montréal, C.O. Beauchemin & Fils, 1886. 43, [1]p. 16cm.

In Roman characters. Contains a vocabulary in French, English, and Cree. Rutherford

943 **Lansdowne**, Henry Charles Keith Petty-Fitzmaurice, 5th marquis of
Canada North-West and British Columbia. Two speeches by His Excellency the Marquis of Lansdowne. Ottawa, Dept. of Agriculture, 1886. cover-title, 32p. fold. map. 21 1/2cm. L.C.

944 **Laurier**, Sir Wilfrid
Speech ... on the Riel question, delivered in the House of Commons at Ottawa, March 16th, 1886. [n.p., 1886] 24p. 21cm. In double column. Shortt

945 **McArthur**, Alexander
Our winter birds. Winnipeg, 1886. 12p. 21cm. (Hist. & Sc. Soc. of Man., no.25) Man. Leg.

946 **McCharles**, A[ngus]
Footsteps of time in the Red River valley, with specific reference to the salt springs & flowing wells to be found in it. [Winnipeg, 1886] 18p. 21cm. (Hist. & Sc. Soc. of Man., no.27) Man. Leg.

947 **Manitoba**. Department of Education
Mémoire préparé par la section catholique du Bureau d'education de la province de Manitoba, en vue de l'Exposition colonial de Londres, 1886. Winnipeg, 1886. 71p. 23cm. N.Y.

948 **Manitoba and North-Western Railway**
Guide book to the lands of the Manitoba and North-Western Railway. Compiled from government township reports and M. & N.W. Railway land examination reports. Winnipeg, McIntyre Bros., 1886. 1p.l., 77p. maps (1 fold.) 25cm. Man. Leg.

949 Manitoba og Nordvesturlandid i Canada. [n.p.] 1886. Broadside 25 x 43cm.

In double column with map showing western Manitoba and eastern Saskatchewan. Icelandic. Denmark

950 **Mercier**, Honoré
Discours prononcé par l'Honorable M. Mercier, député de St-Hyacinthe et chef de l'opposition à l'Assemblée législative de Québec, le 7 mai 1886, sur la question Riel. Québec, Imprimerie de L'Electeur, 1886. 58p. 22 1/2cm. In double column. Shortt

951 **Mousseau**, J[oseph] Octave
Une page d'histoire. Montréal, W.F. Daniel, 1886. 98p. 17 1/2cm.

Relates to the Riel Rebellion. U.B.C.

952 Nya Stockholm, nybildadt skandinaviskt nybygge i Nord-Amerikanska Western. 160 acres land fritt till hvarje person, fyld 18 ar. Enköping, Enköping-Postens tryckeri, 1886. Leaf 28 x 45cm. folding in eight to size of title-page 11 1/2 x 14 1/2cm.

Locations of New Sweden and New Stockholm colonies shown on map. Statements by M.P. Peterson and Emanuel Ohlen of Winnipeg. Sweden

953 **Oliver,** J.W.W.
How to start a farm in the Canadian North West under the auspices of the Manitoba and Northwestern Railway Company. Glasgow [1886?] ... Not seen. Can. Govt. Off.

954 **One Who Knows**
The gibbet of Regina, the truth about Riel; Sir John A. Macdonald and his cabinet before public opinion, by one who knows. New York, Thompson & Moreau, 1886. 200p. ports. 20cm.

Also published in French. Shortt

955 **P., M.**
A winter trip on the Canadian Pacific Railway. Christmas and New Year in the snow, 1885-6. Written for private circulation at the request of his friends, after an absence of 22 years from the old country; by M.P. Cheltenham, copies may be obtained from J.J. Banks [1886?] 1p.l., 29p. 19cm. L.C.

956 **Panton,** James Hoyes
Notes on the geology of some islands in Lake Winnipeg. Winnipeg, 1886. 10p. 21cm. (Hist. & Sc. Soc. of Man., no.20) Man. Leg.

957 **Paquin,** Elzéar
Riel; tragédie en quatre actes. Montréal, C.O. Beauchemin & Fils, 1886. 143p. 17 1/2cm.

A play. Shortt

958 **Presbyterian Church**
Report of the Board of Management of the Church and Manse Building Fund of the Presbyterian Church in Manitoba and the North-West Territories, with statement, by the Superintendent of Missions and Treasurer's report, including list of all subscriptions to the fund received since the organization of the Board. (Presented to the General Assembly, June, 1886) Winnipeg, 1886. self-cover, 32p. illus. Amtmann - 229-653

959 **Richardson,** R[obert] L[orne] comp.
Facts and figures. The highest testimony. What Lord Dufferin, Lorne and Lansdowne say about the Canadian Northwest ... cost of wheat production ... The Indian problem discussed. [Ottawa? 1886?] cover-title, 32p. 23 1/2cm. L.C.

960 **Riel,** Louis
Poésies religieuses et politiques. Montréal, Imprimerie de L'Étendard, 1886. 51p. 17 1/2cm. Shortt

961 [**Riel**, Louis] defendant
The Queen vs. Louis Riel, accused and convicted of the crime of high treason. Report of trial at Regina. - Appeal to the Privy Council, England. - Petition for medical examination of the convict. - List of petitions for commutation of sentence, Ottawa. Ottawa, Printed by the Queen's Printer, 1886. 207p. 25cm. Printed for distribution only as contained, in substance, in sessional papers 43c & 43f. See Entry 903. Shortt

962 **Roman Catholic Church**. Prayers. Cree
Livre de prières en langue crise. Montréal, 1886. 296p. 15 1/2cm. Not seen.

Translated by Rev. A. Lacombe. Morice. Newberry

963 **Ross**, A[rthur] W[ellington]
Pacific railway and North-West Territories. Speech ... in the House of Commons. Ottawa, 1886. 32p. 21 1/2cm. Can. Arch.

964 **Ross**, D.A., & Co. (Ross, Macfarlane & Brewer)
Manitoba farms and land register ... Plan of township. Winnipeg, 1886. 37p. 22cm. Can. Arch.

965 **Rowe**, Lizzie
An old woman's story. Regina, Printed by the Leader Printing Co., 1886. 15p. 20cm. Sub-title: The echoes of the chimes.

Fiction. A ms. note on the title-page of the copy in the Man. Leg. Library: This is the first literary work issued from any press in the North West Territories. [Signed] Nich's Flood Davin. Man. Leg.

966 [**Scudder**, Samuel Hubbard]
The Winnipeg country; or, Roughing it with an eclipse party, by a Rochester fellow ... Boston, Cupples, Upham & Co., 1886. 144p. illus., plates, fold. map. 18 1/2cm.

Inscription on end-papers of the copy in the Shortt Library: Mr. James Fletcher, In pleasant memory of a pleasant trip to another mosquito-land with a pleasant companion, Sam H. Scudder.

Another edition published in New York in 1890. Shortt

967 [**Seton**, Ernest Thompson]
A list of mammals of Manitoba. [1886] 26p. 22cm. (Hist. & Sc. Soc. of Man., no.23) Man. Leg.

968 **Shelford**, W.
The development of North-West Canada by the Hudson's Bay trade route. [n.p., 1886] cover-title, 11p. map. 24cm. Reprinted from The National Review of June, 1886. Printed for private circulation. B.C. Arch.

969 **Skandinaviska National Föreningen**
Skandinaverna i Manitoba och Nord westra Canada. [Winnipeg? 1886] cover-title, 20p. fold. map. 21cm. Map is of the Swedish colony around Stockholm, Sask. Man. Leg.

970 **Skandinaviska National Föreningen**
Skandinaviska National Foreningens hoge beskyddare hans exc. premier ministern af Dominion af Canada Sir John A. McDonald K.C.B. etc. Tillegnas denna bok

vordsamligen af Skandinaviska National Foreningen i Winnipeg. [Winnipeg, 1886?] 20p.

Scandinavian immigration pamphlet. Lande

971 **Society for the Propagation of the Gospel in Foreign Parts**
Rupert's Land. London, The Society, 1886. cover-title, 24p. 18cm. (Historical sketches. Colonial series, no.7) Can. Arch.

972 **Spence**, Thomas
Canada. The resources and future greatness of her great prairie North-West lands. With information for all, of interest to the intending settler and the capitalist seeking profitable and safe investments. Ottawa, Department of Agriculture, 1886. 96p. 22cm.

A 38-page edition was published the same year. Can. Arch.

973 **Tanner**, Henry
Successful emigration to Canada. Rev. ed. Ottawa, Department of Agriculture, 1886. cover-title, 32p. incl. tables. front. (fold. map) 22cm. At head of title: Dominion of Canada.

First edition published in 1885. Shortt

974 **Tassé**, Joseph
La question Riel. Discours ... prononcé devant le 'Cercle Lafontaine' d'Ottawa, le 19 février 1886. [n.p., 1886] cover-title, 13p. 25 1/2cm. In double column. Shortt

975 **Thompson**, John Sparrow David
Discours ... prononcé devant le 'Cercle Lafontaine' d'Ottawa, le 19 février 1886. [Quebec, 1886] 54, [2] p. Ehrlich - 36-15

976 **Thompson**, J[ohn] S[parrow] D[avid]
The execution of Louis Riel. Speech ... Delivered March 22, 1886. [Ottawa? 1886] 31p. 23cm. Can. Arch.

977 **Thompson**, [W.T.]
The city of Winnipeg, the capital of Manitoba and the commercial, railway & financial metropolis of the Northwest, past and present development and future prospects. Thompson & Boyer, editors. Winnipeg, Printed at the office of the Commercial, 1886. [1], ii, [1], [5]-196p. illus. 24cm.

Directory of businesses, p.101-96. Man. Leg.

978 **White**, Thomas
Northwest administration; speech in the House of Commons, Ottawa ... 4th May. [n.p., 1886] caption-title, 19p. 22cm. Can. Arch.

979 Winnipeg, the capital of Manitoba. Winnipeg, 1886. 196p. illus. 23 1/2cm. Not seen. Queen's

980 **Anderson**, Frimann B.
Immigration and settlement of our vacant lands in Manitoba and the North-West. How hindered! How promoted! [Winnipeg, 1887] 19p. 24cm.

Accuses the Dominion government of showing 'little energy, less despatch, and no enthusiasm' in its immigration policy and the settling of the West. Man. Leg.

981 [**Anonymous**]
Elections de 1887. La vraie question. [n.p., 1887] 51p. 22cm.
Relates to the rebellion of 1885. St. Sulpice

982 [**Anonymous**]
La rébellion du Nord-Ouest. [n.p., 1887] cover-title, 18p. 22cm. In double column.
A defence of the Conservative government. Collection Gagnon

983 [**Anonymous**]
Le véritable Riel tel que dépeint dans des lettres de Sa Grandeur Mgr Grandin, évêque de Saint-Albert, du Révd P. Leduc, vicaire-général de Saint-Albert, du Révd P. André, supérieur des missions du district de Carleton, des Révds Pères Touze, Fourmond, Végreville, Moulin et Lecoq, missionnaires du Nord-Ouest, d'une religieuse de Batoche, etc., etc. Suivi d'extraits des mandements de nos seigneurs les évêques, concernant l'agitation Riel. Montréal, Imprimerie Générale, 1887. cover-title, 63p. 21cm.
A ms. note in the copy in the Shortt Library attributes it to J.C. Filteau. Shortt

984 **Archambault**, J[oseph] L[ouis]
Étude politique. Lue devant l'Association conservatrice de Montréal en février 1887. Montréal, 1887. 34p. 22cm.
Relates to the Riel Rebellion. St. Sulpice

985 **Attwood**, P[eter] H[arold]
A jubilee essay on imperial federation as affecting Manitoba and the Northwest ... Part I. Our provincial autonomy. Part II. The question of race. Part III. The final disposition of the C.P. and H.B. railways. Winnipeg, Manitoba Free Press print, 1887. 28p. 21 1/2cm. Man. Leg.

986 **Beaugrand**, Honoré
De Montréal à Victoria par le Transcontinental Canadien. Conférence faite par M. Honoré Beaugrand ... devant la Chambre de Commerce du district de Montréal. Montréal, 23 mars, 1887. [n.p., 1887] 1p.l., [5]-52p. plates. 20 1/2 x 13 1/2cm. Moose Jaw

987 **Bell**, Charles N[apier]
The Selkirk Settlement and settlers. A concise history of the Red River country from its discovery. Including information extracted from the original documents, lately discovered, and notes obtained from Selkirk Settlement colonists. Winnipeg, Printed at the office of the Commercial, 1887. 44p. 23cm. Rutherford

988 **Bell**, Charles N[apier]
Some Red River Settlement history. Winnipeg, Call Printing Co., 1887. cover-title, 8p. 23cm. (Hist. & Sc. Soc. of Man., no.29) Shortt

989 **Bernier**, T[homas] Alfred
Le Manitoba, champ d'immigration. Ottawa, 1887. 144p. front. (fold. map) 22 1/2cm. Shortt

990 **Bryant**, Wilbur F[ranklin]
The blood of Abel. Hastings, Neb., Published, for the author, by the Gazette-Journal Co., 1887. v p., 1 l., [9]-169p. port. 21 1/2cm.

A pamphlet condemning the treatment of Riel. The appendix contains documents.
B.C. Arch.

991 **Canada**. Department of Agriculture
Census of Manitoba, 1885-6. Ottawa, Printed by Maclean, Roger & Co., 1887. 217p. tables. 25cm.

In English and French. Glenbow

992 **Canada**. Department of Agriculture
North West of Canada. A general sketch of the extent, woods and forests, mineral resources and climatology of the four provisional districts of Assiniboia, Saskatchewan, Alberta and Athabasca. Ottawa, 1887. 77, ii p. fold. map. 21cm.
Can. Arch.

993 **Canada**. Department of Militia and Defence
Continuation of appendix no.4 of the report of 18 May, 1886, on matters in connection with the suppression of the rebellion in the North-West Territories, in 1885. Final report of the War Claims Commission. Ottawa, Printed by MacLean, Roger & Co., 1887. 2p.l., 80p. 24 1/2cm. (Canada. Sess. papers, 1887, no.9b) Also published for distribution. U. of S.

994 **Canada**. Department of Militia and Defence
Report of Lieutenant-Colonel W.H. Jackson, Deputy Adjutant-General, principal supply, pay and transport officer of the North-West forces, and chairman of War Claims Commission, on matters in connection with the suppression of the rebellion in the North-West Territories, in 1885. Presented to Parliament. Ottawa, MacLean, Roger & Co., 1887. 44p. 24 1/2cm. (Canada. Sess. papers, 1887, no.9c) Also printed for distribution. Shortt

995 **Canada**. Department of Militia and Defence
Report of Major General Laurie, commanding base and lines of communication, upon matters in connection with the suppression of the rebellion in the North-West Territories in 1885. Ottawa, Printed by MacLean, Roger & Co., 1887. 39p. 24 1/2cm. (Canada. Sess. papers, 1887, no.9d) Also printed for distribution. U. of S.

996 **Canada**. Department of the Interior
The Northwest Rebellion. [Ottawa, 1887?] cover-title, 18p. 21 1/2cm.
Shortt

997 **Canada**. Department of the Secretary of State
Return of the names of those persons, outside of the militia, who have been recommended for scrip for services of whatever kind in the late rebellion. [Ottawa, 1887] 8p. 25cm. (Canada. Sess. papers, 1887, no.59)

Most of the persons named were members of the Prince Albert Volunteers. U. of S.

998 **Canada**. Parliament. Senate. Select Committee on the existing natural food products of the North-West Territories, and the best means of conserving and increasing them

Report and minutes of evidence. [Ottawa, Printed by MacLean, Roger and Co., 1887] 184, [1]p. 25cm. (Senate. Journals, 1887, appendix no.1) U. of S.

999 [**Canadian Manufacturer**, pseud.]
Disallowance. [n.p., 1887?] cover-title, 14p. 22cm. Arkin

1000 **Canadian Pacific Railway**
Facts for farmers. The great Canadian North-West; its climate, crops and capabilities; with settlers' letters. Liverpool, Journal of Commerce Printing Works, 1887. 32p. illus., fold. maps. 21cm. B.C. Arch.

1001 **Clark**, Daniel
A psycho-medical history of Louis Riel. [Baltimore, 1887] 19p. Reprinted from the American Journal of Insanity, July, 1887. Not seen. Toronto

1002 **Conservative Party**
Riel contre l'Eglise catholique. Aux Canadiens français. [s.l., 1887?] caption-title, [4]p. facsim. 20cm. L. of P.

1003 **Costigan**, John
The Riel and Home Rule questions. Hon. John Costigan's speech at Woodstock, N.B. Mr. Costigan's letter to Lord Lorne on Home Rule for Ireland. Gladstone's bill foreshadowed. Opinions of the Irish national newspapers. [n.p.] Curan, Coughlin & Co. [1887?] 27p.

An election pamphlet of 1887 correlating the Riel Rebellion with Irish Home Rule. Lande

1004 **Cumberland**, Stuart C.
The Queen's highway from ocean to ocean. London, S. Low, Marston, Searle & Rivington, 1887. 5p.l., 431p. front., illus. plates, fold. map. 22cm.

The author claimed that he was the first newspaperman to describe the new C.P.R. line from west to east. Shortt

1005 **Drummond**, Lewis [Henry]
The French element in the Canadian Northwest ... Winnipeg, The Northwest Review, 1887. cover-title, 14p. 22 1/2cm. (Hist. & Sc. Soc. of Man., no.28 [i.e. 25]) Shortt

1006 [**Gates**, Edward Wilson]
English emigrants in Canada: a peep at their new homes, by Septimus Scrivener. London, J. Clarke & Co., 1887. 32p. Br. Mus.

1007 [**Gillett**, Walter B.]
Manitoba, Canada. Some of its towns and farming districts ... [Winnipeg] Manitoba Free Press print [1887] cover-title, 20p. 16cm.

A description of several towns and a listing of farms for sale near each. Man. Leg.

1008 **Hudson's Bay Company**
Deed poll, by the governor and company of Hudson's Bay, for conducting their trade in North America, and for defining the rights and prescribing the duties of their officers, 1871. Amended by shareholders, June 27th, 1876; June 24th, 1879. London, Sir Joseph Causton & Sons, 1887. cover-title, 11, [1]p. 25 1/2cm.

A reprint, with two amendments, of the 1871 edition. Shortt

1009 Not used

1010 **Kingston,** W[illiam] H[enry] G[iles]
Snow-shoes and canoes; or, The early days of a fur-trader in the Hudson's Bay Territory. London, S. Low, Marston, Searle, & Rivington, 1887. vi, 336p. front., illus., plates. 19cm.

Juvenile fiction. L.C.

1011 **Liberal Party**
The 'Boodle' Brigade as represented among the members of the Dominion government. [n.p., 1887] 4p. fold. cartoons.

An election pamphlet ridiculing the Macdonald ministry. Lande

1012 **McArthur,** Alex[ander]
A prairie tragedy; the fate of Thomas Simpson, the Arctic explorer ... Winnipeg, G.C. Mortimore, 1887. cover-title, 13p. 21cm. (Hist. & Sc. Soc. of Man., no.26 [i.e. 27]) Shortt

1013 **McMillan,** A[nthony] J.
Life in Canada. [Lecture given in Kenilworth, Warwickshire by A.J. McMillan of Brandon, Manitoba, in 1887] Kenilworth, Warwickshire, 1887. 15p. 21cm. Man. Arch.

1014 **McMillan,** [Donald]
Letters and extracts on the Riel question, with notes. Alexandria, Printed at the office of The Glengarian, 1887. 27p. 21 1/2cm. Can. Arch.

1015 **Manitoba.** Department of Agriculture
2000 free homesteads in Manitoba, 320000 acres of fertile lands open to settlers, all within easy access to railway stations, affording ready market for grain and dairy produce ... [Winnipeg, The Call Printing Co., 1887] folder (12)p.

'Special notice. – The Provincial Government of Manitoba has recently issued no other immigration literature but this, and cannot be responsible for statements made by private parties, or, for their own advantage, by emigration agents abroad.' Amtmann – 189-765

1016 **Morris,** W.J.
The new Northwest. [Perth? Ont., 1887] cover-title, 8p. 21cm. B.C. Arch.

1017 **North West Territories.** Legislative Council
Journals of the Council of the North West Territories, from 1877 to 1887. Regina, Printed by Amédée E. Forget, 1886-87. 9v. in 1. 25cm. No general title-page. Title taken from binder's title. Shortt

1018 **Ontario, Manitoba, & Western Railway**
Synopsis of prospectus of the Ontario, Manitoba, & Western Railway and connections; Manitoba's grand 30,000,000 bushel crop of 1887, and Ontario's unequalled timber, mineral and agricultural wealth, will be more firmly united to the Dominion by this great Canadian enterprise, and is worthy of the warmest attention of every patriot in our fair Canada. [n.p., 1887?] cover-title, 16p. 19cm.

Map on back cover. Toronto

1019 [**Ord**, Lewis Redman]
Reminiscences of a bungle, by one of the bunglers. Toronto, Grip Printing & Publishing Co., 1887. 66p. 18 1/2cm.

The bungler was one of the land surveyors who joined the Dominion Land Surveyors Intelligence Corps. J.L. Doupe, who presented a copy to the Man. Leg. Library, attributed this pamphlet to Lewis R. Ord; F. Anderson, a student of the Riel rebellions, states that the author was T. Russell.

The author, who wrote with great sarcasm, was critical of the generalship in the campaign. Can. Arch.

1020 **Passy**, Louis
Etude sur la colonisation et l'agriculture au Canada. Paris, Georges Chamerot, 1887. 132p. 24cm.

Of a general nature, but the emphasis is on Western Canada, with half the book relating specifically to it. France

1021 **Powell**, T.R.
From Montreal to San Francisco across Canadian territory. Montreal, 1887. 40p. 15cm.

Describes return journey also. Can. Arch.

1022 **Powers**, John Weston
The history of Regina ... Its foundation and growth, with notices of the early pioneer merchants and business men; descriptive notices of the government offices and public institutions; with biographical sketches of Lieut-Gov. Dewdney and principal officials; the Northwest Mounted Police; the Northwest and municipal councils; our churches, schools, &c.; besides a vast amount of other useful information, carefully obtained from reliable and authentic sources. Regina, Printed by The Leader Co., 1887. 93p. front., illus., col. plate, ports. 23cm. Shortt

1023 [**Rickards**, C.D.]
Across America: from Manitoba, to Vancouver [by] C.D.R. of Brighton, England. Brighton, J.G. Bishop, printer, Herald Office [1887] 15p. (incl. cover) 18cm.

Reprinted from The Brighton Herald of 15 Jan. and 22 Jan. 1887. Presentation copy signed by C.D. Rickards, presumed author. Can. Arch.

1024 **Robertson**, F. Beverley
Railway monopoly: letters addressed to the 'Toronto Mail,' by F. Beverley Robertson, and the effects of monopoly, from the 'Manitoba Sun,' now republished by the Conservative anti-disallowance association. Winnipeg, Manitoba Sun, 1887. [10]p. 23cm. Tanghe

1025 **Robertson**, J[ohn] P[almerston]
A political manual of the Province of Manitoba and the North West Territories. Winnipeg, Printed by the Call Printing Co., 1887. 2p.l., [3]-209p. front., plates (part. col.) ports., fold. map, plan. 21cm. Shortt

1026 **Roman Catholic Church**. Prayers. Chipewyan
Prières, cantiques et catéchisme en langue montagnaise ou chipeweyan. Lac la Biche, 1887. 240p. 17 1/2cm. Not seen.

Text in syllabic characters. The printer was the Rev. E.J.B.M. Grouard. Newberry

1027 [**Sheldon**, John Prince]
From Britain to British Columbia; or, Canada as a domain for British farmers, sportsmen, and tourists. [London? 1887?] caption-title, 76p. illus., fold. map. 21 1/2cm. Yale

1028 **Smith**, Goldwin
An address to the electors of Lisgar, delivered at Selkirk, Aug. 18, 1887. Winnipeg, M'Intyre Bros. [1887] 20p. 18 1/2cm. Man. Leg.

1029 **Spragge**, [Ellen Elizabeth (Cameron)]
From Ontario to the Pacific by the C.P.R. [By] Mrs. Arthur Spragge. Toronto, C.B. Robinson, 1887. 2p.l., iv, [5]-186p. front. (fold. map) 14 1/2cm. Shortt

1030 **Taché**, Alexandre [Antonin]
Rapport de Monseigneur Alexandre Taché, vicaire des missions de S. Boniface. Au chapitre général des RR. Pères Oblats de Marie Immaculée, au mois d'avril 1887. [n.p., 1887] 44p. 22cm. Oblates Arch.

1031 **Thomas**, Thomas Henry
Excursion of members of the British Association from Montreal to the Rocky Mountains. Cardiff, 1887. ... Not seen. Can. Govt. Off.

1032 **Watkin**, Sir E[dward] W[illiam]
Canada and the States; recollections, 1851 to 1886. London, Ward, Lock & Co. [1887?] xvi, 524p., 1 l. front. (port.) fold. maps. 19 1/2cm.

Contains information on events relating to the surrender of the H.B.C.'s charter and the beginnings of the C.P.R. Shortt

1033 **Winnipeg**. Board of Trade
An open letter to the shareholders of the Canadian Pacific Railway Co., being an answer to the circular letter of Sir George Stephen, president of the company, addressed to the shareholders, on the subject of the disallowance, by the Dominion government, of railway charters granted by the Legislature of Manitoba. 1st October, 1887. Issued by authority of the Winnipeg Board of Trade and the Brandon Board of Trade. [Winnipeg? 1887] cover-title, 17p. 21cm. Shortt

1034 **Winnipeg**. Board of Trade
Plain facts regarding the disallowance of Manitoba railway charters ... Winnipeg, The Board, 1887. cover-title, 15p. 21cm. Shortt

1035 **Winnipeg**. Joint committee of City Council & Board of Trade
Winnipeg farmlands, cheap lands, good lands, best markets! Most money for produce! Least to pay for merchandise. Facts for intending settlers. A description of lands in the vicinity of Winnipeg. Winnipeg, The Commercial, 1887. cover-title, 8p. 19cm.

See also Entry 1083. Can. Arch.

1036 **Winnipeg and Hudson Bay Railway**
Winnipeg and Hudson Bay Railway. Consolidated act, guarantee act, general by-laws, 1887. [n.p., 1887] cover-title, 24p. 22cm. B.C. Arch.

1037 [**Anonymous**]
The Canadian Pacific Railway; its geographical and financial position. London, Bates, Hendy & Co., 1888. 38p. 21 1/2cm. Shortt

1038 Aukalög fyrir Gimlisveit. Winnipeg, Heimskringlu prentsmidja, 1888. 16p. Fiske

1039 **Bell**, Charles N[apier]
Henry's journal, covering adventures and experiences in the fur trade on Red River, 1799-1801 ... Winnipeg, Manitoba Free Press print, 1888. 9p. 22 1/2cm. (Hist. & Sc. Soc. of Man., no.31) Shortt

1040 **Bible**. New Testament. St. Matthew. Blackfoot
[First ten chapters of St. Matthew's Gospel. Printed by the Canadian Bible Society, n.d.] 48p. 16cm. Title-page in Blackfoot.

Translated by Rev. Harry W.G. Stocken. Failing vision forced him to discontinue the task. Shortt

1041 **Bryant**, W[ilbur] Franklin
Memorial of W.F. Bryant in the matter of Louis Riel. The Senate of the United States, in the matter of Louis Riel. Statement of case. [Washington, 1888] 3p. 23cm. (50th Cong., 2d sess. Misc. Doc., no.11) B.C. Arch.

1042 **Bryce**, George
Holiday rambles between Winnipeg and Victoria. Winnipeg, 1888. 87p. 21cm.

The Indians described are those on the reserves in the Qu'Appelle area. Shortt

1043 **Bryce**, George
Sketch of the life of John Tanner, a famous Manitoba scout. A border type ... Winnipeg, Manitoba Free Press print, 1888. cover-title, 4p. 22cm. (Hist. & Sc. Soc. of Man., no.30) Shortt

1044 **Canada**. Army. Fusiliers
The log, containing an account of the 7th Fusiliers' trip from London, Ont., to Clark's Crossing, N.W.T. Also, the official reports of the officers in charge of boats. London, Ont., Free Press Print. Co., 1888. 47p. 16 1/2cm.

Cover-title: The 7th Fusiliers' trip from London, Ontario, to Clark's Crossing, N.W.T. Includes songs of the regiment, text only. U. of T.

1044A **Canada**. Department of Agriculture
An official leaflet of information relating to the Dominion of Canada. [n.p.] 1888. folder. 16p. illus., map. folds to 15 x 9cm. Can. Arch. (ms.)

1045 [**Canadian Pacific Railway**]
Farming and ranching in the Canadian North-West. General account of Manitoba and the North-West Territories. Superior advantages for agricultural settlers. Unrivalled ranch districts. Free grants and cheap lands, and how to get them. Climate and health. How to go, and what to do at the start. Testimony of actual settlers. [Montreal, 1888] 56p. incl. illus., plates. fold. maps. 21cm. Shortt

1046 **Canadian Pacific Railway**
Free homes for all in Manitoba and the Canadian North-West along the line of the Canadian Pacific Railway. [London, Printed by R. Freeman, 1888?] cover-title, [1], 32p. illus. 21cm.

The same year the railway company also issued pamphlets of 16 pages with 'Manitoba and the Northwest' as a prominent phrase in the title, in the Norwegian, Swedish, and Roumanian languages. (In B.C. Arch.) L.C.

1047 **Canadian Pacific Railway**
Manitoba, the Canadian North-West; a record of the results of the harvest of 1887. [n.p.] 1888. cover-title, 59p. fold. maps, tables. 20cm. Glenbow

1048 **Canadian Pacific Railway**
What actual settlers say of the Canadian North-West as an agricultural country; practical information for intending settlers. [Montreal, 1888?] cover-title, 59p. 2 fold. maps. 20cm. Glenbow

1049 [**Carmichael**, James]
A holiday trip, Montreal to Victoria and return, via the Canadian Pacific Railway, midsummer, 1888. [Montreal? 1888?] cover-title, 32p. illus. 26 1/2cm.
'For private circulation.' Agric.

1050 **Christy**, [Robert] Miller
Sport in Manitoba. Liverpool, Turner and Dunnett, 1888. 23p. illus. 21cm. Reprinted with additions from Field, April 14, 1888. Man. Leg.

1051 **Church of England**. Diocese of Athabasca
Report of the Synod of the Diocese of Athabasca. Held July 6, 1888. Winnipeg, The Call Printing Co., 1888. 24p. 22cm.
The first report of the synod of this diocese to be published. C.M.S. - 41

1052 **Cotton**, L. de
A travers le Dominion et la Californie. Paris, Retaux-Bray, 1889 [1888] 206p. 24cm. Br. Mus.

1053 **Fitzgerald**, J.G., comp.
Alberta, Canada, the great ranching, agricultural and mineral country at the base of the Rocky Mountains. Millions of fertile acres awaiting settlement. Guide to settlers, January, 1888. Published by authority of the Minister of Agriculture of the Dominion of Canada. Ottawa, Citizen Printing and Publishing Co., 1888. cover-title, iv, 82p. fold. table. 21 1/2cm. Shortt

1054 **Great Britain**. Colonial Office
Crofter and cottar colonisation scheme. Memorandum of arrangements entered into with the Canadian government, the principal land companies, &c., for the purpose of starting a colonisation scheme for the crofters and cottars of the western Highlands and islands of Scotland; and relative correspondence. Presented to both Houses of Parliament by command of Her Majesty. London, Printed by Eyre and Spottiswoode, 1888. 10p. 33cm. ([Parliament. Papers by command] c-5403)
See also Entry 1578. U.B.C.

1055 [**Ham**, George Henry]
The new West. Extending from the Great Lakes across plain and mountain to the golden shores of the Pacific. Wealth and growth. Manufacturing and commercial interests. Historical, statistical, biographical. Winnipeg, Canadian Historical

Publishing Co., 1888. [viii], [9]-205p. front., ports., plates (part. fold.) fold. maps. 26 1/2cm.

A directory of places of business in the larger towns along the C.P.R. Shortt

1056 **Hesse-Wartegg**, Ernst von
Kanada und Neu-fundland. Freiburg, Herdersche, 1888. ix, 223p. front., illus., plates, fold. col. map. 24cm.

Pages 104-172 relate to the Prairie Provinces. Bavaria

1057 **Hulot**, Etienne, Baron
De l'Atlantique au Pacifique. A travers le Canada et le nord des Etats-Unis. Paris, 1888. 339p. Br. Mus.

1058 **Ingersoll**, Ernest
The climate of the Canadian West. [n.p., 1888?] 81-101p. 22cm. Reprinted from the Canadian Record of Science. Shortt

1059 **Ingersoll**, Ernest
An excursion to Alaska by the Canadian Pacific Railway. Montreal, 1888. ... illus., fold. map. Montreal Book Auction Cat. no.3, Feb., 1968. No.267

1060 **McDougall**, John, comp.
Cree hymn book, revised and corrected by Rev. John McDougall; also a number of additional translations of the same, and written in Cree syllabic or Cree character by the Rev. E.B. Glass. Toronto, Methodist Mission Rooms, 1888. 153p. 13 1/2cm.

Based on the Cree hymn book translated by Mrs. Hunter. B.C. Arch.

1061 **McDougall**, John
George Millward McDougall, the pioneer, patriot and missionary. With an introduction by Alexander Sutherland. Toronto, William Briggs, 1888. vii, [9]-242p. front. (port.) illus. 19cm.

A second edition was published in 1902. Shortt

1062 **McMicken**, Gilbert
The abortive Fenian raid on Manitoba. Account by one who knew its secret history. Winnipeg, Manitoba Free Press print, 1888. cover-title, 11p. 22cm. (Hist. & Sc. Soc. of Man., no.32) Shortt

1063 [**McPhillips**, Henry Thomas]
McPhillips' alphabetical and business directory of the District of Saskatchewan, N.W.T., together with brief historical sketches of Prince Albert, Battleford, and other settlements in the district. 1888. Qu'Appelle, N.W.T., Printed at The Progress Book and Job Office, 1888. 141 (i.e. 146p.) illus. (incl. ports.) 24 1/2cm. Paging includes advertising.

An invaluable source of information about the settlements in the Saskatchewan valley. Shortt

1064 McPhillips' illustrated Brandon city and country, 1888-89 [Directory]. Montreal, Desbarats [1888] 16p. illus., ports.

Pagination includes advertising. Canner – 474-855

1065 **Manitoba**. Department of Agriculture and Immigration
Facts about Manitoba issued by the Manitoba government. [n.p.] 1888. 31p. illus., fold. map. 22cm. Man. Leg.

1066 **Manitoba and North-Western Railway**
Illustrated guide book (with map) to the lands of the Manitoba & North-Western Railway. Compiled from government township reports, M. & N.W. Railway land examination reports, and corrected up to date by the farmers of the district. 2d ed. Winnipeg, The Call Printing Co., 1888. 96p. illus., plates, maps (1 fold.) diagrs. 24 1/2cm. L. of P.

1067 **Manitoba Central Railway Company**
Correspondence relating to the Manitoba Central Railway. [n.p., 1888] [21]p. 31cm. Tanghe

1068 **Murray**, W[illiam] H[enry] H[arrison]
Daylight land; the experiences, incidents, and adventures, humorous and otherwise, which befell Judge John Doe, tourist, of San Francisco; Mr. Cephas Pepperell, capitalist, of Boston; Colonel Goffe, the man from New Hampshire, and divers others, in their parlour-car excursion over prairie and mountain ... as recorded and set forth by W.H.H. Murray; illustrated ... under the supervision of J.B. Millet. Boston, Cupples and Hurd, 1888. 338p. incl. front., illus., plates. 23cm.

A humorous account bordering on the fictitious. Shortt

1069 **Newett**, W.H.
Farming in Canada, for young men without premiums. Giving cost & particulars for outfit, passage, land, etc. Manchester [England] Y.M.C.A., 1888. 15p. 12cm. Man. Arch.

1070 **Norman**, Henry
The prairies of Manitoba and who live on them; a sketch of the province, its people, agricultural capabilities and climate. [n.p., 1888] 13p. 13 x 17cm. Man. Leg.

1071 North-West brand book. Published under the authority of the Department of Agriculture, N.W.T. [Calgary, Herald Co., 1888-1904] 7v. illus. 15-18cm.

Title varies. 1st ed., 1888: Henderson's Northwest ranchers' directory and brand book. 2d ed. - 3rd ed., 1889-1894: Henderson's North West brand book.

Publisher varies. 1888-1896, Henderson's directory, Winnipeg; 1900-1904, Herald Co., Calgary.

See also Entry 1780. Glenbow

1072 **Palmer**, W.J., comp.
Dennis county, Manitoba, the finest wheat growing and stock raising county in the world. Reliable information concerning the lands in Dennis county ... Winnipeg, Manitoba Free Press [1888] cover-title, 36p. fold. map. 21 1/2cm. Pagination includes advertising. Man. Leg.

1073 **Petitot**, Emile [Fortuné Stanislas Joseph]
En route pour la mer glaciale. Paris, Letouzey [1888] [7], 394, [1]p. illus., port. 20cm.

Xerox copy. Glenbow

1074 **Pocock**, H[enry] R[oger] A[shwell]
Tales of western life; Lake Superior and the Canadian prairie. Ottawa, Printed by C.W. Mitchell, 1888. vii, 164p. illus. 21 1/2cm.

Fiction. B.C. Arch.

1075 **Roman Catholic Church**. Prayers. Beaver
Prières, catéchisme et cantiques dans la langue des Indiens castors. Lac la Biche, 1888. 120p. 14cm.

Translated by the Rev. (later Bishop) E.J.B.M. Grouard. Text in syllabic characters.
A new edition was printed at Hobbema, Alta., in 1926. (In Oblates Arch.)
Newberry. Oblates Arch.

1076 **Schultz**, John
Manitoba. Catalogue of lands for sale, at the office of John Schultz, 609 Main Street, Winnipeg, Manitoba. Issued for information of intending settlers and capitalists. 30 to 50 bushels of wheat per acre in 1887. Winnipeg, 1888. 14, [1]p. illus. Canner - 438-451

1077 **Taché**, [Alexandre Antonin]
Fenian raid. An open letter from Archbishop Taché to the Hon. Gilbert McMicken. [St. Boniface? 1888] 31p. 13cm. Man. Leg.

1078 **Taché**, [Alexandre Antonin]
Rapport ... à messieurs les directeurs de l'Oeuvre de la propagation de la Foi. Saint-Boniface, Imprimerie du Manitoba [1915] 50p. 21 1/2cm. (Soc. Hist. de St-Boniface, no.5, pt.2 [i.e. 1])

The report, made in 1888, surveys the activities of the Roman Catholic Church from the first establishment of the mission at Red River. Shortt

1079 **Tims**, John William, tr.
[Lord's Prayer, the Creed of the Church of England, the Ten Commandments, and prayers for morning and evening in Blackfoot. Blackfoot Reserve, Mission press, 1888?] 8p. Not seen. Heeney, p.74

1080 **Tyrrell**, J[oseph] B[urr]
A brief narrative of the journeys of David Thompson, in north-western America ... Toronto, Copp, Clark Co., Ltd., 1888. 28p. 21 1/2cm.

'Read before the Canadian Institute, March 3rd, 1888. Published in advance of the Proceedings by permission of the council.' Rutherford

1081 **Webster**, W.A.
A Canadian farmer's report. Minnesota and Dakota compared with Manitoba and the Canadian North-West. The facts as personally seen by a Canadian farmer. Ottawa, Printed by the Citizen Printing and Publishing Co., 1888. 16p. 21 1/2cm.

He travelled as far west as Regina. Man. Leg.

1082 **Winnipeg**. Grain and Produce Exchange
By-laws (adopted 26th October, 1888). Rules and regulations for the government of the call board (adopted 18th October, 1888). Rules relating to sales for future delivery (adopted 18th October, 1888). Terms of trade. Winnipeg, Manitoba Free Press, 1888. 24p. 22cm. Nat. Lib.

1083 **Winnipeg.** Joint committee of City Council & Board of Trade
Winnipeg, farm lands! cheap lands! good lands! best markets! facts for intending settlers; a description of lands in the vicinity of Winnipeg. Winnipeg, Robert D. Richardson, 1888. cover-title, 20p. fold. plan. 19cm.

Folding plan has printing on verso. Man. Leg.

1084 **Zero** [pseud.]
One mistake. A Manitoban reminiscence, by Zero. Montreal, Canada Bank Note Co., Ltd., 1888. 120p. 22cm.

The plot of this novel centres on a year's visit by two English girls to an emigrant brother. The heroine made the mistake of falling in love with one young man while engaged to another. U.B.C.

1085 [**Anonymous**]
Dairy farming, ranching and mining in Alberta and Assiniboia. [Winnipeg, 1889] 48p. illus., fold. map. 22cm. Man. Leg.

1086 **Bell,** Charles N[apier]
Continuation of Henry's journal, covering adventures and experiences in the fur trade on the Red River, 1799-1801. Winnipeg, Manitoba Free Press print, 1889. 7p., 15-21p. 21 1/2cm. (Hist. & Sc. Soc. of Man., no.35 & 37) Shortt

1087 [**Bompas,** William Carpenter]
Cree primer. London, Gilbert & Rivington [n.d.] 36p. 16cm. Not seen.

In Cree, except for the headings; includes lessons, prayers, catechism, and hymns. Newberry

1088 **Brandon.** Board of Trade
A handbook of the County of Brandon ... and the City of Brandon ... Brandon, The Sun, 1889. 46p. illus., map. 22cm. Not seen. Acadia

1089 **Bryce,** George
Original letters and other documents relating to the Selkirk Settlement ... by George Bryce and C.N. Bell. Winnipeg, Manitoba Free Press print, 1889. 10p. 22cm. (Hist. & Sc. Soc. of Man., no.33) Shortt

1090 **Canada.** Department of Indian Affairs
Description and plans of certain Indian reserves in the province of Manitoba and the North-West Territories, 1889. [Ottawa? 1889] 1p.l., 113p. fold. maps. 32cm. Nat. Lib.

1091 **Canada.** Privy Council. Committee on Indians
Certified copy of a report of a Committee of the Honourable the Privy Council, approved by His Excellency the Governor-General in Council, on the 17th May, 1889 ... [Ottawa, 1889] 113p. fold. maps. 32cm.

Contains the plans with description of reserves set aside for the Indians. Hudson's Bay House

1092 **Canadian Pacific Railway**
Every-day questions answered in regard to the Canadian West and its opportunities and rewards for farmers. Montreal, 1889. 16p. fold. map. 22cm. Rutherford

1092A **Canadian Pacific Railway**
Manitoba, la meilleur place du Manitoba pour des terres gratuites à present. Le district du Lac des Chenes ... [Winnipeg, 1889]. folder. [?] p. map on verso. 17cm.

Pages not numbered. Can. Arch. (ms.)

1093 **Canadian Pacific Railway**
The North-West farmer in the Canadian North-West, 1889 ... [Montreal, The Company, 1889] cover-title, 80p. illus., fold. maps. 21 1/2cm.

Appendix, p.57-80, contains testimonial letters. Man. Leg.

1094 **Canadian Pacific Railway**
Successful farming in Manitoba. 100 farmers testify. [Winnipeg, The Company, 1889?] 48p. fold. maps. 14 1/2 x 23cm.

Tabulation of questionnaires to farmers. A revised edition was published in 1891. Man. Leg.

1095 **Canadian Pacific Railway**
Tâydellisiâ tietoja Manitoban ja liansipohjais Kanadan maista ja muista seikoista. Siirtolaisille Kanadaan. Montreal, J. Lovell & Son, 1889. cover-title, 13p. maps. 15cm.

Includes letters from Finnish settlers north of Whitewood. B.C. Arch.

1096 [**Church**, Herbert E., & Richard Church]
Making a start in Canada; letters from two young emigrants; with an introduction by Alfred J. Church. London, Seeley, 1889. xx, 224p. 19cm.

The brothers spent a year on a farm in Ontario before settling near Calgary on Sheep Creek. Compare with Herbert E. Church's autobiography published in 1929. Shortt

1097 **Church of England.** Book of Common Prayer. Sioux
Hanhanna qais htayetu cekiyapi token ptecena eyapi kte cin, qa litany, qa nakun dawid tadowan kin etanhan, tonana kahnigapi, qa itancan htayetu wotapi tawa kin, token wicaqupi kin, qa omniciye kin en hoksiyopa baptisma wicaqupi kin, token eyapi kte hecetu. Printed for use at the Sioux mission, Manitoba, Canada, with the approval of the Lord Archbishop of Canterbury, and by direction of the Bishop of Rupert's Land. London, Society for Promoting Christian Knowledge, 1889. 215p. 16 1/2cm. Shortt

1098 **Church of England.** Manual of devotion. Blackfoot
A manual of religious instruction for the use of missionaries and teachers amongst the Blackfoot Indians. Part Second. Blackfoot Reserve, Printed at the Church Missionary Society's Mission Press, 1889. cover-title, [11] p. 18cm.

Roman type; text in Blackfoot, headings in English. C.M.S. - 41

1099 **Davin,** Nicholas Flood
Culture and practical power; an address delivered at the opening of Lansdowne College, Portage la Prairie, November 11, 1889. Regina, Leader Co., Ltd., 1889. 16p. 21 1/2cm. L.C.

1100 **Davin,** N[icholas] F[lood]
The demands of the North-West! A speech delivered in the House of Commons, Ottawa, on Wednesday, February 27th, 1889. Ottawa, A. Senecal, 1889. 27p. 20 1/2cm. Can. Arch.

1101 **Davin**, Nicholas Flood
Eos: an epic of the dawn, and other poems. Regina, Leader Co., Ltd., 1889. viii, [5]-141p. front. (port.) 18 1/2cm. Shortt

1102 **Donkin**, John G[eorge]
Trooper and redskin in the far North-West; recollections of life in the North-West Mounted Police, Canada, 1884-1888. London, S. Low, Marston, Searle, & Rivington, 1889. xi, 289p., 1 l. incl. front. (port.) fold. map. 19 1/2cm.

A satirical vein runs through his observations. Shortt

1103 **Dugas**, G[eorges]
Monseigneur Provencher et les missions de la Rivière Rouge. Montréal, C.O. Beauchemin & Fils, 1889. 331p. 18 1/2cm. Shortt

1104 **Ellis**, George E[dward]
The Hudson Bay Company. [with a critical essay on the sources of information and editorial note] (In Winsor, Justin, ed. Narrative and critical history of America. Boston and New York, 1884-89. 32cm. v.8 (1889) p.1-80. illus.)

1105 [**Goodridge**, Richard E.W., of Headingly]
The colonist at home again; or, Emigration not expatriation, by the author of and as a sequel to 'A year in Manitoba.' London, Wm. Dawson & Sons, 1889. 160p. 18cm.

The author devotes the first forty pages to bringing the reader up to date on family events since the publication of his 'A Year in Manitoba.' The remainder of the book describes a trip to Europe. Shortt

1106 **Grandin**, V[ital Justin]
Un suprême appel. L'évêque du Nord-Ouest supplie tous les amis de la justice au Canada de l'aider à protéger ses ouailles contre les tyrans d'Ottawa. [n.p., 1889?] caption-title, 4p. 26cm. St. Sulpice

1107 **Huleatt**, Hugh
British Columbia, Alaska, and the London artizan colony at Moosomin, Assiniboia. Seven letters. Chilworth & London, Printed by Unwin Bros., 1889. 40p. 13cm. Can. Arch.

1108 **Lake Manitoba Railway and Canal Company**
Development of the North-West. The Lake Manitoba Railway and Canal. With reports, plans, debates and memorials thereon ... Ottawa, 1889. cover-title, 18p. plan. 31cm. Not seen. Can. Arch.

1109 **Lewis**, C.T.
The world's return rebate marriage certificate; or, The want of the West. Qu'Appelle, Printed at the Progress office, 1889. 84p. fold. form. 15cm. At head of title: A revolution. On back cover: a poem 'Cain's Wife' by Sam T. Clover.

A scheme whereby any young man who left for the East in search of a wife received a rebate on his railway ticket if he returned successful. Can. Arch.

1110 **MacArthur**, Duncan
Manitoba; an address, delivered at the Nairn Literary Institute, 29th August, 1889. Nairn, Scotland, Printed at the Telegraph office [1889?] cover-title, 8p. 22 1/2cm. Shortt

1111 **McBean**, A.
A petition and prayer in behalf of the lower animals. Winnipeg, Buckle, Sons, & Co., 1889. ... Not seen. Lib. of Parl., 1889

1112 [**Machray**, Robert]
Some remarks on primary education, by the Bishop of Rupert's Land. December 1889. [n.p., 1889?] cover-title, 14p. 21 1/2cm. Man. Leg.

1113 **Maclean**, John
The Blackfoot sun-dance. Toronto, Copp, Clark Co., Ltd., 1889. cover-title, 7p. 22cm. Reprint from the Proceedings of the Canadian Institute, no.151, 1889. Shortt

1114 **Maclean**, John
The Indians, their manners and customs. Toronto, W. Briggs, 1889. x p., 1 l., [13]-351p. incl. front., illus., plates. 20cm.

A second edition was published in 1907. Shortt

1115 **McLeod**, Malcolm
Memorial to the government and people of Canada ... for indemnity for service in initiating the Canadian Pacific Railway, &c., &c. Ottawa, Printed by A.S. Woodburn, 1889. 24p. 21 1/2cm. Manuscript notes by author. Shortt

1116 **Manitoba**
Manitoba and its resources. Facts for the immigrant. Issued under the patronage of the Manitoba government, January 1st, 1889. Winnipeg, McIntyre Bros., 1889. cover-title, 32p. illus., fold. map. 22cm. St. Sulpice

1117 **Manitoba**
Pamphlet descriptive of Manitoba, showing her attractions for agriculturists, stock raisers, dairymen, and all who desire comfortable homes and prosperity. Issued by authority of the provincial government. [Winnipeg] 1889. 32p. front., illus., tables. 21cm. Not seen. N.S. Arch.

1118 **Manitoba and North-Western Railway**
Close to markets and schools, free homesteads near the present terminus of the M. & N-W. Ry. [Winnipeg, McIntyre Bros., 1889] cover-title, 8p. fold. map. 20 1/2cm.

A description of the Langenburg, Churchbridge, Bredenbury, Saltcoats, and Yorkton districts. Man. Leg.

1119 **Markham**, [Sir] A[lbert] H[astings]
Hudson's Bay and Strait. (In Royal Geog. Soc. Supplementary papers. London, 1889. 24 1/2cm. v.2, p.[615]-660) Shortt

1120 [**Morris**, W.J.]
The Winnipeg and North Pacific Railway. The great highway of the new North-West. The route and its advantages. The country and its resources. Toronto, Spectator Printing Co. [1889?] cover-title, 12p. fold. map., fold. diagr. 25cm.

Prospectus for a line to run from Winnipeg via Prince Albert and Lesser Slave Lake to Port Simpson on the Pacific. Shortt

1121 **Moose Jaw**. Board of Trade
The district of Moose Jaw. North West Territories: a field for emigration. Winnipeg, Call Printing Co., 1889. 24p. 23cm. Man. Leg.

1122 **Ottawa**. Citizens' Committee
Ceremony of unveiling a bronze statue erected on Major's Hill Park, Ottawa, to the memory of Ptes. Osgood and Rogers, of the Guards' Company of Sharp-shooters, who were killed in the North-West Rebellion of 1885. Ottawa, Printed by W.T. Mason, 1889. 38p. 15cm. Can. Arch.

1123 **Ouimet**, Adolphe
La vérité sur la question métisse au Nord-Ouest ... Biographie et récit de Gabriel Dumont sur les événements de 1885 par B.A.T. de Montigny ... Montréal, 1889. 400p. front., port. 23cm.

An English translation by G.F.G. Stanley of Gabriel Dumont's account was published in the C.H.R., v.30, no.3, Sept. 1949. Shortt

1123A **Quebec City**. Board of Trade
Landing of immigrants at Quebec. Copy of correspondence of the Quebec Board of Trade and other details relating to the superior advantages offered to immigrants for landing and transferring luggage to railway trains at Quebec bound for Manitoba and the great North Western Territories. Quebec, Printed by L.J. Demers & Frère, 1889. 14p. 22 1/2cm. Can. Arch. (ms.)

1124 **Regina**. Board of Trade
A few facts respecting the Regina district in the great grain growing and stock raising province of Assiniboia, North-West Territories, Canada. Regina, Printed by the Leader Co., Ltd., 1889. cover-title, 40p. fold. map. 22cm. U. of S.

1125 **Roman Catholic Church**. Saint-Boniface (Ecclesiastical Province) Council, 1st, 1889
Acta et decreta primi concilii provinciae Sancti Bonifacii. [S.L.] 1889. 2p.l., 102p. 21cm.

Texte français: p.[51]-102. St-Jean

1126 **Royal Canadian Mounted Police**
Drill regulations for the North-West Mounted Police. Regina, Barracks print, 1889. 1p.l., ii-v, 228p. 16cm. N.Y.

1127 **Saturday Budget, Quebec**
The Canadian Pacific Railway; an insight into its management and policy. Facts and figures. A series of letters as published in the Quebec (Dominion of Canada), 'Saturday Budget,' March, 1889. [Quebec, 1889] cover-title, 34p. 23cm.

A series of six letters, unsigned. Glenbow

1128 [**Taché**, Alexandre Antonin]
Separate schools. Part of the negotiations at Ottawa in 1870. [n.p., 1889] 12p. 21cm. In double column.

Letters on the subject to J. Taylor. Man. Leg.

1129 **Taché, Alexandre Antonin**
Two letters of Archbishop Taché on the school question. [St. Boniface?] 1889. 8, 9p. 24cm.

Contents: 1, Archbishop Taché thinks his ideas with regard to religious instruction in schools fully corroborated in England; 2, Separate schools; Archbishop Taché answers some statements against Catholic schools. Glenbow

1130 **Tims, J[ohn] W[illiam]**
Grammar and dictionary of the Blackfoot language in the Dominion of Canada. For the use of missionaries, school teachers and others. London, Society for Promoting Christian Knowledge [1889?] xii, 191p. fold. table. 18 1/2cm. L.C.

1131 **United States.** President. Benjamin Harrison, 1889-93
Message: a report on the case of Louis Riel, February 11, 1889. S. Doc. 1 of the special sess., 50th Cong., Cong. serial 2613. ... Not seen. Howard

1132 **Alberta Railway and Coal Company**
A stockman's paradise. Good markets and no taxes on stock. Choice ranch lands in blocks of 10,000 to 100,000 acres. [Buffalo, N.Y., Matthews-Northrup Co., 189–] cover-title, [40]p. illus., double map. 24cm.

A description of grazing lands along the Milk River Ridge. Rutherford

1133 **Allan Steamship Line**
Ffeithiau gwerth eu gwybod. Gwrandewch! Ewch i Canada. Teithiwch gyda'r Allan Line. Liverpool [189–?] cover-title, 11p. 18 1/2cm. Wales

1134 **Allan Steamship Line**
Llawlyfr yr ymfudwr: yn cynwys atebion i gwestiynau ar Manitoba a gogledd-orllewin Canada. 'y gwir, yr holl wir, a dim ond y gwir.' Carnarvon, Wales, Minerva Printing Works [189–] cover-title, 32p. illus. 21cm.

The pamphlet was written in part by William John Williams, a chartered accountant in Carnarvon, who was the local Allan Steamship Line representative. Wales

1135 **Allan Steamship Line**
Skyrslur um hagi Islendinga i Ameriku. (Manitoba og Nordvesturlandinu i Kanada) sumarid 1890. Reykjavik, Sigm. Gudmundsson, 1890. cover-title, 14, [2]p. 18cm. Denmark

1136 **[Anonymous]**
First reading book for schools and families ... Printed at Oonikup, by permission of Geo. Morrish, 1890. 28p. 22 1/2cm.

English and Cree in parallel columns.
Oonikup is Cree for The Pas. The printer was the Rev. Joseph Reader.
Pilling also lists the following in the Roman alphabet; 'First reading book.' [n.p., n.d.] 16p. Shortt

1137 **[Anonymous]**
Free homes. Lands waiting for the settler to go in and occupy them. Fertile homesteads free to all in the Canadian North-West. [Winnipeg, 189–] 48p. map. 24cm. Can. Arch.

1138 **Alexander**, George
The new Canada. Dublin, Daily Express, 1890. 33p. 17 1/2cm. (Daily Express extra, no.4)

Description limited to southern Alberta. Can. Arch.

1139 [**Alexander**, R.L.]
Alphabetical and business directory of the town and district of Moose Jaw in the North West Territories, with a brief historical sketch of the town and district. Moose Jaw, Printed at the Times Printing House, 1890. 45p. fold. plate, ports. 23cm. Sask. Arch.

1140 British settlers in Western Canada. [n.p., n.d.] iv, 57p. illus. 17cm. B.C. Arch.

1141 **Bible**. New Testament. St. Matthew. Blackfoot
The Gospel according to St. Matthew; translated into the language of the Blackfoot Indians, by the Rev. John Tims. London, British & Foreign Bible Society, 1890. 109p. 16 1/2cm. Not seen.

Printed in Roman type. Newberry

1141A **Bible**. New Testament. Galatians
Epistle to the Galatians in Cree syllabics. [Oonikup, 189_] Translated and printed by the Rev. Joseph Reader. See The Beaver, outfit 291, p.48.

1142 **Bible**. Selections. Blackfoot
Readings from the Holy Scriptures in the language of the Blackfoot Indians. Translated by the Rev. J.W. Tims. London, Society for Promoting Christian Knowledge, 1890. 47p. 18 1/2cm.

Consists of Genesis I-III and portions of the Four Gospels. L.C.

1143 **Blaikie**, William Garden
Summer suns in the far West; a holiday trip to the Pacific slope. London, Nelson, 1890. 3p.l., [9]-160p. front. 19cm. Agric.

1144 **Blake**, [Edward]
Mr. Blake to the Owen Sound Reform Association. North-West affairs. Maladministration and rebellion. Strange disappearance of 125,000 immigrants. [n.p., n.d.] caption-title, 22p. 23cm. Amtmann – 176-18

1145 **Blake**, Edward
Speech ... on the Bremner furs, Monday, May 12th, 1890. [Ottawa, 1890] caption-title, 8p. 23cm. (H. of C. Debates) Amtmann – 176-19

1146 **Blake**, Edward
Speech ... on the French language in the North-West, Friday, 14th February, 1890. [Ottawa, Queen's Printer, 1890] caption-title, 9p. 23cm. (H. of C. Debates) Amtmann – 176-21

1147 **Bodard**, A[uguste]
En route pour le Canada. Guide practique du colon et du voyageur. [s.l., 1890?] 36p.

'My first pamphlet in Fr. (50000 c.) was printed by the CPR and distributed by me in 1890.' Interior. Br. Mus.

1148 **Boissevain and Turtle Mountain.** [n.p., 189–] cover-title, [8]p. 18cm.

Largely a listing of farms by local real estate men. Man. Leg.

1149 **Boorne,** [W. Hanson], photographer
Souvenir album of Canadian scenery. From Winnipeg through the Rocky Mountains to the Pacific coast. Calgary, Boorne & May, c1890. [12]l. of plates. 13 x 19cm.

Cover has title: Glimpses of Canadian scenery. Glenbow

1150 **Boyle Brothers' Agency**
Manitoba and the North-West Territories. Messrs. Boyle Brothers' Agency ... London, Phipps & Connor [1890] cover-title, 20p. fold. col. map. 21cm.

The objectives of the agency were stated as:
1. Giving advice and assistance to intending emigrants. 2. Receiving students on a well appointed farm in the vicinity of Winnipeg. 3. Investing for capitalists either in city properties or farm lands. R.E.S.

1151 **Bryce,** George
First recorder of Rupert's Land; sketch of 'Judge Thom,' an early Red River celebrity. [Winnipeg, 1890] 5p. 21 1/2cm. (Hist. & Sc. Soc. of Man., no.40) Man. Leg.

1152 **Bryce,** George
Two provisional governments in Manitoba, containing an interesting discussion of the Riel Rebellion, with an appendix embodying the four Bills of Right verbatim. Winnipeg, Manitoba Free Press print, 1890. cover-title, 11p. 21 1/2cm. (Hist. & Sc. Soc. of Man., no.38) Shortt

1153 **Campbell,** James, and Son, pub.
Manitoba and the North-West. New York, Witteman Bros., 45 Murray St., sole agents for Louis Glaser's souvenir albums. Toronto, [n.d.] 16p. of illus. 13 x 8 1/2cm. Lavallee - 22-211

1154 **Canada.** Department of Agriculture
Manitoba och Nordvest-Territoriet (Nord-Amerika) En skildring af klimat, jordman, hostresultater och forvarfskallor for kapitalister, jordbrukare, handtverkare, vanliga arbetare, tjenstsokande, o.s.v., med speciel hansyn till Skandinaviske kolonister. London, McCorquodale & Co. Ltd., 1890. 47p. illus., fold. map. 21cm.

On cover: 200 millioner acres land for nybyggare i Manitoba.
A German edition with a similarly worded cover-title is in the Canadian Archives.
Sweden

1155 **Canada.** Department of Agriculture
Northern Alberta; its climate and resources. [Ottawa? 189–] cover-title, 7p. 21 1/2cm.

Dept. of the Interior correspondence suggests that the author was T.G. Pearce. Toronto

1156 **Canada.** Parliament. House of Commons. Select Committee on Charles Bremner's furs
Report ... Ottawa, Queen's Printer, 1890. 45p. 25cm. (In H. of C. Journals, 1890, appendix no.1)

The furs were confiscated during the Saskatchewan Rebellion, and distributed among high-ranking officers and government officials. The Can. Arch. has a 9-page printed petition from Bremner to the Governor-General in Council. U. of S.

1156A **Canadian Pacific Railway**
Canada, Manitoba, si nordvest. Consilu pentru ocea care vor sa se aseze acolo. [Liverpool, the Company, n.d.] 15p. illus. 18cm. B.C. Arch.

1157 **Canadian Pacific Railway**
Farming and ranching in Western Canada: Manitoba, Assiniboia, Alberta, Saskatchewan. [Montreal, 1890?] cover-title, 48p. illus., fold. map. 22cm.

Title on page [1]: Western Canada, including Manitoba, Assiniboia, Alberta and Saskatchewan. A pamphlet of 40 pages with the same title is in the British Museum Glenbow

1158 **Canadian Pacific Railway**
Harvest news, 1890; the Calgary district, Alberta. [Winnipeg, The Company, 1890] cover-title, 15p. illus. 16cm.

Testimonial letters from farmers. Man. Leg.

1159 **Canadian Pacific Railway**
La laiterie, la culture, l'élevage du bétail et les mines dans le grand ouest du Canada. [Montreal? 1890?] 1p.l., [3]-60p. illus., maps. 22cm. U. of A.

1160 **Canadian Pacific Railway**
Western Alberta. The sirloin of Canada. Rich in farming, grazing & coal lands ... [n.p., 1890?] folder. [14]p. 25cm. Map on verso. Shortt

1161 **Canadian Pacific Railway**
Wo sich der deutsche Ansiedler eine neue Heimat gründen und bald zu Wohlstand kommen kann. Was die Ansiedler selbst darüber sagen. [Winnipeg? 1890?] cover-title, 16p. illus. 15 x 22 1/2cm. Running title: Manitoba, Assiniboia, Saskatchewan, Alberta. Die grossen Prairieprovinzen des westlichen Canada. L.C.

1162 **Charlton,** John
Speech on the French language in the North-West, House of Commons ... 14th February, 1890. Ottawa, Queen's Printer, 1890. cover-title, 16p. U.C.

1163 **Church of England.** Hymns. Blackfoot
[Blackfoot hymn book in syllabics. Blackfoot Reserve, Mission Press, 189_] 37p. 20cm.

Text in syllabics; title only in English. Rupert's

1164 **Coutlee,** Louis William
A manual of the law of registration of titles to real estate in Manitoba and the North-West Territories. Toronto, Carswell & Co., 1890. xiii p., 1 l., 334p. 23cm. L.C.

1165 **Davin,** Nicholas Flood
For the Leader Company, Limited, *et al.* A speech ... delivered in the Supreme Court of the North-West Territories, His Honour Mr. Justice Richardson presiding, on the 7th July, 1890. Regina, Leader Co., 1890. 11p. 21cm.

Davin's defence in a libel suit filed by Atkinson, editor of the rival paper. Can. Arch.

1166 **Demanche,** Georges
... Au Canada et chez les peaux-rouges ... Paris, Hachette, 1890. 2p.l., 192p. plates, col. map. 25cm. Agric.

1167 [**Dugas,** Georges]
Établissement des Soeurs de Charité à la Rivière Rouge. [n.p., 189–] [3]-16p. 24cm. Shortt

1168 **Dugas,** G[eorges]
Légendes du Nord-Ouest. Montréal, C.O. Beauchemin & Fils [c1890] 3p.l., [7]-142, [1]p. front. 22 1/2cm.

A second series of stories, not another edition of the author's book with the same title published in 1883. Shortt

1169 **Dugas,** G[eorges]
Un voyageur des pays d'en haut. Montréal, C.O. Beauchemin [1890] 142p. front. 23cm.

The travels of Jean-Baptiste Charbonneau in the West, 1812-62.
Reprinted in 1904. Alta. Leg.

1170 **Edmonton.** Board of Trade
The Edmonton district of northern Alberta. Western territories of Canada. Edmonton, Printed at the Bulletin office, 1890. 24p. 15 1/2cm. Not seen. Can. Arch.

1171 **Fisher,** James
The school question in Manitoba. A letter ... to the electors of Russell. [n.p., 1890] 45p. 22cm. Can. Arch.

1172 [**Frank,** Mrs. M.J.]
The Brock family, by A.L.O.M. [pseud.] Toronto, William Briggs [1890] 263p.

A.L.O.M. is A Lady of Manitoba.
Semi-fictional account of early settlement in Manitoba. Nat. Lib.

1173 **Fulthorp,** G.E.
Catalogue of lands for sale, with Torrens titles and on easy terms ... Over 40,000 acres of farming lands. Also a number of market garden plots, and city building lots. Winnipeg, April 1st, 1890. [Winnipeg, McIntyre Bros., 1890] 24p. 22cm.

On cover: Manitoba, cheap homes on easy time and terms. Arkin

1174 **Garçon,** Augustin
Quatre hommes: Skobeleff–Brooke–Grant–Riel. Paris, Henri Charles-Lavauzelle, 1890. 75p. 22cm.

P.65-75 is an essay on Riel on whose behalf the author had petitioned Queen Victoria. St. Sulpice

1175 [**Gates,** Edward Wilson]
Off to Canada, by Septimus Scrivener [pseud.] Self-Help Emigration Society [1890?] 8p. Reprinted from the Christian World. Br. Mus.

1176 **Glass**, E[rvin] B[ird]
Primer and language lessons in English and Cree. Translated by Rev. John McDougall. Toronto, William Briggs, 1890. 109p. 19cm.

English and syllabic Cree on opposite pages. Edmonton

1177 Grande excursion de 'Exploration au Manitoba' cherches de tranquilité dans l'agriculture et l'indépendence. [n.p., 189-] ...

This pamphlet, addressed to French Canadians in New England, is mentioned in Norman Macdonald's 'Canada, immigration and colonization, 1841-1903.'

1178 **Grotty and Cross**
Manitoba lands for sale ... Winnipeg, McIntyre Bros. [189-?] cover-title, 24p. 22cm.

Pagination includes advertising. Arkin

1179 **Hart**, [Thomas]
... Mission work among the Indians of the North-West, a sermon ... Toronto, Presbyterian News Co., 1890. cover-title, 8p. 23cm.

'Sermon preached at the opening of the Synod of Manitoba, North-West Territories and British Columbia, May, 1890. Reprinted from the Presbyterian Review, July 24, 1890.' Man. Arch.

1180 **Hill**, Robert B.
Manitoba; history of its early settlement, development and resources. Toronto, William Briggs, 1890. 3p.l., [iii]-vii, [8]-764p. front., illus., plates, ports. 19cm.

The title is somewhat misleading as much of the history relates to Portage la Prairie. Shortt

1181 **Hurrell**, Charles T.
The statement of a permanently disabled North-West volunteer. [n.p., 1890?] 13, [1]p. 21 1/2cm. Not seen.

A member of the 90th Battalion, at Fish Creek he developed inflammatory rheumatism which hospitalized him until 7 Feb. 1886. His pension was slow in coming and was inadequate. A few references to the case are to be found in Hansard, 1890. Acadia

1182 **King**, John M[ark]
Manitoba college, three great preachers, Vinet, Liddon and Newman, being the opening lecture of the Theological Department, October 30th, 1890. Winnipeg, Manitoba Free Press print, 1890. 14p. 21cm. Can. Arch.

1183 **Lacombe**, A[lbert]
Un nouveau champ de colonisation, la vallée de la Saskatchewan, branche nord, districts d'Alberta et de Saskatchewan, Territoires de l'Ouest. [n.p., 1890?] 13p. illus., fold. map. 22cm. Rutherford

1184 **Lethbridge News**
Railway edition, September, 1890. Published on the occasion of the opening of the Great Falls and Canadian Railway. Lethbridge, 1890. cover-title, [16]p. illus. (incl. ports.) 23 x 31cm. Rutherford

1185 Letters from settlers in Canada. Containing useful information for intending settlers. 1888-90. London, McCorquodale & Co. [1890] 8p. Not seen. Br. Mus.

1186 **Lorne Agricultural Society**
Prince Albert and the North Saskatchewan; a guide to the fertile belt now being opened up by railway from Regina to Prince Albert, the central city and capital of Saskatchewan. [Prince Albert, 1890] 75p. map. Not seen.
Prince Albert Times, Aug. 1, 1890

1187 **McCarthy**, D'Alton
Speech of ... on the French language in the North-West, Tuesday, 18th February, 1890. [Ottawa, Queen's Printer, 1890] 15p. 23cm. (H. of C. Debates)
Amtmann - 176-187

1188 **Maclean**, John
James Evans, inventor of the syllabic system of the Cree language. Toronto, William Briggs [1890] xii, [13]-208p. front., illus. (incl. ports.) 19cm.
Shortt

1189 **McLeod**, Pierre
Mémoire à Son Excellence Mgr Merry del Val, délégué apostolique au Canada. [n.p., 189-?] caption-title, 16p.

Re: Manitoba School Question. U. of A. (Calgary)

1190 **M'Queen**, James
Notes on a trip to America. Castle-Douglas, J.H. Maxwell, Advertiser office [1890?] 72p. 19cm. Queen's

1191 **Manitoba**. Department of Agriculture and Immigration
Manitoba, the prairie province. The finest agricultural country in the world ... Winnipeg, 1890. 40p. illus. 20cm. Illustrated covers. Shortt

1192 **Manitoba and North-Western Railway**
How to start a prairie farm in the Canadian North-West under the 'commercial' colonization system of the Manitoba and North Western Railway Co. of Canada. [Glasgow, 189-] cover-title, 32p. plates, fold. map. 18cm.

'Enlarged edition.' Ayer

1193 Manitoba, the best country in the world for immigrants. The County of Russell and Lake Dauphin district are among the best in Manitoba. Homesteads, timber, grazing lands, wheat lands, forests of timber and rivers of water. Room for all! Come and see for yourselves. [Winnipeg, 1890] 14, [2]p. Ehrlich - 37-20

1194 **Messiter**, Charles Alston
Sport and adventure among the North American Indians. London, 1890. xvi, 368p. incl. plates. front. 21 1/2cm.

The author spent the winter of 1862-63 northwest of Ft. Carlton. Shortt

1195 **Middleton**, Sir Fred[erick Dobson]
Parting address to the people of Canada. Toronto, Printed for the author by Hunter, Rose & Co., 1890. cover-title, 13p. 22cm.

A reply to his accusers re leadership of the Canadian militia during the campaign against Riel.

Amtmann - 168-1616 lists a similar pamphlet under the title General Middleton's Defense. (From the Evening Telegram, Toronto, 21 August 1890.) Toronto

1196 **North Western Coal and Navigation Company, Limited**
Canadian North-West Territories. District of Alberta. [London, Printed by McCorquodale & Co. [189–] folder. 15p. illus. (incl. map) 14 1/2cm. Rutherford

1197 **Oakes**, Christopher
The Canadian senator; or, A romance of love and politics. Toronto, National Book Pub. Co. [1890] 179p.

Novel partly set in Manitoba during the Winnipeg land boom 1880-82.
The author's name may be a pen name. Nat. Lib.

1198 **Oxley**, James Macdonald
[Ti-ti-pu, a boy of Red River. Toronto, Musson, n.d.] 126p. 19cm.

Library copy lacks title-page. Title and imprint supplied from cover. Glenbow

1199 **Ross**, D.A., & Co. (Ross, Macfarlane and Brewer)
Manitoba lands for sale, by D.A. Ross & Co., real estate agents, valuators, etc. Winnipeg, McIntyre Bros. [1890] 39p. 21cm. Man. Arch.

1200 [**Sandison**, J.W.]
A Scotch farmer's success in the Canadian North-West told by himself. With illustrations made from photographs taken on his farm. [Winnipeg, Canadian Pacific Railway] 1890. 12p. illus., fold. map. 14 1/2 x 21 1/2cm. Shortt

1201 **Saxby**, Jessie M[argaret (Edmonston)]
West-Nor'-West. London, James Nisbet & Co., 1890. 4p.l., 154p. front. 19cm.

Describes a visit to the West in 1888.
'A pleasantly and thoughtfully written volume, describing the physical aspects and social conditions of, and the outlook for, settlers in the great North-West.' Morgan, 1898.
B.C. Arch.

1202 Separate schools. Part of the negotiations at Ottawa in 1870. That Bill of Rights. Archbishop Taché's answer to Mr. Fay. 1890. Monseigneur Taché. Rapport les incidents qui ont déterminé l'insertion de la clause des écoles séparées dans l'acte de Manitoba. Refutation des objections de M. James Taylor et autres. [n.p., 1890] 12, 8, 17p. Can. Arch.

1203 **Sutherland**, Hugh McKay
The Hudson Bay Railway; an open letter from the president of the Hudson Bay Railway to the members of the Parliament of Canada. Ottawa, May, 1890. cover-title, 11, [1]p. 23cm. Glenbow

1204 **Taché**, Alexandre Antonin
Pastoral letter of His Grace the Archbishop of St. Boniface, on the new school laws of Manitoba ... [St. Boniface, 1890] caption-title, 14p. Amtmann – 239-553

1205 **Webster**, Geo[rge] H[erbert]
The inland waterways of North-Western Canada. [n.p., 189–] 37p. fold. maps, fold. plans. 22cm. Shortt

1206 **Western Canada Immigration Association**
[Manitoba homesteads. An album containing photographs of homes in Manitoba, together with statements from owners already settled in Canada, as to conditions there] Winnipeg [189–] 18 l. incl. maps, plates. 25cm.

Binder's title: A few Manitoba homes. N.Y.

1207 **Young,** Egerton Ryerson
By canoe and dog-train among the Cree and Saulteaux Indians. With an introduction by Mark Guy Pearse. Toronto, William Briggs [1890] 2p.l., 267p. front, illus., port. 20 1/2cm.

A New York edition by Hunt & Eaton appeared in 1891. Shortt

1208 The advantages of the Prince Albert district, Saskatchewan, are unsurpassed for rich lands. Opinions of disinterested parties on this splendid district. [n.p., 1891] cover-title, 27, [1]p. map, plan. 22cm.

The building of the railway the previous year had raised hopes that large-scale settlement would follow.

A new edition of 24p. published in 1892 is in the Lib. of Parl. Man. Leg.

1209 **Bryce,** George
Older geology of the Red River and Assiniboine valleys. Winnipeg, Manitoba Free Press print, 1891. cover-title, 7, [1]p. diagrs. 22 1/2cm. (Hist. & Sc. Soc. of Man., no.42) Shortt

1210 **Burall,** W.F.
A trip to the far west of British Columbia; a 13,000 mile tour. Wisbech [Eng.] Earl [1891] 26p. illus. 21cm. U.B.C.

1211 **Burman,** W[illiam] A[lfred]
Rupert's Land Indian Industrial School, Middle Church, Man. [Middle Church, Man., Rupert's Land Indian School Press, 1891] cover-title, [4]p. illus. on cover. 18cm.

Imprint from colophon. 'Printed at the school.'

An appeal on behalf of the school. C.M.S. – 43

1211A **Canada.** Department of Agriculture
Adroiddiod [immigration pamphlet in Welsh. Liverpool, Turner & Dunnett, 1891] 32p.

Pamphlet mentioned in a list prepared by the Department. Full title not given.

1212 **Canada.** Department of Agriculture
The visit of the tenant-farmer delegates to Canada in 1890. The reports of Mr. Arthur Daniel, Colonel Francis Fane, Mr. Robert Pitt, and Mr. Henry Simmons on the agricultural resources of Canada ... [Ottawa] 1891. 104p. illus., fold. map. 21cm. Acadia

1213 **Canada.** Department of the Secretary of State
Copies of all correspondence, petitions, memorials, and any other documents submitted to the Privy Council, in connection with the abolition of the official use of the French language in the Province of Manitoba by the Legislature of that province; also copies of reports to or orders in council thereon; also copies of the act or acts relative thereto. Ottawa, 1891. 2p.l., 29p. 25cm. (Canada. Sess. papers, 1891, no.51) Shortt

1214 **Canada.** Department of the Secretary of State
Copies of all correspondence, petitions, memorials, briefs and factums, and of any other documents submitted to the Privy Council in connection with the abolition of separate schools in the Province of Manitoba by the Legislature of that province; also copies of reports to and orders in council thereon; also copies of an act or acts of said Legislature abolishing said separate schools or modifying in any way the system prior to 1890. [Ottawa, 1891] 76p. 25cm. (Canada. Sess. papers, 1891, no.63) 'Return to an address of the House of Commons, dated the 5th May, 1891.'
——Supplementary return. 55p. 25cm. (Canada. Sess. papers, 1891, no.63) Also printed as a separate. Contained the 'factum of case, Barrett vs. city of Winnipeg in connection with the abolition of separate schools.' Shortt

1215 **Canadian Pacific Railway**
The Canadian North-West Territories; dairy farming, ranching, mining. Rev. ed., 1891. [Montreal? The Company, 1891] cover-title, 64p. illus., fold. map. 21cm. Man. Leg.

1216 **Canadian Pacific Railway**
The North West farmer in Manitoba, Assiniboia, Alberta, 1891. Rev. ed. [Montreal? The Company, 1891] 55p. illus., fold. map. 21cm. Man. Leg.

1217 **Canadian Pacific Railway**
The Saskatchewan; northern Alberta. Districts of Edmonton and Battleford reached by the Canadian Pacific R'y. [n.p., 1891?] cover-title, 16p. illus., fold. map. 20 1/2cm. Man. Leg.

1218 **Church of England.** Diocese of Athabasca
Journal of proceedings of the second meeting of the Synod of the Diocese of Athabasca held at Lesser Slave Lake, Athabasca, North West Territories, Canada. September 29, 1891. Including the Bishop's address. Middle Church, Man., Rupert's Land Indian Industrial School Press, 1891. 20p. 18cm. C.M.S. - 43

1219 **[Darnault, J.]**
Excursion de membres du Club Alpin Français au Canada. Paris, Georges Chamerot, 1891. 72p. 23cm.

Seventeen French Alpinists toured Canada in August-September, 1890. A highlight was official entertainment at Saint Boniface. The tour was arranged by Georges Demanche. France

1220 **Davin,** Nicholas Flood
A speech delivered ... in the Regina town hall, Saturday, December 5, 1891. Regina, The Leader Co. Ltd., 1891. 14p. 21cm. Can. Arch.

1221 **Ekru,** Einni
Hveiti-land heimsins hid mesta er Manitoba. Hveiti-uppskeran mest ad vöxtum mest ad gaedum. Manitoba. Frjofsamasta fylkid i hina frjofsama belti Vestur-Canada. [Winnipeg, 1891] 16p. 8 x 22cm.

On the back cover of this Icelandic pamphlet is a coloured map of Manitoba showing the location of Icelandic settlements. Uppsala

1222 An Englishman who has lived twelve years in the country. Canada as a field for emigration. Coventry, Curtis & Beamish, 1891. 40p. Br. Mus.

1223 **Foursin**, Pierre
La colonisation française au Canada; Manitoba – Territoires du Nord-Ouest – Colombie Anglaise. Ottawa, Imprimé par Brown Chamberlin, 1891. 45p. illus. 27cm.

The writer came from France, a member of a delegation of farmers, mostly from the British Isles, which toured Canada in 1890. Shortt

1224 **Globensky**, Emile Auguste [Maximilien]
Le mixed-farming au Manitoba. Une ferme suivant l'expérience du pays. Thèse ... Beauvais, Père, 1891. 160p. map. Tanghe

1224A **Hickman**, Herbert
A two months' tour across Canada. Being a short account of a trip from Liverpool to British Columbia. With notes on the magnificent resources and chances for emigrants in Manitoba and the great North-West. Bridgwater [England, 1891] 23p. 21cm. Can. Arch. (ms.)

1225 **Kenyon**, Charles Richard
Young ranchmen; or, Perils of pioneering in the wild West. London? 1891. 282p. illus. Not seen.

Juvenile fiction. R.E.S.

1226 **McGusty**, H.A.
Two years in Manitoba and the North-West Territory. Frome, Harvey & Woodland [1891] 1 l., 34p. 18cm. Glenbow

1227 **Mackay**, J[ohn] A[lexander] comp. & tr.
Psalms and hymns in the language of the Cree Indians of the Diocese of Saskatchewan, north-west America. London, Printed for the Society for Promoting Christian Knowledge, 1891. 2p.l., 111, [1]p. 19cm. Not seen.

Text in syllabic and Roman characters.
A new edition of 159p. was published in 1927. L.C.

1228 **Maclean**, John
The hero of the Saskatchewan. Life among the Ojibway and Cree Indians in Canada. Barrie, Barrie Examiner Printing and Publishing House, 1891. 4p.l., 49p. front. (port.) 21cm.

On t.-p.: Reprinted from the Barrie Examiner.
Text in double column.
A biography of the Rev. George McDougall. Edmonton

1229 **Manitoba**. Department of Agriculture and Immigration
Map of Manitoba, and a few facts concerning the prairie province. [Winnipeg, 1891] folder. (22p.) in cover. illus. 42 x 67cm. fold. to 14 x 8cm.

Map on one side, text on other. Glenbow

1230 **Morin**, Jean Baptiste
Renseignements sur le Nord-Ouest. [n.p., 1891] ... Not seen. Morice

1231 Nikumoowina. [Oonikup, The Pas, Cumberland, North West Territories, 1891] caption-title, 22p. 15cm.

Imprint from colophon. Hymns in Cree syllabic characters.

Another edition, published the same year, but with a pagination of 10p., is listed in the Yale catalogue.

At least two other publications (See Entries 1136 and 1479) have the Oonikup imprint. The Rev. Joseph Reader, originally with the Church Missionary Society, operated a press near The Pas for a number of years after he joined the Plymouth Brethren. The press was manufactured by Josiah Wade, Halifax, England. Later it was moved to the mission at Onion Lake, Alta. Rupert's

1232 **Osler**, Hammond & Nanton
The Qu'Appelle, Long Lake and Saskatchewan Railroad and Steamboat Co. has 1,000,000 acres of odd numbered sections in the old settled districts between Regina, the capital city of the Canadian Northwest and Prince Albert ... Winnipeg, Commercial print [1891?] folder. (16p.) map. 25 1/2cm. Shortt

1233 **Prince Albert**. Board of Trade
Are you looking for a home? A place to settle?, for yourself, for your sons, your family, your daughters. The advantages of the Prince Albert district of Saskatchewan are unsurpassed for rich lands! Opinions of disinterested parties on this splendid district. Farming, grazing, timber, hay. Read the story of the Saskatchewan. [Winnipeg, 1891] 28p. 2 fold. maps. Ehrlich - 37-18

1234 **Regina**. Board of Trade
An unvarnished tale of Regina and its agricultural and ranching district, in the great Province of Assiniboia, N.W.T., Canada. Regina, Printed by the Leader Co., 1891. 39p. illus., fold. map. L. of P.

1235 **Roper**, Edward
By track and trail; a journey through Canada. With numerous original sketches by the author. London, W.H. Allen & Co., 1891. xii, [2], 455, [1]p. front., illus., plates, fold. map. 23cm.

Chapters 3-8, 25-27 describe the author's experiences on the prairie. Shortt

1236 **Seton**, Ernest Thompson
The birds of Manitoba. Washington, Government Printing Office, 1891. p. 457-643. illus. (music) fold. map. 25cm. (Smithsonian Institute. Proceedings. v.13) U. of A.

1237 Seven Oaks: an account of the affair of Seven Oaks; the circumstances which led up to it; a description of the contestants; the events of the conflict, including the death of Gov. Semple & his followers. Winnipeg, Manitoba Free Press [1891?] cover-title, 38p. illus., map. 22cm. (Hist. & Sc. Soc. of Man., no.43) Shortt

1238 **Tims**, J[ohn] W[illiam]
The Indian missions. Returns to show the state of Indian missions in the Diocese, 1891. Compiled at the request of the Synod by Rev. J.W. Tims. [n.p., n.d.] caption-title, vi p. 18cm. C.M.S. - 43

1239 **Wagstaff,** J.
English lands & English homes in the far West; being the story of a holiday tour in Canada. With an introduction by Joseph Wright. Macclesfield, Claye, Brown, and Claye, Courier Office, 1891. 4p.l., [5]-76p. 20 1/2cm.

An earlier edition was published in Canada. U. of A.

1240 **Winch,** John
A few arguments in favor of adult baptism and close communion as held by the Baptists of Canada. Brandon, Brandon Times Printing and Publishing Co. [1891] 136p. port. 19cm.

Ms. note on end-papers: First book published in Brandon. Arkin

1241 Winnipeg, Manitoba. The prairie city ... Winnipeg, Daily Tribune, 1891. 26p. plates, ports., map. 28cm. Not seen. Acadia

1242 **Baldwinson,** Baldwin Lárus
Hagskyrslur frá Islendingabyggdum i Canada árin 1891-1892. Reykjavik, 1892. 42p. 25cm. U. of M.

1243 **Bjarnason,** Jóhann Magnús
Sogur og kvaedi. Winnipeg, Lögberg Press, 1892. 64p. Not seen. Kirkconnell

1244 [**Bodard,** Auguste]
Emigration en Canada. Description du pays. Ses avantages. La terre promise du cultivateur. Les colonies françaises, belges et suisses. Témoignages et lettres des colons. [n.p., 1892] cover-title, 32p. 23cm.

Map showing C.P.R. railway on back cover.
Inserts: 'Canada informations générales' 4p. signed A. Bodard; 'Voyages maritimes économiques au Canada' 4p. signed L. Desbois. Both printed by Perriaux of Paris. France

1244A **The Bulletin,** Edmonton
The great Saskatchewan valley. Strathcona, the railway town and milling center. Edmonton, Bulletin Co. Ltd., 1892. cover-title, 48p. 27cm.

This pamphlet was printed as a by-product of another of several more pages which had the name of the rival town across the river, Edmonton, in the sub-title. The texts as far as page 48 were identical. Can. Arch. (ms.)

1245 **Calgary.** Board of Trade
The advantages of Alberta. Calgary, 1892. 4p. 20 1/2cm. Not seen. Br. Mus.

1246 **Calgary Tribune**
Irrigation in the Territories. Extracts from the Calgary Tribune. [n.p., 1892?] caption-title, [20]p. 21cm. L. of P.

1247 **Canada.** Department of the Interior
Fiosrachadh 'o'n luchd-riaghlaidh mo Dheighinn Chanada. Inverness, Scotland, The Highland News, 1892. 18p. illus. 21 1/2cm.

Gaelic immigration pamphlet. Can. Arch.

1248 **Canada.** Department of the Secretary of State
Copy of the judgment of the Supreme Court in the appeal case of Barrett vs. the City of Winnipeg, commonly known as the 'Manitoba School Case.' [Ottawa, 1892] 24p. 24cm. (Canada. Sess. papers, 1892, no.46) U. of S.

1248B **Canadian Pacific Railway**
The Edmonton district, northern Alberta. The Canadian Pacific Railway Company has a large area of choice lands in the Edmonton district now open for selection. [Winnipeg, 1892]. folder. 23p. illus. 23cm. Can. Arch. (ms.)

1249 **Canadian Pacific Railway**
Free farms, Manitoba, Assiniboia, Alberta, Saskatchewan, the four great fertile provinces of Western Canada described and illustrated. [n.p.] 1892. folder. (23p.) illus., maps. 23cm. Can. Arch.

1250 **Canadian Pacific Railway**
Free homes in Manitoba. London [1892] 32p. Br. Mus., Supp.

1251 **Canadian Pacific Railway**
The great Canadian North-West. Finest farming lands in the world ... What delegates from various states have to say about it ... [n.p., 1892] 17p. 22 1/2cm.
Descriptions by delegates from Vermont, Maine, and Nebraska, etc. Glenbow

1252 **Canadian Pacific Railway**
Manitoba, Assiniboia, Alberta, Saskatchewan & Athabasca I det store Nordvestlige Amerika 10 til 14 dages reise fra Norge. Gives et frit hjemsted paa 160 acres. Liverpool, Turner & Dunnett, 1892. cover-title, 47p. front. (fold. map) illus. 21cm.
Norwegian immigration pamphlet. Can. Arch.

1253 **Canadian Pacific Railway**
Manitoba och Nordvest-Territoriet (Nord-Amerika) [Liverpool, Turner & Dunnett, 1892] 47p. front. (fold. map) illus. 21cm. Yale

1254 **Canadian Pacific Railway**
Delegates report, being an account of the proceedings of a delegation sent from the Maritime Provinces to examine & report upon Manitoba, Assiniboia, Saskatchewan and Alberta. [London?] 1892. cover-title, 24p. illus., 2 fold. maps. 22 1/2cm. Can. Arch. (ms.)

1255 **Canadian Pacific Railway**
Western Canada. Free homes for all in the great provinces of Manitoba, Assiniboia, Saskatchewan and Alberta. [n.p., 1892?] 64p. illus. 21cm. B.C. Arch.

1256 **Canadian Pacific Railway**
Westliches Canada! Manitoba, Assiniboia, Alberta und Saskatchewan. Wie man dahin kommt. Wie man Land answählt. Wie man anfängt. Wie man Geld verdient. [n.p., 1892?] 24p. illus., fold. map. 20cm.
On cover: Landbau und Viezucht im Westlichen Canada. Map (in English) dated 1890. Includes experiences of German settlers. Glenbow

1257 **Canadian Pacific Railway**
What farmers say. The experience of farmers cultivating the lands of Manitoba, Assiniboia, Alberta, and the Saskatchewan. Letters and reports from farmers who have settled in the provinces of Western Canada, 1892. [London] 1892. 16p. illus. 22cm.

On cover: Canadian North West; what farmers say about Manitoba [etc.] Arkin

1258 **Christy**, Robert Miller
Why are the prairies treeless? London, 1892. 22p. 24cm. Reprinted from Royal Geog. Soc., Proceedings. Not seen. Br. Mus.

1258A **Codd**, J.A.
Great North-West Central Railway Company. Memorandum. Ottawa, James Hope & Co. [1892] cover-title, 8p. 21cm. Can. Arch. (ms.)

1259 **Crissey**, Forrest
Rodney Merton, the young newspaper scout. A story of the Riel Rebellion. Chicago, Mid-continent Publishing Co. [c1892] 194p. front., plates.

Juvenile fiction. U.B.C.

1260 **Davin**, Nicholas Flood, ed.
Homes for millions. The resources of the great Canadian North-West. The reason why agriculture is profitable there and why farmers are prosperous and independent. Ottawa, Government Printing Bureau, 1892. 2p.l., iv, [7]-108p. illus., fold. plate. 24 1/2cm.

The publication of this immigration pamphlet caused a great furore in official circles. An 'inchoate mass' of material was collected by members of the N.W.T. Council, and published by the Dept. of Agriculture in Ottawa. The department had Davin edit it. After it had been printed, Lieut.-Gov. Royal of the N.W.T. objected vehemently to Davin's association with the enterprise.

For the story of the publishing of this pamphlet see Koester, C.B. 'Mr. Davin's pamphlet on the North West; a bureaucratic comedy of errors.' Saskatchewan history, v.16, no.1, winter 1963, p.27-32. Shortt

1261 **Dennis**, J[ohn] S[toughton]
A short history of the surveys performed under the Dominion lands system, 1869 to 1889. (In Canada. Sess. papers, 1892, no.13, pt.vi, p.1-98) U. of S.

1262 **Dwight**, Charles P[rentice]
Life in the North-West Mounted Police and other sketches. Toronto, National Publishing Co., 1892. 139p. 18cm.

Author spent six months in the force as an orderly clerk, stationed at Regina and Maple Creek. Can. Arch.

1263 **Gaetz**, Leo[nard]
Report of six years' experience of a farmer in the Red Deer district. Published by the Department of Agriculture of the Government of Canada. Ottawa, Printed by S.E. Dawson, 1892. 31p. fold. map. 20 1/2cm. At head of title: Alberta, N.W.T.

First printed in 1890. Consists of information furnished by Rev. Leo. Gaetz to a H. of C. committee on agriculture and colonization. Shortt

1264 **Grant**, Alexander
The state; religion; and schools. A lecture delivered in Winnipeg on February 16th, 1892. Published by the Ladies Aid. Winnipeg, Stovel Co., 1892. 1p.l., 20p. 21 1/2cm. Man. Leg.

1265 **The Brandon Times**
Christmas, 1892. [Special issue] no.1. Brandon, 1892. cover-title, 18p. illus., ports. 30cm.

Illustrations on 12 numbered pages.
On Brandon and vicinity. Glenbow

1266 **Hacault**, L[ouis]
Les colonies belges et françaises du Manitoba. Notes de voyage au Canada en 1890. Avec des extraits des rapports des fermiers délégués de Grande Bretagne, chargés de faire en 1890, un enquête sur les ressources agricoles du Canada. Bruxelles, Alfred Vromant, 1892. cover-title, 80p. illus., fold. map. 21cm.

Published in Flemish with title: De Belgische en Fransche colonien van Manitoba (copy in Berkeley Library) Can. Arch.

1267 **Hudson's Bay Company**
Supplemental charter. Special report of the Governor and Committee of the Hudson's Bay Company, to be laid before the shareholders on Wednesday, March 9th, 1892. London, Darling & Sons Ltd., 1892. 22p. 21cm.

This pamphlet was reprinted in 1899 by Causton and Sons. H.B.C.

1268 **Jerome**, Martin
Coup d'oeil rétrospectif sur ce qu'a été la nation métisse dans les affaires politiques lors de l'entrée de la province dans la confédération et ce qu'elle est de nos jours. Winnipeg, Imprimerie du Manitoba Free Press, 1892. cover-title, 12p. 16cm.

A letter to the métis on politics. Man. Leg.

1269 Letters from settlers in Canada, 1891-92. Containing useful information for intending settlers. [London, 1892] 16p. Not seen. Br. Mus.

1270 **Manitoba**
Manitoba. Handbog over provinsen Manitoba, dets klima, jordbrug, regjering, skoler m.m. for kapitalister, jordbrugere, handlende, handvaerkere, arbejdere o.s.v. med saerskildt hensyn til skandinaviske nybygere og udvandrere, udarbejdet af Manitobas regering, 1892. [n.p., 1892] cover-title, 24p. illus. 21cm.

Also issued in Swedish. Man. Leg.

1271 **Manitoba**
Manitoba official hand-book. Issued by authority of the Government of Manitoba. [Liverpool] 1892. 64p. illus. 21 1/2cm. Man. Leg.

1272 **Manitoba**. Department of Agriculture
Homes in Manitoba. [n.p., 1892] cover-title, 36p. plates. 22cm. Arkin

1273 **Manitoba**. Department of Agriculture
Manitoba. Opinions of eminent men and extracts from reports of farmers' delegates. Liverpool, 1892. 15p. Br. Mus., Supp.

1274 Manitoba und die Nordwest-Territorien ... [Winnipeg, Nordwesten] 1892. 51p. illus. 22 1/2cm.

German immigration pamphlet. Can. Arch.

1274A **Ogilvie**, W[illia]m.
Report on the Peace River and tributaries in 1891. Ottawa, Queen's Printer, 1892. 44p. 24 1/2cm. Can. Arch. (ms.)

1275 **Oxley**, J[ames] Macdonald
Fergus McTavish; or, Portage and prairie. A story of the Hudson's Bay Company. Philadelphia, American Baptist Publication Society [c1892] 2p.l., 3-344p. front., plates, map. 18 1/2cm.

Juvenile fiction. An edition with a different sub-title was published in London in 1893. L.C.

1276 **Pennefather**, John P[yne]
Thirteen years on the prairies; from Winnipeg to Cold Lake, fifteen hundred miles. London, Kegan Paul, Trench, Trübner, & Co., Ltd., 1892. viii, 127p. plates, port. 19cm.

Describes his immigration to Manitoba with his sons, and his experiences during the Saskatchewan Rebellion when he served as a medical officer with Strange's column. Shortt

1277 **Plunkett**, Sir Horace Curzon
Report upon emigration to Canada. Dublin, H.M.S.O., 1892. 20p.

Listed in: Carty, James. Bibliography of Irish History, 1870-1911. (Dublin, 1940) No.2618.

1278 **Pritchard**, John
Glimpses of the past in the Red River Settlement, from letters of Mr. John Pritchard, 1805-1836. Notes by Rev. Dr. Bryce. Middle Church, Man., Rupert's Land Indian Industrial School, 1892. 25, [2]p. 21cm. Man. Leg.

1279 **Raine**, Walter
Bird-nesting in North-West Canada. Toronto, Hunter, Rose & Co., 1892. vii, 197p. illus., plates (part col.) 22 1/2cm.

A Toronto ornithologist describes the wild life to be seen on the prairies along the Canadian Pacific Railway. Rutherford

1280 **Ralph**, Julian
On Canada's frontier; sketches of history, sport and adventure and of the Indians, missionaries, fur-traders, and newer settlers of Western Canada. New York, Harper & Bros., 1892. x, 325p. incl. illus., plates. front. 23cm.

Illustrations by Frederic Remington. Most of the chapters appeared originally as sketches in Harper's Magazine. Shortt

1281 **Ritchie**, P.R.
Manitoba and the North-West Territories, being a report ... of a tour extending from April to September, 1892. Ottawa, Printed by S.E. Dawson, 1892. 52p. 22cm. Man. Leg.

1282 Not used

1283 [**Wade**, Frederick Coate]
National schools for Manitoba. Winnipeg, 1892. cover-title, 44p. 22cm.

Written in support of a public school system. For authorship see Morgan's 'Canadian Men and Women, 1898.' Man. Leg.

1284 **Whittier**, John G[reenleaf]
The Red River voyageur, edited and illustrated by the Hudson's Bay Company. Winnipeg, 1892. [16]p. illus. 20cm.

The poet gained his knowledge of Red River from the description given by J. Wesley Bond in his 'Minnesota and its Resources.' The poem was first published in 1859. On 17 Dec. 1891, Whittier's 84th birthday, Archbishop Taché had 'the bells of the Roman mission' rung in the poet's honour. Man. Leg.

1285 [**Young**, Richard]
Diocese of Athabasca. Bishop's annual letter, 1892. St. Luke's Mission, Vermillion, December, 1891. [Middle Church, Man.] Rupert's Land Indian Industrial School Press [1892] caption-title, 8p. 18cm.

Addressed to: My dear friends and fellow workers:- C.M.S. - 43

1286 **Aberdeen and Temair**, Ishbel Maria (Marjoribanks) Gordon, marchioness of
Through Canada with a kodak. Edinburgh, W.H. White & Co., 1893. viii, 249p. front., illus. 19cm.

Three chapters are devoted to the journey across the prairies. U. of S.

1287 [**Anonymous**]
Indian child's book; a primer in English and Cree languages. [n.p., n.d.] 37p. illus. 22cm. Oblates Arch.

1288 [**Anonymous**]
The Manitoba School Case. An independent opinion on the important question. [n.p., 1893?] 4p. 20 1/2cm. Shortt

1289 [**Anonymous**]
The work of a few years among the Indians of Manitoba and the North-West Territories, Canada. [Middle Church, Man.] Rupert's Land Indian Industrial School print, 1893. 17p. 17cm.

Printed for distribution at a booth of Indian exhibits from the Canadian West at the Chicago Exposition. B.C. Arch.

1290 **Anson**, Adelbert John Robert
The church and her work in new settlements of our colonies. The Ramsden sermon for 1893, etc. London, Skeffington & Son, 1893. 16p. Br. Mus.

1291 **Baldwinson**, B[aldwin] L[árus]
Agrip af fyrirlestri um baejalif Islendinga i Canada ... Reykjavik, Felagsprentsmidjan, 1893. 32p. 17cm. U. of M.

1292 **Baldwinson**, B[aldwin] L[árus]
Nokkrar athugasemdir vio Hagskýrslur fra Islendingabyggdum i Canada árin 1891-1892. [n.p., 1893] caption-title, 8p. 24cm. Denmark

1293 **Baldwinson,** B[aldwin] L[árus]
Svar gégn athugasemdum vid Hagskyrslur fra Canada 1891-92. [Reykjavik, 1893] cover-title, 8p. 23cm. Denmark

1294 [**Bodard,** Auguste] supposed author
Le guide du colon dans l'Ouest du Canada. Manitoba, Assiniboia, Alberta, Saskatchewan. [n.p., 1893] cover-title, 32p. 22cm.

Printing on end-papers; illustration on back cover.
Inserts: 'Canada informations générales' 1 leaf, and 'Voyages maritimes économiques au Canada' 4p. Both were printed by Perriaux in Paris. The intending emigrant is referred to M.L. Desbois, 'Agent-général d'Emigration autorisé par le gouvernement français.'
France

1295 **Bouthillier-Chavigny,** [Charles Marie Claude] count de
Our land of promise. A run through the Canadian North-West. Montreal, Gazette Printing Co., 1893. 109p. 17cm.

Two editions in French were published the same year, one with the title 'A Travers le Nord-Ouest Canadien de Montréal aux Montagnes Rocheuses' (205p.), and the other called 'A Travers les Grandes Terres à Blé du Nord-Ouest Canadien' (43p.). See Entry 1304.
Shortt

1296 **British-American**
Canada's fertile plains, containing certain suggestions with the view of awakening public interest in the important subject of a systematic movement of population towards the vacant lands of the western territory of Canada, by a British-American. Toronto, 1893. 82p. 20cm. Man. Leg.

1297 **Canada.** Department of the Interior
Description of the Province of Manitoba published under the authority of the Honourable T. Mayne Daly, Minister of the Interior. Compiled and arranged from the field-notes, plans, and reports of Dominion land surveyors, and published reports of the Geological Survey, Canadian Pacific surveys, and other official reports. Ottawa, Queen's Printer, 1893. iv p., 1 l., 365p. fold. map. 24 1/2cm. Shortt

1298 **Canada.** Department of the Interior
Emigration to North-Western Canada. Information for intending settlers. Ottawa, 1893. 61p. illus., plates, fold. map. 21cm. Can. Arch.

1299 **Canada.** Department of the Interior
Manitoba and North West Territories. Ottawa, Govt. Printing Bureau, 1893. 61p. illus., plates., fold. map. 21cm.

On cover: Emigration to North Western Canada; information for intending settlers.
Br. Mus.

1300 **Canada.** Department of the Interior
En skildring af Manitoba och Nordvest-Territorierna (Nord-Amerika) Dess Klimat ... [etc.] med särskildt afseende fäst på Utvandringslystna svenskar ... Januari, 1893. [Liverpool, Turner & Dunnett, 1893. 47p. illus. 22cm.

On cover: Manitoba, Assiniboia, Alberta, Saskatchewan, och Athabasca i det stora Nordvestliga Amerika. A Swedish pamphlet. Uppsala

1301 **Canada.** Department of the Interior
Western Canada and its great resources. The testimony of settlers, farmer delegates and high authorities, with preface and an appendix on the causes of failure and success in N.-W. farming. Ottawa, Government Printing Bureau, 1893. 38p. plates. 25cm. Shortt

1302 **Canada.** Department of the Secretary of State
Copy of all petitions, memorials, appeals, and any other documents addressed to His Excellency in Council, since the 15th March, 1892, relating to the Manitoba school acts of 1890, and to Section 22 of the 'Manitoba Act' and Section 93 of the 'British North America Act,' also copy of all reports to and of all orders in council in reference to the same; also copies of all correspondence in connection therewith. [Ottawa, 1893] 145p. 24cm. (Canada. Sess. papers, 1893, no. 33-33a) U. of S.

1303 **Canada.** Department of the Secretary of State
Copy of the judgment of the Judicial Committee of Her Majesty's Privy Council in the appealed case of Barrett vs the City of Winnipeg, commonly known as the Manitoba School Case; also copy of factums, reports and other documents in connection therewith. [Ottawa, 1893] 46p. 24cm. (Canada. Sess. papers, 1893, no.33b) U. of S.

1304 **Canadian Pacific Railway**
A travers les grandes terres à blé du nord-ouest Canadien. [n.p., 1893?] cover-title, iv, 43p. 19cm.

Half-title on page I: Aux canadiens-Français qui émigrent aux Etats-Unis.
A note states that this brochure is an extract of four chapters from a book in the course of being published 'A travers le Nord-Ouest Canadien.'
Another edition, tentatively dated 1894 (cover-title, x, 30p.) in Amtmann - 219-1.
See Entry 1295. St. Sulpice

1305 **Canadian Pacific Railway**
Canadian North-West. What settlers from the Maritime Provinces say about Western Canada. [n.p., 1893?] cover-title, 8p. illus. 22cm.
Amtmann - 229-160

1305A **Canadian Pacific Railway**
Fermes gratuites, Manitoba, Assiniboia, Alberta, Saskatchewan. Les quatres grandes provinces fertiles de l'Ouest Canadien décrites et illustrées. [n.p., 1893]. folder. 24p. illus., map. 21cm. Can. Arch. (ms.)

1306 **Canadian Pacific Railway**
Free farms in the fertile districts of Western Canada; Manitoba, Alberta, Assiniboia, Saskatchewan. [n.p., 1893] folder. (15p.) illus., map. 23cm. Can. Arch.

1307 Not used

1308 **Chetlain,** Augustus L[ouis]
The Red River colony. Chicago [Rogerson & Stockton] 1893. 60p. incl. port., map. 22cm.

Substantially the same as his article in Harper's Magazine, Dec. 1878. Devoted largely to the story of the Swiss settlers, their removal to United States, and subsequent history.
Man. Leg.

1309 Cree primer. London, Society for Promoting Christian Knowledge, 1893. 39p. 16cm. Shortt

1310 **Desjardins,** L[ouis] G[eorges]
A true and sound policy of equal rights for all ... Quebec, Morning Chronicle, 1893. 57p. 22cm.

Deals with the Orangist crusade against French influence in Manitoba. Shortt

1311 **Duck Lake Agricultural Society**
The Duck Lake district of Saskatchewan, Northwest Territories of Canada. Winnipeg, Printed by Acton Burrows, at the Western World office, 1893. cover-title, 8p. illus. 31cm. At head of title: In the Saskatchewan country. Facts about the wheat growing, cattle raising and mixed farming of the great fertile belt. Shortt

1312 Facts about grain growing, stock raising and dairying in the midst of the great fertile belt; the district of Kinistino, Saskatchewan, Northwest Territories of Canada. Winnipeg, Burrows, 1893. 8p. illus. Tanghe

1313 **Faucher de Saint-Maurice,** N[arcisse] H[enri] E[douard]
Les Etats de Jersey et la langue française exemple offert au Manitoba et au Nord-Ouest ... Montréal, Senécal, 1893. ix, 83p. 18 1/2cm. Rutherford

1314 **Fisher,** James
The school question. Speech ... in the Manitoba Legislature, 2nd March, 1893. [n.p., 1893?] 23p. 20 1/2cm. Shortt

1315 Free farms: Manitoba, Alberta, Assiniboia, Saskatchewan; the four great fertile provinces of Western Canada described and illustrated. [n.p., 1893?] map. 69 x 81 fold. to 23 x 11cm. U. of A.

1316 **Freemasons.** Saskatchewan. Wascana Lodge No.23, Regina
By-laws of Wascana Lodge No.23, Grand Register of Manitoba, Ancient Free & Accepted Masons, Regina, Assa., N.W.T., Dominion of Canada. Regina, Printed by the Leader Company (Limited) 1892 [i.e. 1893] [1], viii, 23p. 15cm.

'Historical Record of Wascana Lodge No.23 ...' p. i-viii. Glenbow

1317 **Hodgins,** J[ohn] George
Hand book of the Church of England missions in the eleven Dioceses of Selkirk, Mackenzie River, Moosonee, Caledonia, Athabasca, Columbia, New Westminster, Saskatchewan, Calgary, Qu'Appelle, and Rupert's Land; with illustrative extracts from the report of the Indian Department at Ottawa, and from the reports of the four great Church of England missionary societies, etc., in England for the year 1893. Toronto, Rowsell & Hutchison, 1893. 62p. 22cm. Shortt

1318 **Legge,** Alfred O[wen]
Sunny Manitoba, its people and its industries. London, T.F. Unwin, 1893. 297p., 1 l. incl. diagr. front., plates, fold. map. 21 1/2cm.

Based on information gathered while visiting with his sons who had settled in the province. Shortt

1319 **MacBeth**, John
The social customs and amusements in the early days in the Red River Settlement and Rupert's Land. Winnipeg, Manitoba Free Press print, 1893. cover-title, 7p. 22cm. (Hist. & Sc. Soc. of Man., no.44) Shortt

1320 **Manitoba**. Department of Agriculture and Immigration
The great agricultural province of Manitoba. General description and area, population, railway, government, soil and climate, general resources. Winnipeg, The Department [1893] 18p. illus., fold. map. 17 x 26cm. Man. Leg.

1321 **Manitoba**. Department of Agriculture and Immigration
Manitoba; official information for investors and settlers. [Winnipeg] 1893. 32p. illus., map. 21cm. R.E.S.

1322 **Moore**, Thomas
Canada revisited, 1879-1893. A short account of a visit to the Dominion ... [London] 1893. 31p.

See Entry 543. Br. Mus.

1323 **Morin**, J[ean] B[aptiste]
La vallée de la Saskatchewan dans les Territoires du Nord-Ouest. Joliette, Bon Combat, 1893. cover-title, 39p. fold. map. 22cm. At head of title: En avant la colonisation. Rutherford

1324 **Nelson**, Joseph
... Proposed Hudson's Bay and Pacific railway and new steamship route. [London, Economic Printing & Publishing Co.] 1893. 84p. fold. map. 24cm. At head of title: Direct route through the North-West Territories of Canada to the Pacific Ocean.

A 78-page edition was published in 1894. Can. Arch.

1325 **Osler, Hammond, & Nanton**
New homes, free homes in Alberta and Saskatchewan, Western Canada. Winnipeg, The Company [1893?] folder. [32]p. illus., fold. map. 25cm. Shortt

1326 **Prendergast**, James E[mile] P[ierre]
The Manitoba School Question. Speech ... in the Legislative Assembly of Manitoba, on the 10th and 12th day of March, A.D. 1890. [Winnipeg, E.J. Dermody, 1893] 25p. 21cm. Shortt

1327 **Routhier**, Sir A[dolphe] B[asile]
De Québec à Victoria. Québec, L.J. Demers & Frère, 1893. 392p. 21 1/2cm. Rutherford

1328 **Semmens**, J[ohn]
The hand-book of Scripture truths; or, The way of salvation ... Words of admonition, counsel, and comfort. Translated into the language of the Cree Indians by William Isbister, and revised by Rev. John McDougall. Toronto, Methodist Mission Rooms, 1893. 1p.l., 46p. 17 1/2cm.

Text in syllabic characters with captions also in English. L.C.

1329 **Taché,** A[lexandre] A[ntonin]
Les écoles dites écoles publiques de Manitoba sont des écoles protestantes. Saint-Boniface, La Compagnie Canadienne de Publication, 1893. cover-title, 32p. 20 1/2cm.

Also published in English. Shortt

1330 **Taché,** [Alexandre Antonin]
Monseigneur Taché adresse une lettre à M.J. Israel Tarte au sujet des écoles de Manitoba. [n.p., 1893] 4p. 23cm. Shortt

1331 **Taché,** [Alexandre Antonin]
Monseigneur Taché répond à M. Tarte. [n.p., 1893] 6p. 23cm. Shortt

1332 **Taché,** [Alexandre Antonin]
A page in the history of the schools in Manitoba during 75 years. [n.p.] 1893. 52p. 22cm. Shortt

1333 **The Tribune,** Winnipeg
The Luxton expulsion! Why W.F. Luxton has been expelled from the Free Press, and despoiled of the fruits of his life's work. [Winnipeg, 1893] caption-title, [4]p. illus. (port.) 23cm. An article reprinted from The Tribune. Shortt

1334 Why not go to Manitoba. Liverpool [1893] 8p. Br. Mus.

1335 **Young,** Egerton Ryerson
Stories from Indian wigwams and northern campfires. Toronto, William Briggs [1893] 293p. front., illus., plates, ports. 19cm.

A New York edition was published by Hunt. Shortt

1336 [**Young,** Richard]
[Circular letter describing a mission journey through the Athabasca-Peace River country. Athabasca Landing, 1893] 13p. 29cm.

Ms. note on title-page states that it was printed at the mission press. Can. Arch.

1337 **Allan,** Andrew
Manitoba and North-Western Railway Co'y of Canada; letter of the president to the holders of the 540,000 six per cent (1886) first mortgage bonds. Montreal, 1894. 10p. 22cm. Man. Leg.

1337A **Allan Steamship Line**
Allan Line handbook. Concise and useful information for intending emigrants to Canada and the United States. [n.p.] 1894. folder. 16p. illus. 18cm. Can. Arch. (ms.)

1338 **Ancient Order of United Workmen**
Constitution and standing regulations of the Grand Lodge, Ancient Order of United Workmen of Manitoba and North West Territories and by laws of Red River Lodge No.4 A.O.U.W. Winnipeg, 1894. 16p. 14cm. Tanghe

1339 **Bernier,** [Thomas Alfred]
Prêtre, laïque et politique. Incidents de la campagne scolaire au Manitoba. Saint-Boniface, Imp. du 'Manitoba,' 1894. 82p. St. Sulpice

1340 **Bernier**, [Thomas Alfred]
Speeches of Hon. Messrs. Bernier and Scott on the Manitoba and N.W. school questions. Ottawa, April 3rd and 4th, 1894. [Ottawa, 1894] 37p. 23cm. (Canada. Senate. Debates) L. of P.

1341 **Bodard**, Auguste
En route pour le Canada. Description du pays, ses avantages, la terre promise du cultivateur. 2,000,000 de Français, Belges et Suisses. Guide pratique du colon et du voyageur. [Paris, 1894] 36, [1]p. Br. Mus.

1342 [**Bouillat**, J.]
Les contemporains. Mgr Provencher, premier évêque de Saint-Boniface (Canada) (1787-1853) [Paris, Les Contemporains, 189–] caption-title, 16p. port. 26 1/2cm. Glenbow

1343 [**Bouillat**, J.]
Les contemporains. Mgr Taché, Archevêque de Saint-Boniface (Canada) (1823-1894) [Paris, Les Contemporains, 189–?] caption-title, 16p. port. 26 1/2cm. Glenbow

1344 **Brown**, William Foster
The settler's guide, or the homesteader's handy helper. Useful hints and information. How to avoid mistakes in time. Prevention is better than cure. Handy guide to earning a free home. Montreal, William Foster Brown Co., 1894. 52p. illus. 23cm.

An 1896 edition was also published. Agric.

1345 **Bryce**, George
Early days in Winnipeg. Winnipeg, Manitoba Free Press print, 1894. cover-title, 8p. illus. 22 1/2cm. (Hist. & Sc. Soc. of Man., no.46) Shortt

1346 **Canada**. Department of the Interior
Les Belges au Manitoba. Lettres authentiques de colons belges au Manitoba ... Ottawa, 1894. 27p. illus., fold. map. 21cm. Can. Arch.

1347 **Canada**. Department of the Interior
Canada. Le guide du colon français, belge et suisse. [Paris, Perriaux] 1894. cover-title, 32p. illus. 21cm.

Contains a list of French-speaking districts in Western Canada. B.C. Arch.

1348 **Canada**. Department of the Interior
Officiell handbok innehållande underrattelser angående Canada. Med särskild hänsyn till provinsen Manitoba och Nord Vestra Territorierna såsom ett fält för Skandinaviska nybyggare ... Ottawa, 1894. 95p. front., illus., plans (1 fold) fold. table, fold. col. map. 22cm.

On cover: 200 millioner acres land för nybyggare Manitoba i det stora Nordvestliga Amerika. Contains names of Scandinavian settlers and letters from some. Sweden

1349 **Canada**. Department of the Secretary of State
Copies of all petitions, memorials and correspondence, in reference to the appeal made in the name of the Roman Catholic minority of the Province of Manitoba, in reference to the school laws of that province; also copies of reports to and orders in council in reference to the same; also copies of the case submitted to

the Supreme Court of Canada respecting aforesaid appeal, and including factums and all materials in connection therewith, and copies of all judgments rendered and answers given by said court on or to the question referred to them. [Ottawa, 1894] 40p. 24cm. (Canada. Sess. papers, 1894, no.40d) U. of S.

1350 **Canada.** Department of the Secretary of State
Copies of all ordinances, school regulations and amendments thereto, adopted by the Legislative Assembly, the executive, and any board or council of education, in reference to the establishment, maintenance and administration of schools in the North-West Territories since 1885. Also for copies of all petitions, memorials and correspondence thereto. Also for copies of all orders in council, reports of the Governor-General in Council, and all communications and representations to the authorities in the North-West Territories. [Ottawa, 1894] 197p. 24cm. (Canada. Sess. papers, 1894, no.40c) U. of S.

1351 **Canada.** Department of the Secretary of State
School laws and other educational matters in Assiniboia, Prince Edward Island, the North-West Territories and Manitoba including the judgment of the Supreme Court respecting the appeal from the minority in Manitoba. Printed by order of Parliament. Ottawa, Government Printing Bureau, 1894. 2p.l., 16, 35, 197, 40p. 24 1/2cm. Reprint of Canada. Sess. papers, 1894, nos. 40a-d. Shortt

1352 **Canada.** Department of the Secretary of State
Schools in the North-West. [Ottawa, 1894] 16p. 24cm. (Canada. Sess. papers, 1894, no.40a) Running title. U. of S.

1353 **Canada.** Office of the High Commissioner
The advantages of Canada for emigrants. Papers by Rev. John Lightfoot ... the Rev. J. Cavis-Brown ... and the Rev. F.W. Webber ... and appendices containing general information about Canada, and a description of the Canadian exhibits, and the awards they obtained, at Chicago. [London, McCorquodale & Co.] 1894. 40p. illus. 20 1/2cm. L.C.

1354 **Canada.** Royal Commission on the liquor traffic
Minutes of evidence. Provinces of Manitoba, North-West Territories and British Columbia. Ottawa, Printed by S.E. Dawson, 1894. 700p. 24cm. (Canada. Sess. papers, 1894, no.21, v.3 of the evidence) U. of S.

1355 **Canadian Pacific Railway**
Northern Alberta, including the Edmonton, Red Deer, Buffalo Lake, Beaver Lake and other districts. Winnipeg, The Company [1894] folder. 23p. maps. 23 1/2cm. Shortt

1356 **Canadian Pacific Railway**
Western Canada. Manitoba, Assiniboia, Alberta and Saskatchewan. How to get there. How to select lands. How to begin. How to make a home. [n.p., 1894?] cover-title, 56p. illus. 22cm. Shortt

1357 **Church of England.** Diocese of Rupert's Land
Statement put forth by the Executive Committee of the Synod of Rupert's Land. The resources and needs for missions of the church in Manitoba. [n.p., 1894] caption-title, 7p. 18cm. C.M.S. - 44

1358 **Cochin**, Louis
Missionnaire et sauvages pendant la guerre des métis. Lettre du R.P. Cochin, O.M.I., à Mgr Pascal, vicaire apostolique de la Saskatchewan. Paris, A. Hennuyer, 1894. cover-title, 32p. 22cm. Sask. Arch.

1359 **Ewart**, John S[kirving]
The Manitoba School Question, being a compilation of the legislation, the legal proceedings before the Governor-General-in-Council. An historical account of the Red River outbreak in 1869 and 1870, its causes, and its success as shewn in the treaty – the Manitoba Act and a short summary of Protestant promises. Toronto, Copp Clark Co., 1894. vii, 401p. 22cm.

Copy in Arkin collection has a separate section: Addenda, p.403-413. Shortt

1360 **Franklin**, J.T.
English tenant-farmers on the agricultural resources of Canada. The reports of Mr. J.T. Franklin, Mr. R.H. Faulks, and Mr. C.E. Wright on their visit to Canada in 1893. London, McCorquodale & Co. Ltd., 1894. viii, 80p. illus., fold. map. 20 1/2cm. (Part II) Arkin

1361 **Guiry**, Jerome J.
An Irish agricultural delegate on the agricultural resources of Canada. The report of Jerome J. Guiry on his visit to Canada in 1893. London, McCorquodale & Co. Ltd., 1894. viii, 38p. fold. map. 20 1/2cm. (Part VI) Arkin

1362 **Houghton**, C.F.
Houghton to Middleton. The colonel with vigor replies to the general. Long but interesting. Interesting incidents of the campaign of '85. Grave charge explained. Sir Fred. Middleton's conduct towards his second in command as seen by the latter. [n.p.] 1894. 14p. 22 1/2cm. Can. Arch.

1363 **Johnstone**, C[atherine] L[aura]
Winter and summer excursions in Canada. London, Digby, Long & Co. [1894] xv, 213p. illus., plates. 20cm.

The entire book is devoted to describing life in Western Canada. Shortt

1364 **Land Corporation of Canada, Limited**
... Prislista jemte beskrifning. 155,000 acres sorgfälligt utvalda åkerbruks distrikt uti Regina och Long Lake distrikten ... Göteborg, D.F. Bonniers, 1894. cover-title, 21p. fold. map. 21 1/2cm.

On the map the company's land is shown as located in the Regina district and more particularly west of Long Lake. Sweden

1365 **Mackie**, John
The devil's playground; a story of the wild North-West. New York, F.A. Stokes [c1894] 246p. 16 1/2 x 9 1/2cm. (On cover: Twentieth century series) Not seen.

A novel of love and adventure which ran through several English and American editions. L.C.

1366 **Mercier**, Anne
A home in the North-West; being a record of experience, by Anne Mercier and Violet Watt. London, Society for Promoting Christian Knowledge, 1894. 73p. Not seen.

This copy destroyed by enemy action during World War II. Br. Mus.

1367 **Middleton,** Sir Fred[erick Dobson]
Suppression of the rebellion in the North West Territories of Canada, 1885. Edited with introduction by G.H. Needler. Toronto, University of Toronto Press, 1948. xix, 80p. map. 23cm. (University of Toronto studies. History and economics series, v.12)
This account originally appeared in four successive issues of the United Services Magazine (Nov. 1893-Feb. 1894) of London, England. U. of S.

1368 **Morin,** [Jean-Baptiste]
Le Nord-Ouest Canadien et ses ressources agricoles. Témoignages irréfutables recueillis. Ottawa, Imprimerie de l'État, 1894. iv p., 1 l., [7]-31p., 1 l. illus., diagr. 22cm. At head of title: En avant la colonisation.
The testimonial letters are from Morinville and other French settlements in northern Alberta. Shortt

1369 **Morrison,** J.H.
The Manitoba School Question; a paper read before the Junior Liberal-Conservative Association of St. John, N.B., February 13th, 1894. [St. John, The Sun, 1894] caption-title, 8p. 24cm. Can. Arch.

1370 **Osler,** A.
Farming in Canada. Report of the special commissioners of the Dundee Courier and Dundee Weekly News, by Messrs. A. Osler and J. Taylor. Dundee, 1894. ... Not seen. Can. Govt. Off.

1371 **Oxley,** James Macdonald
Archie of Athabasca. Boston, Lothrop, 1893. 262p. Not seen.
Juvenile fiction. An English edition was published in 1894 under the title 'Archie McKenzie.' Horning

1372 **Roberts,** John
Amaethwyr prydeinig ar adnoddau amaethyddol Canada. Adroddiad Mr. John Roberts ... am ei daith i Canada yn 1893 ... [Liverpool, Printed by Turner & Dunnett] 1894. 52p. illus., fold. map. 22cm.
See Entry 1384. Wales

1373 **Schultz,** [Sir] John [Christian]
A forgotten northern fortress. Winnipeg, Manitoba Free Press print, 1894. cover-title, 14p. illus. (incl. map) 22cm. (Hist. & Sc. Soc. of Man., no.47)
Relates to Fort Prince of Wales at Churchill. Shortt

1374 **Schultz,** [Sir] John [Christian]
Old Crow Wing Trail. Winnipeg, Manitoba Free Press print, 1894. cover-title, 32p. incl. plates. 21 1/2cm. (Hist. & Sc. Soc. of Man., no.45) Shortt

1375 **Schultz,** [Sir] John [Christian]
Speech on the occasion of his unveiling the monument erected by the Manitoba Historical Society, near the old King's highway to commemorate the Battle of Seven Oaks, 19th June, 1891. Winnipeg, Manitoba Free Press, 1894. 6p. 22cm. Tanghe

1376 **Shelton,** Reuben
English tenant-farmers on the agricultural resources of Canada. The reports of Mr. Reuben Shelton, Mr. Booth Waddington, Mr. John Cook, and Mr. Joseph

Smith on their visit to Canada in 1893. London, McCorquodale & Co. Ltd., 1894. viii, 96p. illus., fold. map. 20 1/2cm. (Part I) Arkin

1377 **Soullier,** Louis
Voyage du T.R.P. Louis Soullier en Amérique Avril-Octobre 1894. Bar-le-Duc, Imprimerie de l'Oeuvre de Saint-Paul [n.d.] x, 232p., 1 l.

One half of the book relates to the Prairie Provinces. Amtmann - 184-607

1378 **Southwestern Irrigation League**
Irrigation reports and resolutions adopted by the Irrigation Convention held in the city of Calgary on Thursday and Friday March 8 and 9, 1894. Published by the Southwestern Irrigation League of the Northwest Territories. [Calgary] Herald print [1894] 8p. 19 1/2cm. Can. Arch.

1379 **Steven,** John
Scotch tenant-farmers on the agricultural resources of Canada. The reports of Mr. John Steven and Mr. Alex. Fraser on their visit to Canada in 1893. London, McCorquodale & Co. Ltd., 1894. viii, 96p. illus., fold. map. 20 1/2cm. Arkin

1380 **Taché,** [Alexandre Antonin]
Memorial of Archbishop Taché on the school question. In answer to a report of the Committee of the Honorable the Privy Council of Canada. Montreal, C.O. Beauchemin & Son, 1894. 67p. 25cm.

Also published in French. Shortt

1381 **The Times,** London
Manitoba and the Canadian North-West. A reprint of two letters from The Times of January 30th and 31st, 1894. London, Printed and published by George Edward Wright, The Times office, 1894. cover-title, 21, [1] p. 22 1/2cm. Shortt

1382 **Wallace,** Robert
Special report on the agricultural resources of Canada. The report of Robert Wallace on his visit to Canada in 1893. London, McCorquodale & Co. Ltd., 1894. 48p. front., illus. 20 1/2cm. Arkin

1383 **Weeks,** W.
English tenant-farmers on the agricultural resources of Canada. The reports of Mr. W. Weeks, Mr. T. Pitt, and Mr. A.J. Davies on their visit to Canada in 1893. London, McCorquodale & Co. Ltd., 1894. viii, 72p. illus., fold. map. 20 1/2cm. (Part III) Arkin

1384 **Welsh Tenant-Farmers**
Welsh tenant-farmers on the agricultural resources of Canada. The reports of Mr. John Roberts ... Mr. W.H. Dempster ... on their visit to Canada in 1893. [Ottawa, Dept. of the Interior] 1894. viii, 58p. Amtmann - 214-542

1385 **Young,** Egerton Ryerson
Oowikapun; or, How the gospel reached the Nelson River Indians. New York, Hunt & Eaton, 1894. 240p. incl. plates. 19cm.

The following year Wm. Briggs of Toronto and C.H. Kelly of London brought out editions. Shortt

1386 [**Anonymous**]
Prairie agriculture ... Authorized by the Advisory Board of Manitoba. Winnipeg, The Consolidated Stationery Co. [1895?] iv, 259p. illus. 19cm. Shortt

1387 [**Anonymous**]
Provincial government for Alberta, its meaning and necessity. 'Who would be free, themselves must strike the blow.' [Calgary, Alberta Tribune print, 1895] cover-title, 5p. 21cm.

This pamphlet has been attributed to Charles Allan Stuart, later a judge of the Alberta Supreme Court. The copy in the Shortt Library is signed: Compliments R.G.B.

A mass meeting on 22 March 1895 in Calgary discussed the organizing of the western portion of the N.W.T. into a province. A committee was appointed to further the cause. Shortt

1388 **Baird**, Andrew Browning
... The Indians of Western Canada. Toronto, Canada Presbyterian, 1895. 30p. port. 18cm. (Foreign missions of the Presbyterian Church in Canada) Glenbow

1389 **Beck**, H.H.
Improved farms for sale in most of the best districts of Manitoba; cheaper than ever! Apply to H.H. Beck, 208 Main Street, Winnipeg. [Winnipeg] McIntyre Bros., 1895. cover-title, 15p. 22cm. Man. Arch.

1390 **Begg**, Alexander
History of the North-West. Toronto, Hunter, Rose & Co., 1894-95. 3v. front., ports. 22 1/2cm. Shortt

1391 **Benoist**, Charles
Les Français et le Nord-Ouest Canadien. Bar-le-Duc, Imprimerie de l'Oeuvre de Saint-Paul, 1895. 128p. 25cm.

Written from notes taken during a tour made in the winter of 1894-95. Shortt

1392 **Bernier**, [Thomas Alfred]
Speech of the Hon. Senator Bernier on the Manitoba School Question. Ottawa, 25th June, 1895 (Senate. Debates). [Ottawa? 1895] 39p. St. Sulpice

1393 [**Bethune**, Alexander Bernard]
Is Manitoba right? A question of ethics, politics, facts and law: a review of the Manitoba School Question. [Winnipeg] Winnipeg Telegram [1895] 45p. 21 1/2cm.

Another edition with a different subtitle was published in 1896. See R.E.S. Can. Arch.

1394 Calgary, the Denver of Canada, its adaptability as a health resort, and as a site for the Dominion sanatorium for the treatment of consumptives. Calgary, Calgary Herald print, 1895. 38p. fold plate. 22cm. In double column.

W.J. Gage, Toronto publisher, had contributed a sum of money to build a sanatorium in Toronto. In an interview he referred to the fact that hundreds of young men from Eastern Canada went to Denver each year, and that they might be retained in the country by building a sanatorium at Calgary. Calgary set out to prove the salubrity of its climate for consumptives. The pamphlet includes letters from local doctors and from former consumptives living in the area. Toronto

1395 **Canada**
The Manitoba School Case, 1894. Edited for the Canadian government by the appellants' solicitors in London. London, Printed for the Government of the Dominion of Canada, by Reynolds Blogg & Cope, 1895. 2p.l., 286p. 24cm.

An appeal from the Supreme Court of Canada to the Privy Council, 1894. Shortt

1396 **Canada**. Parliament. House of Commons
Papers in reference to the Manitoba School Case presented to Parliament during the session of 1895. Printed by order of Parliament. Ottawa, Printed by S.E. Dawson, 1895. 363p. 24 1/2cm. Shortt

1397 **Canada**. Privy Council
Proceedings in the Manitoba School Case heard before Her Majesty's Privy Council for Canada, February 26th to March 7th, 1895. Ottawa, Government Printing Bureau, 1895. 2p.l., 163p. 24cm. Shortt

1398 **Canadian Pacific Railway**
Farming and ranching in Western Canada. Manitoba, Assiniboia, Alberta and Saskatchewan. [Montreal, 1895?] cover-title, 56p. illus., maps (one fold.) 22cm.

An inside title-page reads: Western Canada, Assiniboia, Alberta, and Saskatchewan. How to get there. How to select Canada. How to begin. How to make a home. R.E.S.

1399 **Church of England**. Diocese of Qu'Appelle
Journal of the twelfth session of the Synod of the Diocese of Qu'Appelle, July 31st, 1895, and an appendix containing reports of the committee and tables of finance. Fort Qu'Appelle, Printed at the Vidette Office, 1895. 12p. 18cm. C.M.S. - 45

1400 **Crissey**, Forrest
The young newspaper scout. An interesting narrative of a boy's adventures in the Northwest during the Riel Rebellion. Chicago, W.B. Conkey Co., 1895. 194p. illus. 20cm.

Juvenile fiction. Americas

1401 **Elkington**, W[alter] M.
Five years in Canada. London, Whittaker & Co., 1895. 138p. 23cm.

After a year at Portage la Prairie, the writer took up farming about forty miles north of Fort Qu'Appelle. He gives an excellent description of homestead life. Man. Leg.

1402 **Ewart**, John S[kirving]
Lecture on the Manitoba School Question in the Congregational Church, Winnipeg, 29th April, 1895. [Winnipeg] Manitoba Free Press print, 1895. cover-title, 18p. 20 1/2cm. Shortt

1403 **Ewart**, John S[kirving]
The Manitoba School Question. A reply to Mr. Wade. Winnipeg, Manitoba Free Press Co., 1895. 63p. 21 1/2cm. Shortt

1404 **Fergusson**, F.W.
Jemförelse mellan Canada och forenta staterna (Ur the Canadian Gazette for den 31 October 1895) Sundsvall, Leon Hallens, 1895. Broadside. 16 x 24cm.

In double column.
A speech made in Chicago by the author. Sweden

1405 **Field**, Septimus
The Canadian Northwest. [Asessippi? 1895] cover-title, 15p. 15cm.

'Small but well written pamphlet' of which 10,000 copies were printed. See annual report of the Dept. of the Interior for 1895. U. of T.

1406 **Fisher**, James
The Manitoba School Question. A series of four letters. [Winnipeg] 1895. 36p. 20 1/2cm. Shortt

1407 **Great Britain**. Privy Council. Judicial Committee
Cause des écoles du Manitoba (1895) Jugement des Lords du Comité Judiciaire du Conseil Privé Impérial, arrêté en Conseil Impérial et arrêté réparateur en conseil. Ottawa, Dawson, 1895. 30p. Canner – 474-548

1408 **Great Britain**. Privy Council. Judicial Committee
Manitoba School Case (1894). The judgment of the lords of the Judicial Committee of the (Imperial) Privy Council, together with the imperial order in council and the remedial order in council. Ottawa, Printed by S.E. Dawson, 1895. 356p. 24cm. (Canada. Sess. papers, 1895, no.20) U. of S.

1409 **Harmony Industrial Association**
Prospectus of the Harmony Industrial Association (co-operative system) [Birtle, Man., Birtle Printing Co., 1895] 19p.

For a history of the Harmony Colony see Saskatchewan History, v.4, no.1, winter 1951. Sask. Arch. (microfilm)

1410 [**Hayes**, Kate E.]
Prairie pot-pourri, by Mary Markwell [pseud. Winnipeg, Stovel Co., c1895] cover-title, 186p. incl. plate. 18cm. At head of title: Souvenir edition.

A collection of stories and verse. Shortt

1411 **Holmes**, O'C.J.
Cause and remedy for the hard times. [n.p., 1895] cover-title, 8p. 22cm.

A report of a meeting at Lorndale School in the municipality of Odanah, Man., on 26 December 1894, at which the subject of economic conditions was discussed and a remedy proposed. Arkin

1412 **Kribs**, Louis P.
The Manitoba School Question considered historically, legally and controversially. Toronto, The Murray Printing Co., 1895. cover-title, iv, [5]-71p. 20 1/2cm. Shortt

1413 **McDougall**, John
Forest, lake and prairie. Twenty years of frontier life in Western Canada, 1842-62. Toronto, William Briggs, 1895. x, [11]-267p. front., illus. 18 1/2cm.

This was the first volume published in a series covering his life as a missionary. A second edition appeared in 1910. Shortt

1414 **McDougall,** John
'Indian wigwams and northern camp-fires,' a criticism. Toronto, Printed for the author by W. Briggs, 1895. 40p. 20cm.

A criticism of the Rev. E.R. Young's 'Stories from Indian wigwams and northern campfires.' Glenbow

1415 **McKellar,** Hugh
Extended notes of an address on the geography of Manitoba. Winnipeg, Hart & Macpherson, 1895. 20p. fold. map., diagrs. 22cm. Man. Leg.

1416 **Mackie,** John
Sinners twain; a romance of the great lone land. 2d ed. New York, F.A. Stokes [c1895] 3p.l., 193p. 16 1/2cm. (On cover: Twentieth century series)

Published also in London by T.F. Unwin. L.C.

1417 **Meek,** Edward
The legal and constitutional aspects of the Manitoba School Question. The statutes, the Privy Council decisions, the remedial orders, and the answer of Manitoba, considered. Toronto, The Hunter, Rose Co. Ltd., 1895. 30p. 19cm. Can. Arch.

1418 **Northwest Territories.** Legislative Assembly
Northwest homesteads. How they are built up. Issued by the authority of the Northwest Legislative Assembly. Saltcoats, Assiniboian News [1895] 22p. 21cm.

Testimonials from Hugh Hamilton, missionary, and other settlers at Yorkton. Man. Leg.

1419 **Oleskiw,** Osyp
O emigratsiyi [On emigration] Lviv, 1895. ... Not seen.

Prof. Oleskiw's favourable report on Western Canada started the great influx of Ukrainians. Yuzyk

1420 **Oleskiw,** Osyp
Pro vilni zemli [On free lands] Lviv, Tovaristo Prosvita, 1895. 38p. 17 1/2cm.

Photostatic copy. Agric.

1421 **Patrons of Industry**
The political position of the Patrons. Rapid City, Man. [1895] ... N.Y.

1422 **Roman Catholic Church.** Diocese of Saint-Boniface
Fêtes de la consécration episcopale de sa grandeur Mgr L.P.A. Langevin, O.M.I., Archevêque de Saint-Boniface. Saint-Boniface, Le Manitoba, 1895. 139p. front. (port.), illus. 20 1/2cm. St-Jean

1423 **Sladen,** Douglas Brooke Wheelton
On the cars and off; being the journal of a pilgrimage along the Queen's highway to the East, from Halifax in Nova Scotia to Victoria on Vancouver's Island ... London, Ward, 1895. xviii, 447p. front., illus., plates, maps. 24cm.

Only thirty pages are devoted to the prairies. Man. Leg.

1424 **Spurr**, J.B.
The Edmonton district directory for the year 1895, containing full and authentic information, statistics, tables, maps and guide to northern Alberta. Edmonton, J.B. Spurr [1895?] 71, [1]p. plan. 15 1/2cm.

Pagination includes advertising.
'First year of publication.' No further editions were published. Printed in Toronto.
Glenbow

1425 **Stewart**, McLeod
Ottawa; an ocean port, and the emporium of the grain and coal trade of the North-West ... A paper read before the Ottawa Board of Trade, on Tuesday, the 7th of November, 1893. 2d ed. Ottawa, Printed by Thorburn & Co., 1895. 23p. 22cm.

Xerox copy. Glenbow

1426 **Van Bruyssel**, Ferd[inand]
Le Canada. Commerce – élevage – exploitation – forestière – colonisation. Bruxelles, 1895. 484p. 22cm.

Pages 286-484 relate to Manitoba and the North-West Territories. Belgium

1427 **Wade**, F[rederick] C[oate]
The Manitoba School Question. Winnipeg, Printed at the Manitoba Institution for the Deaf and Dumb, 1895. 2p.l., 122, [28]p. illus. (incl. facsims.) 20 1/2cm. Shortt

1428 **Watt**, D[avid] H.
Poems on the Manitoba School Question ... Toronto, Stewart Publishing Co. [c1895] 23p. 23cm.

Satirical verse. Man. Leg.

1429 **Young**, Mrs. [Julia Henstley (Harrison)]
Little Marie; or, Marked for God. A true tale of work in Athabasca. [Toronto, W.J. Dickson, printers, 189_] caption-title, 7p. 13cm. Private copy

1430 **[Anonymous]**
The Manitoba School Question. The bishops' view and Mr. Laurier's view. Unanimous opinion of the bishops. [n.p., n.d.] cover-title, 30p. 21cm.

Also published in French. See Entry 1462. Oblates Arch.

1431 **[Anonymous]**
La question des écoles du Manitoba. La minorité sacrifiée au fanatisme. Les Torys sont les ennemis de la paix en Canada. L'orangisme envahissant. Montréal, Imprimé par John Lovell & Sons, 1896. 110p. 20 1/2cm. Shortt

1432 **Aron**, Joseph
Canada-Transvaal. Dédié aux diplomates français qui ont du bon sens. Avec une adresse en français à l'Empereur d'Allemagne. Paris, 1896. 144p. incl. illus., port., facsim., map. 16cm.

(Avec l'appendice sur la question Riel et les denis de justice des Anglais dans cette affaire)
Ouvrage supprimé du marché, libelle contre l'Angleterre; très recherché. L. of P.

1433 **Bible**. New Testament. St. Mark. Cree
The Gospel according to Saint Mark, translated into the Cree. Athabasca Landing, Printed at the Mission press, 1896. 3p.l., 146p. 17cm.

Translated and printed by Bishop Richard Young and the Rev. George Holmes.
Alta. Leg.

1434 **Blais**, Moïse J.
Le Manitoba et le Nord-Ouest canadien. [n.p.] 1896. 100p. Br. Mus.

1435 **Boddy**, Alexander Alfred
By ocean, prairie, and peak; some gleanings from an emigrant chaplain's log, on journeys to British Columbia, Manitoba, and Eastern Canada. London, Society for Promoting Christian Knowledge, 1896. 204p. illus., maps. 18 1/2cm.

Only about one quarter of the book relates to the prairies. B.C. Arch.

1436 **Bryce**, George
Worthies of old Red River. Winnipeg, Manitoba Free Press print, 1896. cover-title, 12p. illus. (incl. ports.) diagr. 21 1/2cm. (Hist. & Sc. Soc. of Man., no.48) Shortt

1437 **Canada**. Department of the Interior
The Edmonton district, northwestern Canada; a description of its soil, climate, products, agricultural capabilities and other resources. [Ottawa] 1896. 10p. 25cm.

Dept. of the Interior correspondence suggests that the author was a Mr. Ruttan.
Glenbow

1437A **Canada**. Department of the Interior
Letters from settlers in Canada. Official and other information for intending settlers in Manitoba, the North-West Territories, British Columbia, and the other provinces of Canada. London, McCorquodale & Co., 1896. cover-title, 47p. 21cm. Can. Arch. (ms.)

1437B **Canada**. Department of the Interior
Official information relating to the Dominion of Canada, including extracts from the reports of the tenant-farmer delegates who visited the country in 1893. London, McCorquodale & Co., 1896. cover-title, 40p. illus., map. 21cm. Can. Arch. (ms.)

1438 **Caron**, Sir [Joseph Philippe René] Adolphe
Discours ... sur le bill réparateur Manitoba, Ottawa, mercredi, 4 mars 1896. [Ottawa, 1896] caption-title, 14p. 25cm.

At head of title: Débats des communes, sixième session, septième Parlement. Can. Arch.

1439 **Church of England**. Hymns and prayers. Cree
Cree hymns and prayers ... [Athabasca Landing, Printed at the house of R. Young] 1896. 11p. 24cm.

A photostatic copy.
'A copy of the first book printed in the province of Athabasca, Canada. Printed in phonetic characters designed to reproduce the sounds of the Cree (Indian) language.' - Ms. note signed: S.W.
Imprint reads: Lesser Slave Lake. Title vignette. Title also in Cree syllabics. Text in Cree with English captions.
See also Entries 1645 and 1678. Americas

1440 **Church of England**. Manual of devotion. Cree
[Manual of religious instruction, by the Bishop of Athabasca and the Rev. George Holmes] Athabasca Landing, Mission Press, 1896. ... Not seen. Rupert's Land

1441 **Colmer**, J[oseph] G[rose]
Across the Canadian prairies. A two months' holiday in the Dominion. London, The European Mail, Ltd. [1896] 85p. incl. front., map. 18 1/2cm.
His sojourn on the prairies described, p.23-57. Shortt

1442 **Dugas**, G[eorges]
L'Ouest canadien. Sa découverte par le Sieur de la Vérendrye. Son exploitation par les compagnies de traiteurs jusqu'à l'année 1822. Montréal, Cadieux & Derome, 1896. 413p. maps. 21 1/2cm.
An English edition was published in Montreal in 1905. Shortt

1443 **Foster**, [Sir George Eulas]
Speech on the Manitoba School Question, delivered in the House of Commons, March, 13th, 1896 ... [n.p., 1896] cover-title, 24p. 21cm.
'From Hansard revised.' Glenbow

1444 [**Gonthier**, Dominique Ceslar]
La question des écoles du Manitoba, par P. Bernard [pseud.] Québec, Léger Brousseau, 1896. 228, 64p. 20 1/2cm. v.2 of Un manifeste libéral. Shortt

1445 **Harman**, Samuel Bruce
'Twas 26 years ago; narrative of the Red River expedition, 1870. Toronto, 1896. 31p. front., illus., ports. 24cm. Reprinted from the Toronto Globe and Empire. Toronto

1446 [**Holmes**, George]
Lesser Slave Lake, Athabasca, North West Canada. [London, 1896] caption-title, [4]p. 20cm.
Description of a Church of England mission field. C.M.S. - 46

1447 **Leduc**, H[ippolyte]
Hostility unmasked. School ordinance of 1892 of the North-West Territories and its disastrous results. Montreal, C.O. Beauchemin & Son, 1896. viii, 78p. 23cm. At head of title: L.J.C. et M.I.
Published also in French. Shortt

1448 **Leibert**, Morris W.
Bruederfeld and Bruederheim. Moravian settlements of German Russians in Alberta, Canada. Extracts from the report of an official visitation, Nov. 4 to Dec. 3, 1895. Bethlehem, Pa., Moravian Publishing Concern, 1896. 33p. 19cm.
An account of an official visit to the newly formed colonies near Edmonton. The pamphlet was published in both German and English. Copy of the German edition in Can. Arch. (ms.) N.Y.

1449 **McCaul**, C[harles] C[oursolles] comp.
Ready reference guide to the ordinances of the North-West Territories. Including the revised ordinances of 1888 and all subsequent ordinances to 1895 (inclusive)

together with a complete index to 'The Judicature Ordinance' (1893), and amendments thereto. Compiled by C.C. McCaul and Horace Harvey. Toronto, Goodwin Law Book and Publishing Co. Ltd., 1896. 3p.l., 54p. 22cm. Shortt

1450 **McDougall**, John
Saddle, sled, and snowshoe; pioneering on the Saskatchewan in the sixties. With illustrations by J.E. Laughlin. Toronto, William Briggs, 1895. ix, [10]-282p. front., plates. 19cm. Shortt

1451 **Maclean**, John
Canadian savage folk; the native tribes of Canada. Toronto, W. Briggs, 1896. viii, [9]-641p. front., illus., port. 22 1/2cm. Shortt

1452 **Maclean**, John
The warden of the plains, and other stories of life in the Canadian North-West. Toronto, Methodist Book & Publishing Co., 1896. 301p. illus. 19 1/2cm.
Fiction. Man. Leg.

1453 **McMillan**, A[nthony] J.
Manitoba and its development. Lecture. Warwick, Evans & Co. [1896] 16p. 17cm. Reprinted from Warwick and Warwickshire Advertiser, Sat., Jan. 11, 1896. Man. Leg.

1454 **McNaughton**, Margaret [(Peebles)]
Overland to Cariboo; an eventful journey of Canadian pioneers to the gold fields of British Columbia in 1862. Toronto, William Briggs, 1896 vii, [xi]-xvi, [19]-176p. incl. front., illus., plates, ports. plates. 19 1/2cm.
Chapters 1-3, p.1-72 describe the journey of the gold-seekers across the prairies. A very general account. Shortt

1455 [**McPhillips**, Albert Edward]
The Manitoba question. True side of the case. Mr. Bodwell's fallacies exposed. Mr. Joseph Martin and his methods. Victoria, Colonist Steam Presses. 1896. cover-title, 15p. 22 1/2cm. Man. Leg.

1456 **Manitoba**. Commissioners appointed to represent the Province of Manitoba on the conference on the school question
Report of the commissioners appointed to represent the Province of Manitoba at the conference held with the representatives of the Dominion government on the school question. [Winnipeg] D. Philip [1896] 24p. 22cm. Shortt

1457 Manitoba School Question! French-Canadian interference with Manitoba. Relation of the Church to civil authority. Direct and indirect expenditure on ecclesiasticism. [Forest, Ont., The Standard, 1896] cover-title, 15p. 23cm.
Printed in double column. Can. Arch.

1458 Manitoba. Ritlingur ... gefinn út af Manitoba-stjorninni, 1896. Winnipeg [1896] cover-title, 34p. illus. Fiske

1459 **Maple Leaf** [pseud.]
My two friends and I; or, The A, B, C of the injustice of forcing separate schools upon Manitoba, by Maple Leaf [pseud.] Ottawa, Taylor & Gilbert [1896?] cover-title, 21p. 20cm. Shortt

1460 **Marriott**, Stephen
To Winnipeg, Manitoba, and back. London, Simpkin, Marshall, Hamilton, Kent & Co., 1896. iii, 112p. illus. Not seen. Amtmann, Oct., 1950

1461 **Mercier**, Anne
The red house by the Rockies. A tale of Riel's rebellion. By Anne Mercier and Violet Watt. Published under the direction of the General Literature Committee. London, Society for Promoting Christian Knowledge [1896] 2p.l., [7]-126p. front. 18 1/2cm. Shortt

1462 **O., A.**
La question des écoles de Manitoba. La doctrine des évêques et la doctrine de M. Laurier. Sentiment unanime des évêques. [n.p., 1896] caption-title, 32p. 22cm.

Ms. note: Par A.O. Can. Arch.

1463 **Power**, [Lawrence Geoffrey]
Remedial bill from the point of view of a Catholic minister. Ottawa, Thorburn & Co., 1896. cover-title, 24p. 20 1/2cm.

A French translation by Hon. Charles Langelier was also published. Shortt

1464 [**Proulx dit Clément**, Jean Baptiste]
Documents pour servir à l'intelligence de la question des écoles du Manitoba, avec quelques notes explicatives. Rome, A. Befani, 1896. 173p. Not seen.

Written by Abbé Proulx, and published in a very limited edition, this volume defended Laurier's stand on the question. Gagnon, v.2, p.93

1465 **Le Quotidien**
Justice à qui de droit. Lévis, Le Quotidien, 1896. 52p. 23cm.

Extracts from Le Quotidien on the Manitoba School Question. Collection Gagnon

1466 **Roman Catholic Church**
Lettre pastorale de nos seigneurs les archevêques et évêques des provinces ecclésiastique de Québec, de Montréal et d'Ottawa sur la question des écoles du Manitoba. Montréal, 1896. 8p. 21cm.

Letter signed by twelve Catholic clergy. L. of P.

1467 **Ruttan**, H[enry] N[orland]
Report on the Assiniboine River and artesian wells as source of supply, and on a system of water works for the city of Winnipeg ... With analyses of waters by Drs. Drown, Girdwood, and Hutton, and report on the condition of Assiniboine River by Dr. Patterson and H.N. Ruttan. Winnipeg, 1896. cover-title, 24p. 22cm. Arkin

1468 **Saxby**, J[essie] M[argaret] E[dmonston]
Brown Jack; a tale of North-West Canada. London, Religious Tract Society, 1896. 80p. front., illus. 14cm.

Fiction. Br. Mus.

1469 **Strange**, T[homas] Bland
Gunner Jingo's jubilee; an autobiography. 3d ed. London, J. Macqueen, 1896. 2p.l., [vii]-xix, 346p., 1 l., 347-546p. incl. illus., plates, maps. plates, fold. plan. 23 1/2cm.

P.380-526 describe the author's experience as a rancher and as commander of the Alberta Field Force in the Saskatchewan Rebellion.
First published by Remington of London in 1893. Shortt

1470 **Swainson,** F[rank]
The Kissock homes, St. Paul's mission, Blood Reserve, Diocese of Calgary, N.W. Canada. Appeal & statement of funds raised. [n.p., 1896?] cover-title, 7p. 17cm. C.M.S. - 45

1471 **Tennyson**, Bertram
The land of Napioa, and other essays in prose and verse. Moosomin, Spectator Printing and Publishing Co., 1896. 3p.l., v, 155, [1]p. 17cm.

The author was a nephew of the great English poet. See also Entry 1746. Shortt

1472 [**Tims,** John William]
Diocese of Calgary. Report on Indian missions with financial statement, list of subscribers and donors, etc. 1895-96. Toronto, Oxford Press, 1896. 22p. illus. 20cm.

Also published for the year 1897-98 by the same publisher. C.M.S. - 45-46

1473 **Turnock,** Francis H.
The Liberals and the North West. What a Grit administration means to us in dollars and cents. [Calgary, 1896] caption-title, [4]p. 21cm.

Written in support of T.B.H. Cochrane, the Conservative candidate for the Alberta seat in the federal election of 1896.
Two related newspaper clippings attached. Glenbow

1474 [**Ward,** B. Peyton]
Roughing it in the North-West Territories of Canada twenty years ago, by B.P.W. London, Worrall and Robey, 1896. 130p. fold. map. 19cm.

An Englishman describes a journey from Winnipeg to Duck Lake, a six-weeks' hunting trip on the plains, and the return journey to Winnipeg in the winter of 1876-77. Man. Leg.

1475 **Western Canada Immigration Board**
A few facts. [Winnipeg] Bulman Bros. & Co. [1896] [95]p. incl. illus., maps, facsims. 24cm.

About half the pamphlet consists of facsimiles of letters and questionnaires answered by farmers. The writer was F.W. Heuback. After the 1st edition of 30,000 was exhausted, a 2nd of 20,000 was printed. Can. Arch.

1476 [**Young,** Richard]
Instructions in the syllabic characters for the use of the Cree Indians in the Diocese of Athabasca. New ed. Printed at the Athabasca Landing, 1896. [7], 106, [1]p. 17cm.

Illustration on title-page.
Probably prepared by Bishop Young and the Rev. George Holmes. Rupert's

1477 [**Anonymous**]
The greatest realistic burlesque farce of the latter part of the nineteenth century. Justice Peg and his justice shop in the city of Win. In four acts. [Winnipeg, 1897?] 19p. 21 1/2cm.

A play issued by the saloon keepers against the temperance campaign of the time. Man. Leg.

1478 **Bernard de Fauconval**, J. de
Le Canada. Provinces d'Ontario et de Manitoba. Richesses, productions, situation économique et commerciale, immigration et colonisation. Brussels, P. Weissenbruch, 1897. ... Lorenz

1479 **Bible**. New Testament. Romans. Cree
The Epistle to the Romans in the Cree language. Oonikup, North West Territory [1897] 67p. 17cm. Title also in Cree. L.C.

1480 **Bible**. New Testament. St. John. Cree
The Gospel according to Saint John, translated into the Cree. Athabasca Landing, Printed at the Mission Press, 1897. 5p.l., 2-190 (i.e. 191)p. illus. 16 1/2cm.

In syllabic characters.
Translated by the Rev. Richard Young, Bishop of Athabasca, and the Rev. George Holmes. Rupert's

1480A **Canada**. Department of the Interior
Hints to settlers. A guide to homesteaders in Manitoba and the North-West Territories. What a settler should do and how he should do it. What he should not do. Ottawa, 1897. 30p. 16cm. Can. Arch. (ms.)

1481 **Canada**. Department of the Interior
Manitoba and the North-West Territories, Assiniboia, Alberta, Saskatchewan, in which are included the newly discovered gold fields of the Yukon. Information as to the resources and climates of these countries for intending farmers, ranchers and miners, 1897. Ottawa, Government Printing Bureau, 1897. 46p. front., illus. 24cm. Arkin

1482 **Courrier du Canada**
La question scolaire des écoles du Manitoba. Quelques observations sur le discours de l'Hon. M. Laurier, au banquet de Montréal. Québec, Édité par Le Courrier du Canada, 1897. [iii]-viii, 32p. 23 1/2cm. Shortt

1483 **Cowie**, Isaac
The grain, grass, and gold fields of south-western Canada. Edmonton, Alberta, Canada. Described as a mixed farming and mining country ... Also a description of the all Canadian routes from Edmonton to the Yukon gold fields. A handbook for agriculturists and gold miners. With information for railway and other capitalists, tourists, sportsmen, big game hunters, scientific explorers and others seeking fresh fields for their energies under the flag. [n.p.] 1897. 54p. illus. Can. Arch.

1484 **Dmytriw**, Nestor
Kanadiyska Rus [Canadian Ruthenia] Jersey City, Svoboda, 1897. 24p. Not seen.

Relates to the Ukrainians. Yuzyk

1485 **Dmytriw**, Nestor
Kanadiyska Rus'; podorozhni vspomyny. Mt. Carmel, Pa. [1897] 56p. 19 1/2cm. (Vydavnytstvo chasopysy 'Svoboda,' ch.4)

A photostatic copy.
Free translation: Canadian Ruthenia; memoirs of a traveler. Agric.

1486 **Fitzpatrick**, Sir Charles
Les écoles du Manitoba. La question du jour, traitée par un avocat constitutionnel. [Québec, 1897] 40p. 19 1/2cm.

The substance of a speech delivered at Toronto. Can. Arch.

1487 **Gordon**, Charles W[illiam]
Beyond the Marshes; a Manitoba idyll. Winnipeg, 1897. 28p. 15cm. Reprinted from The Westminster.

An essay on this Presbyterian missionary's visit to a family whose invalid daughter had great spiritual serenity.
A 19-page edition, with an introductory note by the Countess of Aberdeen, was published in Toronto by Westminster in 1898. A 36-page edition appeared in New York in 1900. Reprints reflect the author's rise as Ralph Connor ('Black Rock' and 'The Sky Pilot')
B.C. Arch.

1488 Not used

1489 **Grey**, Francis Douglas
An appeal from Her Majesty's Court of Queen's Bench in Equity for Manitoba. Between Francis Douglas Grey and Sir John Robert Heron Maxwell, appellants, and the Manitoba and North-Western Railway Company of Canada, respondents. Proceedings and judgement. London, A.P. Blundell, Taylor & Co. [1897?] cover-title, 211p. 28cm. At head of title: In the Privy Council, no.21 of 1896.
Shortt

1490 **Harris**, Josiah
Direct route through the North-West Territories of Canada to the Pacific Ocean. The chartered Hudson's Bay & Pacific Railway route ... London, Spottiswoode & Co., 1897. 3p.l., 66p. fold. map. 25 1/2cm.

Proposed a railway from Edmonton to Churchill via Battleford and Prince Albert. Largely a compilation of evidence. Man. Leg.

1491 **Hart and Company**
From the West. [Winnipeg, Hart & Co., n.d.] cover-title, 9 plates. 11 x 17 1/2cm.

Lithographers, Bulman Bros. & Co. Arkin

1492 **Henham**, Ernest G[eorge]
Menotah, a tale of the Riel Rebellion. London, Skeffington, 1897. xii, 370p. front., plates. 19 1/2cm.

Light fiction. L.C.

1493 **Hering**, Rudolph
Report on a future water supply for the city of Winnipeg, Manitoba. New York, September, 1897. [Winnipeg, McIntyre, 1897] 56p. fold. map, diagrs. 22cm.
Tanghe

1494 **Kaiser**, Georges
Au Canada. Bruxelles, A. Lesigne, 1897. 424p. plates, fold. map. 22 1/2cm.

About one-third of this description of a journey across Canada relates to the Prairies.
Belgium

1495 [**Lacasse**, Pierre Zacharie]
Difficultés scolaires de Manitoba, par questions et réponses à la portée de tous. Québec, Léger Brousseau, 1897. cover-title, 64p. 16 1/2cm. Shortt

1496 [**Lacasse**, Pierre Zacharie]
Une visite dans les écoles du Manitoba, par Jean des Prairies [pseud.] Montréal, Librairie Saint-Joseph, 1897. [87]p. 17cm. Shortt

1497 **Landry**, Auguste Charles Philippe
Le campagne politico-religieuse de 1896-1897 ... par Justitia. Québec, Léger Brousseau, 1897. 2p.l., 175p. 21cm. Contents listed on title-page. Shortt

1498 **Landry**, Auguste Charles Philippe
Les droits de l'Eglise dans la question manitobaine, par Justitia. Québec, Léger Brousseau, 1897. 43p. 21cm. Oblates Arch.

1499 **Leduc**, Hippolyte
'Pouilleux' et 'fossoyeur' ou Souvenir de la consécration épiscopale de Monseigneur Emile Légal, O.M.I., évêque de Pogla et coadjuteur de Saint-Albert. Laval [France] Imprimerie de la Croix de la Mayenne, 1897. 54p. 24cm. McGill

1500 **MacBeth**, R[oderick] G[eorge]
Farm life in the Selkirk colony. Winnipeg, Manitoba Free Press Co., 1897. cover-title, 4p. 21 1/2cm. (Hist. & Sc. Soc. of Man., no.50) Shortt

1501 **MacBeth**, R[oderick] G[eorge]
The Selkirk settlers in real life. With an introduction by Hon. Sir Donald A. Smith. Toronto, W. Briggs [1897] viii, [9]-119p. front. 19cm.

A description of the social life and customs of the settlers. Shortt

1502 **McLean**, Thomas Alexander
A dream of the past, present, and future. Written for the Calgary Tribune, April 3rd, 1889. [Calgary? 1897?] 4p. Not seen.

Ms. note: I have had a few of these printed for our own family and for one or two of our father's oldest & best friends. E.T.F., 31 Dec. 1897. Amtmann, no.24

1503 Manitoba as it is today. [Winnipeg, Stovel Co., c1897] cover-title, 32p. illus. 20 1/2cm. Man. Leg.

1504 **Manitoba Club**
The act of incorporation, constitution, rules and regulations and list of members of the Manitoba Club, established 1874. [Winnipeg] Stovel [1897] 33p. 17cm. Arkin

1505 **Mathers**, C.W., photographer
Souvenir of the Edmonton district. New York, Albertype Co., c1897. [16] plates. 14 x 18cm.

Photographs only, no text. Rutherford

1506 **Mathers**, C.W., photographer
Souvenir – Queen's diamond jubilee celebration at Edmonton, N.W.T., June 22-23, 1897. New York, Albertype Co. [1897] [16] plates. 14 x 18cm.

Photographs only, no text. Rutherford

1507 **Morin,** J[ean] B[aptiste]
La terre promise aux Canadiens-Français; le Nord-Ouest Canadien. Ottawa, 1897. 26p. plates, fold. map. 25cm. Rutherford

1508 **Morton,** James
Polson's probation. A story of Manitoba. Toronto, William Briggs, 1897. v, [7]-368p. 19cm.
Fiction. Shortt

1509 **Newton,** William
Twenty years on the Saskatchewan, N.W. Canada. London, Elliot Stock, 1897. vi, [2], 184p. incl. front. (port.) illus. plate. 20cm.
The Church of England missionary was stationed at Edmonton. Shortt

1510 **Percy,** Algernon Heber
Journal of two excursions in the British North West territory in North America by Algernon Heber Percy and Mrs. Heber Percy, 1877 & 1878. Market Drayton, Eng., Printed for private circulation by Bennion & Horne [1897?] 33p. 13 photos. (incl. front., ports.) fold. map (in pocket) 28cm. Yale

1511 **Perry,** C[harles] E[benezer]
Hon. N. Clarke Wallace, Grand Master Loyal Orange Association of British America. His action on the 'Remedial Bill' and what led up to it. With an appendix by Rev. W.W. Colpitts. Author's edition. [n.p.] 1897. ix, [11]-138p. incl. front., port. 19cm. Cover dated 1901. Shortt

1512 [**Scott,** Sir Richard William]
Synopsis of the Manitoba School Case with appendix of explanatory documents. Ottawa, Government Printing Bureau, 1897. 48p. 24 1/2cm. Can. Arch.

1513 **Thomson Brothers**
Beauties and industries of Alberta, illustrated in photogravure. Calgary, c1897. [17]l. (16 of illus) 14 x 19cm. cover-title: The Alberta Souvenir Album. Glenbow

1514 Not used

1515 **Young,** Egerton R[yerson]
On the Indian trail; stories of missionary work among the Cree and Saulteaux Indians. New York, F.H. Revell Co., 1897. 214p. front. (port.) plates. 20cm. Shortt

1516 **Young,** George
Manitoba memories, leaves from my life in the prairie province, 1868-1884. With introduction by Rev. Alexander Sutherland. Toronto, William Briggs, 1897. 364p. front., illus., plates, port. 19cm.
The most interesting portion of the book deals with the rebellion. The author was Thos. Scott's chaplain. Shortt

1517 [**Anonymous**]
Calgary route to the Klondyke gold fields; description of routes; miners' and prospectors' outfitting guide. [Calgary, 1898] 10p., 1 l. 14cm. N.Y.

1518 **[Anonymous]**
How to get to the Klondike; the safest, best and cheapest route to Yukon gold fields is via the Regina, Prince Albert, Green Lake, and Fort McMurray water routes. Prince Albert, 1898. 29p. illus., 2 fold. maps. 22cm. Can. Arch.

1519 **Atkinson**, George E.
Game birds of Manitoba. Winnipeg, Manitoba Free Press, 1898. cover-title, 21p. incl. illus., plate. 22cm. (Hist. & Sc. Soc. of Man., no.51) Shortt

1520 **Bailey**, J.C.
A synopsis of the Hudson's Bay railways and the capabilities and possibilities of the country traversed by the same. [Toronto, 1898] cover-title, 7p. Amtmann - 92-23

1521 **Begin**, Louis Nazaire
Lettre pastorale de Monseigneur l'Archevêque de Cyrène, administrateur de l'Archidiocèse de Québec, promulgant l'Encyclique 'Affari Vos' sur les écoles du Manitoba ... [Québec, 1898] caption-title, 1 l., 17p. Winnipeg

1522 Binder twine and farmers' interests. [n.p., 1898] cover-title, 6p. 21cm. Tanghe

1523 **Bjarnason**, Jóhann Magnús
Ljódmaeli. Ísafjördur, Skúli Thoroddsen, 1898. 128p. 15 1/2cm. U. of M.

1524 **Blais**, M[oïse] J.
Le Manitoba. Renseignements et conseils aux Canadiens-Français de la Province de Québec et des États-Unis. Ottawa, Imprimerie de l'État, 1898. 52p. illus., map. 19 1/2cm.

A new enlarged edition was published in 1902. See Entry 1671. Can. Arch.

1525 **Bryce**, George
John Black, the apostle of the Red River; or, How the blue banner was unfurled on Manitoba prairies. Toronto, William Briggs, 1898. viii, [9]-159p. front., illus., port. 19cm.

The majority of the Selkirk settlers were Presbyterian but they did not have a minister of their own until the arrival of Rev. J. Black in 1851. In the Ecclesiastical and Missionary Record, v.8-9, 1851-53, are found letters and digests of letters by Rev. J. Black and Alexander Ross on the early struggles of Presbyterianism in the colony. Shortt

1526 **C., A.L.O.**
The story of a dark plot; or, Tyranny on the frontier. By. A.L.O.C. Montreal, Lovell, 1898. 197p. plates, ports. (incl. front.) 20cm.

On the dismissal of William W. Smith, a temperance agitator, from the service of the C.P.R. Br. Mus.

1527 **Canada.** Department of the Interior
Canada; ein oogslag op de verschillende provincie. Aanmerkingen voor Belgische en Hollandsche kolonisten ... uitg voor Belgie en Holland. Ottawa, Drukhij van den Staat, 1898. 35p. illus., fold. map. 21 1/2cm.

This copy bears the stamp of 'D. Treau de Coeli, agent du Gouvernment du Canada en Belgique.' Antwerp

1528 **Canada.** Department of the Interior
A guide to homesteaders in Manitoba and the territories of Western Canada; hints to settlers ... Ottawa, Government Printing Office, 1898. 29, [3]p. illus. 19cm. L.C.

1529 **Canada.** Department of the Interior
Notes from Kansas and Michigan delegates' reports. [Ottawa? 1898] 24p.
30,000 copies printed. Interior, 1899

1530 **Canada.** Department of the Interior
Regulations governing the granting of yearly licenses to cut timber on Dominion lands in Manitoba, the North-West Territories and within 20 miles on either side of the Canadian Pacific Railway in the Province of British Columbia, approved by order in council, dated the 1st of July, 1898. [Ottawa, 1898] 12p. 25cm. Glenbow

1531 **Canada.** Department of the Interior
Reports of the United States delegates on Western Canada. Ottawa, Govt. Printing Bureau, 1898. 80p. 16cm. Can. Arch.

1532 **Canada.** Department of the Interior
Some of the advantages of Western Canada. Practical farmers give their experience. Ottawa, 1898. 16p. 15 1/2cm.
Letters from settlers at Alameda. Can. Arch.

1533 **Canada.** Department of the Interior
The wonders of Western Canada. A U.S. press correspondent's graphic description. Ottawa, Government Printing Bureau, 1898. 38, [1]p. incl. illus. 19 1/2cm. Shortt

1534 **Canada Siftings,** Russell, Man.
... Russell County ... History of its early settlement, soil, timber, water, etc. Convenience to railways. Homesteads open for settlement or for sale. The banner county of the province. Russell, Canada Siftings' print [1898?] [16]p. plates. 21cm. Man. Leg.

1534A Canada as a home for the Scotch agriculturist. The nearest British colony ... Glasgow, John Horn, printer [1898] caption-title, [4]p. 21cm. Can. Arch. (ms.)

1535 **Canadian Pacific Railway**
Going to Western Canada. [n.p., 1898?] cover-title, 16p. illus., fold. map. 16cm.
Gives the intending settler a few tips about his railway journey. Man. Leg.

1536 **Church of England.** Diocese of Calgary
Proceedings of the fifth meeting of the Synod of the Diocese of Calgary held July 13th, 14th and 15th, 1898, at Calgary, Alberta, N.W.T. With appendices. Calgary, Alberta Tribune Job Print, 1898. 42p. fold. table. 17cm. C.M.S. - 46

1537 **The Colonist**, Winnipeg
... Summer souvenir number, 1898; Western Canada illustrated. Winnipeg, Bulman, 1898. cover-title, 84p. illus., port. 31cm.

Contains advertising. Tanghe

1538 **Cuverille**, [Jules-Marie-Armand, Cavelier] de
Le Canada et les intérêts français, par le vice amiral de Cuverille. Paris, Joseph André et Cie, 1898. viii, [9]-79p. 18 1/2cm. Collection Gagnon

1539 **Field**, Septimus
Timely remarks, by Septimus Field; and letters from Western Canadian settlers. Ottawa, Government Printing Bureau, 1898. 24p. illus. 19cm. Shortt

1540 [**Gaire**, Jean M.J.]
Dix années de missions au grand Nord-Ouest canadien. Lille, Imprimerie de l'orphelinat de Dom Bosco, 1898. 216p. 22 1/2cm. (Bibliothèque canadienne)

An account of Father Gaire's colonization activities in southwestern Manitoba, written to persuade more of his compatriots to emigrate. St. Sulpice

1541 [**Gaire**, Jean M.J.]
La question des écoles catholiques et françaises du Manitoba (Canada); appel à la France et la Belgique. Lille, Imprimerie de l'orphelinat de Dom Bosco, 1898. 11p.

Cited in the preface by Mgr Langevin to Cuverille's 'Le Canada et les Intérêts Français.' U.C.

1541A **Girls' Home of Welcome Association**
Annual report. Winnipeg, McIntyre Bros., 1898-1913. 13v. 19cm.

Reports were issued annually. The cover usually carried a photograph of the home for recently arrived immigrant young women. Can. Arch. (ms.)

1542 **Graham**, [Sir] F[rederik] U[lric]
Notes of a sporting expedition in the far west of Canada, 1847. Explanatory footnotes by Jane Hermione Graham. London, Printed for private circulation only, 1898. 4p.l., 120p. col. front. (port.), col. plates, maps. 33 1/2cm.

Author travelled with the fur brigade from Sault Ste Marie to Fort Garry, then overland on horseback to Fort Edmonton and back to Fort Garry. U. of A.

1543 **Hudson's Bay Company**
History of the Hudson's Bay Company. The oldest trading corporation in the world. Its relation to the development of the great Northwest and the gold discoveries of California, British Columbia and Klondike. [Chicago, John F. Higgins] 1898. 101p. illus., plate, map. 24cm. Man. Leg.

1544 **Johnstone**, Catherine Laura
The young emigrants; a story for boys. London, T. Nelson [1898] 171p. plates. 19cm.

Fiction. Prairie setting. Glenbow

1545 **MacBeth**, R[oderick] G[eorge]
The making of the Canadian West, being the reminiscences of an eye-witness. Toronto, William Briggs [1898] x, 11-230p. front., illus., plates, ports. 19cm.

A revised and enlarged edition was published in 1905. L.C.

1546 **McDougall**, John
Pathfinding on plain and prairie; stirring scenes of life in the Canadian North-West. Toronto, W. Briggs, 1898. ix, [10]-277p. front., plates. 18 1/2cm.

Describes the missionary's experiences, 1865-68. Shortt

1547 Manitoba i polnocno zachodnie terytora: Assiniboia, Alberta, Saskatchewan, w ktorych znajduja, sie swiezo odkryte poklady zlota Yukonu; informacye dotyczace zasobow i klimatu tych krajow dla rolnikow, hodowcow bydla i gornikow. Detroit, Mich., Niedzieli, 1898. 31p. illus., fold. map. 24cm.

Polish immigration pamphlet. Can. Arch.

1548 **Martin**, Archer [Evans Stringer]
The Hudson's Bay Company's land tenures and the occupation of Assiniboia by Lord Selkirk's settlers, with a list of grantees under the Earl and the company, by Archer Martin. London, William Clowes and Sons, 1898. ix p., 3 l., 238p. front. (port.) 2 fold. maps, 2 fold. plans. 25 1/2cm.

The author was concerned with the legality of land titles along the Red River. The book contains transcriptions of original documents. Shortt

1549 **Moberly**, Walter, comp.
Eight routes to the Klondyke. With tables of distances, cost of outfits, map of routes, and other information. Winnipeg, Colonist [1898] 56p. fold. map. 22cm.

Advertisements interspersed in paging. B.C. Arch.

1550 [**Murray**, D.L.]
Breezy reminiscences of Manitoba, by an older settler. Glasgow, Murray & Gilchrist [1898?] 100, [4]p. illus. (incl. ports.) 18 1/2cm

A curious collection of sketches and anecdotes about Manitoba. Man. Leg.

1551 [**Patrick**, Thomas Alfred]
Facts bearing on the future of the North-West Territories. Compiled for electors of Yorkton. Yorkton, Printed at the Yorkton Enterprise office, 1898. 10p. fold. map. 22cm. U. of S.

1552 **Russell**, Frank
Exploration in the far north. Being the report of an expedition under the auspices of the University of Iowa during the years 1892, '93, and '94. [Iowa City] The University, 1898. 290p. illus., port., fold. map. 25cm.

While most of the volume relates to the Mackenzie River valley, there is valuable information on the lower Saskatchewan valley, and on southern Alberta. U. of A.

1553 Souvenir of Winnipeg, Manitoba. [Winnipeg? 1898] folder. ([12]p.) of illus. 16 1/2cm.

A folder of views of the city. Shortt

1554 **Virden, Man.** Board of Trade
Manitoba farm lands open for settlement in the districts of Virden, Griswold, Oak Lake, Routledge, Hargrave, Elkhorn, Deleau, Findlay, Pipestone, Reston. [Winnipeg, Bulman Bros. & Co. 1898] [24]p. illus., fold. map. facsims. 22cm. Man. Leg.

1555 **Udden,** Svante
Fran Canada. Rock Island, Ill., Lutheran Augustana Book Concerns, 1898. 92p. 18 1/2cm.

Describes immigrant colonies and religious groups in Western Canada with special emphasis on Lutherans of the Minnesota Conference of the Augustana Synod. Sweden

1556 **Walrond Ranche Company, Limited**
The New Walrond Ranche Company Limited. Letters patent, by-laws, shareholders. Montreal [1898] 19, [1] 21cm. Can. Arch.

1557 **Winnipeg.** City Council
The Winnipeg district; city and farm lands adjacent. Winnipeg, Buckle Printing Co., 1898. [22]p. illus., fold. map. 22cm. Man. Leg.

1558 **Winnipeg.** City Council
Winnipeg distriktet. Staden och kring liggande farmland. Winnipeg, Buckle Printing Co. Ltd., 1898. [24]p. illus., fold. map. 23cm.

On cover: The Winnipeg district, the city and farm lands adjacent, 1898. Swedish edition. Uppsala

1559 **Atkinson,** [George] E.
Manitoba birds of prey and the small mammals destroyed by them. Winnipeg, Stovel Co., 1899. cover-title, 16p. incl. illus., plate. 22 1/2cm. (Hist. & Sc. Soc. of Man., no.53) Shortt

1560 **Benoit,** [Joseph Paul-Augustin]
L'anglomanie au Canada. Résumé historique de la question des écoles du Manitoba. Trois-Rivières, Trifluvien, 1899. 61p. 25.1/2cm. Collection Gagnon

1561 British settlers in Western Canada. [n.p., 1899?] 1p.l., iv, 57, [1]p. illus. Br. Mus.

1562 **Bryce,** Mrs. Marion (Samuel)
Historical sketch of the charitable institutions of Winnipeg. Winnipeg, Manitoba Free Press, 1899. cover-title, 31p. incl. illus., plate. 21cm. (Hist. & Sc. Soc. of Man., no.54) Shortt

1563 **Canada.** Department of the Interior
Delegates' reports and settlers' experiences in Western Canada, 1899. [Ottawa, The Department, 1899] 142, [2]p. illus. 21cm.

A compilation of reports by American farm delegates from the western states. Man. Leg.

1564 **Canada.** Department of the Interior
The resources of Western Canada. Timely remarks and useful information. Ottawa, Govt. Printing Bureau, 1899. 63p. illus.

Cover-title: Ten minutes talk about Western Canada. U. of T.

1565 **Canada.** Department of the Interior
Western Canada and its great resources; the testimony of settlers, farm delegates and high authorities, with a preface on the causes of failure and success in N.-W. farming. [Ottawa, 1899] 38p. Not seen. Higgins

1566 **Canada.** Department of the Interior
Western Canada. Manitoba and the Northwest Territories, Assiniboia, Alberta, Saskatchewan. Information as to the resources and climates of these countries for intending farmers, ranchers, etc. Printed under authority of Hon. Clifford Sifton. Ottawa, 1899. 73, [4]p. incl. illus. 24cm. Shortt

1567 **Canada.** Department of the Secretary of State
Copies of all orders in council, memorials, correspondence and every other document in connection with the granting of 150,000 acres of public lands in favor of the University of Manitoba, and the transfer and patenting of the same to the university. [Ottawa, 1899] 32p. 25cm. (Canada. Sess. papers, 1899, no.48) U. of S.

1568 **The Canadian Colonization Prospecting, Transport and Produce Trading Association**
Canadian colonization scheme. What to do with our sons and daughters; the unemployed; England's poor; and the Irish agrarian questions. The problems solved. [London, 1899] cover-title, 15, [1]p. fold. plan. 25cm.

On back cover: Canadian, West Australian, and South African Land and Colonization Scheme.

Folding plan is a layout for a proposed market town with the plan of a township on verso. 'Settler's contract,' p.13-15. Br. Mus.

1569 **Canadian North-West Irrigation Company**
Irrigated lands in southern Alberta offer a promising field and great opportunity for industrious agriculturists. Lethbridge, Printed at the Lethbridge News, 1899. cover-title, 12p. 21cm. Rutherford

1570 **Canadian Pacific Railway**
Western Canada. Manitoba, Alberta, Assiniboia, Saskatchewan, and Northern Ontario. How to get there. How to select lands. How to make a home. [n.p., 1899] 80p. illus., maps (on end paper, and incl. one fold.) 21 1/2cm. H.B.C.

1571 **Church of England.** Book of Common Prayer. Blackfoot
Blackfoot prayer book. Translated by Rev. J. Hinchliffe and others. [Calgary] Calgary Herald Press, 1899. 59p. 15cm.

In Roman alphabet. Hymns: p.50-59. Glenbow

1572 **Dauphin, Man.** Municipal Office
List of electors of the village of Dauphin, Province of Manitoba, 1899. Persons entitled to vote at municipal elections. [Dauphin, 1899] [5]p. 26cm. Glenbow

1572A **The Edmonton Club, Edmonton**
Constitution, rules and regulations. v.1- 1899- Edmonton, Edmonton Post Print, 1899- v. 15cm.

Title varies. Library has: 1899, 1901, 1913. Glenbow

1573 **Elkhorn, Man.** Board of Trade
Farm lands in the district of Elkhorn, Manitoba, for settlement. Winnipeg, Bulman Bros. & Co. [1899?] cover-title, [23] p. illus., fold. map. 23cm. Man. Leg.

1574 **Fetherstonhaugh,** V.
Mrs. Jim Baker, and Frosts of June. London, Chapman & Hall, 1899. viii, 417p. Not seen.

Fiction. Said to relate to the Fort Qu'Appelle area. Br. Mus.

1575 [**FitzGibbon,** Mrs. Mary Agnes]
The Canadian Doukhobor settlements. A series of letters, by Lally Bernard [pseud.] Toronto, William Briggs, 1899. 69p. front. (map) plates. 21cm.

Letters reprinted from The Globe, Toronto. Toronto

1576 **Ford,** Charles T.
From coast to coast. A farmer's ramble through Canada, and the Canadian Pacific Railway system. Exeter [Eng.] Bearne, 1899. 34p. fold. front., plates. 17cm. B.C. Arch.

1577 [**Gordon,** Charles William]
The sky pilot; a tale of the foothills, by Ralph Connor [pseud.] Toronto, Westminster Co., 1899. 300p. 19 1/2cm.

Fiction. At least five editions and reprints were published in the next nine years in London, New York, and Chicago. Grosset and Dunlap brought out a new edition in 1940. U. of S.

1578 **Great Britain.** Commissioners appointed to carry out a scheme of colonisation in the Dominion of Canada of crofters and cottars from the Western Highlands and islands of Scotland
Crofter colonisation ... Report ... with appendices ... London, Eyre and Spottiswoode, 1890-99. 9v. 33cm. (Command Papers: c-6067, c-6287, c-6693, c-7226, c-7445, c-7738, c-8220, c-8576, c-9140)

These command papers may be found in the series of British Parliamentary Papers, arranged topically and published by the Irish University Press in recent years.

Relate to the crofter settlements at Killarney, Man., and Saltcoats, Sask. Not only do these reports supply general information on the progress of the colonies, but the appendices give very detailed reports on the progress of each individual settler.

See also Entry 1054. Eire

1579 **Lowe,** C.A., comp.
Lowe's directory of the Edmonton district, 1899. Containing full information of towns, villages and country districts, schools, churches, etc. Edmonton, Advertiser Publishing Co. [1899] 185p. 18cm.

At head of title: First year of publication.

For two interesting letters relating to the printing of this directory, see the Edmonton Journal, July 16 and Aug. 18, 1954. Edmonton

1580 **Mackie,** John
The heart of the prairie. [London?] 1899. ... Not seen.

Light fiction. Morgan, 1912

1581 **Mackie,** John
The prodigal's brother; a story of western life. London, Jarrold & Sons, 1899. 259p. Not seen.

Love and adventure at the time of the Saskatchewan Rebellion. Br. Mus.

1582 Manitoba y privnichni-zakhidni terytorii: Asiniboia, Alberta i Saskatchewan. Ynformatsiy pro zasoby i klymat dlia ril'nykiv, hodovtsi v khudoby i hirnykiv. New York, 1899. 30p. illus., fold. map. 23cm.

Ukrainian immigration pamphlet. Can. Arch.

1583 The North-West Territories Medical Register. Printed and published under the direction of the Council of the College of Physicians and Surgeons, N.-W.T. ... Prince Albert, 1899. 52p. 22cm.

'By authority.' Glenbow

1584 Ou [sic] en est exactement la question? [Winnipeg, 1899] 3p. 23cm.

En-tête: Ecoles du Manitoba. Nat. Lib.

1585 [Pesimoo mussinuhikun] 1899. Oonikup [i.e., Prospector, Sask., N.W.T., n.d.] [8]p. 16cm.

Cover-title in Cree syllabic characters. Notes and scripture quotations in Cree syllabic characters, with a calendar for 1899.
Printed by the Rev. Joseph Reader. Tanghe

1586 [**Prud'homme,** Louis Arthur]
Cinq ans après. Mgr Alexandre Taché, O.M.I., premier archevêque de Saint-Boniface. Saint-Boniface, 1899. 16p. 25cm. Can. Arch.

1587 **Willson,** [Henry] Beckles
The great Company; being a history of the Honourable Company of Merchant-Adventurers, trading into Hudson's Bay. With an introduction by Lord Strathcona and Mount Royal ... Toronto, The Copp, Clark Co., Ltd., 1899. xxii, [17]-541p. front., illus. (incl. maps, plans, facsims.) plates, ports. 24cm.

A new corrected edition in two volumes was published in London in 1900. Shortt

1588 **Young,** Egerton R[yerson]
The apostle of the north, Rev. James Evans. New York, Fleming H. Revell, 1899. 262p. front. (port.) plates. 20cm.

Wm. Briggs brought out an edition the following year. Shortt

1589 **Baldwinson,** Baldwin Lárus
Manitoba un aldamótin. [Winnipeg, 1900] cover-title, 32p. illus. Fiske

1590 [**Berns,** Richard]
Ulles van het beste. [Antwerp, n.d.] cover-title, 9p. illus. 14 1/2cm.

In this Flemish pamphlet the answer is given over the page: 'Die beste colonie om zich te vestigen is Canada.' Belgium

1591 The binder twine steal. [n.p., 1900] caption-title, 4p. 23 1/2cm.

An anti-Liberal political pamphlet relating to the sale of binder twine manufactured in Kingston Penitentiary. Can. Arch.

1592 **Bryce,** George
The inner history of Manitoba university ... Inaugural address delivered in Convocation Hall, Manitoba College, Winnipeg, November 17th, 1900. 12p. illus. 24cm.

An address delivered to the college literary society, having the same title, was published as a 10-page pamphlet. A copy of the latter is in the U. of S. Library. Can. Arch.

1593 **Bryce,** George
The remarkable history of the Hudson's Bay Company, including that of the French traders of North-Western Canada and of the North-West, XY, and Astor fur companies ... Toronto, William Briggs, 1900. xx p., 1 l., 501, [1]p. front., plates, ports., maps, facsim., coat of arms. 21 1/2cm.

This history, in contrast to B. Willson's 'Great Company,' stresses the personal struggles on this continent.
Other editions appeared in 1902 and 1910. Shortt

1594 **Burman,** W[illiam] A[lfred]
The present status of natural science in Manitoba and the Northwest. Winnipeg, Manitoba Free Press, 1900. cover-title, 23p. 22cm. (Hist. & Sc. Soc. of Man., no.55) L.C.

1595 **Canada.** Department of the Interior
Delegates' reports on Western Canada, 1900. Ottawa, 1900. 63p. illus., map (on back covers) 14 x 21cm. Agric.

1596 **Canada.** Department of the Interior
L'Ouest Canadien: province du Manitoba et Territoires du Nord-Ouest, Assiniboine, Alberta, Saskatchewan; ressources naturelles et climat de ces régions, renseignements pour les colons, cultivateurs, éleveurs, etc. Ottawa, 1900. 84p. illus. 24cm. Glenbow

1597 Canada. 160 acres fritt land till hvarje Nybyggare. [n.p., n.d.] cover-title, 26, [1]p. illus., fold. map. 22cm.

Swedish immigration pamphlet. Though this pamphlet has the same cover, illustrations and title as the Dutch pamphlet which follows, it has in addition testimonial letters, and a Swedish-English vocabulary. Can. Arch.

1598 Canada. 160 acres vryland voor ieder kolonists. [n.p., n.d.] cover-title, 16p. illus., fold. map. 22cm.

Dutch immigration pamphlet. Can. Arch.

1599 **Canadian North-West Irrigation Company**
Irrigated lands in southern Alberta. [Winnipeg, Printed by Free Press, 1900?] cover-title, 20p. illus. 22 1/2 x 28cm. Rutherford

1600 **Canadian Pacific Railway**
Amit egy tanyan tudnia kell. [n.p., n.d.] ...

Hungarian immigration pamphlet; distributed by the Canadian Pacific Railway. Glenbow

1601 **Canadian Pacific Railway**
Hvad danske Landmaend kunne udrette i Canada. [n.p., n.d.] cover-title, 14p. fold. map. 18cm.

Danish immigration folder.
Folder title freely translated as What Danes can do in Canada. Can. Arch.

1602 **Carre,** William H.
Art work on Winnipeg, Manitoba, Canada. [Winnipeg] 1900. 12pts. in 1v. plates. 35cm. Man. Leg.

1603 **Church of England**
... The traveller's spiritual provision. [Athabasca Landing? 190_?] 1v. 11 1/2cm.

Unpaged volume, one page for each day of the year. Text in Cree syllabic, day of year in English. Printed for use in the Diocese of Athabasca. Rupert's

1604 **Davin,** Nicholas Flood
Strathcona Horse. Speech at Landsdowne Park, March 7th, A.D., 1900, on the occasion of the first parade of the Strathcona Horse. Ottawa, James Hope & Sons, 1900. 20p. illus., ports. 17cm. Acadia

1605 **Ewert,** H[einrich] H.
Plan zur Foerderung des Religionsunterrichtes in den Volkschulen innerhalb der Mennonitischen Ansiedlungen Manitobas. Zu beziehen durch die Mennonitische Bildungsanstalt in Gretna, Man. [n.p., n.d.] 16p. Not seen. Bender

1606 **Fonseca,** W[illiam] G[omez da]
On the St. Paul trail in the sixties. Winnipeg, Manitoba Free Press Co., 1900. cover-title, 14p. illus. 21 1/2cm. (Hist. & Sc. Soc. of Man., no.56) Shortt

1607 **Fraser,** W[illiam] A[lexander]
Mooswa & others of the boundaries. Illustrated by Arthur Heming. New York, C. Scribner's Sons, 1900. xiv p., 1 l., 260p. front., plates. 20 1/2cm.

Fiction. Animal stories.
A revised edition was published in 1923. U. of A.

1608 Free Press, Winnipeg, Canada, 1872-1900. [Winnipeg, Free Press, 1900] cover-title, 16p. illus. 14 x 22 1/2cm. Man. Leg.

1609 **Galbraith,** J.F.
The Mennonites in Manitoba, 1875-1900. A review of their coming, their progress, and their present prosperity. Morden, Man., Chronicle presses, 1900. cover-title, 48p. incl. illus., plates. 22cm. Toronto

1610 **George,** D[avid] Lloyd
Prominent Welshmen on the resources of Western Canada. The report of Mr. D. Lloyd George ... Mr. W.J. Rees ... Mr. W. Llewellyn Williams ... on their visit to Canada in 1899. Published by the Government of Canada. Swansea, Daily Post Printing Works, 1900. cover-title, 18p. illus. 21 1/2cm.

Apparently also published in Welsh. Wales

1611 **[Gordon,** Charles William]
Christian hope, by Ralph Connor. [London] Hodder & Stoughton [n.d.] 31p. 15 1/2cm. (Silent Hour Booklets) Arkin

1612 **Haultain,** [Sir] F[rederick] W[illiam] G[ordon]
Constitutional and financial questions affecting the North-West Territories. Speech ... in the Legislative Assembly on Wednesday, the second day of May, 1900. Printed by order of the Legislative Assembly. Regina, Queen's Printer, 1900. cover-title, 16p. 30cm. In double column. U. of S.

1613 **Hunter,** Francis J[ames]
Colonel Gascoigne, V.C.; a story of travel, adventure & love. [Montreal? 190–] 274p. 19cm.

Fiction; the locale is thirty miles north of Regina. Sask. Arch. (microfilm)

1614 Kanada. Krotkie, zajmujace wiadomosci o tym kraju i o podrozy do tegoz z Europy, zestawione podlug uredowych statystycznych dat rzadu kanadyjskiego. [n.p., n.d.] ...

Polish immigration pamphlet. See note under Entry 1621. Can. Arch.

1615 **Ladies' North-West Conservative League**
Constitution and rules of ... Regina, The West Co., Ltd., 1900. [6]p. 13 1/2cm.

Ms. note on title-page: Founded by Mrs. N.F. Davin. Can. Arch.

1616 **Laut,** A[gnes] C[hristina]
Lords of the north; a romance of the North-West. New York, P.F. Collier & Son [c1900] 6p.l., 5-442p. front. 20 1/2cm.

Fiction; relates to the early fur traders.
Also published the same year by J.F. Taylor of New York. L.C.

1617 The little Manitoban. A child's story-book. Issued ... for the benefit of the Children's Aid Society of Winnipeg. Winnipeg, Manitoba Free Press Co., 1900. 5p.l., [13]-164, [2]p. front., illus. 26 1/2cm.

Stories and poems by local authors. Man. Leg.

1618 **Maclean,** John
Henry B. Steinhauer, his work among the Cree Indians of the western plains of Canada. [Toronto, Methodist Young People's Forward Movement for Missions, 19–?] 51p. illus., ports. 22cm. Rutherford

1619 **MacLeod,** N.W.
Picturesque Cardston and environments; a story of colonization and progress in southern Alberta. Cardston, N.W.T., N.W. MacLeod, 1900. 116p. front., illus., 22 plates at end of text. 21cm. On cover: Souvenir Cardston Golden Jubilee, June 28-July 3, 1937.

This is a reprint of the original pamphlet, even to the title-page. Alta. Leg.

1620 Manitoba in 1900. [n.p., 1900] cover-title, 24p. illus. 20cm. Man. Leg.

1620A **National Editorial Association**
Symposium of ideas and prophecies on the Canadian West, by the members of the National Editorial Association, and what they said in 1900. [Ottawa, Dept. of the Interior, 1900] cover-title, 42p. 7 x 15cm. Can. Arch. (ms.)

1621 **North Atlantic Trading Company, Amsterdam**
Canada. Courtes mais intéressantes informations sur le pays. Moyens de transport et de voyage d'Europe au Canada. Composés d'après des communications statis-

tiques officielles du Gouvernment du Canada. [Amsterdam? 1900?] (12)p. incl. double map. 11 x 14cm.

Also appeared in Italian: Il Canada, brevi ed interessanti comunicazioni ... Polish edition had title: Kanada, krotkie zajmujace wiadomosci ... Probably printed in other languages as well. Can. Arch.

1622 **Martel** (Wm. A.) & Sons
Illustrated souvenir of Souris, Manitoba. Brandon [n.d.] 76p., incl. 64p. of illus. 18 x 24cm.

Probably published in 1902. Glenbow

1623 **Osborn**, Edward Bolland
Greater Canada; the past, present and future of the Canadian North-West. London, Chatto and Windus, 1900. 244p. fold. map.

An English journalist attempts to interpret the West to Englishmen. B.C. Arch.

1624 Plants of Manitoba. [Belfast & London & New York, Marcus Ward & Co. Ltd., 1896?] 40 col. plates bound in a portfolio. 26cm.

Title from portfolio cover. Part II of George Bryce's 'Our Canadian prairies, being a description of the most notable plants of Manitoba.' Trinity

1625 **Saxby**, C.F. Argyll
The call of honour; a tale of adventure in the Canadian prairies. London [190–] 318p. illus. 19cm.

Juvenile fiction. Arkin

1626 **Saxby**, [C.F.] Argyll
The fiery totem; a tale of adventure in the Canadian North-West. London, Religious Tract Society [190–] 222, [1]p. front. 20cm.

Juvenile literature. Br. Mus.

1627 **Somers-Cocks**, Henry Lawrence
Trials of a tenderfoot. [n.p., n.d.] 63p. illus. 19cm.

Reminiscences of working on a farm at Pense, Sask., during 1883-85. Glenbow

1628 **Stovel Company Limited, Winnipeg**
A Winnipeg souvenir. [Winnipeg, 19_ _] [31]p. incl. plates (part. mounted and col.) Hamilton

1629 Vester Canada ... Alit Islendinga a Canada eftir margra ára reynslu. Gefid út ad tilhlutun Canadastjornar. Til útbýtingar. [Winnipeg] 1900. cover-title, 66p. illus., map. Fiske

1630 **Wiebe**, Gerhard
Ursachen und Geschichte der Auswanderung der Mennoniten aus Russland nach Amerika. Von Gerhard Wiebe, Aeltester der Gemeinde zu Bergthal, Russland; gestorben zu Chortitz, Man., am 3, mai 1900. Winnipeg, Der Nordwesten Publishing Co. [1900] 56p. Not seen. Bender (In Goshen College Lib., Goshen, Ind.)

1631 **Wigle**, Hamilton
The life story of Finlay Booth. [c1900] vi, 7-55p. ports. 19cm. Bound with Dezell, R.: A Night on the Prairie.

Booth was caught in a winter storm in Manitoba, and as a result his hands and feet had to be amputated.
Originally published as a separate in 1900; this edition was published in 1907. See Entry 1927. Shortt

1632 **Young**, Egerton R[yerson]
Indian life in the great Northwest. London, S.W. Partridge and Co., 1900. 126p. incl. front., illus., plates. 19cm. L.C.

1633 **Zilliacus**, Konni
Kanada såsom mål för emigranter från den europeiska Norden. Stockholm, Tidskrift Nordisk, 1900. ... Svensk Bokkatalog

1634 **Aikins & Pepler**
List of farm lands improved and unimproved in Manitoba, for sale at low prices and on easy terms of payment. For full particulars and terms apply to Aikins, 451 Main Street, Winnipeg, Manitoba. Winnipeg, Free Press Co., 1901. cover-title, 45p. 21cm. Man. Arch.

1635 **American Land and Loan Company**
The Winnipeg district; farm lands adjacent. [Winnipeg? 1901] cover-title, 24p. illus. 21cm. Man. Leg.

1636 **Bindloss**, Harold
A sower of wheat. London, Chatto & Windus, 1901. vi, 373p.
Fiction. Locale said to be the English colony at Cannington Manor in southeastern Saskatchewan. Exaggerated account. Br. Mus.

1637 **Bryce**, George
Manitoba College thirty years old. Winnipeg, 1901. 15p. illus. Can. Arch.

1638 [**Bryce**, George]
William Silvering's surrender; a story of western experiences. Published under the auspices of the Canadian Forestry Association. Winnipeg, Prepared by Winnipeg Forestry Association, 1901. 96p. front., plates. 18cm.
Written to encourage tree planting. Shortt

1639 **Bryce**, Mrs. Marion (Samuel)
Early Red River culture. Winnipeg, Manitoba Free Press, 1901. cover-title, 16p. illus. (incl. ports.) 22cm. (Hist. & Sc. Soc. of Man., no.57) Shortt

1640 **Campbell**, Roderick
The father of St. Kilda; twenty years in isolation in the sub-Arctic territory of the Hudson's Bay Company. London, W.R. Russell & Co., 1901. xv, 327p. front. 20cm.
The sub-title is deceptive, as the author spent much of his 18 years in the West near Fort Garry and along the Saskatchewan. Relates to the 1860's and 1870's. An unreliable account. Hudson's Bay House

1641 **Canada**. Department of the Interior
Officiell handbok ... [1901 ed. n.p., 1901] 95p.
A Swedish pamphlet. The illustrations are the same as those in the 1894 edition. Uppsala

1642 **Canada.** Department of the Secretary of State
Copies of all memorials, replies thereto and correspondence between the Government of the North-West Territories and any member thereof, and the Government of Canada, and any member thereof, on the subject of the financial status or constitutional status of the said North-West Territories. [Ottawa, 1901] 13p. 25cm. (Canada. Sess. papers, 1901, no.91) U. of S.

1643 **Canadian North-West Irrigation Company**
The age of insurance for farmers, by W.H. Fairfield ... and views of our clergymen, doctors and settlers. Lethbridge [1901] cover-title, 34p. illus. 21cm. Rutherford

1644 **Canadian Pacific Railway**
Western Canada: Manitoba, Assiniboia, Alberta, Saskatchewan and Northern Ontario; how to get there, how to select lands, how to make a home. [Ottawa] 1901. 80p. illus., 2 maps (1 fold., 1 on p.2 of cover) tables. 21cm.

Imperfect: fold. map mutilated. Glenbow

1645 **Church of England.** Hymns. Cree
Hymns in the syllabic characters for the use of the Cree Indians in the Diocese of Athabasca. Athabasca Landing, Printed at St. Matthew's Mission, 1901. 114, [9]p. 17cm.

Illustration on title-page. Rupert's

1646 **De Vos,** Robert
Canada. La colonisation agricole dans l'Ouest. Extrait de Recueil consulaire Belge (T.112). Brussels, P. Weissenbruch, 1901. 112p. 22cm.

Based on a tour of the West made during April 1900. St. Sulpice

1647 **Doukhobors**
Obrashchenie Kanadskykh' Dukhoborov' ko vsiem' liu diam', i druhie dokument' i po stolknoveniu nkh' s' Kanadskym' pravytel' stvom s' predysloviem' P. Byriukov. [Notice of the Canadian Doukhobors to all peoples, and other documents concerning their clash with the Canadian government, with a preface by P. Byriukov] Geneva, Onex, 1901. 64p. 15 1/2cm. Not seen. Br. Mus.

1648 **Fetherstonhaugh,** Mrs. V.
A younger son. London, Downey & Co., 1901. vii, 331p. Br. Mus.

1649 **Fox,** Charles
The land of lasses few; a tale of the Canadian prairies. London, F.R. Henderson, 1901. 91p. 19cm.

Fiction. Story of two Yorkshire girls who find romance and marriage on the bachelor frontier some forty miles north of Regina. U. of Man.

1650 **Hinch & Son, Carman, Man.**
Manitoba, Carman-Winnipeg district; Red River valley lands. [Winnipeg] Manitoba Free Press [1901] cover-title, 32p. illus. 22cm.

Description of the district and a list of farm lands for sale by Hinch & Son. Man. Leg.

1651 **Jonasson,** Sigtryggur
The early Icelandic settlements in Canada. Winnipeg, Manitoba Free Press Co., 1901. cover-title, 15p. 22cm. (Hist. & Sc. Soc. of Man., no.59) Shortt

1652 [**Lacombe,** Albert]
Memoirs on the half-breeds of Manitoba and the territories of the Canadian North West. [n.p., 1901] 11p. 23cm. Author's autographed copy.

This missionary for many years had advocated placing all half-breeds in one large colony under the supervision of the Roman Catholic Church. He retained faith in the project until the settlement he established proved a failure. Shortt

1653 **Law Society of the North-West Territories**
Rules and regulations. Incorporated 1898. Promulgated 1st May, 1901. Regina, Printed at The Leader office, 1901. 35p. 20cm. Shortt

1654 **McCaig,** J[ames]
The story of the climate of southern Alberta, the Colorado of Canada. Lethbridge, Canadian Northwest Irrigation Company [1901] [15]p. illus. 21cm.

Written to prove the mildness of the winters. Man. Leg.

1655 **McLean,** William John
Notes and observations of travels on the Athabasca and Slave Lake regions in 1899, by W.J. McLean. Winnipeg, Manitoba Free Press Co., 1901. cover-title, 7p. illus. 22cm. (Hist. & Sc. Soc. of Man., no.58) Shortt

1656 **Manitoba.** Department of Agriculture and Immigration
Canada's centre is Manitoba, the famous wheat growing and cattle raising province of the North-West. A British colony open to all offers land, liberty, prosperity. [Winnipeg, 1901?] cover-title, 161p. illus., fold. map. 25cm.

Information is arranged by municipality. Man. Leg.

1657 **North West Territories.** Department of Agriculture
The Canadian North-West Territories; an official handbook containing reliable information concerning their resources. Compiled and published under the direction of G.H.V. Bulyea, Commissioner of Agriculture. Winnipeg, Stovel Co., 1901. 72p. illus., double map. 26cm. Rutherford

1658 **Richmond,** W.R.
The life of Lord Strathcona. London, Collins [n.d.] 246p. front. 16cm.

This biography went on sale in London book shops one morning, but by 2:00 p.m. all copies were withdrawn by the publisher under threat of legal action by the biographee who was at that time Canadian High Commissioner. Any copies extant were privately purchased that one morning. The bibliographer has seen two copies. Man. Leg.

1659 **Roblin,** R[odmond] P[alen]
Full text of the Indian Head debate. Held at Indian Head, Assa., on the evening of December 18th, 1901, by the Hon. R.P. Roblin, Premier of Manitoba, and Hon. F.W.G. Haultain, Premier of the N.-W. Territories, at the invitation of four hundred residents of the district, for the purpose of discussing the comparative advantages of union with Manitoba and Mr. Haultain's autonomy policy. [n.p., 1901?] 28p. 24cm. Rutherford

1660 **Société de Colonisation de la Rivière-la-Paix**
Le Nord-Ouest. Athabaska. Préliminaires, site, bornes, sol, étendue, climat, mines, etc. Forêts et rivières, établissements, missions, chemins, communications, conclusion. Montréal, Publié par la Société de Colonisation de la Rivière-la-Paix, 1901. 32p. fold. map. 13cm. Amtmann - 214-617

1661 **Stonewall, Man.** Board of Trade
The Stonewall district; a desirable district for mixed farming. Stonewall, 1901. [32]p. illus. (incl. facsims.) fold. map. 22cm. Man. Leg.

1661A **Stuart**, Charles A[llan]
Our territorial lands; a brief statement of the case for provincial control of the crown domain, being an address delivered before the Young Men's Liberal Club of Calgary. [Calgary, The Albertan, 1901] cover-title, 11p. 20cm. Alta. Arch.

1662 **Territorial Grain Growers' Association**
Constitution and by-laws. Indian Head, Vidette print [1901] cover-title, 6p. 15cm.

The beginning of an important farm movement. Sask. Arch.

1663 **Wetaskiwin, Alta.** Board of Trade
Wetaskiwin, the railway junction town and prosperous commercial centre of Alberta, Canada and district. Published for the information of manufacturers, investors and settlers at The Times, Wetaskiwin, Alberta, N.W.T., Canada [190-?] cover-title, [34]p. illus. 22cm.

Corrigendum slip inserted facing p.[6].
Last 16p. contain advertising matter. Glenbow

1664 **[Anonymous]**
North-West government; a brief review of the political situation. [n.p., 1902] cover-title, 46p. 20cm.

Published in the interests of the Haultain government. Rutherford

1665 **Bach**, R[udolph]
Eine Reise durch das westliche Canada im Sommer 1902. Montreal, 1902. 20p. Not seen. Lehmann

1666 **Barr**, I[saac] M[ontgomery]
British settlements in North Western Canada on free grant lands. Canada for the British. [London, 1902] 15p. Private copy

1667 **Barr**, I[saac] M[ontgomery]
British settlements in North-Western Canada on free grant lands. Canada for the British. Report of my journey to the Saskatchewan Valley, N.W. Canada, to select land for the first British colony ... [London, 1902] cover-title, 24p. incl. map. Lyle

1668 **Barr**, I[saac] M[ontgomery]
British settlements in North-Western Canada on free grant lands. Report on my journey to the Saskatchewan valley. [London, 1902] 24p. map. 21 1/2cm.

A prospectus by the organizer of the famous Barr colony. He is said to have issued five pamphlets and a leaflet. See Wetton: The Promised Land. U. of S.

1669 [**Barr**, Isaac Montgomery]
To the members of the first British colony organized to form a settlement in North-Western Canada. [London, 1902] caption-title, 11p.

In the form of a letter: Oak Lawn, Holly Park, Crouch Hill [London]. Christmas, 1902. Dear Friends. Lyle

1670 **Bellamy**, Herbie
A sketch of the life of Herbie Bellamy. Toronto, Printed by the Women's Missionary Society of the Methodist Church, 1902. 29p. plates.

Relates to the Moose Jaw area. Amtmann - 176-14

1671 **Blais**, Moïse J.
Le Manitoba; renseignements et conseils aux Canadiens-Français de la Province de Québec et des États-Unis. Ottawa, 1902. 74p. illus., fold. col. map. 19cm. B.C. Arch.

1671A **The Bulletin, Edmonton**
The Edmonton district of the Saskatchewan valley. Information for intending settlers. Edmonton, The Bulletin Co. Ltd., 1902. cover-title, 80p. 27cm.

Pagination includes advertising. A 4-page prospectus with the same title was issued to prospective advertisers. Can. Arch. (ms.)

1672 [**Bulman**, William John]
The wondrous West. Winnipeg, Bulman Bros. & Co. [1902] cover-title, [48]p. illus. 17 x 26cm.

Coloured pictorial covers.
Chiefly on Winnipeg and Manitoba. Glenbow

1672A **Canada**. Department of the Interior
Free farms. The land of the future. [Ottawa, 1902?] folder. 16p. illus., map. 23cm. Can. Arch. (ms.)

1673 **Canada**. Department of the Interior
Manitoba. The land of No.1 hard and grass-fed steers. [Ottawa, 1902] 24p. illus. Canner - 474-206

1674 **Canada**. Department of the Interior
Atlas de l'Ouest canadien, contenant les cartes géographiques des provinces ... des districts ... et de la Puissance du Canada. Ottawa [1902] cover-title, 33, [1]p. illus., maps. 28cm. Glenbow

1675 **Canada**. Department of the Interior
Facts relating to Western Canada. [London, 1902] cover-title, 47, [1]p. illus. 19 1/2cm. Can. Arch.

1676 **Canada**. Department of the Secretary of State
Documents relating to payments in connection with Manitoba school lands ... Ottawa, Printed by S.E. Dawson, 1902. 1p.l., 59p. 25cm. (Canada. Sess. papers, 1902, no.83) U. of S.

1676A **Canadian Pacific Railway**
The Saskatchewan valley, Alberta. The undisposed of C.P.R. lands shown on this map of the Saskatchewan valley are for sale at the uniform price of $3 an acre.

Winnipeg, 1902. folder. 14p. large col. map on verso. folds to 26 x 11 1/2cm. Can. Arch. (ms.)

1677 **Church of England.** Ecclesiastical Province of Rupert's Land
The Indian missions ... Fourth triennial report (1899, 1900, 1901), to the provincial synod, 1902, [n.p., 1902] 31p. 21cm.

Other reports in series not seen. Sask. Arch.

1678 **Church of England.** Hymns. Cree
Cree hymns in English characters for use in the Diocese of Athabasca. Athabasca Landing, 1902. [90]p. 17cm.

The Newberry Library has a 1901 edition of 114, [9]p. with a title-page vignette of the mission church. Rupert's

1679 **Conybeare,** C[harles] F[rederick] P[ringle]
Vahnfried. London, Kegan Paul, Trench, Trubner & Co., 1902. 196p. 18cm.

Poetry. Rutherford

1680 **Dugas,** Georges
The first Canadian woman in the Northwest; or, The story of Marie Anne Gaboury, wife of John Baptiste Lajimoniere, who arrived in the Northwest in 1807, and died at St. Boniface at the age of 96 years. Translated by Miss J.M. Morice. Winnipeg, The Manitoba Free Press, 1902. cover-title, 32p. 22 1/2cm (Hist. & Sc. Soc. of Man., no.62) Shortt

1681 Esterház, Magyar colonia, Ejsjak-nyugati Tartományok Kanada. Levelek a telepesektöl s fenykepfelvetelek, melyeket a helyszinén vettek fel 1902, julius havaban. Ottawa, Kormanyzosagi nyomda, 1902. 84p. illus. (incl. group ports.) fold. plan. 22cm.

Written, at least in part, by Count P.O. d'Esterhazy, this pamphlet describes the Hungarian colony at Esterhazy, Sask.
Published also in English as a 67-page pamphlet. L.C.

1682 **Hunt,** Frank L[arned]
Britain's one Utopia. Winnipeg, The Manitoba Free Press, 1902. cover-title, 16p. 22 1/2cm. (Hist. & Sc. Soc. of Man., no.61)

Relates to the Red River Settlement. Shortt

1683 Länsi-Canadan kehitys. [Göteborg, Nyaste Snällposten, 1902] caption-title, [47]p. 30 1/2cm.

In three columns.
This pamphlet was an article reprinted from the Saturday Globe. Sweden

1684 **Leduc,** [Hippolyte]
Oraison funèbre de Mgr V.J. Grandin, premier évêque de St-Albert (Canada) 10 juin 1902. [St-Boniface] Manitoba [1902] 21p. 22cm. Oblates Arch.

1685 **McEvoy,** Bernard
From the Great Lakes to the wide West. Toronto, Wm. Briggs, 1902. 1p.l., 288p. front., plates. 19 1/2cm.

A collection of sketches originally published in the Mail and Empire. Approximately a third of the book is devoted to the prairies. Shortt

1686 **Mackie,** John
Canadian Jack. With illus. by Arthur Twidle. Toronto, Bell & Cockburn [n.d.] 280p. plates (part col.) 20cm. Glenbow

1687 **Maclean,** John
Synopsis of lectures on Manitoba and the Northwest, delivered by Rev. John Maclean, Ph.D., Carman, Man., at the Methodist Young People's Summer School, Victoria College, Toronto, Ont., July 19th to 29th, 1902. [Toronto, 1902] cover-title, 24p. illus. 20 x 10cm. (Methodist Church. Forward movement for missions. Series no.4) Glenbow

1688 **MacPherson,** R[obert] J[ames]
The influence of civilization on the North American Indian. An essay. Submitted to the Board of Studies of the University of Manitoba on the 1st of February, A.D. 1902. [Winnipeg? 1902?] cover-title, 20p. 26cm. Shortt

1689 **Martel,** W[illiam] A., and Son
Illustrated souvenir of Rapid City, Manitoba. Brandon, W.A. Martel & Son [1902] 68p. illus. 18 x 23cm.

The first 12 pages are text, the remainder illustrative plates. Arkin

1690 Representative men of Manitoba. History in portraiture. A gallery of men, whose energy, ability, enterprise and public spirit have produced the marvellous record of the prairie province. Winnipeg, Tribune Publishing Co., 1902. xxxi p. 151 plates (ports.) 24cm. 'Edition de luxe.'

Contains an introduction entitled 'Historical and commercial review of Winnipeg and Manitoba.' No biographical information with the portraits. Shortt

1691 Le serviteur de Dieu, Mgr V.-J. Grandin, Oblat de Marie Immaculée, premier évêque de Saint-Albert, mort en odeur de sainteté le 3 juin 1902. Edmonton [1902] Amtmann – 228-1070

1692 **Territorial Grain Growers' Association**
Report of the proceedings of the annual meeting held at Indian Head, Assa., on Thursday and Friday, December 4th and 5th. [Regina, The West, 1902] [30]p. 22cm. Supplement to The West, Regina. Can. Arch.

1693 En tur igjennem det vestlige Canada. [Göteborg, Nyaste Snällposten, 1902] caption-title, [4]p. 30 1/2cm.

In three columns. Sweden

1694 Vestra Canadas utveckling. [Göteborg, Nyaste Snällposten, 1902] caption-title, [4]p. 30 1/2cm.

In three columns.
This pamphlet is an article reprinted from the Saturday Globe. Sweden

1695 Western Canada. Free homes for all in the great provinces of Manitoba, Assiniboia, Saskatchewan and Alberta. [Winnipeg, 1902] 64p. illus. 21 1/2cm.

Descriptions by American delegates who had toured the West. Man. Leg.

1696 **Western Canada Press Association**
Itinerary program, Winnipeg-California. Third annual excursion, January 5 to 27, 1902. Winnipeg, Telegram Printing Co. Ltd., 1902. cover-title, [16]p. 14 x 22cm.

Mostly advertising. Last three pages describe development of Winnipeg. Sask. Arch.

1697 **Wilson,** Henry Beckles
Lord Strathcona, the story of his life. Forewords by the Duke of Argyll and the Earl of Aberdeen. London, Methuen & Co., 1902. xii, 288p. incl. front., plates, ports. 23cm.

A new edition in two volumes with the title 'Life of Lord Strathcona and Mount Royal' was published in Boston by Houghton Mifflin in 1915. U. of S.

1698 **Winnipeg.** Board of Trade
The wondrous West. [n.p., 1902] cover-title, 45, [3]p. illus. 17 1/2 x 23 1/2cm.

Dept. of the Interior correspondence suggests that the author was Fred W. Heuback. Arkin

1699 **Church of England.** Diocese. Calgary
Report on Indian missions [by Archdeacon J.W. Tims] with financial statements, list of subscribers and donors, etc., 1902. Toronto, Oxford Press, 1903. 24p. illus. 22cm. Glenbow

1700 [**Anonymous**]
The gopher's tail; a good luck bringer. In three chapters. Containing the Cree folk story of the gopher's origin, here set forth in print for the first time. Winnipeg, 1903. 23p. illus. 18cm. Not seen. Can. Arch.

1701 [**Anonymous**]
Ranching in the Canadian Northwest. [n.p., 1903] cover-title, 71p. incl. illus., map. 22 1/2cm.

Attributed in the Canadian Sessional Papers, 1904, no.25, pt.2, p.124, to a Mr. Peterson. Shortt

1702 **Atkinson,** George E.
Insectivorous birds of Manitoba. Winnipeg, Stovel Co., 1903. cover-title, 20p. illus. 22cm. (Hist. & Sc. Soc. of Man., no.60) Shortt

1703 [**Barr,** Isaac Montgomery]
British colony for the Saskatchewan Valley North-Western Canada ... To all members of the British colony who have entered for homesteads. [n.p., 1903] caption-title, 4p. Lyle

1704 [**Barr,** Isaac Montgomery]
British settlements in Canada. The Canadian co-operative home farm no.1. A practical school of training in agriculture and stock-raising. Canada for the British. Prospectus. [London, 1903] caption-title, 12p.

Also a second edition in smaller print. Lyle

1705 [**Barr,** Isaac Montgomery]
Homestead privileges. [London? 1903?] caption-title, 3p.

At head of title: Read this carefully. Lyle

1706 [**Barr**, Isaac Montgomery]
The Saskatoon & Saskatchewan Transport Co. [n.p., 1903?] caption-title, 2p.
At head of title: Provisional prospectus. Lyle

1707 **Biriukov**, Pavel Ivanovich
Dukhoborets Petr Vasil' evich Verigin ... Mezhdunarodnoi ligi antimilitaristovb. [n.p.] Librairie G. Corrtterie, 1903. 16p. 16cm.
A biography of Peter Verigin I, leader of the Doukhobors. L.C.

1707A **The Bulletin, Edmonton**
Edmonton in the great wheat belt of Canada. Information for intending settlers. Edmonton, The Bulletin Co. Ltd., 1903. cover-title, 68p. 21cm.
Can. Arch. (ms.)

1707B **Canada.** Department of the Interior
Canada, the granary of the empire. [n.p., 1903] 15, [1]p. 19cm.
Proof-sheets with note '2nd revise 27/8/03' examined in Can. Arch. No proof that a 2d revision was actually printed. Can. Arch. (ms.)

1708 **Canada.** Department of the Interior
Canada, the granary of the world. [Ottawa, 1903] [32]p. col. illus., map. 18 x 25 1/2cm.
An attractive booklet of coloured cartoons showing John Bull and Uncle Sam inspecting Western Canada. Shortt

1709 **Canada.** Department of the Interior
The evolution of the prairie by the plow. [n.p., 1903] cover-title, 47, [1]p. illus. 17 x 26cm. Man. Leg.

1710 **Canada.** Department of the Interior
Homestead regulations of North-Western Canada with an abridgement of the Dominion Lands Act. [Ottawa, 1903] 31p. fold. map. 24 1/2cm.
Shortt

1711 **Canada.** Department of the Interior
Western Canada farm lands; where and how and all about it. Information and facts for the prospective settler. [Ottawa, 1903] 22p. illus., col. map.
A folder comprising coloured map of the Dominion of Canada with text on verso.
U. of T.

1712 **Canada.** Department of the Interior
Where and how to obtain a home ... [Ottawa, 1903?] [64]p. illus., map. 17cm.
Dept. of the Interior correspondence makes reference to two pamphlets with this title, written about the same time, the one by a Mr. Foran, the other by a Mr. Magurn.
Can. Arch. (ms.)

1712A **Canada.** Department of the Interior
Wo und wie, und alles, was dabée zu wiffen nöthig thut. Informationen und thatsachen fur den landfuchenden unsiedler. Ottawa [1903] folder. 22p. illus., large map on verso. folds to 18 1/2 x 9cm.
Norwegian edition has title: Hvor og hvorledes. Swedish edition has title: Hvarets och huru. Can. Arch. (ms.)

1713 **Canada.** Department of the Secretary of State
Copies of all judgments or opinions delivered by the Supreme Court of Manitoba, touching the alleged rights of exemption from taxation, claimed by the Canadian Pacific Railway Company, in respect to the land of the said company, in the North-West Territories or in Manitoba. [Ottawa, 1903] 12p. 25cm. (Canada. Sess. papers, 1903, no.79) U. of S.

1714 **Canadian Pacific Railway**
Western Canada. Manitoba, Assiniboia, Alberta, Saskatchewan, and New Ontario. How to get there. How to select land. How to make a home. [n.p.] 1903. 80p. illus., fold. col. map. 20 1/2cm. Austria

1715 **Canadian Pacific Railway**
Words from the women of Western Canada. [n.p.] 1903. 39p. illus. Man. Leg.

1716 **Carberry, Man.**
Souvenir views of Carberry and the Big Plain. Carberry, Man., News Print, 1903. cover-title, 48 plates (incl. 2 ports.) 14 x 23cm.

Many pictures identified in manuscript. Glenbow

1717 **Cowie,** Isaac
The western plains of Canada rediscovered. [Winnipeg] 1903. cover-title, 40p. illus., map (on back cover) 8 x 15cm. Glenbow

1718 **Craig,** John R[oderick]
Ranching with lords and commons; or, Twenty years on the range, being a record of actual facts and conditions relating to the cattle industry of the North-West Territories of Canada; and comprising the extraordinary story of the formation and career of a great cattle company. Toronto, Printed for the author by W. Briggs [c1903] vi p., 1 l., 9-293p. front., plates, ports. 19 1/2cm.

The story of the Oxley ranch, written by the manager. The author arraigns the general director, Staveley Hill, an English M.P., for his mismanagement of the company. See Entry 821. Shortt

1719 **Cullum,** Ridgwell
The story of the Foss River ranch; a tale of the North-West. Boston, L.C. Page, 1903. vi, 326p. 20cm.

Fiction. L.C.

1720 **Dufferin and Ava,** Frederick Temple Hamilton-Temple-Blackwood, Marquis of
... Reprint of the 'great' speech delivered by the late Marquis of Dufferin and Ava (Governor-General of Canada) at a farewell dejeuner in the city hall, Winnipeg, in September, 1877. [n.p., 1903?] cover-title, 8p. 22 1/2cm.

At head of title: Compliments of Malcolm Stewart. See also Entry 481. Arkin

1721 **Duncan,** D[avid] M[erritt]
A history of Manitoba and the Northwest Territories for use in public schools. Toronto, W.J. Gage & Co. [1903] 140p. incl. maps. front., illus., ports. 19 1/2cm.

A school text; a revised edition was published in 1908 with the title 'The Prairie Provinces; a Short History ...' Shortt

1722 **The Eastern and Western Land Corporation, Toronto**
Canada, the granary of the world. [Toronto, 1903] 20p. illus., fold. map. 15 x 23cm.

The company's lands were on the Quill Lake plains. B.C. Arch.

1723 **Edmonton, Alta.**
Information for intending settlers. One hundred questions answered on the one hundred and sixty acre free farms in the Edmonton wheat belt. The garden of the north-west is the Edmonton district. Edmonton, Printed by the Bulletin Co., 1903. cover-title, [2], 55, [18]p. incl. covers. plates. 25cm.

The pamphlet entered under The Bulletin, Entry 1753A, is perhaps a later issue. Glenbow

1724 **Elkinton,** Joseph
The Doukhobors, their history in Russia, their migration to Canada. Philadelphia, Ferris and Leach, 1903. viii, 336p. front., plates, ports., maps (1 fold) fold. plan. 20cm.

The author, a Quaker from Philadelphia, visited the Saskatchewan colonies in the summer of 1902. The book was written to raise funds to educate the sect. U. of S.

1725 **Fraser,** William Alexander
The blood lilies. New York, C. Scribner's Sons, 1903. 3p.l., 262p. front., plates. 20cm.

Another edition was published by Briggs of Toronto. Fiction. Prairie setting. L.C.

1726 **German-American Land Co., Limited**
Wegweiser nach der Deutschen Katholischen St. Peters Colonie, im Distrikt Humboldt, Provinz Saskatchewan, Canada. Gegründet im Jahre 1903, unter den Ausspicien der hochiv. Benediktiner-Väter ... St. Cloud, Minn., German-American Land Co., Ltd., 1903? 16p. 22cm.

Relates to the founding of the large German colony around Muenster, Sask. N.Y.

1727 **Iddings,** Daniel W[ilkinson]
Observations on Canada's great West, by Daniel W. Iddings, Andrew S. Iddings, and Elam Fisher. Ottawa, Government Printing Bureau, 1903. cover-title, 32p. illus., fold. map. 20cm. Glenbow

1728 **James,** W.J., photographer
Souvenir of Prince Albert, Sask. Brooklyn, N.Y., Albertype Co. [1903?] 23 plates. 13 1/2 x 18 1/2cm. Arkin

1729 **Jonquet,** E[mile]
Mgr Grandin, Oblat de Marie Immaculée, premier évêque de Saint-Albert. Montreal [Giroux] 1903. 5p.l., v, 531p. incl. illus., plates, ports. front. 23cm. Shortt

1730 **Liberal Party** (North West Territories)
Striking comparisons. A review of the treatment of the Territories by the two political parties. [n.p., 1903?] caption-title, 11, [1]p. 21 1/2cm. Rutherford

1731 **Lloyd**, George Exton
To the members of the British colony of 1902. [Lloydminster?] 1903. caption-title, [4] p.

At head of title: Lloydminster Post Office, Britannia, N.W.T., July 3, 1903.
The letters addressed: My Dear Friends.
The second paragraph is captioned: The British colony is not dead. Lyle

1732 **Lumsden**, James
Through Canada in harvest time; a study of life and labour in the golden West. London, T.F. Unwin, 1903. 3p.l., xi-xix, 363, [1] p. incl. illus., plates. front., fold. map. 21 1/2cm.

About 100 pages are devoted to the journey across the prairies. Shortt

1733 **MacDonald**, P[eter] M[cLaren]
Letters from the Canadian West. [Halifax, Chronicle Publishing Co., 1903] 55p. 19 1/2cm.

These letters first appeared in the Halifax Morning Chronicle. The author mentions by name every Nova Scotian met in his travels. Shortt

1734 **McDougall**, John
In the days of the Red River Rebellion; life and adventure in the far west of Canada (1868-1872) Toronto, Wm. Briggs. 1903. ix, [1], [11]-303p. front., plates, ports. 19cm.

Republished in 1911. Shortt

1735 **MacFarlane**, W.G., pub.
Winnipeg, metropolis of the West; a series of views illustrating the Chicago of Canada as it appears today ... Toronto [190–] [56] p. illus. 18 x 23cm. Glenbow

1736 Manitoba, 1903. Islendingar i Manitoba, shýrslur um hag peirra eftir peirra eigin frásögn og ýms annar fródleikur landinu vidvikjandi. Winnipeg, 1903. 48p. illus. Fiske

1737 **Mathers**, C.W., photographer
Picturesque Edmonton, N.W.T. [Brooklyn, N.Y., Albertype Co., c1903] cover-title, 25 plates (1 fold.) 23 x 29cm.

This is a photograph album. Rutherford

1737A **Mullins**, J.D.
Seven days on the prairie, with Archdeacon Lloyd. London, Colonial and Continental Church Society [1903?] cover-title, 32p. illus. 22cm. B.C. Arch.

1738 **Oxley**, James Macdonald
Won in Western Canada. Illus. by A.H. Hider and J.D. Kelly. [St. John, N.B., Massey-Harris, 1903] [12], 39, [13] p. illus., plates. 24cm.

Unpaged material is the Massey-Harris catalogue for 1903. Glenbow

1739 **Pocock**, Roger
A frontiersman. London, Methuen & Co., 1903. 308p.

An Englishman with the wanderlust describes his adventures in many places. The winter preceding the Sask. Rebellion he joined the N.W.M.P. and when the rebellion broke out marched with Col. Irvine's relief force from Regina to Prince Albert, freezing his feet en route. U. of S.

1740 **Porter,** N[athaniel] J[oseph]
Glimpses through Moose Jaw and district, Moose Jaw, North West Territory, Canada. Photo-gravures. Brooklyn, N.Y., Albertype Co. [c1903] 2p.l., 17 plates. 14 x 18 1/2cm. Sask. Arch.

1741 **Scott,** J[ames] G[uthrie]
Paper on the trans-Canada railway, read before the Literary and Historical Society of Quebec, Tuesday, 13th January, 1903; together with some remarks by Mr. Henry O'Sullivan, on the same occasion. Quebec, Chronicle Printing Co., 1903. 24p. fold. map. 20cm.

The speaker suggested that the line run north of Lake Winnipeg. Can. Arch.

1742 Souvenir of Prince Albert, Sask. [n.p., 1903?] 21 plates 14 x 19cm. Sask. Arch.

1743 **Steen,** [James Elden]
Illustrated souvenir of Winnipeg. An historical and descriptive sketch of its wondrous growth, progress and prosperity. Winnipeg, 1903. ... illus. Ibis – 12-25

1744 **Strathcona, Alta.** Board of Trade
Strathcona, the railway town and manufacturing centre of northern Alberta. [Strathcona, Plainsdealer Co.] 1903. cover-title, 19, [1]p. illus. 22cm.

Strathcona was that section of present-day Edmonton lying south of the Saskatchewan River. Before amalgamation there was bitter rivalry between the two towns.
Rutherford

1745 **Tait,** C[assel] M[orton]
Edmonton illustrated; a practical compendium of illustrative and descriptive information of the town of Edmonton and surrounding parts of northern Alberta in Canada. [Calgary, Herald Co.] 1903. 181, [1]p. illus., fold. plate. 13 1/2 x 20cm.

Illustrations with little text. Man. Leg.

1746 **Weld,** Agnes Grace
Glimpses of Tennyson and some of his friends. With an appendix by the late Bertram Tennyson. London, Williams & Norgate, 1903. 2p.l., 154p. front. 18cm.

Appendix: 'The Blizard' and 'Broncho Days,' by the late Bertram Tennyson, p.123-154. These are extracts from a 'little privately printed volume of prose and verse.' Br. Mus.

1747 **Atkinson,** George E.
Rare bird records of Manitoba. [Winnipeg, 1904] 12p. 22cm. (Hist. & Sc. Soc. of Man., no.65) Man. Leg.

1748 **Bashford,** Henry Howarth
The Manitoban; a romance. London, John Lane, 1904. 4p.l., 304p. 19cm. Not seen. R.E.S.

1749 **Benoit**, [Joseph Paul Augustin]
Vie de Mgr Taché, archevêque de St-Boniface. Montréal, Librairie Beauchemin, 1904. 2v. fronts., illus., plates, ports., fold. maps, plan, fold. table. 24cm.

An effort to furnish a definitive biography of the great prelate. The biographer has quoted from Taché's own statements wherever possible. Shortt

1750 **Bible**. New Testament. Cree
[The New Testament in Plains Cree. Rev. ed.] London, British & Foreign Bible Society, 1904. 453p. 22cm.

The revision was largely by Rev. John A. Mackay. See Entry 1964. Br. Mus.

1751 **Bible**. New Testament. St. Matthew. Cree
[St. Matthew's Gospel in Plains Cree] London, British and Foreign Bible Society, 1904. 60p. 21cm. Rupert's

1752 **Bryce**, George
Among the mound builders' remains. [Winnipeg, 1904] cover-title, 47p. illus. (incl. maps) 22cm. (Hist. & Sc. Soc. of Man., no.66) Shortt

1753 **Bryce**, George
Educational reminiscences of one-third of a century in Winnipeg, 1871 to 1904 ... Inaugural address delivered in Convocation Hall, Manitoba College, Winnipeg, November 18, 1904. cover-title, 12p. illus. 23cm. Reprinted from Man. Free Press. Man. Leg.

1753A **The Bulletin**, Edmonton
Information for intending settlers. One hundred questions answered on the one hundred and sixty acre free farms in the Edmonton wheat belt. The garden of the North-West is the Edmonton district. Edmonton, 1904. cover-title, 55p. illus. 24cm.

The first 20 pages is advertising. Can. Arch. (ms.)

1754 **Calgary**. Fire Department
Historic and illustrated souvenir of the Calgary Fire Department. [Calgary, Herald Co.] 1904. cover-title, 62p. illus., fold. plate, ports. 16 x 23cm. Glenbow

1755 **Camrose**. Board of Trade
Camrose, the rose of Alberta. Edmonton, The Bulletin Co., Ltd. [1904] [32]p. illus., map. 16 1/2 x 25cm. U. of A.

1756 **Canada**. Department of the Interior
Atlas van Westelyk Canada ... Ottawa, 1904. ...

Dutch immigration pamphlet.
This pamphlet was published in several languages. Can. Arch.

1757 **Canada**. Department of the Interior
Le Canada en images. L'Ouest, le Manitoba, l'Assiniboine, la Saskatchewan, l'Alberta, la Colombie Britannique. [Ottawa] 1904. 72p. illus. 20cm. Arkin

1758 **Canada.** Department of the Interior
Conseils aux colons. Terres gratuites. L'Ouest Canadien. Ottawa, 1904. ...

French immigration pamphlet. Can. Arch.

1759 **Canada.** Department of the Interior
Le district de la Saskatchewan. L'Ouest canadien. Fermes gratuites. [Ottawa, 1904] 31p. illus. 21 1/2cm. Can. Arch.

1760 **Canada.** Department of the Interior
European settlers farming in Western Canada. [Ottawa, 1904] cover-title, [33]p. illus., double map, facsims. 18 1/2 x 25 1/2cm.

Letter in settler's native language with translation in parallel column, and illustration of his farmstead on page opposite. Letters in several languages. Can. Arch.

1761 **Canada.** Department of the Interior
Farms and farming in Western Canada. [Ottawa, 1904] cover-title, 32p. col. plates, double map, facsims. 18 x 25cm.

Largely facsimiles of letters from satisfied settlers with a tinted photograph of the writer's farmstead on the opposite page. The most attractive of the turn-of-the-century publications of the Department of the Interior. Glenbow

1761A **Canada.** Department of the Interior
Information for intending settlers regarding the homestead regulations of Western Canada. [Ottawa, 1904] folder. 23p. illus., map. 17 1/2cm. Can. Arch. (ms.)

1761B **Canada.** Department of the Interior
List of Dominion land agents and sub-agents in Western Canada who are authorized to grant homestead entries and prepared at all times to give information to intending settlers. (Corrected to September, 1903) [Ottawa, 1904] cover-title, 4p. 13 1/2cm. Can. Arch. (ms.)

1761C **Canada.** Department of the Interior
Reliable information for use of United States newspaper editors visiting Western Canada. No.1. [Ottawa, 1904] 29p. 15cm. Can. Arch. (ms.)

1762 **Canada.** Department of the Interior
Report on the great landslide at Frank, Alta., 1903. Ottawa, Govt. Printing Bureau, 1904. 17p. diagrs., fold. maps, plates. 25cm.

Extract from part VIII, annual report, 1903. Glenbow

1763 **Canada.** Department of the Interior
Story of a Manitoba farmer. [Ottawa? 1904?] ... Not seen.

10,000 copies printed. Interior, 1905

1764 **Canada.** Department of the Secretary of State
Copies of all orders in council, memorials, letters, telegrams, and other correspondence, and all other documents and communications in writing, between the first day of May, 1903, relating to, or concerning, or in any way having reference to the granting of provincial autonomy to the North-West Territories, or the creation of said territories into a province, or provinces. [Ottawa, 1904] 22p. 25 1/2cm. (Canada. Sess. papers, 1904, no.116a) Shortt

1765 **Christmas**, Walter
Fremtidslande, Canada. Gyldendalkse boghandel forlag. København & Kristiana, 1904. 304, [2]p. illus. (incl. maps) plates. 24 1/2cm.

P.137-236 relates to the Prairie Provinces. L.C.

1766 Commerce has staked the richest claim in the world. [n.p., 1904?] [7]p.

Cartoons relating to Western Canada. Lande

1767 **Cullum**, Ridgwell
The hound of the north; the story of a Canadian farm. London, Chapman & Hall, 1904. 344p.

Fiction.
A 4th edition was published by Wright & Brown in 1933. Br. Mus.

1768 **Grange**, Herbert
An English farmer in Canada, and a visit to the States; being notes and observations by a practical farmer and commercial man on Canada as a field for British capital and labour. London, Blackie & Son, 1904. xii, 150p. plates (part fold.) fold. map. 19cm.

Deals largely with the Prairie Provinces. Man. Leg.

1769 **Herkenrath**, Aug[ust]
Canada und die Hudson's bay-Company. Inaugural-dissertation zur Erlangung der Doktorwurde ... Rheinischen Friedrich-Wilhelms-Universitatzu Bonn ... Bonn, Seb. Foppen, 1904. cover-title, 136, [2]p. 22cm. St. Sulpice

1770 **Kastner**, Frédéric de
... Les La Vérendrye père et fils, Dufrost de La Jemeraye et la découverte du Nord-ouest ... [Québec, La Cie d'imprimerie commerciale, 1904] cover-title, 116p. 22cm. (His Héros de la Nouvelle France. 3.sér.) L.C.

1771 **Lacombe, Alta.** Board of Trade
The district of Lacombe. [Lacombe? 1904] 24p. 15 x 24cm. Alta. Leg.

1772 **Laut**, A[gnes] C[hristina]
Pathfinders of the West; being the thrilling story of the adventures of the men who discovered the great Northwest, Radisson, La Vérendrye, Lewis and Clark. Toronto, William Briggs [1904?] xxv, 380p. front., illus., plates, maps. 21cm.

Reprinted by Ryerson in 1924. Shortt

1773 **Liberal Party**
Sale of land to Saskatchewan Valley Land Co. [n.p., 1904?] caption-title, 16p. 23cm.

Last half of the pamphlet relates to timber berths in Western Canada. See Entry 1881. Sask. Arch.

1774 **McIntyre**, Alexander
The Canadian West, a geography of Manitoba and the Northwest Territories. Toronto, Morang & Co., 1904. iii-xv, 249p. front., illus., double map, diagrs. 19 1/2cm.

A school text. L.C.

1775 **Manitoba Free Press**
A quill from a Canada wild goose, with the Cree legend of Nih-Ka, the wild goose, set forth for the first time in print. Winnipeg, 1904. 16p. illus. 18cm. B.C. Arch.

1776 **Maude,** Aylmer
A peculiar people; the Doukhobors. New York, Funk & Wagnalls Co., 1904. xi, 338p. front., plates, ports., maps. 21cm.

A sympathetic account of the sect by one of those responsible for bringing the Doukhobors to Canada. Shortt

1777 **Mavor,** James
North West of Canada. Report to the Board of Trade on the North West of Canada with special reference to wheat production for export. Presented to both Houses of Parliament by command of His Majesty. London, Eyre & Spottiswoode, 1904. viii, 123p. fold. maps, fold. chart. 33cm. (Papers by command. Cd.2628)

An exhaustive study of the wheat-producing potentialities of the Canadian West. At the time Mavor's conclusions were considered conservative. Shortt

1778 **Moodie,** Marion Elizabeth
Songs of the West. Toronto, Wm. Briggs, 1904. [16]p. illus. 18 1/2cm.

Republished with additional poems as a Ryerson chap-book in 1934.
Private information

1779 **North Alberta Land Company Limited**
Ranching and farming in Alberta, the great Northwest. General information, illustrations, and personal statements. Red Deer [1904] 64p. illus., map. 23cm. Glenbow

1780 **North West Territories.** Department of Agriculture
North West brand book; supplement no.1. Published under the authority of the Dept. of Agriculture, N.W.T. Revised and corrected to Jan. 1st, 1904. [Winnipeg, Stovel Co., 1904] 2p.l., 184p. illus. 17 x 10cm. U. of S.

1781 **Pearson,** W[illia]m, and Co.
Western Canada, the greatest wheat growing country in the world. The last West; a few facts and illustrations of the flower garden of the Northwest. [Winnipeg, 1904] ... Amtmann - 267-296

1782 Reglur og tilskipanir fyrir medhöndlun baendafjelaga i Manitoba. Gimli, Gimli-prentsmidjan, 1904. 14p. Fiske

1783 Souvenir of Winnipeg and Dominion of Canada exhibition. Winnipeg, The Frank Martel Co. [1904?] cover-title, [64]p. illus. 19 x 26cm. Shortt

1784 **Winnipeg.** City Council
Winnipeg, Canada. [Photos by Steele & Co. Winnipeg, Printed by the Telegram Printing Co.] 1904. [48]p. chiefly illus. 26 x 32cm. Glenbow

1785 **Alberta Railway and Irrigation Company**
Irrigated lands in southern Alberta, the 'Colorado of Canada,' with notes on the climate, crops, markets and values, railroad facilities, and the field for the em-

ployment of labor. Lethbridge [ca. 1905] folder. (16, [2]p.) map on verso. 72 x 68cm. Glenbow

1786 **Alberta Railway and Irrigation Company**
Sunny southern Alberta; souvenir letter card. [Lethbridge, Alta., 1905?] cover-title, [24]p., chiefly illus. map (p.3 of cover) 11 x 16cm.

'Intended to draw attention to Lethbridge and to the attractive irrigable lands surrounding the town.' See p.2 of cover. Glenbow

1787 **Atkinson**, George E.
A review history of the passenger pigeon of Manitoba. [Winnipeg, 1905?] 8p. illus. 22cm. (Hist. & Sc. Soc. of Man., no.68) Man. Leg.

1788 Battleford, Sask.: town and district. [Battleford, Saskatchewan Herald, n.d.] leaflet (4p.) 20cm.

Copies are different printings, with copy 2 carrying two small advertisements. Glenbow

1789 **Bible**. New Testament. Selections. Saulteaux
Épîtres et évangiles en sauteux. Québec, 1905. ... Not seen

Translated by the Rev. J.C. Camper. Morice

1790 **Bible**. New Testament. St. John. Blackfoot
... The Gospel according to St. John, chapters 13, 14, 15, 16, 17. Translated into the Blackfoot language and printed in the syllabic characters. Calgary, Printed at the Diocesan Press by the Indian pupils of St. Dunstan's Industrial School [190-?] cover-title, 14p. 23cm.

Title also in Blackfoot syllabics. St. Dunstan's Press operated between 1905 and 1908. Glenbow

1791 **Bible**. Old Testament. Psalms. Cree
The Psalms in Plains Cree. Rev. ed. London, British & Foreign Bible Society, 1905. 136p.

A revision by Rev. John A. Mackay. Br. Mus.

1792 **Bleiler**, William Jennings
Sunny Alberta. [Innisfree? 1905?] ...

Immigration pamphlet mentioned in author's obituary notice, Edmonton Journal, 12 April 1967. Edmonton Journal

1793 **Bole**, J[ames] F[ranklin]
J.F. Bole's address to the electors of Regina city. [n.p., 1905] caption-title, [3]p. port. 27cm.

Dated 9 Dec. 1905. Sask. Arch.

1794 **Borden**, [Sir] R[obert] L[aird]
Speech of ... on the provincial government in the North-West. Ottawa, Wednesday, March 22, 1905. [Ottawa, King's Printer, 1905] caption-title, 20p. 25cm. (House of Commons Debates) Sask. Arch.

1795 **Bourassa**, Henri
Les écoles du Nord-Ouest. Discours prononcé le 17 avril 1905 dans la grande salle du Monument National, à Montréal. Montréal, Le Nationaliste, 1905. cover-title, 29p. 21 1/2cm. Shortt

1796 **Bryce**, George
A great city library. [Winnipeg, 1905] 8p. 22cm. (Hist. & Sc. Soc. of Man., no.70) Man. Leg.

1797 **Bryce**, George
Mackenzie, Selkirk, Simpson. Toronto, Morang & Co., Ltd., 1905. 3p.l., [4]p., 1 l., 305p. incl. ports. 22 1/2cm. (Makers of Canada, v.8)

Another edition was published by the Oxford University Press in 1926. U. of S.

1798 **Calder**, J[ames] A[lexander]
The school question in the new provinces. [n.p., 1905] caption-title, 16p. 11cm. Sask. Arch.

1799 **Calder**, J[ames] A[lexander]
To the electors of South Regina. [n.p., 1905] caption-title, [3]p. 27cm. Sask. Arch.

1800 **Canada**. Department of the Interior
British colony at Lloydminster (Saskatchewan) Ottawa [1905] folder. 22p. illus., fold maps.

Introduction by William Hutchinson, correspondent for the Weekly Telegraph of Sheffield, giving information on the second party leaving for the colony. Contains a few letters from settlers at Lloydminster. Lyle

1801 **Canada**. Department of the Interior
Canada in a nutshell. [London, 1905] cover-title, 32p. illus. 18cm.

Running title: Information about Canada in a nutshell. H.B.C.

1802 **Canada**. Department of the Interior
Farms and farmers in Western Canada. [Ottawa, 1905] [32]p. illus., maps. 18 x 26cm. N.Y.

1803 **Canada**. Department of the Interior
Letters from Scandinavian settlers in Manitoba. [Ottawa? 1905?] ...
Information incomplete. Interior, 1906

1804 **Canada**. Department of the Interior
1905, the biggest crop in the history of the Canadian West. Ottawa, 1905. cover-title, 16p. illus. 19cm. Can. Arch.

1805 **Canada**. Department of the Interior
Prosperity follows settlement in Western Canada. [Ottawa] Canadian Government print, 1905. 112p. incl. illus. 18cm.

First edition published in 1900; another edition in 1903. (In Can. Arch.) Shortt

1806 **Canada**. Department of the Interior
Statement showing the areas of the provisional districts of the North-West Territories. [Ottawa, 1905] 5p. 25cm. (Canada. Sess. papers, 1905, no.97) U. of S.

1807 **Canada**. Department of the Secretary of State
Copies of all correspondence between the Government of Canada, or any member thereof, and the Government of the North-West Territories, or any of its

members, in reference to the granting of provincial autonomy to the said territories, since the date of the last prorogation of Parliament. [Ottawa, 1905] 4p. 25cm. (Canada. Sess. papers, 1905, no.53) U. of S.

1808 **Canada.** Department of the Secretary of State
Copies of all petitions, memorials, and resolutions from Legislative Assembly of Manitoba, the executive of that province, and any correspondence relative to the extension of the boundaries of Manitoba to the west and north. [Ottawa, 1905] 9, 3p. 25cm. (Canada. Sess. papers, 1905, no.102) U. of S.

1808A **Canadian Northern Railway**
A good country for a young man. If Horace Greeley were alive to-day he would amend that oft-quoted advice of his to read: 'Go North-West, young man: go North-West.' ... Winnipeg, Stovel Co. [1905]. folder. 15p. illus., map. 23cm. Can. Arch. (ms.)

1809 **Church of England.** Hymns and prayers. Blackfoot
Atsimoiikanists ki ninniksists. Prayers and hymns (Blackfoot) [Calgary, Printed at the Diocesan Press by the Indian pupils of St. Dunstan's Industrial School, 190–?] cover-title, 23p., 17 l. 23cm. Americas

1810 **Conservative Party** (Saskatchewan)
Haultain declares for national school system. Irreconcilable attitude of Archbishop Langevin forces him to fight conspiracy of church and coercionists ... [n.p., 1905] caption-title, [4]p. 30cm. Sask. Arch.

1811 **Conservative Party** (Saskatchewan)
The public land robbery! How the new provinces are plundered under the Compensation clauses. Are you going to endorse it? Good cause for appeal to the Privy Council. [n.p., 1905] caption-title, 8, [1]p. 20cm. Sask. Arch.

1812 **Cumberland,** Stuart C.
Via Hudson Bay; on the projected Hudson Bay Railway. London, C.W. Stidstone, 1905. 14p. Not seen. Br. Mus.

1813 **Cyr,** [Joseph] Ernest
La prairie. Winnipeg, Typographie de l'Ouest-Canada, 1905. 16p. Not seen. St. Sulpice

1814 [**Denny,** Sir Cecil Edward, bart.]
The riders of the plains. A reminiscence of the early and exciting days in the North West. Calgary, Herald Co., Ltd. [1905] 3p.l., iv, 223p. 19 1/2cm.
See also his posthumous work 'The Law Marches West.' Entry 3677. Man. Leg.

1815 **Dugas,** G[eorges]
Histoire véridique des faits qui ont préparé le mouvement des métis à la Rivière Rouge en 1869. Montréal, Librairie Beauchemin, 1905. ix, 228p. 20cm. Shortt

1816 **Edmonton.** Board of Trade
Fertility and prosperity. [Edmonton] Edmonton Printing and Pub. Co. Ltd. [1905] cover-title, 40p. illus. 15cm. Private copy

1817 **The Enterprise**, Leduc, Alta.
Leduc, Alberta. Leduc, The Enterprise, 1905. 24p. illus. (part fold.) 16cm.

'May number, 1905, of The Enterprise, published expressly for intending settlers.' Rutherford

1818 **Fielding**, W[illiam] S[tevens]
The North-West education question. The compromise reached by the government. An efficient public school system for the new provinces. Speech ... House of Commons, Ottawa, March 24, 1905. [n.p., 1905] caption-title, 16p. 26cm. Sask. Arch.

1819 **Goodloe**, [Abbe] Carter
At the foot of the Rockies. New York, Charles Scribner's Sons, 1905. x p., 2 l., 290p. front., plates. 20cm.

Tales of mounted police life and ranching collected during a summer at Ft. Macleod, Alta. Man. Leg.

1820 **Hapgood**, Ja[me]s
Opinions of ... From Manitoba Free Press, Thursday, Sept. 14. [n.p., 1905] caption-title, 16p. 26cm. Sask. Arch.

1821 **Haultain**, [Sir] F[rederick] W[illiam] G[ordon]
Hon. F.W.G. Haultain outlines his policy. The former premier states his attitude in regard to schools and lands – What his test case policy will result in – the much discussed question of boundaries. [n.p., 1905] cover-title, [3]p. port. 26cm. Sask. Arch.

1822 **Hudson Bay and North West Railway Company**
Momentous announcement. Cheaper, greater, better, safer bread supply in sight for the United Kingdom. Ideal homes for colonists without usual pioneer privations, risks and isolations, all being avoided by unprecedentedly favorable co-operative methods 'in the garden' of the Dominion of Canada. [n.p., 1905] 15p. illus. (incl. ports.) fold. maps. 24 x 30cm.

'The garden' was the Athabasca-Great Slave Lake region. The railway was to connect the latter lake with the navigable portion of the Thelon River. Grain was to be shipped down the river to Chesterfield Inlet, and thence to Europe. Shortt

1823 **Laird**, David
Our Indian treaties. [Winnipeg, 1905] 11p. 22cm. (Hist. & Sc. Soc. of Man., no.67) Man. Leg.

1824 **Landry**, Auguste Charles Philippe
Le bill d'autonomie des provinces d'Alberta et de Saskatchewan devant les Chambres Hautes. Discours ... prononcé le 12 juillet, 1905. Québec, L'Evénement, 1905. 32p. 24cm. Glenbow

1824A **The Leader**, Regina, Sask.
Inaugural number, Sept. 1, 1905. Regina, 1905. 31, [1]p. illus., ports., maps. 35cm.

Running title. Published on the occasion of Saskatchewan and Alberta entering Confederation. Deals chiefly with Regina and district. Glenbow

1825 **Liberal Party** (Saskatchewan)
C.P.R. tax exemptions ... [n.p., 1905] 16p. 21cm. Sask. Arch.

1826 **Liberal Party** (Saskatchewan)
Not an issue of schools but of veracity. False statements made as to the kind of separate schools guaranteed by the Saskatchewan Act. Let electors read for themselves. [n.p., 1905] caption-title, 3p. 27cm. Sask. Arch.

1827 **Liberal Party** (Saskatchewan)
Peace, progress and prosperity. A vote for a Liberal candidate is a vote for Walter Scott, fearless champion of the West. [n.p., 1905] cover-title, [4]p. ports. 27cm. Sask. Arch.

1828 **Liberal Party** (Saskatchewan)
Railway competition for Saskatchewan vs. C.P.R. monopoly. Scott stands for the former; Haultain stands for the latter. [n.p., 1905] cover-title, 8p. 21cm. Sask. Arch.

1829 **Liberal Party** (Saskatchewan)
Splendid lands bargains ... [n.p., 1905] 15p. 21cm. Sask. Arch.

1830 **McInnis**, J[ohn] K[enneth]
The school question. Supplement to the Regina Standard. [Regina, The Regina Standard, 1905] caption-title, 24p. port. 22cm. Sask. Arch.

1831 **Mackie**, John
The rising of the red man; a romance of the Louis Riel rebellion. 2d ed. London, Jarrold & Sons [1905?] 242p. front., plates. 19cm. Shortt

1832 **Motherwell**, W[illiam] R[ichard]
Election address ... to the electors of North Qu'Appelle. [n.p., 1905] caption-title, [4]p. 26cm.

In three columns.
Dated 'Abernethy, Oct. 18, '05.' Sask. Arch.

1833 **Perrier**, Hector J.
Souvenir of Pincher Creek, Alberta; a western town and its people. Copyright by Hector J. Perrier and Charles E. Chatfield. Brooklyn, N.Y., Albertype Co. [1905?] [1], 5, [1]p. 16 plates. 14 x 19cm. Glenbow

1834 **Philippovich**, Eugen von
Im Westen Kanadas. Vienna, Carl Konegen [1905] cover-title, 485-502p. 25cm. (Osterreichischen Rundschau, Band II, heft 24)

Published as a separate.
General description of Western Canada based on his impressions during August 1904.
Austria

1835 Picturesque Calgary. Christmas, 1905. Calgary, The Herald Co., 1905. [102]p. chiefly illus. 23 x 31cm. Glenbow

1836 **Roy**, Philippe
L'autonomie des provinces de l'Ouest. Alberta et Saskatchewan. Situation scolaire. Montréal, 1905. ... Not seen. Morice

1837 **Scott**, Walter
Hon. Walter Scott to the electors of Saskatchewan. [n.p., 1905] cover-title, [3]p. 27cm. Sask. Arch.

1838 **Sherbinin**, Michael Andrew de
The Galicians dwelling in Canada and their origin. [Winnipeg, 1905?] 12p. 22cm. (Hist. & Sc. Soc. of Man., no.71) Man. Leg.

1839 **Tait**, C[assel] M[orton]
The making of a province: Alberta. Together with the urban development and rural advancement of its northern part, in and near the (at least) provisional capital, Edmonton. Edmonton [1905] [32]p. of illus., ports. 18 x 23cm. Glenbow

1840 **Thorgeirsson**, Olafur S.
Handsbok hin yngri. Borgaraleg fraedi fyrir Islenzka borgara i Kanada og Bandarikjum. Winnipeg. Logbergs, 1905. 128p. 16 1/2cm. Denmark

1841 **Waldenström**, P[aul Peter]
Genom Canada; reseskildringar från 1904. Stockholm, Aktiebolaget Normans [1905] 98, [1]p. illus. 22cm.

Impressions travelling across Canada. Two-thirds relates to the prairies. Mentions the colonies of New Stockholm, New Finland, and New Denmark. Sweden

1842 **Wesley College**, Winnipeg
Islendingar vid Wesley-College, 1901-5. [Winnipeg, Prentsmidja Olafs S. Thorgeirssona, 1905. cover-title, 16p. Fiske

1843 Western Canada book of lectures. [n.p., 1905] cover-title, 10, 11, 11, 11, 9p. 27cm.

Five lectures, each separately paged. Can. Arch.

1844 **Western Canadian Immigration Association**
What famous correspondents say about Western Canada. Minneapolis, The Association [1905] [46]p. 22cm.

Reports to papers written by 21 American newspapermen during a tour of the West in the autumn of 1905. Man. Leg.

1845 What famous correspondents say about Western Canada. Grand Forks, N.D., Compliments of Kent Realty & Investment Co. [n.d.] 44p. Lavallee - 34-284

1846 **Wickström**, V[ictor] Hugo
Bland svenskar i Kanada. Separattryck ur arbetet genom sju konungariken. Östersund, Jämt landsposten, 1905. 8p. 21cm.

First published in 1904. Uppsala

1847 [**Wishard**, Luther Deloraine]
The partition of Canada by Anglo-Saxon farmers. Winnipeg [1905?] 13p. fold. map (col.) 20 1/2cm.

Report to a company of American investors on wheat lands in Western Canada by the president of the Wishard Langan Company Ltd. Union

1848 [**Acland**, Frederick Albert]
The Canadian West: its present condition and future possibility. Winnipeg's wonderful growth. How the West has increased in recent years. A great future before Manitoba, Saskatchewan & Alberta. Room for millions more. Ottawa [Dept. of the Interior, 1906?] 78p. illus. 23cm.

Originally appeared as a series of letters to the Toronto Globe by the paper's correspondent. Can. Arch.

1849 Alberta's first parliament, 1906; Edmonton, Alberta's capital. Edmonton, Edmonton Printing & Publishing Co. Ltd. [1906] [48]p. illus., ports. 20 x 23cm. Largely illustrative. Rutherford

1850 **Bain**, George
A run through Canada. Overland to Pacific. Nairn, Printed at the Nairnshire Telegraph Office [1906] 63p. 18cm. Man. Arch.

1851 **Ballantine**, James P.
The golden West; or, Canada at closest quarters. Cumnock, Pub. by James P. Ballantine, 'News' Office, printed by Hunter & Co., 'Standard' Office, Dumfries [1906] vi, 119p. illus. Br. Mus.

1852 **Bashford**, Henry Howarth
The trail together; an episode. London, William Heinemann, 1906. 233p. Not seen.

Fiction. R.E.S.

1853 **Bryce**, George
A history of Manitoba; its resources and people. Toronto, Canada History Co., 1906. x, [3]-692p. front., plates, ports. 28cm. Deluxe edition. Shortt

1854 **Calgary**. Board of Trade
The famous Calgary district. ... illus. Not seen.

Noted in Albertan, 23 May 1906. Glenbow

1855 **Canada**. Department of the Interior
Le Canada du XXe siècle et atlas de l'Ouest Canadien, pour la gouverne des colons intentionnels ... Ottawa [1906] 41p. col. illus., col. maps. 28cm.

Relates exclusively to the Prairie Provinces but contains maps of all the provinces. France

1856 **Canada**. Department of the Interior
Il Canada ed il nuovo secolo ... Ottawa [1906] 42p. plates, fold. map. 19cm.

Italian immigration pamphlet. Can. Arch.

1857 **Canadian Northern Railway**
Through a thousand miles of wheatfields. [n.p.] 1906. 47p. plates, fold. map. 25 1/2cm. Rutherford

1858 **Canadian Pacific Railway**
The Canadian Pacific Railway Company's irrigation project, Alberta, Canada. A handbook of information regarding this undertaking, 1906. [Victoria, Printed by Colonist presses, 1906] cover-title, [40]p. illus., fold. map. 24cm. C.P.R.

1859 **Canadian Pacific Railway**
Western Canada: Manitoba, Alberta, Saskatchewan and New Ontario. How to reach it. How to obtain lands. How to make a home. [Montreal, 1906] 80p. illus., 2 maps (1 fold., 1 on inside front cover) 21cm.

On cover: Western Canada, the granary of the British Empire. Glenbow

1860 **Canadian Pacific Railway**
Western Canada, the granary of the British Empire. [n.p., 1906] cover-title, 80p. illus., fold. map. 20cm.

On a second title-page: Western Canada, Manitoba, Alberta, Saskatchewan and New Ontario. Man. Leg.

1861 **Canadian Pacific Railway**
Women's work in Western Canada. A sequel to 'Words from the women of Western Canada.' [Winnipeg?] 1906. 68p. illus. 17 1/2cm. B.C. Arch.

1862 **Chambers**, Ernest J[ohn]
The 90th Regiment. A regimental history of the 90th Regiment, Winnipeg Rifles. [Winnipeg? c1906] 99p. front., illus., ports. 32cm. Can. Arch.

1863 **Chambers**, Ernest J[ohn]
The Royal North-West Mounted Police, a corps history. Montreal, Mortimer Press, c1906. 160p. front., illus. (incl. ports.) 30 1/2cm. Shortt

1864 **Church of England.** Book of Common Prayer. Blackfoot
The services of morning and evening prayer. Printed in the Blackfoot syllabic characters ... Calgary, Printed at the Diocesan Press by the pupils of the Indian Industrial School at Calgary, 1906. cover-title, 11p. 20cm.

Title also in syllabics.
Translated and written in syllabics by Archdeacon J.W. Tims. Glenbow

1865 **Cockburn, J.A.**
Souvenir views of Alberta, the land of sunshine. Calgary, Published for J.A. Cockburn [1906?] [38]p. chiefly illus. 18 x 23cm. Glenbow

1866 **Compagnie Immobiliere et Agricole du Canada**, Anvers (Belgique) & Winnipeg
Canada, les plus belles terres à froment de l'Ouest Canadien. Canada, de schoonste Tarwevelden van West Canada. Anvers, Impr. cover-title, 1 l., 23p.

Text in French and Flemish. Amtmann - 219-62

1867 **Cullum**, Ridgwell
The night-riders; a romance of Western Canada. London, Chapman & Hall, 1906. v, 330p.

Fiction.
A 5th edition was published by Wright & Brown in 1934. Br. Mus.

1868 [**Dodds**, George Livingstone]
The last West, the latest gift of the lady bountiful, the granary of the greater British Empire. Winnipeg, Winnipeg Printing & Engraving Co., 1906. 138p. illus. (incl. ports.) 23cm. Man. Leg.

1869 **Dugas**, G[eorges]
Histoire de l'Ouest canadien de 1822 à 1869, époque des troubles. Montréal, Librairie Beauchemin [c1906] 154p. 25cm. Shortt

1870 **Dunsford**, J.F.
A holiday trip to Canada. The resources of the Dominion & their development. Information for & advice to intending emigrants. Reprinted from the 'Bridgewater Mercury' & 'Somerset County Gazette' June & July, 1906. [72p.] Antique - 106-51

1871 **Edmonton**. Board of Trade
Edmonton opportunities. [Edmonton, 1906] cover-title, [14]p. tables. 18cm. Glenbow

1872 **Edmonton**. Board of Trade
The last West; Edmonton and opportunities, agricultural, industrial, commercial. Edmonton, Bulletin Company [1906] 48p. illus. 23cm.

—— Information for settlers ... issued as a supplement to 'The last West.' [Edmonton, 1906] fold. ([6]p.) 23cm. Private copy

1873 **Ferrier**, Thompson
Indian education in the North West. [Toronto, Dept. of Missionary Literature of the Methodist Church, 1906] cover-title, 40p. illus., port. 19cm. Rutherford

1874 **Gard**, Anson Albert
The last West. [n.p.] 1906. 63p. illus. 16 1/2cm. Rutherford

1875 **Gladstone, Man**. Board of Trade
Gladstone and surrounding district. Gladstone, Man., 1906. [56]p. (chiefly illus.) 17 x 27cm.

On cover: Gladstone & district illustrated. Glenbow

1876 **Great Britain**. Colonial Office
Canada. Correspondence relating to the complaint of certain printers who were induced to emigrate to Canada by false representations. London, Darling & Son, 1906. iv, 27p. 32cm. ([Parliament, 1906. Papers by command] 2980)

Relates to a printers' strike in Winnipeg in 1906. L.C.

1877 [**Hardy**, John]
Farming in the Canadian North-West, by an old settler. London, H.J. Drane, 1906. 81p. 18 1/2cm. Not seen.

Author's name appears on final page of text.
Describes mixed farming along the Manitoba and Northwestern Railway, northwest of Portage la Prairie. Br. Mus. (subject cat., 1906-10)

1878 [**Hayes**, Kate E.]
Aweena; an Indian story of a Christmas tryst in the early days, by Mary Markwell [pseud.] Illustrated by W. Cotman Eade. Winnipeg, John A. Hart Co., 1906. 60p., 1 l. incl. front., illus., plates. 20cm.

Fiction. Shortt

1879 **Johnstone,** John
A vision of Immanuel. Toronto, Briggs, 1906. 65p.

Poetry. Amtmann - 189-735

1880 **Lethbridge News**
Lethbridge, south Alberta; the Colorado of Canada; centre of the chinook belt. Lethbridge, Lethbridge News [1906] cover-title, [68]p. illus. (incl. ports.) 22 x 30cm. Rutherford

1881 **Liberal Party,** supposed author
Saskatchewan Valley Land Co. [n.p., 1906?] caption-title, 8p. 23cm.

A reply to criticism of the deal between the Dominion government and the company. U. of T.

1882 **Manitoba.** Department of Agriculture and Immigration
[Manitoba - 1906] Publié par autorité du Departément de l'Agriculture et de l'Immigration pour la Province de Manitoba. Winnipeg, 1906. cover-title, 24p. illus. 22cm.

No.1 of a projected series of these pamphlets. Glenbow

1883 **Manitoba.** Legislative Assembly
Resolutions and memorials of the Legislative Assembly of Manitoba respecting public telephones. Speech of Hon. Colin H. Campbell, Attorney-General, introducing the bill respecting government telephone and telegraph systems and respecting municipal systems. Other interesting data, including the acts of the Legislature to construct or acquire and to maintain and operate a public telephone system and respecting municipal telephone systems. Winnipeg, 1906. 59p. 25cm. Can. Arch.

1884 **Marchant,** Bessie
Athabasca Bill; a tale of the far West. Illus. by H. Piffard. London, Christian Knowledge Society [1906] 220p. illus. Br. Mus.

1885 **Marchant,** Bessie
A daughter of the ranges; a story of Western Canada. London, Blackie and Son, 1906. 288p. front., plates. 19cm.

Juvenile literature. Br. Mus.

1886 **Regina.** Board of Trade
Regina, the capital of Saskatchewan, Canada, 1906. Its advantages as a commercial and residential centre. [Regina, Leader press] 1906. [48]p. illus. 18 x 26cm. Shortt

1887 **Salesman Publishing Company,** Winnipeg
Souvenir of Alberta; being a general résumé of the province, with portraits, engravings and biographies of a number of men who have helped to build this great new province of the West. Winnipeg, The Company, 1906. 2p.l., 142p. ports. 26cm. Edmonton

1887A **Saskatchewan**
Memorandum with reference to the claim of the Province of Saskatchewan for an extension of boundaries to Hudson's Bay. [Ottawa? 1906] [1], 13 l. 36cm. Glenbow

1888 **Saskatoon.** Board of Trade
Saskatoon, the hub of the hard-wheat belt of Western Canada. Saskatoon, 1906. cover-title, 28p. illus. (incl. ports.) 28cm. Shortt

1889 **Selkirk, Man.** Board of Trade
Souvenir of Selkirk and the rural municipalities of St. Andrews, St. Clements, Brokenhead and Gimli. Winnipeg, Moore Printing Co. [1906] 31, [1]p. illus. (incl. ports.) double plate, fold. map. 14 1/2 x 22 1/2cm. Man. Leg.

1890 **Sifton,** [Sir] Clifford
Administration of the Canadian West. Speech ... in the House of Commons, Thursday, May 31, 1906. How the country has benefited by the contract of the Saskatchewan Valley Land Company. Remarkable success of the government's policy. A comparison with the Conservative regime. [n.p., 1906] 32p. 25 1/2cm. Can. Arch.

1890A **Soo Line**
1906 settlers' guide via the Soo Line to North Dakota, South Dakota, Manitoba and the Canadian Northwest. Minneapolis, [1906]. cover-title, 32p. map. 23 1/2cm. Can. Arch. (ms.)

1891 **Stokes,** W[illiam] E[dward] H[erbert]
Are our Indians pagan? A plea to the contrary and an appeal for the alteration of this designation. Regina, 1906. 13p. 16cm. Sask. Leg.

1892 **Strathcona, Alta.** Board of Trade
Strathcona, Alberta, invites farmers, homeseekers, and captains of industry to examine her advantages. Victoria, Colonist presses [1906] cover-title, 24p. illus. 21cm. Shortt

1893 **Tait,** C[assel] M[orton] photographer
Beginnings of greatness. Souvenir of Edmonton and Strathcona and their vicinity. Edmonton, C.M. Tait [1906] 24p. largely illus. 17 x 22cm. Arkin

1894 **Tracksell, Anderson & Company, Regina**
Western lands. [Regina, 1906?] cover-title, [30]p. 8 fold. plates. 21cm.

Describes areas in Saskatchewan in which the company offered lands for sale. 'Explanation of crop payment plan' by Tracksell, Price, Anderson & Co., Regina (4 page leaflet) laid in. Glenbow

1895 **Turner,** John P[ercival]
The moose and wapiti of Manitoba. A plea for their preservation. Winnipeg, Manitoba Free Press Co., 1906. cover-title, 8p. illus. 22 1/2cm. (Hist. & Sc. Soc. of Man., no.69) Shortt

1896 **Veterans of the Fur Trade Association**
Pamphlet ordered to be printed by the Veterans of the Fur Trade Association, showing their ownership of 7,455,552 acres of land, being the one-tenth of Lord Selkirk's estate in the country formerly known as the District of Assiniboia. Prince Albert, Advocate office, 1906. cover-title, 23p. 22cm. Prepared by James Taylor, chairman.

1906 Bibliography of the Prairie Provinces

In the deed granting Lord Selkirk a large tract of land, it was specified that one-tenth should be from time to time given to retired servants of the H.B.C. The 'Veterans' unsuccessfully laid claim to the unused portion of the tenth. Shortt

1897 **Whates,** H[arry] R[ichard]
Canada, the new nation; a book for the settler, the emigrant and the politician. London, J.M. Dent & Co., 1906. xvii p., 1 l., 284p. front., plates, map. 19 1/2cm.

A newspaperman, who travelled steerage across the ocean, and worked his way across Canada, describes his experience, and discusses the opportunities for immigrants. About 100 pages are devoted to the prairies. The inconveniences of pioneer life did not appeal to him. Shortt

1898 **Alberta.** Department of Agriculture
An official hand book containing reliable information concerning its resources. Edmonton, J.E. Richards, 1907. 60p. illus., tables. Agric.

1899 **Allan Steamship Line**
Handbook of information ... [Liverpool, 1907] cover-title, 27p. col. illus. 18cm.

Caption-title inside cover is 'Canada. The call of the West.' The pamphlet includes a section entitled 'Letters from settlers. Advice to Englishmen.' Liverpool

1900 **Allan Steamship Line**
Life in Canada; stories of successful settlers. [Liverpool, 1907] cover-title, 20p. 18cm.

The caption-title is 'Canada as British journalists see it.' Excerpts taken from published newspaper accounts of their impressions, and also of interviews they had had with successful settlers. Liverpool

1901 **Anderson,** Charles D.
Claresholm and vicinity. [Calgary, Hammond Lithographing Co., 1907?] cover-title, [16]p. (chiefly illus.) 16 x 23cm. Glenbow

1902 **Associated Boards of Trade of Western Canada.** 4th annual convention, June 18th, 19th, and 20th, 1907.
Memorandum of resolutions to be presented at the fourth annual convention ... to be held in Prince Albert, Sask. ... Convention will meet in Council Chamber, City Hall, Central Avenue ... [n.p., Advocate Press, 1907] cover-title, 16p. 25cm. Sask. Arch.

1903 **Aubert,** Frédéric
L'Ouest canadien et le Jukon (Alaska). Chartres, France, Impr. M. Laffray, 1907. 87p. 24 1/2cm. Rutherford

1904 [**Bezanson,** A.M.]
The Peace River trail. Edmonton, Journal Co., Ltd. [1907] 73p. illus., fold. map. 26cm. Alta. Leg.

1905 **Bryce,** George
Everyman's geology of the three Prairie Provinces of the Canadian West. Winnipeg, 1907. 68p. maps (1 fold.) diagrs. 21 1/2cm. Shortt

1906 **Bryce,** P[eter] H[enderson]
Report on the Indian schools of Manitoba and the North-West Territories. Ottawa, 1907. 21p. fold. map. Errata slip. Can. Arch.

1907 **The Bulletin,** Edmonton
Christmas, 1907. Edmonton, December 25th, 1907. 20p. illus. (incl. ports.) 52cm. Shortt

1908 **Calgary.** City Council
Calgary, the land of plenty. Published by the City Council and Calgary Board of Trade. Calgary, Printed by the Herald Co., 1907. 80p. illus. France

1909 **Canada.** Department of the Interior
A travers le Canada; l'Ouest. Ottawa, 1907. 84p. illus. 22 1/2cm. Arkin

1910 **Canada.** Department of the Interior
Dorus fosgailte do'n Ghaidheal [Doorway plains for the highland Gaels] ... le Ailghinn La Bhruinn ... Ottawa, 1907. 56, [1]p. illus. 18cm.

Title-page in Gaelic. Caption-title at beginning of text: Na Gaidhell Ann an [sic.] Canada [The Highlander Gael in Canada] Toronto

1911 **Canada.** Department of the Interior
English emigrants' experience in Western Canada. [Ottawa 1906?] ... 10000 copies printed. Interior, 1907

1912 **Canada.** Department of the Interior
The last best West. Canada in the twentieth century. Western Canada. Vast agricultural resources. Homes for millions. Ottawa, The Department [1907?] 31, [1]p. incl. illus., maps. 28cm. Shortt

1913 **Canada.** Department of the Interior
Lettres de colons. La vérité sur le Canada. Publié par ordre de l'Hon. Frank Oliver, Ministre de l'Intérieur, Ottawa (Canada) [Paris, France, imprimé par G. Lefebvre, 1907] self-cover, 31p.

Letters from French settlers in Saskatchewan, Manitoba and Alberta. Amtmann - 219-45

1914 **Canada.** Department of the Interior
Papers relating to the holding of homestead entries by members of the Doukhobor community; being part of a return laid on the table of the House of Commons on April 17, 1907; with the final report of the Commission appointed to investigate and adjust claims of Doukhobors as to residence and improvement. Ottawa, Govt. Printing Bureau, 1907. 29p. 25cm. St. Sulpice

1915 **Canada.** Department of the Interior
The story of Western Canada crop. [Ottawa? 1907?] ...

300,000 copies printed. Interior, 1908

1916 **Canada.** Department of the Interior
Western Canada, a land of unequalled opportunity. [Ottawa? 1907?] ...

20000 copies printed. Interior, 1908

1917 **Canada.** Department of the Interior
Western Canada, a land of unprecedented progress. [Ottawa? 1907?] ...
2000 copies printed. Interior, 1908

1918 **Canada.** Department of the Interior
Western Canada, crop prospects. [Ottawa? 1907?] ...
500 copies printed. Interior, 1908

1919 **Canada.** Department of the Interior
Western Canada. Early days. [Ottawa? 1907?] ... Information incomplete.
500 copies printed. Interior, 1908

1920 **Canadian Pacific Railway**
Home life of women in Western Canada. [n.p.] 1907. 40p. illus. 18cm.
Testimonials of women who with their families had settled in Western Canada.
Glenbow

1921 **Church of England.** Church Missionary Society
The North West Canada missions. London, The Society, 1907. 79p.
Br. Mus.

1922 **Church of England.** Literature committee of the Missionary Society
The missionary Diocese of Athabasca. [Toronto, 1907?] cover-title, 24p.
illus., ports. 21cm. Glenbow

1923 **La Compagnie des Colons de l'Ouest**
Emparons-nous du sol! Une prise dans la vallée que nous offrons aux colons.
Les agents de la compagnie inspectant cette région. La Cie des Colons de l'Ouest
Ltée, Valleyfield, P.Q. Valleyfield, Imp. du Progrès [1907] 16p.
Company formed to encourage French-Canadians to settle in the West. Lande

1924 **Conybeare,** C[harles] F[rederick] P[ringle]
Lyrics from the West. Toronto, William Briggs, 1907. iv, [5]-77p. 19 1/2cm.
U. of A.

1925 [**Covey,** Elizabeth (Rockford)]
Comrades two, by Elizabeth Freemantle [pseud.] Toronto, Musson [1907]
245p. front. (port.) 20cm. Cover bears sub-title: A story of The Qu'Appelle
Valley.
Sketches of pioneer life. The American edition, published by G.W. Jacobs of Philadelphia,
had the title 'The One and I.' Rutherford

1926 **Cyr,** J[oseph] Ernest
La colonisation dans l'Ouest. Conférence prononcée ... le 20 mars 1907, devant
l'Institut canadien d'Ottawa. [n.p., 1907] caption-title, 14p. 21 1/2cm.
St. Sulpice

1927 **Dezell,** R[obert]
A night on the prairie. The Meadow Lea tragedy. Toronto, William Briggs, 1907.
xiii, 15-131p. front., ports. 19cm. Bound with Wigle, H.: The life story of
Finlay Booth.

First published under the title 'Fire and Frost.'
During a blizzard in March 1882, fire destroyed a home, leaving the Taylor family and a guest scantily dressed and without shelter. Only one person survived the horrors of that night. Shortt

1928 **Dunsford,** J.T.
Emigration to Canada. British journalists and the Canadian government. Tour through the Dominion. From the Atlantic to the Pacific ... [n.p., 1907] 110p. illus. 18cm. N.Y.

1929 **Edmonton.** Board of Trade
Edmonton, Province of Alberta. Opportunities: agricultural, industrial, commercial. Reached by the Canadian Pacific Ry., the Canadian Northern Ry., the Grand Trunk Pacific Ry. [Montreal, Desbarats & Co., 1907] cover-title, 16p. illus. 23cm. Glenbow

1930 **Edmonton.** Police Department
Regulations for the police of the City of Edmonton. Edmonton, Douglas Co. [190-?] 25, [1]p. form. 14cm. Glenbow

1930A **Edmonton Printing and Publishing Company**
Edmonton, city beautiful, capital of Alberta. Christmas ed. Edmonton, 1907. cover-title, [52]p. illus., ports. 26 x 35cm. Glenbow

1931 **Forestier,** G.
Dans l'Ouest Canadien; la Pointe-aux-Rats. Paris, Librairie Plon [1907] 2p. l., 274p. 19cm. Not seen.

Although written as fiction, the novel was intended to describe conditions in old-country French colonies in the West. A group of colonists in northern Manitoba are unsuccessful farmers, and fall into debt. Some leave to settle in Algeria. R.H.P., 1908

1932 **Fredericksen,** Ditlew M[onrad]
Land laws of Canada and the land experience of the United States. [Canora, Sask? 1907?] cover-title, 19, [1]p. 22cm. Shortt

1933 **High River, Alta.** Chalmers Church. Ladies' Aid
High River cook book, collected and compiled by the Ladies' Aid ... Calgary, Herald Co., 1907. 81p. 17cm.

Unpaged advertising matter (11 pages) at the end. Glenbow

1934 **Kennedy,** Howard Angus
New Canada and the New Canadians. Preface by Lord Strathcona. London, Horace Marshall & Son [1907] 264p. col. front., plates (part col.) map. 19cm. U. of A. (Calgary)

1935 **Larmour,** Robert
Canada's opportunity; a review of Butler's 'Great lone land' in its relation to present day conditions and future prospects. Toronto, W. Briggs, 1907. 32p. 23 1/2cm.

The concluding pages advocate opening Western Canada to Oriental immigration. L.C.

1936 **Lavergne**, Armand [Renaud]
Les écoles du Nord-Ouest. Discours prononcé à Montmagny ... le dimanche 17 septembre 1905. Suivi des différents textes et amendements de la loi, de documents et pièces justificatives. Montréal, Le Nationaliste, 1907. 63p. 22cm. Can. Arch.

1937 Not used

1938 **[Leau, Léopold]**
La terre pour rien. Renseignements pratiques sur la colonisation agricole française au Canada. Par Jean du Saguenay. Paris, Blond, 1907. 128p. fold. maps (one col.) 18 1/2cm.

French-speaking parishes listed and indicated on map. Collection Gagnon

1939 **Lethbridge.** Board of Trade
Lethbridge; a railway centre with the mineral resources of Pittsburg and the agricultural territory of Minneapolis, the commercial and industrial capital of southern Alberta, the western gateway of the Canadian prairie. [Lethbridge] Printed by Southern Alberta News [1907?] [32]p. illus., fold. map. 21 1/2cm.

Largely pictorial. Toronto

1940 **McLean (David M.) Land Company, Chicago**
The story of Western Canada, the last West. The flour barrel of the world. Chicago, The Company [1907] 38p. illus. 24cm. Sask. Arch.

1941 **Melita, Man.** Board of Trade
The County of Arthur and Melita district, the garden of south-western Manitoba. [Melita, Man., The Melita Progress, 1907] folder. (23p.) illus., maps. 21cm.

In red paper covers, with cover-title. Glenbow

1942 **Markússon**, Magnús
Ljóđmaeli eftir M. Markússon. Winnipeg, Prentsmidja Lögbergs, 1907. 125, [3]p. port. 18cm. U. of M.

1943 **[Mitchell, Ross]**
A chronicle of an expedition. [Chicago? 1907?] [36]p. 4 plates on 2 l. 18 1/2cm.

An account of a trip to Canyon Lake, English River, and the Winnipeg River in the summer of 1907. Yale

1944 **Morice**, A[drien] G[abriel]
Aux sources de l'histoire manitobaine ... Québec, Imprimerie de la Compagnie de L'Événement, 1907. 120p., 1 l. 23cm. 'Extrait de la Nouvelle-France.' Shortt

1945 **Okotoks, Alta.** Board of Trade
Okotoks, the Eldorado of south Alberta. Calgary, Hammond Lithographing Co. [1907?] 46p. illus., ports., double map. 20cm. Glenbow

1946 **Partridge**, E[dward] A[lexander]
A farmers' trade union. Winnipeg, 1907? ... Not seen. Morton

1947 **The Prairie Witness**, Indian Head
Indian Head, Saskatchewan ... Published for the Prairie Witness. Toronto, W.B. MacFarlane [1907?] 2p.l. 27 illus. on 10 l. 18 x 23cm. Shortt

1948 **Regina**. Knox Presbyterian Church
Quarter centenary of Knox Presbyterian Church, Regina, Sask. September 15-22, 1907. [Regina] 1907. 24p. plates, ports. 23 1/2cm. At head of title: 1882-1907. Souvenir. Shortt

1949 **Richardson**, E[rnest] L.
Calgary, Alberta, commercial metropolis of Western Canada. Calgary, Hammond Litho Co., 1907. cover-title, [20]p. illus. 16 x 23cm.

'This article won the first prize - fifty dollars in gold - in the essay contest conducted by the Hundred Thousand Club of Calgary, January 1st, 1907.' Glenbow

1950 **St. Germain**, F[rançois] H[yacinthe]
Souvenirs et impressions de voyage du Nord-Ouest Canadien. Arthabaska, 1907. 226p. plates. 20cm. Can. Arch.

1951 **Saskatoon**. Board of Trade
A few facts about the city of Saskatoon; something of its past, present and prospects for the future - a city of opportunities, a railway centre, the hub of the great hard wheat area of central Saskatchewan. [Saskatoon, Phoenix job print, 1907] 36p. illus. 15cm. Toronto

1952 **Saskatoon and Western Land Co., Ltd.**
The heart of the famous Saskatchewan wheat belt. Montreal, Saskatoon & Western Land Co., Ltd. [1907] 89, [1]p. incl. illus. fold. plate, fold map. 20cm. Shortt

1953 **Saxby**, [C.F.] Argyll
Braves white and red; a tale of adventures in the North-West. London, T.C. & E.C. Jack, 1907. vii, 216p. front., plates. 19cm.

Locale 'Qu'Appelle Valley.'
Juvenile literature. Br. Mus.

1954 **Storer**, Effie (Laurie)
Gardiner Presbyterian Church, Battleford, Sask. A short sketch of its history, 1878-1907. A paper read ... on February 14th, 1907. [Battleford] Herald print [1907] 12p. 15 1/2cm. Shortt

1955 **Swan River Valley, Man.** Board of Trade
Swan River Valley; the garden of the Canadian West. [Winnipeg, Bulman Bros., 1907] 31, [1]p. illus. 23cm.

An attractive pamphlet. Man. Leg.

1956 Vestur Canada. Manitoba, Saskatchewan, Alberta. Bezta kornyrkju- og kvikfjarraektarland heimsins. Framtidarland Islendinga. Fródleg og skemtileg bréf frá islenzkum nykyggjum. Gefid út ad tilhlutun Canada-stjórnar. [n.p., 1907] cover-title, 72p. illus., maps. Fiske

1957 **Watt**, Gertrude Balmer
A woman in the West. Edmonton, News Publishing Co., 1907. 52p. plates. 22 1/2cm. Alta. Leg.

1958 **Whitaker**, Herman
The settler. A novel. New York, Harper & Bros., 1907. vi, [1]p., 1 l., 368, [1]p. front. 19 1/2cm.

A novel of the Manitoba park belt. Private copy

1959 **Young**, Egerton R[yerson]
The battle of the bears; life in the North land. Illustrated by the author's photographs and pen and ink drawings. Boston, W.A. Wilde [c1907] 341p. front., illus., plates. 26 1/2cm. Not seen.

Juvenile fiction. Another edition was published by Culley of London. L.C.

1960 **Ames**, [Sir] Herbert B[rown]
Our western heritage and how it is being squandered by the Laurier government. Being a brief summary of the criticisms offered in the House of Commons of Canada during the tenth Parliament as to the manner in which the Laurier government has administered the western lands, as contained in a lecture. Montreal, 1908. 34p. 23cm. Can. Arch.

1961 **Battleford, Sask.** Board of Trade
Battleford and the university. Battleford, 1908. cover-title, 26, [2]p. diagrs. 22 1/2cm.

Arguments in favour of locating the new University of Saskatchewan at Battleford. Regina is said to have published a brochure early in 1909 in support of her claims to the university, but no copies seem to have survived. Shortt

1962 **Bernier**, Joseph
L'instruction obligatoire au Manitoba. Saint-Boniface, Impr. du Manitoba, 1908. 36p. port. Not seen. St. Sulpice

1963 [**Bérubé**, A.Ph.]
Les Canadiens-Français dans l'Ouest. [n.p.] 1908. cover-title, 15p. 20 1/2cm. At head of title: Le gouvernement Laurier devant l'opinion.

Four letters which appeared in the Courrier de l'Ouest for April 1908. The letters speak favourably of prospects and conditions. Can. Arch.

1964 **Bible**. Cree
[The Old Testament in Plains Cree. The New Testament in Plains Cree; revised version] London, British and Foreign Bible Society, 1908. 3p.l., 1512p., 3 l., 453p. 22cm.

The New Testament portion has a separate title-page with the imprint date 1904. See Entry 1750. Rutherford

1965 **Blake**, Samuel Hume
Don't you hear the red man calling? Toronto, W. Tyrrell, 1908. 43p. 19cm.

On the Anglican Indian schools.
Xerox copy. Glenbow

1966 A book of contrasts; illustrating the great development of Western Canada. [n.p., 1908] cover-title, [16]p. illus. 16 x 26cm.

Early and recent views of western cities. Toronto

1967 **Boyle**, James
The sixty of Saskatchewan. [London] 1908. ... Not seen.

Bishop Lloyd appealed in England for catechists to care for the spiritual needs of the settlers from Britain flocking into the Prairie Provinces. This is the story of the catechists told by one of their number. Private information

1967A **Brittain**, Sir Harry Ernest
Canada, there and back. London, 1908. 157p. illus. 19cm. U. of A.

1968 **Burpee**, Lawrence J[ohnstone]
The search for the western sea; the story of the exploration of north-western America. London, Alston Rivers, Ltd., 1908. lx, 651, [1]p. front., plates, ports., fold. maps. 23cm.

A new and revised edition incorporating new material was published in 2 volumes by Macmillan of Toronto, in 1935. Shortt

1969 **Canada**. Department of Agriculture
Canada West, the last best West; homes for millions. Ottawa, 1908. cover-title, 41p. illus., maps (incl. 1 on p.4 of cover) 28cm.

Another edition was published in 1909. Glenbow

1970 **Canada**. Department of the Interior
Correspondence and papers relating to seed grain in Saskatchewan and Alberta. Ottawa, Printed by S.E. Dawson, 1908. 76p. 25cm. (Canada. Sess. papers, 1908, no.25d) U. of S.

1971 **Canada**. Department of the Interior
The last best West is Canada West. Homes for millions. Ottawa [1908?] 33p. illus., double maps.

French edition has title: Le dernier mieux de l'Ouest.
Finnish edition has title: Wuneisin paras lansi. Nebenzahl - 16-274-76

1972 **Canada**. Department of the Interior
Winter wheat is a success in Alberta. Marvellous increase in acreage sown in the past three years. The elevator men and millers are meeting the situation. Farmers are enthusiastic over 'Alberta Red.' Ottawa [1908] 11p. illus. 19cm. Can. Arch.

1973 **Canadian Northern Railway**
A mile a day for twelve years ... How a country within a country has been opened up by a railway that has grown from nothing in 1896, to be the second system in Canada. The Canadian Northern. Toronto, The Company [1908] cover-title, 55, [1]p. illus. 23 1/2cm.

The Can. Arch. has a 15-page pamphlet with the title 'A Mile a Day for Eleven Years.' Shortt

1974 **Canadian Pacific Railway**
Facts concerning the agricultural conditions of southern Alberta and the famous Bow River valley. [n.p.] 1908. 63p. illus. 20 x 10cm. Not seen. R.E.S.

1975 **Church of England.** Literature committee of the Missionary Society
The Diocese of Qu'Appelle. [Toronto? 1908?] cover-title, 31p. illus. 23cm. Sask. Arch.

1976 **Conservative Party** (Canada)
Our western lands. Some transactions of the Laurier administration exposed in the sessions of 1906 and 1907. [n.p., 1908?] 42p. 22cm.

Relates to the Saskatchewan Valley Land Company. B.C. Arch.

1977 **Delaere,** A[chille]
Mémoire sur les tentatives de schisme et d'hérésie au milieu des Ruthènes de l'Ouest canadien. Québec, L'Action Sociale, 1908. 48p. 22cm.

A 42-page English edition was published in Winnipeg, West Canada Publishing Co., 1909. (In Can. Arch.) L.C.

1978 **Dominion Exhibition,** Calgary, 1908
Calgary and sunny Alberta illustrated: the official souvenir of the Dominion Exhibition, Calgary, Alberta, June 29th to July 9th, 1908. [Calgary, Herald Job Printing Co., 1908] [101]p. (chiefly illus.) 21 x 29cm.

On cover: Calgary, Alberta. Glenbow

1979 **Edmonton.** Board of Trade
Edmonton. The agricultural possibilities and resources of the surrounding district. Information issued by the Edmonton Board of Trade, 1908, for the use of those intending to follow agricultural pursuits. Edmonton, Journal Job Printing Co., Ltd. [1908] cover-title, [28]p. illus. (incl. maps) 30cm. Shortt

1980 **Edmonton.** Board of Trade
Membership and by-laws, 1908. [Edmonton, Journal Job Printing Co. [1908] cover-title, 18p. illus. (on cover) 21cm. Glenbow

1981 **Edmonton.** Board of Trade. Committee on the transportation facilities in existence to the Peace, Finlay, and Mackenzie river basins
The all-red route to the Arctic Ocean, via Edmonton. [Edmonton, 1908] [8]p. fold. maps, fold. tables. 17 1/2 x 25cm. Rutherford

1982 **Estevan, Sask.** Board of Trade
Estevan, Saskatchewan, Canada. [Estevan, The Mercury, 1908] cover-title, [32]p. illus. 9 x 15cm. Shortt

1983 **Freemasons.** Alberta. Ashlar Lodge, No.28, Calgary
By-laws. [Calgary, Quick Print, 1908] 16p. 15cm. Glenbow

1984 **Godfrey,** Ernest H.
Settlement and agricultural development of the Northwest provinces of Canada. [London] Journal of the Royal Statistical Society, 1908. cover-title, 8p. 22cm.

Reprinted from the Journal.
Printed for private circulation. Agric.

1985 **Gordon,** Charles W[illiam]
The life of James Robertson, missionary superintendent in Western Canada. Toronto, Westminster Co. [1908] 2p.l., 7-412p. front., plates, ports. 21 1/2cm. Shortt

1986 [**Hugonard**, Joseph]
Cree hymns, with some most useful prayers. [Winnipeg, 1908] 115p. illus. 14cm.

A French edition was published at Indian Head, Sask. Oblates Arch.

1987 **Hume**, Harry, comp.
Prosperous Calgary; a series of articles descriptive of the queen city of Alberta. [Calgary] Issued by the Calgary Daily Herald, 1908. [80]p. illus. 35cm. Glenbow

1988 **Irvine**, J.A.
Souvenir of the Dominion Day pageant held at Calgary, Alberta, July 1st, 1908. Calgary, The author, c1908. 2p.l., 14 plates (incl. ports.) 14 x 19cm.

On cover: Calgary pageant. Souvenir, July 1st, 1908. Glenbow

1989 **Jarvis**, W[illiam] H[enry] P[ope]
The letters of a remittance man to his mother. London, John Murray, 1908. 122p. front. 22cm.

Blunders and tribulations of a remittance man in Western Canada. Fiction. Shortt

1990 **Laut**, Agnes Christina
The conquest of the great Northwest; being the story of the adventurers of England known as the Hudson's Bay Company. New pages in the history of the Canadian Northwest and western states. Toronto, Musson Book Co. [1908] 2v. fronts., plates., ports., maps (part fold.) facsims. 21cm. Shortt

1991 **Law Society of Saskatchewan**
Rules and bylaws of the Law Society of Saskatchewan, adopted and passed by the benchers in convocation the fifth day of June, A.D. 1908. Regina, Printed by J.K. McInnis & Sons, 1908. 31p. 22 1/2cm. Shortt

1992 **Liberal Party** (Canada)
Fact vs. slander; a plain statement of fact in regard to certain matters which the Conservative party in Parliament ... have made the basis of a campaign of slander ... to shake the confidence of the electors in ... the Liberal party. [Ottawa, Ottawa Free Press Print, 1908] 47p. 24 x 13cm.

Relates chiefly to the administration of land and settlement policies in Western Canada. Glenbow

1993 **Liberal Party** (Saskatchewan)
The parliament building site. The actual facts relating to the selection and purchase of the site versus the unfounded statements made by the Haultain candidates. [n.p., 1908] folder. 8p. 19cm.

'Printed from the Regina Leader, August 4, 1908.' Sask. Arch.

1994 **Liberal Party** (Saskatchewan)
Parliament buildings contract. Statement by Premier Scott. ... (Reprinted from the Morning Leader, July 4, 1908) [n.p., 1908] caption-title, 4p. 25cm. Sask. Arch.

1995 **Liberal Party** (Saskatchewan)
Railroads! Roads! Telephones! The Scott government stands pledged to an aggressive railway policy ... [n.p., 1908] cover-title, 7, [1]p. 21cm. Sask. Arch.

1996 **Liberal Party** (Saskatchewan)
The Scott government's record. [n.p., 1908] 46p. 24cm. At head of title: Pluck-Push-Progress. Sask. Arch.

1997 **Liberal Party** (Saskatchewan)
The supplementary Revenue Act. Its successful operation. $145000 for rural schools. Facts vs. misrepresentations. 'The proof of the pudding is in the eating thereof.' [n.p., 1908] 12p. 25cm. Sask. Arch.

1998 **Lionnet**, Jean
Chez les Français du Canada. Les émigrants - Québec - Montréal - le grand Ouest - Vancouver. 4éd. Paris, Plon-Nourrit et Cie, 1908. 2p.l., vi, 284p. 18 1/2cm.

Nearly 120 pages are devoted to his tour of the French settlements throughout the West. Shortt

1999 **Lloydminster, Sask.** Board of Trade
Lloydminster district is the banner district of the West. [Edmonton, The Bulletin, 1908] cover-title, 17, [3]p. illus. 21cm. Sask. Arch.

2000 **McClung**, Nellie L[etitia (Mooney)]
Sowing seeds in Danny. Toronto, William Briggs, 1908. xii p. l., 315p. front. 19cm.

Fiction; a family story set in a small Manitoba town.
Also published in New York. U. of S.

2001 **McDiarmid**, A[rchibald] P.
The right and expediency of independence in university education. An argument presented to the University Commission of the Province of Manitoba on behalf of the Baptist denomination. [Brandon, Brandon Times] 1908. 44p. 21 1/2cm. Shortt

2002 **McDougall**, John
Wa-pee Moos-tooch, or White Buffalo. The hero of a hundred battles. A tale of life in Canada's great West during the early days of the last century. [Calgary, Printed for the author by the Herald Job Printing Co., Ltd.] 1908. 4p.l., 336p. illus. 22cm.

Juvenile fiction. Shortt

2003 **McKenna**, J[ames] A[ndrew] J[oseph]
The Hudson Bay Route. A compilation of facts with conclusions ... Ottawa, Government Printing Bureau, 1908. 54p. front., plates, fold. map. 25cm. Shortt

2004 **Mair**, Charles
Through the Mackenzie basin; a narrative of the Athabasca and Peace River treaty expedition of 1899 ... Also notes on the mammals and birds of northern

Canada, by Roderick MacFarlane. Toronto, William Briggs, 1908. 149p., 1 l., 151-494p. front., plates, ports., fold. map. 23cm.

Also published without the '... Notes.' U. of S.

2005 [**Major**, Mrs. Henniker]
Canadian life as I found it; four years homesteading in the North West Territories, by a homesteader. London, Elliot Stock, 1908. 144p. 19cm.

The Majors, husband, wife, and six-month-old baby, settled on a homestead near Tessier, Sask., in June 1904. The book is a compilation of monthly letters to friends and relatives in England describing the hardships and satisfactions of creating a home in a new country. Toronto

2006 **Marchant**, Bessie
Sisters of Silver Creek; a story of Western Canada. Illus. by Robert Hope. London, Blackie and Son, Ltd. [1908] 368p. front., plates. 20cm.

This copy has on the back end-papers a two-page ms. comment on the plot by Emily F. Murphy, herself a writer using the prairie locale.
Juvenile literature; locale 'Qu'Appelle Valley.' U. of A.

2007 **Marsh**, Edith L[ouise]
Where the buffalo roamed; the story of Western Canada told for the young. With an introduction by R.G. MacBeth. Toronto, W. Briggs, 1908. 246p. illus. 20cm.

A revised and enlarged edition was published in 1923. U. of A.

2008 [**Matheson**, Samuel Pritchard]
Printed letter – His Grace the Archbishop of Rupert's Land, Bishop's Court, Winnipeg, Man. Toronto, 18th Nov., 1908. [Toronto, 1908] 4p. folio.

Relates to Indian schools in the North-West. Antique – 92-105

2009 **Medicine Hat**. Board of Trade
Kipling's town that was born lucky, Medicine Hat, Alberta. [Medicine Hat, The Times, 1908] 32p. 19 1/2cm. Rutherford

2009A **Moore**, O.S.
In the shadow of the Rockies; being some account of the Olds district, its products and possibilities. [Olds, The Olds Gazette, 1908] [24]p. illus. 14 1/2cm.

On cover: Dominion exhibition, Calgary, Alta; June 29th to July 9th, 1908. Alta. Arch.

2010 **Moorhouse**, [Arthur Herbert Joseph]
Deep furrows, which tell of pioneer trails along which the farmers of Western Canada fought their way to great achievements in co-operation, by Hopkins Moorhouse. Toronto and Winnipeg, G.J. McLeod, Ltd. [c1908] 4p.l., 11-299p. 19 1/2cm.

A valuable record of the founding of the Grain Growers' movement. U. of S.

2011 **Morice**, A[drien] G[abriel]
Dictionnaire historique des Canadiens et des métis français de l'Ouest. Québec, J.P. Garneau, 1908. xl p., 1 l., 329p. 22cm.

An accurate and valuable biography of the French and métis connected with the fur trade. Shortt

2012 **New England Company**
Conference on Indian education in Canada convened by the company, April 15, 1908. London, Spottiswoode & Co. Ltd., 1908. 34p. 22cm.

Includes a letter from the Hon. Frank Oliver to the Hon. S.H. Blake, K.C., on the subject of Indian education.

The New England Company was founded in 1649 and incorporated in 1662. Some fifteen years later the company was responsible for printing Eliot's Indian Bible, the first translation into any North American Indian tongue. Sask. Arch.

2013 Det Nordvestlige Canada. [n.p., 1908] cover-title, [13]p. 18 1/2cm.

Danish immigration pamphlet. Ms. note on cover refers to a printing of 1500 copies. Can. Arch.

2014 **Ouellette,** J[oseph] A[lbéric]
L'Alberta-nord, région de colonisation. Edmonton, Le Courrier de l'Ouest, 1908. 31p. illus. 22cm. St. Sulpice

2015 **Ouellette,** J[oseph] A[lbéric]
Le jardin de l'Alberta-Sud. [Montréal, n.p., 1908]. cover-title, 8p.
Canner – 474-993

2016 **Paget,** Edward Clarence
A year under the shadow of St. Paul's; early undergraduate days in Keble College, Oxford, and other papers. Calgary, Herald Job Printing Co., 1908. 212, [1]p. ports. 20cm. Glenbow

2017 **Rice,** Lewis
Interesting scenes in and around Moose Jaw, Saskatchewan. The most important Canadian Pacific Railway centre in the famous new West between Winnipeg and Calgary. Moose Jaw, Lewis Rice [c1908] [32]p. illus. 18 x 23cm.

An album of pictures. Arkin

2018 **Roblin,** R[odmond] P[alen]
Manitoba boundary question. Speech ... in moving a resolution to memorialize the Parliament of Canada on the boundary question. Delivered in the Manitoba Legislature, January 15th, 1908. 61p. Can. Arch.

2019 **Royer,** Marie Albert
Excursion d'un missionnaire en 1907. Clermont-Ferrand, France, 1908. ...
Not seen.

A description of a tour which led to the establishment of old-country French settlements in southwestern Saskatchewan, particularly Ponteix. Morice

2020 Not used.

2021 **Saskatoon.** Board of Trade
Saskatoon. [Saskatoon, Phoenix job print] 1908-16. 6v. illus. 21cm.
Imprint varies.

Descriptive pamphlets, either 24 or 48 pages in extent, issued at frequent intervals bringing Saskatoon's development up to date. The Shortt Library has Spring 1908; 1909; Spring 1910; Summer 1910; 1911; Dec. 1916. Shortt

2022 **Scott**, Walter
The Saskatchewan provincial election campaign of 1908. Premier Scott in a notable speech at Rosthern clearly states the issues which rendered it necessary and analyzes the conduct of the campaign which followed. [n.p., 1908] cover-title, 14p. 20cm. In double column.

Speech delivered 26 Aug. 1908. A 12-page edition is in Sask. Arch. Can. Arch.

2023 **Stovel Company, Winnipeg**
The last of the buffalo, comprising a history of the buffalo herd of the Flathead reservation, and an account of the great round up. [Winnipeg, Stovel] 1908. 32p. incl. illus. 14 x 33cm.

The story of the herd of 250 buffalo bought from Michel Pablo by the Canadian government in 1908. B.C. Arch.

2024 **Strecker**, Carl Christoph
In der Prärie Nordamerikas. Fulda, Verlag der Fuldaer Actiendruckerei, 1908. 106p. Not seen.

A historical sketch of the West and the part played by missionaries. R.H.P., 1908

2025 **Tims**, John William
The call of the red man for truth, honesty, and fair play. [n.p., n.d.] 15p. 22cm.

Written in reply to a pamphlet by S.H. Blake entitled, 'Don't you hear the red man calling?' See Entry 1965. Glenbow

2026 **Tucker**, L[ewis] Norman
Western Canada. Toronto, Musson Book Co., Ltd., 1908. xii, 164p. front., plates, ports., fold. map. 17cm. (Handbooks of English Church expansion [v.2]) Shortt

2027 **Ussel**, Georges d'.
Rapport sur l'agriculture dans l'Ouest Canadien. [Villefranche-de-Rouergue, Société anonyme d'imprimerie, 1908] 78p. 27cm.

In addition to strictly agricultural topics the author has chapters on 'Comment on devient colon,' 'Races immigrantes,' and 'Les français au Canada.' France

2028 **Vegreville, Alta.** Board of Trade
Settlement opportunities on improved and unimproved lands. Vegreville district, Province of Alberta, Canada. [Vegreville, Observer Print [190-] cover-title, 7, [1]p. map. 20cm. Glenbow

2029 **Watt**, Gertrude Balmer
Town and trail. Edmonton, News Publishing Co., 1908. 85p. illus. 22cm.

Essays. Edmonton

2030 **Weijers**, Antoon
De waarheid over Alberta. De algemeene toestand geschetst door Antoon Weijers. [Tilburg] Tilburgsche Handelsdrukkerij [1908] ... illus. 22cm. Not seen.

A Dutch pamphlet entitled 'The Truth about Alberta.' N.Y.

2031 **Wetaskiwin, Alta.** Board of Trade
Wetaskiwin, the elevator city of Alberta. Wetaskiwin, The Times [1908?] [16]p. illus. 11 1/2 x 15cm. Alta. Leg.

2032 **Winnipeg.** Development and Industrial Bureau
A brief history of the City of Winnipeg. [Winnipeg, 1908] 98p.
Hamilton

2033 **Anderson**, Robert T[hompson]
The old timer and other poems. [Edmonton, Edmonton Publishing Co., 1909]
103p. plates, ports. 25 1/2cm. Alta. Leg.

2034 **Athabasca Landing, Alta.** Board of Trade
Athabasca Landing, 1909. The gateway of the last great West. [Athabasca Landing? Northern News print, 1909] cover-title, 28p. illus. 12 x 20cm.
Alta. Leg.

2035 **Blake**, Samuel Hume
Memorandum on Indian work. Toronto, The Bryant Press, 1909. 20p. 23cm.

Xerox copy.
Addressed 'to the members of the Board of Management of the M.S.C.C.'
On Indian schools operated by the Church of England. Glenbow

2036 **British Association for the Advancement of Science**
A handbook to Winnipeg and the Province of Manitoba. Prepared for the 79th annual meeting of the British Association for the Advancement of Science. With notes on some of the chief points to be visited on the western excursion.
Winnipeg, Published by the Local Executive Committee, 1909. 2p.l., [7]-301p.
plates, ports., fold. maps. 18cm. Shortt

2037 **Burlet**, Lucien de
Au Canada. De Paris à Vancouver. Notes d'hier et d'aujourd'hui. [2.éd.] Paris, Librairie Ambert [1909] 286p., 1 l. 18cm.

First edition appeared in 1907. Br. Mus.

2038 **Bryce**, George
The romantic settlement of Lord Selkirk's colonists (the pioneers of Manitoba)
Toronto, Musson Book Co. [c1909] 328p. front., illus., plates, ports., plans.
21 1/2cm. Shortt

2039 **Calgary**. Hundred Thousand Club
... One thousand facts about Calgary, compiled and published by the Hundred Thousand Club, Calgary ... Calgary, Herald-Western Printing Co., Ltd., 1909.
cover-title, 19p. 14 1/2cm. At head of title: 1909 ed.

Lande lists a 1911 edition with the same title. Shortt

2040 **Canada**. Department of the Interior
Correspondence and papers, including financial statement relating to seed grain distribution in 1908 in the provinces of Saskatchewan and Alberta. Ottawa, Printed by S.E. Dawson, 1909. 208p. 24cm. (Canada. Sess. papers, 1909, no.25c) U. of S.

2041 **Canada**. Department of Railways and Canals
Report of the Hudson's Bay Railway surveys. Ottawa, King's Printer, 1909.
22p. plates. 25cm. Shortt

2042 **Canadian Pacific Railway**
Alaska-Yukon-Pacific Exposition, 1909: souvenir. [Montreal, 1909] cover-title, [35]p. incl. covers. illus. 10 x 14cm.

Booklet shaped like a sheaf of wheat, with cover illustrated to look like a sheaf. Chiefly advertising the Prairie region. Glenbow

2043 **Canadian Pacific Railway**
Canada i'r cymry. Rheilffordd y Canadian Pacific. Caerdydd, Wales, Western Mail [1909] cover-title, 60p. illus. 19cm. Wales

2044 **Canadian Pacific Railway**
Gwaith a chyflogau yn Canada, gydag arweiniad i ymfudwyr a'r ffordd oreu i deithio. [n.p., n.d.] cover-title, 10p. illus., fold. map. 24cm.

Numbered pagination includes inside covers. Wales

2045 **Canadian Pacific Railway**
Public opinion concerning the Bow River Valley, southern Alberta, Canada. Calgary, Western Printing and Litho. Co., 1909. 39p. Patrick – 41-169

2046 **Canadian Pacific Railway**
Two blades of grass. Concerning central Alberta. Winnipeg, Canadian Pacific Railway [1909] cover-title, 32p. incl. illus. 19 1/2cm. Shortt

2047 **Church of England.** Catechism. Cree
The Church catechism in the language of the Cree Indians. London, Society for Promoting Christian Knowledge, 1909. 10p. 19cm. Sask. Arch.

2048 **Church of England.** Diocese of Saskatchewan
Indian missions. Diocese of Saskatchewan. Missions, schools, etc. ... Toronto, Oxford Press, 1898-1909. 4v. illus. 21cm.

Archives has: 1898, 1900, 1902, 1909. Sask. Arch.

2049 **Church of England.** Diocese of Saskatchewan
Report on Indian missions. Presented to Synod, June, 1909. Printed by order of the Synod. Toronto, Printed by Geo. Parker & Sons [1909] 24p. illus. (ports.) 21cm. Rupert's

2050 **Clarke,** Annie
Dawnlight and evensong. Poems. [Winnipeg, Hull Printing Co., 190–?] 95p. 16cm. Glenbow

2051 **Directory of Didsbury [Alta.] District**
Directory. Townships between 35 and 28, west 9th, east of Range 26 and west of Red Deer River. [Didsbury] Didsbury Pioneer Print, 1909. 64p. 20cm.

Advertising included in paging. Glenbow

2052 **Dufresne,** A.R.
The St. Andrews lock and dam. [Winnipeg, Public Press, 1909] 11p. illus., fold. maps. 17cm.

On cover: British Association, Winnipeg, 1909. Excursion to St. Andrews Locks on the Red River. Queen's

2053 [**Gordon**, Charles William]
The foreigner; a tale of Saskatchewan, by Ralph Connor [pseud.] Toronto, Westminster Co. [c1909] 384p. 20cm.

The hero is a Ukrainian youth.
Also published in London and New York. Another edition by Hodder & Stoughton in London and New York had the title 'The Settler.' Man. Leg.

2054 **Grand Trunk Pacific Railway**
On the prairie section of the Grand Trunk Pacific Railway, Canada's national transcontinental railway in Manitoba, Saskatchewan and Alberta. For information respecting town sites and farming lands for actual settlers along the Grand Trunk Pacific Railway application should be made to the land commissioner of the railway company at Winnipeg, Man. Montreal, January 1909. folder. 18p. incl. illus. 16 1/2cm.

Large map and illustrations on verso.
Caption reads: On the prairie section of the Grand Trunk Pacific Railway, Manitoba, Saskatchewan, and part of Alberta, showing the Dominion Land Districts.
Amtmann - 241-671

2055 **Grand Trunk Pacific Railway**
7,000 free homesteads in 1909 along the line of the Grand Trunk Pacific Railway in the most fertile section of Western Canada. List of vacant lands, map and homestead regulations. Winnipeg, 1909. 48p. map. 22 1/2cm.
Can. Arch.

2056 **Gray**, Frank M., comp.
Reports of experts on Edmonton water supply, principally Pigeon Lake scheme. [Edmonton, Bulletin Job Print, 1909] cover-title, 14p. illus. 27 x 14cm.
Glenbow

2057 Guide and companion to Edmonton, Alberta; a handbook for everybody: for residents, tourists, intending settlers & others. [Edmonton] Published by Turner & Nutt; printed by the Douglas Co. [1909] cover-title, [4], 63, [9]p. incl. covers. illus., fold. map. 19cm.

Pagination includes advertising matter. Glenbow

2058 **Guttormsson**, Guttormur J[ónsson]
Jón Austfirdingur og nokkur smákvaedi. Winnipeg, Ólafur S. Thorgeirsson prentadi, 1909. 82p. 17cm. U. of M.

2059 **Harwood**, C[harles] A[uguste de Lotbiniere]
The Fort Garry convention. Montreal, C.A. Marchand, 1909. cover-title, 38p. 24cm.

Riel's own account of the convention, Nov. 1869, and Jan.-Feb. 1870. Shortt

2060 **Hope**, Sir Harry
Canada as it appeared to Scotch agriculturists, by Harry Hope, J.P., and Prof. R.B. Greig, F.R.S.E. Being a lecture delivered by Mr. Hope before a meeting of the East Lothian Farmers' Club at Haddington on January 29, 1909, and a series of letters written by Prof. Greig while in Canada, to the 'Aberdeen Free Press.' Ottawa, Department of the Interior, 1909. cover-title, 30p. illus. 18cm.
Can. Arch.

2061 **Hudson's Bay Company**
A visit to Lower Fort Garry. Specially issued on the occasion of a garden party, by the Commissioner of the Hudson's Bay Company and Mrs. Chipman. Thursday, August 26th, 1909. [Winnipeg, Winnipeg Telegram, 1909] cover-title, 8p. 23cm.

At head of title: British Association, Winnipeg, 1909. A second t.-p. has: Lower Fort Garry, 'The Stone Fort'; a retrospect. Arkin

2062 **Hultgren & Davie,** real estate agents
The last best West: Crossfield, the bonanza wheat district in southern Alberta, Canada. [Crossfield, 1909?] cover-title, 4p. 14cm.

Xerox copy on 4 sheets. 22 x 28cm. Includes advertising matter. Glenbow

2063 **Kerby,** George W[illiam]
The broken trail; pages from a pastor's experience in Western Canada. Toronto, William Briggs, 1909. 189p. front., plates. 19 1/2cm. Shortt

2064 **Lowie,** Robert H[arry]
The Assiniboine. New York, The Trustees, 1909. 1p.l., p.1-270. illus., plates. 24 1/2cm. (American Museum of Natural History. Anthropological papers, v.4, pt.1)

Based on a study of the Stoney Assiniboines of Morley, Alberta, and the Assiniboines of Ft. Belknap, Montana. The author discusses their history, material culture, amusements, art, mythology. U. of S.

2065 **McClung,** J[ames] A.
In Dixie and Manitoba; a true story of life. [n.p.] Published by the author, 1909. 13, [1]p. 20cm.

This would appear to be the same booklet as Entry 2070, attributed to J.A. Murray, presumably a pseudonym. Arkin

2066 **Machray,** Robert
Life of Robert Machray, D.D., L.L.D., D.C.L., Archbishop of Rupert's Land, primate of all Canada, prelate of the order of St. Michael and St. George. Toronto, Macmillan Co. of Canada, 1909. xx, 468p. front., illus., plates, ports. 23 1/2cm. Shortt

2067 Manitobans as we see 'em, 1908 and 1909. [Winnipeg] Newspaper Cartoonists' Association of Manitoba [1909] 227 plates on 115 l. 23cm.

Cartoons of prominent Manitobans. Shortt

2068 **Mellick,** H[enry] G[eorge]
The Indians and our Indian missions. Winnipeg, H.C. Stovel, 1909. xi, 142p. plates, ports. 19cm. United College

2069 **Morinville, Alta.** Board of Trade
Morinville, Alberta, 1909. [Edmonton, Courrier de l'Ouest, 1909] 39p. illus. (incl. group photos.) 25cm.

The first part of the text is in French, the second in English. St-Jean

2070 **Murray**, J.A.
In Dixie and Manitoba; a true history of real life. Toronto, Wm. Briggs, 1909. 13p. 18 1/2cm.

Missionary life at Norwood, Man., in the 1890's. Victoria College

2071 **O'Donnell**, John H[arrison]
Manitoba as I saw it from 1869 to date, with flash-lights on the first Riel Rebellion. Winnipeg, Clark Bros. & Co. [c1909] 158p. front., plates, ports. 22cm. Shortt

2072 **Paget**, Amelia [Anne (McLean)]
The people of the plains. Edited with an introduction by Duncan Campbell Scott. Toronto, Ryerson Press, 1909. 199p. front., plates, ports. 20cm.

Relates to the Indians. Shortt

2073 **Parker**, Sir Gilbert
Northern lights. Toronto, Copp, Clark, 1909. [10], 375p. plates. 20cm.

Fiction, set in Western Canada. Glenbow

2074 Pictures of life in Canada; sixty photographs illustrative of everyday life there. London, Gowans & Grady, Ltd., 1909. 64p. front., plates. 15cm.

Nearly half the photographs relate to farm life on the Canadian prairies. The photographs were supplied by the C.P.R. Trinity

2075 **Poirier**, Joseph Emile
... Les arpents de neige; roman canadien, avec une préface de M. Adjutor Rivard. Paris, Nouvelle librairie nationale, 1909. xii, 368p. 22cm.

Fiction. Plot relates to Riel Rebellion of 1885. Toronto

2076 **Reed**, Charles B[ert]
The masters of the wilderness; a study of the Hudson's Bay Company from its origin to modern times. A paper read before the Chicago Historical Society, March 16, 1909. [Chicago, 1909] 1p.l., p.137-73. front. (fold. map) plate. 21cm. Reprint from Chicago Hist. Soc. Proceedings, v.4, pt.3. Shortt

2077 **Regina**. Board of Trade
Regina, the capital of the province of Saskatchewan; a city of beautiful buildings and paved streets, an educational centre. [Regina] Lewis Rice [1909?] [32]p., chiefly illus. 19 x 24cm.

'Many ... illustrations are from copyrighted photos. by Lewis Rice, illustrator & publisher.' Glenbow

2078 **Rohde**, Oscar
Rockies and other things. [Birkenhead, Eng., 1909] cover-title, 12p. 12 plates. 12 x 18cm.

Brief notes on a trip across Canada, with a camping stopover in the Banff area. Glenbow

2079 **Rutherford**, Alexander Cameron
Railway speech delivered ... in the Alberta Legislature, February 24th, 1909. [Edmonton, 1909] [2], 5-20p. 23cm. Glenbow

2080 **Sabourin,** Joseph Adonias
Les Catholiques ruthènes. Leur situation actuelle dans le Diocèse de Saint-Boniface. La paroisse – l'école – le journal. Motifs d'espérer. Québec, Impr. de la Cie de L'Evènement, 1909. 16p. 22cm. St. Sulpice

2081 Saskatchewan, Canada. [n.p., 1909?] 112p. illus., maps (1 fold.) 20cm. Glenbow

2082 **Saxby,** [C.F.] Argyll
The taming of the rancher; a story of Western Canada. London, S.W. Partridge & Co. [1909] 138p. front., plates. 19cm.
Juvenile literature. Br. Mus.

2083 **Scott,** T[homas] R[eid]
A brief history of the Presbyterian church in Oxbow and vicinity. [Hartney? (Man.), 1909] 1p.l., [14]p. 21cm. Sask. Arch.

2084 **Scottish Agricultural Commission**
Canada as seen through Scottish eyes: being an account of a trip taken across the Dominion by the Scottish Agricultural Commission, 1908. Ottawa, 1909. ... Incl. photo.

2085 **Seton,** Ernest Thompson
Life histories of northern animals; an account of the mammals of Manitoba. New York, C. Scribner's Sons, 1909. 2v. fronts., illus., plates, maps. 26 1/2cm. U. of S.

2086 **Tims,** John William
Calgary's appeal on behalf of Calgary's children of the Prairies; being a criticism and reply to the memorandum on 'Indian work,' addressed to the Board of Management of M.S.C.C. by the Hon. S.H. Blake, K.C. [n.p., 1909?] [2], 11p. 21cm.
Xerox copy. See Entry 2035. Glenbow

2087 **Strathcona Collegiate Institute**
Souvenir of the opening of Strathcona Collegiate Institute, Wednesday, February 17, 1909, by His Honor Lieutenant-Governor Bulyea. [Strathcona] Printed by Plaindealer Co. [1909] 16p. illus., ports. 16 x 23 1/2cm. Rutherford

2087A **Trotter,** W.R.
Second report on misrepresentation to undesirable intending immigrants from the British Isles to Canada. Quebec, Trades and Labor Congress of Canada, 1909. 48p. 20 1/2cm. Can. Arch. (ms.)

2087B **United Farmers of Alberta**
Constitution and by-laws. Adopted by the convention, January 14th, 1909. [Edmonton] Alberta Homestead print [1909] cover-title, 16p. 14 1/2cm. Alta. Arch.

2088 **Vegreville, Alta.** Board of Trade
For you! A few facts about the Vegreville district in Central Alberta. Issued by the Vegreville Board of Trade. Vegreville, Observer Print [190–?] folder. 16p. incl. illus., maps. 28cm. Amtmann

2089 **Warner,** W.
Illustrated souvenir of Brandon, Manitoba. [Brandon, 190–?] [44]p. chiefly illus. 26 x 31cm.

Photos by Wm. A. Martel and Sons, Brandon. Glenbow

2090 **Wetaskiwin, Alta.** Alexandra High School
Souvenir, June 1909. [Wetaskiwin, 1909] cover-title, [40]p. 6 plates (incl. ports) 25cm.

Illustrations in margins (decorations)
Includes advertising matter. Glenbow

2091 **Woodsworth,** James S[haver]
Strangers within our gates; or, Coming Canadians. Toronto, F.C. Stephenson [c1909] 356p. incl. tables. front., plates, map. 19 1/2cm. (Methodist Church Missionary Society. Young People's Forward Movement, no.5)
U. of S.

2092 **Yorkton.** Board of Trade
Yorkton. ... The metropolis of northeastern Saskatchewan. The largest grain shipping point in Western Canada. [Yorkton, The Enterprise, 1909] [16]p. 15 1/2cm. Shortt

2093 **Aberdeen, Sask.** Board of Trade
A profitable point for the settler in the last West. Aberdeen, The Board, 1910. 16p. illus. 15 1/2cm. Map on cover. Shortt

2094 **Alberta.** Publicity Bureau
Land and agriculture in Alberta; authentic and reliable information respecting the resources of the new Province of Alberta. Edmonton, Govt. Printer, 1910. 64p. Amtmann - 176-3

2095 **Alward,** Silas
'Our Western heritage' ... 'Then and now; or, Thirty years after' ... Lectures ... Saint John, N.B., The Saint John Globe Pub. Co., 1910. 58p. 22cm.

The first lecture was given to the Mechanics Institute on 23 January 1882; the second lecture was to the Natural History Society of New Brunswick, 8 February 1910. Both lectures describe visits to Western Canada. U. of N.B.

2096 **[Anonymous]**
La langne [sic] française dans l'Alberta et la Saskatchewan. [St-Boniface? 1910] cover-title, 15p. 22cm.

Mostly excerpts from the House of Commons debates at the time of the formation of the new provinces. Shortt

2097 **[Anonymous]**
Something about Edmonton and Canada's richest mixed farming district. Edmonton [1910] 40p. illus., map. R.E.S.

2097A **Athabasca Landing, Alta.** Board of Trade
The northern trek. April, 1910. [Athabasca Landing, Northern News print, 1910] cover-title, [3]p. 26cm. Alta. Arch.

2098 **Bassano, Alta.** Board of Trade
Bassano, the logical and recognized centre of Canada's great inland centre. [n.p., n.d.] cover-title, [8]p. illus., map. 28cm.

One page folds out. Glenbow

2099 **Bible.** New Testament. St. Matthew. Selections. Blackfoot
The Gospel according to St. Matthew, translated into the language of the Blackfoot Indians in the Diocese of Calgary. ... Sarcee Reserve, Calgary, Printed at the Diocesan press, 1910. cover-title, 4p. 21cm.

Text in Blackfoot syllabic. Private copy

2100 **Binnie-Clark,** Georgina
A summer on the Canadian prairie. London, E. Arnold, 1910. viii, 311, [1]p. front., plates. 20cm.

The author spent a summer at Lipton, Sask., on the edge of the Qu'Appelle Valley. She was favourably impressed with the opportunities the West offered, and describes vividly the people in the homesteading community.
Also published by Musson of Toronto. Shortt

2101 **Bird & Antrobus,** pub.
Strome, the garden spot of 'Sunny Alberta.' Strome, Alta. [19--] cover-title, 14, [2]p. illus., map (on back cover) 23cm. Glenbow

2102 **Blackstock Land Co., Regina**
Old Fort Qu'Appelle, Saskatchewan's beauty spot. [Regina, Caxton Press, 191-] 24p. illus. 24cm. Sask. Arch.

2103 **Brinkworth,** G[eorge] W[alter]
Royal Northwest Mounted Police, Canada. Regina c1910. 17 l. of plates, ports. 14 x 24cm.

On cover: Souvenir of the Royal Northwest Mounted Police, Canada. Coat of arms on t.-p. Glenbow

2104 **Calgary.** First Congregational Church
Tried & true cook book; a selection of recipes compiled by the ladies and friends of the First Congregational Church, Calgary, Alta., contributed by the ladies of the congregation. [Calgary, McAra Presses] 1910. 68, [1]p. 18cm.

Includes advertising matter. Glenbow

2104A **Calgary Golf and Country Club, Calgary**
The act of incorporation, constitution, rules and regulations and list of members. v.1- 1910- Calgary, 1910- v. 18cm.

Library has: 1912, 1914-15. Glenbow

2105 **Cameron,** Agnes Deans
The new north; being some account of a woman's journey through Canada to the Arctic ... New York, D. Appleton & Co., 1910. xix, 398p. front., illus. (incl. ports.) map. 23 1/2cm.

Most of the book is devoted to the Mackenzie valley. U. of S.

2106 **Campbell**, Bruce
The garden spot of Western Canada, the town of Selkirk, Manitoba, and its district. Published by the Board of Trade, Selkirk, 1910. Winnipeg, Ransom Engraving Co., Free Press Job Dept. [1910] 24p. plates. Amtmann - 210

2107 Le Canada agricole. L'immigration française. Edmonton, Impr. du Courrier de l'Ouest, 1910. 80p. 21cm.

Emphasizes Saskatchewan and Alberta.
At head of title: Le XXème siècle sera le siècle du Canada. (Sir Wilfrid Laurier)
France

2108 **Canada.** Archives
Red River Settlement. Papers in the Canadian Archives relating to the pioneers; selected by Chester Martin. [Ottawa] The Archives, 1910. cover-title, 27p. 24 1/2cm. Shortt

2109 **Canada.** Department of the Interior
Alberta red, the winning winter wheat; increase in average yield and popularity. Farmers like it. Millers favor it. Climate improves it. Kansas imports it. Ottawa, 1910. 31, [1]p. incl. map. 18 1/2cm. L.C.

2110 **Canada.** Department of the Interior
Canada West, the last best West. Ottawa, The Department, 1910. cover-title, 41p. illus., maps. 27 1/2cm. Shortt

2111 **Canada.** Department of the Interior
Kanada, mulighedernes land. Ottawa, 1910. cover-title, 32p. illus. 19cm.

Coloured map of Canada on back cover; coloured pictures of a stack of sheaves and of a threshing scene on covers.
Contains brief letters from Danish settlers. Denmark

2112 **Canada.** Department of the Interior
Llawlyfr swyddogol Canada. Ottawa, The Department, 1910. cover-title, 56p. illus. 18cm.

Cover has illustration.
On back cover: Picture of a barrel on which is a map of Western Canada and the caption 'The flour barrel of the world.' Wales

2113 **Canada.** Department of the Interior
Prosperity follows settlement in any part of Canada. Letters from satisfied settlers. Ottawa, 1910. 48p. 18cm.

Solely letters and testimonials. Not to be confused with an earlier publication with a similar title but in 'Western Canada.' H.B.C.

2114 **Canada.** Department of the Interior
Silhouettes of the West. The world's last best West. Ottawa [Dept. of the Interior] 1910. cover-title, 14p. 20cm. Reprint from The Globe. Shortt

2115 **Canadian Pacific Railway**
Concerning central Alberta. [London, 1910?] 16p. illus. 18cm. Amtmann - 241-623

2116 **Canadian Pacific Railway**
The heart of the Saskatchewan valley. Winnipeg [1910] 27p. illus. 23cm. Sask. Arch.

2117 **Canadian Pacific Railway**
The staff of life; a story of wheat production in southern Alberta, Canada. [Canadian ed.] Calgary, 1910. cover-title, [2], 2-47 numb. columns on 24p. illus. 20 x 20cm.

Imperfect: section clipped from columns 8 and 11. An edition of 1911, containing 63 pages, is in the New York Public Library. Glenbow

2118 **Canadian Pacific Railway**
Western Canada. Manitoba, Alberta, Saskatchewan. How to reach it. How to obtain lands. How to make a home. [Winnipeg, Canadian Pacific Railway, 1910?] 79p. incl. front., illus. fold. map. 20cm. Shortt

2119 **Canadian Pacific Railway**
Where wheat is king ... Winnipeg [1910] 36p. illus., fold. map. 23cm. Sask. Arch.

2120 **Canadian Townsites Limited**
Cities in the making. [London, Hazell, Watson & Vinery, 1910] 16p. illus., fold. map. 22cm.

The company was sole agent for the Grand Trunk Pacific Development Co. Describes townsites in Western Canada on the G.T.P. R.E.S.

2121 **Carlyle, Sask.** Board of Trade
Carlyle, Saskatchewan, where they grow wheat. [Carlyle, Homes Printery, 1910] cover-title, [36]p. illus. (incl. map) 22cm. Shortt

2122 **Chipman,** George Fisher, ed.
The siege of Ottawa; being the story of 800 farmers from Ontario, Quebec, New Brunswick, Nova Scotia, Manitoba, Saskatchewan, and Alberta; who met the government and members of Parliament in the House of Commons chamber on December 16, 1910, and demanded more equitable legislation. Winnipeg, Grain Growers' Guide [1910] 68p. 23cm. Not seen. L.C.

2123 **Church Missionary Society**
Extracts from the annual letters of the missionaries for the year 1900. Part XIX, North-West Canada. London, The Society [1910] cover-title, 1p.l., [843]-888p. 22cm. Sask. Arch.

2123A **Church Missionary Society**
... The North-West Canada missions. 2d ed. London, The Society, 1910. 79, 1p. incl. double map. 19cm. B.C. Arch.

2124 **Comrades of Equity**
Constitution of ... [191-] 8p. Sask. History, v.18, no.1, p.5

2125 **Conservative Party** (Saskatchewan)
Sessional review, Saskatchewan Legislature, 1909, and statements of the Provincial Rights policy. Regina, Saskatchewan Pub. Co. Ltd., 1910. cover-title, 78p. 22cm. Sask. Arch.

2126 [**Copping**, Arthur Edward]
Seven years ago. The story of a Canadian town. Lloydminster, North Western Territory. [n.p., 1910?] cover-title, 7p. 12 1/2cm. At head of title: With J. Willey's compliments, Brooklands. Reprint from the London Daily News. U. of S.

2127 Cowles' domestic science cook book. Strathcona, Alberta, Published by Frank Cowles, druggist [ca 1910] cover-title, 30p. 18cm.

Includes advertising matter. Glenbow

2128 **Craik, Sask.** Board of Trade
A silent salesman. Craik [Craik Weekly News, 1910] [56]p. incl. front., plates. 20cm. Shortt

2129 **Cran**, [Marion Free (Dudley)]
A woman in Canada, by Mrs. George Cran. Toronto, Musson Book Co., Ltd. [1910] viii, 9-283, [1]p. front. (port.) plates. 22cm.

The author was a keen observer of social conditions, and was concerned with the hardships endured by pioneer women. She was interested in emigration from the British Isles.
U. of S.

2130 **Crean**, Frank J[oseph] P[atrick]
New Northwest exploration. Report of exploration by Frank J.P. Crean in Saskatchewan and Alberta north of the surveyed area, seasons of 1908 & 1909. Ottawa, Government Printing Bureau, 1910. 115p. front., illus. (incl. maps) fold. map. 25cm. Shortt

2131 **Cunard Steamship Company Limited**
Kanada: hogy utazzunk a Cunard Line vöröskéményes gyorsha jóival közvetlenül Kanadaba ... Budapest, Magyarországi Föiroda [1910?] cover-title, 46p. maps. 15cm.

Red line borders on pages.
A handbook for Hungarian immigrants.
Map and back covers missing from this copy. Glenbow

2132 **Dauphin, Man.** Board of Trade
Dauphin – the plentiful. Dauphin, The Board [1910?] [16p.] illus., fold. map. 28cm. Man. Arch.

2133 **Dobry & Large, Limited**
Golden opportunities: 'the Killam district' holds these for you. Read and learn, come and see. Killam, Alberta [1910?] [16]p. illus. 17cm.

On cover: Golden opportunities in Canada's greatest wheat belt. Glenbow

2134 **Du Val**, Frederic B[eal]
The problem of social vice in Winnipeg. Being a reply to a pamphlet entitled 'The attitude of the church to the social evil.' Together with a brief examination of the question in the light of physiology, law, and morality. [n.p., 191–] 32p. 23cm. Sask. Arch.

2135 **Elkington**, E[rnest] Way
Canada, the land of hope. London, Adam and Charles Black, 1910. viii, 239, [1]p. front., illus., plates, fold. map. 20 1/2cm.

Some seventy pages describe his journey across the prairies. Contains some glaring inaccuracies. Shortt

2136 **Evangeliska-lúterska kirkjufélag Íslendinga í Vesturheimi (Hið)**
Gjordabok 26 arsthings hins evangeliska lúterska kirkjufélags Islendinga í Vesturheimi haldid i Winnipeg, Manitoba, 17-20 Juni, 1910. [Winnipeg, 1910] 47p. fold leaf. 21 1/2cm. Denmark

2137 **Evangeliska-lúterska kirkjufélag Íslendinga í Vesturheimi (Hið)**
Minningarrit tuttugu og fimm ára afmaelis Hins ev. lút. kirkjufélags Íslendinga í Vesturheimi, 1885-1910. [Winnipeg, Logbergi, 1910] 78p. illus. 24cm. U. of M.

2138 **Fea**, Samuel
Irish Ned, the Winnipeg newsy. Toronto, Wm. Briggs, 1910. 28p. front. Not seen. Ryerson

2139 **Grand Trunk Pacific Railway**
The big wheat field of Western Canada. [Winnipeg, 191–] folder. ([4]p.) illus. 22cm. Berkeley

2140 **Grand Trunk Pacific Railway**
8,000 free homesteads in 1910 along the lines of the Grand Trunk Pacific Railway in the most fertile section of Western Canada. List of vacant lands, map and homestead regulations. Winnipeg, Grand Trunk Pacific Railway [1910] 52p. incl. illus. fold. map. 23 1/2cm. Shortt

2141 **Grand Trunk Pacific Railway**
The Fort Garry, Winnipeg; the Macdonald, Edmonton. Grand Trunk Pacific hotels. [Winnipeg, 191–] 24p. illus. 21cm. Shortt

2142 **Grand Trunk Pacific Railway**
The Macdonald, Edmonton, Canada. [Winnipeg? 191–] 16p. illus. 21cm. Shortt

2143 **Grand Trunk Pacific Railway**
Purchase farm lands along the lines of the Grand Trunk Pacific Railway in Western Canada. List of lands which may be purchased, maps, prices and information. Winnipeg, 1910. 36p. incl. illus. fold. map. 22cm. Shortt

2144 **Hanley, Sask**. Board of Trade
Hanley. [Regina, University Press, 1910] 47, [1]p. illus. 23 1/2 x 10 1/2cm. On cover: Why Hanley? Wealth. Shortt

2145 **Haydon**, A[rthur] L[incoln]
The riders of the plains, a record of the Royal Northwest Mounted Police of Canada, 1873-1910. Toronto, Copp Clark Co., Ltd., 1910. xvi, 385, [1]p. front., illus., plates, ports., fold. map, fold. diagr. 23 1/2cm. Shortt

2146 **Herrington**, W[alter] S[tevens]
The evolution of the Prairie Provinces. Toronto, Wm. Briggs, 1910. 144p. 19 1/2cm. Shortt

2147 **Huestis**, Charles Herbert
The Indian problem in Alberta. [191-] ... Not seen. Morgan, 1912

2148 **Ingham**, T. Samuel
O arfon i Canada, ymddangosodd yn 'Y Genedl Gymreig,' 1909. Carnarvon, W. Gwenlyn Evans, 1910. 23p. illus. 22cm.

A pamphlet published under the auspices of the Allan Steamship Line. Wales

2149 [**Landry**, Auguste Charles Philippe]
Les écoles du Nord-Ouest. Québec, 1910. cover-title, 35p. 23cm. 'Extrait de la Nouvelle-France.'

At end of text signed: Lex. Rutherford

2150 **Langham, Sask**. Board of Trade
Langham, in the heart of the Saskatchewan valley, Canada's great wheat belt. [Langham] Langham Recorder [1910?] 14 l. illus. 13 1/2 x 20 1/2cm. Shortt

2151 **Lardon**, P[ierre A.]
Poésies de St-Boniface. Winnipeg, Arthur Bontal, 1910. 31p. plates (incl. ports.) 22cm.

In a ms. note the author states that this was the first volume of French poetry published between Ottawa and the Pacific Ocean. Man. Leg.

2152 **Lethbridge**. Board of Trade
Facts for the settler about the Lethbridge district, sunny southern Alberta. [Lethbridge, Daily Herald presses, 1910] 23, [1]p. illus., fold. map. 21cm. Rutherford

2153 **Lethbridge**. Board of Trade
Lethbridge in a nutshell. 4th ed. [Lethbridge, Daily Herald, 1910] cover-title, 16p. 7 1/2 x 12 1/2cm. Rutherford

2154 **Lively**, Gerald J.
The plea of the West, and other poems. London, W. Stewart & Co. [191-] 24p. 18cm. Rutherford

2155 **McClintock**, Walter
The old north trail; or, Life, legends and religion of the Blackfeet. London, Macmillan, 1910. xxvi, 539p. front., illus., plates, fold. map. 22 1/2cm.

The author spent several years among the American branch of the tribe. Shortt

2156 **McClung**, Nellie L[etitia (Mooney)]
The second chance. Toronto, Wm. Briggs, 1910. viii, 369p. col. front. 19 1/2cm.

Fiction; a sequel to 'Sowing Seeds in Danny.' L.C.

2157 **Martel**, W[illia]m A., and Son
Illustrated souvenir of Souris, Manitoba. Brandon [n.d.] 76p. incl. 64p. of illus. 18 x 24cm. Glenbow

2158 **Medicine Hat.** Board of Trade
Medicine Hat, Alberta, Canada. Natural gas, electricity, coal. Medicine Hat, The Board, 1910. 44p. illus. (incl. ports.) fold. plate. 30 1/2cm. Shortt

2159 **Melville, Sask.** Board of Trade
Melville, the West's wonder town. [Melville, Canadian office, 1910] 24p. illus. 10 1/2 x 25cm. Sask. Arch.

2160 **Montgomery,** H[enry] H[utchinson]
The church on the prairie. 2d ed., enlarged. [London] Society for the Propagation of the Gospel in Foreign Parts, 1910. vii, 127p. front., plates. 19cm.

Relates to the Church of England. Sask. Leg.

2161 **Morice,** A[drien] G[abriel]
History of the Catholic Church in Western Canada, from Lake Superior to the Pacific (1659-1895) Toronto, Musson Book Co., 1910. 2v. front., plates, ports., 2 fold. maps, facsims. (1 fold.) 23cm.

A French edition in 3 volumes was published by the author in Winnipeg in 1912, a 4-volume edition in 1921-23. Because of the additional material, the latter is the best to consult. See Entry 2860. Shortt

2162 **Mott,** Lawrence
Prairie, snow and sea. Toronto, Musson Book Co., 1910. 328p. 20cm.

The Prairie Provinces are the setting for several stories. Glenbow

2163 **Murphy,** Emily Gowan (Ferguson)
Janey Canuck in the West, by Emily Ferguson. 3d ed. London, Cassell & Co., Ltd., 1910. viii, 305, [1]p. col. front., illus. 20cm.

Describes the author's experiences on a journey to Edmonton.
A new edition was published by Dent of Toronto in 1919. Shortt

2164 **Pearson, [William] Company, Limited**
Last Mountain Lake, Saskatchewan. [Winnipeg? 1910] caption-title, [3]p. of text and 21 plates. 12 x 17cm. Sask. Arch.

2165 **Prince Albert.** Board of Trade
Prince Albert. 'Europe's easiest way.' [Prince Albert] 1910. 32p. illus., fold. map. 23cm. U. of S.

2166 **Quebec & Western Canada Land Syndicate,** Pierreville, Que.
The Quebec & Western Canada Land Syndicate (Limited) Capital autorise $1,000,000. Bureau Chef: Pierreville, Que. [Montréal, 1910] 1 l., 60p.

Relates to the White Bear Lake district of Sask., near Zealandia. U. of Victoria

2167 **Regina.** Board of Trade
Regina, the capital of Saskatchewan. Official number of the Regina Board of Trade ... Regina, The Board [1910?] 16p. illus., plates. 23cm. Shortt

2168 **Regina.** Greater Regina Club
Regina, the capital of Saskatchewan, Canada. Its commercial & industrial opportunities. Commercial souvenir. Published by The Greater Regina Club, Regina, Saskatchewan, Canada. [1910?] 79, [1p.] illus., 1 fold. diagr. 24cm. Lande

2169 **Regina.** Greater Regina Club
The progress and opportunities of Regina. Souvenir issued ... on the occasion of the visit of the Canadian Manufacturers' Association to Regina, Saskatchewan, September 15, 1910. [Regina, 1910] cover-title, 80p. illus. (incl. map), fold. plan. 23 1/2cm. Arkin

2170 **Robins,** Kingman Nott
The province of Alberta, Dominion of Canada; a report on the rich and varied resources ... With special reference to the opportunities offered for lending on farm mortgages. Rochester, N.Y., Associated Mortgage Investors, 1910. 45p. illus., fold. map, tables. 24cm.

On cover: The province of Alberta, Canada. A descriptive and statistical report. Glenbow

2171 **Saltcoats, Sask.** Board of Trade
Choice lands in the Saltcoats district. [Saltcoats?] The Board [1910] cover-title, 16p. illus., fold. map. 23cm. Shortt

2172 **Saskatoon.** Board of Trade
Saskatoonlets. [Saskatoon, Saturday Press] 1910-11. 2v. 10 x 15cm.

The Shortt Library has Sept., 1910; March, 1911.
These 16-page pamphlets contained latest statistics on the city's growth. Shortt

2173 **Saunders,** William
Manitoba and the Northwest Territories as markets for Ontario and British Columbia fruit. [Ottawa? ca. 1910] caption-title, 7p. 25cm. Glenbow

2174 **Saxby,** [C.F.] Argyll
Comrades three! a story of the Canadian prairies. London, S.W. Partridge & Co. [1910] ix, 11-299, [1]p. front., plates. 19cm.

Locale 'Wascana Valley.'
Juvenile literature. Br. Mus.

2175 **Scott,** Walter
Our land terms. Substance of speech by Hon. Walter Scott at Outlook, October 6, 1910, dealing with Saskatchewan's autonomy land bargain. [Regina, The Leader, 1910] caption-title, 18p. 24cm. Rutherford

2176 **Secretan,** [James Henry Edward]
Out West. Ottawa, The Esdale Press, Ltd., 1910. [206]p. plates. 18cm.

A series of sketches of characters met in the West. Shortt

2177 **Selwyn,** Cecil E.
Prairie patchwork; or, Western poems for western people. [Winnipeg, Stovel Co.] 1910. 96p. illus. 19cm. Shortt

2178 **Semmens,** John
Trials and triumphs of early Methodism in the great North West. 2d ed. Toronto [c1910] 16p. 13cm. Not seen. R.E.S.

2179 **Smith's Book Store**
Souvenir of Edmonton, Alta. Edmonton, Smith's Book Store [n.d.] [1, 31]p. col. illus. 13 x 21cm.

Illustrated from photos signed 'J.V.' U. of A.

2180 Souvenir of Western Canada, its cities, plains & mountains, [Toronto, Hough Litho Co. Ltd. 1910?] cover-title, [31] p. of views in color. 14 x 20cm. Sask. Arch.

2181 **Stead,** Robert J[ames] C[ampbell]
The empire builders and other poems. 4th ed. Toronto, William Briggs, 1910. vii p., 1 l., [11]-100p. 19 1/2cm.

First published in 1908. U. of S.

2182 **Stettler Independent**
Stettler, the heart of Alberta. Stettler 'beats 'em all.' Stettler [1910] cover-title, [12] p. illus. 20cm.

Caption-title: Stettler, 'the busy town.' Glenbow

2183 **Stokes,** W[illiam] E[dward] H[erbert]
The red man's religion and five true tales of my happy career. Regina, Caxton Press, 1910. 77, [1] p. illus. 23cm.

The author's notions on the religion of the Indians served as an excuse for writing a sketch of his life as a remittance man in the West. Shortt

2184 **Valentine and Sons United Publishing Company, Limited**
A souvenir of Calgary, Alta. Montreal [191-] [28] p. chiefly illus. 18 x 23cm. Glenbow

2185 **Vay,** A. P[eter]
Amerikai naplokivonatok, utyegyzetek, leveltoredekek. Budapest, Szent-Istvan-Tars, Stephaneum ny, 1910. 300p. 20cm.

Only about three chapters are on Canada. Hungary

2186 **Vegreville, Alta.** Board of Trade
For you! A few facts about the Vegreville district in central Alberta. Vegreville [191-] 1 sheet, 56 x 42cm., folded to 29 x 12cm. illus. U. of A.

2187 **Vermilion, Alta.** Board of Trade
The Vermilion district of Alberta, a land of promise and fulfilment. Vermilion, Board of Trade [1910] cover-title, 17p. plates. 11 x 17cm. Glenbow

2187A **Walworth,** Bob
On the firing line; or, The North-West Mounted Police on the trail. Cleveland, A. Westbrook Co., c1910. 64p. 17cm. (American Indian series, no.9)

Fiction relating to the Saskatchewan Rebellion. B.C. Arch.

2188 **Ward,** [Mary Augusta (Arnold)]
Canadian born, by Mrs. Humphry Ward; with a frontispiece by Albert Sterner and two landscape illustrations. London, Smith, Elder & Co., 1910. 3p.l., [2], 346p. front., plates. 19 1/2cm.

Fiction. The American and Canadian editions appeared under the title Lady Merton, colonist. U. of A.

2189 **Waugh,** R.D.
Western Canada; the land of opportunity. An address by R.D. Waugh, Esq., city controller of Winnipeg, Man., before the third annual convention of the National

Association of Real Estate Exchanges at Minneapolis, June 15, 16, & 17, 1910. 15p. port. 15cm.

Portrait on title-page. Title at head of address: Development of the great North-West territory. Man. Arch.

2190 **Wilkie Press**
All about the town of Wilkie and surrounding districts. Wilkie, Saskatchewan; the first divisional point on the C.P.R. west of Saskatoon and the hub of the famous Cut Knife, Narrow Lake and Tramping Lake districts. Its phenomenal growth and development. [Wilkie, Wilkie Press, 1910] cover-title, 1p.l., [42]p. illus., fold. map. 22 1/2cm. Shortt

2191 **Winnipeg**. St. Giles' Presbyterian Church
Silver jubilee, 1885-1910, Winnipeg, Man. Winnipeg, Stovel and Company, 1910. cover-title, 23p. illus. 23cm. Man. Arch.

2192 **Wissler**, Clark
... Material culture of the Blackfoot Indians. New York, American Museum of Natural History, 1910. cover-title, 175p. illus., plates. 24 1/2cm. (American Museum of Natural History. Anthropological papers, v.5, pt.1) L.C.

2193 **Wolseley, Sask**. Board of Trade
Wheat wealthy Wolseley; the grain golden city of the central West. [Wolseley, The Sun, 191-?] 2p.l., [18]p. illus. 23 1/2cm. 'Written by W.L.C.' Shortt

2194 **Wilson**, L.C.
Souvenir of Calgary and vicinity. Calgary [1910?] [32]p. of col. illus. 14 x 20cm. Glenbow

2195 **Zealandia, Sask**. Board of Trade
Solid facts about a good point for settlers. Zealandia [The Telegram, 1910] cover-title, [12]p. illus. 15 1/2cm. Shortt

2196 **Aberdeen, Sask**. Board of Trade
Where wheat makes money ... Aberdeen, The Board, 1911. cover-title, 29p. illus. (incl. maps) 15cm. Shortt

2197 **Astley & Shackle**
Investments in Alberta, Canada, and a few facts with reference to Calgary, 'The city of opportunities.' [Calgary? 1911] cover-title, 23p. illus. 22cm. Arkin

2197A **Banff Springs Golf Club**
Constitution, rules and regulations. Banff, Alta., organized 1911. [n.p., 1911] cover-title, 7p. 15cm. Glenbow

2198 **Bramley-Moore**, A[lwyn]
Canada and her colonies; or, Home rule for Alberta. London, W. Stewart & Co., 1911. xi, 185, [1]p. 19 1/2cm.

When Alberta and Saskatchewan were created, the Dominion retained control of the public domain. This book is a vigorous protest. Shortt

2199 **Broadview, Sask.** Board of Trade
All about far-famed Broadview, Saskatchewan, presented at the Dominion Fair, Regina, 1911. [Broadview? 1911] 16p. illus. Sask. Arch. (microfilm)

2200 **Bryce,** George
The Scotsman in Canada; Western Canada, including Manitoba, Saskatchewan, Alberta, British Columbia, and portions of old Rupert's Land and the Indian territories. Toronto, Musson Book Co. [1911] 439p. front., ports. 22cm. (Scotsman in Canada, v.2) U. of S.

2201 **Calgary.** First Baptist Church
Souvenir illustrated; facts of interest, past and present. 1888-1911. [Calgary, 1911] cover-title, 32p. illus., ports. 16 x 23cm.

Printed by Der Deutsch-Canadier.
Advertising matter included in paging. Glenbow

2202 Canada [Arcola-Alameda districts, S.E. Saskatchewan. n.p., 1911?] 32p. illus., double map. 15cm. Sask. Arch.

2203 **Canada.** Department of the Interior
Abstracts from reports on townships west of the fourth meridian received from surveyors between June 30, 1910, and July 1, 1911. [Ottawa, 1911?] 37p. 25cm. Glenbow

2204 **Canada.** Department of the Interior
Le Canada, terre d'initiative et de succès. [Paris, Imprimé par G. Lefebvre, 1911] 48p. illus. 24cm.

About half the pamphlet relates to Western Canada. An earlier pamphlet with the same title and pagination was printed in 1905. France

2205 **Canada.** Department of the Interior
Canada West, the last best West; ranching, dairying, grain raising, fruit raising, mixed farming. Ottawa, 1911. cover-title, 41p. illus., maps. 27 1/2cm. L.C.

2206 **Canada.** Department of the Interior
The country called Canada. [Ottawa, 1911] cover-title, 70, [2]p. incl. covers. 17cm.

Pages 49-64 deal with the prairie region. Glenbow

2206A **Canada.** Department of the Interior
The last best West is Canada West. Ottawa, 1911. 2v. illus., maps. 28cm.

Contents: [1] 160 acres in Western Canada free. [2] Homes for millions. U. of A.

2207 **Canada.** Department of the Interior
What Irishmen say of Canada. Ottawa, 1911. cover-title, 32p. illus., maps. 26 x 14cm. Can. Arch.

2208 **Canadian Pacific Railway**
Coronation. [Winnipeg, 1911] 16p. illus. 8 x 14cm.

Relates to the village of Coronation, Alta. Sask. Arch.

2209 **Canadian Pacific Railway**
Homeseekers excursions to Manitoba, Saskatchewan, Alberta, 1911. [n.p., 1911] cover-title, 15p. illus. 13 1/2cm. Shortt

2210 **Canadian Pacific Railway**
Settlers' guide; complete information, freight and passenger rates to Manitoba, Saskatchewan, and Alberta. [n.p., 1911] 61p. 14 1/2cm. Shortt

2211 **Carrel,** Frank
Canada's West and farther west. Quebec, Telegraph Printing Co., 1911. xvi, 258p. front., plates. 20 1/2cm.

Written in journalistic style by a newspaper editor. Shortt

2212 **Central Alberta Development League**
Central Alberta, Canada's richest mixed farming country ... Edmonton, Printed by The Douglas Co., Ltd. [1911] cover-title, 17p. illus. 25cm. Shortt

2213 **Cherrier,** Alphonse Avila
Mémoire à S.E. Mgr Stagni, délégué-apostolique au Canada, sur la situation religieuse actuelle dans l'Ouest-canadien et sur la question universitaire au Manitoba. St-Boniface, 1911. 50p. with appendix of 12p. 19cm. Oblates Arch.

2214 **Copping,** Arthur Edward
The golden land, the true story and experiences of British settlers in Canada ... London, Hodder and Stoughton [1911] xvi, 263p. col. front., col. plates. 21cm. Shortt

2215 **Curtis,** William E[leroy]
Letters on Canada, by William E. Curtis, special correspondent of the Chicago 'Record-Herald,' and which appeared in that paper from Aug. 23 to Oct. 8, 1911. [Chicago? 1911?] 173, [1]p. illus. (incl. ports.) 23cm.

About half the letters relate to Western Canada. L.C.

2216 **Curwood,** James Oliver
Philip Steele of the Royal North-West Mounted Police. Illus. by Gayle Hoskins. Indianapolis, Bobbs-Merrill Co. [1911] 5p.l., 306 [1]p. front., plates. 19cm.

Fiction; locale forest and prairie region. L.C.

2217 **Farmer,** T[homas] D[evey] J[ermyn]
Where the rivers meet; a retrospect and a contrast. Winnipeg, 1911. [21]p. illus. (incl. 1 on cover) 19cm.

A poem on the history of the Red and the Assiniboine rivers. Glenbow

2218 **Fedyk,** Theodore
Pisni imigrantiv pro stary i novy kray. Winnipeg, 1911. 139p. 17 1/2cm.

Poetry of the old land and the new, originally published in 1908 with the title: Pisni pro Kanadu i Avstriyu (Songs of Canada and Austria). It went through six editions by 1927, and sold 50,000 copies. Yuzyk. Kirkconnell

2219 **Field**, George Blackstone
Rhymes of the survey & frontier. Toronto, Wm. Briggs, 1911. viii, 9-77p. 19 1/2cm. Rutherford

2220 **Fort Saskatchewan, Alta.**
Fort Saskatchewan and district offers opportunities to all. Fort Saskatchewan, Fort Saskatchewan Herald, 1911. ... Not seen. Ream

2221 **Fraser**, Sir John Foster
Canada as it is ... London, Cassell & Co. Ltd., 1911. xii, 303, [1]p. incl. front. 46 plates. 20cm. U. of S.

2222 Galaxy of western editors. [Winnipeg, Toronto Type Foundry Co., Ltd., 1911] 1 v. ports. 13 x 17 1/2cm. Cover-title; loose leaf.

Portraits of editors of country weeklies; no biographical details are given. Shortt

2223 **Gill**, E[dward] Anthony Wharton
Love in Manitoba. Toronto, Musson, 1911. 311, [1]p. 20cm.

Fiction. Man. Leg.

2224 **Grand Trunk Pacific Railway**
Farming, ranching and social conditions in Western Canada. Winnipeg, 1911. 36p. illus. 23cm. Sask. Arch.

2225 **Grand Trunk Pacific Railway**
Land, a living and wealth. The story of farming and social conditions in Western Canada. A series of articles written by practical men on subjects of interest to those looking to better their present condition. Winnipeg, Grand Trunk Pacific Railway [1911?] 53p. incl. illus. 23cm. Shortt

2226 **Grand Trunk Pacific Railway**
Word pictures of the land in townships along the line of the Grand Trunk Pacific Railway. Reports of government land surveyors ... Winnipeg [191–] 47p. 22cm. Sask. Arch.

2227 **Hughes**, Katherine
Father Lacombe; the black-robe voyageur. Toronto, William Briggs, 1911. xxi p., 2 l., 467p. incl. front., plates, map, ports. 21 1/2cm.

A well-written biography of the great missionary. Other editions appeared in 1914 and 1920. Shortt

2228 **Jennings Publishing Company**
Calgary, sunny Alberta, the industrial prodigy of the great West; her phenomenal progress; thriving industries and wonderful resources. Calgary, 1911. 208p. illus., col. fold. plate. 15 x 24cm.

'Merchants and manufacturers record.' Glenbow

2229 **Langevin**, [Louis Philippe Adélard]
Mémoire confidentiel sur la situation religieuse et statistiques de la population catholique de l'archidiocèse de Saint-Boniface. Saint-Boniface, 1911. cover-title, 40p. 19 1/2cm. Oblates Arch.

2229A **Leighton**, Robert
The perils of Peterkin; a story of adventure in North-West Canada. Illus. by Arthur Twidle. London, Jarrold & Sons [1911] ...

Juvenile fiction. Br. Mus.

2230 **Liberal Party**
The grain grower and reciprocity. [Regina, Leader, 1911] caption-title, [4] p. 22cm. Sask. Arch.

2231 **Liberal Party**
Haultain and reciprocity ... [Regina, Leader, 1911] caption-title, [4] p. 22cm. Sask. Arch.

2232 **Liberal Party**
Reciprocity's benefit to Western Canada; some United States views. [Regina, Leader, 1911] caption-title, [4] p. 22cm. Sask. Arch.

2233 **Liberal Party**
The western farmer; opinion of him entertained by leaders of the anti-reciprocity party. [Regina, Leader, 1911] caption-title, [4] p. 22cm. Sask. Arch.

2234 **Liberal Party.** Battleford Constituency
Liberal Farmers Association of the Battleford Constituency. [Battleford? 1911?] caption-title, [3] p. 28cm.

Statement to the electors by a candidate, S.E. McManus. Sask. Arch.

2235 **Linton Bros.**, stationers
The city of Calgary; the commercial capital of sunny Alberta ... Calgary [1911?] [24] p. of illus. 18 x 23cm. Glenbow

2236 **McDougall**, John
On western trails in the early seventies; frontier life in the Canadian North-West. Toronto, W. Briggs, 1911. viii, [9]-279p. front. 19 1/2cm. Shortt

2237 **MacLean**, Donald Alexander
Catholic schools in Western Canada. Their legal status. Toronto, Extension print, 1911. x p., 2 l., 162p. 23cm. L.C.

2238 **McMillan**, Donald M.
Greater Edmonton real estate directory. A complete guide as to the owners of real property in the city of Edmonton. Compiled from the city assessment records of the current year. 3d ed., April, 1911. [Edmonton] 1911. 205p. 16cm.

——Addenda; Sept. 15th, 1911. [Edmonton] 1911. cover-title, 47p. 15cm. Glenbow

2239 **Manitoba.** Department of Agriculture and Immigration
Manitoba, the first province of Western Canada. [Winnipeg, 191-?] 79, [1] p. Amtmann - 176-221

2240 **Manitoba Free Press**
The burden of railway rates. Freight and express charges levied upon the people of Western Canada unjustifiably higher than those in Eastern Canada and in the

adjoining states. Winnipeg, 1911. cover-title, 36p. 22 1/2cm. (Pamphlet no.2) Compiled from articles published in the Manitoba Free Press. Shortt

2241 **Manitoba Free Press**
A piece of buffalo hide. With some account of the buffalo, and particularly of the round-up of the great Pablo herd in Montana and its removal to Western Canada. Winnipeg, 1911. [28]p. illus. 14 x 18cm.

A Christmas souvenir booklet. B.C. Arch.

2242 **Moose Jaw**. Board of Trade
Moose Jaw, Saskatchewan. [Moose Jaw, 1911] [24]p. illus. 14 x 22cm. Sask. Arch.

2243 **Morden, Man**. Knox Church
Twenty-fifth anniversary of Knox Church, Morden, Man. Morden, 1911. 12p. illus. 17 1/2cm. Victoria College

2244 **Newman**, Sara
The prairie altar, 'To trace in nature's most minute design, the signature and stamp of power divine.' – Cowper. [n.p., 1911?] [6p.]

Poetry; privately printed. Locale: the Canadian Prairies. Lande

2245 [**Ney**, Frederick James]
Britishers in Britain, being the record of the official visit of teachers from Manitoba to the Old Country, summer, 1910 ... London, Times Book Club, 1911. xiv, 297, [1]p. front., plates, ports. 22cm. Acadia

2246 **North Battleford, Sask**. Board of Trade
North Battleford, the rising star of northern Saskatchewan ... [Winnipeg, Bulman Bros. Ltd.] 1911. 22p., 1 l. illus. 23 1/2 x 10cm.

The following year a 31-page edition was published in North Battleford. Shortt

2247 **Northwest Territories**. Laws, statutes, etc.
The ordinances of the North-West Territories; being an office consolidation of such of the ordinances of the Northwest Territories in force on August 21st, 1905, as the same appear in the consolidation of 1898, and the amendments thereto, together with the public general ordinances enacted by the Legislature of the Northwest Territories after the year 1898, as have not been replaced by statutes of the Legislature of the Province of Alberta, together with the amendments made thereto by the said Legislature up to and including the second session of the second Legislature, 1910. Edmonton, J.E. Richards, 1911. xxxi, 673p. 26cm.

A new edition was published in 1915 bringing the amendments up to date. Shortt

2248 **Ouellette**, J[oseph] A[lbéric]
L'Alberta, région centrale. Montréal, 1911. 80p. illus., maps. 22cm.

Includes advertising. U. of A.

2249 **Pirot**, Jules
One year's fight for the true faith in Saskatchewan; or, The Hungarian question in Canada in 1910. Toronto, Catholic Register and Canadian Extension, 1911. 24p. 23cm. L. of P.

2250 **Prince Albert.** Board of Trade
Prince Albert, Saskatchewan. 'The easiest way' ... Prince Albert, Prince Albert Times [1911?] folder. (6, [6] p.) illus., map. 23cm. U. of S.

2251 **Prince Albert.** Board of Trade
Prince Albert, Saskatchewan. The ideal spot for the British settler. [Prince Albert, 1911?] folder. ([16] p.) illus. 23cm. U. of S.

2252 **Prince Albert Real Estate and Investment Company**
Prince Albert, Saskatchewan. Toronto [1911] cover-title, 43 columns. illus., map. 21 x 21cm.

Caption-title: Prince Albert – The city-of-entry to the Greater West and to Hudson Bay. U. of A.

2253 **Red Deer, Alta.** Board of Trade
Red Deer, Alberta. [n.p., 1911] 20p. illus. (incl. map) 23cm. Cover has folding flap for mailing. Shortt

2254 **Regina.** Board of Trade
Regina, the queen city of the middle West. Regina, 1911. 10p. illus. 21cm. Sask. Arch.

2255 **Ruse,** Joseph
The story of Calgary ... & Tuxedo Park; compiled under the personal supervision of Joseph Ruse and C.A. Owens. Calgary, J.O.E. Ltd., 1911. [24] p. incl. plates (part fold.) 31cm. Toronto

2256 **Sabourin,** Joseph Adonias
L'apostolat chez les Ruthènes au Manitoba. Québec, L'Action Sociale, 1911. 38p. 19cm. Shortt

2257 **Saskatchewan.** University. College of Agriculture
Report of the first annual convention of the Homemakers' Club of Saskatchewan held at Regina, Sask., Jan. 31, Feb. 1, 2, and 3, 1911. Saskatoon, 1911. 82p. illus. 22 1/2cm. Sask. Arch.

2258 **Savaète,** Arthur
Les écoles du Nord-Ouest canadien. Paris, A. Savaète [1911] 516p. 24cm. (Voix canadiennes: vers l'abîme, v.7) Not seen.

A biased account of the Manitoba School Question. St. Sulpice

2259 **Scott,** Walter
Address to the people of Saskatchewan. [Regina, Leader, 1911] caption-title, [4] p. 22cm.

Relates to the reciprocity issue in the Dominion election. Sask. Arch.

2260 **Sheffield,** T.W.
Facts and opportunities in Regina and Saskatchewan. [Regina] Greater Regina Club [1911] 34, [2] p. illus., fold. plate. 25cm. On cover: The progress and opportunities of Regina. Shortt

2261 **Sheptycky**, Andrey
Address on the Ruthenian question to their lordships the archbishops and bishops of Canada. Leopolis, Ukraine, 1911. 25p. 33cm. Not seen.
Published also in French. Private information

2262 **Sheptycky**, Andrey
Kanadyiskym Rusynam [To the Canadian Ruthenians] Zovkva, Ukraine, 1911. 93p. 20 1/2cm. Not seen. Private information

2263 **Sivell**, Rhoda
Voices from the range. Toronto, T. Eaton Co. Ltd. [1911] 101p. illus. 18cm.
Poetry. A 43-page edition was brought out by Wm. Briggs. U. of S.

2264 **Stead**, Robert James Campbell
Prairie born, and other poems. Toronto, Wm. Briggs, 1911. 95p. Not seen. Ryerson

2265 **Stead**, Robert James Campbell
Songs of the prairie. New York, Platt & Peck Co. [1912] 2p.l., 106p. col. front. 17cm.
First published as a 96-page edition in 1911 by Wm. Briggs, and by Gay and Hancock of London. (In U. of A. Extension) L.C.

2266 **Strathcona, Alta**. Board of Trade
Strathcona, the university city of Alberta. [Strathcona, 1911] 28p. illus. 31cm. Edmonton

2267 **Thomas**, Morris W.
The truth about Canada, with some exciting experiences in Alberta. Haverfordwest, Pembroke County Guardian Office [1911] 50p. 17cm.
The author came to Canada in May 1905, and settled near Stettler, Alberta. This booklet was written when he visited Wales in November 1910. Wales

2268 **Trades and Labour Congress of Canada**
Souvenir of the twenty-seventh annual convention, Calgary, Alta., September, 1911. [Calgary] Published under the auspices of the Calgary Trades and Labour Council [1911] 111p. illus., ports. 23cm.
Includes brief notes on Calgary trade unions. Includes advertising matter. Glenbow

2269 **Transcontinental Townsite Company, Limited**
Mirror, the city beautiful. [Where opportunity awaits the investor, merchant and homeseeker] Winnipeg, The Company [1911] 11p. illus., map. 23cm. Man. Arch.

2270 **Vonda, Sask**. Board of Trade
Some of the reasons why you should consider Vonda when seeking a business location, farm lands or investment in the Canadian West. [Vonda, Vonda News Office, 1911] [38]p. illus. 11 x 16cm. Shortt

2271 [**Witteryck**, Antoon Josef]
Les aventures de Coquelicot au Canada. Bruges, A.J. Witteryck, 1911. 147, [1]p. front., plates. 27cm.

Fictionalized account of the adventures of two friends, Onésiphore Coquelicot and Jérôme Laplume, across Canada as far as Boissevain, Manitoba. Here the former decided to marry and settle, while Laplume returned to Belgium. The last third of the book relates to Coquelicot's experiences in Manitoba as described in letters.

A Flemish edition, 'De lotgevallen van Coquelicot in Canada' was published in 1929. It had 94 pages and no illustrations other than a frontispiece. Belgium

2272 **Yorkton, Sask.** Board of Trade
Facts about the town of Yorkton and the fertile farming district of eastern Saskatchewan in which it is situated and of which it is the commercial, educational, judicial, lands, police and railway centre ... Yorkton, The Board, 1910-11. 2v. illus., fold. map. 20cm. On cover: Yorkton, the commercial centre of eastern Saskatchewan. Shortt

2273 **Adams,** Joseph
Ten thousand miles through Canada; the natural resources, commercial industries, fish and game, sports and pastimes of the great Dominion. London, Methuen & Co. [1912] xx, 310p. front., plates. 20cm.

Very little - about thirty pages - on the prairies. Also published by McClelland & Goodchild of Toronto. Man. Leg.

2274 **Ager,** Paul R.
Life thoughts. Toronto, William Briggs, 1912. 3p.l., 5-36p. 16cm.

Poetry. U. of A. (Extension)

2275 **Alberta, Athabasca & Peace River Land Company, Edmonton**
Dunvegan, an investment safe and sure. [A good place to own a few lots. Edmonton, Alta., 1912?] cover-title, 16p. incl. illus., 2 plans. fold. plan. orig. printed wrappers. 16cm.

Imprint completed from back cover. Amtmann - 241-602

2276 **Bourassa,** Henri
Pour la justice. La législation scolaire au Nord Ouest. Les discours de MM. Monk et Pelletier. Quelques objections. L'esprit de la confédération. Discours prononcé au Monument National, le 9 mars 1912. Montréal, Imprimerie du Devoir, 1912. cover-title, 44p. 22cm. Shortt

2277 Brandon, Man. Brandon [1912?] 32p. illus., map. 11 1/2 x 15cm. Not seen. R.E.S.

2278 **British Empire Agency, Limited**
Canada; collated list of selected lands, timber lands, improved farms, orchard lands, truck farms, market gardens, stock rearing and dairy farms, mixed farms, townsites & investment sites, with a list of desirable mortgages for sale for the autumn of 1912. Offered under instructions of the owners. London, 1912. cover-title, 24p. double map, facsim. 25cm.

Relates chiefly to Western Canada lands. Glenbow

2279 **Brunet,** Edouard
La Moose-Mountain. Le Havre, 1912. ... Not seen. Morice

2280 **Bryce,** George
The life of Lord Selkirk, coloniser of Western Canada. Toronto, Musson Book Co., 1912. vii, 95p. front., illus., ports. 19 1/2cm. Shortt

2281 **Burpee**, Lawrence Johnstone
Scouts of empire; the story of the discovery of the great North-west. Toronto, Musson [1912] v, 104p. 14cm. Glenbow

2282 **Cahan**, C[harles] H[azlitt]
Minority rights in Keewatin. [Montreal, 1912] cover-title, 8p. 22cm.

Relates to expansion of Manitoba's boundaries. Can. Arch.

2283 Calgary. London, Hodder and Stoughton [1912?] xii, 88p. front., plates. 20 1/2cm. (Twentieth century cities) Shortt

2284 **Calgary**. Stampede Committee
The stampede at Calgary, Alberta, 1912. [Calgary, Herald Western Co., Ltd., 1912] cover-title, 64p. illus. (incl. ports.) 23cm.

A collection of articles and poetry on cowboys, ranching, etc.; includes biographical sketches. Alta. Leg.

2285 Calgary, the city phenomenal. [Calgary, c1912] 38p. illus. 30cm. Glenbow

2286 **Canadian Pacific Railway**
Get your Canadian home from the Canadian Pacific; a handbook of information regarding sunny Alberta and the opportunities offered you by the Canadian Pacific Railway in that province. [Canadian ed.] Calgary, 1912. cover-title, [2], 2-63 numb. columns on 32p. illus., double map. 19 x 20cm. fold. to 19 x 10cm. Glenbow

2287 **Canadian Pacific Railway**
... The golden West. A peep into the future. [London?] 1912. 2p.l., [3]-27, [1]p. illus., fold. map. 24cm.

At head of title: April, 1912. Copyright. On title-page: Entered at Stationers' Hall.
A general description of the West, with detailed descriptions of western cities on the C.P.R. Br. Mus.

2288 **Canadian Pacific Railway**
Manufacturing and business opportunities in Western Canada along the lines of the Canadian Pacific Railway. 3d ed. [Winnipeg?] 1912. 161p. fold. map. 21cm. Man. Leg.

2289 Catholic centennial souvenir, 1812-1912; a sketch of the achievements of the Catholic Church in Western Canada. Winnipeg, West Canada Publishing Co., 1912. [97]p. illus. Not seen.

Published in connection with the Selkirk centennial. Consists of a brief sketch of missionary effort followed by biographical sketches of prominent Catholic clergy and laity.
Toronto

2290 **Central Alberta Development League**
Central Alberta; a good country to farm in; the land of big crops and rich pastures; a good country to live in. [Edmonton, The League, 1912] cover-title, 39p. illus., map. Americas

2291 **Cook,** Jim M.
The Canadian North-West as it is to-day. Los Angeles, The Author [1912] 2p.l., 47 (i.e. 52)p. front. (port.) illus., plates. 20cm.

Travel and adventure in northern Alberta. B.C. Arch.

2292 **Copping,** Harold
Canadian pictures; thirty-six plates in colour, illustrating Canadian life and scenery, reproduced from original drawings. Descriptive letterpress by E.P. Weaver. London, Religious Tract Society, 1912. 36 plates. Not seen.

Almost entirely on the West. The artist also illustrated A.E. Copping's 'The Golden Land.' R.H.P., 1912

2293 Crystal City and district, Manitoba, Canada. [Crystal City, Evans Publicity Co., 1912?] cover-title, [24]p. illus. 20cm. Pagination includes advertising. Man. Leg.

2294 Farm lands, Qu'Appelle, Saskatchewan. Qu'Appelle, 1912. 43p. illus. 21cm. Not seen. R.E.S.

2295 **Feilberg,** H[enning] F[rederik]
De derovre en raekke breve fra Canada. Kobenhavn & Kristiana, Glydendalske, 1912. 128p. 20cm.

Experiences and impressions of the Johanne F. Feilberg family, who left Denmark for a Saskatchewan homestead in 1910. Written in letter or diary form, the book covers the period to the summer of 1912. See also Entry 2587. Denmark

2296 **Field,** Edward
Biographical sketch of the late Edward Field. [Wadena, Wadena Herald, 1912] 8p. port. 23cm. Typed copy. Shortt

2297 **Gill,** E[dward] A[nthony] Wharton
A Manitoba chore boy; the experiences of a young emigrant told from his letters. London, Religious Tract Society, 1912. v p., 1 l., 83p. front., plates. 19 1/2cm.

This is really fiction, but the portrayal of Manitoba life is faithful enough to pass as true experience. Shortt

2298 [**Gordon,** Charles William]
Corporal Cameron of the North West Mounted Police; a tale of the Macleod trail, by Ralph Connor [pseud.] New York, Hodder & Stoughton, 1912. 4p.l., 454p. 19 1/2cm. illus. lining-paper.

Fiction. Published also by Westminster of Toronto. U. of S.

2299 **Grand Trunk Pacific Railway**
Land seekers' guide, also free homestead lands along the Grand Trunk Pacific in Western Canada. Winnipeg, The Company, 1912. 24p. illus., fold. map. 23cm. (Pamphlet no.17) Man. Leg.

2300 **Haslam,** J.H.
Problems of the Prairies. [n.p., 1912] cover-title, 30p. 22cm. Sask. Arch.

2301 **Haultain,** [Sir] F[rederick] W[illiam] G[ordon]
The Conservative party is the people's popular policy. The Conservative position on leading provincial issues as declared by the popular Conservative leader ... at Biggar, April 15th, 1912 ... cover-title, [5] p. 23cm. Sask. Arch.

2302 **Haultain,** [Sir] F[rederick] W[illiam] G[ordon]
The public domain, Saskatchewan's rightful heritage ... [n.p., 1912] cover-title, 25p. 22cm. Sask. Arch.

2303 **Heffelfinger,** G.G.
A near view of the New Canadian. [Toronto] Published by the Board of Home Missions and Social Service of the Presbyterian Church in Canada [n.d.] self-cover, 12p. Amtmann - 229-337

2304 **A Homesteader**
Settling on Canada's free land, by a homesteader. Ottawa, Dept. of the Interior, 1912. 32p. illus. 18cm. Sask. Arch.

2305 [**Hotchkiss,** Charles S.]
The International Dry-Farming Congress. [Edmonton?] Published by the Dept. of Agriculture of the Province of Alberta, and the Board of Control of the Seventh International Dry-Farming Congress, 1912. 88p. illus. (incl. ports.) 23cm.

The Congress was held at Lethbridge, Oct. 19-26, 1912. The information in the booklet relates to southern Alberta. Sask. Arch.

2306 Hotel Selkirk, corner First & Jasper, Edmonton, Alberta. [Edmonton, Printed by Edmonton Print. & Pub. Co., 191-?] [16] p. illus. 18cm.

Designed and engraved by McDermid Engraving Company. Glenbow

2307 **Hislop,** Mary
The streets of Winnipeg. Winnipeg, T.W. Taylor Co., Ltd., 1912. 46p. front., plates. 19 1/2cm.

Historical information on the city's streets. Shortt

2308 **Hudon,** Théophile
La Fédération des Catholiques manitobains [St. Boniface, 1912?] self-cover, 24p. Amtmann - 229-361

2309 **Hudson's Bay Company**
The Governor and Company of Adventurers of England trading into Hudson's Bay. London, Printed by William Clowes and Sons, 1912. 12p. 34cm.

Title taken from verso of pamphlet. H.B.C.

2310 **Hudson's Bay Company**
Proposed supplemental charter. Special report of the Governor and Committee of the Hudson's Bay Company, to be laid before the shareholders on Friday, July 12th, 1912. London, Sir Joseph Causton and Sons, 1912. cover-title, 24p. 21cm. H.B.C.

2311 **Hudson's Bay Company**
The supplemental charter. [London, John Parkinson Bland, 1912] caption-title, 8p. 21 1/2cm. H.B.C.

2312 **Hudson's Bay Herald**
A few of the things recently written on the subject of Le Pas and the Hudson Bay Road. The Pas, Hudson's Bay Herald, 1912. 29p. illus. 16 1/2cm. Man. Leg.

2313 **Humboldt, Sask.** Board of Trade
Humboldt, Sask. Humboldt, 1912. 24p. illus. 23cm. Sask. Arch.

2314 **International Realty, Limited**
Bowness, Calgary's finest residential subdivision. [Calgary, 1912] cover-title, [20]p. illus., map. 22 x 29cm. Glenbow

2315 **Jeffery,** John B.
The story of Barney Oldfield's flight, August 10th, 1912. By the Chicago and New York Presses. [by John B. Jeffery and C.E. Ferguson. Calgary, 1912] cover-title, 8 l. illus. 21cm.

Story of the setting of a new world speed record for automobiles on a track at Calgary. Glenbow

2316 **Laurier,** Sir Wilfrid
The Manitoba question. Extension of boundaries. Financial terms. Separate school rights. Sir Wilfrid Laurier, in defeat or in victory, stands for conciliation and mutual respect in religious and educational matters and against coercion in Manitoba. Speech ... House of Commons, March 12, 1912. [Ottawa, 1912] caption-title, 7p. 24 1/2cm. In double column. Arkin

2316A **Leighton,** Robert
Rattlesnake ranch; a story of adventure in the great North West. London, C.A. Pearson, 1912. 288p. (The Scout library, no.17)

Juvenile fiction. The locale is Canmore, Alta. Br. Mus.

2317 **Lethbridge.** Board of Trade
Scenic beauties of Lethbridge. Special souvenir edition. [Approved by the Business Mens' Association and the Board of Trade, illustrated and designed by S. LaFeits] Lethbridge, Printed by the Printers & Stationers, 1912. [40]p. illus., ports. 26cm.

On cover: Lethbridge (illustrated), The city of opportunities. Glenbow

2318 **Liberal Party** (Canada)
How the Macdonald by-election was won. Read the affidavits showing the outrages committed by police and magistrates under the direction of the Rogers-Roblin combination. Publication no.3. Ottawa, Central Information Office of the Canadian Liberal Party [1912?] cover-title, 46p.

Related to the Macdonald electoral district, Manitoba. Amtmann - 192-998

2319 **MacBeth,** R[oderick] G[eorge]
Recent Canadian West letters (historical & descriptive) Brantford, Hurley Printing Co. [1912] 52p.

A series of letters which appeared originally in the Brantford Expositor. R.H.P., 1912

2320 **McClung,** Nellie L[etitia (Mooney)]
The Black Creek stopping-house and other stories. Toronto, Wm. Briggs, 1912. 224p. 20cm. U. of S.

2321 **Machell,** Percy [Wilfrid]
'What is my country? My country is the Empire. Canada is my home.' Impressions of Canada and the new North-West. London, Sifton, Praed & Co., 1912. 45p. illus. 15 1/2cm.

Relates to the Peace River country. B.C. Arch.

2322 **Macleod, Alta.** Industrial Commissioner
Macleod, Alberta, where nature is making a big city. [Macleod, Spectator Presses, 1912] cover-title, 32p. illus., map. 23cm. Glenbow

2323 **MacRae,** Archibald Oswald
History of the province of Alberta. Calgary, The Western Canada History Co., 1912. 2v. front., illus., ports. 27 1/2cm. U. of A.

2324 **Manitoba.** Department of Agriculture and Immigration
Farm, wheat and dairy lands in prosperous Manitoba. Winnipeg, 1912. 54p. illus. Can. Arch.

2325 **Manitoba.** Department of Agriculture and Immigration
Manitoba. True stories of success in farming told by the men themselves. [Winnipeg, 1912?] cover-title, 32p. 16cm. Arkin

2326 **Moosomin, Sask.** Board of Trade
Moosomin. Bountiful, beautiful, progressive. [Winnipeg, Macpherson-McCurdy, 1912] 21, [3]p. illus., fold. map. 15 1/2 x 22 1/2cm. Shortt

2327 **Moosomin, Sask.** Board of Trade
Progressive Moosomin, industrial and commercial centre of eastern Saskatchewan, Canada. Moosomin, Fleming and Welwyn and their environments. [Moosomin, World-Spectator, 1912] cover-title, [52]p. illus. (incl. ports.) 19 x 22cm. Pagination includes advertising.

This pamphlet was issued because it was thought the town was on the eve of important developments. However, the projected branch railway lines, which the Grand Trunk Pacific and the Canadian Northern railways had surveyed, failed to materialize. Shortt

2328 **Murphy,** Emily Gowan (Ferguson)
Open trails, by Janey Canuck [pseud.] London, Cassell & Co , 1912. xi, [1], 291, [1]p. col. front., illus. 20cm.

Also published by Cassell of Toronto. U. of S.

2329 **National Land Company Limited**
Saskatoon, 1912, the fastest growing city in America. [Calgary, McAra Presses, 1912] cover-title, 12p. illus., map, plan (part fold.) 16 1/2cm.

Advertising Victoria Square, a rural subdivision, which forty years later was still prairie. U. of T.

2330 **Paynter,** J[oseph] E[dward]
Spectres of the night and morning light. New York, Everywhere Publication Co. [c1912] 187p. B.C. Arch.

2331 **Penniac Reef Gold Mines, Limited**
Manitoba's first gold mine. [n.p., 1912] cover-title, 9p. illus., fold. plan. 23cm. Arkin

2332 [**Piché**, Marie Anne, Mother]
De Montréal à MacKenzie. Notes de voyage, avril-october, 1912. [Montréal, 1912] 2p.l., 58p. front., plates. 21cm. Glenbow

2332A **Pocock**, Rodger
A man in the open. Toronto, McLeod and Allen, 1912. 352p. 20cm. Br. Mus.

2333 Prince Albert district, Saskatchewan ... [n.p., n.d.] cover-title, 28p. maps. B.C. Arch.

2334 **Pullen-Burry**, B[essie]
From Halifax to Vancouver. Toronto, Bell & Cockburn [1912] xvi, 352p. front., plates. 23cm.
About a third of the book relates to the Prairies. Man. Leg.

2335 **Rathborne**, St. George Henry
Canoe mates in Canada; or, Three boys afloat on the Saskatchewan ... Chicago, M.A. Donohue & Co. [c1912] 238p. incl. front. 20cm. (His Canoe and campfire series)
Juvenile fiction. U. of A.

2336 **Red Deer, Alta.** Board of Trade
Red Deer, Alberta. [Red Deer, 1912] 24p. illus., double map. 23 x 12cm.
Has colored pictorial fold-over cover. Private copy

2337 Regina, before and after cyclone, June 30, 1912. Regina, P.T. Evans & K.L. Fenney [1912] [24]p. illus. 16 1/2 x 26 1/2cm. Shortt

2337A Regina tornado, June 30, 1912. Regina, Saskatchewan, Canada [1912] cover-title, [24]p. chiefly illus. 18 x 25cm.
'Photo[s] by Rossie.' Glenbow

2338 **Regina**. Board of Trade
1000 facts about Regina, Saskatchewan. Regina, 1912. cover-title, 27p. 15cm. Sask. Arch.

2339 **Reid**, W[illiam] D[unn]
Mission work in Alberta. [Toronto. Presbyterian Church in Canada. Board of Home Missions, 1912?] cover-title, [14]p. illus. 16cm. Glenbow

2340 **Reville**, F[rederick] Douglas
A rebellion; a story of the Red River uprising. Illustrated by Paul Wickson. Brantford, Ont., Hurley Printing Co. [c1912] 7p.l., 198p. front., plates. 20cm.
Fiction. Shortt

2341 **Rosthern, Sask.** Board of Trade
Rosthern, where the world's best wheat grows. [Rosthern, The Board, 1912] cover-title, 24p. illus. 21 1/2cm. Shortt

2342 **Sandilands,** John, ed.
Western Canadian dictionary and phrase-book, explaining in plain English for the special benefit of newcomers, the meaning of the most common Canadianisms, colloquialisms and slang, added to which is a selection of items of general information immediately helpful to the newcomer. Winnipeg, Telegram Job Printers, Ltd., c1912. [32]p. 17cm.

The editor claims that the volume is the 'First dictionary ever printed in Canada.' A second edition in 1913 has collation: 52, [1]p. 23cm. Shortt

2342A **Saskatchewan.** Department of Agriculture
Saskatchewan. [Regina, 1912] 112p. illus. 26cm. Glenbow

2343 Saskatoon, Saskatchewan. [n.p., 1912?] 9 plates. 15 x 22cm. Shortt

2344 Stettler, Alberta, the busy town. The heart of Alberta. [Stettler, Stettler Quick print, 1912] 15, [1]p. illus. 19cm. Man. Leg.

2345 **Stock,** A.B.
Ranching in the Canadian West; a few hints to would-be stock-raisers on the care of cattle, horses, and sheep. London, Adam & Charles Black, 1912. x, 84p. 20cm.

The greater part of the book is devoted to technical matters relating to the raising of stock. Shortt

2346 **Sykes,** Ella C[onstance]
A home-help in Canada ... London, Smith, Elder & Co., 1912. xv, 394p. front. 21cm.

The author, an English woman, spent six months in 1911 in Western Canada working in five different positions to investigate opportunities for English women emigrants. Shortt

2347 **Talbot,** Frederick A[rthur Ambrose]
The making of a great Canadian railway; the story of the search for and discovery of the route, and the construction of the nearly completed Grand Trunk Pacific Railway from the Atlantic to the Pacific, with some account of the hardships and stirring adventures of its constructors, in unexplored country ... Toronto, Musson Book Co., 1912. 2p.l., 7-349p. front., plates, fold. map, diagrs. 23cm. U. of S.

2348 **Thwaite,** Leo
The province of Alberta; an account of its wealth and progress. With an introduction by Robert P. Porter. London, George Routledge & Sons, 1912. 250p. front., plates. 20cm. (Porter's progress of the nations) Shortt

2349 **Tofield, Alta.** Industrial League
Tofield & district; sunny Alberta, the place to come to. [n.p., 1912?] 16p. illus. 24cm. Man. Leg.

2350 **Ure,** R. W[alter]
Mortgage investments in Alberta. Calgary, 1912. 60p. Not seen. Br. Mus.

2351 Vegreville district, central Alberta. Vegreville [1912] 23p. illus. 21cm. Not seen. R.E.S.

2352 **Vermilion, Alta.** Ten Thousand Club
Vermilion, Alberta ... [Winnipeg, Public Press, 1912] 32p. illus., map (on inside front cover) 26cm. Glenbow

2353 [**Viel**, Louis]
L'aisance qui vient; vie du colon français dans la prairie canadienne. Par Louis et Jean. Paris, Blond & Cie, 1912. 214p. (Collection canadienne)

First published in 1911. This book, half fiction, half fact, gives a faithful picture of French communities in the West. Written by Louis Viel of Saint-Laurent, Man., and Léopold Leau of Paris, France. Shortt

2354 **Wainwright, Alta.** Board of Trade
Wainwright, the buffalo town; where diversified farming pays. [Wainwright, Wainwright Star, 1912] [8]p. 24cm. Man. Leg.

2355 **Walker**, Eldred G.F.
Canadian trails; hither and thither in the great Dominion ... Toronto, Musson Book Co. [1912?] viii, 11-190p., 1 l. front., plates. 19 1/2cm. Shortt

2356 **Washburn**, Stanley
Trails, trappers, and tender-feet in the new empire of Western Canada. London, Andrew Melrose, 1912. xvi, 350p. front., illus., fold. map. 23cm.

A trip in 1897-98 by pack horse and canoe from Lacombe, Alta., through the Yellowhead Pass, and then down the Athabasca, etc. Dempsey

2357 **White**, Isaac S.
Manitoba muses; or, Gentle Joseph, and other poems, composed in the solitude of the backwoods of Manitoba ... Toronto, Bryant Press, Ltd., 1912. xiv p., 1 l., [17]-327p. front. (port.) 23cm. Shortt

2358 Who's who in Western Canada; a biographical dictionary of notable living men and women of Western Canada. v.1-2, 1911-12. [Vancouver?] Canadian Press Association, 1911-12. 2v. incl. plates. 19cm.

Edited by C.W. Parker. Only 2 volumes were published. U. of A.

2359 **Winnipeg, Selkirk and Lake Winnipeg Railway**
'Picnic time.' [Winnipeg, 1912] [12]p. illus. 9 x 15cm. Glenbow

2360 [**Amy**, William Lacey]
The blue wolf, a tale of the Cypress Hills. Toronto, Musson [1913?] viii, 311p. Not seen.

Fiction. Also published the same year by Hodder and Stoughton of London, and reprinted in 1921 by Herbert Jenkins of London. Can. Imprints

2361 **Anderson**, Robert T[hompson]
Canadian born and other western poems. Edmonton, Esdale Press, 1913. 100p. col. plate. 24cm. Edmonton

2362 **Asselin**, [Joseph François] Olivar.
L'émigration belge et française au Canada. Ottawa, King's Printer, 1913. 33p. 24cm. Can. Arch.

2363 **Bell,** Charles Napier
Lead tablet buried by La Verendrye in 1743. Winnipeg, 1913. caption-title, 7p. 17 x 21cm.

On cover: The story of the lead plate. 'From the Winnipeg Free Press, Saturday, April 12, 1913.' Glenbow

2364 **Bellingham,** Edythe
Canada, the land of hope! Jersey, England, Issued by Bellingham's Ocean Travel Office [1913] cover-title, 13p. 22cm.

'Portions of this article appeared in the "Canadian Gazette" March 27, 1913, issue, and are reproduced by the kind permission of the editor.' Printed by W. de Guerin, Jersey. Describes a tour across Canada in October 1912. Br. Mus.

2365 **Bindloss,** Harold
Prescott of Saskatchewan. With a frontispiece in color by W. Herbert Dunton. New York, Frederick A. Stokes [1913] v, 346p. mounted col. front. 19 1/2cm.

Fiction. Published in Toronto by McLeod and Allen. The edition published in England had the title 'The Wastrel.' L.C.

2366 **Black,** Norman Fergus
English for the non-English ... Regina, Regina Bookshop [c1913] 211p. 20cm. U. of S.

2367 **Black,** Norman Fergus
History of Saskatchewan and the North-West Territories. Regina, Saskatchewan Historical Co. [c1913] 2v. illus., ports. 27 1/2cm.

Includes biographies of prominent citizens. A second edition in 1 volume without the biographical sketches was also published under the title 'A History of Saskatchewan and the Old North West.' Shortt

2368 **Bow City, Alta.** Board of Trade
Bow City, Alberta, Canada, the city of natural resources. [Regina, University Press, 1913?] cover-title, [18]p. illus., diagrs. 22cm. Glenbow

2369 Brandon, Manitoba, Canada. [Brandon, 1913] cover-title, 72p. illus., fold. covers (illus.) 12 x 15cm.

Chiefly illustrations. Glenbow

2370 **Breed,** Elliott, & Harrison
Saskatoon. [n.p., 1913] cover-title, 22p. illus., fold. plate 14 x 19cm.

Designed to interest American capital and business. Shortt

2371 **Broadview, Sask.** Board of Trade
Broadview, the railway town of eastern Saskatchewan. Broadview, Express print, 1913. 32p. illus. (incl. ports.) 21cm. Sask. Arch.

2372 **Buck,** Alanson L.
The outlaw, and other poems. Toronto, William Briggs, 1913. 161p. 19 1/2cm. U. of S.

2373 **Budka**, Nykyta
Dorohovkaz dla Rusyniw shcho yidut do Kanady; pastyrskiy lyst [Guide to the Ruthenians coming to Canada; a pastoral letter] Winnipeg, 1913. 11p. 18 1/2cm. Not seen. Private information

2374 **Burrows**, Clement L[arcom]
Hands across the sea; being memories of a helpful tour in Western Canada. ... Bournemouth, Eng. [Richmond Hill Printing Works Ltd., 1913] 2p.l., 51p. front., plates. 20cm.

The author accompanied Bishop Ingham on the Church of England Mission of Help to Western Canada in the fall of 1912. Edmonton

2375 **Canada.** Department of the Interior
Canada: the Prairie Provinces in 1912. Ottawa, 1913. 48p. illus. 25 x 13cm. Glenbow

2376 **Canada.** Department of the Interior
Canada West, ranching, dairying, grain raising, fruit growing, mixed farming. Ottawa, 1913. cover-title, 41p. illus., maps. 28 1/2cm.

Caption: The last best West, the Canada of opportunity. L.C.

2377 **Canadian Northern Prairie Lands Company, Limited**
Annual report of the board of directors. [Toronto, 1913] 1v. N.Y.

2378 **Canadian Northern Railway**
Peace River country and how to reach it. [Toronto] 1913. cover-title, 15, [1]p. illus., fold. map. 24 x 11cm. Glenbow

2379 **Canadian Northern Railway**
Western Canada has a home for you. Winnipeg [1913] cover-title, 24p. illus., fold. map. 19 x 26cm. Not seen. U. of Texas

2380 **Canadian Pacific Railway**
Erhverv dem et Kanadisk hjem fra Canadian Pacific. En haandbog med oplysninger om Canadian Pacific farme i drift og om laan til nybyggere. [Kobenhavn, 1913] cover-title, 47p. illus. 19cm.

In double column with each column having a page number. The Danish agent for the company was Olaf Lassen. Denmark

2381 **Champion, Alta.** Board of Trade
Grain golden Champion, southern Alberta. The settler's Utopia. [n.p., 1913] 21p. illus. 25cm.

This copy missing title-page; title from half-title. Written by W.L.C. Glenbow

2382 **Charlebois**, Ovide
Débuts d'un évêque-missionnaire: Mgr Ovide Charlebois, O.M.I., évêque de Bérénice, vicaire apostolique du Keewatin. Prise de possession; installation; première visite pastorale des missions sauvages. [Montréal, Impr. des Sourds-Muets, 1913] iv, 102p. front., illus., ports. 18cm. Shortt

2383 **Cowie**, Isaac
The company of adventurers; a narrative of seven years in the service of the Hudson's Bay Company during 1867-1874 on the great buffalo plains; with

historical and biographical notes and comments. Toronto, William Briggs, 1913. 2p.l., 3-515p. front., plates, ports. 22cm. A reprint of articles published in the Manitoba Free Press, Feb. 17-Dec. 14, 1912.

A readable and valuable history of the fur trade as seen by a H.B.C. servant at Qu'Appelle. Gives much information about southern Saskatchewan at that period. Shortt

2384 **Crawford,** Mary E[lizabeth] comp.
Legal status of women in Manitoba as shown by extracts from Dominion and provincial laws. Winnipeg, Political Equality League of Manitoba, 1913. 41p. 23cm. Shortt

2385 **Davidson and McRae**
Industrial and business opportunities in Western Canada; along the lines of the Canadian Northern Railway. 1913 ed. Winnipeg, Davidson and McRae, 1913. cover-title, 172p. illus., map. 22cm.

Incomplete, p.159-172 missing, no map. Man. Arch.

2386 **Dawson & Gowen**
Brandon, the second city of Manitoba is situated on the Assiniboine River, 133 miles west of Winnipeg. It is the most beautiful city in Western Canada and is surrounded by the finest farming country. Photograph by Dawson & Gowen, Brandon. [n.p., 1913?] 72p. 15 x 12cm. Lavallee - 1964-159

2387 **The Edmonton Club,** Edmonton, Alta.
Act of incorporation, constitution, regulations and list of members. With additions and amendments to July 1st, 1913. [Edmonton, 1913] 47, [1]p. 17cm.

'Incorporated 1899.' Glenbow

2388 **Edmonton.** Public Library
... First annual report of the Edmonton Public Library and Strathcona Public Library. With historical sketches by Mrs. Anne Newall and Mr. George M. Hall. Edmonton [Edmonton News Pub. Co. Ltd.] 1913. 31, [1]p. incl. front., illus., tables. 22cm.

Mrs. Newall's four-page sketch relates to library development, Mr. Hall's to that of the city. Miss M. Auxier's copy

2389 **Edwards,** J[ohn] Hugh
Canada: its romance and its call. The County Gentleman, Sporting Gazette, 1913. cover-title, [4]p. illus. (incl. map) 38cm.

Published in the issue of the magazine for June 28, 1913, these pages were later issued as a separate. Wales

2390 **Evalenko,** Alexander M., comp.
The message of the Doukhobors. A statement of true facts by 'Christians of the Universal Brotherhood' and by prominent champions of their cause. New York, International Library Publishing Co., 1913. 3p.l., 9-146p. illus. 20cm. Shortt

2391 **Ferrier,** Thompson
Our Indians and their training for citizenship. Toronto, The Young People's Forward Movement [1913?] 47p. illus., ports. 23cm.

Mostly on Western Canada. Glenbow

2392 **Footner,** [William] Hulbert
Jack Chanty; a story of Athabasca. Garden City, N.Y., Doubleday, Page & Co., 1913. 6p.l., 3-337, [1]p. col. front., plates. 20cm.

Juvenile fiction. L.C.

2393 **Fyfe,** H[enry] Hamilton
Shall I go to Canada? The land of opportunity and hope. London, Associated Newspapers Ltd. [1913] 120p. plates. 22cm.

Over half the book relates to the Prairie Provinces. Netherlands

2394 **Gargas,** Zygmunt
W sprawie emigracyi do Kanady. Kraków, Nakl. Wydawn. 'Przyjaciela Ludu,' 1913. cover-title, 14p. (incl. cover)

On the problem of emigration to Canada. Turek

2395 **Gargas,** Zygmunt
W sprawie wychodźctwa do Kanady. Obbitka ze 'Slowa Polskiego.' Lwów, Nakl. autora, 1913. 16p.

On the problem of emigration to Canada. Turek

2396 **Grand Trunk Pacific Railway**
Bread book; a few terse stories of success and why failure are unheard of along the line of railway through the most fertile districts of Western Canada. 8th ed. Winnipeg, The Company, 1913. 25p. 14 x 22cm. Not seen. R.E.S.

2397 **Grouard, Alta.** Board of Trade
Grouard, the coming metropolis of the great Peace River country, Alberta, Canada. [Edmonton] 1913. 19p. map. Ehrlich - 22-21

2398 **Horden,** J[ohn]
A grammar of the Cree language ... Rev. ed. in Plain Cree. London, Society for Promoting Christian Knowledge, 1913. 2p.l., 209p. 16 1/2cm.

First edition was published in 1881. This edition with Plains Cree terms was revised by Ven. J.A. Mackay, Rt. Rev. J.A. Newnham, and others. Reprinted in 1934. Shortt

2399 **Hornby,** Montague L[eyland]
How to buy land in Canada. London, Adam & Charles Black, 1913. 90p. 20cm. Not seen.

The author advises Englishmen with considerable capital how to secure land in the West. He suggested buying a large estate and dividing it among tenant farmers. R.E.S.

2400 **Hubbard,** Elbert [Green]
Cairns of Saskatoon, being an appreciation. East Aurora, N.Y., The Roycrofters, 1913. 16p. 21cm. Leather binding.

About the city's leading merchant. U. of S.

2401 **Hubbard,** Elbert [Green]
A little journey to Saskatoon. East Aurora, N.Y., The Roycrofters, 1913. 32p. 20cm. Saskatoon

2402 **Ingham,** [Ernest Graham]
Sketches in Western Canada, by Bishop Ingham and Rev. Clement L. Burrows. Toronto, Hodder & Stoughton, 1913. xii p., 1 l., 3-151p. front., plates. 19 1/2cm. Shortt

2403 Interesting facts regarding the development of the city of Moose Jaw. Moose Jaw, 1913. 32p. illus. Not seen. R.E.S.

2404 **Kelly,** L[eroy] V[ictor]
The range men; the story of the ranchers and Indians of Alberta. Toronto, William Briggs, 1913. 468p. front., plates, ports. 23cm.

A compilation of material relating to the early ranching period. U. of A.

2405 **Kennedy,** H.G.
History of the 101st Regiment Edmonton Fusiliers, allied with the Royal Munster Fusiliers, 1908-1913. [Edmonton?] Pierce & Kennedy [1913] 2p.l., 40p. col. front., ports. (incl. group) 23 x 30cm. Rutherford

2406 **Laing,** Hamilton M[ack]
Out with the birds. New York, Outing Publishing Co., 1913. 249p. front., plates. 20cm.

A naturalist studies the birds of Manitoba. Winnipeg

2407 [**Lyttleton,** Edith J.]
The law-bringers, by G.B. Lancaster [pseud.] Toronto, Musson Book Co. [1913] 395p. 19 1/2cm.

Fiction. Two men who fell out for love of a woman meet again in the mounted police force.
Also published in New York by Hodder and Stoughton. R.E.S.

2408 **Manitoba.** Department of Agriculture and Immigration
Greater Manitoba, the home of mixed farming. [Winnipeg] The Department [1913] 64p. illus. 26 1/2cm. Man. Leg.

2408A **The Manitoba Club,** Winnipeg
The act of incorporation, constitution, rules and regulations and list of members of the Manitoba Club. Winnipeg, 1913. 56p. 17cm.

'Established 1874.' Pages 48-56 blank. Glenbow

2409 **Marchant,** Bessie
The youngest sister; a tale of Manitoba. London, Blackie and Son, Ltd., 1913. vi, 9-351p. front., plates. 19cm.

Juvenile literature. Br. Mus.

2410 **Maron,** Gotthard L.
Facts about the Germans in Canada ... Winnipeg, Der Nordwesten Publishing Co. [1913?] 58, [1]p. 23cm. Man. Leg.

2411 [**Mathieu,** Olivier Elzéar]
A page of history; [address] delivered at the Regina Collegiate Institute before the Arts, Literary and Science Association of Regina. [Regina, 1913?] 28p. 2 ports. (1 mounted on cover) 24cm.

Published by Regina Council No.1247, Knights of Columbus. 'Right Reverend Bishop Mathieu': p.5-6. Glenbow

2412 **Maugham,** W[illiam] S[omerset]
The land of promise; a comedy in four acts. London, Bickers & Son, 1913. 78p., 1 l. 18 1/2cm.

This play was printed for purposes of copyright only, in not more than 25 copies. Another edition was printed in Ottawa by Geo. A. Popham in 1914, again only in limited number (Stott, R.T., The writings of William Somerset Maugham. London, 1956). Republished by Heinemann in 1922. (Copy in U. of A.)

The locale of the first act is England; the last three, Manitoba. L.C.

2413 Men and makers of Edmonton, Alta. [n.p., 1913] [58]p. ports. 27cm.
Bound in leather. Edmonton

2414 **Methodist Church**
Report of a preliminary and general social survey of Regina, September, 1913, made by the Department of Temperance and Moral Reform of the Methodist Church, and the Board of Social Service and Evangelism of the Presbyterian Church. [Toronto, 1913] 48p. plan. 27cm.

Report made by J.S. Woodsworth. N.Y.

2415 **Molan,** Adrain
Nagra drag af Kolonisationen i Canada. Stockholm, 1913. (Broschyrer utgifna at Nationalfoereningen mot Emigrationen 6) ... Amtmann - 249-203

2416 **Moose Jaw.** Board of Trade
Moose Jaw, the buckle of the greatest wheat belt in the world. [Moose Jaw, Rice's studio, 1913] 32p. illus. 28cm. Sask. Arch.

2417 **Morris,** Elizabeth Keith
An Englishwoman in the Canadian West. London, Simpkin, Marshall, 1913. 192p. front., plates. 18 1/2cm.

The author, who spent about a year in the Edmonton district, describes the social life of the province. Her book was written to advise Englishwomen who wished to emigrate.
Edmonton

2418 **North Battleford, Sask.** Board of Trade
North Battleford, the centre of new development. [North Battleford, Printed on the North Battleford News presses, 1913] [48]p. illus. 12 x 25cm.

On cover: Views of the city of North Battleford and surrounding country. Glenbow

2419 **North Saskatchewan Land Company, Limited**
North Saskatchewan Land Company, Ltd., owners of 150,000 acres selected farm lands. [Winnipeg? 1913] caption-title, 4p. 36cm.

Letter addressed to the public by the general manager John F. Hansen, setting out the company's land offer. Letter also in Swedish.

Lands located in the Carrot and Saskatchewan river valleys in the vicinity of Melfort.
Sweden

2420 **Partridge,** E[dward] A[lexander]
... Manifesto of the No-Party League of Western Canada ... [Winnipeg, De Monfort Press, 1913] cover-title, 26p. 17cm.

Quotations on front and back covers.
'Prepared by E.A. Partridge, at request of the founders of the League, and revised and endorsed by a committee composed of R.M. Douglas, J. Styon and D Ross, appointed for that purpose.' Sask. Arch.

2421 **Prairie Coal Company, Limited**
Bow City, the Pittsburg of Canada, having coal, natural gas, iron ore, brick clay, water power, rich farm lands ... [Regina, 1913?] cover-title, 16p. maps, diagr. (on back cover) 21cm. Glenbow

2422 Prince Albert, Saskatchewan, 1913. [Prince Albert, Sask., Herald Print. Co., 1913] 2 l., 35, lix p.

'This publication is the outcome of a desire on the part of the author to place before his friends a little information regarding a district which has afforded him, in conjunction with others, excellent opportunities of making good ...' Amtmann - 214-612

2423 **Redcliff, Alta.** Board of Trade
Redcliff, Alberta, Canada's natural gas manufacturing centre. [Redcliff, ca. 1913] cover-title, 16p. illus., map. 26 x 12cm. Glenbow

2424 **Regina.** Board of Trade
Regina, the capital of the province of Saskatchewan, a city of beautiful buildings and paved streets; an educational centre. [Regina, 1913] [32]p. chiefly illus., ports. Hamilton

2425 Regina. [Regina, Published for Canada Drug and Book Co., Ltd., 1913] 1p.l., 12 plates. 11 1/2 x 17cm. Shortt

2425A **Robson,** A. Ritchie
West of the West. A sketch of early mission days in North-Western Canada. Stirling, Scotland, Drummond's Tract Depot [1913] 136p. 18 1/2cm.

Relates to experiences in Saskatchewan. Northland

2426 **Roman Catholic Church.** Liturgy and ritual. Cree
... Grand messe, bénédiction et cantiques en langue crise. Sacred-Heart, Alta. [1913] 232p. 14cm.

Title in Cree syllabic also; text in Cree. Oblates Arch.

2427 **Royal Architectural Institute of Canada**
Souvenir, sixth annual assembly, Calgary, Alberta, Sept. 15 and 16, 1913. [Calgary] Published by Maurice J. Connolly [1913] cover-title, 63p. illus., ports. 18 x 27cm.

Includes advertising matter. Largely pictorial of Calgary. Glenbow

2428 **St. Boniface, Man.** Committee on La Vérendrye monument
A monument to La Vérendrye, the discoverer of the West. St. Boniface, Le Manitoba Print. Co., 1913. 19p. Amtmann - 239-544

2429 **Salter,** E[rnest] J.B.
The Manitoba School Question; being a controversy between the Rev. E.J.B. Salter and the Rev. A.G. Morice, as published in letters to the Winnipeg Free Press. Winnipeg, West Canada Publishing Co., 1913. 86p. 19cm.

Rev. A.G. Morice, who had used the pseudonym Truth, had the letters on both sides published in pamphlet form. The controversy was over whether Catholics should be expected to contribute to the support of public schools as well as their own. Man. Leg.

2430 **Saskatchewan.** Department of Agriculture
Business guide to Saskatchewan. Regina, J.W. Reid, 1913. 54p. 23cm.
Arkin

2431 **Saskatoon.** Board of Trade
... Saskatoon. [Saskatoon] c1913. 60p. illus. 14 1/2 x 20 1/2cm. Shortt

2432 **Savaète,** Arthur
Ecoles du Nord-Ouest canadien (suite) (1880-1913) Paris, A. Savaète [1913]
528p. 24cm. (Voix canadiennes: vers l'abîme, v.8) Not seen. St. Sulpice

2433 **Saxby,** C.F. Argyll
The fiery totem; a tale of adventure in the Canadian North-West. London, Religious Tract Society [1913] 222, [1]p. col. front. 20cm. Glenbow

2434 **Schofield,** F[rank] H[oward]
The story of Manitoba. Winnipeg, S.J. Clarke Publishing Co., 1913. 3v. front., plates, ports., maps. 27cm.

v.1 is a history, v.2-3 are biographical. Shortt

2434A **Stirling,** John T.
The Bellevue explosions, Alberta, Canada: an account of, and subsequent investigation concerning, three explosions produced by sparks from falls of roof; a paper read before the Institution of Mining Engineers, by John T. Stirling and John Cadman. London, Published at the Offices of the Institution, 1913. cover-title, 32p. illus. 25cm.

Annual general meeting at Birmingham, 11 September 1912. Excerpt from the Transactions of the Institution of Mining Engineers, v.54, pt.4, p.740-770. Glenbow

2435 **Stock,** Ralph
The confessions of a tenderfoot; being a true and unvarnished account of his world-wanderings. London, Grant Richards, 1913. 260p. illus. 22 1/2cm.

Describes his ranching experience in the Cypress Hills region; the last half of the book relates to experiences in Fiji and Australia. Shortt

2436 **Teetgen,** A[da] B.
A white passion. London, Wells, Gardner, Darton & Co., Ltd. [1913?]
xv, 329p. 19cm.

A fictionalized account of the hardships of homesteading in Alberta in a district which the author calls 'Finlay' (Islay, Alta.) The book was written to raise funds for a municipal hospital. Shortt

2437 **Wheatley,** E. Perse
Out West, sketches of prairie life. London, T. Murby & Co. [1913] 2p.l., v, 83p. illus., plates. 19cm. N.Y.

2438 **White,** Samuel Alexander
Empery; a story of love and battle in Rupert's Land. Toronto, Musson, 1913. 332p. Not seen.

Fiction. A central character is chief trader at Oxford House. Can. Imprints

2439 **Winnipeg**. Trinity Lutheran Church
Gedenkblatt zum 25-jährigen Jubiläum der deutschen Ev.-Luth. Dreieinigkeitsgemeinde in Winnipeg, Man., 1888-1913. Winnipeg, 1913. 16p. Not seen. Lehmann

2440 [**Anonymous**]
Melfort celebrates the introduction of agriculture to Western Canada by Chevalier de la Corne, 1754-1914. [Winnipeg, J.J. Gibbons Ltd., 1914] cover-title, 12p. illus. 25cm. U. of S.

2440A **Beauvau-Craon**, Charles Louis Juste Elie Marie Joseph Victurnien, prince de ... La survivance, française au Canada, notes de voyage. Préface de M. Maurice Barrès ... Paris, Emile-Paul frères, 1914. 2p.l., xxviii, 233p. 19cm. B.C. Arch.

2441 **Becker**, Heinrich
[The truth about Canada. Edmonton, 1914] ... Not seen.
Title and text in German. Can. Annual Rev., 1914, p.663

2442 **Bennett**, Arthur S.
Chevalier de la Corne and the Carrot River valley of Saskatchewan. [Toronto, Atwell Fleming Pub. Co., 1914?] 39p. illus. (incl. port.) 26cm. Not seen.
Written to advertise the agricultural possibilities of the area. B.C. Arch.

2443 **Bickersteth**, J[ohn] Burgon
The land of open doors, being letters from Western Canada. Foreword by the Right Hon. Earl Grey ... Toronto, Musson Book Co., Ltd. [1914] xxiv, 265, [1]p. front., plates, fold. map. 23cm.
The experiences of a lay missionary of the Church of England in the territory west and north of Edmonton. Shortt

2444 **Binnie-Clark**, Georgina
Wheat & women. Toronto, Bell and Cockburn, 1914. vii, 413p. front., plates. 19 1/2cm.
A vivid description of the author's three-year struggle to make wheat farming pay on a farm near Ft. Qu'Appelle, Sask. A sequel to 'A Summer on the Canadian Prairie.' U. of S.

2445 **Boam**, Henry J., comp.
The Prairie Provinces of Canada; their history, people, commerce, industries, and resources. Edited by Ashley G. Brown. London, Sells, Ltd., 1914. 451p. illus. 32cm. Shortt

2446 **Burpee**, Lawrence J[ohnstone]
Pathfinders of the Great Plains; a chronicle of La Vérendrye and his sons. Toronto, Glasgow, Brook & Co., 1914. ix p., 1 l., 116p. plates, port., map. 18 1/2cm. (Chronicles of Canada) U. of S.

2447 **Byron-May Company**
Pictorial Edmonton. [Edmonton, Edmonton Printing & Publishing Co., Ltd., 1914] [32]p. illus. 18 1/2cm. Rutherford

2448 Calgary social register, 1915. Calgary, Women's Guild of Pro-Cathedral, c1914. 17p. 17cm. Glenbow

2449 **Campbell,** Milton Neil
Reminiscences of pioneer days in the West. Written through the encouragement of the Saskatchewan Archives, Regina, Sask. and covering experiences ... during the years 1902 to 1914. [Hamilton, Ont., n.d.] [12]p. 23cm.

A railway telegrapher tells of experiences in Manitoba and Saskatchewan. Glenbow

2450 Camrose, after seven years. Camrose [c1914] 32p. illus. Not seen. R.E.S.

2451 **Canada.** Department of the Interior
Abstracts from reports on townships west of the fifth and sixth meridians (in the Province of Alberta and the Peace River Block, British Columbia) received from surveyors between July 1, 1913 and July 1, 1914. [Ottawa, 1914?] 61p. 25cm. Glenbow

2452 **Canada.** Department of the Interior
Grand Ouest Canadien. Ottawa, 1914. cover-title, -p. illus., double col. maps. Nebenzahl - 16-200

2453 **Canadian Pacific Railway**
The western provinces of Canada; Manitoba, Saskatchewan, Alberta, British Columbia. [Calgary, 1914] cover-title, 111p. Glenbow

2454 **Coffey,** Claude Cloyd
Directory of oil companies and investor's guide of the Calgary oil field. [Calgary] Compiled and published by C.C. Coffey [c1914] 52p. fold. map. 22cm.

Library copy lacks map. Glenbow

2455 **Conservative Party** (Manitoba)
Record of the Roblin Government, 1900-1914, and the criticisms and pretensions of opponents. [Winnipeg, 1914] 239, viii p. illus., plates, ports., 2 fold. maps, diagr., facsims., tables. 25cm. Glenbow

2456 **Dennis,** J[ohn] S[toughton]
An address on the development of Western Canada and its bearing on the commercial future of the empire. London, London Chamber of Commerce [1914] cover-title, 27p. fold. map. 22cm. C.P.R.

2457 Edmonton, Alberta's capital city. Illustrated with the latest photographs of Edmonton's wholesale and retail districts; park, street, residential, water scenes, etc. Together with a historical review of the city and its standing as a manufacturing, commercial and residential metropolis. Edmonton, Esdale Press Limited and McDermid Engraving Co. Limited, 1914. 180p. of illus. 23 x 31cm.

Several illustrations on each page. Private copy

2458 **Edmonton City Dairy**
Edmonton City Dairy, Edmonton, Alberta, Canada. [Edmonton, 1914] [32]p. of illus. 17 x 26cm. Glenbow

2459 **Gilbert**, Louis
La Saskatchewan; essai de monographie provinciale canadienne. Paris, La Canadienne [1914?] 4p.l., [11]-160p. incl. front. (map) plates, fold. map. 25 1/2cm.

An attempt to gather and interpret data for French readers. U. of S.

2460 **Gill**, E[dward] A[nthony] Wharton
An Irishman's luck; a tale of Manitoba. London, Hodder & Stoughton, 1914. viii, 310p.

Fiction. Br. Mus.

2461 **Giroux**, J.B.H.
La Rivière la Paix pour les Canadiens-français. Venez réclamer une terre fertile de 160 acres dans l'Alberta du Nord, la nouvelle Terre Promise du Canada. Publié sous la direction de l'Honorable W.J. Roche, Ministre de l'Intérieur du Canada. [n.p.] 1914. cover-title, 24p. Amtmann - 214-592

2462 [**Gordon**, Charles William]
The patrol of the sun dance, by Ralph Connor [pseud.] New York, Hodder & Stoughton, George H. Doran Co. [c1914] 2p.l., [7]-363p. 19 1/2cm.

Fiction. L.C.

2463 **Howard**, Henry
Canada, the western cities; their borrowing and their assets. London, Investors' Guardian, 1914. 2p.l., 120p. 19cm. U. of A.

2464 **Jeffs**, Harry
Homes and careers in Canada. With 16 illus. London, J. Clarke, 1914. 199, [1]p. plates. 19cm.

Running title: Making good in Canada. Includes much about the prairie region. Glenbow

2465 **Jolys**, J[ean] M[arie Arthur]
Pages de souvenirs et d'histoire; la paroisse de Saint-Pierre-Jolys au Manitoba. St-Boniface, 1914. xvi, 239p. front., plates, ports. 21cm. Man. Leg.

2466 **Lauritzen**, Fr.
Nybyggerkaar i Canada. Skildringer fra en rejse. Esbjerg, Wedege-Pedersens Bogtrykkeri, 1914. 23p. 21cm. Denmark

2467 **Laut**, Agnes C[hristina]
The 'Adventurers of England' on Hudson Bay; a chronicle of the fur trade in the North. Toronto, Glasgow, Brook & Co., 1914. xi, 133p. plates, ports. (incl. col. front.) maps (part fold.) 18 1/2cm. (Chronicles of Canada) U. of S.

2468 **Legal**, Emile J[oseph]
Short sketches of the history of the Catholic churches and missions in central Alberta. Winnipeg [1914?] 174p. illus. (incl. ports.) 28 1/2cm. Rutherford

2469 **Manitoba.** Department of Agriculture and Immigration
Manitoba: the home of mixed farming; the market; centre province of Western Canada ... [Winnipeg] The Department [1914] 55, [1]p. illus. 25cm. Shortt

2470 [**Mawson,** Thomas Hayton]
Calgary; a preliminary scheme for controlling the economic growth of the city. Published under the auspices of the City Planning Commission of Calgary. London, T.H. Mawson & Sons [1914] 2p.l., vi-viii p., 1 l., 88p. incl. illus., plates (part col., 1 double) plans (1 fold.) col. front. 31 1/2cm. Cover-title: The city of Calgary, past, present and future. Shortt

2471 **Menzies,** J[ohn] H[enry]
The economical condition and resources of the Canadian middle West. Winnipeg, 1914. 12p. Not seen. Br. Mus.

2472 **Methodist and Presbyterian Churches.** Departments of Social Service and Evangelism
Swan River Valley, Manitoba, including the municipalities of Swan River and Minitonas; report on a rural survey of the agricultural, educational, social and religious life. [Toronto, 1914] 73p. plates, fold. map, diagrs. 23cm. Man. Leg.

2473 [**Morice,** Adrien Gabriel]
Edmonton et l'Alberta française, par M. de la Seine. Edmonton, Le Courrier de l'Ouest, 1914. 40p. Not seen.

An appeal to French Canadians to preserve their language in the West, and to send more colonists to the West. R.H.P., 1916

2474 **Morice,** A[drien] G[abriel]
Histoire abrégée de l'Ouest canadien; Manitoba, Saskatchewan, Alberta, et Grand-Nord. Saint-Boniface, The Author, 1914. vii, 162p., 1 l. incl. front., illus. 19 1/2cm.

Although bearing the imprint 1914, this book was not in circulation until 1919. Printed in Lille, France, it remained in that city throughout the German occupation. The book was intended as a school text. Shortt

2475 [**Murphy,** Emily Gowan (Ferguson)]
Seeds of pine, by Janey Canuck [pseud.] New York, Hodder & Stoughton [1914] 6p.l., 307p. col. front., illus. 20cm.

'An impressionistic picture of life on the verge of settlement.' Also published by Hodder in Toronto. L.C.

2476 **Normandeau,** J.A.
L'Alberta centrale. Montréal, 1914. 29p. fold. map. 17cm. St. Sulpice

2477 **The Pas, Man.** Board of Trade
The Pas, capital of new Manitoba and southern terminus of Hudson Bay Railway. [n.p., 1914] 37p. illus., fold. map. 26cm. (Booklet no.1)

On cover: The Pas, the gateway to Hudson Bay. Arkin

2477A **Peace River, Alta.** Board of Trade
Peace River country, the last best West. [n.p.] 1914. 31p. Adelphi

2478 **Perpetual Rights Oil Company**, Calgary
Prospectus, filed with the Registrar of Joint Stock Companies of the Province of Alberta. [Calgary? 1914] cover-title, 20p. Amtmann – 214-382

2479 **Pioneers of Rupert's Land.** Executive Committee
Review of the claims of 'The Pioneers of Rupert's Land,' 1836 to 1870. [Winnipeg, 1914] caption-title, 14p. 22cm. Man. Leg.

2480 **Presbyterian and Methodist Churches.** Departments of Social Service and Evangelism
Turtle Mountain district, Manitoba, including the municipalities of Whitewater, Morton, and Winchester; report on a survey of the agricultural, educational, social and religious life. [Toronto, 1914] 78p. plates, fold map, diagrs. 23cm. Man. Leg.

2481 **Preston,** W[illiam] T[homas] R[ochester]
The life and times of Lord Strathcona. London, Eveleigh Nash, 1914. ix, [2], 13-324p. front. (port.) 23cm. Shortt

2481A **Regina.** Industrial and Publicity Commissioners
Regina, capital of Saskatchewan, Canada. Regina, 1914. cover-title, [32]p. illus. Northland

2482 **Rocky Mountain Oil Fields, Limited**
Prospectus. Issued in accordance with the laws of Alberta June 8th, 1914. Filed with the Registrar of Joint Stock Companies for the Province of Alberta, June 8th, 1914. [n.p., n.d.] 16p. plans (1 fold.) 22cm. Glenbow

2483 **Saskatchewan.** Department of Agriculture
Saskatchewan. Regina, J.W. Reid, 1914. 64p. tables. 26cm.
'... a ... connected story of Saskatchewan's progress and development.' Glenbow

2484 **The Saskatoon Phoenix**
The exhibition harvest edition. Saskatoon, August, 1914. cover-title, 96p. illus. (incl. ports.) 45cm. Shortt

2485 Souvenir of Regina, Sask. Regina, D. Mackinnon [1914] [32]p. of col. illus. 13 1/2 x 20 1/2cm. Shortt

2486 **Stead,** Robert James Campbell
The bail jumper. Toronto, Musson, 1914. ... Not seen.
Fiction. Can. Novel

2487 **Wade,** F[rederick] C[oate]
Experiments with the single tax in Western Canada. [Vancouver, Saturday Sunset presses, 1914] cover-title, 19p. diagr. 18 1/2cm. Paper read before the eighth annual conference on taxation, under the auspices of the National Tax Association, at Denver, Colorado, Sept. 11, 1914. Shortt

2488 **Western Standard Publishing Company**
The story of Calgary – Alberta – Canada; progress – opportunities. [Calgary, Alta., Western Standard Publishing Co., 1914] 65p. illus., ports. 36cm.

Error in paging: no.65 duplicated. 'Issued in Commemoration of the Annual Convention of the International Irrigation Congress, October fifth to ninth, nineteen fourteen.' Includes biographies. Glenbow

2489 **Wilson & Company**
Alberta oil fields. [Calgary, 1914?] cover-title [12]p. illus. 16 x 23cm. Glenbow

2490 **Woodsworth,** J[ames] S[haver] ed.
Studies in rural citizenship, designed for the use of Grain Growers' Associations, women's institutes, community clubs, young peoples' societies and similar organizations and groups desirous of obtaining an intelligent view of rural life in Canada, with its various needs and possibilities. Winnipeg, Canadian Council of Agriculture [1914?] 87, [1]p. 22 1/2cm. Shortt

2491 **Bashaw Extension of Settlement Club**
Bashaw district, Alberta. [Bashaw? 1915] 35p. illus. 15cm. B.C. Arch.

2492 **Bassano Colony Extension of Settlement Club**
Bassano irrigation colony. [Bassano? 1915] cover-title, 32p. illus. 15 1/2cm. B.C. Arch.

2493 **Budka,** Nykyta
Pravyla Rusko-Katolytskoi tserkvy v Kanadi. Winnipeg, Canadian-Ukrainian Publishing Co., 1915. 59, xiv p. 23cm. Not seen. Private information

2494 **Burpee,** Lawrence J[ohnstone]
Sandford Fleming, empire builder. London, H. Milford, 1915. 288p. front., plates, ports., fold. facsim. 22 1/2cm.
Fleming was engineer-in-chief of the C.P.R. during the period of survey. Shortt

2495 [**Campbell,** Thomas Joseph]
Out of the grave; the discovery of Fort St. Charles in 1908. St-Boniface, Le Manitoba print [1915] 22p. illus., map. 21 1/2cm. (Soc. Hist. de St-Boniface, v.5, pt.3) Shortt

2496 **Arnup,** Arthur W.
Résumé of the work and a few opinions on the operation of the Alberta Farm and Colonisation Company. A scheme that is of mutual benefit to the settler and investor. [Edmonton, Art Press, 1915?] cover-title, 1 l., 12, [2]p. 19 1/2cm. Alta. Arch.

2497 **Canadian Pacific Railway**
The granary of the British Empire. The western provinces of Canada: Manitoba, Saskatchewan, Alberta, British Columbia. [n.p., 1915?] 111, [1]p. fold. map. 13 1/2 x 20 1/2cm. Private copy

2498 **Donalda Extension of Settlement Club**
Donalda district. [Donalda, 1915] cover-title, 32p. illus. 15 1/2cm. B.C. Arch.

2499 [**Dubois,** Emile]
Une paroisse d'avenir: Laflèche. Winnipeg, 1915. ... Not seen. Morice

2500 **Edson, Alta.** Board of Trade
Edson, Alberta, Canada. [Edson] 1915. cover-title, [20] p. illus. 15cm.
Glenbow

2501 The engineering works and natural resources of the city of Calgary and the Bow River Valley of Alberta. Presented to the members of the National Engineering Societies of America returning from the International Engineering Congress with the compliments of the city of Calgary and the engineers of Alberta. [Calgary] 1915. cover-title, 24p. illus. 25cm. Glenbow

2502 **Eliot,** Elinor Marsden
My Canada. London, Hodder and Stoughton, 1915. x, 269p. plates. 20cm.
'An inextricable tangle of fact and fiction': foreword. Set in Manitoba and the foothills of southern Alberta. Glenbow

2503 **Goddard,** Pliny Earle
Sarsi texts. Berkeley, University of California Press [1915] cover-title, [189]-277p. 27cm. (University of California. Publications in American archaeology and ethnology, v.11, no.3)
Sarsi and English on opposite pages. L.C.

2504 **Hardisty Extension of Settlement Club**
Hardisty district, Alberta. [Hardisty? 1915] 32p. illus. 15 1/2cm.
B.C. Arch.

2505 **Hines,** J[ohn]
The red Indians of the plains; thirty years' missionary experience in the Saskatchewan. With a preface by Rev. H.E. Fox. London, Society for Promoting Christian Knowledge, 1915. 4p.l., viii, 9-322p. front., plates, ports., maps. 22 1/2cm.
The author was stationed at Sandy Lake, The Pas, and Prince Albert. Shortt

2506 **Hudon,** Théophile
Le conflit des races au foyer, conférence donnée par ... le 14 Novembre 1915 à Edmonton. [n.p., n.d.] cover-title, 24p. Amtmann - 229-360

2507 **Hughenden Extension of Settlement Club**
Hughenden district, Alberta. [Hughenden? 1915] 32p. illus. 15cm.
B.C. Arch.

2508 **Jónsson,** Einar Páll
Öraefaljód. Winnipeg, Thorst. Oddsson, 1915. 96p. port. 15 1/2cm.
U. of M.

2508A **Leighton,** Robert
The red patrol; a story of the North-West Mounted Police. Illus. by Frank Alcock. London, Jarrold & Sons [1915] 348p.
Juvenile fiction. Br. Mus.

2509 **Lone Ridge Extension of Settlement Club**
Lone Ridge district, Alberta. [Lone Ridge? 1915] 32p. illus. 15cm.
B.C. Arch.

2510 **MacBeth**, R[oderick] G[eorge]
Peace River letters ... [Vancouver, White and Bindon, 1915] 31, [1]p. illus. 21cm. Man. Leg.

2511 **McNally**, John T[homas]
Pastoral letter of the Right Rev. John T. McNally, Bishop of Calgary, to the clergy and laity of his diocese. Calgary, Bishop's House, March 1st, 1915. cover-title, 32p. 17cm.

The last 20 pages are an encyclical by Pope Benedict XV on World War I. St-Jean

2512 **Menzies**, J[ohn] H[enry]
Development of the resources of the Canadian middle West. Winnipeg, 1915. 20p. Not seen. Br. Mus.

2513 **Mitchell**, E.B.
In Western Canada before the war. A study of communities. London, John Murray, 1915. xii, 206p. map. 19 1/2cm.

Interested in social problems, the writer divides her book into two parts, 'Impressions' and 'Reflections.' She is concerned with the trend towards urbanization. Shortt

2514 **Mitchell**, Percival H.
The Prairie Provinces, Manitoba, Saskatchewan, Alberta. Ottawa, Dept. of the Interior, Dominion Water Power Branch [c1915] 78, [1]p. illus., fold. maps, diagr. 25cm. At head of title: Water power of Canada. Shortt

2515 **Normandeau**, J.A.
La paroisse Albertaine. Montreal, 1915. 24p. fold. map. 20cm.

Sketch map of the district north of Edmonton showing French-Canadian communities. St. Sulpice

2516 **Norse Extension of Settlement Club of Central Alberta**
Scandinavian colony, central Alberta. [Calgary, West & Brown, 1915] 32p. illus. 15 1/2cm.

The district around Camrose. B.C. Arch.

2517 **Oblates**. Edmonton
Resumé des articles présentés au tribunal ecclésiastique d'Edmonton pour servir au procès informatif dans la cause de béatification et de canonisation du serviteur de Dieu, Monseigneur Vital Justin Grandin, Oblat de Marie immaculée, premier evêque de St-Albert. [n.p., 1915?] 1p.l., 30p. 20cm. St-Jean

2518 **Oliver**, E[dmund] H[enry] ed.
The Canadian North-West; its early development and legislative records; minutes of the Councils of the Red River colony and the Northern Department of Rupert's Land ... Ottawa, Government Printing Bureau, 1914-15. 2v. fold. maps. 25cm. (Publications of the Canadian Archives, no.9)

A valuable collection of documents. Shortt

2519 **Oliver**, Edmund H[enry]
The country school in non-English-speaking communities in Saskatchewan. [Saskatoon, The Author, 1915?] cover-title, 18p. 22cm. Shortt

2520 **Pearce**, William
The absurdity and injustice of single tax as carried out in the western provinces of Canada. Respectfully submitted to students of the subject of taxation. [Calgary, Herald Western Co., Ltd., 1915] 28p. 22cm. Shortt

2521 **Pedley**, J[ames] W[illiam]
Biography of Lord Strathcona and Mount Royal. Introduction by Sir John Willison. Toronto, J.L. Nichols Co., Ltd. [1915] 187p. front., plates, ports. 23cm. U. of S.

2522 **Piper**, Clarence B[rett]
Principles of the grain trade of Western Canada. Winnipeg, The Empire Elevator Co., Ltd., 1915. vii, 179p. 20 1/2cm. Shortt

2523 **Stafford**, J.
The clay god in his hell of a heaven. Present day conditions in Western Canada. Calgary, 1915. 22p. 22 1/2cm. Not seen. Br. Mus.

2524 **Standard Colony Extension of Settlement Club**
Standard colony, Standard, Alberta. [Standard? 1915] 32p. illus. 15 1/2cm. B.C. Arch.

2525 **Steele**, [Sir] S[amuel] B[enfield]
Forty years in Canada; reminiscences of the great North-West, with some account of his services in South Africa. Edited by Mollie Glenn Niblett, with an introduction by J.G. Colmer. London, H. Jenkins Ltd., 1915. xvii p., 1 l., 428p. front., plates, ports. 22cm.

A valuable personal account by an original member of the North West Mounted Police. Published also by McClelland of Toronto. Shortt

2526 **Stringer**, Arthur [John Arbuthnott]
The prairie wife. New York, A.L. Burt Co. [c1915] 4p.l., 316, [1]p. col. front. 19 1/2cm.

Fiction. First of a trilogy; an American society girl on a prairie homestead. See Entries 2745 and 2828. U. of S.

2527 **Trémaudan**, A[uguste] H[enri] de
The Hudson Bay road ... London and Toronto, J.M. Dent & Sons, 1915. xvi, 264p. front. (port.) plates, fold. maps. 21cm. Shortt

2528 **The Western Art Association, Western Branch**
Souvenir of the treaty memorial monument erected at Fort Qu'Appelle, A.D. 1915. [Winnipeg, Public Press Ltd., 1915] 33p. incl. plates, ports. 23cm.

The monument commemorates the Qu'Appelle treaty with the Indians signed in 1874. Shortt

2529 **White**, Isaac S.
Five war poems; a memento of this great, most cruel and atrocious war. Winnipeg, The Author, 453 Flora Ave. [c1915] 23p. 15cm. Man. Leg.

2530 **Wood**, Louis Aubrey [Lorne]
The Red River colony; a chronicle of the beginning of Manitoba. Toronto, Brook & Co., 1915. 5p.l., ix-xi, 152p. plates, ports. (incl. col. front.) fold. map, plan. 18 1/2cm. (Chronicles of Canada, v.21) U. of S.

2530A **Bale**, Florence G.
The pilgrim's trail. Decorations by Elizabeth Farrow. [n.p., 1916?] ... Not seen.
A journey through Western Canada. Specialty 234-714

2531 **Bergmann**, Fridrik J[ónsson]
Hvert stefnir? Erindi flutt i Winnipeg, 4. Marz, 1916 og sioar á ymsum stodum. Winnipeg, Olafur S. Thorgeirsson, 1916. 67p. 18 1/2cm.
Reflections on religion. U. of M.

2532 **Buckskin** [pseud.]
The passing of the buffalo, by Buckskin. Vancouver, The Selkirk Press, Ltd., 1916. iii, 47p. 16 1/2cm. Bound in leather.
A drama in verse; probably published in a limited edition. Shortt

2533 **Canada**. Army. 65th Battalion
65th Overseas Battalion ... Saskatoon, May 31, 1916. Souvenir edition. [Saskatoon, Daily Star Job Department, 1916] cover-title, 28p. ports. 30cm.
Advertising matter included. Running title: The Gazette. Dornbusch

2534 **Canada**. Army. 226th Battalion
226th Overseas Battalion, C.E.F., North-western Manitoba. [Winnipeg, Stovel Co. Ltd., 1916?] 60p. ports. 18 x 26cm. Dornbusch

2535 **Canada**. Army. 79th Highlanders
Souvenir book of the 79th Cameron Highlanders of Canada ... Winnipeg, 1916. 32p. ports. 19 x 26cm. Dornbusch

2536 **Canada**. Army. 90th Winnipeg Rifles
Military vaudeville by 144th Overseas Battalion C.E.F. (3rd Battalion, 90th Winnipeg Rifles) under the patronage of His Honour the Lieutenant Governor, Sir Douglas Cameron and the District O/C M.D. no.10, Col. H.N. Ruttan. Winnipeg Theatre, Winnipeg, Mar. 9th, 10th, 11th, 1916. Winnipeg, Telegram Job Printers, 1916. 95p. port. 18 x 28cm.
On cover: Souvenir 144th Overseas Battalion. Glenbow

2537 **Canada**. Army. 90th Winnipeg Rifles
Standing orders (of the 144th Battalion, Winnipeg Rifles) by Lt.-Col. A.W. Morley. [Winnipeg, 1916] 45p. Br. Mus.

2538 **Canada**. Department of the Interior
The Athabaska River country; a compilation of all authentic information available as to the resources and possibilities of the Athabaska River basin, 1916. [Ottawa, 1916] 36p. front. (map) illus. 25cm. Rutherford

2538A **Canada**. Department of the Interior
Canada West; Manitoba, Saskatchewan, Alberta. 350,000,000 bushels wheat in 1915. [Ottawa, 1916?] cover-title, 40p. illus., maps. 20cm. U. of A.

2539 **Canada**. Department of the Interior
The Peace River country. A compilation of all authentic information available as to the resources and possibilities of the basins of the Peace & Hay rivers.

[Ottawa, Dept. of the Interior, 1916] 47p. incl. illus. front. (map) 24 1/2cm. Shortt

2540 **Canadian Women's Press Club.** Edmonton Branch
Club women's records, Edmonton; Women's Institutes of Alberta; United Farm Women of Alberta. [Edmonton] 1916. cover-title, 120, [14]p. illus., ports. 24cm.

A compilation of the annual reports of all women's organizations in the Edmonton area. Paging includes advertising matter. Glenbow

2541 **Clark, W[illiam] C[lifford]**
The country elevator in the Canadian West. Kingston, Jackson Press, 1916. 23p. 22 1/2cm. (Queen's University. Departments of History and Political and Economic Science. Bull. no.20) Also published in Queen's Quarterly, v.24, no.1, p.46-68. Shortt

2542 **La Compagnie Canadienne de Colonisation, Limitée**
La Saskatchewan; son système économique; ses méthodes et ses avantages. Regina [1916] 35p. illus., fold. map. 23cm.

The preface is addressed 'à nos compatriotes,' and is signed with the initials J.A.L. St. Sulpice

2543 **Conservative Party** (Alberta)
Alberta under Liberal rule; a brief review of provincial affairs, particularly with reference to the administration of the Sifton government. [Calgary, Star Printing Works, 1916] cover-title, 55, [1]p. 20cm.

At head of title: The government of the country concerns every citizen. Rutherford

2544 **Conservative Party** (Alberta)
The provincial Conservative platform. A constructive and progressive policy for the people. Red Deer, News Print [1916?] cover-title, 15p. 21cm. Rutherford

2545 **Deane, R[ichard] Burton**
Mounted police life in Canada; a record of thirty-one years' service ... London, Cassell & Co., Ltd., 1916. 4p.l., 311, [1]p. front., illus., plates, fold. map. 21 1/2cm.

A candid account of the author's experiences in administrative work within the force. Shortt

2546 **Dickson, J[ohn] McK[ay]**
Edmonton's 'original sin'; the story of the city's invisible government. [Edmonton, 1916] cover-title, 15p. illus. 22cm.

'Setting forth the political manipulation which if not stopped will plunge Edmonton in ruin.' Rutherford

2547 **Dickson, J[ohn] McK[ay]**
Edmonton Citizens' League of One Hundred analyzes Edmonton's position. [Edmonton, H.H. Hull Printing Co., 1916] cover-title, 16p. 22 1/2cm.

A severe criticism of the city's government. Edmonton

2548 **Goddard**, Pliny Earle
The Beaver Indians. New York, The Trustees, 1916. 1p.l., p.201-293. illus. 24 1/2. (American Museum of Natural History. Anthropological papers. v.10, pt.4) Ayer

2549 **Houghton**, L[evi]
Verses on everyday life, written chiefly by request, in the Calgary General Hospital; by an impatient patient - a Calgary old-timer. [Calgary, Western Printing & Litho Co., 1916] 20p. 25 1/2cm. Rutherford

2550 **Jerome**, Martin
Souvenirs. Winnipeg, 1916. ... Not seen. Select

2551 **Jonassen**, Jeremias
Vor flyvende; smaahistorier fra Canada-Praerien av Ingvar Olsen. [Winnipeg, December, 1916] cover-title, 64p. illus. 22cm.

In title the name Ingvar Olsen is a signature which may have been written in later. Glenbow

2552 **Laidley**, Frederick W.
The why of the Non-Partisan League. Swift Current, Sask., League Headquarters [1916?] 27 [1]p. illus. 21cm.

See also Entry 2591. Glenbow

2553 **Luse Land & Development Co.**, St. Paul, Minn.
The evidence of one hundred Canadian farmers. [St. Paul? 1916] 80p. illus. 10 x 22cm.

Describes the Tramping Lake area of Saskatchewan. Sask. Arch.

2554 **McEachran**, D[uncan McNab]
Impressions of pioneers, of Alberta as a ranching country, commencing 1881. Ormstown, Que. [1916?] cover-title, 14p. 21cm. Glenbow

2555 **Martin**, Chester [Bailey]
Lord Selkirk's work in Canada. Oxford, The Clarendon Press, 1916. 240p. illus. (maps) 23 1/2cm. (Oxford Historical and Literary Society, v.7) Shortt

2556 **Mavor**, James
Government telephones; the experiences of Manitoba, Canada. New York, Moffat, Yard & Co., 1916. viii, 176p. 19 1/2cm. Shortt

2557 **Morice**, A[drien] G[abriel]
Vie de Mgr Langevin, Oblat de Marie Immaculée, archevêque de Saint-Boniface. St-Boniface, The Author, 1916. xvii, 374p. front., plates, port. 21cm. Shortt

2558 **Morris**, [C.] Keith
The story of the Canadian Pacific Railway. London, W. Stevens Ltd., 1916. 3p.l., 154p. front., plates, ports. 18cm. U. of S.

2559 **Paterson,** Isabel [Mary (Bowler)]
The shadow riders. New York, John Lane, 1916. 379p. 20 1/2cm.
A novel with an Alberta locale. L.C.

2560 **Prud'homme,** L[ouis] A[rthur]
Pierre Gaultier de Varennes Sieur de la Vérendrye, Captain of Marines, Chevalier of the Military Order of St. Louis, discoverer of the North-West, 1685-1749. St-Boniface, Man., Le Manitoba print [1916] 3p.l., [5]-178, iii, [1]p. front. (port.) illus., plates, map. 22cm. (Soc. Hist. de St-Boniface. v.5, pt.2) Shortt

2561 **Saskatchewan Public Education League**
Saskatchewan's great campaign for better schools 1915-1916. This pamphlet has been prepared by the Saskatchewan Public Education League and may be had in English, French, German and Ruthenian. A nonpartisan movement: all citizens, without discussion of party, race or religion, are invited to unite in this good cause. A popular movement: your co-operation is desired and needed, no matter what your occupation may be ... 1916. 24p. 25cm. Can. Arch.

2562 **Stafford & Kent,** photographers
Souvenir album of officers, n.c.o.'s and men of the 50th Overseas Battalion, C.E.F. European War. Calgary [1916?] [28]p. illus., ports. 18 x 25cm.
A southern Alberta battalion. Glenbow

2563 **Stead,** Robert James Campbell
The homesteaders; a novel of the Canadian West. Toronto, Musson [c1916] 319p. Can. Novel

2564 **Stefánsson,** Kristinn
Út um vötn og velli. Ljóðmaeli. Winnipeg, Útgefendur: Rögnvaldur Pétursson og Gísli Jónsson, 1916. 300p. port. 18cm. U. of M.

2565 **Toombs,** Herbert W[esley]
Mormonism. [Toronto?] Board of Home Missions and Social Service. Presbyterian Church in Canada [1916?] cover-title, 50p. 17cm. Shortt

2566 **Trémaudan,** A[uguste] H[enri] de
Pourquoi nous parlons français. Conférence donnée au Manitoba Hall, le 7 mai 1916, sous les auspices de l'Association d'Education Canadiens-Français du Manitoba. [Winnipeg, La Libre Parole, 1916] 32p. 22cm. At head of title: Edition 'Le Canada.' Can. Arch.

2566A **Trémaudan,** A[uguste] H[enri] de
... Les précurseurs ... Adresse donnée à St-Vital, le 13 juillet 1916, sous les auspices de l'Union Métisse St-Joseph, et la présidence de Monsieur Joseph Riel. [Montreal? 1916?] 16p. 22 1/2cm. Private information

2567 **Une soeur de la Providence**
Le Père Lacombe; un apôtre du Nord-Ouest canadien, d'après ses mémoires et souvenirs, par une soeur de la Providence. Montréal, Impr. au Devoir, 1916. xv, 547p. front., plates, ports., fold. map. 23cm. Shortt

2568 **Voligny, L.R.**
Report on the survey of the North Saskatchewan River from Edmonton to Lake Winnipeg, 1910-1915. [Ottawa, 1916?] ...
Microfilm copy. Sask. Arch.

2569 **Western News Agency**
Camp Hughes, 1916. Winnipeg [1916] [48]p. (chiefly illus.) ports. 17 x 23cm.
On cover: Ready for active service. Glenbow

2570 **Polskie Towarzystwo Gimnastyczne 'Sokol,'** Winnipeg
Pamietnik dziesieciolecia Gniazda no.377 Zwiazku Sokolów Polskich w Ameryce Pólnocnej, 3. grudnia, 1906-1916, Winnipeg, Kanada. [Winnipeg, 1916] 32p.
Advertising matter included in paging. Memorial booklet issued on the occasion of the 10th anniversary of the Association. Turek

2571 **Winnipeg Grenadiers**
78th Overseas Battalion (Winnipeg Grenadiers) Winnipeg, Advance Photo Co., 1916. 35p. group ports. 24 x 31cm. Can. Arch.

2572 **Wood,** Ruth Kedzie
The tourist's North-West. With numerous illustrations. Toronto, McClelland, Goodchild & Stewart [1916] 528p. illus., map. 20cm. U. of A.

2573 **Bindloss,** Harold
The girl from Keller's. New York, F.A. Stokes, [c1917] [7], 328p. front. 20cm.
Published in England under title: Sadie's conquest. Story set in the Prairie Provinces. Glenbow

2574 **Calgary.** Board of Trade
Calgary, Alberta, Canada's most progressive city, presenting interesting information regarding Calgary, the industrial metropolis of Alberta. [Calgary? 1917?] cover-title, 16p. Amtmann - 176-39

2575 **Canadian Pacific Railway**
A handbook of information regarding business and industrial opportunities in Western Canada. Get your Canadian home from the Canadian Pacific. Calgary, 1917. cover-title, 47p. illus., fold. map. 23cm. Agric.

2576 **Church of England.** Book of Common Prayer. Cree
... The Book of Common Prayer and administration of the sacraments, and other rites and ceremonies of the church according to the use of the Church of England in Canada. Translated into the language of the Cree Indians by the Ven. Archdeacon Hunter, revised by the Ven. J.A. Mackay. London, Society for Promoting Christian Knowledge, 1917. viii, 299p. 17 1/2cm. U. of S.

2577 **Conservative Party** (Saskatchewan)
The big steal. How the money of the people was wasted to the profit of favorite contractors in the building of the Battleford Asylum ... Moose Jaw, Printed by the News Pub. Co. Ltd. [1917] cover-title, 15, [1]p. 22cm. Sask. Arch.

2578 **Conservative Party** (Saskatchewan)
Cleared? ... What have the royal commissions revealed? ... Bradshaw has been vindicated. [n.p., 1917] cover-title, 8p. 22cm.

Quotations on title-page. Sask. Arch.

2579 **Conservative Party** (Saskatchewan)
Conservative platforms. 'No compromise with wrong.' The Conservative Party of Saskatchewan hereby pledges itself to support the following policies and to put them into effect when returned to power. [n.p., 1917] caption-title, 4p. 22cm. Sask. Arch.

2580 **Conservative Party** (Saskatchewan)
Handbook, campaign, 1917. Regina, Provincial Conservative Association [1917] 32p. 22cm. Sask. Arch.

2581 **Conservative Party** (Saskatchewan)
How Liberal members of the Saskatchewan Legislature were bought. Shameless representatives of people sold themselves for a few hundred dollars to thwart the popular will. The old gang still controls. [n.p., 1917] cover-title, 16p. 22cm. Sask. Arch.

2582 **Conservative Party** (Saskatchewan)
Kindersley Dam. Hon. W.R. Motherwell 'deals the cards.' [n.p., 1917] cover-title, [3]p. 22cm. Sask. Arch.

2583 **Conservative Party** (Saskatchewan)
The liquor traffic and the Saskatchewan government ... [n.p., 1917] cover-title, 16p. 22cm. Sask. Arch.

2584 **Conservative Party** (Saskatchewan)
The patriotic tax; money collected by the assessment of one mill on the dollar goes to pay fat salaries to favored civil servants who have enlisted and the wages of special watchmen on public buildings while the Patriotic Fund suffered ... [n.p., 1917] cover-title, 7, [1]p. 22cm. Sask. Arch.

2585 **Conservative Party** (Saskatchewan)
Phantom roads, fake contracts, false pay rolls. Some facts in the story of the looting of the public treasury through the Highways Department ... [n.p. 1917] cover-title, 22p. 19cm.

Six-line poem on back cover. Sask. Arch.

2586 **Conservative Party** (Saskatchewan)
Weed Lake bridge. Government contracts and political methods. [n.p., 1917] cover-title, [3]p. 22cm. Sask. Arch.

2587 **Feilberg,** H[enning] F[rederik]
Hjemliv pa praerien. De derovre en raekke breve fra Canada. Kobenhavn and Kristiana, 1917. 298p. 19cm.

A continuation of a Danish family's experiences in Saskatchewan, covering the period May 1912 to October 1917.
Other printings appeared in 1918 and in 1927. Denmark

2588 [**Gagnon**, Joseph]
Le Manitoba, ressources et avantages. Winnipeg, 1917. 32p. illus. 17 1/2cm.
On cover: Le Manitoba, vers les belles terres. St. Sulpice

2589 **Goddard**, Pliny Earle
Beaver texts, Beaver dialect. New York, The Trustees, 1917. 1p.l., 295-546p. illus. 24 1/2cm. (American Museum of Natural History. Anthropological papers. v.10, pt.5 & 6) Ayer

2590 **Hewitt**, G.E.
The story of the Twenty-eighth (North-West) Battalion, 1914-17. London, Printed & published for the Canadian War Records Office [1917] 24p. ports. 18 1/2cm. Can. Arch.

2591 **Laidley**, Frederick W.
The why of the Non-Partisan League (Department of Saskatchewan) ... Swift Current, League Headquarters [1917] 24p. illus. (cartoons) 20cm.
On cover: The why of the Farmers N-P. League of Canada. Sask. Arch.

2592 **Lethbridge**. Board of Trade
More and better water for our farms and rural communities; report of a conference called by the Lethbridge Board of Trade at Lethbridge, Alberta, on June 22nd, 1917. [Lethbridge? 1917] 51, [1]p. illus., fold. map, fold. plan. 25cm.
Reprint of articles from the Lethbridge Herald. Glenbow

2593 **Liberal Party** (Saskatchewan)
How Saskatchewan women got the vote. A brief history which every Saskatchewan woman should read. Quotations from speeches made by Hon. W.R. Motherwell and others. [Regina] Provincial Liberal Party [1917] cover-title, 16p. 22cm. Sask. Arch.

2594 **Liberal Party** (Saskatchewan)
The Liberal handbook, 1917. Aim and achievements of Saskatchewan Liberalism. [Regina, Saskatchewan Liberal Party, 1917] 78p. 20cm. Sask. Arch.

2595 **Liberal Party** (Saskatchewan)
Liberalism and progress; the Liberal party and the Martin government alive to Saskatchewan's needs: The big 4: 1. Land settlement. 2. Cheap money. 3. Tariff reforms. 4. Farm machinery. Saskatchewan's economic problems. [Regina] Provincial Liberal Party [1917] cover-title, 14, [2]p. 21cm. Sask. Arch.

2596 **Liberal Party** (Saskatchewan)
Some phases of Saskatchewan's school problem. Facts vs. fiction ... [Regina] Provincial Liberal Party [1917] cover-title, 16p. port. 22cm. Sask. Arch.

2597 **McCaul**, Charles Coursolles
Address ... in opening the case for the prosecution of Sinnisiak, an Eskimo charged with murder, before the Hon. Chief Justice Harvey and a jury, at Edmonton, Alberta, August 14th, 1917. [Edmonton, Douglas Co., 1917?] 15, [1]p. ports. 25cm.
On cover: For private circulation.
Sinnisiak was charged with the murder of the Rev. Père Rouvière at Bloody Fall on the Coppermine River, in November, 1913. Glenbow

2598 **McClung**, Nellie L[etitia (Mooney)]
The next of kin, those who wait and wonder. Boston, Houghton Mifflin, 1917. 4p.l., 256, [2]p. 19cm.

Relates to the war effort, etc., in World War I. L.C.

2599 **MacGregor**, Daisy
The Alberta club woman's blue book, 1917. [Calgary, Albertan job print, 1917] 127p. illus. (incl. ports.) 23 1/2cm.

Sketches on the activities of various women's groups. Published by the Calgary branch of the Canadian Women's Press Club. Alta. Leg.

2599A **Manitoba**
Northern Manitoba; mining, timber and pulp wood, water powers, fish and furs, agriculture, the Hudson Bay route. The Pas, Man., J.A. Campbell, Commissioner of Northern Manitoba, 1917. 47p. illus., maps. 26cm.

'Issued by authority Province of Manitoba.' Glenbow

2600 **Manitoba.** Department of Agriculture and Immigration
Stock raising in Manitoba. Winnipeg, 1917. cover-title, 36p. illus., ports. 24cm. Glenbow

2601 **Marchant**, Bessie
A Canadian farm mystery; or, Pam the pioneer ... London, Blackie & Son, 1917 [1916] 352p. Br. Mus.

2602 **Matheson**, E[dward] K[ing]
The work of the Church of England among the English speaking settlers in the Diocese of Saskatchewan in the earlier years of the diocese. [n.p., 1917] cover-title, 13, [1]p. 21 1/2cm.

'Prepared ... at the request of the members of the rural deanery of Battleford and read ... at the meeting of the rural deanery held in St. Mary's Church, Meota, Sask., on Wednesday, August 29th, 1917.'

This is reprinted in 'Canon E.K. Matheson,' a publication of the Canadian North-West Historical Society, v.1, no.3, 1927. Emmanuel College

2603 **Mathieu**, O[livier] E[lzéar]
Aide au Collège Mathieu, le seul collège Français de la Saskatchewan; appel de S.G. Mgr O.-E. Mathieu ... [n.p., n.d.] 16p. port. Que. Leg.

2604 **Mathieu**, O[livier] E[lzéar]
Eloge funèbre du Rév. P.J. Hugonard, O.M.I., Principal de l'Ecole industrielle de Lebret, Sask., 14 février, 1917. Quebec, Imprimerie Franciscaine missionnaire, 1917. 18 [i.e. 19]p. Que. Leg.

2605 **Normandeau**, J.A.
Culture mixte en Alberta centrale. Montréal, 1917. 12p. 21cm. Glenbow

2606 **Paterson**, Isabel [Mary (Bowler)]
The magpie's nest. New York, John Lane, 1917. 303p. 19 1/2cm.

Fiction with an Alberta locale. L.C.

2607 **Scott**, Walter S[amuel]
Chattel exemptions from writs of execution in Alberta, British Columbia, Manitoba, New Brunswick, Newfoundland, Nova Scotia, Ontario, Prince Edward Island, Quebec, Saskatchewan and Yukon Territory. Edmonton, Atkinson Book Co. Ltd., 1917. 92p. 22 1/2cm. U. of A.

2608 **Scott**, Walter S[amuel]
Homesteads and their exemptions in Western Canada. Edmonton, Books, 1917. 84p. 22 1/2cm. Shortt

2609 **Shortt**, Adam
Canada and its provinces; a history of the Canadian people and their institutions, by one hundred associates. Adam Shortt, Arthur G. Doughty, general editors. Toronto, Glasgow, Brook & Co., 1914-17. v.19-20. fronts., plates. 25 1/2cm.
The above volumes are devoted to the West. U. of S.

2610 **Stead**, Robert J[ames] C[ampbell]
Kitchener, and other poems. With an introduction by William T. Allison. Toronto, Musson [1917] xiv, 161p. 19cm. L.C.

2611 **Sternberg**, Charles H[azelius]
Hunting dinosaurs in the bad lands of the Red Deer River, Alberta, Canada; a sequel to 'The life of a fossil hunter.' Lawrence, Kan., The Author, 1917. xiii, 232p. front., plates. 20cm. U. of A.

2612 **Turner**, J[ohn] P[ercival]
... The prairie chicken; its distribution and need of protection. [Winnipeg] Dept. of Agriculture and Immigration, 1917. cover-title, 16p. illus. 22 1/2cm.
At head of title: Help us protect the game. Glenbow

2613 **Weir**, George M[oir]
Evolution of the separate school law in the Prairie Provinces. [Saskatoon? 1917?] 156p. 19cm. Shortt

2614 **Woodsworth**, James
Thirty years in the Canadian North-West. Toronto, McClelland, Goodchild and Stewart [c1917] xix, 259p. front. (port.) 19 1/2cm.
Covering the period from 1883, it is in a sense a continuation of George Young's 'Manitoba Memories.' Shortt

2615 **Alberta Provincial Police**
The constables' manual. Toronto, Carswell Co., 1918. v, 136p. 17cm.
At head of title: Provincial police, Alberta. Glenbow

2616 **Anderson**, J[ames] T[homas] M[ilton]
The education of the new Canadian; a treatise on Canada's greatest educational problem. Toronto, J.M. Dent & Sons, 1918. 271p. front., plates, ports. 20 1/2cm. U. of S.

2617 **Armstrong**, W.H.G.
Separate schools, introduction of the dual system into Eastern Canada and its subsequent extension to the West. Published by authority of the Provincial

Grand Orange Lodge of Saskatchewan at the session of 1918, held at the City of Weyburn. [n.p., c1918] 92p. 19 1/2cm. On cover: Separate schools in the new provinces. U. of S.

2618 **Bawlf**, William R[ichard]
Marketing of Canadian grain under war conditions. Winnipeg [Winnipeg Grain Exchange] 1918. 12p. 23cm. Not seen. R.E.S.

2619 **Calgary**. Board of Trade
Calgary, Alberta, Canada's most progressive city; presenting interesting information regarding Calgary, the industrial metropolis of Alberta. [Calgary, 1918?] cover-title, 16p. illus., fold. plates, plan (p.3 of cover) 16cm. Glenbow

2620 **Calgary**. Daughters of the Allies. Friday Unit
Conservation cook book; a collection of tested recipes. Calgary, 1918. 159p. 23cm. L.C.

2621 **Canada**. Department of the Interior
The new Manitoba district, Canada; its resources and development, by F.H. Kitto. [Ottawa] 1918. 43p. illus., maps, diagrs., tables. 25cm. Glenbow

2622 **Canada**. Department of the Interior
The Peace River country, Canada; its resources and opportunities, by F.H. Kitto. [Ottawa] 1918. 47p. illus. 25cm.
Various editions were published. Glenbow

2623 **Canadian Council of Agriculture**
The farmers' platform; a new national policy for Canada as adopted by the Canadian Council of Agriculture at Winnipeg, on November 29, 1918. Winnipeg, The Council [1918] cover-title, 8p. 15 1/2cm. Shortt

2623A **The Coal Operators of Northern Alberta**
Coal; where it is and how to get it. [Edmonton, Esdale Press, 1918?] cover-title, 12p. 22cm. Glenbow

2624 **Davidson**, Gordon Charles
The North West Company. Berkeley, University of California, 1918. xi, 349p. 5 fold. maps (incl. front.) 25cm. (University of California publications in history, v.8) Shortt

2624A **Foght**, Harold Waldstein
A survey of education in the province of Saskatchewan, Canada; a report to the government of the province of Saskatchewan. Regina, J.W. Reid, King's Printer, 1918. 183p. illus. (part fold.) maps. 26cm. Glenbow

2624B **Grain Growers' Guide**
History of the Grain Growers, reprinted from the Grain Growers' Guide tenth anniversary number June 26, 1918. [Winnipeg, 1918] caption-title, 16p. illus., ports. 38cm. Glenbow

2625 **Hamer-Jackson Publishing Company**, comp.
Edmonton to Peace River and the north country, 1918-19 guide with map of north country. A pocket guide to Edmonton, Peace River and the north con-

taining accurate and reliable information for benefit of the settlers and tourists seeking pleasure or business opportunities. 5th issue. Edmonton, Douglas [1918] cover-title, 96p. illus., fold. map. 20 1/2cm.

Pagination includes advertising. Private copy

2626 **Holland**, J.A.
The story of the Tenth Canadian Battalion, 1914-1917. London, Printed and published for the Canadian War Records Office by Charles and Son [1918?] [2], 35p. port. 19cm.

Battalion perpetuated by the Canadian Highlanders and the Winnipeg Light Infantry. Glenbow

2627 **Ingersoll**, Will[iam] E[rnest]
The road that led home. New York, Harper, 1918. 5p.l., 307, [1]p. col. front. 19 1/2cm.

Fiction; the hero is a rural school teacher. L.C.

2628 **Jonsson**, Baldur
Leaves and letters. Wynyard, Sask., Wynyard Advance press, 1918. ... Not seen. Select

2629 **MacDonald**, Wilson [Pugsley]
The song of the prairie land, and other poems. [Buffalo, Printed by L.B. Clark] c1918. cover-title, 25 l. 25cm.

Also published in Toronto by McClelland & Stewart in a 144-page edition. A new edition of the latter was published by Ryerson in 1922. (These editions in U. of A. Extension.) L.C.

2630 **Maclean**, John
Vanguards of Canada. Toronto, The Missionary Society of the Methodist Church [c1918] x, 262p. front., plates, ports., fold. map. 19 1/2cm.

A series of sketches of Methodist missionaries. Shortt

2631 **McClung**, Nellie L[etitia (Mooney)]
Three times and out, told by Private Simmons, written by Nellie L. McClung. Toronto, T. Allen, 1918. viii p., 2 l., 247p. front., illus. 19cm.

A soldier from Western Canada, captured by the Germans in the early phases of World War I, narrates the story of his escape from a German prison camp. U. of A. (Extension)

2631A **Manitoba**
Manitoba's northland, including Hudson Bay region and Rice Lake gold area. Minerals, pulp wood, water powers, fish and furs, agriculture. Issued by authority Province of Manitoba. The Pas, 1918. 52p. illus., maps (1 fold.) 26cm. Glenbow

2632 **Medicine Hat, Alta.** Board of Trade
Medicine Hat, Alberta; facts concerning the city and surrounding country. [Medicine Hat] 1918. [16]p. illus. 22cm.

On title-page: 'The town that was born lucky' – Rudyard Kipling. U. of A.

2633 **Morice, A[drien] G[abriel]**
Les droits historiques du Français dans l'Ouest canadien. Winnipeg, La Libre Parole, Ltd., 1918. 19p. 22 1/2cm. Shortt

2633A **Northern Production Company**
The first annual report ... January 16th, 1918, also containing a historical and geological compilation of data on the oil fields of northern Alberta. Edmonton [1918] cover-title, 76, [8]p. illus., ports. 32cm. Glenbow

2634 **Le Patriote de l'Ouest**
Do the French Canadians speak patois? Prince Albert, Le Patriote de L'Ouest [n.d.] ... Amtmann - 228-2515

2635 **Le Patriote de l'Ouest**
The language question in Saskatchewan, translated from 'Le Patriote de l'Ouest' and published by the Committee of Education of L'Association Catholique Franco-Canadienne de la Saskatchewan. Prince Albert, 1918. cover-title, 14p. Amtmann - 229-634

2636 **Le Patriote de l'Ouest**
The question of education in the province of Saskatchewan, translated from 'Le Patriote de l'Ouest' and published by the Committee of Education of L'Association Catholique Franco-Canadienne de la Saskatchewan. Prince Albert, 1918. cover-title, 15p. 22cm. Oblates Arch.

2637 **Peace River Development Corporation Limited.** Transport Department
The Peace River; a great waterway to the far north. [n.p., 1918] folder. ([10]p.) illus., fold. map. 24cm. Shortt

2638 Not used.

2639 **St. Boniface.** Sheptycky Institute
Pershiy richniy zvit bursy im. Mytropolyta A. Sheptyckoho v St. Boniface, 1917-1918. Winnipeg, 1918. 71p. 23cm. Not seen.

Only one report published. Private information

2640 **Sandwell,** Bernard K[eble]
Westing. Printed and published for private circulation. Montreal, 1918. 31p. front. 15cm.

Impressions during a tour of the West. Vancouver

2641 **Silver,** Gerhard Hilarius
[In the age of the wolves] Winnipeg, 1918. 40p. Not seen.

Poetry in Swedish. Kirkconnell

2642 **Speers, Sask.** I.O.D.E. New Ottawa Chapter
New Ottawa, Speers, 1902-1918. [n.p.,] Published by the New Ottawa Chapter, I.O.D.E. [1918?] 2p.l., [7]p. illus. 22cm.

Title taken from cover. A history of settlement at Speers. Sask. Arch.

2643 **Spence,** W[illiam] J., comp.
University of Manitoba. Historical notes, 1877-1917. Winnipeg, 1918. 84p. Wolfe - 26-455

2644 **Stead**, Robert J[ames] C[ampbell]
The cow puncher. Toronto, Musson Book Co., Ltd. [c1918] 4p.l., 341p. front., plates. 19 1/2cm.

Fiction. Published also in New York and London by Harper. U. of S.

2645 **Taverner**, P[ercy] A[lgernon]
Hawks of the Canadian Prairie Provinces in their relation to agriculture. Ottawa, 1918. 14p. illus. (Can. Geological Museum bull. no.28) R.E.S.

2646 **Thorsteinsson**, Thorsteinn Th.
Thaettir. Ljód. Winnipeg, Hecla Press, Ltd., 1918. 91, [2]p. 18 1/2cm. U. of M.

2647 **Trémaudan**, A[uguste] H[enri] de
Le sang français; introduction par le R.P. A.-G. Morice. Winnipeg, Imprimerie de La Libre Parole [1918] xxvii p., 1 l., 240p., 1 l. front. 23cm.

A collection of addresses delivered during 1916-18. Shortt

2648 **Watt**, [Ernest] Frederick Balmer
Boy Blue's verses. Edmonton, 1918. cover-title, 16p. port. on cover. Private copy

2649 **West**, Edward
Homesteading; two prairie seasons. London, T. Fisher Unwin [1918] 302p., 1 l. front., plates. 20 1/2cm.

An excellent description of the homesteading experiences of two Englishmen in the Hafford district of Saskatchewan. Shortt

2650 **Yasenchuk**, Joseph
Kanadiysky kobzar. Edmonton, 1918. 64p. 21cm. Not seen.

Ukrainian poetry. Select

2650A [**Ashall**, William]
Unemployment and the way out, by Cannon Fodder. [Winnipeg, Tank Publishing Co., 1919?] 125p. 22cm.

On cover: No.892681. This was the author's number in the Canadian army in World War I, and led to his identification. Queen's

2650B **Adams**, R[amon] F[rederick]
Poems of the Canadian West. [Vancouver, Evans & Hastings, 1919] 86p. port. 18cm.

Part I: Songs of the Prairie [42p.] U. of A.

2651 **Brown**, Vere C.
The western farmer and the bank. An address given before the annual convention of the United Farmers of Alberta, at Edmonton, 23 January, 1919, in reply to Mr. J.W. Leedy's advocacy of local banks. [n.p., 1919?] 24p. 23 1/2cm. Shortt

2652 **Buck**, Alanson L.
Picardy field and western verse. Regina, University Press, 1919. [6], 144p. plates (incl. port.) 19cm. (Returned soldier series)

Includes poetry descriptive of the Prairie Provinces. Glenbow

2653 **Buller**, A[rthur] H[enry] Reginald
Essays on wheat, including the discovery and introduction of Marquis wheat, the early history of wheat-growing in Manitoba, wheat in Western Canada, the origin of Red Bobs and Kitchener, and the wild wheat of Palestine. New York, Macmillan Co., 1919. xvi, 339p. front. (port.) illus., plates. 20 1/2cm. U. of S.

2654 **Canada**. Army. 11th Canadian Field Ambulance (Western Universities)
Diary of the Eleventh; being a record of the XIth Canadian Field Ambulance (Western Universities) Feb. 1916-May 1919. [n.p., n.d.] 128p. illus. 24cm.

Editorial committee: A.R. Hall, C.T. Best, J.M. Roe. Glenbow

2655 **Canada**. Department of the Interior
The province of Saskatchewan, Canada; its development and opportunities, by F.H. Kitto. [Ottawa] 1919. 153p. illus., diagrs., tables. 25cm. Glenbow

2656 **Canadian National Railways**
Own a 'selected' farm to fit your needs along the line of the Canadian National Railways. Read, think, act. [Chicago? 1919?] cover-title, 39, [1]p. illus., fold. map (in pocket), tables. 23cm.

Promotional pamphlet directed at prospective American immigrants. Glenbow

2657 **Canadian Northern Railway**
Homeseekers and settlers guide to Western Canada. [n.p., 1919?] cover-title, 40p. illus., fold. map. 23cm. N.Y.

2658 **Canadian Pacific Railway**
A handbook of information regarding Alberta, Saskatchewan and Manitoba and the opportunities offered you by the Canadian Pacific Railway in these provinces. Calgary, 1919. cover-title, 64 [i.e. 32]p. illus., fold. col. map (on inside of back cover) 23cm.

Printed in double columns, numbered. Glenbow

2659 Christmas in Regina, 1919. [Regina, 1919] 40p. illus., ports. 35cm.

A compilation of articles about Regina written by citizens. U. of S.

2660 **Curwood**, James Oliver
The river's end; a new story of God's country. Illustrated by Dean Cornwell. New York, Cosmopolitan Book Corp., 1919. 4p.l., 303p. front., plates. 19 1/2cm.

Fiction. Much of the action takes place in Prince Albert. U. of A. (Extension)

2661 **Cyr**, J[oseph] Ernest
Monseigneur Joseph Norbert Provencher. Quelques considérations sur sa vie et son temps. St-Boniface, 1919. 16p. St. Sulpice

2662 **Deachman**, R[obert] J[ohn]
The wheat board fallacy. Calgary, Western Canada Publishing Co. [1919?] 30p. front. (port.) 15cm. Sask. Arch.

2663 **Durkin**, Douglas [Leader]
The heart of Cherry McBain. Toronto, Musson Book Co. [1919] 3p.l., 325p. 20cm.

Fiction. Published by Harper in New York and London in 1920. Man. Leg.

2664 **Edmonds**, W[alter] Everard
Broad horizons; maple leaf sketches from a prairie studio. Toronto, Musson [c1919] 224p. 19cm.

Part II is a collection of historical sketches of people and incidents in Western Canada. Can. Imprints

2665 **Goddard**, P[liny] E[arle]
Notes on the sun dance of the Sarsi, by P.E. Goddard. The sun dance of the Plains-Cree, by Alanson Skinner. Notes on the sun dance of the Cree in Alberta, by P.E. Goddard. The sun dance of the Canadian Dakota, by W.D. Wallis. Notes on the sun dance of the Sisseton Dakota, by Alanson Skinner. New York, American Museum of Natural History, 1919. 1p.l., 271-385p. illus. 24 1/2cm. (American Museum of Natural History. Anthropological papers, v.16, pt.4) L.C.

2666 **Grande Prairie, Alta.** Board of Trade
Grande Prairie and the Peace River district. Grande Prairie, 1919. cover-title, 16p. illus. 22cm. Glenbow

2667 **Great War Veterans' Association of Canada.** Calgary Branch
Southern Alberta yearbook, 3d, 1919. [Calgary] 1919. viii, 244, vi, [2]p. illus., ports. 22cm.

'G.W.V.A. of Lethbridge, yearbook, 1919': p.209-228. 'G.W.V.A. of Medicine Hat, yearbook, 1919': p.229-244. Includes advertising matter. Glenbow

2668 **Hjelt**, Ole
Farmeren og socialismen. Chicago [1919?]

Reference is made to it in his 'Nybyggerliv paa praerien.' This book on socialism, presumably influenced by his farming experiences at Instow, Sask., was confiscated by the Canadian customs as undesirable literature – presumably all copies destroyed.
See Entry 2713.

2669 **Hudson's Bay Company**
Opportunities in Canada's 'success belt.' [Winnipeg, 1919] cover-title, 12p. illus. 21cm. H.B.C.

2670 **Izsak**, George
Mezei virágok [Prairie flowers] Plunkett, Sask., 1919. 202p. 23cm.

Poetry in Hungarian. Shortt

2671 **Jackson**, Thorleifur Jóakimsson
Brot af landnámssögu Nýja Islands. Safnad og samid af Thorleifi Jóakimssyni (Jackson). Winnipeg, Prentsmidja Columbia Press Ltd., 1919. 98p. illus. (ports.) 22cm.

Errata slip. U. of M.

2672 **Jónsson,** Gísli
Farfuglar. Winnipeg, Gísli Jónsson, 1919. 244p. ports. 18cm.
Icelandic poetry. U. of M.

2673 **Kitto,** F[ranklin] H[ugo]
Athabaska to the Bay. Report of a reconnaissance expedition, chiefly by canoe, from Edmonton and McMurray across the northern parts of Alberta, Saskatchewan and Manitoba to Port Nelson and Churchill on Hudson Bay, 1918 ... Ottawa, King's Printer, 1919. 39p. illus., fold. map. 24 1/2cm. Shortt

2674 The language question before the Legislative Assembly of Saskatchewan ... Addresses by Hon. W.M. Martin, Hon. W.R. Motherwell, Hon. S.J. Latta, Hon. C.A. Dunning. Prince Albert, Le Patriote de l'Ouest, 1919. 38, 9, 22, 12p. 21cm.
Relates to the status of the French language. Oblates Arch.

2675 [**Lebel,** Joseph Marc Octave Antoine]
Même sang, tableau historique en deux scènes et deux personnages, par Jean Feron [pseud. Représenté pour la première fois à Arborfield, Sask., au profit de l'Eglise paroissiale les 3 et 4 mars 1919. Arborfield, Sask, 1919?] 28p. Amtmann - 229-31

2676 **Mathieu,** O[livier] E[lzéar]
The social question. Address delivered at the Kiwanis Club of Regina, May the 30th, 1919. Prince Albert, 1919. cover-title, 26p. Amtmann - 229-550

2677 **McCaig,** J[ames]
Alberta: a survey of the topography, climate, resources, industries, transportation and communication, and institutional services of the province of Alberta, by J. McCaig, publicity commissioner. Further information furnished. Issued under the direction of Hon. Duncan Marshall, Minister of Agriculture, Edmonton, Alberta [1919] 96p. illus. 25cm. Lande

2678 **Moose Jaw.** St. Barnabas Church
Souvenir of grand maple leaf bazaar, Dec., 1919. 32p.
Includes historical notes. Adelphi

2679 **Palmer,** George
'Stand to,' by 2751. Calgary, S.A. Hind Litho-Print [c1919] 76p. front. (port.), plates. 20cm.
War poems. U. of A.

2680 **Roy,** Irene
Junette; or, Are women just to one another. Edmonton, Printed by the Douglas Co., 1919. [1], 292p. 20cm.
Novel set in Winnipeg. Glenbow

2681 **Saskatoon.** Board of Trade
Saskatoon, Western Canada. Saskatchewan's university city. Educational, commercial, financial, distributing and railway centre of middle and northern Saskatchewan: situated in the mid-west on the banks of the South Saskatchewan River amid unsurpassed agricultural territory. [Saskatoon] 1919. 40p. 25 1/2cm. Can. Arch.

2682 **Thompson,** Bram
Canada's suzerainty over the West; an indictment of the Dominion and Parliament of Canada for the national crime of usurping the public land of Manitoba, Saskatchewan and Alberta. Toronto, Carswell Co., 1919. 42p. Not seen. C.H.R., 1920

2683 **United Farmers of Alberta**
How to organize and carry on a local of the United Farmers of Alberta. Calgary [1919] 48p. 15cm. U. of S.

2684 **Wheeler,** Seager
Seager Wheeler's book on profitable grain growing. With biographical sketch by Hopkins Moorhouse. Winnipeg, Grain Growers' Guide, Ltd., 1919. xvi p., 1 l., 351p. incl. front. (port.) illus. 20cm. U. of S.

2685 **Winnipeg.** Citizens' Committee of One Thousand
The activities and organization of the Citizens' Committee of One Thousand in connection with the Winnipeg strike, May-June, 1919. Winnipeg, The Committee [1919] 40p. incl. illus (facsims., diagr.) 25 1/2cm. Shortt

2686 **Winnipeg.** Citizens' Committee of One Thousand
An address on the subject of the Winnipeg strike, May-June, 1919. Delivered by a member of the Citizens' Committee of One Thousand to a deputation of citizens from Moose Jaw, Sask. With especial reference to the enunciation therein contained upon the principles of 'collective bargaining.' [n.p., 1919] cover-title, 12p. 25cm. In double column. Shortt

2687 **Winnipeg Strike**
Definition of collective bargaining, a series of statements defining the real status of 'Collective Bargaining,' as it relates to the Winnipeg strike, were issued June 16th, 1919, and are reprinted as a matter of historical record. The statements were made by the Ironmasters engaged in the original dispute, the International officers of the running trades and the officials of the great transcontinental railway corporations at Winnipeg. The record which was the basis of the subsequent settlement of the metal workers' dispute is as follows: Metal Employers define their position. Winnipeg, June 16, 1919. To the citizens of Winnipeg. [Winnipeg, 1919] caption-title, [4]p. 22cm. Private copy

2688 **Winnipeg.** Strike Committee
The Winnipeg general sympathetic strike, May-June, 1919 ... Prepared by the Defence Committee ... composed of delegates from the various labor organizations ... [Winnipeg] Wallingford [1919] 276p. 21cm. Not seen. Acadia

2689 **Woodsworth,** J[ames] S[haver]
Reconstruction from the viewpoint of labor. Winnipeg, Printed by the Hecla Press, Ltd. [1919] cover-title, 15p. 22cm. U. of S.

2690 **Anderson and Brown Consolidated, Limited**
The world's new oil field: Alberta, North West Territories, Mackenzie Basin. Edmonton [Western Veteran Publishing Co., 1920] cover-title, 32p. illus. 19cm. Glenbow

2691 **Anderson**, P[ete]
I, that's me; escape from a German prison camp and other adventures. [Edmonton, Bradburn Printers Ltd., 1920?] 4p.l., 174p. illus. 20cm.

The first section of the book describes his experiences as an Edmonton pioneer. Edmonton

2691A **Bible**. Selections. Cree
Cree daily Bible readings. Compiled by Rev. J.T. Griffin. London, Society for Promoting Christian Knowledge, 1920. [15]p. 19cm. B.C. Arch.

2692 **Bracken**, John
Crop production in Western Canada. Winnipeg, Grain Growers' Guide, Ltd., 1920. xxvi p., 1 l., 423p. incl. front., illus., maps, diagrs. 20cm. U. of S.

2693 **Bramble**, Charles A.
Land of the lobstick; the log of a canoe journey in The Pas district of northern Manitoba; issued by J.A. Macdonald, Publicity Commissioner, Province of Manitoba. [Winnipeg] 1920. 20p. Man. Leg.

2694 **Bridgman**, Wellington
Breaking prairie sod; the story of a pioneer preacher in the eighties, with a discussion of the burning question of today, 'Shall the alien go?' With an introduction by Rev. (Captain) J.E. Hughson. Toronto, Musson, 1920. xv, 265p. port. Shortt

2695 **Buchanan**, Angus
Wild life in Canada. London, J. Murray, 1920. 3p.l., xi-xx, 264p. front., plates, map. 22 1/2cm.

A canoe trip from Prince Albert to Reindeer Lake in the autumn of 1914. L.C.

2695A **Canada**. Department of the Interior
Canada. Where when and how. Ottawa [1920] cover-title, 24p. 14cm. Can. Arch. (ms.)

2696 **Canada**. Department of the Interior
Province of Manitoba list of unoccupied farms for sale east of the principal meridian. Ottawa, 1920. 32, 38p. Can. Arch.

2696A **Canadian National Railways**
Facts about selected farms in Western Canada. Chicago [1920?] folder. 16p. illus. 15 1/2cm. Can. Arch. (ms.)

2697 **Clark**, Archibald Brown
An outline of provincial and municipal taxation in British Columbia, Alberta, and Saskatchewan. Winnipeg, University of Manitoba, 1920. 97p. R.E.S.

2698 **Coaldale, Alta**. Commercial Club
Coaldale, 'the gem of the West' in sunny southern Alberta; a great irrigation project. [Coaldale, 1920] 64p. illus., fold. map. 23cm. Glenbow

2699 **Craik, Sask**. Board of Trade
The centre of the wheat belt, including little stories of success. Craik [1920] [50]p. illus. 20cm. Sask. Arch.

2700 **Cyr**, J[oseph] Ernest
Monseigneur Louis-Philippe Adélard Langevin, O.M.I. St-Boniface, 1920. 20p. St. Sulpice

2701 **Cyr**, J[oseph] Ernest
Monseigneur Alexandre Antonin Taché, O.M.I. St-Boniface, 1920. 28p. port. St. Sulpice

2702 **De Lury**, Justin Sarsfield
... Mineral prospects in southeastern Manitoba, Rice Lake, Maskwa River, and boundary districts. Published by authority of the Government of Manitoba. The Pas [1920] 55p. illus., fold. map. 26cm.

At head of title: Manitoba bulletins. Glenbow

2703 **Dixon**, F[rederick] J[ohn]
Dixon's address to the jury in defence of freedom of speech, considered the most powerful address ever delivered in the courts of Manitoba; and Judge Galt's charge to the jury in Rex v. Dixon. Winnipeg, Defence Committee [1920] 126p. 21cm. Man. Leg.

2703A **Douglas**, David
On the great fur trail; a story of the old trapping days. London, Boy's Own Paper [1920] 252p. 18 1/2cm.

Juvenile fiction. Northland

2704 **Edmonds**, W[alter] E[verard]
Brief history of Edmonton ... compiled from papers read before the Historical Society by M.H. Long, Hon. Frank Oliver, and Dr. D.G. McQueen. Edmonton, 1920. 10p. 29cm. Edmonton

2705 **Edmonds**, W[alter] Everard
In a college library. With a foreword by the Most Rev. S.P. Matheson ... Edmonton, Esdale Press [c1920] [5], 91p. port. 19cm. Glenbow

2706 Edmonton district in central Alberta; Canada's richest mixed country. Edmonton [c1920] 44p. illus., map. R.E.S.

2707 **Edmonton**. Empire Theatre
Souvenir programme. [Grand opening New Empire Theatre, Thursday, Friday, Saturday, December 23rd, 24th and 25th, 1920. Edmonton, 1920] cover-title, 24p. illus. 18 x 27cm.

Pagination includes advertising. 'Fifteen years of Edmonton theatre going,' by A.B. Watt, p. 5-15. U. of A.

2708 **Farney**, Maurice
... Dans les prairies du Canada. Paris, Librairie Larousse [1920] 32p. illus. (incl. map) (Les livres roses pour la jeunesse. no.264)

Juvenile fiction. N.Y.

2709 **Footner**, [William] Hulbert
The fur bringers, a story of the Canadian Northwest. New York, James A. McCann Co., 1920. 4p.l., 7-313p. 20cm. L.C.

2710 **Gravel**, L[ouis Joseph] P[ierre]
La Saskatchewan. Montréal, Bureau de colonisation du gouvernement fédéral [192–] 55p. 17cm.
See also Entry 2928. Collection Gagnon

2711 **Guttormsson**, Guttormur J[ónsson]
Bóndadóttir. Winnipeg, Hecla Press, 1920. 92p. ports. 19 1/2cm.
Icelandic poetry. U. of M.

2712 **Heeney**, William Bertal
John West and his Red River mission. Toronto, Musson Book Co. Ltd. [1920] 3p.l., 45p. front. 20cm. Rutherford

2713 **Hjelt**, Ole
Nybyggerliv paa praerien. [Instow, Sask.] Forfatterens Forlag, 1920. 199p. 19cm.
Printed by Forum Publishing Co. Ltd., Winnipeg. On cover: A picture entitled 'A sod shanty on the plains.' Relates to pioneer experiences of Norwegian homesteaders at Instow, Sask. Norway

2713A **Hudson's Bay Company**
Information about the Company's lands in Western Canada. [Winnipeg, 192_] cover-title, 24p. illus. (part. col.), col. map. 16cm. Can. Arch. (ms.)

2714 **Ingersoll**, William E[rnest]
Daisy herself; a novel. Toronto, Musson, 1920. ... Not seen.
Can. Annual Rev., 1920

2715 **Irvine**, William
The farmers in politics. Toronto, McClelland & Stewart, Ltd [1920] 253p. 20cm. U. of S.

2715A **Johnston**, Thomas
Canadian and Scottish songs and poems. Calgary, 1920. 149p. 20cm.
Glenbow

2716 **Johnstone**, R[obert] C[uthbert]
The story of the Church of England in Rupertsland. With an introduction by the Very Rev. G.F. Coombes. Winnipeg, Bulman Bros., Ltd., 1920. 46p. 20 1/2cm. Shortt

2717 **Lacasse**, Pierre Zacharie
Une mine de souvenirs, pour être exploitée par mes chers compatriotes sous la protection de Marie Immaculée. [St-Boniface? 1920] 180p. 23cm.
Part of the book describes the author's experiences in Western Canada. L.C.

2718 **Lindal**, J.H.
Islendingar i Vatnabygdum. Frumbuar bygdoarinnar. Manntal islendinga i austurparti Saskatchewan-fylkis arid 1919. Winnipeg, Olafs S. Thorgeirssonar, 1920. 14, [2]p. 19cm. Denmark

2719 **Long**, Morden H[eaton]
Knights errant of the wilderness; tales of the explorers of the great North-West. Toronto, Macmillan Co., 1920. xi, 223p. incl. front., illus. (incl. ports.) 21cm. U. of A.

2720 **Lynch-Staunton**, Emma, comp.
A history of the early days of Pincher Creek, of the district and of the southern mountains; which is offered as a tribute to the pioneers of this western country by the members of the Women's Institute of Alberta. [Lethbridge, Herald Printing Co., 1920?] 55p. illus. 24 1/2cm. Shortt

2721 **MacBeth**, R[oderick] G[eorge]
The romance of Western Canada. 2d ed. Toronto, William Briggs, 1920. 12, 309p. illus., ports., facsim. 20cm.
First published in 1918. U. of S.

2722 Not used.

2723 **McCalla**, William Copeland
Wild flowers of Western Canada. Toronto, Musson Book Co. [c1920] 132p. illus. 20 1/2cm. U. of S.

2724 **Macnaughton**, S[arah Brown]
My Canadian memories. London, Chapman and Hall, 1920. vii, 247, [1]p. front. 24cm.
Largely sketches of railway builders, Strathcona, Van Horne, Mackenzie, Mann, and Col. Davidson. These sketches were based on a visit to Canada just before World War I, and were published posthumously. Br. Mus.

2725 **Manitoba**. Department of Education
Education among the New Canadians; by various authors. [Winnipeg] 1920. 20p. illus., diagrs. R.E.S.

2726 **Manitoba**. Department of Education
Manitoba: fifty years a province, 1870-1920. [Winnipeg, 1920] 26, [2]p. illus., ports. 25cm.
On cover: Empire Day, 1920. Glenbow

2727 Manitoba, the key-stone province of the Canadian confederation. [Winnipeg? 1920] 158p. illus., fold. plate, fold. map. 19 1/2cm. Man. Leg.

2728 **Martin**, Chester [Bailey]
'The natural resources question'; the historical basis of provincial claims. Winnipeg, King's Printer, 1920. 148p. 23 1/2cm. On cover: Province of Manitoba. Shortt

2728A **Murray**, S.C.
The challenge of our Prairie Provinces. [Toronto, Presbyterian Church in Canada, 1920] cover-title, [12]p. 16cm. B.C. Arch.

2728B **Nolte**, Joseph
Glimpses behind nature's veil. [Stettler, Alta.] c1920. 32p. 19cm. Glenbow

2729 **Oblates.** St. Boniface
1819-1919: Le Centenaire du R.P. Damase Dandurand, O.M.I., le 23 mars, 1919. Saint-Boniface, Juniorat de la Sainte-Famille [1920] 6p.l., [15]-100p. incl. plates. 25 1/2cm. St-Jean

2730 Opportunities in Edmonton and district. Edmonton [c1920] 20p. illus. R.E.S.

2731 **Owens,** R.C.
Daylight on the money and banking questions and other problems. Edmonton, Western Veteran Pub. Co., 1920. 47p. 19 1/2cm.
Opposed to orthodox money system. Glenbow

2732 Pictorial Edmonton. Edmonton [c1920] 39p. illus. R.E.S.

2733 **Pirot,** Jules
Avant les neiges. Paris, La Maison de la Bonne Presse, 1920. 228p. 10 x 18cm. Not seen. Private information

2734 **Pirot,** Jules
Elle vit. Namur, Belgium, Collection Lavigerie [19--] 208p. 13 x 19cm. Not seen. Private information

2735 **Prest,** J.
Hudson's Bay Company historical pageant in commemoration of the 250th anniversary of the Hudson's Bay Company: By special permission of the Governor and Committee. Programme, under the distinguished patronage of his Honour, Lieutenant-Governor R.G. Brett, Hon. Chas. Stewart, Premier of Alberta, Hon. G.H.V. Bulyea, Hon. Frank Oliver, Joseph A. Clarke, Esq., Mayor of Edmonton. Pageant production Mr. J. Prest, musical direction Mr. Vernon Barford. Empire Theatre, Edmonton, May 6th, 7th, 8th, 1920. [n.p., The Western Publishing Co., 1920] cover-title, 8p. Amtmann - 221-438

2735A **Prince Albert.** Board of Trade
Prince Albert, the marketing and distributing centre of Northern Saskatchewan. Western Canada's finest mixed farming, dairying and stock raising district. Prince Albert, 1920. cover-title, 14p. illus., map. 20 1/2cm. Can. Arch. (ms.)

2736 **Pritchard,** William A.
W.A. Pritchard's address to the jury in the Crown vs. Armstrong. Heaps, Bray, Ivens, Johns, Pritchard, and Queen (R.B. Russell was previously tried) indicted for seditious conspiracy and common nuisance; fall assizes, Winnipeg, 1919-1920. Winnipeg, Defence Committee [1920] 219p. port. 21cm. Man. Leg.

2737 **Saskatchewan**
Some Saskatchewan legislation affecting women and children. Issued under the authority of the president of Council. Regina, King's Printer, 1920. 23p. 25 1/2cm. U. of S.

2738 **Saskatchewan.** Department of Education
From Polish peasant to Canadian citizen; a true story of what Saskatchewan schools are doing for the New Canadians. Regina, King's Printer, 1920. cover-title, 7p. (New Canadian series, no.1) Private copy

2739 **Saskatchewan.** University. College of Agriculture
Homemakers' Club, 1910-1920. [Saskatoon, 1920] 64p. illus. 22 1/2cm.
Consists of historical sketches of individual clubs. Sask. Arch.

2740 **Seaman,** Holly S[kiff]
Manitoba landmarks and red letter days, 1610 to 1920. [Winnipeg, 1920] 1p.l., 5-92p. illus. 23cm. Shortt

2741 [**Schooling,** Sir William]
The Governor and Company of Adventurers of England trading into Hudson's Bay during two hundred and fifty years, 1670-1920 ... London, Hudson's Bay Company, 1920. xvi, 129, [1]p. incl. col. front., illus. plates (part col.) ports. (part col.) maps (part. fold.) facsim. 28cm. Shortt

2742 **Stead,** Robert [James Campbell]
Dennison Grant, a novel of to-day. Toronto, Musson Book Co., Ltd. [c1920] 3p.l., 388p. 19 1/2cm.
Fiction, set in the ranching country. U. of S.

2743 **Stefansson,** Johannes
Love and pride. Winnipeg, 1920. 210p. 22cm.
'Errata' (3p.) inserted after t.-p.
Novel, set partly in Manitoba. Glenbow

2744 **Stocken,** [Henry William Gibbon]
The Gleichen district fifty years ago: the Blackfoot then and now. [Gleichen, Alta., Gleichen Call Print, 1920] caption-title, [8]p. illus., port. 22cm.
Cover gives program arranged by the Gleichen Board of Trade for the visit of the Imperial Press delegates on 19 August 1920. Glenbow

2745 **Stringer,** Arthur [John Arbuthnott]
The prairie mother. Illustrated by Arthur E. Becher. Toronto, McClelland & Stewart [c1920] 3p.l., 359p. front., plates. 19 1/2cm.
Fiction; second in the trilogy. See Entries 2526 and 2828. U. of S.

2746 **Taylor,** William Edington
Our church at work, Canada and overseas; a review of the M.S.C.C. fields. Toronto, Missionary Society, Church of England in Canada [ca. 1920] 188p. illus., maps (1 fold.) plates. 19cm.
First half of book on western and northern Canada. Glenbow

2747 **Tennant,** Joseph F[rancis]
Rough times, 1870-1920 ... A souvenir of the 50th anniversary of the Red River expedition and the formation of the Province of Manitoba. [Winnipeg? 1920] 271p. incl. plates. 23 1/2cm. Shortt

2748 **United Farm Women of Alberta**
The U.F.W.A., the organization for Alberta farm women. [Calgary? 192-?] 15p. 14 1/2cm.

The purpose and the history of the organization. U. of S.

2749 **United Farmers of Canada.** Saskatchewan Section
Do you know this? Saskatoon [192-?] cover-title, 8p. 23cm.

A list of the achievements of farmers' organizations in Western Canada. U. of S.

2750 **Vaughan,** Walter
The life and work of Sir William Van Horne. New York, Century Co., 1920. xiii, 388p. port., illus. 23cm.

Much of the volume is based on material gathered by Katherine Hughes. U. of S.

2751 **Winnipeg.** Board of Trade
Winnipeg, pulse of Western Canada. [Winnipeg, 1920?] 14p. illus. 16cm. N.Y.

2752 **Winnipeg.** Police Department
City of Winnipeg, police department, nineteen hundred and twenty. Winnipeg, E.C. Cleaver [1920] 80p. illus., ports. 31cm.

A description of the work of the force, with a history of notable crimes. Winnipeg

2753 **Winnipeg.** St. Stephen's Church
Silver jubilee, 1895-1920, of St. Stephen's. Winnipeg, 1920. 41p. illus. 24cm. Victoria College

2754 Wonderful Winnipeg, the gateway to the Canadian West. [Winnipeg, 192-] [35]p. illus. 17 x 26cm. Picture album. Man. Leg.

2755 **Woodsworth,** James Shaver, defendant
Court of the King's Bench, fall assizes, 1919. The King vs. J.S. Woodsworth, indictment for publishing seditious libels, six counts, and speaking seditious words. Winnipeg, Defence Committee [1920] cover-title, 14p. ports. 22 1/2cm.

This pamphlet contains the libellous statements on which the charges were based. U. of S.

2756 [**Amy,** William Lacey]
Blue Pete, half breed, by Luke Allan [pseud.] New York, James A. McCann Co. [c1921] 2p.l., 9-284p. 19 1/2cm. Not seen.

Fiction. This was the first of the author's stories about Blue Pete, the half-breed ex-rustler and under-cover investigator for the Mounties in the territory from the Cypress Hills to the Rockies. A new title appeared as late as 1951. Most titles are published by Herbert Jenkins of London. L.C.

2757 **Bible**. New Testament. Gospels. Cree
Les Saintes Evangiles. Vie de Notre Seigneur Jésus-Christ en langue crise. Hobbema, Alta., Journal Cris, 1921. 672p. illus. 18cm.
Translated into Cree syllabic by Rev. L. Balter. Oblates Arch.

2758 **Bible**. Old Testament. Psalms. Cree
[The Psalms in Plain Cree (Revised version)] London, British and Foreign Bible Society, 1921. [6], 917-1052p. 22cm.
In Cree syllabic characters. Glenbow

2759 **Bracken**, John
Dry farming in Western Canada. Winnipeg, Grain Growers' Guide Ltd., 1921. xxi p., 1 l., 386p. incl. front. (map) illus., diagrs. 20cm. U. of S.

2760 **Calgary**. Board of Trade
Calgary, Canada. The city of the foothills. [Calgary, J.D. McAra, 1921?] folder. ([10] p.) maps. Calgary

2761 **Canada**. Department of Immigration and Colonization
Canada. Pa le pa bryd a phafodd. Bangor, North Wales Chronicle Co. Ltd., 1921] cover-title, 23p. 18cm. Wales

2762 **Canada**. Department of the Interior
The lower Athabaska and Slave River district. Prepared under the direction of F.C.C. Lynch ... [Ottawa, 1921] 44p. illus., map. 25cm. Rutherford

2763 **Canadian Pacific Railway**
Canadian Pacific reserve farm lands in the Lloydminster and Battleford districts of central Alberta and Saskatchewan. [n.p.] 1921. 19p. illus. Not seen. R.E.S.

2764 **Canadian Pacific Railway**
Handbook of information regarding Alberta, Saskatchewan and Manitoba, and the opportunities offered you by the C.P.R. in these provinces. Calgary, 1921. 64p. illus., map. 22 1/2cm. Not seen. R.E.S.

2765 **Canadian Pacific Railway**
Irrigation farming in sunny Alberta. Calgary [c1921] 40p. illus., map. 23cm. Not seen. R.E.S.

2766 **Canadian Reconstruction Association**
The Grain Growers and Canada's tariff ... [Toronto] The Association, 1921. cover-title, 16p. 23cm. Shortt

2767 **Clark**, Archibald Brown
Recent tax developments in Western Canada. [Winnipeg] 1921. 22p. 23cm. U. of S.

2768 **Daly**, George Thomas
Catholic problems in Western Canada. Toronto, Macmillan Co. [c1921] 352p. 21cm. U. of S.

2769 **E.P. Ranch**
H.R.H. Prince of Wales 'E.P. Ranch': souvenir. High River, Alta. [192–?] cover-title, [26] plates (incl. 1p. of text) 12 x 18cm. Glenbow

2770 **Edwards**, Henrietta (Muir)
Legal status of women of Alberta as shown by extracts from Dominion and provincial laws. Issued by and under the authority of the Attorney-General. 2d ed. [Macleod] 1921. 80p. 19cm. N.Y.

2771 **Fitzpatrick**, F[rank] J[oseph] E[mile]
Sergeant 331; personal recollections of a member of the Canadian Northwest Mounted Police from 1879-1885. New York, Published by the author, 1921. ii, 126, v p. front., plates, ports., double map. 22cm. Can. Arch.

2772 **Footner**, [William] Hulbert
The woman from 'outside' (on Swan River). New York, J.A. McCann Co. [c1921] [3] 268p. 20cm.

Fiction with northern Canadian setting. Glenbow

2773 **Glendinning**, John C[lements]
'Oh! Canada.' Personal impressions as a delegate to the Imperial Press Conference of 1920. [Londonderry, The Derry Standard, 1921] 86p. front, plates, ports. 19cm.

Describes a trip across Canada and back with quite a few references to the Prairies. Br. Mus.

2774 [**Gordon**, Charles William]
To him that hath; a novel of the West today, by Ralph Connor [pseud.] New York, George H. Doran [c1921] 4p.l., 11-291p. 19 1/2cm. Not seen.

Fiction, based on the Winnipeg general strike of 1919. Published also by McClelland and Stewart of Toronto. L.C.

2775 Guide to Edmonton, Peace River, and the north country, Alberta. 1921. 128p. illus., map. R.E.S.

2776 **Ham**, George Henry
Reminiscences of a raconteur between the '40's and the '20's. Toronto, Musson Book Co. [1921] 3p.l., xi-xvi, 330p. front., plates, ports., fold. map. 21cm.

A newspaperman writes his recollections of people and events; he spent some years in Winnipeg in the 1880's. U. of S.

2777 **Heming**, Arthur Henry Howard
The drama of the forests; romance and adventure; illus. by the author with reproductions from a series of his paintings owned by the Royal Ontario Museum. Garden City, N.Y., Doubleday, Page & Co., 1921. xiii, 324p. col. front., col. plates, col. ports. 25cm.

Fiction. L.C.

2778 **Howarth**, David
The valley of gold; a tale of the Saskatchewan. Illus. by H. Weston Taylor. New York, Fleming H. Revell Co. [1921] 4p.l., 11-272p. front., plates. 19 1/2cm. L.C.

2779 **Jackson**, Thorleifur Jóakimsson
Frá austri til vesturs. Framhald af Landnámssögu Nýja Islands. Winnipeg, Columbia Press, Ltd., 1921. 226p. illus. (ports.) 22cm. U. of M.

2780 **Lefeaux**, Wallis Walter
Winnipeg-London-Moscow. A study in Bolshevism. Winnipeg, Canadian Workers Defense League, 1921. 77p.

Author was assistant defence counsel, Winnipeg seditions conspiracy - General strike trials, 1919-20. Man. Leg.

2781 **Low**, Florence B.
Openings for British women in Canada. London, William Stevens [1921] 96p. plates, map. Br. Mus.

2782 **MacBeth**, R[oderick] G[eorge]
Policing the plains, being the real-life record of the famous Royal North-West Mounted Police. Toronto, Hodder and Stoughton, Ltd., 1921. 320p. front., plates, ports. 23cm. Shortt

2783 **McClung**, Nellie L[etitia (Mooney)]
Purple springs. Toronto, Thomas Allen, 1921. 3p.l., 335p. 19 1/2cm.

Fiction; a crusading young school teacher in a Manitoba community. Another edition was published in Boston in 1922. U. of S.

2784 **McKenzie**, N[athaniel] M[urdoch] W[illiam] J[ohn]
The men of the Hudson's Bay Company, 1670 A.D. - 1920 A.D. Fort William [Times-Journal presses, 1921] 214p. front. (ports.) 21 1/2cm.

An autobiography of a servant of the company in the period after 1876. Stationed at Ft. Ellice, at Ft. Qu'Appelle, near Ft. Pelly, and at Touchwood Hills. Shortt

2785 **MacKinnon**, James N.
A short history of the pioneer Scotch settlers of St. Andrews, Sask. [Regina, Courier, 1921] 30p. 20cm.

The early history of two Scottish settlements south and west of Wapella. Sask. Arch.

2786 **Medicine Hat**. Westminster Presbyterian Church
An historical sketch of Westminster Presbyterian Church, Medicine Hat, Alberta, 1914-1921. [Medicine Hat, 1921] 19p. illus. (incl. ports.) 24cm. United College

2787 **Patrick**, T[homas] A[lfred]
The county system for Saskatchewan; an urgently needed reform. Arguments and data in support of it, by T.A. Patrick and F.J. Pilkington. [Yorkton, Enterprise Publishing Co. Ltd., 1921] 31p. 19cm. Shortt

2788 **Paynter**, W.C.
Canadian money and progress. [Tantallon, Sask., ca.1921] cover-title, 12p. form. 28cm. Glenbow

2789 **Popple**, Arthur E[rnest]
Western Canada law; a concise handbook of the laws of Western Canada, as the same are applicable in the Provinces of Alberta, Saskatchewan and Manitoba,

together with other information of value to business men, farmers, secretaries, justices, police magistrates, and all other persons interested in the laws of Western Canada. 3d ed. Winnipeg, Grain Growers' Guide, 1921. viii, 600p. 19 1/2cm. Shortt

2790 **Raymond**, Mrs. A. Pauline
Gathered sheaves from the National Council of Women, Calgary, 1921. [St. John, N.B., Printed by J. & A. McMillan, 1921] 134p. plates (chiefly ports.) 22cm.

Several plates disfigured. With the author's autograph inscription to Mrs. J.D. Ferguson, Saskatoon. Glenbow

2791 **Rodvik**, Sigv
Fortaellinger fra Canada. Optegnelser fra nybyggerlivet Norske settlementer i Saskatchewan. St. Paul, Munkholm Printing Co. [1921] 160p. front. (port.)., illus. 16 1/2cm.

On cover: Fremtiden Publishing Co. Experiences of a Norwegian homesteader near Canora, Sask. Norway

2792 **Rumball**, Wilfrid G[ladstone]
Manitoba College ... being an account of her achievements past and present, and of her contribution to the growth and development of Western Canada and to the progress of Presbyterianism, including a report of proceedings and addresses of the Jubilee Celebration, Nov. 14th to 20th, 1921. Compiled and edited by W.G. Rumball [and] D.A. MacLennan. [Winnipeg] 1921. 86, [1]p. illus., ports. 16cm.

'Published under the direction of Rev. Principal John Mackay.' Glenbow

2793 **Rupert's Land Historical Society**
Report ... for the year ending June 30th, A.D. 1921. The Pas, The Herald, 1921. cover-title, 14p. 18cm.

Probably the only report published. Shortt

2794 **Sabourin**, J[oseph] Ad[onias]
Les parents, l'Eglise et l'Etat dans leurs rapports avec l'école au Manitoba. [St-Boniface, 1921] 31p. 19 1/2cm. (Etudes et conférences, v.1) Shortt

2795 **Saxby**, C.F. Argyll
The settler of Serpent Creek: a tale of the Canadian prairie. London, The Boy's Own Paper office [1921] 253p. front. 19cm.

Juvenile fiction; locale 'somewhere near Saskatoon.' Shortt

2796 [**Trémaudan**, Auguste Henri de]
Riel et la naissance du Manitoba. Publié sous les auspices de l'Union nationale métisse Saint Joseph du Manitoba. [n.p., 1921] 51p. 22 1/2cm.

Consists of two articles, one by A.H. de Trémaudan, the other by L.A. Prud'homme. Man. Leg.

2797 **Ursenbach**, Octave Frederick
Pearls and broken pinions. Lethbridge, c1921. Private information

2798 **Wilson,** R[obert] N.
Our betrayed wards. A story of 'chicanery, infidelity and the prostitution of trust.' Ottawa, 1921. cover-title, 40p. 24cm.

An attack on the Canadian government for its treatment of the Blood Indians. Private copy

2799 **Alberta.** Publicity Commissioner
Province of Alberta, Canada. Charts of progress. Facts and figures on development in the province of Alberta ... Edmonton [1922] cover-title, 16p. graphs. 23cm. Denmark

2800 Not used.

2801 **Ball,** Geraldine F.
Some extracts and reminiscences of a lifetime. Printed for private circulation. Regina, The Leader Publishing Co., 1922. 165p. group port. 20cm.

Part of Mrs. Ball's life was spent in Grenfell, Sask. Glenbow

2802 **Bateman,** Reginald [John Godfrey]
Reginald Bateman, teacher and soldier. A memorial volume of selections from his lectures and other writings. London, Printed for the University of Saskatchewan and published for the university by Henry Sotheran & Co., 1922. xi, 147, [1]p. ports. 19cm. U. of S.

2803 **Canada.** Department of Immigration and Colonization
Canada west. [Ottawa, 1922] 32p. illus., double maps. 28cm. Glenbow

2804 **Canadian Pacific Railway**
Ako získat' farmu v Kanade. Prague, Rolnická Tiskárna [1922] cover-title, [24p.] 16 1/2cm.

Czech immigration pamphlet; issued for Canadian Pacific Railway. Includes 3p. of advertising. Naprstek

2805 **Durkin,** Douglas [Leader]
The lobstick trail. Toronto, Musson, 1922. 3p.l., 334p. front. 19cm. Not seen.

Fiction, set in Manitoba. Another edition was published by McClurg of Chicago. Can. Imprints

2806 **Edmonds,** W[alter] Everard
The natural resources question. A plea for the completion of Alberta's status as a province of Canada ... Edmonton [Henry Roche Printing Co.] 1922. cover-title, 13p. 23cm. Rutherford

2807 **Evangelical Lutheran Church.** Synod of Manitoba, etc.
Denkschrift zum Silber-Jubiläum der Ev.-luth. Synode von Manitoba und anderen Provinzen, 1897-1922. Winnipeg, National Press, 1922. 32p. Not seen. Lehmann

2808 **Fitzsimmons,** Harry
The sky hoboes; some adventures of two pioneer commercial airmen. [Lethbridge, Alta., 1922] 30p. illus. 23cm.

Xerox copy. Glenbow

2809 **Goerwell,** Sten Wiktor
[A time of breaking] Winnipeg, 1922. 97p. Not seen.

Poetry in Swedish. Kirkconnell

2810 **Grew,** David
Beyond rope and fence. New York, Boni and Liveright [c1922] 4p.l., vii, 240p. col. front. 20cm.

Juvenile fiction. A story of wild horses on the Alberta prairie. U. of W.

2811 **Grouard,** [Emile Jean Baptiste Marie]
Souvenirs de mes soixante ans d'apostolat dans l'Athabaska-Mackenzie. Winnipeg, La Liberté [1922] 4p.l., 440p. incl. illus., plates, ports., maps. front. 24cm. Shortt

2812 **Hasell,** F[rances] H[atton] Eva
Across the prairie in a motor caravan; a 3,000 mile tour by two Englishwomen on behalf of religious education ... In collaboration with J.F.S. London, Society for Promoting Christian Knowledge, 1922. vii, 115p. plates, map. 19cm.

Most of the work of the Misses Hasell and Ticehurst was conducted in west-central Saskatchewan in 1920. Also published by Macmillan of Toronto. Emmanuel College

2813 **Heeney,** [William] Bertal, ed.
Centenary addresses and sermons. The Rupert's Land celebration, held in Winnipeg, October 10th to 17th, 1920. [Winnipeg, 1922] 127p. 23 1/2cm. On cover: The Rupert's Land Centenary, 1820-1920. Shortt

2814 **Hudson's Bay Company**
Hudson's Bay Company's lands in Manitoba, Saskatchewan and Alberta, of particular interest to farmers. Winnipeg, Stovel Co. Ltd. [1922] 17p. illus. 16cm. H.B.C.

2815 **Kipling,** Rudyard
Kipling's advice to 'The Hat' in response to an appeal from an old-timer of Medicine Hat, Alberta. [Dover, Mass., At the sign of The George, 1922] 7 l. 20cm.

The letter to Kipling was signed: Francis F. Flatt. It and Kipling's reply were printed in the Medicine Hat News for Dec. 22, 1910. N.Y.

2816 **Lofty**
Adventures and misadventures, or, An undergraduate's experiences in Canada; a simple narrative. London, J. Bale, Sons & Danielsson, 1922. viii, 219p. illus. 19cm.

Account, with fictitious characters, of the author's sojourn in Canada, including the Prairie Provinces. Glenbow

2817 **Low,** Florence B.
Women out West; life and work in Canada. London, W.T. Cranfield [1922?] 32p. front, illus. 18cm.

Issued by the Society for the Overseas Settlement of British women. Chapters are: The settler's wife; Housekeeping in the West; The household worker; Teachers; The nurse in the West, etc. Br. Mus.

2818 **Macoun**, John
Autobiography of John Macoun, M.A., Canadian explorer and naturalist, assistant director and naturalist of the Geological Survey of Canada, 1831-1920, with an introduction by Ernest Thompson Seton. A memorial volume. [Ottawa] Ottawa Field-Naturalists' Club, 1922. x, 305p. front., plates, ports. 23 1/2cm. Shortt

2819 **Manitoba Agricultural College**
Check list of Manitoba flora, prepared by V.W. Jackson, J.F. Higham, Herbert Groh. [Winnipeg] 1922. 35, [1]p. illus., map. 21cm. Glenbow

2820 [**Mary Agnes**, Sister]
Better than gold; a play for girls, by S.M.A. Winnipeg [1922] 27p.

This authoress wrote at least a dozen plays on religious or moral issues, intended to be produced by girls. See British Museum Catalogue. Br. Mus.

2821 **Oliver**, E[dmund] H[enry]
What the Canadian expects of the New Canadian. Mita Kanadalainen odottaa uudelta Kanadalaiselta. [Translated by] A.I. Heinonen. [n.p., 192–] cover-title, [8]p. 17 1/2cm.

Title-page and text in double column, English and Finnish. Finland

2822 **Petrivsky**, M.
Kavaliysky zhenykh. Winnipeg, Ukrainian Bookstore, 1922. ... Not seen.

A drama in Ukrainian. Select

2823 **Prud'homme**, L[ouis] A[rthur]
Monsieur l'Abbé Louis-Raymond Giroux: Directeur du Collège de Saint-Boniface, Chapelain du gouvernement provisoire. Missionnaire. Curé. 1841-1911. Québec, Charrier & Dugal Ltée, 1922. 94p. illus. (incl. port.) 18 1/2cm. St-Jean

2824 **Ricci**, Victor H.
Ups and downs in Canada. Amersham [Bucks, England] Morland, 1922. 3p.l., ix-xi, 13-54p. 16cm.

Reminiscences written in the form of letters to his mother. U. of T.

2825 **Sabourin**, Joseph Adonias
En face de la persécution scolaire au Manitoba. Saint-Boniface, 1922. p.123-148. 19 1/2cm. (Etudes et conférences, v.1) Series paged continuously. Shortt

2826 **Sabourin**, Joseph Adonias
Précis de l'histoire des Ruthènes et de leurs relations avec les Polonais, et avec Rome. Saint-Boniface, 1922. p.77-118. 19 1/2cm. (Etudes et conférences, v.1) Series paged continuously. Shortt

2827 **Stead**, Robert James Campbell
Neighbours. Toronto, Musson, 1922. 315p.

Fiction. R.E.S.

2828 **Stringer**, Arthur [John Arbuthnott]
The prairie child. Illustrated by E.F. Ward. Toronto, McClelland & Stewart [c1922] 3p.l., 382p. front., plates. 19 1/2cm.

Fiction; third in the trilogy. See Entries 2526 and 2745. U. of S.

2828A **Surrey**, George S.
An outlaw of the plains. London, Herbert Jenkins, 1922. 246p. Br. Mus.

2829 **Tourist Association of South Eastern British Columbia and Southern Alberta**
The scenic heart of the Canadian Rockies, south eastern British Columbia & sunny southern Alberta, a paradise for motorists, anglers, huntsmen and health and vacation seekers. Fernie, B.C. [1922] cover-title, 35, [1] p. illus., fold. map. 24 x 21cm. fold to 24 x 11cm. Glenbow

2830 **Althausen**, Ernest
Zersplitterung oder Verbindung? Bilder aus dem leben der Deutschen in Canada und Wolhynien. Der Reinertrag ist zum vesten der flüchtlinge aus Russland bestimmf. Berlin, Fürsorge-Vereius für Deutsche Ruckwandrer [1922] 66p. 18cm.

Written at a time when many German colonists in Russia were attempting to leave that country and were looking to Western Canada as a place to settle. Book describes many districts in Western Canada. Bavaria

2831 **Vester**, A[nders Jensen]
Blandt Danske paa Kanadas Praerie. Virkelighedsskildring af ni Aars Ophold i Kanada og U.S.A. Viborg, C. Wohlert, 1922. 106p. illus. 20cm. N.Y.

2832 **Wrigley's Directories**
Wrigley's Alberta directory, v.1, 1920; v.2, 1922. Wrigley's Saskatchewan directory, v.1, 1921-22. Edmonton

2833 **Alberta**. Department of Agriculture
Alberta, a land of opportunity. [Edmonton, 1923?] 32p. illus., tables. 22cm. Glenbow

2834 **Bennett**, Arthur S.
Is the West worth while? A candid review of the economic problems of Western Canada, and the urgent need for co-operative action by the east and the west in the interests of national progress. [Swift Current? 1923] [3]-47p. 23cm.

On cover: Is the West worth while; not a new national conscience but a new national conception. Glenbow

2835 **British and Foreign Bible Society**
History of the Cree Indian translation of the Scriptures. [London, 1923?] Pamphlet.

Reference in Boon, T.C.B. 'Centenary of the Syllabic Cree Bible, 1862-1962.' Bulletin of Committee on Archives of the United Church of Canada, no. 17, 1964. p.34.

2836 **Calgary**. Central Methodist Church
Central Methodist Church and the Great War, 1914-1919; memorial service and unveiling of tablet in honor of the 204 who offered their services, 36 of whom gave up their lives, Sunday, July 1st, 1923. [Calgary, McAra Presses, 1923] cover-title, [8] p. illus. 24cm. Glenbow

2837 **Campbell**, John A[rchibald]
The Hudson Bay railway. From speeches ... in December, 1922 and January and February, 1923. The Pas, 1923. 28p. illus. 23cm. Shortt

2838 **Campbell**, R.W.
A policeman from Eton; his prairie diary. London, J. Murray, 1923. vii, 307p. 19 1/2cm.
Fiction. L.C.

2839 **Canada**. Department of the Interior
The Lac la Biche district, Alberta, a guide for intending settlers, compiled from information obtained on land classification surveys by C.P. Hotchkiss. Ottawa, King's Printer, 1923. 26p. illus., 2 maps (1 in pocket) 25cm. (Its Bulletin no.47) Glenbow

2840 **Canada**. Department of the Interior
The Province of Saskatchewan, Canada; its development and opportunities ... Revised ed. Ottawa, The Department, 1923. 114p. incl. illus., maps, diagrs. front. 25cm.
A revised edition of a pamphlet originally written by F.H. Kitto in 1919. Shortt

2841 **Cardston, Alta**. Board of Trade
Official folder of Cardston (the temple city) Alberta, Canada. [Lethbridge, Lethbridge Herald] 1923. cover-title, 8p. illus. (incl. map) 23 1/2cm. U. of A. (Extension)

2842 **Church of the Brethren**. Annual Conference. 125th, Calgary, 1923
Official souvenir of Alberta, Canada. [Calgary, Alberta Job Press, 1923] cover-title, [48]p. illus., ports. 24cm.
Mostly information about Alberta, with a short section on the Church. Glenbow

2843 **Durkin**, Douglas Leader
The magpie. Toronto, Hodder & Stoughton, 1923. 330p. Not seen.
Fiction. N.Y.

2844 **Edmonton**. Board of Trade
The Edmonton district in central Alberta, Canada's richest mixed farming district. [Edmonton] 1923. 47p. illus., fold map. 25cm. Private copy

2845 **Edmonton Morning Bulletin**
A warning from Alberta. Similar disaster impending in Manitoba under existing system of land value taxation unless promptly dealt with by legislation. The Winnipeg tax payers' association call attention to the editorial reprinted ... from the Edmonton Morning Bulletin of 31st October, 1923. [Edmonton, 1923] 6p. 22 1/2cm. Columbia

2846 **Fetherstonhaugh**, Mrs. V.
Aunt Anna's foot; a comedy in three acts. London, A.H. Stockwell, 1923. ... Not seen. Br. Mus.

2847 **Garrioch**, A[lfred] C[ampbell]
First furrows; a history of the early settlement of the Red River country, including that of Portage la Prairie. Winnipeg, The Author, 1923. 3p.l., [2]p., 336p. illus., plates, ports. 21cm. Shortt

2848 **Grove**, Frederick Philip
Over prairie trails; with illustrations by C.M. Manly. Toronto, McClelland & Stewart [1923] 231p. incl. front., plates. 20 1/2cm.

Essays, first published in 1922. U. of S.

2849 **Grove**, Frederick Philip
The turn of the year. Toronto, McClelland & Stewart [c1923] 2p.l., 9-237p. front., illus. 21cm.

Essays. L.C.

2850 **Healy**, William J[oseph]
Women of Red River, being a book written from the recollections of women surviving from the Red River era. A tribute to the women of an earlier day by the Women's Canadian Club. Winnipeg, Russell, Land & Co. 1923. 5p.l., 261, [1]p. col. front., illus. (incl. ports., facsims.) 22cm. Shortt

2850A **Hübscher**, Carl Paul
Die Schweizerkolonie in Kanada. [Montreal, 1923] caption-title, 10p. 22cm.

Describes Swiss settlements in Western Canada. Swiss

2851 **Imperial Order of the Daughters of the Empire.** Jón Sigurdsson Chapter
Minningarrit Islenzkra hermanna [Memorial book of Icelandic service men] Jón Sigurdsson Chapter, I.O.D.E. Winnipeg [Viking Press] 1923. 525, [2]p. illus. (ports.) 28cm. U. of S.

2852 **Innis**, Harold A[dams]
A history of the Canadian Pacific Railway. London, P.S. King, 1923. viii, 364p. 22cm.

Published in Canada by McClelland and Stewart. U. of S.

2853 **Jackson**, Thorleifur Jóakimsson
Framhald á Landnámssögu Nýja Islands. Winnipeg, 1923. 122p. illus. (ports.) 22cm. U. of M.

2854 **Kernighan**, Thomas
Dufferin and Carman, Manitoba; being recollections of an eyewitness. Vancouver, 1923. 74, [1]p. 14 1/2cm. Man. Leg.

2854A **Lawrence**, Henry Frank
Kidnapped. [Pine Lake, Alta., 1923] cover-title, [4]p. 23cm.

Opposing Aaron Sapiro and the proposed Wheat Pool. Glenbow

2855 **Lecompte**, Edouard
Un grand chrétien, Sir Joseph Dubuc, 1840-1914. Montréal, Impr. du Messager, 1923. 270p. 19cm.

Sir Joseph Dubuc was for many years connected with the political and judicial life of the province of Manitoba. Shortt

2856 **Lucas**, Frederick C., ed.
An historical souvenir diary of the City of Winnipeg, Canada. [Winnipeg, Cartwright and Lucas] 1923. 240p. incl. illus., plates (part fold.) 20cm. Shortt

2857 **Lupson**, Arnold. (Eagle Tail)
The Sarcee Indians of Alberta. Calgary [Phoenix Press Co.] 1923. [12]p. ports. 25cm.

Portrait on cover. Rutherford

2858 **McClung**, Nellie L[etitia (Mooney)]
When Christmas crossed 'the Peace.' Toronto, Thomas Allen, 1923. 149p. 17 1/2cm.

Fiction. Shortt

2859 **Magnússon**, H.E.
Lykkjuföll. Nokkur smá kvaedi. Wynyard, Sask., Prentsmidja Wynyard Advance, 1923. 70p. 17cm. U. of M.

2860 **Morice**, [Adrien Gabriel]
Histoire de l'Eglise catholique dans l'Ouest canadien du Lac Supérieur au Pacifique (1659-1915). Saint-Boniface, Chez l'auteur, 1921-23. 4v. plates, ports., fold. map, facsims. (part fold.) 24cm.

Father Morice published an English edition in 1910, and the first French edition in 1912. This much enlarged edition, in addition to being a valuable history of the church, contains much general history, local history, and biographical information. Shortt

2861 **Morrow**, J[ames] W[illiam]
Early history of the Medicine Hat country. [Medicine Hat, The News] c1923. 65p. 22cm. Shortt

2862 **Murphy**, Emily Gowan (Ferguson)
Our little Canadian cousin of the great Northwest. Illustrated by Thelma Gooch. Boston, L.C. Page, 1923. viii, 86p. front., plates. 19 1/2cm. L.C.

2863 **Oliver**, Edmund Henry
The liquor traffic in the Prairie Provinces. [Toronto] Presbyterian Church in Canada, Board of Home Missions and Social Service, 1923. 336p. 17cm.

A survey of the use and regulation of liquor on the prairies from 1670 to 1922. Glenbow

2863A **Pénard**, Jean Marie
... Méditations sur la passion de N.S. J.C. ... Hobbema, Alta., Imprimerie du Journal Cris, 1924. 351p. illus. 17cm.

Title in Chipewyan syllabics and French; text in Chipewyan syllabics.
Copy 2 bound with his Prières, catéchisme, cantiques à l'usage des Montagnais. Glenbow

2863B **Pénard**, Jean Marie
... Prières, catéchisme, cantiques à l'usage des Montagnais du Vicariat Ap. du Keewatin. Hobbema, Alta., Imprimerie du Journal Cris, 1923. 224p. illus. 18cm.

Title in Chipewyan syllabics and French; text in Chipewyan syllabics.
With which is bound his Méditations sur la passion ... Glenbow

2864 **Potter**, Ida Elizabeth
We are coming. Portage la Prairie, The Author, 1923. ... Not seen. Can. Imprints

2865 **Pratt**, Geo[rge] R.
Coal trails. 'Stored Alberta sunshine.' Rev. ed. Winnipeg, 1923. 64p. 17 1/2cm. Northland

2866 [**Reeve**, Winifred (Eaton) Babcock]
Cattle, by Onoto Watanna [pseud.] Toronto, Musson Book Co. [1923] 3p.l., 7-256p. 19 1/2cm.
Fiction. Shortt

2867 **Rondeau**, Clovis
La Montagne de Bois (Willow-Bunch, Sask.); histoire de la Saskatchewan méridionale. Québec, L'Action Sociale, 1923. 2p.l., iii, 291p. port., illus. 19cm. Shortt

2868 **Salverson**, Laura Goodman
The Viking heart. New York, George H. Doran Co. [c1923] viii p.l., 1 l., 326p. 20cm.
Fiction; life among the early Icelandic settlers. U. of S.

2869 **Sapiro**, Aaron
Report of mass meeting addressed by Aaron Sapiro in Third Avenue Methodist Church, Saskatoon, Saskatchewan, on Tuesday, August 7th, 1923. [n.p., 1923] caption-title, 19p. 22cm.
His tour of the West furthered the Wheat Pool movement. Shortt

2870 **Schurck**, Ernest
Kanada. Licht- und Schattenbilder. Bern, Pochon-Jent & Buhler, 1923. iv, 113p. 19cm.
The first half of this little book relates to the Prairie Provinces with quite specific references to Stettler and Wetaskiwin. Swiss

2871 **Scott**, James Guthrie
Canada's grain trade; the diversion of the grain traffic of the Prairie Provinces to U.S. seaports ... and the suggested remedy in the use of the National Transcontinental Railway ... Letters written to the Montreal Gazette. [Montreal? 1923] 24, [1]p. illus., tables, fold. map. 23cm. Glenbow

2872 **Scott**, W[illiam] L[ouis]
Eastern Catholics, with special reference to the Ruthenians in Canada. Toronto, Catholic Truth Society of Canada [1923?] 47p. 18 1/2cm. St. Sulpice

2873 **Steele**, Harwood [Elmes Robert]
Spirit-of-iron (Manitou-pewabic); an authentic novel of the North West Mounted Police. New York, George H. Doran [c1923] viii p., 2 l., 13-358p. 20cm.
Published also by McClelland and Stewart of Toronto. U. of A. (Extension)

2874 **Warwick**, Joseph
Anna of the Troubled Valley; a tale of rural life. Winnipeg, Printed by North Star Publishing Co. [1923] [9], [4]-174p. 17cm.
Locale of the story is principally England. Glenbow

2875 **American Swedish Line**
Svenskar i Canada. [Göteborg, Elanders, 1924] [8]p. 21cm.

Illustrations on covers. The pamphlet lists the names of some Swedish settlers in various districts of Western Canada. Uppsala

2876 **Bernier**, Thomas Alfred
Le pèlerin d'amour; grand poème en cinq actes, par Jean Berthos [pseud.] Québec, Imprimerie Laflamme, 1924. 98p. 25cm. U.B.C.

2877 **Blais**, Telesphore Alexander
An adventurous career; the life of Telesphore Alexander Blais in the wild West. [Edmonton, Western Veteran Pub. Co., 1924] 70p. illus. 17cm.

Xerox copy. Glenbow

2878 **Blue**, John
Alberta, past and present, historical and biographical. Chicago, Pioneer Historical Publishing Co., 1924. 3v. illus. 27cm. U. of S.

2879 **Bridle**, Augustus
Hansen, a novel of Canadianization. Toronto, Macmillan, 1924. viii, 368p. Not seen.

The story of a New Canadian who worked in many parts of Canada, and tried for the Legislature in Alberta. Can. Novel

2880 **Cain**, Sydney C.
Prairie fairies, and other verses. 2d ed. Regina, Leader Publishing Co., 1924. 30p. Not seen. Can. Imprints

2881 **Campbell**, M[ilton] N[eil]
Speech ... on the Hudson Bay Railway. Delivered in the House of Commons on Wednesday, July 16, 1924. [Ottawa, 1924] 5p. 25cm. Shortt

2882 **Canada**. Department of Immigration and Colonization
Canada West. Canada, the new homeland. Ottawa, 1924. cover-title, 32p. Amtmann - 176-73

2883 **Canadian Pacific Railway**
Tell me - why should I leave my farm and home and move to Western Canada. [Winnipeg? 1924?] folder. (8p.) illus., col. map. 34cm.

Text (4p.) on one side; map across 4p. on other side. Glenbow

2884 **Cochrane**, Charles Norris
David Thompson, the explorer. Toronto, Macmillan Co., 1924. 4p.l., 173p. col. front. 18 1/2cm. (Canadian men of action, v.2) Maps on lining-papers. U. of S.

2885 **Constantin-Weyer**, M[aurice]
Manitoba. Paris, F. Rieder et Cie, 1924. 134p., 2 l. 18 1/2cm. (Prosateurs français contemporains)

Another edition was published by Ferenczi et fils in 1930. U. of S.

2886 **Edmonton.** Highlands Methodist Church
Best thoughts, greetings from W.J. and Mrs. Magrath, the Highlands, Edmonton. Arranged by the ladies of the Highlands Methodist Church, Edmonton, Alta. [Edmonton] Norward Print [192–] [28]p. 19cm.

Cover-title: Gleanings from the wheat. A collection of sayings by great writers, each thought in the collection chosen by a member of the congregation. Rutherford

2887 **Hackett,** John A.
Rhymes of the north, and other rhymes. Victoria, Diggon Presses [c1924] 66p. 17cm.

On cover author's name is 'Jack Hackett.' Glenbow

2888 **Hanna,** D[avid] B[lythe]
Trains of recollection drawn from fifty years of railway service in Scotland and Canada, and told to Arthur Hawkes. Toronto, Macmillan Co., 1924. x p., 1 l., 340p. front., ports. 23cm.

Largely the story of the beginnings of the Canadian Northern. Shortt

2889 **Hawkes,** John
The story of Saskatchewan and its people. Chicago, S.J. Clarke Publishing Co., 1924. 3v. fronts., illus. (incl. ports.) fold. plan. 27cm. Shortt

2890 **Jaray,** Gabriel Louis
De Québec à Vancouver; à travers le Canada d'aujourd'hui, par Gabriel Louis Jaray et Louis Hourticq. Paris, Librairie Hachette [1924] 256p. 19cm.

About a quarter of the book is devoted to a description of the prairies. Man. Leg.

2891 **Leys,** J.J.
Nederlandsche kolonisten in Canada. [Amsterdam, 1924] cover-title, 39p. 24cm.

A report to the Governor of Surinam on prospects for Dutch settlers in Western Canada. Netherlands

2892 **Low,** Florence B.
Kvinden i det fjaerne vesten. Liv og gerning i Kanada. Dansk oversaettelse af James W. Savage. Kobenhavn, J.A. Hansen, 1924. 30p. illus. 17cm.

See Entries 2781 and 2817. Denmark

2893 **MacBeth,** R[oderick] G[eorge]
The romance of the Canadian Pacific Railway. Toronto, Ryerson Press [1924] 5p.l., 263, [1]p. front., plates, ports. 21 1/2cm.

A second edition was published in 1926. U. of S.

2894 **McCormick,** J[ames] Hanna
Lloydminster; or, Five thousand miles with the Barr colonists. London, Drane's [1924] 5p.l., 13-254p. front. (port.) plates, maps. 19cm. Shortt

2895 [**MacGregor,** Mary Esther (Miller)]
A gentleman adventurer; a story of the Hudson's Bay Company, by Marian Keith [pseud.] Toronto, McClelland and Stewart [1924] 301p. 19 1/2cm. Not seen.

Fiction. Published also in New York by Doran. Can. Imprints

2896 **McKellar,** Hugh
Presbyterian pioneer missionaries in Manitoba, Saskatchewan, Alberta and British Columbia. Toronto, Murray Printing Co., 1924. 249p. illus. (incl. ports.) 22 1/2cm. Shortt

2897 **Mackintosh,** W[illiam] A[rchibald]
Agricultural co-operation in Western Canada. Toronto, Ryerson Press [c1924] viii, [1], 173p. diagrs. 24cm. (Publications of the Faculty of Arts in Queen's University) U. of S.

2898 **Markússon,** Magnús
Hljómbrot. Winnipeg, City Printing & Publishing Co., 1924. 270p. ports. 17cm.

Icelandic poetry. U. of M.

2899 **Mathieu,** O[livier] E[lzéar]
Lettres pastorales et lettres circulaires de S.G. Mgr O.E. Mathieu, évêque de Regina. 1914-1923. [n.p., 1924?] 3p.l., 9-751p. 23cm. U. of S.

2900 **Church of England.** Missionary Society
'From the East and from the West'; echoes from the triennial report of the Board of Management to the Board of Missions M.S.C.C. and some glimpses of the various fields. Toronto, Literature Dept., Church House [1924?] 88p. illus., ports. 20cm.

About half the book is devoted to Western Canada including missions to Indians and other ethnic groups. Glenbow

2901 **Mitchell,** H[orace] Hedley
Catalogue of the birds of Saskatchewan. Regina, 1924. p.102-19. plates, map. 26cm. Reprinted from The Canadian Field-Naturalist, v.38, no.6, special number, May, 1924. The reprint published for the Saskatchewan Dept. of Agriculture. Shortt

2902 **Neepawa, Man.** Methodist Church
The Neepawa Methodist Church, Neepawa, Manitoba. Neepawa, Church Official Board, 1924. 20p. front., illus. 24cm. Victoria College

2903 **Otto,** Max
In kanadischer Wildnis: Trapper und Farmerleben. Berlin, Paul Parey, 1924. viii, 458p. illus., maps. Not seen.

The author describes his experiences as a trapper and hunter in northern Alta.; violently anti-Canadian; of little value. Later edition published under title: In Kanadas urwaldern und Prärien. 1926. C.H.R., 1924

2904 **Peters,** Klaas
Die Bergthaler Mennoniten und deren Auswanderung aus Russland und Einwanderung in Manitoba. Die wichtigsten Ereignisse vom Jahre 1872 bis auf die Zeit, wo die ersten Ansiedler von ihnen ihr Pionierleben in Manitoba ueberstanden hatten. Zum fuenfzigjaehrigen Jubilaeum. Von Klaas Peters, Waldeck, Sask., zur Zeit in Greenville, Florida. Hillsboro, Kans., Mennonite Brethern Publishing House [1924] 45p. Not seen. Bender

2905 Pioneers and prominent people of Saskatchewan. Winnipeg, Canadian Publicity Co. [c1924] xvi, 343p. 19 1/2cm. U. of S.

2906 **Reformed Church**
Kanada. Geschichte der Deutschen Manitoba-Klassis der Synode des Nordwestens der Reformierten Kirche. Cleveland, Ohio, 1924. ... Not seen. Lehmann

2907 **Rigassi**, Georges
A travers le Canada. Impressions de voyage d'un journaliste suisse. Lausanne, Payot, 1924. 107p. Lorenz

2908 **Runólfsson**, Jón
Thögul leiftur. Winnipeg, Sveinn Thorvaldson, 1924. 270p. port. 17cm.
Icelandic poetry. U. of M.

2909 **Secretan**, J[ames] H[enry] E[dward]
Canada's great highway, from the first stake to the last spike. London, John Lane [1924] 6p.l., 252p. front., plates, ports. 19cm.
The Canadian Pacific Railway. U. of S.

2910 **Stead**, Robert James Campbell
The smoking flax. New York, Doran, 1924. 7-281p. 19cm.
Fiction. Published also in Toronto by McClelland and Stewart. Can. Novel

2911 **United Grain Growers' Limited**
Co-operative cattle selling, a system of marketing cattle of producers in Western Canada for the benefit of producers. Winnipeg, 1924. 20p. 20 1/2cm. Shortt

2912 **Watt**, Edward William
Settling in Canada. Aberdeen, Aberdeen Newspapers Ltd., 1924. 3p.l., [7]-51p. front., illus. 22cm.
Relates largely to impressions of the Prairie Provinces gained during a visit to Canada. Br. Mus.

2913 **Young**, J. Peat
A newcomer in Canada; recollection of work, travel, friendships, & home life in the land of the maple. [London] C. Palmer [c1924] 168p. front., plates. 19 1/2cm.
Includes farm experiences and pioneer life in Saskatchewan. L.C.

2914 **Alberta**. Department of Agriculture
Province of Alberta, Canada, charts of progress; facts and figures on development in the province of Alberta. Edmonton [J.W. Jeffery, King's Printer, 1925] cover-title, 16p. illus. 23cm.
'Published under direction of Hon George Hoadley, Minister of Agriculture, issued from the office of the Publicity Commission.' Glenbow

2915 **Alberta**. Publicity Bureau
A booklet of information in brief form on progress and development of the province of Alberta, Canada. Edmonton, Publicity Commissioner, Dept. of Agriculture, 1925. 48p. illus. Canner – 474-7

2916 **Bellamy**, [Lora (Davis)]
Pioneer days of the first Baptist church in northern Alberta. Edmonton, 1925. cover-title, 15p. 22 1/2cm.

A history of First Baptist Church, Edmonton. Edmonton

2917 **British and Foreign Bible Society**
History of the translation of the Canadian Indian Scriptures. [London, 1925?] Pamphlet.

Reference in Boon, T.C.B. 'Centenary of the Syllabic Cree Bible, 1862-1962.' Bulletin of Committee on Archives of the United Church of Canada, no.17, 1964. p.34.

2917A **Caesar**, Charles E[dward]
Notes on North West Canada, and missionary work among red Indians & Eskimos, carried on by the Bible Churchmen's Missionary Society. London, The Society, 1925. 64p. maps. 18cm. B.C. Arch.

2918 **Campbell**, R.W.
A prairie parson. London, W. & R. Chambers [1925] 4p.l., 260p. 19 1/2cm.

Fiction. L.C.

2919 **Canadian Authors' Association**. Saskatchewan Branch
Saskatchewan, her infinite variety. The Authors' Association pays its respects to debutante province. [Regina? 1925?] 4p.l., 88p. front., plates. 15 x 22cm.

Edited by A.M. Bothwell. Shortt

2920 **Canadian National Railways**
Own your own home in Western Canada. St. Paul, Minn., The Company [1925] cover-title, 31, [1]p. incl. illus. 25 1/2cm. Shortt

2921 **Canadian Pacific Railway**
Irrigation farming in sunny Alberta. [Calgary?] 1925. cover-title, 24p. illus., fold. map. 23cm. N.Y.

2922 **Canadian Pacific Railway**
The Prairie Provinces of Canada. [Calgary? 1925] cover-title, 32p. illus., fold. map. 23cm. N.Y.

2923 **Constantin-Weyer**, M[aurice]
La bourrasque. Paris, F. Rieder et Cie, 1925. 249p., 1 l. 18 1/2cm. (Prosateurs français contemporains)

A new edition was published by Ferenczi et fils in 1929. An English edition under the title 'The half-breed' was published in New York by Macaulay in 1930, while a Polish edition 'Burza nad Kanada' appeared in Warsaw in 1936. U. of S.

2924 **Cropper**, Margaret B.
The caravan; a play about Sunday School work on the prairies, etc., by Margaret B. Cropper and F.H. Eva Hasell. London, Society for Promoting Christian Knowledge, 1925. 30p. port. Br. Mus.

2925 **Cyr**, [Joseph] Ernest
Le Révérend Père Zacharie Lacasse, O.M.I. Conférence donnée sous les auspices de l'Union Canadienne à Saint-Boniface, le 6 novembre 1924. St-Boniface, Maison des Missionnaires Oblats de M.I., 1925. 38p. 21cm.
Bibliothèque de St-Boniface

2926 **Douglas**, William
Freemasonry in Manitoba, 1884-1925. Winnipeg, Grand Lodge of Manitoba A.F. and A.M., 1925. 6p.l., 266, [2]p. front., plates, ports. 21 1/2cm.
Shortt

2927 **Garrioch**, A[lfred] C[ampbell]
The far and furry north, a story of life and love and travel in the days of the Hudson's Bay Company. [Winnipeg, Douglass-McIntyre Printing and Binding Co., Ltd., 1925] 238p. 21cm.

Fiction. The locale is northern Alberta. Shortt

2928 **Gravel**, L[ouis Joseph] P[ierre]
La Saskatchewan; le pays des blés d'or. Montréal, Bureau de colonisation du gouvernement fédéral, 1925. 63p. 17cm.

Illustrations on inside covers. The first section is an address given in Montreal; the last section describes towns where French-Canadian communities were situated. St-Jean

2929 **Grove**, Frederick Philip
Settlers of the marsh. New York, George H. Doran Co. [c1925] 341p. 19 1/2cm.

Fiction; pioneer life in the Manitoba bush country. Also published by the Ryerson Press. U. of S.

2930 **Hudson's Bay Company**
Hudson's Bay Company's historical exhibit at Winnipeg. [Winnipeg, The Company] 1925. cover-title, 76p. illus. 17cm. At head of title: 5th ed.
Shortt

2931 **Kennedy**, Howard Angus
The book of the West. The story of Western Canada, its birth and early adventures, its youthful combats, its peaceful settlement, its great transformation, and its present ways. Toronto, Ryerson Press [c1925] xiii p., 1 l., 205, [1]p., 1 l. front., illus., plates, ports. 19 1/2cm. U. of S.

2932 **Kerby**, G[eorge] W[illiam]
Milestones of Methodism in Calgary and Canada. [Calgary, 1925] cover-title, 14p. 15cm. Calgary

2933 **Kumka**, Michael
[Beginning of gymnastics among the Ukrainians of Winnipeg] Winnipeg, 1925. 32p. Not seen.

Published in Ukrainian. Kirkconnell

2934 **Latour**, [Pierre Zénon] Conrad
Monseigneur Alexandré Taché, Oblat de Marie-Immaculée, premier archevêque de Saint-Boniface, 1823-1894. Montréal, L'Oeuvre des Tracts [1925?] cover-title, 16p. 19cm. (Tract no.51)

Portrait on cover. St-Jean

2935 **Leaver**, H[arold] R.
The mystery of John Jasper. [Edmonton? 1925] 76, 1p. 21cm.

Poetry. Rutherford

2936 **Leslie**, Thomas W.
The legislative building of Manitoba. The keystone province of the Dominion of Canada. Situated in the capital city of Winnipeg ... Winnipeg, Stovel Co. Ltd., c1925. 71p. illus. 23cm. Man. Leg.

2937 **McClung**, Nellie L[etitia (Mooney)]
Painted fires. New York, Dodd, 1925. 316p. 20cm.

Fiction; experiences of a Finnish immigrant girl. Also published by Allen of Toronto. L.C.

2938 **Macdonald**, Adrian
Sir Alexander Mackenzie. Toronto, Ryerson Press, 1925. 32p. 19cm. (Ryerson Can. hist. readers) C.H.R., 1925

2939 **McGregor**, T.F.
Where the great Peace River flows; our Fort Vermilion Mission. From notes by Rev. T.F. McGregor. [Toronto] Presbyterian Church in Canada. Board of Home Missions and Social Work, 1925. cover-title, 11p. illus. 17cm. U. of A.

2940 **Mackie**, George Douglas
A review of local government taxation in Saskatchewan. [Moose Jaw, 1925] 15p. N.Y.

2941 **Mackintosh**, W[illiam] A[rchibald]
The Canadian wheat pools. Kingston, Jackson Press, 1925. 28p. 22 1/2cm. (Queen's University. Departments of History and Political and Economic Science. Bull. no.51) Shortt

2942 **Maclean**, John
Brief sketch of life and work of Rev. James Evans (inventor of Cree syllabics) Winnipeg, The Author, 1925. ... Not seen. Can. Imprints

2943 [**McRaye**, Walter Jackson] ed.
Pioneers and prominent people of Manitoba. Winnipeg, Canadian Publicity Co. [c1925] 3p.l., 353, [13]p. front., illus. 21 1/2cm. Shortt

2944 **Manitoba Economic Conference.** 2d, Winnipeg, 1925
Report of the proceedings. Winnipeg [1925] cover-title, 138p. tables. (1 fold.) 23cm.

Held at Winnipeg, 19 and 20 February 1925. Glenbow

2945 **Maurault**, Olivier
A mari usque ad mare; voyage de l'Université de Montréal à travers le Canada sous la conduite du Pacifique Canadien. Montréal, 1925. 55p. illus. 23cm.

Approximately 20 pages relate to the Prairies. St. Sulpice

2946 **Neufeld**, Dietrich
Kanadische Mennoniten. Bunte Bilder aus dem 50-jährigen Siedlerleben. Zum Jubiläumsjahr 1924. Winnipeg, 1925. 73p. Not seen. Lehmann

2947 **Ontario-Manitoba Boundary Commission**
Report of the commissioners appointed to delimit the boundary between the provinces of Manitoba and Ontario from Winnipeg River northerly. Survey by

J.W. Pierce ... 1921 and 1922, under the direction of the commissioners. Ottawa, Topographical Survey of Canada, 1925. vi, [1], 95p. illus., maps (1 fold. in pocket) tables. 26cm. Glenbow

2948 **Ostenso**, Martha
Wild geese. New York, Dodd, Mead & Co., 1925. 3p.l., 356p. 19 1/2cm.

A prize-winning novel set in a Manitoba Scandinavian community.
Also published by McClelland and Stewart of Toronto. U. of S.

2949 [**Partridge**, Edward Alexander]
A war on poverty; the one war that can end war. Winnipeg, Wallingford Press [1925] iv, xii, 225p. Not seen. Can. Imprints

2950 **Pierce**, H[erbert] C[handler]
Our money system and what it is doing to us (It is sure doing a plenty) The remedy and how to apply it (Inject gently to prevent shock) [Dahlton, Sask., The Author, 1925?] cover-title, 27p. 22cm. Tables on covers. Shortt

2951 **Portage la Prairie.** Board of Trade
Portage la Prairie, the friendly city. [Portage la Prairie, 1925?] [24]p. illus. 20 1/2cm. Man. Leg.

2952 **Ross**, Mrs. Anna
The Presbyterian banner and its battles, 1556-1925, by Mrs. Anna Ross, Strasbourg, Sask. Toronto, The Armac Press [1925] 35p. 17cm.

'Extracts from "The man with the book, or Memoirs of John Ross of Brucefield," with a very little alteration and addition.' Shortt

2953 **Trotter**, Beecham
A horseman and the West ... with Arthur Hawkes assisting. Toronto, Macmillan Co., 1925. 304p. front., plate. 19cm.

Pioneer days at Brandon, Man. Shortt

2954 **Watson**, Robert
Canada's fur-bearers. [2d ed.] Ottawa, Graphic Publishers [c1925] 48p. illus. 22cm.

At head of title: Little nature studies in verse. Glenbow

2955 **Widtsoe**, John Andreas
An examination into the conditions on the Lethbridge northern irrigation district, Alberta, Canada. A report submitted to the Premier of Alberta, February, 1925. [Salt Lake City? 1925] 26p. 26cm.

Photostat (negative) L.C.

2956 **Bennett**, [Annie (Dunlop)]
The Local Council of Women of Regina. Regina, 1926. 64p. 16 1/2cm.

A history of the organization from its foundation in 1895. Local Council

2956A **British Dominions Land Settlement Corporation Limited**
Illustrations of settlers' progress in 1925 and 1926 and their own stories of their success on farm lands bought from British Dominions Land Settlement Corporations Limited. [Winnipeg? 1926?] cover-title, [14]p. illus. 17 x 23 1/2cm.

Illustrations of each farmer's farmstead on one page, his letter in his native language with an English translation on the page facing the illustrations. Alta. Arch.

2957 **Cameron**, William Bleasdell
The war trail of Big Bear; being the story of the connection of Big Bear and other Cree Indian chiefs and their followers with the Canadian North-West Rebellion of 1885, the Frog Lake massacre and events leading up to and following it, and two months' imprisonment in the camp of the hostiles. Toronto, Ryerson, 1926. 256p. front., plates, ports., facsims. 18 1/2cm.

Duckworth of London also published this title, and a revised edition in 1927. An American edition was published in Boston by Small, Maynard and Company the following year. In 1950 a new revised edition under the title 'Blood Red the Sun' was published by the Kenway Publishing Company of Calgary. Shortt

2958 **Canadian Pacific Railway**
Canada, nogle praktiske oplysninger. [Kobenhavn, Triers, 1926] cover-title, 16p. illus. 21cm.

A plain cover with the circular seal of the company. Denmark

2959 **Canadian Pacific Railway**
50,000 harvesters wanted. Excursions to Manitoba, Saskatchewan, and Alberta, 1926. [Montreal, 1926] cover-title, 7p. 14 1/2cm.

Text in English and French. In the days before the introduction of the labour-saving combines, the harvesters' excursion from Eastern Canada was an annual institution. Shortt

2960 **Canadian Pacific Railway**
Successful American settlers in Western Canada invite you to come. Montreal [1926?] cover-title, [24]p. illus. 16cm.

Testimonial letters. Glenbow

2961 **Evans**, William Sanford
The Canadian Wheat Pool: an address, before the Grain Dealers' National Association in convention at Buffalo, October 19th, 1926. [n.p.] Dawson Richardson Publications [1926?] cover-title, 23p. 23cm. Glenbow

2962 **Féron**, Jean
La métisse; roman Canadien. Montréal, Editions E. Garand, c1926. 214p. 19cm. Glenbow

2963 **Innes**, Campbell, ed.
The Cree rebellion of 1884, or sidelights on Indian conditions subsequent to 1876 ... Battleford, Printed by Saskatchewan Herald, 1926. xvi, 69p. illus. (incl. ports.) 23cm. (Battleford Hist. Soc., v.1, no.1) Shortt

2964 **Jackson**, V[incent] W[illiam]
Fur and game resources of Manitoba. Issued and distributed by Industrial Development Board of Manitoba. Winnipeg [Printed by Saults & Pollards, Ltd.] 1926. 55, [1]p. incl. illus., tables, diagrs. plates (incl. 1 map) 23cm. Shortt

2965 **Karger**, Karl
14 Jahre unter Englaendern; ein Auswandererschicksal in Kanada. Breslau, Verfasser, 1926. xv, 218p. illus. (incl. port.) 21cm.

The experiences and observations of a German school teacher who came to Canada in 1915 and was deported in 1919. He worked as a farm hand at Morden and Morris, Man., and as a teacher near Emerson, before moving to Ontario. The author detested everything Canadian. Cf. C.H.R., 1933. Bavaria

2966 **Lewis,** Sinclair
Mantrap. New York, Harcourt, Brace, 1926. 7-308p. 19 1/2cm.

The locale of the novel is Lac la Ronge, Sask., where the author visited about 1924. Some of the characters are thinly disguised portraits of the local inhabitants. U. of A.

2967 **Linck,** Olaf
Kanada det store fremtidsland. Fremtidsmulighederne og udvandrede landsmaends skaebner i Kanada. Copenhagen & Oslo, E. Jespersens, 1926. 191p. plates. 20cm.

Mostly about the prairie region. Denmark

2968 **Local Council of Women of Saskatoon**
Ten years in retrospect, 1916-1926. Saskatoon, 1926. cover-title, 55p. 21cm.

The constitution of the local organization and some history. Local Council

2969 **McCulloch,** John Herries
The men of Kildonan, a romance of the Selkirk settlers. Toronto, McClelland, 1926. xii p., 1 l., 15-276, [1]p. 19 1/2cm.

Fiction. U. of S.

2970 **Martin,** W.
Lord Selkirk. Toronto, Ryerson Press, 1926. 31p. 19cm. (Ryerson Can. hist. readers) C.H.R., 1932

2971 **Merriman,** R[obert] O[wen]
The bison and the fur trade. Kingston, Jackson Press, 1926. 19p. 22 1/2cm. (Queen's University. Departments of History and Political and Economic Science. Bull. no.53) Shortt

2972 **Mézl,** F.
Kanada. Země, lid a hospodářské poměry. Jako prirucku pro vystěhovalce, i turisty a obchodniky. Prague, 1926. 112p. double map. 19cm.

Czech title translated: Canada the country, people and economic conditions. Czech

2973 **Moodie,** Marion E[lizabeth]
Legend of Dryas. [n.p.] c1926. [8]p. front. 18cm.

A fairy tale in prose. Private information

2973A **Moose Jaw, Sask.**
Souvenir book of views, Moose Jaw, Saskatchewan, Canada; the railway capital of Saskatchewan. Ottawa, Printed by Photogelatine Engraving Co. [1926?] 17 l., chiefly illus. 16 x 22cm. Glenbow

2974 **Murchie,** R[obert] W[elch]
Unused lands of Manitoba; report of survey conducted by R.W. Murchie and H.C. Grant. [Winnipeg, 1926] 191p. illus., maps (part fold., part col.) tables, diagrs. 25 1/2cm. U. of S.

2975 **Owens**, R.C.
The bridge to liberty; a plan to evolve from the capitalist system to a co-operative system. Edmonton [The author, 1926] 38p. 17cm. Glenbow

2976 [**Payne**, John Lambert]
The Hudson Bay Railway. What is the truth in this important matter. [n.p., 1926] cover-title, 22p. plates. 22 1/2cm. At head of title: Reprinted from the Calgary Herald. Shortt

2977 **Payne**, J[ohn] L[ambert]
What will it cost? A vital and fundamental question in relation to the Hudson Bay Railway. With supplementary comment on the subject from the Simcoe Reformer. [n.p., 1926] 15p. 23 1/2cm. Shortt

2978 **Pierce**, Lorne
James Evans. Toronto, Ryerson Press, 1926. 30p. 19cm. (Ryerson Can. hist. readers) C.H.R., 1927

2979 **Pierce**, Lorne
John Black. Toronto, Ryerson Press, 1926. 32p. 19cm. (Ryerson Can. hist. readers) C.H.R., 1927

2980 **Pierce**, Lorne
John McDougall. Toronto, Ryerson Press, 1926. 30p. 19cm. (Ryerson Can. hist. readers) C.H.R., 1927

2981 **Pollard**, W[illiam] C[orrell]
Pioneering in the prairie West. A sketch of the Parry Sound colonies that settled near Edmonton, N.W.T., in the early nineties. 3d ed. Toronto, Published for the author by Thomas Nelson [c1926] 4p.l., 92p. front. (port.) plates. 19 1/2cm.

An edition in the library of the Dominion Dept. of Agriculture has imprint and pagination as follows: Uxbridge, Ont., Harold J. Cair, 1924. [31]p. plate. 17cm.

Republished by Stockwell of London in 1930 under the title 'Life on the frontier.' Shortt

2982 **Potter**, Ida Elizabeth
Farmer Maxwell's city niece; a three act drama. [n.p.] c1926. 39p. 20cm. U. of A.

2983 **Regina**. Board of Trade
Regina, centre of the world's hard wheat area. [Regina, 1926] cover-title, 30, [1]p. illus. 23cm. N.Y.

2984 **Sabourin**, J[oseph] Ad[onias]
La coéducation dans les écoles du Manitoba. [St-Boniface, 1926] p.106-34. 19cm. (Etudes et conférences, v.2) Shortt

2985 **Saskatchewan Co-operative Elevator Co., Limited**
A brief record of the history and development of the Saskatchewan Co-operative Elevator Co., Ltd. Regina, The Company, 1926. ... Not seen. Can. Cat.

2986 **Saskatchewan Grain Growers' Association**
A quarter century of progress; a partial record of the activities of the S.G.G.A. from 1901 to the present time. Regina, The Association, 1926. cover-title, 47p. 13 1/2cm. Shortt

2987 **Saskatchewan.** University
University of Saskatchewan. [Saskatoon, 1926?] [26] l., chiefly illus. 12 x 18cm. Glenbow

2988 **Saunders,** Daisy L.
Churnings from a prairie kitchen. Toronto, The Hunter-Rose Co., Ltd., 1926. 3p.l., 83p. 19cm.

Poetry. U. of S.

2989 **Scriven,** George P[ercival]
The story of the Hudson's Bay Company, otherwise of the Company of Adventurers of England trading into Hudson's Bay. Washington, St. Anselm's Priory, 1926. 66p. illus., fold. map. 23cm. Can. Arch.

2990 **Stead,** Robert [James Campbell]
Grain. New York, George H. Doran Co. [c1926] 281p. 19cm.

Fiction. The hero is a farmer who loves the land. U. of S.

2991 **Taverner,** P[ercy] A[lgernon]
Birds of Western Canada. Ottawa, F.A. Acland, 1926. 2p.l., 380p. illus., col. plates. 25 1/2cm. (Canada. Geological Survey. Victoria Memorial Museum. Museum bull. no.41. Biological ser., no.10) U. of S.

2992 **Une religieuse de Notre-Dame des Missions**
... Institut de Notre-Dame des Missions. Petit historique de nos premières fondations au Canada 1898-1923. Lyon, Maison de Recrutement pour les Missions [1926] 185p. illus. (incl. ports.) 24cm.

'Imprimerie des Missions Africaines de Lyon.' In 1901, because of anti-clericalism in France, the entire order moved to Canada. In 1923 it maintained fifteen convents in Western Canada. France

2993 **Vennerström,** Ivar [Teodor]
Kanada och Kanadasvenskarna; studier och reseintryck. Stockhom, Tidens, 1926. 151, [1]p. illus. 20cm. Sweden

2994 **Whitehouse,** Francis Cecil
Plain folks; a story of the Canadian prairies. Ottawa, Graphic Publishers, 1926. 301p.

Fiction. Saskatoon San.

2995 **Williams,** Flos (Jewell)
New furrows; a story of the Alberta foothills. Ottawa, Graphic Publishers, 1926. 7p.l., 303p. 19 1/2cm.

A novel about a Belgian girl and her family in a new country. Shortt

2996 **Woodsworth,** J[ames] S[haver]
'Following the gleam,' a modern pilgrim's progress – to date. [n.p., 1926] cover-title, 20p. 23cm. U. of S.

2997 **Alberta Co-operative Wheat Producers Limited**
Alberta Wheat Pool rally ... Calgary, 1927. cover-title, 46p. 21cm.

A rally held in Calgary on 7 June 1927. St. Sulpice

2998 **L'Association Catholique Franco-Canadienne**
Quinze ans de vie française en Saskatchewan, 1912-1927. [Prince Albert, Imprimerie La Bonne Presse, 1927] cover-title, 135p. illus. 22cm.

'Travaux présentés à la convention conjointe de L'Association Catholique Franco-Canadienne et de L'Association des Commissaires d'Ecole Franco-Canadiens tenue à Regina, les 15, 16 et 17 mars 1927.' Oblates Arch.

2999 **Becket**, Lalie
Peach Davis, the Mountie who thrilled two continents. 2d ed. Calgary, Albertan Job Press [ca. 1927] 32p. port. 17cm.

Deals with Indian troubles in 1881. Glenbow

3000 **Bell**, Charles Napier
The old forts of Winnipeg (1738-1927). Winnipeg, Dawson Richardson Pub., Ltd., 1927. 39p. illus. (incl. maps, double facsim.) 22cm. (Hist. & Sc. Soc. of Man., n.s., no.3) Shortt

3001 **Bell**, Charles Napier
A prehistoric copper hook. Winnipeg, Dawson Richardson Pub., Ltd., 1927. 8p. illus. 22cm. (Hist. & Sc. Soc. of Man., n.s., no.2) Shortt

3002 **Bothwell**, Jessie (Robson)
A health to Regina. [Regina?] 1927. cover-title, 20p. 17cm.

'Women's Canadian Club historical first prizewinning essay in Regina contest.' Glenbow

3003 **Bozyk**, Pantelemon
Tserkov Ukrayintsiv v Kanadi [The Church of the Ukrainians in Canada] Winnipeg, 1927. 335p. illus. 21 1/2cm. Not seen. Select

3004 **Calgary Prophetic Bible Institute**
The Calgary Prophetic Bible Institute [calendar and prospectus] Calgary [1927] 32p. illus., port. 23cm.

William Aberhart, president and founder. Glenbow

3005 **Calgary**. Wood's Christian Homes
A narrative of facts relative to work done for Christ in connection with Wood's Christian Homes for orphans and needy children, Bowness Park, Calgary, Alta. (Formerly of Olds) [Calgary, 1927] cover-title, [8]p. illus., port. 23cm. Glenbow

3006 **Canada**. Department of the Interior
Dominion lands. Hand-book for the information of the public. Ottawa, The Department, 1927. 48p. 20cm. Shortt

3007 **Canadian Pacific Railway**
Canada ... [Helsinki, Tilgmannin Kirjapaino, 1927] 46p. illus. 22cm.

Same pamphlet as seen in other Scandinavian libraries; cover picture of a farmer holding a pitchfork. Finland

3008 **Canadian Pacific Railway**
Canada. [Kobenhavn, Triers, 1927] 72p. illus. 21 1/2cm.

In double column with each column having a page number. Cover illustration of a farmer with a pitchfork in front of a prosperous prairie town. Denmark

3009 **Canadian Pacific Railway**
Opportunity in Canada. Montreal [1927] 72p. illus. 23 1/2cm.

A collection of success stories of immigrants of various nationalities who settled in the Prairie Provinces. U. of A.

3010 **Canadian Wheat Pool**
The truth about grain prices. [Winnipeg, 1927?] cover-title, 8p. graph. 26cm. Glenbow

3011 **Catley**, Elaine M[aud (Clark)]
Ecstacy and other poems. Toronto, Ryerson Press, 1927. 8p. 22cm. (Ryerson poetry chap-books) Not seen. Can. Cat.

3012 **Catley**, Elaine M[aud (Clark)]
Star dust and other poems. Calgary, The Author [1927] 30p. Watters

3013 **Clearwater, Man.** Women's Institute
Clearwater, 1876-1885; being some record of the life and times of Clearwater, Manitoba, from 1876 to 1885. [Pilot Mound, Pilot Mound Sentinel Print, 1927] cover-title, [8]p. illus. 19cm.

Illustration on front and back covers. Compiled by Miss Elna Collins and Miss Ethel Coulthard, March 1927. Man. Leg.

3014 **Cochin**, Louis
Reminiscences ... A veteran missionary of the Cree Indians and a prisoner in Poundmaker's camp in 1885 ... [Battleford, Canadian North-West Historical Society, 1927] 75p. illus. (incl. ports.) 23cm. (Canadian North-West Hist. Soc., v.1, no.2) Shortt

3015 **Davisson**, Walter P.
Pooling wheat in Canada. Ottawa, Graphic Publishers, 1927. 275p. incl. illus., plates, map, tables, diagrs. front., plates, ports. (part fold.) facsim. 23cm. U. of S.

3016 **Douglas**, Mrs. John
Poundmaker's old stamping ground. Being a paper submitted ... in the recent competition under the auspices of the Regina Women's Canadian Club. [Battleford, 1927] caption-title, 6 (i.e. 7) l. 27cm.

Cutknife, Sask. Shortt

3017 **Edmonton.** First Presbyterian Church
Souvenir to commemorate the completion of the fortieth year of the ministry of Rev. D.S. McQueen, B.A., D.D., LL.D. in First Presbyterian Church, Edmonton, Alberta, June 27th, 1887–June 26th, 1927. [Edmonton, 1927] cover-title, 8p. illus. (incl. ports.) 18cm. Sask. Arch.

3018 **Eggleston**, Wilfrid
Prairie moonlight and other lyrics. Privately printed, 1927. 24p. 23cm. Shortt

3019 **Elliott**, T[homas] R[ose]
Hugh Layal; a romance of the up country. New York, Macmillan, 1927. xii, 263p. 19 1/2cm.

A novel about the Red River Settlement. L.C.

3020 **The Farmers' Educational League**
Manifesto ... [n.p., 1927?] caption-title, [4]p. 22cm.

Issued by G.H. Williams, Semans, Sask. At end of manifesto: Left Wing General Convention, Saskatoon, July 12-13-14, 1927. All radicals come.

3021 **Farquharson**, Mrs. James
Recollections of a pioneer minister and his work, by his wife. [n.p., 1927] cover-title, 34p. mounted port. 23cm.

The biography of a Presbyterian minister in Manitoba. United College

3022 **Grande Prairie, Alta.** Board of Trade
Facts worth knowing about the famous Grande Prairie district in the Peace River district. [Grande Prairie, The Herald, 1927] 32p. illus. 23cm. Paging includes advertising. Alta. Leg.

3023 **Hales**, B[enjamin] J[ones]
Prairie birds. Toronto, Macmillan, 1927. xv, 334p. illus. 20cm. Winnipeg

3024 **Hasell**, F[rances] H[atton] Eva
Through Western Canada in a caravan. 2d ed. Westminster, Society for the Propagation of the Gospel in Foreign Parts, 1927. vii, 254p. front., plates. 19cm.

Describes Miss Hasell's second, third, and fourth summers driving a Sunday School van in rural districts. The summer of 1922 was spent in the Calgary diocese, that of 1923 in the Edmonton diocese, and the fourth summer in British Columbia. Shortt

3025 **Healy**, W[illiam] J[oseph]
Winnipeg's early days. A short historical sketch ... And twelve full color prints of early Winnipeg scenes with introduction and descriptive titles, by G.A. Stovel. Winnipeg, Stovel Co., Ltd. [c1927] 3p.l., 9-59p. incl. col. plates. 27cm. Man. Leg.

3026 **Innes**, Campbell, ed.
Canon E.K. Matheson, D.D., Saskatchewan's first graduate; being a history of the development of the Church of England in northwestern Saskatchewan ... [Battleford, Canadian North-West Historical Society, 1927] 86p. illus. (incl. ports.) 23cm. (Canadian North-West Hist. Soc., v.1, no.3)

Articles by several contributors. Shortt

3027 **Kilroe**, William G.B.
Souvenir of Turner Valley oil field, Alberta. [Calgary, 1927] cover-title, [16]p. illus., fold. plates, map. 13 x 17cm.

Chiefly illustrations. Glenbow

3028 **Maclean,** John
McDougall of Alberta; a life of Rev. John McDougall, D.D., pathfinder of empire and prophet of the plains. Toronto [Ryerson Press, 1927] xii, 282p. front., plates, ports. 19 1/2cm. Shortt

3029 **Marwayne, Alta.** Board of Trade
Marwayne, Alberta, Canada, a district which affords splendid opportunities for grain growing or mixed farming. Lloydminster, Lloydminster Times [1927?] folder. (6p.) 16cm. Glenbow

3030 **Mikkelsen,** C.
Canada som fremtidsland; Danske udvandreres vilkaar. Kobenhavn, H. Aschehong & Co., 1927. 126, [1]p. plates. 22cm. Sweden

3031 **Moore,** Irene
Valiant La Vérendrye. Quebec, King's Printer, 1927. 382p. 19cm.

This biography, designed for juvenile readers, was awarded a prize in a historical essay contest sponsored by the Quebec government. U. of A.

3031A **Moose Jaw.** Board of Trade
Moose Jaw, Saskatchewan, Canada, the buckle of the greatest wheat belt in the world. Souvenir of the First Annual Convention of the United Farmers of Canada, Saskatchewan Section. [Moose Jaw, 1927] folder. (26p. in card cover) chiefly illus. 16 x 9cm. Glenbow

3032 **Moose Jaw, Sask.** Moose Jaw Celebration Committee
Diamond jubilee of the Confederation of Canada, sixty years of Canadian progress, 1867-1927. [Moose Jaw, 1927] 80p. illus., ports. 23cm.

On cover: ... 1867-1927. Souvenir programme. Moose Jaw's diamond jubilee celebration, Friday, Saturday and Sunday, July 1, 2 and 3, 1927. Glenbow

3033 **Northwest Grain Dealers' Association**
Facts on grain marketing. Winnipeg [1927] cover-title, 30p. 22 1/2cm.

Arguments against the wheat pools. U. of S.

3034 **Palmer,** [Sir] F[rederick]
Hudson Bay. Report on the selection of a terminal port for the Hudson Bay railway. October, 1927. [London, 1927?] 42p. front., illus., plates, maps (part fold.) 33cm. Shortt

3035 **Poland.** Ministry of Labour and Social Welfare
Wskazowki dla wychodźców do Kanady. Warsaw, 1927. 56p. fold. map. 15cm. (Mala biblioteczka emigranta Polskiego, no.2)

Editions with several more pages but without the map were published in 1928 and 1929. Title in English: Information on emigration to Canada. Poland

3036 **Reid,** Mrs. J.A.
The neighborhood of Battleford by an old time resident. Being a paper submitted ... in the recent competition under the auspices of the Regina Women's Canadian Club. [Battleford, 1927] caption-title, 10, [1] l. 28cm. Shortt

3037 **Saskatchewan.** University
... Student verse. Saskatoon [1927-39] 9v. 20 1/2cm. Shortt

3038 **Saskatoon.** Men of the city
Narratives of Saskatoon, 1882-1912. Prepared by a committee of the Historical Association of Saskatoon. [Saskatoon] University [of Saskatchewan] Book-Store [1927] 96p. incl. front., illus. 22 1/2cm. Shortt

3039 **Scandinavian-American Line**
Breve og avisartikler fra Danske i Kanada. Kobenhavn, Fr. G. Knudtzons [1927] 45p. 15 1/2cm.

Letters and articles by Danes living in Western Canada. Denmark

3040 **Scandinavian-American Line**
Käsikirja henkilöille, jotka aikovat siirtyä Kanadaan. [Kobenhavn, Fr. G. Knudtzons, 1927?] cover-title, 15p. illus., col. double map. 23cm.

Finnish emigration pamphlet though printed in Denmark. Finland

3041 **United Grain Growers' Limited**
A farmers' company comes of age ... Winnipeg, The Public Press [1927] 71p. illus. 28 1/2cm.

Special annual report issued to mark the 21st anniversary of the company. Shortt

3042 **Wade,** M[ark] S[weeten]
Mackenzie of Canada; the life and adventures of Alexander Mackenzie, discoverer. Edinburgh, Blackwood & Sons, Ltd., 1927. xii, 332p. incl. illus. (maps) geneal. tables. front. (port.) plates. 22 1/2cm. Map on front lining-paper. Shortt

3043 **Wallace,** James Nevin
The passes of the Rocky Mountains along the Alberta boundary. Calgary, The Historical Society of Calgary, 1927. cover-title, 8p. 25cm. Glenbow

3044 **Wallis,** J.B.
A colour key to the Manitoban butterflies. (Rev. ed.) [Winnipeg] Natural History Society of Manitoba, 1927. 31p. 25cm. Glenbow

3045 **Winnipeg.** Augustine Church
Augustine Church, Winnipeg, 1887-1927, fortieth anniversary. Winnipeg, The Church, 1927. 32p. front., illus. 23cm. Victoria College

3046 **Winnipeg.** Ukrainian Orthodox Cathedral
Ukrainskiy pravoslawniy sobor Sv. Pokrovy u Winnipegu. Winnipeg, 1927. 30p. illus. 23cm. Not seen. Private information

3047 **Woollacott,** Arthur P[hilip]
Mackenzie and his voyageurs, by canoe to the Arctic and the Pacific, 1789-93. Toronto, J.M. Dent & Sons, 1927. x, 237p. illus. (map) plates. 20 1/2cm. Shortt

3048 **Wrong,** [Humphrey] Hume
Sir Alexander Mackenzie. Toronto, Macmillan Co. of Canada, 1927. 3p.l., 171p. front. (port.) 18 1/2cm. (Canadian men of action, no.4) L.C.

3049 **Alberta Co-operative Wheat Producers Limited**
Pooling Alberta's wheat. Calgary, 1928. 63, [1]p. illus. 22 1/2cm.
Glenbow

3050 Alexander Macdonald; a tribute. Compiled with the kind assistance of Principal John MacKay, Rev. Daniel L. Oliver and Professor Frederick W. Kerr. [Winnipeg, Bulman Bros., 1928] [39]p. incl. ports. 21cm.

Tributes to a prominent Winnipeg businessman, founder of Macdonald's Consolidated.
Glenbow

3051 **[Anonymous]**
Zum Andenken an das Silberne Jubiläum der St. Peters-Kolonie, 1903-28. Münster, Sask., 1928. ... Not seen. Lehmann

3052 **Baker**, Edna
Prairie place names. Toronto, Ryerson Press, 1928. 28p. 18 1/2cm. (Ryerson Can. hist. readers) U. of S.

3053 **Ball**, Augustus H[arry]
Rovers of the valley. London, Dent, 1928. vii, 248p.

Juvenile fiction. Br. Mus.

3054 **Bell**, Charles Napier
The earliest fur traders on the upper Red River and Red Lake, Minn. (1783-1810) A paper read before the Society. Winnipeg, Grain Trade Press, 1928. 16p. incl. map. 21 1/2cm. (Hist. & Sc. Soc. of Man., n.s., no.1) Shortt

3055 **Bindloss**, Harold
The broken net. London, Ward, Locke & Co., 1928. 256p. 19cm.

A novel of the Canadian prairies. Glenbow

3056 **Booth**, J[ohn] F[ranklin]
... Co-operative marketing of grain in Western Canada. Washington, U.S. Govt. Print. Off., 1928. cover-title, 116p. illus., maps, diagrs. 23 1/2cm. (U.S. Dept. of Agriculture. Technical bulletin, no.63) L.C.

3057 **Borel, André**
Croquis du Far-West canadien; gens, bêtes, choses, travaux. Paris, Editions Victor Attinger, 1928. 225p., 1 l. 19cm.

The sketches are based on the author's experiences as a homesteader in the Medicine Hat district during the years 1913 to 1917. Edmonton

3058 **Bryce**, Peter H[enderson]
The value to Canada of the continental immigrant; a series of articles. [Ottawa? 1928] cover-title, 56p. 23cm.

Most of the articles relate to settlements in Western Canada. Private copy

3059 **Buffalo Child Long Lance**
Long Lance, with foreword by Irwin S. Cobb. New York, Cosmopolitan Book Corp., 1928. xv, 1 l., 278p. front., plates, ports. 20 1/2cm.

Went through at least four printings. London edition with different paging by Faber & Gwyer. A German edition was published in Leipzig the following year.
U. of A. (Extension)

3060 **Burpee,** Lawrence J[ohnstone]
Two western adventurers: Alexander Henry and Peter Pond. Toronto, Ryerson Press, 1928. 28p. 19cm. (Ryerson Can. hist. readers) U. of A.

3061 **Canada.** Department of Immigration and Colonization
Kanada; Nový domov. Ottawa, 1928. 29p. col. double map. 12cm.

Czech title translated: Canada, new home. In the form of questions and answers. Naprstek

3062 **Canada.** Geographic Board
Place-names of Alberta. Ottawa, King's Printer, 1928. 138p. fold. map. 25cm. U. of S.

3063 **Canadian Legion.** Saskatchewan Command. Committee on Immigration
Report. Regina, Leader Publishing Co., Ltd., 1928. cover-title, 15p. 25cm. Shortt

3064 **Canadian National Railways**
Familiers bosaettelse i det Vestlige Canada. Kobenhavn, 1928. cover-title, 7, [1]p. 17cm. Denmark

3065 **Canadian Pacific Railway**
Arbetstillfällen och jördforvarv i Canada. Göteborg, Isacsons, 1928. cover-title, 14, [1]p. illus. 21 1/2cm. Sweden

3066 **Canadian Pacific Railway**
Canada. [Kobenhavn, Triers, 1928?] 72p. illus., fold. map. 21 1/2cm.

In double column with each column having a page number. Grey cover without any illustrations. Denmark

3067 **Canadian Pacific Railway**
The prairie farms of Western Canada as the camera sees them. [Montreal, 1928] [20]p. of illus. 14 x 22cm.

Also published with title: Western Canada as the camera sees it. Glenbow

3068 **Compagnie de la Baie d'Hudson**
Société anonyme. Au capital de 250000 francs. Divisé en 500 actions de 500 francs chacune. Siège social à Paris. Statuts. Paris, Imprimerie du Palais, 1928. 20p. 23 1/2cm.

Satire. H.B.C.

3069 **Constantin-Weyer,** Maurice
Un homme se penche sur son passé. Paris, Rieder, 1928. 228p. 19cm.

This novel received the Goncourt award. Several editions by various publishers have appeared in Paris. English editions under the title 'A man scans his past' have been printed by Macmillan of Toronto in 1929, by Macaulay of New York in the same year, and by Holt of New York in 1933. Hungarian, Slovenian, Czech, and Swedish translations have been published. L.C.

3070 **Culliton,** John Thomas
Assisted emigration and land settlement with special reference to Western Canada. Montreal, The Federated Press, Ltd. [1928] 77p. 22cm. (McGill University. Economic studies, no.9) U. of S.

3071 Dodatkowe wskazówki dla wychodźców, wyjeżdżajaeych do Kanady w roku 1928. Warsaw, Druk. Panstwowa [1928] 17, [1]p. 14 1/2 x 10 1/2cm.

Title in English: Additional hints on emigration when on the point of embarkation for Canada. Poland

3072 **Fortin**, Octave
Sixty years and after; an historical sketch of Holy Trinity parish, Winnipeg, written for the most part by the late Venerable Archdeacon Fortin, also an outline of present day activities and possible future developments by Rev. C. Carruthers. Winnipeg, Dawson Richardson, 1928. 138p. illus., plates (1 double fold.) ports., facsims. Man. Leg.

3073 **Fricke**, Arnold
Geschichtlicher Überblick des zwanzigjährigen Bestehens des Canada-Distrikts der Ev.-Luth. Synode von Ohio und andern Staaten. Regina, 1928. 28p. Not seen. Lehmann

3074 **Gardner-Smith**, E.
The call of the West, and other poems. [Calgary, S. Burnard, 1928?] [1], 32p. 18cm. Glenbow

3075 **Gill**, Frank P.
Rhapsody; songs and lyrics. Calgary, Star Printing [1928?] 46p. Watters

3076 **Gockel**, Anton
Die Landwirtschaft in den Prärieprovinzen West-Kanadas. Berlin, Paul Parey, 1928. 140p. incl. maps, tables. 25 1/2cm. U. of A.

3076A **Gordon**, Charlotte
Red gold, a true story of an Englishwoman's development in the West. Vancouver [McBeath-Campbell Ltd.] 1928. 265p. 19cm.

Fiction or semi-fiction, based on the author's experience in the Calgary area. Northland

3077 **Grayson**, Ethel Kirk
Willow smoke. New York, Vinal, 1928. 4p.l., 343, [1]p. 20cm.

Fiction, set in a small Saskatchewan community. Can. Novel

3078 **Grove**, Frederick Philip
Our daily bread, a novel. New York, Macmillan Co., 1928. v, 390p. 20cm.

A prairie farmer's struggle to keep his family on the land. U. of S.

3079 **Hasell**, Frances Hatton Eva
Caravanning through prairie and mountain in Canada. London, S.P.G. Office [1928?] cover-title, 16p. 19cm. ('The King's Business' series) Glenbow

3079A **Hudson's Bay Company**
The Hudson's Bay Company will expose to sale by auction, at their house, Garlick Hill, on Monday and Tuesday, the 30th and 31st January, 1928, at ten o'clock precisely, the following goods ... [London, 1928] [6], 189p. plates. 36 x 17cm.

Copy 243 of a numbered souvenir edition containing reproductions of front pages of auction sales of 1828.

'Presented by the Governor and Company of Adventurers of England trading into Hudson's Bay to D'Alton C. Coleman, Esq. to commemorate the first sale by auction held in their new house on the 30th and 31st January, 1928.' Glenbow

3080 **Innes**, Campbell, ed.
The story of the press ... [Battleford, Canadian North-West Historical Society, 1928] 106p. illus. (incl. ports.) 23cm. (Canadian North-West Hist. Soc., v.1, no.4, pt.1)

Contains sketches of the beginnings of the Nor'-Wester, Saskatchewan Herald, Prince Albert Times, Macleod Gazette, Calgary Herald, Regina Leader, Medicine Hat Times, Lethbridge Times; also H.A. Kennedy's experiences as a war correspondent in 1885. Shortt

3081 **Kennedy**, Howard Angus
The North-West Rebellion. Toronto, Ryerson Press [c1928] 32p. illus. 18 1/2cm. (Ryerson Can. hist. readers) Shortt

3082 **Kennedy**, Howard Angus
Origin of the Canadian Pacific Railway. Toronto, Ryerson Press [c1928] 30p. illus. 18 1/2cm. (Ryerson Can. hist. readers) Shortt

3082A **Kritzwiser**, H.H.
Ten thousand suckers – the Ku Klux Klan in Saskatchewan. Regina, 1928. ...

Three Americans, members of the KKK, or pretending to be, toured the province and accepted personal memberships, then absconded. Private information

3083 **Lloyd**, Cecil Richard Francis
Sunlight and shadow. Toronto, Hunter-Rose, 1928. 83p.

A Manitoba writer who is said to have written four slim volumes of poetry and one of prose essays. Nat. Lib.

3084 **Lloyd**, George Exton
The building of the nation: natural increase and immigration. [A paper read before the Grand Orange Lodge of British America at Edmonton, Alberta, July 26th, 1928. Prince Albert, National Association of Canada, 1928] 29p. 18cm. Glenbow

3084A **Lloydall-Bee**, Alfred
History of the parish of St. Peter, Entwistle, Alberta. [n.p., 1928] cover-title, 16p. plates, ports. 18cm. Glenbow

3085 **Longstreth**, Thomas Morris
The silent force, scenes from the life of the mounted police of Canada. London, Philip Allan & Co., Ltd., 1928. xiv, 383p. front., illus., plates, ports., fold. maps. 23cm. Shortt

3086 **Mathieu**, [Olivier Elzéar]
Gesta dei [Strange fire]. Regina [1928] ... Not seen.

Some account of the day of Monseigneur Mathieu. Amtmann – 277-336

3087 **McWilliams**, Margaret (Stovel)
Manitoba milestones. Toronto, J.M. Dent & Sons, Ltd. [1928] xiv, 249p. col. front., illus. (incl. maps) plates (part col.) ports. 20 1/2cm. Winnipeg

3088 **O'Hagan**, Thomas
Father Morice. Toronto, Ryerson Press, 1928. 31p. 18 1/2cm. (Ryerson Can. hist. readers) Shortt

3089 Not used.

3090 **On-to-the-Bay Association**
The Hudson Bay Route, Western Canada's short outlet to the markets of the world; progress and possibilities, no.1. Winnipeg, The Association, 1928. ... Not seen. Can. Cat.

3091 **Paizs**, Ödön
Magyarok Kanadában (Egy most készülö országról) Budapest, Athenaeum irod. és nyomdai r.-t. [1928] 218p. illus. (map) plates. 18cm. On cover: Korunk mesterei.

Describes all Hungarian settlements in the Prairie Provinces. Shortt

3092 **Patton**, Harald Smith
Grain growers' co-operation in Western Canada. Cambridge, Harvard University Press, 1928. xix, 471p. 22 1/2cm. (Harvard economic studies, v.32) U. of S.

3093 **Peace River, Alta.** Board of Trade
The Peace River country. A booklet of information in condensed form on the topography, development and opportunities for settlement in the most famous farming district in Western Canada. Prepared and issued under direction of the Peace River Board of Trade and the municipal districts of Peace and Fairview. [Peace River, Record Printing Co., Ltd., n.d.] 31, [1]p. illus. 21 1/2cm. Glenbow

3094 **Peace River and Western Development**
Grimshaw district, Peace municipality and the Battle River prairie. Some facts concerning settlement and farming conditions in one of the choicest sections of the Peace River country. Peace River, The Record [1928] cover-title, 12p. illus., map. 21cm. Glenbow

3095 **Peterson**, Charles Walter Christian
Fruits of the earth; a story of the Canadian plains. Ottawa [1928] 304p. Not seen.

Fiction. R.E.S.

3096 **Pick**, Harry
Next year; a semi-historical account of the exploits and exploitations of the far-famed Barr colonists, who, led by an unscrupulous Church of England parson, adventured deep into the wilderness of Canada's great North-West in the early days of the twentieth century. Toronto, Ryerson Press, 1928. xxii, 254p. 19 1/2cm.

Tells the story of the Barr colonists in the form of fiction. Saskatoon

3097 **Pietsch**, Johannes
Bei den Deutschen in Westkanada. Hünfeld, Oblaten der unbefleckten Jungfrau Maria, 1928. 84p. plates, fold. map. 20cm. (added t.-p.: Blüten und Früchte vom heimatlichen und auswärtigen Missionsfelde, dargeboten von den Oblaten der unbefleckten Jungfrau Maria. nr.15) L.C.

3097A **Proby**, William C[arysfort]
Man hunters of the north; being a recital of Captain W.C. Proby's twenty years in the Royal Northwest Mounted Police. As told to J.E. Hansell. Tacoma, Wash., Tacoma Star Pub. Co., 1928. 4p.l., 152p. port., plate. 18cm. Glenbow

3098 **Prud'homme**, L[ouis] A[rthur]
Monseigneur Noël-Joseph Ritchot; vicaire général protonotaire apostolique, curé de la paroisse de Saint-Norbert, 1825-1905. Winnipeg, Canadian Publishers, 1928. 239p. front., plates, ports. 24cm. Bibliothèque de St-Boniface

3099 **Ray**, J[oseph] E[dward]
Things seen in Canada; a description of life in town & country, the glorious scenery & boundless wealth of this great Dominion. London, Seeley, Service, 1928. 153p. plates. 16cm. (The Things seen series)

Several chapters cover Western Canada. Glenbow

3100 **Reeve**, George Joseph
La Vérendrye. Toronto, Ryerson Press, 1928. 32p. map. 19cm. (Ryerson Can. hist. readers) Ryerson

3101 **Regina**. Board of Trade
Regina, Canada. [Regina] 1928. cover-title, 31, [1]p. illus. 23cm. Glenbow

3102 **Roman Catholic Church**. Catechisms. Cree
Catéchisme en langue crise. [Hobbema, Journal Cris, 1928] 93p. illus. 15 1/2cm.

Translated into Cree syllabic by Father Moulin. Oblates Arch.

3103 **Rose**, Hilda
The stump farm, a chronicle of pioneering. With a foreword by Samuel Eliot. Boston, Little, Brown, & Co., 1928. xi, 178p. front., plate, ports. 20 1/2cm.

A series of letters written to friends between 1919 and 1927, and first published in the Atlantic Monthly in 1927. About a third of the book deals with her Canadian experience. Edmonton

3104 **Sabourin**, J[oseph] Ad[onias]
L'évolution dans les écoles du Manitoba; matérialisme et athéisme ... [St-Boniface, 1928] p.137-85, 1 l. 19cm. (Etudes et conférences, v.2) Shortt

3105 **Sabourin**, J[oseph] Ad[onias]
La morale et le nouveau programme des écoles primaires au Manitoba. Québec, L'Université Laval, 1928. 23p. Man. Leg.

3106 **Sutherland**, Alex[ander] H.
Manitoba memories. [Winnipeg, Stovel & Co., Ltd., 1928] 2p.l., 35p. 18cm.

Poetry. Man. Leg.

3107 **Tuckwell**, David Grieve
The kind of old countrymen Canada can absorb. [n.p., 1928] cover-title, 11p. illus. (port.) 16cm. Shortt

3108 **Tuckwell,** David Grieve
Three English emigrants who became premiers of provinces. [n.p., 1928] cover-title, 10p. illus. (port.) 16cm.

Hon. John Oliver of B.C., Hon. Chas. Dunning of Sask., and Hon. Herbert Greenfield of Alta. Shortt

3109 **Tull (G.F.) & Arden, Limited**
Manual of listed and unlisted oil companies of Alberta. April 1928. Calgary, 1928. 14p. 15cm. Glenbow

3110 **Watson,** Robert
The Hudson's Bay Company. Toronto, Ryerson, 1928. 32p. 19cm. (Ryerson Can. hist. readers) Ryerson

3111 **Watson,** Robert
Lower Fort Garry, a history of the stone fort. Winnipeg, The Hudson's Bay Company, 1928. 2p.l., 69p. incl. illus., plates. front., fold. plan. 21cm. Shortt

3112 **Winnipeg Evening Tribune**
Do you know Manitoba? [Winnipeg, The Tribune, 1928?] cover-title, 43p. illus., diagrs. 23cm. Man. Leg.

3113 [**Wollschläger,** Alfred]
Mit zwanzig Dollar in den wilden Westen; Schicksale aus Urwald, Steppe, Busch und Stadt, von A.E. Johann [pseud.] Berlin, Ullstein [c1928] 261p. incl. maps. front., plates. 24cm. Not seen.

Semi-fictional adventures of a German journalist in Western Canada. L.C.

3114 **Adshead,** H[erbert] B[ealey]
Pioneer tales and other human stories. [Calgary, Alberta Job Press Ltd., 1929] 70, [1]p. illus. (incl. ports.) 20cm.

First edition, in 1924, had 48 pages. A copy is in Glenbow. Calgary

3115 Ako ziskat' farmu v Kanade. Prague, Rolnicka'Tisk'rna, 1929. 20, [1]p. illus. 16cm.

Mostly relates to Alberta. Czech

3116 **Ashdown (J.H.) Hardware Co. Ltd.,** Winnipeg
Diamond jubilee ... A short story of the founding of its business, a brief review of the building up of its enormous trade ... together with a brief biography of the late Mr. James Henry Ashdown. [Winnipeg? 1929] 61, [3]p. illus. (incl. ports.) 24cm. Man. Leg.

3117 [**Bergot,** Denys]
Réminiscences d'un pionnier. Jubilé d'argent, St-Brieux, 1904-1929 ... [Cudworth, Sask., The Progress, 1929] 82p. illus. (incl. ports.) 25 1/2cm. Text in French and English.

Written in collaboration with Rev. Lucien Lecomte and Louis Demay. Shortt

3118 **Boyle,** James E[rnest]
Marketing Canada's wheat. Winnipeg, Winnipeg Grain Exchange, 1929. 63p. 23cm. Can. Cat.

3119 **Brendel,** John
Sammlung deutscher Volkslieder der Russlanddeutschen in Amerika im nordwestlichen Teil der Vereinigten Staaten und Kanada. Bismarck, N.D., 1929. Part I. Not seen. Lehmann

3120 **Bugnet,** Georges [Charles Jules]
Nipsya; translated from the French by Constance Davies Woodrow. New York, L. Carrier & Co. [c1929] vi p., 1 l., 9-285, [1]p. 21cm.

Fiction. The heroine is a half-breed girl of the Peace River country. L.C.

3121 [**Bulloch,** Ellen Guthrie]
Pioneers of the Pipestone. [n.p., 1929] 63p. illus. 22cm.

Relates to the Pipestone River district in Manitoba. Man. Leg.

3122 **Burns,** W[illiam] C.
Twenty years of thrilling adventures in the silent places of the North, by W.C. Burns (blind) [with the assistance of Ruby Erwin. Edmonton, Douglas Printing, 1929?] [10], 72p. (incl. 6 col. pages of illus., ports.) 22cm.

Advertising matter, p.49-72. Glenbow

3123 **Burpee,** Lawrence J[ohnstone]
Hudson Bay to the Blackfoot country; journals of Hendry and Cocking. Toronto, Ryerson Press, 1929. 26p. 19cm. (Ryerson Can. hist. readers) Ryerson

3124 **Calgary.** Board of Trade
A trip through Turner Valley with the Young Men's Section of the Calgary Board of Trade, Sept. 12th, 1929. [n.p., n.d.] [6]p. double plan, table. 20cm.

Paging includes p.2 and 3 of cover. Glenbow

3125 **Canada.** Department of Immigration and Colonization
Land settlement in Canada. Winning through; stories of life on Canadian farms told by new British settlers. Ottawa, 1929. 46p. illus. 23cm.

Most of the letters are from settlers on the prairies. C.P.R.

3126 **Canada.** Parliament. House of Commons. Select Standing Committee on privileges and elections
Evidence and report in respect to the Commissioner's reports on the alleged existence of corrupt or illegal practices in the election held in the electoral district of Athabaska in the Province of Alberta, on the 29th of October, 1925. Ottawa, 1929. 2p.l., 83p. 25cm.

The chairman was J.J. Denis. L.C.

3127 **Canadian National Railways**
Canada. [Oslo, 1929?] 80p. illus., fold. map. 21 1/2cm.

On cover: Picture of farmer driving five horses pulling a harrow. Contains information on Norwegian settlements in Western Canada. Norway

3128 **Canadian Pacific Railway**
Canada. [Göteborg? 1929?] cover-title, 36p. illus., fold. map. 22cm.

In double column. The cover has a picture of a man cutting grain with a binder. Sweden

3129 **Church**, H[erbert] E.
An emigrant in the Canadian Northwest. London, Methuen & Co. [1929] ix, 134p. front., plates. 19 1/2cm.

See Entry 1096. Shortt

3130 **Constantin-Weyer**, Maurice
Clairière, récits du Canada. Paris, Stock, 1929. 4p.l., 11-253p., 1 l. plates. 19cm. (On cover: Les livres de nature, 8)

An English translation under title 'Forest wild,' was published by G. Routledge in London, 1932. U. of S.

3131 **Dahlin**, Georg L[udwig]
Canada, skisser och glimtar från en resa. Stockholm, Wahlstrom & Widstrand [1929] 189p. plates, fold. map. 22cm.

Approximately one-third relates to the Prairies. Sweden

3132 **Danylchuk**, Ivan
Svitaye Den. Winnipeg, 1929. 56p. Not seen.

Poetry in Ukrainian. Kirkconnell

3133 **England**, Robert
The central European immigrant in Canada. Toronto, Macmillan Co., 1929. xvii, 238p. illus. (incl. maps) diagr. 20cm. U. of S.

3134 **Faulds**, Mary Jeffrey
Pa-Ke-Noh-Ka, the winner; a dramatization of the life of Rev. John McDougall. (In Stephenson, A.D.S. That they may be one. Toronto [c1929] 19cm. p.[155]-197)

'Based on McDougall of Alberta by Maclean.' Glenbow

3135 **Garrioch**, A[lfred] C[ampbell]
A hatchet mark in duplicate. Toronto, Ryerson Press [c1929] vii p., 1 l., [3]-282p. 19 1/2cm.

Experiences of a missionary in the Peace River district in the 1880's. Shortt

3136 **Heeney**, [William] Bertal
The founding of Rupert's Land and its first bishop. [Winnipeg, Douglass-McIntyre Printing & Binding Co., 1929] 33p., 1 l. 15 1/2cm. Sask. Arch.

3137 **Howay**, F[rederick] W[illiam] ed.
Builders of the West, a book of heroes. Toronto, Ryerson Press [1929] v, 251p. illus. 21cm. Shortt

3138 **Hudson's Bay Company Overseas Settlement**
Brogborough Park Farm. London [1929?] cover-title, 12p. illus. 22cm.

The company maintained a farm in Bedfordshire to train prospective emigrants in agriculture; includes some short letters from pupils who had gone to Western Canada. H.B.C.

3139 **Hull**, J[ohn] T[homas]
The history of co-operation. Regina, Saskatchewan Wheat Pool, 1929. ... Not seen. Can. Cat.

3140 **Hunter**, A[lexander] J[ardine]
A friendly adventure; the story of the United Church Mission among New Canadians at Teulon, Manitoba. Toronto, United Church, Board of Home Missions [c1929] xii, 145p. fronts. (ports.) plates. 20cm. Man. Leg.

3141 **Irwin**, W[illiam] A[rthur]
The Canadian Wheat Pool; a series of articles on the most colossal commercial enterprise of its kind in the world. [Winnipeg] Issued by the Wheat Pool Publicity Department, 1929. 24p. Not seen. C.H.R., 1930

3142 **Janicki**, Stefan
Kanadyjski syndykat sprzedazy pszenicy. (Odbitka z Kwartalnika Nauk. Inst. Emigracyjnego.) Warszawa, Nakl. Naukowego Instytutu Emigracyjnego, 1929. 90p. tables.

Imprint date on cover: 1928. Study on the Canadian Wheat Pool. Poland

3143 **Jefferson**, Robert
Fifty years on the Saskatchewan; being a history of the Cree Indian domestic life and the difficulties which led to serious agitation and conflict of 1885 in the Battleford locality as written by Robert Jefferson after fifty years' research and service. With a foreword by Hon. James G. Gardiner ... Battleford, Canadian North-West Historical Society, 1929. 160p. ports. 23cm. (Canadian North-West Hist. Soc., v.1, no.5) Shortt

3144 **Loeb**, Harold A.
Tumbling mustard. New York, H. Liveright, 1929. 405p. 20cm. Not seen.

Fiction. The central character is 'one of three tumble weeds blown by chance into the frontier town of Medicine Hat.' L.C.

3145 **McLean**, Mrs. Arthur
History of Holy Trinity Church from the year 1893 to 1929. Edmonton [1929] cover-title, 9 l. 20 x 28cm.

Typescript. Private copy

3146 **Mazurkiewicz**, Roman
Polskie wychodźtwo i osadnictwo w Kanadzie. Warsaw, Naukowy Instytut Emigracyjny [1929] 146, [1]p. plates, fold. maps. 23cm.

Title in English: Polish immigration and colonization in Canada. Poland

3147 **Moberly**, Henry John
When fur was king; in collaboration with William Bleasdell Cameron; with illustrations by John Innes. Toronto, J.M. Dent & Sons, 1929. 3p.l., vii-xvii, [1], 237p. incl. plates. front., port., fold. map. 21cm. Shortt

3148 **Morice**, A[drien] G[abriel]
L'Ouest canadien. Esquisse géographique, ethnographique, historique et démographique. Neuchâtel, Paul Attinger, 1929. 98p. illus. 24cm. Shortt

3149 **Nazaruk**, Osyp
Vchasna vesna v Piwnichniy Alberti [Early spring in northern Alberta] Lviv, Ukrainian Christian Organization, 1929. 32p. 16cm. Not seen. Private information

3150 **North-German Lloyd Bremen Line**
Canada, anvisningar för emigranttrafik till Canada för finländska agenturer. [Wasa, A.B. Frams, 1929] 15, [1]p. 23cm.

Emigration pamphlet in Swedish. On cover a small framed picture of a binder. Finland

3151 **North-German Lloyd Bremen Line**
Kanada ohjeet suomalaisille siirtolaisliikennettä varten Kanadaan. [Vaasa, o.-y. Fram'in, 1929] 16, [1]p. 23cm.

Emigration pamphlet in Finnish. On cover a small framed picture of a binder. Finland

3152 **The Pas, Man.** Board of Trade
The Pas and Northern Manitoba. The Pas, 1929. 54p. illus., map (on cover) 22 1/2cm.

On cover: The Pas, gateway to Northern Manitoba where opportunities exist. Also a map in colour. Pagination includes advertising. Glenbow

3153 **Polskie Towarzystwo Bratniej Pomocy**, Coleman, Alta.
Konstytucja opracowana na trzeciej konwencji w dniach od 25-go do 28 października 1929 roku w Coleman, Alberta. [Coleman, Alta, n.d.] 64p.

Text in Polish and English. English section has its own title-page. Constitution of the society. Turek

3154 **Sale**, Charles V.
The winter road. [London, 1929] caption-title, 9p. illus., ports., map. 23cm.

The winter road from Lower Fort Garry to York Factory. Glenbow

3155 **Sapiro**, Aaron
100% control by legislation. Address ... [Saskatoon] United Farmers of Canada (Sask. section), Publicity and Research Department [1929] cover-title, 24p. 23cm. Shortt

3155A The Saskatchewan year book 1929. Regina [Western Printers Assoc.] 1929. 204p. illus. 26cm.

Lists members of the professions in the Legislative Assembly; includes statistics of various kinds; short booster articles on various towns and industries; sports highlights; and curiosities such as an anti-K.K.K. article. Northland

3156 **Strang**, Peter
History of missions in southern Saskatchewan. Regina, The Author, 1929. x, 277p. front., port. 19 1/2cm. Maps on end covers.

United Church of Canada. Shortt

3157 **United Farmers of Canada.** Saskatchewan Section
Facts about 100% control. Saskatoon, U.F.C. [1929?] cover-title, 8p. 23cm. Shortt

3158 **Wagner**, Hermann
Von Kueste zu Kueste; bei deutschen Auswanderern in Kanada. Hamburg, Ev. luth Auswanderermission, 1929. 128p. incl. diagrs., tables. maps. 23cm. N.Y.

1929 Bibliography of the Prairie Provinces

3159 **Wallace,** J[ames] N[evin]
The wintering partners on Peace River from the earliest records to the union in 1821; with a summary of the Dunvegan journal, 1806. Ottawa, Thorburn and Abbot, 1929. 139p. fold. map. 23cm. Shortt

3160 **Woodsworth,** James Shaver
Hours that stand apart. [Ottawa, Mutual Press, 1929?] 40p. 19cm.
Author's autograph on title-page. Glenbow

3161 Alberta poetry year book. v.1- 1930- Edmonton, Canadian Authors' Association, Edmonton Branch, 1930- v. 19 1/2cm.
Published annually since 1930. U. of A.

3162 **Alexander,** Mrs. Mary H.T. (Strachan)
Fort Prince of Wales. Toronto, Ryerson Press [c1930] cover-title, 32p. illus. 19cm. (The Ryerson Canadian history readers)
'Bibliography and authorities': p.32. Glenbow

3163 **Beames,** John
An army without banners. Toronto, McClelland, 1930. 4p.l., [3], 301p. 19cm.
Fiction; the growth of prairie society from the pioneering stage. U. of S.

3164 **Beaubier,** Mrs. Ella L.
History of the Grand Chapter of Alberta, Order of the Eastern Star. Lethbridge, 1930. [3], 8-90p. port. 22cm. Glenbow

3165 **Bloomfield,** Leonard
Sacred stories of the Sweet Grass Cree. Ottawa, F.A. Acland, 1930. 2p.l., 346p. 24 1/2cm. (Canada. Geological Survey. Bull. no.60. Anthropological ser., no.11) Shortt

3166 **Borel,** André
Le Robinson de la Red Deer. Paris, Editions Victor Attinger, 1930. 249p., 1 l. 19 1/2cm.
A Swiss immigrant named Fancey recounts his homesteading experiences in the years before World War I in the area north of Medicine Hat. Probably the experiences were those of the author. Edmonton

3167 **British Medical Association**
The place of meeting. A collection of articles on Canada, Manitoba, and Winnipeg prepared for the 98th annual meeting of the British Medical Association at Winnipeg, August 26, 27, 28, 29, 1930. These articles were prepared for, and appeared in, the British Medical Journal and the Canadian Medical Association Journal. [n.p., 1930] 42p. illus. 23cm. Map: inside back cover. Shortt

3168 **Burpee,** Lawrence Johnstone
Sir Sandford Fleming. Toronto, Ryerson Press [c1930] cover-title, 28p. port. 18cm. (Ryerson Canadian history readers)
'Bibliographical note': p.28. Glenbow

3169 **Burt**, Alfred Lefroy
The romance of the Prairie Provinces. Toronto, W.J. Gage, 1930. viii, 262p. illus. U. of A.

3170 Calgary Albertan oil manual. Issue no.1; Feb. 1930. Calgary, Albertan Pub. Co., 1930. 98p. 23 x 10cm.

A directory of oil companies. Advertising matter (xvi col. pages) inserted between p.50 and 51. Glenbow

3171 **Canada.** National Parks Service
Playgrounds of the prairies. [Ottawa, The Department, 193–] cover-title, 24p. illus. 26cm. U. of S.

3171A **Carey**, Douglas [pseud.]
The raven's feather. Ottawa, Graphic Publishers, 1930. 322p. 20cm.

Author's autograph on title-page. Glenbow

3172 **Charette**, Guillaume [J.]
Manitoba jubilee. Account of events which brought about the formation of the province. [n.p., 1930] caption-title, 11p. 23cm. In double column. Man. Leg.

3173 **Church of England.** Missionary Society
Church hospitals in the Canadian mission field of the Church of England in Canada ... Dynevor hospital, Manitoba ... A nursing centre in the Diocese of Edmonton ... Toronto [193–?] self-cover, 19p. Amtmann - 214-123

3174 **Droonberg**, [Otto] Emil [Muschik]
Die Ansiedler in Canada; Roman. Leipzig, Hesse & Becker, 1930. 265p. 19 1/2cm. Not seen. L.C.

3175 **Frémont**, Donatien
Mgr Taché et la naissance du Manitoba. Winnipeg, La Liberté, 1930. 47p. 24cm. U.B.C.

3176 **Friesen**, George P.
The fangs of Bolshevism; or, Friesen-Braun trials in Saskatchewan, 1924-1929, [by] George P. Friesen. [Saskatoon? c1930] 235p. facsims. 22cm.

A story of intrigue which grew until nearly the whole Mennonite community at Rosthern became involved. Braun obtained H.P. Friesen's signature on a piece of paper and above it filled in a promissory note for $5,000. 'An involved and exasperating affair. In my 25 years' experience in law I have never seen the like of it': Mr. Justice H.Y. MacDonald. Shortt

3177 **Gampell**, Sydney S.
Canada and her wheat pool. Winnipeg, Grain Trade News, 1930. 56p. Not seen. Can. Cat.

3178 **Garczynski**, Leon
Co to jest Kanada? Warsaw, Polskie T-Wo Naukowe, 1930. 84, [1]p. 16 1/2cm.

Title in English: What is Canada? Poland

3179 [**Garvin**, Amelia Beers (Warnock)]
Pierre Esprit Radisson, by Katherine Hale. Toronto, Ryerson Press [c1930] cover-title, 28p. illus. 19cm. Glenbow

3180 **Goodge**, S.H.
History of the parish of St. Mary's and outpoints, Wellsdale, Alberta, Canada. [Vermillion, Standard Print, 1930] [8]p. port. 16cm. Glenbow

3181 **Grande Prairie, Alta.** Board of Trade
Interesting facts about Grande Prairie, a progressive town in the famous Grande Prairie district of the Peace River country. Grande Prairie, Grande Prairie Herald, 1930. 40p. illus. 23 1/2cm. Paging includes advertising. Alta. Leg.

3182 **Grove**, Frederick Philip
The yoke of life. Toronto, Macmillan Co., 1930. vi, 355p. 18cm.
A novel of immigrant life in Western Canada. Can. Cat.

3183 **Gruchy**, Lydia E.
The Doukhobors in Canada. Toronto [n.p., 193_] 64p. illus. 18 1/2cm. Northland

3184 **Gunn**, J[ohn] J.
Echoes of the Red. A reprint of some of the early writings of the author depicting pioneer days in the Red River Settlement. Toronto, Macmillan Co., 1930. ix, [1] 246p. illus., plates, 2 ports. (incl. front.) 18 1/2cm. Shortt

3185 **Guttormsson**, Guttormur J[ónsson]
Gaman og alvara. Winnipeg, Columbia Press, 1930. 190p. 19 1/2cm. Not seen.
Icelandic poetry. U. of M.

3186 **Hamilton**, C[harles] F[rederick]
Royal Canadian Mounted Police. Toronto, Ryerson Press, 1930. 28p. 19cm. (Ryerson Can. hist. readers) C.H.R., 1931

3187 **Harrison**, Marjorie
Go West – go wise! A Canadian revelation. Toronto, Longmans, Green & Co., 1930. xii, 308p. front., plates, ports. 29cm.
Nearly half of this book is devoted to the West. U. of S.

3188 **Herzer**, T.O. F[rancis]
Some recent developments in land settlement. An address ... delivered at luncheons tendered to the officers and representatives of the Canada Colonization Association on the occasion of their annual provincial conventions, by the Regina Board of Trade ... and the Calgary Board of Trade ... [n.p., 1930] cover-title, 11p. 21cm. U. of S.

3189 **Imrie**, John M[ills]
Peace River, an empire in the making. Being a series of articles in the Edmonton Journal based in part on a 3,000 mile tour of Alberta's hinterland ... Edmonton, Edmonton Journal, 1930. 32p. 23cm. Vancouver

3190 **Innis**, Harold A[dams]
The fur trade in Canada; an introduction to Canadian economic history. New Haven, Yale University Press, 1930. 7p.l., 444p. plates, map. 24 1/2cm. U. of S.

3191 **Innis**, H[arold] A[dams]
Peter Pond, fur trader and adventurer. Toronto, Irwin & Gordon, 1930. xi, 153p. fold. map. 23 1/2cm. U. of S.

3192 [**Jan**, Alphonse Marie] comp.
Historic St. Albert, Province of Alberta. Mission park. Official guide book. [Edmonton, W.J. McDonough, 193–?] 24p. illus. Calgary

3193 **Jefferson**, Robert
Saskatchewan verse. Battleford, Printed by the Battleford Press [1930?] 108p. port. 19cm. Shortt

3194 **Kitto**, Franklin Hugo
The Edmonton, Prince George, Peace River triangle: an outing trip of exceptional beauty through majestic wonders of Canadian Rockies. Peace River, Alberta, Record Printing Company Ltd. [n.d.] 17p. illus., map. 21cm.

Xerox copy. Glenbow

3195 **Kvaran**, Einar H[jörleifsson] and **Finnbogason**, Gudm[undur] eds.
Vestan um haf. Ljód, leikrit, sögur og ritgerdir eftir Islendinga í Vesturheimi. Valid hafa Einar H. Kvaran og Gudm. Finnbogason. Reykjavík, Bókadeild Menningarsjóds, 1930. lxiv, 736p. illus. (ports.) 22 1/2cm. U. of M.

3196 **La Chance**, Vernon
Diary of Francis Dickens. Kingston, The Jackson Press [1930] cover-title, 23p. 22 1/2cm. (Queen's University. Departments of History and Political and Economic Science. Bull. no.59) Also in Queen's Quarterly, v.37, Spring, 1930, p.64-79.

Dickens, son of the novelist, was in charge of the detachment of N.W.M.P. at Fort Pitt. The diary covers the abandonment of the post and the trip down the Saskatchewan to Battleford. Shortt

3197 **Laut**, Agnes C[hristina]
John Tanner. Toronto, Ryerson Press, 1930. 32p. 18 1/2cm. (Ryerson Can. hist. readers) Dempsey

3198 **Le Chevallier**, Jules [Jean Marie Joseph]
Saint-Laurent de Grandin; a mission & a shrine in the north-west of America ... Vannes, Lafolye & de Lamarzelle, 1930. 111p., 2 l. illus., plates, ports. 23cm. Shortt

3199 **Little**, R[obert] H.
Reminiscences of my pioneering experiences in tsp.7, range 12, Cypress River locality, during the winter of 1879-80. Treherne, Man., The Times, 1930. cover-title, 36p. port. 20cm. In double column. Man. Leg.

3200 **Lord's Day Alliance of Canada**
Sunday conditions in Western Canada; reports of Rev. George Webber for Alberta and British Columbia, and Rev. J.S. Watson for Saskatchewan and Manitoba, for the year 1929. Toronto [1930?] cover-title, 12, [1]p. 22cm. Glenbow

3201 **Loverove**, A.G.
Poems by a Doukhobor. [n.p., 193–?] 16p. 16cm.

'The purport of this little booklet is to reconcile the divergent principles that prevail so among our youth.' U. of S.

3202 **Macdonald**, J[ohn] S[tuart]
The Dominion telegraph. Battleford, Canadian North-West Historical Society, 1930. 64p. illus. (incl. ports.) fold. map. 23cm. (Canadian North-West Hist. Soc., v.1, no.6)

The story of the building and maintenance of the telegraph line from Red River to Edmonton. Shortt

3203 **MacInnes**, C[harles] M[alcolm]
In the shadow of the Rockies. London, Rivingtons, 1930. viii, 347p. plates, ports., plans (1 fold.) fold. maps. 22 1/2cm.

An excellent history of the development of ranching in southern Alberta. Shortt

3204 **McWilliams**, [Margaret (Stovel)]
All along the river, by Mrs. R.F. McWilliams. [Winnipeg, Russell-Lang's Bookshop, 1930] [12]p. illus. 21 1/2cm.

The text of an address tendered to the ladies of the British Medical Association. Saskatoon

3205 **Manitoba.** Provincial Diamond Jubilee Committee
Manitoba's diamond jubilee, July fifteenth, nineteen hundred and thirty. [Winnipeg] Published for the Provincial Diamond Jubilee Committee by the Government of Manitoba [1930] cover-title, 63, [1]p. illus. (incl. ports. facsim.) map. 22 1/2cm. Shortt

3206 Manitoba's diamond jubilee, 1870-1930. [Winnipeg, Printed by Canadian Publishers, 1930] cover-title, 112p. illus., ports., map. 26cm.

'Special number which has been endorsed by "The Manitoban," "The Brandon College Quill," "The Portage Collegiate Institute Tattler," and other public bodies.' Glenbow

3207 **Mehrhardt-Ihlow**, C.
Ausgerechnet Canada; mit lachenden Jägeraugen durch Prärie und Busch. Mit humoristischen Zeichnungen von Karl Wagner. Berlin, P. Parey, 1930. viii, 211p. illus. 22 1/2cm.

Adventures in Western Canada. Bavaria

3208 **Metzger**, H.
Geschichtlicher Abriss über die Peters-Pfarrei zu Kronau, Sask., und Anlegung der Kolonien Rastatt, Katharinenthal und Speyer. Bei Gelegenheit des 41-jährigen Jubiläums der ersten Ansiedler im Juni 1930 verfasst. 56p. Not seen. Lehmann

3209 **Mooney**, Daniel
The travels and philosophy and life and times of Daniel Mooney, born in the year 1860 on the Dublin road between Banbridge and Drommore, County Down, Ireland. An Irish exile. Winnipeg, The Author, 1930. 442p. 26cm. Printed in double column. Toronto

3210 **Morton**, A[rthur] S[ilver]
David Thompson. Toronto, Ryerson Press [c1930] 32p. illus. 18 1/2cm. (Ryerson Can. hist. readers) Shortt

3211 **Morton**, A[rthur] S[ilver]
The North West Company. Toronto, Ryerson Press [c1930] 30p. illus. 18 1/2cm. (Ryerson Can. hist. readers) Shortt

3212 The mountain school, Banff, Alberta [prospectus. n.p., 193–] [7]p. 1 illus. 14 x 21cm.

Typewritten note by G.H. Gooderham attached to back cover gives further information. Glenbow

3213 **Munday**, Luta
A mounty's wife; being the life history of one attached to the force, but not of it. Toronto, The Macmillan Co., 1930. xi, 217p. plates. 21cm. Can. Cat.

3214 **Niven**, Frederick [John]
Canada west. Illustrated by John Innes. Toronto, J.M. Dent and Sons [1930] viii, 188p. incl. front., illus., plates. 18cm.

'Not a history but rather a series of vivid impressions of the prairies and British Columbia.' C.H.R., 1930. L.C.

3215 **Oblates**. St. Joseph's Colony
Bilder und Blätter zum Silbernen Jubiläum der St. Josephs-Kolonie. Gesammelt von den Patres Oblaten in der Kolonie. [Prince Albert?] 1930. 125p. illus. (incl. maps, ports.) 24cm. N.Y.

3216 **O'Hara**, Mrs. Melita L.
Coast to coast in a puddle jumper. Tessier, Sask., Mrs. H. O'Hara [c1930] 109p. 20cm.

Printed in the U.S.A. Includes a section on the Prairie Provinces. Glenbow

3217 [**Oliver**, Edmund Henry]
Beaver Lodge; a story of frontier settlement in northern Saskatchewan, by Henry Esmund [pseud.] Toronto, Board of Home Missions, United Church of Canada [c1930] 75p. 18 1/2cm.

Fictionalized biography. Shortt

3218 **Peters**, Klaas
Die Bergthaler Mennoniten. [1930?] 128p. Not seen. Select

3219 **Peterson**, Charles Walter [Christian]
Wheat – the riddle of markets; a brief study of the production, sale and consumption of wheat. Calgary, Farm and Ranch Review, 1930. xi, 121p. plates, maps, diagrs. 23cm. Can. Cat.

3220 [**Reid**, William]
Memories of pioneer days at Pilot Mound. [Pilot Mound] Pilot Mound Sentinel print [1930] cover-title, 54p. illus. (incl. port.) 21cm.

The author became interested when the local children began gathering local history as a school project. Man. Leg.

3221 **S., D.L.**
Fifty years in Western Canada, being the abridged memoirs of Rev. A.G. Morice by D.L.S. Toronto, Ryerson Press, 1930. x p., 1 l., 267p. front., illus., plates, ports. 21cm. Shortt

3222 **Saskatchewan.** Royal Commission on immigration and settlement
Report ... Regina, Govt. of Sask., 1930. 206p. illus., maps, tables, diagrs. 26cm. U. of S.

3223 [**Schulze**, Gunnar]
Som emigrant i Kanada. Färder och äventyr. [Stockholm] Lars Hökerbergs [1930] 256p. 21cm.

Experiences of a Swedish immigrant in Manitoba. Sweden

3224 **Schwerla**, C[arl] B[orromäus]
Kanada im Faltboot. Berlin, A. Scherl [c1930] 195, [1]p. plates, fold. map. 19 1/2cm. L.C.

3225 **Une soeur de la Providence**
Une âme de prêtre; l'abbé Louis-Ernest Duchaine, curé de Frenchville, Sask. (1890-1923) ... par Une soeur de la Providence. Montréal, Librairie Saint-François, 1930. 292p. Not seen.

The sister is Soeur Jean-Baptiste. C.H.R., 1930

3226 **Stewart**, David A[lexander]
Early Assiniboine trading posts of the Souris-mouth group 1785-1832. Amplification of a paper read before the Society, November, 1928. [n.p.] 1930. 39, [1]p. illus. (incl. maps) 22 1/2cm. (Hist. & Sc. Soc. of Man., n.s., no.5) Shortt

3226A **Surrey**, George S.
The shack in the coulee. London, Humphrey Milford, 1930. 95p.

This may be autobiographical. Br. Mus.

3227 **Stubbs**, Lewis St. George
The Macdonald will case. [Winnipeg] Wallingford Press [1930] cover-title, 36p. facsims. 22cm.

Relates to litigation over the estate of Alexander Macdonald. See Entry 3050. Arkin

3227A **Sutherland Canadian Lands Company Limited**
Particulars of sale of the irrigable farming property known as the Sutherland Colony, situate near Brooks, in the Province of Alberta ... [London, 1930] 15p. plates, map. 33cm.

'By direction of the Sutherland Canadian Lands Company, Ltd., and the Trustees of the late Duke of Sutherland.' Glenbow

3228 **Swanson**, W[illiam] W[alker]
Wheat, by W.W. Swanson & P.C. Armstrong. Toronto, Macmillan, 1930. xiii, 320p. maps, diagr. 22 1/2cm. U. of S.

3229 **Tavernier**, Father
Les troubles scolaires de la Saskatchewan. Montréal, L'Action Paroissiale [1930?] ... Not seen. L'Oeuvre des tracts, no.147

3230 [**Taylor**, E. Jean]
The lily of Fort Garry, by Jane Rolyat [pseud.] London, J.M. Dent & Sons Ltd. [1930] 2p.l., 7-286, [1]p. 19 1/2cm.

Fiction. U. of S.

3231 **Thomas**, A. Vernon
Main street, Manitoba's historic highway. A panorama of buffalo, Indians, explorers, missionaries, voyageurs, soldiers, pioneers. Portrayed in verse by A. Vernon Thomas, illustrations by E.P. Gibson. [Winnipeg? 193–?] cover-title, 15p. illus. 19cm. Man. Leg.

3232 **Townshend**, C.
The world's best bet. London, A.H. Stockwell [n.d.] 47p. port. (on cover) 19cm.

Fiction; story about a Quaker settlement in northern Alberta. Glenbow

3233 **Uhlenbeck**, C[hristianus] C[ornelius]
An English-Blackfoot vocabulary based on material from the southern Peigans, by C.C. Uhlenbeck and R.H. van Gulik. Amsterdam, K. Akademie van wetenschappen, 1930. 261p., 1 l. 26cm. (K. Akademie van wetenschappen te Amsterdam. Afdeeling letterkunde. Verhandelingen, nieuwe reeks, deel 29, no.4) L.C.

3234 **United Farmers of Canada**. Saskatchewan Section
On immigration. Saskatoon [1930?] 12p. 23cm. U. of S.

3235 **Voorhis**, Ernest, comp.
Historic forts and trading posts of the French regime and of the English fur trading companies. Ottawa, Dept. of the Interior, 1930. 1p.l., ii, 188 l. fold. map (in pocket) 34cm. Shortt

3236 **Watson**, Robert
A boy of the great North West; the rousing experiences of a young Canadian. Ottawa, Graphic Publishers, 1930. 259p. illus.

Juvenile fiction. C.H.R., 1930

3237 **Weaver**, Emily Poynton
Sisters of St. Boniface. Toronto, Ryerson Press [1930] 32p. illus. 19cm. (Ryerson Can. hist. readers)

About the Grey Nuns. Can. Cat.

3238 **Wiegner**, Paul E.
The origin and development of the Manitoba-Saskatchewan District of the Lutheran Church, Missouri Synod, as presented in view of the 35th anniversary

of its founding by the Rev. Paul E. Wiegner, Bruno, Sask., Canada. [n.p., n.d.] 110p. Amtmann - 214-547

3239 **Yates**, Robert L.
When I was a harvester. New York, Macmillan, 1930. 5p.l., 174p. front. (port.) plates. 20cm.

Experiences of a seventeen-year-old youth from the city as a harvester at Sintaluta, Sask. A good description of harvesting in the days of the harvest excursions, but tinctured with bits of fantasy. Shortt

3240 **Bernard**, Harry
Juana, mon aimé; roman. Montréal, Lévesque, 1931. 212p.

Fiction with a Saskatchewan setting. Amtmann - 189-650

3241 **Berry**, J[ames] P.
Clover Bar in the making, 1881-1931. [Edmonton? 1931] 2p.l., 32p. 28cm.

Produced by an off-set printing process, probably in limited numbers. A copy is in the possession of Mr. J.P. Galloway of Fort Saskatchewan. Ream.

3242 **Bindloss**, Harold
The prairie patrol. New York, Frederick A. Stokes Co., 1931. vi, 310p. 19 1/2cm. Not seen.

A novel based on mounted police life in the pioneer period. Published in England under the title 'The Lean Years.' L.C.

3243 Not used

3244 **Canada**. Department of the Interior
Manitoba, Canada; its resources and development by F.H. Kitto. Ottawa, 1931. 191p. illus., maps (1 fold.) tables, diagrs. 23cm.

Originally published about 1923. Glenbow

3244A **Carey**, Douglas [pseud.]
The scorpion; a Limehouse mystery. Ottawa, Graphic Publishers, 1931. 312p. 19cm. Glenbow

3245 **Christen**, Marcel
Feux et frimas [Récits du Far-West Canadien] Avec préface de Robert Guiget et bois gravés de André Christen. Fleurier, Montandon & Co. [1931] iv, 159p. illus. 19 1/2cm.

Sketches relating mostly to Alberta, particularly to Cold Lake area and the village of Cadogan where the writer would seem to have been a Protestant clergyman. Swiss

3246 **Constantin-Weyer**, Maurice
Napoléon. Paris, Rieder, 1931. 216p. 18 1/2cm. (Prosateurs français contemporains)

Fiction. L.C.

3247 **Constantin-Weyer**, Maurice
Toward the West. New York, Macmillan Co. [c1931] 3p.l., 9-253p. 19 1/2cm.

Fiction. This is the English edition of 'Vers l'Ouest,' published in Paris in 1923. L.C.

3248 **Cowan**, Charles L.
Sandy's son. Toronto, J.M. Poole [c1931] 288p. 20cm.

Part of the novel set in Manitoba. Author's autographed presentation copy to Dr. Ross Millar. Glenbow

3249 **Dafoe**, John W[esley]
Clifford Sifton in relation to his times. Toronto, Macmillan Co., 1931. xxix, 552p. front., ports., facsims. 23cm. Shortt

3250 **D'Hauteserve**, L.
Le blé au Canada, conservation et transport. Paris, J.B. Baillière et Fils, 1931. 185p. Not seen. C.H.R., 1933

3251 **Edmonton**. McDougall United Church
Diamond jubilee, 1871-1931. Edmonton, 1931. 24p. illus. (incl. ports.) 23cm. Edmonton

3252 **Fritz**, John
Festschrift und Gottesdienstordnung zum 25. Jubiläum der Ev.-luth. Dreieinigkeitsgemeinde zu Regina. Regina, 1931. 16p. Not seen. Lehmann

3253 **Gostomska**, Z.M.
Z Kanadyjskich szlaków. Lwow, 1931. 120p. 18 1/2cm. Not seen. Br. Mus. (subject index, 1931-5)

3254 **Greene**, David L[eslie]
An historical sketch, Christ Church, The Pas, Man. [n.p., 1931] cover-title, 24p. illus. (incl. ports.) 23cm. Shortt

3255 **Gunter**, Lillian Forbes
Loving memories, and other poems. Regina, Leader Publishing Co. [n.d.] 45p. Watters

3256 **Henderson**, W.R.
Hendy's northern spasms. Flin Flon, Man., Flin Flon Miner, 1931. ...

Poetry. Watters

3257 **Hornby**, Montague Leyland
A plan for British community settlements in Canada. Lethbridge, Alta., The Author, 1931. 45p. Not seen. Contrib. to Can. Ec., v.6

3258 **Huber**, Armin O[tto]
Auf wilden Pfaden im neuen Kanada; Erlebnisse unter Farmern, Trappern, Vagabunden, und Verbrechern des kanadischen Westens. Stuttgart, Strecker und Schroeder [c1931] vii, [1], 239p. front., plates. 20 1/2cm.

The author describes life on a farm near Blaine Lake, Sask., and later in the forest region a hundred miles further north. L.C.

3259 **Hudson's Bay Company**
Charters, statutes, orders in council, &c. relating to the Hudson's Bay Company. London, Hudson's Bay Company, 1931. viii p., 1 l., 248, [2]p. 21 1/2cm. Shortt

3260 **Hurd,** W[illiam] Burton
Agriculture, climate and population of the Prairie Provinces of Canada. A statistical atlas showing past development and present conditions ... Prepared under the direction of W. Burton Hurd and T.W. Grindley. Ottawa, King's Printer, 1931. 102p. maps, diagrs. 26 x 33cm. U. of S.

3261 **Inkyo** [pseud.]
The reflections of Inkyo on the great Company. London, London General Press, 1931. 3p.l., [7]-207p. 22 1/2cm.

The financial history of the H.B.C. since 1863, arranged chronologically by governors. Man. Leg.

3262 **Jamieson,** F[rederick] C[harles]
The Alberta Field Force of 1885 ... Battleford, Canadian North-West Historical Society, 1931. 53p. illus., port., maps. 23cm. (Canadian North-West Hist. Soc., v.1, no.7) Shortt

3263 **King,** Tom
The black ox; or, 'Of the fruits of the earth you shall live.' Moose Jaw, 1931. 76p. 22 1/2cm.

The author's views on the economic conditions of the day. Shortt

3264 **Longstreth,** [Thomas] Morris
Murder at Belly Butte, and other stories from the Mounted Police, by Morris Longstreth and Henry Vernon. Illustrated by Bert Caldwell and E.J. Dinsmore. New York, Century [c1931] xi, 300p. front., plates. 21cm. L.C.

3265 **Lund,** T.
The murder of Dave Brandon; a story of the North West Mounted Police. London, T. Werner Laurie [1931] [3], 7-244p. 19cm.

Story takes place in a lumber camp located some thirty miles northwest of Prince Albert. Glenbow

3266 **MacBeth,** R[oderick] G[eorge]
Sir Augustus Nanton; a biography. Toronto, Macmillan Co., 1931. vi p., 3 l., 3-130p. front., plates, port. 22cm.

Biography of a prominent Winnipeg financier. U. of S.

3266A **McMurtrie,** Douglas Crawford
The first printing in Manitoba. Chicago, Eyncourt Press, 1931. 23p. illus. (facsim., 1 double) 22 1/2cm.

250 copies reprinted from the Printing Review of Canada for October 1930. U. of A.

3267 **Macpherson,** A[ngus] W., ed.
Northern summers. Saskatoon, Saskatchewan Motor Club, 1931. 44p. illus. 23cm. At head of title: Saskatchewan's resorts, sports and cities of 1931. U. of S.

3268 **Mehrhardt-Ihlow**, C.
Auf Bummel und Pirsch in Canada. Mit humoristischen Zeichnungen von Karl Wagner. Berlin, P. Parey, 1931. 4p.l., 208p. illus. 22 1/2cm.

Further adventures in Western Canada. Bavaria

3269 **Morden, Man.** Reunion Organization
Reunion of old timers' and ex-students' souvenir program, Morden, Man., Thursday, Friday, and Saturday, July 9, 10, 11, 1931. [Morden, 1931] cover-title, 44p. illus. 21cm.

Historical sketches in the last half of the volume. Man. Leg.

3270 **Morice**, A[drien] G[abriel]
The Catholic Church in Western Canada. Winnipeg, Canadian Publishers, Ltd., 1931. 26p. 22 1/2cm. Shortt

3270A **Nor'West Farmer and Farm & Home**
Master farmers of Canada. [Foreword by Hon. Robert Weir. Winnipeg, 1931] cover-title, 12p. illus., ports. 28cm.

Awards given in 1930 to ten outstanding Prairie farmers. Glenbow

3271 **Oliver**, Frank
Clover Bar celebration: fifty years of homesteading. Address, August 17, 1931. [Edmonton, 1931] cover-title, 7p. 21cm. Glenbow

3272 **On-to-the-Bay Association**
The Hudson Bay Route; Western Canada's short outlet to the markets of the world. [Winnipeg] The Association, 1931. cover-title, 21p. illus. 22cm. U. of S.

3272A **Paynter**, W.C.
The trumpet call of Canadian money and progress. [Tantallon, Sask.] 1931. 59p. 22 1/2cm.

The author was secretary of the Western Canada branch of the British Banking Reform League. Northland

3273 **Peterson**, Charles Walter Christian
Useful objectives of western agriculture. A reprint of a special article in the April issue of the Farm and Ranch Review. Calgary, Farm and Ranch Review [1931] [1], 17p. 18cm.

Pages 2 and 3 of cover included in paging. Glenbow

3274 **Pinkerton**, Robert E[ugene]
The gentlemen adventurers. Toronto, McClelland & Stewart Ltd. [c1931] viii, 357p. front., plates. 23cm.

Relates to the Hudson's Bay Company. Man. Leg.

3275 **Poirier**, Joseph Emile
La tempête sur le fleuve, roman historique canadien. Paris, J. Tallandier [c1931] 2p.l., [7]-254p. 19cm.

The plot is laid in the West at the time of the Saskatchewan Rebellion. L.C.

3276 **Randall,** C.C.
An historical outline of the see of St. Boniface from the advent of Bishop Provencher, A.D. 1818 to and inclusive of the year A.D. 1930. Prepared and published by C.C. Randall under the direction of the Right Rev. Monsignor Jubinville. [n.p., 1931] 38p. illus. (incl. ports.) 30cm. Man. Leg.

3277 **Rody,** Margaret Ellen [Vance (Strain)]
Gleanings. 2d ed. Kamsack, Sask., Kamsack Times, 1931. 48p. illus. 20cm. Not seen.

Poetry. Can. Cat.

3278 **Sax,** Karl
Der Auswanderer; Roman. Zurich, Letzi-Verlag [1931] 158, [2]p. 21 1/2cm. L.C.

3279 [**Schulze,** Gunnar]
Kamratliv och äventyr; på Kanadas prärier; färder och äventyr. [Stockholm] Lars Hökerberg [1931] 240p. 21cm.

At head of title: Karl Gunnarson [the author's pseud.] Sweden

3280 **Scott,** William Louis
The Ukrainians, our most pressing problem. Toronto, Catholic Truth Society of Canada, 1931. 64p. 15cm. Can. Arch.

3281 **Toronto.** Public Library
The Canadian North-West; a bibliography of the sources of information in the Public Reference Library of the City of Toronto, Canada, in regard to the Hudson's Bay Company, the fur trade and the early history of the Canadian North-West. Toronto, The Public Library, 1931. 52p. 26cm. Shortt

3282 **Troughton,** Felix J.
A bachelor's paradise; or, Life on the Canadian prairie 45 years ago ... London, Stockwell [1931] 32p. plates. Br. Mus.

3283 **United Grain Growers' Limited**
The grain market situation; second annual review of conditions ... Issued on the occasion of the company's twenty-fifth annual meeting at Calgary, November 4th, 1931. [Winnipeg? 1931] cover-title, 15p. 23cm. Shortt

3284 **Wade,** Mark Sweeten
The overlanders of '62. Edited by John Hosie. Printed by authority of the Legislative Assembly. Victoria, Printed by C.F. Banfield, 1931. xiii, 174, [2]p. front., plates, ports. 25cm. (Archives of British Columbia. Memoir no.9)

Based on five diaries of members of the various parties which crossed the prairies to the gold fields. The first 90 pages describe the trek across the prairies as far as Yellowhead Pass. Shortt

3285 **Watson,** Robert
Dreams of Fort Garry. With wood cut illustrations by Walter J. Phillips. Winnipeg, Stovel Co., Ltd. [c1931] 63p. illus. 24 1/2cm.

Poetry. Man. Leg.

3286 **Wilbois,** Joseph
Un pays neuf: l'Ouest canadien. Paris, Librairie Valois [1931] 2p.l., [7]-262p., 1 l. incl. illus. (maps, diagr.) tables. plates. 18 1/2cm. (Enquêtes, vi) U. of S.

3287 **Young,** Charles H[urlburt]
The Ukrainian Canadians; a study of assimilation. Edited by Helen R.Y. Reid. Toronto, Thomas Nelson & Sons, 1931. xiv, 327 (i.e. 329)p. front., illus. (maps) plates, diagrs. (1 fold.) 19 1/2cm. U. of S.

3288 **Anderson,** Robert T[hompson]
Troopers in France. Edmonton, Coles Printing Co., 1932. 123p. ports. 17cm.

A collection of poems written during the period 1914-18 while the poet was serving with an Alberta unit of the Canadian Light Horse in France. Edmonton

3289 **Baptist Union of Western Canada**
Some Baptist pioneers. Edmonton [1932] 64p. 21cm. Glenbow

3290 **Brodie,** Neil
Twelve days with the Indians, May 14–May 26, 1885 ... Being his experience in Poundmaker's camp during the rebellion of 1885. Battleford, Saskatchewan Herald, 1932. 8, [1]p. 22cm. Shortt

3291 **Chaykiwsky,** Peter Basil
Hornya Kavy. Winnipeg, 1932. 32p. 15cm.

Ukrainian poetry. Kirkconnell

3292 **Davidson,** Ida Marion
Gentlemen adventurers. Winnipeg, Manitoba Text Book Bureau, 1932. 36p. illus. 18cm. (Can. history plays, no.2) Can. Cat.

3293 **Davidson,** Ida Marion
Lord Selkirk; with an introduction by S.P. Matheson. Winnipeg, Manitoba Text Book Bureau, 1932. 48p. illus. 18cm. (Can. history plays, no.1) Can. Cat.

3294 [**Davies,** Hilda A.]
Overgrown trails, and other poems, by Tanis [pseud. Calgary, J. Dickmont, 1932] v, [1], 18p. 18cm. Glenbow

3295 **Eschambault,** Antoine d'
Discovery of the Lake of the Woods. Rouseau, Minn., Rouseau County Historical Society, 1932. 16p. Not seen. Can. Cat.

3296 **Ewert,** H[einrich] H.
The Mennonites. Address ... under the auspices of the Historical and Scientific Society of Manitoba, April 18, 1932. [Rosthern, Sask., Printed by D.H. Epp, 1932?] caption-title, 11, [1]p. 22 1/2cm.

At end of text: Issued by the General Conference of the Mennonites of Canada. Arkin

3297 **Farley**, Frank L[egrange]
Birds of the Battle River region; with notes on their present status, migrations, food habits and economic value. Edmonton, Institute of Applied Art, Ltd., 1932. 85p. illus., map. 23cm. Shortt

3298 **Freitag**, Karl W.
Denkschrift zum 30-jährigen Gemeinde-Jubiläum der Ev.-luth. Dreieinigkeitsgemeinde zu Strathcona, 1932. Edmonton, 1932. ... Not seen. Lehmann

3299 **Frémont**, Donatien
Sur le ranch de Constantin-Weyer. Winnipeg, Editions de La Liberté, 1932. 156p., 1 l. 21cm.

A criticism of Constantin-Weyer's writings. Man. Leg.

3300 **Frith**, B.M.
A short history of the Wakaw district. Wakaw, Wakaw Recorder, 1932. cover-title, ii, 60, iii-iv p. illus. (1 fold.) 20cm. Shortt

3301 [**Haegler**, Curt August]
Oh, Canada! Vier Jahre auf und ab [by] Peter Pee. Basel, E. Birkhauser & Cie [1932] iv, 509p. 21 1/2 x 14 1/2cm. Swiss

3302 **Huber**, Armin O[tto]
Roten und weissen Abenteurern in Kanada. Stuttgart, Strecker und Schroeder, 1932. 179p. Not seen.

Although the author publishes his experiences as factual, they must be regarded as largely fictional. The book describes trapping at Big River, Sask., a dog derby at Prince Albert, a killing, and an escape from the R.C.M.P. C.H.R., 1933

3303 **Israelite Daily Press**
The 100th anniversary souvenir of Jewish emancipation in Canada and the 50th anniversary of the Jew in the West, 1832-1932. Winnipeg, Israelite Daily Press, 1932. 60, [60]p. illus., ports. 38 x 27 1/2cm. U. of S.

3304 **Kaufmann**, Hans
Der kanadische Weizenpool. Berlin, Industrieverlag Spaeth und Linde, 1932. x, 234p. Not seen. C.H.R., 1932

3305 **Learned**, William Setchel
Local provision for higher education in Saskatchewan; an advisory memorandum on university policy proposed at the request of the University of Saskatchewan, by W.S. Learned and E.W. Wallace ... with a foreword by Henry Suzzalo ... New York, The Carnegie Foundation, 1932. [30]p. 25cm. U. of S.

3306 **Leigh**, Ursula
Chinook. London, John Heritage, Unicorn Press, 1932. 301p.

Fiction. The tale of a Quebec girl transplanted to a small town along the Saskatchewan River. Can. Cat.

3306A **McClintock**, Gray
The wolves of Cooking Lake and other stories. Albany, N.Y., J.B. Lyon Co. [1932] 224p. front. (port.), plates. 20cm.

Twenty-two stories of famous Indians, mounted policemen, and pioneers of Western Canada. These were first read over a radio station. Northland

3307 **McGibbon**, Duncan Alexander
The Canadian grain trade. Toronto, Macmillan Co., 1932. xiv p., 2 l., 3-503p. front., illus., plates. 21 1/2cm. U. of S.

3307A **McMurtrie**, Douglas Crawford
The early French press in Manitoba. Chicago, Privately printed, 1932. 11p. illus. (facsim.) 21 1/2cm.

250 copies reprinted from the Printing Review of Canada for June 1932. U. of A.

3308 **McMurtrie**, Douglas C[rawford]
The first printing in Alberta. Chicago, Privately printed, 1932. 11p. 22cm. Alta. Leg.

3309 **May**, Sydney
Prairie fairies and other verses. Calgary, The Author, 1932. ... Not seen. Can. Cat.

3310 **Mehrhardt-Ihlow**, C.
Canadisches Nocturno; ein Trapper Idyll in nördlicher Wildnis. Berlin, Paul Parey, 1932. 182p. Not seen.

Adventures along the Churchill River. C.H.R., 1933

3311 **Metcalfe**, J[oseph] H[enry]
The tread of the pioneers; under the distinguished patronage of the Government of the Province of Manitoba, the Corporation of the City of Portage la Prairie, the Council of the Rural Municipality of Portage la Prairie. Portage la Prairie and district Old Timers' Association, 1932. xiii, 305p. plates, ports. 25cm.

A compilation of biographical sketches and reminiscences of local oldtimers. Saskatoon

3311A **Palmer**, George Alfred
Madam Verite at Bath; an original comedy in one act. Regina, 1932. 23p. 16 1/2cm.

A later edition published in 1935 by S. French of Toronto, N.Y. L.C.

3312 **Prince Albert**. Board of Trade
Prince Albert, where progress continues unabated. Gateway to Prince Albert National Park. Prince Albert, Herald Job Print [1932] cover-title, 20p. illus., plan. 20cm. Glenbow

3312A **Rosenberg**, Louis
The land policy of the farmer-labour group, Saskatchewan. Regina [1932?] cover-title, [12]p. 23cm. Glenbow

3313 **Rousseau**, A[lfred]
Les Roux; histoire manitobaine. Cadillac, Sask., Chez l'auteur, 1932. 202p. 18cm.

Historical fiction of French-Canadian settlement in Manitoba. Shortt

3314 **Russenholt**, Edgar Stanford, comp.
Six thousand Canadian men; being the history of the 44th Battalion Canadian Infantry, 1914-1919. Winnipeg, Printed by De Montfort Press, for the 44th Battalion Association, 1932. xii, 364p. front., plates, ports., maps. 24cm. Can. Cat.

3315 **Schäfer**, Theodor
Der schwarze Waldläufer; Lebensbild des Indianerapostels Albert Lacombe, O.M.I. Paderborn, Ferdinand Schoningh, 1932. 328p. front., plates, ports., fold. map. 19cm.

This biography of Father Lacombe is largely based on the one by Katherine Hughes. L.C.

3316 **Stewart**, David A[lexander]
Glimpses at Manitoba history. An address ... to the men's club of the First Lutheran Church. Winnipeg, 1932. 15p. 20cm. Shortt

3317 **Stringer**, Arthur [John Arbuthnott]
The mud lark. Indianapolis, Bobbs-Merrill Co. [c1932] 331p. 19 1/2cm. Not seen.

Fiction; an English girl comes to Alberta to be married. L.C.

3318 **Turner**, Adam
Some rambling historical notes and reminiscences of the early days in Saskatoon with a prelude regarding the formation of the Dominion of Canada. Saskatoon [Modern Press Ltd.] 1932. 27, [1]p. front. 22cm. Saskatoon

3319 **Vestal**, Stanley
Sitting Bull, champion of the Sioux; a biography. Boston, Houghton Mifflin Co., 1932. xvi p., 2 l., [3]-350p. front., illus. (map) plates, ports., facsim. 21 1/2cm. U. of S.

3320 **Villeneuve**, J[ean] M[arie] Rodrigue
Lettres pastorales et circulaires au clergé de Son Excellence Mgr J.M. Rodrigue Villeneuve, O.M.I., premier évêque de Gravelbourg. [n.p., 1932?] 227p. Not seen. C.H.R., 1935

3321 **Watson**, William Ritchie
My desire. Edmonton, University of Alberta Press, 1932. 84p. plates, ports. 20cm.

The autobiography of a physically handicapped youth; describes his boyhood in southern Alberta and his university career. See also Entry 3655. U. of A.

3322 **Young**, Egerton Ryerson, [Jr.]
Three Arrows, the young buffalo hunter. New York, Friendship Press [c1932] 4p.l., [3]-183p. 19 1/2cm.

Juvenile fiction. Shortt

3323 [**Aberhart**, William]
[Coloured leaflet series. Calgary? 1933] 4p. (Series of 6 leaflets)

Brief summaries of Maj. C.H. Douglas's Credit-power and democracy.

3324 [**Aberhart**, William]
The Douglas system of economics: 'Credit-power and democracy'; a system of state credit which will supply purchasing power to the consumer. This is a brief outline of the above system as applied to our Alberta provincial needs. [n.p., n.d.] cover-title, 8p. 23cm.

Yellow paper covers. Glenbow

3325 [**Aberhart**, William]
Study group features. Calgary, 1932-33. 4p. (Series popularly known as 'the white leaflets')

Some titles in the series were the following: 1. The present methods of business. 2. Purchasing power in the hands of the consumers. 3. The necessary flow of credit or; where will all the money come from? 4. The perfect cycle. These leaflets were widely distributed and were important in propagating the Social Credit theory. For a description of these leaflets see Irving, John A. The Social Credit Mòvement in Alberta. Toronto, 1959. p.52-53.

3326 **Alberta**. University
The University of Alberta, 1908-1933. [Edmonton, The University, 1933] 57p. 23cm. U. of S.

3327 **Asseltine**, Robert Whiting
The story of Lodge Progress, no.92, G.R.S., A.F. and A.M., Saskatoon, Saskatchewan, April 15th, 1912, April 15th, 1933. [Saskatoon? 1933] 42p. ports. 23cm. Glenbow

3328 **Buffalo Child Long Lance**
Redman echoes; comprising the writings of Chief Buffalo Child Long Lance and biographical sketches by his friends. Los Angeles, Frank Wiggins Trade School, 1933. 7p.l., 219p. front., plates (ports.) 30cm.

A limited edition of 60 copies. U. of A.

3329 **Canada**. Geographic Board
Place-names of Manitoba. Ottawa, King's Printer, 1933. 95p. 25cm. U. of S.

3330 **Canadian Authors' Association**. Manitoba Branch
Manitoba poetry chapbook, 1933. Winnipeg, Israelite press, 1933. 32p. 21cm.

Poems in several languages by Manitoba poets. Winnipeg

3331 **Clark**, J[eremiah] Simpson
Northern-lights and shadows. Wasagaming, Clear Lake, Riding Mountain National Park. [n.p.] 1933. cover-title, [12] 18cm.

Poetry. Text on end-papers. Half-title: Holiday flights. Glenbow

3332 **Daly**, Denis E.B.
Shooting reminiscences in Manitoba. [Winnipeg, Stovel Co., Ltd., 1933?] 16p. 23cm. Man. Leg.

3333 **Garrioch**, A[lfred] C[ampbell]
The correction line. Winnipeg, Stovel Co., 1933. 5p.l., 414, vi p. front., illus., plates, ports. 24cm.

A history of Portage la Prairie and southern Manitoba; contains much of the material found in his 'First Furrows.' See Entry 2847. Man. Leg.

3334 **Geissler**, A.
Das Land ohne Gnade; Roman der Amerika-Deutschen. Berlin, Drei-Türme-Verlag, 1933. 283p. Not seen. Lehmann

3335 [**Goodchild**, George]
The man from Peace River [by] Wallace Q. Reid [pseud.] London, Wild West Club, W. Collins, Sons and Co. [1933] 249, [1]p. illus. 19cm. Not seen.
Fiction. L.C.

3336 **Grove**, Frederick Philip
Fruits of the earth. Toronto, J.M. Dent and Sons [1933] viii, 335, [1]p. 20cm. Maps on lining-papers.
A novel about a land-hungry farmer in Manitoba. U. of S.

3337 **Higinbotham**, John D[avid]
When the West was young; historical reminiscences of the early Canadian West. Toronto, Ryerson Press [c1933] x, 328p. front., plates, ports., facsims. 21cm.
Experiences in the Macleod-Lethbridge district. Shortt

3338 **House**, John
Old Sun Anglican Residential School, Gleichen, Alberta. Gleichen, 1933. 15p. illus., ports. 23cm.
Imperfect: cover-title missing. Title supplied by the library. Prepared on the occasion of the 50th anniversary of mission work on the Blackfoot Reserve at Gleichen. Glenbow

3339 **Humble**, Harry
Sunday meditations. Calgary, Alberta, Published by the author [1933] cover-title, 64p. port. 17cm.
Originally prepared for a series of radio broadcasts by the same title. Glenbow

3340 **Irving**, S[idney] L[ouis]
Pierre Gaultier Varennes Sieur de la Verendrye, captain of naval troops, knight of the Military Order of Saint Louis, discoverer of the North-West. Born at Trois-Rivières, Que., November 17th, 1685, married October 29th, 1712. Died at Montreal, December 6th, 1749. [Trois-Rivières, S.L. Irving, 1933] cover-title, 48p. 15cm.
Extracts from La Vérendrye's diaries. Dempsey

3341 **Jackson**, Mary [Evangeline] (Percy)
On the last frontier; pioneering in the Peace River block; letters of Mary Percy Jackson. London, Sheldon Press, 1933. viii, 9-117p. illus. 18 1/2cm. Shortt

3342 [**Jamieson**, Heber Carss]
The medical history of Edmonton, with notes on the organization of the Edmonton Academy of Medicine. Issued on the occasion of the thirty-third annual dinner of the Academy, held in the MacDonald Hotel on Wednesday evening, December the sixth, nineteen hundred and thirty-three. [Edmonton] 1933. 8p. illus. 29 1/2cm. Edmonton

3343 **Kenderdine**, [Augustus Frederick La Fosse]
Twelve views of Saskatchewan. Winnipeg, Stovel Co. Ltd. [c1933] 2 l., 12 col. plates. 23cm. Glenbow

3344 **Killarney, Man.** Women's Institute
Stories of pioneer days at Killarney. [n.p., 1933?] 47p. fold. map. 21cm.
A compilation of articles by several old-time residents. Man. Leg.

3345 **Leichner**, Georg
Abenteuerliches Kanada. Reiseerlebnisse. Leipzig, A.H. Payne [c1933] 255p. plates. 19 1/2cm. L.C.

3346 **Longstreth**, T[homas] Morris
In scarlet and plain clothes; the history of the mounted police. Toronto, Macmillan Co., 1933. ix, 365p. 21cm.
Also published in New York. Man. Leg.

3347 **Macphail**, Agnes Campbell
The economic crisis and the C.C.F.; an address to the annual convention of the U.F.A. on January 18th, 1933. [Calgary, West Print., 1933] cover-title, 10p. 22cm. Glenbow

3348 **Mishaegen**, Anne de
Mush! Un hiver en pays Cree. Montréal, Librairie Beauchemin, 1933. 243p. Not seen.
Describes a winter in the country north of The Pas. C.H.R., 1933

3348A **Jennings**, A. Owen
Fools and otherwise. Calgary [Albertan Publishing Co.] 1933. 95p. 20 1/2cm. Northland

3349 **Palmer**, George Alfred
Hail; an original domestic drama in two acts. Regina, 1933. 39p. 17cm. Sask. Arch.

3350 **Rodgers**, Robert Wylie
Dry belt jingles. Cabin Lake, Alta. [193 ?] cover-title, 12p. 18cm.
Many of the jingles are set to familiar tunes. Glenbow

3351 **Rumilly**, Robert
La Vérendrye, découvreur canadien. Montréal, Éditions Albert Lévesque, 1933. 137p. (Figures canadiennes) C.H.R., 1933

3352 **Saskatchewan**. Department of Railways, Labour, and Industries
The Hudson Bay Route and the port of Churchill in the centre of Canada. [Regina, 1933] 63p. illus., maps, diagrs. 23cm. U. of S.

3353 **Sawchuk**, Semen W.
Pyatnatsyat lit pratsi Ukrayinskoyi Hreko-Provoslavnoyi tserkvy v Kanadi [Fifteen years of the work of the Ukrainian Greek Orthodox Church in Canada] Winnipeg, The Consistory, 1933. 23p. 23cm. Yuzyk

3354 **Skinner**, Constance Lindsay
Beaver, kings and cabins; with illustrations by W. Langdon Kihn. New York, Macmillan Co., 1933. 273p. illus., maps. 22cm.
A popular history of the fur trade. U. of A.

3355 **Solloway**, Isaac William Cannon
Speculators and politicians. Westmount, Quebec, Published by the Political and Economic Publishing Co., 1932 [c1933] [7], 3-223p. port., plates. 22cm.

Defense of Solloway, Mills and Company, who were active in promoting Turner Valley oil companies, and aviation in the Canadian north. Glenbow

3356 **Strang**, Peter
Autobiography. [Regina, 1933] 2p.l., 52 l. port. 22cm. Mimeographed.

Experiences of a Presbyterian clergyman. Shortt

3356A **Sutherland**, Alexander Hugh
Red River reminiscences and poems. [Winnipeg, Stovel Co., 1933?] 89p. illus., ports. 19cm. B.C. Arch.

3357 **Sutton**, Francis Arthur
One-arm Sutton. New York, Viking Press, 1933. viii, 277p. front., plates, ports. 21cm.

The author was interested in the development of the Peace River country. L.C.

3358 **Théroux**, Théodore
Impressions de voyage et Histoire de St-Joseph de Végreville. Memoire. [n.p. 1933?] [18]p. 21cm.

A diary kept during the first year of settlement, 1894. A summary of events, 1895-1906, by Madame Poulin. St-Jean

3359 These twenty-five years; a symposium by W.H. Alexander, E.K. Broadus, F.J. Lewis and J.M. MacEachran of the University of Alberta. Toronto, Macmillan, 1933. 4p.l., 133, [1]p. 22cm.

A series of lectures commemorating the 25th anniversary of the University of Alberta. U. of S.

3360 **Tlapnák**, Václav
Situace čsl zemědělců a národnia a kulturni žwot krajanů v Kanadě. Prague, Nákladem Ceskoslovenskeho [1933] cover-title, 18p. 23 1/2cm.

Czech title translated: Situation about Czechoslovakia and the national and cultural life of compatriots in Canada. Naprstek

3361 **Western Broadcasting Bureau**
Commercial broadcasting in the West. Winnipeg, The Bureau [1933] folder. [8]p. Amtmann - 176-386

3362 **Willoughby**, Gerald [Thomas Arthur]
Retracing the old trail. [Saskatoon, 1933] 83p. incl. port. 19cm. Illustrated title-page.

Describes pioneer days in the Temperance Colony at Saskatoon. Shortt

3363 **Winnipeg Rifles**
The Winnipeg Rifles, 8th Battalion, C.E.F., allied with the Rifle Brigade (Prince Consort's Own), fiftieth anniversary, 1883-1933. Winnipeg, 1933. 59p., 3 l. illus. (incl. ports.) 25cm. Man. Leg.

3364 **Woodsworth**, J[ames] S[haver]
A plea for social justice; extracts from the speeches of J.S. Woodsworth, M.P., in the House of Commons, 1930-33. Selected by Grace MacInnis. [Ottawa, Labour Pub. Co., 1933] 80p. 18cm. Glenbow

3365 **The Yorkton Enterprise**
Semi-centennial souvenir number, commemorating the fiftieth anniversary of the founding of Yorkton, Saskatchewan. Yorkton, July 6th, 1933. 36p. illus. 57cm. Shortt

3366 **Alberta**. Legislative Assembly. Agricultural Committee
The Douglas system of Social Credit; evidence, session 1934. Edmonton, King's Printer, 1934. 127p. 26cm. Can. Cat.

3367 **Anderson**, Arthur Antonius
Stoft. Winnipeg, Fofattarens Forlag, 1934. 121p. Not seen.

Poetry in Swedish; title translation, 'Dust.' Kirkconnell

3368 **Baptist Union of Western Canada**
Crusading in the Canadian West; a survey of Baptist missionary endeavor. [Edmonton, Institute Press, 1934] cover-title, 18p. illus. (incl. ports.) 22cm. Glenbow

3368A **Barker**, Bertram
North of 53; the adventures of a trapper and prospector in the Canadian far north. London, Methuen [1934] 242p. plates. 19cm. Map on endpapers.

Much of the book relates to The Pas and northern Man. and Sask. L.C.

3369 **Barritt**, Mrs. R.W.
History of United Farm Women. [n.p.] 1934. cover-title, 8p. 23cm. Glenbow

3370 **Bible**. Old Testament. Psalms. Selections
A birthday book for the Union Jack farm settlement on the Canadian prairie. Compiled from the Psalms of David by a British emigrant. London, Fashion Journals Guild [1934] ... Not seen.

The British emigrant was Georgina Binnie-Clark. Br. Mus.

3371 **Bloomfield**, Leonard, comp.
Plains Cree texts. New York, G.E. Stechert & Co., 1934. viii, 309p. 24 1/2cm. (American Ethnological Society, v.16) 'Printed in Germany.' Shortt

3372 **Canadian Authors' Association**. Calgary Branch
Collected poems. Calgary, John D. McAra for the Association, 1934. 39p. Can. Cat.

3373 **Canadian Legion**. Polish Branch of Winnipeg
15 lat pracy Polskiej Placówki Legjonu Kanadyjskiego B.E.S.L. Winnipeg, 1934. cover-title, 18p. (incl. cover)

Advertising matter included in paging. Commemoration of the 15th anniversary of the Polish branch of the Canadian Legion in Winnipeg.

3374 **Canadian Medical Association**
Sixty-fifth annual meeting, Calgary, Alberta, June 18-22, 1934. [Souvenir booklet. Calgary, J.D. McAra, 1934] [52]p. illus. (2 col.) map, ports. 24cm. Glenbow

3375 **Corbett**, E[dward] A[nnand]
Blackfoot trails. Toronto, Macmillan, 1934. 5p.l., 3-139p. col. front., col. plates. 22cm.

The customs, history, and legends of the Blackfoot Indians. U. of S.

3376 **Corbett**, E[dward] A[nnand]
McQueen of Edmonton. Toronto, Ryerson Press [c1934] vii, 125p. front., plates, ports. 20cm.

The life of Rev. David G. McQueen, Presbyterian minister in Edmonton from 1887 until his death in 1931. U. of S.

3377 **Dawson**, C[arl] A[ddington]
The settlement of the Peace River area; a study of a pioneer area. Assisted by R.W. Murchie. Toronto, Macmillan Co., 1934. xii, 284p. illus. (incl. maps, diagrs.) 26cm. (Canadian frontiers of settlement) U. of S.

3378 **Dunlop**, George Murray
Tales of the Indians of the plains. Edmonton, Institute of Applied Art, 1934. 67p. illus. 21cm. (History readers of the old North-West) B.C. Arch.

3379 **Dunlop**, George Murray
Tales of the North-West Rebellion. [Edmonton] Institute of Applied Art, 1934. 56p. illus., port. 21cm. (History readers of the old North-West) Glenbow

3380 **Dyker**, Bob
Get your man; an autobiography of the North-West Mounted. London, S. Low, Marston & Co. [1934] ix p., 2 l., 3-244p. 22 1/2cm.

The author served in the R.N.W.M.P. from 1907 to 1914. U. of A.

3381 [**Goodchild**, George]
Saskatoon patrol, by Wallace Q. Reid. London, Collins, 1934. 252p. Not seen.

Light fiction about the mounted police. Can. Cat.

3382 **Gray**, Alice Rowan
Kenilworth and other poems. Winnipeg, Printed by Peerless Press for the Author, 1934. 44p. front. (port.) illus. 21cm. Can. Cat.

3383 **Grey Owl**
Pilgrims of the wild; with a foreword by Hugh Eayrs. Toronto, Macmillan Co., 1934. xxii, 282p. front., plate, port. 22cm.

An autobiography. U. of S.

3384 **Hedges**, James B[laine]
The federal railway land subsidy policy of Canada. Cambridge, Harvard University Press, 1934. viii, 151p. 20cm. (Harvard historical monographs, no.3) U. of S.

3385 **Irvine**, William
The forces of reconstruction; a review of world-conditions under capitalism, and the forces working towards the Co-operative Commonwealth. Ottawa, Labour Pub. Co. [1934] 40p. 18cm. Glenbow

3386 **Kells**, Edna
Elizabeth McDougall, pioneer. Toronto, United Church Publishing House [1934] 48p. 19cm. Rutherford

3387 **Leigh**, Ursula
Give me my robe. London, John Heritage [1934] 301, [1]p. 19cm.
Fiction. U. of S.

3388 **McKean**, George Burdon
Making good; a story of North-West Canada. London, H. Milford [1934] 253p. col. front. 20cm.
Story of two English lads' adventures ranching in Alberta. Glenbow

3389 **Mackintosh**, W[illiam] A[rchibald]
Prairie settlement; the geographical setting. Toronto, Macmillan Co., 1934. xv, 242p. incl. illus., plates, maps, diagrs. 26cm. (Canadian frontiers of settlement, v.4) U. of S.

3390 **McNicol**, D[onald]
Louis Riel and the last Indian uprising in the North West. [Perth, Ont., Perth Courier, April, 1934?] caption-title, 8p. 19 1/2cm. In double column. Can. Arch.

3391 **Marchbin**, Andrew A.
Early emigration from Hungary to Canada. [London, 1934] 12p. 24 1/2cm. Reprinted from the Slavonic Review, v.13, no.37, July, 1934. Can. Arch.

3392 **Moose Jaw**. School District
Moose Jaw School District, no.1. Semi-centennial, 1884-1934. Wednesday, Dec. 5th, 1934. [Moose Jaw? 1934] cover-title, 12p. illus 23cm. Shortt

3393 **Morice**, A[drien] G[abriel]
M. Darveau, martyr du Manitoba. Winnipeg, The Author, 1934. 64, [1]p. 22cm.
A biography of an early missionary priest killed by the Indians. Shortt

3394 **Morrier**, Emma
Bon sang ne ment pas. Edmonton, [La Survivance, Ltée] 1934. 20p. 21cm. St-Jean

3395 **Munday**, Albert H[enry]
No other gods; a novel of Saskatchewan. Boston, Meader, 1934. 271p. 19 1/2cm. L.C.

3396 **Napier**, R.M.
Fifty years of St. Barnabas Church (Diocese of Qu'Appelle) in Medicine Hat, Alberta, 1884-1934. [Medicine Hat, Alta., 1934?] 27p. 1 illus. 23cm.
At head of title: Jubilee commemoration. Glenbow

3397 **Oblates.** Le Pas
L'héritier de Mgr Charlebois, O.M.I. Son excellence Mgr Lajeunesse, O.M.I. Le Pas, Maison Provinciale, 1934. cover-title, 102p. plates, ports. 18cm.

Includes an account of Mgr Lajeunesse's first missionary journey by canoe; written by a priest who accompanied him, Father V. Bleau. St-Jean

3398 **O'Neill,** Moira [pseud.]
Collected poems. Edinburgh, W. Blackwood & Sons, Ltd., 1934. xii, 148p. 19 1/2cm. Not seen.

Contents: Songs of the glens of Antrim; Songs from North-West Canada; Translations from Italian poets. L.C.

3399 Pamiatka 30-lecia parafii P.N.K.K. w Ameryce, 1904-1934. Winnipeg, Nakl. Komitetu Jubileuszowego Parafii Matki Boskiej Czestochowskiej P.N.K.K. [1934] 11p.

Memorial album issued to celebrate the 30th anniversary of the parish.

3400 **Peters,** Klaas
Das 60-jaehrige Jubilaeum der Mennonitischen Ost-Reserve, 1874-1934. [1934] ... Not seen. Select

3401 **Riley,** Conrad S[tephenson]
Rowing memories. Winnipeg, 1934. 110p. incl. plates. 16cm.

A history of the Winnipeg Rowing Club, 1883-1932, and the author's association with it. Man. Leg.

3402 [**Saint-Léandre,** Soeur]
L'oeuvre véridique de Louis Riel, 1869-70, 1885. Montréal, Editions Albert Lévesque, 1934. 186, [2]p. 18 1/2cm. At head of title: P. de M. [i.e. Présentation de Marie] Shortt

3403 **Saskatoon.** St. John's Cathedral
Tenth anniversary, 1924-1934. [Saskatoon, Service Printing Co., 1934] 58p. illus. (incl. ports.) 23cm. Pagination includes advertising.

The anniversary marked the tenth year of St. John's as a cathedral, not as a church. Saskatoon

3404 **Shaw,** A[lexander] M[alcolm]
Drought on the Canadian prairies. An address delivered at the Regina Board of Trade luncheon, November 30th, 1934. Saskatoon, University of Saskatchewan, Agricultural Extension Dept., 1934. cover-title, 12p. 22 1/2cm. Shortt

3405 **Stern,** John A.
To Hudson's Bay by paddle and portage. With an introduction by Wallace W. Kirkland. Illustrated from photographs made by Wallace W. Kirkland and Harris Barber. [Chicago] Privately printed, 1934. 54p. front., plates. 21cm. Charts on end-papers. U. of A.

3406 **Street,** Arthur George
Farmer's glory. Toronto, Macmillan Co., 1934. xvii, 294p.

Describes his pioneering experiences at Barloe, Man., from 1911 to 1914. The first edition was published in London in 1932. Reissued as a Penguin book in 1951. (This edition in U. of A.) Can. Cat.

3407 **Uhlenbeck,** C[hristianus] C[ornelius]
A Blackfoot-English vocabulary based on material from the southern Peigans, by C.C. Uhlenbeck and R.H. van Gulik. Amsterdam, Noord-Hollandsche uitgevers-naatschappij, 1934. 12, 380p. 35 1/2cm. (Verhandelingen der Koninklijke akademie van wetenschappen te Amsterdam. Afdeeling letterkunde. Nieuwe reeks, deel 33, no.2) L.C.

3408 **Winnipeg Free Press**
Men of Winnipeg in 'Diamond Jubilee Sketches,' as published in the Winnipeg Free Press during 1934, Winnipeg's Diamond Jubilee Year. Winnipeg, 1934. cover-title, 23p. ports. 25cm.

Biographical sketches of prominent Winnipeggers. Glenbow

3409 **Winnipeg Grain Exchange**
The Winnipeg Grain Exchange, founded 1887, reorganized 1908. Winnipeg, The Exchange, 1934. 20p. illus. 23cm. Can. Cat.

3410 **Aberhart,** William
Social Credit manual; Social Credit as applied to the province of Alberta; puzzling questions and their answers. Calgary, The Author, 1935. 64p. port., facsim. 16cm. Can. Cat.

3411 Aberharts Social Credit Ideen; eine kritische Betrachtung, von K. ... Edmonton, c1935. cover-title, 16p. 27cm. Glenbow

3412 **Alberta.** Legislative Assembly. Agricultural Committee
The constitutionality and economic aspects of Social Credit; evidence of Dean Weir and Prof. Elliott, session 1935. Edmonton, King's Printer, 1935. 20p. 25cm. Can. Cat.

3413 **Baldwin,** Harold
A farm for two pounds; being the odyssey of an emigrant. London, Murray, 1935. viii, 300p. front. 20 1/2cm.

The autobiography of an English immigrant who came to the West in 1908. Can. Cat.

3414 **Baldwin,** Harold
Pelicans in the sky. London, Murray, 1935. 311p. Not seen.

Fiction. Can. Novel

3415 **Bayne,** D[avid] C[alvin]
Calgary School District, no.19, 1885-1935. [Calgary, John D. McAra Ltd., 1935] [3]p.l., [24]p. illus. 24cm. Shortt

3416 **Beck,** Richard
Fimmtíu ára minningarrit hins Evang. Lúterska Kirkjufélags Islendinga í Vesturheimi, 1885-1935. [Golden jubilee memorial volume of Icelandic Lutheran Synod of America] Winnipeg, 1935. 90p. Not seen.
U. of T. Quarterly, 1937-8

3417 **Bjarnason,** Bogi
Sans the grande passion; a collection of short stories in which, contrary to all rules and conventions of short-story writing, love and sex have no part. Treherne, Man., The Times, 1935. 122p. Not seen. Can. Cat.

3418 **Britnell,** George E[dwin]
The western farmer. Toronto, Social Service Council of Canada, 1935. 16p. 23cm. (Machine age series, no.6) U. of S.

3419 **Broadus,** Edmund Kemper
Saturday and Sunday. Toronto, Macmillan, 1935. 7p.l., 3-260p. 22 1/2cm.

Impressions of Edmonton written in 1908 when he first came to the West. The other two-thirds of the book is general essays. U. of S.

3420 **Bugnet,** Georges [Charles Jules]
La forêt, roman. Montréal, Editions du Totem [1935] 2p.l., [7]-239, [1]p. 19cm.

Dr. E.K. Brown, noted Canadian critic, considered this novel of the Peace River country the finest novel to come out of the Canadian West. U. of S.

3421 **Cameron,** Stewart
The Amos and Andy of Social Credit. [Calgary? 1935] cover-title, [16]p. illus. 15 x 23cm.

Chiefly cartoons. Glenbow

3422 **Canada.** Army. North West Field Force Anniversary Re-Union Committee
North West Field Force re-union. 50th anniversary souvenir, July 26th, 27th, & 28th, 1935. [Toronto, 1935] 20p. ports. 24cm. Can. Arch.

3423 **Canada.** Department of Railways and Canals
Churchill and the Hudson Bay Route. Ottawa, King's Printer, 1935. 48p. C.H.R., 1936

3424 **Canadian Wheat Pools**
The wheat pools in relation to rural community life in Western Canada. An account of some of the ways in which the wheat pools have endeavoured to assist the prairie community toward a happier and fuller manner of living. [n.p.] 1935. cover-title, 29, [1]p. 23cm. U. of S.

3425 **Carsley,** Sara E[lizabeth (Keatley)]
Alchemy and other poems. Toronto, Macmillan, 1935. vi, 61p. Can. Cat.

3426 **Cory,** Harper
Grey Owl and the beaver. With two chapters by Grey Owl. Toronto, Nelson, 1935. 140p. illus. 19 1/2cm. Can. Cat.

3427 **Crawford,** J[ohn] W[hite]
A historical sketch of Grace Presbyterian Church, Calgary, Alberta. With a foreword by Rev. James McNeill. [Calgary, A.J. Davis Printing Co., Ltd., 1935] 28p. illus. (incl. ports.) 23 1/2cm. Knox College

3428 **Daly,** Denis E.B.
Days with a gunner and field notes on shooting. [Winnipeg, 1935?] 31p. 23cm. Man. Leg.

3429 **Davidson,** W[illiam] M[cCartney]
The Aberhart plan; a survey and analysis of the Social Credit scheme as placed before the electors of Alberta. Calgary, Issued by the Economic Safety League [1935] 32p. 22cm. Glenbow

3430 **Davidson,** W[illiam] M[cCartney]
The Aberhart proposals; an analysis of the scheme offered Alberta in the name of Social Credit. [Calgary, United Farmers of Alberta, 1935] cover-title, 30p. 21cm.

'Reprinted from the Hanna Herald.' Glenbow

3431 **Ebbell,** Bendix [Joachim]
Eventyrets Land. Oslo, Gyldendal Norsk, 1935. 180p. 19cm.

Approximately one-half of this account of Canada relates to the Prairie region. Juvenile. Nordmanns

3432 **Edmonton.** All Saints' Cathedral
The cathedral church of All Saints, Edmonton, 1875-1935. [Edmonton, 1935] cover-title, 48p. illus. (incl. ports.) 23cm.

Illustration on cover. Pagination includes advertising. Historical sketches by Canon E. Pierce Goulding, Mrs. V.W. Barford, Mr. Vernon W. Barford, and Mrs. W.H. Clark. U. of A.

3432A **Fear,** F.J., comp.
The call of the Northland. Winnipeg, Kingdom Print. [193_] cover-title, 24p. illus. 20 1/2cm.

Short sketches of Nipawin and White Fox, Sask. Includes poetry. Northland

3433 **Fort Qu'Appelle.** Church of S. John the Evangelist
Jubilee momento, 1885-1935. [Fort Qu'Appelle?] 1935. cover-title, 11p. illus. 18cm. Sask. Arch.

3434 Fifty years of dairying in Manitoba. Memorial souvenir presented by the Manitoba Dairy Association on the occasion of the fiftieth annual convention. Winnipeg, 1935. cover-title, 48p. illus. (incl. ports.) 24cm. Man. Leg.

3435 **Frémont,** Donatien
Mgr Provencher et son temps. Winnipeg, Editions de La Liberté, 1935. 292, [2]p., 1 l. incl. front. plates, ports., maps. 19cm. U. of S.

3436 **Gardiner,** James Garfield
Address on the problems of Western Canada ... before the Empire Club of Toronto, Friday, March 8th, 1935. [Toronto, 1935] cover-title, [8]p. port. 23cm. Glenbow

3437 **Gibbon,** John Murray
Steel of empire; the romantic history of the Canadian Pacific, the North-west passage of today. Indianapolis, Bobbs-Merrill Co. [1935] [ii], 423p. front., illus., plates (part col.) ports. (part col.) maps (part fold.) facsims. 24cm. Maps on end-papers. Man. Leg.

3438 **Grey Owl**
The adventures of Sajo and her beaver people. London, L. Dickson & Thompson [1935] xv p., 2 l., 256p. front. (port.) illus., plates. 20cm. U. of A. (Educ.)

3439 **Harrington,** M.A.
25th anniversary, St. Anne's Parish, Blairmore, Alberta. Blairmore, Enterprise Job Print [1935] 35p. illus., ports. 17cm.
Xerox copy. Glenbow

3440 **Herklots,** H[ugh] G[erald] G[ibson]
The first winter; a Canadian chronicle. London, Dent, 1935. xiii, 176p. front. 19cm.
Experiences in and around Winnipeg; an Englishman's impressions. Can. Cat.

3441 **Hudson's Bay Company**
List of books relating to Hudson's Bay Company. [Winnipeg?] 1935. cover-title, 13p. 23cm.
A reprint of two articles which appeared originally in The Beaver. Private copy

3442 **Hudson's Bay Company**
Petit histoire de la Compagnie de la Baie d'Hudson. [n.p., n.d.] cover-title, 46, [1]p. illus., map. 21 1/2cm. Private copy

3443 **Humble,** Harry
Social Credit democracy vs. dictatorship. Calgary, W.D. Stovel [1935] cover-title, 22p. 22cm.
An attack on Social Credit. Glenbow

3444 **Jaques,** Edna
Drifting soil. 2d ed. Moose Jaw, Moose Jaw Times, 1935. 19p. port. 13cm.
Poetry. 'Drifting Soil' and 'Wide Horizons' together sold 10,000 copies in two months when first published in 1932. Can. Cat.

3445 **Jaques,** Edna
My kitchen window. Toronto, Thomas Allen, 1935. ix, 83p. 19cm.
Poetry. Can. Cat.

3446 **Jaques,** Edna
Wide horizons. 2d ed. Moose Jaw, Moose Jaw Times, 1935. 20p. port. 13cm.
Poetry; first published in 1932. See note in Entry 3444. Can. Cat.

3447 **Kirkconnell,** Watson
Canadian overtones; an anthology of Canadian poetry written originally in Icelandic, Swedish, Norwegian, Hungarian, Italian, Greek, and Ukrainian, and now translated and edited with biographical, historical, critical and bibliographical notes. Winnipeg, Printed by the Columbia Press, 1935. 104p. 19cm. U. of M.

3448 **Kudryk,** Wasyl
Chuzha ruka. Winnipeg, Vistnyk, 1935. 208p. 17cm. U. of A.

3449 **Lang,** C[hristopher] D.
Rhymes of a roughneck. Winnipeg, Jackson Trade Publishing Co., 1935. 46p. Not seen. Can. Cat.

3450 **Laurie**, R[ichard] C[arnie]
Reminiscences of early days in Battleford and with Middleton's column ... Recollections of incidents of travel, early surveys, Poundmaker racket in 1884, Fish Creek, Batoche, Frog Lake massacre, pursuit of Big Bear, etc. Battleford, Saskatchewan Herald, 1935. 140p. 21 1/2cm.

Fewer than a hundred copies were printed, and most of these were distributed to friends of the author. Shortt

3451 **Lecky**, Peter [pseud. of Peter Hopegood]
Peter Lecky, by himself. Toronto, Nelson, 1935. 349p. 20 1/2cm. Not seen.

Includes a section describing his experiences as a cowpuncher in Western Canada before World War I. Published by Cape of London and by Scribner of New York. L.C.

3452 **Lehmann**, Heinz
Das evangelische Deutschtum in Kanada. Sonderdruck aus dem Jahrbuch 1935 'Auslanddeutschtum und evangelische Kirche,' herausgegeben von D. Dr. Schubert. Berlin, 1935. 38p. Br. Mus.

3453 **Lloyd**, Cecil Richard Francis
Landfall; collected poems. Toronto, Ryerson Press [1935] 47p. 20cm. U. of A.

3454 **Love**, J.R.
A cross examination of the Alberta Plan of Social Credit. [Edmonton? Reliance Printing Co. Ltd., 1935?] cover-title, [8] p. illus. 29cm. Glenbow

3455 **Lussier**, [J.B.] Rodrigue
La sécheresse dans l'Ouest. Un problème national. [Montréal, L'Imprimerie Modèle Limitée, 1935] 121p., 3 l. incl. maps, table, diagr. 18 1/2cm. Shortt

3456 **McClung**, Nellie L[etitia (Mooney)]
Clearing in the West; my own story. Toronto, Thomas Allen [c1935] 4p.l., 3-378p. 21 1/2cm.

Also published by Revell of New York. U. of S.

3456A **McCollum**, Watt Hugh
Who owns Canada? An examination of the facts concerning the concentration of the ownership and control of the means of production, distribution and exchange in Canada. Regina, Saskatchewan C.C.F. Research Bureau [1935] 60p. illus. 23cm. (Pamphlet no.1)

Pamphlet consists of articles originally published in the C.C.F. Research Review. Glenbow

3457 **McCulloch**, John Herries
Dark acres. Edinburgh, Moray Press, 1935. 318p. 19 1/2cm.

Fiction. U. of S.

3458 **McKee**, G[eorge] A[lbert]
Edmonton School District, no.7, 1885-1935. [Edmonton, Edmonton Public School Board, 1935] 30, [1] p. illus. (incl. ports.) 23cm. Shortt

3459 **Mackintosh,** W[illiam] A[rchibald]
Economic problems of the Prairie Provinces, by W.A. Mackintosh assisted by A.B. Clark, G.A. Elliott, W.W. Swanson. Toronto, Macmillan Co., 1935. ix, 308p. incl. illus. (maps) tables. diagrs. 26cm. (Canadian frontiers of settlement) U. of S.

3460 **MacLeod,** Margaret Arnett
The frozen priest of Pembina. 2d ed. [Winnipeg? Northwest Review, 1935?] [19]p. illus. 22 1/2cm. Reprinted from the Catholic World, New York.
The story of Father Goiffon's journey and misfortune in November 1860. Winnipeg

3460A **McMillan,** Sophia Louise
Manitoba vision and other poems. [n.p., n.d.] 55p. Northland

3461 **Michell,** H[umfrey]
Social Credit; the Alberta experiment. [Montreal, Financial Times, 1935?] cover-title, 7, [1]p. 23 1/2cm. U. of S.

3462 **Moose Jaw.** St. Barnabas Church
Souvenir of consecration, May, 1935. [Moose Jaw, 1935] 24p. illus., ports.
Includes historical notes. Adelphi

3463 **Morice,** A[drien] G[abriel]
A critical history of the Red River insurrection after official documents and non-Catholic sources. Winnipeg, Canadian Publishers, 1935. 375p. plates, ports. 25cm. Shortt

3464 **Niven,** Frederick [John]
The flying years. London, Wm. Collins & Sons, 1935. 284p. 19 1/2cm.
Fiction. U. of S.

3465 **Olafson,** K.K.
The Icelandic Lutheran Synod; survey and interpretation, 1885-1935. [Winnipeg, Art Press Ltd., 1935] 35p. illus. (incl. port.) 23cm.
Relates to the Icelandic Evangelical Lutheran Synod in North America. N.Y.

3466 **Patton,** Harald S[mith]
The Canadian wheat pool in prosperity and depression. [Winnipeg] Canadian Wheat Pools, 1935. cover-title, 18p. 23cm. Reprinted from Economics, sociology and modern world; essays in honor of T.N. Carver. (Harvard University Press, 1935) Shortt

3466A **Peterson,** Charles Walter Christian
The western drought situation and its implications. Calgary, Farm and Ranch Review [1935] cover-title, 19p. tables. 23 x 10cm. Glenbow

3467 **Prince Albert.** Old Timers
Reminiscences of the Riel Rebellion of 1885, as told by old timers of Prince Albert and district who witnessed those stirring days. Prince Albert, Herald Printing Co. [1935] 52p. illus. (incl. ports.) 22cm.
Reprinted from the Prince Albert Daily Herald, 19 March to 26 April 1935. Sask. Arch.

3468 **Radke**, G.D.
Major Douglas's interim report under your microscope. What did Major Douglas say in his interim report to the U.F.A. Government? ... [Fort Macleod, Alta.] Macleod Gazette Print [1935] cover-title, 20p. 19cm. Glenbow

3469 **Ramsay**, Alexander
Coercion; a one act play. Toronto, Samuel French (Canada), 1935. 28p. plan. 19cm. (Can. playwright series)

The setting is a farm in northern Alberta and the effects of the Depression on the lives of the family. Can. Cat.

3470 **Robinson**, Harold
Prairie days and other verse. Printed privately. [n.p., 1935] 67p. Not seen. U. of T. Quarterly, 1935-6

3471 **Rouse**, J[ohn] J[ames]
Pioneer work in Canada, practically presented. Kilmarnock, Scot., John Ritchie, Ltd., Publisher of Christian literature [1935] 181, [1]p. front. (port.) plates. 19cm.

The autobiography of an evangelist of a sect called 'those who gather alone in the name of our Lord Jesus Christ.' About half the book deals with his ministry in Western Canada. Alta. Leg.

3472 **Sandercock**, W. Clark
The dance of the buffalo skull and other poems. Toronto, S.J. Reginald Saunders [1935] 156p. 20 1/2cm. U. of S.

3473 **Saskatoon**. Third Avenue United Church
'Other men have labored and we have entered into their labors.' Third Avenue United Church, Saskatoon, 1902-1935. [Saskatoon, 1935] 36p.

A history of this church. C.H.R., 1935

3474 **Sauvé**, G.
Le crédit social (Douglas et Aberhart) Ottawa, Editions de l'Université d'Ottawa, 1935. 36p. Not seen. C.J.E.P.S., 1936

3474A **Sevareid**, Arnold E.
Canoeing with the Cree. New York, Macmillan, 1935. xii p., 1 l., 201p. illus. (map) plates, ports. 20cm.

A canoe journey from Minneapolis to York Factory by two high-school boys. Northland

3475 **Sinclair**, J[ohn] D.
The Queen's Own Cameron Highlanders of Canada; twenty-fifth anniversary souvenir. Winnipeg, 1935. 99p. plates, ports. 24cm. Winnipeg

3476 **Sinton**, Robert
Looking backward from the eightieth milestone, 1935 to 1854. Memories recalled. [Regina, Paragon Business College, 1935] 2p.l., 102p. ports. 22 1/2cm. Mimeographed. Portraits are photographs mounted on inside covers. Shortt

3477 **Strange,** Henry George Latimer
The Western Canada semi-arid area – its history and probable future. Winnipeg, Wallingford Press, 1935. 30p. Can. Cat.

3478 **Stricker,** Jakob
Erlebnisse eines Schweizers in Kanada. Zürich, Orell Fussli [c1935] 150p. plates, ports. 22 1/2cm. L.C.

3478A **Thomas,** Edgar J[ames]
Three poems. [Winnipeg? 193_] 7p.

Titles of poems: Jubilee ode, Christmas carol, New Year's wassail. Northland

3479 **Thomas,** Lillian (Beynon)
Jim Barber's spite fence; a comedy in one act. Toronto, Samuel French, 1935. 32p. 19cm. (Can. playwright series)

'A character of neighbors and their grown-up children in a western setting.' Can. Cat.

3480 **Tranter,** G[ladys] Joy
Winged words. Winnipeg, Wallingford Press, 1935. 20p. Not seen.

Poetry. Can. Cat.

3481 **Trémaudan,** Auguste Henri de
Histoire de la nation métisse dans l'Ouest canadien. [Montréal] Lévesque, 1935. 448, [2]p. 20cm. (Documents historiques) Man. Leg.

3482 **Walker,** James H.
A Scotsman in Canada. London, J. Cape [1935] 3p.l., 9-381p. 20 1/2cm.

Describes work on harvesting and railroad gangs in Western Canada about 1923; the author spent part of the winter in Ontario. U. of S.

3483 **Watson,** Robert
When Christmas came to Fort Garry; a romance of the early Red River days. Toronto, Ryerson, 1935. 35p. front., illus.

Fiction. Can. Cat.

3484 **Weekes,** Mary [Loretto]
Round the council fires. Toronto, Ryerson, 1935. 113p. illus.

Indians. Can. Cat.

3485 **Western Canada Federation**
Western Canada Federation. Saskatoon, Printed by General Printing & Bookbinding Ltd. [1935?] 16p. double map. 23cm.

The federation favoured the secession of the four western provinces from Canada. R. Roger Smith was secretary. Sask. Arch.

3486 **Winnipeg.** Rosedale United Church
Rosedale United Church, silver jubilee anniversary, 1910-1935. [Winnipeg, 1935] 39, [1]p. illus. (incl. ports.) 25cm. United College

3487 **Woods,** David Scott
Financing the schools of rural Manitoba. Chicago, 1935. 2p.l., iii-xiii, 261p. illus. (maps) diagrs. 24cm. Photolithographed. U. of S.

3488 **Writers' Club of Regina College**
Tuesday night, 1935. Regina, Western Printers, 1935. 32p.

A collection of short stories, plays, and essays. Can. Cat.

3489 **Alberta**. Department of Agriculture. Committee on the drought area
A report on the rehabilitation of the dry areas of Alberta, and crop insurance, 1935-1936. Edmonton, King's Printer, 1936. 80p. illus. (maps) 25 1/2cm. U. of S.

3490 **Alberta Wheat Pool**
Tides in the West; a brief history of the origin, aims and objectives of the wheat pool movement in Western Canada. [Calgary, 1936] cover-title, 45, vi p. incl. port., illus. 23cm. Glenbow

3491 **Battleford**. St. George's Church
St. George's Church, Battleford (Diocese of Saskatoon) Fiftieth anniversary of the first service held in the completed church, October 10, 1886. [Battleford, 1936] 6p. illus. 21cm.

On cover: Golden jubilee celebrations, October 11 and 12, 1936. Sask. Arch.

3492 **Betts**, Mary
Dreams. [Edmonton? 1936?] 33p. Not seen.

Poetry. U. of T. Quarterly, 1936-7

3493 **Bozyk**, Pantelemon
Kanadyska musa. Yorkton, Redemptorist Fathers, 1936. 192p. 18 1/2cm. Not seen.

About 130 poems written in Ukrainian. Can. Cat.

3494 **Brooker**, Bertram
Think of the earth. Toronto, Nelson [1936] 2p.l., 7-288p. 20cm.

A novel set in a Manitoba town about the turn of the century. It won the Governor-General's fiction award. Can. Cat.

3495 Canada. Het rijk van de toekomst. Uitgeg door het Bureau van de Canadeesche Handel-Delegatie, Rotterdam. [n.p., 1936] 79p. plan.

Dutch emigration pamphlet. Leiden

3496 The Canadian Wheat Pools on the air; a series of radio messages broadcast by officials and supporters of the wheat pools of Western Canada. 2d series. Wheat pool organizations of Manitoba, Saskatchewan and Alberta, 1936. 51p. 23cm. Can. Cat.

3497 **Cassap**, William Henry
Winnipeg to London via Hudson Bay. London, Society for Promoting Christian Knowledge, 1936. 48p. ports., map. Can. Cat.

3498 **Chapman**, Ethel
The homesteaders. Toronto, Ryerson, 1936. 252p.

Fiction. The setting is northern Saskatchewan. Can. Cat.

3499 **Church of England.** Missionary Society
Diocese of Athabasca. Toronto, Church House, 1936. cover-title, 20p. illus. 21cm. (Popular information series, no.21) Rutherford

3500 **Church of England.** Missionary Society
Diocese of Calgary. Toronto, Church House, 1936. folder. 8p. illus. 21cm. (Popular information series, no.9) Rutherford

3501 **Church of England.** Missionary Society
Diocese of Edmonton. Toronto, Church House, 1936. folder. 10p. illus. 21cm. (Popular information series, no.20) Rutherford

3502 **Collier,** Wesley H.
Super-money. Edmonton, Alberta, 1936. 24p. 22cm.

A plan to solve all public debt problems. 'Outline of the Collier plan for monetary reform' and accompanying letters laid in. Glenbow

3503 **Dawson,** C[arl] A[ddington]
Group settlement; ethnic communities in Western Canada. Toronto, Macmillan, 1936. xx, 395p. illus. 26cm. (Canadian frontiers of settlement) U. of S.

3504 **Elliott,** Courtland
Report to Alberta Bondholders' Committee; a survey of the fiscal problems of the province of Alberta in relation to the economic and social conditions affecting them [by] Courtland Elliott [and] J.A. Walker. Edmonton, 1936. 1v. (various pagings) tables (part. fold.) 28cm. Glenbow

3505 **Elliott,** Courtland
Say Alberta can pay full interest. [by Courtland Elliott and J.A. Walker. Edmonton, 1936] 16 l. L. of P.

3506 **England,** Robert
The colonization of Western Canada; a study of contemporary land settlement (1896-1934) Toronto, McClelland and Stewart, 1936. 2p.l., 3-341p. front., illus. (maps) plates. 22 1/2cm. U. of S.

3507 **Farm Appraisal Conference,** Winnipeg, 1936
Report. [n.p., n.d.] vi, 20p. 23cm.

'Held under the auspices of Mortgage Loans Association of Manitoba in Winnipeg, Manitoba, February 17th, 18th and 19th, 1936.' Glenbow

3508 **Farmer,** Bernard J.
Go west, young man. London, Nelson [1936] 309p. 20cm.

Manitoba is the setting for several chapters of the novel. Glenbow

3509 **Garrett,** Florence Pearl
Memories. Winnipeg, Wallingford Press [1936] 28p. port. Not seen.

Poetry. Can. Cat.

3510 **Grey Owl**
Tales of an empty cabin. Toronto, Macmillan, 1936. xvi, 335p. front., plates, ports. 22cm. Can. Cat.

3511 **Haver**, Malcolm J.
Social credit explained; a text book for social credit as applied to the province of Saskatchewan and other provinces of Canada. [Saskatoon, The Author, 1936] 59p. 17cm. U. of S.

3511A **Hoffman**, Norman Peter
The book of biologies of life. Regina, [Caxton Press] 1936. [1], 30, [1]p. port. 16 1/2 x 10cm.

The author was blind. Northland

3512 **Hornby**, Montague Leyland
Canada and British immigration; presented to all members of federal Parliament of Canada. Lethbridge, The Author, 1936. 90p. Can. Cat.

3513 **Irvine**, William
Let us reason together; an appeal to social crediters and C.C.F'ers. [Edmonton, Commercial Printers, n.d.] cover-title, ii, 13, [1]p. 17cm.

Written during the early years of the Aberhart government. Glenbow

3514 **Kmeta**, Ivan
Lyra emigranta. Winnipeg, Ukrainian Bookstore Press, 1936 138p. Not seen.

A collection of 243 poems which reflect the author's experiences in the Ukraine and Canada. U. of T. Quarterly, 1937-8

3515 **Kreutzweiser**, Erwin E[lgin]
The Red River insurrection; its causes and events. [Gardenvale, Que., Garden City Press, 1936?] ix p., 1 l., 166p. 19 1/2cm. Shortt

3516 **Laurence**, Frances Elsie Fry
The band plays a march. Linoleum cuts by Bessie A. Fry. [Edson, Alta., The Author, 1936] 4p.l., 3-66p. illus. 19cm.

Poetry. U. of A. (Extension)

3517 **Le Chevallier**, [Jules Jean Marie Joseph]
Esquisse sur l'origine et les premiers développements de Calgary, 1873-1913. (Préparée en 1934) Publiée en 1936 sous les auspices de la Paroisse Sainte Famille. [Calgary, 1936] 164p. illus. 23cm. Pagination includes advertising. Oblates Arch.

3518 **MacKay**, Douglas
The honourable company; a history of the Hudson's Bay Company ... Indianapolis, The Bobbs Merrill Co. [c1936] xii p., 1 l., 15-396p. incl. front. (port.) illus. (maps) plates, ports., plans, facsims. 24cm. U. of S.

3519 **Mackinnon**, Clarence D.
The life of Principal Oliver. A brief appreciation of Dr. Oliver and his work in relation to church and state, the religious and educational life of the Dominion. Toronto, Ryerson Press, 1936. viii, 162p. front. (port.) 21cm. U. of S.

3520 **Magrath**, C[harles] A[lexander]
The Galts, father and son, pioneers in the development of southern Alberta; and, How Alberta grew up, brief outline of development in the Lethbridge district.

Lethbridge, Printed by the Lethbridge Herald [1936?] cover-title, 64p. incl. illus. (incl. maps) ports. 23 1/2cm. Shortt

3521 **Maloney**, John James
Darkness, dawn and daybreak. Vol.1: The story of my life. [Vancouver, 193–?] 40p. 21cm.

About half the pamphlet deals with his anti-Catholic campaigns in Western Canada in the 1920's and 1930's. Glenbow

3522 **Morice**, Adrien Gabriel
The Catholic Church in the Canadian Northwest. Winnipeg, The Author, 1936. 86p. illus., ports. 22cm. Can. Cat.

3523 **Morrier**, Emma
Quatre essais de théâtre national. Va ton chemin. Bon sang ne ment pas. La trahison. Le rêve du poète. Edmonton, La Survivance Ltée, 1936. 113, [1]p. 19cm.

'Cet ouvrage est le premier livre écrit par une Canadienne française en Alberta.' St-Jean

3524 **Murchie**, R[obert] W[elch]
Agricultural progress on the prairie frontier ... Assisted by William Allen and J.F. Booth and others. Toronto, Macmillan Co., 1936. xii, 344p. illus. (incl. maps) diagrs. 26cm. (Canadian frontiers of settlement) U. of S.

3525 **Namao, Alta.** United Farm Women of Alberta, Local no.61
A cameo of the West; story of the pioneers of the Sturgeon River district, 1879-1900. Published by U.F.W.A., Local no.61. [Edmonton, Commercial Printers Ltd.] 1936. 54p. illus. 24cm.

Biographical sketches of pioneers. Alta. Leg.

3526 **Orr**, James Edwin
Times of refreshing; 10,000 miles of miracle through Canada. London, Marshall, Morgan & Scott [1936] 127p. 19cm.

Includes description of travels through the Prairie Provinces. Glenbow

3527 **Pálsson**, Páll S[karphédinsson]
Nordur-Reykir. Kvaedi. Winnipeg, Viking Press, 1936. 176p. port. 18 1/2cm. U. of M.

3528 **Patterson**, Cecil F[rederick]
Hardy fruits; with special reference to their culture in Western Canada. Saskatoon, The Author, 1936. xvi, 321p. illus. 22 1/2cm. U. of A.

3529 **Peterson**, C[harles] W[alter] [Christian]
Immigration and its economic background. Calgary, Farm and Ranch Review, 1936. 54p. 22 x 10cm. Shortt

3530 **Ross**, Hugh R[obert]
Thirty-five years in the limelight; Sir Rodmond P. Roblin and his times. Foreword by Rt. Hon. Arthur Meighen. Summary by Col. Garnet C. Porter. Winnipeg, Farmers' Advocate, 1936. xii, 205p. front., illus., plates, facsims. 22cm. U. of S.

3531 **Russell,** F[rancis] W.
History of St. Mary's Cathedral parish, Winnipeg, Manitoba. Diamond jubilee edition, 1936. [Winnipeg, 1936] 95p. illus. (incl. ports.) fold. plate. 32cm. Man. Leg.

3532 **St. James, Man.** St. James Church
85th anniversary book, 1850-1936. [St. James, Man., St. James Church, 1936] cover-title, 48p. illus., ports. 23 1/2cm. Man. Arch.

3533 **Sanderson,** Charles Rupert
Social Credit. Toronto, McClelland and Stewart, 1936. 27p. 21cm. Can. Cat.

3534 **Saskatchewan.** Bureau of Publications
Tourist trips through Saskatchewan. Regina, The Bureau, 1936. 95p. illus., maps. 23cm. U. of S.

3535 **Saskatchewan Co-operative Wheat Producers Limited**
Via Churchill; a shipment of Saskatchewan wheat to Europe. Regina, The Producers, 1936. 62, [2]p. illus. 22 1/2cm. U. of S.

3536 The Saskatchewan poetry book. v.1– 1936-7– Regina, Saskatchewan Poetry Society, 1936– v. 20cm. annual.

Superseded the Saskatchewan poetry year book published by the Canadian Authors' Association, Saskatchewan Branch. Two issues of the year book appeared, 1934-5 and 1935-6. 'The Crescent Moon, a magazine of original verse by Canadian prairie writers' was published in Moose Jaw by the Prairie Poetry Club. Two issues appeared, Fall 1934 and Spring 1935. Saskatoon

3537 **Saskatoon.** Grace United Church
Golden jubilee, 1886-1936. [Saskatoon, Star-Phoenix, 1936] 40p. illus. (incl. ports.) 23cm. Saskatoon

3538 **Schott,** Carl
Landnahme und kolonisation in Canada am beispiel Sudontarios. Kiel, 1936. 330p. illus., maps, wrappers. (Schriften des Geographischen Institutsder Universitat Kiel. Band VI)

Presentation copy to Herbert Bolton. Agric.

3539 **Schreiber,** Ilse
Die schwestern aus Memel; ein Kanada-roman. Berlin, Zeitgeschichte [1936] 231p. illus., map. 23cm.

Story of the Jeepsche family emigrating to Western Canada, and their experiences there. Austria

3540 **Sigbjornsson,** Rannveig Kristin G.
Pebbles on the beach. Treherne, Man., Treherne Times, 1936. 17p. Not seen. U. of T. Quarterly, 1936-7

3541 **Spence,** Geo[rge]
Co-operation in empire development. A speech ... at the Saskatchewan Immigration and Settlement Convention at Saskatoon on September 23rd, 1936 ... [n.p., 1936?] cover-title, 11p. 25cm. Shortt

3542 **Stanley**, George F[rancis] G[ilman]
The birth of Western Canada; a history of the Riel rebellions. Toronto, Longmans, Green, 1936. xiv, 475p. front., plates, ports., maps. 22 1/2cm.

A scholarly and objective study of two controversial events in Canada's political history. U. of S.

3543 **Stewart**, Charles G.
Social Credit theories exploded! Winnipeg [193–] 23p. 15cm. U. of A.

3544 **Ströme**, Arne
De lange veje. Kobenhavn, Glydendal, 1936. 170p. 21cm.

This book has two sections. The first part is entitled 'Fra Canadas praerie'; a fictionalized account of experiences and people in a typical rural community in the Canadian West. The second part is entitled 'Fra Ruslands steppe.' Norway

3545 **Thomson**, Robert Burns
The poems of Robert Burns Thomson; with introduction, notes, glossary, and index of first lines ... Winnipeg, Wallingford Press Ltd., 1936. xxiv, 387p. 19 1/2cm. L.C.

3546 **Winnipeg**. St. James Anglican Church
85th anniversary book: 1850-1936. [Winnipeg, 1936] cover-title, 48p. illus., ports. 23cm.

Accompanying circular tipped in. Includes advertising matter. Glenbow

3547 **Winnipeg**. St. Nicholas School
Almanakh yuvileyu shkoly Sv. O. Nykolaya ... 1911-1936. Winnipeg, 1936. 96p. illus. 26cm. Not seen.

Compiled by A. Zahariychuk. Private information

3548 **Winnipeg**. St. Vladimir and St. Olga Parish
Yuvileyniy almanakh Ukr. Hr. Kat-tserkvy Sv. Volodymyra i Olhy, 1901-1936. Winnipeg, 1936. 86p. illus. 26cm. Not seen. Private information

3549 **Towarzystwo Sw. Jana Kantego**, Winnipeg
Memorial booklet published on the occasion of the opening of new domicile, December, 13th, 1936. [Winnipeg, 1936] 45p. illus., ports.

On cover: Dedication program. Advertising matter included in paging. P.43-45 left blank for autographs. Text in Polish. Turek

3550 **Zimmermann**, Andreas
Die romisch-catholische Pfarrei, St. Joseph bei Balgonie Saskatchewan. Zum Funfzigjahrigen Jubilaum. 1 Juni 1936. [n.p., 1936] 20p. illus. 18cm. Sask. Arch.

3551 **Alberta Wheat Pool**
The need for a national wheat board; a review of the events in wheat marketing in Canada over the past nineteen years. Calgary [1937] cover-title, 8p. 22cm. Glenbow

3552 **Alberta Women's Institute Girls' Club**
The A.W.I.G.C. magazine. Calgary, Printed by Phoenix Press Co. [1937?] 64p. illus., ports. 23cm.

Title on cover: Year book 1937. Glenbow

3553 Anthology of Y.C. verse; volume of selections from verse contributed by the Young Co-operators and published in the Western Producer from 1932 to 1936. Saskatoon, Western Producer, 1937. 75p. U. of S.

3554 **Canadian Authors' Association.** Calgary Branch
Canadian poems. Calgary, 1937. 46p. 22cm. U. of A.

3555 **Collier,** Herbert B.
Remember when? History of the Viking district. [Edmonton, Commercial Printers Ltd., 1937?] cover-title, 72p. illus. (incl. ports.) 23cm. Pagination includes advertising. U. of A.

3556 **Complin,** Margaret [(Robertson)]
Winged moccasins to winged words. [Regina, Western Printers Association, 1937?] [23]p. 23cm.

Historical sketches of Regina and Ft. Qu'Appelle. Shortt

3556A **Dickson,** [Horatio Henry] Lovat
Grey Owl: a biographical note; and A day at Beaver Lodge. London, L. Dickson, 1937. [16]p. incl. covers. illus., ports. (1 col. on cover) 25cm.

'The material quoted in "A day at Beaver Lodge" is selected from Grey Owl's writings, and is published in this form as a souvenir of his visit to the United Kingdom in the autumn of 1937.'
With Grey Owl's autograph on cover. Glenbow

3557 **Douglas,** Clifford Hugh
The Alberta experiment; an interim survey. London, Eyre and Spottiswoode, 1937. viii, 220p. 18cm. U. of S.

3558 **Economic Safety League**
... The dangers of Douglasism. A one night study of the craze called 'National dividends.' Written in language anyone can understand. Not in the interest of any political party. Farmers, laborers, merchants, all producers, strike a blow for the defense of Alberta and its credit ... Drumheller, The League [1937?] cover-title, 24p. illus. on end papers. 22 1/2cm.

At head of title: 'Come let us reason together' - Isaiah - 1:18. U. of C.

3559 **Erickson,** S.P.
Black blizzards and a lost gold mine. [Ft. Qu'Appelle? 1937] cover-title, 19p. plan. 20cm.

The author advocated tree-planting on the prairies to prevent drought. Sask. Arch.

3560 **Ewach,** Honore
Holos zemli. Winnipeg, Ukrainian Publishing Co., 1937. 92p 24cm.

A novel describing the pioneering experiences of a Ukrainian family living northwest of Dauphin, Man. U. of S.

3561 **Garrett,** Florence Pearl
Life's gleanings. Winnipeg, The Author, 1937. 36p. Not seen.

Poetry. Can. Cat.

3562 **Garrett**, Florence Pearl
Whispering leaves. Winnipeg, The Author, 1937. 32p. port. 13cm.
Not seen.

Poetry. Can. Cat.

3563 **Hattersley**, C[harles] Marshall
Aberhart and Alberta. London, Published for the York Social Credit Conference Liaison Committee [1937] 43p. 22cm. (York pamphlets)

On preliminary leaf as a subsidiary title: The first phase.
Xerox copy. U. of A.

3564 **Hermant**, Léon
L'épopée d'un évêque-missionnaire; le serviteur de Dieu, Vital-Justin Grandin, Oblat de Marie Immaculée. St-Albert, Couvent des Oblats [1937] 173p. illus. 24cm. St-Albert Museum

3565 **Huber**, Armin O[tto]
Helga und der Hermelin; Roman einer kanadischen Liebe. Berlin, Scherl [c1937] 244, [1]p. 19cm. L.C.

3566 **Leacock**, Stephen [Butler]
My discovery of the West; a discussion of east and west in Canada. Toronto, Thomas Allen, 1937. viii, 272p. 21cm.

Jokes and reflections collected during a lecture trip through the West. C.H.R., 1937

3567 **Litterick**, J[ames]
Whither Manitoba? Speech delivered in Manitoba Legislature on Feb. 24th, 1937. Toronto [1937] 32p. port. 16cm. Queen's

3568 **M., J.H.**
Memoirs of Castor and district. Castor, Alta. [Castor Advance] 1937. 60p. illus., map. 21 1/2cm. Glenbow

3569 **McConnell**, William Kennedy
The Alberta fiasco. [Sydney, Printed by W. Horner] 1937. 31p. 21 1/2cm.

Relates to Alberta politics. N.Y.

3570 **MacKay**, Mrs. A.M.
History of Scotia, 1882-1937. [Hamiota, Man., Echo print, 1937] 16p. illus. 22cm.

The history of a church congregation, formerly Presbyterian, near Hamiota.
United College

3571 **Mackenzie**, Cecil Walter
Donald Mackenzie, 'King of the Northwest'; the story of an international hero of the Oregon country and the Red River Settlement at Lower Fort Garry (Winnipeg). Los Angeles, I. Deach, 1937. xviii p., 1 l., 21-210p. front. (port.) illus. (port.) plates. 23 1/2cm. U. of S.

3572 **MacKinnon**, James N.
Moosomin and its pioneers, including humorous incidents and up-to-date sketches. Moosomin, World-Spectator [1937] 2p.l., 67p. illus. 23cm.
Shortt

3573 **McLaurin**, C[olin] C[ampbell]
Sixty years in the ministry. Edmonton, Institute Press, 1937. 13p. Not seen. C.H.R., 1939

3574 **MacLeod**, Margaret Arnett
Bells of Red River. Winnipeg, Stovel Co., 1937. 41p. illus. 23cm.

A second edition was published in 1938. Shortt

3575 **Manitoba**. University
Manitoba essays; written in commemoration of the sixtieth anniversary of the University of Manitoba by members of the teaching staffs of the university and its affiliated colleges. R.C. Lodge, ed. Toronto, Macmillan, 1937. xiii p., 1 l., 432p. incl. plates. front. 22cm. U. of S.

3576 **Marks**, Alfred L[ouis]
Public denied facts by Edmonton Journal ... [Edmonton, United Democrats, 1937] cover-title, [4]p. 28cm.

Letters on the Alberta credit legislation disallowed by the Privy Council. Glenbow

3577 **Morton**, Arthur S[ilver]
Under western skies; being a series of pen-pictures of the Canadian West in early fur trade times. Toronto, Thos. Nelson & Sons Ltd. [c1937] 9p.l., 232p. front., plates., ports., facsim. 21 1/2cm. Maps on lining-papers. Shortt

3578 **Mowery**, William Byron
The black automatic. Boston, Little, Brown, 1937. 4p.l., [3]-284p. 19 1/2cm.

Fiction. The setting is in Winnipeg and the West. L.C.

3579 **Nesbitt**, Leonard D.
The weather in the West. [n.p.] 1937. cover-title, 10p. illus., map. 23cm. U. of S.

3580 **Peterson**, C[harles] W[alter] C[hristian]
The banks and social credit; an address delivered at a meeting of the Kiwanis Club, Calgary, October 4th, 1937. Calgary, Published by the People's League of Alberta [1937] cover-title, 23p. 22 x 10cm. Glenbow

3581 **Peterson**, C[harles] W[alter] [Christian]
Social Credit; a critical analysis. Calgary, The Author, 1937. cover-title, 32p. 23cm. Glenbow

3582 [**Powell**, George P.]
Bankers' toadies – exterminate them. [Edmonton, 1937] caption-title, 1 l. with printing on front and verso.

20,000 copies of this leaflet were printed in September and some distributed, when a charge of defamatory libel (laid by one of the nine prominent Edmonton men named) led to a police raid and seizure of the leaflet. In the trial, 8-15 November, Powell and Joseph Unwin, a member of the Alberta legislature, were found guilty and given gaol terms of six months and three months respectively. Private information

3583 **Salverson,** Laura Goodman
The dark weaver; against the sombre background of the old generations flame the scarlet banners of the new. Toronto, Ryerson, 1937. 415p. 19cm. Not seen.

Fiction. Published in London by Low, Marston & Co. in 1938. Can. Cat.

3584 **Saskatchewan Immigration and Settlement Convention Committee**
British family settlement in Canada: Saskatchewan's standpoint; four addresses delivered at the Saskatchewan immigration and settlement convention. Saskatoon, The Committee, 1937. 16p. U. of S.

3585 **Sinclair,** J[ohn] D.
Westminster Church, the United Church of Canada, Winnipeg, forty-fifth year; souvenir of the silver jubilee of the present church building. Winnipeg, 1937. 101p. plates, ports. 23cm. Man. Leg.

3586 **Smith,** R. Roger
Alberta has the sovereign right to issue and use its own credit; a factual examination of the constitutional problems. Ottawa, 1937. 16p. 22 1/2cm.

'The information contained in this booklet was placed before Premier Aberhart and members of his cabinet by R. Roger Smith in Oct., 1935.' Can. Arch.

3587 **Springett,** Evelyn Cartier (Galt)
For my children's children. Montreal [Printed by Unity Press] 1937. 4p.l., 204p. front., plates, ports. 21cm.

The author's husband was manager of the New Oxley, or Lazy H Ranch, and later of the ranch of the Canadian Land & Ranch Company, better known as the '76.' Lethbridge

3588 **Stark,** James H.
Social Credit in Alberta. Published by the Enterprise, Consort, Alberta. 1st Australian edition. [Brisbane, New World Publishing Co., 1937] cover-title, 16p. 21cm. Glenbow

3589 **Strange,** Kathleen (Redman)
With the West in her eyes; story of a modern pioneer. New York, Dodge, 1937. ix, 292p. 21 1/2cm.

A revised edition with a foreword by Lady Tweedsmuir and an epilogue by the author was published in Toronto, Macmillan, 1945. (In Rutherford) Can. Cat.

3590 **Walker,** Gertrude E.
Romantic Winnipeg. Winnipeg, Farmers' Advocate press, 1937. 48p. C.H.R., 1938

3591 **Weekes,** Mary [Loretto]
The wheatland, by Mary Weekes. Regina, Western Printers Ltd., 1937. [29]p. 22 1/2cm.

Literary sketches. Shortt

3592 **Women's Institutes, Alberta**
A story of the Alberta Women's Institutes, 1909-1937. [Edmonton, 1937] 62p. illus., ports. 17cm. Glenbow

3593 **Yelle**, Emile
La situation des Manitobains de langue française. St-Boniface, La Liberté, 1937. cover-title, 19p. 23cm.

An address delivered at the Congrès de la langue française in Quebec.
Collection Gagnon

3594 **Syndykat Emigracyjny**
Wiadomości o Kanadzie dla użytku wychodźców. Warsaw, 1937. 70p. fold. map. 14cm. (Biblioteczka Syndykatu Emigracyjnego, no.4)

Title in English: Information on Canada of use in emigrating. Poland

3595 **Alberta**
The case for Alberta ... Published by order of the Executive Council. Edmonton, Printed by A. Shnitka, 1938. 2v. in 1. map, tables, diagrs. 29cm.

'Addressed to the sovereign people of Canada and their governments.' Contents: 1. Alberta's problems and dominion-provincial relations. 2. The urgent need for social and economic reform. Glenbow

3596 **Armstrong**, Clara
Stars of happiness. Abbey, Sask., The Author, 1938. 23p. Not seen.

Poetry. Can. Cat.

3597 **Attwood**, C[harles] H.
The water resources of Manitoba, by C.H. Attwood, assisted by D.M. Stephens and B.B. Hogarth. [Winnipeg] Economic Survey Board, 1938. [4], 116p. plates, diagrs. 27 1/2cm. U. of S.

3598 **Bicknell**, Minnie Evans
Relief; a play in one act. Toronto, Macmillan, 1938. 28p. diagr. 16cm.

A story of crop failures on a western farm. Prize-winning presentation by the Marshall, Sask., dramatic club at the Dominion Drama Festival in 1936. Can. Cat.

3599 **Boyd**, Hugh [Ross Cameron]
New breaking; an outline of co-operation among the western farmers of Canada. Toronto, J.M. Dent & Sons Ltd. [1938] 215p. incl. front. plates, ports. 21 1/2cm. Shortt

3600 **Bugnet**, Georges [Charles Jules]
Voix de la solitude. Montréal, Editions du Totem [1938] 145p. 19cm.

Poetry. U. of A.

3601 **Cameron**, S[tewart]
No matter how thin you slice it - 63 cartoons. [Calgary, Calgary Herald, 1938?] cover-title, [64]p. illus. 31cm.

Cartoons on Premier Aberhart and Social Credit which appeared in the Calgary Herald.
Can. Arch.

3602 [**Cameron**, W.B.]
The yarn of the Howling Gale (An Alberta barque with a bad tight) Athabasca, Alta., Cameron Shipyards [c1938] 12p. 17 1/2cm.

Political satire directed at the Social Credit party. Poetry. The author may have been William Bleasdell Cameron. Rutherford

3603 **Campbell,** Marjorie [Elliott] (Wilkins)
The soil is not enough. Toronto, The Macmillan Co. of Canada, Ltd., 1938. 6p.l., 3-285p. 20cm.

Homesteading experiences of the author's father, an Englishman who settled with his family about 40 miles north of Ft. Qu'Appelle, Sask., in 1904. Shortt

3604 **Campbell,** Zola Isabell (Campbell)
A tale of the early years. [Edmonton, n.d.] [16]p. 20cm.

A narrative poem describing the early days of South Edmonton (Strathcona).
Private copy

3605 **Canada.** Army. 1st Canadian Pioneer Battalion
Brief history of the Battalion; France & Flanders, 1916-18. Calgary, 1st Pioneers' Assoc., Calgary Branch, 1938. cover-title, [1] 14 l. illus. 29cm.

At head of title: 1st Canadian Pioneers, C.E.F.
Mimeographed. Glenbow

3606 **Catley,** Elaine M[aud (Clark)]
Canada calling. Calgary, The Author, 1938. 31p. Not seen.

Poetry. Can. Cat.

3607 **Chalmers,** John West
Builders of the West. Edmonton, Institute of Applied Art, 1938. 52p. illus. 23cm. (Grade six social studies. Book 7) Glenbow

3608 **Clay,** Charles
Swampy Cree legends; being twenty folk tales from the annals of a primitive, mysterious, fast-disappearing Canadian race; as told by Kuskapatchees, the Smoky One. Toronto, Macmillan, 1938. xvii p., 1 l., 95p. front. (port.) 20 1/2cm. U. of S.

3609 **Clay,** Charles
Young voyageur. London, Oxford University Press, 1938. viii, 409p. 19 1/2cm. Maps on lining-papers. Not seen.

Juvenile fiction, with the setting east of Lake Winnipeg. L.C.

3610 **Cole,** George E[dwards]
The mineral resources of Manitoba. [Winnipeg] Economic Survey Board, 1938. 201 l. plates, fold. tables, diagrs. 27 1/2cm. U. of S.

3611 **Crocombe,** Leonard
An editor goes West; a holiday notebook. London, Harrap [1938] 255p. front. (port.) 22 1/2cm. Br. Mus.

3612 **Dale,** Arch
$25.00 a month; adventures in Aberhartia with Arch Dale and the Winnipeg Free Press. [Winnipeg, Winnipeg Free Press, 1938] [60]p. illus. 21 x 23cm.

This series of cartoons originally appeared in the Winnipeg Free Press during the first three years of Social Credit government in Alberta. Rutherford

3613 **Davidson,** C[live] B.
Employment in Manitoba. [Winnipeg] Economic Survey Board, 1938. 79 l. diagrs. 27 1/2cm. U. of S.

3614 **Davidson**, C[live] B.
The population of Manitoba; preliminary report, by C.B. Davidson, H.C. Grant, and F. Shefrin. [Winnipeg] Economic Survey Board, 1938. 185 l. maps, diagrs. 27 1/2cm. U. of S.

3615 **Desrosiers**, Léo Paul
Les engagés du Grand Portage. Paris, Gallimard, 1938. 209p., 2 l. 19cm. Not seen.

A novel of the fur trade. L.C.

3616 **Dickson**, [Horatio Henry] Lovat
The green leaf, a tribute to Grey Owl ... London, Lovat Dickson [1938] 100p. front., plates, ports. 22 1/2cm. Glenbow

3617 **Dillabough**, J[ames] V[idal]
Transportation in Manitoba. [Winnipeg] Economic Survey Board, 1938. 145 l. plates, maps, tables, diagrs. 27cm. U. of S.

3618 **Düesberg**, Gerd
Zur wildnis ferner wälder; eine ferienfahrt nach Kanada. Berlin, Hugo Bermühler [1938] 148p. plates, map. 21cm.

Title in English: The wilderness of forests, a vacation trip to Canada.
Describes a trip as far west as Alberta. Austria

3618A **Edmonton**. Chamber of Commerce
Copy of petition for the disallowance of certain acts of the Legislature of Alberta passed at the 1938 session. Edmonton, 1938. cover-title, 12p. 27cm.

The acts in question were: 1. The home owners security act, chap.29. 2. The debt adjustment act, 1937, amendment act 1938, chap.27. 3. The limitation of actions act, 1935, amendment act, 1938, chap.28. 4. The tax recovery act 1938, chap.82. 5. The 1938 securities tax act, chap.7. Glenbow

3619 **Eggleston**, Wilfrid
The high plains. Toronto, Macmillan, 1938. 5p.l., 267p. 21cm.

Fiction. U. of S.

3620 **Ellis**, J[oseph] H[enry]
The soils of Manitoba. [Winnipeg] Economic Survey Board, 1938. [112]p. illus., maps, diagrs. 27 1/2cm. Maps in pocket. U. of S.

3621 **Ells**, S[ydney] C[larke]
Northland trails. [Toronto, Garden City Press, 1938] 1p.l., [5]-189p. illus. (incl. map) 23 1/2cm.

Largely relates to the area around Waterways, Fort McMurray, and Portage la Loche. Dempsey

3622 **Entwistle**, Mary
On trail with the redskins: James Evans, friend of the fur-trappers. Edinburgh, Edinburgh House Press [1938] 32p. 19cm. (Eagle books, no.14)

Also printed in New York by the Friendship Press. Northland

3623 **Fetherstonhaugh**, Robert Collier
The Royal Canadian Mounted Police. Toronto, McClelland & Stewart, 1938. xii, 322p. front., plates, maps. 23cm. U. of A. (Educ.)

3624 **Finsdóttir**, Gudrún
Hillingalond. Reykjavik, Felags Printing Press, 1938. 224p.

A volume of collected stories, most of them with a Western Canadian setting. U. of T. Quarterly, 1938-9

3625 **Gordon**, Charles William
Postscript to adventure; the autobiography of Ralph Connor. New York, Farrar & Rinehart [c1938] xvi p., 2 l., 3-430p. front., plates, ports. 23 1/2cm. U. of S.

3626 **Grant**, H[enry] C[lark]
The commercial fishing industry of Manitoba. [Winnipeg] Economic Survey Board, 1938. 69 l. illus., map, diagrs. 27cm. U. of S.

3627 **Grossman**, Vladimir
The soil's calling. Foreword by Louis Fitch. [Montreal] Eagle Publishing Co., 1938. 128p. 22cm.

Urging Jews to establish agricultural colonies in Canada, particularly in Western Canada. Glenbow

3628 **Halpin**, Barney
Pulpit pounding Bill. Black Diamond, Alta. [1938?] ... Not seen.

Rollicking rhymes mentioned in 'The Rebel' v.2, no.2, 2 Jan. 1939, p.4. Published by J.J. Zubick. 'The Rebel' is in the Glenbow collection.

3629 [**Hermant**, Léon]
Mgr Vital-Justin Grandin, Oblat de Marie Immaculée, apôtre des Indiens du Nord-Ouest Canadien, 1892-1902. Louvain [1938] 32p. 15 1/2cm. (Collection Xaveriana, 15th ser., no.178)

On cover: Un apôtre du Nord-Ouest Canadien, Mgr Grandin, O.M.I. Belgium

3630 **Húnfjörd**, Jóhannes H[alldórsson]
Ómar. Nokkur ljódmaeli af ýmsum efnum og frá ýmsum timum. Winnipeg, Viking Press, 1938. 147p. port. 20 1/2cm.

Icelandic poetry. U. of M.

3631 **Jenness**, Diamond
The Sarcee Indians of Alberta. [Ottawa, King's Printer, 1938] 2p.l., 98p. front., illus. 25cm. (National Museum of Canada. Bull. 90. Anthropological ser., 23) U. of A.

3632 **Kirkconnell**, Watson
The golden jubilee of Wesley College, Winnipeg, 1888-1938 ... Winnipeg, Columbia Press, 1938. 60p. Not seen. U. of T. Quarterly, 1938-9

3633 **League for Social Reconstruction**, Winnipeg Branch
Pioneers in poverty; facts for Western Canadians today. Winnipeg, Printed by The Garry Press Ltd., 1938. 70p. illus., diagrs. 23cm. L.C.

3634 **MacDermot**, Hugh Ernest
Sir Thomas Roddick, his work in medicine and public life. Toronto, Macmillan Co. of Canada, 1938. xiii, 160p. illus., port., map. 22cm.

Chapters 3-4 (p.45-83) deal with Sir Thomas George Roddick and his work in the 1885 Riel Rebellion. Glenbow

3635 **Melven**, J[ohn]
The fur industry of Manitoba. [Winnipeg] Economic Survey Board, 1938. 29 l. maps, diagrs. 27 1/2cm. U. of S.

3636 Mémoires des minorités catholiques de langue française au Canada présentés à la Commission Rowell. Montréal, L'Oeuvre des Tracts, 1938. cover-title, 16p. 19cm. (Tract no.228)

Relates mostly to Manitoba, Saskatchewan and Alberta. St-Jean

3637 **Mewburn**, F[rank] H[amilton] H.
The 25th Battery, Canadian Field Artillery (Canadian Militia, 1908-1914) Reserve of officers. [n.p., 1938?] cover-title, [20]p. illus., ports. 23cm.

'The original of this text was given as an address at a mess dinner of the Gunners' Mess in Edmonton during the summer of 1938.' Glenbow

3638 **Morice**, A[drien] G[abriel]
La race métisse, étude critique en marge d'un livre récent. Winnipeg, L'Auteur, 1938. 91p. 27cm.

A criticism of Trémaudan's 'Histoire de la Nation Métisse.' See Entry 3481. Shortt

3639 **Morton**, Arthur S[ilver]
History of prairie settlement, by Arthur S. Morton; 'Dominion lands' policy, by Chester Martin. Toronto, Macmillan, 1938. xviii, 571p. incl. front., illus., maps, diagrs. 26cm. (Canadian frontiers of settlement, v.2) U. of S.

3640 **Pearson**, R[alph] McN[eille]
Provincial finance in Manitoba. [Winnipeg] Economic Survey Board, 1938. 28 l. diagrs. 27 1/2cm. U. of S.

3641 [**Pénard**, Jean Marie]
Mgr Charlebois, le saint missionnaire [n.p., 1938] caption-title, [28]p.

Portrait of Mgr Charlebois on front cover. Amtmann - 214-649

3642 **Robson**, Albert H[enry]
Paul Kane. Toronto, Ryerson Press [1938] 32p. illus. (part col.; incl. port.) 16 x 12 1/2cm. Rutherford

3643 **Rumilly**, Robert
La Vérendrye; Mackenzie. Montréal, Editions de l'A.C.-F., 1938. 150p. (Albums canadiens pour adolescents) Can. Cat.

3644 **St. Boniface, Man.**
Saint Boniface. [St. Boniface, Imprimerie de la Liberté, 1938] cover-title, 16p. illus., double plan. 18cm. Glenbow

3645 **Savaryn**, Neil [Nicholas]
Rolya otsiv Vasiliyan v Kanadi. Mundare, Alta., Basilian Fathers' Press, 1938. 58p. illus. 17 1/2cm. Not seen. Select

3646 **Smalley**, W[illiam] C[ameron]
Reorganizing for advance in Western Canada. Edmonton, Baptist Union of Western Canada [1938?] cover-title, 20p. illus., double map. 22cm.

Relates to the Baptist Union of Western Canada. Glenbow

3647 **Stevenson**, H[erbert] I[rving]
The forests of Manitoba. [Winnipeg] Economic Survey Board, 1938. 190 l. maps, diagrs. 27 1/2cm. U. of S.

3648 **Stuart**, Duncan
The Canadian desert; an attempt to stay the loss of the West. Toronto, Ryerson Press, 1938. viii, 88p. 19cm. (The new Dominion books, no.2) U. of S.

3649 **Sullivan**, [Edward] Alan
The fur masters. London, John Murray [1938] 320p. 19cm. Maps on end-papers.

Fiction. Man. Leg.

3650 **Sutherland**, Alex[ander] H.
The Selkirk Settlement on Red River. Victoria, The Author [1938] 61p.

Poetry. Man. Leg.

3651 **Tench**, C.W.
Tales of the North-West Mounted Police; daring adventures of the world-famous Canadian force. London, World's Work [1938?] 128p. illus. 24cm. (The Master thriller series, no.23) Glenbow

3652 **Uhlenbeck**, C[hristianus] C[ornelius]
A concise Blackfoot grammar, based on material from the southern Peigans. Amsterdam, Noord-Hollandsche uitgevers-maatschappij, 1938. 3p.l., 240p. 26cm. (Verhandelingen der Koninklijke nederlandsche akademie van wetenschappen te Amsterdam. Afdeeling letterkunde. Nieuwe reeks, deel 41) Not seen. L.C.

3653 **Ukrainian Greek Orthodox Church in Canada.** Consistory
Veliki rokovini, 988-1938. Winnipeg, Ukrainian Publishing Co., 1938. 224p. illus. (incl. ports.) 23cm.

Celebrates the 950th anniversary of the Christianizing of the Ukrainians and the 20th anniversary of the official organization of the Greek Orthodox Church among the Ukrainians of Western Canada. U. of S.

3654 **Watkins**, E[dwin] A[rthur]
A dictionary of the Cree language, as spoken by the Indians in the Provinces of Quebec, Ontario, Manitoba, Saskatchewan and Alberta. Based upon the foundation laid by Rev. E.A. Watkins. Revised, enriched and brought up to date by the late Ven. J.A. Mackay, Ven. R. Faries, Rev. Canon Edward Ahenakew, Rev. R.B. Horsefield, Right Rev. J.G. Anderson. Edited by Ven. R. Faries. Toronto, General Synod of the Church of England, c1938. 1p.l., ix, [1], 530p. 19 1/2cm.

See Entry 251. Shortt

3655 **Watson**, William R[itchie]
I give you yesterday. With a preface by Bernard K. Sandwell. Toronto, Macmillan, 1938. x, 238p. front., plates, ports. 21 1/2cm. L.C.

3656 **Weber**, Aloys
... Der diener Gottes, Bischof Vital Grandin, Oblat der undefleckten jungfrau Maria, erster Bischof von St. Albert, Kanada. Vienna, Ferdinand Schöningh-Paderborn, 1938. 40p. port. 16cm.

At head of title-page: Ein pionier des kreuzes im hohen Norden. Austria

3657 **Winnipeg**. Grace United Church
Three score years and ten; being the 70th anniversary of the founding of Grace Church, Winnipeg, October 30th, 1938. [Winnipeg, 1938] 23p. illus. (incl. ports.) 20cm. Man. Leg.

3658 **Woods**, D[avid] S[cott]
Education in Manitoba ... preliminary report. [Winnipeg] Economic Survey Board, 1938. 2v. maps, tables, diagrs. 27 1/2cm. U. of S.

3659 **Anderson**, A[lvah] J[ohn]
A book of poems. [Saskatoon, 1939?] 93p. 18cm. Shortt

3660 [**Anonymous**]
A historical sketch of the churches of the Evangelical Mennonite Brethren ... (1889-1939) Rosthern, Sask. [1939?] ... Not seen. Francis

3661 [**Anonymous**]
What Aberhart has done for you and me; the record tells the story, by Professor Orthodox Anonymous. Edmonton, Published by Citizens' Slate Committee, 1939? 24 blank leaves. Private copy

3662 **Bell**, J[ames] R[eynolds]
The live stock industry of Manitoba, by J.R. Bell, G. Watkins, and G.W. Wood. [Winnipeg] Economic Survey Board, 1939. 136 l. maps, tables, diagrs. 27 1/2cm. U. of S.

3663 **Bernier**, Noel
Fannystelle; une fleur de France éclose en terre manitobaine. Publié sous les auspices de la Société historique de Saint-Boniface. Québec, Imprimerie Franciscaine missionnaire, 1939. 189p. port. 21cm.

A history of Fannystelle, Man. Man. Leg.

3664 **Blyth**, Alfred, photographer
Royal visit pictorial review, commemorating the Alberta visit of Their Majesties King George VI and Queen Elizabeth, 1939. Calgary-Banff; Edmonton-Jasper. [Edmonton, 1939] cover-title, [40]p. illus., ports. 31cm. Glenbow

3665 **Britnell**, G[eorge] E[dwin]
The wheat economy; editor's preface by H.A. Innis. [Toronto] University of Toronto Press, 1939. xvi p., 1 l., 259, [1]p. illus. (maps) plates. 23 1/2cm. (Political economy series, no.4)

A study of economic conditions in Saskatchewan. U. of S.

3666 **Brouillette**, Benoît
La pénétration du continent américain par les Canadiens Français, 1763-1846; traitants, explorateurs, missionnaires; préface de M. l'abbé Lionel Groulx. Montréal, Librairie Granger Frères, 1939. 2p.l., [7]-242p., 1 l. plates, ports., maps (1 fold.) facsim. 24 1/2cm. Shortt

3667 **Buck**, Tim[othy]
The West and the federal election. A speech delivered ... in the Walker Theatre, Winnipeg, over station C.J.R.C. on Tuesday, April 25th, 1939. Sections of this speech which were censored by the radio station are here printed in full. Toronto, New Era Publishing [1939] 21p. 17cm. Amtmann - 176-35

3668 **Canada**. Department of Transport
Churchill and the Hudson Bay Route. Ottawa, King's Printer, 1939. 50p. illus., map. 20cm. Can. Cat.

3669 **Canadian Pacific Railway**
Agricultural settlement opportunities in the Prairie Provinces of Canada. [Montreal? 1939?] cover-title, 12p. illus., map (double page) 23cm.

A 1934 edition had the title: Agricultural settlement opportunities in Western Canada.
U. of A.

3670 **Church of England.** Diocese of Edmonton. Missionary Society of the Canadian Church. Women's auxiliary
Diocese of Edmonton, 1914-1939. [Edmonton, Douglas Printing Co. Ltd., 1939] 34, [2]p. illus. (incl. ports.) 17cm. U. of A.

3671 **Clarke**, Phyllis Comyn
From the Canadian prairies and other sonnets. Toronto, Copp Clark, 1939. 29p. front. 19cm. Not seen. Can. Cat.

3672 **Conference on Markets for Western Farm Products**, Winnipeg, 1938
Proceedings. [Winnipeg, 1939] 333p. graphs, maps, tables. 26cm.

'Held in Winnipeg, December 12th to 15th inclusive, 1938.' Glenbow

3673 **Connor**, A[braham] J[ames]
The climate of Manitoba. [Winnipeg] Economic Survey Board, 1939. xii, 163p. maps, diagrs. 27cm. U. of S.

3674 **Constantin-Fortin**, Marguerite
Une femme se penche sur son passé, la vie canadienne vue par la soeur de Constantin-Weyer. Paris, Les Livres Nouveaux [1939] 204p. 19cm. France

3675 **Cory**, Harper
Woodland comedy. London, Duckworth [1939] 183p. plates. 20cm.

Describes mammals and birds met while living in the woods in eastern Manitoba.
Liverpool

3676 **Craigie**, J[ohn] H[ubert]
Economic diseases of field crops in Manitoba. [Winnipeg, Economic Survey Board, 1939] 37p. illus., maps. 26cm. U. of S.

3677 **Denny**, Sir Cecil E[dward]
The law marches west; edited and arranged by W.B. Cameron. Toronto, J.M. Dent & Sons [1939] xvi, 319, [1]p. front., plates, ports., fold. map. 23 1/2cm. Illustrated map on lining-papers.

His experiences as one of the original members of the North West Mounted Police.
Shortt

3678 **Douthwaite**, Louis Charles
Royal Canadian Mounted Police. Toronto, Ryerson, 1939. x, 281p. plates, port., map. 21cm. Can. Cat.

3679 **Duggan**, David Milwyn
Review of Premier Aberhart's promises. [Edmonton, 1939] 35, [1]p. 23cm.
Glenbow

3680 **Edmonton.** Collège Saint-François-Xavier
Saint-François-Xavier sous la direction des Pères de la Compagnie de Jésus. 25e anniversaire 1913-1938. Edmonton, 1939. ...

Text in French and English. Amtmann - 228-673

3681 **Grant**, Henry Clark
Agricultural income and rural municipal government in Manitoba, by H.C. Grant, C.B. Davidson, and J.E. Chernick. [Winnipeg] Economic Survey Board, 1939. 124 l. maps, tables, diagrs. 28cm. U. of S.

3682 **Hedges**, James B[laine]
Building the Canadian West; the land and colonization policies of the Canadian Pacific Railway. New York, Macmillan, 1939. vii p., 1 l., 422p. maps (1 fold.) 22cm. Shortt

3683 A history of the rural municipality of South Norfolk, 1879-1939; being essays by Gordon Harland, David Gray and Jas. A. Robson, with a foreword by the present reeve, Dr. J.L. Lamont, and addenda of relevant material. Treherne, Man., Treherne Times, 1939. 2p.l., 79p. ports. 21cm.

The authors were the winners in a local essay contest among pioneers on the occasion of the sixtieth anniversary of the district. Man. Leg.

3683A **Hugill**, John William
Constitutional principle (No. One) in re the office of His Majesty's Attorney General; speech delivered in the Legislative Assembly at Edmonton, Alberta, on Tuesday, February 28th, 1939. Calgary, Published by the author [1939] cover-title, 16p. 23 x 10cm. Glenbow

3684 **Irwin**, Leonard Bertram
Pacific railways and nationalism in the Canadian-American Northwest, 1845-1873. A dissertation in history presented to the faculty of the graduate school of the University of Pennsylvania in partial fulfillment of the requirements for the degree of doctor of philosophy. Philadelphia, 1939. xii, 246p. 23cm.
Shortt

3685 **King**, W[illiam] R[obert]
The history of Alberta, political and financial, 1905-1938. Cochrane [1939] cover-title, 22p. 19cm. Glenbow

3686 **Lehmann,** Heinz
Das Deutschtum in Westkanada. Berlin, Junker und Dunnhaupt Verlag, 1939. 414p. fold. maps. 24cm.

A thorough study of the settlement of Germans in the West, and of their cultural and economic state. U. of M.

3687 **McLaurin,** C[olin] C[ampbell]
Pioneering in Western Canada; a story of the Baptists. Calgary, The Author, 1939. [xvi], 402p. front., plates, ports. 22cm. Shortt

3688 **McTavish,** Douglas Craig
Individualism versus socialism. Thorsby, Alta., c1939. 42p. 23cm.

With author's autograph inscription to H.E. Nichols. Glenbow

3689 **Manitoba.** Department of Agriculture and Immigration
Credit unions in Manitoba. Winnipeg, The Department, 1939. 22p. illus., diagr. 23cm. U. of S.

3690 **Marriott,** Anne
The wind our enemy. Toronto, Ryerson Press, 1939. 8p. (Ryerson poetry chap-books)

A poem describing the tragedy of the drought. U. of S.

3691 **Medicine Hat, Alta.** Junior Board of Trade
Medicine Hat, Alberta, Canada, the city of untold possibilities. [Medicine Hat, Alta.] 1939. cover-title, 32p. illus., maps. 26 x 12cm. Glenbow

3692 **Moose Jaw.** Board of Trade
Brief of the Moose Jaw Board of Trade re: location of a site for a new Saskatchewan mental hospital. [Moose Jaw, 1939] 16p. fold. map. 23cm. Sask. Arch.

3693 **Morton,** Arthur S[ilver]
A history of the Canadian West to 1870-71; being a history of Rupert's Land (the Hudson's Bay Company's territory) and of the North-West Territory (including the Pacific slope) London, T. Nelson & Sons [1939] xiv, 987p. maps (part fold.) 24cm.

An encyclopaedic history of the West to 1870. Shortt

3694 **Oddson,** Asta
Employment of women in Manitoba. [Winnipeg] Economic Survey Board, 1939. 154 l. fold. tables. 27cm. U. of S.

3695 **Page,** John Percy
Unity, the good fight. Reprint of a review of Alberta provincial affairs, and an outline of the basis of the Unity Movement, originally given as a broadcast ... [Edmonton] Edmonton Constituency Unity Association [1939] cover-title, 11p. ports. 23 x 10cm. Glenbow

3696 **Pénard,** Jean Marie
The Vicar Apostolic of Keewatin, Canada; Bishop Ovide Charlebois. Translated from the French by Mary Agatha Gray. Montreal, Beauchemin, 1939. 241p. illus., ports., map. 22 1/2cm. Shortt

3697 **Peterson,** Charles Walter [Christian]
The Canadian railway problem, discussion of the present railway situation from the point of view of western agriculture; submission to the special committee of the Senate, March 29, 1939. Toronto, Citizen's Group for Railway Action, 1939. 29p. 23cm. Can. Cat.

3697A **Putnam,** Ada MacLeod
The Selkirk settlers and the church they built at Belfast. Toronto, Presbyterian publications, 1939. 57p. illus., ports. 21cm. B.C. Arch.

3698 Redemptoristi skhidnoho obryadu: Korotkiy Naris. Yorkton, 1939.
... Not seen.

A short sketch of the Redemptorists of the Eastern Rite.
Sask. History, v.3, no.1, p.3.

3699 **Salverson,** Laura Goodman
Confessions of an immigrant's daughter. Toronto, Ryerson, 1939. 523p. 20cm.

This book won the Governor-General's award for non-fiction. U. of S.

3700 **Saskatchewan Homemakers' Clubs**
Retrospect and prospect. [Saskatoon, 1939] 54p. illus. (ports.) 24cm. Sask. Arch.

3700A **Savage,** Rocke
Prairie trails; a book of verse. London, A.H. Stockwell [1939] 122p. Br. Mus.

3701 **Singer,** H[orace] C[ecil]
History of the Thirty-first Battalion C.E.F., from its organization November, 1914, to its demobilization June, 1919. With nominal roll and information as to all members of the unit. Material compiled and assembled by H.C. Singer. Final revision and writing by A.A. Peebles. [Calgary, Printed by Knight's Bindery, 1939] 515p. maps, plates (1 col.), ports. 23cm.

Battalion recruited in Alberta. Glenbow

3702 **Social Credit Board**
The record tells the story: 1905-1936 – 1936-1939. Read it for yourself. [Edmonton, King's Printer, 1939] 56p. 18cm. Glenbow

3703 **Stapleford,** Ernest William
Report on rural relief due to drought conditions and crop failures in Western Canada, 1930-37. Ottawa, Department of Agriculture, 1939. 130p. illus., maps. 25cm. U. of S.

3704 **Stewart,** Alistair M[cLeod]
The youth problem of Manitoba. [Winnipeg] Economic Survey Board, 1939. 42 l. 27cm. U. of S.

3705 **Stubbs,** Roy St. George
Lawyers and laymen of Western Canada. Toronto, Ryerson Press, 1939. 5p.l., 197p. front., ports. 21cm.

Describes some of the interesting personalities, mostly in the legal profession, found in the West in the early days. U. of S.

3706 Their Majesties' visit to Manitoba; a pictorial record of the visit of King George VI and Queen Elizabeth to the province of Manitoba on May 24 and June 4, 1939. Compiled from pictures taken by Free Press staff and other photographers. Winnipeg, Stovel Co. Ltd. [1939] 48p. illus. (part col.) 27cm. Man. Leg.

3707 **Weekes,** Mary [Loretto]
The last buffalo hunter. As told to her by Norbert Welsh. New York, Thomas Nelson & Sons, 1939. xi, 13-304p. 20 1/2cm.

An aged métis describes incidents in his youth. Shortt

3708 **Williams,** Fred C.
The open road and other poems. [Creelman? (Sask.) 1939] 38p. port. 17cm. Sask. Arch.

3709 **Alberta Wheat Pool**
Story of wheat. Calgary, The Company, 1940. 55p. illus. Can. Cat.

3710 **Anahareo**
My life with Grey Owl. Toronto, Saunders, 1940. x, 230p. front., ports. 22cm. Can. Cat.

3711 [**Anonymous**]
Poems of the prairie. A gift book of verse. [n.p., n.d.] 2p.l., 50p. 16cm.

The writer's maiden name was Evangeline Paula, daughter of R.G. Parks. One poem is entitled 'Dear old Saskatoon' which would suggest that she was, or had been, a resident. Glenbow

3712 **Balter,** L[éon Guillaume]
Courtes instructions en langue crise. Edmonton, La Survivance [1940] 2p.l., 574p. 30cm.

In the Roman alphabet. Oblates Arch.

3713 **Beach,** F[loyd] K[ellogg]
The history of Alberta oil, by F.K. Beach and J.L. Irwin. Issued by the Dept. of Lands and Mines. Edmonton, Publicity and Travel Bureau [1940] 62p. illus., fold. map. 25cm. Private copy

3714 **Bushnell,** David I[ves]
Sketches by Paul Kane in the Indian country, 1845-1848. Washington, Smithsonian Institution, 1940. 1p.l., 25p. front. (port.) illus. (incl. ports.) 24 1/2cm. (Smithsonian miscellaneous collections, v.99, no.1) Not seen. L.C.

3715 **Canada.** Department of Transport
Navigation conditions on the Hudson Bay Route from the Atlantic seaboard to the port of Churchill; season of navigation 1939. Ottawa, King's Printer, 1940. 51p. plate, map. 25cm. Can. Cat.

3716 **Carter,** Ross L.
Rambling rhymes. Edmonton, Douglas Printing Co. [n.d.] ...

3717 **Clay**, Charles
Fur trade apprentice. Illustrated by Nils Hogner. London, Oxford University Press, 1940. viii, 360p. front., illus., plates. 20cm. Map on lining-papers.

Juvenile fiction about the early English traders from Montreal who were on the Saskatchewan in 1775. U. of A. (Extension)

3718 **Dawson**, C[arl] A[ddington]
Pioneering in the Prairie Provinces; the social side of the settlement process, by C.A. Dawson and Eva R. Younge. Toronto, Macmillan, 1940. xiv, 338p. incl. illus. (maps) tables, diagrs. 26cm. (Canadian frontiers of settlement, v.8) U. of S.

3719 **Edmonton**. Commercial Graduates Club
'Sitting on top of the world,' 1915-1940; the amazing record of the Edmonton 'Grads,' official world's basketball champions, covering 25 years of play, 522 official games and over 125,000 miles of travel! [Edmonton, 1940?] 32p. illus., ports., tables. 18 x 26cm. Glenbow

3720 **Fortin**, L. Alphonse
L'âme de ma soeur, Henriette Fortin, cinquante années des souvenirs intimes. St. Boniface, Hôpital St.-Boniface, 1940. 130p. front., port., plate. 24cm.

'The soul of my sister ...' an English translation with the same imprint, appeared in 1946. It was described as a 2d revised edition. St. Sulpice

3721 **Freebairn**, A[dam] L.
Kootenai Brown and other western poems. Pincher Creek, Alta. [194–] 32p. port. 18 1/2cm. U. of A.

3722 **Freebairn**, A[dam] L.
My son and other poems. [Pincher Creek, 194–] 30p. 18cm. Glenbow

3723 **Gardiner**, Mrs. Lue Gillmor
Rhymes from the North West. [Edmonton? The Author? 1940] 39p. 16cm. Glenbow

3724 **Götz**, Karl
Die heimstätter; ein deutsches schidsal in Kanada. Mit einen autobiograpischen nachwort des verfassers. Leipsig, Philipp Reclam [1940] 76, [1]p. 15 1/2cm.

Relates to Saskatchewan. Bavaria

3725 **Hand**, William Henry
The case for Alberta. North Sydney, Australia, Douglas Social Credit Association of New South Wales, 1940. 36p. facsims., diagrs. Not seen. Can. Cat.

3726 **Holmes**, J.W.
Bushels to burn. [Toronto, Canadian Association for Adult Education and Canadian Institute of International Affairs] 1940. 12p. 20 1/2cm. (Behind the headlines series)

About the wheat surplus. U. of S.

3727 **Irvine**, William
The trail of a truth twister; an answer to 'The records tell the story.' [Edmonton, Commercial Printers, 1940] 47p. 17cm. Glenbow

3728 **Kirkconnell,** Watson
The flying bull and other tales; drawings by J.W. McLaren. Toronto, Oxford, 1940. 189p. illus. 19cm.
Poetry. Private copy

3729 **Lamont,** Cecil [Alexander Ralph]
Prairie sentinels. Winnipeg, North-West Line Elevators Association [1940] 63, [1]p. illus. 23cm.
The grain trade. Calgary

3730 **Lamson,** David A[lbert]
Once in my saddle. New York, C. Scribner's Sons, 1940. viii, [3], 289p. 22cm.
Stories, mostly about the Canadian West of the period 1908-14. Glenbow

3731 **Le Chevallier,** Jules [Jean Marie Joseph]
Aux prises avec la tourmente; les missionnaires de la colonie de Saint-Laurent-de-Grandin durant l'insurrection métisse de 1885. [Ottawa? 1940?] 76p. 26cm.
'Extrait de la Revue de l'Université d'Ottawa, livraisons d'octobre-decembre 1939, avril-septembre 1940.' Shortt

3732 **McKitrick,** T[homas] G[eorge]
Corner stones of empire; the settlement of Crystal City and district in the Rock Lake country. Crystal City, Man., Courier Publishing Co. [1940?] 3p.l., 130, [1]p. illus., ports. 21 1/2cm.
Largely a compilation of articles written by pioneer residents of the district. Man. Leg.

3733 **McPhail,** Alexander James
The diary of Alexander James McPhail. Edited by H.A. Innis. Toronto, University of Toronto Press, 1940. xi p., 1 l., 289p. ports. 23 1/2cm.
Diary of the first president of the Canadian Wheat Pool. U. of S.

3734 **Mandelbaum,** David G[oodman]
The Plains Cree. New York, American Museum of Natural History, 1940. 1p.l., p.155-316. illus., fold. map. 24cm. (American Museum of Natural History. Anthropological papers, v.37, pt.2) U. of S.

3735 **Manitoba.** Bureau of Travel and Publicity
Manitoba, Canada. Inside the rim of adventure. [Winnipeg] The Bureau [194–] cover-title, 36p. illus. (part col.) 22cm. U. of S.

3736 **Moose Jaw Writers' Club**
Christmas, 1940. Moose Jaw, 1940. 32p.
Poetry. Can. Cat.

3737 **Nelson,** Hugh S[pence]
Four months under arms; a reminiscence of events prior to, and during the second Riel Rebellion. [Nelson, B.C., Nelson Daily News, 194–] cover-title, 20p. 21cm. Shortt

3738 **Niven,** Frederick [John]
Mine inheritance. London, Collins [c1940] 432p. 20 1/2cm. Map on lining-papers.

Fiction; the Selkirk settlers. U. of S.

3739 **Primeau,** Léonide
Mgr Adélard Langevin, O.M.I., deuxième archevêque de Saint-Boniface. Montréal, L'Oeuvre des Tracts, 1940. cover-title, 16p. 19cm. (Tract no. 252)

Portrait of Mgr Langevin on cover. St-Jean

3740 **Regina Leader-Post**
The Regina Leader-Post presents 'The presses roll'; the story of how thé Leader-Post is produced. [Regina, Regina Leader-Post, 194–] 22p. illus. 15cm. Regina

3741 **Roxburgh,** F[rank] D[ouglas]
History of the Presbyterian Church in Edmonton, 1866-1940. [Edmonton? 1940] 12p. illus. (ports.) 23 1/2cm. Knox College

3742 **Scott,** Robert J.
Birch bark talking; a résume of life and work of the Rev. James Evans. Published by the Board of Home Missions for James Evans Centenary Committee. Toronto, United Church of Canada, 1940. 28p. illus., ports., facsim. 19cm. Can. Cat.

3743 **Searle Grain Company**
How I farm; by 200 prairie farmers. Winnipeg, The Company, 1940. 45p. Not seen. Can. Cat.

3744 **Skov,** S. Adelle
Evening at Waterton Lakes, and other poems. [Cardston, Cardston News Print, n.d.] 17p. 17 1/2cm. Glenbow

3745 **Société Historique de Saint-Boniface**
Saint-Malo; paroisse manitobaine. Saint-Boniface, La Société, 1940. 137p. plates, ports. 21cm.

History of a parish founded in 1900 by Louis Malo. Man. Leg.

3746 **Stegner,** Wallace [Earle]
On a darkling plain. New York, Harcourt, 1940. 4p.l., 3-230, [1]p. 21cm.

Fiction; the background is rural Saskatchewan after World War I. L.C.

3747 **Stephansson,** Stephan G[udmundsson]
Andvökur. Reykjavik and Winnipeg, 1909-1940. 6v. illus., ports. 19cm.

Icelandic poetry. U. of M.

3748 **Stephansson,** Stephan Gudmundsson
Bréf og ritgerdir. [ed. by Rögnvaldur Pétursson] Reykjavik, Gutenberg Press, 1939-40. 2v. Select

3749 **Stewart**, Zaida Mahood
Has published two or three booklets of verse with Alberta imprints.

3750 **Sweeney**, John
Songs and verses of a Peace River pioneer. [Peace River, Printed by the Record-Gazette Press Ltd., 194–] cover-title, 36p. port. 17cm. U. of A.

3751 **Thompson**, Clara Cline
Stairway to the stars. [Has an Alberta imprint.] ... Not seen.
Poetry.

3752 **Ukrainian Teachers' Convention**
Report of the proceedings and addresses of the Ukrainian Teachers' Convention at Mundare, Alta., Nov. 16, 1940. Mundate, Basilian Fathers' Press, 1940. 36p. 21 1/2cm. Not seen. Private information

3753 **United Church of Canada**. Alberta Conference
Rundle in Alberta, 1840-1848. To honour the memory of a pioneer. [n.p.] 1940. cover-title, 32p. illus. (incl. ports.) map, facsim. 21 1/2cm. Shortt

3754 **Unity Council of Alberta**
The truth about the records. Volume 1. [3d ed. Calgary, 1940] 48p. 18cm.
'Here are the facts in answer to "The records tell the story".' Glenbow

3755 **Wright**, J[ames] F[rederick] C[hurch]
Slava Bohu; the story of the Doukhobors. New York, Farrar & Rinehart, Inc., 1940. x, 438p. front. (port.) 22cm. Map on lining-papers. U. of S.

3756 Antologiya Ukrayinskoho pysmenstva v Kanadi. Winnipeg, Canadian-Ukrainian Educational Association, 1941. 158p. ports. 19cm.
An anthology of Ukrainian literature in Canada. Compiled by M. Mandryka. U. of A.

3757 **Arès**, Richard
Nos positions françaises au Manitoba. [St-Boniface] Le Collège Saint-Boniface, 1941. cover-title, 88p. 20cm. St-Jean

3758 **Britnell**, G[eorge] E[dwin]
What about wheat? Toronto, Canadian Association for Adult Education & Canadian Institute of International Affairs, 1941. 26p. (Behind the headlines series, v.2, no.1) U. of S.

3759 **Buck**, Carl E.
Public health in Manitoba; report of a study made by the American Public Health Association. Winnipeg, King's Printer, 1941. 147p. Man. Leg.

3760 **Calgary**. Holy Cross Hospital
Souvenir of the golden anniversary of the Holy Cross Hospital, Calgary, 1891–1941. [Calgary, 1941] cover-title, 15p. illus., ports. 25cm. Glenbow

3761 **Canada**. Army. Rocky Mountain Rangers
Rocky Mountain Rangers. First Battalion C.A.-A.F. 1885-1941. [New Westminster, B.C., Columbian Co., 1941] 60p. illus., ports. 17 x 26cm. Glenbow

3762 **Evans**, William Sanford
How many acres? Canada's immediate wheat problem. Winnipeg, Sanford Evans Statistical Service, 1941. 27p. Not seen. Can. Cat.

3763 **Hinds**, E.M.
Nothing ventured. London, J. Gifford [1941] 319, [1]p. 19cm. Not seen.

This autobiography of an English school mistress includes a description of two years spent in a French-speaking district near Regina. Matthews

3764 How Alberta is fighting finance ... [Liverpool, K.R.P. Publications, Ltd., 1941?] cover-title, 11, [1]p. 18cm. Glenbow

3765 **Le Chevallier**, Jules [Jean Marie Joseph]
Batoche; les missionnaires du Nord-Ouest pendant les troubles de 1885. Montréal, l'Oeuvre de Presse Dominicaine, 1941. 310p. front., illus., ports., maps, facsim. 24cm. Shortt

3766 **Manitoba**. Department of Agriculture
A study of wheat policies in Canada and the United States. Winnipeg, The Department, 1941. 48p. illus. 23cm. Can. Cat.

3767 **Marks**, Alfred L[ouis]
Margaret Anne's wonder book of verse. [Illustrated by Joan Fraser. Edmonton, Printed by Commercial Printers, c1941] 63p. illus. 24cm.

Poetry for children. Glenbow

3768 **Moose Jaw**. Board of Trade
Moose Jaw, tourist centre of Saskatchewan. [Moose Jaw, 1941?] cover-title, [7]p. illus. 23cm. U. of S.

3769 **Moose Jaw Writers' Club**
Verses for you. [n.p., 1941] cover-title, 35p. 16 1/2cm. U. of S. (Regina)

3770 **Philippot**, Aristide
Cinquante ans de vie paroissiale; Morinville (1891-1941) ... Edmonton, La Survivance, 1941. 145, [1]p. illus. (incl. ports.) 24cm.

Title also in English; text in French, with a short summary in English. Private copy

3771 **Pickel**, Weldon U.
Golden jubilee [of] First Baptist Church, Regina, Sask., 1891-1941. [Regina, Commercial Printers, 1941] 22p. illus. (incl. ports.) 28cm. Sask. Arch.

3772 Propamyatna Kniha z nahodi zolotoho yuvileyu poselennya Ukrayinskoho narodu v Kanadi [Commemorative book on the occasion of the golden jubilee of the settlement of the Ukrainian people in Canada] Ulozhena Ukrayinskimi Katolitskimi svyashchenikami pid provodom svoho episkopa [compiled by the Ukrainian Catholic priests under the direction of their bishop] Yorkton, 1941. 81p.l., 338p. illus., ports. 31cm. Shortt

3773 **Roman Catholic Church**. Hymns. Cree
Recueil de cantiques cris. Grouard, Mission St-Bernard [1941] 236, [1]p. 22cm. Errata slips tipped in.

Text in Cree syllabic. Oblates Arch.

3774 **Ross,** [James] Sinclair
As for me and my house. A novel, by Sinclair Ross. New York, Reynal & Hitchcock [c1941] 3p.l., 296p. 21cm.

Set in a small Saskatchewan town in the dry thirties. Saskatoon

3775 **Rumilly,** Robert
Riel. Montréal, Bernard Valiquette [1941] 315p. 20 1/2cm. (Histoire de la province de Québec, v.5) U. of S.

3776 **Schreiber,** Ilse
Kanadische erzahlungen. [Bohm-Leipa] Kaiser [c1941] 117p. 19cm.

Title translated: Canadian stories.
Six stories relating experiences of a German immigrant family in Manitoba. Austria

3777 **Searle Grain Company**
The prairie wheat growers' problems, with some observations upon the nature of parity, the Searle index, and how to give our prairie farmers a reasonable wheat price and still maintain the lower official ceiling price. Winnipeg, The Company, 1941. 23p. diagr. 23cm. Not seen. Can. Cat.

3778 **Schulze,** Gunnar
Åter i Kanada; som cowboy och pälsjägare. Stockholm, Medens Forlags [1941] 252p. 21cm. Sweden

3779 **Social Credit Board**
Alice in Blunderland; a humorous sketch in one act. Edmonton, 1941. cover-title, 12p. 18cm. (Its Educational series, no.2) Glenbow

3780 **Social Credit Board**
Debt legislation passed at the regular session of the Legislative Assembly of Alberta, 1941 (with an introduction on previous legislation). Edmonton, 1941. cover-title, 9, [1]p. 18cm. (Series A, no.1) Glenbow

3781 **Stewart,** Andrew
More farmers for Western Canada; study of possibilities of post-war agricultural settlement in the Prairie Provinces. Toronto, Ryerson, 1941. 32p. 19cm. (Contemporary affairs bulletin, no.9) U. of S.

3782 **Stubbs,** Roy St. George
Men in khaki; four regiments of Manitoba; foreword by the Hon. J.T. Thorson. Toronto, Ryerson Press, 1941. viii p., 2 l., 72p. 20 1/2cm.

History of the Royal Winnipeg Rifles, Winnipeg Grenadiers (M.G.), Queen's Own Cameron Highlanders of Canada and Winnipeg Light Infantry (M.G.) Winnipeg

3783 **Weekes,** Mary [Loretto]
Painted arrows. Illustrated by Orson Lowell. New York, Nelson, 1941. 1p.l., v-ix, 262p. illus. (incl. music) 22 1/2cm.

Juvenile fiction. L.C.

3784 **Wensley,** Amelia
At summer's end. Toronto, Ryerson, 1941. 8p. 22cm. (Ryerson poetry chap-books) Not seen. Ryerson

3785 **Wood**, Thomas
Triple-A for Canada? Saskatoon, 1941. cover-title, 8p. 23cm. Glenbow

3786 **Annett**, R[onald] Ross
Especially Babe. New York, D. Appleton-Century Co., 1942. 3p.l., 263p. 20cm.

Fiction; a small girl on a dust bowl farm. Saskatoon

3787 **Bruce**, Eva
Call her Rosie. New York, I. Washburn [1942] 300p. illus. 20 1/2cm.

Fiction. The scene opens in New Ontario but moves to Western Canada. L.C.

3788 **Calgary Vacant Lots Garden Club**
Rules and regulations. [Calgary, 1942] folder. (6p.) 16cm.

The club was founded in 1914. Glenbow

3789 **Ceuneau**, Augustin
Un compagnon de Mgr Grandin. Le R.P. Alphonse-Hippolyte Leduc, O.M.I. (1842-1918) [Rennes, Nouvelliste de Bretagne, 1942] 103p. port. 24 1/2cm.

Author's presentation copy. France

3790 **Chumer**, Wasyl A.
Spomyny pro perezhyvannya pershykh Ukrayinskykh pereselentsiv v Kanadi, 1891-1941. Edmonton, The Author, 1942. 188p. illus. (incl. ports.) 25cm.

Experiences of the first Ukrainian settlers. U. of S.

3791 **Co-operative Commonwealth Federation**
The first ten years, 1932-1942, commemorating the tenth anniversary of the Co-operative Commonwealth Federation at the seventh national convention, Toronto, Ontario, July 27, 28, 29, 1942. [Ottawa, C.C.F. National Office, 1942] 64p. ports. 30cm.

Includes advertising matter. Glenbow

3792 **Cormack**, Barbara (Villy)
Seedtime and harvest. Toronto, Ryerson Press, 1942. 7p. 21cm. (Ryerson poetry chap-books)

Poetry. U. of A.

3792A **Dent**, Charles L.
Lines from life. [Prince Albert? 194_] 27p. 17cm.

Poetry. Northland

3793 **Dumouchel**, Paul A.
Grammaire saulteuse, rédigée par le R.P. Paul A. Dumouchel ... en collaboration avec le R.P. Joseph Brachet ... St. Boniface, Man., Province Oblate du Manitoba, 1942. xiii, 151, [1]p. 28cm. Glenbow

3794 **Flock**, Elizabeth Burnett
Wild flowers of the Prairie Provinces. Drawings by J.H. Flock. Regina, School Aids & Textbook Publishing Co., 1942. 112p. incl. front., illus. 21cm. U. of S.

3795 **Freebairn**, A[dam] L.
The mountain heights, and other poems. Pincher Creek [194–] 31p. 18cm.
Glenbow

3796 **Freebairn**, A[dam] L.
Rhymes from the foothills. Pincher Creek [194–] 31p. port. 16cm.
Glenbow

3797 **Galloway**, Margaret A[gnes]
I lived in paradise. Winnipeg, Bulman Bros. [1942] 2p.l., [3], 257p. illus., ports. 21cm.

The story of a girlhood in Gladstone where her father ran a general store. Man. Leg.

3798 **Gardiner**, Mrs. Lue Gillmor
Rhymes from ranges. [Edmonton, The Author, 1942] 30p. front. (port.) 17cm. Not seen. Can. Cat.

3799 **Gaudin**, S[amuel] D.
Forty-four years with the northern Crees. Toronto, Published for the author by Mundy-Goodfellow Printing Co. [c1942] 5p.l., 170p. plates. 19cm.
U. of A. (Extension)

3800 **Gordon**, J[ohn] R.
Rhymes of the range. [n.p., n.d.] [9]p. 14cm. Glenbow

3801 **Hamilton**, J.B., comp.
Evidence on the tar sands for the public defenders' court. [n.p., 1942] [16]p. illus. 23cm. Glenbow

3802 **Kraenzel**, Carl F[rederick]
The northern plains in a world of change. A study outline for adult groups in the northern plains of Canada and the United States, by Carl F. Kraenzel ... Watson Thomson ... Glenn H. Craig ... with the collaboration of E.A. Corbett, O.A. Parsons, and Stanley Rands. A preliminary report issued for experimental use. Recommended for distribution by the Northern Great Plains Agricultural Advisory Council of the United States and the Canadian Association for Adult Education. [Winnipeg?] Gregory-Cartwright Ltd., 1942. 190, [8]p. incl. map. 25cm.
U. of S.

3803 **Landstrom**, Oscar
Pioneer homestead stories, from 1868 to present time, written by Oscar Landstrom, Govan, Sask., May, 1942. [Western Printers Association Ltd., 1942] 32p. 23cm.

Illustrated title-page. Shortt

3804 **Lewis**, Oscar
The effects of white contact upon Blackfoot culture, with special reference to the role of the fur trade. New York, J.J. Augustin [1942] vi, 73p. illus. (incl. maps) 24 1/2cm. (American Ethnological Society. Monographs, no.6)
U. of S.

3805 **Mathieson,** George S[impson]
Wheat and the futures market, a study of the Winnipeg Grain Exchange. Winnipeg, Hignell Printing Ltd., 1942. iv, 74p. incl. illus., forms. 21cm. U. of S.

3806 **Matthaei,** Lothar
Irgendwo drüben in Kanada; ein abenteuerlicher Erlebnisbericht. [Nürnberg] Willmy, 1942. 214p. illus. 22cm.

Adventures, mostly in Alberta. L.C.

3807 **Millman,** T[homas] R[eagh]
Publishers of peace. [n.p.] Issued by the joint committee on conferences and summer schools of the Church of England in Canada, 1942. 118p. illus., map.

Details of mission work in the Peace River country, Fort Chipewyan, and Swan Lake, Man. Dempsey

3808 **Moose Jaw Writers' Club**
Christmas, 1942. [Moose Jaw] 1942. cover-title, 24p. 16 1/2cm.

Poetry. Shortt

3809 **Nickle,** C[arl] O[lof]
The valley of wonders; the story of Turner Valley. Calgary, The Oil Bulletin, 1942. 40p. illus., maps, diagrs. 21cm. Can. Cat.

3810 **Orchard,** W[illiam] J[ohn]
The stone age on the prairies. Regina, School Aids and Text Book Publishing Co., Ltd., c1942. 160p. illus. 19cm. Shortt

3811 **Paluk,** William
Canadian Cossacks. Winnipeg, Canadian Ukrainian Review Publishing Co., 1942. 130p. Not seen.

A collection of articles and short stories dealing with Ukrainians in Western Canada. U. of T. Quarterly, 1942-3

3812 **Peterson,** Charles Walter [Christian]
The 'new order' and its problems. Calgary, Farm and Ranch Review, 1942. 79, [1]p. 23cm.

Autographed. Glenbow

3813 **Pritchett,** John Perry
The Red River valley, 1811-1849; a regional study. Toronto, Ryerson Press, 1942. xvii p., 2 l., 295p. incl. front. (map) illus. 25cm. (Relations of Canada and the United States, a series prepared under the direction of the Carnegie Endowment for International Peace, Division of Economics & History) U. of S.

3814 **Roman Catholic Church.** Prayers. Cree
[Prayer book] Winnipeg, Editions de La Liberté, 1942. 324p. illus. 15cm. Not seen. Can. Cat.

3815 **Sallans,** G[eorge] Herbert
Little man. Toronto, Ryerson Press [1942] 5p.l., 420p. 22cm.
This novel won the Ryerson fiction award. U. of S.

3816 **Servants of Mary Immaculate**
Yuvileyna kniha Zhromadzhennya' Sester Sluzhebnits' Presvyatoyi Neporochnoyi Divi Mariyi, 1892-1942. [Jubilee book of the Society of Sisters, Servants of Mary Immaculate], vidana v pyatdesyatu richnitsyu osnuvannya Zhromadzhennya [published on the fiftieth anniversary of the founding of the order] Edmonton, 1942. 208p. illus. 27cm. Not seen. Sask. Hist., v.3, no.1

3817 **Smalley,** W[illiam] C[ameron]
On the western front. Edmonton, Baptist Union of Western Canada [1942] cover-title, 24p. incl. covers. illus., map. 22cm.
On the work of the Baptist Union in Western Canada. Glenbow

3818 **Ukrainian Self-Reliance League**
Scho ye soyuz Ukrayintsiv samostiynykiv. Winnipeg, B. Batycky, 1942. 23p. 23cm. Not seen. Select

3819 **Wallace,** Joseph S.
Night is ended; thoughts in lyrics. Winnipeg, Contemporary Publishers [1942] 95p. port. 20cm. Can. Cat.

3820 **White,** Samuel Alexander
Northwest law. New York, Phoenix Press [c1942] 256p. 19 1/2cm.
Fiction. U. of S.

3821 **Winnipeg.** Holy Ghost Fraternal Aid Society
40-letnia rocznica Bractwa Sw. Ducha, Winnipeg, 2-go maja 1942; 1902-1942. 40th anniversary of the Holy Ghost Fraternal Aid Society, Winnipeg, May 2nd, 1942. [Winnipeg, 1942] cover-title, 24p. illus., ports.
Text partly in English. Advertising matter included in paging.

3822 **Wrigglesworth,** Lew[is John]
Poetical writings of Lew Wrigglesworth. [Calgary? n.d.] cover-title, [32]p. port. 22cm. Glenbow

3823 **Wright,** Laura Moore
Victory verses. Inspired by speeches and events of the World War. [Shaunavon, Sask.] The Author, c1942. cover-title, 36p. 18cm. Shortt

3824 **Achard,** Eugène
La grande découverte de l'Ouest canadien. Montréal, Librairie Générale Canadienne, 1943. 123p. illus. 20cm. Not seen. Can. Cat.

3825 **Alberta.** Post-War Reconstruction Committee
Post-war reconstruction in Alberta. Edmonton, The Committee, 1943. 32p. 19cm. U. of A.

3826 **Bible.** New Testament. Gospels & Acts. Saulteaux
The four Gospels and the Acts of the Apostles, translated from the Latin Vulgate. Saulteaux version. St-Boniface, Oblate Fathers, 1943. iv, 500p. illus. 20 1/2cm. Oblates Arch.

3827 **Buzek**, Karel
Památnik Československé Kanady. [Winnipeg, National Printers, 1943] 197p. illus. 26cm. Naprstek

3828 **Calgary**. Federated Auto Industries
A few thoughts regarding Calgary's transportation system. Calgary [1943] cover-title, 11p. 23cm. Glenbow

3829 **Calgary**. Knox United Church
A souvenir of the diamond jubilee of Knox United Church, Calgary, Alberta. [Calgary, 1943] cover-title, [16]p. illus., ports. 17 x 25cm.
Includes an historical sketch of the church, prepared by Jessie I. Smith. Glenbow

3830 **Canada**. Department of Agriculture
P.F.R.A.; a record of achievement. A report on the activities under the Prairie Farm Rehabilitation Act for the eight-year period ended March 31, 1943. Ottawa [1943] 78p. illus., maps, tables. 25cm. Glenbow

3831 **Canmore, Alta.** Sacred Heart Church
Golden jubilee, 1893-1943. [Canmore, 1943] cover-title, [12]p. illus. (incl. ports.) 17cm. Sask. Arch.

3832 **Complin**, Margaret [(Robertson)]
For remembrance. Regina, The Author, 1943. 22p.
Poetry. U. of T. Quarterly, 1943-4

3833 **Dafoe**, John Wesley
Sixty years in journalism; the text of an address delivered by Mr. Dafoe on the occasion of a dinner tendered him by the Winnipeg Press Club to mark the completion of sixty continuous years of newspaper work in Canada. Winnipeg, Royal Alexander Hotel, Oct. 16. Winnipeg, Winnipeg Free Press, 1943. 13p. illus. 25cm. Can. Cat.

3834 **Dominion Mortgage and Investments Association**
The prairie farmer and his debts. What is in the public interest – more or less debt legislation? [n.p., 1943] cover-title, 11p. 23cm. U. of S.

3835 **Edmonds**, W[alter] Everard
Edmonton, past and present. A brief history. Edmonton, Printed by Douglas Printing Co., Ltd., 1943. 4p.l., 28p. plates. 25cm.
A compilation of facts, figures, and history. Shortt

3836 **Edmonton Bulletin**
Aberhart-Manning; a contemporary account of the life of the late premier of Alberta, leader of the world's first Social Credit government, with a public declaration of policy of his successor in office, the Hon. Ernest Manning, 11th June, 1943, reprinted by permission of the proprietors of the Edmonton Bulletin, in whose pages these two documents appeared concerning the fight for Social Credit in Alberta. Liverpool, K.R.P. Publications, 1943. 23, [1]p. ports. 19cm. Glenbow

3837 **Edmonton.** Holy Trinity Church
A history of Holy Trinity, Edmonton, 1893-1943. [Edmonton, Printed by Douglas Printing Co. Ltd., 1943] cover-title, [24]p. illus. (incl. ports.) 23cm.

Written by the Rev. Winston M. Nainby.
On cover: Illustration of the church. Private copy

3838 **Edmonton.** M. Hrushevsky Ukrainian Institute
Silver jubilee book of the M. Hrushevsky Institute in Edmonton. Winnipeg, Printed by Ukrainian Publishing Co., 1943. 203p., 2 l. illus. 26cm. Added title-page in Ukrainian; text in Ukrainian.

The main article was written by Petro I. Lazarovich, director of the Institute from 1927 to 1932. U. of A.

3839 **Greene,** David L[eslie]
By the swift waters. London, Colonial and Continental Church Society [1943] 31, [1]p. plates. 24cm.

The experiences of a clergyman at Sunkist, Sask., during the homesteading period. Shortt

3840 **Gurney,** F.C.
Soul so dark, and other poems. Didsbury, Alberta, 1943. 86p. Not seen. Watters

3841 **Hansberger,** Clara [and others]
Lighted lanterns. By Clara Hansberger, Evangeline Chapman, Alma Golling Barker [and others.] Moose Jaw, Mrs. C.C. Barker [1943] 22p. 19cm.

Poetry. Can. Cat.

3842 **Highe,** Edward
Maggie abandons the big dough. Calgary, Farm and Ranch Review, 1943. 22p. illus. 17cm. Glenbow

3843 **Hinks,** David
The fishes of Manitoba. [Winnipeg] Dept. of Mines and Natural Resources, 1943. x, 102p. illus., maps, diagrs. 24cm. U. of S.

3844 **Kirkconnell,** Watson
Our Ukrainian loyalists. Winnipeg, Ukrainian Canadian Committee, 1943. 28p. 21cm. U. of S.

3845 **Knox,** Olive [Elsie (Robinson)]
By paddle and saddle. Toronto, Macmillan, 1943. ix, 270p. 20 1/2cm.

Juvenile fiction relating to the fur trade period. A second edition was published in 1945, and a third edition the following year. U. of A. (Educ.)

3846 **Manitoba.** University
The interests of Western Canada and central northwest United States in the peace settlements; a joint preliminary report prepared under the auspices of the University of Manitoba and University of Minnesota ... Minneapolis, University of Minnesota Press, 1943. 43p. plates. 23cm. (Midcontinent and the peace, no.1) U. of S.

3847 **Menzies**, Don, ed.
The Alaska highway, a saga of the North. Rev. ed. [Edmonton, S. Douglas, c1943] cover-title, [48] p. incl. illus. (part col.) ports., map. 26cm. Glenbow

3848 **Moose Jaw Writers' Club**
Prairie poems. [Moose Jaw] 1943. cover-title, 24p. 16 1/2cm. Shortt

3849 **Un Père Trappiste**
Une trappe dans un pays de missions, Notre-Dame des Prairies, St.-Norbert, Manitoba, Canada. Cinquante années de vie contemplative 1892-1942. Par un Père Trappiste. [St. Boniface, Manitoba, 1943] 240p. illus., ports. 20cm. Glenbow

3850 **Saskatchewan.** University
Arthur Silver Morton ... professor of history and librarian in the University of Saskatchewan, 1914-40. Saskatoon, University of Saskatchewan, 1943. 23p. incl. front. (port.) facsim. 25cm. Shortt

3851 **Schreiber**, Ilse
Der gott der fremden erde. Hamburg, Hanseattsche [1943] 381p. 20cm.
A novel, set in Manitoba. Bavaria

3852 **Scott**, Joseph M[orrow]
Story of our Prairie Provinces. Sketches and maps by Lloyd Scott and Kathleen Mair. Toronto, J.M. Dent [1943] viii, 312p. incl. front., illus. 21 1/2cm. U. of A. (Educ.)

3853 **Sovereign**, Arthur Henry
Ambassador of the frozen way, Most Rev. Isaac O. Stringer, D.D., Archbishop of Rupert's Land. [n.p.] Centenary Committee of the Canadian Churches [n.d.] 35p. port. 19cm.
From 'Leaders of the Canadian Church,' edited by Bertal Heeney, 3d ser. (Toronto, 1943) Glenbow

3854 A tribute to William Aberhart; student, teacher, statesman. [n.p., 1943?] 16p. ports., illus. 25 1/2cm. Glenbow

3855 **Ukrainian Canadian Congress.** 1st. Winnipeg, 1943
First all-Canadian congress of Ukrainians in Canada. Winnipeg, Ukrainian Canadian Committee, 1943. 211p. illus. 26cm. U. of S.

3856 **Ukrainian Catholic Youth**
Pyatylitya Ukrainskoho Katolytskoho yunatstva. Yorkton, 1943. 80p. 25 1/2cm. Not seen. Select

3857 **Ukrainian National Federation of Canada**
A program and a record. Saskatoon, The Federation, 1943. 32p. illus. 21cm. Can. Cat.

3858 **White**, Samuel Alexander
Called Northwest. New York, Phoenix Press [c1943] 256p. 18cm.
Fiction; a story of the Saskatchewan Rebellion. Edmonton

3859 **White**, Samuel Alexander
Northwest patrol. New York, Phoenix Press, 1943. 254p. 19 1/2cm.
Fiction. Can. Cat.

3860 **Winnipeg.** Grace United Church
75th anniversary, 1868-1943, and the 60th anniversary of the erection of the present building. [Winnipeg, 1943] cover-title, 43p. illus. (incl. ports.) 21cm.
The history of the 'mother church of Methodism in the West.' United College

3861 **Cantelon,** R[obert] A[lvin]
Edmonton, crossroads of the world; a brief view of the city's development, and its place in the post-war world. Published under the authority of the City of Edmonton, and approved by the council of the Edmonton Chamber of Commerce. [Edmonton] Civic Enterprises, 1944. 80p. illus. 16cm.
Can. Cat.

3862 **Carter,** Eva
Thirty years of progress; history of United Farm Women of Alberta. [Calgary, John D. McAra, 1944] 45p. 18 1/2cm. Glenbow

3863 **Conservative Party** (Saskatchewan)
The policy of the Saskatchewan Progressive Conservative Party. Saskatoon, Provincial Headquarters [1944] cover-title, 7, [1]p. ports. 22cm.
Folder. Sask. Arch.

3864 **Dickson,** [Horatio Henry] Lovat
Out of the west land. Toronto, Collins, 1944. 446p. 21cm.
Fiction; the setting is in Alberta. U. of A.

3865 **Evans,** Allan Roy
All in a twilight. Garden City, N.Y., Doubleday, Doran & Co., Inc., 1944. 6p.l., 3-214p. 20 1/2cm. Not seen.
Fiction. A story of pioneering. Can. Cat.

3866 **Guttormsson,** Guttormur J[ónsson]
Hunangsflugur. Winnipeg, Columbia Press, 1944. 128, iv p. Not seen.
A collection of Icelandic poems. U. of T. Quarterly, 1944-5

3867 [**Hamm,** H.H.]
Sixty years of progress, diamond jubilee, 1884-1944; the rural municipality of Rhineland. [Altona, D.W. Friesen & Son, 1944] 26, [2]p. illus. (incl. ports., map) 23cm.
Rhineland, Manitoba. Man. Leg.

3868 **Horan,** John W[illiam]
On the side of the law; a biography of J.D. Nicholson. With drawings by James Nicoll. Edmonton, Institute of Applied Art Ltd., 1944. vi, 280p. illus. 22cm.
Experiences of the chief of the Alberta Provincial Police Force. U. of A.

3869 **Irvine**, William
Can capitalism survive the war? [Edmonton, Commercial Printers, 194-?] 24p. 17cm.

The C.C.F. platform for a new planned order. Glenbow

3870 John Wesley Dafoe, editor-in-chief, Winnipeg Free Press, 1901-1944. [Winnipeg, Winnipeg Free Press, 1944] 2p.l., 42p. incl. ports. 25 1/2cm. Shortt

3871 **Krumpelmann**, Cosmas W.
In this sign they conquered; being the centenary of the Grey Nuns of St. Boniface, 1844-1944. Muenster, Sask., St. Peter's Press [1944] 33p. illus. (incl. ports.) 18cm. Man. Leg.

3872 **Labor-Progressive Party** (Saskatchewan)
Electors of Saskatoon on June 15th mark your ballot for Nelson Clarke, the man who will fight for your interests in the provincial legislature. [Winnipeg, Universal Printers, 1944] cover-title, 8p. port. on cover. 23cm. Sask. Arch.

3873 **Laviolette**, Gontron
The Sioux Indians in Canada. Regina [Marian Press] 1944. 5p.l., 5-138p. front., plates, ports., fold. map. 23cm. Shortt

3874 **Le Chevallier**, Jules [Jean Marie Joseph]
St. Michael's school at Duck Lake; trials and progress of an Indian school over half a century (1894-1944) [Edmonton, La Survivance Printing Co. Ltd.] 1944 68p. illus. (incl. ports.) 24cm.

Also published in French. Shortt

3875 **Liberal Party** (Saskatchewan)
Facts; a record which is a challenge. Regina, Printed by Western Printers Association Ltd. [1944] cover-title, 47, [1] p. 22cm. U. of S.

3876 **McNaughton**, John
Markets and men, or, The challenge of changing conditions; published as a small contribution to the discussion on post-war problems. [Saskatoon, Printed by Modern Press, 1944] cover-title, 24p. illus. 23cm.

Author's autograph on cover. Glenbow

3877 **Manitoba**. University
The interests of Western Canadian agriculture in the peace settlements; a joint report prepared under the auspices of the University of Manitoba and the University of Minnesota ... Minneapolis, University of Minnesota Press, 1944. viii, 27p. 23cm. (Midcontinent and the peace, no.2) U. of S.

3878 **Mary Murphy**, Sister
St. Boniface heroines of mercy; commemorating the centenary of the Grey Nuns of St. Boniface. 1844-1944. Muenster, Sask., St. Peter's Press [1944] 20p. illus. 18cm. Man. Leg.

3879 **May Guichan**, Soeur
Développement des oeuvres des Soeurs Grises au Manitoba depuis leur fondation à Saint-Boniface, 1844-1944. Causerie donnée le 27 février ... sous les auspices

de la Société historique de Saint-Boniface. [St-Boniface, 1944] 75p. illus. (incl. ports.) 21cm. Man. Leg.

3880 **Methodius**, Brother S., ed.
Canadians on the march. Yorkton, Ukrainian Canadians Cultural Group, 1944. 92p. Not seen.

The text of a series of radio broadcasts stressing patriotism. U. of T. Quarterly, 1944-5

3881 [**Moore**, Helen]
Helen's poems. Collected by Anna M. Walker. Stanger, Alta., 1944. 39p. 20cm. Davies - 1009-1145

3882 **Moose Jaw Writers' Club**
Our autumn offerings. [Moose Jaw, 1944?] cover-title, 23p. 16 1/2cm.

Poetry. Shortt

3883 **Morton**, Arthur S[ilver]
Sir George Simpson; overseas governor of the Hudson's Bay Company, a pen picture of a man of action. Toronto, J.M. Dent and Sons, 1944. xii, 310p. front., plates, ports. 23 1/2cm. Map on lining-paper. U. of S.

3884 **Primeau**, Léonide
Le centenaire des Soeurs Grises. [Montréal, L'Action Paroissiale, 1944] 16p. 19cm. (L'Oeuvre des tracts, no.300)

A series of articles which originally appeared in La Liberté et Le Patriote. Man. Leg.

3885 **Saskatchewan Co-operative Creamery Association Ltd.**
The facts about the Saskatchewan Co-operative Creamery Association Limited. [n.p., 1944] 36p. illus. (incl. ports.) 21cm. U. of S.

3886 **Saskatchewan.** University. College of Agriculture
Soil survey of southern Saskatchewan, from Township 1 to 48 inclusive, by J. Mitchell, H.C. Moss, and J.S. Claxton, with a section on geology by F.H. Edmunds. Saskatoon, 1944. viii, 259p. front., illus. 23cm. (Soil survey report, no.12) Accompanied by a portfolio of 4 fold. maps.

Systematic soil surveys were begun as the outcome of a provincial royal commission to inquire into farming conditions in 1921. Local soil studies were issued as regional surveys were completed. This report is the culmination of twenty years of surveys. U. of S.

3887 **Sinnott**, Alfred A[rthur]
L'Archevêque écrit aux 'chers parents catholiques.' A quel prix la Rédemption. Palais de l'Archevêché, Winnipeg, Man., 1er mai 1944. [Toronto, Le Témoin Evangéline, n.d.] caption-title, [6]p. Amtmann - 176-414

3888 **Sinnott**, Alfred A[rthur]
A letter from Archbishop Sinnott of Winnipeg, Man., March 1st [sic] 1944. [Toronto, Gospel Witness and Protestant Advocate, n.d.] caption-title, 2p. Amtmann - 176-415

3889 **Sisler**, W[illiam] J.
Peaceful invasion. Winnipeg, Ketchen Printing Co. [c1944] 125, [1]p. illus. (incl. group ports.) 21cm.

Deals with the education of non-English-speaking children in Winnipeg. Man. Leg.

3890 **Steen**, Ragna
Pioneer days in Bardo, Alberta. Including sketches of early surrounding settlements, by Ragna Steen and Magda Hendrickson. Introduction by N.N. Ronning. Published by the Historical Society of Beaver Hills Lake, Tofield, Alberta. [Winnipeg, Printed by the Dahl Co., Ltd., 1944] 228p. illus. (incl. ports., maps) 23cm. Shortt

3891 **Storer**, R.H.
I am a lunatic, by R.H. Storer and F. Fowler. Vancouver, R.H. Storer & Co. [1944] vi, 120p. illus. 20cm.

Relates to Social Credit in Alberta. Glenbow

3891A **Taylor**, Mabel Cecilia
My Christmas tree. Moose Jaw, 1944. 68p. port. 21cm.

Poetry. Northland

3892 **Tessier**, Albert
Vers les pays d'en-haut, par A. Tessier et Hervé Biron. Montréal, Fides [1944] 243p. illus. 22cm.

The story of the Grey Nuns of St. Boniface. Man. Leg.

3893 **Underhill**, Frank H[awkins]
James Shaver Woodsworth, untypical Canadian; an address delivered at the dinner to inaugurate the Ontario Woodsworth Memorial Foundation, King Edward Hotel, Toronto, Saturday, October 7th, 1944. Toronto, Woodsworth Memorial Foundation [1944] 34p. illus. 18cm. U. of S.

3894 **United Grain Growers Limited**
The Grain Growers record, 1906 to 1943; an abridged history of Grain Growers' Grain Company, 1906 to 1917, Alberta Farmers' Co-operative Elevator Company, 1913 to 1917 [and] United Grain Growers Limited, 1917 to 1943. [Winnipeg, 1944] 4p.l., 93p. plates, ports. 23 1/2cm. Errata slip inserted. U. of S.

3895 **Winnipeg**. St. Giles' United Church
Diamond jubilee anniversary year (1884-1944), Burrows Avenue and Charles St. Winnipeg [The Church?] 1944. cover-title, 16p. illus. 23cm. Man. Arch.

3896 **Winnipeg**. St. Nicholas Parish
Soroklittia parokhiyi Sv. O. Nykolaya, 1904-1944. Winnipeg, Basilian Fathers, 1944. 39p. illus. 25cm. Not seen. Private information

3897 **Alberta**. Department of Trade and Industry, & Department of Economic Affairs
Your opportunity in Alberta. [Edmonton, Dept. of Economic Affairs, 1945] [64]p. illus., maps. 27cm. U. of S.

3897A **Alberta Hail Insurance Board**
A short history of the development of hail insurance in Alberta. Calgary, 1945. cover-title, 16 l. 32cm. Glenbow

3897B **Alberta Livestock Co-operative Limited**
Alberta co-operative leaders. Edmonton [Hambly Press, 1945?] cover-title, 54p. illus., ports. 26cm.

Messages from the leaders, with a portrait of each. Glenbow

3898 [**Anonymous**]
A northern apostle, Bishop V.J. Grandin, Oblate of Mary Immaculate. Edmonton, La Survivance [1945?] 40p. illus. 16cm. Not seen.
Private information

3899 **Bernier**, A[lfred]
1885-1945, Les dates mémorables du Collège de Saint-Boniface. [Saint-Boniface, 1945] 78p. Amtmann - 214-632

3900 **Berry**, J[ames] P.
Maskepetoon, Alberta's first martyr to peace. Toronto, United Church of Canada, Committee on Missionary Education [1945?] folder. (5p.) 24cm.
Private copy

3901 **Boni**, Armand
Pioniers in Canada; de Belgische Redemptoristen in de provinies Quebec, Manitoba en Saskatchewan. Brugge, De Kinkhoren, 1945. 278p. plates, ports., fold. maps. 21cm. (Missiologische monographieën, nr.4)

The work of the Redemptorists among the Ukrainians. Shortt

3902 **Björnsson**, Sveinn Eiríksson
Á heidarbrún; kvaedi. Winnipeg, Viking Press, 1945. 231p. port. 19 1/2cm.
U. of M.

3903 **Calgary**. Citizens
Welcome home, 14th C.A.(T.)R., Calgary Regiment (Tank). [Calgary, 1945?] 13 l. 22cm. N.Y.

3904 **Calgary Hebrew School**
The yearbook of the Calgary Hebrew High School. Edited by Rabbi A. Horowitz [and others. Calgary] Calgary Hebrew School, June, 1945. cover-title, 46, 54p. 23cm.

Only issue published. English and Yiddish. Yiddish section paged from the back.
Glenbow

3905 Not used.

3906 **Canada**. Army. Loyal Edmonton Regiment
The Loyal Edmonton Regiment memorial booklet including the memorial service, a short history of the Regiment, the roll of honour, by Wm. T. Cromb. [Nijkerk, Drukkerij C.C. Callenbach, 1945] 38p. 20cm.

'Prepared under the direction of Lt.-Col. W.T. Cromb, Jr., officer commanding.' On cover: In memoriam, 1939-1945. Dornbusch

3907 **Canada**. Army. 22nd Canadian Field Battery
Welcome home to 22nd Canadian Field Battery, 13th Canadian Field Regiment, R.C.A., by the citizens of Calgary and Gleichen, Alta. [Calgary, J.D. McAra?, 1945] [8]p. 23cm.

Includes a brief history of the battery and a nominal roll. Title from cover. Dornbusch

3908 **Cowan**, John Bruce
John Innes, painter of the Canadian West. Vancouver, Rose, Cowan & Latta, Ltd., 1945. 2p.l., 7-33p., 1 l. front. (port.) plates. 18cm. Shortt

3909 **Davidson**, Kathleen
Seven sheaves [by] Kathleen Davidson, Amy Downey, Kathleen Dupuis, Borgny Eileraas, Lois Borland, Myra Smith, Jean Sibbald. [Saskatoon, 1945] cover-title, 38p. 25cm.

'Dedicated to The Sheaf.' The contributors of the poetry were university students associated with the U. of S. campus newspaper The Sheaf. U. of S.

3910 **Dionne**, Emil
Men of destiny. Spokane, Wash., Privately printed, 1945. 224p. plates, ports. 21cm.

Locale of the story is The Pas, Manitoba. Glenbow

3911 **Duncan**, Donald Albert
Some letters and other writings of Donald Albert Duncan. [Halifax, Imperial Pub. Co., 1945] [3], 199, [1] p. ports., facsim. 24cm.

Several of the letters were written from Banff, Alta. Glenbow

3912 **East Central Irrigation Association**
[Red Deer River Diversion. Hanna, Alta., Hanna Herald, 1945?] [8] p. double map. 21cm.

Scheme for irrigating areas in east central Alberta. Glenbow

3913 **Eylands**, Valdimar J[ónsson]
Lutherans in Canada. With an introduction by the Most Rev. Franklin Clark Fry. Winnipeg, Icelandic Evangelical Lutheran Synod of North America, 1945. 326, [2], vii p. illus. (incl. ports., maps) 23cm. U. of S.

3914 **Ferguson**, R.T.
We stand on guard. Montreal, Publications (1943) Limited [1945] 55p. 23cm.

An attack on the C.C.F. Glenbow

3914A **Forsyth**, Robert Bell
Fibres of flax. Calgary [1945] 8p. port. 22cm. Glenbow

3915 **Fry**, H[arold] S[tanley]
What's ahead for prairie agriculture? Winnipeg, The Country Guide, 1945. 28p. illus. 23cm. Can. Cat.

3916 **Gard**, Robert E[dward]
Johnny Chinook; tall tales and true from the Canadian West. London, Longmans, Green & Co., 1945. 2p.l., vii-xix, 360p. incl. front., illus. 21cm. Map on lining-papers. U. of S.

3917 **Giraud**, Marcel
Le métis canadien; son rôle dans l'histoire des provinces de l'Ouest. Paris, Institut d'Ethnologie, 1945. lvi, 1296, [3] p., 3 l. plates, fold. maps. 28 1/2cm. (Université de Paris, Travaux et Mémoires de l'Institut d'Ethnologie, no.XLIV) U. of S.

3918 **Glendon, Alta**. Ukrainian Greek Catholic Parish
Pamyatka z posvyachennya parokhialnoyi rezydencyi v Glendoni, Alta., 1945. [Edmonton, 1945] 41p. illus. 22cm. Private information

3919 **Goldfrank**, Esther (S[chiff])
Changing configurations in the social organization of a Blackfoot tribe during the reserve period (the Blood of Alberta, Canada). New York, J.J. Augustin [c1945] vii, 73p. front., plates. 25cm. (American Ethnological Society. Monograph, 8) Bound with the Society's Monograph, 9. L.C.

3920 **Gosselin**, Paul Emile
Radio-Ouest-Française. Québec, Université Laval, Comité Permanent de la survivance française en Amérique, 1945. 47, [1]p. map. 16cm. (Pour survivre, v.7, no.1) St-Jean

3921 **Groulx**, Lionel
Louis Riel et les événements de la Rivière-Rouge. Montréal, Ligue d'Action Nationale [1945] cover-title, 23p. 19cm. Portrait of Riel on cover. Shortt

3922 **Haig**, Kennethe M.
Brave harvest; the life story of E. Cora Hind, LL.D. Toronto, Thomas Allen Ltd., 1945. vii, 275p. front. (port.) 21cm. U. of S.

3923 **Halpert**, Herbert
Tall tales and other yarns from Calgary, Alberta. p.29-49. Reprint from the California Folklore Quarterly, v.4, no.1, Jan. 1945.

Several of the tales are attributed to Dave McDougall, brother of Rev. John McDougall. Calgary

3924 **Hanks**, L[ucien] M[ason]
Observations on northern Blackfoot kinship, by L.M. Hanks and Jane Richardson. New York, J.J. Augustin [1945] 31p. 25cm. (American Ethnological Society. Monograph, 9) Bound with the Society's Monograph, 8. L.C.

3925 [**Henry**, Charles E.]
Regimental history of the 18th Armoured Car Regiment (XII Manitoba Dragoons) Deventer, Nederlandsche Diepdruk Inrichting [1945?] 151p. illus., fold. map. 18 1/2cm.

At head of title: France, Belgium, Holland, Germany, 8 July, 1944 – 4 May, 1945. Man. Leg.

3926 **Horan**, J[ohn] W[illiam]
West, nor' west; a history of Alberta. Edmonton, Northgate Books, c1945. 6p.l., 184p. illus. 24cm. Shortt

3927 **Hoyler**, Clement
In commemoration of the semi-centennial of Bruederheim and Bruederfeld, Moravian colonies in Alberta, Canada, 1895-1945. Edmonton, Moravian Church office [1945] 39p. illus. (incl. ports.) 20 1/2cm. Alta. Leg.

3928 **Jewish Old Folks Home of Western Canada**, Winnipeg
The story of an institution; a report of five years activities on behalf of the Jewish Old Folks Home of Western Canada. Winnipeg, 1945. 74p., incl. back cover. illus., port. 25cm.

Pages 62-74 (including added t.-p.) and front cover in English; text and t.-p. in Yiddish. Pages are numbered back to front. Glenbow

3929 **Kiriak**, Illya
Syny zemli. Edmonton, Institute Press, 1939-1945. 3v. 22cm.

A novel with epic qualities describing the adjustment to Western Canadian life of a Ukrainian community through three generations. An important sociological document. U. of S.

3930 **Line Elevators Farm Service**
Field crop insects in the Prairie Provinces. Winnipeg, 1945. 64p. illus. (part col.) 23cm. (Its Bulletin, no.5) Glenbow

3931 **Local Council of Women of Regina**
The Local Council of Women of Regina, commemorating golden jubilee, 1895-1945. Regina, 1945. 72p. 23cm.

Contents: Part 1, 1895-1925, by Mrs. T.J. Bennett; Part 2, 1925-1945, by Mrs. G.H. Barr. Part 1 is a reprint of a 1926 pamphlet. Shortt

3932 [**McAra**, Peter]
Sixty-two years on the Saskatchewan prairies. [Regina, 1945] cover-title, 48p. 18cm.

Experiences in the Qu'Appelle Valley and in Regina during the pioneer period. Shortt

3933 **McClung**, Nellie L[etitia (Mooney)]
The stream runs fast; my own story. Toronto, Thos. Allen, 1945. xvi, 316p. plate. 21cm.

A sequel to the first volume of the author's autobiography 'Clearing in the West.' U. of S.

3934 **Maltby**, R[ichard] G[rosse], comp.
The Calgary Regiment (14 CAR). [Hilversum, Holland, Printed by De Jong & Co., 1945] cover-title, 17p. 2 double maps. 24cm.

'Compiled by Lt. R.G. Maltby.' In 1958 the Regiment became The King's Own Calgary Regiment (RCAC) Glenbow

3935 **Manitoba**. Bureau of Travel & Publicity
Game birds and animals of Manitoba. [Winnipeg, The Bureau] 1945. 47p. illus. (part col.) 23cm. U. of S.

3936 **Melville**, Tom
Barbed wire ballads. Regina, School Aids and Text Book Publishing Co., 1945. 61p. illus. 20cm. Not seen.

Poetry; written while the author was a prisoner of war in Germany.
U. of T. Quarterly, 1944-5

3937 **Mercure**, André
La Semence; drame historique en 3 actes et apothéose. Centenaire de l'arrivée des missionnaires o.m.i. dans l'Ouest et le Nord Canadien, 1845-1945. [Lebret, Scolasticat du Sacré-Coeur, 1945] cover-title, 1p.l., 43p. 21cm. St-Jean

3938 Not used

3939 **Myers**, C[harles] Vernon
The oil investor. Including a series of articles which appeared in the Calgary Herald [and] the Ottawa Evening Citizen. [Edmonton, Douglas Printing, 1945] 90p. 17cm.

'Published by C.V. Myers.' Emphasizes the possibilities for oil in Alberta. Glenbow

3940 **Oblates**. Edmonton
Le serviteur de Dieu, Mgr V.J. Grandin, Oblat de Marie Immaculée premier évêque de Saint Albert, mort en odeur de sainteté le 3 juin 1902. Edmonton, La Survivance, 1945. 31, [1]p. illus. 16cm.

Portrait on cover. St-Jean

3941 **Oblates**. St. Boniface
Centenary of the Oblate Fathers in Western Canada, 1845-1945. [Winnipeg, Canadian Publishers Ltd., 1945] 84p. illus. (incl. ports.) 28cm. Man. Leg.

3942 **Oblates**. St. Boniface
Exposition missionnaire, 24e juin - 1 er juillet, à l'occasion du centenaire des Pères Oblats de Marie Immaculée dans l'Ouest Canadien, 1845-1945. St-Boniface, Maison provinciale des Pères Oblats, 1945. 104p. illus. 28cm.
St-Albert Museum

3943 **Pacey**, [William Cyril] Desmond
Frederick Philip Grove. Toronto, Ryerson Press [1945] ix, 150p. 20cm. (Canadian men of letters) U. of S.

3944 Le peuplement de l'Ouest Canadien. Paris, Impr. de J. et R. Joly, 1945. 2 fasc. in 4 (Société d'éditions économiques et sociales. Circulaires nos.213-214) Not seen. France

3945 **Priestley**, Norman F[laxman]
Summer fever and other verses. Calgary, 1945. 24p. port. 21 1/2cm.
Private copy

3946 **Primeau**, Léonide
'Soldats conquerants du Christ' (Mgr Antoniutte). A l'occasion du centenaire de l'arrivée des premiers Oblats du Marie Immaculée dans l'Ouest Canadien, 25 août 1845. [St. Boniface, 1945] 62, [2]p. illus., ports. 23cm.

Mostly biographical sketches of prominent members of the order. Glenbow

3947 [**Ringwood**], Gwen[dolyn Margaret] (Pharis)
Dark harvest, a tragedy of the Canadian prairie, by Gwen Pharis. Toronto, Thomas Nelson and Sons, c1945. xi, 143p. illus. 17 1/2cm. (Nelson's collegiate classics)

A play. U. of S.

3948 **Rowe**, W.J.
The West looks ahead. Manitou, Man., The Western Canadian, Sept., 1945. cover-title, 15p. 21cm. Can. Arch.

3949 **Sanders**, Byrne Hope
Emily Murphy, crusader (Janey Canuck) Toronto, Macmillan Co., 1945. xviii p., 1 l., 355p. front., ports. 22 1/2cm. U. of S.

3950 **Saskatchewan.** Bureau of Publications
Saskatchewan plans for progress; a summary of legislation passed at a special session of the Saskatchewan Legislature, October 19-November 10, 1944. Regina, The Bureau, 1945. 40p. illus. 23cm. U. of S.

3951 **Saskatchewan.** Bureau of Publications
The Saskatchewan viewpoint; the seed grain dispute. Regina, The Bureau [1945] 24p. illus. 25cm. U. of S.

3952 **Saskatoon.** Peter Mohyla Ukrainian Institute
Twenty-five years of the P. Mohyla Ukrainian Institute in Saskatoon. Winnipeg, Ukrainian Publishing Co., 1945. 429, [5]p. illus. (incl. ports.) 26cm. Added title-page in Ukrainian; text in Ukrainian. U. of A.

3953 **Saskatoon Light Infantry**
1st Battalion, the Saskatoon Light Infantry MG, Canadian Army Overseas. Honour roll, 10th July, 1943 to 8th May, 1945, Sicily, Italy, Holland. [Aldershot, Gale & Polden Ltd., 1945] 15p. 22cm.

Regimental colours in colour on cover. Dornbusch

3954 **Schaefer,** Paul J.
Heinrich H. Ewert, Lehrer, Erzieher und Prediger der Mennoniten. Zuege aus seinem Leben und Wirken. [n.p.] Verlag der Manitoba Jugendorganisation der Mennoniten-Konferenz von Kanada, 1945. 161p. Amtmann - 176-341

3955 **Segall,** Jean (Brown)
Wings of the morning. Toronto, Macmillan, 1945. 151p. front. 21 1/2cm.

A biography of an R.A.F. pilot, Mark Henry Brown, who was through the Battle of Britain, and was decorated for his services. He was born at Portage la Prairie, and lived in several prairie towns. Man. Leg.

3956 **Shubert,** Bernard
The homesteader; a true story. From the pulpit to the plow; 10 years in Western Canada. Franklin, N.Y. [The author] 1945. cover-title, 129, [1]p. illus., ports. 20cm.

The author homesteaded near Expanse, Sask., from 1909 to 1918. 'The pictures in this book are either photo-graphs or phony-graphs.' Glenbow

3957 **Social Credit Board**
Questions and answers on Social Credit and related subjects. Edmonton, 1945. cover-title, 24p. L. of P.

3958 Stowarzyszenie Polakow W Kanadzie Witajcie rodacy. [Winnipeg, 194-] cover-title, 16p. (incl. covers)

Information for newly arrived Polish immigrants. Turek

3959 **Sykes,** Arthur A.
The story of St. Andrew's United Church, and its place in Manitoba's history. Winnipeg, c1945. cover-title, 42p. illus. (incl. ports.) 23cm. Man. Leg.

3960 **Thorsteinsson,** Thorsteinn Th.
Saga Íslendinga í Vesturheimi. Winnipeg, Thjódraeknisfélag Íslendinga í Vesturheimi, 1945. v.3. (x, 407p.) map. 23cm.

This volume of the history of Icelandic emigration to America deals with settlement in Western Canada. U. of M.

3960A **United Grain Growers Limited**
Presentation to the Royal Commission on Co-operatives. [n.p.] 1945. 41 l. 28cm.

Claimed that the company should be taxed as a co-operative. 'Filed at Ottawa March 1945.' Glenbow

3961 **Usiskin,** Michael
[Oskn un motorn ... Toronto, 1945] 197p. 21cm. Port. on title-page. Not seen.

In Hebrew script. A Jewish settler's pioneer experiences at Edenbridge, Sask. L.C.

3962 Virden days. A partial record of No.19 Elementary Flying Training School, R.C.A.F., Virden, Man. Operated by Virden Flying Training School Ltd., 1941-1944. [Winnipeg, Printed by Saults & Pollard Ltd., 1945?] 94, 2p. illus. (incl. ports.) 26cm. U. of S.

3963 **Wilson,** E[ric] M[ackay]
Vanguard; the Fort Garry Horse in the Second World War. [Doetinchem, Holland, 1945?] 196p. plates, ports., maps (part fold., part double) 25cm. Can. Arch.

3964 **Winnipeg.** St. John's Cathedral. Wardens and vestry
From mission to cathedral. Published by the wardens and vestry of St. John's Cathedral to commemorate the one hundred and twenty-fifth anniversary of the arrival of Rev. John West, first Protestant missionary to the Red River Settlement, October 14, 1820. [Winnipeg, 1945] 12p. illus. 24cm. Man. Leg.

3965 **Winnipeg.** School Board
A visit to our schools; a pictorial review. [Winnipeg, Bulman Bros.] 1945. 48p. illus. 25cm. Winnipeg

3966 **Wood,** [Edgar Allardyce]
Three mile bend, by Kerry Wood; illustrated by Hugh Weatherby. Toronto, Ryerson Press [1945] 4p.l., 170p. illus. 21cm.

Nature stories and sketches. U. of A.

3967 **Wood,** H[enry] E.
Facts about Manitoba, assembled by H.E. Wood ... [Winnipeg] Manitoba, Department of Agriculture and Immigration, 1945. 16p. map. 21cm. U. of S.

3968 **Calgary.** Junior Chamber of Commerce
Calgary, Canada, city of industrial opportunity. [Calgary, F.W. Clark & Co., Ltd., 1946?] cover-title, [16]p. Calgary

3969 **Cameron,** Donald
Community centres in Alberta. Edmonton, University of Alberta, Dept. of Extension [1946] 53p. illus. 23cm. U. of S.

3970 **Clay**, Charles
Muskrat man. Toronto, Ryerson Press [1946] xi, 283p. 21cm.
Fiction; the setting is northern Manitoba. Winnipeg

3971 **Cook**, John Thomas
Nipawin. Moose Jaw, Printed by the Quality Press, 1946. 51p. illus. 22cm.
Shortt

3972 **Coté**, J.B.
Originaux et aventuriers (L'Ouest pittoresque) Ste-Anne-de-la-Pocatière, Fortin & Fils, 1946. 149p. 24cm.
Experiences homesteading in the West. N.Y.

3973 **Crerar**, T[homas] A[lexander]
Canada's wheat problem. Winnipeg, Winnipeg Free Press [1946?] cover-title, 14p. 23cm. (Winnipeg Free Press pamphlet, no.10) U. of S.

3974 **Davis**, Ella
Gift book of sonnets and birthstone rondolettes. Regina, Western Publishers, 1946. 12p. illus. 21cm. Not seen.
Poetry. Private information

3975 **Dick**, Catherine (Bond)
Trails I've ridden; an era in the prairie-foothill country of Alberta. [Calgary, J.W. Dick, 1946] 5-63p. illus., port. 20cm.
On cover: Alberta range rhymes. Glenbow

3976 **Ducks Unlimited** (Canada)
Cooperation unlimited; a conservation manual for Ducks Unlimited Kee-men. [Winnipeg, 1946] [2], 50p. illus., plates (part col.) maps 23cm. Glenbow

3977 **Edmonton**. Comité d'Etablissement Rural
Statistiques relative à l'établissement rural des Franco-Albertains. Le sol albertain offre une part de ses richesses à tout cultivateur désireux de le bien traiter ... [Edmonton, La Survivance, 1946] cover-title, [8]p. illus. 21cm.
St-Jean

3978 **Fahrni**, Margaret [(Morton)]
Third crossing; a history of the first quarter century of the town and district of Gladstone in the province of Manitoba, by Margaret Fahrni & W.L. Morton. Winnipeg, Advocate Printers, 1946. ix, 118p. plates, map. 24cm. U. of S.

3979 **Fiedler**, Arkady
Kanada pachnąca Żywicą. [Warsaw] Spóldzielnia wydawnicza Czytelnik, 1946. 245, [1]p. maps. 21 1/2cm.
Mostly historical information on Canada. Originally published in 1937. A London edition appeared in 1942. A German edition was printed in 1946. Austria

3980 **Gaudet**, Valérien
Pour la formation d'une élite sacerdotale et laïque. Conférence donnée le 12 juillet 1946 au Congrès de l'A.C.F.A., à Edmonton. [Edmonton, La Survivance, 1946] cover-title, [8]p. 23cm.
Printing on inside front cover, illustration on inside back cover. St-Jean

3981 **Grew**, David
The wild dog of Edmonton. Illus. by Ellen Segner. New York, Grosset & Dunlap [c1946] 198p. illus. 22cm.

Fiction. Glenbow

3982 **Grey Nuns**
Hôpital Saint-Boniface; soixante-quinze ans d'apostolat, 1871-1946. [St-Boniface? 1946] 68p. illus. 23cm. Man. Leg.

3983 **Griesbach**, W[illiam] A[ntrobus]
I remember. Toronto, Ryerson Press [1946] 3p.l., 353p. front., ports. 23 1/2cm.

Mostly recollections of early Edmonton. U. of S.

3984 **Grove**, Frederick Philip
In search of myself. Toronto, Macmillan Co., 1946. 6p.l., 457p. front. (port.) 21 1/2cm. U. of S.

3985 **Herzer**, John E.
Homesteading for God; the story of the Lutheran Church (Missouri Synod) in Alberta and British Columbia. [Edmonton, Commercial Printers, 1946?] 70p. illus., ports. 24cm.

On cover: A narrative history of Lutheran mission work in Alberta and British Columbia, 1894-1946. Glenbow

3986 **Honderich**, Beland [Hugh]
The Toronto Daily Star reports on the Saskatchewan government. Regina, Bureau of Publications, 1946. 36p. illus. 22cm. U. of S.

3987 **Hoyler**, Clement, comp.
Heimtal in the making; reminiscences of the beginnings of a Moravian congregation in Alberta, Canada; commemorating the semi-centennial of its organization, July 26, 1896. [n.p., n.d.] 16p. illus., ports. 23cm. Shortt

3988 **Hughes**, Lora (Wood)
No time for tears. Decorations by Edwin Earle. Boston, Houghton-Mifflin Co., 1946. 5p.l., [3]-305p. illus. 21cm. (Life in America series)

Autobiography of a nurse. Only one chapter relates to Alberta, a vivid description of pioneer life near Grande Prairie, Alta. Edmonton

3989 **Hunter**, A[rthur] T[homas]
Chronicle of alcoholic beverages in the Northwest Territories and Saskatchewan. Regina, Commercial Printers [1946?] 32p. illus. (incl. ports.) 23cm. Sask. Arch.

3990 **Kavanagh**, Martin
The Assiniboine basin; a social study of the discovery, exploration and settlement of Manitoba. [Winnipeg, Public Press, 1946] xv, 282p. illus., ports., maps (part fold.) 24cm.

Largely a history of Brandon. Shortt

3991 **Kerr,** Illingworth H[oley]
Gay dogs and dark horses. Illustrated by author. Toronto, J.M. Dent & Sons [c1946] 4p.l., 371p. illus. 21cm.

Literary sketches of a teen-age boy and some of the characters in a town in the Qu'Appelle Valley. U. of S.

3992 **Lesage,** Germain
'Capitale d'une solitude.' Préface de Son Excellence Monseigneur Martin Lajeunesse. Ottawa, Editions des Etudes Oblates, 1946. 185, [6] p. illus., ports. 26cm. (Bibliothèque Oblate II)

History of the Catholic mission at Ile-à-la-Crosse. Glenbow

3993 **Lingard,** C[harles] Cecil
Territorial government in Canada; the autonomy question in the old Northwest Territories. Toronto, University of Toronto Press, 1946. xi, 269p. 23cm. U. of S.

3994 **Luhowy,** Alexander
Bezkhatny. Edmonton, Alberta Printing Co., 1946. 297p.

A novel of Ukrainian immigration to Western Canada. U. of T. Quarterly, 1946-7

3995 **Luxton,** Eric [Charles]
1st Battalion, the Regina Rifle Regiment, 1939-46. [Regina, Commercial Printers, 1946] 70p. illus. (part col.) ports., double map. 30cm. Regina

3996 **Malis,** Oskar
Pouceni z Kanady. Praha, Prazska akciova tiskárna, 1946. ... Not seen. Czech

3997 **Mishaegen,** Anne de
Dans la forêt canadienne. Bruxelles, Renaissance du Livre [c1946] 223p. illus., ports., map. 22cm.

Hunting and trapping experiences in the 1930's. The last half of the book describes experiences at Granville Lake on the Churchill River in Manitoba. L.C.

3998 **Nixon,** John Eric
Morrison's place and other poems. Regina, Printed for the author by Commercial Printers, 194–? [40] p. 20cm. Private information

3999 **Nixon,** John Eric
Selected poems. Toronto, Crucible Press, 1946. [46] p. 20cm. Private information

4000 **Okotoks,** Alta.
Souvenir presented to those men and women of Okotoks and district who served in the armed forces during World War II at a welcome home reception by the town of Okotoks, held on January 7th, 1946. [Okotoks, 1946] cover-title, 16p. chiefly illus. 31cm. Glenbow

4001 **Orchard,** W[illiam] J[ohn]
Prehistoric campsites of Saskatchewan as compared with those found in Denmark, Vancouver, Japan, Nova Scotia, and Scotland. Regina, School Aids and Text Book Publishing Co., 1946. 126p. illus., plates. Can. Cat.

4002 **Osborn,** [Edith Margaret (Camp)]
Frosty-moon, and other poems, by Margot Osborn. Toronto, Ryerson, 1946. 8p. 22cm. (Ryerson poetry chap-books) Not seen. Ryerson

4003 **Pfeifer,** Mrs. Lillian E.
Temperamental moods. [Calgary, Printed by The Times Press, 1946] [14]p. 17cm.

Poetry. 'Dedicated to Con who prodded me on.' Glenbow

4004 **Rashley,** R[ichard] E[rnest]
Voyageur and other poems. [Toronto, Ryerson Press, c1946] 16p. 21 1/2cm. (Ryerson poetry chap-books) U. of S.

4005 **Riddell,** J[ohn] H[enry]
Methodism in the middle West. Introduction by the Right Rev. Jesse H. Arnup. Toronto, Ryerson Press [1946] xii, 371p. front., illus. (maps) plates, ports. 23 1/2cm. Shortt

4006 **Sántha,** Pál
Kanada magyarsága. Winnipeg, Kanadai Magyar Ujsag, 1946. 31p.

Largely a study of the census figures relating to the Hungarians in Western Canada. U. of T.

4007 **Saskatchewan.** Bureau of Publications
Back to Saskatchewan; the inside story of rehabilitation. [Regina, The Bureau, 1946] cover-title, 36p. illus. 16cm. U. of S.

4008 **Saskatchewan.** Bureau of Publications
Progress in health services. [Regina, The Bureau, 1946] cover-title, 16p. illus. 22 1/2cm. U. of S.

4009 **Saskatchewan Wheat Pool**
Twenty-one years of progress, 1924-1945: the Saskatchewan Wheat Pool. [Saskatchewan, Modern Press, 1946] cover-title [12]p. col. illus. 28cm. Glenbow

4010 **Saskatoon.** Board of Trade. Young Men's Division. Hudson Bay Committee
Report ... to the Executive, February 14, 1946. [Saskatoon, Hudson Bay Route Association, 1946] caption-title, 7, [1]p. 23 1/2cm. Shortt

4011 **Shepherd,** Peter
With glowing hearts; true stories of Canadians in the making. Toronto, United Church of Canada, 1946. 138p.

Missionary work among the Ukrainians in Western Canada. Dempsey

4012 **Sigurdsson,** Jónas Ári
Kvaedi. Winnipeg, Columbia Press, 1946. 317p. Select

4013 **Sissons,** Constance (Kerr)
John Kerr. Toronto, Oxford University Press, 1946. ix, 282p. plates. 21cm.

Experiences along the Saskatchewan in the 1880's. Shortt

4014 **Tharp,** Louise Hall
Company of adventurers; the story of the Hudson's Bay Company. Toronto, McClelland and Stewart, 1946. x, 301p. incl. front., illus., plates. 21 1/2cm. Maps on lining-papers. U. of A. (Educ.)

4015 **Ukrainian Canadian Congress.** 2d. Toronto, 1946
Second all-Canadian congress of Ukrainians in Canada. Winnipeg, Ukrainian Canadian Committee, 1946. 190p. illus. 26 1/2cm. U. of S.

4016 **Ukrainian Catholic Council**
Tsentralya Ukraintsiv Katolykiv. Winnipeg, 1946. ... Not seen. Select

4017 **Vrooman,** C.W.
Cattle ranching in Western Canada, by C.W. Vrooman, G.D. Chattaway, and Andrew Stewart. Ottawa, King's Printer, 1946. 80p. illus., diagrs., tables. 25cm. (Canada. Dept. of Agriculture. Pub. 778)

Sets forth the results of a three-year study of ranch management and organization.
U. of A.

4018 **Winnipeg.** Shalom Aleichem School
Finf un zwanzig yor yovel-buch. [Winnipeg, 1946] cover-title, 119p. ports. 27cm.

Anniversary publication of a Jewish school established in 1921. L.C.

4019 **Wood,** [Alexandrina] Gertrude
A handful of lilacs and other poems. [n.p., 1946] 32p. 21 1/2cm.
Shortt

4020 **Yastremskiy,** T.A.
Kanadianizatsiya; politychniy rozvytok Kanadiyskych Ukrayintsiv za poslidnykh 46 rokiw [Canadianization; the growth of the Ukrainian Canadians in the past 46 years] Winnipeg, 1946. 198p. 22cm. Not seen. Private information

4021 **Alberta Teachers' Association**
In memory of John Walker Barnett, General Secretary-Treasurer, Alberta Teachers' Association, 1918-1946. [Edmonton, 1947] cover-title, 23p. ports., fold. facsim. 24cm. Glenbow

4022 **Atkinson,** Isabel
Saskatchewan health policy. Winnipeg, Winnipeg Free Press [1947] cover-title, 18p. 23cm. (Winnipeg Free Press pamphlet, no.18) U. of S.

4023 **Beausejour, Man.** Kosciol Matki Boskiej
Pamietnik z okazji poświecenia nowego Kościola Matki Boskiej Królowej Korony Polskiej w Beausejour, Manitoba, 22-go czerwca R.P. 1947. [Beausejour, Man. 1947] 47p. illus., ports.

On cover: Souvenir of the blessing of St. Mary's Roman Catholic Church, Beausejour, Manitoba. Text in Polish and English. Advertising matter included in paging. Turek

4024 **Bill,** Fred A[delbert]
Life on the Red River of the north, 1857 to 1887, being the history of navigation on the Red River of the north ... Life on the river towns of Fargo and

Moorhead, by J.W. Riggs; introduction and preface by Usher L. Burdick. Baltimore, Wirth Bros., 1947. 122p. illus. 22cm. Man. Leg.

4025 **Binns,** K[enneth] J[ohnstone]
Social Credit in Alberta; report prepared for the Government of Tasmania. Hobart, H.H. Pimblett, 1947. 52, [1]p. facsims. 24 1/2cm. U. of A.

4026 **Bone,** Peter Turner
When the steel went through; reminiscences of a railroad pioneer. Toronto, Macmillan, 1947. 180p. illus. 21cm. U. of S.

4027 **Campbell,** Grace [MacLennan (Grant)]
Fresh wind blowing. Toronto, Collins [c1947] vii, 233p. 20cm.

Fiction. Starting in the Qu'Appelle Valley, the story takes the characters through World War II. Another edition was published in New York. Edmonton

4028 **Camrose Historical Society**
Early history of Camrose, Alberta, and district, 1947. [Camrose? 1947] 36p. illus. (incl. ports.) 24 1/2cm.

Written to commemorate the fortieth anniversary of the town, it consists of chapters contributed by local old-timers; edited by F.L. Farley. Shortt

4029 **Chapman,** H[arold] E[verett]
Progress of co-operative farming in Saskatchewan, by H.E. Chapman and S.L. Medland. Regina, Dept. of Co-operation and Co-operative Development [1947] 15p. 23cm. U. of S.

4030 **Davidson,** Gordon A.
The Ukrainians in Canada; a study in Canadian immigration. Montreal, 1947. 23p. 21 1/2cm. Not seen. Private information

4031 **Douglas,** William
The house of Shea. The story of a pioneer industry. Winnipeg [Printed by Bulman Bros. Ltd.] 1947. xi p., 1 l., 3-109p. incl. front., illus., ports., diagr. 22 1/2cm.

The history of a Winnipeg brewery, the oldest established manufacturing industry in the province. Shortt

4032 **Filles de la Providence**
Cinquantenaire des Filles de la Providence dans l'Ouest Canadien: The golden jubilee of the Daughters of Providence in Western Canada. 1897-1947. [La Prairie, Que., Imprimerie du Sacre-Coeur, 1947] cover-title, 108p. illus. (incl. single & group ports.) 20 x 27cm.

Pagination includes much advertising. Les Filles de la Providence came from St Brieuc in Brittany and established nine convents in Saskatchewan and one in Alberta. St-Jean

4033 **Freedman,** Benedict
Mrs. Mike, the story of Katherine Mary Flannigan, by Benedict and Nancy Freedman. Drawings by Ruth D. McCrea. New York, Coward-McCann [1947] 4p.l., 312p. illus. 21 1/2cm.

Fiction: a Boston girl marries a mounted policeman and lives in Peace River district and around Lesser Slave Lake. L.C.

4034 **Guttormsson,** Guttormur J[ónsson]
Kvaedasafn. Arnór Sigurjónsson gaf út. Reykjavík, Idunnarútgáfan, 1947. 383p. 22cm. U. of M.

4035 **Guttormsson,** Vigfús J.
Eldflugur. Winnipeg, Á kostnad höfundarins, 1947. 199p. Not seen.
Icelandic poetry. U. of T. Quarterly, 1947-8

4036 **Hart,** Walter T.
Sixty-three years of uninterrupted service; Fort Rouge Methodist Church, 1883-1925; Crescent Congregational Church, 1910-1925; Fort Rouge United Church, Crescent United Church, 1925-1935; Crescent-Fort Rouge United Church, 1935-1945. Winnipeg, The Author, 1947. 91p. Man. Leg.

4037 **Hiebert,** Paul G[erhardt]
Sarah Binks. Drawings by J.W. McLaren. Toronto, Oxford University Press, 1947. xix, 181p. illus. 20cm.
A satire on prairie poetry. U. of S.

4038 **Hudson's Bay Company**
Milestones in the progress of the Hudson's Bay Company. Vancouver [1947] cover-title, 31p. illus. 15cm. Glenbow

4039 **James,** Norman B[loomfield]
The autobiography of a nobody. Toronto, Dent [c1947] x, 239p. 21cm.
The latter part relates to the rise of Social Credit in Alberta, and the author's experiences as a member of the legislature. U. of A.

4040 **Jamieson,** Heber C[arss]
Early medicine in Alberta; the first seventy-five years. Edmonton [Canadian Medical Association, Alberta division, 1947] 214p. illus., ports. 22cm. U. of A.

4041 **Jaques,** Florence (Page)
Canadian spring. Illustrated by Francis Lee Jaques. New York, Harper, 1947. xii, 216p. illus. 22cm. Map on end-papers. Saskatoon

4042 **Kohuska,** Natalka L.
Na storozhi kulturi; vidano z prisviachenniam dvadtsiat-littiu kulturnoi pratsi organizatsii soiuzu Ukrainok Kanady. Winnipeg, Ukrainian Women's Association, 1947. 128p. illus., ports. 23cm. U. of A.

4042A **Lent,** D. Geneva
Alberta Red Cross in peace and war (1914-1947) [Calgary? 1947] cover-title, [7], 116, 12, viii p. 28cm.
Mimeographed. Glenbow

4043 **Lysenko,** Vera
Men in sheepskin coats; a study of assimilation. Toronto, Ryerson, 1947. viii, 312p. illus. 21cm.
Ukrainians in Canada. U. of A.

4044 **McAvity** J[ames] M[alcolm]
Lord Strathcona's Horse (Royal Canadians); a record of achievement. [Toronto, Printed by Brigdens Ltd., c1947] 280p. plates, maps. 23cm. Alta. Leg.

4045 **McCourt**, Edward A[lexander]
The flaming hour. Toronto, Ryerson Press, c1947. 3p.l., 170p. 19cm.
Fiction. The setting is southern Alberta at the time of the Riel Rebellion. U. of S.

4046 **McCourt**, Edward A[lexander]
Music at the close. Toronto, Ryerson Press, c1947. 4p.l., 228p. 21cm.
Fiction. The background is the West between two world wars. U. of S.

4047 **MacVicar**, Nell
Tales and trails of Western Canada; stirring stories of personalities and episodes of the trailmaking days in Western Canada, by Nell MacVicar & Irene Craig. Regina, School Aids and Text Book Publishing Co., Ltd. [1947?] 144, [1]p. incl. illus., plates, ports. col. front. 23cm. U. of S.

4048 **Marysburg, Sask.** Assumption Church
Our parish ... interesting facts and pictures about Assumption Parish, Marysburg, Saskatchewan, Canada. Muenster, Sask., St. Peter's Press [1947] 68p. Kapsner

4049 **Maurice**, V[arney]
Fifty years in the Peace River country, and the story of the Alaska Highway. High Prairie, Alberta, 1947. 143, [1]p. 21cm. U. of A.

4050 **Maynard**, [Joseph] Lucien [Paul]
Our education problem. An address ... to the Legislative Assembly on Friday, March 14th, 1947. Edmonton, King's Printer, 1947. cover-title, 23p. 21cm. St-Jean

4051 **Medicine Hat, Alta.** Junior Chamber of Commerce
Medicine Hat, Alberta, Canada: opportunity unlimited in the gas city of the West. [Medicine Hat, Alta., 1947?] cover-title, [48]p. illus. 23cm. Glenbow

4052 **Middleton**, Clara J. [(Russell) Jackson]
Green fields afar, memories of Alberta days, by Clara J. & Jesse Edgar Middleton. Drawings by Thoreau MacDonald. Toronto, Ryerson, 1947. 61p. illus. 21cm. U. of A.

4053 **Mitchell**, W[illiam] O[rmond]
Who has seen the wind. Boston, Little, Brown & Co., 1947. 6p.l., 3-300p. 20cm.
Fiction; life in a prairie town as seen by a little boy. Macmillan of Toronto published an edition in 1948. U. of S.

4054 **Neatby**, K[enneth] W[illiam]
An illustrated guide to prairie weeds, originally prepared by K.W. Neatby, rev. and enl. by F.J. Greaney. Winnipeg, Line Elevators Farm Service, 1947. 78, [2]p. illus. (part col.) 23cm. (The Service's bulletin no.2)
First edition 1941. 'Index of illustrations': p.[2-3] of cover. Glenbow

4055 **Norris-Elye**, L[eonard] T[owne] S[terndale]
The Manitoba museum. [n.p., n.d.] 24p. illus. 24cm. Winnipeg

4056 **O'neil** [sic], Dollie Gray
Rhythm pictures and other poems. [Calgary, J.D. McAra, 1947] [2], 24, [1]p. 21 x 11cm. Glenbow

4057 **Pálsson**, Páll S[karphédinsson]
Skilarétt. Kvaedi. Winnipeg, Viking Press, 1947. 223p. illus. 20cm. U. of M.

4058 **Parsons**, Nell W[ilson]
The curlew cried; a love story of the Canadian prairie. Seattle, Frank McCaffery, 1947. 246p. Not seen.

Fiction. Can. Cat.

4059 **Patterson**, Muriel Beaton
... Messenger of the Great Spirit: Robert Terrill Rundle. New York [1947] 23p. 23cm. (Frontier books, no.4) Northland

4060 **Riley**, R[obert] T[homas]
Memoirs. [Winnipeg? 1947] 119p. ports. 24cm.

An English youth arrived in Manitoba in 1883, and in time became one of the West's leading financiers. The memoirs were found among his papers after his death. Shortt

4061 **[Robertson**, Hugh John]
The story of Knox Church, Winnipeg. Seventy-five years, 1872-1947. [Winnipeg? 1947?] 48p. illus. (incl. ports.) 24cm. Man. Leg.

4062 **Russenholt**, E[dgar] S[tanford] ed.
Meri-ka-chak, his message. [Verses by H.B. Chipman. Edited and illustrated by E.S. Russenholt. 3rd ed. Winnipeg, Kay J. Russenholt, 1947] 31p. illus. 18cm. Glenbow

4063 **Salvation Army**. Calgary Citadel Corps
Diamond jubilee, 1887-1947; souvenir booklet. [Calgary, 1947] cover-title, 24p. illus. (2 on cover) ports. 26cm. Glenbow

4064 **Saskatchewan**. Bureau of Publications
Government in industry; a brief account of Saskatchewan crown corporations. [Regina, The Bureau, 1947] cover-title, 16, [1]p. illus. 23cm. U. of S.

4065 **Saskatchewan**. Bureau of Publications
Progress report from your government; a survey of Saskatchewan government activity, 1944-1947. [Regina, The Bureau, 1947] cover-title, 56p. illus. 26 1/2cm. U. of S.

4066 **Saskatchewan**. Department of Education
Larger school units in Saskatchewan. [Regina, Bureau of Publications, 1947] cover-title, 16, [2]p. illus., map. 21 1/2cm. U. of S.

4067 **Saskatoon.** Board of Trade
Saskatchewan's city of opportunity, Saskatoon. [Saskatoon, General Printing and Bookbinding Ltd., 1947?] cover-title, 16p. illus. 22 1/2cm. Shortt

4068 **Scott,** Duncan Campbell
Walter J. Phillips. Toronto, Ryerson Press [1947] 59p. illus. 19cm. (Canadian art series) U. of A.

4069 **Smye,** Frank Hazle
The Winspear family (1897-1947); an appreciation. [Calgary? 1947?] [38]p. incl. ports., geneal. tables. 24cm. Glenbow

4070 **Swystun,** Wasyl
Kryza v Ukrayinskiy pravoslavniy (Avtokefalniy) Tserkvi. Winnipeg, The Author, 1947. 128p. 20 1/2cm.

Crisis in the Ukrainian Orthodox (Autocephalous) Church. Yuzyk

4071 **Van der Mark,** Christine
In due season. Toronto, Oxford University Press [1947] 363p. 22cm.

A novel of Alberta's northland. U. of S.

4072 **Walker,** D[rayton] E[rnest] comp.
A resumé of the story of 1st Battalion, the Saskatoon Light Infantry (M.G.) Canadian army, overseas. [Saskatoon, General Printing and Bookmending Co. Ltd., 1947] 139, [1]p. incl. ports. (part group) maps. 25cm. Incl. music. Saskatoon

4073 **Walker,** Ella [May] Jacoby
Fortress north. Toronto, Thomas Allen, 1947. xi, 419p. col. front., illus. 21 1/2cm. Map on lining-paper.

A historical novel tracing Edmonton's development. Saskatoon

4074 **Wallis,** Wilson D[allam]
The Canadian Dakota. New York, American Museum of Natural History, 1947. 225p. 27cm. (American Museum of Natural History. Anthropological papers, v.41, pt.1)

A study of Sioux Indians on reservations in Manitoba. U. of S.

4075 **Weekes,** Mary [Loretto]
Great chiefs and mighty hunters of the western plains; stories of daring and resourceful leadership of the Indian chiefs and scouts during the early settlement of the western prairies. Regina, School Aids and Text Book Publishing Co., Ltd. [1947?] 135p. front., illus. (incl. ports.) 22 1/2cm. Shortt

4076 Welfare in Alberta. Winnipeg, Winnipeg Free Press [1947] cover-title, 15p. 23cm. (Winnipeg Free Press pamphlet, no.17) U. of S.

4077 **Wood,** [Edgar Allardyce]
A nature guide for farmers, dealing with the Canadian farmer's pests and pals among birds and animals seen daily on his home acres. By 'Kerry' Wood. Illustrated by Hugh Weatherby and Frank L. Beebe. Saskatoon, H.R. Larson Pub. Co. [c1947] [5], 116p. illus. 23cm. Glenbow

4078 **Wyman**, H.C.
Bissett United Church. Bissett, Man., 1947. 28p. front., illus. 23cm.
Paging includes advertising. Victoria College

4079 **Yates**, S[amuel] W.
The Saskatchewan Wheat Pool; its origin, organization and progress, 1924-1935; with some reference to the Alberta and Manitoba pools, and to the pools' central selling agency. Edited by Arthur S. Morton. Saskatoon, United Farmers of Canada (Sask. section) [1947] 6p.l., 218p. illus. (incl. ports.) 23 1/2cm.
U. of S.

4080 **Yorkton**. Board of Trade
Yorkton, parklands trading centre. [Yorkton, Printed by The Enterprise Publishing Co., Ltd., 1947] cover-title, [48]p. illus. (incl. map) 23cm.
Shortt

4081 **Archer**, John H[all]
Historic Saskatoon; a concise illustrated history of Saskatoon. Written in collaboration with J.C. Bates. [Saskatoon] Junior Chamber of Commerce [1948] 60p. illus. (incl. map, plan) 27 1/2cm.
Illustrated cover. Shortt

4082 **Bagnall**, Lucy Lowe
At the sixtieth milestone; the story of the First Baptist Church, Calgary, Alberta, 1888-1948. Calgary, First Baptist Church, Jubilee Committee, 1948. 81p. front., illus., ports. 23cm. Calgary

4083 **Bartole**, Genevieve
Figure in the rain. Toronto, Ryerson, 1948. 7p. 22cm. (Ryerson poetry chap-books) Not seen. Regina

4084 **Basilian Fathers**
Yuvileyna pamyatka 25-littia novitsiatu otsiv Vasyliyan u Monderi. Mundare, Basilian Fathers, 1948. 112p. illus. 21 1/2cm. Not seen.
Private information

4085 **Catholic Women's League of Canada**. Calgary Diocesan Council
A short history of the Catholic Church of southern Alberta, Diocese of Calgary, 1865-1948 ... Commemorative of the 28th annual convention of the Catholic Women's League of Canada. Calgary, Alberta, November 3rd to 8th, 1948. [Calgary, 1948?] 47p. incl. illus. (part col.) 32cm. Shortt

4086 **Co-operative Commonwealth Federation**. Alberta Section
The story of the Alberta C.C.F., 1932 to 1948, and 1948 provincial convention program, Palliser Hotel, Calgary, November 19th and 20th. [Edmonton, 1948] cover-title, 71, [1]p. ports. 23cm.
Advertising matter and blank 'memo' pages: p.[66-72] Glenbow

4087 **Co-operative Commonwealth Federation**. Saskatchewan Section
C.C.F. program for Saskatchewan. [Regina, The Federation, 1948] cover-title, 19, [1]p. 23cm.
First printed in Nov., 1943. U. of S.

4088 **Co-operative Commonwealth Federation.** Saskatchewan Section
Saskatchewan C.C.F. members' handbook. Regina, The Federation, 1948. 60p. diagr. 14cm. U. of S.

4089 **Co-operative Union of Saskatchewan**
Co-operative principles. [3d ed. Regina, The Union, 1948] 24p. 23cm.
Originally published in 1941 under the title 'The Principles of Consumers' Co-operation.' Shortt

4090 **Cormack,** Barbara (Villy)
Ruth; a tale of new beginnings. Edmonton, The Author, 1948. 11p. 21cm.
Poetry. Watters

4091 **Cullinane,** Eugene Augustine
The Catholic Church and socialism. [Regina, Co-operative Commonwealth Federation (Saskatchewan section) 1948] cover-title, 8p. 25cm.
The article appeared originally in The People's Weekly. Glenbow

4091A **Dickson, Alta.** Bethany Lutheran Congregation
Dickson Koloniens historie et mindeskrift om vore pionerer. Samlet af en komite. Udgivet af Bethania Lutherske Menighed, Dickson, Alberta. Blair, Neb., Lutheran Publishing House, 1948. 45, [1]p. illus. 23cm. Glenbow

4092 **Edmonton.** Saint-Joachim Parish
Fête des pionniers, 1905-1948. 20 juin 1948. [Edmonton, 1948] 19p. illus. 23cm. Pagination includes advertising.
'Notes historiques' par Rev. J.J.M.J. Le Chevallier. Rutherford

4093 **Farmers' action program of Alberta**
Farmers' Union and United Farmers of Canada (Saskatchewan Section) [Edmonton, Commercial Printers, Ltd., 1948?] cover-title, 16p. 21 1/2cm. Shortt

4094 **Ferguson,** George Victor
John W. Dafoe. Toronto, Ryerson, 1948. v, 127p. illus. 20cm. U. of A.

4095 **Gaetz,** Annie L[ouise (Siddall)]
Park country; a history of Red Deer and district. Vancouver, Wrigley Printing Co., 1948. 173p. 22cm. U. of A.

4096 **Garratt,** A[lfred] W[ebster]
History of Milestone, 1893-1910. [Regina, Public Press, 1948] 121p. fold. plate, ports., fold. plan. 19 1/2cm. Shortt

4097 **Gislason,** I[ngvar]
Prairie panorama; a brief study of the Prairie Provinces. Calgary, Western Canada Institute Ltd., 1948. v, 196p. illus. (incl. maps) 23cm. Man. Leg.

4098 **Gradet,** R[oger]
Images du Far-West. Texte et 250 illustrations. Paris, Susse [1948] 172p. illus. 29cm. Br. Mus.

4099 **Grande Prairie, Alta.** Chamber of Commerce
Grande Prairie, Alberta, Canada, the ... centre of the Peace River District. [Grande Prairie, 1948] cover-title, 15, [1]p. illus. 28cm. Glenbow

4100 **Grayson**, Ethel Kirk
Beggar's velvet. Toronto, Ryerson, 1948. vi, 42p. Not seen. Ryerson

4101 **Hayes**, John F[rancis]
Buckskin colonist. Illustrated by Fred J. Finley. Toronto, Copp Clark Co., Ltd. [1948?] vii, 251p. illus. 21cm. Map on end-papers.
Juvenile fiction set in the Red River Settlement about 1812. Saskatoon

4102 **Hermant**, Léon
Thy cross my stay; the life of the servant of God, Vital Justin Grandin, Oblate of Mary Immaculate and first bishop of St. Albert, Canada. [Toronto, Mission Press, c1948] xii, 160p. front., fold. map. 20cm. St-Albert Museum

4103 **Hibbert**, William
Out of the pit. Drumheller, The Drumheller Mail, 1948. 116p. 17cm.
Poetry. Calgary

4104 **Hillsman**, John Burwell
Eleven men and a scalpel. Winnipeg [Columbia Press Ltd., 1948] 144p. 18cm.
No.8 Canadian Field Surgical Unit in World War II. Dornbusch

4105 **Hives**, H[arry] E[rnest]
A Cree grammar; being a simplified approach to the study of the language of the Cree Indians of Canada. Published by authority of the Missionary Society of the Church of England in Canada. [Saskatoon, Modern Press] 1948. 102p. 23cm. Man. Leg.

4106 **Hudson Bay Route Association**
The Hudson Bay Route and port of Churchill, Western Canada's gateway to Europe. Saskatoon, The Association [1948] cover-title, 8p. 15 1/2cm. At head of title: Buy British. Shortt

4107 **Hudson Bay Route Association**
The Hudson Bay Route, Western Canada's shortest ocean outlet to Europe. Saskatoon [Printed by Midwest Litho Printing Co., 1948] cover-title, 16p. illus. 15 x 23cm. Shortt

4108 **Hudson Bay Route Association**
Read the facts about Western Canada's practical and economical ocean trade route to British and continental markets. Saskatoon, The Association [1948] cover-title, 16p. illus. (incl. map) 15 x 23cm. Shortt

4109 **Kenderdine**, [Augustus Frederick LaFosse]
To the youth of Saskatchewan. [Regina] Dept. of Education, 1948. 3p.l., 13 col. plates. 23cm. Mounted col. plate on cover.
Reproductions of the artist's paintings. Private copy

4110 **Knox**, Olive [Elsie (Robinson)]
Red River shadows. Toronto, Macmillan, 1948. viii, 303p. 21cm.
Fiction; the Selkirk settlers. Can. Cat.

4111 **Laing**, Gertrude (Amies)
A community organizes for war; the story of the Greater Winnipeg Co-ordinating Board for War Services and affiliated organizations, 1939-1946. Winnipeg, 1948. 3p.l., 103p. illus. 23cm. Winnipeg

4112 **Lefebvre**, Jean-Jacques
Voyage-éclair dans l'Ouest Canadien et Américain. Montréal, B.D. Simpson, 1948. 35p. 25cm. Lavallee - 1964-10

4113 Lundar diamond jubilee, 1887 to 1947. Saga álftavatns-og grunnavatnsbygoa. Lundar, Man., 1948. 175p. illus. (incl. ports.) 26cm.
Some of the articles are in Icelandic. Contains much biographical material. Man. Leg.

4113A **McDonald**, Mrs. J.R.
Baptist missions in Western Canada, 1873-1948 ... Edmonton, Baptist Union of Western Canada, 1948. 59p., 2 l. illus., fold map. 23cm. B.C. Arch

4114 **MacEwan**, [John Walter] Grant
The sodbusters. Toronto, Thomas Nelson & Sons [1948] 240p. col. front., illus. (incl. ports.) 21 1/2cm.
Biographies of interesting pioneers in the West. U. of S.

4115 [**McIntyre**, William (Billy) Howell, Jr.]
A brief history of the McIntyre Ranch. Lethbridge, 1948? 5-35p. illus., 3 plates (incl. ports.) 19cm.
No proper title-page. U. of A.

4116 **Malov**, Peter N.
Dukhobortsy, ykh ystoryia, zhyzn'y bor'ba; k 50-letyiu preb'ivanyia, Dukhobortsev v Kanada. Knyha pervaia. [Thrums, B.C.] 1948. 605p. illus. (incl. ports.) Vancouver

4117 **Manitoba**. Bureau of Travel and Publicity
Manitoba's romantic northland. [Winnipeg, The Bureau, 1948] cover-title, [32]p. illus. 30cm. U. of S.

4118 **Meilicke**, Emil Julius
Leaves from the life of a pioneer; being the autobiography of sometime senator, Emil Julius Meilicke. (With editorial notes) Vancouver, Wrigley Printing Co., Ltd. [c1948] xv, 168p. incl. maps. front., ports. 21 1/2cm.
Editorial notes by Dr. A.S. Morton. Shortt

4119 **Morrison**, Dorothy
The prairie lily. Regina, School Aids, 1948. 40p. illus. 23cm. Not seen.
Largely poetry. Private information

4120 **Nasir**, George
Fifteen poems. Winnipeg, Dahl Co., 1948. 16p. 24cm. Can. Cat.

4121 **National Research Council of Canada**
Addresses delivered at the official opening of the Prairie Regional Laboratory, Saskatoon, Sask. [n.p., 1948] cover-title, 72p. 22 1/2cm. U. of S.

4122 **Needler**, G[eorge] H[enry]
The Battleford column, versified memories of a Queen's Own corporal in the Northwest Rebellion, 1885. Montreal, Provincial Publishing Co., Ltd. [1948] 92p. illus., ports. 19 1/2cm.
First appeared in Canadian Military Journal in 1947. Private copy

4123 **Orange Benevolent Society of Saskatchewan**
The Protestant Home for Children, Indian Head, Saskatchewan. Questions & answers. [Regina, Central Press Ltd., n.d.] cover-title, 8, [1]p. 15cm. Sask. Arch.

4124 **Orange Benevolent Society of Saskatchewan**
25 years of guarding Canada's greatest asset, 1923-1948. This year the Orange Benevolent Society of Saskatchewan marks its twenty-fifth year of service in the care and education of dependent boys and girls. [Regina, 1948] cover-title, 15, [1]p. illus. 19cm.
Describes the Home maintained at Indian Head. Sask. Arch.

4125 **Rodgers**, Robert Wylie
Dry belt gingles [sic.] No.2. Cabin Lake, Alta. [1948?] cover-title, 8p. 18cm. Glenbow

4126 **Saskatchewan**. Bureau of Publications
The new north. Saskatchewan's northern development program, 1945-1948. [Regina, The Bureau, 1948] cover-title, 38p. 14 1/2cm. U. of S.

4127 **Saskatchewan Co-operative Producers Limited**
The Saskatchewan Wheat Pool and its accomplishments, 1948. [n.p., 1948] cover-title, 39p. illus., diagrs. 20cm. Shortt

4128 **Sharp**, Paul F[rederick]
The agrarian revolt in Western Canada; a survey showing American parallels. Minneapolis, University of Minnesota Press [1948] ix, 204p. 24cm. Shortt

4129 **Swift Current, Sask**. Board of Trade
Swift Current, Saskatchewan, the heart of the grain land. [Swift Current, 1948] cover-title, [28]p. incl. covers. illus. 25cm. Glenbow

4130 **Théoret**, Anatole E.
Sainte-Rose-du-Lac. Winnipeg, Gerald C. Murray, 1948. 138p. illus. 21cm.
The history of a French parish in Manitoba. Man. Leg.

4131 **Thorsteinsson**, Bjarni Frá Höfn
Kvaedi. Preface by Gísli Jónsson. Winnipeg, Columbia Press, 1948. 294p. U. of T. Quarterly, 1948-9

4132 [**Thurn**, Walter Ralph]
The famous Bentleys. [Saskatoon, Modern Press, 1948] 24p. illus. (incl. ports.) 25 1/2cm. Includes advertising.
—— 1949/50 revision. [Saskatoon, Modern Press, 1949] 4p. illus. 25 1/2cm.

Biographical information about a famous hockey family from Delisle, Sask. Shortt

4133 **United Farmers of Canada**. Saskatchewan Section
Rural romance; a story of the Saskatchewan farm movement and its objectives. Saskatoon, The Association [1948?] cover-title, 10, [2]p. 15 1/2cm. Shortt

4134 **Winkler, Man**. Burwalde School District
Diamond jubilee year book of the Burwalde school at Winkler, Manitoba, 1888-1948. [n.p., 1948] cover-title, 48p. illus. (incl. ports.) 25cm. Man. Leg.

4135 **Winnipeg**. Board of School Trustees
Report of the directed self survey, Winnipeg public schools. Chicago, Committee on Field Services, Department of Education, University of Chicago, 1948. xii p., 1 l., 311p. tables. 27cm. U. of S.

4136 **Woodsworth**, J[ames] S[haver]
Toward socialism; selections from the writings of J.S. Woodsworth, edited by Edith Fowke ... [Toronto] Ontario Woodsworth Memorial Foundation [1948] 48p. 17 1/2cm. U. of S.

4137 CFQC, Saskatoon, 1923-1949. [Saskatoon, General Printing and Book Binding Ltd., 1949] cover-title, 41p. illus., plates (1 col.) 28cm.

A history of radio broadcasting in Saskatoon. Shortt

4138 [**Achard**, Eugène]
La caverne des Rocheuses; aventures dans l'Ouest Canadien sur le chemin de fer du Pacifique Canadien [par] Lucien Rivereine [pseud.] Nouv. ed., rev. et complétée. Montréal, Librairie générale Canadienne [1949] 141p. illus. 23cm.

Story set in the Rocky Mountains of Alberta. Glenbow

4139 L'Almanach français de l'Alberta. Edmonton, La Survivance, 1949. 64p. illus. 26cm.

Pagination includes advertising. Publié par le R Père P.-E. Breton. This informative almanac was published over a number of years. St-Jean

4140 **Canadian Association of Social Workers.** Manitoba Branch
The métis of Manitoba. Winnipeg, Published by courtesy of the Winnipeg Foundation, 1949. 24p. 23cm. Man. Leg.

4141 **Canadian Co-operative Wheat Producers, Limited**
Summary of operations of the Canadian Wheat Board, 1935-36 to 1947-48. [Winnipeg] Published by the Canadian Wheat Pools, 1949. cover-title, [12]p. 23cm. Shortt

4142 **Champagne**, Joseph Etienne
Les missions catholiques dans l'Ouest Canadien (1818-1875) Ottawa, Editions des Etudes Oblates; Editions de l'Université, 1949. 208p. 24 1/2cm. (L'Institut de missiologie de l'Université pontificale d'Ottawa) B.C. Arch.

4143 **Charach**, Paul
Power of a woman. Winnipeg, The Author, 1949. 104p. 18cm.
Fiction. Can. Cat.

4144 **Conquest, Sask.** Homemakers' Club
This Conquest of ours, 1904-1948. [Saskatoon, Midwest Litho Ltd., 1949] 51p. illus. (incl. ports., maps) 28cm.
This local history received second prize in the national Lady Tweedsmuir contest.
Sask. Arch.

4145 **Cresswell**, H[enry] C[ooke] P[orter]
The Canadian Pacific and immigration. An address ... at luncheon meeting of the Canada Colonization Association at Winnipeg, February 21st, 1949. [n.p., 1949] cover-title, 19p. 22 1/2cm.
A historical sketch. C.P.R.

4146 **Darwin**, Oliver
Pioneering with pioneers (an autobiography) Toronto, United Church of Canada [c1949] viii, 151p. front., plates, maps (on end-papers) 18 1/2cm.
An early Methodist clergyman's experiences. B.C. Arch.

4147 **Dingwall**, Marjorie McVittie (Saunders)
Now that I am fifty. Edmonton, The Author, 1949. 19p.
Poetry. Can. Cat.

4148 Facts about the new international wheat agreement, 1949-50 to 1952-53. [Saskatoon, Modern Press Ltd., 1949] cover-title, [12]p. 19 1/2cm.
Shortt

4149 **Hamiota, Man.** Women's Institute
The history of Hamiota. Compiled by the Hamiota Women's Institute. Hamiota, Echo print [1949] cover-title, 36p. illus. 22 1/2cm. Pagination includes advertising. Man. Leg.

4150 **Harvey**, Ruth (Walker)
Curtain time. Toronto, Thomas Allen, 1949. 310p. 22cm.
Early theatre in Winnipeg. B.C. Arch.

4151 **Higinbotham**, John D[avid]
Foothill and prairie memories; a group of poems. [n.p., 1949?] 32p. port. 20cm.
The poems are dated 1885 to 1909. Glenbow

4152 **Holmes**, Francis J[oseph] S[loan]
Ducks are different. Caricatures and candid stories of your favorite water-fowl; illustrated by Angus H. Shortt. [Winnipeg, The Author, c1949] cover-title, 38, [1]p. col. illus. 18 1/2cm. Man. Leg.

4153 **Houston**, C. Stuart
The birds of the Yorkton district, Saskatchewan. [Ottawa, 1949] cover-title, p.215-241. illus. 25cm. (Reprinted from the Canadian Field-Naturalist, v.63, no.6) Shortt

4154 **Hudson Bay Route Association**
Operation Bay Route ... Saskatoon [Printed by Midwest Litho Printing Ltd.] 1949. cover-title, 22p. 15 1/2cm. Shortt

4155 **Hudson Bay Route Association.** 6th convention, Prince Albert, Feb. 2d, 1949
Report ... [Prince Albert, Herald job print, 1949] cover-title, 24, [2]p. 19 1/2cm. Shortt

4156 **Jones**, Reg.
The Saskatchewan story. Westview, B.C., 1949. 30p. Canadiana

4157 [**Kirkpatrick**, Mrs. Helen]
Ramblings in verse. By Gemmill [pseud.] Winnipeg, Evans Print, 1949. 59p. Can. Cat.

4158 Ksiazka pamiatkowa z okazji oficjalnego otwarcia nowej siedziby Bractwa SW. Ducha, niedziela, 24 kwietnia 1949, Winnipeg, Manitoba. [Winnipeg, 1949] 36p. illus., ports.

On cover: Grand opening of new club building, Winnipeg, Sunday, April 24th, 1949. Text partly in English. Advertising matter included in paging.

4159 **Link**, Theo[dore] A[ugust]
Oil in Alberta and Western Canada; an address to the Toronto branch of the Canadian Institute of Mining and Metallurgical Engineers. [Edmonton? Alberta Printers, Ltd.] 1949. 35p. illus., maps, charts. 23cm. Glenbow

4160 **Linnell**, J.B.
The story of a pioneer, J.B. Linnell, as told to his daughter-in-law, Ruth Linnell, at Summerberry, Saskatchewan. February, 1949. [Grenfell, Sask., Grenfell Sun print, 1949] 1p.l., [22]p. port. Shortt

4161 **Lobb**, Roy
Plain folks, a book of friendly verse. [Saskatoon, Midwest Litho Ltd., 1949] 10p.l., 146p. port. 16cm. Private copy

4162 **McCourt**, Edward A[lexander]
The Canadian West in fiction. Published under the auspices of the Bibliographical Society of Canada. Toronto, Ryerson Press [1949] vi p., 2 l., 131p. 20 1/2cm. U. of S.

4163 **MacGregor**, James G[rierson]
Blankets and beads; a history of the Saskatchewan River. Edmonton, Institute of Applied Art, Ltd., c1949. 278p. illus. (incl. maps) 22 1/2cm. Saskatoon

4164 **McMahon**, 'Frank' [Francis Murray Patrick]
Brief submitted to the Dinning Commission enquiring into the natural gas resources of Alberta; with a further memorandum regarding the submission. Calgary, 1949. 14p. 25cm. Glenbow

4165 **Magrath, Alta.** Golden Jubilee Celebrations Committee
Magrath's golden jubilee, commemorating 50 years of irrigation. Magrath, July 24th, 25th, 26th, 1949. Official jubilee book. [Magrath? 1949] cover-title, 84p. illus. 20cm. Pagination includes advertising.

Historical and biographical material. Alta. Leg.

4166 **Manitoba.** Bureau of Travel and Publicity
Greater Winnipeg. [Winnipeg, King's Printer, 1949?] cover-title, 19p. illus. (incl. map) 23cm. Shortt

4167 **Manitoba.** Bureau of Travel and Publicity
Guide book to Manitoba. Winnipeg [King's Printer, 1949] 155, [1]p. illus. (incl. maps) 16 1/2cm. Shortt

4168 **Manitoba.** Bureau of Travel and Publicity
Historical Manitoba. [Winnipeg, King's Printer, 1949?] [32]p. illus. 31cm. Shortt

4169 **Minnedosa, Man.** Women's Institute
Minnedosa, Manitoba, 1878-1948; a village history, compiled by the Minnedosa Women's Institute. [n.p., 1949] 50p. plates, ports., map. 22 1/2cm. P.34-50 advertising material. Man. Leg.

4170 **Nasir,** George
New poems. Winnipeg, Dahl Co., 1949. 8p. Watters

4171 **Obodiac,** Stanlee
Pennfield Ridge. [Wembley, Eng., Wembley News Printers, 1949] 100p. ports. (part group) 18 1/2cm.

Experiences of a western lad in a New Brunswick air training school during World War II. Shortt

4172 100 years of medicine, 1849-1949. [Saskatoon, Modern Press Ltd., 1949] 44p. illus., ports. 27 1/2cm.

Edited by Dr. Anna Mary Nicholson and published in connection with the Canadian Medical Association convention in Saskatoon. Devoted largely to women pioneers in medicine. Shortt

4173 The people's guide: Lethbridge business and professional classified directory, 1949. [Lethbridge, Alta., 1949] cover-title, 46, [1]p. illus. 23cm.

Advertising matter only. Glenbow

4174 **Pickel,** Enid
Prairie skyline, by Enid & Vesta Pickel. Regina, c1949. 3p.l., 3-40p. 21cm.

Poetry. Private copy

4175 **Russenholt,** E[dgar] S[tanford]
Selling grain in pigskins; a review of co-operative studies and findings by Dr. E.W. Crampton – in the best way to use Canadian grains to produce top grade market hogs. Published by the Canadian Wheat Pools. [Saskatoon, Modern Press Ltd., 1949] cover-title, 23p. illus. 22 1/2cm. Shortt

4176 **Saskatchewan.** Bureau of Publications
Women and children's rights in Saskatchewan. [Regina, The Bureau, 1949] cover-title, 44p. illus. 21 1/2cm. U. of S.

4177 **Saskatchewan Co-operative Producers Limited**
25 years with the Saskatchewan Wheat Pool. [Saskatoon, Modern Press, 1949] cover-title, [28] p. illus. 25 1/2cm. Shortt

4178 **Saskatoon School District, No.13**
A visit to our public schools; a pictorial review. [Saskatoon, Saskatoon Public School Board] 1949. cover-title, [24] p. illus. (incl. ports.) 26 1/2cm. Shortt

4179 **Smith,** A[lbert] E[dward]
All my life, an autobiography. Toronto, Progress Books, 1949. 224p. 20cm.
A clergyman who served in parishes at Dauphin, Prince Albert, and Winnipeg. He was active in labour movements. Northland

4180 **Tucker,** Walter [Adam]
The C.C.F. record in Saskatchewan examined, by Walter Tucker, and comments by Winnipeg Free Press. [Winnipeg, 1949] cover-title, 37p. 23cm. (Winnipeg Free Press pamphlet, no.27) U. of S.

4181 **Vinet,** [Jean] Lucien
I was a priest. Toronto, Canadian Protestant League [c1949] 143p. ports. 19cm. Private copy

4182 **Weekes,** Mary [Loretto]
Trader King, as told to Mary Weekes; the thrilling story of forty years' service in the North-West Territories, related by one of the last of the old time wintering partners of the Hudson's Bay Company. Regina, School Aids and Text Book Publishing Co. [c1949] 184p. illus., port. 21cm. Hudson's Bay House

4182A **Winnipeg, Man.**
Winnipeg's 75th birthday party, June 5 to 11, 1949. Official program and brief history of Winnipeg ... [Winnipeg, 1949] cover-title, 64p. illus., ports. 23cm.
Advertising matter included in paging. Glenbow

4183 **Winnipeg.** Public Library
A select bibliography of Canadiana of the Prairie Provinces; publications relating to Western Canada by English, French, Icelandic, Mennonite, and Ukrainian authors. Winnipeg, Public Library, 1949. cover-title, 33p. 18cm. Shortt

4184 **Winnipeg.** Ukrainian National Home
Propamyatna knyha Ukrayinskoho narodnoho domu v Winnipegu (Memorial book of the Ukrainian National Home in Winnipeg) Winnipeg, 1949. 863p. illus., ports. 23cm. Added title-page in English; text in Ukrainian. U. of A.

4185 **Wood,** [Edgar Allardyce]
The magpie menace, by Kerry Wood. [Red Deer, Alta., The Author, c1949] 40p. illus., diagrs. 15cm. Glenbow

4186 **Young People's Luther League and Choral Union.** 13th biennial international convention, Saskatoon, June 29-July 3, 1949
Pictorial souvenir book. [Saskatoon, Thams Studio, 1949] [20]p. illus. 28cm.

Consists of nearly 100 photographs of the convention and city. Shortt

4187 **Zelma, Sask.** Homemakers' Club
The community of Zelma, 1904-1949. [Saskatoon, Saskatoon Printers, 1949] [26]p. illus. 23cm. Shortt

4188 **Bronner,** Frédéric
Nouveaux Canadiens. Complete with exercises and French-English exercises. Toronto, J.M. Dent, 1950. iii, 212p. illus. Not seen.

Pioneer farming experiences at Dollard, Sask. Shortt

4189 **Burns,** Dean K.
Little sanctuaries. [Regina, 1950] cover-title, [17]p. 21cm. Mimeographed.

Devotional literature. Private copy

4190 [**Bussard,** Lawrence H.]
Lethbridge public schools, 1950. Issued on the occasion of the formal opening of the Lethbridge Collegiate Institute, Wednesday, November 22nd, 1950. Lethbridge, 1950. 20p. illus. (incl. ports.) 31cm. Shortt

4191 **Cameron,** F[red] J.
The hermit of Chokecherry Creek, and other poems. [Edmonton, Institute of Applied Art, 1950] 113p. illus. 24cm. U. of A. (Extension)

4191A **Galloway,** Christian
Peace River and other verse. London, Mitre Press [1952]. 52p. 23cm. B.C. Arch.

4192 **Campbell,** Marjorie [Elliott] (Wilkins)
The Saskatchewan; illustrated by Illingworth H. Kerr. New York, Rinehart & Co. [1950] 6p.l., 5-400p. illus., double map. 22cm. (Rivers of America) U. of S.

4193 **Canadian Great War Veteran**
The Prince; a Canadian Great War veteran's stories, chiefly concerning his Alberta range horse, as related to his grandson, Christmas day, 1950. [Edmonton, Imperial Publishing Co., 1950] 63, [1]p. illus. 18cm.

Fiction. First published in 1917. On p.3 of cover: Rangeland vocabulary. Glenbow

4194 **Canadian Red Cross Society**
'Call 320'; a documentary record of the 1950 Manitoba flood and Red Cross activities in the disaster. [Winnipeg, 1950] 94p. incl. illus. Hamilton

4195 **Carlson,** William E.
History of Emerson, featuring historical sketches of surrounding districts. Emerson, Emerson Journal, 1950. cover-title, [80]p. illus. (incl. ports.) 24cm.

Originally collected by the Women's Institute in 1928; revised and brought up to date for publication. Man. Leg.

4196 **Doka,** K[alman] C.
Golden jubilee of Békevár, 1900-1950. [Kipling, 1950] 26p. illus. (incl. ports.) 26cm.

The history of a Presbyterian church in a Hungarian community at Kipling, Sask.
Sask. Arch.

4197 **Douglas,** William
The story of Number Four; being a brief summary of the happenings in St. John's Lodge, 1875 to 1950. Winnipeg, The Lodge [1950] 80p. ports. 24cm. Glenbow

4198 **Duddridge,** Hugh
Seen from my seeder step; a volunteer crop of verse from a Saskatchewan farm. [Prince Albert, The Author, 1950] 6p.l., 6-73p. 21 1/2cm. Shortt

4199 **Finlay,** R[obert] E[ddy]
A tour of the old (1871) George McDougall Church. Edmonton [195-] 11p. 21 1/2cm. Illus. on the title-page. Private copy

4200 **Glamis, Sask.** Glamis Memorial United Church
The Glamis Memorial United Church; historical sketch of the church in Glamis district, 1906-1950. [Elrose, 1950] cover-title, 16p. illus. 23cm. Shortt

4201 **Grande Prairie, Alta.** Chamber of Commerce
Grande Prairie, Alberta, Canada, progressive centre of an inland empire. [Edmonton, Reliable Printing Co., 1950] 14, [2]p. illus. 28cm. Glenbow

4202 **Hanks,** Lucien M[ason]
Tribe under trust; a study of the Blackfoot reserve of Alberta, by Lucien M. Hanks, Jr. and Jane Richardson Hanks. Photos by F. Gully. Toronto, University of Toronto Press, 1950. xvi, 206p. plates. 24cm. U. of A.

4203 **Hawarden, Sask.** Homemakers' Club
The history of Hawarden and community. [Saskatoon, Midwest Litho Co., 1950] 1p.l., 32p. illus. 23cm. U. of S.

4204 **High River Times**
This is High River, Alberta, the cowtown capital of the foothills. [High River, 1950] cover-title, [40]p. incl. covers. illus. 23cm.

Each page sponsored by an advertiser. Glenbow

4205 **Jowsey,** [James] Ralph
The first sixty years; a history of Eden School and district from 1890 to 1950. Saltcoats, The Author, 1950. 46p. Mimeographed. Shortt

4206 **Langruth, Man.**
A tribute to soldiers and pioneers of the Langruth district. Published by the Langruth community. [Winnipeg, T.W. Taylor, 1950] 227p. illus. (incl. ports.) 26cm.

Part 1: Biographical sketches of district soldiers who participated in World Wars I & II.
Part 2: p.104-227, is a history of the community. Man. Leg.

4207 **Lipset,** Seymour Martin
Agrarian socialism; the Coöperative Commonwealth Federation in Saskatchewan, a study in political sociology. Berkeley, University of California Press, 1950. xvii, 315p. 23cm. U. of S.

4208 **McClelland,** Lily Coulter
Gems of praise. [Saskatoon, 1950] 47p. 18cm.
Religious poetry. Shortt

4209 **McCourt,** Edward A[lexander]
Home is the stranger. Toronto, Macmillan, 1950. 4p.l., 268, [1]p. 21cm.
Fiction. The story of an Irish war bride's adjustment to the prairie environment. U. of S.

4210 **MacEwan,** [John Walter] Grant
Agriculture on parade; the story of the fairs and exhibitions of Western Canada. Toronto, Thomas Nelson & Sons [c1950] 4p.l., 200p. front., plates. 21cm. U. of S.

4211 **McGrane,** J.E.
The Exeter and the North Saskatchewan. Lac la Biche, Alta., Published by the Exeter sea cadet corps, 1950. 107p. illus. 23cm.
The story of a local branch of the Navy League of Canada and a voyage by youthful sailors down the North Saskatchewan. Alta. Leg.

4212 **MacMillan,** Don[ald] A.
Rink rat. Toronto, Harlequin Books [1950] 192p. 17cm.
Fiction; the story of a Saskatchewan boy who became a national hockey player. U. of A.

4213 **Mantario, Sask.** Homemakers' Club
From oxen to airplane; Mantario, 1908-1950. [Saskatoon, Midwest Litho Co., 1950] cover-title, 91p. illus. (incl. ports., maps, plan) 23cm.
Compiled by C. Evans Sargent. Shortt

4214 **Masters,** Donald Campbell [Charles]
The Winnipeg general strike. Toronto, University of Toronto Press, 1950. xv, 159p. illus. 24cm. (Social Credit in Alberta; its background and development, 2) U. of S.

4215 **Monteith,** George B.
A history of Killarney and Turtle Mountain. [Killarney?] 1950. [8]p. 16 1/2cm. Man. Leg.

4216 **Morrison,** Elsie C.
Calgary, 1875-1950; a souvenir of Calgary's seventy-fifth anniversary, by Elsie C. Morrison [and] P.N.R. Morrison. Calgary, Calgary Publishing Co., 1950. 247, [1]p. illus. (part col.) 29cm. Pagination includes advertising.
A compilation of articles about institutions and people. Calgary

4217 **Morton,** William Lewis
The Progressive party in Canada. Toronto, University of Toronto Press, 1950. xiii, 331p. 24cm. (Social Credit in Alberta; its background and development, no.1) U. of S.

4218 [**Nicol**, John Lennox]
Through the years with Knox; celebrating sixty-five years of service as a pastoral charge, 1885-1950, and the fiftieth anniversary of the opening of the first Knox Church, 1900-1950. Saskatoon, Knox United Church [1950] 59, 1p. illus. (incl. ports.) 27 1/2cm. Shortt

4219 **Obadiac**, Stanlee
The soul speaks. [Yorkton, Redeemer's Voice, 1950] 63p. 17cm.

Most of the poems are based on experiences of a young pilot in England during World War II. Shortt

4220 **Pirot**, Jules
Contes dau lon èt did près. [Tales from far and near] Gembloux, Belgium, Editions Duculot, 1950. 162p. 19 1/2cm. Not seen.

Written in Walloon. Private information

4221 **Rempel**, J[ohann] G.
Die Rosenorter Gemeinde in Saskatchewan in Wort und Bild. Rosthern, D.H. Epp, 1950. 183p. illus., ports. 22 1/2cm. Shortt

4222 River rampant. Published for the benefit of the Manitoba Flood Relief Fund. [Winnipeg, Stovel Press, 1950] [48]p. illus. 28cm.

Relates to the Red River flood of 1950. Man. Leg.

4223 **Rolph**, William K[irby]
Henry Wise Wood of Alberta. Toronto, University of Toronto Press, 1950. xi, 235p. port., plates. 24cm.

A biography of the president of the United Farmers of Alberta. U. of S.

4224 **Russell**, Sheila Mackay
A lamp is heavy. Illus. by Jean McConnell. Philadelphia, Lippincott [c1950] vi, 257p. illus. 23cm.

A novel about nursing. U. of A.

4225 **Steele**, Harwood [Elmes Robert]
Ghosts returning. Toronto, Ryerson Press [c1950] xii, 272p. 21cm.

Fiction. Based on the exploits of the early Mounted Police detachment at Ft. Macleod. Edmonton

4226 **Turner**, John Peter
The North-West Mounted Police, 1873-1893. Ottawa, King's Printer, 1950. 2v. illus. (incl. ports.) fold. map. 25cm. U. of A.

4227 **Tyre**, Robert
Along the highway. Regina, School Aids and Text Book Publishing Co. Ltd. [1950] 124p. illus. 22cm.

On cover: Travel tales and trivia from the log of Galloping Gus; a roving reporter in Saskatchewan. Private copy

4228 **Warren**, Sara Evangeline Matheson
Prairie panels. [Vauxhall, Alta., 1950] cover-title, 22p. 19cm.

Poems. Author's presentation copy to J.D. Higinbotham, inscribed. Glenbow

4229 **Whiteside,** William Carleton
The nomadic life of a surgeon. Edmonton, Douglas Printing Co., 1950. 89p. illus. (incl. ports.) 23cm.

Travels of an Edmonton doctor while a student and later while in the armed services during World War II. U. of A.

4230 **Williams,** Flos (Jewell)
Fold home. Toronto, Ryerson Press [c1950] 3p.l., 265p. 21cm.

Fiction; fortunes of an old-time ranching family in the Calgary-Turner Valley district. Edmonton

4231 **Wood,** [Alexandrina] Gertrude
Through the year with Gertrude Wood. [Aneroid, News Magnet print, 1950] 25, [2]p. 22cm.

Poetry. Shortt

4232 **Yorkton.** St. Joseph's College
Pochatky i pracia Kolegii Sv. Yosypha v Yorktoni. St. Joseph's College. Yorkton [1950?] 8p. illus. 26cm. Not seen. Private information

4233 **Adams,** Mrs. Mary
I married a monk. Toronto, Evangelical Mission [1951?] 67p. ports. 17cm.

Conversion of a Basilian father to a sect of evangelical Protestants. U. of A.

4234 **Alberta Wheat Pool**
The story of the Alberta Wheat Pool, 'farmer owned co-operative.' Calgary, 1951. 22p. tables. 23cm. Canadiana

4235 **Bilecky,** Leonid
Ukrayinski pionery v Kanadi, 1891-1951. Winnipeg, Ukrainian Canadian Committee, 1951. 96p. illus. (incl. ports.) 23cm. U. of A.

4236 **Boily,** Marie-Louis
Nos braves pionniers en terre manitobaine; souvenirs de colonisation. La Broquerie, Man., L'Auteur, 1951. 109p. Mimeographed. Not seen. C.H.R., 1951

4237 **Burnet,** Jean
Next-year country; a study of rural social organization in Alberta. Toronto, University of Toronto Press, 1951. xv, 188p. tables. 27cm (Social Credit in Alberta; its background and development, no.3)

Relates to the district around Hanna, Alberta. U. of A.

4238 **Conklin,** William
Wind blown leaves. [Foleyet, Ont., Macnab Historical Association, 1951] 18p. 23cm. (Carillon poetry chap-books)

Poetry. Shortt

4239 **Cormack,** Barbara (Villy)
Local rag. Toronto, Ryerson Press [1951] ix, 234p. 21cm.

Fiction; life in an Albertan community as recorded in the local newspaper. U. of A.

4240 **Davidson,** W[illiam] M[cCartney]
The life and times of Louis Riel. [Calgary, The Albertan, 1951] cover-title, 114p. illus. (ports.) 23cm. Shortt

4241 **Flipot,** Fernand
Canada, terre d'avenir, vu par un cultivateur normand. Caen, Ozanne, 1951. 48p. illus. (incl. map) 21cm.

The last half of the pamphlet relates to Manitoba, Alberta, and the Peace River country as fields for agricultural settlement. France

4242 **Harrington,** [Eve]lyn [Davis]
Manitoba roundabout. Photographs by Richard Harrington. Toronto, Ryerson Press, 1951. xii, 237p. plates, maps (on lining-papers) 21cm.

Description and travel. U. of A.

4243 **Imperial Order of the Daughters of the Empire.** Military Chapter, Saskatoon, Sask.
Next-of-kin memorial avenue. [Saskatoon, 1951?] 1p.l., 10p. illus. 15cm.

The history of an avenue of trees each of which has a plaque in memory of an individual soldier of World War I. Shortt

4244 **Josephburg,** Alta. Evangelical-Reformed Church
50th anniversary, 1901-1951, Evangelical-Reformed Church, Josephburg, Alberta. [Fort Saskatchewan, Fort Record Office, 1951] [26]p. illus. 22 1/2cm. Private copy

4245 **Kelsey,** Vera
Red River runs north. New York, Harper, 1951. xviii, 297p. maps (1 fold.) 22cm.

A history of the Red River valley. L.C.

4246 **Knox,** Olive [Elsie (Robinson)]
Little giant (Miss-top-ashish); the story of Henry Kelsey. Toronto, Ryerson Press, 1951. [7], 196p. illus., map (on lining-papers) 21cm.

Juvenile. Canadiana

4247 **Kristofferson,** Mrs. Kristine Benson
Tanya. Toronto, Ryerson Press [1951] [2], 250p. 22cm.

The locale of the novel is the lake district of Manitoba. Canadiana

4248 **Lester,** Laela (Ateah)
Cedars of Lebanon. Winnipeg, Columbia Press [c1951] 159p. 21cm.

The story of a Lebanese family who settled at Victoria Beach on Lake Winnipeg. Man. Leg.

4249 **Lethbridge.** Chamber of Commerce
More green acres. [Lethbridge, 1951?] cover-title, 40p. incl. illus. (part. col.) maps, diagrs., tables. Hamilton

4250 **McBeth,** Margaret
The story of Kildonan Presbyterian Church, 1851-1951. Commemorating the coming of Dr. John Black and the organization of the congregation. [Winnipeg, Wallingford Press, 1951] cover-title, 16p. illus. (incl. ports.) 23cm. Man. Leg.

4251 **MacDonald,** [Mary] Christine
Historical directory of Saskatchewan newspapers, 1878-1950. Saskatoon, Saskatchewan Archives, 1951. iv, 114p. 26cm. U. of A.

4252 **McKitrick,** T[homas] G[eorge]
Andrew Stewart of the prairie homesteads. [Altona, Man., Printed by D.W. Friesen & Sons, 1951] 134p. illus. 17cm.

The biography of an early Methodist clergyman in Manitoba who was later principal of Wesley College. Shortt

4253 **McNeill,** Leishman
Tales of the old town; Calgary, 1875-1950. Calgary, Calgary Herald [1951?] 92p. illus. 19cm. In double column. Reprinted from The Calgary Herald. Shortt

4254 **Makowski,** Boleslaw
Polska emigracja w Kanadzie. Z przedm. Melchiora Wańkowicza. Linz, Nakl. Zwiazku Polaków w Austri, 1951. 80p. map, tables.

Bibliography: p.75-76. A study of Polish immigrants in Canada. Turek

4255 **Moore,** Cyril Augustus
The lords of the lakes and forests. Montreal, Privately printed, 1951. 109p. 24cm. Not seen.

Extracts from journals and narratives of the early Nor'Westers. Edition limited to 100 numbered copies. Canadiana, 1952.

4256 **O'Meara,** Walter [Andrew]
The Grand Portage; a novel. Indianapolis, Bobbs-Merrill, 1951. 352p. 22cm.

A fictionalized account of D.W. Harmon of the North West Company. L.C.

4257 **Parker,** William Wilder McKinley
Rhymes from the North-West. Edmonton, The Author, 1951. 47p. illus. 22cm. Edmonton

4258 **Pazulla,** Hans
Canada, deine neue Heimat. Ein Handbuch für Neueinwanderer u. Deutsch-Canadier. Steinbach, Man., 1951. Marburg

4259 **Pickel,** Weldon U.
History of the First Baptist Church, Regina, Sask.; diamond jubilee, 1891-1951. [Regina, 1951] 16p. illus. (incl. ports.) 28cm. Sask. Arch.

4260 **Porcupine Plain, Sask.** High School
The story of Porcupine Plain, compiled by Grade Nine Social Studies class of 1950-51. [Porcupine Plain, 1951] 40 l. illus., fold. maps, diagr. 18 x 23cm. Mimeographed. Shortt

4261 **Raber,** Jessie (Browne)
Pioneering in Alberta. New York, Exposition Press, 1951. 171p. 23cm.

Childhood recollections of life on a homestead near Lacombe, 1895-1905. U. of A.

4262 **Raymond, Alta.**
Golden jubilee of the town of Raymond, Alberta, June 30th, July 1st and 2nd, 1951. [Raymond? 1951] 47p. illus., ports. 23cm. Glenbow

4263 **Roe**, Frank Gilbert
The North American buffalo; a critical study of the species in its wild state. Toronto, University of Toronto Press, 1951. viii, 955p. front. 24cm. U. of A.

4264 **Roy**, Gabrielle
Where nests the water hen; a novel. Translated from the French by Harry L. Binsse. New York, Harcourt, Brace [1951] 251p. 21cm.

Published originally in French in 1950 under the title, 'La Petite Poule d'Eau.' The setting is the Dauphin area of Manitoba. U. of A.

4265 **Rudnyckyj**, Jaroslaw Bohdan
Kanadiyski mistsevi nazvy Ukrayinskoho pokhodzhennya. Winnipeg, Ukrainian Free Academy of Sciences, 1951. 88p. 23cm. (Onomastica, no.2)

Prairie place names of Ukrainian origin. U. of A.

4266 **St. Amant**, J[oseph] Clovis
Histoire de Notre-Dame de Lorette. St-Boniface, 1951. 50p. illus. (incl. ports.) 23cm. Bibliothèque de St-Boniface

4267 **Saskatchewan Herald**
Stories of the old times from the Saskatchewan Herald files. [Battleford, Mrs. J.C. DeGear, 1951] [24]p. 21cm. Shortt

4268 **Saskatoon**. Grace United Church
Grace United Church, Saskatoon, 1886-1951. [Saskatoon, Modern Press, 1951] cover-title, 32p. illus. (incl. ports.) 30cm. Shortt

4269 **Saskatoon**. Third Avenue United Church
Golden jubilee of Third Avenue United Church. 50th anniversary. A record of service and achievement down through the years, 1901-1951. [Saskatoon, Midwest Litho Co., 1951] [32]p. illus. (incl. ports.) 27cm. Shortt

4270 **Schreiber**, Ilse
Canada welt des weizens. Munich, Wilhelm Andermann [c1951] 334p. fold. map. 20cm.

Describes experiences of a German family in coming to Canada about 1929 to settle northwest of Battleford. Would seem to be autobiographical. Bavaria

4271 **Schreiber**, Ilse
Die flucht ins paradies; roman. Munich, Wilhelm Andermann [1951] 364p. 20cm.

Set in the Canadian West. Austria

4272 **Shave**, Harry
Our heritage; commemorating the 25th anniversary of the present (the third) St. John's Cathedral, 1926-1951; and the 131st anniversary of the founding and the birthplace of St. John's mission church, the mother church of the Church of England in Western Canada, 1820-1951. [Winnipeg, De Montfort Press, 1951] 104p. illus. (incl. ports.) 23cm. Man. Leg.

4273 [**Sparling**, Mrs. Reita Bambridge] comp.
Reminiscences of the Rossburn pioneers. [n.p., 1951] 131p. 21cm.

Compiled under the auspices of the Rossburn Women's Institute. Man. Leg.

4274 **Stanley**, G[eorge] D[ouglass]
A round-up of fun in the foothills. [Calgary, Privately printed for the author, 1951] 79p. 26 1/2cm.

Sketches of life in High River, Alta., about the turn of the century. Private copy

4275 **United Church of Canada**. Women's Missionary Society. Alberta Branch
The history of the Women's Missionary Society in Alberta ... [n.p., 1951] 3p.l., 86p. illus. (incl. ports.) 23cm.

Also includes historical sketches of the missionary societies of the early Methodist, Presbyterian, and Congregational Churches. B.C. Arch.

4276 **Watson, Sask**. Pioneers
Fifty years of progress; chiefly the story of the pioneers of the Watson district from 1900-1910. Edited by Ben Putnam, G.H. Sproule, K.F. Zoboski, T.J. Gormican. Watson, Board of Trade, 1951. 111p. illus. Not seen.
Sask. Hist., v.5, no.3

4277 **Wright**, Norman E.
In view of the Turtle Hill; a survey of the history of southwestern Manitoba to 1900. Deloraine, Man., Deloraine Times, 1951. 146p. illus., maps.
Man. Leg.

4278 **Wood**, [Edgar Allardyce]
Cowboy yarns for young folk, by Kerry Wood. Toronto, Copp Clark [1951] ix, 137p. illus. 21cm. U. of A.

4279 **Wood**, [Edgar Allardyce]
Robbing the roost; the Marquis of Roostburg rules governing the ancient and dishonorable sport, by Kerry Wood. Red Deer [Privately printed, n.d.] cover-title, [8]p. illus. 18cm. Glenbow

4280 **Zawadski**, B.A.
Piec lat za oceanem, wspomnienia z Kanady. [Warsaw] Wydawnictwo Ministerstwa Obrony Narodowej [1951] 86, [1]p. 20cm.

Original Russian title: Pięc oryginslu; trans. J. Jakubiszyn, ed. Dorian Plonski. Title in English: Five years over the ocean, recollections of Canada.
The author was sent from Karkov by his widowed mother to live with an aunt near Yorkton. The year was 1927 and he was fifteen. He also lived in Vancouver and Kamloops before returning to Russia. Poland

4281 **Bala**, Joseph
Pershiy Ukrayinskiy epyskop Kanady, Kyr Nykyta Budka. [The first Ukrainian bishop in Canada, Nicetas Budka] Winnipeg, Ukrainian Catholic Council of Canada, 1952. 56p. Rutherford

4282 **Barnwell**, Alberta. [Mormon] Relief Society
Barnwell history. Ann Arbor, Mich., Edwards Bros., 1952. 5p.l., 401p. illus. (incl. maps, ports.) 22cm. Alta. Leg.

4283 **Belton**, Walter L.
Historical sketches of Katrine and Beaver districts. Katrine, Manitoba. [Gladstone] Gladstone Age Press Print, 1952. cover-title, 16p. illus., ports. 22 1/2cm. U.C. Arch.

4284 **Burns**, Mrs. Robert A.
The pioneers' story, 1877-1892-1952; a history of Presbyterianism in Neepawa and district. [Neepawa? 1952] cover-title, [12]p. ports. 23cm. Knox College

4285 **Canada**. Royal Commission on the South Saskatchewan River project
Report. Ottawa, Queen's Printer, 1952. xix, 423p. fold. maps. 26cm. U. of A.

4286 **Chilton**, Vina Bruce
A few more dawns. Toronto, Copp Clark Co. Ltd., 1952. 50p. 20 1/2cm. Not seen.

Poetry. Private information

4287 **Dempsey**, Hugh A[ylmer]
Historic sites of the province of Alberta. [Edmonton, Alberta Dept. of Economic Affairs, 1952] 56p. illus., maps. 25cm.

A preliminary edition of 36 leaves was published a few months earlier. U. of A.

4288 **Dionne**, Emil
Reminiscing. [Spokane, Wash., Evergreen Press, c1952] 64p. illus. (incl. ports.) 22cm.

P.1-37 narrate the experiences of the author as a youth at The Pas. Sask. Arch.

4289 **Edmonton**. Ukrainian Greek Orthodox Cathedral
Pamyatka posvyachennya uholnoho kamenya Ukrayinskoyi Pravoslavnoyi Katedry Sv. Ivana v Edmontoni 1952. Edmonton, 1952. 104p. Not seen. Slavica Canadiana, 1952

4290 **Farley**, Tom
It was a plane. Toronto, Ryerson, 1952. 12p. 22cm. (Ryerson poetry chap-books) Not seen. Ryerson

4291 **Gaetz**, Annie L[ouise (Siddall)]
Trails of yesterday; folklore of the Red Deer district. [Red Deer? 1952] 4p.l., 99p. front. 20 1/2cm. Alta. Leg.

4292 **Gershaw**, F[red] W[illiam]
Medicine Hat; early days in southern Alberta. [n.p., 1952] cover-title, 70p. illus. 21cm. Shortt

4293 **Giscard**, G[aston]
Dans la prairie canadienne. Lyon, Editions des Remparts, 1952. 2p.l., 5-92, [1]p. illus. 18cm.

On cover: Junior. Portrait of author on back cover of this paperback.
The author sent his ms. to a publisher who extracted the more exciting incidents and published as a juvenile book. The author wrote a more detailed sequel which is in the custody of Collège St-Jean. St-Jean

4294 **Gowan**, Elsie Park [(Young)]
Breeches from Bond Street; a comedy in one act. Toronto, French [c1952] 24p. 19cm. U. of A. (Extension)

4295 **Harrison**, Stanley [Gordon]
Gentlemen, the horse! Illustrated by the author. Lexington, Kentucky, The Thoroughbred Press Inc., 1952. 88p. illus. 21cm.
Poetry. Shortt

4296 **Howard**, Joseph Kinsey
Strange empire; a narrative of the Northwest. New York, William Morrow, 1952. xii, 601p. incl. maps. 23cm.
A history of the two Riel Rebellions. U. of A.

4297 **Jennings**, John Edward
The strange brigade; a story of Red River and the opening of the Canadian West. Boston, Little, Brown [1952] 367p. 21cm.
Juvenile fiction. U. of A.

4298 **Johnson**, Gilbert
The history of Fort Ellice. [Russell, Man., Printed by the Russell Banner, 1952] [11]p. 24cm. Shortt

4299 **Kazymyra**, Bohdan
Monsinor Adelyar Lyanzheven i Ukrayinci [Msgr. Langevin and Ukrainian Canadians] Edmonton, Catholic Action, 1952. 31p. illus. U. of A.

4300 **Kennedy**, Fred
The Calgary Stampede story. [Calgary] Published by T. Edwards Thonger, c1952. 236p. illus. 30cm. Pagination includes advertising. Alta. Leg.

4301 **Kerr**, John R.
Other days and other ways; being the early history of Alhambra. [Red Deer, The Author, 1952] 16 l. 36cm. Mimeographed. Rutherford

4302 **Kohuska**, Natalka L.
Chvert' stolittya na hromadskiy nyvi, 1926-1951; istoriya soyuzu Ukrayinok Kanady. [Winnipeg, Trident Press, 1952] 540p. illus., ports. 27cm. Added title-page: Twenty-five years of the Ukrainian Women's Association in Canada. U. of A.

4303 **Kroening**, William F., comp.
In commemoration of the semi-centennial of the Moravian congregation, Calgary, Alberta, Canada, 1902-1952. [n.p., 1952] 20p. plates (incl. ports.) 23cm. Shortt

4304 **Kupsch**, Walter Oscar
Annotated bibliography of Saskatchewan geology, 1823-1951 (incl.) Regina, Queen's Printer, 1952. 106p. diagr. 26cm. (Sask. Geol. Survey. Report no.9) Canadiana

4305 **Laurie**, John Lee
John McDougall, D.D. McDougall memorial service, October 5th, 1952, Morley, Alberta, in aid of the Morley Church Restoration Fund. [n.p., 1952] cover-title, 4p. 19cm. Private copy

4306 **Lawrence**, Edith M., ed.
Glimpses of the past; the history of the American Women's Club, Calgary, Alberta, 1912-1952. [Calgary, 1952] [2], 14p. 21cm. Glenbow

4307 **Liddell**, Ken. E.
This is Alberta. Toronto, Ryerson [1952] x, 190p. plates, map (on lining-papers) 21cm. U. of A.

4308 **MacDonald**, [Mary] Christine
Publications of the governments of the North-West Territories, 1876-1905, and of the Province of Saskatchewan, 1905-1952. Regina, Legislative Library, 1952. 109, [1]p. 26cm.

A preliminary check list in mimeographed form was issued about two years earlier. U. of S.

4309 **MacEwan**, [John Walter] Grant
Between the Red and the Rockies. [Toronto] University of Toronto Press [c1952] x, 300p. 22cm.

A popularized history of prairie agriculture. U. of A.

4310 **MacGregor**, James G[rierson]
The land of Twelve Foot Davis; a history of the Peace River country. Edmonton, Applied Art Products, c1952. 395p. illus., facsim., double map. 23cm. U. of A.

4311 **Macleod Sketch Club**
The story of Macleod. [Calgary, Printed by Kellaway Printing Ltd., 1952?] [26]p. illus. 27 1/2cm. U. of A. (Extension)

4312 **MacMillan**, Mrs. Anne [(Morton)]
Prince of the plains. Regina, School Aids and Text Book Publishing Co. Ltd. [c1952] 204p. illus. 21cm.

A fictionalized account for juveniles of the Currie family who settled in the Regina district in 1882. Private copy

4313 **McTavish**, R. Lorne
For a better tomorrow. Ilfracombe, Eng., Stockwell [1952] 176p. 19cm. Not seen.

Fiction, set mainly in Saskatchewan. Canadiana

4314 **Malkus**, Alida Sims
Little giant of the north, the boy who won a fur empire. Illus. by Jay Hyde Barnum. Philadelphia, Winston [1952] 178p. illus. 22cm. (Winston adventure books)

Juvenile; the story of Henry Kelsey. L.C.

4315 **Morden, Man.** Reunion Organization. Souvenir Book Committee
This is Morden. Morden and district old timers' and students' reunion, July 3-5, 1952. [Morden, Morden Times, 1952] [50]p. illus. 23cm.
Historical sketches by various authors. Man. Leg.

4316 **Moses,** Eva E.
Golden is the wheat. New York, Exposition Press [1952] 302p. 21cm.
Light fiction describing the experiences of an American family who arrived in Saskatchewan in 1911; the latter part of the novel is the adventures of the daughter in Toronto, Montreal, and New York. Private copy

4317 **Nesbitt,** Leonard D.
The case against the speculative marketing of grain. Calgary, Alberta Wheat Pool, 1952. 11p. 23cm. Canadiana

4318 **Nesbitt,** Leonard D.
The farm viewpoint of the Crow's Nest freight agreement. Calgary, Alberta Wheat Pool, 1952. [14]p. 19cm. Canadiana

4319 **Nickle,** Carl Olof
The story of Pincher Creek ['Wet gas' field. Calgary, Lithographed by Commonwealth Press, 1952] [1], 21p. illus., diagrs. 23cm. Glenbow

4320 **Nimchuk,** Ivan
Pochatky orhanizaciynoho zhyttya Kanadiyskykh Ukrayintsiv. Spomyny Albertiyskoho pionera. Memoirs of an Alberta pioneer. Edmonton, Catholic Action, 1952. cover-title, 31p. illus. (incl. ports.) 21cm. U. of A.

4321 **Obodiac,** Stan[lee]
No substitute for victory; the story of the Canadian world hockey victory. [Yorkton, Printed by the Redeemer's Voice, 1952] 150p. illus. 23cm.
The story of the Lethbridge Maple Leafs in Europe in 1951 where they won the world's championship. Private copy

4322 **Okulevich,** G.
Russkie v Kanade. Toronto, 1952. 328p. Not seen.
Slavica Canadiana, 1952

4323 **Peel,** Bruce [Braden]
The Saskatoon story, 1882-1952 [by Bruce Peel and Eric Knowles] Saskatoon, Melville A. East, c1952. 86p. illus. 30 1/2cm. Sub-title on cover: Up the years from the Temperance Colony. Facsim. on cover. Text in double column. Shortt

4324 [**Peltonen,** Emil]
Kulkurina Amerikassa, uutisraivaajana Canadassa. Kirjoittanut Agricola. Duluth, Workers Soc. Publishing Co. [1952] 135, [1]p. 21cm.
The last forty pages describe homesteading experiences near Sylvan Lake, Alta. Author uses pseudonym Agricola. Finland

4325 **Pépin,** Cornélie (Léveillé)
Histoire de St-Paul, Alberta, 1896-1951. [Trois-Rivières, Le Bien Public, 1952] 184p. illus. (incl. ports.) 20cm. Alta. Leg.

4326 **Pratt**, E[dwin] J[ohn]
Towards the last spike; a verse-panorama of the struggle to build the first Canadian transcontinental from the time of the proposed terms of union with British Columbia, 1870, to the hammering of the last spike in the Eagle Pass, 1885. Toronto, Macmillan, 1952. 53p. 24cm. U. of A.

4327 **Redemptorist Order**
The Redemptorists of the Eastern Rite; a brief sketch. Yorkton, 1952. 15p. 12 1/2cm. Not seen. Private information

4328 **Reibin**, Simeon F.
Toil and peaceful life; history of Doukhobors unmasked. San Francisco, Delo [c1952] 338p. port. 21cm. Title in Russian and English. L.C.

4329 **Rimbey, Alta**. Historical Committee
History of Rimbey, Alberta, golden anniversary, 1902-1952. [Rimbey? 1952] cover-title, 49p. illus. 23cm. U. of A. (Extension)

4330 **Ukrainian Catholic Church**. Diocese of Saskatchewan
Almanakh pershoi richnytsi Apostolskoho Eksarkhatu Saskatchewanu, 1952. Yorkton, 1952. 91p. illus. 26cm. Not seen. Private information

4331 **Wilson**, Mabel May
In friendship's name. [Moose Jaw, The Author, 1952] cover-title, 31p. 15cm.

Poetry. Shortt

4332 **Winnipeg**. Holy Ghost Fraternal Aid Society
Golden jubilee of the Holy Ghost Fraternal Aid Society, June 1, 1952, Winnipeg, Canada; 1902-1952. Ksiazka pamiatkowa zlotego jubileuszu Bractwa SW. Ducha, 1-go czerwca 1952 r., Winnipeg, Canada. [Winnipeg, 1952] cover-title, 64p. illus., ports.

Text chiefly in Polish. Advertising matter included in paging.

4333 **Wood**, [Edgar Allardyce]
The sanctuary, by Kerry Wood. Red Deer, The Author [1952] 105p. illus. 19cm.

A bird sanctuary near Red Deer, Alta. Canadiana

4334 **Woodcock**, George
Ravens and prophets; an account of journeys in British Columbia, Alberta and southern Alaska. London, A. Wingate [1952] 244p. illus. 23cm. L.C.

4335 **Zhan**, Josaphat
Pyatdesyat rokiv u Kanadi. 50 years in Canada. [by Rev. Josaphat Zhan and Bohdan Kazymyra] Edmonton, Catholic Action, 1952. 16p. illus. (incl. ports.) 21cm. U. of A.

4336 **Basilian Fathers**
Propamyatna knyha otsiv Vasyliyan u Kanadi (1902-1952) Toronto, Basilian Fathers, 1953. 432p. illus. 23cm. Not seen. Private information

4337 **Bjarnason**, Páll
Fleygar. Winnipeg, Columbia Press, 1953. 270p. Not seen.
Icelandic poetry. U. of T. Quarterly, 1954

4338 **Berry**, Gerald L[loyd]
The Whoop-Up Trail (Alberta-Montana relationships) Edmonton, Applied Art Products, 1953. 143p. illus., ports, maps, plan, tables. 24cm. U. of A.

4339 **Breton**, [Joseph] P[aul] E[mile René]
Forgeron de Dieu; Frère Antoine Kowalczyk, O.M.I., 1866-1947. [n.p., Editions de l'Ermitage] 1953. 223p. front., plates. 20cm. Private copy

4339A **Bruno, Sask**. St. Ursula's Academy
Catholics of St. Peter's colony, we must do something about our academy during this our jubilee year – building fund campaign, Ursuline Academy, Bruno, Sask., Jan.-June, 1953. [Bruno, Sask., 1953] cover-title, [7]p. illus., ports. 28cm. Glenbow

4340 **Calgary**. Ranchmen's Club
A slight historical sketch, 1891-1952. Calgary, 1953. 24, [3]p. illus., mounted col. plate, group ports. 22cm. Glenbow

4341 **Campbell**, Gray
We found peace. Toronto, Thomas Allen, 1953. 244p.
Ranching. The story of an eastern family who bought a ranch near Cowley, Alta., after World War II. U. of A.

4342 **Canadian Mental Health Association**. Saskatchewan Division
The Hutterites and Saskatchewan; a study of inter-group relations. [Regina, 1953] x, 132 l. 28cm.
Bibliography: l. 118-19. Glenbow

4343 **Coleman, Alta**. Board of Trade
Coleman's 50th anniversary booklet. [Lethbridge, Lethbridge Herald, 1953] 70, [1]p. illus., ports. 24cm. Glenbow

4344 [**Cossar**, Mrs. Mary] comp.
Tales of the Touchwoods, from 1880-1953. [Compiled by Mrs. Mary Cossar & Mrs. Stanley Jeal. Regina, Western Printers Association, 1953] cover-title, 112p. illus. 23cm. Sask. Arch.

4345 **DeGroff**, Bert
The early history of Bentley and district. [Red Deer, 1953] 63p. illus. (group ports.) 23cm. Errata slip. Alta. Leg.

4346 **Elson**, Arthur
Origin and history of the Fartown S.D. no.1856; with reminiscences 1903-1948. [Marshall, Sask.] 1953. 63, [1]p. illus., ports. 21cm. Glenbow

4347 **Frémont**, Donatien
Les secrétaires de Riel: Louis Schmidt, Henri Jackson, Philippe Garnot. Montréal, Editions Chantecler, 1953. 205p. 20cm. U. of A.

4348 **Hambley**, George H[enry]
Historical records and accounts of the early pioneers of the district of Swan Lake, Manitoba, from its early settlement, 1873-1950. [Altona, Man., D.W. Friesen & Sons, 1953] cover-title, 280p. illus. 19cm. Man. Leg.

4349 **Hultgren**, Peter
A brief history of Midale and district, 1903-1953. [n.p., 1953] 31, [1]p. illus. 22cm. Pagination includes advertising.
Midale, Sask. Sask. Arch.

4350 [**Hultgren**, Peter]
A short history of First Baptist Church, Midale, Saskatchewan, Canada. Published on the occasion of its jubilee and held in conjunction of the forty-sixth annual assembly of the Central Canada Baptist Conference, June 3-7, 1953. [n.p., 1953] cover-title, [16]p. illus. 21cm. Sask. Arch.

4350A **Humphries**, Thomas Ross
Alberta's wheat. Rev. [ed. Calgary, Alberta Wheat Pool] 1953. cover-title, 11 l. 28cm.
First issued in 1944. Glenbow

4351 **Hutterite Brethren**. Hymnal
Die Lieder der Hutterischen Brüder. Gesangbuch ... 2d ed. Winnipeg, Christian Press, 1953. 632p. Private information

4352 **Legal, Alta**. Paroisse St-Emile de Legal
Cinquante anniversaire, Paroisse St-Emile de Legal. [n.p., 1953] cover-title, 96p. illus. (incl. ports.) 22cm.
Illustration on cover. Pagination includes advertising.
The main section of the history was written by Abbé Normandeau, the first curé, 1903-12. A brief summary appears in English at the end of the book. St-Jean

4353 **Leskiv**, Fylymon
Pionerske zhyttya v Kanadi [Pioneer life in Canada] Saskatoon, Christian Press, 1953. 104p. port. 19cm. Shortt

4354 **Lewis**, S.S., comp.
History of Chumah Church. [Hamiota, Man., 1953] cover-title, [24]p. illus., ports. 24cm. Glenbow

4355 **McMorran**, G[ordon] A[lexander]
Souris River posts, and David Thompson's diary of his historical trip across the Souris plains to the Mandan villages in the winter of 1797-98. Souris, Souris Plaindealer [1953] 43p. double map. 23cm. Man. Leg.

4356 **Macpherson**, C[rawford] B[rough]
Democracy in Alberta; the theory and practice of a quasi-party system. Toronto, University of Toronto Press, 1953. xii, 258p. 24cm. (Social Credit in Alberta; its background and development, 4) U. of A.

4357 **Manitoba**. Archives
Transactions and proceedings of the Historical Society of Manitoba. [Winnipeg, 1953] [9] l. 28cm. Mimeographed. U. of A.

4358 **Methodius**, Brother S.
Reverend Brother Stanislaus Joseph, F.S.C. Yorkton, St. Joseph's College, 1953. 30p. incl. port. 23cm. Shortt

4359 **Middleton**, S[amuel] H.
Kainai chieftainship; history, evolution, and culture of the Blood Indians; origin of the sun-dance. [Lethbridge, Lethbridge Herald, 1953] 178, [1]p. illus. (incl. ports.) 24cm. On cover: Indian chiefs, ancient and modern. U. of A.

4360 **Milne**, Jessie J. (Murray)
Settlers of White Mud River: early pioneers of Mekiwin and nearby districts. [n.p., 1953] cover-title, 23p. 28cm.

Xerox facsim. Original 23cm. Glenbow

4361 **Moon**, Robert [James]
This is Saskatchewan. Toronto, Ryerson Press [1953] xii, 242p. plates, map (on lining-papers) 21cm. U. of A.

4362 **Morley**, Marjorie [Gertrude]
A bibliography of Manitoba from holdings in the Legislative Library of Manitoba. [Winnipeg, Manitoba Legislative Library, 1953] cover-title, 45 l. 28cm. Mimeographed. Private copy

4363 [**Pascoe**, J. Ernest] ed.
Moose Jaw, Saskatchewan, golden jubilee, 1903-1953. [Moose Jaw, Moose Jaw Times-Herald, 1953] cover-title, 50, [2]p. illus. 25cm. Shortt

4364 [**Simms**, Eldon F.]
The story of St. Mary's la Prairie Anglican Church, 1853-1953, commemorating the founding of St. Mary's la Prairie parish by Archdeacon Cochrane, 1853. [Portage la Prairie? 1953] cover-title, 28p. illus. (incl. ports.) 23cm. Man. Leg.

4365 **Stechishin**, Juliyan W.
Mizh Ukrayintsiamy v Kanadi. The Ukrainians in Canada; a brief historical sketch. Saskatoon, Ukrainian Self-Reliance League, 1953. 48p. 21 1/2cm. Not seen. Private information

4366 **Taber, Alta**. Women's Institute
Taber, yesterday and today. [Taber, Taber Times, 1953] 91p. illus. (incl. ports.) 27cm.

In manuscript form this history won second prize in the Alberta section of the Lady Tweedsmuir local history competition. Alta. Leg.

4367 **Tibbits**, Ethel [Caswell] (B[urnett])
On to the sunset. Toronto, Ryerson Press [1953] [5], 155p. 23cm.

Pioneer stories of the Canadian West, based on experiences of the author's family and friends. Glenbow

4368 **Wetton,** Mrs. C[ecilia]
The promised land; the story of the Barr colonists. Lloydminster, Lloydminster Times [1953] 73p. illus. 23cm. Shortt

4369 **Windschiegl,** Peter
Fifty golden years, 1903-1953; a brief history of the Order of St. Benedict in the Abbacy Nullius of St. Peter, Muenster, Saskatchewan. [n.p., n.d.] 3 l., 223p. Amtmann - 176-394

4370 **Yuzyk,** Paul
The Ukrainians in Manitoba; a social history. Issued under the auspices of the Historical and Scientific Society of Manitoba. [Toronto] University of Toronto Press, 1953. xv, 232p. front. 23cm. U. of A.

ADDENDA

4371 **Bible.** O.T. Exodus. Ten Commandments. Cree
[The ten commandments. Rossville, Rossville Mission Press, 1855] Broadside, 44 x 13.8cm.

Each commandment in syllabic characters repeated in the Roman alphabet. The broadside was the Rev. T. Hurlburt's first attempt at printing. Newberry

4372 **Wesleyan Methodist Church.** Catechism. Cree
[No.1 of the Wesleyan Conference catechism, translated into Cree, used in the mission schools in Hudson's Bay. n.p., 185_?] 24p. 17.5cm.

Syllabic type. Newberry

4373 **Lasteyrie du Saillant,** Adrien Jules
La territoire de la Compagnie de la baie d'Hudson. Paris, 1867. ...
Morice

4374 **Soullier,** Louis
Acte de visite du R.P. Soullier, premier assistant général, pour le vicariat de St. Albert, Octobre, 1883. St. Albert, Typographie privée, o.m.i. [1883] [2], 85, [8] p. 20 1/2cm. St-Jean

4375 **Steele,** C.E.
Visitors' guide book and jubilee souvenir giving all places of interest in the vicinity of Winnipeg, with illustrations of the principal public buildings, &c., &c. Winnipeg, C.E. Steele [1887] cover-title, [23] p. port., illus., double map. 21cm.

Pagination includes advertising. U. of A.

4376 **Fort Qu'Appelle**
Fort Qu'Appelle, boating, fishing and shooting club. Organized 9 October, 1888. Qu'Appelle [Vidette office] 1888. 8p. 14 1/2cm. Northland

4377 **Fort Qu'Appelle.** Business Association
Constitution of the Business Association of Fort Qu'Appelle, together with the bylaws and rules of order adopted at a general meeting held on April 19, 1888. Fort Qu'Appelle [Vidette office] 1888. Northland

4378 Cree almanack. Naheyowawe pesimoo mussinuhikun. Oonikup, The Pas, N.W. Territory, 1891-1899. 6v. illus. 16-42cm.

Printed by the Rev. Joseph Reader. The Ayer collection in the Newberry Library has 1891, 1892, 1894, 1895, 1897, 1899. Newberry

4379 **Roman Catholic Church.** Prayers. Cree
Priéres, catéchisme et cantiques en langue crise. Lac Athabaska, Mission de la Nativité, 1895 [1894] 224p. 17.6cm.

Title-page in Roman and syllabic. Text in syllabic.
Presentation copy by Bishop Grouard who was the printer. Newberry

4380 **Roman Catholic Church.** Diocese of Saint-Albert
Règlements, usages et discipline du Diocèse de Saint-Albert, promulgués en l'année 1903, par Mgr Emile Joseph Legal ... Montréal, Beauchemin, 1903. 2p.l., [5]-148p. 23cm. U. of A.

4381 **Canada Congregational Missionary Society**
Our Scandinavian missions, Alberta, N.W.T. Sherbrooke, Que., 1904. cover-title, 7, [1]p. illus., port. 14cm.

On the missions of Rev. G.A. Sanden, who worked out of Wetaskiwin. Glenbow

4382 **Bible.** New Testament. Gospels. Cree
La vie de N.S. Jesus-Christ en langue crise ... [n.p.] 1906. 176p.

Text in Cree syllabic. Amtmann

4383 **Humboldt Realty Company**
Humboldt, Saskatchewan, railway divisional point for the Canadian Northern Railway. [Humboldt? 1910?] 16p. illus. St. Thomas More

4384 **Peake,** Arthur
Ballads of the badlands. [n.p., n.d.] ...

4385 **LaRonde,** Alexandre de
Instructions en Sauteux sur toute la doctrine catholique, traduites de la langue crise par A.D.L. [pseud.] Montreal, Beauchemin [1911] 566p.

Text in Roman alphabet. Amtmann

4386 **Roman Catholic Church.** Diocese of Prince Albert
Règlements, usages et discipline du Diocèse de Prince-Albert, promulgués en l'année 1916, par Mgr Albert Pascal ... Québec, 1916. 2p.l., [7]-254p. 23cm. U. of A.

4387 **Calverley,** Eva
And so Ninette, 1879-1919. Brandon, Leech printing [1919?] ...

(Listed in A. Garland's 'Trials and crossroads to Killarney.' Altoona, 1967)

4388 **Roman Catholic Church.** Catechisms. Blackfoot
Blackfoot catechism and prayers. [Calgary, 1920] [4], 120p. 22cm.

Text in Roman alphabet, the booklet produced by a stencil process. U. of A.

4389 **Oblates.** Montreal
Portraits historiques, Oblats de Marie-Immaculée. Avec notices biographiques. Montréal, 1921. [22 l.] ports. 15 x 21 1/2cm.

The portraits are mostly of clergy who served in the Canadian West. St-Jean

4390 **Roman Catholic Church.** Prayers. Blackfoot
Blackfoot prayers. [n.p., 1921] caption-title, 32p. 21 1/2cm.

Text in syllabic, the booklet produced by a stencil process. U. of A.

4391 Not used

4392 **Roman Catholic Church.** Hymns. Blackfoot
... Blackfoot hymns. [n.p., 1924] caption-title, 72, 26p. 22cm.

Text in Roman alphabet, the booklet produced by a stencil process. U. of A.

4393 **Les Filles de la Providence de Saint-Brieuc**
Les Filles de la Providence de Saint-Brieuc, 1818-1926. St. Brieuc, France, 1926. 83p. illus. St. Thomas More

4394 **Warren,** Clarence Henry
Wild goose chase, being the journal of an intimate adventure into the new world. London, Faber & Gwyer [1927] 251p. 20cm.

Includes several chapters on the Prairie Provinces and the Canadian Rockies. Glenbow

4395 **Calgary.** Holy Cross Hospital
Souvenir of the opening of the new Holy Cross Hospital. Calgary, April 1st, 1929. Calgary [1929] 16p. illus. St. Thomas More

4396 **Edmonton.** Paroisse de l'Immaculée Conception
Souvenir du jubilé d'argent ... Mardi, le 8 Decembre 1931. [Edmonton, 1931] [13]p. incl. illus., ports. 23 1/2cm.

'Notice historique' is signed by P.J. St-Jean

4397 **Edmonton.** Théâtre Français
Souvenir. Vingt années de Théâtre Français à Edmonton. [Edmonton, 1932] 1p.l., 44, [2]p. 22 1/2cm.

Introductory section includes a historical sketch and the names of persons who had acted in amateur theatricals over the years. Following these the remainder of the pamphlet is business advertising, but one of the box advertisements on each page is for one of the thirty-eight plays produced by this organization. St-Jean

4398 **Regina.** St. Matthew's Anglican Church
... Silver jubilee book, 1910-1935. [Regina, 1935] cover-title, 56p. illus. 23cm.

Pagination includes advertising. Northland

4399 **Calgary.** Sacred Heart Parish
A short history of the Sacred Heart Parish in the city of Calgary. Twenty-fifth anniversary. Calgary, 1936. 104p. illus. St. Thomas More

4400 **Libouré**, Théodore
Acte général de visite des missions Indiennes du Nord-Ouest Canadien ... June 1935–Février 1936. Rome, Maison Générale, 1936. 1p.l., [5]-106p. 21 1/2cm. St-Jean

4401 **Trocellier**, J[oseph]
... Consécration of-de Mgr J. Trocellier, o.m.i. Saint Albert, Septembre 8–September 1940. cover-title, [15]p. ports. 18cm.

At head of title: Programme-Souvenir.
Text in English and French on opposite pages. U. of A.

4402 **Labouré**, Théodore
Circulaire ... à l'occasion du centenaire de la fondation de la province du Canada. Marseille, 1941. cover-title, [9]-55p. 21cm.

Each page has double numbering, that of the pamphlet but also of the serial from which it is an excerpt.
Contents largely about Western Canada. St-Jean

4403 **Rousseau**, Joseph
Acte de la visite générale de la province du Manitoba, Mai–Octobre, 1941. [n.p., 1941] 2p.l., 7-99p., 2 l. 21 1/2cm. St-Jean

4404 **Desmoyers**, Anthime
Acte général de la visite de la province d'Alberta-Saskatchewan ... Montréal, 1942. 1p.l., [5]-59p. 22 1/2cm.

Another description of a visitation, with the same title, published in 1947. St-Jean

4405 **Prelate, Sask.** St. Angela's Convent
St. Angela's Convent, Prelate, 1919-1945; Ursulines of St. Angela, 1535-1945. Prelate [1945] 43p. illus. St. Thomas More

4406 **Lethbridge**. St. Patrick's Church
St. Patrick's Church, Lethbridge, Alberta, Canada. Lethbridge, 1952. 20p. illus.

A history of the church issued on the occasion of the opening of a new church.
St. Thomas More

4407 **C., H.**
The western missionary; a sketch of pioneer days in the Northwest Territories, by H.C. Indian Head, Printed at the Prairie Witness Office, 1901. 177p. 15cm.

Covers 'the buckboard stage' of missions in the N.W.T., 1882 to 1900. United College

4408 **Amblad**, Edward E.
The Last Mountain Valley, Saskatchewan, Canada. Hard wheat belt of Western Canada. Where a single crop often pays for the farm on which it was grown. The opportunity of your life time. Winnipeg, Wm. Pearson Co. Ltd. [1913] 40p. illus., fold. map. 25 1/2cm. Sask. Arch.

Also the following listed in R.E. Watters' newly published second edition 'A checklist of Canadian Literature and Background Materials, 1628-1960.'

Sharman, Mrs. Lyon
The horse that educated the children; a Christmas story from the Canadian prairies. Winnipeg, Franklin Press, 1912

Walford, Austin
Confession of the hills. Winnipeg, Middle West Pub. Co., 1915. 313p.

Regan, John Hugh
Valiant heart; a story of a Canadian ranch. London, Hutchinson, 1926. 312p.

Regan, John Hugh
The end of the furrow. London, Hutchinson, 1927. 288p.

Plummer, Norman M.
The goad; a human story of the last great West in the early part of the twentieth century. London, Stockwell, 1930. 180p.

Reynolds, H.T.
The unquenched flax; a story of western Canada. London, Stockwell [1931]. 206p.

Willis, T.K.
The letters of a prairie dog. Victoria, Colonist Print. & Pub. Co., 1945. 65p.

Subject Index

Subject Index

A THE ENVIRONMENT

1 Boundaries

51 Wilcocke, S.H. Notice re the boundary between His Majesty's possessions and the U.S. 1817
412 Dawson, G.M. Report on geology and resources of the 49th parallel. 1875
426 Millman, T. Impressions of the West. 1875
434 Anderson, S. North American boundary. 1876
444 Featherstonhaugh, A. Operations of B.N.A. Boundary Commission. 1876
445 Great Britain. War Office. North-western boundary. 1876
488 United States. Congress. Report upon survey of boundary. 1878
636 Ontario. Prov. Sec. Correspondence 1856 to 1882 re boundaries. 1882
712 Kewaydin. Leg. Assembly. Select Committee on Ontario boundaries. 1884
1806 Canada. Dept. of the Interior. Statement showing provisional districts of N.W.T. 1905
1808 Canada. Dept. of Sec. of State. Copies of petitions re extension of boundaries of Manitoba. 1905
2018 Roblin, R.P. Manitoba boundary question. 1908
2947 Ontario-Manitoba Boundary Commission. Boundary from Winnipeg River northerly. 1925

POSTSCRIPT
Atlas of Alberta. Compiled by the Dept. of Geography, University of Alberta. (Edmonton, 1969)
Atlas of Saskatchewan. Editor, J. Howard Richards, University of Saskatchewan. (Saskatoon, 1969)

2 Geology

195 Canada. Leg. Assembly. Exploration between Superior and Red River. 1858
211 Hind, H.Y. North West Territory. 1859
221 Hind, H.Y. Narrative of Red and Saskatchewan expeditions. 1860
412 Dawson, G.M. Report on geology and resources of 49th parallel. 1875
637 Panton, J.H. Gleanings from outcrops of Silurian strata. 1882
697 Royal Society of Canada. Circular to officers of the H.B.C. 1883
737 Chapman, E.J. Report on coal areas near Medicine Hat. 1884
764 Panton, J.H. Fragmentary leaves. 1884
827 McCharles, A. The extinct cuttle-fish. 1885
946 McCharles, A. Footsteps of time in Red River valley. 1886
956 Panton, J.H. Notes on geology of some islands in Lake Winnipeg. 1886
1209 Bryce, G. Older geology of Red River. 1891
1905 Bryce, G. Everyman's geology of the Prairie Provinces. 1907
2331 Penniac Reef Gold Mines, Ltd. Manitoba's first gold mine. 1912
2482 Rocky Mountain Oil Fields, Ltd. Prospectus. 1914
2611 Sternberg, C.H. Hunting dinosaurs in the bad lands. 1917
2690 Anderson & Brown Consolidated Ltd. The world's new oil field. 1920
2702 DeLury, J.S. Mineral prospects in S.E. Manitoba. 1920
2865 Pratt, G.R. Coal trails. 1923
3801 Hamilton, J.B. Evidence on the tar sands. 1942
4304 Kupsch, W.O. Annotated bibliography of Saskatchewan geology. 1952

3 **Botany**
See also 'Agriculture' and 'Wheat'

83A Douglas, D. Journal. 1827
831 Mennell, H.T. Across Canada to the Rocky Mountains. 1885
998 Canada. Parliament. Senate. Committee on existing food products of N.W.T. Report. 1887
1624 Plants of Manitoba. 1896
2723 McCalla, W.C. Wild flowers of Western Canada. 1920
2818 Macoun, J. Autobiography. 1922
2819 Manitoba Agricultural College. Checklist of Manitoba flora. 1922
3044 Wallis, J.B. Manitoban butterflies. 1927
3528 Patterson, C.F. Hardy fruits. 1936
3794 Flock, E.B. Wild flowers. 1942

POSTSCRIPT
Alberta. University. Alberta trees, shrubs, and flowers, prepared byR.H. Knowles. (Edmonton, 1963)

4 **Birds**

91 Richardson, Sir J. Fauna boreali-americana. 1829
216 Murray, A. Contributions to natural history. 1859
937 Hubbard, J.H. Sport in the Canadian North-West, 1886
945 McArthur, A. Our winter birds. 1886
998 Canada. Parliament. Senate. Select Committee on existing food products of N.W.T. Report. 1887
1236 Seton, E.T. Birds of Manitoba. 1891
1279 Raine, W. Bird-nesting in North-West Canada. 1892
1519 Atkinson, G.E. Game birds of Manitoba. 1898
1559 Atkinson, G.E. Manitoba birds of prey. 1899
1702 Atkinson, G.E. Insectivorous birds of Manitoba. 1903
1747 Atkinson, G.E. Rare bird records of Manitoba. 1904
1787 Atkinson, G.E. History of passenger pigeon. 1905
2004 Mair, C. Through the Mackenzie basin. 1908
2406 Laing, H.M. Out with the birds. 1913
2612 Turner, J.P. The prairie chicken. 1917
2645 Taverner, P.A. Hawks of the Prairie Provinces. 1918
2901 Mitchell, H.H. Catalogue of birds of Saskatchewan. 1924
2991 Taverner, P.A. Birds of Western Canada. 1926
3023 Hales, B.J. Prairie birds. 1927
3297 Farley, F.L. Birds of Battle River region. 1932
3935 Manitoba. Bureau of Travel and Publicity. Game birds and animals. 1945
3976 Ducks Unlimited. Cooperation unlimited. 1946
3966 Wood, E.A. Three mile bend. 1945
4041 Jaques, F.P. Canadian spring. 1947
4152 Holmes, F.J.S. Ducks are different. 1949
4153 Houston, C.S. Birds of the Yorkton district. 1949
4185 Wood, E.A. The magpie menace. 1949
4279 Wood, E.A. Robbing the roost. [n.d.]
4333 Wood, E.A. The sanctuary. 1952

POSTSCRIPT
Salt, W.R. & A.L. Wilk. The birds of Alberta. (Edmonton, 1958)
Houston, C.S. The birds of Saskatchewan. (Regina, 1959)

5 Mammals

91 Richardson, Sir J. Fauna boreali-americana. 1829
216 Murray, A. Contributions to natural history. 1859
937 Hubbard, J.H. Sport in the Canadian North-West. 1886
967 Seton, E.T. A list of mammals of Manitoba. 1886
1111 McBean, A. A petition and a prayer in behalf of the lower animals. 1889
1895 Turner, J.P. The moose and wapiti of Manitoba. 1906
2004 Mair, C. Through the Mackenzie basin. 1908
2023 Stovel Company. Last of the buffalo. 1908
2085 Seton, E.T. Life histories of northern animals. 1909
2241 Manitoba Free Press. A piece of buffalo hide. 1911
2954 Watson, R. Canada's fur bearers. 1925
2964 Jackson, V.W. Fur & game resources of Manitoba. 1926
3438 Grey Owl. Adventures of Sajo. 1935
3675 Cory, H. Woodland comedy. 1939
3935 Manitoba. Bureau of Travel and Publicity. Game birds and animals. 1945
3966 Wood, E.A. Three mile bend. 1945
4041 Jaques, F.P. Canadian spring. 1947
4263 Roe, F.G. North American buffalo. 1951

POSTSCRIPT
Soper, J.D. The mammals of Alberta. (Edmonton, 1964)

6 Climate

885 Bowerman, A. Chinook winds. 1886
1058 Ingersoll, E. Climate of the Canadian West. 1888
1654 McCaig, J. Climate of southern Alberta. 1901
3455 Lussier, J.B.R. La sécheresse dans l'Ouest. 1935
3477 Strange, H.G.L. Western Canada semi-arid area. 1935
3559 Erickson, S.P. Black blizzards and a lost gold mine. 1937
3579 Nesbitt, L.D. Weather in the West. 1937
3648 Stuart, D. The Canadian desert. 1938
3673 Connor, A.J. Climate of Manitoba. 1939

7 Names, Geographical

784 Bell, C.N. Some historical names and places. 1885
3052 Baker, E. Prairie place names. 1928
3062 Canada. Geographic Board. Place-names of Alberta. 1928
3329 Canada. Geographic Board. Place-names of Manitoba. 1933

POSTSCRIPT
Saskatoon. Henry Kelsey Public School. What's in a name? Travelling through Saskatchewan with the story behind 679 place names. (Saskatoon, 1968)
Rudnyts'kyi, J.B. Manitoba mosaic of place names. (Winnipeg, 1970)
Holmgren, Eric & Patricia. 2,000 place-names of Alberta. (Saskatoon, 1972)

B THE PEOPLE

1 Indians
See also 'Indian Languages'

1552 Russell, F. Exploration in the far north. 1898
1632 Young, E.R. Indian life in the great N.W. 1900
1677 Church of England. The Indian missions. 1902
1688 MacPherson, R.J. Influence of civilization. 1902
1699 Church of England. Report on Indian missions. 1903
1752 Bryce, G. Among the mound builders' remains. 1904
1823 Laird, D. Our Indian treaties. 1905
1873 Ferrier, T. Indian education in the N.W. 1906
1891 Stokes, W.E.H. Are our Indians pagan? 1906
1906 Bryce, P.H. Report on Indian schools. 1907
1965 Blake, S.H. Don't you hear the Red Man calling. 1908
2004 Mair, C. Through the Mackenzie basin. 1908
2008 Matheson, S.P. Printed letter. 1908
2012 New England Co. Conference on Indian education. 1908
2025 Tims, J.W. Call of the Red Man for truth. 190_?
2035 Blake, S.H. Memorandum on Indian work. 1909
2048 Church of England. Indian missions of Sask. 1898-1909
2064 Lowie, R.H. The Assiniboine. 1909
2068 Mellick, H.G. Indians and our Indian missions. 1909
2072 Paget, A.M. People of the plains. 1909
2086 Tims, J.W. Calgary's appeal on behalf of Indian children. 1909
2147 Huestis, C.H. Indian problem in Alberta. 1910
2155 McClintock, W. The old north trail. 1910
2183 Stokes, W.E.H. Red man's religion. 1910
2192 Wissler, C. Material culture of Blackfeet. 1910
2391 Ferrier, T. Our Indians and their training. 1913
2503 Goddard, P.E. Sarsi texts. 1915
2528 Western Art Association. Treaty memorial monument. 1915
2548 Goddard, P.E. The Beaver Indians. 1916
2589 Goddard, P.E. Beaver texts. 1917
2665 Goddard, P.E. Sun dance of the Sarsi. 1919
2798 Wilson, R.N. Our betrayed wards. 1921
2857 Lupson, A. Sarcee Indians of Alberta. 1923
2957 Cameron, W.B. War trail of Big Bear. 1926
2963 Innes, C. Cree rebellion of 1884. 1926
3059 Buffalo Child Long Lance. Long Lance. 1928
3143 Jefferson, R. Fifty years on the Saskatchewan. 1929
3165 Bloomfield, L. Sacred stories of the Sweet Grass Cree. 1930
3306A McClintock, G. The wolves of Cooking Lake. 1932
3319 Vestal, S. Sitting Bull. 1932
3328 Buffalo Child Long Lance. Redman echoes. 1933
3338 House, J. Old Sun Anglican School. 1933
3371 Bloomfield, L. Plains Cree texts. 1934
3375 Corbett, E.A. Blackfoot trails. 1934
3378 Dunlop, G.M. Tales of the Indians. 1934
3484 Weekes, M.L. Round the council fires. 1935
3542 Stanley, G.F.G. Birth of Western Canada. 1936
3608 Clay, C. Swampy Cree legends. 1938
3631 Jenness, D. Sarcee Indians of Alberta. 1938
3734 Mandelbaum, D.G. Plains Cree. 1940
3742 Scott, R.J. Birch bark talking. 1940
3799 Gaudin, S.D. 44 years with northern Crees. 1942
3804 Lewis, O. Effects of white contact upon Blackfoot culture. 1942
3810 Orchard, W.J. Stone age on the prairies. 1942

2 Ethnic and Religious Groups

3 Belgians

4 Czechs

5 Danes

6 Doukhobors

1914 Canada. Dept. of the Interior. Papers re holding of homesteads by Doukhobors. 1907
2390 Evalenko, A.M. The message of the Doukhobors. 1913
3183 Gruchy, L.E. Doukhobors in Canada. 193_
3503 Dawson, C.A. Group settlement. 1936
3755 Wright, J.F.C. Slava Bohu. 1940
4116 Malov, P.N. Dukhobortsy. 1948
4328 Reibin, S.F. Toil and peaceful life. 1952

7 **Finns**

1633 Zilliacus, K. Kanada såsom mål för emigranter. 1900
4324 Peltonen, E. Kulkurina Amerikassa, uutisraivaajana Canadassa. 1952

8 **French**

1223 Foursin, P. La colonisation française au Canada. 1891
1538 Cuverille, J.M.A. Le Canada et les intérêts français. 1898
1540 Gaire, J. Dix années de missions. 1898
1931 Forestier, G. Dans l'Ouest canadien. 1907
1938 Leau, L. La terre pour rien. 1907
1998 Lionnet, J. Chez les Français du Canada. 1908
2353 Viel, L. L'aisance qui vient. 1912
2362 Asselin, J.F.O. L'émigration belge et française. 1913
3972 Coté, J.B. Originaux et aventuriers. 1946
4293 Giscard, G. Dans la prairie canadienne. 1952

9 **French-Canadians**

324 Circulaire privée au clergé. 1871
486 Tassé, J. Canadiens de l'Ouest. 1878
1005 Drummond, L. The French element in the Canadian Northwest. 1887
1146 Blake, E. On the French language. 1890
1162 Charlton, J. Speech on French language. 1890
1187 McCarthy, D. On the French language. 1890
1213 Canada. Dept. of Sec. of State. Abolition of the French language. 1891
1313 Faucher de Saint-Maurice, N.H.E. Les États de Jersey. 1893
1391 Benoist, C. Les Français et le Nord-Ouest canadien. 1895
1538 Cuverille, J.M.A. Le Canada et les intérêts français. 1898
1926 Cyr, J.E. La colonisation dans l'Ouest. 1907
1963 Bérubé, A.P. Les Canadiens-Français dans l'Ouest. 1908
1998 Lionnet, J. Chez les Français. 1908
2011 Morice, A.G. Dictionnaire historique des Canadiens. 1908
2096 La langue française. 1910
2473 Morice, A.G. Edmonton et l'Alberta française. 1914
2506 Hudon, T. Le conflit des races au foyer. 1915
2515 Normandeau, J.A. La paroisse Albertaine. 1915
2566 Trémaudan, A.H. de. Pourquoi nous parlons français. 1916
2605 Normandeau, J.A. Culture mixte en Alberta centrale. 1917
2633 Morice, A.G. Les droits historiques du Français. 1918
2634 Le Patriote de l'Ouest. Do French-Canadians speak patois? 191_?
2635 Le Patriote de l'Ouest. The question of education. 1918
2647 Trémaudan, A.H. de. Le sang français. 1918
2674 Language question before Legislative Assembly of Saskatchewan. 1919

2566A Trémaudan, A.H. de. Les précurseurs. 1916?
3481 Trémaudan, A.H. de. Histoire de la nation métisse. 1935
3638 Morice, A.G. La race métisse. 1938
3707 Weekes, M. Last buffalo hunter. 1939
3917 Giraud, M. Le métis canadien. 1945
4013 Sissons, Mrs. C.K. John Kerr. 1946
4140 Canadian Assoc. of Social Workers. Métis of Manitoba. 1949
4296 Howard, J.K. Strange empire. 1952

12 Hungarians

1681 Esterház. 1902
2249 Pirot, J. One year's fight for the true faith in Saskatchewan. 1911
3091 Paizs, O. Magyarok Kanadában. 1928
3391 Marchbin, A.A. Early emigration from Hungary. 1934
4006 Sántha, P. Kanada magyarsága. 1946
4196 Doka, K.C. Golden jubilee of Békevár. 1950

13 Hutterites

4342 Canadian Mental Health Assoc. Hutterites and Saskatchewan. 1953

POSTSCRIPT
Bennett, J.W. Hutterian Brethern; the agricultural, economic and social organization of a communal people. (Stanford, 1967)

14 Icelanders

396 Leidarvisir fyrir vesturfara til Canada. 1874
483 Frá Nýja Islandi. 1878
1038 Aukalög fyrir Gimlisveit. 1888
1221 Ekru, E. Hveiti-land heimsins hid mesta er Manitoba. 1891
1242 Baldwinson, B.L. Hagskýrslur frá Íslendingabyggdum i Canada. 1892
1291 Baldwinson, B.L. Ágrip af fyrirlestri um baejalif Íslendinga i Canada. 1893
1292 Baldwinson, B.L. Nokkrar athugasemdir. 1893
1293 Baldwinson, B.L. Svar gégn athugasemdum. 1893
1458 Manitoba. Ritlingur. 1896
1651 Jonasson, S. Early Icelandic settlements. 1901
1842 Wesley College. Islendingar vid Wesley-College. 1905
1956 Vestur Canada. 1907
2137 Evangeliska-lúterska kirkjufélag Íslendinga í Vesturheimi (Hid). Minningarrit Hins, 1885-1910
2531 Bergmann, F.J. Hvert stefnir? 1916
2671 Jackson, Th. J. Brot af Landnámssögu Nýja Islands. 1919
2718 Lindal, J.H. Islendingar i vatnabygdum. 1920
2779 Jackson, Th. J. Frá austri til vesturs. 1921
2853 Jackson, Th. J. Framhald á Landnámssögu Nýja Islands. 1923
3465 Olafson, K.K. Icelandic Lutheran Synod. 1935
3699 Salverson, L.G. Confessions of an immigrant's daughter. 1939
3960 Thorsteinsson, T.T. Saga Íslendinga í Vesturheimi. 1945

POSTSCRIPT
Lindal, W.J. The Saskatchewan Icelanders; a study of the Canadian fabric. (Winnipeg, 1955)

Kristjanson, W. The Icelandic people in Manitoba; a Manitoba saga. (Winnipeg, 1965)
Lindal, W.J. The Icelanders in Canada. (Ottawa & Winnipeg, 1967)

15 **Jews**

3303 Israelite Daily Press. 100th anniversary of emancipation. 1932
3627 Grossman, V. The soil's calling. 1938
3904 Calgary Hebrew School. Yearbook. 1945
3928 Jewish Old Folks Home. Story of an institution. 1945
3961 Usiskin, M. Oskn un motorn. 1945
4018 Winnipeg. Shalom Aleichem School. Finf un zwanzig yor yovel-buch. 1946

16 **Lebanese**

4248 Lester, L.A. Cedars of Lebanon. 1951

17 **Mennonites**

364 Correll, E.H. Mennonite immigration into Manitoba. 1873
576 Glaubensbekenntniss der Mennoniten. 1881
1605 Ewert, H.H. Plan zur Foerderung des Religionsunterrichtes. 1900
1609 Galbraith, J.F. Mennonites in Manitoba. 1900
1630 Wiebe, G. Auswanderung der Mennoniten. 1900
2830 Althausen, E. Zersplitterung oder Verbindung. 1922
2904 Peters, K. Die Bergthaler Mennoniten. 1924
2946 Neufeld, D. Kanadische Mennoniten. 1925
3218 Peters, K. Die Bergthaler Mennoniten. 1930?
3296 Ewert, H.H. The Mennonites. 1932
3400 Peters, K. Mennonitischen Ost-Reserve. 1934
3503 Dawson, C.A. Group settlement. 1936
3660 Historical sketch of Evangelical Mennonite Brethren. 1939
3954 Schaefer, P.J. Heinrich H. Ewert. 1945
4221 Rempel, J.G. Die Rosenorter Gemeinde in Saskatchewan. 1950
4258 Pazulla, H. Canada, deine neue Heimat. 1951

POSTSCRIPT
Francis, E.K. In search of Utopia; the Mennonites in Manitoba. (Altona, Man., 1955)

18 **Moravians**

1448 Leibert, M.W. Bruederfeld & Bruederheim. 1896
3927 Hoyler, C. Bruederheim & Bruederfeld, 1895-1945
3987 Hoyler, C. Heimtal in the making. 1946
4303 Kroening, W.F. Moravian congregation, Calgary, 1902-52

19 **Mormons**

2565 Toombs, H.W. Mormonism. 1916?
3503 Dawson, C.A. Group settlement. 1936
4282 Barnwell, Alberta. Mormon Relief Society. Barnwell history. 1952

20 Norwegians

2516 Norse Extension of Settlement Club. Scandinavian colony. 1915
2551 Jonassen, J. Vor flyvende. 1916
2713 Hjelt, O. Nybyggerliv paa praerien. 1920
2791 Rodvik, S. Fortaellinger fra Canada. 1921
3890 Steen, R. Pioneer days in Bardo. 1944

21 Poles

2394 Gargas, Z. W sprawie emigracyi do Kanady. 1913
2395 Gargas, Z. W sprawie wychodźctwa do Kanady. 1913
2570 Polskie Towarzystwo Gimnastyczne. Pamietnik, 1906-16. 1916
3146 Mazurkiewicz, R. Polskie wychodźtwo i osadnictwo w Kanadzie. 1929
3153 Polskie Towarzystwo Bratniej Pomocy, Coleman. Konstytucja. 192_
3549 Winnipeg. Towarzystwo Sw. Jana Katego. Memorial booklet. 1936
3821 Winnipeg. Holy Ghost Fraternal Aid Society. 40th anniversary. 1942
4158 Ksiazka pamiatkowa ... nowej siedziby Bractwa Sw. Ducha. 1949
4254 Makowski, B. Polska emigracja w Kanadzie. 1951
4332 Winnipeg. Holy Ghost Fraternal Aid Society. Golden jubilee, 1902-1952

POSTSCRIPT
Turek, V. Polonica Canadiana; a bibliographical list of the Canadian Polish imprints, 1848-1957. (Toronto, 1958)
Turek, V. Poles in Manitoba. (Toronto, 1967) Contains a bibliography bringing his earlier list up to date.

22 Russians

See also 'Doukhobors'

4322 Okulevich, G. Russkie v Kanade. 1952

23 Scottish

See also 'Red River Settlement'

1054 Great Britain. Colonial Office. Crofter and cottar colonisation. 1888
1578 Great Britain. Commissioners appointed to carry out a scheme of colonisation. Crofters colonisation. 1890-99
1200 Sandison, J.W. A Scotch farmer's success. 1890
2200 Bryce, G. The Scotsman in Canada. 1911
2785 MacKinnon, J.N. Pioneer Scotch settlers of St. Andrews. 1921

24 Swedes

952 Nya Stockholm. 1886
969 Skandinaviska National Foreningen. Skandinaverna i Manitoba. 1886
1846 Wickstrom, V.H. Bland svenskar i Kanada. 1905
2875 American Swedish Line. Svenskar i Canada. 1924
2993 Vennerström, I.T. Kanada och Kanadasvenskarna. 1926
3223 Schulze, G. Som emigrant i Kanada. 1930
3279 Schulze, G. Kamratliv och äventyr på Kanadas prärier. 1931

25 Ukrainians

4020 Yastremskiy, T.A. Kanadianizatsiya. 1946
4030 Davidson, G.A. Ukrainians in Canada. 1947
4042 Kohuska, N.L. Na storozhi kulturi. 1947
4043 Lysenko, V. Men in sheepskin coats. 1947
4070 Swystun, W. Kryza v Ukrayinskiy pravoslavniy Tserkvi. 1947
4084 Basilian Fathers. Yuvileyna pamyatka 25-littia novitsiatu. 1948
4184 Winnipeg. Ukrainian National Home. Propamyatna knyha. 1949
4232 Yorkton. St. Joseph's College. Pochatky i pracia. 1950
4233 Adams, M. I married a monk. 1951
4235 Bilecky, L. Ukrayinski pionery v Kanadi. 1951
4265 Rudnyckyj, J.B. Kanadiyski mistsevi nazvy Ukrayinskoho pokhodzhennya. 1951
4280 Zawadski, B. Piec lat za oceanem. 1951
4281 Bala, J. Pershiy Ukrayinskiy epyskop Kanady. 1952
4289 Edmonton. Ukrainian Greek Orthodox Cathedral. Pamyatka posvyachennya uholnoho kamenya. 1952
4299 Kazymyra, B. Monsinor Lyanzheven i Ukrayinci. 1952
4302 Kohuska, N.L. Chvert stolittya na hromadskiy nyvi. 1952
4320 Nimchuk, I. Pochatky orhanizaciynoho zhyttya Kanadiyskykh Ukrayintsiv. 1952
4327 Redemptorist Order. Redemptorists of the Eastern Rite. 1952
4330 Ukrainian Catholic Church. Diocese of Sask. Almanakh. 1952
4335 Zhan, J. Pyatdesyat rokiv u Kanadi. 1952
4336 Basilian Fathers. Propamyatna knyha. 1953
4353 Leskiv, F. Pionerske zhyttya v Kanadi. 1953
4358 Methodius, Bro. S. Rev. S. Joseph. 1953
4365 Stechishin, J.W. Mizh Ukrayintsiamy v Kanadi. 1953
4370 Yuzyk, P. Ukrainians in Manitoba. 1953

POSTSCRIPT

Kaye, V.J. Early Ukrainian settlements in Canada, 1859-1900. (Toronto, 1964)
Marunchak, M.H. Istoriia ukraintsiv Kanady. (Winnipeg, 1968)
MacGregor, J.G. Vilni zemli (Free land) (Toronto, 1969)
Lazarenko, J.M. The Ukrainian pioneers of Alberta. (Edmonton, 1970)
Marunchak, M.H. The Ukrainian Canadians. (Winnipeg, 1970)
Ukrainica Canadiana. (Winnipeg, 1950-   ) Founded by Dr. J.B. Rudnyc'kyj, this annual bibliography is a source of information on the publications of the Ukrainian press in Canada.

26 Biography

87 Wallace, W.S. Documents re N.W.C. 1827
486 Tassé, J. Canadiens de l'Ouest. 1878
1022 Powers, J.W. History of Regina. 1887
1025 Robertson, J.P. Political manual of Manitoba & N.W.T. 1887
1063 McPhillips' alphabetical directory of the Saskatchewan district. 1888
1690 Representative men of Manitoba. 1902
1853 Bryce, G. History of Manitoba. 1906
1887 Salesman Publishing Co. Souvenir of Alberta. 1906
2011 Morice, A.G. Dictionnaire historique des Canadiens. 1908
2067 Manitobans as we see 'em. 1909
2071 O'Donnell, J.H. Manitoba as I saw it. 1909
2200 Bryce, G. Scotsman in Canada. 1911
2222 Galaxy of western editors. 1911

1721 Duncan, D.M. History of Manitoba and N.W.T. 1903
1869 Dugas, G. Histoire de l'Ouest canadien. 1906
2007 Marsh, E.L. Where the buffalo roamed. 1908
2146 Herrington, W.S. Evolution of the Prairie Provinces. 1910
2445 Boam, H.J. The Prairie Provinces. 1914
2474 Morice, A.G. Histoire abrégée de l'Ouest canadien. 1914
2609 Shortt, A. Canada and its provinces. 1914-17
2664 Edmonds, W.E. Broad horizons. 1919
2721 MacBeth, R.G. Romance of Western Canada. 1920
2747 Tennant, J.F. Rough times, 1870-1920. 1920
2931 Kennedy, H.A. The book of the West. 1925
3137 Howay, F.W. Builders of the West. 1929
3148 Morice, A.G. L'Ouest canadien. 1929
3169 Burt, A.L. Romance of the Prairie Provinces. 1930
3577 Morton, A.S. Under western skies. 1937
3607 Chalmers, J.W. Builders of the West. 1938
3693 Morton, A.S. History of the Canadian West. 1939
3852 Scott, J.M. Story of our Prairie Provinces. 1943
3917 Giraud, M. Le métis canadien. 1945
3979 Fiedler, A. Kanada pachnąca Żywicą. 1946
4309 MacEwen, J.W.G. Between the Red and the Rockies. 1952

POSTSCRIPT
Cashman, A.W. An illustrated history of Western Canada. (Edmonton, 1971)

2 Manitoba

532 Gunn, D. History of Manitoba. 1880
535 Historical & Scientific Society of Man. Constitution. 1880
598 Bryce, G. Manitoba, its infancy, growth, etc. 1882
1180 Hill, R.B. Manitoba, history of its early settlement. 1890
1853 Bryce, G. History of Manitoba. 1906
2071 O'Donnell, J.H. Manitoba as I saw it. 1909
2434 Schofield, F.H. The story of Manitoba. 1913
2726 Manitoba. Dept. of Education. Fifty years a province. 1920
2740 Seaman, H.S. Manitoba landmarks. 1920
2855 Lecompte, E. Un grand chrétien, Sir Joseph Dubuc. 1923
3087 McWilliams, M. Manitoba milestones. 1928
3167 British Medical Association. Place of meeting. 1930
3175 Frémont, D. Taché et la naissance du Manitoba. 1930
3205 Manitoba. Provincial Diamond Jubilee Committee. Manitoba's diamond jubilee. 1930
3206 Manitoba's diamond jubilee, 1870-1930
3316 Stewart, D.A. Glimpses at Manitoba history. 1932
4047 MacVicar, N. Tales and trails. 1947
4168 Manitoba. Travel and Publicity Bureau. Historical Manitoba. 1949

POSTSCRIPT
Morton, W.L. Manitoba, a history. (Toronto, 1967)
Jackson, J.A. The centennial history of Manitoba. (Toronto, 1970)

3 Saskatchewan

2367 Black, N.F. History of Saskatchewan. 1913
2889 Hawkes, J. Saskatchewan and its people. 1924

POSTSCRIPT
Russell, R.C. The Carlton Trail. (Saskatoon, 1955)
Wright, J.F.C. Saskatchewan: the history of a province. (Toronto, 1955)
Saskatchewan History (Magazine, published since 1948)

4 **Alberta**

2323 MacRae, A.O. History of the province of Alberta. 1912
2878 Blue, J. Alberta, past and present. 1924
3203 MacInnes, C.M. In the shadow of the Rockies. 1930
3337 Higinbotham, J.D. When the West was young. 1933
3926 Horan, J.W. West, nor'west. 1945
4274 Stanley, G.D. Round-up of fun in the foothills. 1951
4287 Dempsey, H.A. Historic sites of Alberta. 1952

POSTSCRIPT
Alberta Historical Review (Magazine, published since 1953)

D HISTORY, LOCAL

1 **Manitoba**

Assiniboine Valley
1467 Ruttan, H.N. Report on Assiniboine River. 1896
3226 Stewart, D.A. Early Assiniboine trading posts. 1930
3990 Kavanagh, M. The Assiniboine basin. 1946
Beausejour
4023 Beausejour. Kościola Matki Boskiej. Souvenir of the blessing. 1947
Bissett
4078 Wyman, H.C. Bissett United Church. 1947
Boissevain
1148 Boissevain and Turtle Mountain. 189-
Brandon
597 Brandon. 1882
1064 McPhillips' Brandon directory, 1888-89
1088 Brandon. Board of Trade. Handbook of the county of Brandon. 1889
1265 Brandon Times. Christmas, 1892. 1892
2089 Warner, W. Illustrated souvenir of Brandon. 190_?
2277 Brandon. 1912
2369 Brandon. 1913
2386 Dawson & Gowen. Brandon, second city of Man. 1913
2953 Trotter, B. A horseman and the West. 1925
3990 Kavanagh, M. The Assiniboine basin. 1946
Carberry
1716 Carberry, Man., souvenir views. 1903
Carman
1650 Hinch & Son. Carman - Winnipeg district. 1901
2854 Kernighan, T. Dufferin and Carman. 1923
Chumah
4354 Lewis, S. History of Chumah Church. 1953
Churchill
7 Knight, J. The founding of Churchill. 1717

1373 Schultz, Sir J.C. A forgotten northern fortress. 1894
3162 Alexander, Mrs. M.H.T. Fort Prince of Wales. 1930
Clearwater
3013 Clearwater. Women's Institute. Clearwater, 1876-1885. 1927
Crystal City
2293 Crystal City and district. 1912
3732 McKitrick, T.G. Corner stones of empire. 1940
Dauphin
1572 Dauphin. Municipal office. List of electors. 1899
2132 Dauphin. Board of Trade. Dauphin the plentiful. 1910
Dennis County
1072 Palmer, W.J. Dennis County. 1888
Elkhorn
1573 Elkhorn. Board of Trade. Farm lands. 1899
Emerson
514 Armstrong, L.O. Southern Manitoba and Turtle Mountain. 1880
620 Emerson. 1882
4195 Carlson, W.E. History of Emerson. 1950
Fannystelle
3663 Bernier, N. Fannystelle. 1939
Gimli
1038 Aukalög fyrir Gimlisveit. 1888
Gladstone
1875 Gladstone. Board of Trade. Gladstone and surrounding district. 1906
3797 Galloway, M.A. I lived in paradise. 1942
3978 Fahrni, M.M. Third crossing. 1946
Granville Lake
3348 Mishaegen, A. de. Mush! Un hiver en pays Cree. 1933
3997 Mishaegen, A. de. Dans la forêt canadienne. 1946
Hamiota
3570 MacKay, Mrs. A.M. History of Scotia. 1937
4149 Hamiota. Women's Institute. History of Hamiota. 1949
Hudson Bay
3 Tyrrell, J.B. Documents relating to Hudson Bay. 1931
7 Knight, J. The founding of Churchill, 1717
5 Jérémie, N. Relation du Détroit et de la Baie d'Hudson. 1714
6 Jérémie, N. Twenty years of York Factory. 1714
12 Robson, J. Six years residence in Hudson's Bay. 1752
60 McKeevor, T. Voyage to Hudson's Bay. 1819
719 Bell, C.N. Our northern waters. 1884
852 Tuttle, C.R. Our north land. 1885
2467 Laut, A.C. Adventurers of England. 1914
Katrine district
4283 Belton, W.L. Historical sketches. 1952
Killarney
3344 Killarney. Women's Institute. Stories of pioneer days. 1933
4215 Monteith, G.B. History of Killarney. 1950
La Broquerie
4236 Boily, M.L. Nos braves pionniers. 1951
Langruth
4206 Langruth. A tribute to soldiers and pioneers. 1950
Lower Fort Garry
2061 H.B.C. Visit to Lower Fort Garry. 1909
3111 Watson, R. Lower Fort Garry. 1928

Saint Malo
3745 Société Historique de Saint-Boniface. Saint-Malo. 1940
St-Norbert
3849 Un Père Trappiste. Une trappe dans un pays de missions. 1943
Saint-Pierre-Jolys
2465 Jolys, J.M. Pages de souvenirs. 1914
Sainte-Rose-du-Lac
4130 Théoret, A.E. Sainte-Rose-du-Lac. 1948
Selkirk
673 East Selkirk. Board of Trade. East Selkirk. 1883
1889 Selkirk. Board of Trade. Souvenir of Selkirk. 1906
2106 Campbell, B. Garden spot of Western Canada. 1910
Souris
1622 Martel, (Wm. A.) & Sons. Illustrated souvenir. 190–
4355 McMorran, G.A. Souris River posts. 1953
Souris Valley
887 Bryce, G. Souris country; its monuments, etc. 1886
South Norfolk
3683 History of South Norfolk. 1939
Stonewall
1661 Stonewall. Board of Trade. Stonewall district. 1901
Swan Lake
4348 Hambley, G.H. Historical records of Swan Lake. 1953
Swan River Valley
1955 Swan River Valley. Board of Trade. Swan River Valley. 1907
2472 Methodist Church. Swan River Valley, Manitoba. 1914
The Pas
2312 Hudson's Bay Herald. A few things recently written. 1912
2477 The Pas. Board of Trade. The Pas. 1914
2693 Bramble, C.A. Land of the lobstick. 1920
2793 Rupert's Land Historical Society. Report. 1921
3152 The Pas. Board of Trade. The Pas and Northern Manitoba. 1929
3254 Greene, D.L. An historical sketch, Christ Church. 1931
4288 Dionne, E. Reminiscing. 1952
Turtle Mountain
1148 Boissevain and Turtle Mountain. 189–
2480 Presbyterian Church. Turtle Mountain district. 1914
4271 Wright, N.E. In view of the Turtle Hill. 1951
Virden
3962 Virden days. 1945
Winkler
4134 Winkler. Burwalde School District. Diamond jubilee. 1948
Winnipeg
387 Church of England. Diocese of Rupert's Land. Provisional statutes of St. John's Cathedral. 1874
413 Elliott, G.B. Winnipeg as it is. 1875
491 Begg, A. Ten years in Winnipeg. 1879
512 Winnipeg. St. George's Society. Office bearers, etc. 1879
552 Winnipeg. Selkirk Club. Rules. 1880
617 Dart, H.A. Guide to manufacturers in Winnipeg. 1882
648 Steen and Boyce. Winnipeg. 1882
703 Tuttle, C.R. History of the corporation. 1883
708 Agnew, N. Our water supply. 1884
713 Souvenir of Winnipeg. 1884

3548 Winnipeg. St. Vladimir & St. Olga Parish. Yuvileyniy almanakh. 1936
3549 Winnipeg. Towarzystow Sw Jana Kantego. Memorial booklet. 1936
3585 Sinclair, J.D. Westminster Church. 1937
3590 Walker, G.E. Romantic Winnipeg. 1937
3657 Winnipeg. Grace United Church. Three score years and ten. 1938
3821 Winnipeg. Holy Ghost Fraternal Aid Society. 40th anniversary. 1942
3860 Winnipeg. Grace United Church. 75th anniversary. 1943
3889 Sisler, W.J. Peaceful invasion. 1944
3895 Winnipeg. St. Giles' United Church. Diamond jubilee, 1884-1944
3896 Winnipeg. St. Nicholas Parish. Soroklittia parokhiyi. 1944
3959 Sykes, A.A. The story of St. Andrew's United Church. 1945
3964 Winnipeg. St. John's Cathedral. From mission to cathedral. 1945
3965 Winnipeg. School Board. A visit to our schools. 1945
4018 Winnipeg. Shalom Aleichem School. Finf un zwanzig yor yovel-buch. 1946
4036 Hart, W.T. Sixty-three years of service. 1947
4060 Riley, R.T. Memoirs. 1947
4061 Robertson, H.J. The story of Knox Church. 1947
4111 Laing, G. A community organizes for war. 1948
4166 Manitoba. Travel & Publicity Bureau. Greater Winnipeg. 1949
4182A Winnipeg, Man. Winnipeg's 75th birthday party. 1949
4214 Masters, D.C. Winnipeg general strike. 1950
4250 McBeth, M. Story of Kildonan Presbyterian Church. 1951
4272 Shave, Harry. Our heritage. 1951

York Factory

147 Hargrave, L.M. Letters. 1838-52

POSTSCRIPT

For local histories published in Manitoba since 1953 consult the following catalogue:
Morley, Marjorie. A bibliography of Manitoba from holdings in the Legislative Library of Manitoba. (Winnipeg, 1970)

2 Saskatchewan

Aberdeen

2093 Aberdeen. Board of Trade. A profitable point for the settler. 1910
2196 Aberdeen. Board of Trade. Where wheat makes money. 1911

Balgonie

3550 Zimmermann, A. Die romisch-catholische Pfarrei St. Joseph bei Balgonie. 1936

Battleford

681 Laurie, W. Battle River valley. 1883
1788 Battleford, town and district. 1905
1954 Storer, Mrs. E.L. Gardiner Presbyterian Church. 1907
1961 Battleford. Board of Trade. Battleford and the university. 1908
3036 Reid, Mrs. J.A. The neighborhood of Battleford. 1927
3491 Battleford. St. George's Church. Fiftieth anniversary. 1936
4267 Saskatchewan Herald. Stories of the old times. 1951

Broadview

2199 Broadview. Board of Trade. All about far-famed Broadview. 1911
2371 Broadview. Board of Trade. Broadview, the railway town. 1913

Bruno

4339A Bruno, Sask. St. Ursula's Academy. We must do something about our academy. 1953

Indian Head
859 The Albany settlement. 1886
1947 Prairie Witness. Indian Head. 1907
Kipling
4196 Doka, K.C. Golden jubilee of Békevár. 1950
Kronau
3208 Metzger, H. Geschichtlicher Abriss über die Peters-Pfarrei. 1930
Laflèche
2499 Dubois, E. Une paroisse d'avenir. 1915
Langham
2150 Langham. Board of Trade. Langham. 1910
Last Mountain Lake
2164 Pearson, W. Last Mountain Lake. 1910
Lipton
2100 Binnie-Clark, G. A summer on the Canadian prairie. 1910
Lloydminster
1999 Lloydminster. Board of Trade. Lloydminster district is the banner district. 1908
1667 Barr, I.M. British settlements in N.W. Canada. 1902
1669 Barr, I.M. To the members of the British colony. 1902
1703 Barr, I.M. British colony for Saskatchewan. 1903
1704 Barr, I.M. British settlements in Canada. 1903
1705 Barr, I.M. Homestead privileges. 1903
1706 Barr, I.M. Saskatoon and Saskatchewan Transport Co. 1903
1731 Lloyd, G.E. To members of the British colony. 1903
1737A Mullins, J.D. Seven days on the prairie. 1903?
1800 Canada. Dept. of the Interior. British colony at Lloydminister. 1905
2126 Copping, A.E. Seven years ago. 1910
2374 Burrows, C.L. Hands across the sea. 1913
2894 McCormick, J.H. Lloydminster. 1924
3096 Pick, H. Next year. 1928
4368 Wetton, Mrs. C. The promised land. 1953
Mantario
4213 Mantario. Homemakers' Club. From oxen to airplane. 1950
Marysburg
4048 Marysburg. Assumption Church. Our parish. 1947
Melfort
2440 Melfort celebrates the introduction of agriculture to Western Canada. 1914
Melville
2159 Melville. Board of Trade. Melville, the West's wonder town. 1910
Midale
4349 Hultgren, P. Brief history of Midale. 1953
4350 Hultgren, P. History of First Baptist Church, Midale, 1953
Milestone
4096 Garratt, A.W. History of Milestone. 1948
Moose Jaw
1121 Moose Jaw. Board of Trade. District of Moose Jaw. 1889
1139 Alexander, R.L. Alphabetical directory of Moose Jaw. 1890
1670 Bellamy, H. Sketch of the life of Bellamy. 1902
1740 Porter, N.J. Glimpses through Moose Jaw and district. 1903
2017 Rice, L. Interesting scenes in Moose Jaw. 1908
2242 Moose Jaw. Board of Trade. Moose Jaw. 1911
2403 Interesting facts regarding Moose Jaw. 1913
2416 Moose Jaw. Board of Trade. Buckle of the greatest wheat belt. 1913

Regina

841 Regina directory for 1885. 1885
1022 Powers, J.W. History of Regina. 1887
1124 Regina. Board of Trade. A few facts respecting the Regina district. 1889
1234 Regina. Board of Trade. An unvarnished tale. 1891
1886 Regina. Board of Trade. Regina, capital of Saskatchewan. 1906
1948 Regina. Knox Presbyterian Church. Quarter centenary. 1907
2077 Regina. Board of Trade. Regina, the capital. 1909
2167 Regina. Board of Trade. Regina, capital of Saskatchewan. 1910
2168 Regina. Greater Regina Club. Regina, capital of Saskatchewan. 1910
2169 Regina. Greater Regina Club. Progress and opportunities. 1910
2254 Regina. Board of Trade. Regina, queen city of middle West. 1911
2260 Sheffield, T.W. Facts and opportunities in Regina. 1911
2337 Regina, before and after cyclone. 1912
2337A Regina tornado. 1912?
2338 Regina. Board of Trade. 1000 facts about Regina. 1912
2414 Methodist Church. Report of a social survey of Regina. 1913
2424 Regina. Board of Trade. Regina, capital of Saskatchewan. 1913
2425 Regina. 1913
2481A Regina, capital of Sask. 1914
2485 Souvenir of Regina. 1914
2956 Bennett, A. Local Council of Women. 1926
2983 Regina. Board of Trade. Regina, centre of the world's hard wheat area. 1926
3002 Bothwell, J. A health to Regina. 1927
3101 Regina. Board of Trade. Regina. 1928
3252 Fritz, J. 25. Jubiläum der Ev.-luth. Dreieinigkeitsgemeinde zu Regina. 1931
4398 Regina. St. Matthew's Anglican Church. Silver jubilee. 1935
3476 Sinton, R. Looking backward. 1935
3556 Complin, M. Winged moccasins to winged words. 1937
3771 Pickel, W.U. Golden jubilee of First Baptist Church. 1941
3931 Local Council of Women of Regina. Golden jubilee. 1945
3932 McAra, P. 62 years on the Saskatchewan prairies. 1945
4259 Pickel, W.U. History of First Baptist Church. 1951

Rosthern

2341 Rosthern. Board of Trade. Rosthern. 1912
4221 Rempel, J.G. Die Rosenorter Gemeinde. 1950

St. Brieux

3117 Bergot, D. Réminiscences d'un pionnier. 1929

St. Joseph's Colony

3215 Oblates. Bilder und Blätter zum Silbernen Jubiläum. 1930

St. Peter's Colony

3051 Silberne Jubiläum der St. Peters-Kolonie. 1928

Saltcoats

2171 Saltcoats. Board of Trade. Choice lands. 1910
4205 Jowsey, R. The first sixty years. 1950

Saskatchewan River

603 Canada. Dept. of Sec. of State. Tramway around Grand Rapids. 1882
797 Canada. Dept. of Public Works. Improvement of the North Saskatchewan River for purposes of navigation. 1885
1552 Russell, F. Exploration in the far north. 1898
1676A C.P.R. The Saskatchewan valley. 1902
2568 Voligny, L.R. Report on survey of North Saskatchewan. 1916?
4163 MacGregor, J.G. Blankets and beads. 1949
4192 Campbell, M.W. The Saskatchewan. 1950

Willowbunch
2867 Rondeau, C. Montagne de Bois. 1923
Wolseley
2193 Wolseley. Board of Trade. Wheat wealthy Wolseley. 191–
Wood Mountain
2867 Rondeau, C. Montagne de Bois. 1923
Yorkton
779 York Farmers Colonization Co. Guide and record. 1884
1418 Northwest Territories. Leg. Assembly. Northwest homesteads. 1895
2092 Yorkton. Board of Trade. Yorkton, metropolis of northeastern Saskatchewan. 1909
2272 Yorkton. Board of Trade. Facts about Yorkton. 1910-11
3365 Yorkton Enterprise. Semi-centennial souvenir number. 1933
4080 Yorkton. Board of Trade. Yorkton, parklands trading centre. 1947
Zealandia
2195 Zealandia. Board of Trade. Solid facts about a good point for settlers. 1910
Zelma
4187 Zelma. Homemakers' Club. Community of Zelma. 1949

POSTSCRIPT
During Saskatchewan's golden jubilee year as a province, 1955, with the encouragement of the Golden Jubilee Committee some twelve dozen local histories were written. Some prepared by schools were only manuscript books: these were microfilmed to assure preservation by the Saskatchewan Archives. The published histories will be found listed in the issues of *Saskatchewan History* during the years 1955 and 1956.

More recent local histories are regularly listed and reviewed in the above magazine.

3 Alberta

Alberta
1513 Thomson Bros. Beauties & industries of Alberta. 1897
2290 Central Alberta Development League. Central Alberta. 1912
Alhambra
4301 Kerr, J.R. Other days and other ways. 1952
Athabasca
2034 Athabasca Landing. Board of Trade. Athabasca Landing. 1909
2097A Athabasca Landing. Board of Trade. The northern trek. 1910
2538 Canada. Dept. of the Interior. Athabasca River country. 1916
2762 Canada. Dept. of the Interior. The lower Athabaska & Slave River district. 1921
Banff
3911 Duncan, D.A. Some letters and other writings. 1945
Bardo
3890 Steen, R. Pioneer days. 1944
Barnwell
4282 Barnwell. Mormon Relief Society. Barnwell history. 1952
Bashaw
2491 Bashaw Extension of Settlement Club. Bashaw. 1915
Bassano
2098 Bassano. Board of Trade. Bassano. 1910
2492 Bassano Colony Extension of Settlement Club. Bassano. 1915
Bentley
4345 DeGroff, B. Early history of Bentley. 1953

4069 Smye, F.H. The Winspear family. 1947
4082 Bagnall, L.L. At the sixtieth milestone. 1948
4216 Morrison, E.C. Calgary, 1875-1950
4253 McNeill, L. Tales of the old town. 1951
4300 Kennedy, F. Calgary Stampede story. 1952
4303 Kroening, W.F. Moravian congregation, Calgary, 1902-52

Camrose

1755 Camrose. Board of Trade. Camrose, the rose of Alberta. 1904
2450 Camrose, after seven years. 1914
2516 Norse Extension of Settlement Club. Scandinavian colony. 1915
4028 Camrose Historical Society. Early history of Camrose. 1947

Canmore

3831 Canmore. Sacred Heart Church. Golden jubilee. 1943

Cardston

1619 MacLeod, N.W. Picturesque Cardston. 1900
2841 Cardston. Board of Trade. Official folder. 1923

Castor

3568 M., J.H. Memoirs of Castor. 1937

Champion

2381 Champion. Board of Trade. Grain golden Champion. 1913

Claresholm

1901 Anderson, C.D. Claresholm and vicinity. 1907

Clover Bar

3241 Berry, J.P. Clover Bar in the making. 1931
3271 Oliver, F. Clover Bar celebration. 1931

Coleman

3153 Polskie Towarzystwo Bratniej Pomocy, Coleman. Konstytucja. 192_?
4343 Coleman. Board of Trade. Coleman's 50th anniversary. 1953

Coaldale

2698 Coaldale Commercial Club. Coaldale, gem of the West. 1920

Coronation

2208 C.P.R. Coronation. 1911

Crossfield

2062 Hultgren & Davie. The last best West. 1909

Dickson

4091A Dickson, Alta. Bethany Lutheran Congregation. Dickson Koloniens histoire. 1948

Didsbury

2051 Directory of Didsbury townships. 1909

Donalda

2498 Donalda Extension of Settlement Club. Donalda. 1915

Dunvegan

2275 Alberta, Athabasca & Peace River Land Co. Dunvegan. 1912

Edmonton

27 Johnson, A.M. Saskatchewan journals. 1967
1170 Edmonton. Board of Trade. Edmonton district. 1890
1244A The Bulletin, Edmonton. The great Saskatchewan valley. 1892
1248B C.P.R. The Edmonton district. 1892
1424 Spurr, J.B. Edmonton district directory. 1895
1437 Canada. Dept. of the Interior. Edmonton district. 1896
1483 Cowie, I. Grain, grass and gold fields. 1897
1505 Mathers, C.W. Souvenir of Edmonton district. 1897
1506 Mathers, C.W. Souvenir – Queen's diamond jubilee. 1897
1579 Lowe, C.A. Lowe's directory of Edmonton District. 1899

3741 Roxburgh, F.D. Presbyterian Church in Edmonton, 1866-1940
3835 Edmonds, W.E. Edmonton, past and present. 1943
3837 Edmonton. Holy Trinity Church. A history, 1893-1943. 1943
3838 Edmonton. M. Hrushevsky Ukrainian Institute. Silver jubilee book. 1943
3861 Cantelon, R.A. Edmonton. 1944
3983 Griesbach, W.A. I remember. 1946
4092 Edmonton. St-Joachim Parish. Fête des pionniers. 1948
4199 Finlay, R.E. George McDougall Church. 195–

POSTSCRIPT
Cashman, A.W. The Edmonton story; the life and times of Edmonton (Edmonton, 1956)
MacGregor, J.G. Edmonton; a history. (Edmonton, 1967)

Edson
2500 Edson. Board of Trade. Edson. 1915
Entwistle
3084A Lloydall-Bee, A. Parish of St. Peter, Entwistle. 1928
Fort Saskatchewan
2220 Ft. Sask. Ft. Sask. and district. 1911
2981 Pollard, W.C. Pioneering in the prairie West. 1926
Fort Vermilion
3103 Rose, H. Stump farm. 1928
Frank
1762 Canada. Department of the Interior. Report on landslide at Frank. 1904
Gleichen
2744 Stocken, H.W.G. The Gleichen district. 1920
Glendon
3918 Glendon. Ukrainian Greek Catholic Parish. Posvyachennya parokhialnoyi rezydencyi. 1945
Grande Prairie
2666 Grand Prairie. Board of Trade. Grand Prairie & the Peace River district. 1919
3022 Grande Prairie. Board of Trade. Facts worth knowing about the famous Grande Prairie district. 1927
3181 Grande Prairie. Board of Trade. Interesting facts about Grande Prairie. 1930
4099 Grande Prairie. Chamber of Commerce. Grande Prairie, centre of the Peace River country. 1948
4201 Grande Prairie. Chamber of Commerce. Grande Prairie. 1950
Grimshaw
3094 Peace River & Western Development. Grimshaw district. 1928
Hanna
4237 Burnet, J. Next-year country. 1951
Hardisty
2504 Hardisty Extension of Settlement Club. Hardisty. 1915
Heimtal
3987 Hoyler, C. Heimtal in the making. 1946
High River
4204 High River Times. This is High River. 1950
4274 Stanley, G.D. Round-up of fun in the foothills. 1951
Hughenden
2507 Hughenden Extension of Settlement Club. Hughenden. 1915
Killam
2133 Dobry & Large. Golden opportunities. 1910
Lac la Biche
2839 Canada. Dept. of the Interior. Lac la Biche district. 1923

Olds

2009A Moore, O.S. In the shadow of the Rockies. 1908

Peace River Country

1274A Ogilvie, W. The Peace River and tributaries. 1892
1660 Société de colonisation de la Riviere la Paix. Le Nord-Ouest. 1901
1904 Bezanson, A.M. The Peace River trail. 1907
2291 Cook, J.M. Canadian North-West as it is to-day. 1912
2321 Machell, P.W. What is my country? 1912
2378 Canadian Northern Railway. Peace River country. 1913
2461 Giroux, J.B.H. La Rivière la Paix pour les Canadiens-francais. 1914
2477A Peace River, Alta. Board of Trade. 1914
2622 Canada. Dept. of the Interior. Peace River country. 1918
2625 Hamer-Jackson Pub. Co. Edmonton to Peace River. 1918
2637 Peace River Development Corp. Peace River. 1918
2775 Guide to Edmonton, Peace River, etc. 1921
2939 McGregor, T.F. Where the great Peace River flows. 1925
3022 Grande Prairie. Board of Trade. Facts worth knowing about the famous Grande Prairie district. 1927
3093 Peace River. Board of Trade. Peace River country. 1928?
3181 Grande Prairie. Board of Trade. Interesting facts about Grande Prairie. 1930
3341 Jackson, M.E. On the last frontier. 1933
3377 Dawson, C.A. Settlement of Peace River area. 1934
4049 Maurice, V. 50 years in the Peace River country. 1947
4310 MacGregor, J.G. The land of twelve foot Davis. 1952

Pincher Creek

1833 Perrier, H.J. Souvenir of Pincher Creek. 1905
2720 Lynch-Staunton, E. Early days of Pincher Creek. 1920

Raymond

4262 Raymond. Golden jubilee. 1951

Redcliff

2423 Redcliff. Board of Trade. Redcliff, Canada's natural gas centre. 1913

Red Deer

2253 Red Deer. Board of Trade. Red Deer. 1911
2336 Red Deer. Board of Trade. Red Deer. 1912
4095 Gaetz, A.L. Park country. 1948
4291 Gaetz, A.L. Trails of yesterday. 1952

Rimbey

4329 Rimbey. Historical Committee. History. 1952

St. Albert

3192 Jan, A.M. Historic St. Albert. 193-

St. Paul

4325 Pépin, C. Histoire de St-Paul, 1896-1951. 1952

Slave River

2762 Canada. Dept. of the Interior. Lower Athabasca & Slave River district. 1921

Standard

2524 Standard Colony Extension of Settlement Club. Standard. 1915

Stettler

2182 Stettler Independent. Stettler heart of Alberta. 1910
2344 Stettler, Alberta, the busy town. 1912

Strome

2101 Bird & Antrobus. Strome the garden spot. 19_?

Taber

4366 Taber. Women's Institute. Taber, yesterday and today. 1953

Tofield
2349 Tofield. Industrial League. Tofield & district. 1912
Turner Valley
3027 Kilroe, W.G.B. Turner Valley oil field. 1927
3124 Calgary. Board of Trade. Trip through Turner Valley. 1929
3809 Nickle, C.O. Valley of wonders. 1942
Vegreville
2028 Vegreville. Board of Trade. Settlement opportunities. 190–
2088 Vegreville. Board of Trade. For you, a few facts. 190_?
2186 Vegreville. Board of Trade. For you, a few facts. 191_?
2351 Vegreville district. 1912
3358 Théroux, T. Impressions et histoire de Végreville. 1933
Vermilion
2352 Vermilion, Alberta. 1912
Viking
3555 Collier, H.B. Remember when? 1937
Wainwright
2354 Wainwright. Board of Trade. Wainwright, the buffalo town. 1912
Wellsdale
3180 Goodge, S.H. Parish of St. Mary's. 1930
Wetaskiwin
1663 Wetaskiwin. Board of Trade. Wetaskiwin. 190–
2031 Wetaskiwin. Board of Trade. Wetaskiwin, the elevator city. 1908
2090 Wetaskiwin. Alexandra High School. Souvenir. 1909

POSTSCRIPT
For local histories of Alberta communities published since 1953, consult the *Alberta Historical Review* in which new histories are regularly reviewed.

E EXPLORERS, SURVEYORS, AND TRAVELLERS

1 Exploration

1 Kelsey, H. Journal, 1691-1692
2 The Kelsey papers. 1721
13 La Vérendrye, P.G. Journals and letters. 1751
14 Soc. Hist. de St-Boniface. Documents sur la découverte du Nord-Ouest. 1751
15 Henday, A. York Factory to the Blackfeet country. 1755
16 Wales, W. Astronomical observations at Prince of Wales Fort. 1770
17 Cocking, M. Adventurer from Hudson Bay. 1773
22 Hearne & Turnor. Journals. 1792
23 Turnor, P. Result of astronomical observations. 1794
25 Mackenzie, Sir A. Voyages from Montreal. 1801
26 Maclauries, Mr. Narrative or journal of voyages. 1802
34 Thompson, D. Narrative of his explorations. 1812
35 Le Haiye. Diary of trip to Athabasca. 1813
217 Palliser, J. Exploration – B.N.A. 1859
218 Palliser, J. Progress of B.N.A. expedition. 1859
221 Hind, H.Y. Narrative of Red and Saskatchewan expeditions. 1860
222 Palliser, J. Exploration – B.N.A. 1860
223 Palliser, J. Papers of Palliser expedition. 1968
227A Hector, Sir J. Central part of Br. North America. 1861

238 Palliser, J. Exploration – B.N.A. Journals. 1863
660 Bryce, G. Winnipeg country. 1883
1080 Tyrrell, J.B. Brief narrative of D. Thompson. 1888
1770 Kastner, F. de. Les La Vérendrye, père et fils. 1904
1772 Laut, A.C. Pathfinders of the West. 1904
1797 Bryce, G. Mackenzie, Selkirk, Simpson. 1905
1968 Burpee, L.J. Search for the western sea. 1908
2281 Burpee, L.J. Scouts of empire. 1912
2363 Bell, C.N. Lead tablet buried by La Vérendrye. 1913
2428 St. Boniface. A monument to La Vérendrye. 1913
2446 Burpee, L.J. Pathfinders of the Great Plains. 1914
2527 Trémaudan, A.H. de. Hudson Bay road. 1915
2560 Prud'homme, L.A. La Vérendrye. 1916
2719 Long, M.H. Knights errant of the wilderness. 1920
2818 Macoun, J. Autobiography. 1922
2884 Cochrane, C.N. David Thompson. 1924
2938 Macdonald, A. Sir A. Mackenzie. 1925
3031 Moore, I. Valiant La Vérendrye. 1927
3042 Wade, M.S. Mackenzie of Canada. 1927
3047 Woollacott, A.P. Mackenzie. 1927
3048 Wrong, H.H. Sir A. Mackenzie. 1927
3100 Reeve, G.J. La Vérendrye. 1928
3123 Burpee, L.J. Hudson Bay to Blackfoot country. 1929
3179 Garvin, A.B. Pierre Esprit Radisson. 1930
3210 Morton, A.S. David Thompson. 1930
3295 Eschambault, A. d'. Discovery of Lake of the Woods. 1932
3351 Rumilly, R. La Vérendrye. 1933
3643 Rumilly, R. La Vérendrye; Mackenzie. 1938
3666 Brouillette, B. Pénétration du continent américain. 1939
3824 Achard, E. Grande découverte de l'Ouest. 1943

POSTSCRIPT

MacGregor, J.G. Behold the shining mountains; being an account of the travels of Anthony Henday. (Edmonton, 1954)

MacGregor, J.G. Peter Fidler: Canada's forgotten surveyor, 1769-1822. (Toronto, 1966)

2 Overland Journeys to the Arctic

25 Mackenzie, Sir A. Voyages from Montreal. 1801
26 Maclauries, Mr. Narrative, or journal of voyages. 1802
80 Franklin, Sir J. Narrative of a journey. 1823
88 Franklin, Sir J. Narrative of a second expedition. 1828
98 King, R. Narrative of a journey to the Arctic. 1836
108 Simpson, T. Narrative of discoveries. 1843
111 Lefroy, Sir J.H. In search of the magnetic north. 1844
113 Simpson, A. Life and travels of Thos. Simpson. 1845
143 Richardson, Sir John. Arctic searching expedition. 1851
156 Tytler, P.F. Northern coasts. 1853
1073 Petitot, E.F.S.J. En route pour la mer glaciale. 1888
1518 How to get to the Klondike. 1898
1549 Moberly, W. Eight routes to the Klondyke. 1898
1552 Russell, F. Exploration in the far north. 1898
2105 Cameron, A.D. The new north. 1910

3 Overland Journeys to the Pacific

2078 Rohde, O. Rockies and other things. 1909
2129 Cran, M.F. A woman in Canada. 1910
2135 Elkington, E.W. Canada, the land of hope. 1910
2211 Carrel, F. Canada's West & farther west. 1911
2221 Fraser, Sir J.F. Canada as it is. 1911
2273 Adams, J. Ten thousand miles through Canada. 1912
2334 Pullen-Burry, B. From Halifax to Vancouver. 1912
2355 Walker, E.G.F. Canadian trails. 1912
2364 Bellingham, E. Canada, the land of hope. 1913
2440A Beauvau-Craon, C.L.J.E.M.J.V., prince de. La survivance française. 1914
2773 Glendinning, J.C. Oh, Canada. 1921
2890 Jaray, G.L. De Québec à Vancouver. 1924
2907 Rigassi, G. A travers le Canada. 1924
2945 Maurault, O. A mari usque ad mare. 1925
3187 Harrison, M. Go West – go wise! 1930
3216 O'Hara, Mrs. M.L. Coast to coast in a puddle jumper. 1930
3284 Wade, M.S. Overlanders of '62. 1931

4 Overland Journeys from the Pacific

70 Franchère, G. Relation d'un voyage. 1820
89 Ermatinger, E. York Factory express journal. 1828
95 Cox, R. Columbia River. 1831
164 Ross, A. Fur hunters in the far west. 1855
530 Gordon, D.M. Mountain and prairie. 1880
1004 Cumberland, S.C. Queen's highway. 1887
1435 Boddy, A.A. By ocean, prairie and peak. 1896

5 Surveys, Topographical

293 Canada. Dept. of Sec. of State. Instructions to surveyors. 1870
322 Canada. Dept. of Sec. of State. Instructions to Lieut.-Gov. Archibald of Manitoba. 1871
382 Canada. Dept. of the Interior. Annual reports. 1874-1936
493 Canada. Dept. of the Interior. Extracts from surveyors' reports. 1879
602 Canada. Dept. of the Interior. Extracts from surveyors' reports. 1882
728 Canada. Dept. of the Interior. Extracts from surveyors' reports. 1884
893 Canada. Dept. of the Interior. Description of townships. 1886
1261 Dennis, J.S. Short history of surveys. 1892
1297 Canada. Dept. of the Interior. Description of Manitoba. 1893
2051 Directory of Didsbury townships. 1909

6 Description & Travel

A *General*

21 Umfreville, E. Present state of Hudson's Bay. 1790
34 Thompson, D. Narrative of his explorations. 1812
36 Henry, A. New light on history of N.W. 1814
71 Harmon, D.W. Journal of voyages and travels. 1820
77 Simpson, Sir G. Journal of occurrences in Athabasca. 1821
83 Simpson, Sir G. Fur trade and empire. 1825
94 Belcourt, G.A. Mon itinéraire ... à la Rivière-Rouge. 1831
106 Hargrave, J. Correspondence. 1843
110 Lefroy, Sir J.H. Diary of a magnetic survey. 1844

119 Ballantyne, R.M. Hudson's Bay. 1848
141 Laflèche, L.F.R. Lettre. 1851
156 Tytler, P.F. The northern coasts. 1853
165 Ross, A. Letters of a pioneer. 1855
175 Scripps, J.L. Underdeveloped portion of continent. 1856
191 Report on the North West Territories. 1857
196 Ermatinger, E. Hudson's Bay Territories. 1858
207 Dawson, S.J. Exploration between Superior & Red River. 1859
211 Hind, H.Y. North West Territory. 1859
212 Kane, P. Wanderings of an artist. 1859
215 Morris, A. H.B. & Pacific territories. 1859
217 Palliser, J. Exploration – B.N.A. 1859
218 Palliser, J. Progress of B.N.A. expedition. 1859
221 Hind, H.Y. Narrative of Red & Saskatchewan expeditions. 1860
222 Palliser, J. Exploration – B.N.A. 1860
225 Taylor, J.W. Northwest British America. 1860
233 U.S. Treas. Dept. Relations between U.S. and northwest British America. 1862
238 Palliser, J. Exploration – B.N.A. Journals. 1863
4373 Lasteyrie du Saillant, A.J. Territoire de la Compagnie de la baie d'Hudson. 1867
269 Corbett, G.O. Notes on Rupert's America. 1868
288 Taché, A.A. Esquisse sur le nord-ouest. 1869
301 Dawson, A.M. Our strength and their strength. 1870
321 Butler, Sir W.F. Report of his journey. 1871
318 North-West Territories. 1871
342 Butler, Sir W.F. Great lone land. 1872
349 Ross, P.R. Report on the north-west provinces and territories. 1872
356 Butler, Sir W.F. Wild north land. 1873
369 Horetzky, C. North-West of Canada. 1873
370 Langelier, J.C. Étude sur les territoires. 1873
376 Shantz, J.Y. Narrative of a journey. 1873
377 White, T. Our great West. 1873
379 Rupland: Our northern empire. 1874
412 Dawson, G.M. Report on the region of 49th parallel. 1875
426 Millman, T. Impressions of the West. 1875
429 Smyth, E.S. Report on the defences and mounted police. 1875
430 Southesk, Earl of. Saskatchewan and the Rocky Mountains. 1875
441 C.P.R. Description of the country. 1876
444 Featherstonhaugh, A. Operations of B.N.A. Boundary Commission. 1876
487 Trow, J. Manitoba and N.W.T. 1878
489 Chronicles by the way. 1879
501 Dowse, T. Manitoba and the Canadian North West. 1879
503 Fleming, Sir S. Report in reference to C.P.R. 1879
509 Robinson, H.M. Great fur land. 1879
533 Hall, E.H. Lands of plenty. 1880
539 Macdougall's guide to Manitoba and the North-West. 1880
558 Argyil, Duke of. Canadian North-West. 1881
555 Table of distances and description of trails. 1881
571 Chisholm and Dickson. Hand-book for Manitoba and the N.W. 1881
573 Dawson, A.M. North West Territories. 1881
586 Sutherland, A. Summer in prairie-land. 1881
587 Taylor, J.W. Central British America. 1881
591 Anglo-Canadian. Canada. 1882
595 Artigue, J. d'. Six years in the Canadian North-West. 1882
613 Carle, F.A. British Northwest; pen and sun sketches. 1882

632 Macoun, J. Manitoba and the great North-West. 1882
635 O'Halloran, J.S. Five weeks in Canada. 1882
653 Wiedersheim, E. Kanada; Reisebeschreibung und Bericht. 1882
654 Williams, W.H. Manitoba and the North-West. 1882
659 Bryce, G. Notes and comments on Harmon's journal. 1883
666 C.P.R. Official guide book to lands. 1883
667 Corbett, G.O. Vast resources & progress of Christianity. 1883
670 Dionne, N.E. États-Unis, Manitoba et Nord-Ouest. 1883
679 Hind, H.Y. Manitoba and N.W. frauds. 1883
688 Moore, J.G. 15 months round Manitoba & the N.W. 1883
714 Barneby, W.H. Life and labour in the far, far West. 1884
728 Canada. Dept. of the Interior. Extracts from surveyors' reports. 1884
735 C.P.R. Official guide book to lands. 1884
754 Jones, H. Railway notes in the North-West. 1884
760 Morris, A. Nova Britannia. 1884
766 Prance, C.C. Notes on America. 1884
767 Richardson, R.L. Visit of the British Association. 1884
773 Temple, Sir R. Address to the citizens of Winnipeg. 1884
802A Chittenden, N.H. Settlers, miners & tourists guide. 1885
808 Dawkins, W.B. Canada and the great N.W. 1885
812 Family Man. Shall we emigrate. 1885
821 Hill, A.S. From home to home. 1885
842 Ritchie, J.E. To Canada with emigrants. 1885
843 S., A. A summer trip to Canada. 1885
852 Tuttle, C.R. Our north land. 1885
890 Canada. Dept. of Agriculture. Esquisse générale du Nord-Ouest. 1886
893 Canada. Dept. of the Interior. Description of townships. 1886
925 Elliott, C. A trip to Canada & far N.W. 1886
930 Fream, W. Across Canada. 1886
948 Manitoba & N.W. Rly. Guide book to lands. 1886
1031 Thomas, T.H. Excursion of members of British Association. 1887
1055 Ham, G.H. The new West. 1888
1056 Hesse-Wartegg, E. von. Kanada und Neu-fundland. 1888
1102 Donkin, J.G. Trooper and redskin. 1889
1153 Campbell, J. Manitoba and the North-West. 1890
1166 Demanche, G. Au Canada et chez les peaux-rouges. 1890
1169 Dugas, G. Un voyageur des pays d'en haut. 1890
1194 Messiter, C.A. Sport and adventure. 1890
1201 Saxby, J.M.E. West-Nor'-West. 1890
1223 Foursin, P. Colonisation française. 1891
1226 McGusty, H.A. Two years in Man. and the N.W.T. 1891
1260 Davin, N.F. Homes for millions. 1892
1266 Hacault, L. Les colonies belges et françaises. 1892
1280 Ralph, J. On Canada's frontier. 1892
1363 Johnstone, C.L. Winter and summer excursions. 1894
1391 Benoist, C. Les Français et le Nord-Ouest canadien. 1895
1413 McDougall, J. Forest, lake and prairie. 1895
1426 Van Bruyssel, F. Le Canada. 1895
1450 McDougall, J. Saddle, sled and snowshoe. 1896
1460 Marriott, S. To Winnipeg, Manitoba and back. 1896
1474 Ward, B.P. Roughing it in the N.W.T. 1896
1510 Percy, A.H. Journal of two excursions. 1897
1542 Graham, F.U. Notes of a sporting expedition. 1898
1546 McDougall, J. Pathfinding on plain and prairie. 1898

2972 Mézl, F. Kanada. 1926
4394 Warren, C.H. Wild goose chase. 1927
3099 Ray, J.E. Things seen in Canada. 1928
3113 Wollschläger, A. Mit zwanzig Dollar in den wilden Westen. 1928
3131 Dahlin, G.L. Canada, skisser och glimtar. 1929
3171 Canada. National Parks Service. Playgrounds of the prairies. 193-
3187 Harrison, M. Go West - go wise. 1930
3207 Mehrhardt-Ihlow, C. Ausgerechnet Canada. 1930
3213 Munday, Mrs. L. A mounty's wife. 1930
3214 Niven, F.J. Canada west. 1930
3224 Schwerla, C.B. Kanada im Faltboot. 1930
3239 Yates, R.L. When I was a harvester. 1930
3260 Hurd, W.B. Agriculture, climate and population. 1931
3268 Mehrhardt-Ihlow, C. Auf Bummel und Pirsch in Canada. 1931
3286 Wilbois, J. Un pays neuf. 1931
3345 Leichner, G. Abenteuerliches Kanada. 1933
3357 Sutton, F.A. One-arm Sutton. 1933
3389 Mackintosh, W.A. Prairie settlement. 1934
3431 Ebbell, B.J. Eventyrets land. 1935
3478 Stricker, J. Erlebnisse eines Schweizers in Kanada. 1935
3482 Walker, J.H. A Scotsman in Canada. 1935
3526 Orr, J.E. Times of refreshing. 1936
3566 Leacock, S.B. My discovery of the West. 1937
3611 Crocombe, L. An editor goes West. 1938
3618 Düesberg, G. Zur wildnis ferner wälder. 1938
3707 Weekes, M.L. Last buffalo hunter. 1939
3806 Matthaei, L. Irgendwo drüben in Kanada. 1942
4013 Sissons, C.K. John Kerr. 1946
4041 Jaques, F.P. Canadian spring. 1947
4097 Gislason, I. Prairie panorama. 1948
4098 Gradet, R. Images du Far-West. 1948
4112 Lefebvre, J.J. Voyage-éclair dans l'Ouest Canadien. 1948
4334 Woodcock, G. Ravens and prophets. 1952

B *Manitoba*

351 Wagner, W. Einwanderung nach Manitoba. 1872
375 Scott, D.H. Guide-Ontario to Manitoba. 1873
376 Shantz, J.Y. Narrative of a journey. 1873
432 Trow, J. Trip to Manitoba. 1875
446 Hamilton, J.C. The prairie province. 1876
464 O'Leary, P. Travels and experiences. 1877
490 Barnes, H.H. Journal of a trip to Manitoba. 1879
493 Canada. Dept. of the Interior. Extracts from surveyors' reports. 1879
508 Lamothe, H. de. Cinq mois chez les Français. 1879
514 Armstrong, L.O. Southern Manitoba and Turtle Mountain. 1880
525 Currie, D. Letters of Rusticus. 1880
528 Fitzgibbon, M.A. Trip to Manitoba. 1880
541 Macoun, J. Letter to deputy minister. 1880
542 Mitchell, P. West & North-West. 1880
543 Moore, T. Tour through Canada in 1879. 1880
550 Van Dyke, H. Red River of the north. 1880
553 Wyatt, G.H. Journey from Liverpool. 1880
559 Barrette, J.E.T. Récit d'aventures. 1881
564 Canada. Dept. of Agriculture. Canada in 1880. 1881

578 La Londe, A. de. Trois mois au Canada. 1881
582A Munro, W.F. Prairies of the North-West. 1881
584 Rae, W.F. Newfoundland to Manitoba. 1881
641 Pringle, C.A. Manitoba & the North-West. 1882
644 Rae, W.F. Facts about Manitoba. 1882
653 Wiedersheim, E. Kanada. 1882
676 Fraser, H. Trip to the Dominion. 1883
693 Pocock, Sir S.J. Across the prairie lands. 1883
704 Vekeman, G. Lettres d'un émigrant. 1883
718 Begg, A. 17 years in Canadian North-West. 1884
748 Hall, M.G.C. A lady's life on a farm. 1884
803 Christy, R.M. Manitoba described. 1885
932 Galt, F.J. Alia delectant alios. 1886
966 Scudder, S.H. Winnipeg country. 1886
1070 Norman, H. The prairies of Manitoba and who live on them. 1888
1271 Manitoba official hand-book. 1892
1276 Pennefather, J.P. 13 years on the prairies. 1892
1297 Canada. Dept. of the Interior. Description of Manitoba. 1893
1318 Legge, A.O. Sunny Manitoba. 1893
1374 Schultz, Sir J.C. Old Crow Wing Trail. 1894
1415 McKellar, H. Extended notes on geography. 1895
1550 Murray, D.L. Breezy reminiscences. 1898
1606 Fonseca, W.G. da. On the St. Paul trail. 1900
1656 Manitoba. Dept. of Agric. & Immigration. Canada's centre is Manitoba. 1901
1687 Maclean, J. Synopsis of lectures on Manitoba. 1902
1840 Thorgeirsson, O.S. Handsbok hin yngri. 1905
1943 Mitchell, R. Chronicle of an expedition. 1907
2036 British Assoc. for the Advancement of Science. Handbook to Winnipeg and Manitoba. 1909
2297 Gill, E.A.W. A Manitoba chore boy. 1912
2359 Winnipeg, Selkirk & Lake Winnipeg Rly. Picnic time. 1912
2527 Trémaudan, A.H. de. Hudson Bay road. 1915
2599A Manitoba. Northern Manitoba. 1917
2621 Canada. Dept. of the Interior. The new Manitoba district. 1918
2631A Manitoba. Manitoba's northland. 1918
2693 Bramble, C.A. Land of the lobstick. 1920
2848 Grove, F.P. Over prairie trails. 1923
2885 Constantin-Weyer, M. Manitoba. 1924
2965 Karger, K. 14 Jahre unter Englaendern. 1926
3112 Winnipeg Evening Tribune. Do you know Manitoba? 1928
3130 Constantin-Weyer, M. Clairière. 1929
3244 Canada. Dept. of the Interior. Manitoba. 1931
3368A Barker, B. North of 53. 1934
3405 Stern, J.A. To Hudson's Bay by paddle & portage. 1934
3440 Herklots, H.G.G. The first winter. 1935
3474A Sevareid, A.E. Canoeing with the Cree. 1935
3735 Manitoba. Bureau of Travel & Publicity. Manitoba, inside the rim of adventure. 194–
3967 Wood, H.E. Facts about Manitoba. 1945
4117 Manitoba. Bureau of Travel & Publicity. Manitoba's romantic northland. 1948
4167 Manitoba. Travel & Publicity Bureau. Guide book to Manitoba. 1949
4194 Canadian Red Cross Society. Call 320, a record of the 1950 flood. 1950
4242 Harrington, E.D. Manitoba roundabout. 1951

C *North West Territories*

889 Canada. Dept. of Agriculture. Census of N.W.T., 1884-5. 1886

D *Saskatchewan*

422 McLean, J. Notes from the Bishop's journal. 1875
1737A Mullins, J.D. Seven days on the prairie. 1903?
2081 Saskatchewan, Canada. 1909?
2116 C.P.R. Heart of the Saskatchewan valley. 1910
2119 C.P.R. Where wheat is king. 1910
2130 Crean, F.J.P. New Northwest exploration. 1910
2342A Saskatchewan. Dept. of Agriculture. Saskatchewan. 1912
2459 Gilbert, L. La Saskatchewan. 1914
2655 Canada. Dept. of the Interior. Province of Sask. 1919
2695 Buchanan, A. Wild life in Canada. 1920
2919 Canadian Authors' Assoc. Saskatchewan Branch. Saskatchewan, her infinite variety. 1925
2928 Gravel, L.J.P. La Saskatchewan, le pays des blés d'or. 1925
3155A Saskatchewan year book 1929. 1929
3258 Huber, A.O. Auf wilden Pfaden im neuen Kanada. 1931
3267 Macpherson, A.W. Northern summers. 1931
3302 Huber, A.O. Roten und weissen Abenteurern in Kanada. 1932
3343 Kenderdine, G. Twelve views of Saskatchewan. 1933
3534 Saskatchewan. Bureau of Publications. Tourist trips. 1936
4126 Saskatchewan. Bureau of Publications. The new north. 1948
4227 Tyre, R. Along the highway. 1950
4361 Moon, R.J. This is Saskatchewan. 1953

POSTSCRIPT

Baker, E. Bits of Saskatchewan in colour. (Saskatoon, 1955)
Olson, S.F. This lonely land. (Toronto, 1961)
McCourt, E. Saskatchewan. (Toronto, 1968)

E *Alberta*

579 McEachran, D.M. Journey over the plains. 1881
580 McEachran, D.M. Notes of a trip to Bow River. 1881
837 Panton, J.H. Rambles in the North-West. 1885
1042 Bryce, G. Holiday rambles between Winnipeg and Victoria. 1888
1053 Fitzgerald, J.G. Alberta. 1888
1138 Alexander, G. The new Canada. 1890
1552 Russell, F. Exploration in the far north. 1898
1839 Tait, C.M. Making of a province. 1905
1865 Cockburn, J.A. Souvenir views of Alberta. 1906
1981 Edmonton. Board of Trade. All-red route to the Arctic. 1908
2004 Mair, C. Through the Mackenzie basin. 1908
2015 Ouellette, J.A. Le jardin de l'Alberta Sud. 1908
2030 Weijers, A. De waarheid over Alberta. 1908
2115 C.P.R. Concerning central Alberta. 1910?
2130 Crean, F.J.P. New Northwest exploration. 1910
2170 Robins, K.N. Province of Alberta. 1910
2203 Canada. Dept. of the Interior. Abstracts of reports on townships. 1911
2248 Ouellette, J.A. L'Alberta, région centrale. 1911
2267 Thomas, M.W. The truth about Canada. 1911
2305 Hotchkiss, C.S. International Dry-Farming Congress. 1912

2348 Thwaite, L. Province of Alberta. 1912
2443 Bickersteth, J.B. Land of open doors. 1914
2451 Canada. Dept. of the Interior. Abstracts of reports on townships. 1914
2475 Murphy, E.G. Seeds of pine. 1914
2510 MacBeth, R.G. Peace River letters. 1915
2554 McEachran, D.M. Impressions of pioneers. 1916
2611 Sternberg, C.H. Hunting dinosaurs in the bad lands. 1917
2677 McCaig, J. Alberta. 1919
2799 Alberta. Publicity Commissioner. Province of Alberta. 1922
2829 Tourist Assoc. of South Eastern B.C. and Southern Alta. Scenic heart of the Canadian Rockies. 1922
2842 Church of the Brethren. Souvenir of Alberta. 1923
2870 Schurck, E. Kanada. Licht-und Schattenbilder. 1923
2903 Otto, M. In kanadischer Wildnis. 1924
2914 Alberta. Dept. of Agric. Province of Alberta. 1925
2915 Alberta. Publicity Bureau. Booklet of information. 1925
3024 Hasell, F.H.E. Through Western Canada in a caravan. 1927
3043 Wallace, J.N. Passes of the Rocky Mountains. 1927
3057 Borel, A. Croquis du Far-West canadien. 1928
3189 Imrie, J.M. Peace River. 1930
3194 Kitto, F.H. Edmonton, Prince George, Peace River triangle. 1932
3245 Christen, M. Feux et frimas. 1931
3621 Ells, S.C. Northland trails. 1938
3847 Menzies, D. The Alaska highway. 1943
4287 Dempsey, H.A. Historic sites of the province of Alberta. 1952
4307 Liddell, K.E. This is Alberta. 1952

POSTSCRIPT
Liddell, K.E. Alberta revisited. (Toronto, 1960)
Kroetsch, R.P. Alberta. (Toronto, 1968)

F PRO PELLE CUTEM

1 Hudson's Bay Company

8 Dobbs, A. Account of countries adjoining Hudson's Bay. 1744
10 Great Britain. Parliament. H. of C. Committee on Hudson's Bay. Papers. 1749
11 Great Britain. Parliament. H. of C. Committee on Hudson's Bay. Report. 1749
12 Robson, J. Six years residence in Hudson's Bay. 1752
19 H.B.C. Cumberland House journals, 1775-82
21 Umfreville, E. Present state of Hudson's Bay. 1790
22 Hearne & Turnor. Journals. 1792
38 H.B.C. Royal charter of 1670. 1816
55 Gale, S. Notice on the claims of the H.B.C. 1819
72 H.B.C. Instructions relative to administration of justice. 182_?
73 H.B.C. Ordinance for administration of justice. 182_?
75 Garry, N. Diary. 1821
76 H.B.C. Copy of deed poll. 1821
77 Simpson, Sir G. Journal of occurrences in Athabasca. 1821
79 Robertson, C. Correspondence book. 1822
83 Simpson, Sir G. Fur trade and empire. 1825
89 Ermatinger, E. York Factory express journal. 1828

96 Rupert's Land. Northern Dept. Council. Minutes. 1821-31
97 H.B.C. Deed poll. 1834
104 Great Britain. Colonial Office. Hudson's Bay Company ... copy of charter. 1842
106 Hargrave, J. Correspondence. 1843
107 Rupert's Land. Northern Dept. Council. Minutes. 1830-43
114 Isbister, A.K. Few words on the H.B.C. 1847
119 Ballantyne, R.M. Hudson's Bay. 1848
120 Red River Settlement and H.B.C. 1848
123 Thom, A. Charge to Grand Jury. 1848
124 Thom, A. A few remarks on a pamphlet. 1848
127 Fitzgerald, J.E. Examination of the charter. 1849
128 Great Britain. Colonial Office. Hudson's Bay Company. (Red River Settlement) 1849
129 McLean, J. Notes of a 25 years' service. 1849
130 Martin, R.M. Hudson's Bay Territories. 1849
132 Great Britain. Colonial Office. Hudson's Bay Company. 1850
147 Hargrave, L.M. Letters. 1852
177 H.B.C. Canada west, & Indians. 1857
178 Hudson's Bay question. 1857
180 Canada. Gov.-Gen. All lands sold to H.B.C. 1857
181 Canada. Gov.-Gen. Corr. between govt. & Draper. 1857
182 Canada. Gov.-Gen. Return of any charters, etc. 1857
183 Canada. Leg. Assembly. Select Committee on H.B.C. Report. 1857
185 Draper, W.H. Hudson's Bay Company. 1857
186 Financial Reform Assoc. H.B.C. vs. Magna Charta. 1857
187 Freeport, A. Case of the H.B.C. 1857
188 Great Britain. Parliament. H. of C. Select Committee on the H.B.C. Report. 1857
191 Report on the North West Territories. 1857
192 H.B.C. & the late government. 1858
193 Canada. Governor-General. Message on the subject of H.B. Territory. 1858
194 Canada. Governor General. Return on grants of land to H.B.C. 1858
196 Ermatinger, E. Hudson's Bay Territories. 1858
197 Great Britain. Colonial Office. Hudson's Bay Company ... copies of correspondence. 1858
208 A few reasons for a crown colony. 1859
209 Great Britain. Colonial Office. Papers re H.B.C. 1859
215 Morris, A. Hudson's Bay & Pacific territories. 1859
224 Smithsonian Institution. Circular to officers of H.B.C. 1860
228 Synge, M.H. The country v. the company. 1861
234 Canada. Gov.-Gen. Papers on opening of N.W.T. 1863
241 Synge, M.H. Colony of Rupert's Land. 1863
242 Synge, M.H. Rupert Land. 1863
245 Nelson, J. Hudson's Bay Company, what is it? 1864
247 H.B.C. List of Adventurers. 1865
255 H.B.C. A million, shall we take it? 1866
256 Dodds, J. Hudson's Bay Co., its position and prospects. 1866
257 Rawlings, T. What shall we do with H.B. Territory? 1866
268 Canada. Dept. of Sec. of State. Return re H.B. Territory. 1868
269 Corbett, G.O. Notes on Rupert's America. 1868
271 Précis on the H.B.C. 1868
272 Great Britain. Laws, statutes, etc. Hudson's Bay Company. 1868
273 H.B.C. Report of a general meeting. 1868
277 Canada. Delegates on acquisition of Rupert's Land. Report. 1869
281 Great Britain. Colonial Office. Canada (Rupert's Land). 1869

282 Great Britain. Colonial Office. Hudson's Bay Company – letter to the Governor. 1869
283 H.B.C. Correspondence with Government. 1869
284 H.B.C. Report of proceedings. 1869
305 Great Britain. Treasury. Canada (Rupert's Land). 1870
476 Canada. Department of Secretary of State. All correspondence between the H.B.C. and Dominion government. 1878
509 Robinson, H.M. Great fur land. 1879
593 Armit, W. Hudson's Bay Co. report on landed property. 1882
594 Armit, W. Hudson's Bay Co. report on the Company's trade. 1882
599 Brydges, C.J. Hudson's Bay Company. 1882
623 Fleming, Sir S. Observations on the land policy of H.B.C. 1882
697 Royal Society of Canada. Circular to officers of H.B.C. 1883
749 H.B.C. Bye-laws of Adventurers of England. 1884
750 H.B.C. Adventurers of England. Supplemental charter. 1884
1008 H.B.C. Deed poll. 1887
1032 Watkin, Sir E.W. Canada and the States. 1887
1104 Ellis, G.E. Hudson Bay Company. 1889
1267 H.B.C. Supplemental charter. 1892
1280 Ralph, J. On Canada's frontier. 1892
1543 H.B.C. History. 1898
1548 Martin, A.E.S. Hudson's Bay Co's land tenures. 1898
1587 Wilson, H.B. The great Company. 1899
1593 Bryce, G. Remarkable history. 1900
1769 Herkenrath, A. Canada und die H.B.C. 1904
1797 Bryce, G. Mackenzie, Selkirk, Simpson. 1905
1896 Veterans of the Fur Trade Assoc. Ownership of 7,455,552 acres. 1906
1990 Laut, A.C. Conquest of great Northwest. 1908
2076 Reed, C.B. Masters of the wilderness. 1909
2309 H.B.C. Company of Adventurers. 1912
2310 H.B.C. Proposed supplemental charter. 1912
2311 H.B.C. The supplemental charter. 1912
2383 Cowie, I. The company of adventurers. 1913
2467 Laut, A.C. The Adventurers of England. 1914
2479 Pioneers of Rupert's Land. Review of claims. 1914
2481 Preston, W.T.R. Life and times of Strathcona. 1914
2518 Oliver, E.H. Canadian North-West. 1915
2521 Pedley, J.W. Biography of Strathcona. 1915
2735 Prest, J. Hudson's Bay Co. historical pageant. 1920
2741 Schooling, Sir W. Governor & Company of Adventurers. 1920
2784 McKenzie, N.M.W.J. Men of the H.B.C. 1921
2930 H.B.C. historical exhibit. 1925
2971 Merriman, R.O. Bison and the fur trade. 1926
2989 Scriven, G.P. Story of H.B.C. 1926
3079A H.B.C. will expose to sale the following goods. 1928
3068 Compagnie de la Baie d'Hudson. Société anonyme. 1928
3110 Watson, R. Hudson's Bay Company. 1928
3147 Moberly, H.J. When fur was king. 1929
3190 Innis, H.A. Fur trade in Canada. 1930
3226 Stewart, D.A. Early Assiniboine trading-posts. 1930
3235 Voorhis, E. Historic forts and trading-posts. 1930
3259 H.B.C. Charters, etc. 1931
3261 Reflections of Inkyo. 1931
3274 Pinkerton, R.E. Gentlemen adventurers. 1931

3354 Skinner, C.L. Beaver, kings and cabins. 1933
3441 H.B.C. List of books. 1935
3442 H.B.C. Petit histoire. 1935
3518 MacKay, D. The honourable company. 1936
3571 Mackenzie, C.W. Donald Mackenzie. 1937
3577 Morton, A.S. Under western skies. 1937
3693 Morton, A.S. History of the Canadian West. 1939
3883 Morton, A.S. Sir George Simpson. 1944
4014 Tharp, L.H. Company of adventurers. 1946
4038 H.B.C. Milestones in the progress of the Company. 1947
4163 MacGregor, J.G. Blankets and beads. 1949
4182 Weekes, M.L. Trader King. 1949
4192 Campbell, M.W. The Saskatchewan. 1950
4298 Johnson, G. History of Ft. Ellice. 1952

2 North West Company

18 Henry, A. Travels and adventures. 1809
24 M'Gillivray, D. Journal. 1795
25 Mackenzie, Sir A. Voyages from Montreal. 1801
28 Gates, C.M. Five fur traders. 1805
29 Larocque, F.A. Journal. 1805
33 Atcheson, N. Origin and progress of N.W.C. 1811
36 Henry, A. New light on history of Northwest. 1814
42 N.W.C. Memorial of M'Tavish, etc. 1816
43 Selkirk, Earl of. Lord Selkirk and N.W.C. 1816
44 Selkirk, Earl of. Sketch of British fur trade. 1816
61 Masson, L.F.R. Bourgeois de la Compagnie du Nord-Ouest. 1819
71 Harmon, D.W. Journal of voyages and travels. 1820
76 H.B.C. Copy of the deed poll. 1821
77 Simpson, Sir G. Journal of occurrences in Athabasca. 1821
79 Robertson, C. Correspondence book. 1822
84 McGillivray, S. Letter to creditors. 1827
85 Mackenzie, H. Letter to S. M'Gillivray. 1827
87 Wallace, W.S. Documents re N.W.C. 1827
263 Conolly, J. Superior court. 1867
267 Woolrich, J. Testament solennel. 1867?
1169 Dugas, G. Un voyageur des pays d'en haut. 1890
1593 Bryce, G. Remarkable history of H.B.C. 1900
2624 Davidson, G.C. North West Company. 1918
3054 Bell, C.N. Earliest fur traders on upper Red River. 1928
3060 Burpee, L.J. Two western adventurers. 1928
3159 Wallace, J.N. Wintering partners on Peace River. 1929
3190 Innis, H.A. Fur trade in Canada. 1930
3191 Innis, H.A. Peter Pond. 1930
3211 Morton, A.S. North West Company. 1930
3226 Stewart, D.A. Early Assiniboine trading posts. 1930
3235 Voorhis, E. Historic forts and trading posts. 1930
3571 Mackenzie, C.W. Donald Mackenzie. 1937
3693 Morton, A.S. History of the Canadian West. 1939
4255 Moore, C.A. Lords of the lakes and forests. 1951

POSTSCRIPT
Rich, E.E. The fur trade and the Northwest to 1857. (Toronto, 1967)

G RED RIVER SETTLEMENT

201 Minnesota. H. of Representatives. Overland route to British Oregon. 1858
207 Dawson, S.J. Exploration between Superior and Red River. 1859
239 Red River Settlement. Citizens. Memorial. 1863
266 Memorandum in support of an address. 1867
304 Great Britain. Colonial Office. Red River. 1870
315 Taylor, J.W. Correspondence, 1859-70. 1968
328 Hargrave, J.J. Red River. 1871
560 Begg, A. Great Canadian North West. 1881
672 Dugas, G. La première Canadienne. 1883
792 Bryce, G. Old settlers of Red River. 1885
1089 Bryce, G. Original letters re Selkirk Settlement. 1889
1237 Seven Oaks. 1891
1278 Pritchard, J. Glimpses of the past. 1892
1308 Chetlain, A.L. Red River colony. 1893
1319 MacBeth, J. Social customs and amusements. 1893
1375 Schultz, Sir J.A. Speech on unveiling of Seven Oaks monument. 1894
1436 Bryce, G. Worthies of old Red River. 1896
1500 MacBeth, R.G. Farm life in the Selkirk colony. 1897
1501 MacBeth, R.G. Selkirk settlers in real life. 1897
1548 Martin, A.E.S. Hudson's Bay Co's land tenures. 1898
1639 Bryce, Mrs. M.S. Early Red River culture. 1901
1682 Hunt, F.L. Britain's one Utopia. 1902
1797 Bryce, G. Selkirk. 1905
1869 Dugas, G. Histoire de l'Ouest canadien. 1906
1896 Veterans of the Fur Trade Assoc. Ownership of 7,455,552 acres. 1906
1944 Morice, A.G. Aux sources de l'histoire manitobaine. 1907
2038 Bryce, G. Romantic settlement of Lord Selkirk's colonists. 1909
2108 Canada. Archives. Red River Settlement. 1910
2280 Bryce, G. Life of Selkirk. 1912
2518 Oliver, E.H. Canadian North-West. 1915
2530 Wood, L.A.L. Red River colony. 1915
2555 Martin, C.B. Lord Selkirk's work. 1916
2850 Healy, W.J. Women of Red River. 1923
2970 Martin, W. Lord Selkirk. 1926
3184 Gunn, J.J. Echoes of the Red. 1930
3204 McWilliams, M. All along the river. 1930
3571 Mackenzie, C.W. Donald Mackenzie. 1937
3574 MacLeod, M.A. Bells of Red River. 1937
3697A Putnam, A.M. Selkirk settlers and church at Belfast. 1939
3813 Pritchett, J.P. Red River valley. 1942
4024 Bill, F.A. Life on Red River. 1947

H REBELLIONS AND REGIMENTAL HISTORIES

1 Red River Rebellion

289 Red River insurrection. 1870
290 Begg, A. Red River journal, 1869-70. 1956
291 Broadsides of Red River Disturbances, 1869-70
293 Canada. Dept. of Sec. of State. Instructions to surveyors. 1870
295 Canada. Gov.-Gen. Correspondence connected with recent occurrences. 1870
297 Chesson, F.W. Red River insurrection. 1870

299 Corbett, G.O. An appeal to Gladstone. 1870
300 Corbett, G.O. Red River Rebellion. 1870
302 Emslie, J. Journal of expedition to Fort Garry. 1870
303 Great Britain. Colonial Office. Correspondence re recent disturbances. 1870
307 McDougall, W. Red River Rebellion. 1870
308 Major, J.C. Red River expedition. 1870
309 Memorial of people of Rupert's Land. 1870
310 Morton, W.L. Manitoba, birth of a province. 1965
311 Rupert's Land. Legislature. Bills. 1870
312 Rupert's Land. Legislature. Minutes of proceedings. 1870
313 Strathcona, Lord. North-West Territories. 1870
316 Thibault, J.B. North-West Territories. 1870
317 United States. President Grant. McDougall at Pembina. 1870
319 Begg, A. Creation of Manitoba. 1871
323 Canada. Dept. of Sec. of State. Claims consequent upon the insurrection. 1871
326 Dawson, S.J. Report on Red River expedition. 1871
327 Great Britain. War Office. Expedition to Red River. 1871
329 Huyshe, G.L. Red River expedition. 1871
330 Irvine, M.B. Red River expedition. 1871
332 Mills, D. Blunders of the Dominion Government. 1871
335 Riddell, H.S.H. Red River expedition. 1871
337 Sulte, B. Expédition militaire. 1871
339 Canadian who visited Manitoba. Ontario and Manitoba (North West Rebellion) 1872
342 Butler, Sir W.F. Great lone land. 1872
343 Canada. Dept. of Sec. of State. Fenian invasion and Riel. 1872
346 Griffin, J.A. From Toronto to Ft. Garry. 1872
352 Wallace, N.W. Rebellion in Red River Settlement. 1872
366 Denison, G.T. Reminiscences of Red River Rebellion. 1873
368 Great Britain. Colonial Office. Correspondence re question of amnesty. 1873
385 Canada. Parliament. H. of C. Select Committee. Report on causes of difficulties. 1874
388 L'Evénement. Au pilori. 1874
391 Foran, T.P. Trial of Ambroise Lepine. 1874
397 Lepine, A.D. Preliminary investigation and trial. 1874
399 Riel, L. L'amnistie. 1874
400 Taché, A.A. L'amnistie. 1874
401 Taché, A.A. On the amnesty question. 1874
402 Taché, A.A. The Northwest difficulty. 1874
404 Revue de la session parlementaire de 1875
409 Canada. Gov.-Gen. Despatches re Lepine's sentence. 1875
411 Conservative Party. Les Rouges et leurs oeuvres. 1875
414 Exemplification of proceedings re Riel. 1875
427 The Queen vs. Louis Riel. 1875
431 Taché, A.A. The amnesty again. 1875
450 Wood, E.B. Report on claims for apprehension of murderers of Scott. 1876
478 Cinq années d'administration réformiste. 1878
630 McArthur, A. Causes of rising. 1882
884 Boulton, C.A. Reminiscences of rebellions. 1886
987 Bell, C.N. Selkirk Settlement. 1887
988 Bell, C.N. Some Red River Settlement history. 1887
1062 McMicken, G. Abortive Fenian raid. 1888
1077 Taché, A.A. Fenian raid. 1888
1152 Bryce, G. Two provisional governments in Manitoba. 1890

1445 Harman, S.B. 'Twas 26 years ago. 1896
1516 Young, G. Manitoba memories. 1897
1545 MacBeth, R.G. Making of the Canadian West. 1898
1815 Dugas, G. Histoire véridique. 1905
1944 Morice, A.G. Aux sources de l'histoire manitobaine. 1907
2059 Harwood, C.A. de L. Fort Garry convention. 1909
2071 O'Donnell, J.H. Manitoba as I saw it. 1909
2747 Tennant, J.F. Rough times, 1870-1920
2796 Trémaudan, A.H. de. Riel et la naissance du Manitoba. 1921
3172 Charette, G.J. Manitoba jubilee. 1930
3402 Saint-Léandre, Soeur. L'oeuvre véridique de Riel. 1934
3463 Morice, A.G. Critical history of Red River insurrection. 1935
3481 Trémaudan, A.H. de. Histoire de la nation métisse. 1935
3515 Kreutzweiser, E.E. Red River insurrection. 1936
3542 Stanley, G.F.G. Birth of Western Canada. 1936
3775 Rumilly, R. Riel. 1941
3921 Groulx, L. Louis Riel. 1945
4240 Davidson, W.M. Life and times of Riel. 1951
4296 Howard, J.K. Strange empire. 1952
4347 Frémont, D. Les secrétaires de Riel. 1953

2 Saskatchewan Rebellion

780 À la mémoire de Louis Riel. 1885
781 Batoche polka, etc. 1885
782 Adam, G.M. Canadian North-West. 1885
783 Allen, C.W. Volunteer land grants. 1885
785 Bellerose, J.H. Assemblée pour protester contre l'exécution. 1885
786 Blake, E. Disturbance in the North-West. 1885
787 Blake, E. Disturbance in the North-West. 1885
790 Broughall, G. The 90th on active service. 1885
793 Campbell, Sir A. In the case of Riel. 1885
796 Canada. Dept. of the Interior. Papers with respect to commission on half-breed claims. 1885
802 Chapleau, Sir J.A. La question Riel. 1885
809 Deriares, J. Riel. 1885
810 Dunlevie, H.G. Our volunteers in the North-West. 1885
818 Girouard, D. Louis Riel. 1885
819 Gowanlock, T. Two months in the camp of Big Bear. 1885
820 Haultain, T.A. Riel's second rebellion. 1885
822 Irvine, A.G. Official diary. 1885
823 Laidlaw, A. From the St. Lawrence to the North Sask. 1885
825 Logan, J.E. A cry from the Saskatchewan. 1885
826 Louis Riel and the N.W. Rebellion. 1885
832 Le Monde. Insurrection du Nord-Ouest. 1885
833 Montpetit, A.N. Riel à la Rivière-du-Loup. 1885
834 Mulvaney, C.P. History of North-West Rebellion. 1885
838 Pedro, Don. Sketches dedicated to the veterans of _85. 1885?
840 La Presse. Louis Riel, martyr. 1885
846 Sherlock, R.A. Experiences of the Halifax Battalion. 1885
848 Taché, A.A. La situation. 1885
851 Tremblay, E. Riel: réponse à Monsieur Chapleau. 1885
855 White, T. Facts for the people. 1885
856 White, T. North West administration. 1885

857 Winnipeg war sketches. 1885
858 The Witness. The Riel Rebellion. 1885
861 L'histoire d'un crime. 1886?
865 Le mot de la fin. 1886
866 Le peuple vs. Sir John. 1886
867 La question Riel. Les griefs des métis. 1886
868 The Riel Rebellion. 1886
869 True inwardness of North West Rebellion exposed. 1886
872 Bayer, C. Riel; drame historique. 1886
873 Beauregard, G. Le 9me bataillon au Nord-Ouest. 1886
879 Blake, E. Execution of Louis Riel. 1886
880 Blake, E. General review - Riel. 1886
881 Blake, E. Ministers on trial. 1886
882 Blake, E. North-West affairs. 1886
883 Blake, E. North-West Rebellion. 1886
884 Boulton, C.A. Reminiscences of rebellions. 1886
888 Canada. Auditor-General. Expenditures. 1886
895 Canada. Dept. of Militia and Defence. Medical and surgical history. 1886
896 Canada. Dept. of Militia and Defence. Report upon the suppression of the rebellion. 1886
894 Canada. Dept. of the Interior. Claims to land in half-breed grant. 1886
897 Canada. Dept. of Sec. of State. Documents forming record in the cases against the parties tried. 1886
898 Canada. Dept. of Sec. of State. Copies of papers found at Batoche. 1886
899 Canada. Dept. of Sec. of State. Copies of depositions in favor of half-breeds. 1886
900 Canada. Dept. of Sec. of State. Instructions to Major Bell, etc. 1886
901 Canada. Dept. of Sec. of State. Instructions to commissioners reporting on losses. 1886
903 Canada. Dept. of Sec. of State. Epitome of documents. 1886
904 Canada. Privy Council. Committee on pensions. Report. 1886
910 Caron, Sir J.P.R.A. Discours sur la question Riel. 1886
911 Chapleau, Sir J.A. Speech on the motion to blame the government for executing Riel. 1886
916 Comité de collaborateurs. La mort de Riel. 1886?
917 La croisade anti-française. 1886
918 Curran, J.J. Debate on Riel. 1886
919 Daoust, C.R. Cent-vingt jours de service actif. 1886
920 DeMolinari, M.G. Au Canada et aux montagnes rocheuses. 1886
921 Desaulniers, G.L. L'absolution avant la bataille. 1886
922 Dixon, L. Halifax to the Saskatchewan. 1886
923 Documents ... plaintes des métis. 1886?
926 Entragues, L. de St. H. d'. The Soudan campaign. 1886
927 L'Etendard. Polémiques et documents. 1886
928 Faucher de Saint-Maurice, N.H.E. Discours sur la question Riel. 1886
929 Flynn, E.J. Affaire Riel. 1886
933 Girouard, D. Discours sur l'exécution. 1886
939 Jackson, T.W. Views of a Conservative on the rebellion. 1886
944 Laurier, Sir W. Speech on Riel question. 1886
950 Mercier, H. Discours sur la question Riel. 1886
951 Mousseau, J.O. Une page d'histoire. 1886
954 One Who Knows. Gibbet of Regina. 1886
957 Paquin, E. Riel; tragédie. 1886
961 Riel, L. Queen vs. L. Riel. 1886
974 Tassé, J. La question Riel. 1886

975 Thompson, J.S.D. Discours. 1886
976 Thompson, J.S.D. Execution of Riel. 1886
978 White, T. Northwest administration. 1886
981 Élections de 1887. 1887
982 La rébellion du Nord-Ouest. 1887
983 Le véritable Riel. 1887
984 Archambault, J.L. Étude politique. 1887
990 Bryant, W.F. Blood of Abel. 1887
993 Canada. Dept. of Militia & Defence. Continuation of appendix no.4 of report of 18 May, 1886. 1887
994 Canada. Dept. of Militia & Defence. Report of Lieut.-Col. W.H. Jackson. 1887
995 Canada. Dept. of Militia & Defence. Report of Maj.-Gen. Laurie. 1887
996 Canada. Dept. of the Interior. Northwest Rebellion. 1887
997 Canada. Dept. of Sec. of State. Persons recommended for scrip. 1887
1001 Clark, D. Psycho-medical history of Riel. 1887
1002 Conservative Party. Riel contre l'église catholique. 1887
1011 Liberal Party. The 'Boodle Brigade.' 1887
1014 McMillan, D. Letters and extracts on Riel question. 1887
1019 Ord, L.R. Reminiscences of a bungle. 1887
1041 Bryant, W.F. Memorial in the matter of Riel. 1888
1044 Canada. Army. Fusiliers. Log of the 7th Fusiliers. 1888
1122 Ottawa. Citizens' Committee. Ceremony of unveiling a bronze statue. 1889
1123 Ouimet, A. Vérité sur la question métisse. 1889
1131 U.S. President Harrison. Message on case of Riel. 1889
1145 Blake, E. On the Bremner furs. 1890
1156 Canada. Parliament. H. of C. Select Committee on C. Bremner's furs. Report. 1890
1174 Garçon, A. Quatre hommes: (Riel). 1890
1181 Hurrell, C.T. Statement of a disabled N.W. volunteer. 1890
1195 Middleton, Sir F.D. Parting address to people of Canada. 1890
1276 Pennefather, J.P. 13 years on the prairies. 1892
1358 Cochin, L. Missionnaire et sauvages pendant la guerre des métis. 1894
1362 Houghton, C.F. Houghton to Middleton. 1894
1367 Middleton, Sir F.D. Suppression of the rebellion. 1894
1432 Aron, J. Canada-Transvaal. 1896
1469 Strange, T.B. Gunner Jingo's jubilee. 1896
1545 MacBeth, R.G. Making of the Canadian West. 1898
1739 Pocock, R. A frontiersman. 1903
2957 Cameron, W.B. War trail of Big Bear. 1926
3081 Kennedy, H.A. North-West Rebellion. 1928
3143 Jefferson, R. Fifty years on the Saskatchewan. 1929
3196 La Chance, V. Diary of Francis Dickens. 1930
3262 Jamieson, F.C. Alberta Field Force. 1931
3290 Brodie, N. Twelve days with the Indians. 1932
3379 Dunlop, G.M. Tales of the North-West Rebellion. 1934
3390 McNicol, D. Louis Riel and last Indian uprising. 1934
3402 Saint-Léandre, Soeur. L'oeuvre véridique de Riel. 1934
3422 Canada. Army. North West Field Force Anniversary Re-Union Committee. Re-Union. 1935
3450 Laurie, R.C. Reminiscences of early days in Battleford. 1935
3467 Prince Albert. Old Timers. Reminiscences of the Riel Rebellion. 1935
3481 Trémaudan, A.H. de. Histoire de la nation métisse. 1935
3542 Stanley, G.F.G. Birth of Western Canada. 1936

3634 MacDermot, H.E. Sir Thomas Roddick. 1938
3731 Le Chevallier, J.J.M.J. Aux prises avec la tourmente. 1940
3737 Nelson, H.S. Four months under arms. 194-
3765 Le Chevallier, J.J.M.J. Batoche. 1941
3775 Rumilly, R. Riel. 1941
4122 Needler, G.H. Battleford column. 1948
4240 Davidson, W.M. Life and times of Riel. 1951
4296 Howard, J.K. Strange empire. 1952
4347 Frémont, D. Les secrétaires de Riel. 1953

POSTSCRIPT

Osler, E.B. The man who had to hang: Louis Riel. (Toronto, 1961)
Stanley, G.F.G. Louis Riel. (Toronto, 1963)
Bowsfield, H. Louis Riel: rebel of the frontier or victim of politics and prejudice? (Toronto, 1969)
Cerbelaud Salagnec, G. La révolte des métis: Louis Riel, héros ou rebelle? (Tours, France, 1971)
'The life and death of Louis Riel; a study in forensic psychiatry. Part 1 - a psychoanalytic commentary [by] E.R. Markson; Part 2 - Surrender, trial, appeal and execution [by] Cyril Greenland; Part 3 - Medico-legal issues [by] R.E. Turner.' (Canadian Psychiatric Association Journal, v.10, no.4, Aug., 1965. p.244-264)

3 Military History

1604 Davin, N.F. Strathcona Horse. 1900
1862 Chambers, E.J. The 90th Regiment. 1906
2405 Kennedy, H.G. 101st Regiment Edmonton Fusiliers. 1913
2533 Canada. Army. 65th Overseas Battalion. 1916
2534 Canada. Army. 226th Overseas Battalion. 1916
2535 Canada. Army. 79th Cameron Highlanders. 1916
2536 Canada. Army. 90th Winnipeg Rifles. Vaudeville. 1916
2537 Canada. Army. 90th Winnipeg Rifles. Standing orders. 1916
2562 Stafford & Kent. 50th Overseas Battalion. 1916
2569 Western News Agency. Camp Hughes. 1916
2571 Winnipeg Grenadiers. 78th Overseas Battalion. 1916
2590 Hewitt, G.E. The story of the 28th Battalion. 1917
2631 McClung, N.L. Three times and out. 1918
2654 Canada. Army. 11th Canadian Field Ambulance. 1919
2667 Great War Veterans' Association of Canada. Southern Alberta yearbook. 1919
2691 Anderson, P. I, that's me. 1920
2851 I.O.D.E. Jón Sigurdsson Chapter. Minningarrit Islenzkra hermanna. 1923
3314 Russenholt, E.S. Six thousand Canadian men. 1932
3363 The Winnipeg Rifles. 1933
3373 Canadian Legion. Polish Branch in Winnipeg. 15 lat pracy. 1934
3475 Sinclair, J.D. Queen's Own Cameron Highlanders. 1935
3605 Canada. Army. 1st Canadian Pioneer Battalion. Brief history. 1938
3637 Mewburn, F.H.H. The 25th Battery, Canadian Field Artillery. 1938
3701 Singer, H.C. History of Thirty-first Battalion. 1939
3761 Canada. Army. Rocky Mountain Rangers. First Battalion, 1885-1941. 1941
3782 Stubbs, R. St. G. Men in khaki. 1941
3903 Calgary. Citizens. Welcome home, 14th C.A.(T.)R., Calgary Regiment (Tank). 1945
3906 Canada. Army. Loyal Edmonton Regiment. Memorial booklet. 1945

3907 Canada. Army. 22nd Canadian Field Battery. Welcome home. 1945
3925 Henry, C.E. 18th Armoured Car Regiment. 1945
3934 Maltby, R.G. The Calgary Regiment (14 CAR). 1945
3953 Saskatoon Light Infantry. Honour roll. 1945
3962 Virden days. 1945
3963 Wilson, E.M. Vanguard. 1945
3995 Luxton, E. 1st Battalion, Regina Rifle Regiment. 1946
4000 Okotoks, Alberta. Souvenir to those men and women who served in WW II. 1946
4044 McAvity, J.M. Lord Strathcona's Horse. 1947
4072 Walker, D.E. 1st Battalion, Saskatoon Light Infantry. 1947
4104 Hillsman, J.B. Eleven men and a scalpel. 1948
4171 Obodiac, S. Pennfield Ridge. 1949
4206 Langruth, Manitoba. A tribute to soldiers and pioneers. 1950
4243 I.O.D.E. Next-of-kin memorial avenue. 1951

I MAINTIENS LE DROIT: ROYAL CANADIAN MOUNTED POLICE

349 Ross, P.R. Report on the north-west provinces and territories. 1872
449 Royal Canadian Mounted Police. Annual reports. 1876–
429 Smyth, E.S. Report on defences and mounted police. 1875
595 Artigue, J. d'. Six years in the Canadian North-West. 1882
1102 Donkin, J.G. Trooper and redskin. 1889
1126 North-West Mounted Police. Drill regulations. 1889
1262 Dwight, C.P. Life in the N.W.M.P. 1892
1739 Pocock, R. A frontiersman. 1903
1814 Denny, Sir C.E. Riders of the plains. 1905
1863 Chambers, E.J. Royal North-West Mounted Police. 1906
2103 Brinkworth, G.W. Royal Northwest Mounted Police. 1910
2145 Haydon, A.L. Riders of the plains. 1910
2525 Steele, S.B. Forty years in Canada. 1915
2545 Deane, R.B. Mounted police life in Canada. 1916
2615 Alberta Provincial Police. Manual. 1918
2771 Fitzpatrick, F.J.E. Sergeant 331. 1921
2782 MacBeth, R.G. Policing the plains. 1921
2999 Becket, L. Peach Davis, the mountie who thrilled two continents. 1927
3085 Longstreth, T.M. The silent force. 1928
3097A Proby, W.C. Man hunters of the north. 1928
3186 Hamilton, C.F. Royal Canadian Mounted Police. 1930
3213 Munday, L. A mounty's wife. 1930
3264 Longstreth, T.M. Murder at Belly Butte. 1931
3306A McClintock, G. The wolves of Cooking Lake. 1932
3346 Longstreth, T.M. In scarlet and plain clothes. 1933
3380 Dyker, B. Get your man. 1934
3623 Fetherstonhaugh, R.C. Royal Canadian Mounted Police. 1938
3651 Tench, C.W. Tales of the North-West Mounted Police. 1938
3677 Denny, Sir C.E. The law marches west. 1939
3678 Douthwaite, L.C. Royal Canadian Mounted Police. 1939
3868 Horan, J.W. On the side of the law. 1944
4226 Turner, J.P. North-West Mounted Police, 1873-93. 1950

J COMMUNICATIONS

1 Communications with Red River

2 Hudson Bay Route

1812 Cumberland, S.C. Via Hudson Bay. 1905
2003 McKenna, J.A.J. Hudson Bay Route. 1908
2041 Canada. Dept. of Railways & Canals. Report of Hudson's Bay Railway surveys. 1909
2312 Hudson's Bay Herald. A few things recently written. 1912
2527 Trémaudan, A.H. de. Hudson Bay road. 1915
2837 Campbell, J.A. The Hudson Bay railway. 1923
2881 Campbell, M.N. Speech on the Hudson Bay Railway. 1924
2976 Payne, J.L. Hudson Bay Railway. 1926
2977 Payne, J.L. What will it cost? 1926
3034 Palmer, Sir F. Hudson Bay ... selection of a terminal. 1927
3090 On-to-the-Bay Assoc. Hudson Bay Route. 1928
3154 Sale, C.V. The winter road. 1929
3272 On-to-the-Bay Assoc. Hudson Bay Route. 1931
3352 Saskatchewan. Dept. of Railways, Labour and Industries. Hudson Bay Route. 1933
3423 Canada. Dept. of Railways & Canals. Churchill & Hudson Bay Route. 1935
3497 Cassap, W.H. Winnipeg to London. 1936
3535 Saskatchewan Co-op. Wheat Producers Ltd. Via Churchill. 1936
3668 Canada. Dept. of Transport. Churchill & the Hudson Bay Route. 1939
3715 Canada. Dept. of Transport. Navigation conditions on the Hudson Bay Route. 1940
4010 Saskatoon. Board of Trade. Hudson Bay Committee. Report. 1946
4106 Hudson Bay Route Assoc. The Hudson Bay Route & port of Churchill. 1948
4107 Hudson Bay Route Assoc. The Hudson Bay Route, Western Canada's shortest ocean outlet. 1948
4108 Hudson Bay Route Assoc. Read the facts about Western Canada's ocean route. 1948
4154 Hudson Bay Route Assoc. Operation Bay route. 1949
4155 Hudson Bay Route Assoc. 6th convention. 1949

3 Pacific Railway

122 Synge, M.H. Canada in 1848. 1848
131 Smyth, R.S.C. Employment of people and capital. 1849
134 Smyth, R.S.C. Letter to Earl Grey. 1850
136 Wilson, F.A. Britain redeemed and Canada preserved. 1850
140 Doull, A. Employment and colonization for the million. 1851
142 MacDonell, A. Railroad from Superior to the Pacific. 1851
146 Doull, A. Project for opening a north-west passage. 1852
149 Project for construction of a railroad. 1852
151 Synge, M.H. Great Britain one empire. 1852
152 Synge, M.H. Proposal for rapid communication with the Pacific. 195_?
200 MacDonell, A. North-West Transportation, Navigation, and Railway Co. 1858
204 North-West Transportation, Navigation and Railway Co. Prospectus. 1858
231 Fleming, Sir S. Suggestions of inter-colonial railway. 1862
232 Hind, H.Y. Sketch of an overland route. 1862
235 Canada. Gov.-Gen. Opening route to Red River. 1863
237 Fleming, Sir S. Great territorial road to B.C. 1863
250 Rawlings, T. Confederation of B.N.A. 1865
275 Waddington, A. Overland route through B.N.A. 1868
287 Russell, A.J. Red River country. 1869
338 Waddington, A. Sketch of overland railroad. 1871
3684 Irwin, L.B. Pacific railways and nationalism. 1939

4 Canadian Pacific Railway

540 McLeod, M. Problem of Canada. 1880
545 Pacific railway. Speeches by Tupper, etc. 1880
569 Canada. Dept. of Sec. of State. Returns re surveys. 1881
572 Daluaine. The syndicate. 1881
577 Langelier, Sir F.C.S. Le Pacifique. 1881
582 McLelan, A.W. Speech on Pacific Railway Company. 1881
605 Canada. Dept. of Sec. of State. Returns re C.P.R. 1882
606 Canada. Laws, statutes, etc. C.P.R. contract. 1882
610 Canada. Royal Commission on C.P.R. Report. 1882
619 Diogenes. C.P.R. & schemes of syndicate. 1882
622 Fleming, Sir S. Letter to Sec. of State on the C.P.R. 1882
634 Mohawk. The C.P.R. and its assailants. 1882
664 Canada. Dept. of Sec. of State. Sessional papers re C.P.R. 1883
731 Canadian Pacific Co.'s method of financing. 1884
736 C.P.R. Report of special meeting. 1884
743 Foster, Sir G.E. Speech on the C.P.R. resolutions. 1884
752 Ives, W.B. Speech on C.P.R. 1884
753 James, J.C. Western division of the C.P.R. 1884
755 Langevin, Sir H.L. Une question de véracité. 1884
768 Ross, A.W. Speech on C.P.R. 1884
769 Ross, A.W. Speeches on C.P.R. 1884
770 Scott, T. Statement in support of railway act. 1884
776 White, T. Speeches on C.P.R. 1884
788 Blake, E. Speech on the C.P.R. resolutions. 1885
789 Blake, E. Speech on North-Western Coal and Navigation Co. 1885
801 Chapleau, Sir J.A. Discours sur Chemin de Fer Canadien du Pacifique. 1885
870 Argyll, Duke of. Our railway to the Pacific. 1886
874 Begg, A. Canada and its national highway. 1886
963 Ross, A.W. Pacific railway and N.W.T. 1886
1024 Robertson, F.B. Railway monopoly. 1887
1033 Winnipeg. Board of Trade. Open letter to shareholders of C.P.R. 1887
1034 Winnipeg. Board of Trade. Plain facts regarding disallowance. 1887
1037 C.P.R., its geographical and financial position. 1888
1115 McLeod, M. Memorial to the government re C.P.R. 1889
1127 Saturday Budget. Canadian Pacific Railway. 1889
1526 C., A.L.O. Story of a dark plot. 1898
1658 Richmond, W.R. Life of Lord Strathcona. n.d.
1713 Canada. Dept. of Sec. of State. C.P.R. tax exemptions. 1903
1828 Liberal Party. Railway competition for Saskatchewan. 1905
2481 Preston, W.T.R. Life and times of Strathcona. 1914
2494 Burpee, L.J. Sandford Fleming, empire builder. 1915
2521 Pedley, J.W. Biography of Strathcona. 1915
2558 Morris, C.K. Story of the C.P.R. 1916
2750 Vaughan, W. Life and work of Van Horne. 1920
2852 Innis, H.A. History of the C.P.R. 1923
2893 MacBeth, R.G. Romance of the C.P.R. 1924
2909 Secretan, J.H.E. Canada's great highway. 1924
3082 Kennedy, H.A. Origin of the C.P.R. 1928
3168 Burpee, L.J. Sir Sandford Fleming. 1930
3437 Gibbon, J.M. Steel of empire. 1935
3682 Hedges, J.B. Building the Canadian West. 1939
3684 Irwin, L.B. Pacific railways and nationalism. 1939
4326A Pratt, E.J. Towards the last spike. 1952

POSTSCRIPT
Berton, Pierre. The national dream; the great railway, 1871-1881. (Toronto, 1970)
Berton, Pierre. The last spike; the great railway, 1881-1885. (Toronto, 1971)

5 **Other Railways**

K SETTLING THE WEST

1 **Immigration and Settlement**

296 Canada. Parliament. Senate. Select Committee on Rupert's Land. 1870
325 Clarke, H.J.H. Report on Immigration Conference. 1871
333 North West Emigration Aid Society. Second circular. 1871
382 Canada. Dept. of the Interior. Annual reports. 1874-1936
452 Canada. Parliament. H. of C. Select Standing Committee on immigration. Report. 1877
525 Currie, D. Letters of Rusticus. 1880
526 Duffield, A.J. Needless misery at home. 1880
547 Ross, Ross, & Killam. Sixty thousand acres. 1880
561 Begg, A. Letters on the situation. 1881
590 Allen, C.W. Land prospector's manual. 1882
608 Canada North-West Land Co. Memorandum. 1882
614 Charlton, J. Speech on land policy in N.W. 1882
628 Kosmack, A. Beschreibung einer Entdeckungsreise. 1882
632A Manitoba Land Co. Ltd. 1882
651 Temperance Colonization Society. Charter, etc. 1882
689 Munro, W.F. Emigration made easy. 1883
692 Plumb, J.B. Great Canadian North-West! 1883
699 Sask. Land & Homestead Co. Memorial of settlers. 1883
700 A Shareholder. Canadian North West Land Co. 1883
710 A future for the deaf and dumb. 1884
728A Canada. Laws, statutes, etc. Dominions lands act, 1883. 1884
766A Qu'Appelle Valley Farming Co. 1884
779 York Farmers Colonization Company. Guide and record. 1884
783 Allen, C.W. Volunteer land grants. 1885
850 Temperance Colonization Society. Interim report. 1885
875 Begg, A. Emigration. 1886
980 Anderson, F.B. Immigration and settlement. 1887
1006 Gates, E.W. English emigrants in Canada. 1887
1020 Passy, L. Etude sur la colonisation. 1887
1054 Great Britain. Colonial Office. Crofter & cottar colonisation. 1888
1109 Lewis, C.T. World's return rebate marriage certificate. 1889
1123A Quebec City. Board of Trade. Landing of immigrants at Quebec. 1889
1173 Fulthorp, G.E. Catalogue of lands for sale. 1890
1178 Grotty & Cross. Manitoba lands for sale. 1890
1277 Plunkett, Sir H. Report upon emigration to Canada. 1892
1296 British-American. Canada's fertile plains. 1893
1344 Brown, W.F. Settler's guide. 1894
1538 Cuverille, J.M.A. Le Canada et les intérêts français. 1898
1540 Gaire, J. Dix années de missions. 1898
1568 Canadian colonization scheme. 1899
1578 Great Britain. Commissioners on colonization of crofters and cottars. Crofter colonisation reports. 1890-99
1666 Barr, I.M. Br. settlements in N.W. Canada. 1902
1668 Barr, I.M. British settlements in North-Western Canada. 1902
1710 Canada. Dept. of the Interior. Homestead regulations. 1903
1761B Canada. Dept. of the Interior. List of Dominion land agents. 1904
1773 Liberal Party. Sale to Saskatchewan Valley Land Co. 1904
1881 Liberal Party. Sask. Valley Land Co. 1906
1890 Sifton, Sir C. Administration of Canadian West. 1906
1897 Whates, H.R. Canada, the new nation. 1906
1926 Cyr, J.E. La colonisation dans l'Ouest. 1907
1932 Fredericksen, D.M. Land laws. 1907
1934 Kennedy, H.A. New Canada and new Canadians. 1907

2 **Immigration Literature**
For local publicity literature see 'History, Local'

320 Begg, A. Dot it down. 1871
324 Circulaire privée du clergé. 1871
336 Spence, T. Manitoba and the North-West. 1871
376 Shantz, J.Y. Narrative of a journey. 1873
380 Canada. Dept. of Agriculture. Canada et l'emigration Européene. 1874
381 Canada. Dept. of Agriculture. Province of Manitoba. 1874
396 Leidarvisir fyrir vesturfara til Canada. 1874
407A Canada. Dept. of the Interior. Dominion lands, in Man., etc. 1875-78
415 Finney, W. Manitoba. 1875
438 Canada. Dept. of Agriculture. Province of Manitoba. 1876
456 Down, J.W. Manitoba & great N.W. colony. 1877
465 Spence, T. Saskatchewan country. 1877
468 Begg, A. Practical hand-book. 1878
479 Codd, D. Prairie lands of Canada. 1878
481 Dufferin, Marquis of. Canada; Lord Dufferin in Manitoba. 1878
483 Frá Nýja Islandi. 1878
487 Trow, J. Manitoba and N.W.T. 1878
492 Canada. Dept. of Agriculture. Province of Manitoba. 1879
499 Dominion lands in Manitoba, etc. 1879
500 Dominion of Canada, Manitoba and the N.W. 1879
505 H.B.C. Manitoba and the North-West. 1879
507 Lake Winnipeg Land & Colonization Assoc. 1879
511 Spence, T. Prairie lands of Canada. 1879
514 Armstrong, L.O. Southern Manitoba and Turtle Mountain. 1880
518 Burrows, C.A. North western Canada. 1880
519 Canada. Dept. of Agriculture. Reports of tenant farmers' delegates. 1880
527 Dugas, G. Manitoba et ses avantages. 188–
531 Great Britain, Colonial Office. Canada, information for emigrants. 1880
533 Hall, E.H. Lands of plenty. 1880
539 Macdougall's guide to Manitoba and the North-West. 1880
513 Manitoba exhibit of 1879. 1880
542 Mitchell, P. West and North-West. 1880
543 Moore, T. Tour through Canada. 1880
548 The Sun. Manitoba and the North-West. 188–
549 Tassé, E. The North-West. 1880
554 Wyatt, G.H. Manitoba, Canadian North-West, and Ontario. 1880
557 Manitoba and the North-West. 1881
560 Begg, A. Great Canadian North West. 1881
563 Canada. Dept. of Agriculture. Agricultural resources of Canada. 1881
564 Canada. Dept. of Agriculture. Canada in 1880. 1881
565 Canada. Dept. of Agriculture. Manitoba und das Nordwestliche Landergebiet. 1881
566 Canada. Dept. of Agriculture. Puissance du Canada. 1881
567 Canada. Dept. of Agriculture. What farmers say. 1881
570 Chisholm & Dickson. Great Canadian North-West. 1881
589 Wyatt, G.H. Reliable guide for settlers. 1881
601 Canada. Dept. of Agriculture. Canada, free grants of land. 1882
601A Canada. Dept. of Agriculture. Map of Manitoba. 1882
607 Canada North-West Land Co. Manitoba and the Canadian N.W. 1882?
611 C.P.R. Canada veiledning for nybyggere. 1882
612 C.P.R. Land grant. 1882

744 Four Year Resident. Remarks on Manitoba. 1884
751 Imrie, P. Canada as a field for settlement. 188–
759 Moore, J.T. Settler's pocket guide to homesteads. 1884
772 Telfer, J.H. Canadian North-West. 1884
778 Winnipeg Daily Sun. Manitoba and N.W.T. 1884
795 Canada. Dept. of Agriculture. L'agriculture dans le Nord-Ouest. 1885
795A Canada. Dept. of Agriculture. Neu elsass. 1885
799 C.P.R. Plain facts from farmers. 1885
800 C.P.R. Practical hints from farmers. 1885
806 Craigie, P.G. The Canadian North-West. 1885
824 Lennox, G. Guide universel de l'émigrant; Manitoba. 1885
828 Manitoba. 1885
835 Netherlands American Land Co. Official guide to lands. 1885
836 One Who Has Just Returned. Emigrant's prospects in Manitoba. 1885
847 Sykes, R. Guide to the Qu'Appelle Valley. 1885
849 Tanner, H. Canadian North West. 1885
853 200 millioen akkers voor kolonisatie. 1885
854 What British settlers say about the country. 1885
859 The Albany settlement. 1886
862 Manitoba and the N.W.T. 1886
863 Manitoba en het Noord westelyk. 1886
864 Manitoba och Nordvest-territoriet. 1886
876 Begg, A. Great North-West of Canada. 1886
888A Canada. Dept. of Agriculture. Map of the N.W.T. 1886
890 Canada. Dept. of Agriculture. Esquisse générale du Nord-Ouest. 1886
891 Canada. Dept. of Agriculture. 200 millionen Acres in Manitoba. 1886
904A C.P.R. Free grants of land. 1886?
905 C.P.R. Manitoba. Testimony of actual settlers. 1886
905A C.P.R. Letters from actual settlers. 1886?
906 C.P.R. Settler's index to golden Manitoba. 1886
907 C.P.R. Upplysninger om Manitoba. 1886
908 C.P.R. What settlers say of the Canadian N.W. 1886
909 C.P.R. What women say of the North-West. 1886
914 Clark, W. The Canadian North-West. 1886
924 Dominion of Canada, Pacific railway, & N.W.T. 1886
931 Free homes in Manitoba and the N.W. 1886
935 Grogan & Pettit. Settlers' guide to southern Alberta. 1886
943 Lansdowne, Marquis of. Canada North-West & B.C. 1886
948 Manitoba and N.W. Railway. Guide book to lands. 1886
949 Manitoba og Nordvesturlandid i Canada. 1886
952 Nya Stockholm. 1886
953 Oliver, J.W.W. How to start a farm. 1886
959 Richardson, R.L. Facts and figures. 1886
964 Ross, D.A. & Co. Manitoba farms. 1886
969 Skandinaviska National Föreningen. Skandinaverna. 1886
972 Spence, T. Canada. Resources and future greatness. 1886
973 Tanner, H. Successful emigration. 1886
989 Bernier, T.A. Le Manitoba. 1887
992 Canada. Dept. of Agriculture. North West of Canada. 1887
1000 C.P.R. Facts for farmers. 1887
1007 Gillett, W.B. Manitoba, some of its towns. 1887
1013 McMillan, A.J. Life in Canada. 1887
1015 Manitoba. Dept. of Agriculture. 2000 free homesteads. 1887
1016 Morris, W.J. The new Northwest. 1887

1044A Canada. Dept. of Agriculture. Official leaflet. 1888
1045 C.P.R. Farming and ranching. 1888
1046 C.P.R. Free homes for all. 1888?
1047 C.P.R. Manitoba, the Canadian N.W. 1888
1048 C.P.R. What actual settlers say. 1888
1053 Fitzgerald, J.G. Alberta. 1888
1065 Manitoba. Dept. of Agric. and Immigration. Facts about Manitoba. 1888
1066 Manitoba and N.W. Rly. Illustrated guide book to lands. 1888
1069 Newett, W.H. Farming in Canada. 1888
1072 Palmer, W.J. Dennis county, Manitoba. 1888
1076 Schultz, J. Manitoba, catalogue of lands for sale. 1888
1081 Webster, W.A. A Canadian farmer's report. 1888
1083 Winnipeg. Joint committee. Winnipeg, farm lands. 1888
1092 C.P.R. Every-day questions answered. 1889
1092A C.P.R. La meilleur place du Man. 1889
1093 C.P.R. North-West farmer in Canadian North-West. 1889
1094 C.P.R. Successful farming in Manitoba. 1889
1095 C.P.R. Taydellisia tietoja Manitoban. 1889
1085 Dairy farming, ranching and mining. 1889
1107 Huleatt, H. British Columbia, Alaska, & London artizan colony. 1889
1108 Lake Manitoba Railway & Canal Co. Development of the North-West. 1889
1110 MacArthur, D. Manitoba. 1889
1116 Manitoba. Manitoba and its resources. 1889
1117 Manitoba. Pamphlet descriptive of Manitoba. 1889
1118 Manitoba and N.W. Railway. Close to markets and schools. 1889
1121 Moose Jaw. Board of Trade. District of Moose Jaw. 1889
1124 Regina. Board of Trade. Few facts respecting Regina district. 1889
1132 Alberta Railway and Coal Co. A stockman's paradise. 189-
1133 Allan Steamship Line. Ffeithiau gwerth eu gwybod. 189_?
1134 Allan Steamship Line. Llawlyfr yr ymfudwr. 189_?
1135 Allan Steamship Line. Skyrslur um hagi Islendinga. 1890
1137 Free homes. Lands waiting. 189-
1140 British settlers in Western Canada. 189-
1150 Boyle Brothers' Agency. Manitoba and the N.W.T. 1890
1154 Canada. Dept. of Agriculture. Manitoba och Nordvest-Territoriet. 1890
1155 Canada. Dept. of Agriculture. Northern Alberta. 189-
1156A C.P.R. Manitoba, si nordvest. 189-
1157 C.P.R. Farming and ranching in western Canada. 1890
1158 C.P.R. Harvest news. 1890
1159 C.P.R. La laiterie, la culture. 1890
1160 C.P.R. Western Alberta. 1890
1161 C.P.R. Wo sich der deutsche Ansiedler. 1890
1170 Edmonton. Board of Trade. Edmonton district. 1890
1175 Gates, E.W. Off to Canada. 1890
1177 Grande excursion de 'Exploration au Manitoba.' 189_?
1183 Lacombe, A. Un nouveau champ de colonisation. 1890
1185 Letters from settlers, 1888-90
1191 Manitoba. Dept. of Agric. and Immigration. Manitoba, the prairie province. 1890
1192 Manitoba & N.W. Rly. How to start a prairie farm. 189-
1193 Manitoba, the best country in the world. 1890
1196 North Western Coal & Navigation Co. Canadian N.W.T. 189-
1199 Ross, D.A. Manitoba lands for sale. 1890
1200 Sandison, J.W. A Scotch farmer's success. 1890
1206 Western Canada Immigration Assoc. Manitoba homesteads. 189-

1208 Advantages of Prince Albert. 1891
1211A Canada. Dept. of Agriculture. Adroiddiod. 1891
1212 Canada. Dept. of Agriculture. Visit of tenant-farmer delegates. 1891
1215 C.P.R. Canadian North-West Territories. 1891
1216 C.P.R. North West farmer. 1891
1217 C.P.R. The Saskatchewan; northern Alberta. 1891
1221 Ekru, E. Hveiti-land heimsins hid mesta er Manitoba. 1891
1222 An Englishman who lived twelve years in the country. Canada as a field for emigration. 1891
1223 Foursin, P. Colonisation française. 1891
1229 Manitoba. Dept. of Agriculture. Map of Manitoba. 1891
1230 Morin, J.B. Renseignements sur le Nord-Ouest. 1891
1232 Osler, Hammond & Nanton. Qu'Appelle, Long Lake & Sask. Railroad. 1891
1233 Prince Albert. Board of Trade. Are you looking for a home. 1891
1234 Regina. Board of Trade. An unvarnished tale of Regina. 1891
1239 Wagstaff, J. English lands & English homes. 1891
1244 Bodard, A. Emigration en Canada. 1892
1245 Calgary. Board of Trade. Advantages of Alberta. 1892
1247 Canada. Dept. of the Interior. Fiosrachadh 'o' n luchdriaghlaidh. 1892
1249 C.P.R. Free farms. 1892
1250 C.P.R. Free homes in Manitoba. 1892
1251 C.P.R. Great Canadian North-West, finest farming lands. 1892
1252 C.P.R. Manitoba ... fra Norge. 1892
1253 C.P.R. Manitoba och Nordvest-Territoriet. 1892
1254 C.P.R. Report of delegates from Maritime Provinces. 1892
1255 C.P.R. Western Canada. 1892
1256 C.P.R. Westliches Canada. 1892
1257 C.P.R. What farmers say. 1892
1260 Davin, N.F. Homes for millions. 1892
1263 Gaetz, L. Report of six years in Red Deer district. 1892
1269 Letters from settlers, 1891-92
1270 Manitoba. Handbog. 1892
1271 Manitoba official hand-book. 1892
1272 Manitoba. Dept. of Agriculture. Homes in Manitoba. 1892
1273 Manitoba. Dept. of Agriculture. Opinions of eminent men. 1892
1274 Manitoba und die Nordwest-Territorien. 1892
1281 Ritchie, P.R. Manitoba and N.W.T. 1892
1291 Baldwinson, B.L. Agrip af fyrirlestri um baejalif Islendinga. 1893
1292 Baldwinson, B.L. Nokkrar athugasemdir. 1893
1293 Baldwinson, B.L. Svar gégn athugasemdum. 1893
1294 Bodard, A. Le guide du colon dans l'Ouest. 1893
1298 Canada. Dept. of the Interior. Emigration to North-Western Canada. 1893
1299 Canada. Dept. of the Interior. Manitoba and the N.W.T. 1893
1300 Canada. Dept. of the Interior. En skildring af Manitoba. 1893
1301 Canada. Dept. of the Interior. Western Canada and its great resources. 1893
1304 C.P.R. A travers les grandes terres à blé. 1893
1305 C.P.R. Canadian N.W., what settlers from the Maritimes say. 1893
1305A C.P.R. Fermes gratuites. 1893
1306 C.P.R. Free farms in fertile districts. 1893
1311 Duck Lake Agricultural Society. Duck Lake district. 1893
1312 Facts about grain growing. 1893
1315 Free farms. 1893
1320 Manitoba. Dept. of Agric. and Immigration. Great agricultural province. 1893
1321 Manitoba. Dept. of/Agric. and Immigration. Manitoba; official information. 1893

1537 The Colonist. Summer souvenir number. 1898
1538 Cuverille, J.M.A. Le Canada et les intérêts français. 1898
1539 Field, S. Timely remarks. 1898
1547 Manitoba i polnocno zachodnie terytora. 1898
1554 Virden. Board of Trade. Manitoba farm lands. 1898
1558 Winnipeg. City Council. Winnipeg distriktet. 1898
1561 British settlers in Western Canada. 1899
1563 Canada. Dept. of the Interior. Delegates' reports and settlers' experiences. 1899
1564 Canada. Dept. of the Interior. Resources of Western Canada. 1899
1565 Canada. Dept. of the Interior. Western Canada and its great resources. 1899
1566 Canada. Dept. of the Interior. Western Canada. 1899
1569 Canadian North-West Irrigation Co. Irrigated lands in southern Alberta. 1899
1570 C.P.R. Western Canada. 1899
1582 Manitoba y privnichni - zakhidni. 1899
1589 Baldwinson, B.L. Manitoba un aldamótin. 1900
1590 Berns, R. Ulles van het beste. 190_?
1595 Canada. Dept. of the Interior. Delegates' reports on Western Canada. 1900
1596 Canada. Dept. of the Interior. L'Ouest canadien. 1900
1597 Canada. 160 acres fritt land. 1900?
1598 Canada. 160 acres vryland. 1900?
1599 Canadian North-West Irrigation Co. Irrigated lands in southern Alberta. 1900
1600 C.P.R. Amit egy tanyan tudnia kell. 1900
1601 C.P.R. Hvad danske Landmaend kunne udrette. 1900?
1610 George, D.L. Prominent Welshmen on Western Canada. 1900
1614 Kanada. Krotkie ... 1900?
1620 Manitoba in 1900. 1900
1620A National Editorial Association. Prophecies on the Canadian West. 1900
1621 North Atlantic Trading Co. Courtes mais intéressantes informations. 1900
1629 Vester Canada. 1900
1633 Zilliacus, Konni. Kanada såsom mål för emigranter. 1900
1635 American Land & Loan Co. Winnipeg district. 1901
1641 Canada. Dept. of the Interior. Officiell handbok. 1901
1643 Canadian North-West Irrigation Co. Age of insurance for farmers. 1901
1644 C.P.R. Western Canada. 1901
1646 De Vos, R. Canada, la colonisation agricole. 1901
1654 McCaig, J. Story of climate of southern Alberta. 1901
1656 Manitoba. Dept. of Agric. and Immigration. Canada's centre is Manitoba. 1901
1657 N.W.T. Dept. of Agriculture. Canadian N.W.T. 1901
1660 Société de colonisation de la Rivière la Paix. Le Nord-Ouest. 1901
1671 Blais, M.J. Le Manitoba. 1902
1672 Bulman Bros. The wondrous West. 1902
1672A Canada. Dept. of the Interior. Free farms. 1902?
1673 Canada. Dept. of the Interior. Manitoba, land of No.1 hard. 1902
1674 Canada. Dept. of the Interior. Atlas de l'Ouest canadien. 1902
1675 Canada. Dept. of the Interior. Facts relating to Western Canada. 1902
1683 Länsi Canadan kehitys. 1902
1693 En tur igjennem det vestlige Canada. 1902
1694 Vestra Canadas utveckling. 1902
1695 Western Canada, free homes for all. 1902
1698 Winnipeg. Board of Trade. The wondrous West. 1902
1701 Ranching in the Canadian Northwest. 1903
1707B Canada. Dept. of the Interior. Canada, granary of the empire. 1903
1708 Canada. Dept. of the Interior. Canada, the granary of the world. 1903
1709 Canada. Dept. of the Interior. Evolution of the prairie by the plow. 1903

1911 Canada. Dept. of the Interior. English emigrants' experience. 1906
1912 Canada. Dept. of the Interior. Last best West. 1907
1913 Canada. Dept. of the Interior. Lettres de colons. 1907
1915 Canada. Dept. of the Interior. Story of Western Canada crop. 1907
1916 Canada. Dept. of the Interior. A land of unequalled opportunity. 1907
1917 Canada. Dept. of the Interior. A land of unprecedented progress. 1907
1918 Canada. Dept. of the Interior. Western Canada, crop prospects. 1907
1919 Canada. Dept. of the Interior. Western Canada early days. 1907
1920 C.P.R. Home life of women in Western Canada. 1907
1923 Compagnie des colons de l'Ouest. Emparons-nous du sol. 1907
1928 Dunsford, J.T. Emigration to Canada. 1907
1938 Leau, L. La terre pour rien. 1907
1940 McLean (David M) Land Co. Story of Western Canada. 1907
1952 Saskatoon and Western Land Co. Heart of famous wheat belt. 1907
1956 Vestur Canada. 1907
1966 A book of contrasts. 1908
1969 Canada. Dept. of Agriculture. Canada West. 1908
1971 Canada. Dept. of the Interior. The last best West. 1908
1972 Canada. Dept. of the Interior. Winter wheat is a success. 1908
1974 C.P.R. Facts concerning agricultural conditions. 1908
2013 Det nordvestlige Canada. 1908
2014 Ouellette, J.A. L'Alberta-nord. 1908
2015 Ouellette, J.A. Le jardin de l'Alberta-Sud. 1908
2042 C.P.R. Alaska-Yukon-Pacific exposition. 1909
2043 C.P.R. Canada i'r cymry. 1909
2044 C.P.R. Gwaith a chyflogau yn Canada. 190_?
2045 C.P.R. Public opinion concerning Bow River Valley. 1909
2046 C.P.R. Two blades of grass. 1909
2055 Grand Trunk Pacific Railway. 7,000 free homesteads. 1909
2057 Guide & companion to Edmonton. 1909
2060 Hope, Sir H. Canada as it appeared to Scotch agriculturists. 1909
2084 Scottish Agricultural Commission. Canada as seen through Scottish eyes. 1909
2094 Alberta. Publicity Bureau. Land & agriculture in Alberta. 1910
2107 Le Canada agricole. 1910
2109 Canada. Dept. of the Interior. Alberta red. 1910
2110 Canada. Dept. of the Interior. Canada West. 1910
2111 Canada. Dept. of the Interior. Kanada, mulighedernes land. 1910
2112 Canada. Dept. of the Interior. Llawlyfr swyddogol Canada. 1910
2113 Canada. Dept. of the Interior. Prosperity follows settlement. 1910
2114 Canada. Dept. of the Interior. Silhouettes of the West. 1910
2115 C.P.R. Concerning central Alberta. 1910?
2116 C.P.R. Heart of the Saskatchewan valley. 1910
2117 C.P.R. The staff of life. 1910
2118 C.P.R. Western Canada. 1910
2119 C.P.R. Where wheat is king. 1910
2120 Canadian Townsites Ltd. Cities in the making. 1910
2131 Cunard Steamship Co. Kanada. 1910
2139 Grand Trunk Pacific Railway. The big wheat field. 1910
2140 Grand Trunk Pacific Railway. 8,000 free homesteads. 1910
2143 Grand Trunk Pacific Railway. Purchase farm lands. 1910
2148 Ingham, T.S. O arfon i Canada. 1910
2170 Robins, K.N. Province of Alberta. 1910
2173 Saunders, W. Manitoba and N.W.T. markets. 1910
2180 Souvenir of Western Canada. 1910?
2189 Waugh, R.D. Western Canada, the land of opportunity. 1910

2553 Luse Land & Development Co. Evidence of one hundred Canadian farmers. 1916
2575 C.P.R. Handbook of information. 1917
2588 Gagnon, Joseph. Le Manitoba. 1917
2600 Manitoba. Dept. of Agric. and Immigration. Stock raising in Manitoba. 1917
2656 Canadian National Railways. Own a selected farm. 1919
2657 Canadian National Railways. Homeseekers and settlers guide. 1919
2658 C.P.R. Handbook of information. 1919
2669 H.B.C. Opportunities in Canada's success belt. 1919
2695A Canada. Dept. of the Interior. Where when and how. 1920
2696 Canada. Dept. of the Interior. Manitoba unoccupied farms. 1920
2696A Canadian National Railways. Facts about selected farms. 1920?
2706 Edmonton district in central Alberta. 1920
2710 Gravel, L.P. La Saskatchewan. 192-
2713A Hudson's Bay Company. Information about Company's lands. 192_
2727 Manitoba, the key-stone province. 1920
2730 Opportunities in Edmonton. 1920
2761 Canada. Dept. of Immigration. Pa le pa bryd a phafodd. 1921
2763 C.P.R. Canadian Pacific reserve lands. 1921
2764 C.P.R. Handbook of information. 1921
2765 C.P.R. Irrigation in sunny Alberta. 1921
2775 Guide to Edmonton. 1921
2803 Canada. Dept. of Immigration and Colonization. Canada West. 1922
2804 C.P.R. Ako získat' farmu v Kanade. 1922
2814 H.B.C. Lands of particular interest to farmers. 1922
2833 Alberta. Dept. of Agriculture. Alberta, land of opportunity. 1923
2840 Canada. Dept. of the Interior. Province of Saskatchewan. 1923
2875 American Swedish Line. Svenskar i Canada. 1924
2882 Canada. Dept. of Immigration and Colonization. Canada West. 1924
2883 C.P.R. Tell me – why should I move to Western Canada. 1924
2892 Low, F.B. Kvinden i det fjaerne vesten. 1924
2920 Canadian National Railways. Own your own home. 1925
2921 C.P.R. Irrigation farming in sunny Alberta. 1925
2922 C.P.R. Prairie Provinces of Canada. 1925
2956A British Dominions Land Settlement Corporation Limited. Illustration of settlers' progress. 1926
2958 C.P.R. Canada, nogle praktiske oplysninger. 1926
2960 C.P.R. Successful American settlers invite you. 1926
3006 Canada. Dept. of the Interior. Dominion lands. 1927
3007 C.P.R. Canada (Finnish). 1927
3008 C.P.R. Canada (Danish). 1927
3009 C.P.R. Opportunity in Canada. 1927
3035 Poland. Ministry of Labour. Wskazowki dla wychodźców do Kanady. 1927
3039 Scandinavian-American Line. Breve og avisartikler fra Danske i Kanada. 1927
3040 Scandinavian-American Line. Käsikirja henkilöille. 1927
3061 Canada. Department of Immigration. Kanada, nový domov. 1928
3064 Canadian National Railways, Familiers bosaettelse i det Vestlige Canada. 1928
3065 C.P.R. Arbetstillfällen och jördforvarv i Canada. 1928
3066 C.P.R. Canada (Danish). 1928
3067 C.P.R. Prairie farms as the camera sees them. 1928
3071 Dodatkowe wskazówki dla wychodźców. 1928
3107 Tuckwell, D.G. Kind of old countrymen Canada can absorb. 1928
3108 Tuckwell, D.G. Three English emigrants. 1928
3115 Ako ziskat farmu v Kanade. 1929
3125 Canada. Dept. of Immigration & Colonization. Land settlement in Canada. 1929

3127 Canadian National Railways. Canada. (Norwegian). 1929
3128 C.P.R. Canada (Swedish). 1929
3146 Mazurkiewicz, R. Polskie wychodźtwo i osadnictwo w Kanadzie. 1929
3150 North-German Lloyd Bremen Line. Canada, anvisningar för emigranttrafik. 1929
3151 North-German Lloyd Bremen Line. Kanada ohjeet suomalaisille siirtolaiśliikennettä. 1929
3178 Garczynski, L. Co to jest Kanada. 1930
3495 Het rijk van de toekomst. 1936
3594 Zyndykatu Emigracyjnego. Wiadomosci o Kanadzie. 1937
3669 C.P.R. Agricultural settlement opportunities. 1939
3958 Stowarzyszenie Polakow w Kanadzie Witajcie rodacy. 194_
4241 Flipot, F. Canada, terre d'avenir. 1951

ADDENDA

The annual reports of the Department of the Interior and of the Auditor-General contain passing references to other pamphlets. Unfortunately the description of these is too incomplete to warrant inclusion as proper entries in the body of the Bibliography. The titles are listed here in the hope that bibliographers and collectors may provide fuller descriptions of them.

Erikson's (Swedish) pamphlet. 1892. 20,000 copies

Manitoba (Danish-Norwegian) Ottawa, 1893. 28p. 10,000 copies
Manitoba (German) Ottawa, 1893. 47p. 5,000 copies
Manitoba (Finnish) England, 1893. 'a small folder'
Meyer's (Danish) folder. 1893
Kanada (German) folder. 1893

Free farms (English, French, German) 1894. 'a large folder' (Entry 1315 would appear to be the English edition)
Long, Professor James. Report of his visit of 1893. 1894
Manitoba (Danish-Norwegian) Liverpool, 1894. 47p.

Dr. Brisson's report of 1894. 1895

Canadian North West. 1896. 15p. (The following year a French edition 'Le Nord Ouest Canadien' was listed)

Advantages of Canada (compiled by clergymen) 1897
Canada (Danish) Ottawa, C.C. Meyer, 1897. 16p. 10,000 copies
Canada (Swedish) Ottawa, 1897. 76p. 10,000 copies (Perhaps the same pamphlet as the one attributed to Wendlebo below)
Canada (Swedish) Liverpool, 1897. 47p.
Canada, the country for farmers. London, McCorquodale, 1897. 27p. 50,000 copies
Frit land (Danish-Norwegian) London, McCorquodale, 1897. Pamphlet issued by C.P.R.
Fritt land (Swedish) London, McCorquodale, 1897. Issued by the C.P.R.
Gold in grain, cattle and nuggets. Ottawa, 1897. 5p. 20,000 copies
Le guide du colon. 1897. 100p.
Meyer, Charles C. Canada (Danish) 1897
Smith, Hedley. Canada as a field for emigration. 1897
Swanson, C.O. Swedish letters. 1897
Wendlebo's (Swedish) pamphlet. 1897. Also published in Danish-Norwegian
Western Canada. Ottawa, 1897. 47p. 20,000 copies

Kanada (Bohemian, German, Italian, Swedish) 1898. Entry 1597 may be the Swedish edition
Le Manitoba (French). May have been a reissue of the Blais 1896 pamphlet (Entry 1434)
Zapadni Canada (Bohemian) Omaha, Nebraska, Pokrok zapadu, 1898. 32p. 5,000 copies

Akerlindh (Swedish) pamphlet. 1899
Canada (Finnish) pamphlet. 1899
Canada (Swedish) pamphlet. 1899. 87p. 10,000 copies
de Coeli (Flemish) 1899. 35p. 10,000 copies
Kanada (Hungarian) New York, Singer Printing, 1899. 79p. 5,000 copies
Saskatchewan leaflet (French) 1899
Western Canada. Montreal, Montreal Herald, 1899. 77p. 100,000 copies (This pamphlet may be Entry 1570)

Frei heim (Danish-Norwegian) Chicago, Rand McNally, 1900. 34p. 20,000 copies
Gouin, Rev. Father. pamphlet. 1900
Moose Mountain district. 1900
Swanson's (Swedish) folders, Nos.1 & 2. Winnipeg, 1900

British settlers in Western Canada. 1901
Broadview described. 1901
Calgary illustrated. 1901
Hungarian circular. New York, 1901. 4p. 5,000 copies
Osborne's Manitoba and the North West Territories. 1901
Russell county illustrated. 1901
Virden Board of Trade pamphlet. 1901

Bach's (German) pamphlet. 1902
Guerin. Pour le colon. 1902
Ribout's pamphlet. 1902
Warwick Brothers. Free homes in Canada. 1902

Canada in harvest time. 1903
Chromos. Sixty years after. 1903
Guerin. Voyage d'exploration au Nord-Ouest. 1903
Hard wheat belt. 1903
Saginaw Delegates. Report of. 1903
Story of a Manitoba farmer. 1903
Von Rajcs (Hungarian) pamphlet. 1903
Wheat growing in Canada. 1903

Asked and answered. 1904
Lacombe (Alta.) pamphlet. 1904
Selkirk. Board of Trade. Souvenir. 1904

Letters from successful settlers (in French) 1906

3 Pioneer Life

575 Galbraith, J.F. Sketch of both sides of Manitoba. 1881
626 Goodridge, R.E.W. A year in Manitoba. 1882
675 Ffolkes, E.G.E. Letters from a young emigrant. 1883
739 Cockburn, J.S. Canada for gentlemen. 1884

748 Hall, M.G.C. A lady's life on a farm. 1884
1096 Church, H.E. Making a start in Canada. 1889
1105 Goodridge, R.E.W. The colonist at home again. 1889
1172 Frank, Mrs. M.J. The Brock family. 1890
1224 Globensky, E.A. Le mixed-farming au Manitoba. 1891
1226 McGusty, H.A. Two years in Manitoba and the N.W.T. 1891
1276 Pennefather, J.P. 13 years on the prairies. 1892
1401 Elkington, W.M. Five years in Canada. 1895
1627 Somers-Cocks, H.L. Trials of a tenderfoot. 190_?
1877 Hardy, J. Farming in the Canadian North-West. 1906
1925 Covey, E. Comrades two. 1907
1927 Dezell, R. A night on the prairie. 1907
2005 Major, Mrs. H. Canadian life as I found it. 1908
2074 Pictures of life in Canada. 1909
2100 Binnie-Clark, G. A summer on the Canadian prairie. 1910
2267 Thomas, M.W. The truth about Canada. 1911
2271 Witteryck, A.J. Les aventures de Coquelicot. 1911
2295 Feilberg, H.F. De derovre en raekke breve fra Canada. 1912
2296 Field, E. Biographical sketch. 1912
2332A Pocock, R. A man in the open. 1912
2437 Wheatley, E.P. Out West. 1913
2444 Binnie-Clark, G. Wheat & women. 1914
2449 Campbell, M.N. Reminiscences of pioneer days. 191_?
2587 Feilberg, H.F. Hjemliv pa praerien. 1917
2649 West, E. Homesteading; two prairie seasons. 1918
2713 Hjelt, O. Nybyggerliv paa praerien. 1920
2733 Pirot, J. Avant les neiges. 1920
2734 Pirot, J. Elle vit. 19–
2791 Rodvik, S. Fortaellinger fra Canada. 1921
2801 Ball, G.F. Extracts of a lifetime. 1922
2824 Ricci, V.H. Ups and downs in Canada. 1922
2854 Kernighan, T. Dufferin and Carman, Manitoba. 1923
2877 Blais, T.A. An adventurous career. 1924
2953 Trotter, B. A horseman and the West. 1925
2967 Linck, O. Kanada det store fremtidsland. 1926
3030 Mikkelsen, C. Canada som fremtidsland. 1927
3057 Borel, A. Croquis du Far-West canadien. 1928
3076A Gordon, C. Red gold. 1928
3103 Rose, H. Stump farm. 1928
3114 Adshead, H.B. Pioneer tales. 1929
3122 Burns, W.C. Twenty years of thrilling adventures. 1929
3129 Church, H.E. An emigrant in the Canadian Northwest. 1929
3166 Borel, A. Le Robinson de la Red Deer. 1930
3184 Gunn, J.J. Echoes of the Red. 1930
3199 Little, R.H. Reminiscences of pioneering experiences. 1930
3223 Schulze, G. Som emigrant i Kanada. 1930
3245 Christen, M. Feux et frimas. 1931
3282 Troughton, F.J. Bachelor's paradise. 1931
3301 Haegler, C.A. Oh, Canada; vier Jahre auf und ab. 1932
3306A McClintock, G. The wolves of Cooking Lake. 1932
3341 Jackson, M.E. On the last frontier. 1933
3377 Dawson, C.A. Settlement of Peace River area. 1934
3406 Street, A.G. Farmer's glory. 1934
3413 Baldwin, H. Farm for two pounds. 1935

3456 McClung, N.L. Clearing in the West. 1935
3476 Sinton, R. Looking backward. 1935
3603 Campbell, M.W. The soil is not enough. 1938
3674 Constantin-Fortin, M. Une femme se penche sur son passé. 1939
3718 Dawson, C.A. Pioneering in the Prairie Provinces. 1940
3724 Götz, K. Die heimstätter. 1940
3730 Lamson, D.A. Once in my saddle. 1940
3778 Schulze, G. Åter i Kanada. 1941
3803 Landstrom, O. Pioneer homestead stories. 1942
3839 Greene, D.L. By the swift waters. 1943
3932 McAra, P. 62 years on the Saskatchewan prairies. 1945
3956 Shubert, B. The homesteader, a true story. 1945
3988 Hughes, L.W. No time for tears. 1946
3997 Mishaegen, A. de. Dans la forêt canadienne. 1946
4049 Maurice, V. 50 years in Peace River country. 1947
4052 Middleton, C.J. Green fields afar. 1947
4114 MacEwan, J.W.G. The sodbusters. 1948
4118 Meilicke, E.J. Leaves from the life of a pioneer. 1948
4160 Linnell, J.B. Story of a pioneer. 1949
4188 Bronner, F. Nouveaux Canadiens. 1950
4220 Pirot, J. Contes dau lon èt did près. 1950
4261 Raber, J.B. Pioneering in Alberta. 1951
4293 Giscard, G. Dans la prairie canadienne. 1952
4324 Peltonen, E. Kulkurina Amerikassa, uutisraivaajana Canadassa. 1952
4367 Tibbits, E.C. On to the sunset. 1953

POSTSCRIPT
MacGregor, J.G. North-west of 16. (Toronto, 1958)
Shepherd, Geo. West of yesterday. Edited with a commentary by John H. Archer. (Toronto, 1965)
A number of other reminiscences of pioneer life have been published since 1953

4 Women in the West

See also 'Pioneer Life'

909 C.P.R. What women say of the Canadian North West. 1886
1541A Girls' Home of Welcome Association. 1898-1913
1680 Dugas, G. First Canadian woman in the Northwest. 1902
1715 C.P.R. Words from women in Western Canada. 1903
1861 C.P.R. Women's work in Western Canada. 1906
1920 C.P.R. Home life of women in Western Canada. 1907
1957 Watt, G.B. A woman in the West. 1907
2129 Cran, M.F. A woman in Canada. 1910
2384 Crawford, M.E. Legal status of women in Manitoba. 1913
2444 Binnie-Clark, G. Wheat & women. 1914
2540 Canadian Women's Press Club. Club women's records. 1916
3592 Women's Institutes, Alberta. Story of ... 1909-1937
2599 MacGregor, D. Alberta club woman's blue book. 1917
2642 Speers. I.O.D.E. New Ottawa chapter. 1918
2737 Saskatchewan. Legislation affecting women and children. 1920
2748 United Farm Women of Alberta. U.F.W.A. 192–
2770 Edwards, H. Legal status of women of Alberta. 1921
2781 Low, F.B. Openings for British women. 1921
2790 Raymond, Mrs. A.P. Gathered sheaves from the National Council of Women. 1921

2817 Low, F.B. Women out West. 1922
2850 Healy, W.J. Women of Red River. 1923
2956 Bennett, A. Local Council of Women of Regina. 1926
2968 Local Council of Women of Saskatoon. Ten years in retrospect. 1926
2992 Une religieuse de Notre-Dame des Missions. Petit historique de nos fondations au Canada. 1926
3164 Beaubier, Mrs. E.L. Order of the Eastern Star. 1930
3369 Barritt, Mrs. R.W. History of United Farm Women. 1934
3552 Alberta Women's Institute Girls Club. The A.W.I.G.C. Magazine. 1937
3589 Strange, K.R. With the West in her eyes. 1937
3694 Oddson, A. Employment of women in Manitoba. 1939
3700 Saskatchewan Homemakers' Clubs. Retrospect and prospect. 1939
3763 Hinds, E.M. Nothing ventured. 1941
3862 Carter, E. Thirty years of progress; United Farm Women of Alberta. 1944
3931 Local Council of Women of Regina. Golden jubilee. 1945
3933 McClung, N.L. The stream runs fast. 1945
3949 Sanders, B.H. Emily Murphy. 1945
3997 Mishaegen, A. de. Dans la forêt canadienne. 1946
4176 Saskatchewan. Bureau of Publications. Women and children's rights. 1949
4275 United Church of Canada. Women's Missionary Society. Alberta Branch. History. 1951
4302 Kohuska, N.L. Chvert' stolittya na hromadskiy nyvi. 1952
4306 Lawrence, E.M. Glimpses of the past, American Women's Club. 1952

POSTSCRIPT

Ukrainian Catholic Women's League. Liga Ukpains'kykh Katolyts'kykh Zhinok Edmontons'koi eparkii, pochatky i diial'nist; Ukrainian Catholic Women's League of the Edmonton Eparchy. (Edmonton, 1967)

Gray, J.H. Red lights on the Prairies. (Toronto, 1971)

L RANCHING

616 Craig, J.R. Grazing country of Canada. 1882
821 Hill, A.S. From home to home. 1885
1071 North-West brand book. 1888-1904
1132 Alberta Railway & Coal Co. A stockman's paradise. 189-
1469 Strange, T.B. Gunner Jingo's jubilee. 1896
1556 Walrond Ranche Co. Ltd. New Walrond Ranche. 1898
1718 Craig, J.R. Ranching with lords and commons. 1903
1701 Ranching in the Canadian Northwest. 1903
1780 N.W.T. Dept. of Agriculture. North West brand book; supplement no.1. 1904
2284 Stampede at Calgary. 1912
2345 Stock, A.B. Ranching in the Canadian West. 1912
2404 Kelly, L.V. The range men. 1913
2435 Stock, R. Confessions of a tenderfoot. 1913
2554 McEachran, D.M. Impressions of pioneers. 1916
2769 H.R.H. Prince of Wales 'E.P. Ranch.' 192_?
3129 Church, H.E. An emigrant in the Canadian Northwest. 1929
3203 MacInnes, C.M. In the shadow of the Rockies. 1930
3451 Lecky, P. Peter Lecky. 1935
3587 Springett, E.C. For my children's children. 1937
4017 Vrooman, C.W. Cattle ranching in Western Canada. 1946

4115 McIntyre, W.H., Jr. Brief history of McIntyre Ranch. 1948
4340 Calgary. Ranchmen's Club. Slight historical sketch. 1953
4341 Campbell, G. We found peace. 1953

POSTSCRIPT
MacEwan, J.W.G. John Ware's cow country. (Edmonton, 1960)
MacEwan, J.W.G. Blazing the old cattle trail. (Saskatoon, 1962)
McCallum, W.S. A Scot in Canada: adventures on a ranch. (Calgary, 1963)
MacEwen, J.W.G. Hoofprints and hitching posts. (Saskatoon, 1964)
Russell, Andy. Trails of a wilderness wanderer. (New York, 1971)

M THE WHEAT ECONOMY

1 Agriculture

296 Canada. Parliament. Senate. Select Committee on Rupert's Land. Report. 1870
679 Hind, H.Y. Manitoba and North-West frauds. 1883
756 McNeill, R. Practical tests on gardening. 1884
794 Canada. Dept. of Agriculture. Agricultural statistics for Manitoba and N.W.T. 1885
814 Fream, W. The prairie. 1885
831A Meyer, R. Co-operative society for cheese and butter. 1885
1190 McQueen, J. Notes on a trip to America. 1890
1246 Calgary Tribune. Irrigation in the Territories. 1892
1386 Prairie agriculture. 1895
1522 Binder twine and the farmer's interests. 1898
1591 The binder twine steal. 1900
1777 Mavor, J. Report to Board of Trade. 1904
1782 Reglur og tilskipanir fyrir medhöndlun baendafjelaga. 1904
1970 Canada. Dept. of the Interior. Seed grain. 1908
2027 Ussel, G. d'. Rapport sur l'agriculture. 1908
2030 Weijers, A. De waarheid over Alberta. 1908
2040 Canada. Dept. of the Interior. Seed grain distribution. 1909
2458 Edmonton City Dairy. 1914
2592 Lethbridge. Board of Trade. More and better water for our farms. 1917
2684 Wheeler, S. Seager Wheeler's book. 1919
2692 Bracken, J. Crop production. 1920
2759 Bracken, J. Dry farming in Western Canada. 1921
2955 Widtsoe, J.A. Examination of northern irrigation district. 1925
2959 C.P.R. 50,000 harvesters wanted. 1926
3076 Gockel, A. Die Landwirtschaft in den Prärieprovinzen. 1928
3227A Sutherland Canadian Lands Company, Ltd. Sale of irrigable farming property. 1930
3260 Hurd, W.B. Agriculture, climate and population. 1931
3263 King, T. The black ox. 1931
3270A Nor'West Farmer and Farm & Home. Master farmers of Canada. 1931
3273 Peterson, C.W.C. Useful objectives of western agriculture. 1931
3312A Rosenberg, Louis. Land policy of the farmer-labour group. 1932?
3389 Mackintosh, W.A. Prairie settlement. 1934
3404 Shaw, A.M. Drought on the Canadian prairies. 1934
3418 Britnell, G.E. The western farmer. 1935
3434 Fifty years of dairying. 1935

2 **Wheat**

3 **Grain Trade**

2941 Mackintosh, W.A. Canadian wheat pools. 1925
2985 Saskatchewan Co-op. Elevator Co. A brief record. 1926
3010 Canadian Wheat Pool. Truth about grain prices. 1927
3015 Davisson, W.P. Pooling wheat in Canada. 1927
3033 Northwest Grain Dealers' Assoc. Facts on grain marketing. 1927
3041 United Grain Growers' Ltd. A farmers' company comes of age. 1927
3049 Alberta Co-operative Wheat Producers. Pooling Alberta's wheat. 1928
3118 Boyle, J.E. Marketing Canada's wheat. 1929
3141 Irwin, W.A. The Canadian Wheat Pool. 1929
3155 Sapiro, A. 100% control by legislation. 1929
3157 U.F.C. (Sask. Sect.) Facts about 100% control. 1929
3177 Gampell, S.S. Canada and her wheat pool. 1930
3219 Peterson, C.W.C. Wheat, the riddle of markets. 1930
3228 Swanson, W.W. Wheat. 1930
3250 D'Hauteserve, L. Le blé au Canada. 1931
3283 United Grain Growers' Ltd. Grain market situation. 1931
3304 Kaufmann, H. Kanadische Weizenpool. 1932
3307 McGibbon, D.A. The Canadian grain trade. 1932
3409 Winnipeg Grain Exchange. 1934
3466 Patton, H.S. The Canadian wheat pool. 1935
3496 Canadian Wheat Pools on the air. 1936
3729 Lamont, C.A.R. Prairie sentinels. 1940
3733 McPhail, A.J. Diary. 1940
3766 Manitoba. Dept. of Agriculture. Study of wheat policies. 1941
3777 Searle Grain Co. Prairie wheat growers' problems. 1941
3805 Mathieson, G.S. Wheat and the futures market. 1942
3894 United Grain Growers' Ltd. Grain Growers record. 1944
3973 Crerar, T.A. Canada's wheat problem. 1946
4079 Yates, S.W. Saskatchewan Wheat Pool. 1947
4127 Saskatchewan Co-op. Producers. Saskatchewan Wheat Pool. 1948
4141 Canadian Co-op. Wheat Producers. Summary of operations of Canadian Wheat Board. 1949
4148 Facts about the wheat agreement. 1949
4177 Saskatchewan Co-op. Producers. 25 years. 1949
4317 Nesbitt, L.D. Case against the speculative marketing of grain. 1952
4318 Nesbitt, L.D. Farm viewpoint of the Crow's Nest freight rate. 1952
4350A Humphries, T.R. Alberta's wheat. 1953

4 Economic Conditions

721 British North American Fire Insurance Co. Prospectus. 1884
1411 Holmes, O'C.J. Cause & remedy for hard times. 1895
2197 Astley & Shackle. Investments in Alberta. 1911
2350 Ure, R.W. Mortgage investments in Alberta. 1912
2385 Davidson & McRae. Industrial and business opportunities. 1913
2434A Stirling, J.T. The Bellevue explosions. 1913
2463 Howard, H. Canada, the western cities. 1914
2471 Menzies, J.H. Economical condition and resources. 1914
2478 Perpetual Rights Oil Co. Prospectus. 1914
2489 Wilson & Co. Alberta oil fields. 1914
2512 Menzies, J.H. Development of the resources of the Canadian middle West. 1915
2623A The Coal Operators of Northern Alta. Coal; where it is. 1918?
2633A Northern Production Company. 1918
2651 Brown, V. The western farmer and the bank. 1919

2690 Anderson & Brown Consolidated, Ltd. The world's new oil field. 1920
2834 Bennett, A.S. Is the West worth while? 1923
2865 Pratt, G.R. Coal trails. 1923
2944 Manitoba Economic Conference. Report. 1925
2950 Pierce, H.C. Our money system. 1925
2975 Owens, R.C. The bridge to liberty. 1926
3050 Alexander Macdonald, a tribute. 1928
3109 Tull & Arden. Manual of oil companies. 1928
3170 Calgary Albertan oil manual. 1930
3263 King, T. The black ox. 1931
3266 MacBeth, R.G. Sir A. Nanton. 1931
3272A Paynter, W.C. Trumpet call of Canadian money. 1931
3389 Mackintosh, W.A. Prairie settlement. 1934
3459 Mackintosh, W.A. Economic problems of the Prairie Provinces. 1935
3466A Peterson, C.W.C. Western drought situation. 1935
3504 Elliott, C. Report to Alberta Bondholders' Committee. 1936
3507 Farm Appraisal Conference. Report. 1936
3613 Davidson, C.B. Employment in Manitoba. 1938
3665 Britnell, G.E. The wheat economy. 1939
3672 Conference on Markets for Western Farm Products. Proceedings. 1939
3703 Stapleford, E.W. Report on rural relief. 1939
3713 Beach, F.K. History of Alberta oil. 1940
3801 Hamilton, J.B. Evidence on tar sands. 1942
3802 Kraenzel, C.F. The northern plains in a world of change. 1942
3812 Peterson, C.W.C. The new order and its problems. 1942
3834 Dominion Mortgage & Investments Assoc. Prairie farmer and his debts. 1943
3897 Alberta. Dept. of Trade & Industry. Your opportunity in Alberta. 1945
3939 Myers, C.V. The oil investor. 1945
4060 Riley, R.T. Memoirs. 1947
4065 Saskatchewan. Bureau of Publications. Progress report from your government. 1947
4097 Gislason, I. Prairie panorama. 1948
4159 Link, T.A. Oil in Alberta and Western Canada. 1949
4164 McMahon, F. Brief ... natural gas resources of Alberta. 1949
4319 Nickle, C.O. Story of Pincher Creek. 1952

POSTSCRIPT
Schwartz, Charles. The search for stability. (Toronto, 1959)
Gray, J.H. The winter years; the Depression on the Prairies. (Toronto, 1966)
Gray, J.H. Men against the desert. (Saskatoon, 1967)

5 Taxation

2487 Wade, F.C. Experiments with single tax. 1914
2520 Pearce, W. Absurdity and injustice of single tax. 1915
2697 Clark, A.B. Provincial and municipal taxation. 1920
2767 Clark, A.B. Recent tax developments. 1921
2845 Edmonton Morning Bulletin. A warning from Alberta. 1923
2940 Mackie, G.D. Review of local government taxation in Saskatchewan. 1925

N CO-OPERATION

1 Co-operation

1409 Harmony Industrial Assoc. Prospectus. 1895
2010 Moorhouse, A.H.J. Deep furrows. 1908
2624B Grain Growers' Guide. History of the Grain Growers. 1918
2854A Lawrence, H.F. Kidnapped. 1923
2869 Sapiro, A. Report of mass meeting. 1923
2897 Mackintosh, W.A. Agricultural co-operation in Western Canada. 1924
2911 United Grain Growers' Ltd. Co-operative cattle selling. 1924
2941 Mackintosh, W.A. Canadian wheat pools. 1925
2961 Evans, W.S. The Canadian Wheat Pool. 1926
2975 Owens, R.C. Bridge to liberty. 1926
2997 Alberta Co-operative Wheat Producers Ltd. Alberta wheat pool rally. 1927
3033 Northwest Grain Dealers' Assoc. Facts on grain marketing. 1927
3056 Booth, J.F. Co-operative marketing of grain. 1928
3092 Patton, H.S. Grain growers' co-operation. 1928
3139 Hull, J.T. History of co-operation. 1929
3141 Irwin, W.A. Canadian Wheat Pool. 1929
3142 Janicki, S. Kanadyjski syndykat sprzedazy pszenicy. 1929
3155 Sapiro, A. 100% control by legislation. 1929
3157 U.F.C. (Sask. Sect.) Facts about 100% control. 1929
3177 Gampell, S.S. Canada and her wheat pool. 1930
3304 Kaufmann, H. Kanadische Weizenpool. 1932
3424 Canadian Wheat Pools. Wheat pools in relation to rural community life. 1935
3466 Patton, H.S. The Canadian wheat pool. 1935
3490 Alberta Wheat Pool. Tides in the West. 1936
3551 Alberta Wheat Pool. Need for a national wheat board. 1937
3496 Canadian Wheat Pools on the air. 1936
3599 Boyd, H.R.C. New breaking. 1938
3689 Manitoba. Dept. of Agric. and Immigration. Credit unions. 1939
3733 McPhail, A.J. Diary. 1940
3791 Co-operative Commonwealth Federation. First ten years, 1932-1942. 1942
3876 McNaughton, J. Markets and men. 1944
3885 Saskatchewan Co-op. Creamery Assoc. Facts. 1944
3894 United Grain Growers' Ltd. Grain Growers record. 1944
3897B Alta. Livestock Co-operative Ltd. Alberta co-operative leaders. 1945?
3960A United Grain Growers Ltd. Presentation to Royal Commission. 1945
4009 Saskatchewan Wheat Pool. Twenty-one years of progress, 1924-1945. 1946
4029 Chapman, H.E. Progress of co-op. farming. 1947
4079 Yates, S.W. Saskatchewan Wheat Pool. 1947
4089 Co-operative Union of Saskatchewan. Co-operative principles. 1948
4127 Saskatchewan Co-op. Producers. Saskatchewan Wheat Pool. 1948
4177 Saskatchewan Co-op. Producers. 25 years. 1949
4234 Alberta Wheat Pool. Story of the Alberta Wheat Pool. 1951

2 Agricultural Societies

758 Manitoba and Northwest Farmers' Union. Resolutions. 1884
829 Manitoba and Northwest Farmers' Union. Statement of claims. 1885
1662 Territorial Grain Growers' Assoc. Constitution. 1901
1692 Territorial Grain Growers' Assoc. Report of annual meeting. 1902
2010 Moorhouse, A.H.J. Deep furrows. 1908
2087B United Farmers of Alberta. Constitution & by-laws. 1909
2490 Woodsworth, J.S. Studies in rural citizenship. 1914

2623 Canadian Council of Agriculture. Farmers' platform. 1918
2683 United Farmers of Alberta. How to organize. 1919
2715 Irvine, W. Farmers in politics. 1920
2748 United Farm Women of Alberta. U.F.W.A. 192-
2749 U.F.C. (Sask. Sect.) Do you know this? 192-
2986 Saskatchewan Grain Growers' Assoc. A quarter century of progress. 1926
4093 Farmers' action program of Alberta. 1948
4128 Sharp, P.F. Agrarian revolt in Western Canada. 1948
4133 U.F.C. (Sask. Sect.) Rural romance. 1948
4210 MacEwan, J.W.G. Agriculture on parade. 1950

O POLITICS AND GOVERNMENT

1 General

485 Taché, A.A. Pastoral letter concerning the elections. 1878
561 Begg, A. Letters on the situation in the North West. 1881
760 Morris, A. Nova Britannia. 1884
1028 Smith, G. Address to electors of Lisgar. 1887
1144 Blake, E. North-West affairs. 1890
1421 Patrons of Industry. The political position of the Patrons. 1895
1824 Landry, A.C.P. Le bill d'autonomie des provinces. 1905
1946 Partridge, E.A. A farmers' trade union. 1907?
1992 Liberal Party. Facts vs. slander. 1908
1960 Ames, H.B. Our western heritage. 1908
2122 Chipman, G.F. The siege of Ottawa. 1910
2124 Conrades of Equity. Constitution. 191_?
2230 Liberal Party. Grain grower and reciprocity. 1911
2231 Liberal Party. Haultain and reciprocity. 1911
2232 Liberal Party. Reciprocity's benefit to Western Canada. 1911
2233 Liberal Party. The western farmer. 1911
2234 Liberal Party. Liberal Farmers Association of Battleford. 1911
2259 Scott, W. Address to people of Saskatchewan. 1911
2330 Paynter, J.E. Spectres of the night. 1912
2420 Partridge, E.A. Manifesto of No-Party League. 1913
2552 Laidley, F.W. The why of the Non-Partisan League. 1916
2591 Laidley, F.W. The why of the Non-Partisan League. 1917
2668 Hjelt, O. Farmeren og socialismen. 1919
2689 Woodsworth, J.S. Reconstruction from the viewpoint of labor. 1919
2715 Irvine, W. Farmers in politics. 1920
2731 Owens, R.C. Daylight on money. 1920
2766 Canadian Reconstruction Assoc. Grain Growers and Canada's tariff. 1921
2788 Paynter, W.C. Canadian money and progress. 1921
2949 Partridge, E.A. A war on poverty. 1925
3126 Canada. Parliament. H. of C. Select Standing Committee on privileges and elections. Evidence re illegal practices in Athabaska. 1929
3160 Woodsworth, J.S. Hours that stand apart. 1929
3249 Dafoe, J.W. Clifford Sifton in relation to his times. 1931
3347 Macphail, A.C. Economic crisis and the CCF. 1933
3355 Solloway, I.W.C. Speculators and politicians. 1933
3364 Woodsworth, J.S. A plea for social justice. 1933
3385 Irvine, W. Forces of reconstruction. 1934

3436 Gardiner, J.G. Problems of Western Canada. 1935
3485 Western Canada Federation. 1935
3456A McCollum, W.H. Who owns Canada. 1935
3502 Collier, W.H. Super-money. 1936
3511 Haver, M.J. Social credit explained. 1936
3566 Leacock, S.B. My discovery of the West. 1937
3633 League for Social Reconstruction. Pioneers in poverty. 1938
3667 Buck, T. The West & the federal election. 1939
3688 McTavish, D.C. Individualism versus socialism. 1939
3914 Ferguson, R.T. We stand on guard. 1945
3893 Underhill, F.H. Woodsworth, untypical Canadian. 1944
4025 Binns, K.J. Social Credit in Alberta. 1947
4128 Sharp, P.F. Agrarian revolt in Western Canada. 1948
4180 Tucker, W.A. C.C.F. record in Saskatchewan examined. 1949
4217 Morton, W.L. The Progressive party in Canada. 1950

2 Manitoba

322 Canada. Dept. of Sec. of State. Instructions to Archibald. 1871
372 Manitoba. Executive Council. Report on claims of Manitoba. 1873
354 Plea for early development of our resources. 1873
463 O'Donnell, J.H. Manitoba matters. 1877
556 Letters on the anomalous position of Manitoba. 1881
551 Winnipeg Conservative Party. Constitution and by-laws. 1880
747 Greenway, T. Province of Manitoba. 1884
763 Norquay, J. Memoranda by the provincial treasurer. 1884
765 Plumb, J.B. Opposition press on Manitoba & N.W. 1884
774 Tuttle, C.R. Open letter on the agitation in Manitoba. 1884
775 Veritas Vincit. Manitoba and confederation. 1884
829 Manitoba & Northwest Farmers' Union. Claims of the province. 1885
985 Attwood, P.H. Jubilee essay on imperial federation and Manitoba. 1887
1025 Robertson, J.P. Political manual of Manitoba and N.W.T. 1887
1213 Canada. Dept. of Sec. of State. Abolition of the French language. 1891
1268 Jerome, M. Coup d'oeil rétrospectif. 1892
2282 Cahan, C.H. Minority rights in Keewatin. 1912
2316 Laurier, Sir W. The Manitoba question. 1912
2318 Liberal Party. How the Macdonald by-election was won. 1912
2455 Conservative Party. Record of the Roblin government. 1914
2687 Winnipeg Strike. Definition of collective bargaining. 1919
2780 Lefeaux, W.W. Winnipeg-London-Moscow. 1921
3530 Ross, H.R. 35 years in the limelight. 1936
3567 Litterick, J. Whither Manitoba? 1937

POSTSCRIPT
Donnelly, M.S. The government of Manitoba. (Toronto, 1963)

3 North West Territories

451 Canada. Dept. of Sec. of State. Instructions to Lieut.-Gov., etc. 1877
902 Canada. Dept. of Sec. of State. Memorial to N.W. Council. 1886
1017 N.W.T. Leg. Council. Journals, 1877-87
1025 Robertson, J.P. Political manual of Manitoba and N.W.T. 1887
1100 Davin, N.F. Demands of the North-West! 1889
1387 Provincial government for Alberta. 1895

POSTSCRIPT

Thomas, L.H. The struggle for responsible government in the Northwest Territories, 1870-97. (Toronto, 1956)

4 Saskatchewan

2579 Conservative Party. Conservative platforms. 1917
2580 Conservative Party. Handbook, campaign, 1917. 1917
2581 Conservative Party. How Liberal members were bought. 1917
2582 Conservative Party. Kindersley Dam. 1917
2583 Conservative Party. Liquor traffic. 1917
2584 Conservative Party. Patriotic tax. 1917
2585 Conservative Party. Phantom roads. 1917
2586 Conservative Party. Weed Lake bridge. 1917
2593 Liberal Party. How Saskatchewan women got the vote. 1917
2594 Liberal Party. Liberal handbook, 1917. 1917
2595 Liberal Party. Liberalism and progress. 1917
2596 Liberal Party. Some phases of Saskatchewan school problem. 1917
2787 Patrick, T.A. The county system for Saskatchewan. 1921
3020 Farmers' Educational League. Manifesto. 1927
3082A Kritzwiser, H.H. Ten thousand suckers. 1928
3312A Rosenberg, L. Land policy of the farmer-labour group. 1932?
3863 Conservative Party. Policy. 1944
3872 Labor-Progressive Party. Electors of Saskatoon [vote] Nelson Clarke. 1944
3875 Liberal Party (Sask.) Facts, a record which is a challenge. 1944
3950 Saskatchewan. Bureau of Publications. Saskatchewan plans for progress. 1945
3951 Saskatchewan. Bureau of Publications. Saskatchewan viewpoint. 1945
3986 Honderich, B.H. Toronto Daily Star reports. 1946
4065 Saskatchewan. Bureau of Publications. Progress report from your government. 1947
4087 C.C.F. (Sask. Sect.) C.C.F. program for Saskatchewan. 1948
4088 C.C.F. (Sask. Sect.) C.C.F. members' handbook. 1948
4207 Lipset, S.M. Agrarian socialism. 1950

POSTSCRIPT

Tyre, Robt. Douglas in Saskatchewan; the story of a socialist experiment. (Vancouver, 1962)

Higginbotham, C.H. Off the record: the C.C.F. in Saskatchewan. (Toronto, 1968)

Ward, N. Politics in Saskatchewan. (Don Mills, Ont., 1968)

Saskatchewan Archives. Directory of members of Parliament and federal elections for the N.W.T. and Saskatchewan, 1887-1966. (Regina, 1967)

Saskatchewan Archives. Saskatchewan executive and legislative directory 1905–1970. (Regina, 1971)

5 Alberta

1849 Alberta's first parliament. 1906
2543 Conservative Party (Alberta). Alberta under Liberal rule. 1916
2544 Conservative Party (Alberta). Provincial Conservative platform. 1916
2806 Edmonds, W.E. Natural resources question. 1922
2975 Owens, R.C. The bridge to liberty. 1926
3323 Aberhart, W. Coloured leaflet series. 1933
3324 Aberhart, W. Douglas system of economics. 1933
3325 Aberhart, W. Study group features. 1932-33
3366 Alberta. Leg. Assembly. Agricultural Committee. Douglas system of Social Credit. 1934
3410 Aberhart, W. Social Credit manual. 1935
3411 Aberharts Social Credit Ideen. 1935
3412 Alberta. Leg. Assembly. Agricultural Committee. Constitutionality & economic aspects of Social Credit. 1935

3421 Cameron, S. The Amos and Andy of Social Credit. 1935
3429 Davidson, W.M. The Aberhart plan. 1935
3430 Davidson, W.M. The Aberhart proposals. 1935
3443 Humble, H. Social Credit democracy. 1935
3454 Love, J.R. Cross examination of Social Credit. 1935
3461 Michell, H. Social Credit. 1935
3468 Radke, G.D. Major Douglas's interim report under your microscope. 1935
3474 Sauvé, G. Le crédit social. 1935
3505 Elliott, C. Say Alberta can pay full interest. 1936
3513 Irvine, W. Let us reason together. 193_?
3533 Sanderson, C.R. Social Credit. 1936
3543 Stewart, C.G. Social Credit theories exploded. 193_?
3557 Douglas, C.H. The Alberta experiment. 1937
3558 Economic Safety League. The dangers of Douglasism. 1937
3563 Hattersley, C.M. Aberhart and Alberta. 1937
3569 McConnell, W.K. The Alberta fiasco. 1937
3576 Marks, A.L. Public denied facts by Edmonton Journal. 1937
3580 Peterson, C.W.C. Banks and Social Credit. 1937
3581 Peterson, C.W.C. Social Credit. 1937
3582 Powell, G.P. Bankers' toadies – exterminate them. 1937
3586 Smith, R.R. Alberta has the sovereign right. 1937
3588 Stark, J.H. Social Credit in Alberta. 1937
3595 Alberta. The case for Alberta. 1938
3601 Cameron, S. No matter how thin you slice it. 1938
3612 Dale, A. $25.00 a month. 1938
3618A Edmonton. Chamber of Commerce. Disallowance of certain acts of legislature. 1938
3628 Halpin, B. Pulpit pounding Bill. 1938
3661 What Aberhart has done for you and me. 1939
3679 Duggan, D.M. Review of Premier Aberhart's promises. 1939
3683A Hugill, J.W. Principle re office attorney general. 1939
3685 King, W.R. History of Alberta, political & financial, 1905-1938. 1939
3695 Page, J.P. Unity, the good fight. 1939
3702 Social Credit Board. The record tells the story. 1939
3725 Hand, W.H. Case for Alberta. 1940
3727 Irvine, W. The trail of a truth twister. 1940
3754 Unity Council of Alberta. The truth about the records. 1940
3764 How Alberta is fighting finance. 1941
3779 Social Credit Board. Alice in Blunderland. 1941
3780 Social Credit Board. Debt legislation. 1941
3836 Edmonton Bulletin. Aberhart-Manning. 1943
3842 Highe, E. Maggie abandons the big dough. 1943
3869 Irvine, W. Can capitalism survive the war. 194–?
3891 Storer, R.H. I am a lunatic. 1944
3957 Social Credit Board. Questions and answers. 1945
4039 James, N.B. Autobiography of a nobody. 1947
4223 Rolph, W.K. Henry Wise Wood. 1950
4356 Macpherson, C.B. Democracy in Alberta. 1953
4086 C.C.F. Story of the Alberta C.C.F., 1932 to 1948. 1948

POSTSCRIPT

Mann, W.E. Sect, cult, and church in Alberta. (Toronto, 1955)
Thomas, L.G. The Liberal party in Alberta; a history of politics in the province of Alberta, 1905-1921. (Toronto, 1959)

Mallory, J.R. Social Credit and the federal power in Canada. (Toronto, 1954)
Irving, J.A. The Social Credit movement in Alberta. (Toronto, 1959)
Macpherson, C.B. Democracy in Alberta; Social Credit and the party system. (Toronto, 1962)
Nichols, H.E. Alberta's fight for freedom. 5 pamphlets. (Edmonton, 1963)
Hooke, A.J. 30 + 5; I know, I was there. (Edmonton, 1971)

6 Natural Resources Question

561 Begg, A. Letters on the situation in the North West. 1881
556 Letters on the anomalous position of Manitoba. 1881
1661A Stuart, C.A. Our territorial lands. 1901
2198 Bramley-Moore, A. Canada and her colonies. 1911
2682 Thompson, B. Canada's suzerainty over the West. 1919
2728 Martin, C.B. The natural resources question. 1920

P LAWS, STATUTES, ETC.

1 Assiniboia

210 Great Britain. Laws, statutes, etc. An act for the regulation of trade. 1859
230 Assiniboia Laws, statutes, etc. Laws of Assiniboia. 1862
311 Rupert's Land. Provisional govt. Bills. 1870

2 North West Territories

322 Canada. Dept. of Sec. of State. Instructions to Archibald. 1871
384 Canada. Laws, statutes, etc. Acts re administration of justice. 1874
439 Canada. Dept. of the Interior. Laws and ordinances of N.W.T. 1876
451 Canada. Dept. of Sec. of State. Instructions to Lieut.-Gov. 1877
471 Canada. Dept. of the Interior. Copy of ordinances of N.W.T. 1878
494 Canada. Dept. of Sec. of State. Copies of ordinances of N.W.T., 1878. 1879
1164 Coutlee, L.W. Manual of registration of titles. 1890
1449 McCaul, C.C. Ready reference guide to ordinances of N.W.T. 1896
2247 N.W.T. Laws, statutes, etc. Ordinances, 1905. 1911

3 General

2607 Scott, W.S. Chattel exemptions. 1917
2608 Scott, W.S. Homesteads and their exemptions. 1917
2789 Popple, A.E. Western Canada law. 1921

Q MEDICINE AND NURSING

1583 North-West Territories Medical Register. 1899
2436 Teetgen, A.B. A white passion. 1913
3173 Church of England. Church hospitals. 193_?
3342 Jamieson, H.C. Medical history of Edmonton. 1933
4395 Calgary. Holy Cross Hospital. Souvenir of the opening. 1929
3634 MacDermot, H.E. Sir Thomas Roddick. 1938
3760 Calgary. Holy Cross Hospital. Golden anniversary, 1891-1941

3871 Krumpelmann, C.W. In this sign they conquered. 1944
3878 Mary Murphy, Sister. St. Boniface heroines of mercy. 1944
3879 May Guichan, Soeur. Développement des oeuvres des Soeurs Grises. 1944
3884 Primeau, L. Le centenaire des Soeurs Grises. 1944
3892 Tessier, A. Vers les pays d'en-haut. 1944
3982 Grey Nuns. Hôpital Saint-Boniface. 1946
4008 Saskatchewan. Bureau of Publications. Progress in health services. 1946
4022 Atkinson, I. Saskatchewan health policy. 1947
4040 Jamieson, H.C. Early medicine in Alberta. 1947
4042A Lent, D.G. Alberta Red Cross in peace and war. 1947
4172 100 years of medicine. 1949
4229 Whiteside, W.C. Nomadic life of a surgeon. 1950

POSTSCRIPT

Tyre, Robt. Saddlebag surgeon; the story of Murrough O'Brien, M.D. (Toronto, 1954)

Saskatchewan. Legislative Assembly. Library. The medicare crisis in Saskatchewan, Jan. 1, 1960-July 31, 1962: a bibliography. (Regina, 1963)

Thompson, W.P. Medical care: programs and issues. (Toronto, 1964)

Tollefson, E.A. Bitter medicine; the Saskatchewan medicare feud. (Saskatoon, 1964)

Cashman, A.W. Heritage of service, the history of nursing in Alberta. (Edmonton, 1966)

Banfill, B.J. Pioneer nurse. (Toronto, 1967)

R THE SPIRITUAL LIFE

Some religious history is to be found under 'The People,' e.g., Doukhobors, Mennonites, etc.

1 Baptist Churches

1240 Winch, J. In favor of adult baptism. 1891
2068 Mellick, H.G. Indians and our Indian missions. 1909
2201 Calgary. First Baptist Church. Souvenir. 1911
2916 Bellamy, L. Pioneer days of first Baptist church, Edmonton. 1925
3289 Baptist Union of Western Canada. Some Baptist pioneers. 1932
3368 Baptist Union. Crusading in the Canadian West. 1934
3573 McLaurin, C.C. 60 years in the ministry. 1937
3646 Smalley, W.C. Reorganizing for advance. 1938
3687 McLaurin, C.C. Pioneering in Western Canada. 1939
3771 Pickel, W.U. Golden jubilee of First Baptist Church, Regina. 1941
3817 Smalley, W.C. On the western front. 1942
4082 Bagnall, L.L. At the sixtieth milestone. 1948
4113A McDonald, Mrs. J.R. Baptist missions in Western Canada. 1948
4259 Pickel, W.U. History of First Baptist Church, Regina. 1951
4350 Hultgren, P. History of First Baptist Church, Midale. 1953

2 Calgary Prophetic Bible Institute

3004 Calgary Prophetic Bible Institute. Calendar. 1927

3 **Church of the Brethren**

2842 Church of the Brethren. Official souvenir of Alberta. 1923

4 **Church of England**

81 West, J. Substance of a journal. 1824
112 Mountain, G.J. Journal during visit to north-west mission. 1845
126 Church Missionary Society. Historical notice of formation of N.W. mission. 1849
137 Anderson, D. Charge to clergy. 1851
138 Anderson, D. Seal of apostleship. 1851
144 Tucker, S. Rainbow in the north. 1851
157 Anderson, D. Charge to clergy. 1854
158 Anderson, D. Children instead of fathers. 1854
168 Anderson, D. Charge to clergy. 1856
169 Anderson, D. Winner of souls. 1856
173 Goodwin, J. North-west-America mission. 1856
219 Anderson, D. Charge to clergy. 1860
226 Anderson, D. Truth and the conscience. 1861
243 Anderson, D. Charge to clergy. 1864
254 Brief sketch of life of Archdeacon Cockran. 1866?
261 Church of England. Report of Diocese of Rupert's Land. 1867
262 Church of England. Diocese of Rupert's Land. 2d conference, 1867. Report. 1867
274 Machray, R. Christian privilege and duty. 1868
279 Church of England. Rupert's Land. Report of Synod. 1869
298 Church of England. Rupert's Land. By-law of clergy widow & orphan's fund. 1870
331 McLean, J. Circular letter to clergy and laity. 1871
371 Machray, R. Memorandum on the present state of the mission. 1873?
387 Church of England. Diocese of Rupert's Land. Provisional statutes of St. John's Cathedral. 1874
410 Church of England. Rupert's Land. Journal of Provincial Synod. 1875
417 Johnson, M.E. Dayspring in the far west. 1875
420 Machray, R. Bishop submits statement. 1875
422 McLean, J. Notes from the Bishop's journal. 1875
442 Church Missionary Society. Memorandum of N.W. America financial system. 1876
454 Church of England. Diocese of Saskatchewan. 1877
497 Church of England. Diocese of Rupert's Land. 1879
498 Church of England. Memorandum of the Bishop to the church societies. 1879
615 Church of England. Saskatchewan. Report of Synod. 1882
646 Society for the Propagation of the Gospel. North-west Canada. 1882
667 Corbett, G.O. Vast resources & great progress of Christianity. 1883
684 McLean, J. Principles of church action. 1883
804 Church of England. Diocese of Qu'Appelle. Constitution. 1885
912 Church of England. Diocese of Rupert's Land. Report of Synod. 1886
971 Society for the Propagation of the Gospel in Foreign Parts. Rupert's Land. 1886
1051 Church of England. Athabasca. Report. 1888
1218 Church of England. Athabasca. Journal of second Synod. 1891
1238 Tims, J.W. The Indian missions. 1891
1285 Young, R. Diocese of Athabasca. 1892
1290 Anson, A.J.R. The church and her work. 1893

1317 Hodgins, J.G. Hand book of Church of England missions. 1893
1336 Young, R. Circular letter describing a mission journey. 1893
1357 Church of England. Rupert's Land. Resources & needs for missions. 1894
1390 Church of England. Qu'Appelle. Journal of 12th Synod. 1895
1429 Young, J.H. Little Marie. 189_?
1446 Holmes, G. Lesser Slave Lake. 1896
1470 Swainson, F. The Kissock homes. 1896
1472 Tims, J.W. Diocese of Calgary. 1896
1509 Newton, W. Twenty years on the Saskatchewan. 1897
1536 Church of England. Calgary. Proceedings of fifth Synod. 1898
1677 Church of England. The Indian missions. 1902
1699 Church of England. Report on Indian missions. 1903
1921 Church of England. North West Canada missions. 1907
1922 Church of England. Missionary Diocese of Athabasca. 1907
1967 Boyle, J. The sixty of Saskatchewan. 1908
1975 Church of England. Diocese of Qu'Appelle. 1908
2008 Matheson, S.P. Printed letter. 1908
2016 Paget, E.C. A year under the shadow of St. Paul's. 1908
2026 Tucker, L.N. Western Canada. 1908
2048 Church of England. Indian missions of Saskatchewan. 1898-1909
2049 Church of England. Saskatchewan. Report on Indian missions. 1909
2066 Machray, R. Life of Robert Machray. 1909
2123 Church Missionary Society. Extracts from letters of missionaries. 1910
2123A Church Missionary Society. North-West Canada missions. 1910
2160 Montgomery, H.H. Church on the prairie. 1910
2374 Burrows, C.L. Hands across the sea. 1913
2402 Ingham, E.G. Sketches in Western Canada. 1913
2443 Bickersteth, J.B. Land of open doors. 1914
2505 Hines, J. Red Indians of the plains. 1915
2602 Matheson, E.K. Work of Church of England. 1917
2712 Heeney, W.B. John West. 1920
2716 Johnstone, R.C. Church of England in Rupertsland. 1920
2746 Taylor, W.E. Our church at work. 1920
2812 Hasell, F.H.E. Across the prairie in a motor caravan. 1922
2813 Heeney, W.B. Centenary addresses. 1920
2847 Garrioch, A.C. First furrows. 1923
2900 Missionary Society of the Church of England. From the East and from the West. 1924
2917A Caesar, C.E. Missionary work among red Indians. 1925
3024 Hasell, F.H.E. Through Western Canada in a caravan. 1927
3026 Innes, C. Canon E.K. Matheson. 1927
3072 Fortin, O. Sixty years and after. 1928
3079 Hasell, F.H.E. Caravanning through prairie and mountain. 1928
3084A Lloydall-Bee, A. Parish of St. Peter, Entwistle. 1928
3135 Garrioch, A.C. Hatchet mark in duplicate. 1929
3136 Heeney, W.B. Founding of Rupert's Land. 1929
3145 McLean, Mrs. A. History of Holy Trinity Church. 1929
3173 Church of England. Church hospitals. 193_?
3180 Goodge, S.H. Parish of St. Mary's, Wellsdale. 1930
3254 Greene, D.L. Christ Church, The Pas. 1931
3333 Garrioch, A.C. Correction line. 1933
3338 House, J. Old Sun Anglican School. 1933
3396 Napier, R.M. Fifty years of St. Barnabas Church. 1934
3403 Saskatoon. St. John's Cathedral. Tenth anniversary, 1924-1934

3433 Ft. Qu'Appelle. Church of S. John the Evangelist. Jubilee memento. 1935
3432 Edmonton. All Saints Cathedral. The cathedral church, 1875-1935
4398 Regina. St. Matthew's Anglican Church. Silver jubilee. 1935
3491 Battleford. St. George's Church. Fiftieth anniversary. 1936
3499 Church of England. Diocese of Athabasca. 1936
3500 Church of England. Diocese of Calgary. 1936
3501 Church of England. Diocese of Edmonton. 1936
3532 St. James. St. James Church. 85th anniversary book, 1850-1936
3546 Winnipeg. St. James Anglican Church. 85th anniversary book, 1850-1936
3670 Church of England. Diocese of Edmonton, 1914-1939
3807 Millman, T.R. Publishers of peace. 1942
3837 Edmonton. Holy Trinity Church. A history, 1893-1943
3839 Greene, D.L. By the swift waters. 1943
3853 Sovereign, A.H. Ambassador of the frozen way, 194_?
4272 Shave, H. Our heritage. 1951
4364 Simms, E.F. Story of St. Mary's la Prairie Anglican Church. 1953

POSTSCRIPT
Boon, T.C.B. The Anglican Church from the Bay to the Rockies. (Toronto, 1962)
Church Missionary Society. [Records and correspondence] 52 reels of microfilm. (This important source material for early western history is available in several Canadian libraries)

5 Congregational Church

4381 Canada Congregational Missionary Society. Our Scandinavian Missions. 1904

6 Hutterite Brethren

4351 Hutterite Brethren. Hymnal. Die Lieder der Hutterischen Brüder. 1953

7 Lord's Day Alliance

3200 Lord's Day Alliance. Sunday conditions in Western Canada. 1930

8 Lutheran Churches

1555 Udden, S. Fran Canada. 1898
2136 Evangeliska-Luterska Kirkjufelag Islendinga. Gjordabok 26 arsthings. 1910
2137 Evangeliska-Lûterska Kirkjufélag Íslendinga. Minningarrit Hins, 1885-1910
2439 Winnipeg. Trinity Lutheran Church. Gedenkblatt zum 25-jährigen Jubiläum. 1913
2531 Bergmann, F.J. Hvert stefnir. 1916
2807 Evangelical Lutheran Church. Synod of Manitoba. Denkschrift zum Silber-Jubiläum, 1897-1922
3073 Fricke, A. Canada-Distrikts der Ev.-Luth. Synode von Ohio. 1928
3208 Metzger, H. Geschichtlicher Abriss über die Peters-Pfarrei. 1930
3238 Wiegner, P.E. Man.-Sask. District of Lutheran Missouri Synod. 193_
3252 Fritz, J. 25. Jubiläum der Ev.-luth. Dreieinigkeitsgemeinde zu Regina. 1931
3298 Freitag, K.W. Denkschrift ... Ev.-luth. Dreieinigkeitsgemeinde zu Strathcona. 1932
3416 Beck, R. Evang. Lúterska Kirkjufélags Íslendinga, 1885-1935
3452 Lehmann, H. Das evangelische Deutschtum in Kanada. 1935
3465 Olafson, K.K. Icelandic Lutheran Synod. 1935

4146 Darwin, O. Pioneering with pioneers. 1949
4179 Smith, A.E. All my life. 1949
4199 Finlay, R.E. George McDougall Church. 195–
4252 McKitrick, T.G. Andrew Stewart of prairie homesteads. 1951
4305 Laurie, J.L. John McDougall. 1952

10 **Presbyterian Church**
See also 'United Church of Canada'

373 Moore, W. Report on Prince Albert mission. 1873
407 Bryce, G. Presbyterian Church in Canada. 1875
723 Bryce, G. Presbyterianism. 1884
839 Presbyterian Church. Man. and N.W.T. Home mission work. 1885
958 Presbyterian Church. Report on church building fund. 1886
1179 Hart, T. Mission work among the Indians. 1890
1388 Baird, A.B. The Indians of Western Canada. 1895
1487 Gordon, C.W. Beyond the Marshes. 1897
1525 Bryce, G. John Black. 1898
1948 Regina. Knox Church. Quarter centenary. 1907
1954 Storer, E.L. Gardiner Presbyterian Church, Battleford. 1907
1985 Gordon, C.W. Life of J. Robertson. 1908
2070 Murray, J.A. In Dixie and Manitoba. 1909
2083 Scott, T.R. Presbyterian Church in Oxbow. 1909
2191 Winnipeg. St. Giles' Presbyterian Church. Silver jubilee, 1885-1910. 1910
2243 Morden, Man. Knox Church. 25th anniversary. 1911
2339 Reid, W.D. Mission work in Alberta. 1912
2728A Murray, S.C. Challenge of our Prairie Provinces. 1920
2753 Winnipeg. St. Stephen's Church. Silver jubilee, 1895-1920
2786 Medicine Hat. Westminster Church. An historical sketch. 1921
2896 McKellar, H. Presbyterian pioneer missionaries. 1924
2939 McGregor, T.F. Where the great Peace River flows. 1925
2952 Ross, A. Presbyterian banner. 1925
2979 Pierce, L. John Black. 1926
3017 Edmonton. First Presbyterian Church. Fortieth year of ministry of Rev. D.S. McQueen. 1927
3021 Farquharson, Mrs. J. Recollections of a pioneer minister. 1927
3045 Winnipeg. Augustine Church. 40th anniversary. 1927
3140 Hunter, A.J. A friendly adventure. 1929
3156 Strang, P. Missions in southern Saskatchewan. 1929
3356 Strang, P. Autobiography. 1933
3376 Corbett, E.A. McQueen of Edmonton. 1934
3427 Crawford, J.W. Grace Presbyterian Church, Calgary. 1935
3519 Mackinnon, C. Life of Principal Oliver. 1936
3697A Putnam, A.M. Selkirk settlers and church at Belfast. 1939
3741 Roxburgh, F.D. History of Presbyterian Church in Edmonton. 1940
4196 Doka, K.C. Golden jubilee of Békevár. 1950
4250 McBeth, M. Story of Kildonan Presbyterian Church. 1951
4284 Burns, Mrs. R.A. The pioneers' story, Neepawa. 1952

11 **Reformed Church**

2906 Reformed Church. Geschichte der Deutschen Manitoba-Klassis. 1924
4244 Josephburg, Alta. Evangelical-Reformed Church. 50th anniversary, 1901-1951

12 **Roman Catholic Church**
For the Ukrainian Catholic Church and the Greek Orthodox Church see also 'Ukrainians'

2567 Une soeur de la Providence. Le Père Lacombe. 1916
2604 Mathieu, O.E. Eloge funèbre du Rév. P.J. Hugonard. 1917
2729 Oblates. St. Boniface. Le centenaire du R.P. Dandurand. 1920
2661 Cyr, J.E. Mgr Provencher. 1919
2700 Cyr, J.E. Mgr Langevin. 1920
2701 Cyr, J.E. Mgr Taché. 1920
2717 Lacasse, P.Z. Une mine des souvenirs. 1920
2768 Daly, G.T. Catholic problems in Western Canada. 1921
4389 Oblates. Portraits historiques. 1921
2811 Grouard, E.J.B.M. Souvenirs. 1922
2860 Morice, A.G. Histoire de l'Eglise catholique. 1921-23
2823 Prud'homme, L.A. L'Abbé Louis-Raymond Giroux. 1922
2867 Rondeau, C. Montagne de Bois. 1923
2899 Mathieu, O.E. Lettres pastorales et lettres circulaires. 1924
2925 Cyr, J.E. Père Lacasse. 1925
2934 Latour, P.Z.C. Mgr A. Taché. 1925
4393 Les Filles de la Providence de Saint-Brieuc. Les Filles, 1818-1926
2992 Une religieuse de Notre-Dame des Missions. Petit historique de nos fondations au Canada. 1926
3014 Cochin, L. Reminiscences. 1927
3086 Mathieu, O.E. Gesta dei. 1928
3088 O'Hagan, T. Father Morice. 1928
3097 Pietsch, J. Bei den Deutschen in Westkanada. 1928
3098 Prud'homme, L.A. Mgr N.J. Ritchot. 1928
3198 Le Chevallier, J.J.M.J. Saint-Laurent de Grandin. 1930
3221 Fifty years in Western Canada. 1930
3225 Une soeur de la Providence. Une âme de prêtre. Abbé Duchaine de Frenchville. 1930
3237 Weaver, E.P. Sisters of St. Boniface. 1930
4396 Edmonton. Paroisse de l'Immaculée-Conception. Souvenir. 1931
3270 Morice, A.G. Catholic Church in Western Canada. 1931
3276 Randall, C.C. Historical outline of see of St. Boniface. 1931
3315 Schäfer, T. Der schwarze Waldläufer ... Albert Lacombe, O.M.I. 1932
3320 Villeneuve, J.M.R. Lettres pastorales. 1932
3393 Morice, A.G. Darveau, martyr. 1934
3397 Oblates. L'héritier de Mgr Charlebois. 1934
3399 Pamiatka 30-lecia parafii P.N.K.K. w Ameryce, 1904-1934
3435 Frémont, D. Mgr Provencher. 1935
3439 Harrington, M.A. 25th anniversary, St. Anne's Parish, Blairmore. 1935
4399 Calgary. Sacred Heart Parish. A short history. 1936
4400 Labouré, T. Visite des missions indiennes. 1936
3517 Le Chevallier, J.J.M.J. Origine de Calgary. 1936
3521 Maloney, J.J. Darkness, dawn and daybreak. 193_
3522 Morice, A.G. Catholic Church in Canadian Northwest. 1936
3531 Russell, F.W. History of St. Mary's, Winnipeg. 1936
3550 Zimmermann, A. Die romisch-catholische pfarrei, St. Joseph bei Balgonie. 1936
3564 Hermant, L. L'épopée d'un évêque-missionnaire. 1937
3629 Hermant, L. Mgr Grandin. 1938
3636 Mémoires des minorités catholiques de langue française. 1938
3641 Pénard, J.M. Mgr Charlebois, le saint missionnaire. 1938
3656 Weber, A. Der diener Gottes, Bischof Grandin. 1938
3680 Edmonton. Collège Saint-François-Xavier. 25e anniversaire, 1913-1938
3696 Pénard, J.M. Vicar Apostolic of Keewatin. 1939

3731 Le Chevallier, J.J.M.J. Aux prises avec la tourmente. 1940
3739 Primeau, L. Mgr Langevin. 1940
4401 Trocellier, J. Consécration. 1940
4402 Labouré, T. Centenaire du Canada. 1941
3765 Le Chevallier, J.J.M.J. Batoche. 1941
3770 Philippot, A. Cinquante ans de vie paroissiale, Morinville. 1941
4403 Rousseau, J. Visite du Manitoba. 1941
3789 Ceuneau, A. Un compagnon de Mgr Grandin. 1942
4404 Desmoyers, A. Visite d'Alberta-Saskatchewan. 1942
3831 Canmore, Alberta. Sacred Heart Church. Golden jubilee. 1943
3849 Un Père Trappiste. Une trappe dans un pays de missions. 1943
3874 Le Chevallier, J.J.M.J. St. Michael's school. 1944
3887 Sinnott, A.A. L'Archevêque écrit aux 'chers parents catholiques.' 1944
3888 Sinnott, A.A. A letter from Archbishop Sinnott. 1944
3898 A northern apostle, Bishop Grandin. 1945
3937 Mercure, A. La Semence; l'arrivée des missionnaires o.m.i. dans l'Ouest. 1945
3940 Oblates. Edmonton. Le serviteur de Dieu, Mgr Grandin. 1945
3941 Oblates. Centenary of Oblate Fathers. 1945
3942 Oblates. Exposition missionnaire. 1945
4405 Prelate, Sask. St. Angela's Convent, 1919-1945
3946 Primeau, L. Soldats conquerants du Christ. 1945
3992 Lesage, G. Capitale d'une solitude. 1946
4023 Beausejour. Kosciol Matki Boskiej. Souvenir of the blessing. 1947
4032 Filles de la Providence. Cinquantenaire dans l'Ouest Canadien. 1947
4048 Marysburg. Assumption Church. Our parish. 1947
4085 Catholic Women's League. History of Catholic Church of southern Alberta. 1948
4091 Cullinane, E.A. Catholic Church and socialism. 1948
4092 Edmonton. St-Joachim Parish. Fête des pionniers, 1948
4102 Hermant, L. Thy cross my stay. 1948
4142 Champagne, J.E. Les missions catholiques dans l'Ouest canadien. 1949
4181 Vinet, J.L. I was a priest. 1949
4406 Lethbridge, St. Patrick's Church. 1952
4339 Breton, J.P.E.R. Forgeron de Dieu. 1953
4352 Legal, Paroisse St-Emile de Legal. Cinquante anniversaire. 1953
4369 Windschiegl, P. Fifty golden years. 1953

POSTSCRIPT

Tremblay, Emilien. Le père Delaere et l'Eglise ukrainienne du Canada. (Berthierville, Que., 1961)

Kazymyra, Bohdan. Relihiino-hromads'ke zhyttiia v Ukrains'kii Katolyts'kii mytropolii v Kanadi; Development of the Ukrainian Catholic group in Canada. (Toronto, 1965)

13 Salvation Army

4063 Salvation Army. Calgary Citadel Corps. Diamond jubilee, 1887-1947

14 'Those Who Gather Alone'

3471 Rouse, J.J. Pioneer work in Canada. 1935

15 United Church of Canada

3156 Strang, P. Missions in southern Saskatchewan. 1929

3251 Edmonton. McDougall United Church. Diamond jubilee. 1931
3473 Saskatoon. Third Avenue United Church. Other men have labored. 1935
3486 Winnipeg. Rosedale United Church. Silver jubilee. 1935
3519 Mackinnon, C. Life of Principal Oliver. 1936
3537 Saskatoon. Grace United Church. Golden jubilee. 1936
3570 MacKay, Mrs. A.M. History of Scotia. 1937
3585 Sinclair, J.D. Westminster Church, Winnipeg. 1937
3657 Winnipeg. Grace United Church. Three score years and ten. 1938
3829 Calgary. Knox United Church. Diamond jubilee. 1943
3860 Winnipeg. Grace United Church. 75th anniversary. 1943
3895 Winnipeg. St. Giles' United Church. Diamond jubilee, 1884-1944
3959 Sykes, A.A. Story of St. Andrew's United Church. 1945
4036 Hart, W.T. 63 years of uninterrupted service. 1947
4061 Robertson, H.J. Story of Knox Church, Winnipeg. 1947
4078 Wyman, H.C. Bissett United Church. 1947
4179 Smith, A.E. All my life. 1949
4200 Glamis, Sask. Memorial United Church; historical sketch. 1950
4218 Nicol, J.L. Through the years with Knox. 1950
4268 Saskatoon. Grace United Church, 1886-1951
4269 Saskatoon. Third Avenue United Church. Golden jubilee. 1951
4275 United Church of Canada. Women's Missionary Society. Alberta Branch. History. 1951
4354 Lewis, S. History of Chumah Church. 1953

S EDUCATION

1 General

74 On the civilization of the Indians. 182_?
176 Aborigines' Protection Society. Memorial to Secretary of State for Colonies. 1857?
1211 Burman, W.A. Rupert's Land Indian Industrial School. 1891
1818 Fielding, W.S. North-West education system. 1905
1873 Ferrier, T. Indian education in the N.W. 1906
1936 Lavergne, A.R. Ecoles du Nord-Ouest. 1907
2012 New England Co. Conference on Indian education. 1908
2149 Landry, A.C.P. Ecoles du Nord-Ouest. 1910
2237 MacLean, D.A. Catholic schools in Western Canada. 1911
2366 Black, N.F. English for the non-English. 1913
2391 Ferrier, T. Our Indians and their training. 1913
2432 Savaète, A. Ecoles du Nord-Ouest canadien. 1913
2613 Weir, G.M. Evolution of the separate school law. 1917
2616 Anderson, J.T.M. Education of new Canadian. 1918
2617 Armstrong, W.H.G. Separate schools. 1918
2768 Daly, G.T. Catholic problems in Western Canada. 1921
3005 Calgary. Wood's Christian Homes. Work done for orphans and needy children. 1927

2 Manitoba

447 Manitoba. Laws, etc. Acte pour établir un système d'éducation. 1876
459 Libertas. National schools for Manitoba. 1877

1464 Proulx, J.B. Documents. 1896
1466 Roman Catholic Church. Lettre pastorale de les archevêques de Québec. 1896
1465 Le Quotidien. Justice à qui de droit. 1896
1482 Courrier du Canada. Question scolaire du Manitoba. 1897
1486 Fitzpatrick, Sir C. Les écoles du Manitoba. 1897
1495 Lacasse, P.Z. Difficultés scolaires de Manitoba. 1897
1496 Lacasse, P.Z. Une visite dans les écoles. 1897
1497 Landry, A.C.P. Campagne politico-religieuse. 1897
1498 Landry, A.C.P. Droits de l'Église. 1897
1511 Perry, C.E. Hon. N. Clarke Wallace. 1897
1512 Scott, Sir R.W. Synopsis of Manitoba School Case. 1897
1521 Begin, L.N. Lettre pastorale sur les écoles. 1898
1541 Gaire, J. La question des écoles catholiques. 1898
1584 On en est exactement la question. 1899
1560 Benoit, J.P.A. L'anglomanie au Canada. 1899
1676 Canada. Dept. of Sec. of State. Manitoba school lands. 1902
1753 Bryce, G. Educational reminiscences. 1904
1962 Bernier, J. L'instruction obligatoire. 1908
2213 Cherrier, A.A. Mémoire à S.E. Mgr Stagni. 1911
2258 Savaète, A. Ecoles du Nord-Ouest. 1911
2276 Bourassa, H. Pour la justice. 1912
2429 Salter, E.J.B. Manitoba School Question. 1913
2639 St. Boniface. Sheptycky Institute. Pershiy richniy zvit bursy. 1918
2725 Manitoba. Dept. of Education. Education among the New Canadians. 1920
2794 Sabourin, J.A. Les parents, l'Eglise et l'Etat. 1921
2825 Sabourin, J.A. En face de la persécution scolaire. 1922
2984 Sabourin, J.A. La coéducation. 1926
3104 Sabourin, J.A. L'évolution dans les écoles. 1928
3105 Sabourin, J.A. La morale et le nouveau programme des écoles. 1928
3487 Woods, D.S. Financing the schools of rural Manitoba. 1935
3547 Winnipeg. St. Nicholas School. Almanakh. 1936
3658 Woods, D.S. Education in Manitoba. 1938
3889 Sisler, W.J. Peaceful invasion. 1944
3965 Winnipeg. School Board. A visit to our schools. 1945
4018 Winnipeg. Shalom Aleichem School. Finf zwanzig yor yovel-buch. 1946
4134 Winkler, Man. Burwalde School District. Diamond jubilee. 1948
4135 Winnipeg. Board of School Trustees. Report of directed self survey. 1948

POSTSCRIPT
Manitoba. Royal commission on education. Report. (Winnipeg, 1959)

3 North West Territories

690 N.W.T. Council. Proposed school ordinance. 1883
1350 Canada. Dept. of Sec. of State. Schools in N.W.T. 1894
1351 Canada. Dept. of Sec. of State. School laws. 1894
1352 Canada. Dept. of Sec. of State. Schools in the North-West. 1894
1447 Leduc, H. Hostility unmasked. 1896
1795 Bourassa, H. Ecoles du Nord-Ouest. 1905
1836 Roy, P. L'autonomie des provinces. 1905
2276 Bourassa, H. Pour la justice. 1912

2001 McDiarmid, A.P. The right and expediency of independence in university education. 1908
2213 Cherrier, A.A. Mémoire à S.E. Mgr Stagni. 1911
2643 Spence, W.J. University of Manitoba. 1918
2792 Rumball, W.G. Manitoba College. 1921
2987 Saskatchewan. University. University of Saskatchewan. 1926
3212 The Mountain school, Banff. 193-?
3305 Learned, W.S. Local provision for higher education. 1932
3326 Alberta. University. University, 1908-1933
3519 Mackinnon, C. Life of Principal Oliver. 1936
3575 Manitoba. University. Manitoba essays. 1937
3632 Kirkconnell, W. Golden jubilee of Wesley College. 1938
3899 Bernier, A. 1885-1945, Les dates mémorables du Collège de Saint-Boniface. 1945

T INDIAN LANGUAGES

1 Bible

139 Bible. N.T. St. John. Cree. (Mason) 1851
153 Bible. N.T. St. Matthew. Cree. (Hunter) 1853
4371 Bible. O.T. Exodus. Ten Commandments. Cree. 1855
159 Bible. N.T. St. Mark. Cree. (Hunter) 1855
160 Bible. N.T. St. John. Cree. (Hunter) 1855
161 Bible. N.T. St. John, First epistle general. Cree. (Mrs. Hunter) 1855
171 Bible. N.T. St. John, First epistle general. Cree. (Mrs. Hunter) 1856
179 Bible. N.T. Selections. Cree. (Mason) 1857
206 Bible. N.T. Cree. (Sinclair, Steinhauer, Mason) 1859
227 Bible. Cree. (Sinclair, Steinhauer, Mason) 1861
341 Bible. N.T. Cree. (Lacombe) 1872
436 Bible. O.T. Psalms. Cree. (Hunter) 1876
437 Bible. N.T. Cree. (Horden) 1876
469 Bible. Paraphrases. Chipeweyan. (Faraud) 1878
877 Bible. N.T. St. Mark. Beaver. (Garrioch) 1886
878 Bible. O.T. Psalms. Tukkuthkutchin. (McDonald) 1886
1040 Bible. N.T. St. Matthew (10 chapters) Blackfoot. (Stocken) n.d.
1141 Bible. N.T. St. Matthew. Blackfoot. (Tims) 1890
1141A Bible. New Testament. Galatians. Cree. 189_
1142 Bible. Selections. Blackfoot. (Tims) 1890
1433 Bible. N.T. St. Mark. Cree. (Young) 1896
1479 Bible. N.T. Romans. Cree. 1897
1480 Bible. N.T. John. Cree. (Young & Holmes) 1897
1750 Bible. N.T. Cree. (Mackay) 1904
1751 Bible. N.T. Matthew. Cree. 1904
1790 Bible. N.T. John. Blackfoot. 1905
1791 Bible. O.T. Psalms. Cree. (Mason; rev. by Mackay) 1905
1789 Bible. N.T. Selections. Saulteaux. (Camper) 1905
4382 Bible. N.T. Gospels. Cree. 1906
1964 Bible. Cree. (rev. by Mackay & others) 1908
2099 Bible. N.T. St. Matthew. Selections. Blackfoot. 1910
2691A Bible. Selections. Cree daily Bible readings. 1920
2757 Bible. N.T. Gospels. Cree. (Balter) 1921
2758 Bible. O.T. Psalms. Cree. 1921
3826 Bible. N.T. Gospels & Acts. Saulteaux. 1943

2 Devotional Literature

1678 Church of England. Hymns. Cree. 1902
1809 Church of England. Hymns and prayers. Blackfoot. 190-?
1864 Church of England. Morning and evening prayers. 1906
1986 Hugonard, J. Cree hymns, with some useful prayers. 1908
2047 Church of England. Catechism. Cree. 1909
4385 LaRonde, A. de. Instructions en Sauteux sur toute la doctrine catholique. 1911
2426 Roman Catholic Church. Liturgy and ritual. Cree. 1913
2576 Church of England. Book of Common Prayer. Cree. (Hunter, rev. by MacKay) 1917
4388 Roman Catholic Church. Catechisms. Blackfoot. 1920
4390 Roman Catholic Church. Prayers. Blackfoot. 1921
4392 Roman Catholic Church. Hymns. Blackfoot. 1924
2835 British & Foreign Bible Society. Cree Indian translation of the Scriptures. 1925
2863A Pénard, J.M. Meditations sur la passion. 1924
2863B Pénard, J.M. Prieres, catechisme, cantiques a l'usage des Montagnais. 1923
3102 Roman Catholic Church. Catechisms. Cree. (Moulin) 1928
3622 Entwistle, M. On trail with the redskins; James Evans. 1938
3773 Roman Catholic Church. Hymns. Cree. 1941
3814 Roman Catholic Church. Prayers. Cree. Prayer book. 1942

3 Dictionaries, Grammars and Primers

4 Bowery, T. Dictionary of H.B. Indian language. 1701
100 Belcourt, G.A. Principes de la langue sauteux. 1839
109 Howse, J. Grammar of the Cree language. 1844
121 Smithurst, J. English-Cree-Ojibway word book. 1848
199 Hunter, J. First reading book. 1858
251 Watkins, E.A. Dictionary of Cree language. 1865
347 Lacombe, A. Dictionnaire ... de la langue crise. 1872
394 Lacombe, A. Dictionnaire de la langue des Cris. 1874
395 Lacombe, A. Grammaire de la langue des Cris. 1874
416 Hunter, J. Lecture on the Cree language. 1875
470 Bompas, W.C. Beaver Indian primer. 187-
661 Burman, W.A. Sioux language. 1883
816 Garrioch, A.C. Vocabulary of the Beaver Indian language. 1885
815 Garrioch, A.C. Beaver Indian primer. 1885
941 Lacombe, A. First reader in English and Blackfoot. 1886
942 Lacombe, A. Petit manuel en langue crise. 1886
1087 Bompas, W.C. Cree primer. 188-
1130 Tims, J.W. Grammar and dictionary of the Blackfoot language. 1889
1136 First reading book for schools and families. 1890.
1176 Glass, E.B. Primer and language lessons in English and Cree. 1890
1287 Indian child's book. 189-
4378 Cree almanack. 1891
1309 Cree primer. 1893
1476 Young, R. Instruction in syllabic characters. 1896
2398 Horden, J. Grammar of the Cree language. 1913
2589 Goddard, P.E. Beaver texts. 1917
3233 Uhlenbeck, C.C. English-Blackfoot vocabulary. 1930
3407 Uhlenbeck, C.C. Blackfoot-English vocabulary. 1934
3652 Uhlenbeck, C.C. Concise Blackfoot grammar. 1938
3654 Watkins, E.A. Dictionary of the Cree language. 1938
3712 Balter, L.G. Courtes instructions en langue crise. 1940
3793 Dumouchel, P.A. Grammaire saulteuse. 1942
4105 Hives, H.E. Cree grammar. 1948

U LITERARY WORKS

1 Fiction

285 Kingston, W.H.G. Rob Nixon. [n.d.]
320 Begg, A. Dot it down. 1871
562 Bryan, M.E. Wild work; story of Red River tragedy. 1881
600 Butler, Sir W.F. Red Cloud, the solitary Sioux. 1882
805 Collins, J.E. Story of Louis Riel. 1885
807 Daunt, A. In the land of the moose, bear, and beaver. 1885
871 Ballantyne, R.M. Red man's revenge. 1886
915 Collins, J.E. Annette, the métis spy. 1886
965 Rowe, L. An old woman's story. 1886
1074 Pocock, H.R.A. Tales of western life. 1888
1084 Zero. One mistake. 1888
1172 Frank, Mrs. M.J. The Brock family. 1890
2174 Saxby, J.M. Comrades three. 1910.
1365 Mackie, J. Devil's playground. 1894
1366 Mercier, A. A home in the North-West. 1894
1410 Hayes, K.E. Prairie pot-pourri. 1895
1416 Mackie, J. Sinners twain. 1895
1452 Maclean, J. The warden of the plains. 1896
1461 Mercier, A. The red house by the Rockies. 1896
1468 Saxby, J.M. Brown Jack. 1896
1471 Tennyson, B. Land of Napioa. 1896
1492 Henham, E.G. Menotah. 1897
1508 Morton, J. Polson's probation. 1897
1574 Fetherstonhaugh, V. Mrs. Jim Baker. 1899
1577 Gordon, C.W. The sky pilot. 1899
1580 Mackie, J. The heart of the prairie. 1899
1581 Mackie, J. The prodigal's brother. 1899
1607 Fraser, W.A. Mooswa & others of the boundaries. 1900
1613 Hunter, F.J. Colonel Gascoigne, V.C. 190–
1616 Laut, A.C. Lords of the north. 1900
1636 Bindloss, H. Sower of wheat. 1901
1648 Fetherstonhaugh, V. A younger son. 1901
1649 Fox, C. Land of lasses few. 1901
1686 Mackie, J. Canadian Jack. [n.d.]
1719 Cullum, R. The story of Foss River ranch. 1903
1725 Fraser, W.A. The blood lilies. 1903
1746 Weld, A.G. Glimpses of Tennyson and some of his friends. 1903
1748 Bashford, H.H. The Manitoban. 1904
1767 Cullum, R. The hound of the north. 1904
1819 Goodloe, A.C. At the foot of the Rockies. 1905
1831 Mackie, J. The rising of the red man. 1905
1852 Bashford, H.H. The trail together. 1906
1867 Cullum, R. The night-riders. 1906
1878 Hayes, K.E. Aweena. 1906
1931 Forestier, G. La Pointe-aux-Rats. 1907
1958 Whitaker, H. The settler. 1907
1989 Jarvis, W.H.P. Letters of a remittance man to his mother. 1908
2000 McClung, N.L. Sowing seeds in Danny. 1908
2053 Gordon, C.W. The foreigner. 1909
2073 Parker, Sir G. Northern lights. 1909

2075 Poirier, J.E. Les arpents de neige. 1909
2156 McClung, N.L. The second chance. 1910
2162 Mott, L. Prairie, snow and sea. 1910
2187A Walworth, B. On the firing line. 1910
2188 Ward, M.A. Canadian born. 1910
2216 Curwood, J.O. Philip Steele. 1911
2223 Gill, E.A.W. Love in Manitoba. 1911
2298 Gordon, C.W. Corporal Cameron. 1912
2320 McClung, N.L. Black Creek stopping-house. 1912
2340 Reville, F.D. A rebellion. 1912
2360 Amy, W.L. The blue wolf. 1913
2365 Bindloss, H. Prescott of Saskatchewan. 1913
2392 Footner, W.H. Jack Chanty. 1913
2407 Lyttleton, E.J. The law-bringers. 1913
2436 Teetgen, A.B. A white passion. 1913
2438 White, S.A. Empery. 1913
2460 Gill, E.A.W. An Irishman's luck. 1914
2462 Gordon, C.W. Patrol of the sun dance. 1914
2486 Stead, R.J.C. The bail jumper. 1914
2502 Eliot, E.M. My Canada. 1915
2526 Stringer, A.J.A. The prairie wife. 1915
2559 Paterson, I.M.B. The shadow riders. 1916
2563 Stead, R.J.C. The homesteaders. 1916
2573 Bindloss, H. The girl from Keller's. 1917
2606 Paterson, I.M.B. The magpie's nest. 1917
2627 Ingersoll, W.E. The road that led home. 1918
2628 Jonsson, B. Leaves and letters. 1918
2644 Stead, R.J.C. The cow puncher. 1918
2659 Christmas in Regina. 1919
2660 Curwood, J.O. The river's end. 1919
2663 Durkin, D.L. The heart of Cherry McBain. 1919
2680 Roy, I. Junette. 1919
2709 Footner, W.H. The fur bringers. 1920
2714 Ingersoll, W.E. Daisy herself. 1920
2742 Stead, R.J.C. Dennison Grant. 1920
2743 Stefansson, J. Love and pride. 1920
2745 Stringer, A.J.A. The prairie mother. 1920
2756 Amy, W.L. Blue Pete, half breed. 1921
2772 Footner, W.H. The woman from outside. 1921
2774 Gordon, C.W. To him that hath. 1921
2777 Heming, A.H.H. The drama of the forests. 1921
2778 Howarth, D. The valley of gold. 1921
2783 McClung, N.L. Purple springs. 1921
2805 Durkin, D.L. The lobstick trail. 1922
2827 Stead, R.J.C. Neighbours. 1922
2828 Stringer, A.J.A. The prairie child. 1922
2838 Campbell, R.W. A policeman from Eton. 1923
2843 Durkin, D.L. The magpie. 1923
2858 McClung, N.L. When Christmas crossed the Peace. 1923
2866 Reeve, W.B. Cattle. 1923
2868 Salverson, L.G. The Viking heart. 1923
2873 Steele, H.E.R. Spirit-of-iron. 1923
2874 Warwick, J. Anna of the Troubled Valley. 1923
2879 Bridle, A. Hansen. 1924

3417 Bjarnason, B. Sans the grande passion. 1935
3420 Bugnet, G.C.J. La forêt. 1935
3457 McCulloch, J.H. Dark acres. 1935
3464 Niven, F.J. The flying years. 1935
3483 Watson, R. When Christmas came to Fort Garry. 1935
3488 Writers' Club of Regina College. Tuesday night. 1935
3494 Brooker, B. Think of the earth. 1936
3498 Chapman, E. The homesteaders. 1936
3508 Farmer, B.J. Go West, young man. 1936
3539 Schreiber, I. Die Schwestern aus Memel. 1936
3544 Ströme, A. De lange veje. 1936
3560 Ewach, H. Holos zemli. 1937
3565 Huber, A.O. Helga und der Hermelin. 1937
3578 Mowery, W.B. The black automatic. 1937
3583 Salverson, L.G. The dark weaver. 1937
3591 Weekes, M.L. The wheatland. 1937
3615 Desrosiers, L.P. Les engagés du Grand Portage. 1938
3619 Eggleston, W. The high plains. 1938
3624 Finsdóttir, G. Hillingalond. 1938
3649 Sullivan, E.A. The fur masters. 1938
3738 Niven, F.J. Mine inheritance. 1940
3746 Stegner, W.E. On a darkling plain. 1940
3756 Antologiya Ukrayinskoho pysmenstva. 1941
3774 Ross, J.S. As for me and my house. 1941
3776 Schreiber, I. Kanadische erzahlungen. 1941
3786 Annett, R.R. Especially Babe. 1942
3787 Bruce, E. Call her Rosie. 1942
3815 Sallans, G.H. Little man. 1942
3820 White, S.A. Northwest law. 1942
3851 Schreiber, I. Der gott der fremden erde. 1943
3858 White, S.A. Called Northwest. 1943
3859 White, S.A. Northwest patrol. 1943
3864 Dickson, H.H.L. Out of the west land. 1944
3865 Evans, A.R. All in a twilight. 1944
3929 Kiriak, I. Syny zemli. 1945
3970 Clay, C. Muskrat man. 1946
3991 Kerr, I.H. Gay dogs and dark horses. 1946
3994 Luhowy, A. Bezkhatny. 1946
4027 Campbell, G.M. Fresh wind blowing. 1947
4033 Freedman, B. Mrs. Mike. 1947
4037 Hiebert, P.G. Sarah Binks. 1947
4045 McCourt, E.A. The flaming hour. 1947
4046 McCourt, E.A. Music at the close. 1947
4053 Mitchell, W.O. Who has seen the wind. 1947
4058 Parsons, N.W. The curlew cried. 1947
4071 Van der Mark, C. In due season. 1947
4073 Walker, E.M.J. Fortress north. 1947
4110 Knox, O.E. Red River shadows. 1948
4138 Achard, E. La caverne des Rocheuses. 1949
4143 Charach, P. Power of a woman. 1949
4193 Canadian Great War Veteran. The Prince. 1950
4224 Russell, S.M. A lamp is heavy. 1950
4209 McCourt, E.A. Home is the stranger. 1950
4212 MacMillan, D.A. Rink rat. 1950

4225 Steele, H.E.R. Ghosts returning. 1950
4230 Williams, F.J. Fold home. 1950
4239 Cormack, B.V. Local rag. 1951
4247 Kristofferson, K.B. Tanya. 1951
4256 O'Meara, W.A. Grand Portage. 1951
4264 Roy, G. Where nests the water hen. 1951
4270 Schreiber, I. Canada welt des weizens. 1951
4271 Schreiber, I. Die flucht ins paradies. 1951
4313 McTavish, R.L. For a better tomorrow. 1952
4316 Moses, E.E. Golden is the wheat. 1952

ADDENDA
Connor, Ralph. The Swan Creek blizzard. (New York, 1904)
Fraser, W.A. Brave hearts. (Toronto, 1904)
Fraser, W.A. Bulldog Carney. (Toronto, 1919)
Leighton, Robt. The perils of Peterkin; a story of adventure in North-West Canada. (London, 1911) 2229A
Leighton, Robt. Rattlesnake ranch; a story of adventure in the Great North West. (London, 1912) 2316A
Leighton, Robt. The red patrol; a story of the North-West Mounted Police. (London, 1915) 2508A
Pocock, Rodger. A man in the open. (Toronto, 1912) 2332A
Surrey, G.S. An outlaw of the plains. (London, 1922) 2828A
Surrey, G.S. The shack in the coulee. (London, 1930) 3226A
The bibliographer's attention was drawn to several of the above books on reading a thesis written for the University of Alberta in 1971. Ference, Mrs. Ermeline A. 'Literature associated with ranching in Southern Alberta.'

POSTSCRIPT
Stegner, Wallace. Wolf willow; a history, a story, and a memory of the last plains frontier. (New York, 1962)
Wiebe, R.H. Peace shall destroy many. (Toronto, 1962)
Laurence, Margaret. A jest of God. (London, 1966)
National Library. Manitoba authors: Ecrivains du Manitoba. (Ottawa, 1970)

2 **Fiction, Juvenile**

170 Ballantyne, R.M. Snowflakes and sunbeams. 1856
202 Mueller, K. Die jungen Pelzjaeger. 1858
276 Ballantyne, R.M. Away in the wilderness. 1869
340 Ballantyne, R.M. The pioneers. 1872
537 Kingston, W.H.G. The frontier fort. 188–
618 Daunt, A. The three trappers. 1882
1010 Kingston, W.H.G. Snow-shoes and canoes. 1887
1198 Oxley, J.M. Ti-ti-pu, a boy of Red River. 189_
1225 Kenyon, C.R. Young ranchmen. 1891
1259 Crissey, F. Rodney Merton. 1892
1275 Oxley, J.M. Fergus McTavish. 1892
1371 Oxley, J.M. Archie of Athabasca. 1893
1400 Crissey, F. The young newspaper scout. 1895
1544 Johnstone, C.L. The young emigrants. 1898
1617 The little Manitoban. 1900
1625 Saxby, C.F.A. The call of honour. 190–
1885 Marchant, B. Daughter of the ranges. 1906

1953 Saxby, C.F.A. Braves, white and red. 1907
1959 Young, E.R. The battle of the bears. 1907
2002 McDougall, J. Wa-pee Moos-tooch. 1908
2006 Marchant, B. Sisters of Silver Creek. 1908
2082 Saxby, C.F.A. The taming of the rancher. 1909
2138 Fea, S. Irish Ned, the Winnipeg newsy. 1910
2174 Saxby, C.F.A. Comrades three. 1910
2229A Leighton, R. The perils of Peterkin. 1911
2316A Leighton, R. Rattlesnake ranch. 1912
2335 Rathbone, St. G.H. Canoe mates in Canada. 1912
2409 Marchant, B. The youngest sister. 1913
2433 Saxby, C.F.A. The fiery totem. 1913
2508A Leighton, R. The red patrol. 1915
2601 Marchant, B. Canadian farm mystery. 1917
2703A Douglas, D. On the great fur trail. 1920
2708 Farney, M. Dans les prairies du Canada. 1920
2795 Saxby, C.F.A. Settler of Serpent Creek. 1921
2810 Grew, D. Beyond rope and fence. 1922
2828A Surrey, G.S. An outlaw of the plains. 1922
3053 Ball, A.H. Rovers of the valley. 1928
3226A Surrey, G.S. The shack in the coulee. 1930
3236 Watson, R. A boy of the great North West. 1930
3310 Mehrhardt-Ihlow, C. Canadisches Nocturno. 1932
3322 Young, E.R. Three Arrows. 1932
3388 McKean, G.B. Making good, a story of North-West Canada. 1934
3609 Clay, C. Young voyageur. 1938
3717 Clay, C. Fur trade apprentice. 1940
3783 Weekes, M.L. Painted arrows. 1941
3845 Knox, O.E. By paddle and saddle. 1943
3981 Grew, D. Wild dog of Edmonton. 1946
4101 Hayes, J.F. Buckskin colonist. 1948
4246 Knox, O.E. Little giant. 1951
4278 Wood, E.A. Cowboy yarns for young folk. 1951
4297 Jennings, J.E. The strange brigade. 1952
4312 MacMillan, A. Prince of the plains. 1952
4314 Malkus, A.S. Little giant of the north. 1952

3 Poetry

308 Major, J.C. Red River expedition. 1870
741 Davin, N.F. Eos. 1884
746 Grant, J.C. Prairie pictures. 1884
762 Nicholl, M.A. Lays from the West. 1884
825 Logan, J.E. A cry from the Saskatchewan. 1885
1101 Davin, N.F. Eos; an epic of the dawn. 1889
1284 Whittier, J.G. Red River voyageur. 1892
1428 Watt, D.H. Poems on Manitoba School Question. 1895
1679 Conybeare, C.F.P. Vahnfried. 1902
1778 Moodie, M.E. Songs of the West. 1904
1879 Johnstone, J. Vision of Immanuel. 1906
1924 Conybeare, C.F.P. Lyrics from the West. 1907
2033 Anderson, R.T. The old timer. 1909
2050 Clarke, A. Dawnlight and evensong. 190_
2154 Lively, G.J. The plea of the West. 191-

3425 Carsley, S.E. Alchemy and other poems. 1935
3444 Jaques, E. Drifting soil. 1935
3445 Jaques, E. My kitchen window. 1935
3446 Jaques, E. Wide horizons. 1935
3447 Kirkconnell, W. Canadian overtones. 1935
3449 Lang, C.D. Rhymes of a roughneck. 1935
3453 Lloyd, C.R.F. Landfall. 1935
3460A McMillan, S.L. Manitoba vision. 193-
3470 Robinson, H. Prairie days. 1935
3472 Sandercock, W.C. Dance of the buffalo skull. 1935
3478A Thomas, E.J. Three poems. 193_
3480 Tranter, G.J. Winged words. 1935
3492 Betts, M. Dreams. 1936
3509 Garrett, F.P. Memories. 1936
3516 Laurence, F.E.F. The band plays a march. 1936
3536 Saskatchewan poetry book, 1936-
3545 Thomson, R.B. Poems. 1936
3553 Anthology of Y.C. verse. 1937
3554 Canadian Authors' Assoc. Calgary Branch. Canadian poems. 1937
3561 Garrett, F.P. Life's gleanings. 1937
3562 Garrett, F.P. Whispering leaves. 1937
3596 Armstrong, C. Stars of happiness. 1938
3602 Cameron, W.B. Yarn of the Howling Gale. 1938
3604 Campbell, Z.I. A tale of the early years. n.d.
3606 Catley, E.M. Canada calling. 1938
3650 Sutherland, A.H. The Selkirk Settlement on Red River. 1938
3659 Anderson, A.J. A book of poems. 1939
3671 Clarke, P.C. From the Canadian prairies. 1939
3690 Marriott, A. The wind our enemy. 1939
3700A Savage, R. Prairie trails. 1939
3708 Williams, F.C. The open road. 1939
3711 Poems of the prairie. 193_?
3716 Carter, R.L. Rambling rhymes. [n.d.]
3721 Freebairn, A.L. Kootenai Brown. 194-
3722 Freebairn, A.L. My son and other poems. 194-
3723 Gardiner, L.G. Rhymes from the North West. 1940
3728 Kirkconnell, W. The flying bull. 1940
3736 Moose Jaw Writers' Club. Christmas, 1940
3744 Skov, S.A. Evening at Waterton Lakes. 194_
3749 Stewart, Z.M. Booklets of verse. [n.d.]
3750 Sweeney, J. Songs and verses of a Peace River pioneer. 194-
3751 Thompson, C.C. Stairway to the stars. [n.d.]
3767 Marks, A.L. Margaret Anne's wonder book of verse. 1941
3769 Moose Jaw Writers' Club. Verses for you. 1941
3784 Wensley, A. At summer's end. 1941
3792 Cormack, B.V. Seedtime and harvest. 1942
3792A Dent, C.L. Lines from life. 194-
3795 Freebairn, A.L. The mountain heights. 194-
3796 Freebairn, A.L. Rhymes from the foothills. 194-
3798 Gardner, Mrs. L.G. Rhymes from ranges. 1942
3800 Gordon, J.R. Rhymes of the range. 194_
3808 Moose Jaw Writers' Club. Christmas, 1942
3819 Wallace, J.S. Night is ended. 1942
3822 Wrigglesworth, L.J. Poetical writings. [n.d.]

3823 Wright, L.M. Victory verses. 1942
3832 Complin, M. For remembrance. 1943
3840 Gurney, F.C. Soul so dark. 1943
3841 Hansberger, C. Lighted lanterns. 1943
3848 Moose Jaw Writers' Club. Prairie poems. 1943
3881 Moore, H. Helen's poems. 1944
3882 Moose Jaw Writers' Club. Our autumn offerings. 1944
3891A Taylor, M.C. My Christmas tree. 1944
3909 Davidson, K. Seven sheaves. 1945
3936 Melville, T. Barbed wire ballads. 1945
3945 Priestley, N.F. Summer fever. 1945
3974 Davis, E. Gift book of sonnets. 1946
3975 Dick, C. Trails I've ridden. 1946
3998 Nixon, J.E. Morrison's place. 194–
3999 Nixon, J.E. Selected poems. 1946
4002 Osborn, E.M. Frosty-moon. 1946
4003 Pfeifer, Mrs. L.E. Temperamental moods. 1946
4004 Rashley, R.E. Voyageur. 1946
4019 Wood, A.G. Handful of lilacs. 1946
4056 O'neil, D.G. Rhythm pictures. 1947
4062 Russenholt, E.S. Meri-ka-chak. 1947
4083 Bartole, G. Figure in the rain. 1948
4090 Cormack, B. Ruth. 1948
4100 Grayson, E.K. Beggar's velvet. 1948
4103 Hibbert, W. Out of the pit. 1948
4119 Morrison, D. The prairie lily. 1948
4120 Nasir, G. Fifteen poems. 1948
4125 Rodgers, R.W. Dry belt jingles. No.2. 1948
4147 Dingwall, M.M. Now that I am fifty. 1949
4151 Higinbotham, J.D. Foothill and prairie memories. 1949
4157 Kirkpatrick, H. Ramblings in verse. 1949
4161 Lobb, R. Plain folks. 1949
4170 Nasir, G. New poems. 1949
4174 Pickel, E. Prairie skyline. 1949
4191 Cameron, F.J. Hermit of Chokecherry Creek. 1950
4191A Galloway, C. Peace River & other verse. 1952
4198 Duddridge, H. Seen from my seeder step. 1950
4208 McClelland, L.C. Gems of praise. 1950
4219 Obodiac, S. The soul speaks. 1950
4228 Warren, S.E.M. Prairie panels. 1950
4231 Wood, A.G. Through the year. 1950
4238 Conklin, W. Wind blown leaves. 1951
4257 Parker, W.W.M. Rhymes from the North-West. 1951
4286 Chilton, V.B. A few more dawns. 1952
4290 Farley, T. It was a plane. 1952
4295 Harrison, S. Gentlemen, the horse. 1952
4331 Wilson, M.M. In friendship's name. 1952

4 Poetry, French

921 Desaulniers, G.L. L'absolution avant la bataille. 1886
960 Riel, L. Poésies religieuses et politiques. 1886
2151 Lardon, P.A. Poésies de St-Boniface. 1910
3600 Bugnet, G.C.J. Voix de la solitude. 1938

5 Poetry, Hungarian

2670 Izsak, G. Mezei virágok. 1919

6 Poetry, Icelandic

1243 Bjarnason, J.M. Sogur og kvaedi. 1892
1523 Bjarnason, J.M. Ljódmaeli. 1898
1942 Markússon, M. Ljódmaeli. 1907
2058 Guttormsson, G.J. Jón Austfirdingur. 1909
2508 Jónsson, E.P. Öraefaljód. 1915
2564 Stefánsson, K. Út um vötn og velli. 1916
2646 Thorsteinsson, T.T. Thaettir. 1918
2672 Jónsson, G. Farfuglar. 1919
2711 Guttormsson, G.J. Bóndadóttir. 1920
2859 Magnússon, H.E. Lykkjuföll. 1923
2898 Markússon, M. Hljómbrot. 1924
2908 Runólfsson, J. Thögul leiftur. 1924
3185 Guttormsson, G.J. Gaman og alvara. 1930
3195 Kvaran, E.H. Vestan um haf. 1930
3527 Pálsson, P.S. Nordur-Reykir. 1936
3630 Húnfjörd, J.H. Ómar. 1938
3747 Stephansson, S.G. Andvökur. 1909-40
3866 Guttormsson, G.J. Hunangsflugur. 1944
3902 Björnsson, S.E. Á heidarbrún. 1945
4012 Sigurdsson, J.A. Kvaedi. 1946
4034 Guttormsson, G.J. Kvaedasafn. 1947
4035 Guttormsson, V.J. Eldflugur. 1947
4057 Pálsson, P.S. Skilarétt. 1947
4131 Thorsteinsson, B. Kvaedi. 1948
4337 Bjarnason, P. Fleygar. 1953

7 Poetry, Swedish

2641 Silver, G.H. [In the age of the wolves] 1918
2809 Goerwell, S.W. [A time of breaking] 1922
3367 Anderson, A.A. Stoft. 1934

8 Poetry, Ukrainian

2218 Fedyk, T. Pisni imigrantiv pro stary i novy kray. 1911
2650 Yasenchuk, J. Kanadiysky kobzar. 1918
3132 Danylchuk, I. Svitaye Den. 1929
3291 Chaykiwsky, P.B. Hornya Kavy. 1932
3493 Bozyk, P. Kanadyska musa. 1936
3514 Kmeta, I. Lyra emigranta. 1936

9 Drama

790 Broughall, G. 90th on active service. 1885
872 Bayer, C. Riel; drame historique. 1886
886 Broughall, G. Tearful and tragical tale. 1886
957 Paquin, E. Riel; tragédie. 1886
2412 Maugham, W.S. The land of promise. 1913

2536 Canada. Army. 90th Winnipeg Rifles. Vaudeville. 1916
2675 Lebel, J.M.O.A. Même sang. 1919
2707 Edmonton. Empire Theatre. Souvenir programme. 1920
2820 Mary Agnes, Sister. Better than gold. 1922
2822 Petrivsky, M. Kavaliysky zhenykh. 1922
2846 Fetherstonhaugh, V. Aunt Anna's foot. 1923
2924 Cropper, M.B. The caravan. 1925
2982 Potter, I.E. Farmer Maxwell's city niece. 1926
3134 Faulds, M.J. Pa-Ke-Noh-Ka, the winner. 1929
3292 Davidson, I.M. Gentlemen adventurers. 1932
3293 Davidson, I.M. Lord Selkirk. 1932
4397 Edmonton. Théâtre Français, Souvenir de vingt années. 1932
3311A Palmer, G.A. Madam Verité at Bath. 1932
3349 Palmer, G.A. Hail. 1933
3394 Morrier, E. Bon sang ne ment pas. 1934
3469 Ramsay, A. Coercion. 1935
3479 Thomas, L.B. Jim Barber's spite fence. 1935
3523 Morrier, E. Quatre essais de théâtre national. 1936
3598 Bicknell, M.E. Relief. 1938
3937 Mercure, A. La Semence. 1945
3947 Ringwood, G.P. Dark harvest. 1945
4294 Gowan, E.P. Breeches from Bond Street. 1952

About theatre

4150 Harvey, R.W. Curtain time. 1949

10 Satire

712 Kewaydin. Leg. Assembly. Select Committee on Ontario boundaries. 1884
1428 Watt, D.H. Poems on the Manitoba School Question. 1895
1477 Greatest realistic burlesque. 1897
3601 Cameron, S. No matter how thin you slice it. 1938
3602 Cameron, W.B. Yarn of the Howling Gale. 1938
3628 Halpin, Barney. Pulpit pounding Bill. 1938
3661 What Aberhart has done for you and me. 1939
3779 Social Credit Board. Alice in Blunderland. 1941

11 Legends and Folklore

671 Dugas, G. Légendes du Nord-Ouest. 1883
1168 Dugas, G. Légendes du Nord-Ouest. 1890
1700 The gopher's tail. 1903
1775 Manitoba Free Press. Quill from a Canada wild goose. 1904
3165 Bloomfield, L. Sacred stories of Sweet Grass Cree. 1930
3371 Bloomfield, L. Plains Cree texts. 1934
3608 Clay, C. Swampy Cree legends. 1938
3916 Gard, R.E. Johnny Chinook. 1945
3923 Halpert, H. Tall tales from Calgary. 1945

V JOURNALISM

1165 Davin, N.F. For the Leader Company. 1890
1333 The Tribune. The Luxton expulsion. 1893

1608 Free Press, Winnipeg, 1872-1900
1876 Great Britain. Colonial Office. Correspondence re complaint of certain printers. 1906
2222 Galaxy of western editors. 1911
2776 Ham, G.H. Reminiscences of a raconteur. 1921
3080 Innes, C. The story of the press. 1928
3308 McMurtrie, D.C. First printing in Alberta. 1932
3740 Regina Leader-Post. Regina Leader-Post presents 'The presses roll.' 194–
3833 Dafoe, J.W. Sixty years in journalism. 1943
3870 John Wesley Dafoe. 1944
3922 Haig, K.M. Brave harvest; E. Cora Hind. 1945
4094 Ferguson, G.V. John W. Dafoe. 1948
4251 MacDonald, M.C. Historical directory of Saskatchewan newspapers. 1951

W BIBLIOGRAPHY

669 Dennis, W. Sources of north-western history. 1883
2835 British and Foreign Bible Society. Cree Indian translation of the Scriptures. 1923
2917 British and Foreign Bible Society. Translations of Canadian Indian Scriptures. 1925
3266A McMurtrie, D.C. First printing in Manitoba. 1931
3281 Toronto. Public Library. Canadian North-West. 1931
3307A McMurtrie, D.C. Early French press in Man. 1932
3441 H.B.C. List of books relating to Hudson's Bay Company. 1935
4183 Winnipeg. Public Library. Select bibliography of Prairie Provinces. 1949
4304 Kupsch, W.O. Annotated bibliography of Saskatchewan geology. 1952
4308 MacDonald, M.C. Publications of the N.W.T. & Sask. 1952
4357 Manitoba. Archives. Transactions and proceedings of Historical Soc. of Manitoba. 1953
4362 Morley, M.G. A bibliography of Manitoba. 1953

POSTSCRIPT

Lande, L.M. The Lawrence Lande collection of Canadiana in the Redpath library of McGill University. (Montreal, 1965)
Morley, Marjorie. A bibliography of Manitoba from holdings in the Legislative Library of Manitoba. (Winnipeg, 1970)
Lande, L.M. Rare and unusual Canadiana. (Montreal, 1971)
Amtmann, Bernard. Contributions to a short-title catalogue of Canadiana. (Montreal, 1971) multivolumed.

Title Index

Author Index
with Biographical Notes

SOURCES CITED IN BIOGRAPHICAL NOTES

Biographical details of authors were not infrequently collected from scattered references; only the more important of these are given as sources.

Agric. Inst. of Canada. Agricultural Institute of Canada. Who's who in the Agricultural Institute of Canada. (Ottawa, 1948)
Allaire. Allaire, J.B.A. Dictionnaire biographique du clergé canadien-français. (St. Hyacinthe, Que., 1906-34)
Alta. Hist. Rev. Alberta Historical Review (periodical)
Assoc. of Ont. Land Surveyors. Annual report, 1943. (Toronto, 1943)
Atlantic Monthly. (Boston, 1857-)
Ayer's. Ayer (N.W.) & son's directory, newspapers and periodicals, 1952. (Philadelphia, 1952)
Beaver. The Beaver (periodical published by H.B.C.)
Beck. Beck, R. History of Icelandic poets, 1800-1940. (Ithaca, N.Y., 1950)
Begg. Begg, A. Ten years in Winnipeg. (Winnipeg, 1879)
Biog. clipping. Scrap book of biographical clippings from newspapers in the Manitoba Legislative Library; also clipping file in the Library of the Free Press, Winnipeg
Black. Black, N.F. History of Saskatchewan and the North West Territories. (Regina, 1913)
Blue. Blue, J. Alberta, past and present. (Chicago, 1924)
Boon. Boon, T.C.B. The Anglican Church from the Bay to the Rockies. (Toronto, 1962)
Brandon direct. Henderson's Brandon directory
Br. army lists. Great Britain. War office. A list of officers of the army, etc. (London, 18-)
Br. Mus. British Museum. Catalogue of printed books. (London, 1881-1900) Supplement. (London, 1900-1905) Also General catalogue of printed books. (London, 1931-)
Bryce. Bryce, G. History of Manitoba. (Toronto, 1906)
Bull. M 'n N Canadiana. Bull, W.P. M 'n N Canadiana. (Brampton, Ont., 1933)
Bulletin. Edmonton Bulletin (newspaper)
Burke's landed gentry. Burke, Sir J.B. A genealogical and heraldic history of the landed gentry. 12th ed. (London, 1914)
Bussard. Bussard, L.H. Lethbridge public schools. (Lethbridge, 1950)
Calgary direct. Henderson's Calgary directory
Calgary Herald. (newspaper)
Can. Agric. Ec. Assoc. Proc. 9th annual meeting., June 28-30, 1937
Can. almanac. Canadian almanac & directory. (Toronto, 1848-)
Can. ann. rev. The Canadian annual review of public affairs, ed. by J.C. Hopkins. (Toronto, 1901-38)
Can. Church Historical Soc. Offprint series
Can. lib. direct. Canadian library directory, 1952. In Canadian Library Association Bulletin, September, 1952
Can. Library. Canadian Library (periodical)
Can. Med. Assoc. J. Canadian Medical Association Journal (periodical)
Can. novel. Thomas, C. Canadian novelists. (Toronto, 1946)
Can. N.W. Hist. Soc., v.1, no.4, pt.1. Canadian North West Historical Society. The story of the press. (Battleford, 1928)
Can. parl. comp. The Canadian parliamentary companion. (Ottawa, 1864-)
Can. parl. guide. The Canadian parliamentary guide. (Ottawa, 1898-)
Can. who's who. The Canadian who's who. (London, 1910; Toronto, 1937-)

Cath. direct. of Can. Catholic directory of Canada; Le Canada écclesiastique. (Montreal, 1887-)
C.H.R. The Canadian Historical Review (periodical)
Church Missionary Gleaner. (periodical)
Civil service lists. Civil service lists. In Canadian sessional papers, 1869-1921
C.L.A. biographies. Canadian biographies; artists, authors and musicians. Loose-leaf volume compiled by the Canadian Library Association. (Ottawa, 1952)
Cleverdon. Cleverdon, C.L. Woman suffrage movement in Canada. (Toronto, 1950)
Cochrane. Cochrane, W. The Canadian album. (Brantford, 1891-95)
Colonist. Daily Colonist, Victoria (newspaper)
Colquette. Colquette, R.D. The first fifty years. (Winnipeg, 1957)
Country Guide. (periodical)
Coyle. Coyle, Wm. Ohio authors & their works. (Cleveland, 1962)
Crockford's. Crockford's clerical directory. (Oxford, 1870-)
Current biog. Current biography. (New York, 1940-)
Cyclopaedia of Methodism. Cornish, G.H. The cyclopaedia of Methodism. (Toronto, 1881-1903)
D.A.B. Dictionary of American biography. (New York, 1928-35)
Dayspring. Dayspring in the far West. (London, 1875)
Direct. of Am. scholars. Directory of American scholars. (Lancaster, Pa., 1942 & 1951)
D.N.B. Dictionary of national biography. (London, 1885-1912) Supplements. (1912-)
Dom. A.R. The Dominion annual register, ed. by H.J. Morgan. (Ottawa, 1878-86)
Edmonton direct. Henderson's Edmonton directory
Free Press. Winnipeg (formerly Manitoba) Free Press (newspaper)
Gaetz. Gaetz, A.L. Park country. (Vancouver, 1948)
Green and White. (periodical of the Alumni Association of the University of Saskatchewan)
Greene. Greene, D.L. Christ Church, The Pas. (n.p., 1931)
Ham. Ham, G.H. The new West. Winnipeg, 1888
Hargrave. Hargrave, J.J. Red River. (Montreal, 1871)
Hargrave, L. Letters. Hargrave, L. Letters. (Toronto, 1947)
Hawkes. Hawkes, J. The story of Saskatchewan and its people. (Chicago, 1924)
Hedges. Hedges, J.B. Building the Canadian West. (New York, 1939)
Higinbotham. Higinbotham, J.D. When the West was young. (Toronto, 1933)
Hist. & Sc. Soc. of Man. Annual reports. (Winnipeg, 188--)
Hist. direct. of Sask. newspapers. MacDonald, M.C. Historical directory of Saskatchewan newspapers. (Saskatoon, 1951)
Hist. of Can. journalism. Canadian Press Association. A history of Canadian journalism. (Toronto, 1908)
Hodge. Hodge, F.W. Handbook of American Indians north of Mexico. (Washington, 1910-12)
H. of C. Committee on Agric. & Colon., 1886. Canada. House of Commons. Committee on Agriculture and Colonization. Proceedings, 1886. In Canadian sessional papers
Howay & Scholefield. Howay, F.W., & E.O.S. Scholefield. British Columbia from the earliest times to the present. (Vancouver, 1913)
Journal. The Edmonton Journal (newspaper)
Kirkconnell. Kirkconnell, W. Canadian overtones. (Winnipeg, 1935)
L.C. official. Library of Congress official card catalogue (consulted in Washington, D.C.)
Leader. Regina Leader (later the Regina Leader-Post)

Leader-Post. Regina Leader-Post (newspaper)
Legal. Legal, E. History of the Catholic churches in central Alberta. (Winnipeg, 1914)
Le Jeune. Le Jeune, L. Dictionnaire général. (Ottawa, 1931)
Lethbridge direct. Henderson's Lethbridge directory
Lethbridge Herald. (newspaper)
London Times. The Times (newspaper of London)
McKellar. McKellar, H. Presbyterian pioneer missionaries. (Toronto, 1924)
Mackinnon. Mackinnon, J.N. Moosomin and its pioneers. (Moosomin, 1937)
McLaurin. McLaurin, C.C. Pioneering in Western Canada. (Calgary, 1939)
Maclean's. Maclean's Magazine
MacRae. MacRae, A.O. History of the province of Alberta. (Calgary, 1912)
Man. & N.W.T. direct. Henderson's Manitoba, Northwest Territories & British Columbia gazeteer and directory. (Winnipeg, 1880-1905)
Matthews. Matthews, W. Canadian diaries and autobiographies. (Berkeley, Cal., 1950)
Medical register, 1952. Great Britain. General Medical Council. Medical register. (London, 1952)
Medicine Hat News. (newspaper)
Metcalfe. Metcalfe, J.H. The tread of the pioneers. (Portage la Prairie, 1932)
M.L.A. Manitoba Library Association. Pioneers and early citizens of Manitoba. (Winnipeg, 1971)
Moose Jaw direct. Henderson's Moose Jaw directory
Morden reunion. Morden, Man. Reunion Organization. Reunion of old timers. (Morden, 1931)
Morgan, 1898. Morgan, H.J. The Canadian men and women of the time. (Toronto, 1898)
Morgan, 1912. Morgan, H.J. The Canadian men and women of the time. (Toronto, 1912)
Morice. Morice, A.G. Histoire de l'Eglise catholique dans l'Ouest canadien. (St. Boniface, 1921-23)
Morice, Dictionnaire. Morice, A.G. Dictionnaire historique des Canadiens et des métis français de l'Ouest. (Québec, 1908)
Morin. Morin, J.B. La vallée de la Saskatchewan. (Joliette, 1893)
Morton. Morton, A.S. A history of the Canadian West to 1870-71. (London, 1939)
National. National reference book on Canadian men and women (Title varies) (Montreal, 1922?-)
New Trail. (alumni magazine of the University of Alberta)
Nor'West Farmer. (periodical) (Winnipeg, 1882-1936)
Nouveau Larousse. Larousse du XXe siècle. (Paris, 1928-33)
N.Y. obit. New York Times obituaries index, 1858-1968. (New York, 1970)
Obit. clipping. Scrap book of biographical clippings from newspapers in the Manitoba Legislative Library; also necrology file in the Library of the Free Press, Winnipeg
Official Cath. direct. Official Catholic directory. (New York, 1886-) Volume consulted, 1953
Pépin. Pépin, C. Histoire de St-Paul, Alberta. (Trois-Rivières, 1952)
Pilling. Pilling, J.C. Bibliography of the Algonquin languages. (Washington, 1891)
Pioneers & prominent people of Man. McRaye, W. Pioneers and prominent people of Manitoba. (Winnipeg, 1925)
Prince Albert direct. Henderson's Prince Albert directory
Province. The Province (Vancouver newspaper)
Regina Daily Post. (later the Regina Leader-Post)
Regina direct. Henderson's Regina directory

R.E.S. Royal Empire Society, London. Subject catalogue of the Library (v.3, Canada, etc.) (London, 1932)
Rhodenizer. Rhodenizer, V.B. Canadian literature in English. (Montreal, 1965)
R.H.P. Review of historical publications relating to Canada. (Toronto, 1897-1919)
Riddell. Riddell, J.H. Methodism in the middle West. (Toronto, 1946)
Robertson. Robertson, J.P. A political manual of the province of Manitoba and the North-West Territories. (Winnipeg, 1887)
Robertson, Correspondence. Robertson, C. Correspondence book. (Toronto, 1939)
Rondeau. Rondeau, C. La Montagne de Bois. (Québec, 1923)
Rose. Rose, G.M. A cyclopedia of Canadian biography. (Toronto, 1888)
Roy. Soc. of Can. Trans. Royal Society of Canada. Transactions. (Ottawa, 1883-)
Sask. Arch. Biog. file. Saskatchewan Archives, Regina Division. Biographical file.
Sask. Arch., 2d report. Saskatchewan Archives. Second annual report, 1946-47. (Regina, 1947)
Sask. Herald. Saskatchewan Herald (early Battleford newspaper)
Sask. Hist. Saskatchewan History (periodical)
Saskatoon direct. Henderson's Saskatoon directory
Saskatoon Phoenix. (later Saskatoon Star-Phoenix)
Saskatoon Star (later Saskatoon Star-Phoenix. See Star-Phoenix)
Schofield. Schofield, F.H. The story of Manitoba. (Winnipeg, 1913)
Shave. Shave, H. Our heritage. (Winnipeg, 1951)
Sissons. Sissons, C. John Kerr. (Toronto, 1946)
Souvenir of Alberta, 1906. Salesman Publishing Co. Souvenir of Alberta. (Winnipeg, 1906)
S.P.G. records. Society for the Propagation of the Gospel. Classified digest of the records of the Society, 1701-1892. (London, 1893)
Star-Phoenix. Saskatoon Star-Phoenix (newspaper)
Telegram. Winnipeg Telegram (early newspaper)
Toronto Star. (newspaper)
Tribune. Winnipeg Tribune (newspaper)
United Church yearbook. United Church of Canada yearbook. (Toronto, 1927-)
U. of S. register. University of Saskatchewan election register, 1952. (Saskatoon, 1952)
U. of T. Quarterly. University of Toronto Quarterly. (Toronto, 1931-)
Vancouver Sun. (newspaper)
Walford's county families. Walford, E. Walford's county families of the United Kingdom. 60th ed. (London, 1920)
Wallace. Wallace, W.S. The dictionary of Canadian biography. 2d ed. (Toronto, 1945)
Wallace, D.N.A.A. Wallace, W.S. A dictionary of North American authors deceased before 1950. (Toronto, 1951)
Washington Post. (newspaper)
Watters. Watters, R.E. A check list of Canadian literature and background materials, 1628-1960. (Toronto, 1972)
Western Producer. (weekly newspaper published in Saskatoon)
Who knows – and what. Who knows – and what. (Chicago, 1949)
Who was who. Who was who, 1897-1960. (London, 1920-62)
Who was who in Am. Who was who in America. (Chicago, 1968)
Who's who. Who's who. (London, 1849-) Volumes after 1898 consulted.
Who's who among N.A.A. Who's who among North American authors. (Los Angeles, 192--) Volume consulted, v.6, 1933-35

Who's who and why. Who's who and why. (Toronto, 19 -21) Volumes consulted, 1917-18 & 1921
Who's who in Am. Who's who in America. (Chicago, 1899-)
Who's who in Australia. (Melbourne, 1922-)
Who's who in Can. Who's who in Canada. (Toronto, 1922-) Formerly Who's who and why
Who's who in Germany. (Munich, 1956-)
Who's who in lit. Who's who in literature. (Liverpool, 1924-) Volume consulted, 1933
Who's who in Sask. Who's who in Saskatchewan. (Saskatoon, 1959)
Who's who in Switzerland. (Zurich, 1951)
Who's who in Western Can. Who's who in Western Canada. (Vancouver, 1911-12)
Winnipeg direct. Henderson's Winnipeg directory
Wolfenden, Begg vs. Begg. Wolfenden, M. 'Begg vs. Begg.' (In B.C. Historical Quarterly, 1937)
Wright. Wright, J.F.C. Slava Bohu. (New York, 1940)
Wrigley's Alta. direct. Wrigley's Alberta directory
Young. Young, G. Manitoba memories. (Toronto, 1897)
Yuzyk. Yuzyk, P. The Ukrainians in Manitoba. (Toronto, 1953)

AUTHOR INDEX

A.L.O.M.
see Frank, Mrs. M.J.

Aberdeen and Temair, Ishbel Maria (Marjoribanks) Gordon, Marchioness of, 1857-1939
Wife of Canada's Governor-General whose term of office was 1893-99. (D.N.B.)
Through Canada with a kodak. 1286

Aberdeen, Sask. Board of Trade
A profitable point for the settler. 2093
Where wheat makes money. 2196

Aberhart, William, 1878-1943
Came from Ont. to Calgary, 1910; taught public and high school in Calgary, 1910-35; taught a Sunday School class which became the Prophetic Bible Institute, opened in 1927; leader of the Social Credit party and Premier of Alta., 1935-43. (Bulletin, 24-5-43; Wallace)
Coloured leaflet series. 3323
Douglas system of economics. 3324
Social Credit manual. 3410
Study group features. 3325

Abernethy, W.J.
Saskatchewan Fife wheat. 707

Aborigines' Protection Society
Canada West & H.B.C. 167
Memorial to Labouchere. 176

Achard, Eugène, 1884-
Montreal librarian, writer and publisher. (Can. who's who, 1967-69; Who's who among N.A.A.)
La caverne des Rocheuses. 4138
La découverte de l'Ouest. 3824

Acland, Frederick Albert, 1866-1950
Journalist in Eastern Canada; became a Dominion civil servant. (Morgan, 1912; Who's who in Can., 1922; Who was who, 1951-60)
The Canadian West. 1848

Adam, Graeme Mercer, 1839-1912
Toronto newspaper editor and author. (Wallace)
The Canadian North-West. 782

Adams, Joseph
English nature writer. (Br. Mus.)
10,000 miles through Canada. 2273

Adams, Mrs. Mary, 1928-
Born at Waskatenau, Alta.; married Father Hilarion (Henry Gregory Adams), a Basilian monk, her pastor in the Ukrainian Catholic Church; both joined an evangelical Protestant church.
I married a monk. 4233

Adams, Ramon Frederick, 1889-
Writer of books on the cowboy life in the early American West; resident of Dallas, Texas; spent some time in Western Canada as a young man.
Poems of the Canadian West. 2650B

Adshead, Herbert Bealey, 1862-1932
Arrived in Alta., 1898; began farming near Olds, Alta., 1899; moved to Calgary, 1912; on city council for three terms; in H. of C., 1926-30. (Can. parl. guide, 1929; Can. ann. rev., 1931-32)
Pioneer tales. 3114

Ager, Paul R.
Machinist who lived in Edmonton, 1912-13. (Edmonton direct., 1912-13)
Life thoughts. 2274

Agnew, Niven, 1826-1905
Prominent Winnipeg eye, ear, and nose doctor who came from Toronto in 1879. (Bryce; Cochrane)
Our water supply. 708

Agricola
see Peltonen, Emil

Aikins & Pepler
List of farm lands. 1634

Alberta
Case for Alberta. 3595

Alberta. Dept. of Agriculture
Alta., land of opportunity. 2833
Official hand book. 1898
Province of Alberta. 2914

Alberta. Dept. of Agriculture. Committee on Drought
Rehabilitation of dry areas. 3489

Alberta. Dept. of Trade & Industry
Your opportunity in Alberta. 3897

Alberta. Legislative Assembly. Agricultural Committee
Aspects of Social Credit. 3412
Douglas system of Social Credit. 3366

Alberta. Post-War Reconstruction Committee
Post-war reconstruction. 3825

L'Association Catholique Franco-Canadienne
15 ans de vie française. 2998

Astley & Shackle
Investments in Alberta. 2197

Atcheson, Nathaniel, 1771-1825
Sec. of the Committee of British North American Merchants formed in London in 1811. (Br. Mus.)
Origin and progress of N.W.C. 33

Athabasca Landing, Alta. Board of Trade
Athabasca Landing. 2034
Northern trek. 2097A

Atkinson, George E., d. 1913
Taxidermist; lived in Brandon from 1898; drowned in Assiniboine River when he suffered an epileptic seizure while in a row boat. (Obit. clipping)
Game birds of Man. 1519
History of the passenger pigeon. 1787
Insectivorous birds of Man. 1702
Manitoba birds of prey. 1559
Rare bird records. 1747

Atkinson, Isabel
Saskatchewan health policy. 4022

Attwood, Charles H.
Engineer with the Dominion Dept. of the Interior stationed at Winnipeg, 1920-30; with Man. civil service, as deputy minister of mines and director of water power, 1930-48. (Winnipeg direct., 1920-48)
Water resources of Man. 3597

Attwood, Peter Harold, 1828-1902
Came to Winnipeg where he engaged in real estate and loan business, 1880-90; resided in U.S.A. for several years before moving to Neepawa where he acted as police magistrate. (Telegram, 23-1-02)
A jubilee essay. 985

Aubert, Frédéric
Traveller from France.
L'Ouest canadien. 1903

Bach, Rudolph, 1851-
Came from Germany to Montreal where he was Canadian correspondent to German papers, 1891-1905; editor of Der Nordwesten, a German language newspaper in Winnipeg, 1905-13. (Morgan, 1912; Winnipeg direct., 1913)
Eine Reise. 1665

Bagnall, Lucy Ann (Lowe), 1883-1969
With her husband, Rev. H.S. Bagnall, came from Maritimes to Calgary; settled on homestead in Grande Prairie district, Alta., while her husband did missionary work, 1912-16; stationed at Medicine Hat where he was killed in a motor accident; high school teacher in Calgary, 1923-44; author of several social science texts for schools; awarded an honorary degree by her alma mater, Acadia. (McLaurin; Calgary direct., 1923-50; Calgary Herald, 22-8-69)
At the sixtieth milestone. 4082

Bailey, J.C.
Hudson's Bay railways. 1520

Bain, George
Scottish writer.
A run through Canada. 1850

Baird, Andrew Browning, 1855-1940
Born in Ont.; Presbyterian minister, Edmonton, 1881-87; for many years lectured at Manitoba College; first minister at Augustine Church, Winnipeg, 1887-92. (Can. who's who, 1936-37; Obit. clipping)
Indians of Western Canada. 1388

Baker, Edna
Prairie place names. 3052

Bala, Joseph
Ukrainian Catholic clergyman in Man. (Official Cath. direct., 1953)
Pershiy Ukrayinskiy epyskop Kanady. 4281

Baldwin, Harold, 1888-
Came to Canada, 1908; worked at various occupations including farming; resident of U.S.A. on two occasions; a journalist in Swift Current, Sask. (Can. novel; Can. who's who, 1967-69)
Farm for two pounds. 3413
Pelicans in the sky. 3414

Baldwinson, Baldwin Lárus, 1856-1936
Came from Iceland to Winnipeg where he entered business, 1882; became immigration agent and made a number of trips to Iceland; instrumental in bringing 7000 persons to Canada; owned an Icelandic language newspaper Heimskringla, 1898-1913; for 12 years an M.L.A. for Gimli; deputy provincial treasurer, 1913-22; died in California. (Free Press, 9-12-36)
Ágrip af fyrirlestri. 1291
Hagskýrslur frá Íslendingabyggdum. 1242
Manitoba un aldamótin. 1589
Nokkrar athugasemdir. 1292
Svar gégn athugasemdum. 1293

Benoist, Charles, d. 1895
Lieut. in French navy; died shortly after visiting the West and his notes were published by a sorrowing father.
Les Français et le N.-O. Canadien. 1391

Benoit, Joseph Paul Augustin, 1850-1915
Scholarly member of the regular clergy of the O.M.I. who came from France with three brothers in 1891; founder of the Man. parish of Notre Dame de Lourdes which was settled by old-country French and by Swiss. (Morice)
L'anglomanie au Canada. 1560
Vie de Mgr Taché. 1749

Bergmann, Fridrik Jónsson, 1858-1918
Clergyman of Icelandic Lutheran Church; taught Icelandic at Wesley College.
Hvert stefnir? 2531

Bergot, Denys, 1863-1933
A Breton; lived in the old-country French settlement of St. Brieux, Sask., 1904-33; collected much anecdotal material to illustrate the difficulties experienced by immigrants in adjusting to a new country, but unfortunately this was destroyed after his death. (Letter from Louis Demay)
Réminiscences d'un pionnier. 3117

Bernard, Harry, 1898-
Quebec journalist. (Can. who's who, 1969-70)
Juana, mon aimé. 3240

Bernard, Lally
see FitzGibbon, Mrs. Mary Agnes

Bernard, P.
see Gonthier, Dominique Ceslar

Bernard de Fauconval, J. de
Belgian consul-general in Ottawa.
Le Canada. 1478

Bernier, Alfred, 1882-1961
Clergyman and teacher at St. Boniface College for many years; died 17-5-61. (Winnipeg direct.; Free Press Library)
Les dates mémorables. 3899

Bernier, Joseph, 1874-1951
Son of T.A. Bernier; member of Man. Leg., 1901-15, 1922-32; later appointed a judge of surrogate court; died 9-6-51. (Morgan, 1912; Who's who in Western Can.; Can. parl. guide, 1932; Free Press Library)
L'instruction obligatoire. 1962

Bernier, Noel, 1879-1944
Son of T.A. Bernier; called to Man. bar, 1902; editor of Le Manitoba, 1900-18; contributed many political and historical articles to French language papers. (Tribune, 1-7-44)
Fannystelle. 3663

Bernier, Thomas Alfred, 1844-1908
Came from Que. to Man., 1880; supt. of education (Cath. section), 1881-90; first mayor of St. Boniface; senator, 1892-1908. (Morgan, 1898; Can. parl. guide, 1907)
Le Manitoba. 989
Le pèlerin d'amour. 2876
Prêtre, laïque et politique. 1339
Speeches of Messrs. Bernier and Scott. 1340
Speech, on Man. School Question. 1392

Berns, Richard
A Dutch emigration agent for the Allan and other steamship lines in Antwerp.
Ulles van het beste. 1590

Berry, Gerald Lloyd, 1915-
Head, dept. of secondary educ., faculty of educ., Univ. of Alta.
The Whoop-up Trail. 4338

Berry, James P., 1867-1953
Born in Ont.; ordained in Methodist ministry, 1898; came to Langdon, Alta., 1907; served in several Alta. communities over the next 30 years; died in Edmonton. (Journal, 15-1-53)
Clover Bar in the making. 3241
Maskepetoon, Alberta's first martyr. 3900

Berthos, Jean
see Bernier, Thomas Alfred

Bérubé, A. Ph., d. 1913
Catholic clergyman; stationed at Vonda, Sask., 1908-13. (Can. almanac, 1908-13)
Canadiens-Français dans l'Ouest. 1963

Bethune, Alexander Bernard, 1855-1932
Resided in Winnipeg, 1881-1905; a student of the economic and transportation problems of the West, his ideas found voice in the columns of the Winnipeg Tribune of which he was one of the founders. (Free Press, 23-12-32)
Is Manitoba right? 1393

Betts, Mary
Dreams. 3492

Bezanson, A.M., 1878-
Owner and promoter of Bezanson townsite in the Peace River district, 1913. (Edmonton direct., 1913)
Peace River trail. 1904

Church, Regina, 1949. (United Church year-book, 1927-51)
Little sanctuaries. 4189

Burns, Mrs. Robert A.
Resident of Neepawa, Man.
The pioneers' story. 4284

Burns, Thomas S.
Born in Scotland; after a few years in Western Canada arrived in Calgary, August 1883; established himself as auctioneer, valuator, and justice of the peace.
Calgary, her industries, etc. 811

Burns, William C., 1857-1929?
Born in London, Ont.; some time before 1886 was on a freighter which sank 400 miles off Melbourne, Australia, and was one of two men who survived on a raft for 72 hours; was a boxer in the U.S.A. and attended the big fights as a sparring partner; a member of John L. Sullivan's troupe for several tours; frontispiece of book contains quotations about Burns by Mark Twain and Upton Sinclair; employed on construction of G.T.P. in 1910; homesteader and woodcutter for river steamers in the country around Lesser Slave Lake and along the Athabasca River; home town Mirror Landing; blindness forced him to retire to Edmonton where he was a non-paying guest at the Selkirk Hotel, 1927; began writing to raise money; apparently published a booklet in 1928, giving first-hand accounts of John L. Sullivan's fights.
Twenty years of adventures. 3122

Burpee, Lawrence Johnstone, 1873-1946
Canadian sec. of the International Joint Commission; outstanding Canadian historian.
Adventurer from Hudson Bay. 17
Hudson Bay to Blackfoot country. 3123
Larocque's journal. 29
La Vérendrye's journal. 13
Pathfinders of the Great Plains. 2446
Sandford Fleming. 2494
Scouts of empire. 2281
Sir Sandford Fleming. 3168
Search for the western sea. 1968
Two western adventurers. 3060
York Factory to Blackfeet country. 15

Burrows, Charles Acton, 1853-1948
Worked as reporter and editorial writer on Winnipeg papers, 1879-82; first provincial deputy minister of agric., 1882-1887; first editor of the Nor'West Farmer, 1882, and pres. of the company until 1895; editor of the Manitoban, 1885-87; editor of the Morning Call, 1887-89; editor of the Western World, 1890-98; returned to Ont., 1898. (Tribune, 15-11-48; Morgan, 1898)
C.P. telegraph route. 517
North western Canada. 518

Burrows, Clement Larcom, 1858-
Church of England clergyman; vicar of St. Paul's, Bournemouth, Eng.
Hands across the sea. 2374
Sketches in Western Canada. 2402

Burt, Alfred Lefroy, 1888-1971
Professor of history, Univ. of Alta., 1913-30; joined Univ. of Minnesota staff. (Direct. of Am. scholars, 1951)
Romance of the Prairie Provinces. 3169

Bushnell, David Ives, 1875-
American anthropologist connected with the Smithsonian Institution.
Sketches by P. Kane. 3714

Bussard, Lawrence H.
Supt. of Lethbridge schools, 1951-
Lethbridge public schools. 4190

Butler, Sir William Francis, 1838-1910
British soldier; participated in Wolseley's Red River expedition as an advance scout, 1870; sent across the prairies to report on the smallpox epidemic, 1870-71; made a trip to Lake Athabasca and on to Victoria via the Peace River, 1872-73. (Who was who, 1897-1916)
Great lone land. 342
Red Cloud, the solitary Sioux. 600
Report of his journey. 321
Wild north land. 356

Buzek, Karel
Památnik Československé Kanady. 3827

Byron-May Company
Pictorial Edmonton. 2447

C., A.L.O.
The story of a dark plot. 1526

Cadman, John
The Bellevue explosions. 2434A

Caesar, Charles Edward
Missionary work among red Indians. 2917A

Cahan, Charles Hazlitt, 1861-1944
A Montreal lawyer, later Sec. of State for Canada, 1930-1935. (Wallace)
Minority rights. 2282

Christmas, Walter, 1861-1924
Danish writer who flourished at the beginning of the 20th century.
Fremtidslande, Canada. 1765

Christy, Robert Miller, 1861-
English writer. (Who's who in lit., 1933)
Manitoba described. 803
Sport in Manitoba. 1050
Why are the prairies treeless? 1258

Chumer, Wasyl A., 1883-
Arrived in Canada, 1905; after teaching school for some years, entered the wholesale business in Edmonton.
Spomyny. 3790

Church, Herbert E., 1868-
Arrived in Canada from England with his brother, 1886; spent a year as apprentice farmer near Owen Sound, Ont.; settled on Sheep Creek, 27 miles from Calgary, 1888, where he farmed and ranched until moving to B.C., 1897.
Emigrant in the Northwest. 3129
Making a start in Canada. 1096

Church, Richard, 1869-1897
Younger brother of H.E. Church; lost his life crossing the Athabasca River while on a prospecting trip.
Making a start in Canada. 1096

Church Missionary Society
Extracts from annual letters. 2123
Formation of N.W. mission. 126
Mem. on N.W. America financial system. 442
North-West Canada missions. 2123A

Church of England. Beaver texts
Manual of devotion. Beaver. 524, 913

Church of England. Blackfoot texts
Hymn book in syllabics. 1163
Manual of religious instruction. 1098
Morning & evening prayer. 1864
Prayer book. 1571
Prayers & hymns. 1809

Church of England. Cree texts
Book of Common Prayer. 162, 172, 220, 2576
Cree hymns for use in Athabasca. 1678
Church catechism. 2047
Hymns in syllabic characters. 1645
Hymns & prayers. 1439
Manual of religious instruction. 1440
Traveller's spiritual provision. 1603

Church of England. Sioux texts
Book of Common Prayer. Sioux. 1097

Church of England. Diocese of Athabasca
Journal of Synod. 1218
Report of Synod. 1051

Church of England. Diocese of Calgary
Fifth meeting of Synod. 1536
Report on Indian missions. 1699

Church of England. Diocese of Edmonton
Diocese of Edmonton. 3670

Church of England. Diocese of Qu'Appelle
Constitution and canons. 804
Journal of 12th Synod. 1399

Church of England. Diocese of Rupert's Land
Clergy widow & orphan's fund. 298
Diocese of Rupert's Land. 497
Indian missions. 1677
Journal of provincial Synod, 1875. 410
Memorandum of Bishop to church societies. 498
Provisional statutes. 387
Report of Diocese, 1865. 261
Report of Diocese, 1867. 262
Report of Synod, 1869. 279
Report of Synod, 1886. 912
Resources and needs for missions. 1357

Church of England. Diocese of Saskatchewan
Diocese of Saskatchewan. 454
Indian missions of Sask. 2048
Report of Synod. 615
Report on Indian missions. 2049

Church of England. Missionary Society
Church hospitals. 3173
Diocese of Athabasca. 3499
Diocese of Calgary. 3500
Diocese of Edmonton. 3501
Diocese of Qu'Appelle. 1975
From the East & from the West. 2900
Missionary Diocese of Athabasca. 1922
North West Canada missions. 1921

Church of the Brethren
Conference. Calgary, 1923. 2842

Clark, Archibald Brown
Professor of political economy, Univ. of Man., 1912-31. (Winnipeg direct., 1912-31)
Economic problems. 3459
Provincial and municipal taxation. 2697
Recent tax developments. 2767

Haultain declares. 1810
How Liberal members were bought. 2581
Kindersley Dam. 2582
The liquor traffic. 2583
The patriotic tax. 2584
Phantom roads. 2585
Policy of the party. 3863
Public land robbery! 1811
Sessional review. 2125
Weed Lake bridge. 2586

Constantin-Fortin, Marguerite, 1891-
At age 16 with her mother came to Man. to join her brother Constantin-Weyer and her fiancé; describes life on a farm which they lost in buying a stallion from a dishonest horse trader; lived on a homestead; her husband, Marcell, and her brother immediately enlisted in the French army in 1914; with her mother moved to Winnipeg, Montreal, and back to France.
Une femme se penche. 3674

Constantin-Weyer, Maurice, 1881-1964
Came to Canada and settled in an old-country French settlement, Saint-Cloude, Man., 1904; married a métis girl, 1910, by whom he had three children; after failing at farming, worked briefly in a store in Morris, on a survey gang, and as a real estate agent at Hudson Bay Junction; returned to France when war broke out, 1914; in WWI received 58 wounds, one of France's most decorated soldiers; became a successful novelist, basing most novels on his Canadian experiences; received award from Académie Goncourt for his 'Un homme se penche sur son passe,' 1928; author of 46 novels, three plays, and two movie scripts. (Journal, 19-10-64)
La bourrasque. 2923
Clairière. 3130
Manitoba. 2885
Napoléon. 3246
Toward the West. 3247
Un homme se penche. 3069
About:
Frémont, Sur le ranch. 3299

Conybeare, Charles Frederick Pringle, 1860-1927
Came to Canada, 1880; called to the N.W.T. bar, 1885; practised law in Lethbridge, 1885-1927; versed in Indian lore. (Morgan; Wallace)
Lyrics from the West. 1924
Vahnfried. 1679

Cook, Jim M., 1858-
A rancher from New Mexico who spent 20 months in the Peace River country, 1911-12. (L.C. official)
Canadian North-West. 2291

Cook, John
Resident of Cleobury Mortimer, Shropshire, Eng.
English tenant-farmers. 1376

Cook, John Thomas
Graduate of Univ. of Sask., 1930; taught at St. John's College, Winnipeg, and later at Calgary.
Nipawin. 3971

Co-operative Commonwealth Federation (Alberta)
Story of Alberta C.C.F. 4086

Co-operative Commonwealth Federation (Sask.)
Sask. C.C.F. members' handbook. 4088
C.C.F. program for Sask. 4087
First ten years. 3791

Co-operative Union of Sask.
Co-operative principles. 4089

Copping, Arthur Edward, 1865-1941
English author and traveller. (Who was who, 1941-50)
The golden land. 2214
Seven years ago. 2126

Copping, Harold, d. 1932
English artist. (Who was who, 1929-40)
Canadian pictures. 2292

Corbett, Edward Annand, 1887-1964
Connected with the dept. of extension, Univ. of Alta., after 1920; director of the dept., 1928-37; moved to Toronto. (Can. who's who, 1936-37; Who's who in Can. 1943-44)
Blackfoot trails. 3375
McQueen of Edmonton. 3376

Corbett, Griffith Owen
Medical missionary; came to Canada from England, 1851; at Red River, 1852-55; built Headingly Church, 1854; appeared before the Select Committee on H.B.C. in England, 1857; one of a party of five who made an exploratory trip southeast as far as Lake of The Woods to test practicability of road between Red River and Lake Superior; scandal, famous trial and imprisonment, 1863; returned to England, 1864; there held many short-term appointments as a curate and was listed in Crockford's as late as 1904; his wife and family remained in the Red River Settlement, where Mrs. Corbett was living as late as 1910. (Hargrave; Biog. clipping, 18-10-10)
Appeal to Gladstone. 299
Few reasons for a crown colony. 208
Notes on Rupert's America. 269

Craigie, Patrick George, 1843-1930
Sec. of central Chamber of Agriculture in Britain, 1878-90. (Who was who, 1929-40)
Canadian N.W. & its development. 806

Craik, Sask. Board of Trade
Centre of the wheat belt. 2699
A silent salesman. 2128

Cran, Mrs. Marion Free (Dudley), 1879-1942
English author; commissioner for the Canadian govt. to report on conditions for prospective Br. women emigrants to Western Canada, 1908. (Who was who, 1941-50)
A woman in Canada. 2129

Crawford, John White, 1883-1962
Born in Illinois, came to Calgary, 1906; studied law on his own, and was called to the bar, 1914; appointed a K.C., 1943; sec. of Alta. Conservative party. (Can. who's who, 1949-51; Calgary Herald, 24-9-62)
Grace Presbyterian Church, Calgary. 3427

Crawford, Mary Elizabeth, 1876-1953
Began medical practice in Winnipeg, 1903; school physician and chief medical inspector of schools, 1918-41; prominent in the movement to obtain the franchise for women. (Morgan, 1912; Who's who in Can., 1947-48; Free Press, 6-6-53)
Legal status of women. 2384

Crean, Frank Joseph Patrick, 1875-
Civil engineer employed in the Dept. of the Interior for several years after 1908. (Civil service lists, 1910-14)
New Northwest exploration. 2130

Crerar, Thomas Alexander, 1876-
Came West with his parents to a homestead, 1881; taught school for several years; pres. of the Grain Growers' Grain Co., later the United Grain Growers' Ltd., 1909-29; in H. of C., 1917-19, 1921-22, 1930, 1935-45; Minister of Mines, Immigration and Colonization, and the Interior, 1935, until these depts. were amalgamated as Mines & Resources in 1936, then minister of the latter dept. until appointed to the Senate, 1945. (Who's who in Can., 1969-70)
Canada's wheat problem. 3973

Cresswell, Henry Cooke Porter, 1892-
Chief commissioner, dept. of immigration and colonization of the C.P.R. (Can. who's who, 1949-51)
Canadian Pacific & immigration. 4145

Crissey, Forrest, 1864-1943
American writer.
Rodney Merton. 1259
Young newspaper scout. 1400

Crocombe, Leonard
An editor goes West. 3611

Cropper, Margaret B.
The caravan. 2924

Cullinane, Eugene Augustine, 1907-
Catholic clergyman, ordained in 1936
Catholic church & socialism. 4091

Culliton, John Thomas
Economist; graduate of Univ. of Sask., 1926; later on staff of McGill Univ. (U. of S. register)
Assisted emigration. 3070

Cullum, Ridgwell, 1867-1943
Englishman who travelled in many countries, ranched in Montana, hunted in Canada; turned writer in 1904, using Canada as the locale of several of his short stories. (Morgan, 1912; Who was who, 1941-50)
Foss River ranch. 1719
Hound of the north. 1767
Night-riders. 1867

Cumberland, Stuart C.
The pseud. of an Australian journalist named Charles Garner.
Queen's highway. 1004
Via Hudson Bay. 1812

Cunard Steamship Company Limited
Kanada: hogy utazzunk. 2131

Cunningham, Robert, 1836-1874
Newspaper correspondent to Toronto papers during the Red River Rebellion; with William Coldwell owned and edited the Manitoban, 1870-74; in H. of C., 1872-74; died at St. Paul, Minn., while returning to Man. (Can. parl. comp., 1874-75)
Speeches on Indian difficulties. 365

Curran, John Joseph, 1842-1909
Quebec judge & politician. (Wallace)
Debate on Riel. 918

Currie, David, d. 1916
Newspaperman on the staff of the Montreal Witness, who visited Man. in 1879; wrote under the pseud. Rusticus. (Can. ann. rev., 1916)
Letters of Rusticus. 525

Curtis, William Eleroy, 1850-1911
American journalist and traveller; with the Chicago Record Herald.
Letters on Canada. 2215

Curwood, James Oliver, 1878-1927
American writer; for some years received an honorarium from the Canadian govt. to write articles, etc., to publicize the Canadian West and North; used the Canadian wilds as the setting for adventure stories.
Philip Steele. 2216
The river's end. 2660

Cuverille, Jules Marie Armand, Cavelier de, 1834-1912
French admiral. (Nouveau Larousse suppl.)
Le Canada et les intérêts français. 1538

Cyr, Joseph Ernest, 1854-1929
In Man. Leg., 1883-87; mayor of St. Boniface, 1885; in H. of C., 1904-08; police magistrate in St. Boniface; supt. of Dominion public works in Winnipeg, 1910. (Who's who in Western Can.)
La colonisation dans l'Ouest. 1926
Mgr Langevin. 2700
Mgr Provencher. 2661
Mgr Taché. 2701
Père Lacasse. 2925
La prairie. 1813

Dafoe, John Wesley, 1866-1944
On the staff of the Manitoba Free Press, 1886-92; worked on eastern papers for several years; editor-in-chief of the Free Press, 1901-44. (Free Press, 10-1-44; Wallace)
Clifford Sifton. 3249
60 years in journalism. 3833
About:
J.W. Dafoe. 3870
Ferguson, Dafoe. 4094

Dahlin, Georg Ludwig, 1889-
Swedish traveller and author who visited Canada about 1928; not living in 1969; used pseud. J.L. Kessel.
Canada, skisser och glimtar. 3131

Dale, Arch, 1882-1962
Cartoonist with papers in Gt. Britain, before homesteading in Sask.; with the Winnipeg Free Press from 1927. (Can. who's who, 1949-51)
$25.00 a month. 3612

Daluaine
A pseud.
The Syndicate. 572

Daly, Denis E.B.
Winnipeg real estate dealer, 1918-30; retired. (Winnipeg direct., 1918-41)
Days with a gunner. 3428
Shooting reminiscences in Man. 3332

Daly, George Thomas, 1872-1956
Catholic clergyman, in the West as rector of Holy Rosary Cathedral, Regina, 1917-21; his name was proposed as Bishop of Prince Albert; moved east. (Saskatoon Star, 14-1-21)
Catholic problems. 2768

Dane, Barry
see Logan, John Edward

Danylchuk, Ivan, 1901-
Born at Canora, Sask.; taught school for a number of years; later director of extension at P. Mohyla Ukrainian Institute, Saskatoon. (Kirkconnell)
Svitaye Den. 3132

Daoust, Charles Roger, 1865-1924
Quebec journalist who saw service in the Sask. Rebellion, 1885. (Wallace)
Cent-vingt jours. 919

Darnault, J.
Member of French Alpine Club in 1891.
Excursion de membres du Club Alpin. 1219

Dart, H.A.
Winnipeg printer in 1880s.
Guide to Winnipeg. 617

Darveau, Jean Edward, 1816-1844
Early Catholic missionary. (Morice)
About:
Morice, Darveau. 3393

Darwin, Oliver, 1860-1961
Emigrated from England to Canada, 1884; started as a Methodist lay preacher in Winnipeg, and served parishes mostly in the Prairie Provinces until 1923; missionary supt. for the Methodist, and later of the United, Church in B.C., 1923-28
Pioneering with pioneers. 4146

Daunt, Achilles
English novelist.
In the land of the moose. 807
Three trappers. 618

Dauphin, Man. Board of Trade
Dauphin – the plentiful. 2132

Dauphin, Man. Municipal Office
List of electors. 1572

Deachman, Robert John, 1878-1955
Ont. journalist interested in agricultural and economic problems; member of H. of C., 1935-40. (Can. parl. guide, 1937)
Wheat board fallacy. 2662

Deane, Richard Burton, 1848-1930
A member of R.N.W.M.P., 1883-1914; rose to be senior supt. (Wallace)
Mounted police life. 2545

DeGroff, Bert
Pioneer resident of the Blindman valley near Bentley, Alta., where he homesteaded about 1908; retired in Red Deer.
Early history of Bentley. 4345

Delaere, Achille, 1868-1939
Catholic clergyman; a Belgian; member of the Redemptorist order; came to Canada as a missionary among the Ukrainians, 1899; by permission of the Vatican transferred from the Latin rite to the Greek (Ruthenian) rite, 1906; his work and influence radiated from Yorkton, Sask. (Sask. Hist., v.3, no.1)
Mémoire sur Ruthènes. 1977

Delaney, Annie
Batoche polka. 781

Delaney, 'Theresa' Mary (Fulford), 1865?-1913
Wife of a settler killed in the massacre at Frog Lake, 1885; prisoner of Big Bear's Cree band for some weeks; died at Aylmer, Que.
In the camp of Big Bear. 819

De la Seine
see Morice, A.G.

DeLury, Justin Sarsfield, 1884-1968
Associated with the Univ. of Man. as professor and head of the geology dept., 1915-27, 1928-44. (Can. who's who, 1955-57; Free Press Library)
Mineral prospects in S.E. Man. 2702

Demanche, Georges, 1855-
Traveller from France.
Au Canada et chez les peaux-rouges. 1166

De Molinari, M.G.
Traveller from France.
Au Canada et aux Montagnes Rocheuses. 920

Dempsey, Hugh Aylmer, 1929-
Journalist, later provincial editor of the Edmonton Bulletin, 1948-51; with the Alta. Dept. of Economic Affairs, 1951-55; archivist, later director, of the Glenbow Foundation, Calgary; editor, Alta. Historical Review.
Historic sites of Alta. 4287

Dempster, W.H.
Welsh tenant-farmer.
On agricultural resources. 1384

Denison, George Taylor, 1839-1925
One of founders of the 'Canada First' group, he was active in stirring up Ont. during Red River Rebellion; commanded Governor-General's Body Guard during Sask. Rebellion; for many years a Toronto police magistrate. (Morgan, 1912)
Red River Rebellion. 366

Dennis, John Douglas Carey
see Carey, Douglas, pseud.

Dennis, John Stoughton, 1856-
Civil engineer who came to the West as a surveyor, 1872; served for four years as surveyor with H.B.C.; commanded Dennis's Scouts during Sask. Rebellion; inspector of surveys for Dominion govt., 1887-94; chief engineer with the irrigation branch, 1894-1902; deputy-commissioner of public works for the N.W.T., 1897-1902; joined the C.P.R. in charge of immigration branch, 1902; appointed asst. to the pres. of the C.P.R., 1911. (Morgan, 1912; Who's who in Can., 1922; MacRae)
Development of Western Canada. 2456
Short history of surveys. 1261

Dennis, William, 1856-1920
Journalist on the Winnipeg Sun, 1882-83; later editor of the Halifax Herald. (Cochrane; Wallace)
Sources of N.W. history. 669

Denny, Sir Cecil Edward, 1850-1928
Member of N.W.M.P., 1874-1881; Indian agent; in later years archivist of the province of Alta. (Wallace)
The law marches west. 3677
Riders of the plains. 1814

Dent, Charles L.
Resident of Prince Albert.
Lines from life. 3792A

Deriares, Jules
Riel. 809

Desrosiers, Léo Paul, 1896-
Montreal writer and librarian.
Les engagés du Grand Portage. 3615

Desaulniers, Gonzalve Lesieur, 1863-1934
L'Absolution avant la bataille. 921

Desjardins, Louis Georges, 1849-1928
Journalist and M.P.P. of Que. (Rose).
True and sound policy of equal rights. 1310

Dodds, James
Shareholder in H.B.C.
H.B.C., its position & prospects. 256

Doka, Kalman C., 1918? -
Born at Kipling, Sask.; school teacher; Presbyterian clergyman; resident of Abbotsford, B.C.
Golden jubilee of Békevár. 4196

Dominion Exhibition, Calgary
Calgary & sunny Alberta. 1978

Dominion Mortgage & Investments Association
Prairie farmer & his debts. 3834

Donalda Extension of Settlement Club
Donalda. 2498

Donkin, John George, 1853-1890
Englishman who emigrated to Man., 1884; joined the N.W.M.P. and was stationed at Regina, Prince Albert, Wood Mt., and Estevan; purchased his discharge, 1888; returned to England. (Leader, 2-3-90)
Trooper and redskin. 1102

Doughty, Sir Arthur George, 1860-1936
Dominion archivist and prominent historian. (Wallace)
Canada & its provinces. 2609
Cheadle's journal. 236
Kelsey papers. 2

Douglas, Clifford Hugh, 1879-1952
English engineer and economist. (Who's who, 1952)
Alberta experiment. 3557

Douglas, David, 1798-1834
English botanist who travelled in North America, mostly on the Pacific coast, collecting botanical specimens from 1823 to 1827; killed in Hawaii when he fell into an animal pit in which an enraged bull was trapped.
Journal in North America. 83A

Douglas, David
On the great fur trail. 2703A

Douglas, George, 1825-1894
Memorial of Rev. George McDougall. 443

Douglas, Mrs. John
Pioneer of Rockhaven, Sask., who settled about 1905.
Poundmaker's stamping ground. 3016

Douglas, Robert, 1881-
Twenty years of York Factory. 6

Douglas, William, 1878-1963
Winnipeg business executive interested in historical research; died 11-12-63. (Winnipeg direct., 1915-51; Free Press Library)
Freemasonry in Man. 2926
House of Shea. 4031
Story of Number Four. 4197

Doukhobors
Obrashchenie Kanadskykh' Dukhoborov'. 1647

Doull, Alexander
English civil engineer; associated with the Canadian Land & Rly. Assoc.
Employment and colonization. 140
Opening a N.W. Passage. 146

Douthwaite, Louis Charles, 1878-
Royal Canadian Mounted Police. 3678

Down, J.W.
Manitoban & great N.W. colony. 456

Downey, Amy Louise
Graduate of the Univ. of Sask.; wife of W.D. Marsland. (U. of S. register)
Seven sheaves. 3909

Dowse, Thomas
Resident of St. Paul, Minn.; newspaper correspondent and later real estate salesman who in early 1880s was salesman for land dept. of the St. Paul, Minneapolis, and Manitoba Rly. Co. (Letter from Minnesota Hist. Soc.)
Manitoba & the N.W. 501

Draper, William Henry, 1801-1877
Ontario politician & jurist. (Wallace)
Hudson's Bay Company. 185

Droonberg, Otto Emil Muschik, 1864-
German novelist, some of whose novels have their setting on this continent.
Die Ansiedler in Canada. 3174

Drummond, Lewis Henry, 1848-1929
Jesuit priest and author; for a number of years on the staff of St. Boniface College. (Free Press, 21-11-08; Wallace)
French element. 1005

Dubois, Emile, 1882-
Catholic clergyman; arrived from France, 1911; stationed in 1914 at Lafleche, Sask., where he served for several years before moving to the Maritimes. (Morice; Rondeau)
Une paroisse d'avenir. 2499

Farley, Frank Legrange, 1869-1949
Came to Alta. and homesteaded at Red Deer, 1892; resident of Camrose, 1905-49; an amateur ornithologist. (Journal, 25-10-49)
Birds of Battle River. 3297
Early history of Camrose. 4028

Farley, Tom 1917-
A resident of Lloydminster.
It was a plane. 4290

Farm & Home
Master farmers of Canada. 3270A

Farm Appraisal Conference
Report. 3507

Farmer, Bernard J.
Go west, young man. 3508

Farmer, Thomas Devey Jermyn
Where the rivers meet. 2217

Farmers' Educational League
Manifesto. 3020

Farney, Maurice
A French writer of children's stories.
Dans les prairies du Canada. 2708

Farquharson, Mrs. James
Wife of pioneer Presbyterian clergyman, whom she married in Ont. in 1881; resident of Man.
Recollections. 3021

Faucher de Saint-Maurice, Narcisse Henri Edouard, 1844-1897
Quebec author and politician. (Wallace)
Le chemin de fer. 928
Les Etats de Jersey. 1313

Faulds, Mary Jeffrey
Pa-Ke-Noh-Ka. 3134

Faulks, R.H.
Resident of Langham, Oakham, Rutland, Eng.
English tenant-farmers. 1360

Fea, Samuel, 1872-1943
Church of England clergyman in Man.
Irish Ned. 2138

Fear, F.J.
Druggist in Nipawin, Sask., in the 1930s.
Call of the Northland. 3432A

Featherstonhaugh, Albany
Capt. in the Royal Engineers and asst. astronomer of Br. section of Br. American Boundary Commission engaged in surveying the 49th parallel, 1872-76. (Br. army lists, 1875)
B.N.A. Boundary Commission. 444

Fedyk, Theodore, 1873-1949
Came from the Ukraine to Canada about 1905; worked first as a labourer then as a storekeeper. (Kirkconnell; Yuzyk)
Pisni imigrantiv. 2218

Feilberg, Henning Frederik, 1831-1921
Danish folklorist, author of a number of books.
De derovre en raekke. 2295
Hjemliv pa praerien. 2587

Ferguson, C.E.
New York journalist.
Barney Oldfield's flight. 2315

Ferguson, George Victor, 1897-
On the staff of the Winnipeg Free Press, 1925-46; editor of the Montreal Daily Star. (Can. who's who, 1967-69)
John W. Dafoe. 4094

Ferguson, R.T.
We stand on guard. 3914

Fergusson, F.W.
Senior official of the Commercial Bank of Manitoba in the 1890s.
Jemförelse mellan Canada. 1404

Fernon, Thomas Sargent
American pamphleteer interested in railway expansion.
No dynasty in North America. 482

Feron, Jean
see Lebel, Joseph Marc Octave Antoine

Ferrier, Thompson
Methodist clergyman; joined Man. conference, 1897; associated with Brandon Indian residential school for many years until 1930. (Can. almanac, 1906-20; Brandon direct., 1923-29)
Indian education in the North West. 1873
Our Indians & their training. 2391

Fetherstonhaugh, Robert Collier, 1892-1949
Montreal historian. (Wallace, D.N.A.A.)
Royal Canadian Mounted Police. 3623

Fetherstonhaugh, Mrs. V.
Said to have been an early resident of Ft. Qu'Appelle.
Aunt Anna's foot. 2846
Mrs. Jim Baker. 1574
A younger son. 1648

Canada and became interested in bringing French immigrants to Canada; as a result the Foncier Society of Canada was formed which established a colony of old-country French at Montmartre, Sask. (Sask. Hist., v.7, no.1)
La colonisation française. 1223

Fowke, Edith (Fulton)
Toward socialism. 4136

Fox, Charles
English settler in the Qu'Appelle Valley north of Regina.
Land of lasses few. 1649

Franchère, Gabriel, 1786-1863
Fur-trader. (Wallace)
Relation d'un voyage. 70

Frank, Mrs. M.J.
An early Manitoba settler who wrote under the pseud. A.L.O.M. (i.e. A Lady of Manitoba)
Brock family. 1172

Franklin, J.T.
Resident of Towcester, Northampshire, Eng.
English tenant-farmers. 1360

Franklin, Sir John, 1786-1847
Arctic explorer. (Wallace)
Narrative of a journey. 80
Narrative of a 2d expedition. 88

Fraser, Alexander
Resident of Balloch of Culloden, Inverness, Scot.
Scotch tenant-farmers. 1379

Fraser, George B.
Early editor of the Morris Herald.
Morris, Man. 625

Fraser, Hugh
A farmer from Clune, Scotland, who toured the Canadian North West.
Trip to the Dominion. 676

Fraser, Sir John Foster, 1868-1936
English journalist and traveller; visited Canada in 1903 and 1904. (Who was who, 1929-40)
Canada as it is. 2221

Fraser, William Alexander, 1859-1933
Born in N.S.; lived for seven years in India, and then for five years in Western Canada; used these two regions for some of his stories. (Wallace)
Blood lilies. 1725
Mooswa. 1607

Fream, William, 1854-1906
Entomologist at Edinburgh Univ.
Across Canada. 930
The prairie. 814

Fredericksen, Ditlew Monrad, 1866-
American connected with the Scandinavian Canadian Land Co. which held 40,000 acres in eastern Sask. (Who was who in Am., 1961-68)
Land laws. 1932

Freebairn, Adam L., 1881-
Came from Scotland to Pincher Creek, 1899; cowboy, drugstore clerk, and merchant after 1906. (Maclean's, 1-7-54)
Kootenai Brown. 3721
Mountain heights. 3795
My son. 3722
Rhymes from the foothills. 3796

Freedman, Benedict, 1919-
American author and mathematician. (Current biog., 1947)
Mrs. Mike. 4033

Freedman, Lois Nancy (Mars), 1920-
American author; wife of above. (Current biog., 1947)
Mrs. Mike. 4033

Freemantle, Elizabeth
see Covey, Elizabeth (Rockford)

Freemasons. Alberta. Ashlar Lodge, No.28, Calgary
By-laws. 1983

Freemasons. Saskatchewan. Wascana Lodge, No.23, Regina
By-laws. 1316

Freeport, Andrew
A pseud.
Case of the H.B.C. 187

Freitag, Karl W.
Pastor of Evangelical Trinity Lutheran Church, Edmonton, 1929-34. (Edmonton direct., 1929-34)
Dreieinigkeitsgemeinde. 3298

Frémont, Donatien, 1881-
Came to Canada from France, 1904; associate editor of Le Patriote de l'Ouest at Prince Albert, 1916-23; editor of La Liberté, Winnipeg, 1923-41; moved to Montreal. (Can. who's who, 1967-69)
Mgr Provencher. 3435
Mgr Taché. 3175
Le ranch de Constantin-Weyer. 3299
Les secrétaires de Riel. 4347

German, Orrin, d. 1905
Methodist missionary stationed at Oxford House, 1873-79; at Norway House, 1879-85; Whitefish Lake, 1885-92; at Battle River & Bear Hill, 1892-1905; translated some of the sermons of evangelist Dwight L. Moody into Cree. (Riddell; Young; Blue)
Methodist hymns. 817

German-American Land Company, Limited
Wegweiser nach der Colonie. 1726

Gershaw, Fred William, 1883-1968
Born and educated in Man.; after graduation practised medicine at Medicine Hat; elected to represent Medicine Hat in the H. of C., 1925, 1926, 1930; summoned to the Senate, 1945. (Can. parl. guide, 1950; Journal, 28-6-68)
Medicine Hat. 4292

Gibbon, John Murray, 1875-1952
Publicity agent for C.P.R. (Can. who's who, 1949-51)
Steel of empire. 3437

Gilbert, Louis
Resident of France.
La Saskatchewan. 2459

Gill, Edward Anthony Wharton, 1858-1944
Came from England to Man., 1885; ordained as a Church of England clergyman, 1889; stationed at Minnedosa, 1889-1910; associated with St. John's Cathedral and St. John's College, Winnipeg, for many years; retired from active ministry, 1934. (Free Press, 2-9-10 & 10-1-44)
Irishman's luck. 2460
Love in Man. 2223
Man. chore boy. 2297

Gill, Frank P.
Rhapsody. 3075

Gillett, Walter B.
Winnipeg land agent, 1885-90. (Winnipeg direct., 1885/86-90)
Manitoba. 1007

Giraud, Marcel
French historian and sociologist who visited Western Canada in the 1930s to study the métis; professor of the history of North American civilization at the Collège de France in Paris. (Sask. Hist., v.7, no.1)
Le métis canadien. 3917

Girls' Home of Welcome Association
Annual reports. 1541A

Girouard, Désiré, 1836-1911
For many years a Quebec M.P.
L'éxecution de Riel. 933
Louis Riel. 818

Giroux, J.B.H.
La Rivière la Paix. 2461

Giscard, Gaston, 1886-1969
Arrived in Western Canada from France, 1910; homesteaded at Jack Fish Lake, Sask.; opened a general store; moved to Edmonton where he was one of the founders of a company called the Franco-Canadien Realty Co.; returned to France when WWI broke out; returned for a visit to Western Canada, 1957; killed in an automobile accident in his home city of Toulouse, 1969. (Private information)
Dans la prairie canadienne. 4293

Gislason, Ingvar
Teacher at Western Canadian High School, Calgary, 1947- (Calgary direct., 1947-50)
Prairie panorama. 4097

Gladstone, Man. Board of Trade
Gladstone & surrounding district. 1875

Glamis, Sask. Memorial United Church
Historical sketch. 4200

Glass, Ervin Bird, 1852-1927
Methodist clergyman, ordained in 1887; spent sixteen years in Indian missionary work, seven of these at Battle River, nine at Whitefish Lake; stationed at Snowflake, Man., 1902. (Riddell; United Church yearbook, 1930)
Cree hymn book. 1060
Primer in Eng. & Cree. 1176

Glazebrook, George Parkin de Twenebrokes, 1899-
Professor of history at the Univ. of Toronto. (Direct. of Am. scholars, 1951)
Hargrave correspondence. 106

Glendinning, John Clements, 1866-1949
Journalist, and senator in the parliament of Northern Ireland. (Who was who, 1941-50)
Oh! Canada. 2773

Glendon, Alta. Ukrainian Greek Catholic Parish
Posvyachennya parokhialnoyi rezydencyi. 3918

Globensky, Emile Auguste Maximilien, 1830-1906
Seignior of St. Eustache and Mille-Isles in Que. (Wallace)
Le mixed-farming au Manitoba. 1224

Grogan and Pettit
Settlers' guide to southern Alberta. 935

Grossman, Vladimir, 1884-
Born in Russia and educated at St. Petersburg and Berlin universities; came to Montreal, 1919; author of non-fiction books of international interest. (Can. who's who, 1952-54)
The soil's calling. 3627

Grotty and Cross
Manitoba lands for sale. 1178

Grouard, Emile Jean Baptiste Marie, 1840-1931
Catholic missionary; came from France to the Peace River-Athabasca region, 1862; vicar apostolic of Athabasca, 1910-30; brought first printing press to Alta., and on it printed a number of religious works in Indian languages (see Entries 469, 696, 1026, 4379); the press now in the St. Albert Museum. (Le Jeune; Morice)
Souvenirs. 2811

Grouard, Alta. Board of Trade
Grouard. 2397

Groulx, Lionel, 1878-
Professor of history at the Univ. of Montreal. (Can. who's who, 1964-66)
Louis Riel. 3921

Grove, Frederick Philip, 1872-1948
Born in Sweden; educated in European universities and travelled extensively in Europe; came to the U.S.A. in 1892 and to Western Canada in 1893; worked as a farm-hand for many years, with full-time writing his goal; later taught school in Man.; in his last years received recognition as a major Canadian novelist.
Fruits of the earth. 3336
In search of myself. 3984
Our daily bread. 3078
Over prairie trails. 2848
Settlers of the marsh. 2929
Turn of the year. 2849
Yoke of life. 3182
About:
Pacey, Grove. 3943

Gruchy, Lydia E.
The Doukhobors in Canada. 3183

Guichon, Sister May
see May Guichon, Sister

Guiry, Jerome J.
Resident of Fethard, Clonmel, Ire.
An Irish agricultural delegate. 1361

Gunn, Donald, 1797-1878
In service of H.B.C., 1813-23; became a judge at Red River Settlement; member of Leg. Council of Man., 1871-76. (Robertson)
History of Manitoba. 532

Gunn, John J., 1861-1907
Grandson of Donald Gunn; farmer and apiarist on the banks of the Red River; gored to death by a bull on his farm.
Echoes of the Red. 3184

Gunnarson, Karl
see Schulze, Gunnar

Gunter, Lillian Forbes
Loving memories. 3255

Gurney, F.C.
Resident of Didsbury, Alta.
Soul so dark. 3840

Guttormsson, Guttormur Jónsson, 1878-
Born at Riverton, Man.; after a variety of jobs homesteaded at Shoal Lake; became a partner in a general store; finally bought his father's original farm at Riverton, 1910; a leading Icelandic poet. (Kirkconnell)
Bóndadóttir. 2711
Gaman og alvara. 3185
Hunangsflugur. 3866
Jón Austfirdingur. 2058
Kvaedasafn. 4034

Guttormsson, Vigfús J.
Icelandic resident of Lundar, Man.
Eldflugur. 4035

Gwynn, Grace (Mrs. Kenneth H.)
see Leigh, Ursula

Hacault, Louis, 1843-1921
Belgian journalist and lawyer; as a correspondent for the Courrier de Bruxelles and of the Handelsblad of Anvers toured Man. in 1890; in search of health, emigrated with his family and settled at Bruxelles, Man., 1891. (Morice)
Les colonies belges. 1266

Hackett, John A.
Resident of Grouard, Alta., and of the Slave Lake area, in the period prior to World War I; later a resident of B.C. (Preface)
Rhymes of the north. 2887

Haegler, Curt August
Oh, Canada! 3301

Hahn, Otto
Canada. 677

Hattersley, Charles Marshall, d. 1952
English Social Credit theorist who settled in Edmonton in 1952. (Journal, 27-12-52)
Aberhart and Alberta. 3563

Haultain, Sir Frederick William Gordon, 1857-1942
Prominent in the political and judicial life of the N.W.T., and later of Sask. (Morgan, 1912; Wallace)
The Conservative party. 2301
Constitutional & financial questions. 1612
Haultain outlines his policy. 1821
Indian Head debate. 1659
The public domain. 2302

Haultain, Theodore Arnold, 1857-1941
Toronto writer. (Wallace)
History of Riel's 2d rebellion. 820

Haver, Malcolm J., d. 1968
Social service worker in Saskatoon, 1930-37; school teacher, 1937-45; in business after 1945; prominent advocate of Social Credit in Sask.; unsuccessful candidate in several provincial elections. (Star-Phoenix, 1-10-68)
Social credit explained. 3511

Hawarden, Sask. Homemakers' Club
History of Hawarden. 4203

Hawkes, Arthur, 1871-1933
In Western Canada 1885-88; returned to Eng.; prominent journalist; in charge of publicity for the Canadian Northern Rly. for a few years before 1910; moved to Toronto. (Morgan, 1912)
Horseman & the West. 2953
Trains of recollection. 2888

Hawkes, John, 1851-1931
Came to the West about 1887; taught school, and worked for Dept. of Indian Affairs; candidate for N.W.T. Leg., 1888, and for H. of C., 1896; organized Whitewood Creamery Co., 1896; edited Whitewood Herald, 1896-99; edited Carnduff Gazette, 1899-1905; legislative librarian in Sask., 1907-29; organized travelling libraries in the province. (Leader, 5-3-31; Sask. Arch., 2nd report)
Sask. & its people. 2889

Haydon, Arthur Lincoln, 1872-
English writer. (Who's who, 1952)
Riders of the plains. 2145

Hayes, John Francis, 1904-
Spent childhood in Ft. William; received secondary education in Winnipeg; later resident of Toronto.
Buckskin colonist. 4101

Hayes, Kate E., 1856-1945
Arrived in the West, 1879; married C. Bowman Simpson, 1882, but obtained legal separation, 1889; librarian of N.W.T. legislature, 1891-98; wrote under pen name Mary Markwell; joined editorial staff of Winnipeg Free Press, 1899, on which paper she organized the women's page, and with which she was associated for many years; organized the Canadian Women's Press Club; sent to England on special immigration work, 1906; died in B.C. (Tribune, 16-1-45; Morgan, 1912)
Aweena. 1878
Prairie pot-pourri. 1410

Healy, William Joseph, 1867-1950
Arrived in Winnipeg, 1899; associate editor of the Free Press, 1901-20; provincial librarian of Man., 1920-37; died in San Francisco. (Regina Leader-Post, 25-8-50)
Winnipeg's early days. 3025
Women of Red River. 2850

Hearne, Samuel, 1745-1792
Fur-trader and explorer; built Cumberland House, the first permanent settlement in the future province of Sask., 1774. (Wallace)
Journals. 22

Hector, Sir James, 1834-1907
Scottish-born geologist who accompanied the Palliser expedition as surgeon and geologist; subsequent career was in New Zealand. (Wallace)
Central part of Br. North America. 227A

Hedges, James Blaine, 1894-1965
American history professor. (Direct. of Am. scholars, 1951; Who was who in Am., 1961-68)
Building the Canadian West. 3682
Federal railway land subsidy policy. 3384

Heeney, William Bertal, 1873-1955
Church of England clergyman; rector of St. Luke's Church, Winnipeg, 1909-42; moved to Ottawa. (Wallace; Free Press, 22-6-42)
Centenary addresses & sermons. 2813
Founding of Rupert's Land. 3136
John West. 2712

Heffelfinger, G.G.
Near view of the New Canadian. 2303

Heinonen, A.I.
Finnish immigrant.
What the Canadian expects. 2821

Heming, Arthur Henry Howard, 1870-1940
Canadian traveller and illustrator. (Wallace)
Drama of the forests. 2777

Hickman, Herbert
Two months' tour across Canada. 1224A

Hiebert, Paul Gerhardt, 1892-
Born at Pilot Mound, Man., and grew up at Altona; took an M.A. degree in Gothic and Germanic philology at the Univ. of Toronto, then changed to physics and chemistry; professor of chemistry, Univ. of Man. (Tribune, 27-12-47)
Sarah Binks. 4037

High River, Alta. Chalmers Church
High River cook book. 1933

High River Times
This is High River. 4204

Highe, Edward
Maggie abandons the big dough. 3842

Higinbotham, John David, 1864-1961
Pioneer druggist who began business in Macleod, 1884, moved to Lethbridge, 1885; Lethbridge postmaster, 1886-1910; prominent in local organizations; spent his declining years in Guelph; died 15-4-61. (Blue; Souvenir of Alberta, 1906)
Foothill & prairie memories. 4151
When the West was young. 3337

Hill, Alexander Staveley, 1825-1905
Prominent English politician, who was one of the promoters of the Oxley ranch in 1882; the ranch was named after his English estate. (Who was who, 1897-1916)
From home to home. 821

Hill, Robert Brown, 1838-1900
Born in Scotland; settled at Portage la Prairie in early 1870s, where he was a carriage maker, and later a journalist with the Portage newspapers. (Free Press, 12-12-00)
Manitoba. 1180

Hillsman, John Burwell
A Winnipeg physician who served in a field surgical unit in northwest Europe in WWII.
Eleven men and a scalpel. 4104

Hinch, Herbert H., 1872-
Entered real estate business in Man., 1900; pres. of Manitoba and Western Colonization Co., interested in settling American farmers in the Red River valley; son of Ogden Hinch. (Schofield)
Carman – Winnipeg district. 1650

Hinch, Ogden, 1851-1908
Real estate dealer in Winnipeg after 1900.
Carman – Winnipeg district. 1650

Hinchliffe, Joshua, 1868-1954
Came to Canada, 1890; ordained a Church of England priest, 1894; missionary to Peigan Indians, 1893-99; co-operated with Canon Stocken in devising a syllabic form of writing for the Blackfoot Indians; Red Deer, 1899-1907; moved to B.C. where active in politics. (Who's who in Western Can.; Can. who's who, 1949-51; Province, 10-5-54)
Blackfoot prayer book. 1571

Hind, Ella Cora, 1861-1942
Agricultural editor of the Free Press for many years; won fame for her skilful prediction of the total annual crop yield of the prairies.
About:
Haig, Brave harvest. 3922

Hind, Henry Youle, 1823-1908
Geologist who was a member of the Red River exploratory expedition sent out from Canada, 1857; in command of the Assiniboine-Sask. exploratory expedition, 1858. (Wallace)
Exploration, Superior & Red River. 195
Man. & N.W. frauds. 679
Narrative of Red & Sask. expeditions. 221
North West Territory. 211
Report on canoe route. 198
Sketch of an overland route. 232

Hinds, E.M.
English school mistress who spent two years teaching school in a French-speaking community near Regina; later published a novel 'Victorious venture' which may have a Canadian locale. (Matthews)
Nothing ventured. 3763

Hines, John, 1850-1931
Church of England missionary; came to the West, 1874; ministered to the Sandy Lake and Mistawasis Indian bands, 1874-88; stationed at The Pas, 1888-1902; supt. of Indian missions in Prince Albert area, 1902-11; died in Winnipeg. (Tribune, 25-2-31)
Red Indians of the plains. 2505

Hinks, David, d. 1942
Biologist on staff of the Man. fisheries branch; enlisted in the R.C.A.F., 1940; killed over Germany.
Fishes of Man. 3843

Hislop, Mary
Streets of Winnipeg. 2307

Historical and Scientific Society of Manitoba
Agnew, N.
Our water supply. 708

Hives, Harry Ernest
Church of England missionary, graduate of Emmanuel College; stationed at Cumberland

Janicki, Stefan
Syndykat sprzedazy pszenicy. 3142

Jaques, Edna, 1891-
Born in Ont.; came with her parents to a homestead in Moose Jaw district about 1902; married W.E. Jamieson and with him homesteaded near Tisdale, Sask., 1924; lectured for Homemakers' Clubs in Sask., 1933-39; popular poet. (C.L.A. biographies)
Drifting soil. 3444
My kitchen window. 3445
Wide horizons. 3446

Jaques, Florence (Page), 1890-
American author; wife of F.L. Jaques. (Who's who in Am., 1950-51)
Canadian spring. 4041

Jaques, Francis Lee, 1887-
American artist. (Who's who in Am., 1950-51)
Canadian spring. 4041

Jaray, Gabriel Louis
Traveller from France.
De Québec à Vancouver. 2890

Jarvis, William Henry Pope, 1876-1944
Engaged in journalism for a time in the West. (Morgan, 1912; Wallace, D.N.A.A.)
Letters of a remittance man. 1989

Jeal, Mrs. Stanley
Tales of the Touchwoods. 4344

Jean, Josaphat
see Zhan, Josaphat

Jean-Baptiste, Soeur
see Soeur de la Providence

Jefferson, Robert, 1856-1934
Came from England to Man., 1876; moved to Battleford, 1878; teacher on Red Pheasant reserve, 1878-85; Poundmaker's prisoner during the Sask. Rebellion; married Poundmaker's sister; later deputy sheriff at Battleford and an employee of the provincial mental hospital. (Colonist, 8-8-34)
Fifty years on the Sask. 3143
Sask. verse. 3193

Jeffery, John B.
A major and 'dean' of Chicago press.
Barney Oldfield's flight. 2315

Jeffs, Harry, 1860-1938
English journalist and editor of religious journals; at the time of his visit to Canada was editor of the Christian World Pulpit. (Who was who, 1929-40)
Homes and careers in Can. 2464

Jenness, Diamond, 1886-1969
Canadian ethnologist. (Can. who's who, 1936-37)
Sarcee Indians of Alberta. 3631

Jennings, John Edward, 1906-
American novelist.
Strange brigade. 4297

Jennings Publishing Company
Calgary, sunny Alberta. 2228

Jérémie, Nicolas, 1669?-1732
Fur-trader from New France employed by Compagnie du Nord at posts on Hudson Bay, 1694-1714. (Wallace)
Détroit et la Baie d'Hudson. 5
Twenty years of York Factory. 6

Jerome, Martin, 1850-
Métis member of Man. Leg., 1888-1903; later on staff of federal immigration branch in Winnipeg; living as late as 1932. (Morice, Dictionnaire)
Coup d'oeil rétrospectif. 1268
Souvenirs. 2550

Jewish Old Folks Home of Western Canada
Story of an institution. 3928

Johann, A.E.
see Wollschläger, Alfred

Johnson, Alice M.
Archivist of the Hudson's Bay Co. in London for many years until her retirement in 1968. (The Beaver, Autumn, 1971)
Saskatchewan journals. 27

Johnson, Gilbert
Grain buyer at Marchwell, Sask.; author of articles on local history. (Sask. Hist., v.4, no.1)
History of Fort Ellice. 4298

Johnson, M.E.
Dayspring in the far west. 417

Johnston, Thomas
Came from the Orkney Islands to Alta.; settled at Ghost Pine Creek.
Canadian & Scottish songs & poems. 2715A

Johnstone, Catherine Laura, 1838-1923
Scotswoman who visited Canada.
Winter & summer excursions. 1363
Young emigrants. 1544

Kavanagh, Martin, 1895-
Born 'at the turn of the century' in County Wicklow, Ireland; came to Canada, 1923; principal of Tummel consolidated school and later of Treherne high school; teacher of Latin and commercial geography at Brandon Collegiate after 1930.
The Assiniboine basin. 3990

Kazymyra, Bohdan, 1913-
Born in the Western Ukraine; educated at Lviv, and the Universities of Louvaine and Vienna; came to Canada, 1950; journalist with Ukrainian News, Edmonton; librarian at Univ. of Sask. (Regina). (Edmonton direct., 1951)
Monsinor Lyanzheven i Ukrayinci. 4299
Pyatdesyat rokiv u Kanadi. 4335

Keating, William Hypolitus, 1799-1840
Geologist and historian of the expedition under Maj. S.H. Long sent out in 1823 by the American govt. to explore the headwaters of the Mississippi River.
Expedition to St. Peter's River. 82

Keith, Marian
see MacGregor, Mary Esther

Kells, Edna, 1880-
On staff of Edmonton Journal, 1910-33, during the latter part of the period as editor of the women's page. (Edmonton direct., 1910-33)
Elizabeth McDougall. 3386

Kelly, Leroy Victor, 1880-1956
Homesteaded near Dickson, Alta., 1902-05; reporter, and for a time news editor, on the Calgary Herald, 1905-10; marine editor on the Vancouver Daily Province, 1915-49. (Private information; Province, 9-1-56)
The range men. 2404

Kelsey, Henry, d. 1729
H.B.C. employee. (Wallace)
Journal. 1
Kelsey papers. 2

Kelsey, Vera, 1891?-1961
Born in Winnipeg; resident in the U.S.A.
Red River runs north. 4245

Kenderdine, Augustus Frederick La Fosse, 1870-1947
Received art training in England; farmed and ranched near Lashburn, Sask., 1908-20; held a one-man art show in Saskatoon, 1920; joined Univ. of Sask. as art instructor; organized Summer Art School at Emma Lake; director of fine arts at Regina College from 1934 until his death. (Green & White, Fall, 1954)
To the youth of Sask. 4109
Twelve views of Sask. 3343

Kendrick, Edward
Man. & the Canadian N.W. 627

Kennedy, Fred
Born in Scotland; came to Alta. as a boy; arena director of stampedes at different western centres, 1925-27; journalist on Calgary Herald.
Calgary Stampede story. 4300

Kennedy, H.G.
101st Regiment Edmonton Fusiliers. 2405

Kennedy, Howard Angus, 1861-1938
Prominent Montreal journalist who was a war correspondent in the Sask. Rebellion, 1885. (Wallace)
Book of the West. 2931
New Canada & New Canadians. 1934
North-West Rebellion. 3081
Origin of the C.P.R. 3082

Kenney, James Francis, 1884-1946
Dominion archivist and historian. (Can. who's who, 1936-37)
Founding of Churchill. 7

Kenyon, Charles Richard
English novelist. (Br. Mus.)
Young ranchmen. 1225

Kerby, George William, 1860-1944
Pastor of Calgary Central Methodist Church, 1903-10; principal of Mount Royal College, Calgary, 1910-42. (Morgan, 1912; United Church yearbook, 1944; Letter from Calgary Library)
Broken trail. 2063
Milestones of Methodism. 2932

Kernaghan, William
Chicago merchant who appeared before the Br. Select Committee on the H.B.C. in 1857; was interested in having the trade in Rupert's Land declared free.
H.B. & Red R. Settlement. 189

Kernighan, Thomas
Homesteaded in 1878 near Carman, Man., where he lived for a number of years on S.33-T.6-R.4. (Man. & N.W.T. direct., 1885-87)
Dufferin and Carman. 2854

Kerr, Frederick William, 1881-1945
Born in Ont.; school teacher in Edmonton, 1901-02; Presbyterian clergyman; professor at Manitoba College, Winnipeg, 1920-28, and

minister of Knox Church, 1925-32; moved to Montreal; died 7-6-45. (Who's who in Can., 1936-37; Free Press Library)
Alexander Macdonald. 3050

Kerr, Illingworth Holey, 1905-
Born at Lumsden, Sask.; spent some years in England and Vancouver; art instructor on staff of Calgary Institute of Technology and Art.
Gay dogs & dark horses. 3991

Kerr, John Andrew, 1851-1940
Town clerk of Perth, Ont.; came West with Wolseley expedition, 1870; spent more than a decade in the West, part of the time as a hunter and trader along the Sask. River, before returning to Ont.
About:
Sissons, John Kerr. 4013

Kerr, John R.
Pioneer in Alhambra district of Alta.; retired in Red Deer.
Other days and other ways. 4301

Kessel, J.L.
see Dahlin, Georg Ludwig

Kewaydin. Select Committee
Boundaries of Ontario. 712

Killam, Albert Clements, 1849-1908
Moved to Man. and practised law, 1879; member of H. of C., 1883-85; appointed a judge, 1885; chief justice of Man., 1899, appointed to Supreme Court of Canada, 1903; chief commissioner of the Bd. of Rly. Commissioners, 1905. (M.L.A.)
(See entries under Ross, Ross, & Killam)

Killarney, Man. Women's Institute
Stories of pioneer days. 3344

Kilroe, William G.B., d. 1927
Appeared in Calgary directory for only one year, 1927, as an insurance agent.
Souvenir of Turner Valley. 3027

King, John Mark, 1829-1899
Presbyterian clergyman; principal of Manitoba College, 1883-99. (Wallace)
Manitoba College. 1182

King, Richard, 1811?-1876
Surgeon and naturalist on Back's expedition to the Arctic, 1833-35. (D.N.B.)
Journey to the Arctic. 98

King, Tom
Came from Minnesota in 1906 to Pasqua, Sask., where he farmed for many years; was also a road contractor; later a resident of Moose Jaw. (Moose Jaw direct., 1929-31)
Black ox. 3263

King, William Robert, 1888-
Born in Ont.; director of Sunset Ranche Ltd. near Calgary; represented the constituency of Cochrane as a Social Credit M.L.A., 1935-40. (Can. parl. guide, 1939)
History of Alberta. 3685

Kingston, William Henry Giles, 1814-1880
English author of boys' adventure stories. (D.N.B.)
The frontier fort. 537
Rob Nixon. 285
Snow-shoes & canoes. 1010

Kipling, Rudyard, 1865-1936
English poet who visited Western Canada in 1906.
Kipling's advice to 'The Hat.' 2815

Kiriak, Illya, 1893-1955
Came to Canada from the Ukraine, 1906; educated at the Univ. of Alta.; a school teacher; director of the Michael Hrushevsky Institute, Edmonton, 1940-42. (Journal, 30-12-55)
Syny zemli. 3929

Kirkby, William West, 1827-
Arrived at Red River and took charge of the Model Training School, 1852; ordained a Church of England clergyman by Bishop Anderson, 1854; served in the Mackenzie River district, 1859-68; returned to England to recuperate his health. (Dayspring)
Manual of devotion. 524
Manual of prayer & praise. 506

Kirkconnell, Watson, 1895-
Professor of English at Wesley College, Winnipeg, 1922-40; later professor at McMaster Univ.; pres. of Acadia Univ. (Can. who's who, 1948)
Canadian overtones. 3447
Flying bull & other tales. 3728
Jubilee of Wesley College. 3632
Our Ukrainian loyalists. 3844

Kirkpatrick, Mrs. Helen, 1877-
Used pseudonym Gemmill.
Ramblings in verse. 4157

Kitto, Franklin Hugo, 1880-
Dominion civil servant in the Dept. of the Interior.
Athabaska to the Bay. 2673
Edmonton, Prince George, Peace River triangle. 3194
Manitoba. 3244
New Manitoba district. 2621

Parliament buildings contract. 1994
Peace, progress and prosperity. 1827
Railroads, roads, telephones. 1995
Railway competition. 1828
Scott government's record. 1996
Some phases of school problem. 2596
Splendid lands bargains. 1829
Supplementary revenue act. 1997

Liberal Party Battleford Constituency
Liberal Farmers Association. 2234

Libertas
Pseudonym.
National schools for Man. 459

Liddell, Ken E., 1912-
Born and educated in Regina; on staff of Regina Leader-Post, 1930-49; on Edmonton Bulletin, 1949; on Calgary Herald, 1950-
This is Alberta. 4307

Lightfoot, John
Clergyman from Cross Stone, Yorks, England.
Advantages of Canada for emigrants. 1353

Linck, Olaf, 1874-
Danish traveller and author who visited the U.S.A. and Canada in the 1920s.
Kanada. 2967

Lindal, J.H.
Islendingar i Vatnabygdum. 2718

Line Elevators Farm Service
Field crop insects. 3930

Lingard, Charles Cecil, 1901-
Born at Carnduff, Sask.; school principal at Kincaid and Macklin, Sask., 1920-30; history teacher in a Regina collegiate, 1930-40; chief librarian, Regina Public Library, 1940-45; editor of the International Journal, 1945- (C.L.A. biographies)
Territorial government. 3993

Link, Theodore August, 1897-
Born in American mid-West; held several senior posts as a geologist; asst. chief, and chief, geologist for Imperial Oil Ltd., 1944-48; consulting geologist resident in Calgary. (Who's who in Can., 1969-70)
Oil in Alberta & Western Canada. 4159

Linnell, J.B.
Homesteader who settled at Summerberry, Sask. in 1885.
Story of a pioneer. 4160

Linton Bros.
Stationers in Calgary in 1911.
City of Calgary. 2235

Lionnet, Jean, 1872-
Writer from France who visited Canada in 1906. (L.C. official)
Chez les Français. 1998

Lipset, Seymour Martin
American sociologist who spent a year in Sask. studying provincial govt. under the C.C.F.
Agrarian socialism. 4207

Litterick, James, 1901-1961
Came from Scotland to Canada, 1925; a miner in Man.; sec. of the Man. branch of the Communist Party of Canada; member of Man. Leg., 1936-41; died 10-2-61. (Can. parl. guide; Free Press Library)
Whither Manitoba. 3567

Little, Robert H., 1859?-
Came from Brussels, Ont., to homestead near Cypress River, Man., 1879-89. (Man. & N.W.T. direct., 1885/86-88)
Reminiscences. 3199

Lively, Gerald J.
Plea of the West. 2154

Livingston, William Guy
Farmer vs. Livingston. 538

Lloyd, Cecil Richard Francis, 1884-1938
Born in England; educated at Queen's Univ. and at London Univ.; employed in a business firm in Winnipeg, 1917-30. (Wallace)
Sunlight and shadow. 3083
Landfall. 3453

Lloyd, George Exton, 1861-1940
Church of England clergyman; chaplain of Queen's Own Rifles during Sask. Rebellion, and wounded at Cut Knife Hill, 1885; chaplain of Barr Colonists, 1903; Bishop of Saskatchewan, 1922-31. (Wallace)
Building of the nation. 3084
To members of British colony. 1731
About:
Mullins, Seven days. 1737A

Lloydall-Bee, Alfred
Parish of St. Peter, Entwistle. 3084A

Lloydminster, Sask. Board of Trade
Lloydminster district. 1999

McCaig, James, d. 1921
Came from Ont. to Lethbridge; principal of Lethbridge high school, 1899-1904; appointed to staff of provincial Normal School, Edmonton, 1915; supt. of schools for Edmonton; publicity commissioner for the govt. of Alta. for several years until his death.
Alberta, a survey. 2677
Climate of southern Alta. 1654

McCalla, William Copeland, 1872?-1962
Born at St. Catharines, Ont.; a botanist; instructor at Edmonton Normal School, 1913-15; at Calgary Normal School, 1915-38; collected an extensive herbarium now at the U. of A. (Calgary direct.)
Wild flowers of W. Can. 2723

McCarthy, D'Alton, 1836-1898
Ontario lawyer & politician. (Wallace)
On the French language. 1187

McCaul, Charles Coursolles, 1858-1928?
Came to N.W.T., and practised law at Ft. Macleod and Calgary, 1883-99; during that period edited the N.W.T. Law Reports; in the Yukon, 1899-1902; after spending a short time in Vancouver, settled in Edmonton where he practised until his death. (Morgan, 1912)
Ordinances of N.W.T. 1449
Prosecution of Sinnisiak. 2597

McCharles, Angus
Extinct cuttle-fish. 827
Footsteps of time. 946

McClelland, Lily Coulter
Resident of Saskatoon for many years; her husband was chief engineer at Univ. of Sask. power house.
Gems of praise. 4208

McClintock, Gray
The wolves of Cooking Lake. 3306A

McClintock, Walter, 1870-1949
American ethnologist. (N.Y. Times, 27-3-49)
The old north trail. 2155

McClung, James A.
Methodist clergyman and father-in-law of Nellie McClung, the novelist; joined Man. conference, 1888; supt. of conference, 1914. (Can. almanac, 1908-15)
In Dixie & Manitoba. 2065

McClung, Nellie Letitia (Mooney), 1873-1951
Came to Man. from Ont. with her family, 1880; taught school, 1888-96; married R.W. McClung, 1896; early identified with the women's rights and temperance movements in Man., until moving to Edmonton in 1913; represented Edmonton in the Alta. Leg., 1921-25; the McClungs moved to Victoria, B.C., 1937; did much newspaper work as well as writing books.
Black Creek stopping-house. 2320
Clearing in the West. 3456
Next of kin. 2598
Painted fires. 2937
Purple springs. 2783
Second chance. 2156
Sowing seeds in Danny. 2000
The stream runs fast. 3933
Three times and out. 2631
When Christmas crossed 'the Peace.' 2858

McCollum, Watt Hugh
Who owns Canada. 3456A

McConnell, William Kennedy
Australian.
The Alberta fiasco. 3569

McCormick, James Hanna
Barr colonist; went overseas during World War I, and after the war remained in Ireland.
Lloydminster. 2894

McCourt, Edward Alexander, 1907-1972
Born in Ireland; came to Kitscoty, Alta., with his parents, 1909; Rhodes scholar from Alta.; taught in Eastern Canada until 1944; professor of English at Univ. of Sask.; author of eight additional titles. (Can. who's who, 1967-69)
Canadian West in fiction. 4162
The flaming hour. 4045
Home is the stranger. 4209
Music at the close. 4046

McCulloch, John Herries, 1892-
Scottish writer.
Dark acres. 3457
Men of Kildonan. 2969

MacDermot, Hugh Ernest, 1888-
Sir Thomas Roddick. 3634

McDiarmid, Archibald P., 1852-
Baptist minister who came to the West to organize Baptist educational work, 1899; founded Brandon College, and served as principal, 1899-1912; retired to Robson, B.C. (Morgan, 1912; McLaurin)
Independence in univ. education. 2001

Macdonald, Adrian
Sir Alexander Mackenzie. 2938

McKenna, James Andrew Joseph, 1862-1919
In Dept. of Indian Affairs, 1886-1917; helped to negotiate treaties with the Indians in northern Alta. and Sask.; on the commission for settlement of half-breed claims, 1900-01; at the time of his retirement he was inspector of Catholic Indian schools on the prairies. (Can. who's who, 1910; Civil service lists, 1917)
Hudson Bay Route. 2003

Mackenzie, Sir Alexander, 1763-1820
Explorer and fur-trader. (Wallace)
Voyages from Montreal. 25
About:
Bryce, Mackenzie, etc. 1797
Macdonald, Mackenzie. 2938
Rumilly, Mackenzie. 3643
Wade, Mackenzie of Canada. 3042
Woollacott, Mackenzie. 3047
Wrong, Mackenzie. 3048

Mackenzie, Cecil Walter. 1860-
American telephone executive; grandson of Donald Mackenzie. (L.C. official)
Donald Mackenzie. 3571

Mackenzie, Charles, 1774-1855
Fur-trader. (Wallace)
Mississouri Indians. 61

McKenzie, Daniel, 1769?-1832
Fur-trader. (Wallace)
Letter to Selkirk. 52

Mackenzie, Donald, 1783-1851
Fur-trader; governor of Assiniboia, 1825-33.
About:
Mackenzie, D. Mackenzie. 3571

Mackenzie, Henry, 1781?-1832
Brother of Roderick; member of firm of McTavish, McGillivrays & Co., 1814-25; during Selkirk trials was in charge of N.W.C. publicity. (Wallace)
Letter to S. M'Gillivray. 85

McKenzie, Nathaniel Murdoch William John, 1856-1943
Joined the H.B.C., 1876; served at Ft. Ellice, Riding Mt., Qu'Appelle, Shoal River, Touchwood Hills, Winnipegosis, 1876-1909; fur trade inspector in Athabasca, and later in Lake Superior district, 1909-16. (Wallace)
Men of the H.B.C. 2784

Mackenzie, Roderick, d. 1844
Fur-trader; cousin of Sir A. Mackenzie. (Wallace)
Mackenzie's voyages from Montreal. 25
Reminiscences. 61

Mackie, George Douglas, 1878-
Local government taxation. 2940

Mackie, John, 1862-1939
After a sojourn in Australia, came to Canada and joined the N.W.M.P., 1888-93; returned to Gt. Britain, and became a writer; experiences in the Canadian West furnished material for many of his stories. (Morgan, 1912)
Canadian Jack. 1686
Devil's playground. 1365
Heart of the prairie. 1580
Prodigal's brother. 1581
Rising of the red man. 1831
Sinners twain. 1416

Mackinnon, Clarence D., 1868-1937
United Church clergyman; principal of Halifax Theological College, 1909-27. (Can. who's who, 1936-37)
Life of Principal Oliver. 3519

MacKinnon, James N., 1871-1946
Came from Scotland and settled south of Wapella, Sask., 1884; later moved to Moosomin where he was on the staff of the provincial gaol; joined the staff of the land titles office at Moosomin, 1913, and became chief clerk before his retirement, 1937.
Moosomin & its pioneers. 3572
Pioneer Scotch settlers. 2785

Mackintosh, William Archibald, 1895-
Taught economics at Brandon College, 1917-19; principal of Queen's Univ., 1951-61. (Can. who's who, 1967-69)
Agricultural co-operation. 2897
Canadian wheat pools. 2941
Economic problems. 3459
Prairie settlement. 3389

McKitrick, Thomas George, 1873-1952
Came to Man. with his family, 1880; farmed south of Crystal City but later took over the Crystal City Courier which his father had edited; editor for 40 years. (Free Press, 13-4-52)
Corner stones of empire. 3732
Stewart of the homesteads. 4252

McLagan, John Campbell, 1838-1900
Came from Ont. and resided in Winnipeg during the boom of the 1870s when he was part owner of the Winnipeg Sun; moved to Vancouver a few years later. (Morgan, 1898)
Man. & the great N.W. 632

Maclauries, Mr.
Fictitious name used in plagiarizing Mackenzie's 'Voyages.'
Narrative of voyages. 26

scrip commission which concluded Peace River treaty with the Indians, 1899; died at Victoria. (Free Press, 9-7-27)
Through the Mackenzie basin. 2004

Major, Mrs. Henniker
An Englishwoman, who with her husband and baby took up a homestead southwest of Saskatoon, 1904.
Canadian life as I found it. 2005

Major, J.C.
Member of the Wolseley expedition, 1870.
Red River expedition. 308

Makowski, Boleslaw
Polska emigracja w Kanadzie. 4254

Malis, Oskar
Pouceni z Kanady. 3996

Malkus, Alida Sims, 1895-
Little giant of the north. 4314

Maloney, John James
Trained for the Catholic priesthood but turned violently anti-Catholic; in the late 1920s toured Western Canada as a Klu Klux Klan lecturer and organizer.
Darkness, dawn & daybreak. 3521

Malov, Peter N.
Doukhobor living at Thrums, B.C.
Dukhobortsy. 4116

Maltby, Richard Grosse
Calgary Regiment. 3934

Mandelbaum, David Goodman, 1911-
Anthropologist connected with Univ. of Minnesota.
The Plains Cree. 3734

Manitoba
Manitoba and its resources. 1116
Manitoba's northland. 2631A
Northern Manitoba. 2599A
Pamphlet descriptive of Man. 1117
Why not go to Manitoba. 1334

Manitoba. Archives
Transactions of Hist. Soc. of Man. 4357

Manitoba. Bureau of Travel & Publicity
Game birds & animals. 3935
Greater Winnipeg. 4166
Guide book to Man. 4167
Historical Manitoba. 4168
Inside the rim of adventure. 3735
Manitoba's romantic northland. 4117

Manitoba. Commissioners on the School Question
Report. 1456

Manitoba. Dept. of Agriculture & Immigration
Canada's centre is Man. 1656
Credit unions in Man. 3689
Facts about Man. 1065
Farm, wheat & dairy lands. 2324
Great agricultural province. 1320
Greater Manitoba. 2408
Homes in Manitoba. 1272
Manitoba. 1882
Man., home of mixed farming. 2469
Man., information for investors. 1321
Man. the first province. 2239
Man., the prairie province. 1191
Opinions of eminent men. 1273
Stock raising in Manitoba. 2600
Study of wheat policies. 3766
True stories of success. 2325
2000 free homesteads in Manitoba. 1015

Manitoba. Dept. of Education
Education among New Canadians. 2725
Man., 50 years a province. 2726
Mémoire par la section catholique. 947

Manitoba. Executive Council
Report on claims of Man. 372

Manitoba. Laws, statutes, etc.
Pour établir un système d'éducation. 447

Manitoba. Legislative Assembly
Resolutions re telephones. 1883
Select committee on H.B. Route. 757

Manitoba. Provincial Diamond Jubilee Committee
Manitoba's diamond jubilee. 3205

Manitoba. University
Interests of Western Canada. 3846
Manitoba essays. 3575
Western Canadian agriculture. 3877

Manitoba Agricultural College
Check list of Manitoba flora. 2819

Manitoba & Northwest Farmers' Union
Claims of the province. 829
Resolutions. 758

Manitoba and North-Western Railway
Appeal from Court of Queen's Bench. 1489
Close to markets & schools. 1118
Guide book to lands. 948
How to start a prairie farm. 1192
Illustrated guide book to lands. 1066

Melville, Tom
Sports writer on the Regina Leader-Post. (Regina direct., 1946-51)
Barbed wire ballads. 3936

Melville, Sask. Board of Trade
The West's wonder town. 2159

Mennell, Henry Tuke
English botanist.
Across Canada. 831

Menzies, Don
The Alaska highway. 3847

Menzies, John Henry
At one time collaborated with Goldwin Smith before settling in Winnipeg, where he was an accountant for some years before 1918. (Who's who in Western Can.)
Development of resources. 2512
Economical condition. 2471

Mercator
see Ellice, Edward

Mercier, Mrs. Anne
English writer.
Home in the N.W. 1366
Red house by the Rockies. 1461

Mercier, Honoré, 1840-1894
Premier of Que., 1887-91. (Wallace)
La question Riel. 950

Mercure, André
Catholic clergyman of the Oblate order; ordained, 1948; stationed at Jack Fish mission, Sask. (Cath. direct. of Can., 1968-69)
La Semence. 3937

Merk, Frederick, 1887-
Professor of history at Harvard Univ.
Fur trade and empire. 83

Merriman, Robert Owen, 1894-
Bison & the fur trade. 2971

Messiter, Charles Alston, 1841-
A young Englishman who came to the Canadian West in 1862, travelling in the company of Milton and Cheadle; spent the winter of 1862-63 northwest of Ft. Carlton in the Thickwood Hills; lived in the American West, 1863-78. (Burke's landed gentry, 1914)
Sport and adventure. 1194

Metcalfe, Joseph Henry, 1870-1938
Came to Man. from England, 1890; after farming for some years moved to Portage la Prairie early in the century, where he was manager of the Farmers' Trading Co.; at one time mayor of Portage. (Free Press, 3-1-38)
Tread of the pioneers. 3311

Methodist Church
Regina, a social survey. 2414
Swan River Valley, Man. 2472
Turtle Mountain district. 2480

Methodius, Brother S., 1904-
Religious name of William H. Koziak; born at Leeshore, Alta.; taught high school in Yorkton, Edmonton, and Eastern Canada; first person of Ukrainian origin to join the Brothers of the Christian Schools; principal successively of Ukrainian Catholic Institute, Edmonton, St. Joseph's College, Yorkton, and the Sheptytskey Institute, Saskatoon.
Canadians on the march. 3880
Rev. S. Joseph. 4358

Metzger, H.
Peters-Pfarrei. 3208

Mewburn, Frank Hamilton H., 186–?-1954
Surgeon with Winnipeg Light Infantry, 1885; surgeon for N.W.M.P. at Fort Macleod; later a surgeon in Edmonton. (Morgan, 1912)
25th Battery. 3637

Meyer, R.
Co-op. for cheese & butter. 831A

Mézl, F.
A Czech writer.
Kanada. 2972

Michell, Humfrey, 1883-
Taught school in Man., 1910-13; professor of political economy at McMaster Univ. 1919-48. (Can. who's who, 1964-66)
Social Credit. 3461

Middleton, Clara J. (Russell) Jackson, 1872?-1955
Born near London, Ont.; married Homer Jackson, and settled in North Dakota; settled 20 miles east of Carstairs, Alta., 1904; married Jesse Edgar Middleton, 1934.
Green fields afar. 4052

Middleton, Sir Frederick Dobson, 1825-1898
English soldier who commanded the Canadian militia, 1884-1890; general in charge of the suppression of the Sask. Rebellion, 1885. (Wallace)
Parting address to people of Canada. 1195
Suppression of the rebellion. 1367
About:
Houghton, Houghton to Middleton. 1362

Monteith, George B.
History of Killarney. 4215

Montgomery, Henry Hutchinson, 1847-1932
English clergyman who was sec. of the Soc. for the Propagation of the Gospel. (Who was who, 1929-40)
Church on the prairie. 2160

Montgomery, Sir James, bart., 1766-1839
Selkirk's brother-in-law.
Substance of a speech. 62

Montigny, Benjamin Antoine Testard de, 1838-1899
Montreal lawyer. (Wallace)
Biographie de Gabriel Dumont. 1123

Montpetit, André Napoléon, 1840-1898
Quebec journalist. (Wallace)
Riel à la Rivière-du-Loup. 833

Montreal and Western Land Company
Manitoba lands. 634A
Prairie farms in Qu'Appelle Valley. 634B

Moodie, Marion Elizabeth, 1867-1958
Graduated from Calgary General Hospital, 1898, the first nurse to graduate from any Alta. hospital; held nursing positions in Calgary, Manitoba sanatorium at Ninette, and in Montreal; retired to Calgary; a botanist, early in the century she was commissioned to prepare a collection of native plants and grasses for the Alta. govt.; other botanical collections were sold to the Smithsonian Institution, N.Y. City Botanical Gardens, Harvard Univ., Stanford Univ., and the Field Museum, Chicago. (National, v.5; Journal, 12-3-53)
Legend of Dryas. 2973
Songs of the West. 1778

Moon, Robert James, 1925-
Born in Sask.; a graduate in economics from Univ. of Sask.; member of editorial staff of the Regina Leader-Post, 1947-
This is Saskatchewan. 4361

Mooney, Daniel, 1860-
Travels & philosophy. 3209

Moore, Cyril Augustus, d. 1951
Lords of the lakes & forests. 4255

Moore, Helen, d. 1941
Educated and later taught at Stanger, Alta.; taught for many years at Greencourt. (Preface)
Helen's poems. 3881

Moore, Irene, 1876-1947
Taught school in Ont., Alta., and Sask.; a resident of Sask. after 1905; went into journalism; editor of the women's page of the Saskatoon Phoenix; women's editor of the Regina Leader for 30 years; collaborated on a book for war brides distributed after World War II, and left an unfinished manuscript about the Sask. River.
Valiant La Vérendrye. 3031

Moore, J.G.
May have been the John Green M. who was a railway mail clerk in Man. at this time. (Civil service lists, 1886)
Fifteen months round Man. 688

Moore, John Thomas, 1844-1917
Toronto businessman interested in the West; lived in Red Deer, Alta., for a decade after 1901; member of Alta. Leg., 1905-09; returned to Toronto.
Settler's guide to homesteads. 759

Moore, O.S.
Resident of Olds, Alta.
In the shadow of the Rockies. 2009A

Moore, Thomas
A farmer delegate from Britain, 1879.
Canada revisited. 1322
A tour through Canada. 543

Moore, William, 1838-1915
Presbyterian clergyman in Ottawa for many years; sent by the church to investigate charges of mismanagement in the affairs of the Prince Albert mission. (Morgan, 1912)
Report on Prince Albert mission. 373

Moorhouse, Arthur Herbert Joseph, 1882-
Sec. to the Premier of Man., 1907-10; member of Man. Dept. of Agric., part of the time as deputy minister, 1910-16; employee of United Grain Growers, 1917; engaged in journalism in Winnipeg, 1918-23; moved to B.C.; author of at least two novels. (Who's who among N.A.A.; Winnipeg direct., 1907-23)
Deep furrows. 2010
Seager Wheeler's book. 2684

Moorhouse, Hopkins
Author above wrote under this name.

Moose Jaw
Book of views. 2973A

Moose Jaw. Board of Trade
Buckle of the greatest wheat belt. 2416, 3031A

Morrison, Dorothy, 1909-
Born in Sask., the daughter of a pioneer school teacher; taught school before her marriage; resident of Regina.
The prairie lily. 4119

Morrison, Elsie C.
Wife of Peter N.R. Morrison.
Calgary, 1875-1950. 4216

Morrison, J.H.
Manitoba School Question. 1369

Morrison, Peter N.R.
Calgary collegiate teacher.
Calgary, 1875-1950. 4216

Morrow, James William, 1869-1932
Came to Alta., 1894, to serve in Presbyterian mission fields in the Edmonton area; settled in Medicine Hat, 1896, where he remained pastor of the Presbyterian church and outlying fields until ill-health forced his retirement, 1918. (McKellar; Letter from Medicine Hat Library)
Early history of Medicine Hat. 2861

Morton, Arthur Silver, 1870-1945
Born in Trinidad of Nova Scotian missionary parents; after a distinguished scholastic career in Europe and teaching experience in Eastern Canada, came to the Univ. of Sask., 1914; professor of history, and librarian, 1914-40; during these years delved into the early history of the West, particularly that of the fur-trade period, gathered documents for the library, and wrote numerous articles and books; upon his retirement from the Univ. of Sask., the chancellor and senate conferred upon him an honorary degree of doctor of laws, while the Royal Society of Canada presented him with the Tyrrell gold medal; first provincial archivist of Sask., 1941-45.
David Thompson. 3210
History of Canadian West. 3693
History of prairie settlement. 3639
M'Gillivray's journal. 24
North West Company. 3211
Sir George Simpson. 3883
Under western skies. 3577
About:
Sask. Univ., Morton. 3850

Morton, James, 1869-
An early Manitoba resident who moved to B.C. where he wrote a biography of Premier Oliver. (L.C. official)
Polson's probation. 1508

Morton, William Lewis, 1908-
Born at Gladstone, Man.; professor of history, Univ. of Man., 1935-64; at Trent Univ. after 1964. (Can. who's who, 1967-69)
Manitoba: the birth of a province. 310
Progressive party in Canada. 4217
Third crossing. 3978

Moses, Eva E. (Mrs. Wm. A. Plecity)
Born in U.S.A., but spent her girlhood in Sask. before returning to U.S.A.; resident of Los Angeles.
Golden is the wheat. 4316

Motherwell, William Richard, 1860-1943
Came from Ont. to the West, 1881; farmed at Abernethy from 1881; founded first Grain Growers' Assoc. in Sask.; M.L.A. and Minister of Agric. and Provincial Sec., 1905-18; M.P., 1921-35; Dominion Minister of Agric., 1921-30; died in Regina. (Wallace; Morgan, 1912)
Election address. 1832

Mott, Lawrence, 1881-1931
American novelist.
Prairie, snow & sea. 2162

Moulin, Pierre Marie Celestin, 1877-1950
Catholic clergyman from France, a member of the O.M.I.; in 1903 came to the Cree mission at Hobbema, Alta., where he spent the remainder of his life.
Catéchisme en langue crise. 3102

Mountain, George Jehoshaphat, 1789-1863
Third Anglican Bishop of Quebec. (Wallace)
Journal during visit to N.W. 112

Mousseau, Joseph Octave
Montreal medical doctor.
Une page d'histoire. 951

Mowery, William Byron, 1899-
American author. (Who's who among N.A.A.)
Black automatic. 3578

Mueller, Karl
German writer of boys' books.
Die jungen Pelzjaeger. 202

Mullins, J.D.
Seven days on the prairie. 1737A

Mulvaney, Charles Pelham, 1835-1885
Church of England clergyman and writer; associated with Bishop's College, Lennoxville, Que. (Dom. ann. reg., 1885; Wallace)
North-West Rebellion. 834

Munday, Albert Henry, 1896-1957
Began journalistic work in Moose Jaw; moved to Toronto; a writer. (Can. who's who, 1955-57)
No other gods. 3395

Munday, Mrs. Luta
A mounty's wife. 3213

Munro, William F.
Lived in Ont. and on the prairies before 1881; later immigration agent in Scotland acting on behalf of the C.P.R. and the Canadian North West Land Co.
Emigration made easy. 689
Prairies of the North-West. 582A

Murchie, Robert Welch, 1883-1937?
Pioneered in the field of rural social surveys in Canada when he made two surveys before 1914; on staff of Man. Agricultural College, 1915-31; head of dept. of agricultural economics, 1925-31; on staff of Univ. of Minnesota, 1931-37. (Can. Agric. Ec. Assoc. 9th annual meeting, June, 1937)
Agricultural progress. 3524
Settlement of Peace River. 3377
Unused lands of Manitoba. 2974

Murdoch, W.
Civil engineer.
Winnipeg & H.B. R'y. 761

Murphy, Mrs. Emily Gowan (Ferguson) 1868-1933
Her husband, a clergyman, transferred from Ont. in 1904 to Swan River, where she engaged in journalism; moved to Edmonton, 1907; became active in various social and humane organizations, and a champion of women's rights; appointed police magistrate to deal with cases of juvenile delinquency, 1912, and in this field some of her finest work was done; one of five women who carried the fight for admission of women to the Senate before the Privy Council, 1929, and won their case; wrote as Emily Murphy and under the nom de plume Janey Canuck. (Who was who, 1929-40; Wallace)
Janey Canuck in the West. 2163
Open trails. 2328
Our little Canadian cousin. 2862
Seeds of pine. 2475
About:
Sanders, E. Murphy. 3949

Murray, Andrew, 1812-1878
Scottish naturalist.
Contributions to natural history. 216

Murray, D.L.
A Scot who spent eight years in Man., part of the time at Napkina. (Man. & N.W.T. direct., 1894)
Breezy reminiscences. 1550

Murray, J.A.
May be a pseudonym used by the Rev. James A. McClung.
In Dixie & Manitoba. 2070

Murray, S.C.
Challenge of Prairie Provinces. 2728A

Murray, William Henry Harrison, 1840-1904
American clergyman and writer.
Daylight land. 1068

Myers, Charles Vernon, 1912-
Journalist; oil editor of Calgary Herald for many years.
Oil investor. 3939

Namao, Alta. U.F.W.A., Local no.61
A cameo of the West. 3525

Nanton, Sir Augustus, 1860-1925
Prominent Canadian financier who lived in Winnipeg, 1884-1924. (Wallace)
About:
MacBeth, Nanton. 3266

Napier, R.M.
Medicine Hat resident; warden of the church, 1913-15.
St. Barnabas Church. 3396

Nasir, George
Described as a writer in the directory. (Winnipeg direct., 1950)
Fifteen poems. 4120
New poems. 4170

National Editorial Association
Prophecies on the Canadian West. 1620A

National Land Company Ltd.
Saskatoon, 1912. 2329

National Research Council of Canada
Prairie Regional Laboratory. 4121

Nazaruk, Osyp, 1883-1940
Lawyer, novelist, and publisher in the Ukraine; lived in Western Canada, 1920-23.
Vchasna vesna v Piwnichniy Alberti. 3149

Neatby, Kenneth William, 1910-
Director of science service for the Dominion Dept. of Agric. (Can. who's who, 1955-57)
Illustrated guide to prairie weeds. 4054

Palmer, George Alfred, 1869-1954
Came from London, Eng., to Red Deer with his family about 1890; chief clerk for C.P.R. in Calgary; edited a weekly magazine 'The Bond'; moved to Sask. to help organize bridge and ferry services and continued as chief clerk of the Dept. of Highways until retirement, 1934; wrote verse and short stories. (Letter from Sask. Leg. Library)
Hail. 3349
Madam Verite at Bath. 3311A

Palmer, W.J.
Lumber merchant and real estate agent who lived at Virden for a few years. (Man. & N.W.T. direct., 1887-88)
Dennis county, Man. 1072

Pálsson, Páll Skarphédinsson, 1882-
Emigrated to Canada from Iceland, 1897; advertising manager of the Viking Press, Winnipeg. (Winnipeg direct., 1929-51)
Nordur-Reykir. 3527
Skilarétt. 4057

Paluk, William, 1914-
Graduate of United College, Winnipeg; an editor of Opinion, 1947-50; writer of short stories in Ukrainian. (Yuzyk)
Canadian Cossacks. 3811

Pambrun, Pierre Chrysologue, 1792-1841
Entered H.B.C. service, 1815; taken prisoner at Qu'Appelle by N.W.C. men, 1816 (Wallace)
Narratives. 63

Panton, James Hoyes, 1847-1898
For many years on the staff of Ont. College of Agric. at Guelph, except for 1883-84 spent in Winnipeg. (Wallace)
Fragmentary leaves from geol. records. 764
Gleanings from outcrops. 637
Notes on geology. 956
Rambles in the North-West. 837

Paquin, Elzéar, 1850-1947
French-Canadian medical doctor. (Wallace, D.N.A.A.)
Riel: tragédie. 957

Parage, E.
Riel: drame historique. 872

Parker, C.W.
Who's who in Western Canada. 2358

Parker, Sir Gilbert, 1862-1932
Canadian-born author. (Wallace)
Northern lights. 2073

Parker, William Wilder McKinley, 1894-
Rhymes from the N.W. 4257

Parks, Evangeline Paula
Poems of the prairie. 3711

Parsons, Nell Wilson, 1898-1968
The curlew cried. 4058

Partridge, Edward Alexander, d. 1931
Settled at Sintaluta, Sask., as a homesteader and school teacher, 1883; a member of the Yorkton Rangers, 1885; an early apostle of farmer co-operative movements; organizer and first pres. of Grain Growers' Grain Co., 1906, but later lost the leadership because of his visionary and radical ideas; first editor of the Grain Growers' Guide, 1908; lost his foot in a binder accident; resigned from G.G.G. Co. board of directors, 1912; organized Square Deal Grain Co. which soon failed; founded a magazine to advance agrarian ideas; endeavoured to change the farmers' political philosophy; many of his ideas anticipated the C.C.F.; sobriquet 'That man Partridge.' (Colquette, R.D. The first fifty years)
Farmers' trade union. 1946
Manifesto of No-Party League. 2420
A war on poverty. 2949

The Pas, Man. Board of Trade
The Pas. 2477
The Pas and Northern Man. 3152

Pascoe, J. Ernest, 1900-1972
Farmed in Moose Jaw district for many years; retired in Moose Jaw. (Moose Jaw direct., 1951-52)
Moose Jaw golden jubilee. 4363

Passy, Louis
Etude sur la colonisation. 1020

Paterson, Isabel Mary (Bowler) d. 1961
Spent childhood on a ranch in Alta.; journalist in B.C. and U.S.A. (Who was who in Am., 1961-68)
Magpie's nest. 2606
Shadow riders. 2559

Patrick, Thomas Alfred, 1864-1943
Pioneer doctor; arrived in Yorkton, 1890; in N.W.T. Leg., 1894-1904; advocated formation of two provinces rather than one out of the territories. (Morgan, 1912)
County system for Sask. 2787
Facts bearing on the N.W.T. 1551

Rich, Edwin Ernest, 1904-
Professor of history at Cambridge Univ., Eng., who has edited several volumes relating to the early history of the H.B.C.
Cumberland House journals. 19
Robertson's corresp. book. 79
Simpson's Athabasca journal. 77

Richards, Alfred Bate, 1820-1876
English dramatist and journalist. (D.N.B.)
Britain redeemed & Canada preserved. 136

Richardson, Ernest L., 1876-
Manager of the Calgary Exhibition and Stampede from about 1912-1940. (Calgary direct., 1912-40; Who's who in Can., 1936-37)
Calgary, commercial metropolis. 1949

Richardson, Sir John, 1787-1865
Explorer; accompanied Sir John Franklin on Arctic journeys of 1819-22 and 1825-27; in command of the search party for Franklin, 1848-49. (Wallace)
Arctic searching expedition. 143
Fauna boreali-americana. 91
Progress to the eastward. 88

Richardson, Robert Lorne, 1860-1921
Born in Ont.; came to Winnipeg where he participated in the founding of the Winnipeg Sun, 1882; this paper became the Winnipeg Tribune which he owned and edited, 1890-1921; in the H. of C., 1896-1901. (Who's who in Western Can.; Wallace)
Facts & figures. 959
Report of visit. 767

Richmond, W.R.
Life of Lord Strathcona. 1658

Rickards, C.D.
A resident of Brighton, Eng.
Across America. 1023

Riddell, Henry Som. Hutton
Lieut. in 60th Rifles of Br. regular army garrisoned at Quebec; member of the Wolseley expedition to Red River. (Br. army lists, 1875)
Red River expedition. 335

Riddell, John Henry, 1863-1952
Methodist clergyman; came to Man., where he first served at Cartwright, 1890-91; served in Winnipeg churches, 1892-1902; professor of classics, Wesley College, 1896-1902; founder and first principal of Alberta College, Edmonton, and of St. Stephen's Theological College on the Univ. of Alta. campus; principal and later pres. of Wesley College, 1917-38; died 9-11-52. (Morgan, 1912; Can. who's who, 1948; Free Press Library)
Methodism in the middle West. 4005

Riel, Louis 'David,' 1844-1885
Métis leader; pres. of provisional govt. at Red River, 1869-70; escaped with arrival of Wolseley's force; elected to H. of C. to represent Provencher, in 1873 and 1874, but unable to sit; declared an outlaw, 1875; lived in Montana until invited by métis to the Sask. country, 1884; led second rebellion, 1885; executed at Regina, 16 Nov. 1885.
L'amnistie. Mémoire. 399
Poésies religieuses et politiques. 960
Queen vs Louis Riel. 961

Rigassi, Georges, 1885-
Prominent Swiss journalist. (Who's who in Switzerland, 1968-69)
A travers le Canada. 2907

Riley, Conrad Stephenson, 1875-1960
Prominent Winnipeg businessman; died 21-11-60. (Can. who's who, 1958-60; Free Press Library)
Rowing memories. 3401

Riley, Robert Thomas, 1851-1944
Born in Yorkshire; after a few years in Ont., arrived in Man., 1881; became one of Winnipeg's leading businessmen. (Who's who in Western Can.; Morgan, 1912)
Memoirs. 4060

Rimbey, Alta. Historical Committee
History. 4329

Ringwood, Gwendolyn Margaret (Pharis), 1910-
Born in Alta.; graduate of Univ. of Alta.; wife of an Edmonton doctor; in addition to the title below, has written other successful plays which have been published in collections.
Dark harvest. 3947

Ritchie, James Ewing, 1820-1898
English author who visited Canada in 1884. (L.C. official)
To Canada with emigrants. 842

Ritchie, P.R.
Scottish farmer settled in Essex, England, who toured the Canadian N.W.
Manitoba & N.W.T. 1281

Ritchot, Joseph Noël, 1825-1905
Catholic clergyman; parish priest at St. Norbert, Man., for many years.
About:
Prud'homme, Mgr Ritchot. 3098

St. Paul, Minneapolis & Manitoba Railway Company
Fourth annual report. 698

Sale, Charles V.
The winter road. 3154

Salesman Publishing Company
Souvenir of Alta. 1887

Sallans, George Herbert, 1895-1960
Came to the prairies at age eight; after serving in World War I worked on various newspapers in Winnipeg, Saskatoon, and Vancouver; general manager of British United Press, Montreal; won the Governor-General's fiction award for his novel, 1943. (Free Press, 27-5-43)
Little man. 3815

Saltcoats, Sask. Board of Trade
Choice lands. 2171

Salter, Ernest J.B., 1871-1942
Methodist clergyman; sec. of the Man. district of the British and Foreign Bible Soc. for 36 years. (Riddell; Obit. clipping, 1942)
Manitoba School Question. 2429

Salvation Army. Calgary Citadel Corps.
Diamond jubilee. 4063

Salverson, Laura Goodman, 1890-1970
Canadian author of Icelandic descent; resident of Winnipeg. (Can. who's who, 1949-51; Journal, 14-7-70)
Confessions. 3699
The dark weaver. 3583
Viking heart. 2868

Sandercock, W. Clark, d. 1938
Came to Pilot Mound, Man. as a child, 1880; for 38 years taught in schools in Man. and Sask.; interested in poetry, history, and nature science, and a frequent contributor to periodicals. (Obit. clipping, 16-2-38)
Dance of the buffalo skull. 3472

Sanders, Byrne Hope, 1902-
Toronto editor. (C.L.A. biographies)
Emily Murphy. 3949

Sanderson, Charles Rupert, 1887-1956
Chief librarian, Toronto Public Libraries. (Can. who's who, 1949-51; Wallace)
Social Credit. 3533

Sandilands, John
Early Winnipeg printer.
Western Canadian dictionary. 2342

Sandison, J.W.
Came from Scotland to Man., 1884; bought land near Brandon, 1884, and became a success story which reached its zenith about 1890 when he farmed 2800 acres; owned 30 binders with other machinery in commensurate scale; his methods of finance were unorthodox, and by 1893 he was hopelessly in debt; disappeared along with the hired girl in May 1893. (Western Producer, 1-5-52)
A Scotch farmer's success. 1200

Sandwell, Bernard Keble, 1876-1955
Writer and editor of Toronto and Montreal. (Can. who's who, 1949-51)
Westing. 2640

Sántha, Pál
Resident of Stockholm, Sask.
Kanada magyarsága. 4006

Sapiro, Aaron, 1884-1959
San Francisco lawyer, specialist in co-operative organizations and rural credits; toured Western Canada in 1923 and again in 1929; his first tour influenced the development of the Canadian wheat pools. (Who was who in Am., 1951-60)
Report of mass meeting. 2869
100% control by legislation. 3155

Sargent, C. Evans
From oxen to airplane. 4213

Saskatchewan
Claim for extension of boundaries. 1887A
Legislation affecting women and children. 2737

Saskatchewan. Bureau of Publications
Back to Sask. 4007
Government in industry. 4064
New north. 4126
Progress in health services. 4008
Progress report from your govt. 4065
Sask. plans for progress. 3950
Sask. viewpoint. 3951
Tourist trips through Sask. 3534
Women & children's rights. 4176

Saskatchewan. Dept. of Agriculture
Business guide. 2430
Saskatchewan. 2342A, 2483

Saskatchewan. Department of Education
From Polish peasant. 2738
Larger school units. 4066

Saskatchewan. Dept. of Railways, Labour, & Industries
Hudson Bay Route. 3352

About:
Bryce, Selkirk. 1797, 2280
Martin, Selkirk. 2970
Martin, Selkirk's work. 2555

Selkirk, Man. Board of Trade
Souvenir of Selkirk. 1889

Selwyn, Cecil E.
Winnipeg bookkeeper about 1913-28.
Prairie patchwork. 2177

Semmens, John, 1850-1921
Methodist missionary; arrived at Winnipeg as assistant to Rev. G. Young, 1872; moved to Norway House, 1873; opened Methodist mission at remote Nelson House, 1874; later at Berens River; after his return to southern Man. stationed at Carberry and in Winnipeg; pres. of Methodist conference of Man., 1892; principal of the new Brandon industrial institute for educating Indian children, 1895-1900; retired from principalship and ministry due to ill-health; inspector of Indian agencies for Canadian govt.; secured surrender of 133,000 sq. miles in 10 adhesions in Indian Treaty No. 5; translated four works into Cree. (Obit. clipping; Cochrane; Who's who in West Can.; Riddell; Wallace)
The field & the work. 771
Hand-book of Scripture truths. 1328
Trials of Methodism. 2178

Servants of Mary Immaculate
Yuvileyna kniha. 3816

Seton, Ernest Thompson, 1860-1946
Arrived in Man. in 1881, and lived near Carberry for varying periods over several years; later a famous naturalist.
Birds of Manitoba. 1236
List of mammals. 967
Northern animals. 2085

Sevareid, Arnold E.
Canoeing with the Cree. 3474A

Shantz, Jacob Yost, 1822-1909
Citizen of Berlin (Kitchener), Ont., sent to Man., 1872, by members of the Mennonite sect in Russia to report on lands; his favourable report led to the founding of the first Mennonite settlements in the West; interested himself in the welfare of these immigrants, and made a total of thirty trips to Man., usually on business connected with the settlers.
Journey to Manitoba. 376

Shareholder, A.
Canada North West Land Co. 700

Sharp, Paul Frederick, 1918-
Professor of history at Iowa State College.
The agrarian revolt. 4128

Shave, Harry
Winnipeg businessman. (Winnipeg direct., 1934-52)
Our heritage. 4272

Shaw, Alexander Malcolm, 1885-
With dept. of animal husbandry, Univ. of Sask., 1913-15; livestock commissioner of Sask., 1918-19; professor in dept. of animal husbandry, Univ. of Sask., 1919-30; dean of agric., 1930-37; joined Dominion Dept. of Agric. (Can. who's who, 1967-69; Agr. Inst. of Can.)
Drought on the prairies. 3404

Sheffield, T.W., 1882-
Born in England; came to Canada, 1905; commissioner of Greater Regina Club, 1910-12. (Who's who in Western Can.)
Opportunities in Regina. 2260

Shefrin, Frank, 1913-
Born and educated at Winnipeg; agricultural economist with the Dominion Dept. of Agric.
Population of Man. 3614

Sheldon, John Prince, d. 1913
Professor of agriculture in England. (Who was who, 1897-1916)
From Britain to B.C. 1027
To Canada & through it. 845

Shelford, W.
Development of N.W. Canada. 968

Shelton, Reuben
Resident of Ruddington, Nottingham, Eng.
English tenant-farmers. 1376

Shepherd, Peter
Church of England clergyman.
With glowing hearts. 4011

Sheptycky, Andrey, 1865-
Metropolitan of the Ukrainian Catholic Church who visited Canada in 1910 and 1921.
Address on the Ruthenian question. 2261
Kanadyiskym Rusynam. 2262

Sherbinin, Michael Andrew de, 1856-
Educated in Russia; a friend of Tolstoy, he was mentioned in 'War and Peace' as a cavalry officer named Tsherbinin; became a preacher in the Russian Evangelical Church; came to Canada and worked among the Doukhobors near Saskatoon as a teacher, first under auspices of the Quakers, later of the Presbyterians; professor

Stewart, David Alexander, 1874-1937
First licensed in Man. as a doctor, 1906; supt. of the sanatorium at Ninette, Man., for many years. (Free Press, 17-2-37)
Assiniboine trading posts. 3226
Glimpses at Man. history. 3316

Stewart, McLeod, 1847-1926
Ottawa lawyer. (Wallace)
Ottawa; an ocean port. 1425

Stewart, Zaida Mahood
Booklets of verse. 3749

Stirling, John T.
The Bellevue explosions. 2434A

Stock, A.B.
Englishman who apparently ranched for a time in southern Alta.
Ranching in the Canadian West. 2345

Stock, Ralph, 1882-
English writer who tried ranching in the West, then went to Australia.
Confessions of a tenderfoot. 2435

Stocken, Harry William Gibbon, 1858-1955
Church of England missionary; served at Blackfoot reserve, 1885-88; Sarcee reserve, 1888-95; Blackfoot reserve, 1895-194-?; he began translating the Gospel of St. Matthew into Blackfoot syllabic but was prevented from completing the task by failing eyesight; retired to Esquimalt, B.C. (Private information)
Bible. N.T. St. Matthew. Blackfoot. 1040
Gleichen district. 2744

Stokes, William Edward Herbert, 1869-1948
Arrived in the West as a 'remittance man,' 1892; in the next ten years spent most of his time in Alta., following 14 occupations, 13 of which he considered failures; worked as a telegrapher on C.P.R., 1902?-05; joined N.W.T. Dept. of Public Works and continued in the dept. after formation of the province of Sask.; clerk of Dept. of Agric., 1913-18; editor of Public Service Monthly, 1919-27. (Letter from Sask. Arch.)
Are our Indians pagan? 1891
Red man's religion. 2183

Stonewall, Man. Board of Trade
Stonewall district. 1661

Storer, Effie (Laurie), 1867-1951
Member of the Laurie family of Battleford, founders of the Saskatchewan Herald; married in 1889 to a member of the N.W.M.P., who was killed in France, 1917; worked as journalist on Regina and Moose Jaw papers. (Star-Phoenix, spring of 1951)
Gardiner Presbyterian Church. 1954

Storer, R.H.
I am a lunatic. 3891

Stovel Company
Last of the buffalo. 2023
Winnipeg souvenir. 1628

Strachan, John, 1778-1867
Anglican Bishop of Toronto. (Wallace)
Letter to Selkirk. 45
McDonald's reply. 41

Strang, Peter, 1856-1934
Arrived in Man., where he homesteaded, 1884; returned to university, 1893, and graduated in theology, 1897; stationed in the Presbyterian field at Virden, Man., 1897-1911; supt. of missions in southern Sask. for Presbyterian Church, 1911-25; for United Church, 1925-28.
Autobiography. 3356
Missions in southern Sask. 3156

Strange, Henry George Latimer, 1882-1964
After a varied career came to Canada and farmed in Alta., 1919-30; director of agricultural research for Searle Grain Co., 1930; died 2-11-64. (Can. who's who, 1948; Free Press Library)
Western Canada semi-arid area. 3477

Strange, Kathleen (Redman), 1896-
Wife of H.G.L. Strange; came to Canada from England with her husband and with him won the world wheat championship in 1923. (Can. who's who, 1967-69)
With the West in her eyes. 3589

Strange, Thomas Bland, 1831-1925
After serving in the Imperial forces in Canada, and in the organization of the Canadian artillery, left the army and established the Military Colonization Company ranch near Calgary, 1881; in command of the Alberta Field Force in 1885, and fought the battle of Frenchman's Butte. (Morgan, 1898; Wallace)
Gunner Jingo's jubilee. 1469

Strathcona & Mount Royal, Donald Alexander Smith, 1st Baron, 1820-1914
Canadian financier and statesman prominent in H.B.C. and C.P.R. (Wallace)
North-West Territories. 313
Speeches on Indian difficulties. 365
About:
Pedley, Biography. 2521
Preston, Life of. 2481

White, James, 1863-1928
Geographer in Dominion civil service. (Wallace)
York Factory express journal. 89

White, Samuel Alexander, 1885-1956
Ontario writer of adventure stories. (Morgan, 1912)
Called Northwest. 3858
Empery. 2438
Northwest law. 3820
Northwest patrol. 3859

White, Thomas, 1830-1888
Dominion Minister of the Interior, 1885-88. (Wallace)
Facts for the people. 855
Northwest administration. 856, 978
Our great West. 377
Speeches on the C.P.R. 776

Whitehouse, Francis Cecil, 1879-
Came to Canada from England; employed by the Canadian Bank of Commerce; bank manager at Red Deer, Alta., 1904-16; held other posts before retiring to B.C. (Gaetz)
Plain folks. 2994

Whiteside, William Carleton, 1900-1967
Son of an early Methodist missionary stationed in Edmonton; surgeon in Edmonton; moved to Victoria, 1956. (Can. Med. Assoc. J., 18 Mar. 1967)
Nomadic life of a surgeon. 4229

Whitney, Mrs. John E.M.
Otter grand march. 781

Whittier, John Greenleaf, 1807-1892
American poet.
Red River voyageur. 1284

Wickstrom, Victor Hugo
Bland svenskar i Kanada. 1846

Widtsoe, John Andreas, 1872-1952
Mormon leader in Utah. (L.C. official)
Examination into irrigation. 2955

Wiebe, Gerhard
Auswanderung der Mennoniten. 1630

Wiedersheim, Eduard
Official in Hohenheim, Germany.
Kanada. 653

Wiegner, Paul E.
Lutheran Church, Missouri Synod. 3238

Wigle, Hamilton, 1858-1934
Methodist clergyman; sec. of Man. conference of the Methodist Church, 1900; of Sask. conference, 1904; represented Sask. at the World Sunday School Convention in Jerusalem, 1904; moved to the Maritimes, 1910. (Morgan, 1912; Wallace)
Life story of Finlay Booth. 1631

Wilbois, Joseph, 1874-
Resident of France.
Un pays neuf. 3286

Wilcocke, Samuel Hull, 1766?-1833
Came to Canada in service of N.W.C. as a propagandist during the Selkirk trials. (Wallace)
Death of B. Frobisher. 61
Narrative of occurrences. 50
Notice re the boundary. 51
Report of proceedings. 67, 68
Report of trials. 53

Wilkie Press
All about the town of Wilkie. 2190

Williams, Flos (Jewell), 1893-
Born in Ont.; married and settled in Calgary, 1915. (Can. who's who, 1948)
Fold home. 4230
New furrows. 2995

Williams, Fred C.
Editor of The Commonwealth in Regina, 1936-51; hardware merchant in Carlyle, Sask. (Hist. direct. of Sask. newspapers)
The open road. 3708

Williams, W.H.
Newspaperman connected with Toronto Globe.
Manitoba & the N.W. 654

Williams, W. Llewellyn, 1867-1922
Welsh writer and member of Br. parl. (Who was who, 1916-28)
Prominent Welshmen on Western Canada. 1610

Willoughby, Gerald Thomas Arthur, 1866-1933
One of the Temperance Colonists who founded Saskatoon in 1883; later in real estate and insurance business in Saskatoon.
Retracing the old trail. 3362

Willson, Henry Beckles, 1869-1942
Born in Canada; became a London journalist. (Wallace)
The great Company. 1587
Lord Strathcona. 1697

Wilson, Eric Mackay, 1901-1960
Lieut.-col. of Ft. Garry Horse during WWII; director of advertising for Montreal Star. (Free Press, 6-7-60)
Vanguard. 3963

Yuzyk, Paul
Graduate of Univ. of Sask.; professor in the depts. of history and Slavic studies at the Univ. of Man.
Ukrainians in Manitoba. 4370

Zawadski, B., 1912?-
Ukrainian immigrant; sent to Canada by his widowed mother in 1927 when he was fifteen; lived with an aunt at Yorkton and later worked in Vancouver and Kamloops before returning to Russia about 1932.
Piec lat za oceanem. 4280

Zealandia, Sask. Board of Trade
Solid facts. 2195

Zelma, Sask. Homemakers' Club
Community of Zelma. 4187

Zero
A pseud.
One mistake. 1084

Zhan, Josaphat, 1885-1972
Ukrainian form of the name of Rev. J. Jean; born in Eastern Canada; joined the Basilian Fathers, 1913; an interpreter in the diplomatic service of the Ukrainian Republic, 1918-23; immigration agent directing Ukrainian settlers into the Peace River district, 1925; organized the Ukrainian-Canadian museum at Mundare, Alta. (Journal, 10-6-72)
Pyatdesyat rokiv u Kanadi. 4335

Zilliacus, Konni, 1855-1924
Finnish writer who visited Canada about 1900; his given names were Konrad Viktor. (L.C. official)
Kanada såsom mål för emigranter. 1633

Zimmermann, Andreas
Die romisch-catholische Pfarrei. 3550

Zyndykatu Emigracyjnego
Wiadomosci o Kanadzie. 3594

Initials, Pseudonyms,
and Religious Names

Older settler *see* D.L. Murray
One of the bunglers *see* Lewis Redman Ord
One of themselves ...
One who has just returned from the great North-West ...
One who knows ...
O'Neill, Moira pseudonym of Mrs. Agnes Shakespear Higginson Skrine

P., M. ...
Pedro, Don *see* Nehemiah Jones
Pee, Peter *see* Curt August Haegler
Père Trappiste *see* François Nicol
Prairies, Jean des *see* Pierre Zacharie Lacasse

R., C.D. *see* C.D. Rickards
Reid, Wallace Q. *see* George Goodchild
Religieuse de Notre-Dame des Missions, Une ...
Retired officer *see* Richard E.W. Goodridge
Rivereine, Lucien *see* Eugene Achard
Rochester fellow *see* Samuel Hubbard Scudder
Rolyat, Jane *see* E. Jean Taylor
Rusticus *see* David Currie

S., A. ...
S., D.L. ...
Saint-Léandre, Soeur (religious name) *see* Mariette Nöel
Scrivener, Septimus *see* Edward Wilson Gates
Shareholder, A. ...
Sister of Charity of Montreal ...
Soeur de la Providence *see* Soeur Jean-Baptiste
Soeur de la Providence ...

Tanis *see* Hilda A. Davies
Truth *see* Adrien Gabriel Morice
'2751' *see* George Palmer

Veritas Vincit pseudonym of Henry T. Burgess
Vestal, Stanley pseudonym of Walter S. Campbell

Watanna, Onoto *see* Winifred (Eaton) Babcock Reeve

Young emigrant in Manitoba *see* Edward G.E. Ffolkes

Zero ...

www.ingramcontent.com/pod-product-compliance
Lightning Source LLC
LaVergne TN
LVHW080403090826
844660LV00054B/1253

* 9 7 8 1 4 8 7 5 7 9 0 9 8 *